ARTHURIAN STUDIES LXXXII

THE COMPLETE STORY OF THE GRAIL

ARTHURIAN STUDIES

ISSN 0261–9814

General Editor: Norris J. Lacy

Previously published volumes in the series
are listed at the back of this book

Other translations by Nigel Bryant

The High Book of the Grail:
A translation of the thirteenth century romance of Perlesvaus

Robert de Boron: *Merlin and the Grail*

The Legend of the Grail

Perceforest:
The Prehistory of King Arthur's Britain

The True Chronicles of Jean le Bel 1290–1360

The Medieval Romance of Alexander

The History of William Marshal

THE COMPLETE STORY OF THE GRAIL

Chrétien de Troyes' *Perceval* and its continuations

Translated by Nigel Bryant

D. S. BREWER

© Nigel Bryant 2015

All rights reserved. Except as permitted under current legislation no part of this work may be photocopied, stored in a retrieval system, published, performed in public, adapted, broadcast, transmitted, recorded or reproduced in any form or by any means, without the prior permission of the copyright owner

The right of Nigel Bryant to be identified as the author of this work has been asserted in accordance with sections 77 and 78 of the Copyright, Designs and Patents Act 1988

First published 2015
D. S. Brewer, Cambridge
Paperback edition 2018

ISBN 978 1 84384 400 6 hardback
ISBN 978 1 84384 498 3 paperback

D. S. Brewer is an imprint of Boydell & Brewer Ltd
PO Box 9, Woodbridge, Suffolk, IP12 3DF, UK
and of Boydell & Brewer Inc.
668 Mt Hope Avenue, Rochester, NY 14620–2731, USA
website: www.boydellandbrewer.com

The publisher has no responsibility for the continued existence or accuracy of URLs for external or third-party internet websites referred to in this book, and does not guarantee that any content on such websites is, or will remain, accurate or appropriate

A CIP catalogue record for this book is available from the British Library

Typeset by
www.thewordservice.com

Contents

INTRODUCTION

Chrétien's Intention	xviii
The First Continuation: the Unimportance of the Holy Grail	xxii
The Second Continuation: Wandering Astray	xxvi
Gerbert's Continuation: the Crusading Knight	xxxii
The Third Continuation: Revenge	xxxix
The Elucidation Prologue and Bliocadran	xlv
Reading Aloud	xlvi
Dates	l
Manuscripts	l
Modern Editions	li
Further Reading	li

CHRÉTIEN DE TROYES: *PERCEVAL*

Line numbers refer to *Le Roman de Perceval ou Le Conte du Graal*, ed. William Roach (Geneva, 2nd edition, 1959)

Chrétien's Prologue — 1
  Chrétien dedicates his work to Count Philip of Flanders (1–68)

The Welsh Boy — 2
  The boy's first encounter with knights; he leaves his mother (69–634)

A Pie, a Ring and a Kiss — 7
  The boy meets a girl at a pavilion and takes her ring (635–833)

The Red Knight — 8
  The boy arrives at Arthur's court; he kills the Red Knight and takes his arms (834–1304)

Training in Arms — 13
  The boy is knighted by Gorneman (1305–1698)

The Siege of Beaurepaire The new knight defends Blancheflor against her enemies (1699–2975)	16
A Grail and a Lance The new knight comes to a castle where he sees a mysterious procession (2976–3421)	27
No Questions Asked The new knight realises his mistake; he guesses his name; he is warned about his sword (3422–3690)	30
The Proud Knight of the Glade Perceval breaks his sword (3691–4143)	33
Blood in the Snow Perceval breaks Kay's arm; Gawain leads him back to Arthur (4144–4602)	37
The Price of Perceval's Failure Perceval vows to search for the grail and the lance; Gawain is accused of murder (4603–4815)	41
The Tournament at Tintagel Gawain sets out to defend himself against the charge; on the way he takes part in a tournament (4816–5655)	42
Sir Gawain is Besieged A mob besieges Gawain in a tower; he must go in search of the bleeding lance (5656–6216)	49
Perceval and his Hermit Uncle Perceval meets his hermit uncle on Good Friday (6217–6518)	54
Gawain and the Haughty Girl Gawain's horse is stolen; he has to fight to win it back (6519–7370)	57
The Castle of the White-haired Queen Gawain lies on the Bed of Marvels and is offered lordship of the castle (7371–8371)	63
The Perilous Ford Gawain crosses the Perilous Ford; Guiromelant challenges him to combat (8372–9234)	71

THE FIRST CONTINUATION

Line numbers refer to *The Continuations of the Old French Perceval of Chrétien de Troyes, Volume II*, ed. William Roach and Robert H. Ivy (Philadelphia, 1950)

Arthur and his court set out to see the combat (1–503)	79
King Arthur's Mother Arthur goes in secret to the castle of the white-haired queen (504–944)	83
Preparing for Battle Guiromelant arrives for his combat with Gawain (945–1440)	86

CONTENTS　　　　　　　　　　　　　　　　　　　　　　vii

Gawain's Battle with Guiromelant　　　　　　　　　　　　　　　90
　　Gawain and Guiromelant engage in a furious duel (1441–1739)

Gawain's Anger　　　　　　　　　　　　　　　　　　　　　　93
　　Clarissant intervenes; she marries Guiromelant without Gawain's knowledge
　　(1740–1955)

The Maiden of the Ivory Horn　　　　　　　　　　　　　　　　94
　　Gawain recovers a stolen horn; he rescues twenty maidens from captivity (1956–3630)

The Broken Sword　　　　　　　　　　　　　　　　　　　　107
　　Gawain sees the grail and the lance; he tries to mend a broken sword (3631–3969)

Gawain's Adventure at Montesclaire　　　　　　　　　　　　　110
　　Gawain frees the damsel of Montesclaire; he takes the Sword of the Strange
　　Belt (3970–4828)

Gawain is Accused Again　　　　　　　　　　　　　　　　　116
　　Dinadaret accuses Gawain of having killed his father (4829–4951)

A Double Duel　　　　　　　　　　　　　　　　　　　　　117
　　Gawain is forced to fight two enemies at once (4952–5508)

The Siege of Branlant　　　　　　　　　　　　　　　　　　121
　　King Arthur lays siege to Brun's city of Branlant; Gawain is wounded in
　　a raid (5509–6151)

The Portrait of Gawain　　　　　　　　　　　　　　　　　　126
　　A maiden identifies Gawain by his portrait; it leads to seduction and killing
　　(6152–6670)

Eliavret the Enchanter　　　　　　　　　　　　　　　　　　131
　　An enchanter lies with Arthur's niece and fathers a son (6671–6784)

Carados is Knighted　　　　　　　　　　　　　　　　　　　132
　　The son, Carados, comes to Arthur's court and is trained in arms and
　　knighted (6785–7136)

The Beheading Game　　　　　　　　　　　　　　　　　　135
　　An unknown knight offers to exchange beheading blows; Carados accepts
　　the challenge (7137–7425)

Carados Exposes his Mother　　　　　　　　　　　　　　　　137
　　Carados reveals the truth about his conception; his mother Ysave is
　　imprisoned (7426–7551)

Carados Rescues Guinier　　　　　　　　　　　　　　　　　138
　　Carados rescues a maiden from a rejected suitor (7552–8078)

The Great Tournament　　　　　　　　　　　　　　　　　　142
　　Carados excels in a mighty tournament (8079–9612)

The Enchanted Serpent　　　　　　　　　　　　　　　　　　154
　　The enchanter Eliavret fixes a serpent to Carados's arm; Guinier has to
　　save him (9613–11948)

The Healing of Guinier's Breast Guinier's breast, wounded in saving Carados, is healed with a golden shield-boss (11949–12270)	173
The Drinking Horn An ivory horn arrives at court; it turns water into wine, but exposes infidelity (12271–12506)	175
The Mission to Rescue Girflet Arthur declares that Girflet must be rescued from imprisonment in the Proud Castle (12507–12920)	177
Kay, the Dwarf and the Peacock Kay is humiliated with a roasted bird (12921–13283)	180
Bran de Lis and Gawain's Child Gawain does battle with Bran de Lis; his own son intervenes (13284–15181)	183
The Jousts at the Proud Castle Lucan, Bran and Kay challenge the castle's champions (15182–15778)	198
The Rich Soldier Gawain defeats the castle's lord, but pretends to have been beaten; Girflet is rescued (15779–16614)	202
The Search for Gawain's Son Gawain's son is kidnapped (16615–16836)	209
The Death of the Unknown Knight A knight is mysteriously killed at the queen's pavilion; Gawain takes up his mission (16837–17114)	211
The Black Hand Gawain takes refuge in a chapel and sees a terrifying black hand (17115–17226)	214
The Grail and the Lance Again The grail and bleeding lance appear again to Gawain; he learns it is the lance of Longinus (17227–17880)	215
The Challenge at the Ford Gawain is challenged to combat at a ford; he discovers that the youth is his son (17881–18374)	220
The Swan-Boat Arthur sees a boat arrive, pulled by a swan; on board is a slain knight, awaiting vengeance (18375–18688)	224
Guerrehés and the Little Knight Gawain's brother Guerrehés is humbled by a little knight (18689–19154)	227
Guerrehés Takes Revenge Guerrehés avenges the knight on the swan-boat (19155–19606)	231

CONTENTS

THE SECOND CONTINUATION

Line numbers refer to *The Continuations of the Old French Perceval of Chrétien de Troyes, Volume IV*, ed. William Roach (Philadelphia, 1971)

The author returns us to Perceval as he leaves his hermit uncle (19607–19653) — 237

The Lord of the Horn — 237
Perceval fights the Lord of the Horn (19654–20006)

The Castle of the Magic Chessboard — 240
A damsel tries to drown Perceval; a magic chessboard defeats him; a maiden lends him her dog to hunt a white stag (20007–20303)

The Knight of the Tomb — 243
Perceval kills the white stag, but the dog and the white stag are stolen; he fights with a knight from a tomb (20304–20772)

The Murdered Boy — 246
Perceval avenges a murdered boy; his killer refuses to ask for mercy (20773–20908)

The Search for the Stolen Dog — 247
Perceval learns why the stag's head and the dog were stolen; he does battle with a lion and defeats Abrioris (20909–21578)

The Dead Knight Odinial — 253
Perceval finds a slain knight, and has to tell the knight's sweetheart of his death (21579–21658)

Perceval and the Giant — 253
Perceval rescues a maiden from a murderous giant (21659–21955)

The Amorous Ford — 256
Perceval defeats the defender of the Amorous Ford (21956–22224)

The Fair Unknown — 258
Perceval meets Sir Gawain's son, 'the Fair Unknown' (22225–22551)

Perceval Returns to Blancheflor — 260
Perceval finds himself back at Beaurepaire; he spends the night with Blancheflor (22552–23120)

The Handsome Knight and the Ugly Damsel — 265
Perceval meets 'the Fair Bad Knight'; he sends him to Arthur's court to tell of his love for an ugly damsel (23121–23532)

Perceval Returns to his Sister — 268
Perceval finds himself at his mother's house; he reveals his identity to his sister; they go together to visit his hermit uncle (23533–24221)

The Castle of the Maidens — 274
Striking a brass table earns Perceval lodging at a castle inhabited only by maidens (24222–24731)

Recovering the Dog and the Stag's Head — 278
Perceval wins back the stag's head and the maiden's dog; the knight of the tomb is explained (24732–25432)

Crossing the Bridge of Glass — 283
Perceval sees a strange light in the forest; a maiden tells him that it comes from the grail; she lends him a mule and a ring; he has to cross a bridge of glass (25433–26193)

The Unfinished Bridge — 289
Briol urges Perceval to prove himself at a tournament at the Proud Castle; to reach it Perceval must cross an unfinished bridge (26194–26824)

The Tournament at the Proud Castle — 294
Perceval twice fights in the tournament against King Arthur's knights; both times he goes unrecognised (26825–27373)

Trapped in the Tomb — 298
Perceval is tricked into being trapped in a tomb; he returns the maiden's mule and ring (27374–27600)

The Magic Chessboard — 300
Perceval delivers the dog and the stag's head; the maiden tells him the story of Morgan the Fay and the magic chessboard (27601–28238)

The Madness of Mount Dolorous — 305
Perceval rescues a knight hung up in a tree by Sir Kay; he hears about the pillar on Mount Dolorous (28239–28408)

Revenge upon Sir Kay — 306
The rescued knight, Bagomedés, goes to Arthur's court seeking revenge upon Sir Kay; the knights of the court set out in search of Perceval (28409–29208)

The Little Knight's Shield — 312
Sir Gawain meets a tiny knight, the guardian of a shield that tests the prowess of a knight and the true love of his sweetheart (29209–29953)

The Tournament in the Blanche Lande — 317
At the tournament only Gawain can carry the shield (29954–30507)

Sir Gawain and the Pensive Knight — 321
Gawain recovers a maiden abducted from her beloved, the Pensive Knight (30508–31040)

The War against King Carras — 325
Gawain tells his son, 'the Fair Unknown', of his search for the Fisher King; his son tells him of King Carras's aggression against Arthur; Gawain returns to resolve the conflict (31041–31420)

The Pillar on Mount Dolorous — 328
A child in a tree directs Perceval to Mount Dolorous; he tethers his horse to Merlin's pillar (31421–32027)

Perceval Nears the Grail Castle . . . 333
Perceval comes to the tree of candles and the chapel of the Black Hand; he is directed to the Fisher King's castle (32028–32264)

Perceval and the Fisher King . . . 335
Perceval returns to the Grail Castle, and asks the Fisher King the meaning of his adventures and the truth about the grail and the lance; but he repairs the broken sword imperfectly (32265–32594)

GERBERT'S CONTINUATION

Line numbers refer to *Gerbert de Montreuil: La Continuation de Perceval, Volumes I–III*, ed. Mary Williams and Marguerite Oswald (Paris, 1922, 1925, 1975)

Perceval is not yet worthy to know all the secrets of the grail; a voice tells him to seek his mother's house (1–102) . . . 339

Perceval Breaks his Sword . . . 340
Perceval hears rejoicing inside a ring of wall; he breaks his sword on the gate; he is given a healing letter (103–286)

The Forge on the Lake . . . 341
Perceval finds he has restored the land; he battles past serpents to the smith Trebuchet, who repairs his broken sword (287–898)

The Healing Letter . . . 346
Perceval uses the healing letter to save Agravain and Sagremor, driven mad on Mount Dolorous (899–1158)

The Perilous Seat . . . 348
Perceval returns to Arthur's court and sits in the Perilous Seat (1159–1612)

The Faithless Lover . . . 352
Perceval's cousin is about to be jilted by the faithless knight Faradien, who plans to marry another damsel; Perceval forces him to keep his promise (1613–2482)

A Demon in the Shape of a Girl . . . 358
Perceval wards off a demon by making the sign of the cross (2483–2586)

The Meaning of the Broken Sword . . . 359
Perceval and his sister visit his hermit uncle, who explains the significance of a sword's two edges (2587–2861)

Perceval Learns his Mother's Name . . . 361
Perceval repels Mordred's attack on his sister; he returns to the Castle of the Maidens, where he learns his mother's name and her connection with the grail (2862–3247)

A Stranger Challenges Arthur's Knights . . . 365
Faradien and Mordred arrive at court to submit to Arthur; the king's knights are challenged to combat by a stranger; he is recognised as Tristran (3248–3692)

CONTENTS

Tristran's Disguise — 368
Tristran goes to King Marc's court to see Yseut, disguised as a minstrel; she recognises him by the tune he plays (3693–4110)

Beaten by Minstrels — 372
Tristran and his companions shame their opponents by turning the tide of the tournament while disguised as minstrels; Perceval arrives and defeats them in turn (4111–4726)

Tristran Forgiven — 377
Gawain makes peace between Tristran and King Marc (4727–4868)

Gorneman and the Demon Knights — 378
Perceval defends Gorneman, who had knighted him, against forty demon knights (4869–5496)

The Healing Balm — 383
A hag restores the knights to life with a potion; Perceval wins it from her and heals Gorneman and his sons (5497–6154)

Perceval Marries Blancheflor — 388
Perceval returns to Beaurepaire and keeps his promise to marry Blancheflor (6155–7020)

Dragonel the Cruel — 395
Perceval prevents a knight forcing a girl to marry him against her will (7021–7526)

The Knight of the Cart — 399
Perceval saves a knight who has been robbed, stripped and abused (7527–8291)

The Shield with the Red Cross — 405
Perceval sees two hermits beating and worshipping a cross, and a beast devoured by her offspring; he is given a white shield with a red cross (8292–8905)

The Knight of the Dragon — 410
With the aid of the red cross shield Perceval defeats the Knight of the Dragon and rescues the Maiden of the Circle of Gold (8906–10192)

Mordrain — 420
At an abbey Perceval sees King Mordrain, his wounds still fresh after three hundred years; he hears the story of Mordrain, Crudel and Joseph of Arimathea (10193–10613)

The Ivory Chest — 423
Perceval opens a chest to reveal himself the killer of the Red Knight long before; he defends himself against the Red Knight's sons; a minstrel saves his life; he releases the captive Gawain (10614–12380)

The Hidden Knife — 437
A damsel is about to murder Gawain, but then falls in love with him; she saves him from death at her father's hands, and then saves her father from Gawain (12381–14078)

CONTENTS xiii

The Worm in the Stone 450
    A hermit gives Perceval instruction; Perceval frees a demon worm from a block of marble (14079–14571)

Lugarel the Jealous 454
    Perceval defeats a murderous knight unable to forgive his sweetheart's killer (14572–14998)

The Maiden in the Spring 457
    Perceval rescues a girl who has been forced to stand naked in a pool; but she then tries to betray him (14999–15268)

The Brigands' Girl 459
    A second girl betrays Perceval, luring him into an ambush; he destroys a band of brigands (15269–15738)

The Hermit's Injunction 463
    A hermit tells Perceval that a knight's purpose is to defend Holy Church; he engages in violent combat with the Knight of the Ill-cut Coat, who is honoured to be defeated by him (15739–16049)

The Black Giant 466
    Using his lance like a javelin, Perceval defeats a black giant seeking vengeance for his brother's death; he is given fine new arms (16050–16556)

The Search for Perceval 470
    Arthur's knights set out to find Perceval; Kay's discourtesy costs him dear again (16557–16839)

The Repair of the Broken Sword 473
    Perceval returns to the Fisher King and perfectly repairs the broken sword (16840–17086)

THE THIRD CONTINUATION

    Line numbers refer to *The Continuations of the Old French Perceval of Chrétien de Troyes, Volume V*, ed. William Roach (Philadelphia, 1983)

Perceval, as repairer of the broken sword, must take revenge upon Partinal, the murderer of King Goondesert, and so heal the Fisher King (32595–33183) 477

Perceval and Sagremor 481
    Perceval meets Sagremor, whose horse has been stolen; together they battle the knights who stole it, and rescue an abducted maiden (33184–33757)

Sagremor and the Robber Knight 486
    Sagremor pursues the thief and wins back his horse (33758–34080)

Sagremor at the Castle of the Maidens 488
    Sagremor raises the siege of the Castle of the Maidens (34081–34725)

Sagremor Rescues a Damsel 493
    Sagremor saves a damsel from rape, but is wounded (34726–35050)

Gawain's Unfinished Mission   495
    The sister of Silimac, the knight killed at the queen's pavilion, reminds Gawain of his promise to complete her brother's mission (35051–35299)

Gawain Rescues Dodinel   498
    Gawain saves a maiden from a pyre, and frees Dodinel from prison, refusing to believe him guilty of murder (35300–35745)

King Margon   501
    Gawain defends Silimac's sister against King Margon's siege; she charges Gawain to take revenge upon Kay for her brother's death; Margon, known as the King of One Hundred Knights, saves his sister (35746–36363)

Gawain's Battle with Kay   506
    Gawain is attacked as the killer of Silimac; Silimac's sister explains that Kay, not Gawain, was to blame; at Arthur's court Gawain, disguised, does battle with Kay (36364–36916)

Gawain and Agravain   511
    Gawain aids his brother Agravain against five knights (36917–37140)

The Chapel of the Black Hand   513
    Perceval battles with the black hand; he is shown Queen Brangemore's graveyard (37141–37862)

The Devil Horse and the Demon Maiden   518
    A black horse tries to drown Perceval; a demon appears to him as Blancheflor (37863–38409)

A Toll is Demanded   522
    A knight demands that Perceval pay a toll or accept imprisonment; Perceval defeats him and sends him to Arthur (38410–38545)

Perceval and Dodinel   523
    Perceval saves Dodinel's sweetheart from her abductor; he hears that Blancheflor is under attack (38546–38922)

Perceval Returns to Beaurepaire   526
    Perceval has his horse re-shod and his sword repaired by the smith Trebuchet's son; he defeats Blancheflor's attacker Aridés; Blancheflor pleads with him to stay (38923–39359)

Perceval's Prisoners Submit to Arthur   530
    The knights defeated in Perceval's latest adventures surrender at Arthur's court (39360–39576)

The Coward Knight   531
    Perceval meets a handsome knight who is terrified of combat; but as Perceval rides to the rescue of two maidens, the cowardly knight is transformed (39577–39969)

The Vow to Search for Perceval   534
    Arthur is downcast when Perceval fails to arrive at Pentecost; the knights vow to go in search of him (39970–40182)

Boort Abandons his Brother Boort sees his brother Lionel in dire straits, but abandons him to go to the rescue of a maiden; it is Gawain instead who saves Lionel (40183–40513)	536
Boort's Combat with Lionel A demon disguised as a hermit tries to make Boort despair; Lionel attacks Boort in a rage and kills Calogrenant when he intervenes; a cloud descends to stop the battle (40514–40974)	538
The Fair Bold Knight Joining Perceval in a tournament, the Coward Knight displays such courage that he earns a new name (40975–41317)	542
The Healing Grail Perceval finds Ector in a wretched state; they fight and almost kill each other, but are healed by the holy grail (41318–41606)	545
Revenge for the Fisher King Perceval takes revenge upon Partinal as he had promised the Fisher King (41607–41860)	547
The Healing of the Fisher King The Fisher King is healed at the sight of Partinal's head; the grail serves food in abundance; the Fisher King bequeaths his kingdom to Perceval (41861–42101)	549
Perceval Returns to Arthur Perceval jousts against six knights with arms of every colour; he returns to Arthur's court and recounts his adventures; news arrives of the Fisher King's death (42102–42468)	551
The Grail and the Lance Depart Perceval is crowned; he reigns and retires from the world and dies, and the grail goes with him; Manessier dedicates his work to Jeanne, countess of Flanders (42469–42668)	554
Appendix 1: The Elucidation Prologue	557
Appendix 2: Bliocadran	562
Appendix 3: Independent conclusion to the Second Continuation in the Bern manuscript (Burgerbibliothek 113)	569
Glossary	571
Index	573

Introduction

Chrétien de Troyes 'began the story of Perceval till death overtook him and prevented him completing it': so we are told by Gerbert.[1] Unfinished at his death – suspended almost in mid-sentence – Chrétien's last Arthurian romance, *Perceval: the Story of the Grail*, was evidently seen as too good and too intriguing to leave; not only did its tantalising theme inspire quite separate works, but his own incomplete poem was taken up, expanded and finally brought to a conclusion in four continuations.

This, *The Complete Story of the Grail*, is a translation of Chrétien's romance and all four of those continuations. Written throughout in verse, in rhyming couplets of eight-syllable lines, they have survived in fifteen manuscripts: some of these contain only Chrétien's poem; others contain Chrétien and one, two or three continuations; only two contain all four; and the First Continuation exists in three redactions which, although telling essentially the same stories in the same order, are of vastly differing lengths: the long redaction – translated here – is more than twice as long as the short. This apparently erratic copying of *The Story of the Grail* might suggest that it was held in less esteem than other Arthurian works. And indeed, the scholarly attention given to the *Perceval* Continuations has been considerably less than that devoted to the great Arthurian prose cycle, the *Lancelot-Grail*. There seems to have been a worry and preoccupation with assessing how far the Continuations consistently develop the strands introduced by Chrétien; and because in many respects they don't – they go their own sweet ways in massive digressions, introducing narratives that have nothing whatever to do with the Grail (or with Perceval, who barely features in the First Continuation) – they seem to have been deemed of little serious consequence, a relatively minor body of work, the more so since the last two Continuations in particular borrow numerous episodes from other existing romances.

This is very strange. To object to the lack of 'continuity' in the Continuations, or to their tendency to borrow, is to object to much of the development of Arthurian romance and indeed to most artistic endeavour in the Middle Ages.

Even more glaringly, it is to object to our own inclinations in our own time. How we love soap operas, with their endless interlacing of story-lines and introduction of new strands and new people! How we love long-running television series, and the box sets of DVDs that preserve them in collections we can cherish like the finest Arthurian manuscripts! How we love movie sequels that turn into rambling franchises! And do we expect continuity? Up to a point, perhaps; but if there is inconsistency in character, relationship or narrative detail between one *Pirates of the Caribbean* movie and another, are we really that concerned? Do we even remember? We may well be watching them at an interval of months or years. And can we guarantee that we will see or hear every episode of a long-running television or radio series, which we may likewise be watching

---

[1] Below, p. 394.

or hearing with days or weeks in between? Do we not rather enjoy and value each episode for itself?

This surely applies also to the reception of these romances. Phrase after phrase suggests that they were predominantly heard, read aloud, rather than read in private silence – a notably vivid image is given in the First Continuation when the author suggests that 'we should all say a *Pater Noster* for the deceased, and before I continue the story you will call for the wine'.[2] In such circumstances, an episode heard on a particular day (some previously having even been missed), while perhaps appreciated more in the context of a whole, essentially stood or fell on its own merits.

And so it does now. *The Story of the Grail* is a rich compendium of narratives which, as much as any other Arthurian cycle, was setting out to develop, following the example of Geoffrey of Monmouth's inspirational *History of the Kings of Britain*,[3] a whole past world; and though the theme which supposedly holds it all together is the Grail, it would be rash to expect a single-minded commitment to it. Rather, each day's episode in this beguiling world should be enjoyed and understood for its own distinct quality, content and resonance.

Chrétien's Intention

And resonate these stories did – and do. We cannot of course be sure how Chrétien intended to develop and conclude his last poem, but his intention in beginning it is resonantly clear. He was writing about what it is to be a knight – or, in broader terms, what it is to be a human being. With brilliant boldness, he creates for us in Perceval an emblematic Everyman. He introduces us at the outset to a boy who knows nothing of the world but what his mother has taught him – in piecemeal fashion, easily misunderstood; and she has brought him up in cushioned isolation, trying to protect him from all knowledge of life's dangers. She has tried to keep him in particular from the world of knights; so that when he first encounters a knight he mistakes him for an angel and then for God, about which he knows just as little. But dazzled by the shining glamour of this grown-up world, the youth finds it – to his mother's horror – irresistible, and his mother is now an irrelevance, rejected and abandoned. Everymother's pain as this Everychild leaves home without a second backward glance is a scene that haunts the reader, and comes back to haunt the boy.

Then, as he ventures into the complicated outside world, everything he sees is new and a thing of wonder, so that, on first setting childlike eyes upon a castle, he naïvely 'saw the castle's towers being born – for in his eyes they were being born, emerging from the rock'.[4] And his naïve misunderstanding of his mother's advice leads – as in life it so often can – to comic and embarrassing error, especially in his first encounter with a girl; and his blundering, childlike single-mindedness to have the accoutrements that he wants makes him fearless: he will challenge and kill the Red Knight, of whom Arthur's court are all in awe, without a second thought. Everyyouth is in a hurry.

But he's discovered an innate talent, and when the noble Gorneman gives him instruction in horsemanship and the use of weapons, the boy takes to it like a fish to

---

[2] p. 214.
[3] Geoffrey's *Historia Regum Britannie* (c. 1135) created a history of Britain spanning nearly two thousand years, and was hugely influential in introducing the first major narratives of King Arthur.
[4] p. 13.

water. He is duly knighted, taking on a role for which he was evidently born, and promptly meets his first great challenge and succeeds in it quite brilliantly, rescuing the maiden Blancheflor from the terrible siege of Beaurepaire and restoring joy to her people. He is growing up quickly, and after this first great chivalrous deed and his first awakening to love, his growing maturity is reflected in the change in his style of speech: gone is the comic naivety of his responses, exploited with aplomb by Chrétien; now he starts to talk in adult fashion, and with an adult understanding of responsibility for past actions, as he addresses the monks and nuns on his departure from Beaurepaire.

But how far can Everyknight go before he realises there's more to life? Now he encounters things with which he is wholly unequipped to cope – things, that is, beyond the worldly and the everyday. He sees a man fishing from a boat on a river – in a profound and haunting image he's sitting dead still in midstream, dropping a line and hook beneath the visible surface; and this man takes one look at the young knight and says:

'You've need of lodging and more beside, I'd say.'[5]

And that night he does indeed take lodging in the hall of the fisherman, who proves to be a crippled king, and he does indeed see more beside. It's no ordinary hall: it 'was square, being as long as it was wide. In the middle of the hall ... was a great fire of seasoned logs, blazing brightly... Four hundred men could have sat around that fire and all would have had a good place... And in that hall was the brightest light that could ever be created by candles.'[6] It is, then, huge, and a symmetrical centre of warmth and light. And what he sees in it is extraordinary: in the awesome glow of blazing candles appears a procession of mysterious objects including a grail – a serving dish, golden and bejewelled, at the appearance of which 'so radiant a light appeared in the hall that the candles lost their brightness like the stars at the rising of the moon or sun'[7] – and a lance that, wondrously, sheds blood from its head in a never-ending flow.

And what is Everyknight's response to these mysteries? He's intrigued, certainly; but whereas, in his childhood, he couldn't stop asking questions of the knight he encountered in the forest ('He asks the name and use of everything he sees'),[8] he has now, as part of his training as a grown-up knight, been conditioned not to enquire too far: 'he remembered the warning of the one who'd knighted him, who'd taught him to beware of talking too much; he was afraid it might be frowned upon, so he didn't ask at all'.[9] Heeding the most banal – albeit well-meant – advice of a grown-up, courtly knight, the youth asks no questions whatever. He, like so many, is quite content not to enquire into wonders.

This surely has potent, timeless resonance. And it would have had a very specific one for Chrétien's own audience. The marvellously lit objects that process past the youth would have carried radiant significance. Brought into such a singular atmosphere, it is inconceivable that a lance shedding blood from its tip would not instantly have prompted thoughts of the most sensational of holy relics, famously, melodramatically and dubiously discovered at Antioch during the First Crusade: the Holy Lance that pierced Christ's side on the cross. Chrétien doesn't even hint at this connection because he doesn't need to: he is writing for an audience obsessed with relics – streams of them were returning to Northern Europe from the Holy Land, many of them ludicrous and their provenance

[5] p. 27.
[6] pp. 27–8.
[7] p. 29.
[8] p. 3.
[9] p. 28.

lightly questioned – and listeners' imaginations would have been running riot at the serving dish and the trencher that follow the lance, the whole procession suffused with light. It's no surprise to discover in due course that the dish, the grail, carries something sacred: a host – communion bread. Nor is it at all surprising that another poet, Robert de Boron, was inspired to write a 'prequel' to Chrétien's poem, *Joseph of Arimathea (Le Roman de l'Estoire dou Graal)*, in which he created a provenance for the mysterious dish, identifying the grail as the vessel used by Christ at the Last Supper and by Joseph of Arimathea to gather Christ's blood at the crucifixion.[10]

If Chrétien was unspecific about the identity of the lance and the grail, he was anything but equivocal about the consequence of the young knight's failure to ask. It's calamitous. No sooner has he left the Fisher King's castle than he meets a girl – a cousin, it transpires – who tells him that it's 'a disaster that you failed to ask all this! You would have healed the good crippled king – he would have regained the use of his limbs and the rule of his land – and you would have profited greatly! But now, I tell you, many ills will beset both you and others.'[11] These ills are specified later by the ugly damsel who appears at Arthur's court and tells the young knight: 'Do you know what will happen, now that the king won't be healed and rule his land? Ladies will lose their husbands, lands will be laid waste, maidens will be left in distress and orphaned, and many knights will die: all these woes will strike because of you.'[12] By failing to ask questions, by failing to investigate wonders, Everyyouth creates a wasteland.

And Chrétien's audience would not have missed the implication of the other mishap that befalls the young knight after asking nothing: he breaks his sword with the very first blow he strikes. The significance of the broken sword is to be expanded upon later, in Gerbert's Continuation; but explication is barely necessary, when a sword is so central to a knight's function.

And what *is* a knight's function? The young knight – Perceval – realises how much he's missed the point about his function when, five years later, plodding forlornly across a wilderness, he meets his hermit uncle. For five years he's been 'seeking deeds of chivalry: he went in search of strange, daunting, gruelling adventures, and encountered so many that he tested himself well. In five years he sent sixty fine knights as prisoners to King Arthur's court.' But in all that time he's been 'without a thought for God'.[13] He tells his hermit uncle:

'I was once at the house of the Fisher King and saw the lance with the head that assuredly bleeds, but asked nothing about the drop of blood I saw hang from the tip of that shining head. And truly, I've done nothing since to make amends. Nor do I know who was served from the grail I saw. Since then I've been in such a dismal state I wish I were dead! I've forgotten God because of it! Never since have I asked Him for mercy – and I don't think I've done anything to earn it!'[14]

This episode comes strikingly after Sir Gawain suspends his chivalrous gallivanting – embroiling himself in judicial combats and philandering himself into dire scrapes – to go and seek the Bleeding Lance. Chrétien, without crudely saying so, is making plain that there is much more to knighthood than the worldly and the martial. That this should be a crucial theme of his last romance is not surprising. He was writing it, his prologue

---

[10] See Robert de Boron, *Merlin and the Grail*, trans. Bryant (Cambridge, 2003).
[11] Below, p. 32.
[12] p. 41.
[13] p. 54.
[14] p. 55.

tells us, for Count Philip of Flanders, and although the precise date of composition is uncertain, it must have been before Philip's departure on the Third Crusade, for during it he died at Acre in 1191. That a knight should be thinking about God would have been at the forefront of Chrétien's crusading patron's mind – as would holy relics, under serious threat in the Holy Land, where the True Cross itself was lost to Saladin in 1187 at the catastrophic battle of Hattin. To this crusading theme we shall return.

But to it Chrétien does *not* return. Instead he turns for the rest of his unfinished romance to the adventures of Sir Gawain. And although he has supposedly set out to seek the Bleeding Lance, Gawain's adventures have nothing to do with the grail and its attendant mysteries. But they do reflect on knighthood. In contrast to the young knight Perceval, at the start of his career, we are shown an accomplished, experienced, mightily admired knight in Gawain. And to what do his adventures and his attitudes lead him, if not into endless difficulty?

Firstly, Gawain's promise to fight a judicial combat to defend himself against a charge of treachery prevents him taking part in a tournament for fear of being injured (and thus unable to honour his promise); this leads to a volley of embarrassing mockery: 'He must be a pacifist!'… 'He's a tradesman!'… 'He's a money changer!'… 'He may look like a knight but he's not: he's disguised himself as one to dodge duties and tolls!' Gawain resists the provocation – until tempted by a pretty face who begs him to fight as her knight next day; he duly wins the tournament, but has been willing, for a pretty girl, to risk much greater dishonour than mockery.[15]

In the next episode, after his horse – with evident symbolism – has lost a shoe and begun to hobble, he rapidly responds to another pretty face, the sister of the lord of Escavalon. Within moments of being left without a chaperone 'they talked of love'; and it is tempting to read as sardonic Chrétien's following comment: 'had they talked of anything else, what a waste of time it would have been!' In no time this leads him into even greater trouble: he ends up besieged in a tower by a mob.[16]

How quickly, too, in his next adventure, he spurs his horse and goes to flirt with the 'Haughty Maiden', whose endlessly scornful words deter him not in the least. Despite repeated warnings, he sets off with her on a journey that leads to him losing his horse and having to ride a humiliatingly wretched nag – provoking the Haughty Maiden's delighted derision; and she later lies to him in the hope of drowning him in the Perilous Ford. And why has she become so haughty, scornful, cold and malicious? It's because of her treatment at the hands of another accomplished, experienced knight, Guiromelant, who had killed the one she truly loved so that he could woo her himself, and '"ever since Death robbed me of my first love,"' she says, '"I've been mad and spoken haughtily and acted wickedly and crazily, not caring who I crossed – [every knight who sought my company] I deliberately tormented, hoping to find one whose temper was such that I could drive him wild with rage so he'd cut me to pieces!"'[17]

At every turn the actions and attitudes of accomplished knights lead to trouble and pointless strife. At every turn it's possible to see or to sense doubt and irony in Chrétien's view of the courtly knight and of knightly endeavours.[18]

---

[15] pp. 44–9.
[16] pp. 49–54.
[17] p. 76.
[18] Similarly, thinking back to Perceval's childlike perceptions at the beginning, and to his misunderstanding of what the shining, ironclad figures in the forest may be, Matilda Bruckner observes that 'we can laugh at Perceval's naïveté because we know that knights are neither devils

But the question is: did his continuators see and sense it? The answer is: not necessarily. Each continuator had his own response to the unfinished poem, and his own purpose in carrying it on.

The First Continuation: the Unimportance of the Holy Grail

The anonymous author[19] of the First Continuation, unlike Chrétien, shows no misgivings whatever about conventional chivalry. Directly continuing the unfinished last episode of Chrétien's romance, the first continuator has Gawain almost instantly acclaimed as 'the finest knight who ever rode horse or bore lance and shield… He's free and clear of all baseness – he hasn't the slightest blemish… He's the model of all good qualities.'[20] There is no apparent irony in this lack of reservation. The eulogies for Gawain come thick and fast. We are well aware, in Chrétien, that his impending combat with Guiromelant has been sparked by past knightly havoc, Gawain having previously killed Guiromelant's cousin and Gawain's father having killed Guiromelant's; but as his combat with Guiromelant approaches, the first continuator unreservedly assures us that 'Gawain's custom was that, if he knew he was in the wrong, he would admit it even if he was being challenged by the feeblest of men, which only enhanced his reputation as one who deplored wrongdoing: he was humble and kind towards the worthy; but he was full of fierce courage when confronting the wicked, the oppressive, the proud.'[21] He leaves us in no doubt, in fact, that Gawain is nothing short of flawless: 'Gawain more than anyone despised wickedness and sin and crime and vice, and avarice and spite; he more than anyone was devoted to courtesy and placed his faith in God.'[22]

Chrétien, bringing young Perceval to confront Clamadeus at the siege of Beaurepaire, says 'I could tell you all about [the battle] if I wanted to go down that road, but I'm not going to spend my energies on that – one word's as good as twenty!'[23] How different this is from the first continuator, who revels in chivalrous combat, lavishing many lines in recounting the duel between Gawain and Guiromelant in vivid detail. The combat later fought between Carados and Alardin is so admirable in the continuator's eyes, so engrossing, that it borders on fun: 'no one,' he assures us, 'who'd seen that fight would have wanted to leave!'[24] And fun is the predominant tone of the mighty tournament that follows this; as King Cadoalan and King Ris and their forces batter and hew (despite the fact that they deal 'cleaving blows that left some crippled and others lacking arms'[25]), the overall sense is of a boisterous romp:

> you'd have seen the earth shake, lances smashed, shields pierced, great blows struck with whetted blades, men crashing down and leaping up, the strong battering the weak, knights laid out on the ground and empty horses running wild: it must be said, it wasn't the prettiest sight! Anyone who

---

nor angels, but that comic polarisation introduces more searching questions about what knights really are and do'. Bruckner, *Chrétien Continued* (Oxford, 2009), p. 124.

[19] Or authors: there may well have been more than one; there were certainly a number of redactors influencing its content. But for convenience I shall refer to 'the first continuator'.
[20] Below, pp. 79–80.
[21] p. 90.
[22] p. 91.
[23] p. 24.
[24] p. 140.
[25] p. 145.

couldn't defend himself was soon forced to dismount – and not with any decorum! Those who weren't up to it really came a cropper, and I can assure you the cowardly didn't dare go near!²⁶

In his brilliant description of a twelfth-century mêlée, it is clear that the first continuator has bought fully into the values and customs of the tournament, qualmlessly observing that 'family loyalty and friendship don't stop knights dealing blows!'²⁷

If the author of the First Continuation does not pick up the questioning tone of Chrétien's poem, what *does* he pick up? He doesn't even pick up the first protagonist: the Welsh boy-turned-knight, Perceval, and his failure to ask all-important questions, are not of the slightest consequence. Perceval, in fact, appears in the First Continuation only once, and briefly, as a participant in a tournament. Instead, the continuator devotes two huge sections of his work to virtually independent stories – the splendid tale of Carados, his mother and the enchanter Eliavret, and the tale of Gawain's brother Guerrehés and his adventure with the Little Knight. These have nothing whatever to do with the grail. 'Nevertheless,' writes William Roach in the introduction to his edition, 'every manuscript which contains the First Continuation places it immediately after Chrétien's *Perceval*. It seems certain, therefore, that to the men who rewrote and copied the First Continuation, it was a Grail poem.'²⁸ With all respect to the outstanding editor of the Continuations, this is missing the point. To the author and redactor-copyists of the First Continuation, the grail was quite clearly just another adventure – albeit a particularly good one ('God save me, sirs,' the first continuator says as Gawain's visit to the grail castle draws near, 'there's been a long digression in the story; but now you'll hear what you've long been waiting for.'). ²⁹ In our present times, when the Holy Grail has become a cherished journalistic cliché³⁰ and, in the bizarre belief that it really exists, the object of actual quests by fantasists, we may assume that it must be at the heart of any romance with 'grail' in the title; but the apparently 'independent', grail-free Carados and Guerrehés stories are just as entitled as the holy vessel to inclusion in the work – for the simple reason that they involve Arthur's court. Carados is not only a member of Arthur's court but related to Arthur, his mother being Arthur's niece Ysave. Guerrehés likewise is a member of the court and Arthur's own nephew.

Arthur, exemplary king, and his court of exemplary knights are the heart and focus of the work, not the grail. The author of the First Continuation is working with narratives, regardless of any grail connection, that illuminate knighthood – or, more broadly, worthy human behaviour, as in the marvellous story of Carados, which centres on the selfless love of Guinier who risks herself for the knight horribly stricken by the enchanter. Just as Chrétien had the hermit uncle give Perceval 'spiritual' guidance, so the first continuator impresses chivalrous qualities upon his audience. When Arthur knights Carados,

> the good King Arthur told Carados to have prowess as his watchword; sense and moderation as his motto; if he did so it would be much to his advantage,

---

[26] p. 146.
[27] p. 152.
[28] *The Continuations of the Old French* Perceval *of Chrétien de Troyes*, Vol. I, ed. W. Roach (Philadelphia, 1949), p. xiii.
[29] Below, p. 214.
[30] See Appendix 4 of Richard Barber's *The Holy Grail – Imagination and Belief* (London, 2004), detailing the astonishing number of uses of the term 'Holy Grail' in major newspapers between 1978 and 2002.

for excess and presumption were incompatible with honour and valour, but if he were courteous and civilised he would win honour and praise indeed and all, of every degree, would love him.[31]

The stories are a constant illustration of what it means to be 'courteous and civilised', of how to win 'honour and praise'. The lengthy story of Gawain and the Rich Soldier of the Proud Castle, apart from being richly entertaining, is most striking as a moral tale of courtesy and sympathy towards a defeated foe; Gawain is willing to feign defeat out of pity for his adversary's plight, and the author concludes: 'I'm going to leave them now; but I must say this: Gawain should be admired and loved and honoured indeed, for vanquishing the knight in combat and then treating him with such great courtesy.'[32] Time and again the first continuator shows and tells us what is expected of knights, in terms of courage and mercy – and the importance, quite simply, of *doing*. In the chivalric world vision, *deeds* are at the centre of life: 'Carados, endowed as he was with all fine qualities, said he had no need of rest: he wanted to be involved in deeds of arms – and rightly so: no knight wishing to earn praise can afford to do otherwise; no knight wins a reputation by being idle.'[33]

Deeds and correct behaviour are especially important, these stories show, in relation to women. In the First Continuation the first maiden to be rescued by Gawain, the Maiden of the Ivory Horn, establishes women as creatures to be protected and revered: when Gawain recovers her horn, stolen by the 'wicked and treacherous Macarot of Pantelion' who is guilty of 'outrageous wrongs' and 'overweening pride', she tells Gawain that 'I cherish and treasure [this horn]… Its power is such that anyone possessing it will be free of cold and thirst and hunger, even in the wildest land.'[34] With such a cornucopia, her status as a near-goddess is plain. And all maidens should be treated with such respect. The author makes an immediate, startling juxtaposition between the good Maiden of the Ivory Horn and a wicked damsel who has induced a knight to kill or capture any other who enters her castle; but her wickedness is less a reflection on her than on *knights*, for it is prompted solely by a desire to avenge her rape by another knight, Greoreas. The behaviour of knights towards women, the author shows, can have disastrous consequences. Gawain treats this raped damsel with understanding and courtesy, and as he liberates the girls imprisoned by her he shows them every possible care, 'concerned above all that the girls should be properly served'.[35]

And what of the behaviour of an ideal king? King Arthur in these stories *does* very little; but he presides as the exemplary epitome of mercy: he repeatedly pardons the knights sent to him as prisoners and retains them in his household, and shows pity to the people starving as he lays siege to Branlant. And – vital, at a time when a king was the source and repository of so much wealth – he shows outstanding largesse: 'The court lasted three days. Then the king gave the knights so much gold and silver and so many horses and Eastern silks and costly brooches and fine rings and belts and hounds and birds that they returned to their lands in the highest spirits.'[36]

All the same, the grail episodes are, the continuator recognises, 'what you've long

---

[31] Below, p. 133.
[32] p. 209.
[33] p. 138.
[34] p. 98.
[35] p. 106.
[36] p. 177.

been waiting for'. So how does he continue Chrétien's intriguing theme? Many critical observations have been made about inconsistency of detail between Chrétien and his continuators in relation to the grail; but it should be noted in fairness that anyone continuing his poem had a problem: in terms of the grail and the other mysteries of the Fisher King's castle, there was actually little mystery left. One question – who was served from the grail? – had already been answered in Chrétien's own poem by the hermit uncle; and for many in the audience the grail's identity had been clearly established – a 'spoiler' if ever there was one! – by Robert de Boron in his *Joseph of Arimathea*. It's true that Perceval had been told that if he'd asked questions about the 'mysteries' he'd witnessed, then all would have been well – the Fisher King would have been healed and other calamities set right – and we surely want to see that happen; but to resolve this suspended narrative, all a continuator had to do was bring an experienced knight like Gawain (never slow to come forward, forthright and bold in giving his name to anyone who asks and surely bound to pose the required questions) into the presence of the grail and lance. He would ask the questions, and hey presto! But knowing the size, shape and colour of the rabbit that will come from the hat is not very thrilling. The 'mystery' of the grail is not in fact the greatest gift to a story-teller. And sure enough, the first continuator has Gawain find the grail quite early and he duly asks the questions… but our anonymous author ingeniously – though of necessity, if he wants the story to have further mileage – introduces a new element: a broken sword. The Fisher King

> took it and handed it to Gawain who was so eager to fathom the mysteries; but all he would say was this: that if he could join the sword and fuse one part of the blade to the other to make it whole again, 'then you can learn the truth and meaning of the bier and the grail and the lance, and why the maiden weeps'.
>
> Without more ado Gawain took the pieces and joined them. They fitted together as one, and everyone who saw it thought it was whole again. Then the lord said:
>
> 'Take the blade by the point and pull. If you don't pull it apart, then you will learn the whole and perfect truth about the mystery of the grail and the lance and the bier.'
>
> So Gawain took the sword and pulled; and at the very first tug he parted one piece of the blade from the other.
>
> 'You have not yet achieved enough as a knight,' said the lord, 'to know the truth about this mystery. The one who comes to know it will be deemed the finest knight in the world, I promise you. But you may yet come to know, and by your chivalry win esteem and pre-eminence over all the world.'[37]

The mending of the broken sword – the full significance of which is to be suggested in due course by Gerbert, as we shall see – is a new and vital motif, far more important to the ongoing story than the grail itself.[38]

So unimportant, relatively speaking, is the grail that its very nature can change. When, later in the First Continuation, Gawain makes a second visit to the Fisher King's castle,

---

[37] p. 109.
[38] Note that the broken sword takes up a full half of the manuscript illumination reproduced on the cover.

the grail turns into a kind of magic feeding vessel, zipping around the tables serving food and drink all by itself 'with perfect, brisk and wondrous ease'. And the terms and conditions of the story change, too; the continuator moves the goalposts yet again: Gawain again fails to repair the broken sword, but despite this, he *is* this time given answers to all his questions about the lance and the grail, the Fisher King telling him of their identity and provenance in accordance with Robert de Boron's *Joseph of Arimathea* – they are the lance, he says, with which Longinus stabbed Christ in the side and the vessel used by Christ at the Last Supper and by Joseph of Arimathea to gather Christ's blood at the foot of the cross. Instead of keeping him from the truth (already known to many of the audience thanks to Robert de Boron), Gawain's failure to mend the sword now keeps him from completing the mission he's undertaken on behalf of a knight mysteriously killed at Queen Guinevere's pavilion. And, splendidly, we don't yet know what the mission is. Just as splendidly, Gawain falls asleep before we can hear the story of the blow that caused the sword to be broken – a blow so devastating that 'the whole land and realm of Logres, which had been held in such high regard, was laid waste'.[39] The story-teller's bobbing and weaving here is very nimble, very deft. If we really imagine the Holy Grail to be important we should maybe think again: it has already, with three continuations yet to come, revealed all its mysteries and become nothing more than a catalyst for adventures. But what great adventures they are. This series can run and run.

The Second Continuation: Wandering Astray

While the first continuator almost wholly overlooked Chrétien's first protagonist, the second continuator returns the focus to Perceval, reintroducing him at the exact point where Chrétien had left him with his hermit uncle. There is initially a sense that this new author – usually identified as Wauchier de Denain[40] and for convenience I shall call him this – is going to be attentive to the premises of Chrétien's work, as in his opening passage he repeats almost verbatim two memorable sentences from Chrétien's poem: 'Perceval, so the story says, had lost his memory to such a degree that he'd quite forgotten God. April and May passed by five times – that's five whole years – without him setting foot inside a church or worshipping God or His cross.' So what was his understanding of the premises of Chrétien's work, and how deep are his reflections upon them?

Bearing always in mind the caveat already given – that each episode in this long-running series is first and foremost to be enjoyed and understood for itself and on its own merits – it is possible to detect an overall purpose behind the work attributed to Wauchier. A frequently recurring motif is Perceval's tendency to stray from a given path. Having established him at the very start of the Second Continuation, merely by the blast he blows on a horn, as 'the finest of all knights living in the world… This one will vanquish every foe he meets!', Wauchier brings him almost immediately to a river beyond which, he is convinced, is

> the place where he'd first met the Fisher King… He was instantly reminded
> of that noble man who'd given him lodging, and of the lance and the grail

---

[39] p. 219.
[40] But see footnote 37, below, p. 328.

he'd seen pass before him but had failed to ask anyone about, which since had caused him so much grief. He longed to cross the river and go again to that king's court... He prayed to God to help him find some crossing-place, some ford or bridge.

He promptly meets 'a girl sitting beneath an almond tree, combing her hair' who immediately offers to ferry him across, and 'Perceval, distracted by the sight of her and his eagerness to cross the river, asked her nothing' – an interesting variation on the theme of his failure to ask questions – and is about to board her boat when

> his horse baulked, snorting and whinnying in alarm: it wouldn't board the boat for anything... And then, from further off, a ferryman cried at the top of his voice: "Stay off that boat, sir knight! The girl means to drown you! It's all she ever does! If you board that boat you're a dead man!"

It is interesting to note that the drama of the situation is barely exploited – we are simply told that the ferryman 'kept appealing to Perceval to flee, and said he'd come and fetch him; and so he did, and ferried him across, telling him the dreadful truth about the girl'. This may seem anti-dramatic, but Wauchier's emphasis falls not on the rescue but on what follows – or at least, it does if delivered with insightful stress by one skilled at reading aloud – as the ferryman then 'showed him the exact, clear way that would take him straight to the court of the Fisher King. But truly, Perceval wandered off it, because there beside the river he saw the pretty little castle he'd spotted before. He found the wide, handsome gates unlocked, and decided to go inside and explore its beauties.'[41]

How easily Perceval is distracted! How easily led astray! He's proving himself to be 'the finest of all knights living in the world', he's heard and understood the guidance of his hermit uncle, he's been shown 'the exact, clear way that would take him straight' to what he seeks, but a 'pretty little castle' and 'its beauties' are all it takes to lead him off it and into new adventures. And in these adventures he is constantly and chaotically changing direction. After he has been comprehensively outplayed by a magic chessboard, a damsel (who, we are told, is 'good at turning the heads of fools') sends him with her dog to hunt a white stag.[42] He is robbed of both dog and the captured stag's head and then tricked by a knight in a tomb.[43] He then meets a huntsman who 'told him to take the path to the right if he wanted to get out of the forest... [But] as he followed the huntsman's directions and was about to turn to the right, he heard a cry away to his left and headed off towards it.'[44] Responding to the cry, he avenges the brutal murder of a boy, and then meets 'a very aged knight... mounted on a handsome and perfectly white mule'. The information he's given by this image of experience and rectitude is worth considering at length. He tells him:

> 'I know you're looking for the lance that bleeds at the Fisher King's court, and due to suffer much before you find it. So it may have been you the other night who found his daughter, a comely damsel, at a castle up ahead. I met her on

---

[41] pp. 240–1.
[42] pp. 242–3.
[43] p. 244.
[44] p. 246.

> her way to his court; and she mentioned a little dog that she'd arranged for a girl to carry off, along with a stag's head, because she wanted to test and trouble a much-praised knight who'd been to the court of the Fisher King but failed to ask the question he should: who was served from the grail. So while he was dealing with the stag he'd killed, this girl robbed him of the dog. He asked her to return it, but she gave it back only when he agreed to go to a vaulted tomb where a knight would fight anyone the moment he was called. But while he was embroiled in combat with him, he laid the dog and the stag's head on the ground there in the field, and another knight, passing by, carried off both dog and head! All this was the damsel's doing!... I heard all about it from the damsel herself, who made it clear that if it hadn't been for the business with the grail she'd have given the knight no trouble or grief.'[45]

It is, then, the Fisher King's own daughter who is putting all these obstacles and distractions in Perceval's way, because of 'the business with the grail': it is, in a sense, a penance imposed for the failures of his youth.[46] He accepts this willingly and indeed with delight, but still he doesn't learn from past mistakes:

> Perceval was so delighted at hearing this that he failed to ask anything about the one who'd killed the boy – the knight he'd slain with his own hands: either which land he came from, or where he'd been or where he was going. So he was none the wiser.[47]

And then, when the wise old knight tells him the way back to the Fisher King's daughter, lo and behold...

> Perceval rode on alone along the good, broad, well-made road that the knight had shown him, but... then, most unfortunately, he became so distracted, so deep in thought about his quest and all he'd been told, that he wandered off the path... [48]

These endless strayings can of course be seen merely as a convenient way for the writer to make the series ever more long-running; but it may be seen also as a return to the Everyman quality of Chrétien's protagonist, giving a potent image of us all, too busy with life and immediate challenges to learn from the past or to make sense of anything in particular. Similarly, the routine regularity with which Wauchier describes the reception of the knight for lodging, his disarming and dressing, the stabling of his horse, the washing of hands, the serving of a meal, the preparation of beds, the going-to-sleep and the waking next morning, might be seen as pedestrian, unimaginative and even unnecessary punctuation of a story; but it may be seen also as an image of Everylife, punctuated as it is by routine needs before the wonders and adventures of each succeeding day.

---

[45] p. 248.
[46] Significantly, the aged knight is none other than the brother of the Red Knight slain by Perceval with his javelin early in Chrétien's poem. Perceval expresses his sorrow for the deed, and the knight forgives him 'since you've admitted it'. With penitence, the author implies, forgiveness is possible.
[47] Below, p. 248.
[48] p. 248.

There are times when Wauchier is 'faithful' to Chrétien's work but 'continues' it in a rather functional manner – he brings Perceval back, for instance, to his sister's home and has him revisit his hermit uncle, but without developing or advancing much at all. But there are also times when he shows a real awareness of Chrétien's essential theme of what it means to be a knight. Nowhere is this better seen than in the sequence of episodes beginning at the bridge of glass. Perceval encounters an intriguing damsel who knows a great deal about the grail and the Fisher King, and he asks her if she knows his castle.

> 'Yes, before God,' she replied, 'I know it well, and I'll tell you how to find it – if you'll keep to the way and not stray from it… If you'll lead your destrier by the reins and ride my mule, whiter than any living creature, she'll go straight to the glass bridge over the river Marsonde, which is swift and wide and deep… And take this ring of mine: its stone is fine and precious indeed; as long as you have it on your finger my white mule will carry you safely, unerringly, wherever you wish to go. And you'll need have no fear of crossing the bridge of glass.'[49]

Perceval duly rides the white mule to this daunting bridge, which is

> made of glass, and two and a half feet wide. It was perfectly transparent: through it the water could be seen below, roaring like a tempest. But Perceval dallied on the bank no longer: he gave the mule free rein and she climbed straight on to the fragile bridge. He pulled his fine destrier after him by the reins… The white mule didn't falter: she walked on as surely and confidently as if she'd been on solid ground. But the destrier crossed with difficulty, most fearfully, and behind him the bridge, so perilous and daunting to cross, was crumbling all away… But Perceval was undismayed: he had faith in the mule, who bore him fearlessly and calmly and safely to the other side, so that he felt no pain, discomfort, fear or doubt or dread.[50]

The white mule, then, crosses 'fearlessly and calmly and safely', but his destrier – his warhorse, a warrior's mount – crosses 'with difficulty, most fearfully'. Being a great warrior, it is implied, is not enough. But true to form, no sooner has Perceval crossed than he allows himself – far from following the path to the Grail Castle – to be distracted into yet more feats of martial prowess, proving his outstanding worth as a warrior in a great tournament at the Proud Castle. When, therefore, he comes to return the mule to the damsel, and blithely tells her that he hasn't been to the Fisher King's court but 'got delayed!', her reaction borders on speechless contempt:

> He climbed from the mule at once and returned her to that fair-faced girl. With barely a word she promptly mounted and, without taking leave, rode swiftly away… Perceval was left bewildered – and lost: he'd no idea which path or direction to take if he was to find the way to the king called the Fisher.[51]

---

[49] p. 287.
[50] pp. 288–9.
[51] p. 300.

It is very tempting to point to a clear 'meaning' in this sequence of events, to see it as an indication of Perceval's martial prowess being insufficient to make him worthy of a return to the grail, his martial endeavours being an endless distraction. But looking for a neat, systematic progression in the author's work, or for neat, systematic interpretations, is a mistake. It is vital, as ever, to read and interpret each episode *for itself*; for between these incidents – the crossing of the bridge of glass and the maiden's disdainful reaction to his failure to keep to the path – are two further episodes that emphasise Perceval's exceptional qualities and do so without any reservation. Firstly, to reach the tournament – which the maiden evidently feels is such an unworthy distraction – he has to cross another challenging bridge, an unfinished bridge, which 'no man would ever be able to cross unless he were the most praiseworthy knight in the whole wide world', not merely 'in combat and in chivalry' but also, most importantly, 'in largesse and in courtesy, in honouring and serving God and in respect for Holy Church, and in all the virtues that a man born of woman can possess'.[52] It is to such a knight that the deep mysteries of the grail are to be revealed – and cross this qualifying bridge Perceval does. Even more strikingly, the episode immediately prior to the damsel treating him with disdain sees him survive an adventure that is nothing short of an echo of Christ's resurrection from the dead. Having freed a knight from a tomb, Perceval is cheated (betrayed, one might say) into taking his place, as the knight

> barged into him, knees and arms and ribs together, to send him tumbling into the grave. Then back down crashed the marble slab, so hard that the ground around it quaked, for it was truly colossal. And that was that! The knight cried:
>
> 'Now you'll have to guard this place, just as I've done all this while! Pursue folly and the chances always are you'll come to grief! I've bequeathed you a home where you'll have little comfort! I've a feeling you'll die before you ever escape!'
>
> And he strode up to the mule [given by the maiden to Perceval] and mounted at once, intending to ride off. But the mule stood firm as if tied to a stake. The knight was enraged, speechless with fury. He jumped from the mule and ran to the horse, and mounted at once… He beat and kicked at the horse, trying to ride away. But no amount of thrashing would make it stir.
>
> 'What's going on?' he cried. 'The nag won't move! Either it holds me in contempt or the knight's cast a spell on it! He's charmed the mule he brought, as well!'
>
> In a terrible rage he dismounted and strode back to the tomb. For a moment he paused. Then, with all his malice ebbing away, he raised the marble slab and said:
>
> 'Come out, sir. It would be wicked and wrong of me to do you harm. And I couldn't even if I wanted to: I know in truth you're the most worthy, refined, accomplished knight, the best endowed with chivalry, alive …'
>
> Then Perceval stepped from the tomb and the knight jumped back inside without another word.[53]

[52] p. 293.
[53] pp. 298–9.

Interestingly, both the white mule (with its echoes of the entry into Jerusalem) and the warrior's destrier (despite its struggle to cross the bridge of glass) are the allies of the good knight Perceval, here the type of the grave-conquering Christ.

If Wauchier had wanted to progress neatly and meaningfully to a conclusion, he could surely have brought this peerless knight back to the Grail Castle at this point, to ask the all-important questions, mend the broken sword, heal the Fisher King and learn all the mysteries. But why bring a successful series to an end, when there are so many potential story-lines, offering such exciting insights into what it means to be a knight? And how many listeners, in any case, are interested in neat meanings and parables? Are most listeners not more like the people of Beaurepaire who, flocking to church where Perceval and Blancheflor are going to hear mass, 'were stunned and said you could search every land and sea and never find such a handsome couple. They looked so fair indeed that people went more to see them than they did to hear the mass of the Holy Spirit.'[54] There is no hint of censure in this remark, for in the end enjoyment is the key: 'people,' Wauchier comments as they celebrate, 'who most commit themselves to being happy, and don't refrain from merriment, tend to find it's for the best'.[55]

Wauchier is intent not upon bringing Perceval's questing journey to a neat and meaningful end, but upon adding to the fund of beguiling stories, to create an ever-richer Arthurian world. But that is not to say that the tales are superficial and mere diversions. They do carry meaning, but not in a systematic way. And the listener should be ever alert to the meaning of each episode, to what it has to illustrate and demonstrate about values and behaviour: faithfulness in love, explored in the story of the shield carried by Gawain at the tournament in the Blanche Lande; the deceptiveness of appearances in the story of the handsome knight and the ugly damsel; avoiding unnecessary loss of life by treating defeated enemies with the grace and mercy shown by Arthur to the rebellious kings Claudas and Carras; and the importance of a woman allowing her knight to do his duty and fulfil his life's mission, recognised by Blancheflor who, distraught though she is to see Perceval leave her and resume his quest, acknowledges that 'it isn't right for such a worthy man as you to abandon what he's vowed to do… I'll do exactly as you wish, since I can't keep you here by force or pleading! And even if I could it would be very wrong of me to do so and anger you, for a damsel should do nothing to displease and vex her love. If she's come to love him with a noble love that's true and sure, she should bear the pain that wrings her heart.'[56]

So the adventures weave entertainingly on, accumulating reflections upon life, until Wauchier at last decides it's time to bring Perceval back to the Fisher King's court. Surely now we've reached the end: this outstanding knight will mend the broken sword, ask the questions and hear the truth about the grail and the lance, and heal the Fisher King – won't he? In one manuscript he does indeed, and the whole story gallops to a crashing conclusion – see Appendix 3; but the journey is so much more interesting than the arrival, and other manuscripts contain the work of at least one more poet, as Wauchier, leaving the way delightfully open for a further journey and more adventures, has Perceval repair the broken sword, yes… but *imperfectly*:

---

[54] p. 264.
[55] p. 264.
[56] p. 263.

>It looked as handsome, new and shining as the day that it was made – except that, just by the join, there remained a tiny notch, not big at all. The king, so kind and courteous, said:
>
>'Listen, sir. You've devoted much to the practice of arms, I think – indeed I'm sure you have. And this test proves to me that of all men now living in the world none can surpass you in combat or in battle; but you've not yet done enough to have God bestow on you the honour and perfect courtesy, the wisdom and the chivalry, to enable us to say with confidence that of all knights you're the most endowed with all high qualities.'[57]

Despite all Perceval's previous feats, including his crossing of the unfinished bridge which seemed to have shown that he was 'the most praiseworthy knight in the whole wide world… in all the virtues that a man born of woman can possess', Wauchier doesn't want him to score and end the game and has moved the goalposts yet again: there is still more, he says, for Perceval to do before he can repair the final notch in the symbolic sword.

Gerbert's Continuation: the Crusading Knight

The majority of manuscripts follow the Second Continuation with the Third, written by Manessier (of whom we know nothing but this work); but two precede Manessier's by inserting a fourth, whose author is identified as Gerbert[58] and is generally assumed to be Gerbert de Montreuil, author of the thirteenth-century *Roman de la Violette*. At several points there are strong suggestions that Manessier and Gerbert were writing their continuations more or less simultaneously, with no knowledge of each other's work;[59] and they certainly had very different responses to the work of their predecessors, and different ideas of what prevented Perceval mending the sword with complete perfection.

In some ways it's ironic that only two scribes chose to include Gerbert's Continuation. Not only is it substantial in length – almost twice as long as Chrétien's poem and almost as long as the fullest redaction of the First Continuation; it is also the most considered and purposeful adoption and exploration of Chrétien's main themes. Chrétien had Perceval's hermit uncle tell him that

>'a sin of which you're unaware has done you great harm: it's the grief you caused your mother when you left her. She collapsed in a faint at the foot of the bridge outside the gate, and of that grief she died. It's because of the sin you committed there that you came to ask nothing about the lance and the grail, and many misfortunes have befallen you in consequence.'[60]

This is one of very few uses by Chrétien of the word 'sin'. In Gerbert's Continuation, however, the word appears with striking regularity. The very first passage tells us that Perceval

>acutely felt himself a sinner, being unfit to know the truth about the grail…
>He wondered what offence or sin barred him from learning the grail's secrets.

---

[57] p. 337.
[58] p. 394.
[59] See, for example, footnotes 31 and 38, below, pp. 526 and 529.
[60] p. 55.

But the king would reveal nothing more, except that he made him keenly aware that he was gravely burdened by the sin he'd committed towards his mother, who'd fallen dead at the foot of the bridge outside the gate on the day he left her; and he said that until he'd atoned for that sin – and others – the secrets of the grail would never be fully disclosed to him.[61]

'And others'. As soon as he leaves the Fisher King he is barred entry to a walled enclosure inside which he can hear great rejoicing, and the gatekeeper tells him: 'You're seeking something so sacred that it will never be attained by any man unless he's clean of all sins – and you are sorely stained with them.'[62] In hammering on the gate of this ring of wall, demanding entry, Perceval breaks his sword, and when he comes to the smith who can repair it for him, he is told: 'You've greatly sinned in breaking your sword, which I made long ago. You broke it at the gate of Paradise, I see.'[63]

Gerbert was evidently very struck by the potent image of a broken sword. This had been partly introduced by Chrétien, who had had Perceval break the sword given him by the Fisher King with the very first blow he struck; and the First Continuator then made the repair of another broken sword a key test of a knight's worthiness to know the secrets of the grail and the lance. Gerbert not only has Perceval break yet another sword 'at the gate of Paradise', but takes Perceval back to his hermit uncle – feeling, perhaps, that Wauchier in the Second Continuation had done little with that scene – to make the significance of the broken sword absolutely plain. It is not a long scene, but the focus is intense. The hermit gives just a brief exhortation, telling Perceval that a knight needs 'suffering, fasting, prayer and true repentance, and wearing a hair-shirt in penitence, and unburdening oneself of every sin in confession to a priest. Such are the arms with which a knight should arm himself if he seeks to love God and to be valiant and worthy'; then he launches straight into the crucial question:

> 'A knight's sword has two cutting edges: do you know why? It should be understood, truly, that one edge is for the defence of Holy Church, while the other should administer earthly justice, protecting Christian people and upholding justice without deception or self-interest. But I tell you this: Holy Church's edge is broken, while the earthly edge cuts indeed! Every knight hacks and hews the poor and holds them to ransom, though they've done him no wrong at all! So *that* edge of the blade is very sharp, and a knight who carries such a sword is deceiving God! And if he fails to mend his ways, the gate of Paradise will be closed to him. God keep you, dear friend,' the hermit said, 'from such a sword, which would condemn your soul.'[64]

'Holy Church's edge is broken', Perceval is told, just as, in Chrétien, he'd been brought to realise that in his five long years of pursuing knightly deeds he'd quite 'forgotten God'. And Gerbert's notion of how a knight's energies should be directed for the sake of 'Holy Church' is made abundantly clear when he has Perceval accept from a maiden a very special shield: a white shield with a red cross.

---

[61] p. 339.
[62] p. 341.
[63] p. 346.
[64] p. 361.

> All white it was, with a red cross, and in the cross was a relic that certainly mustn't go unmentioned, for in it was embedded a piece of the holy wood on which the flesh of Jesus Christ, the son of God, was tortured... No one could find the holy grail or the lance with the ever-bleeding head except the first to be able to take the shield from this beautiful maiden's neck. But it was at his peril that any man touched it or tried to take it unless he was the bravest in the world, both in word and deed, and confessed of all his sins; were he not, he'd instantly be destroyed in a hail of a thousand stones, and nothing could protect him. There was an inscription upon it to that effect for the benefit of all who saw the shield and were able to read.
>
> The girl ... had been scouring many lands, both day and night, but no one who read the inscription would lay a hand upon the shield: they didn't dare – it was too fearsome a test. Without a moment's hesitation Perceval ran to help the damsel from her horse. And first he took the shield from her neck: it weighed little, but was made of such fine stuff that it feared no blow from any lance. When she saw he'd taken the shield she threw herself to the ground: she knew now he was the finest knight in all the world, for confession, which washes sin away, had greatly increased his worth.[65]

Perceval, unmistakably, is here becoming a crusader. Crusading, for Gerbert, is the essential purpose and function of the knight if both sides of his sword are to be notch-free. Chrétien's patron Philip of Flanders had answered the call and taken up the crusader's shield – and died at Acre on the Third Crusade.[66] And now Gerbert lays the challenge before his audience – and a daunting challenge it is: a knight has to be 'the bravest in the world' (and 'confessed of all his sins'), and for many it was 'too fearsome a test'; but if he follows the example of Perceval and goes 'without a moment's hesitation' to take the shield, a knight will show himself to be 'the finest in all the world'.

With this white shield with the red cross, Perceval goes to confront the Knight of the Dragon, who is laying siege to Montesclaire, whose lady is the Maiden of the Circle of Gold. The significance of this would not have been lost on an audience familiar with this episode's source, the prose romance *Perlesvaus*, in which the Circle of Gold is identified as the crown of thorns set in gold and adorned with gems.[67] And this precious holy relic is under threat (as were so many in the late twelfth and early thirteenth centuries) from an infidel; for the Knight of the Dragon, Perceval is told,

> 'had built a city in the isles of the sea, superbly fortified with towers and walls, and filled it with people who refused to believe in God... And this lord, the Knight of the Dragon, devoted himself... to the Devil, who'd endowed him in return with such power that no one could withstand him in battle or any combat. The Devil brought him a terrible, ghastly shield, blacker than any berry: a dragon's head is fixed in it, by such demonic art that it burns and engulfs in flame anyone who fights him! ... He's been laying siege for some time now to the peak of Montesclaire. No one dares go out to face him; there are three hundred and ten knights inside the castle, but

---

[65] pp. 406–7.
[66] Philip, in fact, went on crusade twice: he had previously been to the Holy Land in 1177–9.
[67] See *The High Book of the Grail (Perlesvaus)*, trans. Bryant (Cambridge, revised edition 2007), pp. 125, 159–61.

none has the courage to confront him. The evil tyrant, with a vast army, is besieging the lady within because he wants her for his wife. But she – the Maiden of the Circle of Gold – swears she would sooner kill herself...'[68]

But the crusader has no need to fear, Gerbert says, for the power of the sign of the cross is too great for the Devil's dragon. When Perceval confronts the Dragon Knight in awesome battle, and shield comes face to face with shield,

> the demon in the dragon's head, hurling the fire and flame, now saw the cross and was filled with dread, for Jesus Christ the King won the battle on the cross and so broke into Hell and freed His friends who were suffering dire torment; and in terror of the cross on which Christ was crucified, the demon howled and bellowed like a bull... and when the cross clashed with the demon it created mighty chaos: the cross's power made the demon leap from the dragon – it had no strength against the cross and dared abide no longer![69]

Gerbert is suggesting that a knight armed with the crusader's shield need have no fear of fighting the infidel: unlike any ordinary shield in these romances, of which we see countless pierced, shattered and hacked to pieces, the red cross shield is unbreakable, and the infidel Dragon Knight is helpless and defeated and dies of his wounds – though only after Perceval has converted him.

And how could a knight resist the call to crusade and stay at home when reminded by Gerbert that 'a man disgraces and demeans himself if he lets softness or idleness stop his pursuit of honour: faint-hearted softness strips a man of prowess, making him stay quietly at home and earn a reputation as a glorified watchman! It's brought shame on many a man – and will continue to, I tell you!' Typically, he adds that 'It's the work of the devil and sin.'[70]

Obsessed as Gerbert is by this concept, it's interesting to note that, in considering the 'sin' that stops Perceval knowing the grail's secrets, he changes the emphasis from his abandonment of his mother to his failure to marry his sweetheart Blancheflor. Meeting Gorneman again – the nobleman who'd knighted him in Chrétien's poem – Perceval tells him:

> 'The Fisher King said I could ask as much as I liked, but I'd learn nothing till I repaired the notch in the sword. He also said I'd done something that made me unworthy of knowing the secrets... and it worries me that I don't know what wickedness or sin of mine's to blame: I can't think of any sin, great or small, that I haven't confessed and done penance for – except one: I gave a pledge of marriage to a fair and lovely girl – she was your niece, I know... it's Blancheflor of Beaurepaire I mean. It's only right that I acknowledge that sin. I brought an end to a war being waged against her, and she loved me with a true heart and said I should take her and make her

[68] Below, pp. 410–11.
[69] pp. 415–6.
[70] pp. 352–3.

my wife; I promised to be her love and marry her and to do no wrong with any other. I remember now! I'm sure that's the sin that taints me most.'[71]

In rectifying this 'sin', Gerbert takes a striking attitude. In the Second Continuation Wauchier had been quite happy to have Perceval and Blancheflor, although unmarried, consummate their love:

> Perceval took her in his arms, hungry for the solace of her embrace: he had loved her for so long; he smothered her with kisses – a hundred in a row without a pause. I don't wish to reveal the rest of what followed; but if Perceval didn't fail to go further, Blancheflor didn't object: gracious-hearted soul that she was, she wouldn't resist any desire of his. And so they took their pleasure; they didn't sleep much that night.[72]

And indeed, Wauchier had no apparent reservations about Perceval having full relations also with the damsel of the Chessboard Castle:

> Perceval didn't fall asleep as quickly as usual: he was thinking of that damsel of fairy-like beauty. And as he was deep in those very thoughts she came to his bed and lay down and fulfilled her promise to him, just as he'd asked and she'd vowed to do... They lay together all that night, until the day dawned bright and fair across the land.[73]

Gerbert absolutely disapproves! In the face of his predecessor's stories, very early in his Continuation he insists that Perceval is not only chaste but a virgin.[74] When the maiden Escolasse comes to his bed he declines her kind offer, saying: 'Fair damsel, I've no need of that just now. But truly, I refuse you only because it would be a dreadful sin to ruin your virginity or mine. And I've never really yearned for such pleasure in my life – I don't see what purpose it serves.'[75] And Gerbert has Perceval and Blancheflor keep their virginity even when he rectifies his 'sin' and marries her. In a passage which would surely have startled Wauchier, and perhaps raised the eyebrows of many of his audience, Gerbert tells us that on their wedding night the couple

> lay together beneath the sheets, arm against arm, skin against naked skin. And Blancheflor began to shake and tremble, and so did he, like an aspen leaf, for they felt unsure: they were both afraid that through bodily pleasure they might lose what the elect have in the bliss of Heaven, and they wanted to save themselves from the perils and dread torment of Hell.

And agreeing that 'virginity surpasses all: as topaz is worth more than crystal and fine gold more than other metal, so it is with virginity', they

---

[71] p. 380.
[72] pp. 262–3.
[73] p. 304.
[74] Matilda Bruckner may well be right that this is – in part at least – because Gerbert, writing after the composition of *The Quest of the Grail*, is 'under the influence of the prose romances and cannot allow any sexual taint to sully his Grail hero'. Bruckner, *Chrétien Continued* (Oxford, 2009), p. 66.
[75] Below, p. 344.

> rose from their bed and went down on their knees with clasped hands and faced the east … and begged Jesus to keep them in such a state that they might come to a good end, to preserve them with their virginity inviolate. They lay back down together then, but didn't touch each other in such a way as to have carnal love: they fell asleep without delay.[76]

They are, however, then woken by a 'voice' who tells them that their virginity will not be permanent – they are to beget an important line.

> 'I have come from God to declare to you that no man should touch his wife except in a virtuous way and for two things only: to beget children, and to avoid sin… I tell you this: from your line will come a girl who'll… beget a daughter who'll bear the choicest fruit, most pleasing to everyone, for she'll have three sons who'll conquer Jerusalem, the sepulchre and the true cross.'[77]

So back to the crusades Gerbert comes. And the true knight Perceval – the knight with the proper function, the crusading knight – is, Gerbert implies, the type of Christ Himself. He gives Perceval a lineage which relates him to Jesus on his mother's side, albeit distantly,[78] and then gives a derivation of his name that makes him a clear Christ figure: defending Gorneman against a band of demon knights who are endlessly restored to life by a hag who possesses a healing balm, he is told by the hag: '"You're rightly called 'Perceval', for you've *pierced the vale*: you've penetrated the place where the balm is kept."'[79] This balm is none other than the potion with which 'God, who delivers those He loves from Hell, was anointed and embalmed when He was laid in the sepulchre',[80] and in winning it Perceval now holds, like Christ, the key to eternal life; and when he proceeds to use the balm to heal the grievously wounded Gorneman, Gerbert says: 'If God had descended from Heaven and appeared in bodily form He wouldn't have been embraced more fervently than Perceval was by Gorneman and his sons.'[81] That's not to say that He represents (or is) Christ, but he's *like* Him.

And so, Gerbert implies, are *all* good knights who are willing to crusade and confront the infidel. It is notable that the distinctly heathen, pagan hag figure who has tried to keep the balm from Perceval tells him that '"you'll learn nothing about the grail – not the merest jot – as long as I'm alive, I swear it!"';[82] and Gorneman had been attacked by the demon knights, the hag explains, at the command of '"the King of the Waste City, who cannot and will not believe in God"' and who wanted to destroy Gorneman for one reason only: '"*because it was he who made you a knight*, and because through his guidance you'll do a deed that will undo the Devil's work: by you God's friends, whom the Devil has been working to destroy, will be restored to joy and well-being."'[83] Gerbert is implying that the making of the knight – and the work of *any* knight – is an essentially holy act with a holy purpose; and in his description of Perceval's fight against one of the demons, he shows how holy, how godlike, is the mercy a true knight will show to a defeated enemy:

[76] p. 393.
[77] p. 394.
[78] See below, p. 364 and footnote 19.
[79] Below, p. 384.
[80] p. 384.
[81] p. 387.
[82] p. 384.
[83] p. 384.

> The demon knight reeled back, struggling to defend himself, but refused to cry for mercy – it would certainly have been granted, but he was sure he'd done Perceval too much harm to be forgiven: he was too full of despair to have the capacity or heart to appeal for mercy. Now you can see that a sinner who abandons hope, who cares not a jot for confession and doing good and thinks he's committed too many sins to have forgiveness, is a fool to give way to despair; for God is full of pity and mercy for any man who seeks accord with Him and craves His forgiveness with a sincere heart and seeks His peace and love.[84]

The crusading knight, at war with the heathen, the infidel, is for Gerbert godlike, the type of Christ.

But it must be stressed again that, as with the other Continuations, this theme in Gerbert's work is not systematically developed. The episodes referenced here are not sequential; they do not form an organised progression. Each episode is still to be enjoyed and understood for itself. Gerbert is quite happy to digress into an entertaining story about Tristran which is almost as 'independent' as the first continuator's tale of Carados – though unlike the latter it does significantly feature Perceval, who despite his battered arms and exhausted mount is still able to unhorse the lord-deceiving lover Tristran, sending him crashing: 'everyone in the tournament saw him with his heels in the air and measuring his length in the grass'.[85] Significantly, too, Gerbert has Perceval voice his disapproval of Tristran's disguise and ploy on which the whole episode depends:

> Gawain told him the whole story: how Tristran had taken them to King Marc and engaged as his personal spy.
> 'It's not a good idea,' said Perceval, 'keeping watch on people if they're true and loyal friends. It can all go horribly wrong: it makes even the wisest lose all sense, breeding suspicion and jealousy.'[86]

The Tristran episode is not the only 'independent' tale in Gerbert's Continuation to be appreciated on its own terms on a given day. Gerbert retells the well-established story of the Perilous Seat, for instance, and exploits it to rail against 'those deviants who prefer young men to girls', as knights who've sat in the seat and been swallowed by the earth return to report what lies in wait for 'anyone tainted with that vice. On the great Day of Judgement they'll be deep down in the pit of Hell, blacker than ink or iron!'[87] Then towards the end of his Continuation, Gerbert gives us a series of episodes in which a demon worm tricks Perceval into freeing it from a stone, and then two maidens, Dyonise and Felisse, each in a very different way, likewise try to deceive him and take his life. So many dangers lie in a good knight's path! Before that sequence, Gerbert tells two parallel tales of Perceval and Gawain confronting the consequences of past misdeeds: Perceval finds himself embroiled with descendants of the Red Knight he'd slain with his javelin early in Chrétien's poem, and Gawain is embroiled with Urpin, whose kinsmen he has killed in numbers. In both cases, crucially, there is finally mercy, peace and reconciliation; the futility of killing and blood-feuds is plain: all that chivalric chaos,

[84] p. 385.
[85] p. 375.
[86] p. 376.
[87] p. 351.

Gerbert is implying, is a distraction from knights' proper function. As the Continuation nears its close, Gerbert introduces another hermit to tell Perceval that

> some men's way of life was madness.
> 'I don't consider any man wise who spends his life in such a way that he wastes his body and loses his soul. God didn't make knights to wage war and kill, but to uphold justice and defend Holy Church: God loves not presumptuous pride… It's a shame that a noble youth like you has chosen such a path: you'd be better devoted to the Church! Put your trust in God, and always remember that He suffered death for us in His sacrifice on the cross. Keep Him ever in your mind and you will win God's glory.'[88]

Has Perceval now learnt the lesson? Is the symbolic notch in the broken sword still there? It's not long before Gerbert returns Perceval to the Grail Castle to try his hand at repairing the sword. And sure enough, Perceval's understanding of a sword's two edges and a knight's true function – the defence of Holy Church, crusading against the infidel – has in Gerbert's eyes done the trick:

> He came straight to the sword and grasped it boldly. Then he looked and saw the notch in the blade and was distraught. He rubbed his hand up and down the blade – no one intervened or bade him stop – and then brandished it four times, so violently that he almost broke it. And thereupon the notch was repaired: he had joined it perfectly.[89]

Now the grail's secrets can be revealed.

The Third Continuation: Revenge

But, as noted previously, there are barely any secrets to be revealed. Manessier, the poet commissioned by Countess Jeanne of Flanders to continue and complete the story of Perceval, was confronted with the ending of the Second Continuation (he almost certainly had no knowledge of Gerbert's work)[90] and realised, like Gerbert, that the secrets were already well known to the audience thanks to Robert de Boron, and that the real narrative potential lay not in the grail but in the story of the broken sword. So Manessier, carefully but briskly, has the Fisher King tell Perceval the already-known 'secret' story of Joseph of Arimathea, the grail and the lance of Longinus, and then has Perceval proceed to the far more exciting *new* question (left unanswered in the First Continuation thanks, as noted above, to Gawain falling asleep):

'Good sir, please don't object: I'd love to hear how the sword I've twice repaired was broken.'[91]

And so it is that, from the very outset of the Third Continuation, Manessier focuses, not like Gerbert on crusading, but on *revenge*. For the answer to the question is that the

---

[88] p. 464.
[89] p. 474.
[90] It is very possible, though by no means certain, that Gerbert wrote his own conclusion to the romance, and that the scribes who incorporated his work into the whole series of continuations edited out his ending so that the Third Continuation could still be added.
[91] Below, p. 478.

sword had broken in half in the striking of a dreadful, treacherous blow which had killed the Fisher King's own brother. And the Fisher King now tells Perceval that his niece – his slain brother's daughter – had told him that

> 'if I kept the sword till the coming of a knight who took it in his hands and made the two halves join again, "then know this," she said. "By the one who repairs the sword, my dear father will be avenged." I, crazed with grief, took the broken blade she gave me and, that very instant, made a cut through my thighs, severing every nerve. Truly, I've been helpless ever since, and will remain so till I'm avenged upon the false traitor who slew the finest of all knights born since God was crucified.'[92]

So yet again the goalposts move: the Fisher King will no longer be healed by the asking of the questions, but by a completely new condition – the avenging of his brother's death at the hands of a knight named Partinal.

And revenge is a dominant theme of Manessier's whole Continuation. First he launches Gawain and Sagremor into a series of adventures that see them righting and avenging wrongs. It is no surprise that the character of Sagremor, nicknamed with good reason 'the Rash', appeals so much to Manessier, who has a noticeable penchant for the boisterous action into which the impulsive Sagremor so readily charges. Manessier is a straightforward but vigorous story-teller, keen to resolve unfinished, vivid adventures like the story of the dread Black Hand, and he does so with a good deal of aplomb.[93]

And his treatment of the revenge theme is not at all crude. When, for example, Sagremor defeats Tallidés, the knight besieging the Castle of the Maidens, Tallidés begs him not to send him there as a prisoner, convinced that the castle's lady would be vengeful:

> 'Send me somewhere else, I beg you: you'd have to truly hate me to condemn me to imprisonment with her! She'd have my head if she had me in her power... You may as well behead me now, good sir! Send me there and you're sending me to the slaughter!'[94]

But when Sagremor insists, Tallidés finds himself not only forgiven by the lady of the castle but allowed to marry the girl who'd been the object of his siege.

> Hearing his words the lady felt deep pity in her heart; she realised his love for the girl was true, and that, because he knew she doubted him, he wouldn't dare let her down.
>
> 'Tallidés, good sir,' she said, 'you know full well you've done me much harm and wrong and caused me all manner of grief and woe: you've burnt my castles, ravaged my land and besieged me here. Day and night you've done all in your power to hurt me!'

---

[92] p. 479.
[93] I entirely share Corin Corley's puzzlement that Manessier's work 'has been the subject over the years of the almost universal opprobrium of scholars'. Corley, 'Manessier's Continuation of Perceval and the Prose Lancelot Cycle', *Modern Language Review* 81 (1986), p. 574.
[94] Below, p. 492.

'I know, lady, I know!' he said. 'But I'll make amends for all the strife and injuries, indeed I will!'

'And I,' she said, 'tomorrow, out of love for you, will give you the girl you love so much, have no fear.'[95]

This forgiveness is not gratuitous: crucially, it has been earned by his honourable behaviour. Despite all the harm he'd done, Tallidés has shown himself to be a man of honour as he prepares to do battle with the castle's champion, Sagremor. Addressing his followers he says:

> 'I want you to stay well back and keep your distance; I've accepted a challenge to battle today in which I'll achieve my goal with the edge of my whetted sword! By all the saints, if I see any one of you move, no ransom will save his head…! If I vanquish this champion of theirs, I'll have my beloved girl – I ask no more; but if he defeats me I'll go back to my land, leave the castle alone and the girl in peace: never more will I trouble them, on my honour. Those are the terms I've agreed and I'll honour them, come what may.'[96]

There has, significantly, been no such mercy or forgiveness for the villains of the previous adventures, because they showed no honour: knights intent on raping a damsel are duly slaughtered by Perceval and Sagremor; one who'd sleazily stolen Sagremor's horse while he was asleep ends up with a severed arm and throws himself down a well.[97]

The story of King Margon[98] piles revenge upon revenge. The sister of Silimac – the knight mysteriously killed at the queen's pavilion in the First Continuation – is under siege from Margon because she has rejected the advances of his son Cargrilo. Margon has treacherously hanged the knight she truly loves, and she, in revenge, has catapulted the captive Cargrilo over her castle walls to die at Margon's feet. Gawain now fights as her champion and defeats Margon; he shows mercy and sends him as a prisoner to King Arthur rather than to her, and this appears well earned by Margon, who – like Tallidés at the Castle of the Maidens – behaves with all honour: vanquished and crestfallen, he

> returned to his men and, with many a sigh, told them how Gawain, Arthur's nephew, had outfought and defeated him: he told them everything.
>
> 'Quickly now,' he said. 'Go and mount. A hundred knights will come with me: it's only right that a king should yield as a prisoner and avoid reproach.'[99]

But while Gawain is merciful, Silimac's sister is as vengeful in spirit as ever, and cries: 'If only you'd taken his head! That would have been the better deed! God help me, it's a shame you spared him death!' Despite this vengefulness, though, she admits to having been 'a wretched fool' in exacting revenge for her lover's hanging by killing Margon's

---

[95] p. 493.
[96] p. 491.
[97] pp. 483–4, 487.
[98] pp. 501–6.
[99] p. 505.

son: revenge, she evidently feels, has to be right and appropriate – the sin of the father should not have been visited on the son.[100]

She's convinced, however, that it's wholly appropriate to take revenge on Kay for the murder of her brother Silimac. Gawain argues that 'I could never be sure it was Kay who killed him – no one could.' But she insists, on the basis of astrology, that

> 'It was, sir, have no doubt. I've read in the stars that Kay killed him with his knife: he drew it from his mantle without anybody seeing, taking him unawares and condemning me to grief… That faithless man, driven by spite, robbed him of his life when he'd done him no wrong.'[101]

Revenge is right and proper, she feels, because of the dishonourable, unworthy nature and motivation of the killing. And because her brother was murdered while under Gawain's protection, '"that vengeance," she says, "pertains to you, too"', and she presents Gawain with a lance 'to which she'd tied a wondrously handsome pennon of red silk emblazoned with a white lion; she implored him to stain it with Kay the seneschal's blood, wherever he might find him'.[102]

Gawain, 'horrified by the whole affair', has to go through with this dreadful mission of revenge. He does battle with Kay and overcomes him and has him at his mercy. He stands with sword aloft, weeping, praying that the king will intervene; the whole palace is filled with wailing. Silimac's vengeful sister, however, is

> brimming with joy… and couldn't care less about the crushing, crazing agony the others felt! Instead she cried aloud to her champion:
> 'In the name of the crucified God, dear friend, look to avenge my brother! Go on! Cut off his head! Heal me of my pain!'

The queen prays to the Virgin to save Kay's life, and Arthur prays to the damsel herself, saying:

> 'Have pity on me, I beg you! Don't kill my seneschal – it would be a wicked sin! I implore you now, show charity, and I and all my men will be at your service!'

'Charity' here is an attempt to translate the difficult word *franchise*, implying noble-hearted generosity and openness. And Silimac's sister, to the joy of all and the relief of Gawain, responds to the king's appeal in the name of *franchise* and says:

> 'So help me God, good sire, I don't know what to say. I don't see how I can ignore and refuse your plea: I'd be sorely reproached.'[103]

In a matter of moments charity, compassion, *franchise* wins out over vengefulness, and Kay is forgiven for a crime witnessed by no one but allegedly revealed by astrology.

[100] p. 502.
[101] p. 502.
[102] p. 504.
[103] p. 510.

INTRODUCTION

Shortly after this we return to Perceval, who has recovered from wounds so effectively that 'if anyone had wronged him he could have taken revenge without any risk'.[104] This knee-jerk assumption that revenge is the right response is, however, tempered by his encounter with a hermit who tells him in no uncertain terms that he's following a wildly mistaken path:

> 'I can't believe what I'm hearing! You say you win honour and esteem by vanquishing knights? So help me God, you rather win the surest damnation for your soul!'
> Perceval was dumbfounded by the worthy man's words...
> 'If you want to save yourself you must abandon the paths you've followed so long and control your proud heart: unless you have pity on yourself it'll lead you to damnation soon, indeed it will! ... It's plain to see that a man who kills and murders others and devotes himself to doing ill wins only his own misfortune, grief and downfall: he'll be in Hell eternally, for as long as God is in Paradise!...'
> Perceval was deeply shaken by the worthy man's words, and took them very much to heart.[105]

But it's not in his heart for long. No sooner has he left the hermitage than he's robbed of his horse by a knight who fells him, unprovoked, and Perceval says:

> 'This morning I unburdened myself of all my sins, wanting to make amends for the wrongs I've done, and now I've lost my horse! It's maddening! That knight who stole him has played a rotten trick on me – how it pains my heart! I'd gladly break my promise to that God-devoted priest: if I knew where to find the wretch who robbed me and left me without a mount – not even a nag! – I'd take revenge!'[106]

That, however, and perhaps significantly, immediately leads him to mounting a demon horse that almost leads him to his death; and certainly, the following episodes see Perceval engaging in combats as ever, but to all of the knights he vanquishes – to the knight who demands a toll of him; to the abductor of Dodinel's sweetheart; and to Aridés, besieger of his own beloved Blancheflor – he shows mercy, sending them to submit as prisoners to King Arthur. And it's notable that the scene that follows – the arrival of the defeated knights, one after another, to surrender at Arthur's court – is entirely repetitive and serves no purpose other than to show the king being repeatedly magnanimous and forgiving.

Although it would, as ever, be an overstatement to say there is a neatly developing theme of mercy versus vengefulness, Manessier's attitude is certainly consistent: the following episode, Perceval's 'conversion' of the Coward Knight, sees killing a-plenty, with no mercy shown to the knights they fight – because those knights are planning the most dishonourable and despicable of crimes: the abuse and cruel burning of two girls. Boort likewise kills knights to save a girl from rape; Gawain kills knights who are

[104] p. 513.
[105] pp. 517–8.
[106] p. 518.

shamefully abusing Lionel. But as for knights fighting and killing *without* good cause, Manessier gives us two memorable scenes condemning such violence – one on either side of a vigorous tourney in which the Coward Knight proves himself and changes his name forever (what a fine training ground for knights the tournament is). In the first of these scenes, a battle between the brothers Boort and Lionel (tragically leading to the death of the good Calogrenant) is halted by the intervention of an engulfing cloud and a voice from heaven; in the second, Perceval and a fellow knight of the Round Table, Ector, batter one another to such a state of exhaustion that they're both on the point of death, but are saved and healed by an angel bearing the Holy Grail. The healing grail brings an end to this misdirected energy and strife at home: if there is to be violence, the real cause to which the good knight Perceval should be devoting himself lies in another land – the avenging of the Fisher King's brother.

And this he now achieves. He finds and does battle with Partinal, 'the one who's caused such grief to the king who guards the holy grail', and

> victory went to Perceval by the will of the king of glory. He brought Partinal to the ground before him and said the battle was over if he'd surrender as his prisoner. But the one who didn't believe in God said he'd never stoop to yielding captive to any knight: he shouldn't imagine for a single moment that he'd ever ask for mercy.
>
> 'Then may God never forgive me if I refrain from killing you.' Perceval raised his sword and threatened to slay him there and then if he didn't yield.
>
> 'I swear,' Partinal replied, 'I'll not surrender to my dying breath. If you want to kill me, go ahead: I'll never plead for mercy or submit to being a prisoner.'
>
> 'Then kill you I shall,' said Perceval, 'though it grieves me.'
>
> And he struck him a blow that severed head from trunk.[107]

Partinal, then, 'didn't believe in God', and rejects all offer of mercy. The two concepts, as noted previously, are linked. And the killing of this infidel leads to the instant and total healing of the maimed Fisher King. As Perceval returns to the Grail Castle with the infidel Partinal's severed head,

> a servant ran straight to tell the king that a knight had arrived with a slain knight's head on his saddle; the king that instant sprang to his feet in joy and jubilation: he felt healed in body and spirit alike.[108]

The Fisher King has been healed, then, not by Perceval's asking of the questions about the grail and the lance as Chrétien had suggested, nor directly by the mending of the broken sword, but by revenge for the treacherous wrong committed by the infidel. But this is not a contradiction. Chrétien, writing for his crusading patron Philip of Flanders, would surely have approved. A knight's true duty, at a time when affairs in the Holy Land were less than happy for the forces of Christendom, was to be conscious of the meaning of the two edges of his sword and to fight for the defence of Holy Church; and the vision of the lance and the grail, with their resonance – seen instantly by Robert

---

[107] p. 549.
[108] pp. 549–50.

de Boron – of relics under threat, were reminders of that need and call, and a knight who didn't ask the question and was content to let the vision pass was no true knight.

But a true and complete knight Perceval has now become; and as he makes his way to King Arthur's court for the final time, we see him joust against six knights with shields of every colour under the sun: the first is white, the second green, the third yellow, the fourth indigo, the fifth red, and the sixth is 'striped with a mixture of all their colours' – and he defeats them all.

The Elucidation Prologue and Bliocadran

So beguiling was Chrétien's unfinished romance that continuators looked backwards as well as forwards. Two anonymous preludes to Chrétien's *Perceval*, translated and included here as Appendices 1 and 2, have survived, *The Elucidation Prologue* in just one manuscript and *Bliocadran* in two. The former is an intriguing curiosity, worthy of attention, but the text clearly baffled the scribe at times and contains some severely garbled passages. Interestingly, it makes the rape of maidens the dreadful act that turned the land to waste: 'no tree ever bore leaf again; the meadows and the flowers withered; the rivers dried to a trickle. And from that time forth no one could ever find the court of the wondrous Fisher King.'[109] But much of what follows makes its title 'the Elucidation' a misnomer, referring (in no coherent order) partly to narratives in Chrétien and the Continuations and partly to tales which don't exist in them at all, in such a way as to suggest that it may in fact have been wrongly attached to *Perceval* and have been intended rather as a prologue to some other compendium of Grail-related stories, now lost.

Bliocadran, however, is a different matter. This is a well written and very thoughtful addition to the work, showing in a most interesting way the response of another writer to Chrétien's poem – not, like the continuators, to its unfinished ending, but to its beginning. The author of *Bliocadran* was evidently intrigued by Perceval's mother having hidden the boy away from the world, desperate to keep him from contact with knights, and wanted to explore and develop this theme. For him (as for the continuators), consistency of detail was far less important than narrative theme, and like them he felt quite free to change details and move goalposts to serve his purpose. Chrétien had the mother tell Perceval that his father, a great knight, had been crippled by a wound in the leg and retreated to their house in the forest, where he died of grief when Perceval's two elder brothers were later killed in battle. But the *Bliocadran* author changes and expands the story: Perceval's father – Bliocadran by name – is the last of twelve brothers to survive, the other eleven having all been killed in unspecified ways, and he himself is then killed in a tournament, prompting his wife to retreat to the forest with their new-born baby (Perceval) to ensure that the same fate cannot befall him. The fact that the father is killed in a tournament can be seen as significant: the modern editor of *Bliocadran*, Lenora D. Wolfgang, has suggested that 'the underlying theme is that the chivalric practice of the tournament can be a brutal and destructive activity. This was a contemporary concern. The Church at times bitterly condemned the tournament… The tournament at the time Chrétien was writing was a live and serious issue…'[110] It is true that a major theme in Chrétien's poem is a disapproval of misdirected knightly energies, and Perceval's wandering for five years, endlessly and randomly vanquishing knights

[109] p. 558.
[110] *Bliocadran*, ed. Wolfgang (Tübingen, 1976), pp. 9–11.

'without a thought for God', is very much akin to Bliocadran and his brothers frequent travelling 'to other lands to engage in tournaments and wars, seeking to win renown and reputation'.[111] But there is no detectable disapproval of tournaments in Chrétien's description of the tourney at Tintagel, and other continuators positively revel in them. Wolfgang may be right: the shocking reality of the tournament's dangers (Bliocadran's death is horribly graphic) and the brief, blunt recounting of his burial may, it's true, have been intended as a sobering (and unsympathetic) warning about throwing life away in a reckless misdirection of knightly effort. But they can equally be seen as a way of emphasising the daunting, awesome lot of the knight and the perilous nature of the world to which Perceval, like so many youths, is irresistibly drawn. Much will depend, as we shall discuss in a moment, on the way in which key passages are delivered.

What is certain is that *Bliocadran* is a fine prelude to this great corpus of tales, for it raises in striking fashion the crucial questions: what is the true purpose of this daunting calling? Is it right for the mother to stop her son even learning about knights, simply because of the dangers? Whether right or not, what decisions about staying at home or venturing abroad should the father have made? If, as is very possible, *Bliocadran* was written before *Perlesvaus*, it is interesting that the anonymous author of the latter changed the details yet again, having Perceval's father and his eleven brothers die specifically 'in battle in the service of the Holy Prophet who renewed the Law by His death... Each lived no more than twelve years as a knight before dying in battle in their great ardour to advance the New Law.'[112] There are no doubts or reservations about *these* deaths: such valiant knights, the author of *Perlesvaus* says, gave Perceval a worthy lineage indeed; for crusading, in that author's eyes, is the true function of the knight.[113] The *Bliocadran* author, perhaps, had that very thought in mind, and understood it to be the implication of Chrétien's tantalising last, unfinished, poem.

Reading Aloud

But much depends, as ever, on interpretation. And for a medieval audience that interpretation was not simply their own but was channelled through the delivery of a reader. Reading aloud was far more common in the Middle Ages than private, solitary reading to oneself.[114] These works are essentially scripts for performance, and that must be borne in mind at every point. In *Bliocadran*, for instance, when Perceval's father is dead and newly buried, the reader-aloud is presented with the innocuous statement: 'But that's the last I'll say of him – his story's done'. The *delivery* of this is crucial: in the absence of the much clearer indications that a modern novelist would give, delivery alone determines whether this line is cold and dismissive, emphasising the foolish, pointless waste of his death in the tournament, or gently regretful, ruefully conveying the loss that is ever likely in the grimly dangerous world of knights. The same could be said about the delivery of the passage describing his death and burial:

> the youth's lance flashed over the rim of Bliocadran's shield and struck him full in the face – and right through it: the whole lance-head burst through

---

[111] Below, p. 562.
[112] *The High Book of the Grail (Perlesvaus)*, trans. Bryant (Cambridge, revised edition 2007), p. 2.
[113] In *Perlesvaus* the Grail Castle itself has to be recaptured from a heathen king.
[114] See Evelyn Birge Vitz, *Orality and Performance in Early French Romance*, Cambridge, 1999.

the back of his neck. He couldn't help but reel from the blow – it was a mortal wound; and he fell to the ground unconscious. His men came rushing to gather him up, wailing with shock and grief; and they made a bier, and in it they carried him to the castle where they'd lodged the previous night. They did all they could to comfort him, laying him gently in a chamber well away from everyone; and they saw that he was shriven. He lived for only two more days – there was nothing they could do to save him. He was carried to a church, his knights all grieving terribly, tearing at their clothes and hair. There they held a fine service for him, and then took him away to be buried.

It would be quite possible for a reader-aloud, with a blunt or wry delivery that these phrases potentially invite, to imply futility in all the wailing, grieving and tearing (and emphasise the pointless loss of life in an irresponsible, reprehensible tournament, as Wolfgang suggests); if, however, he wants to induce sympathy, then gentle, emotionally engaged delivery could make the simplicity of these sentences moving, conveying a true sense of shock. The manner adopted might well determine an audience's response to, and their very understanding of, *Bliocadran*.

The crucial importance of a reader-aloud's delivery applies at every turn. Modern novelists tend to paint vivid characters, and openly tell their silent, private reader how to hear a voice by adverbs defining speech at a given moment, or by describing facial expressions or body language. Medieval writers rarely do that – because they didn't need to: they knew that an intelligent and imaginative reader-aloud would create the voice and insinuate the meanings of moments and whole passages.[115] There are characters such as the acerbic Kay and impetuous Sagremor who are gifts for the performer, their voices and manner implicit in every word they utter; far more often, however, it needs creativity and clear understanding on the performer's part to make sense of many a passage. When, for example, Perceval takes his broken sword to Trebuchet the smith, Trebuchet knows that repairing the sword will signal his own death. So when Perceval arrives

> the old man, white with age, flew into a rage and cried: 'Curse your coming! I know exactly what you want! Did you enter here on wings?'
>
> 'No,' said Perceval. 'I overcame the two crested serpents: I battled with them till I slew them both. Now show me where I can find the smith who used to forge here.'
>
> 'What do you want with him?'
>
> 'God save me,' Perceval replied, 'I need him to repair my sword.'
>
> When the lord heard this he leapt to his feet; he trembled and turned pale; he saw the sword at Perceval's side which he himself had made; and he knew exactly where it had been broken.
>
> 'Sir knight,' he said, 'you've greatly sinned in breaking your sword, which I made long ago. You broke it at the gate of Paradise, I see, and truly, I must

---

[115] There is a parallel difference between modern and early playscripts: whereas modern playwrights give many a guiding indicator for the actor or director, anything from a pause to elaborate, explanatory paragraphs, Shakespeare and his contemporaries, for example, wrote hardly a single stage direction of any kind (not least because they would often be personally involved in rehearsal and performance).

repair it, or it will never be repaired.' With that he unlocked a wicket-gate and said: 'Dismount, sir knight, and give me your sword. I'll join the pieces together, and there'll be no risk of it ever breaking again, no matter what blow is struck with it. This sword is meant for a worthy man, truly; it's never to be in a coward's hands.'

Initially, then, the writer (Gerbert) gives the reader-aloud – just as a modern novelist would give the silent reader – one or two simple directions: Trebuchet 'flew into a rage' and later 'trembled and turned pale'; but it's up to an intelligent performer to convey, without any further directions, the change of mood and manner – stoical, subdued – in what follows. It is crucial, certainly, to conjure stoicism and resignation – through pace and timing as well as tone – if there is to be any power in the superficially bland phrases a moment later:

> He burnished the blade immaculately and repaired the inscription on it; then he returned the sword to its scabbard and said:
> 'I'll tell you now, sir: you should be counted the finest knight in the world. You've been through many perilous tests, I know, and many winters and summers, too, for the sake of the grail – and have more to go through yet, I think. And I can tell you this for certain: I've not much longer to live.'[116]

Time and again speeches on the page may appear clumsy. With no authorial interjections to indicate changes of mind, it's up to a performer to bring speeches alive, as with Yseut's, for instance, as she sees through Tristran's disguise:

> 'Ah!' she thought. 'Holy Mary! That must be Tristran, my beloved! He's come here disguised, for my sake, I'm sure of it! But no – what nonsense! Tristran has two eyes in his head – this man's lost his left. It can't be him, of course not – and he's nothing to me now: he's lied to me and betrayed me, teaching someone else the lay that he and I composed! But it must be Tristran – he's never been untrue to me! It is! I see it now, I'm sure it's him! And how could I think ill of him, when he's disguised himself like that for me? He's acted like a faithful lover, putting himself through so much for my sake!'[117]

As with lines in many a play, this may be clumsy on the eye, but it's potentially effective and amusing to the ear.

Sometimes the demands made of a performer – as with any script – are considerable. There is nothing easy, for example, about conveying the emotions of a girl who lures Gawain into her bed where she's concealed a knife, ready to murder him to avenge his killing of her brother, but then comes to be so taken with him that, after he's had his way with her,

> she sighed and wept and howled and wailed. But then she said: 'Sir, I won't lie: you'd better get up quickly or you're dead! Arm right now – my cousins'll be here and they'll show no mercy: they'll kill you on the spot! You've slain my brother and abused my body, but I don't want you killed now – though

[116] pp. 345–6.
[117] p. 371.

by the Holy Spirit, when I first lay down with you I'd have liked to rip your heart out with my hands!... Love has taken hold of me: all hatred's gone – henceforth you'll have my total love!'[118]

And there is nothing exceptional in this: the demands made of the performer are, in fact, constant. The modern, private reader of *The Story of the Grail* needs to be ever alert to apparently banal but hugely suggestive phrases that the medieval authors expected their readers-aloud to spot and exploit. In the Second Continuation, for instance, as he approaches a ruined castle, Perceval sees 'a girl sitting beneath an almond tree, combing her hair'. The last three words could hardly be simpler; how easily they can be glanced past and taken for granted; but their intelligent delivery – accompanied by the performer's suggestive enactment (it would frequently have been a visual as well as an aural experience) – can create character, atmosphere, suspicion; and it's a suspicion that will prove well founded, as moments later she tries to drown Perceval in a river.

It's on the bank of a river that one of the most atmospheric scenes in Chrétien's poem is set, when Perceval first encounters the Fisher King; but that atmosphere, the strange and haunting quality, depends entirely on delivery. It depends on a performer finding the right pace, timing and tone, and appropriate voices for the king and for Perceval – even the manner of people calling across water – as Chrétien's script gives us:

> 'Oh, almighty Lord!' said Perceval. 'If only I could cross this river I'd find my mother on the other side, I'm sure, if she's still alive.'
>
> He rode along the bank till he neared a rocky crag; the river washed right up to it: there was no further he could go. But suddenly he saw a boat coming downstream. There were two men on board. He drew rein and waited, thinking they'd keep sailing till they reached him; but they stopped and stayed dead still in midstream, anchored fast. The man in the bow was fishing with a line, baiting his hook with a little fish slightly bigger than a minnow. The boy, not knowing what to do or where to find a crossing, hailed them and asked:
>
> 'Tell me, sirs, is there any bridge across this river?'
>
> The one who was fishing replied: 'No, brother, I promise you; and I don't think there's a boat bigger than the one we're in – which wouldn't carry five men. You can't cross on horseback for twenty leagues upstream or down: there's no ferry or bridge or ford.'
>
> 'Then tell me, in God's name,' he said, 'where I might find lodging.'
>
> And the fisherman answered: 'You've need of that and more beside, I'd say. I'll give you lodging tonight...'[119]

It is with a performer's eye that any reader, silent or aloud, needs to read every line of these romances. They are scripts.

---

[118] pp. 439–40.
[119] p. 27.

Dates

Precise and certain dating of these poems is impossible, and most of the following suggestions should be prefaced with the word 'probably'. Chrétien's *Perceval* must have been written in the 1180s before Count Philip of Flanders, to whom Chrétien dedicates the poem (referring to him in the present tense), set off on the Third Crusade, during which he died at Acre in 1191.

The anonymous First Continuation – in its initial shorter form, the Long Redaction translated here almost certainly post-dating the Short – was written in the 1190s, but late enough for Robert de Boron to have already composed his 'prequel', *Joseph of Arimathea (Le Roman de l'Estoire dou Graal).*

The Second Continuation, attributed to Wauchier de Denain, followed in the early 1200s. Many manuscripts of this continuation contain an interesting reference to the count of Poitiers's fondness for a particular story,[120] and they speak of him in the past tense; this must surely be a reference to Richard Lionheart, who was count of Poitiers for most of the period from 1169 until his death in 1199 (and had a reputation among poets, to whom he was always generous, for having a good knowledge of the romances and a talent himself as a writer of songs).

Judging by their extensive borrowings from the prose romances *Perlesvaus* (probably written in the first decade of the thirteenth century) and the *Lancelot-Grail* (c. 1215–30),[121] it is likely that Manessier and Gerbert wrote their continuations – probably at the same time as one another, with no knowledge of each other's work – in the late 1220s or shortly after 1230: Manessier dedicates his work to Countess Jeanne, the 'lady and mistress of Flanders',[122] a description which applies to her best during the years when she was ruling alone, between 1214 and 1227 while her husband Ferdinand was imprisoned following his defeat at the battle of Bouvines, and between his death in 1233 and her remarriage in 1237; and Gerbert makes a reference (though it could of course be a scribal interpolation) to the splendour of the castle of Coucy in Picardy,[123] the building of which was not begun until about 1225.

Manuscripts

There are fifteen surviving manuscripts,[124] three of which contain only Chrétien's poem, others one, two or three continuations; only two contain all four. One of these two, MS français 12576 of the Bibliothèque Nationale, Paris, is of outstanding quality and was copied with a high degree of care, having very few obvious errors or accidental omissions, and its scribe took great pains to retain continuity and consistency of detail as he incorporated the continuators' work.[125] This manuscript was used by William Roach for his edition of Chrétien, and it is that text which is

---

[120] See below, p. 313 and note 32.
[121] For a detailed discussion of the 'series of parallels between Manessier's Continuation and the Prose Lancelot, too close and too numerous to be attributed to coincidence', and the 'high degree of skill' with which Manessier incorporated elements of the latter, see Corin Corley's article in *Modern Language Review* 81 (1986) listed in *Further Reading* below.
[122] Below, p. 556.
[123] p. 413.
[124] To be precise, there is a sixteenth which contains only the Second Continuation (and gives an independent conclusion to it – see Appendix 3), and fragments of Chrétien's poem have survived in four more.
[125] See, for example, p. 529, footnote 38.

translated here; it was also the base manuscript for the edition of Gerbert's Continuation by Mary Williams and Marguerite Oswald, likewise followed in this translation. However, MS 12576 does not contain the fullest version of the First Continuation; for the Long Redaction of that continuation, translated here, Roach took as the base manuscript for his edition MS 19.1.5 of the National Library of Scotland, Edinburgh; he used this also as the base manuscript for his editions of the Second and Third Continuations, and this translation follows those texts. But in the Edinburgh manuscript there are 'cases – and they are unfortunately much more numerous than in [MS 12576] – where the scribe has blundered through inattention';[126] and on those frequent occasions (too frequent to be footnoted), or where there are significant omissions, this translation has always followed a clearly better or fuller reading in other manuscripts.

Modern editions

Chrétien de Troyes, *Le Roman de Perceval ou le Conte du Graal*, ed. William Roach, Textes Littéraires Français, 2nd edition (Geneva and Paris, 1959).
Chrétien de Troyes, *Le Roman de Perceval ou le Conte du Graal: édition critique d'après tous les manuscrits*, ed. Keith Busby (Tübingen, 1993).
The Continuations of the Old French Perceval of Chrétien de Troyes, Vols. I-V, ed. William Roach (Philadelphia, 1949–83).
Gerbert de Montreuil, *La Continuation de Perceval*, ed. Mary Williams and Marguerite Oswald, Classiques Français du Moyen Âge (Paris, 1922–75).
Manessier, *La Troisième Continuation du Conte du Graal* (bilingual edition, text edited by William Roach with modern French translation by Marie-Noëlle Toury), Champion Classiques (Paris, 2004).
The Elucidation Prologue, ed. A. W. Thompson (Chicago, 1931).
Bliocadran: a Prologue to the Perceval of Chrétien de Troyes: edition and critical study, ed. Lenora D. Wolfgang (Tübingen, 1976).

Further Reading

Barber, Richard, *The Holy Grail – Imagination and Belief* (London, 2004).
Baumgartner, Emmanuèle, *Chrétien de Troyes: Le conte du graal* (Paris, 1999).
Bruckner, Matilda T., *Chrétien Continued: A Study of the Conte du Graal and its Verse Continuations* (Oxford, 2009).
Busby, Keith, *Chrétien de Troyes: Perceval (Le Conte du Graal)* (London, 1993).
Corley, Corin, 'Réflexions sur les deux premières Continuations de Perceval', *Romania*, 103 (1982), pp. 235–58.
Corley, Corin, 'Manessier's Continuation of Perceval and the Prose Lancelot Cycle', *Modern Language Review* 81 (1986), pp. 574–91.
Corley, Corin, *The Second Continuation of the Old French 'Perceval': A Critical and Lexicographical Study* (London, 1987).
Grigsby, J. L., 'Heroes and their Destinies in the Continuations of Chrétien's Perceval', *The Legacy of Chrétien de Troyes*, ed. Lacy, N. J., Kelly, D. and Busby, K. (Amsterdam, 1988), Vol. II, pp. 41–53.

---

[126] Roach, ed., *Continuations of the Perceval, Vol. II*, p. vii.

Haidu, Peter, *Aesthetic Distance in Chrétien de Troyes: Irony and Comedy in 'Cligés' and 'Perceval'* (Geneva, 1968).

Hinton, Thomas, *The Conte du Graal Cycle: Chrétien de Troyes's 'Perceval', the Continuations, and French Arthurian Romance* (Cambridge, 2012).

Keen, Maurice, *Chivalry*, New Haven and London, 1984.

Lacy, Norris J. and Grimbert, Joan T. (eds.), *A Companion to Chrétien de Troyes* (Woodbridge, 2005).

Lancelot-Grail: The Old French Vulgate and Post-Vulgate in Translation, 10 vols., ed. Norris J. Lacy (Cambridge, 2010).

Le Rider, Paule, *Le chevalier dans le 'Conte du Graal' de Chrétien de Troyes* (Paris, 1978).

Perlesvaus (The High Book of the Grail), trans. Nigel Bryant (Cambridge, revised edition 2007).

Robert de Boron, *Merlin and the Grail: Joseph of Arimathea . Merlin . Perceval*, trans. Nigel Bryant (Cambridge, 2003).

Stephens, Louise D., 'Gerbert and Manessier: the Case for a Connection', *Arthurian Literature* 14 (Cambridge, 1996), pp. 53–68.

Tether, Leah, *The Continuations of Chrétien's 'Perceval': Content and Construction, Extension and Ending* (Cambridge, 2012).

Vitz, Evelyn B., *Orality and Performance in Early French Romance,* (Cambridge, 1999).

Chrétien de Troyes: *Perceval*

Chrétien's Prologue [1]

He little reaps who little sows, and anyone wishing for a worthwhile harvest spreads his seed in such a place that God repays a hundredfold; for on worthless ground good seed will parch and fail.

Chrétien now sows the seed of a romance that he begins, and sows it in so good a place that he is bound to reap reward: his work is for the worthiest man in the empire of Rome – Count Philip of Flanders,[2] who is of even greater worth than Alexander. Alexander is deemed to have been so good, but I shall prove that the count's worth quite surpasses his; for Alexander had amassed within him all the vices and all the faults of which the count is clean and clear. The count will never listen to base jokes or spiteful words, and hates to hear ill spoken of a man, whoever he may be. The count loves justice and loyalty and holy church, and despises all baseness. And he is more generous than any man known: he gives according to the Gospel, without hypocrisy or guile, for it says: 'Let not your left hand know the good deeds done by your right';[3] let the knowing be left to the receiver – and to God, who knows every secret and sees every hidden working of men's innermost beings. And why does the Gospel say 'hide from your left hand your good deeds'? Because the left, according to the scriptures, signifies the pride that goes with false hypocrisy. And what does the right signify? Charity, which does not boast of its good works but does them covertly, so they're known only to the one whose names are God and Charity. For God is charity; and Saint Paul says – I read it there[4] – that the man who lives in charity according to the scriptures lives in God, and God in him. So know this, truly: the gifts bestowed by good Count Philip are given in charity, prompted only by his kind, fair heart which bids him do good. So is he not of greater worth than Alexander, who gave no thought to charity or other good deeds? Indeed he is; never doubt it!

So Chrétien's labour will not be vain as he strives by the count's command to put into rhyme the finest tale ever told in a royal court: the story of the grail, of which the count gave him the book.[5] Hear how he acquits himself.

---

[1] Two manuscripts feature an additional prologue, the anonymous *Bliocadran*. In one of them this is preceded by yet another, *The Elucidation Prologue*. These are given below (pp. 557–68) as Appendix 1 and Appendix 2.

[2] Philip I, count of Flanders from 1168 till his death during the epidemic that struck the crusader army at the siege of Acre in 1191. Chrétien refers to 'the empire of Rome' because the counts of Flanders held part of their land as a fief of the Holy Roman Empire.

[3] A paraphrase of Matthew 6: 3.

[4] Chrétien is presumably referring to Corinthians, chapter 13.

[5] This tantalising allusion to a written source has been the subject of much conjecture. Nothing is known for certain about what 'the book' may have been.

The Welsh Boy

It was in the time when trees burst into leaf, and fields and woods and meadows turn green, and the birds in their Latin sing so sweetly in the morning, and every being is fired with joy, that the son of the widowed lady of the lonely Waste Forest rose, and with all eagerness he saddled his hunting horse and took three javelins and set out from his mother's house.

He thought he'd go and see the harrowers who sowed her crops – twelve oxen they had, and six harrows. So into the forest he rode; and how his heart then leapt within him at the sweetness of the season and the singing of the joyful birds: how everything delighted him! The weather was so fair and mild that he took the bridle from his hunting horse and let him wander free to graze upon the fresh, green grass.

He was very skilled with his javelins, and went throwing them all around, backwards and forwards, high and low, for hours – till he heard, coming through the wood, five armed knights: all fully armed from head to foot. And their arms made a terrible din as they came, as oak- and elm-branch crashed against them; their lances clashed upon their shields, the mail-rings of their hauberks*[6] ground; wood and iron, shield and mail, all alike resounded. The boy could hear but couldn't see them as they came towards him at a walk. He was filled with awe and said:

'Upon my soul! My mother wasn't lying when she told me demons were the foulest things in the world! She taught me that to counter them a man should make the sign of the cross – but never mind that! I'm not going to cross myself – no, I'm going to hit the strongest with one of my javelins: then the others'll stay well away, I think!'

So he said before he saw them; but when he saw them openly, no longer hidden by the trees, and saw their hauberks shimmering, their burnished helmets dazzling, saw the red and the white shining brightly in the sun, and all the gold and blue and silver, he thought it handsome and glorious indeed and said:

'Oh, lord God, thank you! These are angels I see here! And truly, I've sinned terribly and done great wrong, saying they were demons! My mother was telling me no fable when she said angels were the fairest things there are – except God, who's fairer than anything. But there, I think, I see God Himself! I see one so fair that – God preserve me! – the others aren't a tenth as beautiful! My mother told me we should worship God above all things, and pray to Him and honour Him, so I'm going to worship that one there, and all the angels after Him!'

And he threw himself to the ground and spouted all the creed and prayers that he knew – taught him by his mother. The foremost of the knights saw him and said:

'Stay back! A boy has seen us and dropped to the ground in fear! If we all advanced on him at once he'd be scared to death, I think, and wouldn't be able to answer any of my questions!'

So the others drew rein while the foremost knight rode quickly up and greeted the boy and reassured him, saying: 'Don't be frightened, lad.'

'I'm not, by the Saviour I believe in,' he replied. 'You're God, aren't you?'

'No indeed!'

'Who are you, then?'

'I'm a knight.'

---

[6] An asterisk in the text indicates that the word appears in the Glossary, below, pp. 571–2.

'I've never met a knight before,' the boy said, 'or ever seen or heard of them, but you're more beautiful than God! How I wish I were the same – made like you, and shining so!'

And he drew close up to the knight, who asked him: 'Have you seen five knights and three maidens pass through this glade today?'

But the boy had other news to seek and questions of his own to ask. He reached for the knight's lance and, taking hold, said: 'Good sir, who call yourself "knight", what's this thing you're holding?'

'I see I'm to have fine guidance here!' the knight replied. 'I'd thought to learn news from you, my friend, but you want some from me! And I'll tell you: it's my lance.'

'Do you launch[7] it, then,' asked the boy, 'as I do my javelins?'

'No, lad! What a simpleton you are! You strike with it directly.'

'Then one of my javelins is far more use: I kill whatever I want with them – animals, birds – from the same range as a crossbow!'

'That's not really what concerns me, boy; answer my question about the knights. Do you know where they are? And did you see the girls?'

The boy grabbed the bottom of his shield and said, straight out: 'What's this? What's it for?'

'You're having me on, lad, aren't you?! You keep changing the subject, avoiding my question! By God, I thought you'd *give* me news rather than get it *from* me! But you want *me* to tell *you* what's what! And so I shall, come what may, for I've taken a liking to you. This thing I'm carrying is called a shield.'

'A shield?'

'And truly,' said the knight, 'I shouldn't undervalue it: it's such a faithful friend that if anything's thrown or thrust at me it sets itself against the blows – that's the way it serves me.'

Just then the knights who'd stayed behind rode briskly up to join their lord and said: 'What's this Welshman saying, sir?'

'He doesn't quite know his manners,' the lord replied. 'So help me God, he won't give me a straight reply to anything I ask! Instead he asks the name and use of everything he sees!'

'Truly, sir, the Welsh are all by nature dumber than the beasts in pasture! And this one's pretty beastly! Only a fool would dally with him – unless he wanted to fritter his time in drivelling babble!'

'Perhaps,' the first knight said, 'but truly, before I carry on I'll tell him whatever he wants to know; I'm not leaving till I do.' And he asked him yet again: 'If you don't mind, lad, tell me about the five knights and the girls: have you met or seen them today?'

The boy grabbed him by his mail coat and started tugging. 'Tell me, sir: what's this thing you're wearing here?'

'Don't you know, boy?'

'No, I don't.'

'It's my hauberk, lad, and it's heavy as iron – because it's made of iron, as you can see.'

'I wouldn't know,' he said, 'but by God it's handsome! What do you do with it? What's it for?'

---

[7] There is an untranslatable play on words here, the noun '*lance*' being echoed by the third person singular of the verb '*lancer*' (to throw). The boy hears the noun and asks: 'Are you saying you *lance* (throw) it…?'

'That's easily answered. If you aimed a javelin or an arrow at me you couldn't do me any harm.'

'Oh, sir! God keep stags and hinds from having hauberks! I'd never be able to kill one – I'd have to give up hunting them!'

'God bless you, boy,' the knight said yet again, 'can you tell me news of the knights and maidens?'

But he, in his simplicity, asked him: 'Were you born like that?'

'No, boy, that's impossible! No man could be born like this!'

'Who was it, then, made you that way?'

'I can tell you that indeed.'

'Go on, then.'

'Gladly. Not five years ago I was given all these arms by King Arthur, who dubbed me knight. But now you tell me: what became of them – the knights who passed this way with the three girls? Were they riding fast or slowly?'

And the boy replied: 'Look up there, sir: the highest wood that you can see, circling the mountain – that's where the passes of Valbone are.'

'What of it, lad?'

'My mother's harrowers are there, ploughing and sowing her land. If those people passed that way and they saw them, they'll tell you.'

The knights said they'd follow if he'd show them the way to the folk who worked the land; so the boy mounted his hunting horse and rode to where they were harrowing a field sown with oats. But when they saw their young master they trembled with alarm. Do you know why? Because of the knights they saw with him, fully armed; for they knew very well that if the knights had told him of their life and ways, then he would want to be a knight, and his mother then would lose her mind – they'd been trying to keep him from ever seeing knights or learning anything of their business. The boy asked the men who drove the oxen:

'Have you seen five knights and three girls ride this way?'

'They went through the pass this very day,' the ox-drivers said.

So the boy said to the knight who'd talked to him so long: 'Sir, the knights and girls did come this way. But tell me more about the king who makes men knights: where does he usually live?'

'I'll tell you, boy,' he said. 'The king's staying at Cardoil. He was there not five days ago – I was there, too, and saw him; and if you don't find him there now, someone will give you news of him for sure, wherever he may have gone.'

With that the knight rode off at a gallop, anxious to catch up with the others. And the boy wasn't slow to ride home, where his mother was waiting, her heart black with worry because he'd been away so long. But the moment she saw him she was filled with joy; she couldn't hide her relief – she loved her son so much – and ran to meet him, crying:

'Dear son! Dear son!' a hundred times and more. 'Dear son, I've been so afraid! You've been gone so long! I was so beset with worry I nearly died! Where have you been all day?'

'I'll tell you where, mother, and without a word of a lie: I've seen something that made my heart soar! Didn't you always tell me that the angels and our Lord God were more beautiful than any of Nature's creatures? That there was nothing fairer in the world?'

'I say so still, dear son. I said so, truly, and still do.'

'Mother, say so no more! Haven't I seen the fairest things alive, riding through the Waste Forest? They're more beautiful than God and all His angels!'

His mother took him in her arms and said: 'Oh, God preserve you, dear son! I'm so afraid for you! I do believe you've seen the angels who cause such grief, killing whoever they catch!'

'No I didn't, mother, truly, no! They say they're called knights.'

His mother collapsed and fainted at the word, hearing her son say 'knights'; and when she came to, she cried, now filled with anguish: 'Oh, alas! What blows Fate deals me! My good, dear son, I'd planned to guard you so well from knights that you'd never hear of them or see one! You should indeed have been a knight, if God had looked after your father and others close to you. In all the isles of the sea, dear son, there was no knight so renowned and feared and respected as your father. You can be proud indeed of your lineage – both on his side and on mine, for I too was born of a line of knights, the finest in the land: in all the ocean's isles there was no better lineage than mine in my time. But now the greatest of my line have fallen: it's often the case that misfortunes strike the worthy men who strive to live in honour and prowess. Iniquity and shame and sloth, they never fall, for they can sink no lower, but the good, it seems, must always be brought down! Your father – though you've never known this – was crippled by a wound in the leg, whereupon his land and all his treasures, held by him as a noble man, went to perdition and he fell into utter poverty.

'Then, after the death of King Uther Pendragon, father of the good King Arthur, worthy men were wickedly robbed of their inheritances, ruined and impoverished; the lands were laid waste and the poor folk left destitute – they took to flight, all those who could. Your father had this manor out here in the Waste Forest; he couldn't flee, so he had himself brought here on a litter, not knowing where else to go. You were just a little boy, barely weaned, little more than two years old; but you had two very dear brothers, and when they grew older, at your father's advice and prompting they went to two royal courts to receive arms and horses. The elder went to the king of Escavalon, and served him for a long while till he was dubbed a knight; and the other, born after him, went to serve King Ban of Gomorret. On one and the same day both boys were dubbed and knighted, and on one and the same day they both set out to come home to please me and their father; but he never saw them again, for they both fell in combat. Yes, both were killed in battle, and it grieves and pains me deeply. A dreadful fate befell the elder: when his body was found, crows and rooks had pecked out his eyes. Your father died of grief for his sons, and I've endured a bitter existence ever since. You've been my only treasure and consolation – all that remained to me! God left me nothing else to give me joy and comfort.'

The boy had hardly listened to a word of this. 'Give me something to eat,' he said. 'I don't know what you're on about! I'd love to go to the king who makes knights – and go I shall: I don't care what anyone says.'[8]

His mother delayed his leaving as long as she could. She fitted him out in a baggy canvas shirt, and breeches made in the Welsh style, where shoes and leggings, I believe, are made together in one piece; and he had a tunic of deerskin with a tight-fitting hood. That's how his mother dressed him! She kept him back for just three days; after that all her ploys were vain. Then terrible grief possessed her; in floods of tears she hugged and kissed him, saying:

---

[8]   Literally 'no matter who it hurts'.

'It's agony to see you go, dear son! You'll go to the king's court and bid him give you arms – and there'll be no refusal: he'll give you them, I know he will! But when it comes to using them, what'll happen then? How will you fare at something you've never done and never seen others do? Badly, I fear, indeed: you'll be hopeless! And no wonder: you can't know what you've never been taught – the wonder's when a man fails to learn what he often hears and sees.

'Dear son, I want to give you advice that you'd do well to heed: keep it in mind and it'll be much to your advantage. You'll soon be a knight if it please God – I'm sure you will. If you encounter, near or far, a lady in need of help or a maiden in distress, be ready to aid them the moment they ask: all honour lies in such deeds, and when a man fails to honour ladies his own honour is surely dead. Serve ladies and maidens and you'll be honoured everywhere. But if you should request a maiden's love, take care not to upset her by doing anything she doesn't want. And a girl who kisses gives a lot – if she consents to kiss you, I forbid you to take more! For love of me, leave it at that! But if she has a ring on her finger or a purse at her waist, and for love – or in answer to your pleas – she gives it to you, then I'm happy for you to take her ring; yes, I give you leave to take the ring or purse.

'Dear son, here's another piece of advice: on the road, or when taking lodging, share no man's company for long without asking him his name; for know this, in short: by the name he acquires one knows the man.

'Speak with worthy men, and seek their company, for a worthy man never gives false counsel to his fellows.

'Above all, I beg you go to minster or to church, to pray to our Lord to give you honour in this world and to grant that you so lead your life that you come to a good end.'

'Mother,' he said, 'what's a church?'

'It's where service is paid to God, my son, who created heaven and earth and put men and women here.'

'And what's a minster?'

'The same, my son: a beautiful and holy house where sacred relics and treasures are kept, and where we make a sacrament of the body of Jesus Christ, the holy prophet so wickedly treated by the Jews: He was betrayed and unjustly condemned, and suffered death for men and women – their souls went to Hell when they left their bodies, but He set them free. He was bound to a stake and scourged, and then crucified and crowned with thorns. To hear masses and matins, and to worship this Lord, I urge you to go to church.'

And that was that. He took his leave, his mother wept, and on went his saddle. He was dressed in the style and manner of the Welsh, and had shoes of coarse hide on his feet. He carried three javelins wherever he went, and wanted to take them now, but his mother took two of them away because he would have looked too Welsh – she'd have taken all three if she could! In his right hand, as a goad for his horse, he carried a simple stick. The mother who adored him, tears streaming, kissed him as he departed, and prayed to God to keep him safe.

'God guide you, dear son!' she cried. 'May He send you more joy than is left to me, wherever you may go!'

When the boy had gone a pebble's throw he looked back, and saw his mother collapsed at the bridge's foot; she lay there unconscious, as if she'd fallen dead. But he beat his hunting horse on the rump with his stick and rode on. His mount was sure of foot and bore him swiftly away through the forest, great and dark. He rode from early morning till the day drew to a close, and slept that night in the forest, till the bright new day appeared.

A Pie, a Ring and a Kiss

In the morning when the birds began their chorus the boy rose and mounted. On he rode until he caught sight of a pavilion pitched in a lovely meadow beside the stream from a spring. The pavilion was so fair it was a wonder: one side was vermilion and the other decked with orfrey,* and on top was a gilded eagle, beaten by the rays of the bright and blazing sun, so the whole meadow shimmered with the pavilion's light. All around this tent, the most beautiful in the world, were leafy bowers, and lodges made in the Welsh manner, of interwoven branches. The boy headed for the pavilion, and as he drew near he said:

'God, I see your house! It'd be wrong of me not to go and worship you. My mother was right: she always said a church was the fairest thing there is; and she told me that whenever I found one I should go and worship the Creator in whom I believe. Indeed I will: I'll go and pray he sends me food – I could really do with some!'

He came up to the tent and found it open; and inside he saw a bed spread with a rich silken coverlet, and in the bed, all alone, lay a young girl, sleeping. Her companions were out in the wood: her maids had gone to pick fresh flowers to strew the pavilion as they always did. As the boy entered the tent his horse neighed so loudly that the girl heard it and woke with a start; and the boy, simple soul that he was, said:

'I give you greeting, girl, like my mother taught me! She told me to greet girls whenever I met them!'

The girl trembled with fear, thinking he was mad – and charged herself with madness for letting him find her alone.

'Be off with you, boy!' she cried. 'Away, before my sweetheart sees you!'

'No, by my life! I'm going to kiss you, whatever anyone says! My mother told me to!'

'I'll never kiss you, truly I won't, not if I can help it!' cried the girl. 'Be off before my lover finds you – if he does, you're dead!'

The boy had strong arms and embraced her – gauchely, knowing no better way. Then he laid her down full-length beneath him; she struggled with all her might to get away, but she fought in vain: whether she liked it or not the boy kissed her seven times without stopping, so the story says – till he saw a ring on her finger crowned with a brilliant emerald.

'My mother also told me,' he said, 'to take the ring from your finger, but to do no more with you. So let's have the ring! I want it!'

'You'll never have my ring, I swear,' she cried, 'unless you tear it from my hand by force!'

He grabbed her hand, forced her fist open, snatched the ring from her finger and slid it on his own. Then he said: 'All the best, girl! I'm off now, and with rich reward! And it's much better kissing you than the chambermaids in my mother's house: your mouth doesn't taste sour!'

She burst into tears and said: 'Boy, don't take my ring – I'll be sorely punished, and sooner or later it'll cost you your life, I promise you!'

He didn't take in a word of this, but he knew he hadn't breakfasted: he was dying of hunger, horribly. He found a cask full of wine and beside it a silver goblet, and then saw a fresh white cloth on a bundle of rushes; he lifted it, and underneath found three lovely, new-baked venison pies – far from unappealing! To quell the hunger that beset him he broke open one of the pies and tucked in with a vengeance; then he filled the silver cup with wine: it wasn't bad – he drank great and frequent draughts. Then he said:

'I can't eat all these pies myself, girl! Come and eat – they're really tasty! We can have one each and there'll still be a whole one left!'

But for all his calls and urgings, the girl just sobbed and couldn't say a word. She wrung her hands and wept piteously, while the boy ate and drank till he'd had his fill. Then he covered up what was left and took his leave without more ado, commending her to God – not that his good wishes pleased her.

'God preserve you, dear girl!' he said. 'And don't be upset that I took your ring – before I die I'll repay you for it. I'm off now, by your leave.'

The girl, in tears, swore she'd never commend him to God: because of him she'd suffer greater shame and distress than any hapless girl had ever known; and she didn't want any help from him as long as he lived – he should realise he'd betrayed her. And so she was left there, weeping.

It wasn't long before her lover returned from the wood; and when he saw the hoof-prints left by the boy he was most aggrieved. Then he found his sweetheart in tears and said:

'Damsel, from the signs I see I'd say a knight's been here!'

'No, sir, no, I promise you! But a Welsh boy has – a bothersome, base and foolish youth who drank as much of your wine as he fancied and ate some of your pies!'

'And that's what's made you cry, my dear? I'd gladly have let him eat and drink the lot!'

'But that's not all, sir,' she said. 'There's also my ring: he grabbed it from me and carried it off! I'd rather have died than have had him take it!'

Her love was most put out at this, his heart incensed. 'In faith,' he cried, 'this is an outrage! Since he's taken it, let him keep it – but I think he did more! If he did, don't keep it from me!'

'Sir,' she said, 'he kissed me.'

'Kissed you?'

'Yes indeed, but against my will!'

'No!' he cried, in a ferment of jealousy. 'It was as you wished, and pleased you well! He met with no resistance! You think I don't know you? Indeed I do – I know you well! I'm not so blind or boss-eyed that I can't see through your falseness! You've taken a wicked course – a course that'll bring you pain! Your horse will have no oats to eat or any care till I've had revenge: if he loses a shoe he'll go without – and if he drops dead you'll have to follow me on foot! And you'll have no change of clothes: what you're wearing now you're stuck with! You'll follow me on foot and naked if need be, till I have that Welsh boy's head – I'll settle for no less!'

And with that he sat down and began to eat.

The Red Knight

Meanwhile the boy went riding on, until he saw a charcoal burner coming, driving an ass before him.

'Worthy donkey-driver,' he said, 'tell me the quickest way to Cardoil. I want to see King Arthur: they say he makes knights there.'

'Carry on this way, lad,' he replied. 'There's a castle overlooking the sea. You'll find King Arthur there, my friend, filled with joy and sorrow.'

'Joy and sorrow? Why's that? Do tell me.'

'I will. In short, King Arthur and his whole army fought against Rion, king of the Isles, and Rion was defeated – hence King Arthur's joy. But he's upset that his companions have gone to stay at whichever castles they thought best, and he's no news of them at all – that's what's caused his sorrow.'

The boy cared little for the charcoal burner's news, only for his directions; he carried on the way he'd shown till he caught sight of a castle overlooking the sea, superbly positioned, and fine and strong. And then he saw, riding out of the gate, an armed knight carrying a golden cup: in his left hand he held his reins and lance and shield, and in his right the cup of gold. His arms looked splendid, and were entirely red. The boy gazed at these handsome, brand new arms and was very taken with them.

'In faith,' he said, 'I'll ask the king for those! I'd love it if he gave them to me! A curse on the man who'd seek any different!'

With that he hurried on towards the castle: he couldn't wait to reach the court. But as he drew near, the knight stopped him and asked:

'Where are you off to, lad? Tell me.'

'To the court,' he said, 'to ask the king for those arms!'

'And well you might, boy!' said the knight. 'Off you trot, then, quickly, and then come back. And tell this to that worthless king: that if he doesn't want to hold his land as my vassal he should surrender it to me or send a champion to defend it against me, for I say it's mine. To prove the point, I just took this cup from under his nose, with the very wine he was drinking!'

He should have looked for a different messenger – the boy hadn't heard a word. He rode straight on to the court, where the king and his knights were seated at dinner. The hall was on ground level so the boy went in on horseback. It was paved with flagstones, and as long as it was wide. King Arthur was sitting at the head of the table, deep in thought; all the knights were laughing and joking, but not the king: he was silent, troubled. The boy came forward, but didn't know which one to hail – he'd know idea who was the king. Then Yvonet came up to him, holding a knife in his hand.

'Vassal,' said the boy, 'you with the knife – show me which of these men is the king.'

The courteous Yvonet replied: 'There he is, friend.'

The boy rode straight up to the king and hailed him, in his own way. But the king was still lost in thought and didn't say a word. So the boy addressed him a second time; the king mused on and said nothing.

'By my life,' said the boy, 'this king never made a knight! How could he, when you can't get a word out of him?'

So he made to go, and turned his hunting horse about; but he pulled his mount so near the king, like the rude soul that he was, that, without a lie, he sent the king's hat flying from his head to the table. The king turned his bowed head to the boy and abandoned his musing and said:

'Welcome, dear brother. Please don't take it amiss that I didn't return your greeting: grief and outrage stopped my tongue, for my worst enemy, the one who hates and troubles me most, is now contesting my land – he's madly claiming he'll have it all, unconditionally, whether I like it or not! The Red Knight of the Forest of Quinqueroi, that's his name. And the queen had come to sit here beside me, to see and to comfort the knights who are wounded; I wouldn't have cared about the Red Knight's bluster, had he not taken my cup from before me, and snatched it up so recklessly that he tipped the whole cupful of wine over the queen! It was a rude, base, disgraceful act; the queen ran off to her chamber, burning with rage, suicidal with anger – by God, I don't think she'll get over it: I think it's going to kill her!'

The boy cared not a jot about the king's story or his upset or his shame – and just as little about the queen.

'Make me a knight, lord king,' he said. 'I want to be off!'

The eyes in the head of this untaught youth were bright with excitement. No one who saw him thought him wise, but all who saw him thought him handsome and charming.

'Dismount, friend,' said the king, 'and give that hunting horse of yours to a page: he'll look after him as you wish. Shortly you shall be a knight, to my honour and your advantage.'

But the boy replied: 'The ones I met in the glade never dismounted – why do you want *me* to? By my life I'll not step down! Just hurry up, then I can go!'

'Ah, my dear friend!' said the king. 'I'll do so gladly, to your advantage and my honour.'

'By the faith I owe the Creator, my good lord king,' said the boy, 'I'll not be a knight for long without being a *red* knight! Grant me the arms of the one I met outside the gate – the one who's taken your golden cup.'

Kay the seneschal,* who was one of the wounded, was angered by these words and said: 'How right you are, friend! Go at once and take his arms – they're yours! How wise of you to come and ask!'

The king heard this and was annoyed; he said to Kay: 'It's wrong of you to mock the boy, and it ill becomes a worthy man. Just because the boy's naïve, it doesn't mean he's not a noble youth: his upbringing may be to blame, at the hands of a poor master; he may yet prove a worthy knight. It's base to mock others – as it is to promise without giving. No worthy man should promise anything that he cannot or will not give, lest he incur the resentment of one who was his friend before the pledge and who, since it was made, expects it to be honoured. It's clearly better to refuse from the start than to raise false hopes. The fact is, a man who makes a pledge and fails to keep it is deceiving and fooling himself: he's robbing himself of a friend's goodwill.'

As the king said this to Kay, the boy, turning to leave, saw a fair, most comely girl and greeted her; she returned his greeting, and then laughed, and as she laughed she said:

'If you live long, boy, my heart tells me that in all the world there will never be – nor will there ever have been known – a finer knight than you: so I think and feel and believe.'

This girl – who hadn't laughed for more than six years – said these words loud enough for all to hear, and they enraged Kay; he leapt forward and slapped her so hard on her tender cheek that he laid her full length on the floor. And turning back from hitting the girl he ran into a court fool standing by a chimney, and in his raging temper he kicked him into the blazing fire, because this fool had always said:

'That girl will never laugh till she sees the one who's destined to be the greatest of all knights.'

The fool howled, the girl wept, and the boy delayed no longer: without a word from anyone he set off after the Red Knight. Yvonet, who knew his way around and was a keen purveyor of news to court, slipped away all on his own through a garden beside the hall and down through a postern gate and out to the path where the knight was waiting for adventure and a trial of chivalry, the golden cup placed on a block of grey stone beside him. The boy was racing towards him to take his arms, and when he'd ridden within earshot he cried:

'Lay down those arms! King Arthur commands that you bear them no more!'

The knight asked: 'Well, boy, does anyone dare come and defend the king's right? If so, out with it!'

'What the devil? Are you making fun of me, sir knight, not taking off those arms of mine? Off with them, quick! I command you!'

'I'm asking you, boy,' said the knight, 'if anyone's coming to fight me on the king's behalf.'

'Sir knight, take those arms off right away or I'll take them off you! I'm not letting you have them any more! I'm warning you: I'll hit you if you make me say it again!'

The knight was angered then; with both hands he swung his lance and gave the boy such a blow across the shoulders with the shaft that he rocked forward over his horse's neck. The pain of the blow incensed the boy. He aimed straight for the knight's eye, and let fly his javelin so fast that the knight neither heard nor saw it; it went clean through the eye and into the brain, and out through the nape of the neck the blood and brain came spilling. The knight's heart burst with agony, and he pitched over and crashed to the ground, stone dead. The boy dismounted, and laid the knight's lance to one side and took the shield from his neck. But he didn't know how to tackle the helm on his head: he couldn't think how to remove it; and he wanted to ungird his sword but didn't know how – nor could he draw it from its scabbard: he just grabbed the sword and yanked and heaved. Yvonet began to laugh when he saw the boy's bewilderment, and said:

'What's going on, friend? What are you doing?'

'I don't know. From what your king said I thought he'd given me these arms, but I'll have to chop the knight to bits before I get them! They're so tight to the body that inside and out are all one piece, it seems – they're stuck together solid!'

'Don't worry,' said Yvonet. 'I'll separate them if you like!'

'Go on, then,' said the boy, 'and let me have them, quickly.'

So Yvonet set to work and stripped the knight right down to his toes: he left him neither hauberk nor chausses,* nor the helm on his head nor any other piece of armour. But the boy wouldn't lay aside his own clothes: for all Yvonet's pleas he wouldn't take the gorgeous tunic of quilted silk that the knight had worn beneath his mail; nor could Yvonet talk him out of the rough cloth boots tied round his feet.

'The devil!' said the boy. 'You must be joking! Change the fine clothes my mother made me just the other day for this knight's stuff? My nice thick canvas shirt for his, all soft and thin? Give up my tunic that never leaks for this thing, that wouldn't keep out a drop? Hang anyone who'd swap good clothes for bad!'

Teaching a fool's not easy. All pleas were vain: he wouldn't take a thing except the armour. Yvonet helped him into it: he fastened the spurs over his ankle-boots, which the boy kept on over the chausses; then he clad him in the hauberk – a finer one was never seen; and over the mail hood he placed the helm, which fitted him perfectly; and he showed him how to gird the sword so that it hung loose and well. Then he set the boy's foot in the stirrup and helped him mount the knight's destrier:* he'd never seen stirrups before and knew nothing of spurs – he'd only used sticks and switches. And lastly Yvonet brought the shield and the lance and handed them to him. Before Yvonet turned back, the boy said to him:

'Have my hunting-horse, friend – take him with you: he's really good but you can have him – I don't need him any more. And take the king's cup back to him with my regards. And say this to the girl Kay slapped on the cheek: that if I can, before I die I mean to deal with him so that she can count herself avenged.'

Yvonet said he'd return the king's cup and deliver his message faithfully. With that they parted and went their ways.

Through the door of the hall where the barons sat came Yvonet; he carried the cup to the king and said: 'Rejoice, sire! That knight of yours who was here just now has sent you back your cup!'

'Which knight do you mean?'

'The one who just left,' said Yvonet.

'What? You mean the Welsh boy,' said the king, 'who asked me for the red[9] arms of the knight who's done all in his power to shame me?'

'Yes indeed, sire!'

'And how did he get my cup? Did the knight feel so well disposed to him that he returned it of his own free will?'

'On the contrary! The boy made him pay dearly for it: he killed him!'

'How did that happen?'

'I don't know, sire – except I saw the knight hit him with his lance and hurt him, and the boy struck back with a javelin, right through the eye, so that blood and brain spilled out behind, and laid him out dead on the ground.'

'Ah, Kay!' said the king to the seneschal. 'You've done me no favour! With your offensive tongue, ever spouting abuse, you've robbed me of the boy who's served me so well this day!'

'And truly, sire,' said Yvonet, 'he gave me a message for the queen's maid, slapped by Kay out of bile and spite: he says he'll take revenge if he has the chance.'

The fool, who was sitting beside the fire, heard this and came bounding to the king, hopping and skipping for joy, and said: 'By God, lord king, adventures are about to come our way – and many will be forbidding and tough! And I promise Kay this: he'll rue the work of his hands and his feet and his base, daft tongue! Before a fortnight's out the knight will have avenged the kick he gave me, and the slap he gave the girl will be well repaid and dearly bought, for he'll break his right arm between elbow and armpit! He'll carry it in a sling for half a year, indeed he will; he can avoid it no more than death!'

Kay was so incensed by this that he nearly burst with rage and fury; he'd have killed the fool in front of everyone, but refrained from attacking him for fear of incurring the king's wrath.

'Ah!' cried the king. 'Ah, Kay! You've upset me today, indeed you have! If the boy had been given guidance in the use of arms, so he knew something about handling a shield and lance, he'd have made a good knight for sure. But he knows nothing about arms or anything else – he couldn't even draw his sword if he had to! So now he's sitting, armed, on his destrier, and he's bound to meet a knight who'll have no qualms about maiming him to win his horse! He'll be killed or crippled in an instant: he won't know how to defend himself! He's such a simple, untaught soul he'll soon be done for!'

Such was the king's lament for the boy. He looked crestfallen; but worrying would do no good, and he said no more.

---

[9] '*sinople*': see Glossary.

Training in Arms

The boy went riding through the forest without a stop, till he came to open ground beside a river. It was wider than a crossbow's range, but all the water that ebbed and flowed stayed within its banks. He rode right across a meadow towards this great, roaring river, but he didn't venture in: he saw that it was dark and rushing, a good deal deeper than the Loire. So he rode along the bank. On the opposite side rose a great crop of rock, the water beating at its foot, and on one side of the rock, where it sloped down to the sea, stood a splendid, mighty castle. As the river opened into a bay the boy turned to his left and saw the castle's towers being born – for in his eyes they were being born, emerging from the rock. In the middle of the castle stood a great, strong tower, and a mighty barbican faced the bay and made its stand against the sea that pounded at its foot. At the four corners of the castle wall, made of great, square, solid stones, were four turrets, handsome and strong. The castle was finely positioned indeed, and well arranged inside. Before the round gatehouse a bridge spanned the river: it was tall and strong, built of stone and sand and lime and crenellated; and half way across was another tower, with a drawbridge in front, designed and built to serve as it should: as a bridge by day and a gate by night. Towards it the boy now headed.

Dressed in a rich and deep-hued gown, a nobleman was strolling on the bridge, carrying a cane for appearance's sake and followed by two servants, lightly dressed. Up rode the boy. He was very mindful of his mother's advice, for he gave the nobleman his greeting and said:

'My mother taught me that, sir!'

'God bless you, dear brother,' the noble said, seeing from his words he was a simpleton. 'And where have you come from?'

'Where? From King Arthur's court!'

'And what have you been up to there?'

'The king – God send him good fortune – made me a knight!'

'A knight? God bless me, I thought he'd forgotten such matters for now – I thought he'd other things on his mind than making knights. But tell me, good brother, who gave you those arms?'

'The king did.'

'Really? How was that?'

So the boy told him, just as you've heard in the story: to repeat it would be a bore and pointless – no tale gains from repetition. The nobleman questioned him further, asking him about his horsemanship.

'I run him up and down all right, just like I did the hunter that I took from my mother's house.'

'And how do you manage with your arms, my friend?'

'I know how to get them on and off: I watched the lad put them on me and strip them off the knight I killed. They're very nice and light to wear – no bother at all!'

'By my life, that's good,' the noble said. 'I'm glad of that! So tell me, if you will, what's brought you here?'

'Well, sir, my mother told me to sound out worthy men wherever I found them, and to trust in what they said, for there was much to gain by heeding them.'

'God bless your mother, friend,' the noble said. 'She gave you good advice! Have you anything else to tell me?'

'Yes.'
'What's that?'
'Just one thing: give me lodging tonight.'
'Gladly,' said the nobleman, 'if you'll do me a favour that'll help you, too.'
'What's that?'
'Trust your mother's advice, but also mine.'
'In faith,' said the boy, 'I promise you that!'
'Dismount, then.'

And the boy stepped down. One of the two servants who'd come there took charge of his horse while the other helped him from his armour. That left him in his ridiculous get-up: in the ankle-boots and ill-made, ill-cut deerskin tunic given him by his mother. They fitted the noble with the sharp steel spurs that the boy had brought, and he mounted the boy's horse, hung the shield round his neck by its strap and took up the lance and said:

'Now learn about arms, my friend: observe how to hold a lance and how to spur and control a horse.'

And he unfurled the pennon and showed the boy how a shield should be held, making it hang forward a little till it was touching the horse's neck; then he set the lance in its rest and spurred the horse on. It was worth a hundred marks, that horse: none ever charged with more will, more speed or more power. The nobleman was highly skilled with shield and horse and lance, having practised the art since childhood, and everything he did thrilled and delighted the boy. When he'd finished his fine mock-combat, watched by the boy with rapt attention, he returned to him with lance raised and asked him:

'Well, friend, could you handle the lance and shield like that, and spur and control your mount?'

The boy declared outright that he didn't want to live another day or acquire the slightest wealth unless he was able to do those things.

'My dear friend,' said the nobleman, 'what a man can't do he can learn to do, if he's willing to work and apply himself. All skills need heart and effort and practice: with those three they can be learnt. And you shouldn't be ashamed or blamed if you can't do what you've never done and never seen another do.'

Then he told him to mount, and the boy began to bear the lance and shield as perfectly as if he'd spent his life in tournaments and wars and roamed every land in search of battle and adventure; for it came to him quite naturally, and with nature instructing him and his whole heart committed he was bound to have no trouble – not when nature and heart strove together. He gave such a fine account of himself that the noble was delighted, and said to himself that if the boy had spent his whole life in the practice of arms it would still have been impressive.

When the boy had finished he came back to the nobleman with lance raised, just as he'd seen him do, and said: 'Did I do all right, sir? Do you think it's worth my while to keep working at it? I've never set eyes on anything I've wanted quite so much! I'd love to be as good at it as you!'

'Don't worry, friend,' said the nobleman. 'If you set your heart on it, you will.'

Three times he mounted and three times taught him everything he could, until he'd taught him a good deal, and three times he bade the boy do likewise. After the final time he asked him:

'If you met a knight and he struck you, what would you do?'
'I'd hit him back!'

'And if your lance broke?'
'Then there'd be nothing else for it: I'd lay into him with my fists!'
'No you wouldn't, friend!'
'What should I do, then?'
'Join combat with the sword.' And he planted the lance bolt upright in the ground, eager now to show the boy how to defend himself with the sword if he were attacked, and to go on the offensive if the chance arose. Gripping the sword he said to the boy: 'This is how you defend yourself if anyone attacks you.'

'Before God,' said the boy, 'I know more about that than anyone: I learned all about it at my mother's, practising with cushions and bucklers – often till I was quite worn out!'

'In that case let's go straight inside!' the noble said. 'I've nothing more to tell you! Tonight we'll enjoy the finest hospitality[10] – no one shall stand in our way!'

They both set off then side by side, and the boy said to his host: 'Sir, my mother taught me not to go with a stranger and share his company for long without knowing his name. If she was right I'd like to know yours.'

'Dear friend,' he replied, 'my name is Gorneman de Gorhaut.'

So they walked into the castle, hand in hand. As they climbed the steps to the hall a page came eagerly to meet them bearing a short mantle, in which he hurriedly dressed the boy in case he caught some harmful cold after being so hot. Gorneman's house was rich and grand and handsome and his servants very able: dinner was already prepared, and a fine and appealing spread it was indeed. The knights washed and sat down to dine. Gorneman sat the boy next to him, and had him eat with him, sharing the same bowl. But I shan't go on about the meal – how many dishes they had or what they were; suffice it to say that they ate and drank their fill. And when they rose from the table Gorneman, courteous soul that he was, asked the boy who'd sat beside him to stay a month; he'd gladly keep him a whole year if he wished, and in that time he'd teach him, if he cared to learn, things that would be of great use in time of need. But the boy replied:

'Sir, I don't know if I'm near my mother's house, but I pray that God may lead me there so I can see her again; I saw her fall in a faint at the foot of the bridge outside the gate, and I don't know if she's alive or dead. She fainted with grief at my leaving her, I know it. So I can't stay long, not till I know how she is; I'll leave tomorrow morning.'

Gorneman could see it was no use pleading with him. They said no more, and retired to rest without another word, the beds being already made.

Early next morning Gorneman rose and went to find the boy still abed. He had a shirt and breeches of fine linen brought to him as a gift, and hose dyed with brazil-wood, and a tunic of violet silk woven and made in India; all these things he gave him, and said:

'Take my advice, friend, and wear these clothes.'

'You can't be serious, sir!' said the boy. 'Aren't the clothes my mother made me better? You want me to wear *these*?'

'By my life and the eyes in my head, lad, these are better by far!'

'Much worse, you mean!'

'You promised, friend, when I brought you in, you'd do everything I told you!'

---

[10] '*l'ostel Saint Juliien*': a reference to the legend of Saint Julian the Hospitaller (the patron saint of travellers seeking lodging), implying total hospitality.

'And so I will,' said the boy. 'I shan't break my word in any way.'

So he delayed no longer and donned the clothes, abandoning the ones his mother had made. Then Gorneman knelt and fastened the boy's right spur; for it was the custom that whoever made a knight should fix his spur. There were a good number of other boys present, and all who could lent a hand to arm him. And Gorneman took the sword and girded it on the boy and kissed him, and said that with the sword he'd bestowed upon him the highest order created and ordained by God: the order of knighthood, which should be entirely free of baseness. Then he said:

'Good brother, be ever mindful of this: if you have to fight a knight and you gain the upper hand, so that he can resist no longer and is forced to beg for mercy, then I pray and entreat you, be sure to grant it: don't kill him.

'Another thing: don't be too keen on talking. Anyone who talks too much will often say things that make him look a fool; in the words of the wise: "Speaking too much is a grave mistake." So I advise you, friend, not to have too loose a tongue.

'I ask this of you, too: if you find a man or woman, orphan or lady, in any kind of distress, you'll do well to lend them aid if you can see a way and it's in your power.

'And one more lesson I have for you, and don't disparage it – it's not to be scorned: go willingly to church and pray to the one who created all, that He may have mercy on your soul hereafter, and in this world guard you as His Christian.'

The boy replied: 'May all the apostles of Rome, good sir, bless you for your advice: my mother said the same!'

'Never say, dear brother,' said Gorneman, 'that your mother taught you such and such: say it was me. I don't blame you for having said so hitherto, but from now on please refrain – if you keep on saying it, people will think you're mad.'

'What shall I say, then, sir?'

'You can say that the vavasor* who fastened your spur taught and instructed you so.'

And the boy promised that as long as he lived he wouldn't mention anyone but him, for he trusted his advice.

Then Gorneman raised his hand and blessed him with the sign of the cross and said: 'Since you don't wish to stay and are determined to go, go with God and may He guide you.'

The Siege of Beaurepaire

So the new knight left his host, impatient now to return to his mother and to find her alive and well. He headed into the lonely forests, being more at home there than in open country, knowing the ways of the woods.

He kept riding till he caught sight of a castle. It was strong and well sited, but outside the walls there was nothing but sea and river and wasteland. He pressed on towards it till he neared the gate, but before he could reach it he had to cross a bridge so weak he wasn't sure it would take his weight; but he ventured on, and crossed without harm or mishap. But when he came to the gate he found it locked. He didn't hammer gently, and his cries were none too soft. He pounded away till a thin, pale girl came running to the windows of the hall and cried:

'Who's calling?'

He looked up and saw her and said: 'I'm a knight, dear girl, asking you to let me in and give me lodging tonight.'

'Lodging you shall have, sir,' she replied, 'though you'll give me little thanks for it! But we'll show such hospitality as we can.'

The girl drew back from the window then, and the boy, left below at the gate, felt he was being made to wait too long and started to shout again. Then four retainers, each with a stout sword in his belt and an axe in hand, came and unlocked the gate and said:

'Come this way.'

If they'd been in a happy state they'd have been fine figures of men; but they'd suffered so much from lack of food and sleep that they were a piteous sight. And just as he'd found the land outside deserted and bare, so he found precious little within. Everywhere he went he found the streets empty and the houses in ruins, with not a man or woman to be seen. There were two churches in the town that had both been abbeys: one of nuns, now lost and fearful, the other of monks, bereft, bewildered; these churches were adorned with neither ornament nor tapestry – instead he saw their walls cracked and crumbling, their towers roofless. And the doors of the houses hung open at night as they did by day. No millstone ground, no oven baked in any part of the town; there wasn't a drop of wine or a scrap of bread – not a pennyworth of anything. The castle he'd found was devoid of all: there was no bread or any other dough;[11] and no wine, no cider, no ale.

The four retainers led him to a slate-roofed hall and helped him dismount and disarm. Then a boy came down the steps with a grey mantle which he draped across his shoulders, while another stabled his horse – though there was hardly any corn or oats or hay: it had all run out. The others ushered him up to the hall, which was handsome indeed, and two noblemen and a girl came to meet him. These gentlemen were grey with age but not altogether white – indeed they'd have been in the prime of health and strength had it not been for their troubles and their woe; and the girl was more elegant, comely and graceful than a hawk or popinjay. Her bliaut* and mantle were of dark purple* spangled with gold; there was no trace of wear on the ermine lining, and the neck of her mantle had a border of sable, black and grey, of a perfect length and breadth. And if I've ever described the beauty bestowed by God upon a woman's face or body I must do so once more, and not a single word will be a lie: her head was bare, and the hair revealed was so fair and shining that anyone who saw it would have thought it was made of pure gold, if such a thing were possible; her forehead was high and white and smooth, as if carved by hand from stone or wood or ivory; her eyebrows were fine and perfectly spaced, and her eyes were clear, well set and bright with life; her nose was smooth and straight; and in her cheeks the red blended with the white more perfectly than sinople* with argent* in heraldry. Truly, God had made in her a prodigy for stealing men's hearts! He'd never made her like before and has never done so since! When the knight saw her he greeted her and she greeted him, as did the two knights with her. Then she took him by the hand most courteously and said:

'Good sir, your lodging tonight will certainly not be such as befits a worthy man: if I told you the full extent of our plight, you might think it was a base attempt to make you leave! But come now, please, and take lodging, such as it is, and may God grant you better tomorrow!'

And she led him by the hand to a chamber with a painted ceiling, spacious and most handsome. They sat together on a quilt of samite spread across a bed. Knights crowded into the room in groups of four and five and six and sat down quietly, looking at the

---

[11]   '*paste*', essentially related to modern pasta.

one who was seated beside their lady not saying a word. He was refraining from talking because he was mindful of the advice that Gorneman had given him, and all the knights began whispering to each other about his silence.

'God,' they all said, 'I wonder if this knight's a mute? It would be a great pity: never was such a handsome knight born of woman! He looks so well beside our lady, and our lady beside him – if only they weren't both struck dumb! He's so handsome, and she's so fair, that no knight and maiden were ever so well matched: they look as if God made them for each other and planned to join them all along!'

They couldn't stop talking about it. And the girl kept waiting for him to speak to her about something or other, till she realised he wasn't going to say a word unless she did so first. So she said, very charmingly:

'Where have you come from today, good sir?'

'Damsel,' he replied, 'I've been staying at the castle of a nobleman where I had very fine lodging indeed. It has five strong, splendid towers, one big and four small; I could describe it all but I don't know its name – though I do know the name of the worthy noble: Gorneman de Gorhaut.'

'Oh, dear friend!' said the girl. 'That's well and courteously said! May God the King bless you for calling him worthy: you never said a truer word! A worthy man he is indeed, by Saint Richier – I can testify to that. I'm his niece, you know, but I haven't seen him for a very long time. I'll swear you won't have met a finer man since you left home. He'll have given you delightful lodging, good and kindly soul that he is – and powerful, too, and well served and rich. But here we have only five small loaves which an uncle of mine, a prior, a most devout and holy man, sent me for supper tonight, and a little cask of sour wine. There's no other food here but a roebuck that one of my servants shot this morning with an arrow.'

She gave orders then for the tables to be set; her bidding was done and everyone sat down to supper. They didn't sit eating long, but the food was taken eagerly. When they'd finished they parted: those who'd kept watch the night before stayed behind to sleep, and those who were on guard that night went and made ready. Fifty servants and knights kept watch that night, while the others did all they could to see to their guest's comfort. He was bedded in white sheets and a costly spread with a fine pillow beneath his head: he had that night all the comfort and pleasure imaginable in bed – except the enjoyment of a girl, had it been his wish, or a lady, had it been allowed. But he knew nothing about love or anything else, and in no time he fell asleep, untroubled and free of all cares.

But his hostess, shut up in her chamber, could get no rest. While he slept at ease she was burdened with worry: she was defenceless in the face of an imminent battle. She tossed and turned, back and forth, in terrible anxiety. Finally she threw a mantle of scarlet silk over her shift, summoning up her courage to take the risk; it was no easy decision – she'd go to her guest and tell him something of her plight. She rose from her bed and left her chamber, in such trepidation that she shook in every limb and broke into a sweat. Out of her chamber she came, weeping, and made her way to the bed where he lay sleeping. She sobbed and sighed deeply, and went down on her knees and wept until her tears spilt over his face, but she couldn't bring herself to do more. She wept so much that at last he woke, startled and bewildered to find his face all wet, and saw her kneeling beside his bed, hugging him tightly about the neck. He responded kindly, taking her in his arms and drawing her to him, saying:

'What's the matter, dear girl? Why have you come?'

'Oh, gentle knight, have pity on me! In the name of God and His son, don't think ill of me for coming here: I may be almost naked but I had no foolish, base or wicked thought! There's not a living soul as burdened with grief and misery as I: nothing brings me pleasure or comfort, and I don't have a day free of care, so unfortunate am I! But I'll see no night beyond tonight, nor any day beyond tomorrow: I'm going to kill myself by my own hand! Of three hundred and ten knights who used to man this castle only fifty now remain: two hundred and sixty have been dragged away and killed or imprisoned by an evil knight named Engygeron, the seneschal of Clamadeus of the Isles. I grieve as much for the captured as the slain – I know they'll die: they'll never escape. So many worthy men have died for me: I've every reason to despair! Engygeron has besieged us here for a whole winter and summer, never moving; and his strength increases constantly, while ours has waned and our provisions are exhausted: we've not enough left to feed one man properly! We're now in such a plight that tomorrow, unless God intervenes, this castle will be surrendered – it can hold out no longer – and I'll be surrendered with it as a wretched captive. But I'll kill myself before he takes me alive, truly I will: he'll have me dead – then I won't care if he carries me off! Clamadeus expects to have me, but he never will, not at all – except bereft of life and soul! In a casket I keep a knife of finest steel – I'll bury it in my heart! That's what I had to tell you; I'll go now and let you rest.'

The knight could soon earn praise indeed if he had the courage, for whatever she might have given him to understand, the only reason she'd come and wept on his cheeks was to inspire him to take up the battle to defend her land, if he had the courage to be her champion. He said to her:

'Cheer up, my dear; take comfort now and stop your weeping. Come up here beside me and wipe the tears from your eyes. If it be God's will, he'll send you better fortune tomorrow than you think. Come and lie beside me on this bed – it's wide enough for us both. You'll not leave me tonight.'

'Very well,' she said, 'if that's your wish.'

And he kissed her and held her fast in his arms, and drew her gently and softly under his blanket. She let him kiss her – and I don't think she minded! They lay like that all night, side by side, lip to lip, till morning and the approach of dawn. She found great comfort that night as they slept lip to lip, arm in arm, till daybreak. At dawn the girl returned to her chamber, and without the help of a maid or waiting-woman she dressed and made herself ready, waking no one.

As soon as they saw day break, those who'd been keeping watch that night woke the sleepers, rousing them from their beds; they rose without delay. At the same time the girl returned to her knight and said to him most courteously:

'God give you a good day, sir. I'm sure you won't be staying long: what would be the point? You'll leave, I know, and it would be wrong of me to object, for we've done you no honour or service here. I pray God has better lodging in store for you, with more bread and wine and everything else than you've had from us!'

'Fair damsel,' he replied, 'I shan't be looking for other lodging today; I'll be bringing peace to all your land instead, if I possibly can. If I find your enemy outside I'll not abide his staying there to harass you in any way. But if I kill and vanquish him I ask as my reward that your love may be mine. I'll take no other payment.'

Then she answered him, most graciously: 'Sir, you've asked of me a small, poor thing, and if it were denied you'd take it as pride, so I won't refuse. But don't say that the condition of having my love is that you go and die for me! That would be a grievous shame! Be sure of this: you're not yet strong or old enough to survive a battle against so great and tough and forbidding a knight as the one who waits outside.'

'You'll see if that's so today,' he said, 'for I'm going to fight him. Nothing you can say will stop me.'

She'd fashioned her speech very cleverly, pretending to plead against his plan when it was just what she wanted! People often belie their wishes when they see a man eager to do their will, so as to fire his keenness even more! And that's what she did so skilfully – inspiring him to do what she staunchly deplored!

He called for his arms and they were brought; they armed him and mounted him on a horse made ready in the courtyard. But everyone present looked daunted as they said:

'Sir, may God send you His aid today, and heap misfortune on Engygeron the seneschal who's laid waste all this land!'

Such was the prayer of every man and woman. They led him in a convoy to the gate; and seeing him outside they all cried with one voice: 'Good sir, may the true cross on which God allowed His son to suffer guard you today from mortal peril, misfortune and capture, and bring you safely back to where you may rest at ease in happiness and comfort.' Such was the prayer of all.

Men in the besieging army saw him coming. They pointed him out to Engygeron, who was sitting outside his tent, chausses already laced, expecting the castle to be surrendered before nightfall, or that someone would come out to engage him in single combat. And his men were in high spirits, thinking they'd conquered the castle and the whole country. He mounted a mighty, sturdy charger and came calmly up to the knight at a walk, and said:

'Who sent you here, boy? Tell me your business: have you come in search of peace or battle?'

'You'll tell me first,' he replied, 'what are you doing in this land? Why have you been killing their knights and ravaging the country?'

Engygeron answered, like the haughty, arrogant man he was: 'I want that castle cleared forthwith and the keep surrendered. It's been held too long against me. And my lord will have the girl.'

'Damn that decree,' cried the boy, 'and the one who uttered it! You'll renounce every claim you've made!'

'What drivel's this you're spouting? By Saint Peter, the innocent often pay the price!'

The boy was incensed at this and levelled his lance, and they charged at each other as fast as their mounts could bear them. With their furious rage and the strength in their arms they made their lances shatter and fly into pieces. But Engygeron was the only one to fall, and he was wounded through his shield, in terrible pain in his arm and side. The boy dismounted, not knowing how to attack him on horseback; down he jumped, sword in hand, and advanced upon Engygeron. I don't know what more to tell you: I shan't describe what befell each man or give you a blow-by-blow account, but the battle lasted a long while and the blows they dealt were fearsome, till at last Engygeron fell. The boy assailed him fiercely till he cried for mercy. He said he'd have no mercy at all – but then remembered Gorneman's injunction never deliberately to kill a knight once he'd vanquished him and had mastery.

'Good, gentle friend!' Engygeron cried. 'Don't be so cruel as to refuse me mercy! I freely admit defeat – victory's yours! You're a truly splendid knight, but listen: no one who knew us both would believe you could have killed me in single combat, not unless he'd seen it with his own eyes; but if I testify, in the presence of my men outside my tent, that you've vanquished me, my word will be believed and your honour much enhanced, more than any other knight's. And if you've a lord who's done you some boon or service and you've yet to repay him, send me to him: I'll go and report on your behalf how you defeated me in battle, and yield to him as his prisoner, to do with me as he will.'

'Damn anyone,' said the boy, 'who'd sue for more! You want to know where to go, then? To the castle – and you'll tell the fair girl who's my love that never, as long as you live, will you trouble her again, and you'll put yourself entirely, wholly, at her mercy.'

'Then kill me!' said Engygeron. 'For she would have me killed! She desires nothing so much as my shame and pain, for I was a party to her father's death, and I've made her suffer this year, killing and capturing all her knights. Sending me to her would be a dreadful sentence – the worst possible! If you've any other friend or sweetheart who's not so set against me, send me there! She would take my life for sure if she ever got her hands on me!'

So he told him to go to a castle belonging to a worthy nobleman, and gave him his name. And no mason in the world could have described the castle better! He spoke glowingly of the river and the bridge, and the turrets and the tower and the mighty surrounding walls, till Engygeron realised all too well that he was sending him as a captive to where he was hated most!

'Good brother,' he said, 'that's no safe haven! God help me, if you send me there you're putting me in the worst plight and worst possible hands! I killed one of his brothers in this war! Kill me yourself, dear friend, rather than make me go to him: if you force me there, it'll be my death!'

'Then go,' said the boy, 'as a captive to King Arthur. Give the king my greetings, and tell him from me to point out the girl who was struck by Kay the seneschal because I made her laugh. You're to submit as her prisoner, and tell her, if you please, that I pray God will let me live long enough to avenge that blow.'

Engygeron replied that he'd carry out that service to the letter. Then the victorious knight headed back towards the castle, while Engygeron set off to his imprisonment, giving orders for his banner to be taken down. The besieging army departed, till not a fair- or a dark-haired head remained.

The people of the castle came pouring forth to meet the returning knight. But they were most upset that he hadn't beheaded the knight he'd defeated or brought him back to them; as they joyously helped him dismount and disarm at a mounting-block they all said:

'If you haven't brought Engygeron back, why didn't you take his head?'

'Truly, sirs,' he replied, 'I don't think that would have been right: he's killed your kinsmen, and I couldn't have protected him – you'd have killed him in spite of me. And it wouldn't have been good of me to refuse him mercy when I had the better of him. And do you know what that mercy was? He's to submit as a captive to King Arthur, if he keeps his word.'

Just then the girl appeared and greeted him with the utmost joy, and took him to her chamber to rest and take his ease. She put up no resistance to his kisses and embraces: rather than eating and drinking they played and kissed and embraced and exchanged sweet words.

Meanwhile Clamadeus, obsessed with his foolish plan, was expecting the castle imminently to be his, uncontested – till he met a boy along his path, lamenting bitterly, who told him the news about his seneschal Engygeron.

'Oh, by God, sir, it's all gone wrong!' cried the boy, in such a state that he was tearing his hair out with both hands.

'What's happened?' said Clamadeus.

'Truly, sir, your seneschal's been defeated; he's to surrender as a prisoner to King Arthur – he's already on his way!'

'Who did this, boy? Speak up! How could it happen? Where could he have come from, a knight capable of making such a worthy, valiant warrior submit?'

'I don't know who he was, good sir,' said the boy. 'But I know this much, for I saw it myself: he came out of Beaurepaire, armed all in red.'

'What do I do now, boy? Tell me!' Clamadeus cried, nearly going wild.

'Now, sir? Go back the way you came: there's no point carrying on.'

At this a knight with greying hair, who'd always been Clamadeus's mentor, intervened and said: 'That's shameful, boy! We need better, wiser words than that! He'd be a fool to listen to you: if he takes my advice he'll carry on. Sir,' he continued, 'do you want to know how to get the knight and the castle? I'll tell you right enough, and it couldn't be easier! Inside the walls of Beaurepaire there's nothing to eat or drink and the knights are weak, while we are strong and fit, safe from hunger and thirst, and could endure a mighty battle if they dared come out and face us. We'll send twenty knights to offer a fight outside the gate. The knight, sporting with his fair love Blancheflor, will want to prove his chivalry, but he won't stand a chance – he'll be captured or killed: the rest will be too weak to be much help; our twenty will do nothing except draw them out and keep them occupied while we creep up this valley and entrap them from behind!'

'Oh yes!' said Clamadeus. 'I approve of that! We've four hundred armed knights here, all outstanding warriors, and a thousand footmen well equipped: our foes are all as good as dead!'

So Clamadeus sent twenty of his knights to the castle gate, with pennons and banners of every description unfurled in the wind; and when the men of the castle saw them they rashly flung open the gates at the boy's command, and under the watching eyes of everyone he rode out to confront the knights. Bold and strong and confident, he met them all together – and no one on the end of his onslaught thought him an apprentice in the art of arms! He showed great skill that day: he gutted many with his lance, pierced chests and breasts, broke arms and collars, some he killed and others crippled, some he toppled, others seized, and sent the captured knights and horses to those who needed them.

But suddenly they caught sight of the great battalion who'd come up through the valley: four hundred armed knights and a thousand foot. The men of the castle drew up close to the open gate, while their attackers beheld the loss they'd suffered of their wounded and slain companions, and came charging towards the gate in wild disorder. The defenders were ranged in serried ranks at their gate and received them boldly; but they were few in number and weak, while their attackers were reinforced by the infantry behind them, and at last they could resist no more and fell back into the castle. Above the gate were archers shooting into the huge, seething press that burned and raged to break inside, till finally, and violently, one band forced their way in. But the men above sent a portcullis crashing on to those below, killing and crushing all it caught as it fell. Clamadeus couldn't have seen a more painful sight: the falling gate had killed a huge number of his men and locked him out. There was nothing for it but to go and rest: to continue with a rushed assault would be futile now.

But his mentor and counsellor told him: 'Sir, there's nothing surprising in misfortune striking a worthy man: good and ill befall everyone according to God's will and pleasure.

The long and the short of it is: you've lost! But every saint has his feast day! The tempest's fallen on you – your men have taken a battering and the men of the castle have come off best. But they'll lose yet, be sure of that! Tear out both my eyes if they hold out three days longer! Castle and keep will be yours. They'll put themselves entirely at your mercy. If you can just stay here today and tomorrow – that's all – the castle will be in your hands; even the girl who's refused you so long will beg you in God's name to take her!'

Those who'd brought tents and pavilions had them pitched, while the rest made lodges and shelters as best they could. Meanwhile the men of the castle disarmed the knights they'd captured; but they didn't lock them in towers or irons, provided they promised as loyal knights to stay in captivity honourably and to do their captors no harm. Such was their imprisonment.

Now, that very day a mighty wind had blown a vessel across the sea with a great cargo of wheat and other supplies. By God's will it arrived safe and sound below the castle, and as soon as the people saw it they sent down to enquire who the sailors were and what they wanted. Down they came from the castle to the ship and asked where they were from and where they were going. They replied:

'We're merchants carrying provisions to sell: bread and wine and salted bacon; and we've plenty of cattle and pigs to slaughter if need be.'

'God be praised,' the people cried, 'for giving the wind the power that blew you adrift and brought you here! You're very welcome! Start unloading – you can sell the lot, as dear as you dare! Quickly now and take your payment – you won't know what to do with it all! Bars of gold and silver we'll give for your wheat; and for the wine and meat you'll have a cartload – more if we must!'

The buyers and sellers went about their business with a will, unloading the ship and sending all the goods ahead to fortify the people in the castle. When they saw them coming laden with supplies you can well imagine the jubilation! And they didn't dally preparing dinner! Clamadeus, skulking outside, could sit there now as long as he liked: inside the castle they had cattle, pigs and salt meat in abundance, and wheat enough to last till the next harvest! And the castle cooks weren't idle: soon the kitchen fires were blazing, ready to cook the dinner.

Now the young knight could revel with his love at their ease; she embraced him, and he kissed her, delighting in each other's company. And the hall was far from silent now: it rang with sounds of celebration. The thought of food made everyone rejoice – they'd longed for it so much! The cooks beavered away with all their might till at last they announced they could sit down to dine – and how they needed it!

When they'd eaten they happily rose. But Clamadeus's men were none too jolly: they'd heard the news of the castle's fortune and said they'd have to leave; there was no way now of starving them out – their siege was all in vain! But Clamadeus was incensed at this, and without anyone's counsel or agreement he sent a messenger to the castle to tell the red knight that till noon next day he could come and meet him alone on the plain to fight him if he dared. When the girl heard this message to her love she was desperately upset; but he returned word that, come what may, Clamadeus would have battle if that was what he wanted. At this her distress was deeper still, but no amount of tears from her, I think, would ever have made him stay. Every man and woman there was begging him not to go and fight a knight that none had yet withstood in battle; but the boy said:

'It's best you say no more, sirs; no man in the world could hold me back.'

This stopped their tongues: they dared say nothing more; instead they took to their beds and rested till the sun rose in the morning.

But still they were most distressed about their lord: however much they implored him they couldn't change his mind. His sweetheart, too, had been begging him that night not to go to battle but to stay there in peace, for they'd nothing more to fear from Clamadeus and his men. But all her pleas were vain – which is strange and quite amazing, for her coaxing words were as tender as could be, and accompanied by kisses so soft and sweet that she slid love's key into the lock of his heart. Yet still she found no way of dissuading him; he called for his arms, and those to whom he'd entrusted them brought them with all speed. There was much unhappiness as he armed: men and women alike were all downcast. He commended them to the king of kings, his swarthy horse was brought to him, he mounted and in a moment he was gone. As he swept away he left them sorely grieving.

When Clamadeus saw his enemy coming he arrogantly imagined he'd have him out of his saddle in no time. The plain was fine and level, and there was no one there but the two of them: he'd disbanded his army and sent them away. Both knights had their lances lowered, fixed in their rests before their saddle-bows, and they charged at each other without a challenge or wasting words. Both had piercing heads on ashwood shafts, stout and good to handle, and the knights were strong and their chargers swift, and they were filled with mortal hatred. They exchanged such blows that they smashed their shields and shattered their lances and brought each other down; but up they leapt in an instant and straight to the attack, and fought with swords for a long while, and it was an even contest. I could tell you all about if I wanted to go down that road, but I'm not going to spend my energies on that – one word's as good as twenty! In the end Clamadeus, against his will, had to plead for mercy. But just like his seneschal he swore most earnestly that on no account would he submit to imprisonment at Beaurepaire; nor, for the whole empire of Rome, would he go to the noble who owned the fine castle. But he did willingly promise the boy that he'd surrender as a prisoner to King Arthur and relay his message to the girl so basely struck by Kay: that he was determined to avenge that blow, whatever anyone said, if God gave him the power. Then the boy made him swear that before dawn next day all those held captive in his dungeons would be set free, safe and sound, and that as long as he lived, if ever an army threatened Beaurepaire he'd do his best to drive them off; and that the girl would never more be troubled either by him or by his men.

So Clamadeus returned to his own land; and as soon as he arrived he ordered the release of all his prisoners: they could go their ways, completely free. His bidding was no sooner said than done: out came all the captives, who set off at once with all their gear, for nothing was kept from them.

Then Clamadeus set out on a different path, travelling all alone. It was the custom at that time – so I find written in my source[12] – that a knight had to yield himself prisoner dressed just as he'd been when he left the combat: in the state he'd been at the moment of defeat, without removing or donning anything. Clamadeus did just this as he set off after Engygeron, who was heading for Disnadaron where the king was due to hold court.

Meanwhile, back at Beaurepaire, there was mighty jubilation as those who'd spent so long in grim captivity returned. The hall and the knights' lodgings rang with celebration, and all the bells in the chapels and churches pealed with joy. Every monk and nun sent

---

[12] i.e. the 'book' referred to in the prologue above, p. 1.

thanks to God, while through the streets and squares all the people danced their rounds. What rejoicing there was in Beaurepaire, now they were free from attack and war!

And meanwhile Engygeron journeyed on, and Clamadeus behind him: three nights in a row he lodged at the house where Engygeron had stayed. He followed him from lodging to lodging to Disnadaron in Wales, where Arthur was holding a packed court in his halls. They saw Clamadeus coming, armed as custom required, and he was recognised by Engygeron, who'd delivered the boy's message at court on his arrival the previous night, and been taken into the king's household and confidence. He saw his lord now covered in crimson blood, but knew him nonetheless; and he said at once:

'Sirs! Sirs, this is amazing! Trust me, that knight's been sent here by the boy with the red arms! He's vanquished him, I'm sure of it – he's covered in blood! I know that blood well, and the man himself, for he's my lord and I'm his vassal. Clamadeus of the Isles is his name; I thought there was no finer knight in the empire of Rome, but misfortune befalls even the worthiest.'

So said Engygeron; and then Clamadeus arrived, and they ran and met each other in the middle of the courtyard.

It was Pentecost, and the queen was seated beside King Arthur at the head of the table, and there were a good many kings and counts, dukes and queens and countesses present; all the masses had been sung, and the ladies and knights had returned from church. Kay came striding through the hall, without a cloak or mantle, a stick in his right hand and a hat of rich cloth on his fair-haired head. There wasn't a more handsome knight in the world, and his hair was plaited in a braid; but his looks – and his prowess – were devalued by his wicked, mocking tongue. His tunic was of a rich cloth coloured with a deep red dye, a gorgeous colour, and girdled with a finely wrought belt of which the buckle and all the links were gold – I can say that with confidence, for so my source-book testifies. Everyone stepped out of his path as he strode through the hall, avoiding him for fear of his cruel jibes and vicious tongue. Anyone with any sense fears spiteful words, whether they're spoken in jest or earnest. The whole court feared his mockery, and no one said a word to him.

In view of them all he stepped up to where the king was seated and said: 'If you wish, sire, you may dine at once.'

'Leave me be, Kay,' he replied. 'By the eyes in my head, I'll not eat on so high a feast day, in a plenary court, until some news arrives.'

It was while they were talking thus that Clamadeus entered, ready to submit as a prisoner and armed as custom required; he said: 'God save and bless the finest king alive, the most generous and most noble: so he is judged by all who know of his great deeds. Hear me now, good sire,' he said. 'I have a message to deliver. Much as it pains me, I acknowledge I am sent here by a knight who vanquished me, and on his behalf I must submit as your prisoner, whether I like it or not. If I were asked if I knew the knight's name I'd have to say no, but I can tell you that his arms are red and he said you gave them to him.'

'Before God, my friend,' the king replied, 'tell me truly: is he fit and well, in good health and spirits?'

'You may be sure he is, sire,' said Clamadeus. 'He's the most valiant knight I've ever known. And he told me to speak to the girl who laughed on seeing him, which made Kay give her a shameful slap: he says he'll avenge her if God grants him the power.'

The court fool, when he heard these words, jumped for joy and cried: 'God bless me, lord king, that blow will be avenged indeed, without a word of a lie! Kay's going to have a broken arm and his shoulder out of place – there's nothing he can do to stop it!'

Kay heard this and thought it offensive drivel; it wasn't cowardice that stayed his hand from giving the fool a clout, but the presence of the king and the risk of shame. The king shook his head and said to Kay:

'It pains me deeply that he's not here with me. It was you and your foolish tongue that made him go, and it saddens me.'

Then Girflet rose at the king's command, along with Sir Yvain, from whose company no one failed to profit, and the king bade them escort Clamadeus to the chambers where the queen's maids were amusing themselves. Clamadeus bowed to the two knights, and they led him to the chambers and pointed out the girl who'd been slapped by Kay; he told her the news that was music to her ears, still smarting as she was from the shame inflicted on her cheek. She'd recovered well enough from the buffet she'd received, but the shame was not forgotten – or forgiven. And no one of worth forgets a shame or injury: the pain passes but the shame remains in a strong and vigorous man; only in one of little worth does it cool and die away.

So Clamadeus had delivered his message, and the king retained him in his court and his household for life.

Meanwhile the one who'd fought him for the land of the girl – and for the girl herself, his fair love Blancheflor – was now taking his pleasure and ease at her side. The land would now have been wholly his, undisputed, had his heart not been set elsewhere; but his mind was more on someone else, his heart-strings pulled by thoughts of his mother and the sight of her collapsed in a faint, and he longed more than anything to go and see her. He didn't dare ask his sweetheart's leave: she was dead set against it, and ordered all her people to plead with him to stay. But nothing they said was of any use, except that he made them a promise: if he found his mother alive he would bring her back with him, and from that day on would be lord of the land; and if she were dead he'd return likewise: they had his word to that.

And so he set off, promising to return, leaving his fair love filled with sorrow and anguish, as was everyone. There was such a procession to escort him from the town that it was like Ascension Day or a Sunday: all the monks were there in their silken copes, and all the nuns in their veils; and they were saying:

'Sir, you've saved us from ruin and restored us to our homes: it's no wonder we grieve when you leave us so soon! Our sorrow's bound to be great – and it couldn't be greater!'

'There's no need,' he replied, 'to weep any more. With God's guidance I'll return, and what cause is there for tears? Don't you think it's right that I should go and see my mother, when I left her all alone in the woods called the Waste Forest? I'll come back, whether it's her wish or not – I shan't fail on any account. And if she's alive, I'll have her take the veil as a nun in your church; and if she's dead, I'll have a service sung for her soul each year, that God may set her with the souls of the pious in the bosom of the holy Abraham. Worthy monks, and you, good ladies, this should be no cause for grief: I'll endow you richly for her soul's sake, if God leads me back here.'

With that the monks and nuns and all the rest turned back into the castle. And he departed, lance in rest and fully armed, just as he had come.

A Grail and a Lance

All day long he rode, without meeting a Christian soul who could guide him on his way. And all the while he prayed to God the sovereign Father to grant that he might find his mother full of life and health, if it were His will.

He was still praying so when into view came a river, flowing down a hill. He could see that the water was swift and deep, and he didn't dare venture in; but he said:

'Oh, almighty Lord! If only I could cross this river I'd find my mother on the other side, I'm sure, if she's still alive.'

He rode along the bank till he neared a rocky crag; the river washed right up to it: there was no further he could go. But suddenly he saw a boat coming downstream. There were two men on board. He drew rein and waited, thinking they'd keep sailing till they reached him; but they stopped and stayed dead still in midstream, anchored fast. The man in the bow was fishing with a line, baiting his hook with a little fish slightly bigger than a minnow. The boy, not knowing what to do or where to find a crossing, hailed them and asked:

'Tell me, sirs, is there any bridge across this river?'

The one who was fishing replied: 'No, brother, I promise you; and I don't think there's a boat bigger than the one we're in – which wouldn't carry five men. You can't cross on horseback for twenty leagues upstream or down: there's no ferry or bridge or ford.'

'Then tell me, in God's name,' he said, 'where I might find lodging.'

And the fisherman answered: 'You've need of that and more beside, I'd say. I'll give you lodging tonight. Ride up through the cleft that's cut in that rock, and when you reach the top you'll see a house in a valley ahead of you: that's where I live, close to river and close to woods.'

So he made his way up the rock; but when he reached the top he looked all around and saw nothing but land and sky and said:

'What was the point of coming here? It's a wild goose chase! Shame on the joker who sent me here! A fine guide he was, telling me I'd find a house when I reached the top! It was most unworthy of you, fisherman, if you meant it to cause mischief.'

But suddenly, in a valley close by, the top of a tower caught his eye. From there to Beirut you wouldn't have found one more handsome or impressive: it was square and built of stone, and flanked by two smaller towers; and a hall stood before the tower and a range of chambers before the hall. He headed down towards it, saying he'd been well guided after all; he praised the fisherman who'd sent him there, no longer calling him treacherous or false or a liar, now that he'd found a place to stay.

He came up to the gate, and before it found a drawbridge; it was lowered, so over the bridge and in he rode. Four boys came to meet him: two helped him disarm while the third led his horse away to be given oats and hay; the fourth dressed him in a fresh, new mantle of scarlet.* Then they led him to the living quarters; and truly, you could have searched from there to Limoges and found no more splendid chambers.

The boy stayed there till two servants were sent to escort him to their lord. He went with them to the hall – which was square, being as long as it was wide. In the middle of the hall, on a bed, leaning on his elbow, he saw a handsome nobleman with greying hair; on his head he wore a chaplet of sable, berry-black, covered on top with the purple cloth from which his whole gown was made. Before him was a great fire of seasoned logs, blazing brightly, surrounded by four columns. Four hundred men could have sat around that fire and all would have had a good place. The columns were very strong, supporting a tall, wide chimney of heavy bronze. The two servants led their guest forward, one on each side, and brought him before their lord. As he saw him approach, the lord greeted him at once; then he said:

'Forgive me, friend, if I don't stand to greet you: I'm unable.'

'Don't mention it, sir!' he replied. 'As I pray God will grant me joy and health, it doesn't bother me at all.'

But out of respect for his guest the nobleman forced himself as upright as he could, and said: 'Come here, friend. Don't be afraid of me: I bid you sit down here beside me – you're quite safe.' So the boy sat at his side, and the nobleman asked him: 'Where have you come from today, my friend?'

'This morning I set out from Beaurepaire – that was its name.'

'So help me God, that's a long way you've travelled! You must have left before the watch sounded the dawn.'

'No indeed,' said the boy. 'Prime* had already been rung, I promise you.'

While they were talking a boy came through the door; he was carrying a sword hung round his neck, and presented it to the nobleman. He half drew it from its scabbard; and from an inscription on the blade he learned where it was made, and that it was of such fine steel that there was only one way it could ever be broken, known only to the one who had forged and tempered it. The boy who'd brought it said:

'My lord, the beautiful fair-haired girl, your niece, has sent you this gift; you never saw a finer sword as long and as broad as this. You may give it to whoever you wish but, wherever it's bestowed, my lady dearly hopes it'll be put to good use. The one who forged the sword only ever made three, and he's about to die, so this is the last he'll ever make.'

Thereupon the lord presented the sword to his guest with its belt – which itself was worth a fortune. The sword's pommel was made of the finest Arabian or Grecian gold, and the scabbard of Venetian orfrey. This handsome sword the lord gave to the boy, saying:

'Good brother, this sword was intended and destined for you, and I very much want you to have it. Come, gird it on and draw it.'

The boy thanked him; he fastened it so that it wasn't too tight, and then drew it, naked, from the scabbard. After gazing at it for a while he sheathed it again; and truly, it sat splendidly at his side and even better in his hand, and it seemed indeed that in time of need he would wield it like a man of valour. Behind him he saw a group of boys gathered round the blazing fire; among them was the one who was caring for his arms, and he entrusted the sword to him. Then he sat down again beside the lord, who treated him with the greatest honour. And in that hall was the brightest light that could ever be created by candles.

While they were talking of one thing and another, a boy came from a chamber holding a gleaming lance by the middle of the shaft, and he passed between the fire and the pair who were sitting on the bed. Everyone in the hall saw the bright lance and its shining head. And from the tip of the lance's head came a drop of blood; and right down to the boy's hand this red drop ran. The lord's guest gazed at the wonder that had appeared that night, but refrained from asking how it came to be, because he remembered the warning of the one who'd knighted him, who'd taught him to beware of talking too much; he was afraid it might be frowned upon, so he didn't ask at all. Then two other boys appeared, holding candlesticks of fine gold, inlaid with niello;* they were handsome boys indeed, and in each of the candlesticks they bore were at least ten burning candles. A girl who entered with the boys, fair and graceful and beautifully attired, was holding a grail[13] between her hands. And as she entered with the grail, so radiant a light appeared in the hall that the candles lost their brightness like the stars at the rising of the moon or sun. After her came another girl, holding a silver trencher. The grail, which went ahead, was made of fine, pure gold, inlaid with many kinds of jewels, the richest and most precious in earth or sea: the stones in the grail surpassed all other gems, without a doubt. They passed before the bed as the lance had done, and entered another chamber. The boy saw them pass, but didn't dare ask who was served from the grail: he'd taken the words of wise Gorneman to heart. I fear he may suffer for doing so: I've heard it said that sometimes a man can talk too little as well as too much! But whether it was to bring him good or ill – I don't know which – he asked nothing.

The lord bade the servants bring water and set the tables. Those whose job it always was did as they were bidden, and the lord and the boy washed their hands in warm water. Then two servants brought a wide table of ivory – according to my source it was all one solid piece – and held it for a moment before the lord and his guest until two others came with a pair of trestles made of a wood with two fine qualities: it would never rot and never burn, for it was ebony, which is proof against both, so the trestles would last forever. On them the tabletop was set and the cloth was spread – and what should I say of the cloth? No legate, cardinal or pope ever dined on one so white! The first dish was a roasted haunch of venison, seasoned with hot pepper. There was no shortage of clear, delicious wine to drink from golden cups. Before them a servant carved the peppered venison, drawing the haunch to him on the silver trencher, and presented portions to them on a whole flatbread. And meanwhile the grail passed before them again – but still the boy didn't ask who was served from it, refraining because of Gorneman's well-meant warning not to talk too much: he'd taken it to heart and had it ever in mind. But he held his tongue more than he should, for as each course was served he saw the grail pass before him, right before his eyes, and he didn't know who was served from it and he longed to know. He told himself that before he left he'd be sure to ask one of the boys of the court, but he'd wait till morning when he took his leave of the lord and the rest of the household. So he put it off till later, and turned his attention to eating and drinking.

They weren't mean with the wines or the dishes – and they were delicious, quite delectable! The food was fine indeed: the nobleman was served that night with all the dishes befitting a king or a count or an emperor, and the boy with him. And after they'd dined they stayed up together and talked, while the servants prepared the beds and brought fruit to eat – fruit of the dearest kind: dates and figs and nutmegs, and cloves and pomegranates; and to finish there were electuaries and digestives, including Alexandrian ginger and *pliris archonticum*, restorative and settling for the stomach.[14] Then there was an array of drinks to sample: sweet and aromatic wine, but flavoured with neither honey nor pepper, and well-aged mulberry wine and clear syrup. The boy was amazed by it all – he'd no idea any of this existed!

[13] The use of the indefinite article on the grail's first appearance is not at all as strange as it may seem. A medieval audience would have been perfectly familiar with grails: derived from the Latin *gradalis*, a *graal* was a broad, shallow dish or platter.
[14] The references to various tonics and electuaries (digestive medicines made into a paste with syrup or honey) evidently caused the scribes some difficulty: they vary greatly from manuscript to manuscript.

Then the lord said: 'My friend, it's time to retire for the night. I'll go now, if you don't mind, and sleep there in my chambers, and whenever you wish you can sleep in here. I've no strength in my body: I'll have to be carried.'

At that four strong and able servants came from the chamber, took hold of the four corners of the blanket that lay across the bed on which the lord was sitting, and carried him where bidden. Other boys stayed with his guest to serve him, attending to his every need: as soon as he wished they took off his shoes and clothes and saw him to bed in sheets of fine white linen.

He slept till morning. Day had broken and the household had risen; but he could see no one as he looked about him, and he had to get up alone whether he liked it or not. Seeing that he had no choice he made the best of it, pulling on his shoes without waiting for help, and then went to don his arms again, finding they'd been brought and laid at the end of a table. Once he'd fully armed he went to the doors of the chambers that he'd seen open the night before – but to no avail: they were shut fast. He called and pounded and barged a good deal; but no one opened up for him or said a word. After calling for quite a while he went and tried the door of the hall; this did open, so he went down the steps to find his horse saddled and his lance and shield propped against a wall. He mounted and went searching everywhere, but couldn't find a living soul. There wasn't a squire or a servant to be seen. He rode up to the gate and found the drawbridge lowered: it had been left like that so that, whenever he came to leave, nothing should stop him passing straight across. Seeing that the bridge was down, he guessed the boys must all have gone into the woods to check their traps and snares. He'd no wish to stay longer, and decided to go after them and see if any of them would tell him why the lance bled, if it was all right to ask, and where the grail was taken. So he rode out through the gate. But before he was across the bridge he felt his horse's hooves swept upward; the horse made a great leap – and if he hadn't jumped so well both he and his rider would have been in trouble: the boy looked back to see what had happened, and saw that the bridge had been raised. He called out, but there was no reply.

'Hey!' he cried. 'Whoever raised the bridge, speak to me! Where are you? I can't see you! Come out and let me look at you – there's something I want to ask!'

But he was wasting his time calling out like this: nobody wanted to answer.

No Questions Asked

He headed for the forest, and came upon a path where he found fresh hoofprints and said:

'I think the ones I'm after went this way.'

So he pressed on swiftly through the wood as far as the tracks led him, till he chanced upon a maiden sitting beneath an oak, weeping and wailing in piteous grief.

'Alas!' she cried. 'Wretch that I am, I was born in an evil hour! Curse the hour I was conceived and the hour of my birth! I've never known such misery! Would to God my love weren't dead here in my arms – better by far that I should have died and he had lived! Why did Death deal me such a blow, taking his soul rather than mine? What's the point of living when I see the one I loved most dearly lying dead? Now he's gone I care nothing for my life or for my body! Come, Death, and take my soul! Let it be the chambermaid and companion to his, if he'll accept it!'

Such was her lament for a knight she was holding, his head severed. As soon as he saw the girl the boy rode right up to her. As he drew near he greeted her, and she greeted him, but her head stayed bowed, her grief unremitting. He asked her:

'Damsel, who killed that knight who's lying in your lap?'

'Another knight, good sir,' she said, 'this very morning. But there's something that quite amazes me: they say you could ride forty leagues the way you've come and find no decent, proper lodging, yet your horse is well fed and groomed. Had he been washed and brushed and given a trough of oats and hay he wouldn't have a fuller belly or a sleeker coat! And you look as if you've had a good night's rest yourself!'

'Indeed, dear girl,' he said, 'I was as comfortable as could be last night – if it shows, it's with good reason! But if you gave a loud shout from where we are, they'd hear it clearly where I stayed last night! You don't know this country very well – you can't have explored it much: it was the finest lodging I've ever had, without a doubt!'

'Oh, sir – then you lodged at the house of the great Fisher King!'

'By the Saviour, girl, I don't know if he's a fisherman or a king, but he's very wise and courteous. I don't know what more to tell you – except that, late last evening, I came across two men in a boat. They were bobbing along, and one of them was fishing with a hook and line, and he told me the way to his house and gave me lodging.'

And the girl said: 'He *is* a king, good sir, I can assure you. But he was wounded in battle and wholly crippled: he's helpless now – he was struck by a javelin through both his thighs. He still suffers so badly that he can't even mount a horse. But when he wants some sport and pleasure he's carried to a boat and goes fishing with a hook: that's why he's called the Fisher King. He finds enjoyment that way – he couldn't manage any other sport at all: he can't go hunting in the woods or marshes. But he has his men to hunt the wildfowl, and archers and huntsmen who go shooting in his forests. That's why he's chosen to live just here: in all the world he couldn't find a retreat better suited to his needs, and he's had a house built befitting a great king.'

'Truly, damsel, it's true what you say, and I wondered at it when I came before him last night. I was standing a little back, and he bade me come and sit beside him and not to think him haughty if he didn't stand to greet me: he didn't have the strength or power. So I went and sat at his side.'

'Truly, he did you great honour when he seated you beside him. And tell me now: as you sat with him, did you see the lance with the point that bleeds, though it has neither flesh nor veins?'

'Did I see it? Indeed I did!'

'And did you ask why it bled?'

'I didn't say a word, so help me God.'

'I tell you, that was a grave mistake. And did you see the grail?'

'I saw it clearly.'

'Who was holding it?'

'A girl.'

'Where did she come from?'

'From a chamber.'

'And where did she go?'

'To another chamber.'

'Did anyone go ahead of the grail?'

'Yes.'

'Who?'

'Two boys, that's all.'

'What were they holding?'
'Candlesticks full of candles.'
'And who came after the grail?'
'Another girl.'
'Holding what?'
'A little silver trencher.'
'Did you ask where they were going?'
'Not a word crossed my lips.'
'God help me, so much the worse. What's your name, friend?'

And the boy, who didn't know his name, guessed and said it was Perceval the Welshman – not knowing whether it was true or not. But it was true, though he didn't know it. And hearing this, the girl stood up before him and said, bitterly:

'Your name is changed, my friend.'

'To what?'

'Perceval the Wretched! Oh, hapless Perceval! What a disaster that you failed to ask all this! You would have healed the good crippled king – he would have regained the use of his limbs and the rule of his land – and you would have profited greatly! But now, I tell you, many ills will beset both you and others. And know this, too: this misfortune has befallen you because of the wrong you did your mother – she has died of grief on your account. I know you better than you know me: you don't know who I am, but I was raised with you at your mother's house for a long, long time – you and I are cousins. And I grieve no less for your tragic failure to learn what was done with the grail or where it's taken, than I do for your mother's death, or for this knight I loved and adored because he called me his dear sweetheart and loved me like a noble, loyal knight.'

'Oh, cousin!' said Perceval. 'If what you've told me is true, tell me how you know!'

'I know it to be true,' she said, 'because I saw her laid in the ground.'

'May God in His goodness have mercy on her soul,' said Perceval. 'It's a cruel tale you've told me. And now that she's been buried, what would be the point of going on? I was heading home only because I wanted to see her – I'll have to take a different course. I'd gladly have you come with me if you wish: the one who lies here dead will be of no service to you now. The dead with the dead, the living with the living: let's journey on together. I can't see any sense in staying here on your own watching over his body; let's go after the one who slew him. And this I swear and promise: if I can track him down, we'll fight till one of us is forced to submit.'

But she, unable to staunch the grief in her heart, said: 'Dear friend, I won't go with you and leave him – not at any price, not until I've buried him. If you'll take my advice you'll follow this cobbled road – the cruel, wicked knight who slew my sweetheart went this way. But truly, I don't say that because I'd have you pursue him – though I wish him as much ill as if it were me he'd killed! But listen: where did you get that sword that hangs at your left hip? It's never spilled a man's blood and has never been drawn in battle. I know exactly where it was made and who forged it. Beware! Never trust it! It'll let you down, I promise you, when you find yourself locked in mighty combat: it'll fly into pieces!'

'Dear cousin, it was sent to my good host last night by a niece of his, and he gave it to me and I consider it a fine gift – but you worry me if what you say is true! Tell me: if it came to be broken, do you know if it could be repaired?'

'It could, but it would be a challenging journey for anyone to the lake below Cothoatre.

There you could have the sword beaten and tempered anew and made whole again – if chance[15] were to lead you there. You must go to a smith named Trebuchet, and to him alone: he was its maker and will make it anew – it will never be repaired by anyone else. Make sure no other tries his hand – he'd be sure to fail.'

'Truly,' said Perceval, 'I'd be very sorry if it broke.'

He set off then, and his cousin stayed behind, not wanting to leave the one whose death weighed so heavy on her heart.

The Proud Knight of the Glade

Along the path rode Perceval, ever following a horse's tracks, till he came upon a palfrey, scrawny and exhausted, plodding along before him – such a skinny, wretched specimen that he thought it must have fallen into bad hands. It looked well worked and poorly fed – like a borrowed horse: overtaxed all day and neglected all night. This palfrey was so thin that it shivered as if frozen stiff; its neck was mangy, its ears drooped; it would soon be fodder for mastiffs and mongrels: its hide was all that covered its bones. But on its back was a woman's saddle and on its head a bridle to match, and in the saddle was a girl – the most wretched ever seen. She'd have been fair and comely enough if she'd been in a decent state, but far from it: there wasn't a hand's breadth of her gown untorn – her breasts showed through the rips; it was held together here and there with knots and rough stitches; and her skin looked as if it had been slashed with a lancet, cracked and burnt by heat and gale and frost. She was bare-headed, without a veil or wimple; so her face was clearly visible, with many an ugly stain left in the paths of her endless tears, which flowed to her breast and over her gown and right down to her knees. She had every reason to be heavy-hearted, being in such distress.

As soon as Perceval saw her he rode swiftly on to meet her. She clasped her clothes about her to cover up her skin – but she was bound to open other holes: whenever she covered one spot, one gap shut and a hundred opened! So Perceval found her pale and wan and wretched, and as he drew near he heard her bitterly bewailing her suffering and woe.

'God!' she cried. 'Let me live no longer! I've endured misery too long, suffered too much privation – and through no fault of mine! You know I've done nothing to deserve it, God, so send me, I pray you, someone who'll free me from this torment; or deliver me Yourself from the one who makes me live in shame, for I can find no pity in him: I can't escape him with my life, yet he won't put me to death! I don't know why he wants my company when he keeps me so – unless he relishes my shame and misery! Even if he knew for sure I'd done something to deserve it, he should have had mercy now that I've paid so dearly – if I meant anything to him; but it's clear I don't please him at all, when he makes me endure such a hard life in his wake and doesn't care.'

Perceval had reached her now, and said: 'Dear girl, God save you.'

Hearing him she bowed and answered softly: 'May you, sir, who have greeted me,

---

[15] '*aventure*', a word which in medieval French meant a great deal more than the modern 'adventure'. In many contexts it means a remarkable phenomenon or happening, or, as here, something closer to chance or fortune or destiny. It was frequently – and importantly – a sign of divine intervention in the world, and sometimes of God's grace, in that a knight would not even encounter an '*aventure*', let alone succeed in whatever test it might present, if he were unworthy of doing so, or unable to recognise it as a sign of divine presence and guidance.

have all that your heart desires – but I shouldn't be wishing you that.'

Perceval, flushing with shame, replied: 'In God's name, damsel, why? Truly, I don't think I've ever seen you before or done you any wrong!'

'Yes, you have!' she cried. 'I mustn't be greeted by anyone – that's the torment I have to bear, wretch that I am. I break into a dreadful sweat when anyone speaks or looks at me!'

'Truly, I didn't realise,' said Perceval. 'I didn't come here to cause you shame or trouble: it's just the way my path led me. But once I'd seen you in such a plight, so poor and naked, I couldn't rest content till I'd learned the truth: what's brought you to such woe and hardship?'

'Oh, sir!' she said. 'Have pity! Ride on! Fly from here and leave me be! It's sin that makes you stop here – do the right thing and fly!'

'I'd like to know,' he answered, 'what fear or threat should make me fly, when no one's chasing me?'

'Don't be offended, sir,' said the girl, 'but go while you can, before the Proud Knight of the Glade finds us together! All he ever wants is battle and combat, and if he found you here he'd kill you on the spot! If anyone stops to talk to me he's so enraged that, if he arrives while they're still at it, it'll cost them their heads – he slew one a short while ago! But first he tells each one why he keeps me in such a shameful, wretched state.'

And just as they were talking thus, the Proud Knight burst from the wood and galloped like a thunderbolt across the sand and dust, roaring: 'You there, beside the girl, you've made a big mistake! For detaining her a single step your time has come, I tell you! But I shan't kill you till I've explained the wrong she's done to make me keep her in such a shameful state; so listen now, and hear the story.

'A while ago I'd gone into the wood and left this girl in my pavilion. I loved no one but her. But then a Welsh boy turned up there; I don't know who he was or where he was going, only that he went so far as to kiss her – by force, so she told me! And if she was lying, what was to stop him doing more? And even if it *was* against her will, wouldn't he then have done all he wanted? Of course he would! No one would believe he kissed her and left it at that – the one always leads to the other! If a man and a woman are alone together and he kisses her and goes no further, then I think it's *his* decision; for a woman who yields her lips gives the rest quite easily to anyone who makes the effort! And though she may resist, we all know, without the slightest doubt, that a woman wants to win in all matters but one: that struggle in which she grabs the man by the throat and scratches and bites and wrestles, but wants to be overcome! She struggles, but she longs for it! Too cowardly to grant it, she wants it to be taken by force – but then shows no gratitude or thanks! That's why I'm sure the Welsh boy lay with her. And he took from her a ring of mine that she wore on her finger – he went off with it, much to my rage; and before he left he had his fill of good strong wine and lovely pies that were being kept for me! So now my love has a charming reward, as you can see! All who commit acts of folly must pay the price, so they take care not to reoffend. I'd every reason to be angry when I returned and learned what had happened; and I swore, and rightly so, that her palfrey would have no oats to eat and wouldn't be groomed or shod again, and that she'd have no tunic or mantle but the ones she was wearing then, until I'd got the better of the boy who'd raped her, and taken his life and his head.'

When Perceval had heard him out he answered in these very words: 'Know this, my friend, without a doubt: her penance is done. It was I who kissed her, and it was against her will and upset her deeply. And it was I who took the ring from her finger, but that was all: I did no more – though I admit I ate one of the pies and half the other, and drank my fill of your wine! But I did nothing stupid.'

'By my life!' the Proud Knight cried. 'What an incredible confession! You've deserved death, that's for sure, now that you've admitted it!'

'My death's not as near as you think,' said Perceval.

Without another word they sent their horses charging at each other, and met with such a fearsome clash that their lances flew into shards. They emptied both saddles as they brought each other down, but leapt to their feet at once and drew their swords and exchanged almighty blows. Perceval struck his opponent first with the sword that he'd been given – he wanted to put it to the test – and landed such a blow on his helm of steel that he broke the Fisher King's fine sword in two. The Proud Knight wasn't cowed: he paid him back in full on his burnished helm, smashing off gems and gilding. Perceval was distraught that his sword had failed him; but he gathered up the pieces and slid them in the sheath, and drew the sword that had belonged to the Red Knight. Then they came at each other on equal terms and began a bitter battle – you never saw one greater. It was a tough and mighty contest, but I've no desire to describe it further: in my view it's a waste of effort. They fought on till the Proud Knight of the Glade admitted defeat and asked for mercy. And Perceval, ever mindful of Gorneman's plea that he shouldn't kill a knight once he'd called for mercy, said:

'Truly, knight, I'll not have mercy on you till you have mercy on your love: she hasn't deserved the treatment you've made her suffer, I swear.'

And the knight, who loved her more than his own eyes, replied: 'Good sir, I'll make amends to her as you wish; I'll do whatever you command. My heart is dark and heavy for the suffering I've made her bear.'

'Then go,' said Perceval, 'to the nearest house you have in these parts, and let her bathe and rest and be tended back to health. Then make ready and take her, in her very best dress and finery, to King Arthur; greet him on my behalf and surrender to his mercy clad exactly as you are when you leave here. If he asks who sent you, tell him it was the one he made a red knight at the advice of Sir Kay the seneschal. And you must tell the court of the penance and suffering you've made your girl endure: proclaim it aloud to all present, so that everyone hears, including the queen and the ladies – there are many lovely damsels in her household. I hold one in special regard: because she laughed on seeing me, Kay gave her a blow that knocked her out. I want you to find her and give her this message from me: that on no account shall I come to any court held by King Arthur till I've avenged her to her joy and satisfaction.'

The knight replied that he'd go most willingly and say everything as bidden, and without delay – though he'd first let his beloved rest and clothe her as she needed. He would gladly have taken Perceval with him, too, to rest and heal and dress his wounds, but Perceval said:

'Go now, and good luck to you; just take care of her – I'm going to look for other lodging.'

The talking ended there, and neither party dallied longer: they set off without more ado. And that evening the knight had his sweetheart bathed and richly dressed, and cared for her so lovingly that she regained her former beauty.

Then they both set out and went straight to Carlion where King Arthur was holding court – and a most intimate affair it was, with a mere three thousand knights of high repute! Before them all he went to submit as King Arthur's prisoner, bringing his sweetheart with him; and coming before the king he said:

'My good lord king, I am your captive, to do with as you will, which is only right and proper, for so I was commanded by the boy who asked you for red arms and was granted them.'

The moment the king heard this he knew exactly who he meant. 'Disarm, good sir,' he said. 'May the one who's sent you to me have joy and all good fortune! You're very welcome: for his sake you'll be cherished and most honoured in my house.'

'Sire, I've other news to tell you before I disarm; and I'd like the queen and her maids to come and hear it, for it won't be told till the one is here who was struck on the cheek for no other crime than uttering a single laugh.'

Then the knight paused, and the king realised he should call the queen; so he sent to her and she came, and all her maids with her, hand in hand. Once the queen was seated beside her lord King Arthur, the Proud Knight of the Glade addressed her, saying:

'Lady, I bring you greetings from a knight I hold in high esteem, who vanquished me in single combat. I don't know what else to say about him, but he sends you my beloved – the girl you see here.'

'My thanks to him, friend,' said the queen.

Then he told her of the shame and abuse he'd inflicted on her so long, and of the suffering she'd endured, and the reason why: he told her everything, concealing nothing. When he was done they showed him the girl who'd been struck by Kay the seneschal, and he said to her:

'The knight who sent me here, young lady, asked me to greet you on his behalf; and he told me not to take off my boots till I'd told you this: he swears to God that, come what may, he'll never enter King Arthur's court till he's avenged you for the slap, the blow, you received on his account.'

When the fool heard this he leapt to his feet and cried: 'Kay! Kay! By God, you're going to pay for it, you really are – and soon!'

And the king followed on from the fool by saying: 'Ah, Kay! How courteous you were to mock that boy! You've robbed me of him with your scornful tongue: I don't think I'll ever see him again.'

And he seated his captive knight before him, and pardoned him imprisonment and bade that he be disarmed.

Sir Gawain, sitting at the king's right hand, asked: 'In God's name, sire, who ever was he, who vanquished such a fine knight in single combat? In all the isles of the sea I've never met or heard of anyone to match the Proud Knight of the Glade in arms and chivalry!'

'Good nephew,' said the king, 'I don't know who he is. I saw him once, but at the time I didn't have a chance to ask him anything at all. He just told me to knight him there and then, and I saw what a fine-looking youth he was and said: "Gladly, brother, but dismount while they fetch you golden arms!" But he said he'd not accept them, and wouldn't dismount till he had *red* arms! And what was more amazing still, he said the only arms he'd take were those of the knight who'd stolen my golden cup! Then Kay, offensive as he's always been and ever is and will be, never seeking to say a kind word, said: "Brother, the king grants you the arms – they're all yours – off you go and take them!" Not realising it was a joke, thinking he meant it, the boy went after the knight and killed him with a throw of a javelin! I don't know how the mess and clash began except that, for some reason, the Red Knight of the Forest of Quinqueroi gave him a haughty blow with his lance, so the boy flung a javelin clean through his eye and struck him dead and took his arms! Since then he's done me such fine service that – by my lord David, the saint they worship and revere in Wales – I shan't lie in any chamber or hall for two nights in a row till I know if he's alive, on land or sea! I'm setting out to search for him right now!'

And once the king had made that vow, they all knew there was nothing for it but to go!

Blood in the Snow

Then you'd have seen sheets and blankets and pillows packed, and chests filled, and packhorses laden and carts and wagons piled high: they weren't sparing with the number of pavilions and tents they took. A bright and able clerk, had he taken all day, couldn't have listed all the harness and equipment that were rapidly prepared: the king rode from Carlion as if he were going on campaign, with all his barons following. Not even a single girl remained: the queen took them all as a display of power and authority. They camped that night in a meadow beside a forest.

By morning it had snowed heavily, and the country round about was freezing cold. Perceval had risen early as he always did, eager to seek adventure and knightly deeds, and was heading straight towards the frozen, snow-covered meadow where the king's host was encamped. But before he reached the pavilions, a flock of wild geese, dazzled by the snow, came flying overhead. He saw and heard them as they fled, honking wildly, from a falcon that swooped after them till it found one of them alone, cut off from the flock, and swept down and struck the bird so hard it sent it plummeting to the ground. But it was very early in the morning and the falcon flew away, with no appetite to press home its attack. Perceval spurred ahead to where he'd seen the goose fall. It was wounded in the neck, and bled three drops of blood that spilled on to the whiteness of the snow; it looked like a natural colouring. But the goose wasn't hurt badly enough to keep it grounded, and by the time Perceval arrived the bird was already flown. And when he saw the crushed snow where the goose had lain, and the blood drops here and there, he leaned on his lance to gaze at the vision; for the blend of blood and snow appeared to him as the fresh hues in the face of his beloved: he became quite lost in the thought that in her face the red was set upon the white like those three drops of blood on the whiteness of the snow. He was so enraptured as he gazed that he thought he was looking at the fresh complexion of his fair love's face. As Perceval mused upon the drops, all the early morning passed him by.

At length some squires emerged from the tents, and seeing him in his contemplation they thought he was asleep. Outside the royal pavilion, before the king, still slumbering inside, had woken, the squires ran into Sagremor, who because of his impetuous nature was called the Rash.

'Come on!' he said. 'Don't hide it: what brings you here in such a hurry?'

'Sir,' they said, 'we've seen a knight outside the camp, asleep astride his charger!'

'Is he armed?'

'Yes indeed!'

'I'll go and speak to him,' said Sagremor, 'and bring him back to court.' He hurried into the king's tent and woke him, and said: 'Sire, outside on the open ground there's a knight who's fast asleep!'

The king commanded him to go and bring the knight back without fail. Sagremor immediately called for his arms and his horse; his bidding was done and he had himself well and swiftly armed. Then he left the camp and rode on till he reached the knight.

'Sir,' he said, 'you must come to the king!'

The knight didn't move; he seemed not to have heard. He addressed him again but he made no reply. Sagremor was annoyed and said:

'By Saint Peter the apostle, you'll come whether you like it or not! I'm sorry I ever deigned to ask – it was a waste of breath!'

Then he unfurled the pennon that was rolled around his lance, and the horse beneath him leapt away to take up charging distance; he called to the knight to defend himself, and Perceval looked up and saw him coming full tilt. He snapped out of his reverie and spurred ahead to meet him. Sagremor smashed his lance as they clashed, but Perceval's neither broke nor bent; instead he struck him with a force that sent him crashing to the ground. His horse didn't linger but fled away, head high, back to camp.

Those who were now rising saw the horse from their tents and were most upset. But Kay, who could never resist a cruel barb, made a joke of it, saying to the king:

'Oh, look, sire, Sagremor's back! He's got the knight by the reins and is dragging him back against his will!'

'Kay,' said the king, 'it's wrong of you to mock worthy men. Go yourself – let's see you do better.'

'I'm only too glad you'd have me go!' said Kay. 'And I'll bring him back by force, whether he likes it or not, oh yes! And I'll make him give his name!'

He had himself armed with great aplomb, and then mounted and headed for the knight, who was so intent on gazing at the three drops of blood that he was oblivious to all else. Kay shouted to him from a distance:

'Vassal! Vassal! Come to the king! You'll come right now, indeed you will, or you're going to pay dearly!'

Perceval, hearing the threat, turned his horse's head about; and with thrusts of his spurs of steel he came galloping at Kay – who wasn't riding slowly himself. Both knights meant business and clashed whole-heartedly. Kay struck with all his force, so hard that his lance smashed and shattered like bark; nor did Perceval hold back: he hit Kay just above the boss and sent him crashing on a rock, dislocating his shoulder and breaking his right arm between elbow and armpit like a stick of kindling – just as the fool had often foretold! The fool's prediction had come true! Kay passed out with the pain, while his horse went prancing back to camp.

The Britons saw the horse return without the seneschal, and boys and knights and ladies rode out to find him still unconscious. They were sure he was dead, and all began to mourn most dreadfully. Meanwhile Perceval was leaning on his lance again over the three drops of blood.

The king was distraught about his wounded seneschal, grieving and anguished – till he was told not to be alarmed, for Kay would recover well if he just had a surgeon who could put a shoulder back in place and mend a broken arm. So the king – who was very fond of Kay: he was very close to his heart – sent an able doctor with two girls who were pupils of his, and they reset his shoulder and bound his arm and joined the broken bone. Then they carried him back to the king's tent and did all they could to comfort him, assuring him he'd recover well and had no need to worry.

Then Sir Gawain said to the king: 'Before God, sire, it isn't right – as you've always said and rightly judged – that a knight should disturb another's thoughts as these two have done, no matter what. I don't know if they were in the wrong, but they've come to no good, that's for sure! The knight was thinking, maybe, of some loss he's suffered, or perhaps his sweetheart's been stolen from him and it's upsetting him and weighing on his mind. But if you wish I'll go and see how he looks, and if I find he's finished musing I'll ask him to come back here to you.'

Kay was incensed by this and said: 'Oh yes, Gawain, you'll lead him back by the reins whether he likes it or not, of course you will – if victory's handed to you on a plate! You've taken loads of prisoners like that! When the knight's worn out and has fought long enough, then the valiant champion asks permission to try his hand – and of course he goes and triumphs! Oh, Gawain, you're no fool! There's plenty to learn from you – a hundred curses on me if there's not! And you're good at spinning smooth and silky phrases, aren't you? Are you going to lay into him with harsh and haughty words? Damn any fool who thinks so – *I* can't see it! You could do this job in a silk shirt! You won't have to draw a sword or break a lance! Rest assured: if you can just get your tongue round "God save you, sir, and send you joy and health", he'll do your will! Oh, far be it from me to give you lessons: you'll cosset and coax him like a cat, while everyone's thinking "Sir Gawain's locked in mighty battle!"'

'Ah, Sir Kay,' said Gawain, 'there's no need to speak so harshly. Do you mean to vent your rage and spleen on me? Truly, my friend, I'll bring the knight back if I can – without a broken arm or a dislocated shoulder: that's not my idea of a reward!'

'Go now, nephew,' said the king. 'You've spoken most courteously. Bring him back if possible – but take all your arms with you: you're not to go unarmed.'

Gawain, renowned and esteemed for all virtues, mounted a good, strong horse and rode straight to the knight who was leaning on his lance, still not tired of his delightful musing. But the sun had dried up two of the blood-drops that had lain on the snow and was fast erasing the third, so he was less absorbed than before. Sir Gawain ambled up to him with no hint of aggression, and said:

'Sir, I'd have greeted you if I'd known your heart as well as my own. But I can tell you I'm a messenger of the king, who bids me request you to come and speak to him.'

'There have already been two,' said Perceval, 'who threatened my life and tried to lead me off a captive. I was musing so deeply on a blissful thought that whoever tried to interrupt was asking for trouble! There were three drops of fresh blood here, gleaming in the whiteness of the snow, and as I gazed I imagined I was looking at the fresh hues of my fair love's face, and didn't want to leave.'

'Truly,' said Sir Gawain, 'there was nothing base about that thought! It was courtly and sweet indeed, and the one who turned your heart from it was insensitive and rude. But I'd like to know what you mean to do now: I'll gladly take you to the king if you've no objection.'

'Tell me first, dear friend,' said Perceval, 'if Kay is there, the seneschal.'

'Indeed he is. And I tell you, he was the one who jousted with you here just now – and it cost him dear: you've broken his right arm, though you may not know it, and dislocated his shoulder.'

'Then I think I've avenged the girl he struck!'

When Gawain heard this he was taken aback; he gave a start and said: 'God save me, sir, it's you the king's been seeking! What's your name, sir?'

'Perceval, sir; and yours?'

'Truly, I was baptised with the name of Gawain.'

'Gawain?'

'Indeed, good sir.'

Perceval was overjoyed and said: 'I've heard a great deal about you, sir, and longed to make your acquaintance! I hope it may please you, too.'

'Truly,' said Sir Gawain, 'it pleases me no less than you, but more, I think!'

'In faith,' said Perceval, 'then I'll gladly go wherever you wish – it's only right. I'm honoured to be your companion.'

With that they embraced, and unlaced their helms and ventails* and opened their mail hoods; then they happily headed back. From the crest of a hill some boys saw them returning in genial mood and came running to the king.

'Sire! Sire!' they cried. 'Sir Gawain's bringing back the knight, and they seem the best of friends!'

All who heard this dashed from their tents and went out to meet them. And Kay said to his lord the king: 'Now your nephew Gawain has won honour and praise! My word, he's had a tough and perilous battle! He's coming back in the same shape that he left: he hasn't had a blow from anyone, and no one's felt a blow from him! He hasn't uttered a word of challenge! How right that he should be esteemed and lauded! And that people should say he's done what we all failed to do, for all our might and effort!'

So, rightly or wrongly, Kay spoke his mind as he always did.

Sir Gawain didn't want to take his companion to court in his armour, so he had him disarmed in his tent, where one of his chamberlains took a robe from a coffer and presented it to Perceval. Once he was well and handsomely dressed, in a tunic and mantle that suited him perfectly, he and Gawain came hand in hand to the king, who was sitting outside his pavilion.

'Sire,' said Sir Gawain, 'I bring you the one you've been longing to meet for fully a fortnight past: the one you've spoken of so much, the one you've been out searching for; I present him to you – here he is!'

'Thanks indeed, dear nephew!' said the king, so overjoyed that he leapt to his feet to greet him, saying: 'Welcome, sir! Now tell me, please, what name I should call you.'

'I shan't keep it from you, truly,' he said. 'My good lord king, my name is Perceval the Welshman.'

'Ah, Perceval, my good, dear friend, now that you've come to my court I'd never have you leave! I've been very troubled on your account: when I first saw you I didn't know what a great future God had planned for you! Yet it was clearly foretold, as all my court heard, by the girl and the fool whom Kay the seneschal struck – and you've verified their prediction perfectly! No one now can be in doubt that reports about your chivalry have been true.'

As he said this the queen arrived, having heard the news about the knight who'd come. As soon as Perceval saw her and was told that it was she, and saw the girl behind her who'd laughed when he'd looked at her, he went straight up to meet them and said:

'May God grant honour and joy to the fairest and finest of all ladies living, as all who have ever seen her testify.'

And the queen replied: 'It's a joy indeed that you've been found: you're a proven knight of high and fine prowess!'

Then he greeted the girl who'd laughed at him, and embraced her, saying: 'Dear girl, if ever you need me, I shan't fail to come to your aid.'

And the damsel gave him thanks.

The Price of Perceval's Failure

The king and queen and barons gave the most joyous welcome to Perceval the Welshman, and led him back to Carlion, returning there that day. They celebrated all that night and all the day that followed.

And then, on the third day, they saw a girl coming, mounted on a tawny mule, a whip in her right hand. Her hair hung in two tresses, twisted, black; and if my source is to be believed, there was no such utterly hideous creature even in Hell. You've never seen iron as black as her neck and hands, but that was nothing compared to the rest of her ugliness: her eyes were just two holes, as small as a rat's; her nose was like a cat's or monkey's, her lips like an ass's or a cow's; her teeth were discoloured to the shade of egg-yolk and she had a billy-goat's beard. With a hump in her chest and a crook in her back, her loins and shoulders were a dancer's dream: her back curved and her legs bent and buckled like willow wands – just right for dancing! Never was such a girl seen in a royal court.

She rode her mule right up to the knights, and hailed the king and all his barons together – all, that is, except Perceval. Sitting there on her tawny mule she said:

'Ah, Perceval! Fortune has fair locks before but is bald behind! A curse on anyone who greets you or wishes you well, for you didn't grasp Fortune by the hand when you met Her! You entered the house of the Fisher King and saw the lance that bleeds, but it was such a strain for you to open your mouth and speak that you couldn't ask why that drop of blood sprang from the tip of the lance's bright head; nor did you ask who the worthy man was who was served from the grail you saw. How wretched is the man who sees the perfect chance and waits for a better one! And you, you are the wretched one: you could see it was the time and place to speak and yet said nothing; you had ample opportunity! It was a disaster that you held your tongue: if you had asked, the great king who is so distressed would now have been quite healed of his wound and would have held his land in peace, which now he'll never do! And do you know what will happen, now that the king won't be healed and rule his land? Ladies will lose their husbands, lands will be laid waste, maidens will be left in distress and orphaned, and many knights will die: all these woes will strike because of you.'

Then she said to Arthur: 'Forgive me, king, if I leave now, but I must lodge tonight far from here. I don't know if you've heard of the Proud Castle, but that's where I must go tonight. In that castle are five hundred and sixty six knights of worth; and I tell you, each of them has his love with him, a noble, fair and courtly lady. I'm telling you this because anyone who goes there is sure of a joust or battle: anyone eager for chivalrous deeds is bound to find them if he seeks them there. But if anyone aspires to be deemed the finest in the world, I think I know the very place where he could win that name – if he dared. On the peak of Montesclaire a damsel is besieged; whoever could raise the siege and free the girl would win the greatest honour and all possible praise; and the one to whom God granted such good fortune could safely gird the Sword of the Strange Belt.'

With that she fell silent: she'd said all she wished. Off she rode without another word.

Then Sir Gawain leapt up and said he'd go to Montesclaire and do all in his power to rescue the girl. And Girflet the son of Do said for his part that with God's aid he would go to the Proud Castle.

'And I,' said Kahendin, 'am going to climb Mount Dolorous: I shan't rest till I've done so.'

But Perceval spoke quite differently: he said that as long as he lived he wouldn't sleep in the same place for two nights together, nor hear word of any perilous test but he would undertake it, nor hear of any knight greater than others but he would go and fight him, until he knew who was served from the grail and had found the bleeding lance and learnt the certain truth about why it bled; he would never give up, come what may.

Fully fifty of them rose and pledged and vowed to each other to seek out any marvel or adventure that they heard of, in no matter how daunting a land.

And then, while they were arming and preparing in the hall, through the door came Guigambresil, bearing a gold shield with a blue bend* that covered a full third of its face. Guigambresil recognised the king and greeted him in proper fashion; but he didn't greet Gawain: instead he accused him of a treacherous act, saying:

'Gawain, you killed my lord! And you did so without issuing a challenge, for which you should be shamed, reproached and censured: I charge you with treachery! And know this, all you noble knights: every word I've said is true.'

At this Sir Gawain leapt to his feet, burning with shame; but the proud Agravain, his brother, jumped up and pulled him back, saying: 'In God's name, sir, don't disgrace your line! I'll defend you against the shameful charge this knight has made against you, I swear.'

But Gawain answered: 'Brother, no man but I will defend me from it; I *must* defend myself, for he accuses no other but me. If I knew I'd wronged the knight I'd gladly sue for peace and make amends acceptable to all his friends and mine. But his charge is an outrage, and I offer my gage* and will defend myself here or wherever he likes.'

Guigambresil said he'd prove his foul and wicked treachery in forty days before the king of Escavalon, who in his view was more handsome even than Absalom.[16]

'I'll follow you straightway, I swear,' said Gawain, 'and there we'll see who's in the right!'

With that Guigambresil set off, and Sir Gawain prepared to follow him without delay. Whoever had a good horse or lance, a fine helm or sword, offered it to him; but he wouldn't carry anything belonging to another. He took seven squires with him, and seven horses and two shields. But before he'd left the court there was bitter grieving, with much beating of breasts and tearing of hair and clawing of faces in anguish: even the most level-headed of ladies mourned for him quite desperately. Crowds of men and women wailed as Sir Gawain took his leave.

You'll hear me tell at length now of the adventures he encountered.

The Tournament at Tintagel

First he saw a band of knights riding across a heath. A squire was following them on his own, with a shield slung round his neck and leading a Spanish horse by the bridle, and Gawain asked him:

'Tell me, who are those knights who passed this way?'

'It's Meliant de Lis, sir,' the squire replied, 'a worthy and courageous knight.'

'Are you in his service?'

---

[16] King David's third son; 'in all Israel there was none to be so much praised as Absalom for his beauty: from the sole of his foot to the crown of his head there was no blemish in him.' 2 Samuel, 14: 25.

'No, sir. Dröés d'Avés is my lord's name; he's no less worthy a knight.'

'Indeed,' said Sir Gawain, 'I know Dröés d'Avés well. Where's he heading? Tell me all.'

'He's going to a tournament that Meliant de Lis has undertaken against Tibaut of Tintagel. I wish *you*'d go, too, sir, and help the men of the castle against the outsiders!'

'By God!' said Sir Gawain. 'Wasn't Meliant de Lis brought up in Tibaut's house?'

'God save me, sir, he was indeed. His father loved Tibaut dearly; he considered him such a faithful friend that, as he lay on his death-bed, he entrusted his little son to him, and Tibaut raised and cared for him as lovingly as he could. In time Meliant craved the love of one of Tibaut's daughters, but she said she'd never grant him her love while he was still a squire. So Meliant, passionately eager, had himself knighted and then returned with his request. But the girl then said: "It can never be, till I've seen you fight and joust well enough to earn my love; for things that are given free of charge are never so pleasant and sweet as those that are paid for! Challenge my father to a tournament if you want my love, for I want to know for sure that my love would be well bestowed if I granted it." So he's undertaken the tournament as she asked; for Love holds such sway over those who are in Her power that they never dare refuse whatever She demands! You'll not shirk supporting the men of the castle, sir? That would be plain lazy! If you were willing to help they could certainly do with you!'

'You'd better ride on, brother,' said Sir Gawain, 'and follow your lord, and say no more of this.'

So the squire left him, and Sir Gawain rode on: he headed straight for Tintagel – there was no other way to go.

Tibaut had gathered together all his kin and called upon his neighbours, and they'd all arrived now – tall and short and young and old. But when Tibaut spoke in private with his counsellors they urged him not to engage in the tourney: they were very afraid that Meliant meant to destroy them utterly. So Tibaut had every entrance to his castle blocked: all the gates were soundly filled with solid stone and mortar – no need now for a gatekeeper! The only entrance left unblocked was a little postern – and its door certainly wasn't made of glass but of copper, made to last forever, barred with a great beam, and there was enough ironwork on the door to fill a cart.

Sir Gawain, with all his gear before him, came up to the gate – he had to go through the castle or turn back: there was no other path or road for seven long leagues around. When he saw the postern shut he rode into a meadow below the keep, enclosed by a fence, and dismounted beneath an oak and hung his shields upon it.

The people of the castle spotted him. Most of them were very sad that the tourney had been abandoned, and among them was an old vavasor, a wise and well respected man, with substantial lands and powerful kin, whose every word, whatever its outcome, was trusted by everyone in the castle. He'd seen Gawain and his squires coming – they were pointed out to him in the distance before they reached the fenced meadow – and he went to speak to Tibaut and said:

'God save me, sir, I do believe I've seen two knights coming,[17] companions of King Arthur! Two worthy knights make a big difference: just one can win a tournament. For my part I say we should go to the tourney with confidence: you have good knights and good sergeants – and good archers to kill their horses! Your foes are bound to come

---

[17] He thinks there are two rather than one because Gawain has hung up two shields: when he left court 'he took seven squires with him, and seven horses and two shields' (above, p. 42).

seeking combat outside the gate; if their pride brings them here, the gain will be ours, the loss and damage theirs!'

Tibaut took his advice, and gave leave for all who so wished to arm and ride forth. The knights were elated, and squires rushed to fetch arms and saddle horses, while the ladies and girls went to the highest points to watch the tournament. In the field below they saw Sir Gawain's baggage train, and thought at first that there were two knights, as they could see a pair of shields hung on the oak. They said they were lucky to have such a good view: they would see the two knights don their arms right there before them! So said some; but there were others who said:

'Dear lord God, that knight has enough gear and horses for two, but he's no companion with him! What will he do with two shields? No knight's ever been seen bearing two shields at once!' It would be amazing, they thought, if this lone knight were to carry both shields together!

While they were discussing this, and the knights rode out of the castle, Tibaut's daughter – who'd caused the tournament to be held – climbed to the top of the tower. Her younger sister was with her, too, who dressed in a style that had led her to be known as the Girl of the Little Sleeves, as they fitted so tightly to her arms; and all the girls and ladies joined Tibaut's daughters at the tower-top.

The tourneyers now gathered before the castle. And there was no knight there as handsome as Meliant de Lis – so said his beloved, who called to the ladies about her:

'Truly, I've never seen a knight – I don't see why I should lie to you – as pleasing to my eye as Meliant! Isn't it a joy to see one so handsome? He was made to sit astride a horse and to bear a lance and shield! See how well he handles them!'

But her sister, sitting at her side, said there was one even more attractive! The elder daughter was furious, and stood up ready to slap her; but the ladies pulled her back and restrained her, much to her annoyance.

The tournament began. Many lances were smashed, many sword-blows dealt, many knights unhorsed. And I tell you, all who clashed with Meliant paid the price: anyone who faced his lance was sent crashing to the ground – and if his lance broke he doled out mighty sword-blows, performing better than anyone on either side.

His sweetheart was so ecstatic that she couldn't keep quiet! 'What an amazing display! You've never seen or heard of the like! Look at him: the finest knight you ever beheld! He's more handsome and performing greater deeds than any at the tournament!'

But the younger daughter said: 'I can see one who may prove finer and more handsome still!'

Her sister came at her, blazing with rage, and cried: 'You bitch! You've the nerve to disparage the one I've praised? You'll be sorry! Take this – and never do it again!'

And she gave her such a slap that she left the stamp of her fingers on her face. The ladies rebuked her hotly and pulled her away. Then they started talking among themselves about Sir Gawain.

'God!' said one of the girls. 'That knight beneath the oak, what's he waiting for? Why doesn't he arm?'

Another, more impertinent, said: 'He must be a pacifist!'

And another: 'He's a tradesman! Don't tell me he means to take part: he's brought all those horses to sell!'

'No,' said a fourth, 'he's a money changer! And he's no intention of sharing his wealth with the poor young knights today! I'm not making it up, you know: it's all cash and silver in those bags and chests of his!'

'Really! You've got wicked tongues!' said the younger sister. 'And you're wrong. You think a tradesman carries a great lance like his? You've mortally hurt me with your devilish words! By the Holy Spirit, he looks far more like a jouster than a tradesman or money changer. He looks every inch a knight.'

'He may look it, my dear,' all the ladies said, 'but he's not. He's disguised himself as one to dodge duties and tolls! He thinks he's clever, but he's a fool: he'll be arrested as a thief and charged with a base and stupid crime, and end up with a noose around his neck.'

Sir Gawain heard their mocking words quite clearly, and was upset and ashamed. But he was mindful, rightly, that he'd been charged with treachery and had to go and defend himself; and if he failed to appear and do battle as he'd sworn, he'd bring shame upon himself and all his line. It was fear of being wounded or captured that stopped him taking part in the tourney – keen though he was to do so, seeing the fray growing ever fiercer and more intense. And Meliant de Lis was calling for stout lances to deal still greater blows.

All day long till nightfall the tourney raged outside the gate. Those who won booty were carrying it off to where they thought it safest. The ladies saw a squire, very tall and bald, holding the broken stump of a lance and carrying a horse's head-stall round his neck. One of the ladies called him a witless fool, saying:

'God help me, squire, you've lost your mind, scrabbling around for lance-heads and head-stalls and cruppers and lumps of wood! Call yourself a squire? To aim so low – have some self-respect! Right near you, in this meadow below, I can see unguarded riches! You'd be mad not to take advantage! That knight's the most soft-natured ever born – you could pluck every hair of his moustache and he wouldn't move! So don't settle for that cheap loot of yours: if you've any sense you'll take all the horses and the other stuff there – no one's going to stop you!'

So the squire went straight to the meadow, smacked one of the horses with his stump of lance and said to Gawain: 'Vassal, are you feeling all right, sitting here watching all day? You haven't done a thing – you haven't pierced a shield or broken a lance!'

'Be off!' he said. 'What's it to do with you? You may come to know the reason in time, but by my life it won't be yet, for I don't care to tell you! Get you gone – be about your business.'

The squire left Gawain instantly, not daring to rile him more.

The tournament now drew to a halt, but there'd been many knights captured and many horses killed. Meliant's men had come out on top, but the men of the castle had taken more booty, and as they parted they exchanged pledges to reassemble in the field next day and resume the contest. So they separated for the night, and all who'd come from the castle made their way back. Sir Gawain, too, entered the castle behind the main body, and outside the gate he met the worthy vavasor who'd advised his lord to begin the tourney. He kindly offered Gawain lodging, saying:

'Lodging's ready for you here in the castle! Do stay here, please: if you carry on you'll find nowhere good to stay tonight.'

'Thank you, sir,' Gawain replied, 'I'll gladly stay. I've heard worse suggestions than that today!'

The vavasor led him to his lodging, talking of one thing and another as they went, and asked him what had stopped him taking up arms in the tournament. Sir Gawain explained exactly why: he was being accused of treachery, and rightly feared capture or wound or injury until he could clear himself of the charge, feeling he'd bring shame on himself and his kin if he failed to appear on time for the battle he'd pledged to fight. The vavasor admired him for that and said he approved, and that he'd done right to avoid the tourney if that had been the reason. So he led him to his house and they dismounted.

But the people of the castle were very resentful, and hotly discussed how their lord should seize Sir Gawain. And the lord's elder daughter did everything she could to spite her sister, saying:

'Father, I know you've suffered no loss today – in fact you've won more than you think! I'll tell you how: make no mistake, but have that stranger arrested – the one who's brought him into the town won't dare defend him – for he lives by criminal deception! He has shields and lances carried before him, and horses led by the bridle, and so avoids paying levies because he looks like a knight! He goes around trading, disguised as a nobleman, scot-free! So give him what he deserves! He's at the house of Garin, the son of Berte – he's given him lodging: I saw him take him there just now.'

Thus she strove to have him brought to shame. And the lord her father mounted right away – he wanted to go in person – and headed straight for the house where Gawain was staying. When the younger daughter saw him leave like this, she slipped out of a back door, not wanting to be seen, and hurried to Sir Gawain's lodging at the house of Garin, the son of Berte. Garin had two lovely daughters, and when they saw their young lady coming they greeted her with sincere delight; they took her by the hands and kissed her on the eyes and lips and joyfully led her inside.

Meanwhile Sir Garin – who lacked neither wealth nor largesse – had remounted along with his son Herman; they were heading for court, as was their custom, wishing to speak to their lord. They met him in the middle of the street, and when Garin greeted him and asked where he was going, he said he was on his way to Garin's house in search of entertainment.

'Truly,' said the worthy Garin, 'nothing would please me more! There you'll meet the finest figure of a knight on earth!'

'That wasn't quite what I had in mind!' said the lord. 'I'm going to arrest him – he's a trader, by God! He leads a train of horses to sell and makes out he's a knight!'

'Come now! What base words are these?' said Garin. 'I'm your vassal and you're my lord, but I'll withdraw my homage and defy you here and now, in my own name and for all my kin, before I'll let you act so dishonourably in my house!'

'So help me God,' the lord replied, 'I didn't want to do this, but I've been strongly urged and advised to seize him. But your house and your guest I'll treat only with respect.'

'Thanks indeed,' said Garin. 'It will be a great honour to introduce you to my guest.'

And with that they rode together, side by side, to Garin's house. When Sir Gawain saw them he rose like the courteous knight he was and said: 'Welcome!'

They both greeted him and sat down at his side. Then the worthy lord of the land asked him why, having come to the tourney, he'd refrained from taking part. Sir Gawain didn't deny it was wrong and shameful, but explained at once that a knight had accused him of treachery and he was on his way to defend himself at a royal court.

'Then you had a worthy reason, truly,' said the lord. 'Where's this battle to be?'

'I must appear before the king of Escavalon, sir; I mean to go straight there.'

'I'll provide you with an escort,' said the lord. 'And since you'll be passing through very poor land I'll give you food to take with you and horses to carry it.'

Sir Gawain said there was no need for that: if he could find any for sale he'd have all the provisions he needed and good lodging wherever he went; he wanted nothing of his. So the lord rose to leave. But as he was going he saw his younger daughter coming the other way, and she rushed up and clasped Gawain by the leg, saying:

'Hear me, good sir! I've come to appeal against my sister who's hit me: defend my cause, I pray you!'

Sir Gawain, wondering who she was speaking to, said nothing; he just patted her on the head. She tugged at him and said:

'I'm talking to you, sir! I'm appealing to you against my sister – I don't love her at all – for she's shamed me today on your account!'

'What has it to do with me, dear girl?' said Gawain. 'How can I defend your cause?'

The lord, who'd been about to leave, heard her plea and said: 'Daughter! Who told you to come and make appeals to knights?'

'Is she your daughter, then, good sir?' said Gawain.

'She is, but take no notice of what she says! She's a child – a foolish, simple thing.'

'Then truly,' said Sir Gawain, 'it would be ungracious of me not to find out what she wants.' And turning to her he said: 'Tell me, dear child, how can I help you regarding your sister?'

'Just for tomorrow, sir,' she said, 'for my sake, please, take part in the tourney!'

'Tell me, my dear, have you ever made a request of a knight before?'

'No, sir.'

'Take no notice,' said the lord, 'of anything she says. Don't listen to her nonsense!'

But Sir Gawain said: 'No, sir! God help me, she's a young girl but has spoken well in her childish way, and I shan't refuse her plea. Since it's her wish, tomorrow I'll be her knight for a while!'

'Thank you, kind sir!' she said, so overjoyed that she bowed down to his feet.

Then they left without another word. The lord carried his daughter home on his palfrey's neck, and asked her how the quarrel had arisen. She told him the whole story, saying:

'I was very upset because my sister kept saying that Meliant de Lis was the best and most handsome of them all, but I'd seen that knight in the meadow below and couldn't help but contradict her, saying I'd seen one finer than Meliant! So my sister called me a silly bitch and gave me a hiding: damn anyone who thought it funny! I'd let both my tresses be cut off, much as it might spoil my looks, if it meant my knight would unhorse Meliant in tomorrow's tourney! That would put paid to my sister's claims! She's gone on about him so much today that she's irritated all the ladies! But the weather can quickly turn!'

'Dear daughter,' said the lord, 'I'll let you – no, I bid you, for courtesy demands – send the knight some token: a sleeve, perhaps, or wimple.'

And she, in her innocence, said: 'Gladly, if you say so, but my sleeves are so small: I wouldn't dare send them – he might not think much of them at all!'

'Leave it to me, daughter,' said the lord. 'I'll see to it, don't worry.'

So saying he carried her home, hugging and kissing her fondly, till they arrived outside his hall. When the other daughter saw him coming with her sister in his arms, her heart was filled with anger and she said:

'Where's my sister been, then, sir, the Girl with the Little Sleeves? She's full of tricks and ruses – she may be young but she's learnt them fast! Where did you fetch her from?'

'What does it matter to you?' he replied. 'You be quiet. She's a great deal better than you – you've pulled her hair and beaten her! That's no way to behave – I'm very upset!'

Her father's reproach and reprimand stunned her into silence. Then he called for a length of red samite to be brought from one of his chests and had it made into a long, wide sleeve; then he called his younger daughter to him and said:

'Rise early tomorrow morning, child, and go to the knight before he sets out. Give him this new sleeve as a token of love, and he'll wear it when he rides to the tourney.'

She replied that as soon as she saw day break she'd be up and washed and dressed. With that her father left her; and she, filled with excitement, begged her companions not to let her sleep long in the morning, but to wake her the moment they saw the sun rise if they wanted her to be their friend.

They did so faithfully: they woke and dressed her at the crack of dawn. So the girl was up early, and off she went alone to Sir Gawain's lodging – but not early enough to arrive before they'd risen and gone to hear mass. She waited at Garin's house till they'd prayed a long while and heard all that they should; then when they returned from church she jumped up to meet Gawain and said:

'God keep you and grant you honour today! And wear this sleeve for me, I pray you.'

'Gladly! Thank you, my dear,' Sir Gawain said.

The knights now armed without delay, and gathered outside the town. All the girls and ladies of the castle went up and lined the walls again, and watched the bands of strong, brave knights assemble. Meliant de Lis charged ahead of them all against the opposing line, leaving his companions hundreds of yards[18] behind; and when the elder daughter saw her beloved she couldn't hold her tongue.

'Ladies!' she cried. 'Here comes the finest of all knights!'

Sir Gawain charged to meet him as fast as his horse could go. Meliant didn't fear him, but shattered his lance as he struck him; and Gawain returned a blow that did real damage, sending him crashing head first to the ground. Then he reached out for Meliant's horse and took it by the bridle and gave it to a boy, telling him to go to the one for whom he was fighting and to say he was sending her the first booty he'd won that day, for he wanted her to have it. So the boy led the horse, complete with its saddle, to the girl, who from a window of the tower had had a perfect view of Sir Meliant de Lis's fall. And she said:

'Sister, now you can see Meliant de Lis, whose praises you were singing, flat out on the ground! To anyone with any sense what I said yesterday is clear: now, God save me, it's plain to see there's a knight of greater worth than he!'

She deliberately taunted her sister till she drove her wild! 'Hold your tongue, you bitch!' she cried. 'If I hear another word from you today I'll give you such a battering you'll not have a leg to stand on!'

'Shame on you, sister!' the younger replied. 'Remember God! Just because I've told the truth you shouldn't go beating me! I saw him well and truly felled, and so did you – as well as I! I don't think he's the strength to stand! I'd say so even if it killed you: every lady here saw him sent flying, head over heels and flat on his back!'

Her sister would have slapped her if she'd had the chance, but the ladies in their company wouldn't let her. And then they saw the squire coming, leading Meliant's horse by the reins. He found the girl sitting at a window and presented the horse to her. She thanked him more than sixty times! Then she bade that the horse be taken for her, while the squire returned to convey her thanks to Gawain, who seemed to be lord and

---

[18] Literally 'two and a half arpents'; in medieval France the *arpent* was roughly equivalent to 70 metres.

master of the tourney: there was no knight, however dashing, who could face Sir Gawain's lance and keep his stirrups. He'd never been so eager to win horses. He made presents of four that day, won by his own hand: the first he sent to the little girl; with the second he thanked Garin's wife, who was delighted with the gift; one of Garin's two daughters received the third and the other the fourth.

Then the tournament broke up, and Sir Gawain rode back through the gate, carrying off the prize in the judgement of both sides, though it wasn't yet noon when he left the fray. As he returned he was accompanied by such a throng of knights that the town was packed; they all followed him, eager to find out who he was and from what land.

He met the young damsel right at the door of his lodging, and this is what she did: she took hold of his stirrup there and then and greeted him and said: 'Five hundred thousand thanks, good sir!'

He knew just what she meant, and replied like the courteous knight he was: 'I'll be grey and white with age, dear girl, before I fail to serve you, wherever I may be. However far I may be from you, if I hear you're in need of help, nothing will stop me coming as soon as I have word.'

'Thank you indeed!' she said.

They were talking thus when her father arrived, and he tried with all his might to have Sir Gawain stay that night and accept his hospitality; and he asked him first, if he would, to tell him his name. Gawain declined to stay, but said: 'Sir, my name is Gawain. I've never withheld my name when it's been requested – but neither have I given it unless first asked.'

When the lord heard he was Sir Gawain his heart filled with joy, and he said: 'Oh, stay, sir! Accept my service tonight, for yesterday I gave you none at all! Never in my life, I swear, have I seen a knight I so desired to honour!'

He implored him to stay, but Gawain refused all his pleas. Then the little girl – neither bad nor foolish – kissed his foot and commended him to God. He asked her what she'd meant by this, and she said she'd kissed his foot so that he'd remember her wherever his feet should tread. He replied:

'Have no fear, my dear: I'll never forget you when I'm gone, so help me God.'

And with that he departed, taking leave of his host and the others, and they all commended him to God.

Sir Gawain is Besieged

Sir Gawain slept that night at an abbey where he was given all he needed, and set off on his way again early next morning. As he rode along he saw deer grazing at the edge of a forest. He told Yvonet[19] – who was leading one of his horses, the finest, and holding a strong, stout lance – to stop and to bring him the lance, and to tighten the girths of the horse he was leading and to exchange it for his palfrey. The squire didn't hesitate, giving him the lance and the horse without delay, and Gawain rode off after the hinds, chasing them with such trickery and guile that he trapped a white one against a thorn bush, laying his lance across her neck. But the hind leapt like a stag and escaped him; off he went in pursuit, and was on the point of catching her when one of his mount's front shoes came clean away. Feeling him hobble he was much put out, and set off back

---

[19] Gawain set out on his journey with seven squires. Yvonet, who'd helped young Perceval deal with the Red Knight's armour (above, p. 11), is evidently among them.

to his baggage-train; he couldn't think what was making him limp, unless he'd caught his hoof on a tree-stump. He called to Yvonet to dismount and take care of his horse – he was hobbling badly; he did as bidden, and immediately lifted a hoof and saw the shoe was missing.

'Sir, he needs to be shod,' he said. 'We'll just have to walk him gently till we find a smith who can fit a new shoe.'

They journeyed on till they caught sight of a party coming from a castle and along the road. At the front was a lightly clad group, boys on foot with dogs on leashes, and behind them huntsmen with bows and arrows; and last of all came knights. At the very rear were two riding destriers, one of them a young man, the most striking and most handsome of them all. He alone greeted Gawain and took him by the hand and said:

'Let me entertain you a while! Carry on the way I've come and dismount at my house. It's time you found lodging, if it please you: I've a charming sister who'll make you very welcome. My companion, sir, will take you. Dear friend,' he said, 'I'm sending you with this gentleman: escort him to my sister. Greet her first, then tell her that I bid her, by the love and trust we rightly share, that if she ever cared for a knight she should lovingly care for this guest of ours and do as much for him as she would for me, her brother, and give him all the company and pleasure that he wishes till we return. Once she's received him graciously, make haste and follow us: I want to be back to keep him company as soon as I can.'

With that the knight set out – leaving Gawain to be taken to where he was mortally hated by all! But he wasn't recognised, for he'd never been seen there before; nor did he know he was in danger.

He noted the castle's fine position, overlooking an arm of the sea, and saw the walls and tower, so strong that it feared nothing. And then he saw the town, filled with fine-looking folk, and the money-changers' tables piled with gold and silver and all manner of coin, and the squares and streets filled with skilled craftsmen of every kind: one made helms and another hauberks, one saddles, another shields, this one bridles and that one spurs; some furbished swords, some fulled cloth while others wove it, others combed it, others sheared it; some melted gold and silver and others worked them into rich and handsome goods – cups, goblets, bowls, enamelled jewellery, rings, belts, buckles. You might well have thought there was a permanent fair in town, brimming as it was with so many riches: wax and pepper and spices and furs and every kind of merchandise. They rode on, gazing here and there at all this wealth, until they reached the tower, where boys came out to take charge of the horses and the other gear.

The knight entered the tower alone with Sir Gawain, and led him by the hand to the girl's chamber. He said to her: 'My dear, your brother sends you greetings and bids you serve and honour this knight – and not grudgingly, but with as much good will as if you were his sister and he your brother. Be unstinting in answering his every request: be generous, free, warm-hearted! See to it now, for I need to go: I must follow your brother to the wood.'

The girl was delighted and said: 'Bless him for sending me such company! To lend me such a fine companion shows how much he loves me: I thank him dearly! Come, good sir,' she said, 'and sit beside me. You seem a most worthy and charming guest, and since my brother has bidden me, I'll give you sweet entertainment!'

The knight stayed no longer and set off. Sir Gawain had no complaints about being left with the girl: she was so fair and so agreeable – and so well raised that she was sure no one would send a chaperone, even though she was alone with him. They talked of love – had they talked of anything else, what a waste of time it would have been! Sir Gawain sought and implored her love, promising to be her knight all his life; and she didn't refuse: she granted it gladly! But just then a vavasor entered – much to their cost, for he recognised Gawain, and when he found them kissing and cavorting he couldn't hold his tongue but loudly cried:

'Shame upon you, woman! God destroy and confound you! Letting yourself be kissed and caressed by the man you should hate most in all the world! Wretched, foolish woman, how typical this is of you! You should have stolen his heart with your hands, not your lips! Your kisses have taken hold of his heart, no doubt, and drawn it from his breast, but you'd have done better to rip it out with your hands! And so you should! There's no good in a woman: a woman's not a woman if she spurns evil and loves good – it would be wrong to call her a woman then: if she's devoted to good she loses the name! But you're a woman, plainly: the man beside you killed your father, yet you kiss him! When a woman has her pleasure she cares little for the rest!'

With that he dashed away before Gawain could say a word; and the girl fell to the floor where she lay a long while in a faint. He lifted her up, aggrieved and upset at her fear. When she came to she said:

'Ah, we're dead! Because of you I'll die today – and so will you, I think, because of me! The people of the town will be here in an instant, I'm sure of it – there'll be ten thousand massed outside this tower! But there are plenty of weapons in here: I'll have you armed in no time! One worthy knight could defend this tower against a whole army.'

And she ran, fearful as she was, to fetch the arms. Once she had him properly armed both she and Gawain were less worried; but as ill chance would have it there was no shield to be had, so he took a chessboard as a shield, saying:

'My love, there's no need to look further!'

And he tipped the chessmen on the floor; they were of ivory, ten times bigger than other chessmen and of harder bone. Come what may, he now felt sure he could hold the door and entrance to the tower, for at his belt hung Escalibor, the finest sword there was: it sliced through iron as easily as wood.

The vavasor meanwhile had run from the tower and found a town assembly in session: the mayor and the aldermen and a crowd of other citizens – and they certainly hadn't been purging themselves: they were all well fed and corpulent. He dashed up, yelling:

'To arms, sirs! Let's go and seize Gawain, the treacherous killer of my lord!'

'Where is he? Where is he?' they all cried.

'I found that proven traitor in the tower,' he replied. 'He's taking his ease, fondling and kissing our lady – and she's not complaining! She's enjoying it, and only too willing! So come, let's go and seize him! If you can deliver him to your lord, how grateful he'll be! The traitor's deserved to be brought to shame – but take him alive; my lord would rather have him alive than dead, and rightly so: a dead man fears nothing. Raise the whole town, and do your duty!'

With that the mayor rose, and all the aldermen after him. Then you'd have seen a host of raging townsfolk snatch up whatever they could: axes and gisarmes[20] and makeshift

---

[20] The gisarme was a pole weapon similar to a halberd, combining a hook with a point or axe-blade. Its origin was the crude fixing of a hand tool to a long pole, and the implication here is that the weapons grabbed by the commoners are less than sophisticated.

shields: one grabbed a door, another a winnowing fan! The town crier bellowed and all the bells clanged to raise the whole commune and see that no one stayed behind; even the most wretched rogues snatched up a pitchfork, a flail, a pick or a club. A pack of Lombards out to kill a slug never made such a racket![21] Even the basest curs came rushing, clutching some weapon or other. Sir Gawain was a dead man unless God came to his aid!

The girl bravely made ready to help, and cried to the mob: 'Away! Be off, you rabble, you mad dogs, you slavish scum! What devil's sent you here? What are you after? What do you want? God heap misery on you! You'll never take this knight in here, so help me God: there'll be countless of you dead and maimed instead! He didn't fly here or sneak inside – my brother sent him to me as a guest, and begged me to treat him as I would my own brother. Do you think me base for entertaining him, for offering him pleasure and comfort as my brother bade? Think what you like, but that's the only reason I gave him such a welcome – I'd nothing foolish in mind. I'm outraged that you shame me so, drawing swords upon me at my chamber door without good cause – or if you have a cause you haven't told me what it is! You've shown me the vilest disrespect!'

While she was speaking her mind, the mob were smashing the door down with hatchets, splitting it in two. But the doorman fought back well! Gawain wielded his sword and dealt with the first man in such a way that the others were all aghast, and no one dared go forward: each of them feared for his own skin – or rather for his head! No one had the courage to attack, such was their dread of the doorman! No one raised a hand against him or advanced a single step! Then the girl took the chessmen that were scattered on the floor and started flinging them at the mob in fury. She hitched up her clothes and swore in her rage that, before she died, she'd destroy the lot of them if she could! The mob drew back, and threatened to bring the tower down on top of them if they didn't surrender; but they mounted an even fiercer defence, bombarding them with the ivory chessmen. Some of the rabble couldn't take it and turned tail; they started undermining the tower with steel picks, aiming to bring it down, not daring to attack and fight at the door that was held so well against them. And believe me, one valiant knight could hold and defend it well, for the doorway was so narrow and low that two men would have struggled to enter abreast; and you couldn't have asked for a doorman more adept at splitting helmless heads to the teeth and scattering their brains.

The lord who'd given him lodging knew nothing of all this, but he was now returning swiftly from the wood where he'd been hunting. And still the mob were hacking away at the tower with their picks.

It was at this very moment that Guigambresil – unaware of the goings-on – came galloping into the castle. He was bewildered by the racket and the hammering of the mob. He'd no idea that Gawain was there; but when he heard the news he forbade anyone, if he valued his life, to dare dislodge a stone. But they said they wouldn't stop because of him: they'd bring the tower down on top of *him*, too, if he were inside with Gawain! Guigambresil, seeing his command ignored, decided to go and meet the king,[22]

---

[21] A passing jibe at the Lombards for their supposed cowardice. 'Slaying the slug' was a proverbially derisory act, and the bitterness towards Lombards was intensified by their resented success as money-lenders, and also by the challenge of the Lombard League – an alliance of Northern Italian cities formed in 1167 – to the authority of the Emperor (to whom, as noted above, p. 1, Chrétien's patron Count Philip of Flanders paid homage).

[22] It is only now that the knight who'd been hunting and had sent Gawain to be entertained by his sister – 'the lord who'd given him lodging' – is revealed to be none other than the king of Escavalon, before whom Gawain is due to present himself to answer the charge made by Guigambresil.

returning from the wood, and bring him back to the riot that the townsmen had begun. He told him:

'Sire, your mayor and your aldermen have done you a great disgrace! They're attacking your tower and knocking it down! I'd like to see you make them pay! I've charged Gawain with treason, as you know, and it's Gawain you were lodging at your house! And it's only right, if you've made him your guest, to see that he suffers no harm or shame!'

'He won't,' the king replied, 'once we get there. I'm most aggrieved. I'm not surprised my people wish him dead, but I'll protect him if I can from capture or harm, since I've given him lodging.'

So they rode on to the tower, and found the people thronging round, making a great commotion. The king told the mayor to leave and to take the people with him; and they all moved off – not a single one remained since that was the mayor's wish.

Now, there was a vavasor present, a native of the town, who, being a man of great wisdom, gave advice to the whole country; and he said to the king:

'My lord, you need clear and honest counsel. It's no wonder that the man who treacherously killed your father has been besieged here: he's mortally hated as you know, and rightly so. But the fact that you've given him lodging should protect him from being slain or taken captive. And it must be said, Guigambresil there should guard and save him, for he went to King Arthur's court and accused Gawain of treachery. There can be no doubt that Gawain was coming here to defend himself against the charge at your court; but I advise that this combat be postponed for a year, and that Gawain should go in search of the lance with the ever-bleeding head – it can never be wiped clean of a drop of blood. He should either deliver that lance to you or submit to such imprisonment as he's suffering here; then you'd have a better reason for holding him captive than you have now. I don't think you could ever impose a task upon him, however hard, that he'd fail to accomplish brilliantly! But it'll be tough – and you should make those you hate suffer all the hardship that you can: I can think of no better way of punishing your foe!'

The king took the vavasor's advice. He went into the tower and up to his sister, and found her in quite a state. She rose to meet him, as did Sir Gawain, who showed no sign of fear – no trembling, no pallor. But suddenly Guigambresil came striding forward and greeted the girl – who certainly *had* changed colour – and said these vain words:

'Sir Gawain, Sir Gawain, because of my charge of treachery you're under my protection; but I warned you never to be so bold as to enter any castle or city belonging to my lord but to avoid it if you would.[23] So you've no cause to complain of what you've suffered.'

But the wise vavasor said: 'By God, sir, there's no need for all that! Who's he to appeal to if the mob have assaulted him? The debate would go on and on till Judgement Day! No, let it be settled according to the will of my lord the king: he commands through my lips that if you and Gawain have no objection, you're to postpone your battle for a year and let Sir Gawain go; but first my lord will have an oath from him: that within that year – no longer – he will deliver to my lord the lance whose head sheds tears of the clearest blood: it is written that the time will come when the whole kingdom of Logres – once the land of giants – will be destroyed by that lance. My lord the king wants that pledge and assurance.'

---

[23] This wasn't specifically mentioned when Guigambresil made his challenge (above, p. 42); perhaps Chrétien means us to understand that more words passed between them than simply those quoted.

'Truly,' said Sir Gawain, 'I'd rather let myself die or languish here for seven years than swear such an oath or make such a pledge! I'm not so scared of dying: I'd sooner suffer death with honour than perjure myself and live in shame!'

'Good sir,' said the vavasor, 'it won't be to your shame and you'll be none the worse for it; let me explain why: your pledge will be to do your best to find the lance, but if you fail to bring it back you'll return to imprisonment in this tower, and thus be absolved of the oath.'

'In that case,' said Sir Gawain, 'I'm prepared to make the pledge.'

Then a precious reliquary was brought to him, and he vowed to devote all his energies to finding the bleeding lance. And so the battle between Gawain and Guigambresil was postponed for a year; he'd escaped from great peril in being thus freed.

Before he left the tower he took his leave of the girl; and he told his squires to return to his land, and to take back all his horses except Gringalet. So the boys left their lord and departed; but I've no wish to say more about them or the grief they felt. The story leaves Sir Gawain here and turns to Perceval.

Perceval and his Hermit Uncle

Perceval, my source-book tells us, had lost his memory to such a degree that he'd quite forgotten God. April and May he passed five times – that's five whole years – without setting foot in a church or worshipping God or His cross: he lived liked this for five years. That's not to say that he stopped seeking deeds of chivalry: he went in search of strange, daunting, gruelling adventures, and encountered so many that he tested himself well. In five years he sent sixty fine knights as prisoners to King Arthur's court. That was how he spent five years, without a thought for God.

At the end of these five years he happened to be riding across a wilderness, fully armed as ever, when he met three knights and ten ladies with them, their heads covered by their hoods and all of them on foot, in hairshirts and bare-footed. The ladies, for the salvation of their souls, were doing penance on foot for the sins they'd committed, and were astonished to see him coming clad in armour and holding a lance and shield. And one of the three knights stopped him and said:

'Dear friend, don't you believe in Jesus Christ, who laid down the New Law and gave it to the Christians? Truly, it's neither right nor proper, but very wrong, to bear arms on the day when Jesus died.'

And the one who had no sense of day or hour or season, so troubled was his heart, said: 'What day is it, then?'

'What day, sir? Don't you know? It's Good Friday, the day when a man should worship the cross and weep for his sins, for on this day the one who was sold for thirty pieces of silver was hung upon the cross. Clean of all sins, He saw the sins with which the whole world was stained and bound, and became a man to save us from them. Truly, He was God and man, for the Virgin bore a son conceived by the Holy Spirit, a son in whom God assumed flesh and blood, so that deity was housed in the flesh of man. That is certain; and those who won't believe it will never see Him face to face. That son born of the Virgin Lady, who assumed the form and the soul of man with His holy deity, on this day was nailed to the cross, truly, and freed all His friends from Hell. It was a holy death indeed: it saved the living and brought the dead from death to life. The false Jews, who should be put down like dogs, did themselves great harm and us great good when they wickedly raised Him on the cross: they damned themselves and wrought our salvation! And all who believe in Him should be spending today in penance; no man who believes in God should bear arms today, either in the field or on the road.'

'Where have you just come from?' Perceval asked.

'From a worthy man, sir, a holy hermit who lives here in the forest – such a holy man that he lives solely by the glory of God.'

'In God's name, sir, what did you do there? What did you ask? What were you looking for?'

'What did we ask and do?' said one of the ladies. 'We asked him for guidance from our sins and we made confession – the greatest thing any Christian can do if he wants to come to God.'

What Perceval had heard made him weep, and he longed to go and speak to the worthy man. 'I'd dearly love to go there,' he said, 'if I were sure of the way.'

'Sir, anyone wishing to go to him should head straight along the way we've come, through the deep, dense wood, and look out for the branches we tied together as we came: we left them as signs so that no one seeking the holy hermit should lose his way.'

With that they commended each other to God and no more questions were asked. Perceval set off along the path, sighing from the depths of his heart: he felt very guilty in the eyes of God, and repented deeply. He rode on, weeping, right through the wood.

When he arrived at the hermitage he dismounted and disarmed and tethered his horse to an elm. Then he went inside. In a little chapel he found the hermit and a priest and a clerk who, truly, were beginning the highest, sweetest service that can be held in holy church. Perceval went down on his knees the moment he entered the chapel; and the good man, seeing him humbly weeping, with tears streaming from his eyes to his chin, called him to draw near. Deeply afraid that he'd offended God, Perceval clung to the hermit's foot, bowing right down before him; then with clasped hands he begged him to give him guidance, for he had great need. The good man told him to make confession, for he'd never have remission if he didn't confess and repent.

'Sir,' said Perceval, 'fully five years ago I lost my bearings, and stopped loving God and believing in Him; and since then I've done nothing but ill!'

'Oh, dear friend!' said the worthy man. 'Tell me why you did this, and pray to God to have mercy on His sinner's soul.'

'Sir, I was once at the house of the Fisher King and saw the lance with the head that assuredly bleeds, but asked nothing about the drop of blood I saw hang from the tip of that shining head. And truly, I've done nothing since to make amends. Nor do I know who was served from the grail I saw. Since then I've been in such a dismal state I wish I were dead! I've forgotten God because of it! Never since have I asked Him for mercy – and I don't think I've done anything to earn it!'

'Oh, dear friend,' the hermit said, 'tell me your name.'

And he said: 'Perceval, sir.'

At that the worthy man gave a sigh, for he recognised the name, and said: 'Brother, a sin of which you're unaware has done you great harm: it's the grief you caused your mother when you left her. She collapsed in a faint at the foot of the bridge outside the gate, and of that grief she died. It's because of the sin you committed there that you came to ask nothing about the lance and the grail, and many misfortunes have befallen you in consequence. And know this: you wouldn't have survived this long had she not commended you to God. But her prayer had such power that God has watched over you for her sake, and kept you from death or capture. It was sin that cut off your tongue and stopped you asking the reason when you saw the lance-head with its endless flow of blood; and folly seized you when you failed to learn who was served from the grail. The one who's served from it is my brother. My sister, and his, was your mother. And as for the wondrous Fisher, I believe he's the son of the king who's served from the grail.[24] And don't imagine he's given pike or lamprey or salmon; he's served with a single host[25] which is borne to him in that grail: it comforts and sustains his life, such a holy thing is the grail. And he, so spiritual that he needs no more for life than the host that comes in the grail, has lived there for twelve years without ever leaving the chamber that you saw the grail enter. Now I wish to give you direction and penance for your sin.'

'I want that with all my heart, dear uncle!' Perceval said. 'If my mother was your sister, you should call me nephew and I should call you uncle – and love you the more.'

'That's true, dear nephew! But listen now: have pity on your soul and repent in all sincerity, and each morning, before going anywhere else, go in a spirit of penitence to church and you'll benefit greatly; don't fail to do so on any account. Wherever there's a minster, chapel or parish church go there when you hear the bell ring – or sooner if you're up; it won't do you any harm: it'll be much to your soul's benefit! And if mass is begun there'll be still more profit in being there: stay till the priest has said and sung it all. If you do this with a will, you may enhance your reputation all the more, and win honour and a place in Paradise.

'Love God, believe in God, worship God; honour men and women of religion; and stand before priests – it's a service that costs little, and God truly loves it as a sign of humility.

'And if a girl or widow or orphan appeals to you for help, be sure to grant it: it'll be the better for you – it's a worthy act of charity, so you'll do well to give them your aid; make sure you do so, without fail. I'd have you do this to atone for your sins, if you want to recover your former virtues. Now tell me if you'll do so.'

'I shall, sir, most willingly.'

'Then stay here with me, please, for the next two days, and in penance eat the same food as I.'

Perceval agreed to all of this. Then the hermit whispered a prayer in his ear, repeating it till he'd learnt it. Many of the names of Our Lord appeared in this prayer, including the greatest, which the tongue of man should never utter except in fear of death; and when he'd taught him the prayer he forbade him ever to use those names except in times of utmost peril.

'I shan't, sir,' said Perceval.

So he stayed and heard the service, which delighted him; and after the service he worshipped the cross and wept for his sins. That night he ate what the hermit chose; but there were only beets, chervil, lettuce and cress and millet, and bread made of barley and oats, and clear spring water. And his horse was given a bed of straw and a basin full of barley.

So it was that Perceval came to recognise that God accepted death and was crucified on the Friday. And at Easter, in most worthy fashion, Perceval received communion.

The story says no more about Perceval for now. You'll have heard a good deal about Sir Gawain before I tell of him again.

[24] The Fisher King is thus revealed to be Perceval's cousin; Perceval's mother was the Fisher King's aunt.
[25] i.e. communion bread. Given that a 'graal' was a broad, shallow dish or platter (see note 13, above, p. 29), the reference to fish is not at all as strange as it may appear.

Gawain and the Haughty Girl

Sir Gawain, after his escape from the tower where the mob had attacked him, wandered on until one morning, between terce* and noon, he approached a hill and saw a tall, spreading oak tree, thick with leaves, giving plenty of shade. He could see a shield hanging on the oak, and beside it a good, straight lance. He hurried on towards the tree till beside it he saw a small, dark palfrey; he was very surprised by this – it didn't seem right: arms and a palfrey didn't go together. Had it been a destrier he'd have supposed that some knight, roaming the land in search of honour and renown, had climbed to the top of the hill. But just then he looked beneath the oak and saw a girl sitting there, who'd have been fair indeed had she been happy – but her fingers were thrust in her tresses to tear out her hair and she was wailing wildly, grieving for a knight, kissing him over and over on the eyes and lips and forehead. Gawain rode closer and and saw the knight was wounded, with gashes to his face and a dreadful sword-cut in his head; down both his sides blood poured in streams. He'd passed out many times with the pain and now at last lay still, and when Gawain arrived he couldn't tell if he was alive or dead.

'How does he seem, dear girl,' he said, 'that knight you're holding?'

She replied: 'You can see his wounds are grave indeed: he'd die of the very least.'

'Wake him if you will, dear friend,' said Gawain. 'I want to ask him about the affairs of this land.'

'I'll not wake him, sir!' she said. 'I'd rather be flayed alive! I've never loved a man so much, nor shall I ever as long as I live. Now that he's sleeping and at rest I'd be a wretched fool to disturb him!'

'Then truly, *I'll* wake him if I can!' said Gawain, and swinging his lance around he nudged him on the spur with the butt. It didn't trouble the knight to be woken – Sir Gawain knocked his spur so gently that it didn't hurt him. Instead the knight thanked him, saying:

'A thousand thanks, sir, for shaking me awake so gently that I suffered no harm. But for your own sake I beg you go no further – you'll be a fool if you do: take my advice and stop here!'

'Stop? Why should I?'

'I'll tell you, truly, since you want to know. No knight who's ever gone that way, by road or field, has ever come back; for this is the border of Galvoie,[26] and no knight can cross it and return. I'm the only one who's ever done so – and now I'm in such a state I don't think I'll last till nightfall! For I met a knight, bold and valiant, mighty and fierce: I've never encountered one of such valour or tested myself against one so strong. That's why you'd do better to turn back than cross this hill – returning's a cruel business!'

'Truly,' said Sir Gawain, 'I didn't come here to go back again. I should be deemed a base coward if I turned back now that I've taken this path. I'll carry on till I see for myself why no one can return.'

'I see there's nothing for it,' said the wounded knight. 'You'll go, for you're eager to enhance your honour. But I'd ask this of you if you'll let me: if God should grant you the honour which no knight has ever had – and never will, I think, neither you nor any other – please return this way and see if I'm alive or dead, or any better or worse. And if I'm dead, then in the name of charity and the holy trinity I beg you take care of this

---

[26] A place-name possibly based on Galloway (south west Scotland).

girl, and see she suffers no harm or shame. Please do so, for God never made, or thought of making, one more noble or good-hearted.'

Sir Gawain granted his wish, promising that, unless he were prevented by capture or other mishap, he'd return to him and give the girl such assistance as he could. With that he left them and rode on without stopping, over plains and through forests, till he caught sight of a mighty castle, on one side of which was a great seaport with a fleet of ships to match: this noble city almost rivalled Pavia. On its other side lay vineyards, and beneath it flowed the great river that girded its walls all around before opening into the sea, protecting the castle and the town on every side. Gawain crossed the bridge and rode in.

When he'd climbed to the citadel he found, beneath an elm tree in a courtyard, a charming girl, whiter than snow, gazing at her face and lips in a mirror. She'd made a crown around her head with a narrow band of orfrey. Sir Gawain gave his horse a spur and rode smartly up towards the girl, but she called out:

'Easy, sir! Go easy! You're riding like a madman! There's no need to hurry and wear out your horse: it's daft to rush for nothing!'

'God bless you, girl,' said Gawain. 'But tell me, dear friend, what did you mean – telling me to go easy for no good reason?'

'Oh, I had good reason, knight, indeed I did! I know exactly what's on your mind!'

'What's that?' he said.

'You want to take me and carry me off across your horse's neck!'

'True enough, girl!'

'I knew it,' she said. 'But curse whoever would think such a thought! You can forget about putting me on your horse! I'm not one of those simple women knights sport with and carry off when they go adventuring – you'll not take me! And yet, if you dared, you *could* take me with you: if you'd risk fetching my palfrey from that garden I'd go with you – and misfortune, hardship, grief and shame and woe would strike you in my company!'

'Is anything needed but courage, my dear?'

'I don't think so, vassal,' the girl replied.

'Ah, but damsel: where shall I leave my horse if I go? He couldn't cross that plank into the garden.'

'No, knight – give him to me and cross on foot. I'll look after him as long as I can hold him. But you'd better hurry back: I couldn't keep hold if he refused to be calm – or if he were taken by force before you returned.'

'True enough,' he said, 'but I shan't hold you responsible if he escapes or is snatched from you. And I won't go back on that.'

So he gave her his horse and set off – but decided to take all his arms with him: if there were someone in the garden who refused him the palfrey and forbade him to take it, there'd be kerfuffle and combat before he brought it back! So he crossed the plank – and found a sizeable crowd of people who stared at him in dismay and cried:

'May a hundred demons burn you, girl, for the wickedness you've done! Misfortune strike you! You've never shown love for a worthy man! You've sent so many to lose their heads – it's a grievous shame! You mean to take the palfrey, knight, but don't realise what'll befall you if you touch it! Oh, knight, why don't you turn back? You wouldn't go anywhere near if you knew the shame and harm and pain in store if you take the palfrey!'

So said all the men and women, desperate to steer him away from the palfrey, wanting him to go back. He heard them well enough, but nothing was going to change his mind; on he went, greeting the crowd, and they all returned his greeting, but didn't hide their anguish and distress. Then he stepped up to the palfrey and reached for the reins – it was fully saddled and harnessed. But a tall knight, sitting beneath a lush, green olive tree, said:

'It's no use trying to take that palfrey, knight. Don't lay a finger on it: it would be an act of the vainest presumption. I'll not forbid or stop you if you're really keen to take it, but I'd advise you to be gone: if you take that palfrey you'll find a fearsome challenge elsewhere!'

'That's not going to stop me, sir,' said Gawain. 'I was sent by that girl beneath the elm, looking at herself in the mirror – and if I don't take the palfrey back, what was the point of coming? I'd be in disgrace – I'd be thought a cowardly failure!'

'It'll cost you, brother!' the tall knight said. 'By God the sovereign Father to whom I hope to deliver my soul, no knight has ever taken the palfrey and escaped a dismal fate: beheading! I fear the same will befall you. I meant you no harm when I told you not to take it: you can do so if you wish – neither I nor anyone here will stop you – but you're making a big mistake if you take it from this garden. I don't recommend it – it'll cost you your head!'

But Sir Gawain wouldn't dally a moment longer. He drove the palfrey – its head black on one side and white on the other – across the plank. And it knew the way well enough – it had crossed it many times and was well trained and schooled in it now. Then he took it by its silken rein and came straight to the elm where the girl was absorbed in her mirror; she'd dropped her mantle and wimple on the ground so that she could see her face and body freely. Gawain presented the saddled palfrey to her and said:

'Come now, girl: I'll help you mount.'

'God forbid,' she replied, 'it should ever be said, in any court you take me to, that you held me in your arms! If you ever held any part of me, or touched me with your bare hand, I'd think myself disgraced! If it were ever known and spread abroad that you'd laid hands on me – what horror! I'd rather my skin and flesh were stripped from my bones, I swear! Come – leave me the palfrey: I can mount perfectly well by myself – I don't need help from you. And God grant I see what I expect: great shame befall you before the day is out! Go where you will, you'll never touch my body or my clothes; but I'll be constantly behind you till you've suffered some disaster because of me! I know I'll make you come to grief – you can't escape it any more than death!'

Gawain heard every word the haughty girl had said, but he made no reply; he simply gave her the palfrey and she handed back his horse. Then he bent down, meaning to pick up her mantle from the ground and drape it round her; but she, never slow or afraid to say shameful words to a knight, watched him and said:

'Vassal! What business have you with my mantle or my wimple? I'm not half as simple as you think, by God! I've no desire at all to have you serve me: your hands aren't clean enough to touch anything I wear on my body or head. You shouldn't handle anything that touches my body, my lips, my forehead or my face! God send me shame if I ever accept your service in any way!'

So the girl mounted, having donned and fastened her clothes herself, and said: 'Now, knight, go where you like, and I'll follow you everywhere till I see you shamed because of me – and that'll be today, please God!'

Sir Gawain was silent, saying not a word in reply. He mounted, abashed, and they set off; and with head bowed he returned towards the oak where he'd left the girl and the knight in urgent need of a doctor for his wounds. Gawain knew more than any man about healing wounds, and saw a herb in a hedge that was very good for relieving pain. He went and picked it, and then carried on till he found the girl beneath the oak, lamenting; and the moment she saw him she said:

'Ah, dear sir, I think this knight is dead now: he hears and is aware of nothing any more.'

Gawain dismounted, and found that the knight had a firm pulse, and his lips and cheeks were not too cold.

'He's still alive, girl, you may be sure: his pulse is good and his breath is strong and he has no mortal wound. I've brought a herb that'll greatly help, I think; it'll relieve some of the pain as soon as it's applied: it's written that no finer herb can be laid upon a wound, and that its power is such that were it tied to the bark of a blighted tree, then – unless it were completely withered – the roots would recover and the tree would return to leaf and flower. Your sweetheart need fear death no more, girl, once we've applied this herb to his wounds and bound it on; but we'll need a wimple of fine cloth to make a bandage.'

'I'll give you the one I'm wearing,' she said without hesitation. 'It's the only one I've brought.'

So she took the wimple from her head, and fine and white it was indeed; and Sir Gawain cut the lengths required and bound the herb on all the knight's wounds, the girl helping as best she could. Gawain didn't move till the knight gave a sigh and spoke, saying:

'God reward the one who's restored my speech – I was very afraid I'd die without confession. A procession of demons came here, seeking my soul! I dearly want to make confession before I'm laid in the ground. There's a chaplain I know close by; if only I had a mount I'd go and confess my sins to him and take communion – then I'd no longer fear death. Do me this service if you will: give me the rouncey[27] of the squire who's trotting this way.'

At this Sir Gawain turned and saw a squire approaching – and of most unpleasant appearance he was. What was he like? I'll tell you: his hair was red and tousled, and stood on end like the spines of an angry porcupine; his eyebrows were the same, and covered his face and nose right down to his moustache, which was long and twisted; he had a great slit of a mouth and a broad beard, forked and knotted, and a short neck atop a bloated chest. Gawain was keen to go and ask for the horse, but first he said to the knight:

'Truly, sir, I don't know who he is, that squire, but whoever he may be I'd rather give you seven destriers, if I had them here to hand, than that nag of his!'

'I tell you,' said the knight, 'he's intent on one thing only: to do you harm if he can.'

Sir Gawain went to meet the squire and asked him where he was heading; and he, being far from pleasant, answered:

'What's it to do with you, vassal, where I've been or where I'm going? Whatever my path may be I hope you come to grief!'

At that Sir Gawain gave him what he deserved: a blow with his open palm; and his arm being armoured and his will to strike keen, he bowled him over and emptied his

---

[27] The rouncey ('*roncin*') was a tough, multi-purpose horse, lacking the *cachet* of the finest warhorse (the '*destrier*') – and costing only a fraction as much. It was still a very useful mount, sometimes used in combat by squires or less wealthy knights, but here the implication clearly is that this one's a bit of a nag: it's about to be described as a sorry sight.

saddle. When the squire tried to stand he reeled and fell down flat again – he fell seven times or more, I jest not, in less than the length of a pinewood lance! When he did find his feet again he said:

'You hit me, vassal!'

'Indeed I did,' Sir Gawain said, 'but I've done you no great harm. I'm sorry I hit you, before God I am, but you spoke most offensively.'

'Well you'll pay for it, and I'll tell you how! You'll lose the hand and arm that dealt that blow: it'll never be forgiven!'

While this was going on, the wounded knight's heart, which had been so weak, returned to him and he said to Gawain: 'Leave that squire, good sir – you'll never have a courteous word from him! Yes, you'd do best to leave him now; but bring me his rouncey, and take this girl here at my side, fasten the girths of her palfrey and help her mount: I don't want to stay here longer. I'll mount the rouncey if I can, and look for somewhere to make confession: I shan't stop till I've confessed and taken communion and received the last rites.'

Gawain took the rouncey there and then and gave it to the knight. His sight had now returned and cleared, and he saw Sir Gawain and recognised him for the first time. Gawain took the girl and, like the kind and courtly knight he was, he helped her on to the dark palfrey. And while he was setting her in the saddle, the knight took Sir Gawain's horse and mounted, and sent him charging in all directions! Gawain saw him galloping about the hill and laughed in amazement; but as he laughed he called out:

'Truly, sir knight, it's not a good idea to make him leap about! Dismount and give him to me: you could easily hurt yourself and reopen your wounds.'

But he said: 'Hold your tongue, Gawain! You'd better take the rouncey – you've lost the horse! I like the way he runs – I'm taking him for my own!'

'What! I come here to help you and you'd do me wrong? Don't you dare take my horse – it would be treachery!'

'I'd go further, Gawain, given half a chance – I'd like to rip your heart out with my two bare hands!'

'This reminds me of a proverb,' said Gawain. '"Do some men a good deed and your throat'll bleed!" I'd like to know why you'd have my heart! And why you're taking my horse! Never in my life have I wished or done you any harm! I'm sure I've done nothing to deserve it – I've never seen you before, to my knowledge.'

'Oh yes, you have, Gawain! You saw me all right – and shamed me terribly! Don't you remember the man you tormented by forcing him to eat with the dogs for a month, with his hands tied behind his back? What a mad, foolish deed that was – and now the shame is yours!'

'Are you, then, Greoreas, who abducted the girl and had your way with her? Yet you knew full well that maidens are protected in King Arthur's land: the king has guaranteed their safety – he watches over them, ensuring their safe conduct. I can't believe you hate me or seek to do me harm for what I did to you: I did it for the sake of justice, which is established and exacted throughout the king's land.'

'Yes, Gawain, you exacted justice – I remember it well! And now you must suffer the justice that *I'll* exact: I'm taking Gringalet – it's the best revenge I can have for now. You'll have to switch to the nag from which you felled that squire – there's no other swap you can make!'

With that Greoreas left him and raced off after his sweetheart; she was riding swiftly away and he followed with all speed. The wicked girl laughed at Gawain then and said:

'Oh, vassal, vassal! What will you do? It may well be said of you now: "There's one born every day!" By God, it's great fun trailing you – I'll gladly follow wherever you go! If only the nag you've taken from the squire had been a mare! I wish it were, I really do – then your disgrace would be greater still!'[28]

So Sir Gawain, having no choice, mounted the stupid, trotting rouncey. It was an ugly beast, with a scrawny neck and a fat head and long, limp ears, and all the imperfections of age: its lips were shrunk a finger's length apart, its eyes were dim and cloudy, its hooves covered in sores, its flanks leathery and slashed to bits by spurs. It was long and thin, with a skinny rump and a sagging back. The reins and headstall were made of cord and there was no blanket beneath the saddle – which had seen much better days; and the stirrups were so short and frail that he didn't dare put any weight on them.

'Oh, truly,' cried the girl, tormenting him, 'this is going splendidly! I'll happily go where you like – for a week or a fortnight, three weeks or a month: who wouldn't, when you're so finely harnessed and mounted on that handsome charger! You're a fitting escort for a girl indeed! But now I want to see you come properly unstuck: what fun! So give your horse a spur and test him – but watch out, and don't be alarmed: he's like lightning! I'll be right behind: I'm not leaving till disgrace has truly struck you – as it surely will!'

'You can say what you like, dear friend,' he replied, 'but it's not right for a girl to speak so rudely when she's more than ten years old; she should be well-mannered and courteous and civil, if she's the wit to learn.'

'What! You want to teach me lessons, Sir Hapless? I don't need instruction from you! Ride on and hold your tongue: I've got you just the way I wanted!'

So on they rode together till evening, and neither said a word. Sir Gawain went ahead and she rode behind. He didn't know what to do with his nag – he couldn't get it to canter or gallop, however hard he tried; it plodded along whether he liked it or not, for if he dug in his spurs he had a dreadful ride: it shook up his insides so much that he couldn't bear to have it go beyond a walk.

On he plodded on the nag, through wild, deserted forests, till he came to open country beside a deep river, so wide that no sling of catapult or mangonel could have thrown a stone across, and it was well beyond a crossbow's range. On the other side, overlooking the river, stood a castle of great size and strength and splendour. It was built upon a cliff, and without a word of a lie, no man alive ever set eyes on so fine a fortress, with a great hall, all of grey marble, set upon a sheer rock. And in the hall were fully five hundred open windows, all filled with girls and ladies gazing out before them at the meadows and flowery gardens. Many of the girls were dressed in samite and many in silk of various colours, all brocaded with gold. From the waist up they could all be seen, with their shining hair and comely bodies, as they leaned there at the windows.

The most hateful creature in the world, now riding ahead of Gawain, came straight down to the river. Then she stopped and stepped down from her little white-stockinged palfrey, and on the bank she found a boat; it was fastened and padlocked to a stone, but there was an oar in the boat and on the stone lay the key to the lock. The cruel-hearted girl climbed into the craft and the palfrey stepped in after her – as it had done many times before.

---

[28] In the 14th-century romance *Perceforest* there is a lengthy passage revolving around the perceived disgrace of a knight being forced to ride a mare. See *Perceforest*, tr. Bryant (Cambridge, 2011), pp. 74–9.

'Dismount now, vassal,' she said, 'and climb aboard with me and bring that nag of yours – it's as skinny as a chicken! – and haul in the anchor; you'll be in a sorry plight unless you cross the river quickly – or can swim fast!'

'What, girl? Why?'

'You haven't seen what I see, knight: if you had you'd get a move on!'

Gawain now turned and saw a knight approaching across the meadow, fully armed. 'Would you mind telling me,' he said to the girl, 'who that knight is? He's riding my horse, stolen from me by the traitor I healed of his wounds this morning!'

'Oh yes, I'll tell you,' the girl said gleefully, 'by Saint Martin I will! But you can be sure I wouldn't, not for all the world, if I thought you'd be pleased! But since I'm certain his coming's bad news I shan't keep it from you: he's Greoreas's nephew – he's sent him after you, and I'll tell you exactly why: to track you down and kill you and take him back your head! So you'd better dismount and climb aboard and flee – unless you want to die here!'

'I certainly shan't flee because of him, girl. I'll wait.'

'Well I certainly won't stop you!' she replied. 'I'll say no more! Oh, what a splendid charge, what a stirring gallop you'll make before those lovely girls, leaning at the windows! They're only there because of you – it's because of you they've come! So charge! They'll love it, with you mounted on that mighty steed – you look all set to go and joust!'

'Come what may, girl, I'm not backing out. I'm going to meet him: I'd dearly love to recover my horse.'

So he turned about and steered his nag towards the knight who was spurring along the sandy riverbank. Gawain prepared to meet him, bracing himself so firmly in the stirrups that he snapped the left one off; so he let the right one go and just waited for the knight – the nag wouldn't move: however hard he spurred he couldn't make it budge.

'Alas!' he cried. 'A packhorse is no steed for a knight when he wants to go and do battle!'

And the knight came charging on Gawain's own horse – which wasn't one to hobble! He gave Gawain such a blow with his lance that it bent like a bow and snapped clean across, leaving the head buried in the shield. And Sir Gawain struck him above the boss, with such force that it smashed through his shield and right through his hauberk and sent him crashing down in the fine sand. Gawain reached out and seized his horse and leapt into the saddle. The outcome was so sweet to him and his heart so filled with joy that he'd never felt so happy in his life! Then he rode back to the girl who'd climbed aboard the boat – but there was no sign of either boat or girl. He was very put out: he didn't know what had become of her.

The Castle of the White-haired Queen

While he was puzzling about the girl he saw a skiff coming from the castle, guided by a boatman. When he reached the bank he said:

'I bring you greetings, sir, from the damsels yonder; and they send you word not to withhold my rightful possession: return it to me if you will.'

Gawain replied: 'God bless all the company of maidens, and you, too. You'll lose nothing on my account that you can claim to be rightly yours – I've no wish to wrong you. What is it you'd have from me?'

'I saw you topple a knight here, sir, whose horse I should rightfully have. If you've no wish to wrong me you should hand it over.'

'That's a lot to ask, my friend,' said Gawain. 'I'd have to continue on foot.'

'Shame upon you, knight!' said the boatman. 'The girls will think you dishonest and wicked now, if you won't return what's mine by right! Whenever I've known a knight has been unhorsed here on this bank, I've always had his mount. And if I haven't had the horse I've never failed to have the knight!'

And Sir Gawain said: 'I'll not refuse you the knight, my friend: take him – he's all yours!'

'In faith, sir, that's no gift!' replied the boatman. 'I think you'd have trouble taking him yourself if he decided to resist! But if you've got it in you, go and take him prisoner and bring him back to me – then you can keep what's rightly mine.'

'Friend, if I dismount and go on foot, can I trust you to hold my horse in all good faith?'

'Indeed you can. I'll guard him for you faithfully, and willingly give him back: I'll never do you any wrong as long as I live, I swear.'

'I'll trust you, then,' Sir Gawain said, 'on your word of honour.'

So he climbed from his horse and entrusted it to the boatman, who took it and promised to guard it faithfully. Then Gawain set out, with sword drawn, towards the knight – who had no need of further trouble: he was so badly wounded in the side that he'd lost a deal of blood. As Gawain came up to him he said, in some distress:

'I can't hide it, sir: I've such a grievous wound that I can do without receiving worse! I've lost a gallon of blood – I crave your mercy.'

'Arise, then,' said Sir Gawain.

And the knight struggled up and Gawain led him back to the boatman, who thanked him deeply. Then Gawain asked him to tell him about the girl he'd brought there: did he know where she might have gone? And the boatman answered:

'Forget her, sir! Who cares where she's gone? She's not a girl – she's worse than Satan! She's caused many a knight to be beheaded on the bank here! Take my advice and come with me and accept such lodging as I can offer – it's no use staying here on the riverbank: it's a wild place, full of strange wonders.'

'If that's your advice I'll take it, friend, whatever may befall me.'

So he did as the boatman said. His horse was led aboard the boat and Gawain climbed in after, and they pushed off and crossed to the other bank. The boatman's house was close to the water, and offered every comfort: it was fit to receive a count! The boatman led his prisoner and his guest inside, and gave them the warmest welcome that he could. Sir Gawain was served with everything befitting a noble man: he supped on plover and pheasant and partridge and venison, and the wines were strong and clear, white and red and new and old. The boatman was delighted with his prisoner, and with his guest. They supped at length, till finally the table was cleared away and they washed their hands again. Sir Gawain's host and lodging that night were greatly to his liking: he appreciated the boatman's hospitality, and it pleased him very much.

Next morning, as soon as he saw day break, he duly rose as he always did, and the boatman rose likewise to look after his guest. They went together and leaned at the windows of a turret, and as Sir Gawain gazed out at the countryside, which was fair indeed, he saw the forests and the plains and the castle on the cliff.

'Host,' he said, 'I'd like to ask if you don't mind: who is the lord of this land and that castle?'

But his host replied: 'I don't know, sir.'

'You don't know? You astonish me: you're a retainer of the castle and it brings you a handsome income, yet you don't know who is its lord?'

'I can tell you in all honesty,' he said, 'I don't know and have never known.'

'Then tell me, host, who defends and guards the castle?'

'It's guarded well indeed, sir: there are five hundred bows and crossbows always at the ready. If the castle were ever threatened they'd shoot ceaselessly and never tire, so ingeniously are they contrived. And I'll tell you this much: there's a queen at the castle, a most noble, wise, illustrious lady of the highest lineage. She came to live in this land with her great store of gold and silver, and made the mighty residence you see before you. With her she brought a lady she dearly loves, whom she calls queen and daughter; and this other lady has a daughter, too, who does nothing to debase or shame her line: I don't think there's a girl of fairer looks or manners under heaven!

'And the hall is guarded well – by magic and enchantment, as I'll explain if you wish to hear. In that great hall a clerk, well versed in the stars and brought here by the queen, has created such marvels that you've never heard their like: no knight can enter and live as long as it takes to ride a league, if he's tainted with such vices as cupidity, dishonesty or greed. No coward or traitor can endure; liars and perjurers can't survive – they all die in an instant!

'But there are many squires, gathered there from many lands, serving at the castle and preparing for knighthood: well over five hundred, some bearded, others not; a hundred have neither beard nor moustache, a hundred more have beards just starting, a hundred shave and trim each week, a hundred are turning grey and a hundred are whiter than wool! And there are elderly ladies without husbands or lords: they've been wrongly deprived of their lands and possessions since their husbands died. And with the two queens are orphaned girls who are kept with great honour.

'All these people go about their lives at the castle, nursing a wild and impossible hope: they're waiting for a knight to come and be their protector, who'll restore the ladies to their domains, give husbands to the maidens and knight the squires. But all the sea will turn to ice before they find a knight who can stay in the hall! He would have to be handsome and wise, wholly free of covetousness, brave and bold, noble-hearted, loyal, and clean of all wickedness and baseness. If such a knight were to come he could be lord of the castle; he'd restore their lands to the ladies and bring an end to the deadly wars, and marry off the girls and knight the squires, and cast out the enchantments of the hall forthwith.'

This news thrilled Sir Gawain: it appealed to him greatly! 'Host,' he said, 'let's go down. Have my arms and my horse brought to me at once: I don't want to dally here – I want to be off!'

'Where to, sir? Oh, stay – God bless you – today and tomorrow and longer still!'

'Bless your house, host, but that shall not be. I'm going, with God's help, to see those maidens and the marvels of the hall!'

'Hush, sir! Please God, you'll do nothing so foolish! Listen to me and stay!'

'Hush, host! Do you take me for a faint-hearted coward? God forsake my soul if I follow your advice!'

'Very well, I'll hold my tongue: I can see I'll be wasting my breath! Go if you're so keen, though it grieves me. But I must guide you there – truly, you could have no better escort than I. But I'd like to ask a favour.'

'What's that, host? Tell me.'

'Grant it first.'

'I'll do as you wish, host – as long as it won't shame me!'

Then he ordered his horse to be brought from the stable, ready to ride, and called for his arms again. They were duly brought and he armed and mounted and set off, and the boatman likewise mounted his palfrey – wanting to lead Gawain faithfully to where he'd prefer he didn't go!

On they rode until, at the foot of the steps outside the hall, they found a one-legged man sitting alone on a bundle of rushes. He had a false leg made of silver – or silver-plated – inlaid here and there with gold and precious stones. His hands weren't idle: he had a knife and was busy sharpening an ashwood stick. He didn't address the two as they passed, and they said nothing to him. The boatman drew Gawain to him and said:

'What do you make of that one-legged man, sir?'

'His false leg isn't made of poplar, that's for sure!' said Gawain. 'It looks a splendid thing to me.'

'By God,' replied the boatman, 'he's rich indeed, with great and handsome revenues. You'd have been in a spot of bother if I hadn't been escorting you!'

On they went to the hall. Its entrance was lofty indeed and the doors were grand and beautiful: the hinges and bolts were of pure gold, so my source-book says. One of the doors was of ivory, superbly carved, and the other was of ebony, carved likewise, and both doors glittered with gold and wondrous gems. The hall was paved in many colours – green and red, deep blue and indigo – perfectly laid and smooth.

And in the middle of the hall stood a bed. Not a single part of it was wooden: every bit was made of gold – except the cords, which all were silver. This is no lie! Wherever the cords were interlaced there hung a little bell; the bed was spread with a great swathe of samite; on each of the posts was mounted a garnet, yielding more light than four brightly burning candles; the bed stood on grotesque carved dogs with snarling faces: these sat on four casters, so smooth and swift that the bed could be sent from one end of the hall to the other with a nudge of a single finger. The like of this bed was never made for a king or count, believe me, and never will be; and there it stood in the middle of the hall.

And trust me, no part of that hall was made of limestone: the walls were all of marble, with windows above so clear that, through the glass, anyone keeping watch could see all who entered as soon as they stepped through the door. The walls were painted in the finest, richest colours that can ever be imagined or made. I don't want to describe every detail now, but in that hall were a good four hundred windows closed and a hundred open.

Sir Gawain went up and down, this way, that way, gazing at every inch of the hall. Having looked all around he called to the boatman and said:

'Dear host, I see nothing to make a man fear this place! What have you to say? Why did you insist I shouldn't come? I'm going to sit on this bed and rest a bit – I've never seen one so luxurious!'

'Ah, sir! God forbid you go anywhere near! Touch that bed and you'll die the most dreadful death that any knight's ever known!'

'What should I do, then?'

'I'll tell you, since I see you're keen to stay alive! Just before we left my house, I asked of you a favour, though I didn't say what. Now I'll ask you to grant it: return to your own land, and tell your friends and the people there that you've seen the most splendid hall that you and they have ever known.'

'Then I'll say God hates me and I'm damned! I'm sure you mean me well, but I tell you, nothing's going to stop me sitting on the bed and seeing the maidens I saw last night, adorning all the windows!'

The boatman took a dramatic step back to drive home his point, saying: 'You won't see a single one of them! Return the way you came – you've no chance of seeing the girls! But God save me, they and the queens and ladies can see you even as we speak – through those glass windows, from their chambers on the other side.'

'In faith,' said Sir Gawain, 'if I can't see the girls I'll at least sit on the bed! It was surely made for just one reason: to have a worthy man or noble lady lie on it! And so I shall, upon my soul, whatever may befall me!'

The boatman saw he couldn't stop him, and said no more; but he didn't want to stay in the hall and see him sit on the bed – he headed off, saying:

'Your death distresses me terribly, sir! No knight has ever sat on that bed and left alive! It's the Bed of Marvels, in which no one sleeps, slumbers, rests or sits and rises from it alive and well! It's a dreadful pity that you mean to put your life in pledge, never to be redeemed or ransomed! Since nothing I say will drag you away, may God have mercy on your soul – it would break my heart to see you die!'

And with that he left the hall. Sir Gawain, armed as he was, and with his shield slung round his neck, sat down on the bed. As he did so, the bedcords made a mighty din as all the bells upon them rang till the whole hall resounded; and then suddenly all the windows opened and the marvels and enchantments were revealed, for down through the windows flew arrows and crossbow bolts – more than seven hundred smashed into Sir Gawain's shield. But he didn't know what had hit him: the enchantment was such that no man could see where the bolts had come from, or who was shooting! And you can well imagine the deafening sound of all those bows and crossbows! Gawain wouldn't have been there now for a thousand marks! But suddenly the windows shut, without anyone touching them. Then Gawain began to pull out the bolts imbedded in his shield, and they'd wounded him in several places and he was losing blood. But before he'd drawn out all of them he was confronted with another test: a villein kicked open a door, and a ravening lion, mighty, huge and fierce, sprang from a vault and in through the door and attacked Gawain with savage fury. Its claws tore through his shield as if through wax and drove him to his knees; but Gawain leapt up instantly, drew his naked sword from its sheath and dealt the creature such a blow that he cut off its head and both its feet. He was jubilant: the feet were left hanging on his shield by the claws – one on the inside and one on the front.

Having killed the lion he sat down on the bed again, and his host came running back into the hall, his face beaming, and found him sitting on the bed.

'Sir,' he said, 'you've no more to fear, I promise you! Take off all your armour now: you've cast out the hall's enchantments forever! You'll be served and honoured here by young and old – God be praised!'

Then squires came streaming in, all clad in the finest tunics, and went down on their knees and said: 'Good, dear, gentle sir, we offer you our service: how we've yearned and longed for your coming!'

'I was later than you'd have wished, it seems!'

Then some began to disarm him and others went to stable his horse, left standing outside. And while he was being disarmed a most beautiful and comely girl appeared, with a circlet of gold upon her head; and her hair was as bright as the gold, or brighter. The whiteness of her face was illumined by Nature with a pure red hue, and she was lithe and fair, with a graceful body, tall and straight. Behind her came other maidens, comely and fair indeed. Just one boy appeared with them, carrying a gown, a tunic, a mantle and a surcoat; the mantle was lined with ermine and with sable, berry-black, and the cloth was a rich red scarlet.* Sir Gawain gazed in wonder at this great array of maidens; he couldn't contain himself, and sprang to his feet and said:

'Welcome, girls!'

The first of them bowed to him and said: 'My lady the queen sends you greetings, good sir, and bids all her people hold you as their rightful lord and come and serve you. I shall be the first to offer you my service in all faithfulness, and these girls here all hold you as their lord and have long desired your coming; they're overjoyed to see you now, the finest of all worthy knights. There's nothing more to say, sir: we're at your service!'

And with that the maidens knelt and bowed, committed to serving and honouring him. He bade them rise again at once and be seated; he gazed at them with delight – partly because of their beauty, and more because they were making him their prince and lord! He rejoiced more than he'd ever done at this honour that God had granted him! Then the girl stepped forward and said:

'My lady has sent you this gown to don before she sees you; she supposes, wise and thoughtful soul that she is, you'll have suffered much toil and heat and hardship, so put it on and see if it fits: wise men guard against the cold after being hot – it can chill and deaden the blood. That's why my lady the queen has sent you this ermine gown, to protect you from harmful cold; for just as water turns to ice, so blood can freeze and stop its flow when a man starts shivering after heat.'

And Gawain, the most courteous knight in the world, replied: 'May the Lord in whom all good resides protect my lady the queen – and you likewise, fair maiden that you are, so kind and gracious: the lady's most discerning, I'd say, to have such courteous messengers! And she knows a knight's needs, certainly, sending me such a gown to wear! I'm grateful indeed; give her my deepest thanks.'

'I shall most gladly,' she said. 'In the meantime you can dress, sir, and view the lie of the land from the windows here, or climb the tower if you wish and look at the forests and meadows and rivers till I return.'

With that she left him, and he donned the gown, which was rich indeed, fastening the neck with a clasp that hung at the collar. Then he decided to go and see the view from the tower; so he set off with his host the boatman, and they climbed a spiral stairway at the side of the vaulted hall till they reached the tower's top and saw the country all around. It was indescribably beautiful; Sir Gawain gazed at the river and the meadows and the forests, teeming with game, and looked at his host and said:

'By God, I'd love to live here and go hunting and shooting in those forests!'

'You'd better say no more of that, sir,' the boatman said. 'It's established and decreed – so I've often heard tell – that whoever was so loved by God that he came to be called master and lord and protector of this place would – rightly or wrongly – never be able to leave the castle! So it's no good talking of hunting and shooting! This is where you stay – you'll never leave again!'

'Enough!' Sir Gawain cried. 'Say no more or you'll drive me mad! I tell you, if I couldn't go out when I wished I could no more live here for a week than for seven score years!'

And with that he strode down from the tower and back into the hall. Fuming and troubled he sat down on the bed again, his face morose and grim. At last the girl returned, and when he saw her he rose to greet her, angry as he was. She saw his manner and speech had changed and that something had upset him, but she didn't dare say so; instead she said:

'Sir, my lady will come and see you whenever you please. But dinner is ready and you may eat if you wish, either down here or up above.'

'I'm not interested in food, dear girl!' he replied. 'Blast my body if I eat or make merry till I hear what I badly need: words of reassurance!'

She returned at once in grave concern, and the queen asked what had happened, saying: 'Grand-daughter dear, how did you find the good lord that God has sent us?'

'Oh, lady, honoured queen, I'm dying of worry for that good and kindly lord! The only words he'll utter are of anger and distress! I can't tell you why – he didn't say and I didn't dare ask! All I know is this: when I first saw him today he was so happy and gracious and pleasant of speech that one could never tire of listening to his words or gazing at his smiling face! But suddenly he's changed and would gladly be dead, I think – everything he hears displeases him!'

'Don't worry, grand-daughter: he'll calm when he sees me. However great his rage may be, I'll soon cast it out and set joy in its place.'

Then the queen set out and came to the hall, and with her went the other queen, who was only too pleased to go; and with them they took fully two hundred and fifty girls and at least as many squires.

The heart often guesses aright, and the moment Sir Gawain saw the queen coming, holding the other by the hand, his heart told him she was the queen of whom he'd heard – it wasn't hard to guess, seeing her white hair hanging to her hips, and the gorgeous white silk she wore, finely embroidered with golden flowers. He wasn't slow to go and meet her, and they exchanged greetings and she said:

'I am lady of this castle, sir, but under you: I yield to you the lordship, for you have well deserved it. But tell me: are you of King Arthur's household?'

'I am indeed, lady.'

'And are you one of the knights of the watch, who've done many feats of prowess?'

'No, lady.'

'Very well. Then tell me, are you one of the Round Table, the most esteemed in all the world?'

'Lady,' he said, 'I wouldn't dare say I'm among the most esteemed: I don't claim to be one of the finest – nor do I think I'm one of the worst!'

'A most courteous answer, sir,' said the queen, 'claiming neither the credit of the best nor the censure of the worst. But tell me now about King Lot: how many sons did he have by his wife?'

'Four, my lady.'

'Tell me their names.'

'Gawain was the eldest, lady, and the next was Agravain, the proud one with strong hands; the other two are Gaherïet and Guerrehés.'

'So help me God, sir, those are their names indeed, I think. Would to God they were here with us now! But tell me, do you know King Urien?'

'Indeed I do.'

'Has he a son at court?'

'Yes, lady – two, of great renown. One is named Sir Yvain, most gracious and courtly – I'm happier all day if I see him in the morning, I find him so bright and pleasant! The other's name is also Yvain, but he's not his full brother – that's why he's known as the Bastard. He outfights any knight who engages him in battle. They're both at court, and valiant, wise and courteous they are.'

'And King Arthur, good sir,' she said, 'how is he faring?'

'Better than ever: in finer health and spirits, and ever stronger.'

'Indeed, sir, that's as it should be, for King Arthur is a child – he can't be more than a hundred, surely! But I'd like you to tell me just one more thing, if you will: how is the queen? How is she faring?'

'Truly, she's courteous, wise and beautiful – God never made a race or land where you'd find so fair a lady! There's been no lady of such renown since God formed the first from Adam's rib! And her reputation is deserved: just as a wise teacher instructs little children, so the queen directs and teaches others – she's the source and fount and wellspring of all goodness. No one leaves my lady without good guidance. She knows so well each person's worth and what she needs to do to please him. No man does a good or honourable deed unprompted by my lady; and no man, however forlorn, leaves her with his mind still troubled.'

'Nor will you, sir, leave *me* so.'

'I'm sure of that, lady,' Sir Gawain said, 'for before I saw you I didn't care what became of me, such were my despair and grief. But now I'm as joyful and as happy as could be!'

'By God who gave me life,' said the white-haired queen, 'your happiness will double yet and your joy will increase constantly and never fail. Since you're now at ease and happy, dinner is ready: you may eat when you wish and wherever you please – up above if you like, or if you prefer you can come and dine in the chambers below.'

'Lady, I'd rather have this hall than any room: I've been told no knight has ever sat or dined here before.'

'No, sir – none that ever left again, or stayed alive as long as it takes to ride a league!'

'Then I'll dine here, lady, by your leave.'

'I grant you that, sir, gladly. You'll be the first knight who ever ate in this hall!'

With that the queen departed, leaving two hundred and fifty of her loveliest girls with him. They dined there with him in the hall, and served him and ensured his comfort, providing for his every wish. Squires were serving joyfully at dinner – some of them white-haired, some greying and others not; some, too, had yet to grow a beard or moustache, and two of these youngest knelt before him, one of them cutting meat and the other pouring wine. Sir Gawain seated his host beside him.

The dinner wasn't short: it lasted longer than a day around Trinity![29] It was dark, black night and many huge torches were burning before the meal was over. There was lively talking over dinner, and then they danced for a long while before taking to their beds: they rejoiced for their beloved lord till they were quite worn out! When he decided to retire he lay on the Bed of Marvels. Beneath his head one of the maidens laid a pillow which made him sleep most peacefully.

Next morning when he woke, a gown of ermine and sable had been made ready for him, and the boatman came and attended as he rose and dressed and washed his hands. Clarissant was present, too, the noble, comely, honourable, bright and courteous girl; and she went then to the chambers of her grandmother the queen who asked her:

'By the faith you owe me, grand-daughter, has your lord risen yet?'

'Yes, lady, a while ago.'

'Where is he, my dear?'

'He went up to the turret, lady; I don't know if he's come down again.'

'I'll go to him; and if it please God he'll have no cause to be other than happy today!'

---

[29] A week after Pentecost, so always in late May or early June when days are long.

With that the queen rose, eager to go and see Gawain. She spotted him high up at the windows of a turret, where he was watching a girl and a fully armed knight approaching across a meadow. The two queens came side by side to where Gawain stood watching, and found him and his host at two windows.

'Sir,' said the queens together, 'a happy rising to you – may this day be a joyous one! May that glorious Father grant it so, who made His daughter His mother.'

'May the one who sent His son to earth to establish Christianity send you great happiness, ladies. But come here to the window if you will, and tell me who that girl can be, heading this way: there's a knight with her, carrying a quartered shield.'

The lady looked down at them and said: 'I'll tell you here and now: it's the one who came with you last night – may the fires of Hell consume her! Don't concern yourself with her – she's a haughty, malicious woman; and forget about the knight she's brought, I pray you – I tell you truly, he's the bravest of all knights! He doesn't fight for sport: I've seen him kill many a knight there on the riverbank!'

But Gawain answered: 'Lady, by your leave, I wish to go and speak to that girl.'

'God forbid I give you leave to go and court disaster! Let her go her way – she's a dreadful girl! Please God you'll never leave for such a senseless cause – and you must never leave at all unless you mean to wrong us!'

'Oh, come now, good-hearted queen! That's an awful thing to say! I'd think myself ill rewarded here if I could never leave! God grant I be not a captive here so long!'

'Ah, lady!' said the boatman. 'Let him do as he wishes! Don't keep him here against his will – he might die of grief.'

'Then I'll let him go,' the queen replied, 'on condition that he'll return tonight – if God preserves his life.'

'Don't worry, lady,' Gawain said. 'I'll return if I can. But I beg of you a favour: if you've no objection, please don't ask my name till seven days have passed.'

'If that's your wish, sir,' said the queen, 'I'll refrain from asking: I don't want your ill will. But if you hadn't forbidden it, your name would have been the first thing I'd have asked!'

So they came down from the turret, and squires hurried to arm Gawain and fetch his horse. He mounted, fully armed, and rode down to the landing-place accompanied by the boatman. They boarded the boat together, and oarsmen rowed them from the bank and across to the other side, and Sir Gawain went ashore.

The Perilous Ford

The other knight said to the pitiless girl: 'Tell me, my dear, this knight heading towards us armed – do you know him?'

'Not at all,' she replied, 'but he's the one who brought me here last night.'

'God save me!' he said. 'He's the very man I've been looking for! I was worried he'd escaped me, for no knight of woman born crosses the border of Galvoie and goes and boasts he's come from this land if I see him and have him within my reach! And since God has led him to me, this one shall be seized and caught!'

Then the knight, without issuing a threat or challenge, braced his shield, thrust in his spurs and charged. Sir Gawain headed to meet him and struck him a blow that wounded him gravely in the arm and side; it wasn't fatal, his hauberk holding well enough to stop the whole lance-head breaking through, but a full finger's length of the tip pierced his body and bore him to the ground. He got to his feet and was dismayed to see the blood from his arm and side flowing down his burnished mail. He attacked Gawain with his sword, but was soon too tired to carry on and had to cry for mercy. Sir Gawain received his assurances, and then handed him to the boatman who was waiting to take him.

Meanwhile the wicked girl had climbed from her palfrey; Gawain came up and greeted her and said:

'Mount again, my dear: I'm not leaving you here. You're coming with me where I have to go – back across the river.'

'Oh, knight!' she cried. 'How high and mighty you are now! You'd have had a proper battle on your hands if my sweetheart hadn't been weakened by old wounds. He'd have put paid to your boasts and stopped your crowing! Have you ever been checkmated in the corner of the board? That's how humbled you'd have been! Tell me truly: do you really think you're better than him because you've unhorsed him once? You've surely often seen that the weak will sometimes beat the strong. But listen: you've put my sweetheart in the boat; if you left this landing-place and came with me beneath that tree and did something he's always done for me when I so desire, then I'd admit you were his equal and wouldn't disdain you any more.'

'If it's only that far, girl,' he said, 'I've no reason to refuse.'

And she murmured: 'God grant I never see you return!'

And they set off, she in front and he behind. The girls and ladies, watching from the hall, tore their hair and rent their clothes in anguish, crying:

'Oh, alas! Alas! How can we live, seeing the one who was to be our lord going to his death and downfall? That wicked, cruel girl is leading him to the place from where no knight returns! Alas! We're accursed when we thought our luck was blessed! God had sent us a lord endowed with courage and every other virtue, lacking none!'

Such was their lament for their lord as they watched him go with the hateful girl.

When she and Gawain reached the tree he called to her, saying: 'Tell me, my dear, have I done my duty now, or is there something more you want from me? I'll do it if I can, rather than lose your favour.'

Then the girl said: 'Do you see the deep ford ahead, where the banks are so high? My sweetheart always crosses there, and I don't know any easier place.'

'But that's impossible, I fear! The bank's so high all the way along that no one could get down it!'

'I knew it – you daren't cross!' she said. 'I didn't think you'd have the heart to try, for this is the Perilous Ford, which none but the truly exceptional dares cross at any price!'

At that Sir Gawain led his horse to the bank – and saw the deep water below and the sheer bank beyond. But the river was narrow, and seeing this he said to himself that his horse had cleared many wider ditches; and he'd often heard that whoever could cross the deep water of the Perilous Ford would be deemed the finest knight in the world. So away from the bank he drew and came galloping back to leap across. But he failed; he didn't take the jump well, and came down right in the middle of the ford. But his horse swam on till he had four hooves on land; then he gathered himself for a leap, launched himself forward and sprang on to the great, high bank. Once there he stood stock still, unable to go another step, and Gawain had to dismount: he could see his horse was exhausted. So he climbed down at once and took off his saddle and turned it upside down to dry; then he removed the saddle-cloth and wiped the water from his horse's back and flanks and legs.

At last he put the saddle back on and remounted, and rode on at a walk till he caught sight of a knight out hunting with a sparrowhawk, and two retrievers in the field before him. He was the most handsome figure imaginable. Gawain rode up and greeted him and said:

'Good sir, may God who made you fairer than any man alive send you joy and good fortune!'

The knight was quick to reply, saying: 'You are good and worthy and gracious, sir; but tell me if you will: how did you come to leave the wicked girl alone on the other bank? What's happened to her companion?'

'Sir,' replied Sir Gawain, 'a knight with a quartered shield was with her when I met her.'

'And what did you do?'

'I defeated him in combat.'

'What became of him then?'

'The pilot took him away: he said he should be his prisoner.'

'Indeed, dear brother, he told you the truth. That girl was once my love, but she would never deign to love me or call me her sweetheart. And I swear I never kissed her except by force, and never had my way with her for I loved her against her will. I'd robbed her of a lover of hers whose company she used to share: I killed him and led her off and strove in every way to serve her. But I was wasting my time: she sought to leave me at the first chance she had, and took for her love the knight from whom you've just parted her. And he's no joke, that knight! He's valiant indeed, so help me God – though from that day forth he never dared come near me! But today you've done what no knight has ever attempted before; and in doing so your valour has made you the finest and most praised knight in the world. It took the greatest courage to leap into the Perilous Ford, and I tell you truly, no knight has ever come through it.'

'Then the damsel lied to me!' said Gawain. 'She gave me to believe that her sweetheart crossed it every day for love of her!'

'Did the traitress tell you that? Oh, would that she'd drowned there! She must be possessed by a host of demons to tell you such a tale! She hates you, there's no denying it! That devil – God confound her! – meant to see you drown in the deep, roaring water! But promise me something now, and in return I give my word you can ask me anything – whether it upsets me or not! – and I'll give you the honest answer if I know it. You likewise must promise to tell me truthfully, without any evasion, whatever I wish to know.'

They exchanged these pledges, and Gawain started the questioning, saying: 'Tell me, sir, about yonder city: who does it belong to, and what's it called?'

'I can certainly tell you that, my friend, for it belongs to me entirely: I owe no part of it to any man born – I am vassal to God alone. It's called Orqueneseles.'

'And what's your name?'

'Guiromelant.'

'I've heard of you often, sir: that you're most valiant and worthy, and lord of a very great land. And what's the name of the girl of whom no good is spoken near or far, including by you?'

'I can testify indeed,' he said, 'that she's much to be feared: she's full of malice and scorn. That's why she's known as the Haughty Maiden of Nogres – which is where she was born, though she was taken thence when very young.'

'And what's the name of her sweetheart, now the boatman's prisoner whether he likes it or not?'

'I tell you, friend, he's a remarkable knight; he's known as the Proud Knight of the Narrow Pass: he guards the borders of Galvoie.'

'And what's the name of the noble, handsome castle I left today, where I ate and drank last night?'

At that Guiromelant turned his back in sorrow and began to move away. But Gawain reminded him:

'Sir! Sir! Remember your promise and answer me!'

Guiromelant stopped and turned his head and said: 'Curse the hour I saw you and made that pledge! Be gone! I release you from your vow, and you absolve me of mine! I meant to ask you news of the place, but it seems you know as much about that castle as you do about the moon!'

Sir,' said Gawain, 'I was there last night and lay upon the Bed of Marvels. There's none to match it – no man has ever seen the like!'

'By God,' he replied, 'you amaze me! It's a joy to hear your fantasies – as entertaining as a story-teller! I see it now – you're a minstrel! Why, I thought you were a knight and had done some feat of prowess yonder! But come now, tell me honestly: did you really do some valiant deed there? What did you see at the castle?'

Then Sir Gawain told him: 'Sir, when I sat on the bed there was a dreadful commotion in the hall. Trust me, I'm not lying: the bed-cords groaned and the bells upon them rang, and closed windows opened all by themselves and crossbow bolts and flashing arrows smashed into my shield! And in it stuck the claws of a massive, ferocious, bristling lion, long kept chained in a vault! A villein sent it to attack me – he set it loose and it came with such a mighty leap and struck at my shield and plunged in its claws so hard that it couldn't pull them free! If you don't believe me, see the claws still hanging here! I cut off its head, thank God, and its feet, too. What do you make of these marks of proof?'

At this Guiromelant jumped from his horse and went down on his knees and clasped his hands and begged Gawain to forgive his foolish words.

'They're forgiven entirely,' Gawain said. 'Remount now.'

Guiromelant did so, filled with shame for his foolishness, and said: 'God save me, sir, I didn't think there was any knight, near or far, who'd ever have the honour that's befallen you! But tell me: did you see the white-haired queen? Did you ask her who she was and where she was from?'

'I didn't think to ask,' said Gawain. 'But I saw her and spoke to her.'

'Then I'll tell you,' said Guiromelant. 'She's King Arthur's mother.'

'By the faith I owe God and His power, I don't believe King Arthur's had a mother for ages – not for sixty years or more, I think!'

'But it's true, sir: she's his mother. When his father Uther Pendragon was buried, Queen Ygerne came to this country, bringing all her treasure, and built that castle on the rock with the rich and handsome hall that you've described. And I'm sure you'll have seen the other queen: that fair and noble lady was the wife of King Lot and the mother of the one I wish every misfortune – Gawain.'

'Gawain, sir, is one I know well, and I've heard he's not had a mother for twenty years at the very least.'

'But she's his mother, sir, you may be sure. She came to live with the white-haired queen – *her* mother – and was with child. That child was the noble, beautiful girl who is my love – and, I shan't deny it, the sister of Gawain – God send him deepest shame! I tell you, he wouldn't escape with his head if I had the upper hand and he was within my reach as you are now! I'd behead him on the spot! And his sister wouldn't stop me tearing his heart from his chest with my bare hands, I hate him so!'

'Upon my soul,' Sir Gawain said, 'then you don't love as I do! If I loved a girl or lady, I'd love and serve her kinsmen for her sake!'

'You're right – I agree. But when I recall how Gawain's father killed mine, I can't wish him well! And Gawain himself, with his own hands, killed one of my closest cousins, a valiant and worthy knight. And I've never had a chance to take revenge. But do this favour for me now: return to the castle and take my beloved this ring. Present it to her as a gift from me, and tell her I believe and trust that her love is such that she'd rather her brother Gawain died a dismal death than that I should hurt my smallest toe! Send her my greetings and give her this ring from me, her sweetheart.'

Sir Gawain placed the ring on his little finger and said: 'In faith, sir, you have a wise and courteous girl for your love, a noble woman of high lineage, fair and comely – and devoted to you, if she agrees with what you've said!'

'You'll be doing me a great favour, I swear,' said Guiromelant, 'if you take this ring as a gift to my beloved, for I love her deeply. In return I'll tell you the name of the castle as you asked. You may not know of it: it's called the Rock of Canguin. Many fine, rich cloths are woven there, green and red and fine scarlet, bought and sold in great quantities. Now I've told you all you wished to know – and without a word of a lie – and you've done likewise for me. Is there anything else you'd like to ask?'

'No, sir – just your leave to go.'

'Before I let you,' said Guiromelant, 'tell me your name if you will.'

'So help me God, sir,' he replied, 'my name shall never be kept from you. I am the one you hate so much. I am Gawain.'

'You are Gawain?'

'Indeed I am – King Arthur's nephew.'

'In faith, then you're very bold or an utter fool to tell me your name when you know I hate you mortally! Oh, if only I had my helmet and my shield! If I were armed as you are, I'd cut off your head this instant – nothing would stop me! But listen: if you've the nerve to wait for me I'll fetch my arms and return to do battle, and bring three or four men as witnesses. Or if you're willing, we'll wait seven days and return here on the seventh fully armed; you'll summon King Arthur and his queen and all their people while I gather the forces from all my kingdom – then our battle won't be fought in secret: all who come will see it. For a battle between such worthy men as we are deemed to be shouldn't be fought without witnesses; it's only right that ladies and knights should be present in numbers: when one of us is vanquished and everybody knows it, the victor will have a thousand times more honour than if he alone knew!'

'Sir,' said Sir Gawain, 'I'd gladly do without all this, if you'd agree to avoid battle. If I've done you any wrong I'll willingly make amends acceptable both to your friends and to mine, so that all is just and proper.'

But Guiromelant said: 'I can't see any way to justice unless you're brave enough to do battle. I've given you two options: choose which you prefer. Either wait for me now if you dare, while I go and fetch my arms, or summon all the people of your land to come here in seven days. At Pentecost King Arthur will be holding court at Orquenie, so I've heard, which is only a two-day ride from here; your messenger could find the king and his people there, all equipped and ready. Send for him: that would be best – a day's respite is a precious thing.'[30]

---

[30] Literally 'is worth a hundred sous'.

'God save me,' said Gawain, 'the court will indeed be there – you've heard quite rightly. And I swear by this hand I'll send to him tomorrow – or before I sleep a wink!'

Then Guiromelant said: 'Gawain, I'm going to take you to the finest bridge in the world. The river is very deep and swift – no man alive could cross it or jump to the other bank.'

But Sir Gawain replied: 'I'm not going to seek any ford or bridge, come what may – that treacherous girl will think it cowardice! I'm going to conclude my deal with her and go straight over!'

So saying he thrust in his spurs, and his horse sprang nimbly over the water, quite untroubled. When the girl who'd so misled him saw him coming, she tethered her mount to the tree and came to meet him on foot. And her attitude and heart had changed completely: she greeted him in meek, crestfallen fashion, and said she'd come to plead for mercy, admitting her guilt, knowing she'd caused him a deal of trouble.

'Good sir,' she said, 'listen now, and I'll tell you why I've been so haughty with every knight who's made me his companion. Please, I want to explain. That knight – God damn him! – who was talking to you yonder, he ill bestowed his love on me, for he loved me and I hated him because – I shan't conceal it – he'd caused me bitter pain by killing the knight I loved. He thought he'd do me the honour then of wooing me! But he was wasting his time – at the first opportunity I escaped from him and joined company with the knight you took me from today. Losing him doesn't bother me at all, but ever since Death robbed me of my first love I've been mad and spoken haughtily and acted wickedly and crazily, not caring who I crossed – I tormented them deliberately, hoping to find one whose temper was such that I could drive him wild with rage so he'd cut me to pieces! I've yearned for death for a long while now! So mete out justice, sir – such justice that no girl who ever hears of me will dare speak basely to a knight again!'

'Dear girl,' said Sir Gawain, 'why should I punish you? If it please the son of God you'll never suffer harm from me. Mount now, without delay, and we'll go to that grand castle. The boatman's at the landing place, waiting to take us across.'

'I'll do whatever you wish, sir,' said the girl; and she climbed into the saddle of her little palfrey with its flowing mane and tail, and they rode to the boatman who calmly ferried them over the river.

The ladies and maidens, who'd been grieving bitterly for Gawain, saw them coming. All the squires at the hall, too, had been crazed with worry, but now their jubilation was the greatest ever seen. The queen sat outside the hall, awaiting him, and bade all her girls take one another by the hand to dance and celebrate. And so they began their rejoicing to greet Sir Gawain on his return, singing and dancing their rounds, and he came and dismounted in their midst. The girls and ladies and both the queens embraced him and welcomed him with joyous greetings, and amid great celebration they took the armour from his legs and arms and breast and head. The damsel he'd brought with him was welcomed, too: everyone served her willingly – but for his sake, not for hers. They moved on, celebrating, into the hall and all sat down together.

Sir Gawain took his sister and seated her beside him on the Bed of Marvels, and whispered to her softly: 'Damsel, I bring you a golden ring from across the river, mounted with an emerald, glittering green. A knight sends it to you as a love token with his greetings, and says that you're his sweetheart.'

'I'm sure he does, sir,' she replied. 'But if I love him at all it's from a distance – he's never seen me, nor have I seen him, except from across the river! He's sworn his love for me for a long time now, for which I thank him – yet he's never come to the castle.

He kept sending messengers to beg for my love till I granted it, I confess; but that's all the sweetheart I am to him as yet.'

'Oh, dear girl! He's already boasting that you'd rather your brother Sir Gawain were dead than that *he*'d hurt a single toe!'

'What, sir? I'm amazed he could say such a foolish thing! By God, I never dreamt he'd be so ill-mannered – and ill-advised, sending such a message! Alas, my brother doesn't even know I'm born; he's never seen me. Guiromelant's quite wrong: upon my soul, I wouldn't have my brother suffer harm, any more than myself.'

As they talked together and the ladies waited, the white-haired queen said to the other queen, seated at her side:

'What do you make, my dear, of the lord sitting beside your daughter, my granddaughter? He's been whispering to her for an age! I don't know what he's saying but I'm delighted, as we both should be: it's a mark of great nobility that he's drawn to the fairest and the wisest in the hall! How fitting! I wish to God he would marry her, that she was as pleasing to him as Lavinia to Aeneas!'

'Oh, lady,' said the other queen, 'may God so incline his heart that they may be as brother and sister – that they may love each other so dearly that they be one flesh!'

The lady meant by her prayer that Gawain should love her and take her for his wife – she hadn't recognised her son; they would indeed be as brother and sister: there'd be no other kind of love between them once they knew they were related, and their mother wouldn't be happy for the reason she imagined!

After speaking with his fair sister for quite a while, Sir Gawain turned and called to a boy at his right, the one who seemed most diligent and willing and the brightest and most able of all the squires in the hall. Then he went downstairs to a chamber, followed by the boy alone. When they were both inside he said:

'You look a trusty soul, boy, resourceful and sharp. I'm going to tell you a secret, and I advise you to keep it – you'll profit greatly if you do. I'm sending you where you'll be received with joy.'

'Sir, may my tongue be torn from my mouth before a word you wish to keep hidden leaves my lips!'

'In that case, brother, you're to go to my lord King Arthur – I am his nephew, Gawain. The way is neither long nor hard: he's holding court for Pentecost at the city of Orquenie; but if the journey costs you dear I'll repay you well. When you come before the king you'll find him in low spirits, but when you greet him on my behalf he'll be filled with joy! The whole court will be cheered when they hear you bring news from me! You're to tell the king that by the faith he owes me – he being my lord and I his vassal – he mustn't fail on any account to appear before me, encamped in the meadow below this tower, on the fifth day of Pentecost; and he's to bring the whole company that's gathered at his court, nobility and common folk alike, for I'm committed to do battle with a knight who respects neither me nor the king – he thinks him a man of little worth! The knight is Guiromelant, who hates him mortally. You're to tell the queen that she must come, too, by the great faith there should be between us, she being my lady and my friend; and when she hears the news she won't fail, for my sake, to bring all the ladies and girls who're at court that day. But one thing worries me: have you a good hunting horse to bear you there swiftly?'

The boy replied there was a fine one, big and fast and strong, that he could take for his use.

'Excellent!' said Sir Gawain.

The boy took him quickly down to the stables and brought out some strong, well-rested hunting horses, one of which was ready to ride: he'd had it newly shod and it lacked neither saddle nor bridle.

'My word, boy,' Sir Gawain said, 'you're all set! Go now, and may the lord of all kings guide you on the right path and bring you safely there and back.'

He saw the boy on his way, taking him down to the river and bidding the boatman ferry him across. He did so – and it wouldn't tire him: he had a good crew of oarsmen. So the boy crossed the river and was soon on the right road for the city of Orquenie – anyone with the wit to ask the way can go anywhere in the world.

Meanwhile Sir Gawain returned to the hall, where he passed the time in joy and delight, for everyone loved and served him. And the queen had baths of hot water prepared in five hundred tubs, and bade all the squires go in to wash and bathe. Robes specially made for them were ready when they left the baths: the cloth was woven with golden thread and lined with ermine. Then the squires spent all night in the chapel till after matins, standing all the while, never kneeling. And in the morning Sir Gawain, with his own hands, fastened the right spur for each of them and girded their swords and gave them the accolade. He now had a company of fully five hundred new knights.

In the meantime the boy had reached the city of Orquenie, where the king was holding a court befitting such a high feast day. The crippled and the sick, watching the boy ride past, said:

'He's in a hurry! I reckon he's bringing news or a message to the court from far away. Whatever it is he'll find the king deaf and dumb, he's so lost in grief and woe. He'll be beyond all help when he's heard what the messenger has to say!'

'What are you prattling about?' said others. 'What do you know of the king's affairs? You should be distraught, dismayed that we've lost the one who defended us all in the name of God, and out of love and charity brought us so many blessings.' Throughout the city the poor folk lamented so for Gawain: they loved him dearly.

The boy rode on till he found King Arthur sitting in his hall, with a hundred counts palatine and a hundred kings and a hundred dukes seated around him. Arthur was mournful, downcast, seeing the great host of nobility but no sign of his nephew; his distress was such that he fainted and fell. The first to reach him and help him up must have been pretty nippy, for everyone rushed to his aid!

The lady Lores was sitting in a gallery, and saw the panic that had gripped the hall; she ran down from the gallery and came to the queen in a terrible fluster. When the queen saw her she asked what was wrong.[31]

---

[31] In the majority of manuscripts there is no indication of a change of author: the text continues without any break – as indeed it does from one Continuation to another. But in the Bibliothèque Nationale (Paris) MS fonds français 794 appear (preceded and followed by a black line) the words '*Explycyt Percevax le viel*' ('Here ends the old Perceval'), and in the Berne manuscript, at the same point, '*Explicit li romanz de Perceval*' (the Berne manuscript does not contain the Continuations at all).

The First Continuation

'Dear sister!' she said. 'Why are you in such a state? So upset? Tell me!'

'Oh, lady! I've just seen a boy come clattering through the doors on an iron-grey horse, and before he'd even dismounted the king collapsed in a swoon among his men! Then I saw countless lords do likewise – they couldn't bear to see his grief!'

When the queen heard that the king had fainted *she* passed out as well – and she can hardly be blamed for that. Then ladies and damsels came thronging and started wailing like you've never heard!

Meanwhile, back in the hall, the boy they'd seen charge in jumped down and handed his horse to a dwarf. I'll spare you the details of the wailing commotion and tell you about Sir Gawain's boy: he grabbed his mantle and thrust it at the dwarf behind him and then came coatless to the king and, seeing his woebegone expression, hailed him thus:

'May God who dwells in heaven on high, His power and glory all-pervading and ruling all, protect and keep the good King Arthur! So says the finest knight who ever rode horse or bore lance and shield: he's lived – by God's grace – long enough to win the whole wide world's esteem; I do believe the knight I serve has proved himself quite peerless!'

'God bless you and him,' the king replied, 'whoever he may be. But we'd better know his name and more about him if he's so famous! Tell me, dear friend.'

'The one who sent me here, my lord, is King Lot's son, Gawain. He's well deserving of all praise: there's not a trace of weakness in him!'

The king leapt up and embraced and kissed the boy, overjoyed by every word he'd said – as were they all. The whole court thronged around him: no one wanted to be left out – all degrees of rank and wit came flocking to his side. The king asked the messenger if his nephew was in good health and heart, and the boy, like the courteous soul he was, replied:

'Yes indeed, sire! I can assure you my lord is well and in good spirits. And he's achieved greater honour than any knight before him: he's gone where no knight born in this kingdom has ever ventured and managed to return – a feat indeed! He's gone beyond the borders of Galvoie, which none but he has ever crossed and kept his body and life intact! But he, resourceful man that he is, made it across quite effortlessly, painlessly and unscathed! And he vanquished the Proud Knight of Rogal[1] who attacked him, and leapt across the Perilous Ford[2] where many a knight has drowned. It was effort well spent: he's won the kind of glory that many good knights have tested their prowess to win – and none but he has lived to tell the tale.'

The barons listened in delight as he told them Gawain had performed so many feats of prowess that he couldn't recount a tenth of them!

---

1   'l'Orgueilleux dou Rogal'. This is the 'Proud Knight of the Narrow Pass, who guards the borders of Galvoie' defeated by Gawain in Chrétien's *Perceval*, above, pp. 71–2, 74.
2   In Chrétien, above, p. 72.

'I don't know what to say of him, except that he's free and clear of all baseness – he hasn't the slightest blemish; no, he's the model of all good qualities. And he bids you and your people come in three days' time to the meadows below the castle where he's staying: he bids the whole court, without exception – tall and short, young and grey-haired! – go there together and nowhere else, for he's engaged to do battle with a knight who's filled with spite and mortal hatred towards you as well as him. His name's Guiromelant,[3] and he's most aggrieved about his father's death at Gawain's hands. And I know, by God, that if he could get the better of my lord he'd bring him to shame indeed: neither you nor Gawain – nor anyone who sides with you – has a more implacable enemy. So he begs you as his lord to do him honour and lend him aid, for he sorely needs it. I've often heard it said that in the hour of need you find out who your friends are, and it's an urgent need that sends me here to a king who always supports those threatened by the proud.'

Such joy was never seen at any court: at the news of Gawain everyone rejoiced. And the king told the boy that he wouldn't miss the battle for the whole of Cornwall – when the court was all assembled he'd bring such a train as would cover a whole league of meadow, field and riverbank with their silk tents and pavilions! And no one disagreed: they all declared they longed for nothing more than to go and see Gawain, and that all their wishes were fulfilled in knowing he was still alive, the knight who would restore courtesy to the world if every trace of it was lost. The whole court came flocking then, and the hall rang as harps and hurdy-gurdies played and songs were sung and lays performed. No man alive could describe to you the sweetness of the music there. The celebrations went on and on. That doesn't happen without cause, and they had the best cause in the world, inspired as they were by love and joy, a fine cause for celebration indeed: I can think of none better.

When Kay the seneschal heard the news he made all the right noises, but really he was his usual resentful self. But so what? When it comes to the crunch a malcontent can sometimes be worth two men, while sweet-tongued flatterers vanish like froth. 'My lord,' he said to Arthur, 'it's a weight off our mind to know Sir Gawain's alive! God be praised! Our fears and worries about him outweighed all other joys. What a godsend! Now you can see how much a man gains by being truly worthy: the very thought that he might have died by some misfortune had us all distracted! It's true what they say, by God: you don't realise a good man's worth until you've lost him. God has mightily blessed our lord King Arthur – and all of us, I'd say: there were fully four thousand of us lost in gloom, and now the sun's come out again, knowing the one so rich in chivalry is alive and well! Our former worries don't compare with the joy we all now feel for that good, fine, worthy, noble knight so immeasurably well-disposed to all! We owe him all the help he needs.'

So said the seneschal in the hearing of everyone – he made sure of that. And the king sent him with Girflet and the boy messenger straight to the chambers to take the news to the tearful, anguished queen. 'Go, friend,' he told the boy, 'and tell her your news that has cheered me so. I'd rather she heard it from you than from anyone, even me.'

And without more ado the boy went upstairs to where the grieving was in full flood. The like was never seen: the queen was weeping and sighing, wringing her hands and tearing her hair, beside herself with woe.

---

[3] Guiromelant challenged Gawain to single combat towards the end of Chrétien's *Perceval*, above, p. 75.

Meanwhile one of her maids, the lady Ysave, had been sitting in an antechamber and heard the rejoicing and the singing of songs and lays in the hall. She hurried to the queen and said: 'Lady, I do believe you're about to hear good news! The king's making a huge fuss of a messenger who's cheered and heartened him greatly. Please God you're about to have joyful news of Gawain: the sweet music below seems to herald it! Truly, my heart tells me you'll soon be hearing joyous tidings of Gawain, the king's nephew!'

'May God hear your prayer, my dear!' said the queen. 'It's my prayer, too, and the wish of all these maids and ladies. God send us good news!'

In her excitement she gave no thought to her dress, and without stopping to don a mantle or cloak she jumped up and headed straight for the hall; all the damsels, maids and ladies cast aside their mantles and raced after her. Ladies never left their chambers in such utter disarray! You never saw damsels venture out in such a state!

But just as she was about to leave, the queen ran into Girflet, the seneschal and the messenger boy as they came ambling in. She'd calmed down a little, but the boy could see that her eyes and face were still wet with tears; and he knelt before her and repeated his whole story, perfectly from start to finish. I won't go through it all again – that would be a waste of time – but to conclude he said:

'Lady, through me Sir Gawain appeals to you, by the great faith you owe him and he owes you, to retain all the ladies, maids and damsels who've come to court and bring them with you without fail: a true friend makes true efforts – a curse on those who make shows of friendship and fail to act! For the first time now, in his hour of need, he's going to find out if he has real friends: until he's in need no one ever knows if his friendship goes one way! For true friends can't go missing when they see one another in trouble; and only by going through trouble, by God, do you discover what someone feels for you.'

Hearing the boy's words the queen stepped up and kissed him joyfully. The cloud of woe he'd met with was now lifted: the ladies and damsels made a joyous fuss of him, all eager to serve and honour him as they stopped their weeping and hung on his every word – and he spoke with such eloquence that no one interrupted; he needed no guidance: he was a bright lad indeed, for sure.

'Lady,' he said to the queen, 'to repeat: my lord begs you in God's name not to forget him, for he loves you dearly; come with the king – don't fail, on any account – and bring with you all your ladies, maids and girls: the young, the old, the fair and the not so fair! That was his most insistent wish.'

And the queen replied that he needn't fear: she would go indeed, and take with her such a company of ladies and damsels that so many beauties would never have been assembled in one place! 'And we'll keep riding through any weather – snow or rain or frost – till we reach the fields below the castle that he's taken.'

With that the boy took his leave of the queen, and he and Kay and Girflet didn't dally but left the chamber, a chamber where the ladies had woven many a rich cloth of gold and scarlet. But I'll leave these three now, and tell you about the court where all the lords had flocked from all parts of the city.

When they heard the news about Gawain the whole court, it seems, was overcome with joy. Terce*[4] had rung, I think, by the time they were all assembled, and the king called for the water.[5] The kings of Ireland and Northumberland hurried to take charge of the basin,

---

[4] An asterisk in the text indicates that the word appears in the Glossary, below, pp. 571–2.
[5] i.e. for the washing of hands before a meal.

and King Mark, lord of Cornwall, held the towel. Then the king sat down, and with everything in perfect order they all took their places at the tables. Beside the king at the high table sat many a duke and prince, and kings were present, too; and before him at the other tables sat Yvain and Count Quinable and the knights of the Round Table, the most accomplished and most chivalrous in the world. What a noble company it was: so many barons, princes, counts. I don't intend to maunder on about how many dishes they had and what they all were, but they ate and drank their fill before rising from the table, and I know, without a word of a lie, that such splendid fare was never gone so swiftly or consumed in such high spirits in any court! No meal was ever so appealing, delicious and brief!

The king then called for the constable;* he was promptly fetched and the moment he arrived the king ordered him to spread the word that every squire at court was to be packed first thing next morning, for they'd be heading straight for Galvoie. The constable sent the crier through the streets; everyone got cracking and by midnight every squire had packed and was mounted and ready to go before the watchman sounded the dawn. They loaded all the wagons and carts – of which there was no shortage – and took to the road with all the gear, including their silk pavilions.

Then about prime* the king rose with the barons and the queen, and all went together to the church of Saint Catherine and found a chaplain in his vestments to celebrate the mass. There was a great crowd of kings and counts and ladies at the offering: so many lovely women hadn't been seen together in a church for many a day! And when they'd heard the service the whole company went and mounted their horses: no one stayed behind – every last man at court, the long-haired and the bald alike, followed the king; and with him he took a lengthy train of destriers* and palfreys. The queen had heard mass with the lords, and she too now mounted; and in her company were five hundred girls, not counting the ladies and the damsels who numbered more than two thousand. Two by two they rode from the city, each mounted in comfort on a handsome mule or fine palfrey with a good wide girth and a steady pace. And all were richly harnessed, with elegant saddles and brand-new bridles; they were such a noble sight as they rode that people flocked from their houses to gaze at the girls, and couldn't take their eyes off the procession, such was the ladies' beauty.

They rode and journeyed on till late in the afternoon. What more should I tell you? The barons had now dismounted: their pavilions had been pitched for them in an encampment covering the whole of a lofty hill. The queen didn't take long to join them; to one side an array of fine tents had been made ready for her, too, and she entered with her great company of maids. I don't think there's anything to add; the horn blew at the king's pavilion for the washing of hands, and all – lords and ladies alike – took supper, and then slept all night till daybreak. Then the horses and gear were made ready again and they set off somewhat earlier than before.

They headed straight for the borders of Galvoie, and made such good speed that before none* sounded they all arrived in the meadow below the Castle of Marvels. Many pavilions of silken cloth, red and green, were unfolded and laid out, and once they'd been erected the barons all dismounted and relaxed there on the green sward, strolling through the meadows in twos and threes and fours and looking up at the castle on its high crag, where it had nothing to fear from mangonel or catapult, surrounded as it was by the great river, deep and swift and wide. From the meadow they gazed up at the great hall and impressive keep surrounded by mighty walls, baileys and huge ditches. Meanwhile the queen was in her tent with her many fair, elegant, courtly maids. The king's men were lodged further off, away from the ladies.

King Arthur, then, was camped with his great host between the river and the woods. And the messenger boy came smartly to the king and took his leave, which the king gladly granted; and he swiftly left the camp and rode along the riverbank until, beside a rock, he found a boat with an oar. He clambered in along with his horse, and pushed off and kept rowing hard till he'd crossed the river; then he moored the boat and pulled his horse on to the bank. Having rowed across he went to deliver his message to his master, and found him in the keep with an impressive company of at least five hundred newly-dubbed knights, clad in silk most handsomely. He spotted his lord and went to him and gave his message in confidence, keeping it between just the two of them. The moment he heard it Sir Gawain went up to the windows and leaned out and saw the riverbank, meadows and wooded slopes covered in silken tents. The other knights, too, now gathered round him and peered out from the windows.

King Arthur's Mother

The ladies for their part were ranged along the upper windows of the hall; they too could see the tents pitched between the river and the woods, and were dismayed, convinced that such a host could be encamped there only to besiege them! An alarming sight indeed! Seeing the array of tents filled the ladies with fear. King Arthur's mother was among them, and as she looked down at the host in the meadow she was aghast, her heart weak and trembling. She took her daughter by the hand and said:

'Morcadés my daughter, we've lived a long while – and now our time has come! We're being besieged! I've never seen so many men, such a great gathering of knights in arms! Look at all those shields, poleaxes, lances, swords! And the women! Whether they're ladies or fairies I'm not sure, but I've never seen damsels and maidens and ladies form an army like this and go to war!'

She left the hall at once, taking her grand-daughter Clarissant and Gawain's mother with her, and hand in hand they went to find Gawain. As soon as he saw them he jumped up and greeted all three of them most courteously and happily. He took his grandmother by the hand and asked her how she was.

'Sir,' she said, 'along the riverbank we've seen so many banners, such a vast encampment! We're very afraid: we don't know if this horde has come with good or bad intentions!'

'Lady,' Gawain replied, 'you need have no fear: I know exactly who they are and who's in charge! I know all of them, and where they're from and where they're going.'

Then one of the ladies, King Arthur's mother, said: 'By God and His power, sir, you're ahead of us if you know why they've landed here! But listen: I've patiently waited to learn your name; tell me now, this instant, I beg and implore you. I've waited the allotted time, this is a good moment, and my eyes will never be free of tears till I know it!'

'First,' he said, 'I'll tell you who those people are and where they're going and why.'

'Tell me then,' she said, 'and quickly!'

'It's King Arthur, with all his forces – the fair company you can see in the meadows! He's not here to besiege the castle – he's come to make sure I'm in good shape! He's my uncle: my name is Gawain – my father was King Lot.'

When the two older ladies heard this, even the more stressed of them was filled with joy! Neither was slow to smother him with kisses; Queen Ygerne embraced him and kissed his eyes and lips, and her daughter, even more affected, couldn't restrain herself:

her heart was leaping, just as it had leapt and kept her from sleep on the day when he was born: she kissed his eyes and breast.

'My dear, sweet man!' said Queen Ygerne. 'By Almighty God, I am King Arthur's mother! And this is my daughter: she is your mother – her husband was the king your father!'

The two ladies, then, were making a joyous fuss of Gawain, kissing and embracing him. But his sister Clarissant was anything but happy about the news: she was deeply embarrassed at having told him that she and Guiromelant were in love.[6] She was so upset she'd have gladly died there on the spot; she hated and berated herself for having told him: she thought it would be the death of her. While the others kept celebrating, Clarissant left the keep and ran weeping to a private chamber, and as she went to sit on the bed she collapsed in a swoon. She was beside herself, her heart overcome with anguish: she tore her hair and wrung her hands.

Meanwhile Sir Gawain, in happy conversation with the queens, was saying: 'If you wished, ladies, to cheer you even more I'd gladly bring King Arthur to you, and the finest and most worthy of his barons – the queen and her ladies, too.'

His grandmother bowed and thanked him deeply. So Gawain went down from the keep and called for his horse and bade his companions mount; there must have been thirty, all clad in rich silk, and they set out joyfully from the castle, each mounted on a fine horse from Gascony, Germany or Spain. They rode straight down to the river where a boat was waiting to carry them across. They didn't need to exert themselves with rowing or steering: they clambered in and pulled their horses aboard, and then oarsmen and tillerman set to work and took them to the other side. Out they jumped and mounted again, and rode together to the meadow. They approached the encampment at an amble; and Sir Kay the seneschal, emerging from King Do's pavilion, looked up and saw them all come riding side by side. He recognised Sir Gawain instantly, and came to King Arthur and said:

'Have I got news for you, by God! I've just seen thirty knights coming, I'd say, and among them is a tall knight, mounted on his destrier but quite unarmed, who looked like Sir Gawain! The others are riding in a line abreast, with him on his own in front.'

At that very moment the leading rider dismounted before the king's tent, and all the others followed suit. When the king heard it was Sir Gawain, he leapt up and made straight for the entrance; he met him there in a joyous embrace: he felt as if he would take off and fly, such were his joy and relief at being able to hold once more that noble, courteous knight, so free and clear of all wickedness. Everyone else came flocking to see him; young and old, they honoured and served him – his companions, too – for they knew him to be endowed with all good qualities.

When the celebrating was done, the noble Sir Gawain spoke up, saying: 'Flower of all kings, I bear greetings from a lady who asks nothing of God but your presence! Your coming has brought her joy and comfort, truly. I speak of the mother who carried you inside her for nine months.'

When the king heard this he thought it a far-fetched fantasy! He swore by Saint Cosmas that he hadn't had a mother for fifty years! He feared Gawain had been bewitched, and the barons shared his worry! But Sir Gawain started telling them the whole story of his adventure, and every king and noble lord thronged together to hear it – though I don't need to repeat it for you. And at the end of it he took the king his uncle by the hand and said:

---

[6] Near the end of Chrétien's romance, above, pp. 76–7.

'My lord, I swear by Saint Germain: when Uther Pendragon died your mother, truly, crossed the borders of Galvoie with a company of knights and girls, including many fair and well-bred noble damsels. My mother came with them, too: she and your mother are together now. She abandoned all our lands and fended for herself; and she was left with child, and gave birth to a daughter who's there in the castle – a beautiful and comely girl indeed, in a company of many more. They brought with them to this land a great treasury of gold and silver, and had this castle built here – strong and handsome, as you can see. No one could lay siege to it – it's too well defended with walls and moats, and a great river runs right round it. With its mighty keep and outer baileys it fears no siege or army. For a long time a trap lay in wait for any passing knights who came to visit: there's a hall in the castle, the most splendid you'll ever see, which was the downfall of many men; no one who ever entered it and tried to stay there left the place alive – except me! I sat there in the hall and survived, thanks be to God!'

The king was thrilled to hear about the castle: he'd never heard a tale with such delight. He begged Gawain to tell them more about the hall, and exactly why no one could stay there; the other kings and lords all asked the same. So Gawain explained that there was a bed in the hall, the most gorgeous ever seen, but anyone who ever lay on it was killed in an instant: the moment anyone sat on it he saw the hall raining javelins, darts and crossbow bolts, flying at him from every side – but couldn't see where they were coming from, or the archers who were loosing them! The king was amazed when he heard of this marvel: he couldn't understand it; but mystified though he was, he believed what Gawain said.

And Sir Gawain now insisted that he come to the castle and let nothing detain him, and bring three knights with him if he wished. The queen was to come, too, with three girls to attend her. They had horses saddled at once, and the king and three chosen vassals mounted without any of the other barons being aware they'd gone. The king, Gawain and his companions shook their reins and away they went on their fine and handsome mounts. The king rode straight to the queen's tent where they all dismounted; and when the queen heard that the king had come to see her with his nephew, her heart was filled with joy and she went to meet them, elegantly dressed in red samite: it was the richest ever seen, embroidered with golden thread; the mantle was worth a fortune, studded with stones imbued with special powers.[7] When she saw King Arthur holding his nephew by the hand she stepped swiftly up to Gawain and gave him a joyous welcome, delighted to see him in good health and spirits. He explained the whole situation eloquently, and she mounted at once, riding a horse whose harness was worth a hundred pounds.[8] She took with her three of her fairest girls, splendidly dressed and mounted.

The queen and the knights rode over hill and dale till they reached the boatman waiting for them at the river's edge, and with oars working swiftly they were soon on the other side. Once across the river, the people of the castle came to meet them in a fittingly great procession: monks carrying silver censers were followed by a great crowd

---

[7] Stones of power are found in many medieval narratives. As Corinne Saunders has written, 'the many protective rings of romance function through the simple but immensely influential notion of the stone of special power... Repeatedly, rings are said to contain gems "of swich vertu" that they give marvellous protection, usually from wounds and other kinds of harm... The ring is an object of peculiar potency: it combines the figure of the circle, repeatedly used in magic rituals, with the notion of the stone with occult powers...' Saunders, *Magic and the Supernatural in Medieval English Romance* (Cambridge, 2010), p. 125.

[8] Literally 'a hundred *livres* minted at Chartres'.

– all the townsfolk, as well as the newly-dubbed knights and orphaned girls and the two disinherited queens. They'd adorned and bedecked the streets behind them: the whole castle was draped with silken cloth to celebrate the coming of the king. So out the people of the castle came, and the king and his company were thrilled to see them. They all dismounted, including the king and queen, and returned together with the whole procession – all the folk, of every rank and degree of wit – into the resounding castle: I don't believe it had ever heard such roars of jubilation.

They all went to church together to hear the service sung most pleasingly: what a fine and noble congregation they were! And what an offering they made! The king gave thirty bezants,* while the queen had a rich purple* robe taken from one of her chests and given by way of offering; the two queens of the castle made offerings, too.

As soon as compline* was over they left the church and went up to the hall. What celebrations followed there! Were I to describe them with total honesty you wouldn't believe me! But you may be sure of this: when the king saw his mother and she saw him, and brother saw sister and uncle saw niece, the rejoicing lasted a long while! But I shan't go on – I don't want to lengthen the story or embellish it with what's not true.

But another thing you must believe: however joyful they may have been, across the river there was such alarm as you've never seen, because to welcome the king with even greater splendour the queen of the castle had told the newly-dubbed knights to hang their arms from every chamber window – and their arms were truly wondrous, covered as they were with magical jewels that shed such a light over King Arthur's camp that it was as bright as noon! They were aghast, fearing some imminent attack, and Kay ran half-dressed to the king's pavilion to report to him in confidence; and when he discovered he was missing, panic spread like wildfire: they all thought they'd lost their lord King Arthur who'd kept them in such illustrious state. They were beside themselves, overwhelmed by grief and woe. Such lamentation was never seen; there was no stopping it – it was desperate. Sir Yvain passed out, as did the Count of Wales, known as the Bald. Sir Kay the seneschal wailed and bemoaned his lost lord: you've never seen such grief. And had it been daybreak they wouldn't have armed more speedily than they did now at nightfall; in panic-stricken confusion they all flung on their brigandines[9] – even the bravest, the most daring, rushed to arms. They didn't know who the enemy might be, but were sure they were about to be attacked; not that their fear lessened the grieving throughout the camp, which had started the moment they'd found the king was gone. What a contrast! On one side there was singing, on the other, wailing! On one side, laughter, on the other, tears! And the cause of the singing and the weeping was the same: in the castle, all the singing was for the king, and so was all the panic in the camp.

Preparing for Battle

When day broke next morning the king set out from the castle followed by a great company of knights, ladies and attendants. They crossed the river by boat, and once they were on the other side the whole camp came flocking when they recognised King Arthur. Had it been a moment later his companions and most of the rest would have had their horses harnessed and been on their way, but as soon as the king rode into camp their elation matched their former grief. All the barons, young and old, flocked

---

[9] '*broignë a clox sarcite*' – literally 'nail-studded leather tunics'. The brigandine was a form of body armour, usually of leather or cloth lined with small, riveted steel plates.

to meet him, and King Arthur's heart was filled with joy; and the queen's girls, too, went to meet her at the riverbank. Their happiness was complete: they wanted for nothing in the world; the whole company was overcome with joy at the return of their king and queen. But I'll leave it at that: I'll say no more or you'd think I was exaggerating.

The king dismounted at his pavilion and all the others at theirs: the queen, so gracious and elegant, rode to her tent and dismounted there with all her maids. For his part Sir Gawain went straight to make confession to the bishop of Carlion. And when he'd confessed and unburdened himself of the sins that negate all virtues, the holy bishop embraced him and gave him many a guiding and reassuring word: fine instruction indeed. Sir Gawain accepted his words of censure in all humility; and when the bishop realised he repented in all sincerity, he gave him full absolution in the name of God and Holy Mary and the company of saints. Then he blessed him with the sign of the cross and bade him trust in God entirely: since he'd made true confession he need never fear; whenever he called upon God with a true heart He would come to his aid. With that their talking ended.

Then every horse in the camp – from the finest to the poorest – was offered to Gawain by its owner! And he could fairly claim that every good sword was brought to him likewise; and anyone who had a good lance or helm offered it to him if he deigned to accept. He said he had no need of them; but he had his eye on two splendid horses that were being tended by Yvonet,[10] and called for one of them to be fitted with a brand new saddle from among his gear: it was a fine steed, black in colour, so strong and sleek that they added no blanket. Then he had a great swathe of samite spread on the floor before a bed and called for his arms. Those he'd commanded brought them at once: two bright, handsome pages came and laced his knee-pieces, and fastened strong, light iron chausses* with bands of gold. Over these they laced sharp, golden spurs, and then dressed him in a gambeson* of quilted silk and cotton. They didn't stop there, but clad him in a coat of mail so strong that he needn't have the slightest fear of any blow from sword or lance. Without more ado his ventail* was laced by Tristan, the king of Cornwall's nephew who suffered so much pain and shame on account of the fair Yseut; and on top they placed a helmet fit for King Solomon. Then they girded on a sword: it was such a sword that any woman in labour – even if her life hung in the balance – would be delivered of her child at once if struck on the head with the flat of the naked blade.

Thus armed, Gawain didn't hesitate; without a hint of trepidation he strode out to where they'd carpeted the ground with silken cloth.[11] There so many tears were shed – everyone present was weeping; the knights and maidens, the queen and damsels were beside themselves with worry for him. But more distressed than anyone was the fair and comely Clarissant: she was knotted with anguish, so distraught about her brother and her lover that she wept and wailed and clawed her face and collapsed against the queen in a swoon. When she came to, she howled and bawled quite frantically, weeping and wailing so frenziedly that no creature so distracted was ever seen in all the world. Love – the cause of so much trouble! – drove her to grieve for her sweetheart, and thought it right and proper that she should. But Nature argued and made the case that her grief should be for the good and fine and worthy Gawain, 'for he is my brother – sharing father and mother – and I am his sister likewise'. She was torn in both directions

---

[10] The squire who accompanied him from court in Chrétien; see above, p. 49.
[11] The Edinburgh manuscript refers to ground 'paved with marble', which is hard to picture in an encampment.

– for her brother, for her lover. All the barons were shocked and amazed by her distress.

Meanwhile Gawain was calling to Girflet and Sir Yvain: 'Go together, sirs, to Guiromelant, and tell him I'm ready for battle and to be sure he's ready likewise – there'll be no delay on my account. Don't bother asking anyone to point him out: just make straight for the most handsome and impressive of them all! Then give him my message and speak on my behalf.'

They mounted two fine palfreys and set off, while Gawain had his horse prepared and leapt straight from the ground into the saddle, not deigning to use the stirrup! He looked ready to vanquish the finest warrior. He fixed himself so firmly in the stirrups, gleaming with gold, that he almost broke them. All eyes were on him: great crowds of knights were there, ready to support him. They handed him a good strong shield, and he, the most esteemed of all knights in the world, took it by the strap. In his right hand Yder placed a mighty, stout, smooth-shafted lance. Then in an instant he was gone. A tall, fine figure he was indeed, poised in the saddle as he spurred his horse over hill and dale and then set out along a cobbled road.

Meanwhile his messengers had ridden through valley and over hill and plain and now arrived at the camp of Guiromelant, who was on his way to confront Sir Gawain. They didn't find him on his own: any proven knight, in all the isles of the sea, who was fit for battle and had any desire to wage war on Arthur, would have had support from Guiromelant; so every enemy of Arthur had come now to his aid. And if the host of barons supporting him was great, three times greater, truly, was the host of ladies: there were even more with him than with King Arthur. So the messengers arrived; and they knew at once, without asking, which one was Guiromelant: he was standing on an elegant new carpet of luxurious red samite, his arms resting on the shoulders of two squires. Two more were kneeling at his feet, fitting and tightly lacing his chausses followed by his spurs. When this was done to the satisfaction of the attendant barons he promptly donned an haqueton* embroidered all over with lion cubs: it had been brought to him from Venice. There was nothing loutish or weedy about him! There was no finer-looking specimen in the world! A handsome face with bright and shining eyes; broad shoulders and chest, a powerful frame; strong arms and big fists: you'll never find a better-built man. And truly, his hands were permanently clenched from gripping weapons! One of his squires, standing before him, now clad him in a costly hauberk,* and pages, who knew their business well, inspected him on every side, making sure all was as it should be. It was perfect: they reported to the squire that all was in order.

The two messengers came forward as soon as they saw Guiromelant: they realised it must be him from the way he was being armed; and they saw, too, the pleasure he displayed at the prospect of that day's fight – he was clearly convinced he was going to vanquish Sir Gawain in the battle. They went straight up and hailed him, and delivered Gawain's message eloquently. He asked them their names and who they were, and Sir Yvain replied:

'I shan't hide my name from you, good sir: I am Yvain; and my companion's name is Girflet, a bold-hearted man indeed, and the son of Do, no less.'

'I'm grateful to Sir Gawain,' said Guiromelant. 'I'm heartily glad to see you here – you're widely esteemed as men of worth. I'm most impressed that he should send you two: it shows his calibre! I know now, Sir Yvain, that it's true what people say of him: he's a courteous man indeed, sending no lesser men than you to be his messengers. God give me strength, there are no two barons I'd rather he'd sent than you! I've heard glowing reports of you – were God Himself to send me some great blessing, I'd think myself honoured if He sent it via such envoys!

'But listen: by God on high I swear, Sir Yvain – I place my hands between yours in solemn oath – I'm thrilled at having to test myself against the finest knight in all the world. Everyone knows his reputation: no one doubts his worth, and nor do I – I know he's the flower of chivalry, honour and courtesy, and his courtesy has won him the love of many. But no one loves him as much as I hate him! If I can get the better of him, nothing will stop me having his head – I'll accept no lesser tribute! Then I'll carve the heart from his breast – unless he's got a spell on him to make him blade-proof! By this hand that's holding yours, if I prevail he's a dead man!'

'God forbid, good sir,' said Yvain, 'that it should come to that. He'd be striking us a heavy blow if He let harm befall Sir Gawain: what a loss he'd be to the world – he's worth more than all other men put together!'

'That's the plea of one who loves him, Yvain! By the being we call God, Gawain wouldn't be worth a lot if the whole world hated him as much as I – we'd soon be rid of him, and gladly!'

Yvain's reply was immediate: 'The good in him outweighs all the ill that may be said of him – out of spite or anger – by any man alive!'

'You're a credit to yourself, Yvain. You've done your duty most ably. I trust you and I can be on good terms. Don't be upset by what I've said: my words are prompted by the wrath in my heart, which I assure you won't be purged till I've taken revenge!'

'Then prepare, sir,' said Yvain, 'for battle.'

'Right!' cried Guiromelant. 'I'll have my ventail laced and then I'll be off! And I'll be bringing this mighty army with me!'

The messengers didn't dally; they took their leave at once and set off back to where they'd left Gawain, leaving the others to finish arming Guiromelant with all speed. A helmet, shining, hard and strong, they laced securely on his head. Then they brought him a sword: none finer was ever forged[12] – not even Roland's Durendal;[13] he girded it at once. Then a mighty horse was brought to him, and he could have been a picture, he was so handsome: berry-black, with flaring nostrils, and completely clad in iron. Guiromelant leapt straight up – no need of the stirrup – a man ablaze with courage. As he sat proudly on this awesome horse, they brought him a shield, wonderfully strong and light, and placed a stout, red lance in his right hand: he took it by the grip and brandished it so violently that he almost shattered it! What a splendid sight he was when fully armed!

He set off in fine array towards the king's camp, dividing his great host into three companies: there were two thousand fine knights in the first and as many in the second, and the third comprised three thousand more, imposing indeed and mighty. And behind them rode Guiromelant, fully armed. How fierce was his bearing! And his arms shone with a dazzling light that lit up the whole host! The gems on his helm alone were worth the cities and kingdom once defended by William![14] What a helm it was, with a circle of gold braid studded with jaspers, rubies and other glittering gems. With him, too, came the company of fair ladies richly attired in gorgeously bedecked gowns, all mounted on palfreys with matching harness, riding two by two towards the Perilous Ford.

All together, then, Guiromelant's great host made its way to the ford. And from the other direction came the queen, the barons and the rest of Arthur's host, a vast company

---

[12] Literally 'tempered'.
[13] The famous sword of Charlemagne's nephew, the hero of *The Song of Roland*.
[14] Guillaume d'Orange, hero of another epic *chanson de geste*, the 12th-century *Song of William*.

of lords and ladies and knights. And at their head rode Sir Gawain on his prancing horse. The two valiant knights he'd sent as his messengers arrived and said:

'Welcome, sir! You'll have your battle right away, of that you can be sure! Your enemy sends word that he means to keep his oath without fail.'

'As I do mine, good sirs. And God grant me the honour of victory.'

To which a thousand added with one voice: 'Amen to that, good sir!'

He remounted without a moment's delay and took the shield proffered by his liegemen and slung the strap over his neck. There were ten pages each holding a lance, uncertain which of them he'd choose; but they soon found out, as Yvonet, King Yder's son, who'd served him for many years, handed him a stout and mighty lance that had been the death of many a knight with its sharp steel head and solid applewood shaft. A pennon embroidered with orfrey,* emblazoned with his arms, they fastened to the lance with golden nails – and if you're wondering where it had come from, it was a love-token.

Gawain was elated and gave thanks to God that battle was imminent. And he looked towards the Perilous Ford and saw, appearing over the crest of a hill, four thousand armed knights, shields braced, and then three thousand more, and a further four, all ready for combat, side by side; and without more ado these three great companies dismounted by a tree facing the king's host. Gawain saw them and remained composed – indeed, courage swelled within him; his custom was that, if he knew he was in the wrong, he would admit it even if he was being challenged by the feeblest of men, which only enhanced his reputation as one who deplored wrongdoing: he was humble and kind towards the worthy; but he was full of fierce courage when confronting the wicked, the oppressive, the proud.

The three companies who'd come and dismounted by the tree were now gathered together as one. Under that tree, right opposite King Arthur's host, many a mighty warrior could be seen, and many a horse of every colour: sorrel, bay, white-stockinged. For the greater safety of his host King Arthur bade four thousand of his own men arm and be prepared to guard them: all of them were knights of worth. Then Gawain, as he looked towards the ford, saw an approaching company of three thousand ladies, damsels, girls, all richly dressed, accompanied by minstrels playing tunes on hurdy-gurdies, pipes and all manner of instruments. He said to Kay, who was at his right hand:

'That's where my enemy will be, I do believe.'

'I'd say so, sir.'

And this final company dismounted on the flowered ground where the battle was to be fought. All of them would have a perfect view – if they wished, and their hearts could bear it.

Gawain's Battle with Guiromelant

When Gawain saw all the companies gathered he called his party together, as did his opponent, and rode swiftly forward from King Arthur's host. So did Guiromelant from his host likewise, superb gold shield slung from his neck, his horse splendidly caparisoned in red and yellow – red at the fore and yellow at the crupper – and a great, stout, mighty lance in hand, its strength filling him with confidence. There was no delay or exchange of oaths: like the expert warriors and bold knights they were they braced their shields and turned to face the foe, and gripping tight with their knees and pricking hard with their spurs they charged in full view of the king and his barons, who raised their hands to the skies in prayer. The horses galloped full tilt; the knights levelled their lances. Big and bold and strong they were and they hated each other mortally; with their lances huge and stout, tipped with the sharpest heads of steel, they struck each other with all the strength in their mighty arms, and drove both heads and shafts clean through shields and flashing past skin, bringing red blood gushing forth. The lances shattered, but the knights couldn't stop their ferocious charge and they and their horses smashed together, girths and collars sundering, unable to hold their saddles on, and down they crashed full length on the ground. Such a fearsome clash was never seen. Their mounts were sprawled beneath them, but the knights, afire with rage, leapt straight up and went at each other wildly with their swords. You should have seen the blows they unleashed, standing toe to toe, raining blows on each other in passionate fury: denser than hail those blows descended in a wild and brutal assault on body and head. God, what a battle it was! On their helms they dealt such stunning blows that they stove and smashed them utterly; from their shields the tempered, shining blades hacked and hewed great wedges. They were at each other mercilessly, pressing and giving ground in turn. No battle so fierce between two knights had ever been seen since Christ was born; both were utterly bent on inflicting damage and shame; both returned every blow in kind; it was impossible to say who was on top. Thick and fast, from right and left, the attacking blows came, and many of them landed; they were testing each other to the full, and shedding each other's blood with their blades of steel.

It carried on all morning till terce was rung. Gawain was a wise knight: he didn't fight willingly unless someone demanded battle of him; but when he struck a blow his opponent knew it – his moves were as devastating as a queen's in chess! And once terce was past his strength and ferocity doubled. After that, I promise you, with each passing hour his force waxed ever greater, and you've never seen fighting like it. Gawain's sword had been slashing and hewing, and so had his enemy's, cruelly, as they dealt each other awesome blows; but once terce was rung all those watching saw the combat intensify as they launched still mightier attacks upon each other: it was a wonder they could keep going at all, let alone with such ferocity. I can't describe the dismay of the people watching: they feared for them both, no matter who was the better man. But everyone, of course, supports those dear to him: even a man of little worth, if he matters to you, is the equal of the noblest lord! But forgive me: I'm not referring to these two – they were both exceptional.

Pity tore and seared the hearts of those who watched them fight and wound each other. And there's no need to ask if the king was upset: he was speechless with distress. Seeing his nephew in such a plight he'd have given anything to see it end with honours even and neither party suffering shame. He dearly wished it might be so – as long as his nephew escaped with honour unscathed; for Gawain more than anyone despised wickedness and sin and crime and vice, and avarice and spite; he more than anyone was devoted to courtesy and placed his faith in God.

It was a sight to see the two knights driving each other this way and that, giving ground and taking it. Gawain didn't harangue his foe but boldly assailed him with his blade of steel; and back at him came Guiromelant, sword in hand: they struck each other on the helm, every blow that landed doing damage, and mighty blows they rained on their shields, hacking off chunks with every strike. There was nothing fake about any of this – they hated each other mortally! Their hauberks, fine and strong, they couldn't breach at all, but so fierce and grim were the blows they dealt that dark red blood was streaming beneath their mail from broken flesh and sinew. Their helms were battered utterly, their shields so smashed to pieces that neither had a foot of shield left. And still they drove each other back and forth. God! it was a piteous sight: there was never a more distressing battle between two knights.

But now for every blow dealt by Guiromelant, Sir Gawain hungrily dealt two. Guiromelant's strength had so far lasted all day, as had his prowess, courage, heart and hostile wrath: it was a wonder that he still had breath; but no human body, however tough, could have failed to be weary from such exertion, and I tell you, as noon passed Guiromelant tired indeed. But Gawain's strength still grew, redoubled: now he was twice as strong! For such was his custom: he was always at his strongest between noon and three.[15] Now he gave his enemy more blows than he could handle: Guiromelant ceased to defend himself or even move – Gawain was in complete control. The giving now was all one way: the blows he lavished on him were not repaid! Guiromelant's host were horrified to see him in such a plight, and wept for his noble qualities and the God-given beauty of his body and face: all were grieving bitterly. But while they wept and wailed, on the king's side there was delight and laughter as they rejoiced to see Gawain in such fine shape: the ladies joyously declared he was bound to win; their spirits soared.

But as for Clarissant, she didn't know what to think: should she side with her sweetheart as urged by Love, or with the worthy, accomplished Gawain? For Reason was insisting that her brother Gawain was of greater worth, arguing that she could always find another lover, but if she lost her brother he could never be replaced, and he was the finest man in all the world. Back came Love, reminding her that her sweetheart loved her dearly:

'Your every wish is his command! Your heart is his and his is yours!'

Such was Love's insistent plea; and, rightly or wrongly, Love swayed her! Clarissant wept and wrung her hands and cried and wailed and flung herself to the ground and tore her clothes and hair. She didn't know what to say or do: there was no way of winning – if she saw her brother brought to shame she'd want to die, and if she saw her sweetheart killed she'd be in misery and woe for the rest of her life. Truly, she was in a shocking state, her heart wracked with pain. But now she hauled herself from the ground, beating her hands and crying, and came running to the king and fell at his feet. The king was alarmed and shocked to see her weeping so, and asked her what was wrong. Wailing loud, she kissed his foot and begged him to have pity, saying:

'Good king, most noble lord, I've heard it said you've never rejected a plea for help; if you reject mine I don't know what I'll do! For God's sake, have pity! I see my brother and my sweetheart fighting each other here: I pray you in God's name, settle this battle for me! Don't refuse my plea! Do me the honour of giving me Guiromelant for my husband: he loves me – I've given him my love and he's given me his. It's the first time, noble king, this niece of yours has asked you for any favour! Grant it, sire: it would be a great boon!'

'Dear niece, it's not in my gift! Gawain is fighting against a charge of treachery: it would be wrong of me to interfere in such a combat now that my court's assembled. I can't do as you ask – and I'm only too sorry: by God the son of Mary, nothing in the field of chivalry has given me such pain! From the moment he fastened his left spur for battle, it was beyond my power and right to intervene. By God all-seeing and all-knowing, niece, you'd have a fine lord if you took that knight for your husband! And it would be a relief to me indeed – I'd be sorrier to see him suffer than any knight I've known; by the faith I owe the Creator, I've never seen a finer, more handsome man – at least, that's

---

[15] Literally 'from midday till the ninth (canonical) hour'.

what I've heard from those who've seen him out of armour! Go, niece, with all speed, and appeal to your brother to have mercy and end this battle; and in the name of God and His grace ask him for that knight's hand in marriage, that they may be friends henceforth. God bless me, it would be splendid if you could reconcile them so, for I can't intervene – it's not within a king's power; but if you can persuade your brother to make the knight your husband I'll be overjoyed.'

Gawain's Anger

The anguished girl rushed away from the king and headed to where her brother was locked in battle. The damsel Clarissant's courage was amazing – and came from her noble heart. Flinging aside her mantle she ran, in full view of everyone, straight into the fighting and fell at Gawain's feet. With the utmost kindness he asked what she wanted, and she begged him, as a man with a good and generous heart, to do as she'd asked the king. He replied:

'Dear sister, I'll never grant you that till he withdraws his scandalous charge against me. In any case, listen: I can tell *you*'re speaking from the heart but I know nothing of *his* intentions – after all, many a girl finds that her sweetheart's love's not genuine, that she's being deceived and toyed with. So, sir knight,' he called across, 'have you been listening to this?'

'I have, good sir.'

'Tell us your mind, then: how do you respond to her request?'

'God bless me, what do you expect me to say? We've been fighting all this while and we're still at it! If you give me your sister it'll be no dishonour to you or to her: she'll be endowed with seven cities.'

Now, Sir Gawain was never one to insult a knight or to say anything haughty or foolish, and he had no desire to put down or belittle Guiromelant. So showing him the utmost respect he said:

'By God, sir knight, you could have asked me for her this morning and you'd have had your wish then! But perhaps you *wanted* it this way – the path to true love should never be easy! And it always needs God to smile kindly! But if it may be done with my honour safe, you alone shall have the sweet gift of her hand, for it's clear to me she'll have a noble marriage: you, good sir, are quite the finest knight in all the world.'

'Come, come, Sir Gawain!' he replied at once. 'If there weren't one finer than me right here, your reputation would be belied! But I've seen ample proof of its veracity, and thanks be to God I consider myself honoured to have held out so long against the world's finest knight. I thank you deeply for saying she can be mine and I her lord, for I love her dearly as she loves me.'

'I say so indeed,' said Gawain, 'on condition, that is, that you retract your charge against me. I shan't withhold what I've promised, provided you withdraw, in the hearing of everyone, that egregious slur.'

The king delayed no longer now, but hurried to join his niece, and the discussion continued a long while with Clarissant weeping constantly. Sir Gawain repeated his promise that if Guiromelant withdrew his charge he would gladly, saving his honour, grant him his sister's hand, and would be only too pleased that peace should be thereby made. But if he refused to retract the charge that so aggrieved him, he should lace his ventail again next day and return to battle with the arms he was bearing now. This was accepted by both parties, and with that the talking ended. Gawain rode slowly back to his lodgings where he was swiftly disarmed, and there was much celebration all night long.

The companies guarding the watching hosts disarmed likewise, and the king supervised the disarming of Guiromelant and had him mounted on a palfrey and took him back with him and Clarissant. What celebration there was that night!

And then, first thing next morning, King Arthur sent for his niece, and as soon as she was ready they took her to church, beautifully dressed and adorned. Her husband received her from the hand of an archbishop, with many bishops in attendance. What a joyous service it was, accompanied by the merry music of minstrels and the happy acclamation of the court.

But while they were still in church Sir Gawain arrived at the king's lodgings, fully armed. Kay hurried to meet him and asked him why he was armed at such a time.

'I'm ready to do battle,' he replied. 'Why else? Is the king up yet?'

'You don't need to worry, sir! Peace is made, that's certain! Your sister's just been married – they're still in church, listening to the service!'

'What? Has my uncle done me such a shameful wrong as to give my sister to the man who's charged me with treachery? Married her without my consent and approval? You can go and tell the king that I shall never be his vassal, and never return to his land, till he comes and finds me in some distant country with three thousand knights of worth, properly clad and well equipped!'

And with that Sir Gawain galloped away. Kay raced to the church and blurted out: 'Here's news for you, sire: you've lost your nephew! He's forsaken your court because you've given his sister to his enemy before the charge against him has been withdrawn, against his express wishes. He no longer holds you as his friend or his uncle or his lord!'

At these words the king felt more bitter grief than any in his life: he was almost crazed with anguish. The barons were just as distressed; all the jubilation vanished – suddenly everyone was plunged in woe. Guinevere and Ygerne fainted, while Clarissant cursed the day she was born, distraught that her brother had stormed from court. The king called for his palfrey to be saddled at once. The squires set to work that instant, fetching and saddling all the horses: not a soul stayed behind, knight or girl or lady. Guiromelant and his new wife and the three queens mounted, and princes, barons, kings and counts set off with King Arthur, their horses led by the bridle and their arms and shields carried behind. If I named them all I'd make the story overlong, but I can assure you no one in all the host was smiling – they couldn't have been more downcast: they were inconsolable, distraught, thinking they'd lost Gawain. I don't think anyone had ever seen so many lords go together in search of a single knight: all the nobles of the land went with the king. No one stayed behind – it was a huge company, numbered at nine thousand when they left the city, not counting the fair ladies and damsels: I don't know how many of them there were, and I don't want to lie or make things up. And the whole vast company, you may be sure, were desperately dejected, and there's no need to ask why. So the king rode on his way distracted, with all the barons and the queen likewise deeply troubled.

The Maiden of the Ivory Horn

But we'll leave the king's host now and tell of Gawain. He rode through wood and over plain, through glade and spinney, this way and that way, all day long. He followed no path of any kind but gave his horse free rein, up hill and down dale, wherever he fancied; he didn't try to steer him because he didn't care: his anger at the marriage arranged by the king against his wishes had wiped all other thought from his mind. So he didn't care where he went, which path he took or where he ended up.

He rode all day without eating or drinking – he didn't give food a thought. Then the sun set and night fell – and what a beautiful night it was: none so fair was ever seen, before or since. Gawain rode on by the light of a brilliant moon, and didn't care about stopping anywhere when the going was so pleasant. And he was riding with all the speed he could, spurred on by the thought of the king behind him: he didn't want him to catch up until he'd reached a far-flung land. That thought, and the fair, fine weather, kept him riding on.

But about midnight things took a turn for the worse: the moon stopped shining as the sky was covered in a blanket of dense, black cloud laden with rain and hail. He was alarmed to see lightning flash in sheets and bolts on every side, accompanied by crashing thunder. He started spurring harder than before, to see if he could escape the rain and storm, but he'd not gone far before the weather turned worse than he'd ever seen. He was a good deal less than comfortable, bombarded by rain and hail and lightning bolts. Soon it was impossible to ride on, and he dismounted beneath a tall, spreading oak. He propped his ashwood lance against the tree and covered himself with his shield, swearing he'd never seen rain so dense or such terrible thunder and lightning in all his life. He could see just a few yards[16] with each lightning flash before he was plunged in gloom again. The storm raged on incessantly till it was almost dawn, without any break or easing; Sir Gawain coped with the discomfort as best he could – he had no choice.

But as day broke the dreadful weather passed, and the sky that had been so black and grim was now serene and clear. Then Gawain, having suffered the storm all night, slept a little, his head on his arm, and when he woke he found the sun was shining brightly. He'd no wish to dally, and mounted at once and set off along a path till he came upon a charming wood. On he rode – all alone on his horse Gringalet, accompanied by no squire or page – until he emerged from the wood into a beautiful glade: you couldn't ask for one more fair and lush and decked with flowers. On every side was the tall, thick forest, where the birds were singing their sweet, high morning song. Gawain, revelling in the lovely place where he found himself, and delighting in the birds' dulcet melodies, ambled along till noon without meeting a living soul.

Then he saw a girl approaching at a similar pace, mounted on a mule. None fairer or more finely dressed was ever seen in any land: even if I had a hundred tongues I couldn't describe her beauty, if my source is to be believed! The mule, which was completely black, was heading towards Sir Gawain. Its rider was holding an ivory horn in her right hand and the reins, embroidered with flowers of golden thread, in her left; and she was singing a delightful love song. As Sir Gawain drew near he greeted her thus:

'Damsel, may the one who presides over all the world send you every joy and fortune your heart desires.'

'God bless you, good sir,' she replied, clearly needing no instruction, 'and grant you everything I'd wish for myself. But I'd love to know what brings you here, for this is the domain of the hateful damsel whose house and abode are here beside the Glade of Marvels.[17] I fear you'll have to stay as her prisoner.'

'What? Is she really so wicked?'

---

[16] Literally 'the distance a shout would carry'.
[17] '*Lande Aventureuse*', called a few lines later the '*Lande Merveilleuse*'.

'Yes, sir! And the land hereabouts is hers entirely; and this glade, so broad and fair, is called the Glade of Marvels. You'll encounter many perilous adventures before you leave – which you may, if you keep to the right path. But tell me, if you will, where you took lodging last night: I can't believe you had much comfort – I don't know of any house or dwelling for twenty leagues in any direction except the damsel's.'

'True enough, young lady!' said Gawain. 'My lodging and my bed last night had little to commend them! I lay armed like this in the forest back there, and it rained on me all night long.'

'I can believe it, by God,' the girl replied. 'You and your horse could do with some rest, I'd say. Don't go further till you've dined, I pray you, for you've a lot to get through if you're to find your way out of this glade.'

Gawain accepted: the thought of food was very welcome. And thereupon she put her horn to her lips and blew it once and then again – as if sounding the end of a hunt; then she hung it round her neck by a Frisian lace and dismounted. Suddenly a hundred or more young men and girls sprang forth, all handsome and fair and elegantly dressed in the richest clothes. When Gawain saw them he dismounted and tethered his horse to an oak beside him and propped his lance against it; then he hung his shield from a branch, unlaced his ventail, took off his helm and greeted the girls. The damsel came and took him by the hand and made a great fuss of him, and ordered the boys to prepare for them to dine; they smartly set about it. In the glade stood a handsome tree, tall and spreading wide, providing ample shade for a hundred knights to dine in comfort, truly; the sun at its midday zenith wouldn't have troubled them. Without more ado they headed there. Those responsible for serving dinner had spread tablecloths over the grass with everything laid ready, and said:

'Dinner is served, my lady, if it please you.'

The damsel stood and told Gawain to disarm, but he said at once that he wouldn't – he would dine just as he was, for as soon as he'd had a little to eat then with her leave and approval he'd be on his way again.

The damsel agreed. Then they washed their hands and sat down. But while they were sitting eating, they saw a knight come riding, fully armed, on a horse blacker than any berry, though the surcoat above his arms was white and his shield was red. Lance in hand, helm on head, the knight rode up before them and then drew rein; but he didn't dismount, nor did he greet them or utter a word of any kind. He came right up beside the damsel, bent down, threw his arms round her neck, took the horn and instantly rode away. She was left beating her palms in anguish and crying:

'Alas, was this my destiny? Oh, curse the hour I was born! That my horn should be snatched away like this – I've lost it now for the rest of my life!'

Gawain was upset by her distress, and leapt to his feet and vowed that the knight wouldn't escape without a fight. He laced his ventail and then his helm, and two boys brought him Gringalet and he mounted without delay. He took up his shield and lance and rode straight off, and galloped after the knight till he caught him up. The knight heard him in hot pursuit and turned and said:

'What brings *you* here, knight? Tell me: by my life, I want to know.'

'Oh, you'll know, don't worry! I've come to ask you in courtesy to return the horn you took from the girl.'

'That wasn't very bright of you! If you'd had any sense you'd have carried on with your dinner! Go and throw your weight around elsewhere: by Saint Luke, there's no way you're having this horn! Go on – be off with you!'

'Come now, noble knight,' said Gawain, 'please don't take that attitude. It's not the mark of a chivalrous knight to snatch things from a defenceless girl who can respond with nothing but tears and curses. Do the decent thing and send back her horn, on the understanding that if in future she ever wrongs you I'll make amends for her.'

'I'll do nothing of the kind, by God!' said the knight. 'Be off with you and leave me in peace, or you'll regret it before we're through!'

'I promise you,' Gawain replied, 'if you won't return it with good grace you'll have to fight me for it!'

'By God! You're a fool to take me on! It wouldn't bother me if there were four of you!'

'By Saint Paul!' said Gawain. 'I don't know what'll come of this, or who'll have the worse of the blows and the fight, but come what may, I challenge you!'

Hearing this, the knight took the horn from his neck and hung it on a branch; then he returned to the field. There was to be no stopping either of them, more's the pity: they drew back from each other half a bowshot's length,[18] gripped their shields, levelled their lances and thrust in their sharp steel spurs, sending their horses into a faster charge than a sparrowhawk's swoop on quail! At each other they came in fury, shield slung from neck, lance in rest, and exchanged such blows on their quartered shields that their steel lance-heads smashed clean through. The knight with the red shield struck first, to no little effect: his lance went straight through Gawain's shield like a sheet of old parchment; but it found his hauberk more resistant – far from piercing the mail, the lance broke clean in half. And Sir Gawain, that paragon of valour, strength and intelligence, returned a like blow, and such was the momentum of his charge that neither shield nor hauberk could stop him driving the steel lance-head right through the knight's body below the left breast: the head and fully six feet of shaft burst through. He sent him crashing dead from his horse, and there he left him lying. Then he seized the black horse and led him away by the reins, and rode to the horn hanging from the oak and took it down and carried it off, rejoicing in his heart.

When the damsel saw him coming she jumped straight up and went to meet him. Gawain greeted her and handed her the horse and horn. She received them with the utmost joy and hung the horn round her neck once more. Then Gawain dismounted and took off his helm and laid it down, and ten or so boys came running and took his shield and lance, and unbridled his horse and tethered it by the halter and left it to graze. Then Gawain and the damsel resumed their dinner, and there were no glum looks or cross words, only laughter and merriment from everyone. They went out of their way to fête and serve and honour Gawain, saying:

'Bless the hour you came here, sir! The aid you've given us today is your finest service ever!'

With everyone at ease again, they dined at leisure and at length and in the best of spirits, untroubled and at peace. You won't hear me say how many dishes they had or what they were, but they ate and drank their fill before the servants duly cleared the cloths; and a most comely girl came with water in a pair of silver bowls, and they washed. Then Gawain called for his helm at once, without more ado, saying:

'I'll be on my way now, damsel, if it please you.'

'No more of that, good sir!' she replied. 'God bless you, stay with us for what's left of the day, and make yourself at home – all that's ours is at your command. The

---

[18] '*un arpant*': the *arpent* was a unit of length roughly equivalent, in medieval France, to 70 metres.

light is failing, look – noon's long past; and you must surely be tired after fighting the most fearsome man there's ever been! If you leave now you'll be too late to find any lodging tonight.'

'By my life, damsel, I really can't stay – I've a long journey ahead of me. It's no use insisting! But tell me your name, I pray you: I'd dearly like to know it.'

'I shall, if you wish,' she said. 'It would be wrong of me to keep it from you. The truth is, I'm known in this land as the Maiden of the Ivory Horn. But I should have asked the same of you, indeed! So tell me your name, if you will.'

'By God and His power, I've never kept my name from anyone. I am Gawain, King Arthur's nephew and son of King Lot.'

When the damsel heard this her heart soared. She was upset, though, that she hadn't honoured him all the more, but how could she have done, when she hadn't known who he was? She said:

'Oh sir, sir, I can quite believe you're Gawain – yes, by God! There's no doubting your strength and courage when you vanquish such a knight: he's lived long and won many a battle – he killed every knight he met who took him on! His self-regard was huge – you don't realise how much you achieved! You defeated him in combat, yes, but you don't yet know his name or who he was. That wicked and treacherous knight was Macarot of Pantelion. Maybe you've never heard anything – fact or fiction – about the outrageous wrongs he committed; so let me tell you: if he heard of any knight coming this way he would force him to do battle – he didn't care a jot if there were three or four of them! He couldn't have enough of fighting! He guarded this path constantly. And he did me many wrongs, all of them unpunished – but now, thank God, I've lived to see his overweening pride pricked and burst! By Saint Julian, at last I'm avenged! If that wicked man had carried off my horn and I'd lost it for good I'd never have been happy again – I cherish and treasure it for the sake of the dear knight who gave it to me as a love token, and its power is such that anyone possessing it will be free of cold and thirst and hunger, even in the wildest land.'

'By Saint Luke,' said Gawain, 'such a horn should be treasured indeed! It sounds priceless! But enough now: I must be on my way. But be assured that, wherever I am, if ever you're in need of help I'll be at your command.'

The damsel thanked him graciously and said: 'Take this ring from my finger, sir, and don't refuse, for you'll be needing it, that's certain – and sooner rather than later, I think you'll find. I assure you, sir, while you're wearing this ring you needn't fear five enemy knights, even the strongest in the world – even if each was as big as a mountain! Have no doubt: you'll defeat them all.'

She proffered the ring which he accepted without protest, thanking her most courteously. Then he donned his helm and jumped straight on his horse, slung his shield round his neck and collected his lance. The damsel stepped up and took hold of his reins and said:

'Before God, sir, I give you my ring on condition that if I ever ask for it you'll return it without demur.'

'It's surely only right, damsel, that I return it if you wish. I would never be so base as to refuse.'

They said no more; with that they parted. She remained, and Gawain rode swiftly away. He was delighted that chance had brought him to that glade of such renown: he'd heard about it often, but had never come across it in all his wanderings through many lands in search of chivalry.

He pressed on all that day till none;* then, as he looked ahead along the path, he saw a dwarf approaching. He was deformed, hunch-backed, squat – so small that it was hard to believe he was one of God's creations – and this ugly dwarf was seated on a skinny, clapped-out horse. If I didn't think it would bore you I'd take the time to describe him to the best of my powers – though even at my sharpest I don't think I could convey what a wretched specimen he was! But as a special treat I'll do my best to pass on what I gather from my source: he was so ugly, in all honesty, that in all the world you wouldn't have found a more hideous, misshapen creature. His head was long and pointy, with hair sticking up on end like a bristling boar. He had huge, flapping ears, and bushy red eyebrows that completely covered his eyes – which were sunk four inches[19] into his head. And believe me when I say his nose was a tiny, stubby, hairy thing – you've never seen one so small. His great fissure of a mouth was as long as a man's hand, and the teeth inside were giant fangs the colour of egg yolk. He had lips like a donkey or an ox and, rather horribly, he'd lost the upper one – it looked as if it had been burnt off; it was all curled up so the top and bottom of his mouth were permanently stuck two inches apart. You couldn't call what he had a beard – it was more like the stuff on a witch's chin. As for his neck, it was a mystery: he didn't seem to have one. And truly, he had a hunch on his front as well as his back. His arms were all right, though – for a dwarf – and looked good dangling from his hunched-up shoulders. With a body and legs and feet like his, what a figure he'd have cut in a dance! A better-proportioned dwarf you couldn't find! No carver or mason in the land could have sculpted a better example! What made him look worse was his worthless nag: plodding along was the best it could manage. And the dwarf was hidden by the front of his saddle – which had seen better days: it was ancient, falling apart, held together in a dozen places with straps and bits of string. But still he beat the poor nag, which was so far gone that every dog in the district was expecting it for supper; nobody would have bought it, even for its hide, covered in sores as it was.

Anyway, this dwarf, just as I've described him, was plodding along and Sir Gawain was riding fast towards him. Gawain couldn't wait to meet him, hoping he might have some news; but when he drew near and could see him up close he was shocked, and swore he was the ugliest creature Nature ever made. He drew rein and said:

'Where have you come from, dwarf?'

He didn't reply at all; he just rode on by as quickly as he could. Sir Gawain hailed him again, a little louder this time, saying:

'In God's name tell me where you've come from, and if I'd have lodging if I went there.'

The dwarf muttered something to himself and then said, irritably: 'I say a fig for you, Gawain! Dashing here, dashing there, dashing off your promises! No one should take you seriously.'

'Eh? What are you talking about, dwarf?'

'You really want to know? You're all talk! You sit at King Arthur's table, puffed up, lording it over everyone, but you're the worst knight in the world! A proper knight's courageous, dependable, sincere. Your courage isn't in doubt, but dependable and sincere? In the past year you've shown yourself to be anything but! Anyone who knows anything of your words and deeds and behaviour will testify to that! You used to be the flower of chivalry, but now you've changed: now you're the worst of the lot – and going

---

[19] Literally 'four fingers' widths'.

downhill by the day! You don't give a thought to sincerity now. I don't suppose you recall a promise you made this year – a promise you've made no attempt to keep? People have been waiting for you to honour it, but they're going to have to go on waiting – it seems you've no intention of keeping your word! At King Arthur's table you said – and appeared to mean it – that you'd go and rescue the damsel besieged on the peak of Montesclaire, and gain supreme praise by girding on the Sword of the Strange Belt.[20] That was what you vowed to do.'

'You're right, dwarf,' Gawain replied. 'It's true I promised to go to her aid. But I've done nothing about it yet because I've had so much else to deal with that it's been driven from my mind. Bless the one who gave you birth! Your reminding me has done the damsel and her castle no end of good!'

And he swore by Saint Marcel that until he'd been to Montesclaire he wouldn't sleep in any house for more than a single night.

'Well, we'll see, won't we?' said the dwarf. 'If you do as you say you'll erase your bad record! I assure you, you'll be there within three days if you keep to the right path. The siege has still not lifted: the damsel's still hemmed in, quite unable to leave. And let me tell you, she rests her hopes on you alone: when she heard you were coming to her rescue, well, you've never seen joy and celebration like it!'

'And by my life, she's right to rejoice!' said Gawain. 'If I get there and find the siege still on I'll do all in my power to raise it, of that she can be sure.'

With that he galloped away from the dwarf, while the dwarf set off in the other direction, his duty done. And so they parted; and Gawain rode on swiftly, delighted that he'd chanced to meet the dwarf and been reminded of the mission he'd undertaken: he hadn't given it a thought – it had gone completely from his mind.

He pressed on for a fair while. Then he looked ahead and saw a tent topped with a golden pommel, which reflected the sun so dazzlingly that it seemed to light the whole surrounding land. He couldn't wait for a closer look, and loosed the reins and spurred towards it. But as he drew near he heard such wails and cries within that they'd have been heard by an attentive ear a league[21] away. He dismounted and took a peep inside; and there he saw a knight lying stiff upon a bier. He'd clearly been killed that very day, but he didn't know who he was. He stepped softly inside, hoping to ask who the knight was and from what land, to find out if he knew him. But by my life, if he'd known he would never have entered – not if he had any sense! I fear he'll be in trouble before he leaves unless he's careful! But enter the tent he did, and immediately launched into his Paternoster, praying that God the son of Holy Mary would have pity on the dead man's soul. And he'd hardly begun when the corpse's wound started shedding great gouts of blood. But only Gawain noticed – and knew then exactly who it was! He asked no questions – he didn't need a word from anyone! He went straight back to his horse, mounted, took up his lance and rode off. But he'd gone no more than two bowshots, so the story says, before he heard four knights galloping after him, armed to the teeth. And they were crying:

'Traitor! You're not leaving without paying – with your head, whether you like it or not! You slew Macarot, but he's going to be avenged right now! You're for it, and there's no way out!'

[20] The Edinburgh MS accidentally (but consistently) changes the name that appears in Chrétien – *'l'Espee as Estranges Renges'* – to *'l'Espee o les Estroites Ranges'*: 'the Sword with the Narrow (or Tight) Belt'. Gawain made his vow in Chrétien, above, p. 41.

[21] A league is a notoriously vague medieval measurement, not least because it varied from country to country. In France it was just over two miles.

When Gawain heard this he rode no further; he drew rein and turned his horse about, resolved to stay and face them. As they drew near he asked them what they wanted and who they were. They said not a word in reply; they rode straight up and all together struck him on the shield with their ashwood lances. But it was strong and they didn't pierce it – no, each of the lances broke! And that valiant knight lost neither saddle nor stirrup; instead he spurred his horse a little ahead, then quickly turned and charged them. Clutching his lance he struck one so hard that he thrust it clean through his body; the knight crashed from his horse and his soul departed, unable to stay – Gawain had nothing to fear from him any more! The others, enraged, gripped their swords of steel and launched a furious attack with their shining blades. On his gleaming helm they rained blows thick and fast, hammering like smiths on an anvil. But he, afire with courage, drew his sword likewise and defended himself so valiantly that they could inflict no damage: you'd have seen him wield his burnished, shining blade this way, that way. But he had his hands full: they were attacking him from front and side and back, and he couldn't find a way to fend off all three. He was paying back their blows with interest, but there was a problem: the day was waning, and with it his strength, as was his custom – as you heard earlier,[22] his strength redoubled as noon approached, but after noon it steadily waned till night was done and morning came when his power and strength would rise again. He needed God to make day dawn once more! But he had to put up with it and carry on the uneven battle; he defended himself as best he could, experienced swordsman that he was. He taught one of them a lesson with his steel blade, striking him dead, parting head from body so deftly that he never felt a thing! God's truth, how Gawain rejoiced at this! Whatever trouble he might still face, at least it was less than before! The other two knights, incensed, gave him no rest but attacked together, vowing the tide would turn and counting themselves wretched if they couldn't have his head and avenge Macarot and their fellows. They blazed with hatred – but found Gawain afire and ferocious, too. They sent great sparks leaping from his helm; with their honed blades they battered it till it was dented and split all over. God! How awful that he had no companion to help him, if only to occupy *one* of his foes! Then he'd have given them a hiding! But the fact was he was on his own, and he had to mount such defence as he could, in the certain knowledge that he was a dead man if they got the better of him. Then you'd have seen his courage and vigour and fury return, and the attack he launched upon them then was such that they could have said with all conviction that no finer, bolder, braver knight was ever seen. He wasn't playing this time! He dealt one of them a blow on the crown of the head that clove through the helm and down to the teeth: he was dead and done for – no need to worry about *him* any more! And Gawain, with three of them killed, didn't think the fourth would be any trouble if he tried to fight on man to man. But to his surprise the fourth wanted only an end to the battle; he proffered and surrendered his sword, crying:

'Mercy! Mercy, sir! You've vanquished and killed three knights who were the pride and protectors of the land; now you've crushed them – their strength and power are gone. I've no desire to fight on: I'd have done so gladly if I could see any point – I'd love to avenge the deaths of those you've killed, all three of them my brothers, born of the same womb – but I know I couldn't compete with you! So I surrender as your prisoner: take my sword! I acknowledge you the victor, but in the name of God I crave your mercy: I'm entirely in your power, to do with as you will.'

[22] Above, p. 92.

Gawain heard his earnest plea and submission and took pity on him. He put an end to the battle, saying:

'I grant you mercy indeed, my friend – on condition that you take heed of what I say: I swear I'll kill you here and now if you baulk at it, now that you've surrendered.'

'I have, it's true, sir, I know. So what's your command? I'll do all in my power to fulfil it.'

'Right, then!' said Gawain. 'If you want to live, give me your word that you'll never again attack any man, as you did me, without issuing a challenge in person or via a messenger – to do so is very wrong. Furthermore, you must surrender to the one with whom I dined today – the Maiden of the Ivory Horn. It was for her sake that I killed Macarot of Pantelion, that ill-natured, treacherous-hearted man who rashly snatched the horn from her neck before my very eyes. He treated me with contempt when I asked him to return it and told him it was a foolish deed; I offered to make amends if the damsel had ever wronged him, but he was having none of it. It's no wonder I was riled and fought so hard to win back the horn, and recovered it for the damsel.'

The knight, hearing he was placing him at the damsel's mercy and in her hands as her prisoner, replied in dismay:

'God's truth, sir, cut off my head rather than condemn me to that! No one hates me as much as she! And she's reason enough, God knows, for I've done her nothing but wrong! Send me captive to anyone, I beg you, anywhere you like, but not to her! I'd never escape alive: she'd have me hanged, I swear, or burnt!'

'If it's as you say,' said Gawain, 'and she hates you mortally, it'd be cruel to send you captive to her – hardly an act of compassion or mercy. But tell me truly, who are you and what's your name?'

'By my life, sir, I'm Clarinon of the high forest of Ateine. I used to spend my time revelling by the shining Fountain of Love, its waters glistening with gold; I kept close guard, defeating anyone who came near.'

'Indeed, I've heard a lot about you, far and wide: I believe you're one of the finest knights alive. So I'll have mercy and let you go free; but you're to promise me you'll go at once wherever I send you in future, no matter how perilous, and accept imprisonment wherever I choose, however hard you find it, short of it causing you harm or shame.'

'If that's your wish, sir, I'll concur. But tell me truthfully your name: I'd like to know it.'

'By holy charity, my name is Gawain.'

'Gawain, good sir, I've heard many fine reports of you! You're deemed to be the finest knight in the world. By my life, I think better of myself now, having done battle with you! I don't mind yielding as your prisoner! I'll keep my promise faithfully, so help me God.'

And with that they parted and went their separate ways. I'll leave Clarinon now: I'll say no more about where he went or what became of him. But as for Gawain, he kept riding across the open land till he came upon a path that turned to the right and led into the forest. Day was drawing to a close and mingling with night, and Gawain decided to follow the path and see if he could find a house where he might take lodging. So off he went along the path and kept riding till night had fully fallen. But the moon was shining, and by its light he saw, in a deep valley, a house well defended by moats, drawbridges, walls and palisades – everything a fortified house should have. Gawain headed down and found the gate open and the entrance unguarded, so in he rode. But he hadn't passed through before the gate flew down: it would have skinned the hide off his horse's rump if he hadn't leapt ahead! Now he was well and truly trapped – and far more dangerously than he thought: he was going to need to defend himself more than ever before! He looked all around and up and down to see if he could spot anyone to tell him about the house and what was going on: why had the gate dropped shut behind him? He rode quickly to the door of the hall, and propped his lance outside and jumped from his horse and tethered him. Then he entered the hall, shield slung from neck and sword at his side. No man or woman or living thing did he find inside; but at the far end of the hall he saw a table set, spread with a beautiful white cloth, two brightly shining candles and an appealing array of food. Seeing this he stood there in the middle of the hall and said:

'Well, the table's laid, I see. Since it's almost time to eat, surely some boy or knight or damsel's about to come, and they'll talk to me.'

So he stood there – for a long while, girded with the sword that had served him in so many battles. But still no man or woman appeared.

'By my life, I'm not going to hang about! There's a door: I'll call and see if anyone answers, if there's a boy or knight or maid through there.'

So he went to the door and called – several times; but he didn't hear a word. He swore, by God, he'd had enough of calling, and strode back to the entrance to the hall, intending to fetch his horse inside – but when he reached the door he couldn't find him: he wasn't there. He was very upset, and little wonder! He stamped on the threshold and said:

'I think I've been bewitched! There's no one here, but someone's had my horse! I don't know what's going on!' And crossing himself with his right hand he said: 'But whatever it is, I'll have to look on the bright side till there's a reason not to! At least I've got decent board and lodging! And if I've lost my horse I'll find another before too long, God willing.'

So saying, he went back inside the hall and took off his helm and laid it on a couch along with his sword. Then, as he looked around, he saw two silver basins filled with hot water for washing his hands. So he went and washed and sat down at the table, very taken with the spread of food. But just as he began to eat he heard a door crash open, and through it strode a huge and powerful knight, armed to the teeth. He stormed towards him and thundered:

'Vassal! Vassal! Who gave you leave to eat my food? By Saint Denis, I forbid it! Just for sitting at the table without leave I'll make you pay so you never do it again: it's going to cost you your head – a high price for your supper!'

'Oh, my good, dear sir!' said Gawain, staring at him. 'Am I guilty of so great a crime? I didn't think I was wronging anyone: in my country no knight is denied food anywhere – nor should he be; no, it's deemed only right and proper that he should take it if he finds it. So that's what I did, not knowing your custom. And it's surely not a terrible crime! If I've wronged you I'm ready to make what amends you wish, saving my honour.'

'It's no good,' the knight replied. 'Your words mean nothing here. To make amends you must do battle with me forthwith. Rightly or wrongly, I want your head and it'll be mine! I'll accept no other payment – that's the custom here.'

'What nonsense!' Gawain said. 'This is a wicked and outrageous custom, and I'll cast it out! If that means fighting, I'll give it my all! You're not having my head if I can help it!'

He jumped up, laced his helm, girded his fine blade of steel and turned to face the knight. He was clutching his sword in his right hand, so Gawain drew his own. They didn't mount and joust – they went straight into combat with the sword, and none so ferocious was ever seen. The contest raged for a very long while, and they both inflicted many a wound: it was a piteous, dreadful sight. But the upshot was that Gawain outfought and defeated the knight, and he had to cry for mercy. As he did so, from the very door through which he'd appeared came a fair and charming girl. If I tried for the rest of my life I couldn't describe her beauty! She came and knelt before Gawain, wetting his feet with tears, and said:

'Noble knight, have mercy on my sweetheart – don't kill him! I'll repay you however you wish, but grant my request, I pray you in God's name!'

Gawain saw the damsel weeping bitterly on one side and the knight submitting and begging for mercy on the other. He was filled with pity and said:

'Cry no more, girl. I grant your wish and his – on condition that he will never again refuse hospitality to any knight who needs it, no matter where; rather he'll serve him willingly to the best of his ability. This he must swear if he's to be spared.'

'Ah!' she said. 'He'll swear it for sure! I know he cares about nothing so much as acting honourably; but I, wretch that I am, forced him to all these wicked deeds: I told him he would never fully have my love unless he made all who came to this house end up on a bier! It pained and tormented his heart – but as you know, a man is no longer lord of himself when he becomes Love's subject! He loved me, and didn't dare question my command. He would gladly have done otherwise if he could: before he fell in love with me there was no knight in the land so endowed with all fine qualities. I know he'd gladly forgo this torment and return to doing good.'

That was what she told Sir Gawain; and she implored him to have mercy, in God's name, and let her have her sweetheart, and he would willingly do whatever he asked in return.

'I shall indeed return him to you,' he replied, 'on condition that he does what I said before: that's all I ask.'

'My good, dear sir,' the damsel said, 'may the sovereign king reward you.'

The knight made the oath and Sir Gawain released him. Then four handsome boys came smartly up and disarmed them both and clad them in mantles, and they sat on a bed together like good friends. The damsel sat between them, and did all she could to honour Gawain, repeatedly calling him 'lord' and saying:

'Sir, you've fared better than anyone before: no other knight who's come here has ever left; they've stayed here, either alive or dead – and if his sweetheart was with him she had to stay here, too. Rightly or wrongly they never left this house but remained here in my power; that was the way I wanted it, and I'll tell you why.

'One morning, some three or four years ago, I was out on my own, riding happily on my mule, wandering this way and that as chance took me, when I came to a tower about half a league from here. At the foot of a rock I saw a young man lying dead, stripped of his arms. He'd only just been killed. I stopped – and what a mistake that was: I was looking so intently at the youth that before I knew it a knight was suddenly before me – a knight of great renown named Greoreas.[23] He'd long been wooing me but I'd always rejected his advances: I'd no desire for him; I wouldn't give him my love at any price – I'd sooner have killed myself. This Greoreas rode up to me and took my mule by the reins, and said he had all he desired now that I was in his power, and that I should welcome it, because if I were willing to be his sweetheart and his lover he

---

[23] This is the Greoreas encountered by Gawain in Chrétien, above, p. 61.

would love me dearly: if I loved him he would love me a hundred times more than his own life! I'd recognised him instantly, and said:

'"Sir Greoreas, make sure you don't get carried away! You have me in your power, but that doesn't mean you should force your will upon me. I know you've loved me for a long while and have often begged for my love, but I've always resisted – simply because I've yet to see anything in you to make me feel I should be yours. I'm not saying you lack chivalry, but I'm not yet inclined to love anyone. Don't be upset or bear me ill-will if I ask you to wait till a year from today; then I'll accept your love and you shall have mine."

'God knows I said this just so I could get away! But the treacherous knight looked at me and said:

'"God curse me if I agree to delay when I have you in my power! If I let you slip away I'll just be prolonging my pain!"

'Then he seized me and – I'm not ashamed to admit it – raped me. As soon as I could get away I went and protested to the king who has the power to deal with such matters – but he exacted little punishment, it seemed to me. I returned here downcast, depressed, enraged! I went to Greoreas, who'd sought my love so long, and gave myself to him on condition that he'd do whatever I said; he was delighted and promised he would. So I told him that if he wanted to have my love he'd have to go along with me in all things, for better or for worse, and if any knight came to take lodging here he'd have to fight him without demur, with all his might, until he'd killed him or taken him captive. He's done so now for a long time, and all the while I've been convinced that someone would turn up and take revenge! But in the meantime he's killed many knights.'

'Truly, damsel,' Gawain said, 'that was very wrong. The knight was tried for his heinous crime by the king's household, and he suffered disgrace enough: for a whole month he was made to eat nothing but bread and water from the floor between his feet, with his hands tied.'[24]

'What?' said the girl. 'You saw it with your own eyes?'

'I did – and I was the one who imposed the punishment for his grave misdeed.'

'Really? What's your name, then, sir?'

'Gawain, damsel, King Arthur's nephew and son of King Lot.'

Hearing this she spoke with courteous eloquence, saying: 'Bless the hour, sir, I gave you lodging here! My heart yearned for nothing so much as to entertain and honour you and offer comfort and joy and courtesy, in return for the honour you paid me at court, where you saw me rather gauche and foolish, unable properly to put my case. You're not hard-hearted: you took pity on me and spoke for me and helped me achieve my aim. I love you for it and I always shall: this house and all within it is yours!'

At that a line of twenty girls entered, one after the other, who'd have looked elegant and fair indeed had they been properly dressed; and all twenty knelt before Gawain and begged his mercy and told him all about themselves and what they were enduring.

'Sir,' they said, 'we're imprisoned here against our will, though all of us are of noble line. We've all lost our sweethearts in this house, but now at last the one who killed them has been defeated and forced to submit! He used to be lord of this place, but he has found his master in you, and the lordship now is yours. Our life and death depend on you, and we have come to beg you, in the name of holy charity, to have pity on us

---

[24] See above, p. 61, where we are told he was made to eat 'with the dogs for a month, with his hands tied behind his back'.

and free us from this place where we dwell in deep distress and torment. There's no escape from here; and we have to weave and sew all day. If we ever chance to take a nap – not having slept even half the night! – and fail to fulfil our work for the week, we're stripped and birched three times until we bleed! And we're given nothing to eat but bread and water, however hard we work – even if we've avoided napping! It's not the life we long for, that's for sure! So we've come to beg you, sir: free us from this dreadful torment, or for the love of God kill us right here and now! Every one of us would rather die than continue to live as we've done so long!'

Sir Gawain heard their clamorous appeal and it pained his heart. He turned to the damsel and implored her on the girls' behalf: 'Damsel, if ever in my life I've done you any service I ask that you reward it now by letting all these girls – who'd look fair indeed if they were properly dressed – go freely and happily home to their lands in the morning.'

'By Saint Martin, sir,' she replied, 'I would never refuse the boon you ask if I were lady of the house – but by my soul I'm not! I have no authority over you – to give or deny them leave is entirely up to you!'

'Then truly, lady, I'll gladly give them leave, if you agree.'

'I do, sir; in all humility I grant them leave for your sake. I'll be happy to see each girl return to her own land tomorrow morning.'

Sir Gawain was very glad, and said: 'Young ladies, when morning comes you're free to go wherever you wish: no one will stand in your way!'

Hearing this the damsels showered him with thanks. Then ten boys came with cloths and set up the tables and laid them perfectly; another boy brought water, and Gawain and the damsel and the vanquished knight washed their hands and sat down at the table. The three of them sat on their own, apart from the others: Gawain had the girls sit separately but right where he could see them. They were served by two fine, handsome, charming youths who provided for their every wish; but Gawain was concerned above all that the girls should be properly served. After eating at length and leisure they rose at once and the beds were prepared, and as soon as they wished they lay down and slept till morning.

At first light, as the sun's bright rays came shining down, Sir Gawain woke and was into his clothes and shoes very early; but he entered the hall to find all the girls already up! They wished him good day and he replied:

'Girls, may God send you all the honour I would wish.'

Then he saw the damsel appear from a chamber: she, too, had already risen. They exchanged greetings, and then he asked her for his arms, and she said:

'What, sir? What do you mean? You're lord of this house and all its land: you should stay and maintain it – if you're willing.'

'Truly, I can't,' he said. 'I'd be breaking an oath.[25] Don't be upset: I promise you, if I achieve my present mission and you ever need my help, you may send for me with confidence, secure in the knowledge that I'll never fail to bring you aid.'

The damsel thanked him, and Gawain asked her to send for his arms at once. She knew there was no dissuading him, so she called for his arms and he began to don them. As soon as he was armed he asked for his horse, saying he would then be gone; but first, if it pleased her, he would like to ask a favour in return for his service, and was

---

[25] Gawain is under more than one obligation: he has to find the lance that bleeds and return it to the king of Escavalon, and the dwarf has reminded him of his earlier vow to raise the siege at Montesclaire.

sure that she would grant it. She told him to feel free, for she was his to command, and he asked her in God's name to return to the girls the palfreys they'd been riding when they first arrived at the house, so that they could all be on their way. The damsel did exactly as he asked and had their mounts returned. Then Gawain took up his weapons and mounted his horse, and all the girls, too, mounted their palfreys in the courtyard, blessing the hour they were born now that they were free to leave that place. Gawain took his leave, delighted to have such fair company, and set off. But he sent all the girls out first, still fearing as he did some trickery; then he rode out behind them, and on they went, rejoicing and happy, till they came to the edge of the open land where paths forked away in three directions. There he commended them to God and they feelingly returned his wish, thanking him deeply for restoring them to happiness. Then they all went their separate ways.

The Broken Sword

Until about noon, I tell you truly, Gawain kept riding at a good, swift pace, all alone through the dark forest, over hill and plain, through wood and valley, this way and that, until he came at last to a great river, deep and swift and wide. He looked along the high, rocky banks but could see no plank or bridge or ford where it would be possible to cross. So he wandered along beside the river, hoping to find a path or track or crossing-place.

As he did so his mind turned to the lance he was meant to be seeking; but he didn't know where – or even to which land – chance had brought him, and he felt very foolish, thinking he'd been dallying too long. He was fiercely anxious now to fulfil his oath – and then there was the matter of his promise to go to the aid of the damsel besieged at Montesclaire. He wondered what to do: he didn't know which way to go, or who to ask for directions. He decided to ride on until he found some knight or damsel who could give him news or guidance. So he turned away from the river and headed for a rocky height. He lashed and spurred his horse till he reached the top; but then Gawain, that knight so full of fine qualities, rode for a whole fortnight without finding anything but flat, open land,[26] and he was nearly mad with frustration at seeing no way to further either of his missions.

'Truly,' he said, 'I've never known anything like this: I've never felt so utterly thwarted!'

Then he looked towards a wood and saw something to cheer him: at the edge of the forest was a great, tall tower. He himself vouched for its impressiveness: he was full of praise for the fortress. Sir Gawain, greatly heartened, headed that way and came to the gate, where a drawbridge was lowered and he rode straight into the hall and dismounted from Gringalet. More than a hundred boys came running to attend him, and entrusted his horse to the mareschal* who provided him with oats and hay. The boys disarmed Sir Gawain in the plushest, most handsome suite of lodgings you'd find from here to Limoges: the lord had had them built of shining new marble. Equally new was the gown

---

[26] There is possibly a scribal error here. All the details – the uncrossable river and the riding to the rocky height, followed in a moment by spotting a tower (and even the coming reference to Limoges) – are echoes, presumably designed to appeal to the memories of sharp readers and listeners, of Perceval's first sighting of the Fisher King's castle in Chrétien (above, p. 27). This mention of a fortnight's journey is therefore inappropriate, and is perhaps a scribal misreading of a line which may originally have said something like 'he could see nothing for many miles [i.e. the distance ridden in a fortnight] but flat, open land'.

of fur-lined samite that they brought him; and that knight of proven valour took it and donned it at once, whereupon, without more ado, they led him back to the hall. Dressed in that rich attire as he was, he looked anything but drab!

Escorted by the boys he came into the hall; and there he found a distinguished, somewhat grey-haired nobleman sitting on a bed. He was no shabby penitent or idle rogue: his gown alone was worth a hundred marks,* and his hat wasn't made of straw but of black sable covered with rich Alexandrian purple;* and the hat was crowned with a beautiful golden coronet laden with jaspers and sardonyx and glittering jewels, the most perfect imaginable. He was a wealthy man indeed, that lord seated on the bed; and his joy and pleasure would have been as great as his riches had he not been maimed and helpless – but I'm not going to explain just yet how that had come to be. As Sir Gawain came up to the rich lord with his fine household of retainers, well-bred and well-spoken, the worthy man greeted him at once. Gawain promptly returned the greeting, and the lord, with no thought for his own discomfort, invited him to sit at his side. Once he was seated the worthy man asked him where he was from, and from which land, and Gawain, with no reason to conceal it, told him everything. They were completely at ease – it was a place lacking nothing a lord or knight could wish – and they spoke of many things. The cooks had the food ready, and boys promptly brought basins full of warm water for the washing of hands, while others brought a towel to dry them. As soon as they were washed and dried two boys smartly brought trestles of cypress wood and laid a table on top – but if I told you what it was made of you'd think I was making it up! Another boy spread a cloth upon it, the finest and whitest you'd find anywhere from here to Aleppo.[27] The hall wasn't plunged in barn-like gloom: there were so many candles burning that it was bathed in a beautiful light.

They hadn't been seated long at dinner when they saw a boy emerge from a chamber, the most handsome, I think, that any man ever beheld: anyone who saw him would have deemed him the fairest youth in all the world. In his hand he was holding a smooth, shining lance. He passed right before Sir Gawain. And the head of the lance was bleeding in a ceaseless flow. Straight through the hall the boy passed. Then, through the door of another room, Gawain saw a most fair and comely girl appear: he gazed at her intently and thought her very beautiful. She was holding in her hand a little silver trencher. She walked past everyone, following the lance. After this Sir Gawain saw two more boys carrying candlesticks filled with burning candles. Gawain yearned and longed to ask who these people were and where they were from. And while he was thinking this he saw, passing through the hall after the boys, a girl of notable grace and beauty, but she was weeping in great distress; and in her hands she was holding aloft a grail for all to see. Gawain saw it very clearly. And he wondered why she was weeping so much, and where she was going and what she was carrying; he was very puzzled that she should be so upset and unable to stop crying. She passed before them swiftly and went straight into another room. As soon as she'd disappeared with the grail, four boys entered carrying a bier covered with a rich, regal cloth, and in the bier lay a body. And on top of the cloth lay a sword which was broken across the middle, though anyone who hadn't known would never have noticed that the sword wasn't in one piece. The four boys carried the bier right through the hall; none of those assembled there addressed them in any way; nor did the boys utter a single word to them. Gawain was mystified by it all, and longed to ask who they were and why they were there and where they'd come

---

[27] 'Halape'.

from and where they were going. The four boys with the bier disappeared into a chamber. But little more than a moment later the boy reappeared with the shining lance whose tip shed blood though it had neither flesh nor vein; then the girl returned and passed before them with the silver trencher; after her came the two boys with the candlesticks; then came the bejewelled grail, carried by the weeping girl; and only just behind them was the bier. Three times they processed through the house like this, and everyone present in the hall had a clear and open view. Sir Gawain saw them just like all the others, and was completely mystified. Then it dawned on him and he knew for sure, without a doubt, that they were the grail and the lance he was meant to be seeking. He drew himself closer to the worthy lord and asked him the significance of the grail and the lance and why the girl was weeping. He went straight on and asked why the bier was being carried so: he dearly wished the lord would tell him, if he could – and also why the burnished sword was placed upon the bier. And that lord endowed with all noble qualities replied that he would tell him indeed, if he were worthy to know. He called four boys and said:

'Go and bring me that good sword of mine.'

They ran and fetched it; but it was broken across the middle, and they delivered it to their lord in pieces. This broken sword, I should tell you, had been sent to him by a niece of his as a token of affection. He took it and handed it to the knight who was so eager to fathom the mysteries; but all he would say was this: that if he could join the sword and fuse one part of the blade to the other to make it whole again, 'then you can learn the truth and meaning of the bier and the grail and the lance, and why the maiden weeps'.

Without more ado Gawain took the pieces and joined them. They fitted together as one, and everyone who saw it thought it was whole again. Then the lord said:

'Take the blade by the point and pull. If you don't pull it apart, then you will learn the whole and perfect truth about the mystery of the grail and the lance and the bier.'

So Gawain took the sword and pulled; and at the very first tug he parted one piece of the blade from the other.

'You have not yet achieved enough as a knight,' said the lord, 'to know the truth about this mystery. The one who comes to know it will be deemed the finest knight in the world, I promise you. But you may yet come to know, and by your chivalry win esteem and pre-eminence over all the world.'

While the lord was speaking thus, Gawain listened and hung on his every word – until he slumped asleep over the table. And don't think I'm making up stories now – I won't tell you a word of a lie if I can help it: he slept solidly all night till morning came, when he woke and was astonished to find himself in a marsh with his arms and his gear beside him and his horse tethered to a tree by a hedged enclosure. He was alarmed and bewildered to find himself there, and full of vexation and self-recrimination at having failed to learn the secrets that he so longed to know. He'd have given anything to have succeeded: he was shaking and trembling with rage.

He took up his arms and donned them, and when he was armed he came to the elm where his horse was tethered and mounted at once and rode away, head bowed, deeply troubled.

But after much thought he raised his head again and said: 'Well, what of it? Whether I like it or not there's nothing I can do: I need to take up another challenge, and make sure I see it through to the end. It's no use carrying on with a task you can't accomplish: it's better to move on.'

Gawain's Adventure at Montesclaire

While he was saying this he passed into a great forest. All day long without a break he rode swiftly through this dark forest, finding no end to it that day and having to sleep there all night and wait for morning. He took off his horse's bridle and fastened a halter and left him to graze, while he lay down beneath a beech tree; but he slept very little that night, and I'm not surprised.

When the sun rose and it grew light next morning he mounted again, took up his lance and set off. But he rode all day without a stop and didn't meet anyone worth mentioning. On he pressed till none* when he finally came to open ground. Then to his delight he heard a loud blast on a horn, and out of the forest he saw a vavasor* come riding, a man in the prime of life; he'd been hunting in the woods that day, and behind him was tied a roebuck that he'd caught in the forest. This vavasor, of high repute, seeing Sir Gawain approach, rode straight up and greeted him with a heartfelt 'Welcome, sir!' And Gawain, courteous man that he was, replied just as warmly.

'Sir, sir,' said the vavasor, 'I'm delighted to meet you! If you wish and have no objection, come and lodge with me tonight: my house is a good place and ready to receive a guest: please don't decline.'

Sir Gawain thanked him for the offer and said he'd accept with pleasure, very gladly.

'In that case, sir, you're welcome indeed! I haven't been so pleased to have a guest for a long while: you seem a most worthy man.'

So off they rode together, talking of one thing and another until Gawain asked the vavasor his name, wishing very much to know.

'Truly, sir,' he said, 'my name is Galehés de Bonivant; and what is yours, good sir?'

And he, never slow to give his name, replied: 'I am Gawain, sir.'

When Galehés heard that name his heart leapt with joy and he said: 'Now I'm more pleased than ever, by God! I'm glad I didn't fail to ask your name! This is the best news I could have had! I've heard such fine reports of you that I've always longed to serve you. I'm so pleased you've accepted my hospitality!'

Talking of this and that they rode together to a handsome manor house, very strong and commodious, well fortified with walls of stone and impressive towers, and wide, deep, water-filled moats. The drawbridge was down and they rode straight over and into the courtyard. Then the worthy lord blew a loud blast on his horn, whereupon ten boys came running; they dismounted at once, and handed their horses to the boys to take care of. Without more ado Galehés took Gawain and led him up to the hall, where two boys disarmed him with deft efficiency and a third dressed him in a mantle of samite lined with vair.*

Just then a lady entered through the open door of a chamber, and you never heard tell of a fairer woman. When Gawain saw her he greeted her most courteously and she greeted him likewise. And she wasn't unattended: with her came four girls, hand in hand. The lord and lady of the house now went aside with Gawain and sat together with him on a couch, where they spoke of many things till it was time to eat. Then four boys came and set up the tables and laid the cloths, and the three of them stood and washed their hands before taking their seats. They were served with at least five or six dishes, I believe, before they rose from the table, and when they did so the tables were cleared and they washed their hands once more.

Then the lord asked Sir Gawain where he was headed – if it wasn't a secret he would be very glad to know. Hearing his interest in his mission and trusting in his integrity, Gawain replied:

'God save me, sir, I'll gladly tell you. Some nine months ago my lord the king was at Carlion, holding a great celebration for a dear friend of his;[28] and in the middle of the feast a maiden arrived at court with all manner of news. And she swore that any knight who wanted to be deemed the finest in the world should go, if he was brave enough, straight to the peak of Montesclaire where a damsel was besieged: if he could raise the siege he could count himself the most praiseworthy of all knights in the whole wide world; and she gave us to believe that he'd be able to gird on the Sword of the Strange Belt.'

'By my life, sir,' said Galehés, 'she told you the truth. The castle's so near here that if you took the right path you'd be there by prime tomorrow. But it's not an easy ride! The castle stands on a solid crag, the most imposing and perfectly formed in the world and so high that no shot from sling or bow, however strong, could ever reach the top; and the path up is so narrow, truly, that no horse can make the climb. At the foot of the peak, at the very bottom of the narrow path, springs a gentle fount called the Spring of the Laurel; three knights stand guard there constantly, night and day, and they've ravaged the land so utterly that nothing grows there. Those besieged on the peak can get no supplies from outside: it's taken just the three knights to blockade the castle, and they've been sat there for a long time now, and I'll tell you why.

'At about this time of year, some while ago, one of them declared his love for the damsel and asked for her love in return, but she was adamant that she would never love him and didn't want a lover. When he heard her refusal he warned her to beware of him, for no one was going to stop him laying siege to her castle and he'd carry on till she bowed to his will. They've been there ever since; they haven't moved. They've caused the people of the castle no end of trouble: no one and nothing gets in or out. If any knight chances to pass that way he's forced to fight the three till they strike him dead. And before they do battle they sound a horn: they want the suffering people in the castle to come and watch, and see how they deal with anyone who tries to get past them; this makes their grief and torment worse. That's how they carry on, those three: they're brothers, and they call themselves the three black knights of the desolate waste.'

'By my life,' said Gawain, 'this is an outrage! It would be a great deed to get rid of them when they're so wicked and cruel! I've no intention of doing anything else! I came on their account and no one's going to see me shirk the mission! I wouldn't give up this battle for anything, by God – not even if you offered me a city!'

'Ah, by the holy trinity,' said Galehés, 'don't say that! You'd be mad to take on those three! If you fight them on your own you'll never escape alive! I wouldn't want to see you killed, no, not for all the riches in the world: I'd rather see the castle reduced to soot and ash! Just wait three days and I'll give you knights of the highest calibre – a good eight or ten or twelve – to help you pull it off.'

'Come now!' replied Sir Gawain. 'What do you take me for? Truly, if I had companions in the battle and we came out on top, what praise and credit would it bring me? Thanks, but I'll decline your offer: when I leave here I'll have no companion to help me except God. I undertook this mission alone, I'll see it through alone, and I alone shall have the praise if it be God's will – or else I'll come off the worse. Nothing's going to change my mind.'

Galehés could see that the matter was settled and they said no more. Instead he called for wine; and they had, I believe, great handfuls of cloves, and sweetmeats and electuaries.*

---

[28] i.e. Perceval; above, pp. 41–2.

Then all the beds were made and they lay down to sleep. But before Sir Gawain took to his bed Galehés asked him to grant a harmless favour; Gawain agreed to do so, provided it would incur no reproach or shame. With that they parted.

Gawain went to bed, in urgent need of rest, and enjoyed unbroken sleep till day had fully dawned; then seeing the brightness of the sun he rose and dressed and left the chamber where he'd slept and went into the hall. There he saw Galehés already up and on his way to wake him. He greeted him, and Galehés wasn't slow to return the greeting, saying:

'Sir, may the one who made and shaped the world as He saw fit guard and protect you this day and grant you all success. I can see you're set and ready to be on your way.'

'Indeed I am, sir,' Gawain replied. 'Bid them bring my arms.'

'By God, I shall, sir, with pleasure,' said Galehés. 'But first hear the favour you promised me, if you will. It's this: I dearly wish to go with you if you'll let me. I want it more than anything – I know the way exactly. And I want to be there when you fight them, so that if you win I can bear witness far and wide that I saw them defeated and you victorious!'

'Truly, I shan't refuse you that,' said Gawain. 'It's granted – as long as you promise not to help me.'

Galehés gave his word and thanked him for the boon; then he called for new armour and Gawain armed himself splendidly. Once he was armed he mounted his horse and was handed a white shield which he hung round his neck before taking his lance. Then Galehés armed in turn and leapt on his horse without using the stirrup, and they both took their leave and set off.

They kept riding till they were within two bowshots of Montesclaire. Then Gawain saw the tent pitched by the spring, and turned and eagerly asked if it was the one he sought: the tent of the three knights who were plaguing the land. Galehés assured him that it was.

'In that case,' he said, 'I pray you go no further: stay here and wait for me.'

'Gladly, sir,' said Galehés, and without another word Gawain set off, hungry for battle.

It didn't take long for the knights to see him, and as soon as he was spotted they blew a mighty blast on a horn, enough to make the very ground shake; and high up on the castle walls people could be seen lining the battlements, hoping against hope for deliverance. The three knights mounted at once and charged up to Gawain without drawing rein, and without a single word of warning they smashed their spears into his shield with all their force, shattering and splintering them. But they breached neither shield nor hauberk, and galloped past leaving Gawain still upright in the saddle. He spurred forward a little, then turned to face them, and delivered such a charge that he struck one right through the chest, driving him from his stirrups and dead to the ground: against Gawain's lance neither shield nor mail had been worth a jot. Now he had fewer enemies: now they were one down! Seeing their fellow fall, they drew their swords and came at Gawain, vowing they'd count themselves shamed indeed and worthless wretches if the death he'd dealt wasn't dearly bought. They attacked him again, those insatiable knaves, though their efforts were doomed to fail. They rained and hammered blows upon him, but that accomplished knight dealt two for every one of theirs, delivering blow after furious blow with his scything sword, hacking through shields and slicing through mail, his blade soon drenched from drawing blood. But they were inflicting heavy damage, too: they'd left him with less than a foot of shield, and breached his hauberk and stove his helm and battered him till blood was pouring from his nose – his shield had started white but now was crimson. Two against one was no even fight, that's for sure; but Gawain was undaunted, and fought back fearsomely. He struck from right and left, and his fine blade bit deep;[29] but his blows were growing weaker than before, and his two foes noticed this and pressed him all the harder. But he summoned up a blow with his whetted blade that severed the head of one and sent it flying: it was whipped clean off – he knew nothing about it; and the other, seeing this, burned and blazed with rage: he clutched his sword with both hands and came at Gawain and struck out at him, but Gawain, primed and on his mettle, dodged aside. The blow completely missed, and the unstoppable momentum plunged the sword into the ground; and as the knight twisted it to try and pull it out, the blade broke in his hands. He was aghast, horrified – now he was in trouble, bereft of a sword! He turned to Gawain and begged for mercy in God's name; and Gawain, cruelty being a stranger to his nature, granted it on condition that he would do exactly as bidden.

'That's all I ask, sir!' said the knight. 'Command, and I'll obey.'

When the people above on Montesclaire saw the three brothers had been vanquished they were overwhelmed with joy, and rushed to tell their lady what had happened. When she heard the news she ordered them to make ready, for she was going to the mountain's foot to see the finest knight in the world who had brought them salvation at last.[30] Then you'd have seen no end of horses saddled in the city: fully two thousand, I believe, rode out – no maiden ever left a castle with such a great and raucous company as she did then! The damsel's complexion was neither pale nor ruddy, but a perfect blend of white and rose; and I assure you, she was the finest figure of a woman ever seen: so she was deemed wherever she went. She rode swiftly down to the mountain's foot, and Galehés, jubilant after seeing the battle, hurried up to Gawain and said:

'Sir, here comes the damsel – my niece, she is – who's lady of all the surrounding land! She comes to you now as her long-awaited lord! She wants to hold this land as your vassal. She's coming to find you and take you back to the castle.'

'Only too glad!' said Gawain. 'I want to go there very much.'

So he mounted, and bade his defeated foe mount likewise, and the three of them rode to the mountain's foot where they met the damsel. Gawain, delighted at the meeting, stepped down from his horse; the damsel dismounted, too, and came to him, and they exchanged most fair and courteous greetings. Gawain delivered the vanquished knight to her, and asked her to forgive him her wrath for his sake and to spare his life.

'Truly, sir,' she replied, 'if that's your wish I'll temper my wrath. But come now, I pray you, up to the castle; no people in all the world love you as much as they, that's certain. Come and see them!'

'Indeed I shall,' said Gawain. 'I have business there.'

So the company led him back up the mountain, doing all they could to serve and honour him; but I'm not going to spend time describing all their celebrations. The damsel, though, was making a great fuss of her uncle Galehés, for at All Saints it would be a year since she'd seen him; and she asked him if he knew the knight's name.

'I'd be lying if I said I didn't!' he replied. 'And why would I keep it from you? His name is Gawain, the son of King Lot.'

When the damsel heard this she was overjoyed.

---

[29] Literally 'did not rebound'.
[30] Literally 'had freed them from orphanhood [i.e. defencelessness]'.

They pressed on swiftly to the great walled city. The whole town was festooned with silk, even the narrowest streets: Gawain could safely say it had been a good day for him! And as they made their joyous arrival at the castle, he asked for someone to bring him the sword he'd come to find:[31] it was the very reason he'd left his own land – he'd been told it would be given to the one who raised the siege, and he trusted the promise would be honoured. The damsel heard his request, but said:

'Good sir, we have to tell you: the sword isn't in our gift. It's true that it's rightly yours – everyone knows that; but we don't know how it's to come to you. But we'll gladly show you where it's kept: it's been there at least a hundred years. God grant that you have it now in safety, without trouble.'

'By my life,' said Gawain, 'wherever it is I'll go there, lady, come what may.'

There was nothing she could do to stop him; she took him there with a heavy heart, greatly fearing it would be his death. There was a garden below the keep, enclosed by high, high walls, and in it, dug deep in the ground, was a grotto. At the entrance to this was an iron door which by all accounts had never been opened for a hundred years or more; and here, in this secret grotto, was the Sword of the Strange Belt. That supremely praised knight, handsomely and nobly armed, followed by a great host of people, marched straight to the grotto. And amazingly, the door swung open before him, much to the excitement of everyone, and the damsel was filled with new heart and hope that her longed-for deliverance would be complete. Gawain, thrilled to see the door swing open, went through and down the stairway that led to the grotto's depths; he was clutching his drawn sword, ready to fight if anyone tried to attack him – not that he was worried. When he reached the bottom he looked ahead and saw, according to all accounts, the most dazzling light he'd ever seen; but still he was undaunted, and strode forward down another flight of steps and into a chamber. It wasn't panelled with wood like all the rest: from floor to ceiling the walls were made of pure, gleaming gold, and I'm amazed to say the ceiling itself was silver. It was the most splendid, beautiful place he'd ever seen, and the source of light was a vast array of precious stones dotted all around: as Gawain, looking eagerly for what he sought, peered across the chamber he saw a golden pillar standing in the middle, and from it shone a golden carbuncle shedding a light as bright as any sunbeam. And hanging on this pillar he could see a wondrous sword – I'd be wasting my time if I tried to describe it – and above it was an inscription saying:

> Knight, in constant search of prowess and renown,
> Behold! On this pillar hangs
> The Sword of the Strange Belt.
> If you trust in yourself enough
> You may take it without hindrance.

Gawain, who knew how to read, thrust out his right hand and grasped the sword, unhooked it from the pillar and hung it at his left side. He was utterly, irrepressibly elated! He turned and headed straight back out of the grotto to where everyone was waiting. They were very afraid that he wouldn't return; and when they saw him safe and sound and bearing back the sword they were overcome with relief and joy, for in truth they hadn't expected to see him ever again. The damsel, rejoicing, thrilled by the

---

[31] i.e. the Sword of the Strange Belt.

wondrous outcome, came and took his hand and led him up to the hall and had him disarmed. Then ladies, knights and serving-boys alike began to dance and sing, accompanied by all manner of priceless instruments. Greater jubilation couldn't be imagined or described! They threw themselves into their songs and dances with a passion! But what's the point of piling words on words? The damsel, overcome with joy, took Gawain aside and asked him his name. She'd been waiting for him for a very long time, she said, but, thank God, he'd now thoroughly fulfilled his promise.[32]

'Oh, God help me, lady, I'm sorry I was a long time coming! Put it down to sheer foolishness! And forgive me, I pray, for the trouble I've caused.'

'Enough of that, sir!' she replied. 'Think nothing of it! Consider me your friend now, truly, in every way; your every honourable wish I'll strive to fulfil.'

Hearing this, Gawain gave her sweet and courteous thanks and said: 'That's good enough for me! So tell me, if it's no trouble, the truth about the Sword of the Strange Belt – if it's a truth you can reveal. Its fame has spread far and wide.'

'By my life, sir,' she replied, 'it would be wrong of me to hide it from you when you're clearly worthy to have the sword. You should certainly know how it came to be here. You've no doubt heard, like many here, how Joseph of Arimathea – a very fine knight – came to this land after the death of Our Lord, who'd been wrongly crucified by the treacherous Jews. When Joseph landed here he brought with him this sword, which had belonged to Judas Maccabeus; and it's said that when that worthy soul died he sent the sword straight to this castle, with instructions that it should be placed in the grotto and never hang at any knight's side unless he'd proved himself to be of greater courtesy, honour, chivalry and valour than any other. So the sword was taken there, and as soon as its bearer left the grotto the solid iron door shut fast behind him, and no one since could ever open it. I've seen many great men of high renown, reputed to be valiant knights indeed, come and try to open the door, but in vain: they came back in a sorry state, in body or in mind. No man of woman born, I've always been told, has ever had any success but you – and you've brought back the sword! And this you should know: anyone bearing that sword in battle when right is on his side will be invincible; but if his cause is unjust it'll be sure to work against him, and he'll turn coward, unable to fight on.'

'My word,' said Sir Gawain, 'it's no worse a sword for that! No, by God, I'd say it's all the better!'

They spent a long while talking together, and when at last they rose it was time to eat – and they dined at leisure, most happily.

Gawain stayed a whole week at Montesclaire while he had his wounds examined and treated. But once they'd healed, so the story says, as he lay in bed one morning his thoughts turned to the lance he'd seen shed shining blood from its sharp tip. It led him to remember the promise he'd made at Escavalon almost a year before: to deliver the bleeding lance on the appointed day or to defend himself in combat against the charge levelled against him.[33] He rose at once and went straight to the hall. He found the damsel already up and asked for his arms and that his horse be saddled.

'What do you mean, good sir?' she said. 'Sir, tell me.'

'Truly, lady,' he replied, 'there's a matter I need to address: a mission that I can't neglect at any price if I'm to avoid lasting shame for myself and all my kin. It's no use

---

[32] i.e. the promise he'd made in Chrétien's romance to raise the siege at Montesclaire.
[33] Guigambresil's charge of treachery. To be precise, Gawain had promised to bring back the bleeding lance or submit to imprisonment: see Chrétien, above, p. 54.

trying to stop me – nothing will make me stay. Send for my arms quickly and I'll be gone: nothing anyone says will change my mind.'

'Ah! By the true cross, good sir,' she said, 'stay with us! Will you leave this city bereft, abandoned? Our only hope is in God and you! You've saved Montesclaire from disaster: will you leave so soon? In God's name, don't! Stay and defend the land! It's yours now: you've won it – I relinquish it and bequeath it to you: it means nothing to me now!'[34]

The damsel and everyone else implored him to stay and take the land as his own and be its lord; but he insisted that he couldn't and wouldn't.

She saw there was nothing else for it, and bade two boys bring him new arms; and when he was armed he called for the sword he'd won: the damsel had it ready, and gave it to him, and he girded it at his side. Then they brought him his horse and he mounted at once and hung his shield from his neck; and he took his leave of all the people, especially of the damsel and of his host the worthy Galehés who was at his side, and then left without more ado. Then you'd have seen everyone throughout the town weeping all together, so bitterly that you'd have thought they'd all just lost a father; they were saying:

'Sir, you've saved us from imminent death and harm and orphanhood and ruin! What shall we do, now you're leaving us? We'll never find such a worthy lord!'

Such was their lament.

And meanwhile Gawain rode for a whole fortnight, this way and that way, without furthering his mission in the slightest: he was nearly going out of his mind.

Gawain is Accused Again

As he remembered the vow he'd made he shook in every limb with tortured worry, fearing he was going to miss the appointed day of battle.

One morning he rose from sleep in a hermitage where he'd spent the night, and as soon as he was dressed and armed he left the hermitage and rode on swiftly till he came to a forest. He saw nothing to cheer him – in fact everything displeased and vexed him, as he had to scale a mountain, high and steep and massive. But beyond it lay a beautiful open plain, dotted with trees, and Gawain saw a knight and a maiden riding across it towards him. He politely asked them where they were going, but they replied very haughtily, saying:

'What's it to do with you? You'd be better keeping your mouth shut than sounding off. What does it matter to you where we're going?'

'Come now!' said Sir Gawain. 'Don't be so ill-mannered. Answer my question and have done – I mean no harm.'

'By God the Father,' said the knight, 'are you some kind of idiot? I'm not telling you a thing about myself, but you're going to tell me your business – and whatever it may be I'll know your name. Out with it, and tell me straight – I insist!'

Gawain didn't hesitate; he said: 'Since you're so keen to know I'll not keep my name from you. I'll tell you gladly: the Britons call me Gawain, and I'm King Arthur's nephew.'

'By God and His might!' said the knight. 'It's Gawain I've been looking for! And now I've found him, thanks be to God! Know, then, I defy you! You're going to pay for my father's death right here and now! I'll never rest as long as you prosper! I yearn to shame and humble you – right is plainly on my side – and God give me the power!'

---

[34] Literally 'it's of no more value to me now than a hawthorn berry'.

He drew back and set his lance in its rest; then they charged straight at each other in such a fury that they sent a yard and a half of their lances rasping through their wooden shields, and stout and sturdy though they were, both shafts shattered. So they came back at each other with their swords of tempered steel and exchanged tremendous blows to head and body, wasting none: no king or count ever saw a better-fought battle; none so fine indeed will ever be seen, as each strove with all his might to bring the other to grief and humble him. But finally the point came when the knight, who wearied sooner, said:

'That's enough, Gawain! And I'll tell you why: if you kill me (or I kill you) your renown won't be enhanced in any way – nor will you be believed, for no one's present to witness it. So I say we postpone our battle for now on the following terms – I know I can count on you: as soon as I meet you at any court, be it in the near or the distant future, if I summon you to fulfil your promise you'll do battle with me immediately, and seek no excuse.'

Gawain gave his word, saying: 'If that's your wish and you want to postpone, I'd like to know your name before you leave.'

'Truly, sir, my name's Dinadaret. I've known warfare more than I've known peace: I never tire of battle! But tell me now, where are you heading from here?'

'I shan't be dallying: I've business to see to – a battle I have to fight before the king of Escavalon. But by the worthy Saint Ladre,[35] I fear I've already delayed too long: I've been under oath to go there since last summer, and I'm afraid I shan't be there in time – I must be on my way! So I'm going – I commend you to God.'

And Dinadaret commended him to the Lord God, too.

A Double Duel

Then Gawain set out across the plain down a well-made road and pressed on day by day till he reached Escavalon, where he dismounted at a mounting-block right below the tower.[36] He kept his shield and all his arms except his lance: he was feeling wary and cautious, knowing he was little loved there. Into the hall he strode, fully armed, and greeted the king and said:

'In faith, sire, I have come to keep my oath. I've striven hard to find the grail and lance: I haven't stopped searching for a whole winter and summer; but since I've failed to find the lance I've come to submit as your prisoner, for I've no wish to act dishonestly.'

He fell silent then and said no more. But Guigambresil[37] leapt up and came before the king and said: 'Gawain has returned, my lord, and come what may I pray you let me do battle with him: I'll be denied no longer!'

'I'll see what my barons have to say about this,' the king replied. 'I know they'll judge the matter fairly for both parties.'

He rose at once and took his barons aside in private. The king was superbly dressed in rich red silk; if my source is to be believed he was a handsome and a courtly man indeed.

But while the king was consulting his barons a mighty knight arrived at court with a train of three warhorses clad in iron right down to the ground. Their reins and bits

---

[35] Like other lesser-known saints referred to in *The Story of the Grail*, Saint Ladre has particular connections with Picardy and Flanders.
[36] i.e. the tower at the centre of his adventure when he was besieged by the mob in Chrétien's romance, above, pp. 51–3.
[37] Who had charged him with treachery.

were so well fixed that no one could have seized either bit or rein;[38] and at his side a pair of serving-men carried two stout, sharp-headed ashwood lances, and another bore his shield, the finest ever made. It was thus he made his entrance to the court, and people flocked to see him. But he didn't stop or take a seat; the moment he set eyes on Gawain he brusquely cried:

'I summon you to keep your promise!'

The king hurried back from his deliberations, and the knight explained his business; and in the presence of all the court, as soon as they were assembled, he demanded that Gawain honour the vow he'd made on the heath three days before in the presence of the girl. But Guigambresil, too, was reminding Gawain of his oath and promise, saying he must either deliver the lance as he'd vowed or do battle with him forthwith. On the one side, then, was Dinadaret, demanding he be made to keep his pledge to him: he'd vowed to fight him as soon as they met at any court, regardless of any objection, so he wanted him to do battle now; and on the other side was Guigambresil, equally loud in his demand that Gawain must do battle with *him*. He wanted the decision in his favour – but so did Dinadaret. So the king ordered the most eminent men of the land to step aside and discuss whether Sir Gawain should fight on his own against both of them together or against each one in turn. The barons duly went to decide; one of them said:

'Sirs, I say he should fight them each in turn.'

Three or four said otherwise, and the one who was most learned in law argued and reasoned that, since Gawain was under oath to each, he should fight them both together at once, without delay, respite or excuse. Other barons were shocked by this and wouldn't agree; but he, well versed in law, explained the matter, saying to them all:

'Will he not be breaking his oath if he's unable to fight Guigambresil? But he swore to Dinadaret that he'd do battle as soon as he found him at any court – and behold, he's found him here. The right judgement, I think I've proved, is that he should fight them both together.'

Then all the barons, I understand, were persuaded that Gawain should fight both knights and returned to their seats, agreeing with his decision without dispute or fuss; and the one who'd made the judgement boldly reported their verdict to the king, saying:

'My lord, the court's view is that, since neither will defer his battle with him, this knight, alone though he is, should fight them both together.'

'Let's be about it then,' said the king, 'and quickly!'

Guigambresil armed with all possible speed, as boys rushed to fetch his arms and armed him from top to toe, finally lacing his helmet on his head; then, without a moment's delay, around his neck they slung a good, strong shield emblazoned with a leopard. Dinadaret, too, was splendidly armed, greatly impressing the crowd around him. Then everyone went to the windows of the tower to sit and watch the battle.

But there was a boy at the court who was a kinsman of Gawain, and he raced away to tell his uncle King Arthur the news that alarmed him so. He knew that neither the king nor any of Gawain's friends would be aware that he was committed to battle against two men of such esteem as the knights who were to fight him that very day, with no question of deferral. The boy was beside himself with worry and rushed to fetch help. He left the castle and galloped away on a strong, swift horse.

Just a league from the city, at the mouth of a little valley, he met Kay the seneschal

---

[38] i.e. avoiding the danger of losing control of the horse in combat.

riding along on a mighty destrier. Kay hailed him at once, and the boy drew rein as soon as he saw him and stopped there in the open field. Kay asked him:

'If you can spare the time, my friend, would you mind telling me who owns that splendid castle? It's strong enough to fear no assault.'

'Before God, sir,' the boy replied, 'it belongs to the king of Escavalon. There's none finer or stronger from here to Avalon, that's for sure! And there's about to be a battle there: one knight against two!'

'An unfair contest!' retorted Kay. 'And unchivalrous! No man with any decency should let a battle of one against two be held at his court! May the Lord God stand by the knight who's on his own and take his side!'

'He's a very fine knight, sir,' said the boy.

'Tell me, friend,' Kay said to him, 'who are the two who're joining forces?'

'One is named Dinadaret, a fierce, aggressive knight indeed, and the other is Guigambresil, who's thought to be rather more affable.'

'In faith, I know both of them well. I'd say the knight who's on his own has got his hands full! Who is he?'

'Gawain, sir, the son of King Lot. Tear out both my eyes if I've told you a word of a lie!'

'I'm sorry to hear that, indeed I am!' said Kay. 'So where are you off to now?'

'To find King Arthur, sir, and bring him here to intervene.'

'Keep going, then – he's not far off. God guide you on your way and see you safely back with him.'

Then Kay, with a hundred cries of 'alas!', rode straight off with the boy as he took the news that Kay found so distressing; and they didn't stop till they reached the camp where they found the king and his great company who'd been in search of Gawain ever since he'd left Guiromelant:[39] they were camped in a fine meadow beside a fast-flowing river. Kay didn't dally but went straight to the king and told him of his nephew Gawain's plight. The king realised how grave it was, and sweating with dismay and rage he said:

'When's this battle to be fought?'

'Imminently, sire!' said the boy who'd brought the news.

'And where, friend?'

'At Escavalon. We have to go now, quickly! There's no time to lose: when I left them earlier they were about to set to it!'

The king, trembling with fear and anger, sent word throughout the camp bidding everyone come straight after him: no one was to stay behind. As the good king of Britain mounted, so did all his people down to the very last page and servant, and as soon as they were ready they rode swiftly away behind their king.

Sir Yvain, alarmed by the news of Gawain's plight, instantly called for his horse to be saddled; it was done at once, without further debate, and that worthy, valiant knight mounted and set off ahead of the rest and pressed on to Escavalon, not stopping for anything till he came before the king. And the moment he saw him he said:

'Sire, I am King Arthur's man; he's sent me here on an urgent mission, indeed he has, for we've heard you mean to have Sir Gawain do imminent battle with two knights! He asks you not to take offence, but bids you through me: have mercy and postpone the battle.'

The king instantly ordered the lords presiding over the field to delay the start of the contest; and it wasn't long before King Arthur arrived – he certainly hadn't been dragging

---

[39] Above, p. 94.

his heels! The king of Escavalon went to meet him along with a mighty company, and gave him a splendid welcome: he was incapable of doing otherwise – it was ever his custom and he was a master at it! I praise him most of all for that: he was always pleased to meet worthy men and relished their company. And a man who serves and honours the worthy will soon have his reward; but those who serve the wicked will find their service and their efforts wasted. But by the saints, you're hard pressed to find worthy men – they're few and far between! How often it is that you take to a man and feel sure he's a truly worthy soul, and he proves to be a bag of wind! It's so easy to be deceived! But the king of Escavalon, putting heart and soul into serving King Arthur to the utmost of his powers, knew he'd found a worthy man and was bound to be rewarded. And you may be sure his service would be well repaid indeed, if God kept King Arthur from harm.

Into the court he came, and Sir Gawain's heart was filled with joy: he thought he would take wing when he saw the king his uncle! He would surely make peace and stop the perilous battle which Dinadaret and Guigambresil were so keen to fight. As Arthur entered he was served and honoured by young and old alike; and then he withdrew and summoned Guigambresil and Dinadaret to discuss peace terms. Agreement was duly reached, for Arthur gave them the hands of his nieces: they were married by the bishop of Escavalon. All the lords rejoiced at the making of peace and concord: not a single voice was raised against the plan proposed by the king who ruled all Britain.

And so it was that peace was made: Dinadaret took Autandre as his wife, and Guigambresil took another of Arthur's nieces – a maiden of high lineage, young and bright and spirited and fair: her name was Tanete la Petite. She was a girl of perfect beauty, and he had given her a very fine marriage. The weddings were held at Escavalon with many mitres and crosiers present, summoned by King Arthur; and every knight in all the isles of the sea attended: Arthur was delighted to see them all responding to his call and assembled there. What a great and glorious gathering! What joy and celebration! I've certainly never seen the like or heard tell of it in any tale.

And Arthur shrewdly took the chance to receive the homage and allegiance of all the barons, of every degree. I can't name them all and don't wish to try; but the king of Escavalon paid homage to Arthur immediately, much to his delight, and Dinadaret, a knight he respected highly, promptly followed suit, receiving his land as his vassal; so too did Guigambresil, which gave Arthur much joy and pleasure. What more should I tell you? They all became his liegemen, holding all they possessed as his vassals: every prince in all the isles of the sea became his man that day either willingly or by force, the king duly accepting their allegiance. How the king rejoiced in his heart as so many knights and barons – I can't name every one – received their lands as his vassals and he received their homage.

They were all united, all of a mind, it seems – all except just one: Brun de Branlant, a knight of high degree. He wouldn't show any respect to Arthur, and rode away most offensively. All at that court had sworn fealty, receiving their lands from the king; every knight from all the isles of the sea had paid him homage and vowed allegiance without demur; he could rejoice that every man in the land of Logres was prepared to do his will; yet one man alone, Brun de Branlant, rejected him. King Arthur was aggrieved indeed: not for all of France or Normandy would he fail to launch an attack on him before harvest time! He sent missives to all his lords throughout his lands, informing every last one of his intention to besiege and ensnare Brun de Branlant who had treated him so shamefully. Kings and counts flocked to his call, and I'll give you their names in a moment.

It was at Pentecost, sirs, that good King Arthur summoned his barons. He chose to hold court at Escavalon; it was there he called and assembled them, planning to go straight from there to lay siege to Brun de Branlant, for whom he felt no love at all. I can give you the names of the many lords from numerous lands who came there to the court: I'll name them one by one, and make sure I list them all and overlook none. Hear now which barons came: first of them all was King Mark, followed by Lot of Orkney, who should certainly not be forgotten; Guiromelant was there, a worthy and valiant knight indeed; so too was the courtly King Ebrox of Gomeroit, and King Camandans of Norgoise, so fun-loving and fond of sport; from Ireland came Meraugins, a king to be reckoned with; and King Yder came, and Caradoc, who was more inclined to hauberk than to cowl; and King Gandon of Veline, in love with a fair lady of a neighbouring land; and Marguïs, an Irish king who never sought or asked for peace; and King Menadoc came, and the king of Madoc, and Lost of Loënois – I shan't forget him at any price. Now I've named all the kings who gathered at the court – except the worthy king of Escavalon: I omitted him from the list but he shouldn't be overlooked. And after them came Gawain, so full of fine qualities; Sir Yvain came too, and his father Urien, and with them Count Quinable and Bedivere the constable; and Guerrehés whose arms were grey, without any blazon, and Agravain, a proud man with mighty hands: these last two were sons of Lot of Orkney and had great influence at court. And the harsh-tongued Kay the seneschal was there, as was the fine knight Lucan the butler. So too was Lancelot of the Lake, who had a high position at court, and Tristan, who never laughed, and Tors the son of Arés, and Sagremor the Rash who never tired of fighting. And the lord of the White Glade, lover of the beautiful Golden-haired Maiden of the White Forest, he came to the court without demur.

Now I've given you, I think, the names of all the eminent men who came to that court – much to King Arthur's delight. I think I should also name some of the ladies who came to the queen's chamber, though I shan't list them all as I did with the lords. The damsel of Montesclaire was there, and Blancheflor of Beaurepaire, and the three lovely maidens of the Sparkling Springs, and the charming, beautiful Golden-haired Maiden. There was also lady Ysave de Carahés, who proved to be wily indeed, and the admirable damsel Guinier, who later came to have a breast of gold – she was the sister of the good Cador of Cornwall and, I can say with certainty, wife of Carados Shortarm.[40] Spirits among them all were high – but I'll say no more about that now, for I find no more details in my source.

King Arthur was overjoyed to see the lords he'd summoned gathered all around him; and he complained to them of the outrageous offence committed by Brun de Branlant, relating exactly what had happened. I tell you, they were most displeased, and declared they'd join in attacking Brun if he wouldn't plead for forgiveness: so said the whole great throng of barons, counts and others who'd flocked, the story says, to Arthur. What noble celebrations followed among those worthy lords and knights! But I shan't describe the festivities at court – they would delay my telling of the story.

The Siege of Branlant

When day broke next morning the king set out in fine array, heading straight to lay siege to Branlant and swearing he'd be there till he captured the one who'd so shamefully wronged him. Out from Escavalon he rode with many a distinguished

---

[40] This last sentence refers to characters and events later in the First Continuation: below, pp. 131–77.

lord, all eager to start their attack on Brun, and they pressed on until, at vespers, they arrived outside the city. It was very long established, with no fewer than five bishops; and its walls were finely fortified, with ditches beneath fully forty yards wide: the gates were the only possible entrance. And it was well garrisoned and provisioned from its fields, vineyards, great rivers and woods: the city of Branlant was exceptionally fine. An arm of the sea beat at its walls, surrounding it on every side: what a splendid city it was, its ancient walls as high as any arrow would carry, the battlements beyond the reach of any siege engine. And it had grown rich and powerful indeed from all the wealth it attracted.

King Arthur now arrived with all his host; the newly-dubbed knights were especially excited. As they drew up outside the city they pitched a vast array of splendid tents and pavilions of silk and the finest cloth all across the surrounding land, covering every hill and vale and plain. Those who didn't have tents built huts of branches. By the time the whole host had dismounted and made camp it stretched an incredible distance; no one anywhere had ever seen so many fine, swift chargers, so many shields and banners, so many handsome, elegant tents.

Brun de Branlant can't have been too pleased! But he'd rallied all his men and allies there to support him: in the city were fully seven hundred knights and a great body of fine, tough soldiers who would hold and defend the city against their king without complaint for two years or even three.

As soon as the king arrived the knights of his army rushed to arms. Without any command from the king, those who were fired by love and the desire for honour went spurring forward to engage the foe – in no order, every man for himself – and rode up to the gate to skirmish. The moment they saw them coming the men of the city flung open the gates and rode out to meet them: a good two hundred shields there were, the finest, most highly rated men, fully armed, their helmets laced – not to mention the guards ranged along the gates and walls – and they fixed lances in rests and levelled them straight at their hated foe. The king's newly dubbed knights, seeing them charge, met them in the fiercest combat ever, lowering their lances and driving their horses forward and smashing through shields and piercing hauberks, shattering shafts from lance-heads, killing and gutting till the living were stumbling over the dead. Their lances broken, they exchanged mighty blows with their swords. The new knights had the better of the contest and all the credit, taking many of the city men captive. They maimed and killed scores of horses and won a lot more, and broke many a stout lance in many a fierce joust; and they toppled and captured a host of fine knights and later delivered them to Arthur. They performed a good many deeds of prowess, so many indeed that they drove the enemy back into the city in a confused and wretched retreat. They followed them, baying, and before they could get through the gates Arthur's men captured nearly fifty knights and more than sixty horses, and wounded and killed still more. But finally the gates were shut and both sides withdrew; the fray was over.

King Arthur's knights gathered together and rode straight back to camp. The king came to meet them as soon as he saw them, and there was great celebration throughout the camp. He summoned the surgeons to tend those who needed treatment, and they came and saw to the sick and wounded. The king commanded that they give them their very best attention, and they applied themselves with a will – they had no choice after the king's insistent prayers! Then he sent a party to find and bury those who'd been killed in the fighting. They were laid in the cemetery, and everyone wept and lamented for those dear to them.

They left it at that for the night; but when they rose in the morning everything was soon abuzz again. The king gave orders for mangonels and catapults to be prepared and positioned: he was going to mount an assault; and those commanded rushed to get the engines ready and deployed: they were determined to take the city and deliver it to their good lord King Arthur.

But the men in the city were little daunted; they mounted a stout defence, responding with piercing darts and bolts. The besiegers pelted and bombarded them likewise, but for all their efforts they made no impression: the men on the siege engines strove and laboured mightily, keeping at it all day, not stopping till they saw the approach of night and the day draw to a close. But then they all returned to camp, unable to carry on in the dark and in any case very weary.

They spent the night bewildered by their failure. As for the king, his heart was sorely vexed, and he summoned his foremost lords to discuss what he should do and how he could take the city. Once they'd gathered he said:

'You must give me sound advice now: you can see I need it! This city's so strong it'll never be taken by storm: we'll have to starve them out. They're well protected by their mighty walls, and they've clearly no thought of surrender – they've made provision for a staunch resistance.'

Such was the king's appeal for guidance. The king of Ireland was the first to respond, saying: 'It's a fine, strong city indeed. If we were joined by every man from here to Limours we still couldn't take it by force. And as things stand they could survive for seven years, I think, before we starve them out. We need to consider how best to proceed. The problem is the sea: we need to blockade the port in strength and numbers or you'll never take the city in your life; it's their major asset – it's from the sea that they're constantly supplied. Decide who's to be sent to block and guard the port.'

The king agreed with this; and he swore by all the powers in earth and heaven that he wouldn't leave on any account till he'd captured the city and punished those who'd resisted him unless they all submitted.

So King Arthur vowed to maintain the siege, swearing he wouldn't leave till the city was taken. He had three castles built to careful plans: one was positioned on the seaward side under the command of Sir Gawain and called the Look-out Castle;[41] the second, watching over the river, was called Pancrist, and was held by Girflet the son of Do, one of those I rate most highly; and the third to be built was guarded by Tors the son of Arés, and could have resisted any mangonel. All three castles, indeed, were good and strong.

But you'd still have seen the assaults on the city rage on, and the knights and lords massed inside the towers – the latter defending, Arthur's men attacking. Time and again they pounded and battered at the walls, but nothing they threw at them made any impression. The king besieged the city for fully seven years without success: that's at least how long the siege lasted – so we've discovered in the book we've read. And in that time you may be sure the city's defenders mounted numerous sorties and performed many great deeds of chivalry. Meanwhile the king, each year at the start of Lent, dismissed his whole army so that they could return to their own lands and rest, except those guarding the three castles he'd built; and then, a week after Pentecost, he reassembled his forces outside the city and carried on the siege all summer, till he'd ravaged the surrounding country so completely that there were no crops or fruit to provision the city.

---

[41] *'li Chastiaux de l'Angarde'*.

But they wouldn't have held out against the king and his men for so long, I can assure you, had it not been for two girls there in the city; most courtly and beautiful they were: one was named Lore de Branlant, a brave and spirited girl indeed; the other was Ysave de Carahés, and a fairer girl could not be found from here to Rohais. When food in the city was exhausted and they were in agonies of hunger, these two girls were leaning at the windows of their chamber in a turret high atop the walls. A fair meadow lay below them – between the city and the king's host – where Sir Gawain and Sir Yvain would often go and pass the time in conversation with the girls. They asked if there was anything they needed that they could provide; the girls appealed to them, telling of their suffering and distress, and they rode straight back to the king and pleaded on their behalf, craving his mercy and begging him to send them provisions without delay. Then that noble king, so valiant and courteous, sent abundant supplies of bread and wine and meat and fish and poultry and venison to the city – which led to them holding out for four years longer than they would have done had it not been for those two girls! And finally the king forbade any knight in the army to be so bold as to ask for food to be sent there! No one dared suggest it!

Then the king lined his catapults before the walls and had the gates closely guarded so that no one could get in or out and no supplies could reach the city. And so he starved them out: they were in such straits, so desperate, that they were willing to surrender forthwith if their lives would be spared.

They'd eaten nothing for two days when, one morning at the crack of dawn, Sir Yvain mounted a fine, strong horse to go for a ride. He was making his way round the city and came to the flowery meadow below the tower, where he stopped on hearing the girls in their chamber above, lamenting and weeping and wailing. He called up and asked them why they were crying, and the fair Lore replied that it was because of their hunger. When Sir Yvain heard this he was so overcome with pity that he couldn't speak; instead he thrust in his spurs and went galloping back through the camp to the king's pavilion, and without bothering to see to his horse he jumped down and strode straight in. He knelt before the king and humbly implored his mercy in the name of the One who never lies. The king took his hand and bade him rise and said:

'What's wrong, Sir Yvain? Tell me! If someone's wronged you he'll have no love from me, regardless of his rank, till he's made amends! Or if you desire some gift from me, be it some honour or money or land, I'll not refuse it, you can be sure.'

'Thank you, sire!' he replied. 'My request is this: that you send food at once to those girls in the city – nothing's passed their lips for two whole days!'

'Gladly,' said the king, 'since I offered you a favour and that's your wish – though if anyone else had asked for it I wouldn't have let him stay at court or anywhere I could lay my hands on him!' Then he called for Kay and said: 'Seneschal, go and have a packhorse loaded with food – bread and kegs of wine and fresh meat and fruit and every delicacy, and send it to the girls there in the city.'

Just as Yvain had requested, so it was done; and Kay didn't see to it grudgingly: indeed, he handled it with more courtesy than he'd ever done in his life! I really must tell you: as soon as he received the king's command he had the camp searched high and low for the biggest, strongest horse to carry the load; and with everyone watching he had a fit, lean packhorse promptly charged with an immense pile of light, white, wheaten bread, hefty kegs of strong, clear wine, fresh birds and venison and all kinds of fruit; they kept loading till the beast could scarcely take the weight, packing and piling till it was near to collapse. When they could finally load no more, they sent an able hand to take it to the city. But the poor beast struggled to move: the load was so heavy it could hardly lift its hooves; it hadn't gone far before it stopped and stretched out on the ground, and overcome by the colossal weight its heart gave out. Burdened by all the food, it dropped dead in full view of the city gate; and don't imagine the people watching from the walls were sorry! They rushed straight out and accepted the present joyfully! Now they had plenty to eat in the city for three whole days!

Brun de Branlant was a daring, fierce, courageous knight; nothing daunted him, nor was he slow to seek an advantage. Despite the gift he realised he was done for unless he acted quickly. One morning, just before daybreak, he ordered a body of his men to arm; then he had the gate opened and, leaving the others behind to guard the city, he rode out with those he'd picked. With a company three hundred strong he pressed on to King Arthur's camp, where he found the knights all fast asleep in bed; but he didn't kill or capture them – he had something else in mind: before any in the camp could arm he had a string of fine rounceys* and destriers piled high with food, and then set off back to the city with his booty, following his men at a walk. Loud cries were raised throughout the camp, and everyone rushed to arms. Sir Gawain, quite unarmed, leapt on a destrier; with no thought for donning armour – all he had was a shield, and what a fool he'd later think himself! – he snatched up a lance and spurred his galloping horse towards the noise to find out what was happening. The moment he was clear of the tents he saw the raiding party lumbering away unscathed, laden with plunder. He charged straight off in pursuit – a rash deed that almost cost him his life. Brun de Branlant saw him coming, and immediately turned his horse about and headed for him boldly, with a will. The fine and valiant Gawain charged to meet him likewise, as fast as a crossbow bolt; and as their horses hurtled together he thrust his lance through Brun de Branlant's shield and through his hauberk, too, the head and a fair length of shaft flashing past his skin and out the other side; but the noble-hearted Brun thrust likewise, and didn't miss: he struck Gawain above the shield, sending the bright, sharp lance-head clean through his shoulder – along with a stump of broken shaft. Leaving him speared with more than a yard of lance, he headed back to the city, sending his men inside and seeing the gates shut fast behind them.

   The illustrious knights who came riding up in a body from Arthur's camp gathered around Gawain, and when they saw him unconscious and limp, they howled in anguish. They didn't dare remove the lance; they cut it off at both ends and then carried him back to his pavilion, wailing – such grieving spread throughout the camp as had never been heard before. And when the king heard what had happened he was so beside himself that he collapsed four times. As soon as he recovered speech he sent for all his surgeons, bidding them attend to his nephew and see if they could save him. He summoned the priest, too, who heard his confession; and as soon as he was shriven the surgeons carefully, gently pulled the stump of lance from his body, and washed the wound with white wine and drew out all the blood. Once it was cleansed they probed and examined the wound with care, and declared he would recover well and that the king had nothing to fear: Gawain was not in mortal danger; they'd have him fit and well again. The king was much relieved by this; and the surgeons, able men indeed, tended Gawain with such assiduous care that a week later he was clearly on the mend. The king, greatly comforted, his fears assuaged, deployed his engines and started bombarding the city's walls and towers with his mighty catapults. But Sir Gawain was laid up for another three and a half months before his wound was healed.

He was lying one morning all alone in his tent, with the sides rolled up so that he could enjoy the weather and the light, when he saw one of his pages leading Gringalet back from the river where he'd taken him to drink. He called to the boy, who dismounted and came straight to him and knelt before his bed. Gawain quietly bade him put a saddle on his horse and make it good and tight, and the boy set about it at once. Then Gawain asked his chamberlain to fetch him linen breeches and a shirt, and he promptly brought them, spotlessly clean. Gawain dressed in bed, and then stood up and called for a buckram tunic to go under armour; he donned it quickly and then had his armour smuggled in. With pounding heart he armed superbly, splendidly, and as soon as he was armed he went to his horse and mounted. He took up a strong, stout lance and hung his shield from his neck and then set off through the camp as quietly as he could. But he was spotted by Kay the seneschal, who went running to the king and said:

'You've lost your nephew!'

At this the king cried: 'Holy Mary! Why, what's happened to him, Kay? Tell me!'

'My guess is he's not worried about his wound any more, so he's riding out of camp, my lord, fully armed on his destrier, and galloping off in search of adventure! But if he gets involved in combat or has any exertion you'll never set eyes on him again! If there's any strain on his wound it'll split wide open: the new flesh is too young and soft.'

Without more ado the king, mounted on his dappled bay Brüellet, switch in hand, went spurring away from the tents and out of camp full tilt. He caught up with Gawain and cried:

'Dear nephew, stop! Tell me where you're going, and why you're armed like this!'

'Forgive me, sire,' he replied. 'Don't think I've donned my armour to go in search of chivalry or combat. I'm just going out to enjoy myself and to see the green fields and the leafy woods! I know I've been very sick, for sure; and that's why I'm armed, my lord: to see if I could bear them if need arose. I shan't go far, sire – I'll be back before it's time to eat.'

'I'm pleased to see you up and about, dear nephew. But promise me as you love me that you'll be sure to come back quickly.'

'I shall, sire,' said Gawain, 'have no fear.'

With that the king left him and returned to camp at a walk, while Sir Gawain rode away across fair meadowland.

The Portrait of Gawain

Here a new strand of the story begins. Gawain wandered on all morning till he crossed a river – it wasn't very wide or deep, but as pretty as any in the world – and carried on across the meadows and found himself in a flowery sward, lovelier and more fragrant than any he'd seen in his life, filled with an abundance of every plant there is. On he rode towards a thick, lofty, deeply green wood, its floor carpeted with flowers. The air was pure and fresh and still, the sky was perfectly bright and clear, and the birds were filling the woods with their high, sweet song. He stopped to listen to their delightful melodies, and his heart was so uplifted by the sound that he thrust in his spurs and leapt into a charge, lance levelled. He finally drew rein in the middle of a glade feeling fit and lithe and strong, no longer sensing that his wound should stop him bearing arms or riding all day long – though the flesh was still a little tender. So on he rode, and swiftly, right through the wood and straight through another, and then a third and a fourth without a backward look or any thought of turning. Indeed he decided not to return to camp at all until he'd heard some rare news or encountered an adventure.

As he rode on, pondering this, he saw in the middle of a glade a magnificent pavilion pitched beside a spring. Its every panel was awash with colour, richly decorated in silken birds and beasts and flowers, and on its pommel was perched an eagle made of dazzling gold. This pavilion, wondrously splendid in every way, was surrounded by bowers and lodges of interwoven branches. And the floor within was strewn with fresh, sweet-smelling flowers. Sir Gawain headed towards it with all speed and dismounted; he hung his shield from the branch of an oak, propped his lance against it, and without more ado, still in his armour and with his helmet laced, strode into the tent through the open door. Inside he saw a bed covered with a great spread of samite. On the bed a girl was sitting; and so exceptional was her beauty that there was no lovelier creature in all the world: Nature had excelled in making her – she was flawless, peerless. For a moment Sir Gawain stood astounded by her beauty; but then he stepped up to her and courteously said:

'May the king of glory who never lies keep you always, my dear, sweet lady.'

She bowed her head and made no reply, and he instantly realised his mistake in having said 'lady'; so with great poise and style he corrected himself, saying:

'May God who made you so gracious and fair guard and keep you, maiden!'

'May the one who made the night and morning guard and keep Sir Gawain, and bless you likewise, sir.'

'Fair girl, sweet friend, tell me for the love of God: why do you mention Gawain before me?'

'Why? Truly, sir, I do the same when I bless my father – and my brother, who's a most valiant knight.'

'I'd love to know why that's your custom, gentle friend!'

'I'll tell you, then, and without a word of a lie. It's a good three years, I think – even more – since I first heard tell of Sir Gawain; and such glowing reports: that he's endowed with more prowess, honour, courtesy and largesse than any knight alive! That's why I refer to him first when greeting my father or anyone else.'

'Gracious girl, I've never given my name to anyone without being asked, but nor will I keep it from anyone who cares to know it.'

'Then I pray you, in all courtesy, don't keep it from me, sir: I'd like to know.'

'Truly, my dear, I am Gawain!'

'Gawain!' she said. 'I don't believe it!'

'I am, sweet friend! It's God's truth!'

'Then take off your armour, sir! I want to see your face and figure!'

'So help me God in whom I trust, I shall, my dear! What harm could it possibly do?'

He was out of his armour in an instant; and she said most graciously: 'Good sir, I'm just going to my chamber. I'll come straight back, and then I'll be able to tell at once whether you're Gawain or not.'

He nodded assent, and she went and raised the gorgeous swathe of cloth that screened her chamber and passed through. Inside was a Saracen girl from the chambers of Queen Guinevere. With great skill, in Saracen style, this courtly, worthy girl had embroidered a portrait of Sir Gawain. She hadn't made him hunchbacked or deformed; no, she'd depicted him so accurately, both in armour and unarmed, that no man alive would have failed to see the likeness if he'd viewed the portrait and Gawain together, so close was the resemblance. As soon as the girl had seen it she went straight back and looked at the knight, who'd now donned a mantle, and from his face and his whole aspect she knew he was Gawain indeed. She came and embraced him, kissing his eyes and face a hundred times without stopping; then she said:

'I surrender my body to you, sir! I give you my love forever, faithfully!'

'Sweet friend, this rich gift I accept with joy and pleasure, in all honour! In return I give my love sincerely, if it please you to accept it.'

And he swept her up and kissed her. Of the pleasures of noble love they spoke together – and indeed indulged therein, until she replaced the name of maiden with that of lover and damsel. And before he left her he set a time by which he'd return to find her and take her away with him. Then he took his leave and donned his armour, and mounted and left her, setting off at a gentle pace.

It was rather faster that Norroiz de Lis, the damsel's father, came riding up to the tent.
'Maiden,' he said, 'may the true God who dwells in Heaven on high guard and keep you.'

I get the impression that she bowed her head and said nothing. After a moment her father repeated: 'Dear daughter, God keep you.'

'Dear father, may the one who made you bless you and give you long life. I'm your daughter indeed – but maiden I'm not!'

'Ah! Daughter, who's responsible?'

'Sir Gawain! He's riding away right now: he's only just left, taking my maidenhead with him! I always said I'd let him have it unhindered the moment I set eyes on him, if time and place allowed!'

When her father heard this he turned his horse's head about and left the pavilion and spurred away, following the trail of hoofprints as best he could. He pressed on at such speed that beyond a wood, in open ground, he caught up with Sir Gawain who was ambling along, lost in thoughts of his sweetheart. The moment he saw him he cried:

'Traitor! You're not leaving! I'll make you pay for killing my brother[42] and for the shame you've now done me, robbing my daughter of her maidenhead!'

Sir Gawain didn't appreciate this; he smiled to himself and then replied: 'There's no need for that, sir knight: I've done you no shame or wrong. If I have, I'm willing to make whatever amends you please that are acceptable to your friends and mine. But the charge of treachery I reject.'

He fiercely turned to face him and set his shield before his breast as the father, enraged, came charging at him. They met with all the force they could summon, Norroiz de Lis striking such a blow that his lance bent like a bow and shattered, flying into pieces; and Gawain returned a furious blow through shield and hauberk – it made quite an impression: he wounded him mortally, and the force of the blow was such that he sent him over his horse's crupper and crashing to the ground. He didn't linger a moment longer: he left him there and rode away.

Meanwhile the damsel's brother Bran de Lis, an outstandingly fine knight, had arrived at the pavilion.

'Maiden,' he said, 'God send you honour and good fortune.'

She didn't respond to this, so he repeated: 'Sweet sister, may God grant you all the happiness your heart desires.'

---

[42] In Chrétien's romance Gawain unhorsed Meliant de Lis at a tournament (p. 48), though there is no suggestion at the time that it was a mortal blow.

'Dear brother,' she replied, 'I'm your sister indeed, but I assure you I'm no maiden!'

'Don't say such a thing, my dear!'

'I'm telling you the truth, brother!'

'Who deflowered you, then?'

'Dear brother, it was Sir Gawain!'

Bran went wild with rage; he whipped his horse's head about and spurred away from the pavilion, galloping right through the wood and into the open plain. There he found his father, and when he saw the blood on the ground, pumping from his side, he asked him who'd dealt that mortal wound.

'Dear son,' he said, 'I met Gawain just a moment ago, and he unhorsed me here. Go and fetch my horse and I'll mount – I'm not too badly hurt.'

'No, dear father: I'm going after that traitor to avenge the shame he's dealt my sister. He'll pay dearly for the harm he's done you!'

With that he raced away, galloping through woods and over plains till he caught up with Gawain at the edge of a copse and cried:

'Proven traitor, you'll not escape! You're going to pay for the wrongs you've done: you've killed my father, my uncle too, and robbed my sister of her maidenhead! You'll wish you'd never set eyes on her: it's going to cost you your life!'

Sir Gawain, drawing rein, replied: 'Come now, good sir knight! There's no need for such offensive words, so help me God. If I've ever wronged or harmed you or your kin, I'm ready to make amends to the satisfaction of your friends, barring dishonour or discredit or any shame to mine; but I'll defend myself right here and now against your charge of treachery.'

Without another word they braced their shields, set their blazoned shields before their breasts and lowered their lances. Then both knights thrust in their spurs and sent their brave, swift horses into an unstoppable charge, a charge so thunderous that they made the ground shake and sparks fly from the stones. This was no sporting joust in lists below a castle; these two knights, the lesser of them a worthy warrior indeed, charged at each other from a mighty distance, lances levelled. All the force of the charge they put into their blows, their piercing lance-heads smashing through their shields, the shafts bending on the mail of their bright hauberks and shattering, shards flying skyward. The horses didn't stop nor their riders flinch: they collided, bodies and shields together, with such force that they sent each other crashing, emptying both saddles. So violent was the clash that they skinned their left knees and their faces, and lay stunned and battered on the ground, showing no sign that they'd ever stand again. But in their fervent desire to do each other damage they hauled themselves to their feet as soon as they could, pulled the broken lances from their shields and clutched their whetted swords. Bran de Lis was a fine young knight and fully half a foot taller than Gawain; and they advanced on each other, swords at the ready, and exchanged such fearsome, weighty blows on their shining helms that they smashed off the golden hoops[43] and stove in the helms completely. Down came the blades on the shields, cleaving off chunks every time a blow landed, for these two weren't holding back but dealing blows thick and fast till they were both exhausted, gasping for breath. So intense were the efforts and the strain they endured that the flesh around Sir Gawain's wound split again and reopened, and his chest was covered by the hot, red blood that came pouring forth. When he realised this he was horrified, knowing that if the battle lasted any longer he

---

[43] i.e. the reinforcing bands around the helmets.

was going to die there. And seeing Bran de Lis unhurt and free of blood but weak with exhaustion, reeling from the blows he'd given and received, he said:

'In God's name, friend, don't you think we've fought enough? Let's make peace now.'

'Forget it, Gawain! In your pride you criminally slew my father and my uncle, and this very day deflowered my sister when you found her alone! But I'll postpone this battle till another day if you wish – on certain conditions.'

'Go on, then, sir: say what they are.'

'Gladly,' said Bran. 'You must promise that the very next time we meet, you'll fight me exactly as I chance to find you – either armed or unarmed, no more, no less.'

'Indeed,' said Sir Gawain, 'I promise that faithfully. I can see you've a bold and strong and vigorous heart, but you're not yet old enough to engage with me or anyone in lengthy combat.'

So their battle was postponed, but both exchanged vows to observe the set conditions: Gawain was still under obligation to Bran de Lis. With that they parted, remounting and going swiftly their separate ways.

Sir Gawain rode on till he came to the wood and passed through, and as he emerged on the other side he dismounted on the grass beneath an oak. He took off his tunic and tore off a strip to bind his reopened wound. It staunched the bleeding straight away, and he struggled back into the saddle.

Meanwhile Bran de Lis, in poor shape himself, collected the body of the valiant Norroiz, his dead father, and carried him, grieving bitterly, to an abbey that stood near open grassland on a hill beside the forest. There the monks buried him with all due rites in a grave they dug for him. But we'll say no more for now about Bran de Lis and his fair-faced sister – who was left with child.

Sir Gawain headed straight back to rejoin the king's army besieging Branlant. He was very weak and ill, and dismounted at his tent and took to his bed. The news spread swiftly through the camp, and the king summoned his surgeons urgently to see to the wound; even the most skilled was alarmed to see the tender new flesh split open. Gawain was confined to bed for six whole months before it healed. The king, very upset, sent him to stay at Pancrist,[44] where he could enjoy most creature comforts, until he had fully recovered.

It's well known, sirs, what manner of man King Arthur was, and how for seven years he continued the mighty siege of Branlant, which involved a good many adventures. But I don't want to spend more time on that; I'll draw these matters to a close by telling you that the city was finally starved out, and Brun de Branlant surrendered and placed himself at Arthur's mercy. The siege at last was broken up and everyone departed. God, what rich rewards the king bestowed upon the other kings and counts and lords! Then all returned to their native lands. The knights of the Round Table, the most esteemed in all the world, didn't linger, nor did the peers and the knights of the watch;[45] after so long at the siege they all resorted to their favoured pastimes, some going hunting in the woods and rivers, others courting girls and ladies in the women's quarters. As for the king, he left the siege and went to Quineli, a great city of his, taking with him Brun de Branlant. Within a week he'd released him from captivity and presented him with

---

[44] One of the three castles mentioned above, p. 123.
[45] 'The knights of the watch' are mentioned in Chrétien (above, p. 69). There appear to have been thirty peers (below, p. 178). The implication is that there were a number of select groups of knights in Arthur's court and household.

Quineli, to hold it as his vassal. Brun became his liegeman there and then, and rendered him such service in his household that it's still spoken of today. His sister Lore became Sir Kay's sweetheart.

And the king stayed at Quineli with his privy household in happiness and contentment.

Eliavret the Enchanter

It was while the king was here at Quineli that there came to his court a tall, strapping, powerful, striking knight by the name of Caradoc, the lord and king of the realm of Verne.[46] He was young and Fortune was smiling on him, except that he didn't have a wife; and he came to King Arthur now to ask for a spouse, feeling sure he'd be all the better if the king were to provide him with a wife: he said he'd rather be unmarried for fourteen years than be given a wife by anyone other than the sovereign of kings! He wanted the gift to be bestowed by him alone. It wasn't long before Arthur gave Caradoc his own niece, the fair Ysave de Carahés, a bright and gracious woman indeed.

On the appointed wedding day the king summoned all his barons and most able and deserving courtiers. Ladies and maids and the damsels of the queen's chambers came, along with kings, dukes, princes, emirs,[47] barons, castellans, vassals: so many people came that the city shook! So loud was their celebration that you wouldn't have heard God's thunder! It would take too long to list all who were present at the marriage and what they ate and what they drank, and I've no intention of trying: I'll move on and tell you that God brought them to their joyous wedding one Tuesday morning. They duly bedecked the fair Ysave, and I can assure you no one could have matched her beauty in body and face, and her nature and her bearing were just as fair; and how her dress became her! The good king took her by the hand, and then without further ceremony they made their way to the church for the wedding, which took place to the joy of a huge congregation. It was followed by mass, and after the offertory and the mass had been sung and said, the king left the church along with all his knights while the queen took the bride back to her chambers.

Then Sir Kay bade a trumpet sound for the bringing of the water, and once the king had washed he took his seat at the top table. But I'm not going to describe the dishes that were served – there were so many! And after they'd eaten and drunk their fill they went out to the meadows and started jousting.[48] But I'm not going to dwell on that, either, for I've something else to tell you which fills my heart with rage: I'd gladly go to prison, truly, if it would expunge this dreadful wrong and mean it had never happened! What a worthy achievement that would be! It would free ladies from a good deal of the blame unfairly levelled at them. What happened was this.

There was a knight at court who was an enchanter, the most skilled you'll ever see. His name was Eliavret. All day long his eyes had been fixed on the fair Ysave in her gorgeous attire, and he fell utterly in love with her: if he didn't have her he would languish incurably. He stalked her here, there and everywhere, and with his enchantments, charms and conjurations he brought her under his spell and made her betray her husband.

---

[46] A place-name possibly based on Vannes, as Caradoc is about to feature prominently in a story set partly in Brittany.
[47] *'aumaçor'*: a high-ranking title from the East.
[48] *'behorder'*. The *behourd* tended to be associated with young men training to be knights; it was usually 'an informal sport frequently occurring on the spur of the moment'. Juliet Barker, *The Tournament in England, 1100–1400* (Woodbridge, 1986), pp. 148–9.

On that first night, as Caradoc went to lie with Ysave, he was quite unaware that he was lying with a greyhound bitch: the enchanter's deception was so complete that he didn't realise – he thought he was lying with his wife and that she was a virgin! Meanwhile the enchanter spent the whole night with Ysave. And the next night, I'm distressed to say, he made Caradoc lie with a sow while he enjoyed the lady's embraces all night long. And the third night, truly, he made him lie with a mare while he freely took his pleasure with Ysave. And it was from that night's business, I believe, that she was left with child. And for the moment at least, the deception was undiscovered.

Carados is Knighted

That splendid court at last broke up with the bestowal of many fine gifts, and King Caradoc and his wife returned to his realm. The enchanter went his separate way, and I shan't tell you what became of him till the appropriate time. When Caradoc saw that Ysave had conceived he loved her all the more, not realising who the father was. And when she came to term and gave birth, she was delivered of a fine son. There was celebration throughout the land – and no one could describe her lord Caradoc's joy. He had the child baptised with all due ceremony, and because he cherished him so dearly he named him after himself, Carados.

The boy was given a series of nurses, and once he was five years old a tutor was appointed for his greater improvement and instruction. Four years later he'd learnt so much that he was regarded more highly than his master! He certainly had a way with words; and when he was ten he came to his father the king and said that, if he would let him, he would very much like to join the fine knights of his uncle[49] King Arthur's household. So Caradoc and Ysave equipped and prepared him, and as soon as he was ready he was gone: he took his leave of his father and set off. He was amply supplied with gold and silver, and took with him his tutor and a fine company of worthy men and servants: Caradoc sent a good number with him. He was too upset to escort him himself, but the one who was bound to love him most rode with him as far as the sea – his mother Queen Ysave, that is, who shed many a bitter tear and kissed him, weeping. But the boy didn't linger.

'Lady,' he said, 'your leave.'

'I commend you to God, dear son. May he keep you from all harm.'

With that they parted. His ship set out from the shore, and carried by a fair wind sailed swiftly and calmly over the sea and landed at Hantone.[50] As for the lady Ysave, she didn't move a step from the shore; her eyes stayed with them all the way, and only when the ship was lost to view did she leave the harbour along with her company, and they went by highways and byways and escorted her to Nantes, a very fine city that belonged to her and her husband. He'd been in residence there for quite some time, and he stayed there a good while longer, and the queen with him. They didn't leave Nantes at all: they stayed there pining for their son Carados, who'd now landed at Hantone.

He journeyed on with his companions right across England, and found King Arthur's court at Cardoil. I'm not going to dwell on the joyous reception he was given, led by Arthur himself. Everyone made a great fuss of the boy, but that'll do: I'm not going to hold things up by describing it all.

---

[49] It should strictly be 'great-uncle', his mother Ysave being Arthur's niece.
[50] A name probably based on Southampton.

King Arthur, then, was in residence at Cardoil, a city of his realm that stood on the border between Wales and England in a fine position, surrounded by forest and river. He was with his privy household, and several days a week, you may be sure, he would go hunting or spend his time in sport along the river, and he took Carados with him to teach and train him in the art of trapping game; and later he gave him fine instruction in how to carry a hawk and fly it when the time came. He also showed him the importance of being courteous and temperate, and the ins and outs of chess and dice[51] and the various other pastimes which gentlemen should master; and he taught him to honour ladies and damsels and to champion maidens, to be sure not to fail them if they ever needed help; and to cherish and support poor worthy knights, and to shun the malicious and insincere; to seek the company of the good and avoid the wicked, for there's no lasting pleasure to be gained from the latter; and when he became a knight he should never boast of his own deeds – he should strive to do more than anyone when the need arose but to speak the least when the deeds were done, for a knight who brags about his prowess will end up choking on his boastfulness – it'll be his downfall. The good King Arthur told Carados to have prowess as his watchword; sense and moderation as his motto; if he did so it would be much to his advantage, for excess and presumption were incompatible with honour and valour, but if he were courteous and civilised he would win honour and praise indeed and all, of every degree, would love him.

Carados was most attentive to his words, and young though he was he became so set on winning respect that before his fifteenth year was out he'd won higher regard than anyone else in King Arthur's household. Sir Gawain loved him dearly, as did Sir Yvain and the king and all the other knights, and with every reason.

But now we'll return to King Arthur himself. It was several years since the siege of Branlant, and in all that time he'd never worn his crown or held a court of any note or carried arms in war; instead he'd spent his time in sport and entertainment with his privy household, the most distinguished in the world.

One day he'd gone hunting with his companions with great success, and returned laden with game towards Cardoil, the good king's residence – he'd hardly moved from there, being so agreeably placed amid woods and rivers on the border of his land between England and Wales. As they made their way home they weren't restrained but celebrating raucously, horns blasting. In these high spirits they went prancing on their way and didn't notice that the king was lost in thought; on they raced and spurred and galloped and had soon left him far behind, following at a walk. But it wasn't long before Gawain realised: he saw them riding swiftly on and looked back to see the king in the distance, all alone, deep in thought, plodding along with his head bowed. Gawain drew rein, very puzzled to see the king apparently so troubled, and called to his companions to stop. When the king realised they'd all stopped for him he started riding a little faster and cantered on till he caught up.

'You've been riding alone for quite a while, sire,' said Sir Gawain. 'It was very bad of us – forgive us, please! But tell us, if you will, why you're so preoccupied when you're surrounded by friends and liegemen who all love you, and have destroyed, defeated and confounded every foe in all directions! We don't like to see you look so downcast and worried – we want you to rejoice, sire, loud enough for all the world to hear!'

---

[51] '*tables*': a dice game related to backgammon.

The king smiled and placed his hand on Sir Gawain's head and said: 'I'll tell you what's been on my mind. I've been thinking that it's many winters and summers since I last held proper court. I've decided to bear my crown at Pentecost, and to hold the finest court from here to Constantinople, a court whose renown shall ring throughout the world, eclipsing any other I've ever held, where I'll distribute gifts greater than I've ever bestowed before. What's more, I shall knight my dear nephew[52] Carados.'

'Truly,' said Sir Gawain, 'that's a noble plan indeed – not the musings of a miserly man but of a brilliant, valiant king!'

They passed that night most happily, and next morning the king sent messengers throughout the land summoning everyone, of every degree, to attend court at Cardoil. So many flocked from far and wide that it was a wonder; I shan't give you all the names – there were far too many to list them all, so many that only a fool would have tried to count them!

It was in the summer, in the month of May, on that peerless, God-given day called Pentecost; and as the king returned from hearing mass, you should have seen the excitement of his nephew Carados! He was accompanied by fifty other youths that King Arthur, out of love for him, was about to knight that day, all of them the sons of counts and barons, young and tall and stalwart, courteous and brave and well instructed. They'd been washed and bathed; and the noble Queen Guinevere had been anything but mean, sending Carados and his fellows beautifully made shirts of finest linen: you wouldn't have found better anywhere. On top of these they donned raiment worthy of the greatest duke: all of them were clad in silk from the land of Greece, adorned with golden thread; their mantles were lined with squirrel-fur and bordered with sable; their surcoats were lined with gold-spangled ermine. They were richly garbed indeed, those youths, not least Carados: his mantle was so superb that Charles Martel[53] would have been proud to wear it at his coronation! His tunic suited him wonderfully; and what a supremely handsome youth he was: slim and slender in the waist but with well-developed arms and shoulders. Nature had excelled in his making: he was perfect in body and face. What more need I say? Carados and his companions, many a duke's and baron's son, hadn't had a wink of sleep – they'd spent the whole night in song and celebration. Sir Gawain fastened Carados's right spur and Sir Yvain his left, and the king girded his sword and gave him the accolade, saying:

'Dear nephew, may God by His grace make you a worthy knight.'

And a hundred of the court's most illustrious knights fastened the spurs of all the rest with loving care, and girded their swords and gave them their accolades. And so they were all dubbed knights. Now on with my story.

They all went to church to hear the divine service. The Archbishop of Canterbury began the mass of the glorious Holy Spirit; the offertory was great and wondrous to behold, attended by so many people. King Arthur bore his crown that day, a splendid crown indeed. And when the service was done they withdrew to the hall, where the servants had spread the cloths and laid the tables with bread and wine and fine knives and cups and vessels of gold and silver. Cut off my nose but I couldn't describe the rich beauty of that ware! The tables were gloriously decked indeed. As that illustrious company of knights made their joyous entry with the king, each honouring him in turn, Sir Kay came from a chamber and strode through the panelled hall to the king and, staff of office in hand, his cloak removed, said:

---

[52] Strictly speaking it should be 'great-nephew': see note 49, above, p. 132.
[53] Charlemagne's grandfather, heroic victor of crucial battles against the Moors.

'When it please you, sire, I'll bring you the water.'

But the king replied: 'No hurry, Kay. By all God's saints, you know that whenever I've held a court as king I've never washed my hands or eaten till some marvel has appeared to us, and I don't intend to start now.'

The Beheading Game

While they were talking a knight on a grey horse came clattering through the door, singing a little song. His head was covered with a simple hood to protect him from the heat, but he was dressed in an ermine gown on top of which, with a silken belt, was girded the sword with which he would shortly be beheaded. He rode straight up to the king and said:

'God save you, king, the finest and noblest king alive on Earth! I've come to ask a favour of you, if you'll deign to grant it.'

'Welcome, friend,' the king replied. 'I'll return your greeting when I've heard the boon you crave, which I'm sure won't be refused.'

'King,' said the knight, 'I shan't deceive you. The favour I ask is to receive a blow and give another in return.'

'How's that? You'll have to explain!'

'Explain it I shall, king! I'm going to give this sword to one of the knights here before you. Let him strike with a will, and see if he can cut my head off with one blow! And if I recover from being beheaded, a year from today hand me back my sword and I'll return the blow!'

'By Saint John!' cried Kay. 'I wouldn't do that for all the wealth of Normandy! You'd have to be mad to get involved in this!'

The knight stepped down from his horse and said: 'King, I've asked you for this boon. If you refuse, all the world shall hear of it! I'll let it be known that I was refused a trivial favour at your court – and I've been seeking you for ages!'

He drew the sword from its scabbard. The king looked aghast, and everyone of every degree was dumbstruck, wondering what honour could be gained by striking the knight. But Carados, newly dubbed, could bear it no longer: he cast off his mantle and ran to the knight and took the brand of steel in hand and addressed him thus:

'Are you the finest of all knights?'

'No indeed – the maddest!'

And the knight stretched out his neck and laid his head on a table. The king and all the lords were horrified! Sir Yvain was about to rush and snatch the sword from Carados's hands, but the moment passed and he made no move. Carados raised the sword on high and gave the knight a blow indeed: it sliced clean through to the table. The head went flying a fair old way – but the body was quick to catch up: before anyone could grasp what was happening the body collected its head again and restored it to its proper place! Then back came the knight before the king, perfectly hale and hearty!

'Now, king,' he said, 'don't break your word! I've received a blow, so let me give mine a year from today, right here in your court.'

The king didn't hesitate: he commanded all his lords, of every degree, to attend his next court just as they'd attended that, at exactly the same time and place. And the knight said:

'Carados, you've given me a mighty blow before the king. You'll have mine in return, a year from today!'

With that he left the court and went on his way, leaving the king deep in troubled thought. The distress of the knights and ladies is indescribable; there was little laughter there at dinner: the whole court was in a state of shock. But Carados was unperturbed and said:

'Stop worrying, uncle! Everything's in the hands of God.'

But many tears were shed for Carados.

So the court was summoned to gather at Cardoil the following year at Pentecost. And meanwhile the deeply troubling news reached Caradoc the king of Verne and his wife the lady Ysave. So dreadful was their grieving for their beloved son that no one could describe the anguish and the suffering they endured all year. But Carados stayed at his uncle's court, and far from being cautious and withdrawn he went out seeking new adventures: you've never heard of any one knight achieving so many feats of chivalry in such a short time as Carados did that year. Everyone was talking of him – and all who saw him wept and grieved.

The year's end inevitably came, and the court was due to assemble. As the word spread, people came flocking over land and sea to watch the extraordinary events unfold. But many a girl and lady, and King Caradoc and his wife, were too distressed to go – though they weren't idle: they made all manner of gifts and charitable bequests in the hope that God, creator of all, would protect their son from harm that day.

The day of Pentecost came. The fearful event was imminent. The whole court had assembled; they'd processed to church and heard the mass; the water was brought and they were about to eat. And in came the knight on his horse, sword at his waist; he didn't look cool but flushed from the heat.

'Lord king,' he said, 'God save you.'

'And God bless you, friend.'

'I can't see you, Carados. Step forward and let's have fun! Lay your head before me now – I once did the same for you, and it's only fair that I show I can strike a blow and return the one you gave.'

Carados realised his time had come. He took off his mantle and stepped forward. He bowed his head before the knight and said:

'Now you have me, good sir. Strike as best you can.'

'Sir knight!' cried the king. 'You'll not be so discourteous as to refuse a ransom!'

'A ransom? Name it, then.'

'Oh, gladly! I'll give you a huge ransom! I'll give you, I swear, all the plate to be found here at my court, whoever may have brought it – and every bit of this knight's equipment – he's my nephew – I love him dearly!'

'Not interested! I'm having his head, and no one's going to stop me!'

'No, wait – there's more! I'll give you all the treasure – jewels, silver, gold – to be found in all my land: in Britain, in England, wherever I hold sway!'

'Not interested! I'm cutting off his head! You think I'm stupid! I'm having his head right now: he can't escape, and no one's going to stop me!'

'No, wait – there's more!'

But the knight raised his hand and held his sword high, poised to strike. The king saw this and fainted with horror. Carados cried out in anguish:

'Why don't you strike, sir? You're making me die a double death, hesitating so! I think you're a coward!'

The queen now came to make an appeal, running from her chamber with a hundred fair maids and ladies.

'Don't touch him, sir knight!' she said. 'It would be a shame and a sin if he were slain! Have mercy on him, for God's sake! If you grant me his reprieve you'll be well rewarded! Please consider! Would you do me any favour? Do this much for me: absolve Carados, the king's nephew, of this blow – it'll earn you a wondrous ransom: see all these fair and comely girls? You can have them all! Do the wise thing and pardon him!'

'Not for all the women in the world! I'll have no other payment than his life! If you're not brave enough to watch, go and sort out your room!'

The queen covered her head and began lamenting bitterly; she retreated to her chamber with the ladies, all grieving with her so desperately it was very nearly the death of them. The king and all his knights were beside themselves, helpless with distress: no man alive could describe it. Carados stepped up to a table and laid his head upon it. The knight raised his sword, and then struck him – with the flat of the blade, not hurting him at all.

'Get up, Carados,' he said. 'It would be a dreadful wrong and shame were I to kill you. Step aside and speak with me a moment: I want to talk in private.'

So he spoke to him in confidence, saying: 'Do you know why I didn't kill you? You're my son. I'm your father.'

'I'll defend my mother from any such claim!' said Carados. 'She's not your lover and never was! She's never behaved improperly!'

But the knight told him to be quiet and listen. He told him the whole story and exactly what had happened: how he'd lain with his mother for three nights – but I shan't bore you by repeating it all. Carados was terribly upset and protested, saying:

'Knight, these are empty boasts and lies! You never tricked my father or lay with my mother! You never sired me or anyone else on her! Say so again and you'll be sorry!'

The knight said no more; he mounted his horse at once and took his leave and went his way. The court was left in jubilation: the trumpet sounded, the king called for the water which was duly brought, and knights and ladies washed and sat down to eat, King Arthur taking his place at the high table. But I'm not going to give you a list of the dishes – I'd wear myself out before I'd finished! And when the time came for the court to part, there was such a distribution of gold and silver and splendid, handsome birds and horses that no one arrived at court so poor but he was a rich man when he left! They all returned to their own lands, but the king and his privy household chose to stay.

Carados Exposes his Mother

Carados headed for Brittany – he hadn't been there for a long while – and came at last to Nantes where he found his mother and King Caradoc residing. When the king heard of his arrival his heart leapt, and he came to meet him and embraced him and kissed him and tenderly said:

'Welcome indeed, my dear, beloved son! Seeing you, I know for sure that God is on my side!'

'Oh, good sir! Why do you make such a fuss of me when I'm not your son?'

'Not my son?'

'No indeed! You want to know the truth?'

'That I do!'

'I'll tell you, then, no word of a lie.'

And they drew aside and Carados told him the whole story in detail: how his mother had been bewitched by the cunning enchanter, who'd admitted that on their wedding night he'd put a greyhound bitch under the king's blanket for him to lie with while he'd been the first to enjoy the king's bride.

'Don't imagine I'm deceiving you,' he said. 'The next night he made you lie with a sow! And the third night you lay with a mare, truly! And you never knew! And all the while the enchanter was having his way with my mother! It was on that third night, I believe, that she was left pregnant with me. That's why I don't consider you my father – but she is still my mother, and there's still no man in the world I love as much as you.'

The king's heart was so distressed that he nearly went out of his mind. And when the queen heard what Carados had said she didn't hold back but rushed to embrace him. He kissed her eyes and face and said:

'I can't help kissing you, lady, because you're my mother, I know. But it doesn't mean I love you or hold you dear. Do you know why? You've betrayed the king – your good lord and mine. You know very well what happened.'

The king couldn't contain himself. 'Lady,' he said, 'how can you stand there in my sight after what you've done? Be gone, and quickly, or anger might make me go too far and you'll be the one to feel it!'

The queen went away in dreadful distress, and wasn't slow to leave the palace. But I'll say no more about her grief: I'll return to the raging king. It was looking bad for the queen, that's for sure: the king took Carados aside at once and said:

'Well, my friend: what's to be done with your mother? Tell me. We'll do whatever you say. Your wish will be mine.'

'My lord,' Carados replied, 'nothing in the world would make me want to see my lady suffer in any way: she's still my mother. But to make sure the enchanter never consorts with her again, I say you should build a tower, tall and slender – not at all wide. Have my mother imprisoned there, so that no heir of the enchanter can ever claim your inheritance – I assure you, it shouldn't come to me!'

The king devoted money to the building of just such a tower and had the queen imprisoned there, and only he and those he permitted could enter. No other men, only women, were ever with her: that's the long and the short of it.

Once the queen was locked in the stone tower at Nantes, Carados didn't linger there but rejoined the illustrious court of his uncle the good King Arthur: there was no finer king in all the world, save God. And Carados, endowed as he was with all fine qualities, said he had no need of rest: he wanted to be involved in deeds of arms – and rightly so: no knight wishing to earn praise can afford to do otherwise; no knight wins a reputation by being idle. Such was his heart, and such was his thought: Carados returned to England, fiercer than a lion.

Carados Rescues Guinier

In May, when the roses bloom, the king had sent messengers to decree that all who held lands as his vassals and owed him homage should attend his court at Carlion. From both sides of the water, over land and sea, they came to honour his court; everyone made their way there, down to the very last maid.

Among them, from Cornwall, came a youth of great valour named Cador, bringing with him his sister, the worthy and comely Guinier.[54] She wasn't one to tart herself up – she never applied anything that God hadn't put there! – for she was such a lovely

---

[54] Guinier and her brother Cador were mentioned above, p. 121.

creature that if Nature had spent seven years in her making She couldn't have made her fairer than she was! But for all that, her beauty was surpassed by her loyalty: she was ever faithful and steadfast in true love. I shan't go on about her, but in hair and eyes and face and figure she had absolutely everything that could be wished for in a girl. As for her brother Cador, he was a fine and handsome knight. Their father, who'd been king of Cornwall, had died the previous summer, and so they came now to King Arthur's court as they held their land from him.

They came on their own, just the two of them, for in those days girls could travel in more confidence than they would do now. But as they made their way, a well-armed knight emerged from a valley and rode towards them. Cador was armed, too, apart from his helmet: he'd taken it off and let it hang from his shoulders, for it was very hot and he was expecting no attack. The approaching knight kept spurring forward till he drew near; and when he saw Guinier he realised she was the one who'd refused him her love. I don't think I've mentioned this yet – I can't tell you everything at once: I have to tell you one thing at a time, but it'll all make sense in the end! This knight who'd just appeared was known in his country as Alardin of the Lake, and he'd loved the maiden Guinier deeply and asked her brother and her father (before his death) for her hand, wanting to take her as his wife and make her lady of his land. But she said she wished to be neither his wife nor his sweetheart: she wouldn't have him at any price, even though he was more handsome and endowed with more prowess than any knight of her own land. Alardin's heart was so set on her that, before her father died, he tried fervently to win her by entreaty and every possible ploy, but without the slightest success. Seeing her now, he thrust in his spurs all the harder and cried to her brother Cador:

'Truly, knight, you'd better leave your sister to me: you're taking her no further! If you don't you'll have me charging at you! I'd don your helm if I were you, or by Saint Paul you'll have a blow from me that'll send you to a higher place!'

Cador's reply was no less bold; he came straight back with: 'Come on, then! Do you know who I am? I'm Cador, and I wouldn't stoop to giving you my sister for your whole weight in gold – what a proof of my love for her that would be!'

So saying, Cador donned his helm, and the two knights drew apart and then spurred their horses into a charge, letting their lances do the challenging; they smashed and shattered them utterly, and their mounts were bearing them at such a speed that their collision brought knights and steeds together crashing to the ground in a heap. Disastrously for Cador, his horse landed on top of him – he was beneath it, on his back; and the rear saddle-bow smashed down on his leg and broke it – he couldn't have been blamed if he'd passed out with the pain: he was in such agony that he lay there as still as a tree-stump. Seeing this, Alardin wickedly said:

'Whether you like it or not, Sir Cador, now your sister will be ours – mine first, then I'll pass her on to my companions! It was a big mistake you made, denying me her hand! If you'd given her to me she'd have had my complete love: I'd have taken her as my wife and made her my lady. But now things have worked out better than I could have dreamt!'

Without another word he leapt on his horse and went and seized Guinier. What more can I say? He led her off by force, while she howled in greater anguish than you've ever heard. And Cador was left helpless, lying in the road, pouring loathing on his life and on himself. You can well imagine his distress when his sister, his to protect, was dragged away before his very eyes and he was powerless to help himself or her. Only a heartless wretch could have heard him willing Death to take him and not felt pity. For her part Guinier was beating and clawing herself in grief, wailing and fainting repeatedly.

'Ah, God! Sweet Holy Mary! What will my dear mother say when she hears of this? She'll be beside herself! Death has robbed her of my father, and now this demon has robbed her of my brother and me! Truly, he's no knight who wants to take a woman by force: it's a flagrant act of evil!'

While Guinier thus wailed and cried, Carados was heading swiftly to his uncle King Arthur's court. He was coming down a hill, fully armed upon his horse, when he heard the maiden's strident cries; he looked down a valley and saw her just a short way off and realised she was in trouble. He thrust in his spurs and set off towards her as fast as he could. As soon as she saw him she begged him to take pity, crying:

'Ah! Noble, valiant knight! In God's name save me from this cursèd devil! He's mortally wounded my brother before my very eyes and now he's abducting me! Truly I'd rather be dead – burned alive, drowned, destroyed – than have him treat me as he intends! Anyone who saves me from him will win me utterly! I beg you, sir knight, have pity on me for the love of God – help me – don't let him take me another step!'

Carados confronted him and said: 'Come, friend: leave the girl with me.'

'Leave her with you? Are you mad? Hang me if I do any such thing! Don't push it! She's nothing to do with you – be about your business!'

Sir Carados answered: 'Nothing in the world would make me leave her with you: I wouldn't shame myself by letting you take her now that she's appealed to me for help.'

With his lance in one hand he grabbed Guinier's bridle by the other. Alardin struck out with his sword and almost severed the hand that held the lance; as it was, it was such a blow that it cut clean through the lance's shaft. Carados struck him back with the stump, full on the head: Alardin couldn't keep his seat, but crashed from his horse with his legs in the air. And now it really started.

'Sir knight,' said Carados, 'how dare you show us your backside!'

And he leapt from his horse while Alardin, filled with shame, jumped up. They went at each other fiercely with their sharp steel blades: no idle threats – their blows were real. No one who'd seen that fight would have wanted to leave! You'd have seen many a keen sword-blow exchanged: they rained blow after blow on the tops of their shields, hacking them to pieces, along with their fine-meshed hauberks. Whoever could deal the most blows did so, striving to gain the upper hand. They struck, they parried, driving one another back and forth; they knew they were in a proper battle as they hammered away at each other: the combat was ferocious – and very long. Both knights had dealt so many blows that, I promise you, before the first assault was over they'd smashed their shields to bits – they weren't worth a light; and their hauberks, fine and strong though the mail had been, were well and truly sundered, and they'd drawn blood from each other's body by the time the first bout was done. Then Alardin drew back, and Cador didn't pursue him: he was boiling hot from the sweat and exertion.

But when the two knights had recovered breath they clutched their swords once more and dealt each other mighty strikes to head and neck and wherever else they could land a blow, till they'd stained the ground with their blood: it was flowing in torrents – the grass had turned crimson. Their hauberks now were hanging in shreds, dark with the blood that boiled through the mail. Then Carados delivered such a blow that, if Alardin hadn't dodged aside, it would have been the end of him; it was such a telling blow that if the sword hadn't turned in his hand or Alardin had been slower to move it would have cloven him to the teeth; and although he dodged it, Carados still managed to smash away the whole right side of his helm. It was a loss for Alardin, certainly: his head was now protected by the mail hood alone. But I promise you, if it hadn't been for that grave loss he mightn't have come off worse: he'd been keeping his end up in the contest, that's for sure: but for that grave mishap he would never have lost. Alardin was enraged – the odds were now stacked against him! But still he was bent on revenge, and aimed a blow at Carados's hand. But sometimes it rebounds on you, not knowing when you're beaten, and so it was with Alardin: the blow flashed down and missed the hand, and now his plight was even worse, for his blade landed on the cross-piece of Carados's sword and shattered clean in two. There was nothing else for it now: Alardin surrendered; and he proffered him the hilt of his broken sword, knowing further resistance was futile, saying:

'I surrender to you and your mercy, sir, the finest knight who ever rode a charger! I am your prisoner. But tell me who you are, now you've given me such a hiding!'

'My name is Carados; I'm King Arthur's nephew. And tell me yours, sir.'

'My name shall never be hidden: in my own country I'm called Alardin of the Lake. I'd met this maiden who'd refused me her love – though I wanted to make her lady of my lands and estates. I've been at constant war with her father – a wealthy man indeed – and now I've robbed her of her brother. I'd have taken her from you, as well, for sure, had it turned out better for me! But you're such a fine knight that you've outfought me, and the long and the short of it is: I surrender.'

'Friend,' said Carados, 'don't argue now: go and yield to the maiden.'

'I shall, sir, willingly, if so you command.'

'Ah, Carados, dear friend,' the girl replied, 'not for all the world! I can never find it in my heart to forgive him for robbing me of my brother, unless he returns him to me safe and sound. And even then I'd rather hang myself than take him as my husband!'

'Truly, girl,' said Alardin, 'I'm ready to deliver him to you safe and well – if he's alive, that is!'

With that, all three mounted and rode on till they found Cador close by, just where he'd jousted. There he lay, so badly wounded that he'd never have risen again – he was barely breathing; and the two knights, exhausted from their fighting and loss of blood, struggled to lift him from the ground and put him on a horse. Then they set off down a valley, Carados carrying Cador with him on the same horse, gently supporting him, as he couldn't have stayed upright without help. And the maiden's grieving was wondrous and terrible to hear.

They rode on till they came upon a pavilion pitched beside a river. It was quite magnificent, so covered in gold and silver that if I described it in detail no one would believe me. The meadow around it was green and lush and the river was delightful. This lovely spot appealed to Carados greatly, and the joyous birdsong he could hear in the trees began to soothe away all his cares.

'Ah, God!' he said. 'Sweet heavenly king! What a glorious place this is – its lord must be loved by God indeed.'

Just as he said this he heard the sound of girls singing, pining for their sweethearts. But what surprised and delighted him even more, and what really drew his attention, were two gold and silver statues at the entrance to the tent: by magic they acted as doormen, one of them opening the door and the other closing it. And that wasn't their only role: one of them played the harp with amazing skill, while the other held a dart to thrust clean through any rogue who tried to enter. And the one that played the harp had another gift: it could see through any girl who claimed to be a virgin after she'd lost her maidenhead, and as soon as she came to the entrance the harp would break a string and sound a discord. The floor of the pavilion was strewn with herbs, rushes and aromatic flowers to freshen the air in readiness for the lord of the place. No man alive could describe that pavilion's beauty. Carados could hear the revelry of all the people inside: ladies and knights were singing, while the boys and maids – some of them fair indeed – were making merry in the meadow. He asked Alardin if he knew who the pavilion belonged to.

'Sir,' he replied, 'no one's closer to the owner than I – for I'm the man himself! I'm welcoming you now to my own abode: all those people singing are my vassals and my men. And when you enter the pavilion you'll see my great wealth; and you'll see my sister, too – God grant her joy and honour – I love her like my own life.'

Everyone, of every degree, came from the pavilion then to pay honour to their lord. The maiden his sister held his stirrup, while the others went to help the wounded Cador to dismount: they gently helped him down and carried him into the pavilion. How comforted he was then: without a word of a lie, as soon as he heard the harp's melody it was as if he was waking and reviving from a dream. Everyone was amazed: the sweet sound filled him with such joy that his pain was quite forgotten. Then Alardin called to his beautiful sister, the Maiden of the Pavilion (I've never heard her referred to by any other name), and said:

'Dear sister, I pray you attend to these knights and this maiden as you would to me: do all you can to heal their wounds as you would your brother's – I'm hurt myself, and badly, so help me now.'

She responded to his plea and gave their wounds her full attention, and within a week had healed them all – but I don't want to lengthen and slow the story by describing exactly how. She showed the fair Guinier every honour and became very fond of her, but again I'd be exhausted if I told you all the details, so I'll just say they spent that week most happily: you'll often have heard of more tiresome stays! And the long and the short of it is that Carados and Alardin and Cador pledged lifelong friendship, and Alardin made amends to fair Guinier for the wrong he'd done her.

Then, it seems, they all resolved to go next day without further delay to the court of the good King Arthur. When they were ready they all set out together, Carados riding at the right hand of his dear and comely Guinier, and the Maiden of the Pavilion beside Cador. The valiant Carados, lightly dressed because of the heat, was a handsome figure indeed and delightful company, and in the heart of the fair Guinier the flame of love now burned for him; she didn't dare even look his way: she loved him more than her own life but didn't dare show it, and you wouldn't expect the maiden rather than the man to be the first to declare her love. But I'll leave them now, riding swiftly on.

The Great Tournament

The king had been holding court at Carlion, attended by people from Normandy and England, from many distant lands: so many knights, so many ladies, that Alexander of Allier[55] never assembled such numbers in his life. As the court broke up, the kings

---

[55] i.e. Alexander the Great. The name 'Alexander of Allier' first appears in the 12th-century Alexander romance *Li Fuerre de Gadres*, and there are references to Alexander as *'le roi d'Alier'* at several points in the verse *Roman d'Alexandre*. *'Allier'* may have derived from 'Illyricum'.

Cadoalan and Ris, two fierce rivals, engaged in a great tournament. Cadoalan was the king of Ireland and Ris came from Valen, an area enclosed by forest not far from Carlion. Alardin and Carados rode to join in, accompanied by Cador; they arrived just in time: the tourney was about to begin. They dismounted under some elms and unpacked their arms, and laid them out on fine rugs and set about arming: they laced their chausses and hauberks and hoods, girded their swords of steel and laced their helms and took up their sturdy shields; then they clad their horses – one sorrel, one bay and the third dapple grey – in iron, and then the three knights mounted, each with a pennon on a lance tipped with a piercing head. As for the shields they bore, Carados had a shield of gold so dazzling that it lit the surrounding land, handsomely emblazoned with three red lions rampant; Alardin had a red[56] shield decorated with a flying eagle of white ermine; and Cador had a blood-red[57] shield bordered with gold. Thus armed they rode on till they neared the tourney ground. The girls stayed a little way off in lovely bowers they'd made; they left them there with two knights and other vassals and members of Alardin's household to keep them company. Then without more ado the three knights thrust in their spurs and rode swiftly on till the castle's keep came into view.

They now decided that Alardin should enter the tourney first and have the first joust; so off he went and positioned himself in full view of everyone. He was right below the tower; and to a window on the side with the finest view had come a most attractive girl who beautified the tower more than anything could have done. She looked down and saw the knight who'd stopped below on his horse; and it wasn't a glance she gave him: it was her full attention! She called out, clear as a bell:

'God save you, sir knight!'

Alardin looked up and replied most courteously: 'May the ever-truthful one bless you, damsel! I trust you're not alarmed to see me here?'

'I'd be happier if I knew your name! But if it bothers you and you'd rather keep it secret I won't tell anyone! And tell me why you're dallying here so long.'

'Indeed I shall, girl, and I won't lie – making your acquaintance won't trouble me at all! My name is Alardin of the Lake, and I've come here for no other reason than to take part in the tournament. But to be honest, I want to go incognito if I can.'

'And you're going on your own?'

'Yes indeed. But tell me, girl, do you know if Sir Gawain and Sir Yvain are at the tourney?'

'The finest knights in the world? They will be for sure! I heard them say no amount of money would stop them coming to the tournament and delivering some decent blows!'

Alardin was elated to hear this news of those valiant knights, and he sent his horse prancing up and down – much to the delight of the girl: her heart leapt and she turned pale and perspired and then flushed red as she gazed at him! Her heart was now entirely his – she'd none left for herself: she'd given it all to him! And in the hope that he'd love her in return, she gave him a courtly, loving gift of her sleeve of rich oriental silk to turn into a pennon. She addressed him by his proper name and said:

'I shan't deny it, sir: God love me and grant me honour, there's no one in the world I'd rather know better than you – and you're from this country. King Ris seeks to have

---

[56] *'de gueules vermoilles'*: literally, coloured red with pieces of skin cut from an animal's throat, just as the eagle blazon is made from a piece of ermine.
[57] *'sinople'*. See Glossary.

me, as does King Cadoalan, but never in a month of Sundays would I choose either of them – not for anything! It's you I love, sir, not them! I want them to know I've set my heart on you, my love, for they vainly want to claim me and I don't want either of them! In their haughty pride they've set up this contest today in the presence of the king and me, thinking I'll wed whichever of them wins! If only their pride could be crushed, my heart would be saved from torment!'

Alardin could see the knights were ready to begin, and said: 'Damsel, tell me your name if you will – but don't feel you must.'

'My name, sir, ends in the word for gold:[58] it's Guingenor; and I'm the great-niece of King Arthur – my mother was his niece, being Sir Gawain's sister. My father's name's Guiromelant and my mother's name is Clarissant – it was she who intervened and made peace in the bloody battle between Gawain and my father.[59] Now I've told you my position; and I pray that God who gave me birth will let me see the day when we can talk at greater leisure!'

'All you need to know, girl,' said Alardin, 'is that I'm wholly yours!'

With that he turned away, and to one side he saw a noble, most imposing figure who looked as if he wanted the first joust. Backed by a mighty company and superbly armed and equipped, he came riding proudly before the girl, seeking to have the first joust of the day. It was King Ris, let me tell you, who along with all his entourage had his base inside the castle bailey. King Cadoalan of Ireland had his base elsewhere on the tourney ground, because, as I should explain, it was enclosed by a ditch, high and deep and broad, with a special crossing-place. These were the two kings who'd arranged the tournament. But let me carry on and tell you that King Ris, fully armed, rode from before the castle gate seeking the first joust. Alardin, sporting the maiden's sleeve on his lance, spurred his horse forward and they came at each other full tilt, braced in their stirrups, ramming in their spurs, clutching their blazoned shields tight and charging to meet with all their force. King Ris struck Alardin so hard that he destroyed his lance! And Alardin's blow in return was such that Ris and White Lion-Cub – that was his horse's name – were brought irresistibly crashing in a heap. But King Ris was a valiant knight indeed, and as Alardin came to renew the attack it wasn't clear who would land the first blow, for King Ris had plenty of men determined to see Alardin defeated who rushed to try and remount their king. But as Alardin returned, clutching his drawn sword, he dealt King Ris a mighty blow to the helm: nothing – not the offer of all his kingdom! – would have stopped him felling the king. Now twenty knights burst in between them, assailing Alardin and battling to put their king back in the saddle. One knight against twenty was hardly an even contest! But he did himself proud nonetheless! For all their efforts, and despite their numbers, they couldn't sufficiently wear him down and would never have seen their king remounted had it not been for reinforcements flocking to him from the castle.

But before I say any more I want to tell you about the most illustrious knights in the world, those of the Round Table, and how according to the story they were divided between the two sides. The two most valiant of all, Sir Gawain and Sir Yvain, were with King Cadoalan. So was Kay the seneschal, a fine knight indeed, and Lucan the butler, and thousands more I shan't bother to name. On his side the Welsh king Ris had the king of Estregales and the Rich Soldier and Idier the son of Nu and a hundred other

---

[58] The last syllable being '*or*'.
[59] i.e. earlier in the First Continuation, above, pp. 92–3.

knights. Now, I don't know which of the thousands it was, but as happy chance would have it, although they didn't recognise Alardin they came charging from the other side to help him, and in the process there were casualties, some sorely wounded, some killed. The battle now raged around Alardin. It was a great day for him, that's for sure! What praise he won! They came at him from every side but he fought back mightily.

And then he saw his companion Cador coming from the tower. Cador was sure he could handle whoever first took him on. This proved to be the Rich Soldier, who advanced upon him, seeking a joust, and they clashed so hard that the Rich Soldier's lance shattered as it bent to the utmost, and Cador met him with such force that he brought him and his horse to the ground in a heap. Cador called on him to yield, but he had no intention of surrendering, preferring to sell himself dear. They both drew their swords, and were about to set to when Sagremor the Rash, superbly armed and with a mighty entourage, came charging at Cador with levelled lance. They struck him from all sides, thick and fast, attacking him all together, but still they couldn't unseat him! You should have seen how he fought! Fiercer than a tiger or a leopard, with naked sword in hand he delivered blows on every side. What a ferocious ringing and clashing you'd have heard, as they hammered at him and he struck back with hewing, cleaving blows that left some crippled and others lacking arms. He cut through the press with his blade of steel, dismaying even the bravest. All the same, they came to the Rich Soldier's rescue and managed to get him back in the saddle.

But Cador's mind was now on Alardin: King Cadoalan would have to wait[60] – nothing was going to stop him riding to Alardin's aid. And when the two companions joined forces they offered such fierce resistance that they made all the rest tremble before them. The maidens in the tower couldn't believe their eyes – except the one who'd spoken to Alardin from the window: she wasn't surprised at all, for she'd seen him before – though she hadn't realised he was *quite* so brave! What she saw in him now pleased her more than ever! He'd looked good before – and now he proved it! She knew now that he was a fine knight indeed, and pretty much all of her now was devoted to him: her eyes to gaze upon him, her sweet lips to speak of him, her heart to think of him, and her body – which would be shared with no other! And Alardin, dealing blow after blow, was throwing many a glance her way, and keeping himself where she could see him, all the while hoping in his heart that God in His mercy would do all in His power to protect him.

Meanwhile a very fair and comely girl had taken a shine to Cador and couldn't take her eyes off him – though she knew nothing about him: who he was, from what land he came or who his parents were. It pained her terribly that she didn't know, and she was determined to find out, for she could see how keenly he gave and parried blows, how strong he was in attack and defence alike. No man indeed could have fought better: his deeds were unmatchable. All her heart and mind were set on him, and she swore she'd never be happy till she learned his name. This girl was a sister of the worthy Cahadis, and a cousin of Carados; she'd been born in Britain of Sir Yvain's line, and her name was the fair Ydain. She came to the lovely Guingenor to talk to her of Cador, saying:

'Damsel, do you see those two amazing knights fighting valiantly with their swords against all the rest? Have you ever seen a pair like them? If they were to die, would there ever have been such a tragedy? Don't you think he's really handsome, that knight

---

[60] i.e. Cadoalan's entry into the tournament was being delayed by Alardin's great combat.

on the sorrel horse, with the gold-cotticed* shield? How bravely he bears himself! He's the one my heart is set on!'

'He's brave indeed,' the other girl replied. 'But the one with the red shield blazoned with the eagle of ermine[61] is performing wonders! He'll better the lot of them – he'll scatter all the rest!'

So each girl heaped praise on her knight. But they didn't dare say all that was on their minds: they admitted only the half of it!

While they were talking, into the fray rode King Cadoalan and with him Sir Kay, along with that fine knight Perceval, the good Welshman,[62] and the most splendid company ever led by a king in a tournament: there were many great men at the tourney that day. And as they joined the mêlée you'd have seen the earth shake, lances smashed, shields pierced, great blows struck with whetted blades, men crashing down and leaping up, the strong battering the weak, knights laid out on the ground and empty horses running wild: it must be said, it wasn't the prettiest sight! Anyone who couldn't defend himself was soon forced to dismount – and not with any decorum![63] Those who weren't up to it really came a cropper, and I can assure you the cowardly didn't dare go near! King Cadoalan of Ireland was no laggard: the first knight he met had a tough time of it, being unseated as they clashed – and that was the good King Yder. Sir Kay the seneschal performed bravely, too: in his first charge he challenged the most aggressive knight of all, the proud Agravain. It was a well-matched contest: they vied with each other for haughtiness, and both were querulous men indeed, full of taunts and insults. They charged at each other furiously, as fast as their horses could go, and sent one another crashing with fearsome blows. I'd rather not go into what happened when they got up: anyone who tried to come between them was out of his mind! As for the good Perceval the Welshman, he brought down three in a single charge, felling Cligés first, then Arés's son, and do you know who the third was? It was Idier the son of Nu. All the rest of Cadoalan's company performed well, too, but I'd be worn out by the time I'd listed all who were felled and all who did the felling!

And all the while the two companions, Alardin and Cador, were showing their abundant qualities, still locked in combat without a moment's rest. They were praised more than anyone, and rightly so: they gave King Ris rich entertainment, driving and forcing back his men; all the efforts of the Rich Soldier, Sagremor, Bedivere and all the other knights were vain – they couldn't return King Ris to his destrier, White Lion-cub. The king, indeed, would surely have been taken captive, despite all his supporters, had it not been for the Fair Good Knight[64] who rode to his rescue with a huge number of his company and did him the great favour of mounting him on another horse. No one could describe how hard-pressed now were Alardin and Cador – or the courage and the prowess they displayed. They brought down Sagremor, though he was remounted by Bleheris. Then King Ris came charging at the two loyal companions. Now Sir Perceval arrived and struck the Fair Good Knight to the dismay of his followers, for he couldn't stop the blow bringing him to the ground. Bleheris had nothing to smile about: he was the next to be felled by Perceval. Everyone feared to be his target, for anyone he struck was done for!

Alardin saw Perceval taking care of the fine horse that his prowess had won him. It prompted him to send his good companion Cador to the maiden Guingenor with the

---

[61] This is Alardin's shield: see above, p. 143 and footnote 56.
[62] Perceval's participation in this tournament is his only appearance in the First Continuation.
[63] Literally 'without his stirrup being held'.
[64] '*li Biaux, li Boens*'.

horse he'd won from King Ris. Cador fought his way out of the mêlée with many a mighty blow, and rode up to the window.

'Damsel!' he said. 'May the one who gave you birth bless and keep you and your fair company! So says your knight with the red shield riding yonder, who's done wonders in the tourney; you saw him here earlier, and made him a pennon of your elegant sleeve! He's sent me to present you with this destrier: he won it today from your enemy King Ris. It's his prize, certainly, the first of the tournament!'

'Sir,' she replied, 'may God, who bequeaths all knowledge and made all living things, send great good fortune to the knight who draws my heart to love him more than any other! I've seen today that the great reports I've heard of him are true! It fills my heart with joy to see he's an even finer knight than I'd been led to believe! He deserves to have a sweetheart – and he'll have his just deserts: he has a sweetheart sure enough, right here! Thank him for his present, and tell him that I'm his to command, and shall be all my life! But I hope you won't mind, sir, if I ask your name and if you're his companion, for you're a valiant knight indeed and seem to be of noble birth.'

'Damsel, my name is Cador of Cornwall, and he and I are companions indeed. I'll go now by your leave: I've been gone too long!'

The fair Ydain, tormented now by love for him, presented him with a lance with a silk pennon, saying: 'Take this lance, sir, and bring me back that knight I see, riding up the valley to join the tourney. He's a most presumptuous man called Guigambresil – and he's a foe of yours.'

Cador didn't dally an instant: to prove his courage he charged at him with such fury that he unhorsed him as they clashed. It was a speedy answer to the girl's request! Whether Guigambresil liked it or not Cador forced him to go to her as her prisoner. He didn't go back himself; no, he plunged straight back into the fray. Clutching the lance bestowed by the fair Ydain, he sent the first knight he met flying to the ground; then he used his sword to send the next in the same direction. He did likewise with fully seven or eight, much to the fair Ydain's delight: all day she kept saying how well her lance had been bestowed on Cador, boasting to Guingenor that her sweetheart was mindful of her indeed! He was performing so many deeds of chivalry on her account that it would take all day to recount a half, no, a third, no, a quarter of them!

Now the king of Estregales advanced with his company. Alardin, gripping a strong, stout, mighty lance, charged at him so furiously that the king left his saddle! His men came to his rescue, and he fought fiercely till they managed to remount him. Then three knights came riding up, Sir Girflet the son of Do, and Lucan and Sir Madoc, joined by Perceval the Welshman and Cador and King Cadoalan, who drove into the king of Estregales' men and sent them reeling back, hammering them irresistibly, raining blows on them thick and fast with their whetted swords and forcing them to give ground. But Alardin wasn't finished with the king! They'd fought so long with the sword that the king was exhausted, and his men intervened, trying to rescue him; but Perceval came to support Alardin and beat the throng away. Now Alardin piled pressure on the king; and he looked up at his sweetheart, and called to the king:

'Nothing will save you unless you go and surrender to that girl!'

The king was sure he could defend himself and escape from Alardin. But he was cut off from all support: the Welshman Perceval, along with King Cadoalan and Cador, had his men well occupied, gutting them and their horses! And Alardin, seeing King Ris now isolated, dealt him a blow to the head that sent him unconscious to the ground without uttering a word. When he finally came to, he placed himself entirely at Alardin's mercy, and that was the end of the matter. Alardin let him remount on condition that he promise to surrender to his sweetheart at the window of the tower; and with that Alardin and his prisoner left the fray.

But the Fair Good Knight and the Rich Soldier were set on gaining from their day's work and earning plenty of booty, and thought they'd make short work of Alardin! But they came unstuck when they took him on: it all rebounded on them! While King Ris headed for the window where the girl was seated, and greeted her and surrendered to her quite properly and courteously (and she received him gladly), Alardin was embroiled again with his enemies, who were determined to make him pay for what he'd made them suffer that day! The Fair Good Knight and the Rich Soldier came at him with drawn swords, filled with animosity, and rained blows at him, driving him this way and that. Given half a chance they'd have cut him to pieces! But his helm was intact, his blade was sharp and his strength was undiminished, and before his eyes was his sweetheart to inspire him all the more! He fought back so ferociously that he clove through the Rich Soldier's helm and hood of mail; there was nothing cack-handed about that blow! The blade didn't stop till it bit into the head and almost to the brain: down the Rich Soldier tumbled to the ground. Now the Fair Good Knight was on his own, with no support: he certainly couldn't count on further help from the battered Soldier! He and Alardin went at it furiously. What should I tell you? Right below the tower Alardin ended victorious against both assailants and forced them to surrender to his sweetheart, and the maiden received them graciously.

The tournament had now turned completely against King Ris: his company was in disarray. King Cadoalan of Ireland had almost driven them from the tourney ground; all were reeling from him.

It was now that Carados came charging up; he couldn't see his companions and didn't know where to look for them, but was hungry to win honour. As fast as his horse could bear him he went to give heart to the captive knights, thinking he'd win all the more honour by helping the most hard-pressed. And help them he did indeed: right before them he first unhorsed Cadoalan and then Sir Madoc and then Girflet the son of Do – all three he felled in a single charge! Sir Kay then wanted to take him on, and Carados saw him. I'll tell you what transpired: Sir Kay was a bold knight but loud and abrasive in speech – his rash haughtiness often got him into trouble; and he found himself in trouble now: he charged at Carados and was sent flying, crashing to the ground and dislocating his arm, and Carados rode right over him, battering him almost senseless. He called to him:

'By my life, Kay, you're a bigger fool than I ever was! I've not forgotten how you treated me: not three years ago, at my uncle's court at Cardoil, you ridiculed and mocked me and tried to make life difficult – you'd have done better to keep your mouth shut! And now you've made a fool of yourself, jousting with me here! I do believe it's death for you unless you surrender right away!'

'I surrender, sir, and willingly!'

Carados made him swear that without delay or demur, grumble or gripe, he would go and surrender to his sweetheart, the fair Guinier, at the bower she'd made in the wood. Sir Kay set off at once and made his way as he'd promised and surrendered to the maiden in the name of her beloved Carados. She received him most graciously, and when she realised it was Kay she was all the more delighted, because of his reputation for rudeness.

The tournament raged on, and Carados was having a high old time, delivering blows on every side. And now Sir Bran de Lis arrived with a host of companions, and the contest intensified wondrously; but still Carados displayed more strength and daring than anyone, and I promise you, he battered them so with his sword and fought so tirelessly that he made the great King Cadoalan and all his men turn tail – though I exclude Alardin and Cador and the good Welshman Perceval. Those three most noble knights took the following prisoners from King Ris's side: Sir Perceval took Cligés, and Alardin captured Sir Tors, the son of Arés, a noble youth indeed; and Cador dealt so convincingly with Sagremor the Rash that he sent him captive to his sweetheart whether he liked it or not. These three, as I say, each had a prisoner, Alardin taking his to Guingenor, and Cador delivering his by his own hand to his beloved Ydain. But Perceval didn't have his sweetheart[65] present at the moment, so let me tell you how he nobly behaved.

You've already heard how Kay submitted to the mercy of the fair and courteous Guinier, having been sent to yield to her by her sweetheart Carados. After she'd graciously received him she began to ask him about the tournament and which knight was winning most acclaim.

'Truly, damsel,' Sir Kay replied, 'the one who sent me captive to you is winning more praise than anyone – and he proved his worth when he vanquished me: no one's ever outfought me in King Arthur's presence!'

Guinier was delighted by Kay's words, thrilled to hear such reports of her sweetheart's prowess, and she longed now to see him at the tourney. She set off at once, accompanied only by the Maiden of the Pavilion,[66] that worthy, comely, fair and courteous damsel. They asked Sir Kay if it was far to the tournament, and he said:

'If you need to go, get going – it's no distance.'

So they left Sir Kay at their bower and rode on till they came in sight of the tourney ground and the tower and all the rich display. They sat down in pleasant shade and watched the knights' performance with delight. But I said I'd tell you about Sir Perceval. He'd spotted the girls and rode swiftly up to where they were sitting, taking his prisoner with him. He addressed the Maiden of the Pavilion first, saying:

'God save you, damsel, and your fair companion.'

'God bless you, kind sir, and yours!'

'What brings you, damsel,' Perceval asked, 'wandering through these woods and valleys?'

'Our keenness, sir, to see this tournament!'

While they were talking Lucan the courteous butler rode up, and he knelt before the fair Guinier and surrendered to her.

'I bring you greetings, damsel, from a dear friend of yours who's sent me here to you: he's the valiant knight with the shield of fine gold emblazoned with three lions rampant,[67] but I don't yet know his name. I surrender to you freely as your prisoner, to do with as you please.'

The maiden received him most kindly, saying: 'Sit you down, sir, here; I accept you most gladly for the sake of the one who took you captive, and may God send him honour and praise.'

Meanwhile Perceval was addressing the Maiden of the Pavilion; as a token of friendship he made his prisoner, Cligés, surrender to her. Now Cligés had someone to

---

[65] i.e. his beloved Blancheflor.
[66] Alardin's sister: see above, p. 142.
[67] Carados: his shield was described above, p. 143.

natter with! He had Lucan the butler for company – and they both marvelled at the beauty of the two girls.

The good knight Perceval was in pleasant conversation with Guinier and the Maiden of the Pavilion when he saw Cador and Alardin, who'd left their prisoners with their sweethearts, come galloping up. They hadn't realised who the two maidens were who'd received Cligés and Lucan as captives, and when they arrived they were amazed to find they were their sisters! Then they heard about the captures of Kay and Lucan the butler and understood, and all they could think about then was returning to the tourney. As for Perceval, let me tell you that the Maiden of the Pavilion had offered him her love, and in return he sent her ten captive knights from the tournament that day. But you'll have to forgive me if I don't name all those captured by Carados – I'd probably get them wrong, for I promise you, truly, he took twenty or thirty prisoners, and sent them all to his sweetheart as tokens of his love.

But we'll leave the maidens now. The three knights, Alardin and Perceval and Cador, thrust in their spurs and rode away and charged back into the tournament. But they didn't find their companions as they'd left them: their side was getting a battering, with King Ris driving King Cadoalan exactly where he pleased. Not that Ris could take the credit for that: it was all down to Carados and Sir Bran de Lis, who were enjoying themselves no end, sending countless opponents tumbling: no one could mock their performance that day!

Meanwhile there was one knight who'd been taking it too easy – though he was certainly no fool or idler – and that was Sir Gawain. And now, seeing his companions in retreat, he began to boil with rage; he could bear it no longer, and into the fray he rode and Sir Yvain with him. Valiant knights both, they unhorsed the first two they met, and the knights who followed them did splendidly, each felling an opponent – until, that is, Carados came charging into them and laid out Sir Yvain before Gawain's very eyes. He carried straight on and dealt the Bold Ugly Knight such a blow on his shield that it was almost the death of him – he fell unconscious from his horse. On he rode and struck Perceval; but Perceval met him fearlessly, returning like for like, and I assure you neither knight could keep his seat: knights and horses alike came crashing to the ground. But they were both soon back in the saddle, one remounted by that fine knight Bran de Lis and the other by Sir Gawain. Perceval was furious that Carados had unhorsed him, and pursued him hither and thither, seeking another joust – and again they brought each other down along with their horses, all in a heap. But again they remounted instantly, for they were both valiant knights indeed. And their swords were sharp; there'd have been some blows exchanged had they not been separated by the throng!

But Carados wasn't going to rest for a moment. He wanted to test the very bravest; and indeed he posed many a question that day to which he received no answers! He probed the very strongest and found no convincing response! He piled on the pressure and had them completely on the run! To the dismay of King Cadoalan even his bravest had deserted him. Sir Bran de Lis was in hot pursuit and won great credit there, dealing Cador such a blow that he knocked him from his sorrel horse; if Perceval hadn't come to his rescue Bran would have taken him captive. Bran was enraged as Perceval came out on top, pulling Cador from his grasp, and to avenge his loss he charged at Perceval and drove him from his horse – but Perceval delivered a like blow and they both found themselves on the ground. They'd have started battering each other's bones had Carados and other knights not ridden up and returned them to their mounts. Perceval was incensed at being unhorsed, and longed to take revenge on Carados; he grabbed a lance and headed straight to where he was busy dealing blows. As soon as Carados saw him coming he made ready to receive him; and receive him he did – so fiercely that as they clashed it was impossible to tell who had come off worse. If they wanted to know where each other was, they had only to look on the ground! They'd dismounted without using their stirrups! Perceval was fuming: he drew his sword from its scabbard, bent on instant revenge. But Carados didn't fear him, and drew his sword and drove him back. So fearsome was their combat then that they did each other real damage, hacking their shields to pieces, smashing mail rings from their hauberks and battering in their helms. For all their strength they were soon exhausted, and one of them would surely have been humbled – and what a dreadful pity that would have been – had Alardin and Cador not arrived, heads bowed beneath their helms. When Carados saw these two he feared Perceval now had the upper hand and was about to inflict a crushing defeat – but to his joy he suffered no harm: Cador and Alardin separated them and he rode away.

But he didn't rest: he kept challenging and answering challenges, dealing and receiving blows, attacking and repelling attacks. I don't know what more to tell you about his feats of prowess, but I can assure you he forced King Cadoalan and all his side to retreat; and without a word of a lie he sent his sweetheart Guinier a stream of prisoners including Kay the seneschal and Girflet and Galles the Bald and Lucan the courteous butler; but there are fully thirty-three more whose names I'd rather not record, as there are some whose reputations would suffer if I told you, so I'll leave them out of the list and save them the disgrace! But if the story's to be believed, Carados's prisoners included some of the most valiant knights of all King Arthur's household. Carados, with his amazing strength, won soaring praise that day for capturing so many knights and putting the king to flight.

Sir Gawain was far from pleased by this; he said it had pained him to see his companions defeated before his eyes – and he'd done nothing to help them. He'd seen Carados's feats in the tourney, and provoked by his displays of prowess he charged at him now in a fury. But they clashed three or four times without either bringing the other down, awesomely strong knights that they were.

Now King Cadoalan mounted a recovery; he and his men fought back hard and regained ground, and I'll tell you how it happened. Perceval confronted Carados and so did Yvain and Sir Gawain; they all wanted the first joust, willing to risk all in order to unhorse him, knowing what a worthy knight he was. They charged full tilt from three directions and finally brought him down; and in felling him they struck a mighty blow for Cadoalan in his fight-back against King Ris. But Carados was back on his feet in an instant and came at Perceval. He realised he'd lost his horse, so all he could do in self-defence was kill Perceval's in return. But Perceval and Gawain and Yvain hemmed him in and called on him to yield and not fight on, for they knew him to be such a very fine knight that they'd no wish at all to hurt him. With great respect Sir Gawain kept summoning him to yield, not yet realising who he was; but Carados declared he would never surrender: he would fight on as long as he could. How brave he was to mount a defence against three such knights as they, more daunting than any others in the world! He resisted for a long, long time and put up a mighty fight, admirably giving as good as he got, dealing blows so thick and fast that they couldn't lay a hand on him from any side. But it was no use: sooner or later he'd have been killed or captured, had not Cahadis seen his plight – and not Cahadis alone but also the valiant Idier, son of Nu, and the Bold Ugly Knight, and the Fair Coward made a fourth and that excellent knight Sir Bran de Lis a fifth: all five of them, seeing Carados in trouble, rode nobly to the rescue, and with them you'd have seen a hundred knights from King Ris's side go charging to his aid. They were in earnest: they said they'd have lost their reputations if they allowed him to be taken!

'Better give our all than have him captured! He means everything to us: without him we're nothing!'

That's what they said; now I'll tell you what they did. To his rescue they came, each clutching a well-honed blade of steel. Bran de Lis headed straight for Gawain, naked sword in hand, and cried:

'You'll not take this knight prisoner, sir! It would be a mistake to try!'

'Well he won't be surrendered freely! You'll have to fight for him – and hard!'

Then you'd have seen knights clash and the ground shake, lances shatter, swords strike, severing arms and hands; lances piercing shields and hauberks, iron heads plunging through; steel helms were stove and cloven, knights sent sprawling on the ground, some wounded, others dead. Even the strongest were in trouble. This rescue of Carados had started something that would lead to pain for all! King Cadoalan for one lost out, for sure, for Carados was seized from his supporters and from his grasp, much to the fury of Sir Gawain who'd been about to lead him away a captive. King Ris's men fell on him from all sides, dealing blows thick and fast as they fought to rescue Carados. But truly, Carados fought fearlessly in his own defence, more so than anyone; when he saw support arriving he struck without mercy, wreaking havoc with his sword, making his opponents recoil in dismay. Sir Gawain, Yvain and Perceval were distraught to see him escaping them; and he and Bran de Lis, his excellent companion, killed the horses of all three, bringing them to the ground.

Cador and Alardin knew nothing of all this: they'd been performing wonders in another part of the field, winning much honour, praise and glory and taking numerous prisoners and sending them to their girls. But now they split up and galloped away, racing to be the first to the mighty fray they saw surrounding Carados. When they saw he was escaping they were most aggrieved; they were determined to catch him, and rode in hot pursuit. They didn't realise who he was, for he'd changed shields after losing his own, and with his own horse killed he was now mounted on another he'd won, a much-prized steed from Hungary. Cador charged him first, lance levelled; but Carados, too, had a good stout lance, and once they'd clashed, Cador's horse was there for the taking – he'd have been none the wiser – as he landed head first, legs in the air: he couldn't have told you where he was, not for all the world. Alardin was horrified to see his companion sprawling in the dust; he'd lose all self-respect if he didn't take revenge on the spot. He set himself on his swift charger; he gripped his lance of apple wood; and Carados saw him and knew exactly who he was – but that wasn't going to stop him charging! That's the custom of the tournament: family loyalty and friendship don't stop knights dealing blows! They came at each other with a will, in a raging fury, and smashed into each other so violently, chest to chest, that they were both sent flying from their saddles. But up they leapt, and battered one another with their whetted blades till they both drew blood and bit into flesh and bone. But Carados had the better of it and seized hold of Alardin; but up came Sir Gawain, blazing mad with Carados, convinced he'd take him captive this time – but it still wasn't to be, for Carados, brimming with courage, mounted a bold defence again. Sir Gawain attacked him, sure he'd beat him, and dealt him such a blow on the helm that his head was reeling; Alardin struck, too, from the other side, and Carados almost fell under the weight of their blows. If they could have pressed home their attack they would surely have struck him down, but in the nick of time Sir Bran de Lis came to his rescue. And he wasn't half-hearted as he laid into Alardin, striking him full on the helm with his well-honed blade, steel ringing on steel; he followed this with two more blows that almost brought him down, a third that stove his helm right down to the head, and a fourth that would have felled him if it had landed. But Carados had recognised Alardin and blocked the blow; but in doing so he turned his back on Gawain, and Gawain, seeing him turn, delivered a blow that all but felled him. But Carados didn't give short change: he sprang up and paid him back in full, right on the helm – a fair transaction, to be sure! What a combat started then! By the time they finished they'd exchanged so many blows that they were both worn out: they didn't hold back – they delivered blows at every chance. Each in turn had the upper hand as mighty blows fell this way and that. Back and forth they drove one another, in awe of each other's strength, striking wondrous blows and shedding a deal of blood. Their hauberks were cut to pieces, their shields hacked to bits, their helms smashed open; they were exhausted, spent. Sir Gawain had never been so drained by any test in all his life; he was hungry to know where the knight was from who'd resisted him so long – and not just resisted him, but worn him out completely! He longed to know his name, for no man had ever given him such a tough and testing time.

He couldn't expect any of his companions to appear: they had their hands full, all needing to defend themselves or be killed or beg for mercy, as King Ris's side proved the worthiest. But if anybody won praise that day it was Carados: he was deemed the outstanding performer at the tourney; no one else had done as much or won as much honour as Carados. The contest had to finish now as darkness descended on them – but as they parted accounts were settled with blades and fists alike! But the side who came off worse and had less credit was King Cadoalan's.

It was plain to Gawain that Carados feared nothing – and equally clear that his companions were on the losing side. So he said: 'Tell me truly, sir knight: where are you from, and what's your name?'

Carados made no reply: he didn't want to reveal his identity yet. But Sir Gawain pressed him for an answer, courteously asking:

'Most noble sir, I beg you kindly tell me your name: to refuse would be thought uncivil.'

'Know then, good sir, my name is Carados; I'm from Brittany. Now don't think you can get away without telling me yours!'

'Truly, friend, I've no desire to keep it from you. I am Gawain: I've never concealed my name.'

'I knew that, Gawain!' said Carados. 'And I can't tell you how much I wanted to test you and your renowned courage!'

Gawain was taken aback by this – and greatly impressed by his conduct. Then he said: 'King Arthur's niece the fair Ysave: is she anything to you? Do you know her?'

'Yes, indeed, quite well: she's my mother!'

'Ah, you're really that Carados! I know you now! You're a valiant knight indeed – and my kinsman!'

With that they both threw down their shields and swords and unlaced their helms, pulled back their hoods of mail and embraced most warmly. Their joy was mixed with tears – tears for what they'd made each other suffer, and joy at their meeting. And so the two knights, who'd given each other such a hard time that day, were now acquainted – and because of all the harm they'd done their joy was all the greater, as was their delight at finding each other so full of prowess.

Everyone else was delighted, too, when they recognised Carados – especially Alardin and his companion Cador: they were thrilled when they realised who he was, and rightly so. They were puzzled that they'd failed to know him all day, but he'd fooled them by hiding his identity with a succession of different arms: he hadn't wanted them to recognise him and hold back for fear they might prove stronger than him – and the upshot was that he could now be truly deemed the very best. Now he was plainly recognised as the finest of all at the tournament. The knights had come flocking in scores, hundreds, thousands, when they saw Sir Gawain's joyful greeting of Carados! They wanted to know who the knight was who'd done one side so much damage and the other side so much good! King Ris and Cadoalan disengaged and came from their separate sides, calling an end to the tournament amid all the celebration.

And let me tell you, at the tournament's close and parting, my lord King Arthur gave his great-niece, lady Guingenor, to the courtly Alardin and the fair Ydain to Cador: they were the maidens who'd been stationed at the window of the tower. As for the Maiden of the Pavilion, it pleased both the king and her brother Alardin to give her to the fine and worthy young Perceval the Welshman.[68] So all three found the happiest of marriages. And Carados didn't miss out! He had his beloved, the fair Guinier. So, then, I've told you who they married, but I'm not going to give details of the weddings, of the place or day or time. I want to press on, for I've lots more to tell!

Everyone went their separate ways as the tournament broke up. Alardin and Cador and their companion Carados divided their spoils between them; they were now united, and exchanged embraces and pledges of lifelong friendship. Then they went to take their leave of King Arthur; but he wouldn't give them leave at any price, having seen what fine knights they were! He insisted they stay with him for a good long while; and they stayed, I believe, for almost a year, and had a fine and pleasant time as the king enjoyed a long and leisurely residence.

But I can no longer refrain from telling you about his niece, Carados's mother the lady Ysave. I've been putting it off, but now I must tell you the unpalatable truth. It gives me no pleasure – and if anyone does take pleasure in telling adverse stories of noble ladies, then he's most ungallant. Just because one lady's guilty of a foolish act, it doesn't mean it's typical! They're not all the same! For every one who misbehaves, a dozen are blameless! So it pains me that I have to tell of one of the former: would to God I could end my story here before it takes a turn for the worse! But I'm pleased to say that if the beginning of what follows reflects badly on noble ladies, they come out better by the end! For one of their number expunges and negates any blame they may incur, and that's the worthy and beautiful Guinier. I shan't tell you about her just yet: I'll come to her in due time and place.

The Enchanted Serpent

I want to go back now and pick up the story where I left off. I think I'd told you about the lady Ysave, and how she came to be locked up in the lofty tower at Nantes. But the fact is that Eliavret the enchanter, who'd fathered Carados, was still hovering around, knowing she'd been locked away on his account. Unfortunately for King Caradoc and all the people of his land, the enchanter was undeterred! Driven on by

---

[68] A clear indication that the First Continuation was composed before any development and resolution of Perceval's relationship with Blancheflor.

his love for Ysave, and empowered by his knowledge of magic, he would surely find a way in! Not even the boldest of lovers would have dared, but Eliavret undertook the challenge. And little wonder: being adept at the dark arts as he was, he could hardly resist the chance to impress his beloved! And so he did: in no time at all he was in the tower! But in one respect he went too far, and it was to rebound on him. He cast a spell to fill the tower with harpers and minstrels playing harps and hurdy-gurdies, dancers dancing and acrobats tumbling – it went on like this the whole time he was there!

Now, King Caradoc decided to make an agreeable circuit of the other cities in his land, thinking all was secure, and that no one could do mischief behind his back. But while he was about his business Eliavret came to the queen and they cavorted and took their pleasure as I've just described. So riotous was the carry-on that all the neighbours were kept awake from the moment the king departed! So they sent secret messages to the king; and when he heard the news he was distraught and sighed from the depths of his heart. He ordered that the tower be closely guarded, but it made no difference: they could find no way to stop the goings-on; and so loud were the sounds of roistering that rang from inside it every night that the tower came to be called the Rumpus[69] – and so it is still called in those parts. King Caradoc heard for himself the amazing racket wrought by the enchanter, and you can imagine how upset he was. So he sent for his son Carados.

The messenger set off at once and made his way straight to England. He soon found Arthur's noble court, and asked for Carados and found him there. He greeted him in his father's name and told him the distressing news. Carados asked leave of the king at once, explaining how urgent the business was, and the king granted him leave but made him promise to return as soon as it was sorted out, and to let nothing else detain him. Alardin took his leave of the king at the same time, and so did his companion Cador, and Arthur opened his treasury to them and bade that they be given however much they wished to take. They didn't dally but took their leave of their companions and set off at once. Sir Gawain and Sir Yvain escorted them a long way, until they reached the place where Carados had found Alardin trying to abduct the fair and comely girl Guinier. From there ran roads that would take each to his own land; but it was a tearful parting: they dismounted and took their leave of each other and exchanged kisses before returning to their mounts. Then that good knight Sir Gawain and his companion Sir Yvain rode with Carados down to the coast and saw him safely put to sea on a strong, fine ship. They were very concerned for their friend, and downcast as they watched him go; they returned then to court and rejoined the king.

Meanwhile Cador went back to Cornwall with the fair Ydain, and took his sister Guinier with him: Carados didn't want to take her to Brittany; he preferred that she should stay with her brother, who loved her dearly, than go with him and hear unsavoury news of his mother. But I can assure you, wherever he might be his heart and his mind were with her in Cornwall – no matter that he'd crossed the sea! But I can tell you this as well: their hearts were to suffer much before they saw each other again.

As soon as he landed, Carados, richly clad in gold-embroidered silk, rode swift and straight to Nantes, where he found his lord King Caradoc in great distress. The king was overjoyed to see him and gave him a glorious welcome, making a great fuss of him; and then, once they'd eaten and drunk, he told Carados all that had happened.

---

[69] *'le Bofois'*.

So Carados kept close watch and finally, one night, he caught his father the enchanter in the tower with his mother. And I tell you, the enchanter was made to pay! By way of revenge, the king forced him to couple first with a greyhound bitch and then with a sow; and then, to make the revenge complete, he made him take a mare! As he coupled with the bitch he sired a great hound called Guinaloc – so the hound was Carados's brother; on the sow he sired a huge boar called Tortain; and on the mare a strong, fierce, mighty destrier, Loriagort. All of these were brothers to Carados, being his father's sons. Carados would have had him hanged and flayed as well, but took pity on him, for he really was his father, and he greatly feared offending God if he treated his father as terribly as he might have done. So the king had his revenge, as you've heard me tell, but then they let him go.

Eliavret was seething. I tell you, he wasn't slow to find a way back to Queen Ysave, still lodged in the tower; and he complained bitterly to her about their son and the wrong he'd done him. She wept and wailed when she heard what Carados had made him suffer.

'Oh, my love!' she said. 'You'd be mad not to find a way to take revenge!'

'Lady! It would be a dreadful sin and cruelty to kill my own child!'

'What are you talking about? Did he have pity on you? Not in the least! So why do you care? Are you too weak-willed to take revenge? Oh, I knew it! How short-lived was our happiness! Our joy is over – he's taking it from us and we're too feeble to stop him! I hope you can see how you're letting me down, not paying him back for the harm he's done us – what a coward you are to have pity on him!'

'Listen – I'm his father! I couldn't find it in my heart to kill him! But just to please you, with your help I'll let him live – but make it a life not worth living!'

'I'll do whatever you want: I'm ready! Plan your revenge, and quickly!'

Eliavret promptly left, and came back with an enchanted snake: he'd cast a special spell upon it. Then he told Ysave what to do with the serpent; weaving yet more magic he placed it in a cabinet, and once it was safe inside he told her of his plan.

'Lady,' he said, 'with this serpent we'll have our revenge.'

'How, sir?'

'How? Like this. I beg you, for God's sake don't touch that cabinet whatever you do – don't go near it. Anyone who does will be in trouble! But the next time your son comes up here to chat and relax with you, start to let your hair down and ask him to fetch your comb from the cabinet. As soon as he opens it you'll see the hidden serpent: it'll go straight for him and coil itself around him – so tight that his dearest friends could try for two and a half years and still not get it off! And eventually it'll be the death of him!'

'Oh thank you, sir!' she said. 'What a sweet revenge! He'll suffer more with a lingering death than with a quick one! I may be his mother, but it'll make me no less cruel! I'll do exactly as you say, and bring him to his death.'

With that the treacherous enchanter left her.

It wasn't long before Carados decided to visit his mother. Alas! How could he have guessed the terrible, cruel plan she had in store? It didn't occur to him! Up the tower he softly climbed and said:

'Lady, may the Creator of the world, who purges the good of evil, guard and bless and keep you!'

The queen's reply was quite counter to her heart as she said: 'God protect you, too, dear son! I wasn't expecting you – I haven't seen you for ages! You took me by surprise!

What a state I'm in with my hair undone! It's been bothering me – I was about to dress it with a lovely comb that was brought to me from Caesarea. It's over there in that cabinet – would you fetch it for me? Do stay and spend the day with me – I'd love to share some time together: it's so tiresome being up here alone.'

As soon as he heard his mother's wish he rose and went to the cabinet. He opened it and reached inside. And the serpent plunged its fangs in his arm and wound itself around it. Carados leapt back. He was sure he could rid himself of the snake and repel its attack, and he shook his arm, trying to throw it off – but the serpent bit and clung on all the harder. Carados began to flush hot and cold, shuddering and sweating with the pain: he didn't know what to do. His mother – his enemy! – jumped up, pretending to be shocked by what had happened: she made a great display of wailing and howling and wringing her hands and wishing she was dead.

'Ah, misery!' she cried. 'Why doesn't Death come and take me now? Why has this monstrous serpent[70] seized my son and not me? This evil snake, planted here by demons, it should have attacked *me* – my life means nothing! Oh, dear son, make confession: unburden yourself of the great wrongs you've done your father and me, your mother. For your sinful deeds against us both, the Lord God is exacting vengeance! Suffer it patiently, and beg loud and long to God for mercy, that He may free you from this evil creature!'

Such was his mother's sermon to him – and Carados made no reply at all, but sighed from the depths of his heart, feeling sure, in spite of what she said, that she was inwardly rejoicing. No man could describe the agony he felt.

Nor could anyone describe the grief and wrath that filled the king's heart when he heard the news. He raced to the tower and it was all he could do to stop himself killing the queen: she had to be taken to another chamber in case rage overcame him and he throttled her with his own hands. The king saw Carados, writhing in agony in the serpent's grip, and collapsed in distress, cursing his life and sighing deeply and tearing at his hair and beard. He gave orders for Carados to be carried from the tower, and swore the enchanter would pay dearly: if he could get his hands on him no trickery or spells would stop him inflicting every conceivable pain; nothing would save him from an agonising death.

At least fourteen knights took hold of Carados and carried him down from the tower. A perfect bed was prepared for him in a chamber richly decked with silk, and there they laid him down. But he couldn't rest or find any relief as the serpent wound and coiled itself ever more tightly and painfully round his arm. At last the king sent for doctors from all parts of his land, to see if any could find a way to prise the serpent off. They all had a go, but none succeeded or dared keep trying, and the king began to despair, not knowing what to do to rid Carados of the creature that tortured him. He sent messengers to England, France, throughout the world, begging all who knew anything about medicine – healing stones or herbs, roots or charms or incantations – to come with all speed, for he'd handsomely reward anyone who could free Carados from the snake: he'd give whatever anyone asked. A great many doctors came, but none, regardless of their skill, could apply or strap on anything to make the evil serpent uncoil itself at all.

In her chamber the queen was exultant, ever mindful of the trouble and pain her son had caused her.

---

[70] Literally 'this serpent, this wyvern' – i.e. no ordinary snake.

'Well, boy!' she said. 'God's clearly taking revenge on you for making your mother and father suffer! Now you'll do penance indeed! You'll live out the rest of your days in pain, and die in it, with no relief!'

She went on gloating like this most days of the week. A lot of people heard her, but none of them wanted to disturb the king and risk making him twice as angry – it doesn't take much to double a man's wrath. If anyone had told the king, his rage towards the queen would have soared to the point where he'd have banished her from the kingdom. His temper was so fierce that, had she not been King Arthur's niece, he would already have banished or even killed her.

Rumour travels fast; and soon the news spread far and wide, till King Arthur himself heard about Carados and the serpent that had fixed itself to his arm and couldn't be removed by any medicine or charm. He was in a wood, beneath an elm, when he was told; he was blind with grief, his heart so filled with anguish that he collapsed and sprawled on the ground, unconscious. When he came to, he cursed and berated himself for having let his dear nephew[71] Carados depart all on his own.

'Death should take me,'[72] he said, 'for letting him leave like that! I should have gone with him myself, or sent Gawain or Yvain as an escort. I swear this: if God lets me live, I shan't stay more than one night in any town till I find dear Carados!'

Such was King Arthur's vow; and he leapt up and set out with all speed. I promise you, it was with a bitter heart that he crossed the sea, his whole body racked with agonies of worry for Carados. And the sea was racked, too: hostile winds buffeted and blasted them and blew them off course, so that they landed not in Brittany but Normandy, the ship making landfall at a port named Oustreport. The king and his lords set out from there and rode without rest till they came to Brittany.

But I'm going to leave them for the present and tell you about Cador. The news of Carados, you may be sure, had found its way to Cornwall – to Cador, who was so fond of him, and to his fair beloved Guinier; and when she heard the news she fell flat on her back, so overcome by grief that she was utterly helpless – she might as well have been dead. She lay there in a faint for a long while,[73] bathed in sweat, all colour lost, unable to stand. When she finally came round, she started gabbling senselessly, flushing hot and cold, her heart near breaking. Then she burst into bitter tears and cursed the day her father sired her.

'Dear God, how cruel you are if you take my sweetheart from me! I've every right to curse you – damn me if I don't! Oh, dear Lord God, if I'd seen him just once before he died, my faith in you would have doubled – but now it's weak and shaken! Oh, wretched Death, base and vile! You're taking such a worthy man! Why do you seize on him so soon? What pleasure do you think I feel, seeing you rob me of my love?'

And she grabbed her hair and clawed at it with both hands, tearing it apart; then she collapsed again, grief nearly crushing her heart. When she came to, she wrung her hands and cried:

'Oh, Death, the iniquity! You prey upon the good and let the wicked live! Death, oh Death, how you hate the good, pouncing on them the moment they flourish! Why do you want to take my love? If you're intent on robbing me of him, take *my* life, too – it's a torture

---

[71] See note 52, above, p. 134.
[72] Literally 'my soul should leave my body'.
[73] Literally 'the time it takes to travel a league'.

to me! If he must die, don't leave me out! *I* should die, too, for with my sweetheart gone there'd be no consolation – not for a single day, in any season! It would be better by far that we die together – anyone left when her love has died lives her whole life in sorrow; but love's true servants should have their devotion repaid: God should let us die together!'

And with those words she fainted again. And when she came round she set to work on her face as if her permanent image would be a mask of grief: she tried to tear out her eyes and all her hair – it was truly shocking: she seemed to be going mad.

'Ah, God! I appeal by your most holy name: dear Lord, I beg you intercede with this monstrous, demon serpent, bent on consuming my love! Ah! Foul serpent, loose the arm of Carados! Uncoil yourself from my sweetheart's arm and come and cling to mine! Ah, dear brother Cador, take me to Carados, that I may see him before he's dead, and then die with him in happiness!'

In such grief and distress as I've described – far more, indeed, than I could tell you in a day and a half – did Guinier lament her beloved. Cador, too, was so beside himself that his worthy servants and vassals could find no way to console him.

Then he had a ship made ready, and embarked with his sister and set sail to find the one they loved so dearly. On they sailed and landed in Brittany, and rode day after day over hill and plain until they arrived at Nantes.

Meanwhile ever-swift rumour had flown before them; it was now so rife that Carados himself had heard the news: King Arthur of Britain was coming to see him with a mighty company, and Cador was coming from Cornwall with the fair Guinier, who loved him beyond all words, to tend and comfort him in his sickness. But this news only made him worse: it distressed him so much that he didn't know what on earth to do; he dismissed everyone around him, and stayed all alone in his chamber, distraught beyond description and bitterly protesting:

'Dear Lord God, the one I love most in all the world will be disgusted when she sees my face and flesh so wasted and the serpent clinging to me! And she'll have every right – I'm not worthy to have her as my love: I never was and never will be! Lord God, dear God, what shall I do? How can I go on living? And how can I bear to have the loveliest creature Nature ever made see me here in this wretched state? Alas! What torment! What torture! I dread to have the very thing I long for! I'd love to see my sweetheart if I were flourishing and happy – but I know the moment she sets eyes on me she'll hold me in contempt! I can't bear to have her see me! I know what I'll do: God help me, I'll run away. Run away? What am I saying? True love forbids me to act so basely towards my beloved! So what if she sees me in this state? If she truly loves me she won't hold me in contempt – in the words of the proverb: "Anyone who truly loves is slow to forget". Ah, but on the other hand we read in *Sayings for the Common Man*:[74] "You have so much, you're worth so much: that's how much I love you!" Alas! I'm one who has nothing, is worth nothing: I'm off!'

Carados spent the whole day with his face pointedly turned to the wall, so that if he saw anyone coming he could trick them into thinking he was asleep.

Then, that evening, King Caradoc and a courtly messenger sent the previous night by Cador came to him; and when Carados saw the messenger he wisely hid what he was thinking: it's always best to conceal your thoughts till the right time comes – and if you're thinking foolish thoughts it's best not to reveal them at all! Carados certainly didn't risk it. The messenger stepped up to him and said:

---

[74] '*Diz au Vilain*'. Composed c.1175–90, this was a kind of commentary on popular proverbs.

'Sir, your dear friend Cador has crossed the sea with his sister the fair Guinier, who loves you more than her own heart. She sends you greetings, and promises that before noon tomorrow you'll see them here: your beloved Guinier and your companion Cador, who'd gladly give his own weight in gold, indeed his whole inheritance, to have your return to health sung and celebrated – which it shall be, have no fear!'

'Dear friend, my beloved is welcome indeed, as is my companion! But oh, alas! How wretched I am, unable to go and meet them!'

That was all he said, and he turned pale, reflecting on his miserable state; and as he thought of his sweetheart he trembled with anguish in every limb; as he thought of his love he was so stricken with pain that it seemed Death was about to rob him of his heart – he fell unconscious; but Death resisted taking him, fearing grave reproach if Carados died for love. And love indeed was torturing him, inflaming him with desire to see his sweetheart, but with the desire came fear – fear that when she saw him she'd feel nothing but contempt. But then, it's often the case that you fear what you love – and so now did Carados, as he yearned to see the fair Guinier: with that longing came fear, the dread that her seeing him in such a wretched state would bring nothing but grief. This fear took such a hold of him that all he could think of, rightly or wrongly, was running away: what could he hope to gain from letting her see him as he was? So he turned back to the messenger and said:

'You've brought me great comfort with this news, my friend, assuring me the maiden won't despise me when she sees this evil serpent fixed to me. But I don't know how that's possible! I despise myself – still resisting Death when I'd rather be dead than alive! In God's name, sire,' he said to the king, 'look after this messenger – see that he's comfortable – and leave me with just a servant, for it's not decent or proper for me to mix with other people now. Leave me alone to rest, and to wrangle with myself! My troubles aren't improved by company – it kills me to have people milling around.'

Beside the king stood a servant who'd come with Carados from England.

'He's the one,' said Carados, 'I'd have you leave with me. You go off and have something to eat.'

'But *you* must eat!'

'Not I – be gone now, and let me rest.'

So the king left him and went to sup, taking the messenger with him. And when they'd finished they took to their beds, not wanting to disturb Carados or wake him. So, leaving him with just the servant, everyone went to bed.

They might have slept, but I assure you Carados didn't; instead he called to his servant, saying:

'Don't be surprised or troubled, friend, if I make you my counsellor and put all my trust in you. I've been unwell for some time and I've no confidence in my health, so I'm depending on you. Please keep this plan of mine secret: not far from here there's a chapel where a most devout hermit spends his life in prayer, and I very much want to go to him. I hope you don't mind, friend, but I want to go this very night, for I believe that once he's prayed for me this cruel serpent will be driven from my body. But money won't lure the good man from his bed! That's not his way! Take whatever you brought with you from England – there's no point looking for more.'

'I'll do whatever you ask, sir. I'm ready to do your will.'

So they made ready. Then they unbolted a door that opened on to a garden, enclosed by high walls. They looked everywhere but couldn't find a way out, so they spent all night making a hole in the wall and clambered through. Once they were out Carados knew every twist and turn of the surrounding country, and off he went, burdened with anguished thoughts: I tell you, he wouldn't have turned back for a thousand bezants* – if he stayed any longer his sweetheart might find him, and he couldn't have borne the shame.

He followed a cart track till at last, deep in a wood, he found the house of the worthy hermit. I don't know the hermit's name or the name of his house, but it stood surrounded by nothing but fine woodland packed with more wild beasts, great and small, than you'd ever believe. Carados went straight up and entered the chapel, and the hermit hailed him cheerfully and they exchanged warm greetings. He said a short prayer, for the serpent was hurting him terribly; then once he'd prayed they sat down together. Carados was very weary from his journey, and the soles of his feet were an agony after walking all the way from Nantes when he wasn't used to walking at all. The holy man was the first to speak, asking his name and the land of his birth and what had brought him to the hermitage. Carados told him who he was and explained the whole story, and then he made confession. He showed him the dreadful torture he was suffering with the serpent, and described everything: how his father and mother had surprised him with their trick. Then he prostrated himself before the hermit, blaming and accusing himself for the wrongs he'd done his father and mother, and declaring it only right that he should suffer even more than he was. That was why he'd run away: he didn't want happiness or pleasure in his life till he was sure he'd done penance for the suffering he'd caused them. He wept, sighing from the depths of his heart, and said:

'Truly, I'm the worst man who ever walked the earth!'

He was so distressed that he collapsed on the ground. The good man saw how contrite he was; he imposed a penance, but because of the remorse he showed he gave him absolution.

Then Carados begged him in God's holy name that, if he came across anyone looking for him, he would tell them nothing or give any sign that he'd ever seen him in his life.

And I tell you, Carados stayed there at the hermitage and lived in the woods with the holy man for a long while; the holy life pleased him and he duly served his penance. The hermit freely shared with him whatever food he had, and sent for more sustenance from the houses he knew of in the country round about, for Carados couldn't get used to living on such very poor fare as the good man could provide. And because he lived so far from others, the hermit had a servant who patiently saw to his needs, and Carados had his servant, too, who did all he could to serve and please his master faultlessly. Carados followed a strict regime: he fasted three days every week by way of abstinence and penance. They lived like this for a long time without anybody knowing, for the hermitage was remote indeed: it was a good ten or twelve leagues from that wood to Nantes, down very narrow paths, and at least four leagues to the nearest house.

Here the story leaves Carados, confined with the hermit, sharing his austere and arduous life, and returns to King Arthur, who'd crossed the sea to visit him with a great number of his household, very distressed by the news of his affliction.

King Caradoc was thrilled when he heard that Arthur was coming. The messenger had taken all night to get there: he'd lost his way and had often had to dismount and walk, after leaving King Arthur at Mont Saint Michel the previous morning. In his hand was a letter from Arthur to the king of Verne,[75] sending word that he was coming to his

---

[75] Caradoc is the king of Verne: see above, p. 131.

land to see him, both in friendship and also because of his concern at the news about Carados and the serpent fixed to his right arm. The messenger arrived at Nantes at the crack of dawn, utterly exhausted. King Caradoc, because of his worry and distress, had woken very early, and the messenger came before him and hailed him and delivered the letter. Caradoc had it read at once, and as soon as he heard it he bade that his horse be saddled and said he'd go and meet Arthur. He went straight to where he imagined Carados was asleep and resting, to tell him the news. He came to his door and called to him; but when he heard no reply, then, loving him dearly as he did, he decided not to disturb him, assuming that he was sleeping.

So he went to his horse and mounted with a great escort of nobles of high degree (I couldn't tell you how many), and set off to give a joyful welcome to their lord King Arthur – for Arthur was their lord indeed, as he was of so many lands:[76] on neither side of the sea could any man claim lordship of a land but he did so as King Arthur's vassal and paid him due service for it. They all rode to meet him, and down one hill they went and up a mountain, and there it was they found Arthur of Britain. When the kings saw each other approach they ran to meet, laughing and weeping: laughing for joy at their meeting (and because it was their nature), and weeping for their shared distress. And indeed, it's often the way: when friends meet laden with grief and worry, their heartache and sorrow intensify. And that's what happened now: when they saw one another they started weeping before either could say a word – and if they'd known the whole story they'd have wept all the more! If they'd known that Carados had run away you wouldn't have seen them laughing.

But no one knew at all – not even his beloved Guinier or her brother Cador, who were likewise on their way to see him. They arrived at Nantes at a fateful hour: they were received with all honour, but alas! what a shock awaited them – they didn't find the one they'd come for. They asked at once how Carados was and where he lay, and were shown to his chamber. But the door was shut tight – Carados had seen to that when he and his servant left. Guinier was the first to call:

'My love,' she said, 'open the door! If you won't come out, open up and your love will enter! It's not right to hide when you hear your sweetheart call! Open, open, my dear sweet love! I've been so worried about you – I haven't known a moment's rest since I heard of your affliction!'

When she saw he wouldn't open, and didn't seem to trust that he could come to her, she started crying louder:

'Oh my love! What wrong have I done, that you treat me so? Why are you hiding from me? Do I need the king's authority to open this door? I'll get his key if I have to, by God I will! I don't understand it: I know if my love were alive – or even if he were in Paradise – nothing would stop him coming to see me if he heard me at his door! I fear he must be dead! Dear brother, is this door too strong to be broken down?'

Then Cador found the wherewithal to force the door open, and they plainly saw that Carados wasn't there – and found the door to the garden open wide. Gripped now by alarm, they scoured the garden and all the ground around the house and found nothing at all – except the hole through which he'd escaped. They could wail as much as they liked, but he was ever more distant: if they wanted to find him, they'd have to look further afield. They were all stunned; their blood froze in fear and bewilderment.

'Ah, ah, my love!' cried the fair Guinier. 'What trick is this you're playing, running off without me? I won't let you! I think you mean to die alone! Well it won't work! I

---

[76] Literally 'lord of them and of all the empire'.

won't live a single day in this world after you! You shouldn't have run away, no, you should have sent me a message the moment the serpent struck, bidding me come and join you in your plight – a trouble shared is a trouble halved.' Then she lamented: 'Alas! Why was I born, when my sweetheart turns his back on me and flees? I should be burnt alive – I see it now: the only reason he's run away is he couldn't bear to stay and hear me weep and wail! And now, alas, he's gone, taking my heart with him! If he dies it'll be the death of me, too – I can't live without a heart! If he dies, I die – and it'll be a godsend!'

Lovers among you, judge for yourselves whether there's still such love in the world. Indeed there's not; a different kind of love prevails now: some women love men solely for what they can give them, and when such women give their love it's just by way of payment, not really love at all. Others, though, don't care about gain – they love men solely for their looks! And what faithlessness results: when such a woman sees a more handsome prospect she has a new lover instantly! And there's another kind of woman, too, who loves a man for what he does for her, but the moment his service fails it's the end of her love. But what about men? I shouldn't let them off! A man's way tends to be to turn a woman's head and heart with his beguiling tongue, but if he finds she's not the brightest he'll make a total fool of her, leaving her confused and bewildered, rejected and rebuffed, while he goes off to chase another. Tricksters like that do love a grave disservice. Other men are fickle and capricious, their love a fleeting lunacy, boundless and baseless! And if they don't quickly get what they want, it's tantrum time! They abandon love and pour scorn upon it, suddenly despising what they'd just been mad about. And if they do get their way, well – even worse – as soon as they find someone to tell, they'll tell it! That's not the way of true love – it shouldn't start or end like that; a true lover must expect to take the rough with the smooth, and make sure, upon his soul, that Love doesn't find him guilty of pride. And if he's lucky in love and it all works out he needs to keep it quiet! The moment love starts being blabbed about, it quickly turns into a joke. Those of you who are faithful lovers, I commend you to the Lord of heaven; those who make a mockery of love, I commend to the ones who stoke Hell's fire.

As for Carados and his beloved Guinier, I don't commend *them* to the latter! How could I? For in them could be found all the qualities to be looked for in true lovers – and how they suffered for it! So much for love's delights – one was in tears, the other in flight! And the one who'd fled was grieving for the one he'd left behind, and you can well imagine her pain at being left. Their hearts, I tell you, were inseparable: one might flee, the other remain, but they were really still together: Carados's heart was with Guinier, and Guinier's heart was with him in the wood.

Meanwhile King Arthur had arrived at Nantes, and had heard the woeful news. Before he'd even got there a messenger had come and told him that Carados had gone – he'd run away from them and nobody knew where. The king was less than happy at the news: if he'd been worried before, now he was even more so.

'By God our Lord,' he said, 'words fail me – I don't know which way to turn. Oh, God! What's the point of going to Nantes when I know my nephew's gone? Is this really true, boy? I hope you're not deceiving me!'

'By my life, sire, it's the truth! Come and see, and then you'll believe me!'

So to Nantes he came, and Carados was nowhere to be seen; but he found his sweetheart Guinier in terrible distress, earnestly praying for death. They didn't dally, I can assure you: they set off at once in search of Carados, and scoured every castle and town, every field and wood. They even came to the hermitage where he was staying! But they didn't realise he was there, so thorough was his disguise. To avoid being caught he'd donned the hermit's voluminous, sleeveless cloak and a white smock, and his face was completely hidden in a hood. His footwear was as rough as the rest of his garb. So for the moment, by guile and trickery, he avoided recognition.

In short, King Arthur and all the barons and counts, castellans, princes and lords searched the whole of Brittany and left no stone unturned, but they didn't find Carados. The king was distraught. Touraine, Anjou, Poitou, Maine, Normandy, France and Burgundy, the Thiérache,[77] Germany, Saxony – all the lands on this side of the sea – they searched in the hope of finding him. Already weary, they crossed the sea and went scouring the whole of England to its furthest tip. How distressed they were when they didn't find him – the king more than anyone: he was sick with grief and said he would gladly die; Sir Gawain was almost as bad, as were Yvain and Tors the son of Arés and all the rest of the royal household. For the king's sake, and in their depression at failing to find Carados, they didn't move from Cardigan when their search was done but stayed there, in such a state that it's a wonder there was life left in their bodies. But when they could bear it no longer, and realised grieving would do no good, they picked themselves up and went their separate ways across the country, feeling helpless but tired of mourning. So matters stayed for two years or more, with no news at all of Carados – no one heard a thing.

But I can assure you Cador kept searching for his friend through many lands, accompanied by his sister Guinier. He combed all Brittany before crossing back to Cornwall, and though others might have abandoned the search Cador set out and carried on alone, leaving his sister in Cornwall, well provided for. Then he scoured England and Ireland, Wales and Northumberland; from there he crossed to Spain before returning to Brittany. And by the time he'd hunted everywhere, achieving nothing but toil and hardship, more than two years had passed and Cador had searched for Carados without respite. Yet still he swore he wouldn't break his word or fail in his promise: he'd keep on till he found him, wherever he might be. And let me tell you how he asked for news as he roamed the land.

'In God's name,' he would say, 'tell me, good people, have you seen a man with a serpent clinging fast to his arm?'

But all they'd do, the people he asked, was commend themselves to God and cry: 'God have mercy! We've never seen him here – there's no one like that in these parts!'

So Cador carried on in his hunt for his companion.

For his part, Carados was living by foraging.[78] He'd left the hermitage that summer and gone in search of other holy men, wandering the woods and grazing on wild plants, doing penance through this harsh existence. And still the serpent tortured him, sucking blood and flesh from him. It was no joke, I assure you: he was in such a state, so sapped and drained, that even if Cador had seen him he might well not have known him: he was very nearly broken.

He found himself at last in a patch of woodland close to a delightful hermitage, where a company of good men conducted services to Our Lord in a chapel, small but handsome, beside the stream from a spring that ran down into a valley little visited

---

[77] '*Tiesche*'. The Thiérache is the area of North-East France and modern Belgium including Lille, Douai, Cambrai and Valenciennes.
[78] Literally 'solely on herbs'.

by anyone. It was a solitary, charming spot, where God was most worthily served. Carados had taken shelter in a thicket in this wood, living out his days and waiting for his life to end. He harboured no further hope of cure, and was living on roots and on water from the spring. And every day of the week he would take a narrow path down to the chapel to pray and hear the divine service. The good men – in their generosity and for love of the Creator – kindly provided him with such food and clothing as they had; and they saw for themselves the evil serpent that clung fixedly to his arm, and heard the poor unfortunate, suffering such a bitter penance, cry in pain. After eating a little he would return to his thicket, seeking no greater comfort than that God should grant him death.

Cador had searched for him through many lands, and was at a loss to know where to look for him next, when he came by chance to the hermitage where poor Carados was staying. Night was falling, and he asked the good men for lodging, which they granted, giving him such food as they had. He asked them if they knew or had ever seen a noble man with an agonising, hideous serpent on his arm that was killing him, and one of them replied:

'Dear sir, he comes here every day! You'll see him here tomorrow when he comes to hear mass.'

Cador, his hopes raised, said: 'Good sir, is he well-built, and dark-haired?'

'Well, dear friend, you might say so. He was well-built when he was in health, but now he's reduced to skin and bones. And I don't know his name.'

Cador's heart was soaring. He went and lay down – but the night seemed endless: he never stopped complaining about the bed, which was rather less than comfortable, though the good men had made it the best they could. But night passed and day came, and Cador couldn't wait to complete his mission. And Carados, sure enough, came early to chapel. Cador had hidden in a corner out of sight, so that Carados would be unaware of him till the moment he held him in his arms. So Carados, expecting nothing untoward, calmly entered the chapel and prayed most feelingly to God. Cador saw him and couldn't believe it was him, but came forward nonetheless. Carados was intent on praying, but Cador stepped in and interrupted, saying:

'Ah, God help me! Brother, brother, what ever brought you here? I've worn the soles off my feet[79] searching for you! I've scoured so many lands I'm quite worn out! It's a good two years since I saw you last, my dear, gentle friend! But who ever put you in this get-up? They didn't do you any favours, dressing you like this!'

Carados was wearing two tunics and a pair of thick, coarse boots, with a hooded cloak slung over the top. As Cador looked at him he wept with pity – but at the same time he was filled with joy that his search was over, for he would otherwise never have stopped till he found his friend. As for Carados, to put it bluntly he was filled with shame at the sight of his companion: not for a valley-full of gold – not for the whole world! – would he have said a word to him. He pulled his hood over his face and fell prostrate on the rush-strewn chapel floor. Cador stepped forward and picked him up and kissed him.

'Ah, friend,' he said, 'you've suffered so long with the serpent that shrivels and wastes your body. Don't deny it – there's no point trying to hide! Here we are in church, so don't conceal the truth but tell me: why were you so determined to leave your land? And why have you abandoned your beloved Guinier?'

---

[79]   Literally 'I've made my legs and feet bleed'.

At the name of Guinier, Carados started to weep and sigh, and said: 'Truly, dear friend, I was afraid her heart would harden and she'd despise me when she saw what had become of me. That's why I've run away – I'd sooner be dead and buried! In fact that's all I want – my life means nothing to me now.'

What bitter tears and sighing followed, as Cador wept at Carados's despair. He begged him to think otherwise but he refused; he tried to approach but he rebuffed him – Carados couldn't bring himself to be embraced. They carried on like this till their sorrowful cries brought all the good men running. They pleaded with Carados, but nothing – fond prayers, appeals in the name of God and His dear mother, the apostles and the martyrs – would persuade him to leave that place. When Cador saw there was no alternative, that for the moment he'd have to leave him there and find some other way, he begged and bade that the good men care for Carados and give him what he needed, 'and I promise you, truly, everything you do for him will be well rewarded'. And with that he departed, leaving his companion with the good men at their house.

He went to Nantes and found Carados's mother – she could hardly be anywhere else.[80] He came before her and greeted her, but then fiercely rebuked and berated her for doing nothing to help her son when she'd caused him to suffer so much and for so long.

'Everyone, lady – from the wisest man to the most drunken sot! – agrees that it's all your doing: it's through your deliberate wickedness that the snake's fixed to his arm! Everyone blames and accuses you! But let me tell you: you could redeem your reputation by saving him. A mother should discipline her child through punishment, sure enough, but after a beating she should console him, not leaving him to bear a grudge but seeking reconciliation: after punishment there should be warmth.'

Ysave knew perfectly well that Cador was pleading for Carados, but she pretended not to understand and said: 'My dear Cador, what's got into you?'

'I'll tell you, lady! It's Carados I'm talking about, your forgotten son! It's a cruel and heartless mother that lets her child suffer so much when she could prevent it – God forbid that Paradise should ever be lumbered with such a woman!'

'What? Is Carados alive, then?'

'Indeed he is, lady!'

'Upon my soul, I didn't know! He's alive – and I thought he was dead: I've been blaming myself for it! I'd be blamed indeed, and deemed most cruel, if people heard my child had died in agony when I could have saved him. Come back tomorrow, and I'll tell you if he can be cured or if the snake will kill him.'

Cador left the lady then and waited till next day. When he saw it was time to go and speak to the queen he came to her, and she summoned him to follow her to a chapel on one side of the house. They went there alone.

'Cador,' she said, 'my heart grieves terribly for my child. I feel such pity that I've sought a way to heal him.'

'Let's hear it, then,' he said.

'Oh truly,' she replied, 'it's not going to be straightforward. Listen: a girl would need to be found who was clearly his equal in nobility and beauty and loved him as much as her own life; then, at the time of the Full Moon, two tubs – not too big and not too small – should be set beside each other, three feet apart, one full of vinegar and the other

---

[80] i.e. because she was still imprisoned there, in the tower called the Rumpus: see above, p. 155.

full of milk; once that's done, Carados, so withered and thin, should get in the vinegar and, without qualm or hesitation, the girl should get in the milk with her right breast leaning on the rim of the tub; then she must call upon the serpent to leave her sweetheart and fasten on her breast. When it hears the maiden's plea – and smells the vinegar – and sees the girl, so white and tender, offering her breast, it'll leap from one to the other; and as it does so a man with a drawn sword, if he's brave enough to strike, will kill it before it can recoil. I promise you, it's the only way Carados can be rid of the monstrous creature; find such a girl and see for yourself.'

The lady proffered this advice – but gave no hint of where the idea had come from. The truth was that the fiend Eliavret had visited her that night, and while they were romping and cavorting in bed she'd said:

'My sweet one, I fear terribly for my soul – that it'll be utterly damned for the cruel fate we've inflicted on our son: we're destroying him, and it's all my doing! I beg you, find some remedy: tell me how to make it loose its hold, the serpent that's drained him so horribly.'

It was then that the enchanter gave her the idea I've told you; and he said: 'You don't realise, lady, but by God the king on high, Carados had only three months left before he'd have died – he could have done nothing to prevent it.'

So that's where the lady had got the idea she put to Cador. He took his leave and returned to Carados and consoled him with the good news, telling him about the cure in every detail.

'Stay here, my dear companion,' he said, 'with heart and hope, and I'll go and see how your beloved Guinier responds: she'll surely not refuse to risk herself for you.'

With that Cador departed, leaving Carados with the good men at their hermitage in the woods.[81] He bade them take good care of him and make sure he had everything he craved or needed. 'I'll be back very soon,' he said, 'and reward you well.' Then that loyal friend Cador set off and rode to the sea and embarked and sailed straight to Cornwall, where he found his sister, the unhappy Guinier, most forlorn. The moment she saw him she longed to know what had happened. She was glad to see him looking well, and then he told her the news that made her heart soar:

'Dear sister,' he said, 'I've found the one you love most in all the world.'

'You've found him? You can't mean it!'

'Sister, I swear: I wouldn't be so cruel as to joke. I've found Carados.'

'Where, brother?'

'In a wood, living on herbs and roots. And there's no way he can be cured, dear sister, except by you.'

'By me? How?'

And he told her. He explained the idea that had been put to him, and how she could rid her beloved of the fiendish serpent if she would surrender her own body to the creature.

'Truly,' she said, 'I'll put my body at stake to rescue him: I've not forgotten how he risked his life for me.'

They didn't tarry long; next day at the crack of dawn they made ready and headed for the sea. They took ship and made the crossing, rode through Brittany and came to the wood where the path forked and led them to the hermitage.[82] Such friends are to

---

[81] Literally 'abbey in the wooded enclosure'.
[82] Here again the hermitage is referred to as an 'abbey'.

be treasured indeed, when they suffer toil and hardship for the sake of their companion – as is a girl who will risk her very life for her beloved. God would hardly be merciful if he failed to reward this girl, Guinier, who was submitting herself to such torment for her sweetheart's sake – it's hard indeed for a woman to suffer death for her beloved: a woman is a soft, weak thing when it comes to facing death; but Guinier wasn't made like other women: she was endowed with greater qualities than I could ever tell you. The hearts of false lovers should feel nothing but remorse and shame, for they don't understand the meaning of love! Anyone willing to be Love's true servant, be he never so unhappy, will find joy for sure; for nobody serves Love in vain – he'll be well rewarded. But as for false lovers, feigning love, true love will always find them out. Love always sees through all pretence, but those who love without deception will find that a rich reward lies in store. And these two, who'd endured so much for love, had certainly not been faking!

In the name of love and companionship they came at last to the hermitage, and as soon as they were spotted they were warmly welcomed: the good men did all they could to honour them. Then they led them to the chapel; and when Carados saw Guinier, his rose-cheeked sweetheart, he was beside himself with joy. He began to weep with happiness, laughing through his tears. Shame gave way and let him find his tongue, and Love kept urging him to give the girl a joyful greeting – and he followed the advice! He resisted no longer! No one was going to stop him, ailing though he was, from rising to greet her as fast as he could manage. But when he was standing, let me tell you, he was tall and thin and pale. He was wearing three heavy, shabby, grubby cloaks like a hermit, and clumping boots – without spurs! – on his feet and two hoods on his head to keep out the cold. He was a sorry sight: his brow was wan, his eyes sunken, his nose and cheekbones jutting from his drawn and haggard face; his voice was rough and croaky, and his beard, dark and tangled, came down to his waist and his long and tousled hair right down his sides. His whole body, honestly, was tinder-dry, for the serpent wound around his arm had drained him, as surely as if he'd been starved, of all the strength and beauty he'd been given by Nature. But now Carados came to his beloved, and as he looked at her, all the ills he'd suffered so long were quite forgotten. I can't put into words the joy they felt: how could anyone describe the happiness of two such lovers? But I can tell you this much: despite his haggard face and his beard and hair, the girl thought no less of him – no, she held him tightly in her arms and kissed him tenderly. But what's the point of keeping on, when I couldn't convey half the joy and suffering their love was causing them? Joy they felt at being together, but they suffered, too, knowing how much pain they were inflicting on each other: Carados was in agony that his beloved Guinier was willing to risk death to free him from the serpent.

'Have no fear, my love,' she said. 'I've come here to save you – to put my life at stake for yours, by Saint Peter the apostle; and there's nothing else for it but to make ready.'

He set about dissuading her, saying: 'That can't happen. I'd rather die alone than have you die with me.'

'My sweet love, by the faith I owe God the celestial king, I'll have it no other way! I couldn't bear to see you die when I have a chance to save you or at least die at your side! My heart would be in agony if I were left and you were gone. If you die, I die: I couldn't live without you!'

Cador spoke now, too; he embraced and kissed his companion and said: 'Dear friend, she's my sister, and I wouldn't have either of you die at any price! But do this much for us, I pray you, and to preserve yourself from death: in one of two tubs you're about to see, take off your clothes and climb in; your sweetheart Guinier will climb in the other and entice the serpent to her. The evil creature will leap for her, and as it does I'll cut off its head and rid you of it and set you free.'

And Guinier said to Carados: 'Do as Cador says.'

'I shan't!'

'You shall!'

'I'd rather die!'

'No, die you won't, so help me glorious God! I'll never do anything for you if you won't do this for me!'

'Go to it, then, my love,' he said. 'Make your preparations. But be sure of this: if you die in saving me, I'll have to die on your account! Truly, I couldn't bear to live if my life had cost my sweetheart's death!'

When Cador heard Carados assent to the plan he called for the tubs and had them filled – one with vinegar, the other with milk. Then he bade his sister climb straight in the milk, naked, and lay her breast on the rim of the tub; and into the other, set three feet away and filled with clear vinegar, free of dregs, stepped the valiant Carados. He sank in right up to the neck, so that the snake was plunged in the vinegar, making it writhe in pain. Then hear what Guinier said, as she enticed the evil creature:

'Look at my breasts! How white they are, how soft and comely! Look at them, whiter than may blossom! And how bitter is the vinegar! And how thin is Carados – there's nothing left to take from him! There's no point clinging there – you'd do better to leave him and come and take hold of me! I conjure you, serpent, by God the almighty king, let go of my beloved's arm and fasten to my breast! For I am white and plump and soft – you'll be well off with me!'

Meanwhile the godly hermits had said the mass of the Holy Spirit with great devotion, and came now in procession to where Guinier was summoning and appealing to the serpent; there they made their prayers to God, begging Him to destroy the evil creature there and then, before it could do any more harm to Carados or the girl. For its part, the serpent felt the vinegar burn and sting, and saw the milk and the damsel luring and enticing it, and could find nothing more to suck from Carados; it unwound itself from him and leapt across, darting at the girl's right breast, but her brother was right beside her, naked sword in hand, and he struck the serpent a well-aimed blow, severing its head – but with it he took the tip of his sister's breast, which was in the serpent's maw: in severing the serpent's head he also cut off the nipple. The serpent crashed to the floor and Cador fell upon it, hacking it to pieces, avenging his companion in full. Then Carados leapt from the tub, distressed for Guinier and the hurt to her breast, but elated to find himself cured and free of the monstrous snake.[83] Cador, beside himself with joy, took him in his arms, and Carados hugged and kissed him in return, over and over, before running to Guinier and taking her in his embrace. The fair girl wept. Cador lifted her from the tub, stark naked, and dressed her in fine, rich clothes; and Carados, too, donned his – but not the poor, wretched garments the hermits had lent him: they brought him others, much finer and more handsome. Then the hermits and Cador and Carados attended to Guinier, and looked to her wound. One of the godly hermits had some knowledge of medicine and applied a healing poultice; and he also drew from Carados the poison that the serpent, so long bound to him, had leached into his body. They

---

[83] As above (p. 157) the word used is '*guivre*' (from which the English 'wyvern' is derived), implying an unnatural creature.

bathed and took such care of Carados and Guinier that within a week they were both healed – though they could think of no way to restore the tip of her breast.

How could Carados be unhappy now, when he could hold and kiss the one he loved? In the joyous company of his beloved he revelled, and Guinier, too, was deeply happy, holding her sweetheart once again. They found much comfort and pleasure – though all of it innocent – in the joys of love.

Carados was well tended – he was shaved and washed and his hair was dressed; and so strong was his constitution that, truly, in less than a month he'd recovered from all the harm inflicted by the serpent. But one trace of it did remain: where the snake had clung to him, I promise you, one bone was now half the length of the other; and because of the size of this arm he came to be known as Carados Shortarm. It was perfectly clear where the snake had been, though the arm was no less strong. Meanwhile Cador roamed the surrounding land to find them food, and so they carried on happily.

Gradually word of what had happened spread till it reached King Caradoc. He couldn't believe it, and rode through the forest seeking further news, till he came by chance to the hermitage where Carados Shortarm was staying. Carados didn't try to hide: the moment he saw him in the distance he went running to meet him and took him in his arms in a warm embrace, kissing and holding him tight. The king's escort were filled with joy to see Carados and his fair-haired sweetheart and his companion Cador – such joy indeed that I shan't linger and spend time describing it! Then the king bade everyone make ready, and as soon as they'd done so they were off; and as they departed they bestowed such riches on the hermitage that they left it the wealthiest abbey in Brittany: for Carados's sake they gave so much gold and silver and revenues, fiefs and holdings that there was none better off in all the world.

They made their way straight back to court, arriving there one morning. And then, in short, all the barons and counts of Normandy, Brittany, Anjou, Poitou and Maine[84] were so thrilled and happy at the news that none except the sick could bear to stay in city, town, manor, fort or castle: they wouldn't rest or be content till they'd seen Carados for themselves. They flocked to see him, and wouldn't even let him sit in peace! He had to stand and greet every nobleman who came, and I tell you, he was so worn out he couldn't bear it! When night came he left the throng and went off on his own, for the serpent had sapped his strength so much that he couldn't cope with it all.

The king had been honouring Cador and his sister highly – indeed, he conducted her at his right hand – and they set off with Carados to Nantes; for Carados wanted to see his mother who, thanks to him, had been long imprisoned there. She was still locked in the Rumpus;[85] but her son now set her free, and knelt before her and humbly begged forgiveness for the harm he'd caused her. She did forgive him and, to conclude, he ensured she was a prisoner no more; now she could walk and go riding up and down the land at will. And in saying that, I don't mean to imply that she was still seeing another man and loved anyone other than the king. But I'm going to leave her now, for I've much else to tell.

Carados didn't rest; he prepared in earnest to go and see King Arthur. King Caradoc was similarly inclined, and they did as they planned and crossed the sea and landed in England. They didn't have to go far to find the court, for King Arthur had already heard

---

[84] All the extant MSS read '*Alemeigne*' (Germany), but geography suggests a scribal error in an early copy.
[85] '*Bofoi*', the name given to the tower where she was imprisoned: see above, p. 155.

that Carados had been found and was fully recovered, and he was eagerly making his way to see him. When he heard he'd landed he was happier than he'd ever been in his life; he couldn't wait to see him and vowed he'd ride until he found him. On they rode till the two parties met, and the moment they caught sight of each other they spurred their horses forward to greet one another joyfully: so joyful was the meeting indeed that no man in the world could describe it. Everyone in King Arthur's household flocked to join the celebration, weeping with happiness. They were making up for all their grief and worry, their relief being even greater than their previous distress: it's often the case that depths of sorrow lead to heights of joy. But I'm not going to pile words on words describing it all: that would be tiresome!

In short, they spent a long while in England with the good King Arthur, and the bold, valiant knights went in search of adventures: Carados Shortarm, I assure you, tested his prowess in a fair number. Then the time came when his lord Caradoc, king of Verne, died, and left him his kingdom as his heir. Before he died he summoned Carados to his side, and in the presence of his uncle King Arthur he bequeathed the realm to him, with Arthur's full approval. But Carados began by protesting:

'Ah, my good lord, my dear friend, I told you a long time ago that I'm not your son! I'm sorry you're not my father, truly I am, but I have to tell you I've no desire to take another man's land or possessions. Indeed I don't wish to have any land unless I win it myself: people would think ill of me if they heard I'd usurped another man's rights.'

Such were his words in a staunch refusal; but he was finally persuaded to accept this fine inheritance in the presence of King Arthur. Then King Caradoc died, his days were done, and he was given most honourable burial. Carados Shortarm mourned him deeply for the full forty days of Lent, King Caradoc having passed away at the beginning, I believe.

King Arthur then proclaimed his intention to hold court at Nantes on Rogation Day; and so many people gathered there that I wouldn't like to guess the number: when they heard the king's proclamation, and that he planned to crown Carados there, they came flocking from all parts without delay, along with men of every craft and trade who hoped to serve the court and win reward. Knights and ladies and maidens – of every degree of beauty – all assembled. Cador of Cornwall's sister, the fair Guinier, was there for sure: Carados had no intention of being crowned without her, for she was his love as he was hers, and both had risked their lives for each other, so it was only right and proper that they should now know joy together – and so they would, I do believe.

When the day dawned Carados dressed in the richest garb: a tunic and mantle of silken cloth superbly embroidered with little golden doves. He was a noble, handsome sight indeed, pleasing to every eye. And the ladies bathed Guinier and washed and combed her hair and carefully set it in its band, and beneath her cloak, lined with gorgeous ermine, they dressed her in the very same silk that Carados Shortarm wore. Her handsome mantle, lined with squirrel fur and edged with sable, bore two special stones that made the wearer irresistible: she would be hated by no one; she would be loved and adored by all. In this they clad the fair Guinier; then that noble maiden was escorted to church by King Arthur on the one hand and on the other by Sir Gawain. Her cheeks aglow with a bashful flush, anyone who saw her might have thought she was made for stealing hearts. Carados, too, was handsome indeed: he'd changed, I assure you, from the figure he'd been in the woods, and all the common folk were saying he didn't look much like a hermit! The chapel wasn't far away, and a bishop was there, devoutly clad in his godly vestments, ready to confirm the union of Carados and his beloved. Never, in any age, was a marriage seen of two people so matched in beauty and demeanour: everyone declared that God had made them for each other. And so they were joined in marriage, and then crowned and anointed, he as king and she as queen. King Arthur himself set a magnificent crown on the maiden's head: in the front was mounted a most precious, priceless onyx that came from the river that runs through Paradise, and clustered around it were a sapphire, a topaz and jaspers and more onyx, stones of high nobility, and emeralds and amethysts and jacinths and chrysolites and carbuncles and beryls; it also bore a host of high, most holy relics. No man ever saw in any age a king – or anyone – wear such a majestic crown, and to conclude I'll add, without a word of a lie, it was made of purest gold. The reliquary that it bore was reverently wrought of gold likewise, and inlaid with the aforementioned gems, the finest of them all. I could go on about the crown, but I think it would be tiresome! And King Arthur it was who placed it on the head of the fair Guinier, his impeccably raised niece. Then he crowned his nephew Carados with a golden crown, elegant and rich beyond price. Everyone agreed they'd never seen a coronation of such splendour. After the reading from the gospel and the singing of the creed, the people flocked to the altar with so many offerings that the priests were kept busy collecting it all!

When the services were over in all the main churches of the city, everyone went to dine, and food was provided in abundance. I don't know what more to add – to describe it at more length would be tedious. When they'd eaten and drunk their fill, young knights keen to establish themselves started jousting,[86] while others played games – some chess, some dice.[87] Then the light passed with the day as it always does, and darkness fell. But Carados and Guinier weren't sorry to see the day end: they were both longing for the joy and pleasure of bed. Who can blame them? They'd waited so long for the sport they desired. And now they wanted for nothing and wished for nothing else. They had no complaints: both had their desires fulfilled.

So now I've told you of the marriage of the faithful-hearted Guinier and the good Carados Shortarm who'd so long borne the serpent, and how they were crowned and began their reign. And God! what gifts were given there! Never at any king's coronation will you see such bounteous giving as there was at that court: even the smallest gift made its recipient wealthy for the rest of his life! What more can I say? Everyone was more than satisfied!

The wedding festivities lasted a full week. Then everyone departed, this way and that, each heading home to his own land. But the king didn't stir from Brittany; he and his privy household stayed a long while with his nephew and niece. But after this lengthy stay he crossed the sea once more, taking Carados with him – but that took some persuasion: it was reluctantly indeed that Carados left the good lady who was as dear to him as his own life. He could hardly bear to go, but his good uncle chid him, warning him not to stay with his wife so long that people would say he was letting his chivalry go to waste because of jealousy! So he didn't dally, but set off with his uncle and sailed with him to England. They had a fine time there, roaming the forests of the land in search of adventures to win renown, and taking part in tournaments so notably that Carados came to be deemed one of the finest knights of Arthur's court. He performed wonders, accomplishing so many noble deeds that his reputation soared: soon Carados was said to be the most praiseworthy, and the mightiest, of all King Arthur's household.

---

[86] '*behorder*': see note 48, above, p. 131.
[87] '*tables*': see note 51, above, p. 133.

The Healing of Guinier's Breast

One Ascension Day the king was at Carlion. He was holding a court of notable splendour: many people had come to witness the magnificence. But after dinner the king gathered his most valiant companions about him and said:

'At Pentecost, sirs, I mean to hold a finer court than any I can ever recall! And tomorrow I want you to meet at the break of day to go hunting in the woods: we won't dally – we'll go as soon as we've heard mass.'

They were all delighted by this. They returned to their lodgings and went to bed and slept till they were woken by the watch. Up they got and heard mass and then they were on their way.

Through the forest they rode till they spotted a boar. They pursued it all day long, on and on till night drew in – but they didn't care: they were sure they could hunt it down and toy with it till they had it at their mercy. But the boar outwitted them, taking refuge in a dense thicket where it plunged in a marsh and lay wallowing. I'm not going to labour describing the boar when those who'd laboured to hunt it accomplished nothing; for the fact is that, partly because of the darkness but also because of the fearful booms and flashes of the terrible storm that broke upon them as night fell, they took to flight in earnest. The thunder and lightning were such that they thought the sky had split asunder, and it was now so dark that none of them could see a thing except here and there when the lightning flashed. In fear of calamity they longed to be back in the city, and the king and all his barons spurred towards Carlion where they knew they'd be safe.

But Carados got split up from them: he found himself on a different path. On he went till he caught sight of a knight riding along all alone. He was a strapping, handsome figure, and surrounded by an amazing number of birds all singing their various songs – all those birds that have the sweetest tunes were flocking round him, singing so delightfully that Carados had never heard such melodious birdsong in his life. And the knight was lit as if by a sunbeam – it wasn't raining on him at all: he was bathed in gorgeous weather; and the shaft of light beamed all along his path. Carados was astonished – by the mighty, elegant, handsome knight and by the light and the birds surrounding him. He began to press his horse onward, wanting to join him if he could; but no matter how hard he spurred he couldn't get any nearer. He kept on till almost midnight, and you can imagine how vexed he was, chasing so hard and not catching up – and still being soaked by the rain! He was even more annoyed at seeing the knight quite dry!

On they rode till they came to a very fine house. The door was open; a warm fire blazed within: it was an inviting place indeed! The knight rode in and Carados followed. It was a handsome hall and filled with people. Servants sprang forward as soon as they saw their lord, and ran to hold his stirrup. He dismounted to a joyous welcome. They were puzzled that Carados didn't do likewise, and the knight was the first to address him, saying:

'Come, friend: dismount!'

'Hear me, sir knight: I shan't dismount till you tell me your name, and who you are.'

'My name is Alardin, friend. My father was called Guiniacalc, and I go by the name of Alardin of the Lake. This house belongs to me. In fairness now you should tell me *your* name.'

'I shan't keep it from you: my name is Carados Shortarm, the one the serpent gripped by the arm for two whole years and more; I'm King Arthur's nephew.'

When Alardin heard this he took him in his arms and straight out of his stirrups and down from his horse, which a bevy of servants led away and saw comfortably bedded and given plenty of oats. The two companions greeted each other with joyful embraces and kisses, overcome and lost for words. Alardin was the first to speak, as he kissed and held Carados and said:

'My dear companion, you've kept yourself well hidden from me! But God has answered my prayers: it seems He's taken pity – had it not been His will, and had He not led you astray and away from the city, I'd never have had you here in my house! But here you are now in my arms, praise be to God! And I tell you, you're a fair way from Carlion – there's no man on God's earth who could ride there in less than two days. Please stay here with me for a good long while, for I love you dearly, so help me God, and it's a delightful place as you'll see tomorrow.'

Then he led him by the hand and the servants took his cloak and draped him in a mantle. There was a roaring fire and a table laden with food. A company of knights and beautiful ladies stood ready to receive Carados and they gave him a joyful welcome; and then Alardin's wife Guingenor, fairest of them all, appeared from a chamber in elegant array and greeted him with joy. I could go on all day about the words they exchanged and I'd never be done; let's just say their happiness was total, unalloyed, and they told each other everything that had befallen them since their last meeting.

Supper was ready, and the knights and ladies rose and took their places at the table to eat and drink. They were ably served with a whole array of dishes. When their eating and drinking were done it was almost time for bed; they called for wine which was duly served, and then took to their beds and slept till morning. Carados stayed there for a whole week, and King Arthur was in great distress, fearing that he'd lost him.

Now, Alardin had a shield that bore a boss of purest gold. Finer gold indeed could be found in no treasury: it was truly as malleable as wax; believe me when I say that if a man had lost an ear or a nose, this gold could have been made into a replacement as fine as Nature could have forged! Alardin called Carados aside in private and said to him:

'I love you truly, dear companion, and would suffer all manner of toil and loss for you if the need arose. I've heard that your lovely wife, the fair Guinier, has lost the tip of her breast, cut off by her brother as he took revenge on the monstrous snake. Don't worry: take this golden boss and place it on her breast, that's all you need to do; you'll see the gold fuse and mend the wound as well as Nature could ever do.'

He called for the shield, which was gold with a horizontal band of azure, and its strap was of rich, deep blue silk.

'Carados, dear friend,' he said, 'no craftsman in this land could make such a boss as this, however hard he tried; for just as gold is worth more than silver, so the gold of this shield's boss is worth more than any other. It has such power that if a knight had half his nose cut away and he replaced it with the gold, it would fix at once and never fall: it would be irremovable. And you shall have it, if it please you, sir.'

'I accept it gladly, my dear, kind sir! A thousand thanks!'

'A wise decision, Carados! I know where it'll be of use!'

Then Alardin had the boss removed and graciously gave it to Carados, who took it and set off at once and rode all the way to the court, where Arthur was beside himself, fearing he'd been imprisoned: he'd sent men to scour the whole forest for news of him. The moment Carados arrived the king was the first to rush and kiss him, and everyone greeted him with joy unparalleled: now all was well again!

His wife Guinier now arrived there, too, having been summoned to the great court that was about to be held: it was certainly not diminished by her presence, but all the more enhanced. Holding the edge of her ermine mantle, Carados led her to a chamber, and there he said:

'Lady, show me where you lost the tip of your breast when you freed me from that wicked serpent.'

She did so at once; and Carados looked at the breast and straightway took the tip of the golden boss and gently, carefully laid it on the wound. In an instant the gold moulded itself to the white and tender flesh and took the very shape it had had before. When King Carados saw this, his heart filled with joy; then he said:

'It would be best, lady, to let no one know your breast is tipped with gold – please don't, dear love. I tell you this: if anyone but the two of us ever found out it would grieve my heart forever, for you'd have gone against my command and wish.'

'But tell me, sir, in God's name, I pray you, how can I ensure it's not discovered?'

'I'll tell you, my love: I'll wrap your breast in a band I'll make, and not even your closest maid or damsel must help you with it, either when you rise or when you go to bed. I'll unwrap it at night – happily, with pleasure! – and wrap it again in the morning, gently and lovingly.'

The queen thanked him for this fine solution.

The Drinking Horn

King Arthur had sent letters throughout his empire summoning his knights and barons to join him at Pentecost, and all the lords duly gathered at Carlion. After the great procession and the singing of mass, the worthy, courtly Arthur, in the great hall filled with knights and maidens and fair and elegant ladies, took his place at the high table as was his custom. Kay appeared from a chamber and came to the king and said:

'If it please you, sire, I'll bid the trumpets sound for the washing of hands, for dinner is ready.'

'No you won't, Kay, my dear man; don't think of bringing the water yet. You know what my custom's always been, and I don't mean to change it now, please God: I've never yet eaten at any court I've held till I've seen some marvel or adventure.'

And just as he said this, into the hall on a mighty horse burst a knight, sword at waist, without a cloak but richly, handsomely dressed in scarlet.* From his neck hung a horn of ivory bound with rich bands of gold and inlaid with wondrous jewels. He rode up to the king and then dismounted and said, loud enough for all to hear:

'Dear lord, I present you with this horn, whose name is Beneoiz.[88] It's richly wrought of finest gold, but has a greater value still, I promise you. Fill it from a spring or with any other pure, sweet water, and it will turn to the finest, clearest wine in all the world! And everyone in this hall could drink in turn and it would provide for them all!'

'By the Lord who never lies,' said Kay, 'what a splendid gift!'

But then the knight said: 'Before God, good sir, no knight will drink from it if his wife has ever deceived him or he's deceived his wife; the wine will spill all over him.'

---

[88] This would appear to mean 'Blessed'; but of the many variant spellings of the name in the MSS of the different redactions of the First Continuation, one, '*Boënet*', makes clearer sense in the light of the story that follows, as it could be translated as something like 'Drink-clean'.

'Oh, what!' cried Kay the seneschal. 'God help me, sir knight, your gift's not so appealing now!'[89]

The king quickly had the horn filled in the presence of everyone. But Guinevere couldn't help herself and said, in the whole court's hearing:

'My good, dear lord, don't drink from it! It's some enchantment, meant to bring disgrace to many! No man with any sense would drink from it: he'll make a fool of himself or someone else – it'll just cause shame and trouble!'

But the king merely laughed and said: 'Lady, by the faith I owe to everyone I'm going to be the first to have a go – before all these good knights here!'

The queen was aghast at hearing this; but she smiled and said good-humouredly: 'I pray to almighty God – if He's ever approved of a prayer I've made – that if you try and drink from the horn you'll get a soaking!'

The king took up the horn at once and made to drink; but he slopped the wine all over him, before the watching gaze of the whole hall! The queen hung her head in shame and rage, and Kay said:

'This isn't going well.'

The king was fuming; but he managed to hide his wrath and vexation – not wanting to disturb the assembled throng – and said with great restraint: 'My dear seneschal, it was foolish of me to try my hand against the queen's wishes: nothing would make me want to upset her! She clearly has God on her side, judging by the way He answered her prayer! But come, seneschal – don't let me be the only one to be made to look a fool! By the love and faith you swore to me when you became my liegeman, you must have a go now!'

So saying, he handed him the horn. Kay was less than pleased but took it, not daring to refuse. Seething, livid, he put it to his lips, and the wine poured down all over him. Everyone in the hall dissolved in laughter and carried on ribbing him. The king laughed more than anyone and said:

'Well, Kay, that makes two of us!'

'Indeed it does, sire. But there'll be more of us yet, you mark my words!'

'By the soul of my father Pendragon, whether this thing's real or an elaborate joke, every knight here's going to have a go!'

'Come on, then, sire!' said the seneschal. 'I'll give it to whoever you like! But I'd say your nephew Gawain should be the first one after me!'

'Take it to him, then,' said the king; and Kay went straight to Sir Gawain and placed the horn in his hand, brim-full of wine, and said to him, laughing:

'There's no getting out of it, Gawain! Drink, by the love you owe the king: that's his order!'

'I'll try, if my lord so commands, Sir Kay, and see if I can drink from it.'

So saying, he put the horn to his lips – and the moment they touched it he spilled and slopped the wine right down him.

'Pass it on, sir!' said Kay, and roared with laughter, as did everyone the length and breadth of the hall – not least the king and Sir Kay, who were delighted. Then Sir Gawain handed the horn to Sir Yvain, seated at his right hand, and said:

'Now, sir, let's see how *you* get on!'

---

[89] Curiously, two of the three MSS of this redaction imply the opposite: they have Kay say that the horn is now 'of even greater worth'. This makes no sense of his initial exclamation '*Ostez!*', which means literally 'Take it away!' The scribes evidently misread '*mainz*' ('less') as '*miauz*' ('better').

'It'll be better than you, for sure,' said Yvain as he took it, 'if faithfulness counts for anything!'

And he raised the horn and went to drink – but failed: the wine splattered and splashed all over his gorgeous robe of rich Byzantine cloth. Then every noble knight of the Round Table, truly, tried his hand and, whether they liked it or not, ended up sodden! On went the horn till it came to Carados. As he took it he was filled with trepidation, you can be sure! He looked at his wife Guinier, sitting beside the queen, and she clearly saw that her husband doubted her; and the moment she realised this she said:

'Drink, sir, with confidence.'

And he drank with ease, not spilling the slightest drop.

'Thank you, lady!' he said. 'Truly, no lady ever did her husband a greater honour than you've done me, sweet love!'

The horn carried on right round the hall, and one knight after another tried to drink; and I promise you, every single one got wet – and every single one was enraged that Carados had drunk and was dry! The queen was deeply aggrieved, as were many other noble ladies, and they took against Guinier, resenting the way she'd said 'drink with confidence'; indeed they hated her more intensely than any living being.

Then the trumpets sounded and they washed and sat down to eat, and were served with great pleasure and at leisurely length.

The court lasted three days. Then the king gave the knights so much gold and silver and so many horses and Eastern silks and costly brooches and fine rings and belts and hounds and birds that they returned to their lands in the highest spirits.

The king was left with just his privy household, and you may be sure they included Carados; so he sent Guinier home as soon as he could – a wise move, I'd say – for he knew the queen harboured a mortal hatred for her because she'd said he could drink 'with confidence'.

The king now spent a long time in great contentment, relaxing and sporting all winter long in his finest hunting grounds.

The Mission to Rescue Girflet

It was May, the fresh, new season when the birds sweetly sing, and the king had gone riding in the woods. He'd taken with him his closest companions, for he always enjoyed company: he wasn't one for being alone, like the miserable souls so mean of spirit who avoid all kinds of pleasure for fear it might cost a few pence. The good king wasn't like that; the more he spent and gave, the happier he was. So, as I say, he'd been in the woods, hunting with his companions, and as evening fell he was heading for home with his knights all in high spirits. The king was mounted on a swift, strong hunter; he'd thrown off his cloak and was clad in a handsome green tunic. But he was riding behind the others, and hunched over, as if weighed down by thought. Sir Gawain noticed him lagging behind, pensive and alone, and called to his companions to stop and wait till he caught up. Then he reached out and took the king's bridle and said:

'Tell us, sire, in God's name, what's on your mind? It can surely be only good: there's no prince in the world with such power and honour as you – you've no reason to be other than happy!'

The king, wise man that he was, replied: 'Dear nephew, I've reason to be happy indeed, and I tell you, I was thinking that no king living in this world is as well served by his men as I am by mine, and it's only right that I repay them for all the efforts they've made to win me my position. And it struck me, too, dear nephew, that my wealth would be of little use if I failed to reward the fine service of the worthy men who've won me the love and honour I enjoy. I'll tell you here and now, at Pentecost I'm going to hold a greater feast than I've ever done, and bestow such gifts that everyone will be happy and satisfied, and well disposed for evermore.'

Sir Gawain was the first to reply, saying before all the rest: 'Bless you for that thought, dear lord! A fine and courteous plan indeed! No count or king or emperor could conceive of better!'

'Tell me, nephew, right away: where should I hold that court?'

'At Carahés, sire. Let all your knights assemble there: there's no finer place or more splendid hall anywhere in your kingdom, and it's on the border between Wales and England.'

The king and all his company happily made their way home; and that very night King Arthur bade that letters be sent summoning all the knights and barons throughout his lands to join him at Carahés at Pentecost.

Ah, God! So many fine knights from far-flung lands came and gathered at that court! They came from Ireland and Northumberland, from Wales and Galvoie – a land where many a man's been lost[90] – and Logres and Escavalon, Norway, Brittany, Denmark and Orkney. So many knights had never gathered at any court as were mustered by the good King Arthur on that illustrious day.

After wearing his crown in the grand procession, the knights and barons led him to his hall amid great celebration. Kay the seneschal straightway called for two trumpets to sound for the bringing of the water. The king was the first to wash, and then he took his seat at the high table so that everyone at the feast could see him and the twelve score knights of the Round Table – though three were missing. The thirty peers were seated at the second table, but all the other knights were packed together on benches, settles and on the floor! Kay the seneschal promptly fetched the first course and duly served it to all.

And the king, as he ate, surveyed the Round Table, attentive to all as he always was, and his eye fell on the empty seat of a valiant, worthy knight; he was filled with such emotion that tears rose straight from his heart to his eyes and burst forth, and he let out a piteous sigh as he remembered the missing knight. He took a knife from Quirier, King Yder's nephew, who always cut his meat for him; and hunched over, lost in thought, he plunged the knife through his bread and into the table. He sat with his chin in one hand, downcast and perturbed, and was so far away that he let the other hand slip on to the blade of the knife. He cut his palm, and saw the blood and came to; so he let go of the knife and took the tablecloth and quickly wrapped his hand in it so that nobody feasting in the royal hall would notice. Then down went his head once more and he was lost in thought again; and as he mused tears began to flow, and Gawain, seeing this, bowed his own head in shame, and rightly so, for everyone in the hall thought the king's behaviour very odd. Then Gawain got up and made his way through the ranks of knights and up to the high table. He could see the king still deep in thought, and didn't want to say a word till he saw him raise his head; but the moment he looked up he addressed him courteously, saying:

---

[90] See above, p. 79: 'the borders of Galvoie, which none but he has ever crossed and kept his body and life intact!'

'Sire, sire, so help me God, it's unbecoming to behave like this, to look so worried and distracted in the presence of all these worthy knights. You should be thrilled and cheered to have their company.'

'Gawain, shall I tell you what's troubled and upset me so?'

'Yes, sire, please do!'

'I'll gladly tell you, dear nephew, yes indeed, and all these good knights before me. I was thinking about you and many others here: how full of wickedness you are, and how you've long harboured envy and flagrant treachery!'

That was all he said: he fell silent then. And Sir Gawain flushed red with anger and hurt. Everyone in the hall was stunned, shocked that the king should so shamefully, in the hearing of all, have called Gawain a proven traitor. They were all dismayed. The target of the insult was the first to reply, saying:

'Sire, that's most offensive. For your honour's sake, just think about what you've said in the presence of all this company.'

'It wasn't said idly, Gawain. I say it again, indeed I do. And I'd have Yvain know I was thinking the same about him! In fact I accuse every single knight here of grievous wrong and treachery!'

I can't tell you how many sprang to their feet; there was uproar in the hall.

'Sirs!' cried Tors the son of Arés. 'I summon you on your honour, join with me in answering King Arthur as we should. He charges us all with treachery – it's shocking!'

Sir Yvain agreed, and Sir Gawain cried: 'Ah, God! This noble gathering met so joyously – how dismally it'll part!'

The king heard this and sighed and said: 'Gawain, I've told you the truth.'

'Tell us, dear lord, for the love of God, in what way, shape or form are we guilty of baseness or treachery? I'm shocked, and so are all you've wrongly called unworthy.'

'I'll tell you, since you ask,' the king replied. 'Listen: you know full well that a year or so ago a host of men waxed mighty and built castles and citadels and fortresses against us, including the great Proud Castle. You insisted on confronting them before I did, and I wasn't happy about it! I still grieve for the numbers of men lost there, many killed and others captured – in particular a companion of mine they've held captive for three whole years. It pains my heart: I never knew a better knight – amazingly brave, a fine figure of a man and the wisest of counsellors. And just now, as all these lords were sitting feasting, I noticed that knight's seat left empty. The pain and pity of it gripped and cast a shadow on my heart. I was nearly out of my mind – which is why, sirs, I accused you all of treachery. That fine and noble knight is Girflet, the son of Do; he's been locked in a tower for three whole years, and you're all treacherous indeed, letting three years pass without going to find him! But I, your accuser, am plainly more treacherous still: that I should ever have borne my crown or feasted and made merry before seeing if I could rescue him, or finding out if he's alive or dead! And now, by the faith I owe the king of high heaven who has given me earthly honour and lands and kingship, I'm resolved, whatever might befall me and however far off he may be, to go and find him! I tell you this, decidedly: a king who basely, idly, accepts the loss of such a worthy man has no right to lands or station – he shouldn't live another day without rescuing his knight when he's suffering imprisonment in his cause. I vow before you all I'll sleep nowhere longer than one night till I win him back or discover he's dead.'

Then all the knights together answered: 'Damned be anyone who denies the charge of treachery, sire: you're right! How feeble we've been! We should have gone long ago and searched for him at the Proud Castle!'

'Then listen, sirs,' said the king. 'I'm leaving tomorrow, by God and Saint Germain. And I need to proceed with thought and guile – might alone won't serve us here.'

'True enough, my lord,' said Gawain. 'It's a tough road from here to the Proud Castle: it'll take a good fortnight, and there's no harder journey, it must be said. And when you get there, sire, you'll face a battle every day, that's certain, and they'll match you for numbers, however many you throw at them. You need to consider carefully who to take.'

'Eat now, sirs,' said the king, 'and then with your advice I'll decide who's to go and who's to stay and look after my land and people.'

Everyone in the hall, of every degree, ate with eager pleasure. Then as soon as he saw it was time to talk the king called for the tables to be cleared. This was done at once; then the water was brought[91] and wine was served in rich goblets of finest gold. When everyone in the hall had drunk, more than three thousand knights sprang to their feet and implored the king in God's name to take them with him on the mission, for they dearly wished to go; and the king replied:

'I'll follow my barons' advice, good sirs, on who's to come. The others I shall command to keep my realm in peace.'

King Urien was the first to respond, a man of notable wisdom; he said: 'It's best, my lord king, not to take too great a force on a long expedition. Far better, I think, to take a small but chosen body of men: that way you'll sooner rescue the prisoner, the much-valued Girflet. Take your very finest knights; you'll win more honour – and a swifter victory – if you fight in single combat. Have no fear whatever: you'll carry the day and set him free, the valiant, worthy Girflet! I don't know what more to say: just tell those who're to go with you to prepare!'

'What do the rest of you think, sirs?' said the king. 'I'm eager to hear.'

King Yder was the first to speak, saying: 'Dear lord, we must all give the best advice we can: damn anyone who steers you towards anything but honour! Almost everyone, I'm sure, would want to go with you if you asked them to, but that would not be wise. Do as King Urien advised; he was quite right.'

'Indeed,' said Sir Gawain, 'anyone who says otherwise is a villain and a fool!'

They all said: 'Let the king decide! He can take who he wishes and leave the others here in peace.'

'You've spoken well,' the king replied. 'Go to your lodgings now and make ready to ride. I'll have a silken pennon given to each man who's to come.'

They did as bidden, returning to their lodgings to prepare. And the king sent the pennons with an order to be mounted and ready to leave at the crack of dawn.

Kay, the Dwarf and the Peacock

What shall I tell you next? At dawn next day the knights were armed as the king had bidden, and all those who'd been sent the pennons gathered, mounted, outside the hall. I'll name them for you: foremost among them were Sir Gawain, King Yder, Gosoain, Kay and Lucan the butler. The sixth knight was Tors, and then there were Sagremor and King Urien's nephew, Maboagran. That's eight of them. King Urien's son makes nine – he was one of their number, that's for sure; and Idier, son of Nu, makes ten. The Bold Ugly Knight was the eleventh, and with Count Doon l'Anglain they were

---

[91] i.e. for the washing of hands after the meal.

twelve, all of them eminent knights indeed. There was Galegentin the Welshman, too; with the valiant Carados Shortarm, a very good man to have on your side, the number reached fourteen. And the good Taules de Rougemont was there, I know: he was the fifteenth and last – for that was the number, no more and no less. And as they waited, armed, outside the hall, King Arthur came riding forth; and I truly don't think any man was ever so magnificently armed or ever will be. The queen accompanied him to the door of the hall before she took her leave and left. Then the king bade his companions take to the road, and they set out as fast as they could – but so many people escorted them and crowded round that they had trouble getting out of the city! After riding three leagues they stopped in a meadow, and there Arthur bade the crowd farewell; they were very distressed to see him go but they made their way back to the city, while the king and his fifteen companions rode on, right across the country.

All the land they passed through now was barren, which made the going tough. One day the king, having eaten nothing, passed out of a great forest and into a heath of broom. The sun was blazing hot, the wasteland stretched for miles, and the king, worn out with heat and hunger, longed to rest if he could find a good place. They rode on till they found a big tree and halted there. There was a spring at its foot; and hot and tired, they removed the armour from their hands and heads and washed. They'd have eaten with relish if they'd had any food, but I assure you they had nothing at all, and they were very worried about the king who was feeling the hunger acutely. Then Sir Gawain, peering across the heath towards a valley below the forest, pointed out to the seneschal a sturdy house of cob.

'Kay,' he said, 'I'd say there are people living in that cottage.'

'Indeed,' said Kay. 'I'll go and see if I can find some food. Wait here.'

So saying, he left the others and headed straight to the house. He found an old woman inside, but not what he was hoping for – there wasn't a thing to eat. The old woman told him:

'God help me, sir, there's nothing but barren heath for twenty leagues around! Except, yes, there's a house up there in the forest, built by the count of Melioirant. He often stays there, just him and his hunting dogs. You'd be well lodged there if you found him, sir; from that tree over there you can see the house on the side of the hill.'

The seneschal went straight to where she pointed and saw the house, surrounded by gardens, trees, fields, mills, pools and fishponds, and enclosed by earthworks and palisades; and in the middle stood the finest tower you could ever wish to find. On he rode towards it, and across a great causeway and through a gate and over the main drawbridge. He came to the foot of the tower and dismounted; but he couldn't find a living soul to speak to, or to ask who and what was there. He stepped inside a hall; it was lofty, long and wide, and in a tall chimney he saw a beautiful fire lit; but there was no one there – except a dwarf roasting a lovely plump peacock, the best you've ever seen, skewered on a long applewood spit. The dwarf was turning it expertly; but when Kay strode towards him, all he was met with was a scowl.

'Tell me, dwarf,' he said, 'is there anyone here but you?'

But the rascal wouldn't say a word. Kay would have killed him on the spot if he hadn't feared dishonour, but he knew it would be shameful, so he said:

'Look here, you vile, hunchbacked dwarf, I can't see anyone in the house but you and this peacock and I'm going to have it for my dinner – I and others I'll share it with.'

'So help me the ever-truthful king,' said the dwarf, '*you*'re not going to eat it! And you're going to pay dearly if you don't clear off!'

'Shut your mouth, you jumped-up rogue! How dare you challenge me? If you try and stop me I'll bash your head on that pillar so hard it'll send your eyeballs flying!'

'God help me,' said the dwarf, who was a nasty piece of work, 'you're not having this peacock and nor is anyone else! You'd better shift, I'm telling you, or you'll be out on your ear!'

Kay was enraged; he strode forward and kicked him smack into the chimney pillar, so hard that blood flew everywhere. The heat from the fire made the wound keep bleeding, and the dwarf yelled out in fear of death. But suddenly, to his left, the seneschal heard a door crash open, and through it came a mighty, fearsome knight, a fine, strapping figure, though he can't have been more than twenty. He was clad in a brand new tunic of samite warmly lined with ermine, of no great length but ample and beautifully made and it suited him well. He had fine shoes, too, and a handsome belt of gold rings, the finest there ever was in any treasury. In he strode, ready for action, looking stern, and holding the green silk collar of a dog that followed at his heels; and when he saw the dwarf bleeding he cried:

'So, you've come into my hall, fully armed: why have you killed my servant? Damn anyone who thinks it's funny!'

Kay the seneschal replied that the dwarf was the biggest rogue in the world – but also the smallest and most deformed.

'By all the saints,' said the knight, 'that's a wicked thing to say!'

'And you're no better, my dear sir!' said Kay. 'I've seen loads of worthy vassals as high-born as you, and you're just a disagreeable, ill-mannered wretch! If I've kicked this oik who was roasting the peacock, you might politely ask me why.'

The knight replied then civilly, saying: 'I don't care for your manner of speaking, sir. But I pray you, kindly tell me your name.'

'Oh, gladly! By God, I've told five hundred better knights than you! Truly, sir, my name is Kay.'

'I can well believe it! Everyone knows you just by your tongue! The dwarf refused you the peacock, did he? It's not the custom in my house to refuse food to anyone who asks. You'll have a share of the bird at once, I promise.'

And he grabbed the peacock in both hands, lifted it high and brought it crashing down on Kay with such force and weight that he nearly killed him. Do you know where it caught him? In the neck! His legs gave way and he crumpled to the floor, while the peacock split and splattered to pieces. The hot blood oozed through the mail of his hauberk, leaving Kay with an ugly burn-mark on his neck, by the ear, for the rest of his days. The knight tossed the bird to two of his dogs and said:

'Get up, Sir Kay. You've had your share – that's all you're getting! Now for God's sake go: I can't stand the sight of you!'

Then two well-armed sergeants came and threw him out. He climbed on his horse and rode away across the bridge and over the heath, straight to where the king had dismounted. The companions asked him:

'Well, seneschal, did you find what you went looking for?'

'No, sirs: it's a useless place for foraging! I've been told you'll have to go miles to find lodging or anything to eat.'

But Gawain answered: 'Surely whoever you spoke to lives on food the same as us! He can't survive on nothing in this vast, desolate waste.'

'No, by the saints!' said Kay. 'But so help me God, I swear the knight I met's so haughty he won't give us lodging whatever you say!'

'Then he's a base rogue,' said the king. 'I suggest Gawain should go and see him. Go, dear nephew; we'll wait for you here.'

Gawain mounted at once; and to come straight to the point he rode to the house, and the moment the knight saw him he gave him a joyful welcome! He asked his name, and he replied that all who knew him called him Gawain; then he told him the situation, saying:

'The king's not far away and would gladly come and lodge with you.'

The knight was delighted and said: 'Go and fetch the king, good sir, and bring him here!'

So Gawain rode swiftly to the king and led him back to the house; and before they even got there, the fishponds had been emptied as the knight made elaborate preparations to receive the king with joy and honour. He escorted him to the tower where the dogs were still busily munching the peacock. The king looked at Taules[92] and said:

'By the body of Saint Thomas, those two hounds have been better fed than we have today!'

The knight heard this and laughed; Kay heard it, too – and kept very quiet. They carried on into the hall, and once they'd disarmed supper was prepared, the knight ordering white linen for the tables and a serving of delicious pies. After they'd eaten he saw them bathed from travel-weary head to foot, and then provided them with delightful beds with coverlets of samite, and they slept without a blink till morning.

When they awoke their host gladly laid on the most generous dinner, and they sat straight down and were splendidly served: to list all the dishes would be tiresome. They all laughed about the burn to the seneschal's neck – the dwarf couldn't resist telling them; if it hadn't been for him it would never have been known: you can be sure Kay kept it quiet, and so did the knight. The mark he was left with, which as I say was permanent, made people think he had a skin disease. It was a constant source of embarrassment that day – they ribbed him about it day and night till bedtime.

Next morning the king rose at the crack of dawn, and so did the others without delay, arming at once. He thanked their host most heartily for providing such fine lodging, and, to cut the story short, said:

'Please don't keep your name from me.'

'Sire,' he replied, 'my name is Yders the Fair, and this castle is mine.'

He earnestly asked the king to take him with him, but Arthur replied that he could take only those he'd brought with him from his land. Then he took his leave of the knight and set off; his stay there was over, and he rode away with his companions.

Bran de Lis and Gawain's Child

The story at this point is very long, but I'll make it more concise for you. They now went another whole day without food, finding nowhere to eat or take lodging. Instead they had to carry on to the Garden of Tombs, a place beset by many wonders, where they ate with all the hermits there – there were a hundred or more. It's not possible to describe to you the marvels of the cemetery, for marvels they were indeed: no man on earth would believe how the graveyard had come to be created. You won't yet hear whose tombs they were, or what the hermits' custom was – and indeed, it may be a

---

[92] Taules de Rougemont, one of the fifteen knights listed in Arthur's company, above, p. 181.

while before it's the time and place to tell you. All I'll say is this: the king spent the day exploring the cemetery before he went and ate.

When he left next day he rode on till he came to the fairest land you could wish to find, with meadows, woods and orchards planted with all kinds of beautiful trees. In the woods the grass grew thick and green and reached up to their horses' bellies and breast-straps. But as evening fell they came to a place where the long grass had been flattened, trampled down by horses, to form a path more than a bowshot wide: the kings' companions reckoned it must have been done by a band of a hundred or more. Sir Gawain said to the king:

'Quick, my lord! Bring your men and let's follow their trail! I'll ride ahead and ask if there's any lodging to be had nearby: we could certainly do with it! Don't leave the path whatever you do, no matter what anyone says.'

With that he thrust in his spurs and went galloping off, swiftly following the trail ahead. He hadn't gone far before he came out of the woods, and on a hill in the distance he saw the riders he was after: a good hundred of them were jousting[93] on the hilltop. He hurried onward, down the valley and up the hill – and found no one there. But beyond, at the foot of the hill, beside a great river, he saw the most handsome city he'd ever seen. I could spend all night describing it – and I'm not sure I'd know how: all I'll say is that no man ever set eyes on one so fine. Then Gawain spotted the band of knights heading straight towards it: they were on the point of crossing the bridge and riding in; so down the valley he rode to where the city stood. At the foot of the bridge, on the right hand side, there was a spring among four olive trees; two damsels were there: most beautiful they were, and dressed in gowns of rich purple, and they were holding a pair of golden pitchers filled with water they'd drawn from the spring. Sir Gawain called to them:

'God save you, damsels!'

And they both replied: 'God bless you, too, sir.'

'Tell me, what have you got in your pitchers?'

'Water, sir: we're taking it to the good knight we follow; he washes his hands in no other.'

'Truly,' said Sir Gawain, 'you speak of him most courteously.'

'We do indeed, in faith,' replied one, 'because he's the finest and most handsome I've ever seen. There he is now, entering his castle.'

Sir Gawain said no more to them but hurried on, straight into the city. No man's eyes ever beheld the like: all the streets he passed through were draped with richly woven tapestries. He was astounded, filled with wonder. And all through the streets he saw money-changers' tables piled high; spread on cloths of many colours were vessels of gold and silver, finer than in any treasury – the most beautiful goblets, cups and bowls he'd ever beheld – filled with coins from every land: from Normandy, Byzantium, from Arabia, from Africa, so many different currencies that he could hardly believe his eyes. And inside the houses there were furs of every kind – he couldn't imagine the worth of them all – and every door, he saw, was open. And the wonder of it was that he couldn't see a living soul! He could only think they'd gone to honour their lord and escort him to the castle after he'd entered the city with the band of knights I've mentioned. So up to the castle Gawain went. And there, in a wide and lofty hall that stretched the length of a crossbow shot, he saw the tables spread with linen: no count or king ever dined on

---

[93] 'behorder': see note 48, above, p. 131.

such gorgeous cloths. The food was ready, and the bread and wine were set on the tables – but there was no one to be seen. In an anteroom ahead he could see more than a hundred boars' heads laid on silver grails,[94] with pepper beside them, ground and ready, served out into bowls. Sir Gawain gazed in wonder; and he raised his hand and crossed himself, and didn't want to stay there when he found no one to speak to. Back through the city he rode. He expected to find the damsels with the pitchers of water they'd drawn from the spring as you heard just now; but there was no sign of them, much to his disappointment. He was sure they'd told him the absolute truth about where the lord had gone, and he'd seen him riding in; he was very frustrated that he hadn't been able to find out more. He didn't know what to do; he couldn't help thinking that if he left that place he couldn't expect to return. He would have loved his companions and King Arthur to see the wonders of the city, but he was worried that if he stayed there any longer he might cause the king to lose his way and never find it again. He chose the better course, and set off swiftly back to the king.

He gave his horse its head and rode back to the hilltop; then he looked ahead and saw the king and his companions at the edge of the wood. He thrust in his spurs and galloped all the way back.

'So, dear nephew,' Arthur said, 'are we going to have lodging tonight? We could do with it, that's for sure! In God's name, what have you found? I tell you, I'm fainting and worn out with hunger!'

'Truly, sire,' Gawain replied, 'you needn't worry: you're going to have plenty, and lodging tonight the like of which you've never had in all your life! All you need do is wash your hands!'

'Sounds good to me!' said Kay. 'I'll serve the king with the first course the moment we get there, and then the rest of you straight after!'

'Kay,' Gawain replied, 'you won't believe the wonders I've seen.'

And as he led them to the city he told them all exactly what he'd found. When they reached the streets the king was astounded by the riches they beheld. And Kay found something civil to say:

'Anyone who could win you, city, should never let you go!'

Fully armed, they rode up to the castle. Straight into the hall they went – and found not a living soul. They were baffled, but couldn't see anyone, so there in the hall they dismounted without more ado and took off their helms. But they couldn't find a thing to give their horses, and said it would be bad to make them go hungry. So the king said:

'If you like, once we've supped we'll go out and sleep in the meadows: the grass is long and thick and lush.'

They all agreed. They tethered their horses to a row of antlers along a wall, and opened the hoods of their hauberks and washed in a pair of silver basins. King Arthur sat down first and all the others after him; then Kay went straight to serve the first course to the king, happily presenting him with a huge boar's head and then promptly bringing one to each of the others. He said anyone who wasn't satisfied could have plenty more!

'No trouble at all – I'll give you as much as you like! And I'll tell you this: if our horses could eat boars' head we'd be going nowhere else tonight – I can see lovely beds in that chamber with gorgeous blankets!'

---

[94] The word is used casually, unremarkably, because a grail was a perfectly familiar item for its medieval audience: a broad, shallow dish or platter, suitable here for serving a boar's head. See note 13, above, p. 29.

Just then Sir Gawain peered through a half-open door and saw a shield hanging on a peg, and in it was fixed the stump of a great, stout lance with a rich pennon. I tell you, the moment he set eyes on it the blood stirred throughout his body. Without saying a word he leapt up from the table, throwing down the knife he held, and swiftly donned his helm and tightened his saddle-straps. Then he sat down on a bench next to the king and put his shield beside him. The king was bemused, and all the rest were muttering:

'God! What's got into Gawain?'

They all wanted to know why he'd armed so hurriedly. They thought his brain must be addled from fasting and the heat – it had been very hot that day. They were all bewildered – they'd seen and heard no reason to arm and couldn't think what had worried him. The king gently said:

'Dear nephew, please tell me why you've stopped eating. We can't imagine why you've armed like this. Tell me, I pray you: is there something wrong?'

'Not at all, sire,' he replied. 'If you love me, I just want you to hurry up and eat!'

'What?' said the king. 'How can I eat without you, when you've gone hungry as long as the rest of us? By God and Saint Thomas, I'll do no such thing! I couldn't stomach it!'

'It's no good, by God,' Gawain replied. 'I'm not going to eat, not for anything in the world, and that's the end of it! I hate this place – I'm sorry I ever set foot in here! I can't wait to be gone, so for God's sake, sire, hurry up and eat!'

But Arthur swore blind before everyone, by the glorious king who never lies, that he wouldn't eat on any account until he knew exactly why Gawain had donned his helm.

'In that case, sire,' he said, 'it would be quite wrong of me not to say. So I'll tell you, and without a word of a lie.

'You'll remember how ten years ago your mighty, fearsome army was laying close siege to Branlant.[95] You had a good many dukes and counts and barons with you there, and more than twenty thousand troops. There were many fine knights defending the city, too: the lord of the place had garrisoned it well. One morning, at the crack of dawn, they launched a surprise raid, and in the confusion I didn't have time to arm – I jumped straight on a horse and charged towards the clamour armed only with my shield and a lance. As I rode from camp I saw the men of the city heading back with their booty; they were already near the gate and many were inside. I went after them, fool that I was! It almost cost me my life: I was wounded in the shoulder with a lance, and taken for dead and carried back on my shield. The army was in great distress, and you sent for your surgeons – it was a good four months before I was healed and recovered.

'Then one morning I was lying, frustrated, in my pavilion. I'd had the sides of the tent rolled up so that I could see what the day was like, and I spotted one of my pages who'd been exercising Gringalet. I called him and he came to me, and I bade him saddle my horse at once. He set about it, while I quickly dressed and had my arms fetched quietly; then I armed and mounted and slipped away from camp all on my own. But you, my dear lord, rushed after me and caught up with me a little way from camp and told me to return. But I persuaded you to go back while I went wandering for two whole days without finding anywhere to take lodging or be fed.

---

[95] Gawain is about to refer to events recounted above, pp. 121–30.

'On the morning of the third day I was riding along when, to my right, I heard a bell ring in a hermitage close to the path, so I gladly turned aside to hear the mass. The holy man saw me arrive; and after he'd sung the mass he went straight and fetched me cider to drink, and some very black barley bread – though I know he'd have preferred to give me whiter bread if he'd had it. As soon as I'd eaten, sire, I took my leave of the holy man and carried on; and I tell you, it was the loveliest morning I'd ever seen or have ever seen since, and the trees soared high and thick with green, a delight to behold, and the forest was filled with joyous birdsong. It wasn't just the weather and the lushness of the green: the forest had a scent that made my heart rejoice; truly, no man ever saw fairer woodland than around that hermitage. The mass I'd heard had filled me with a deep resolve, sire, to change my life. If the same spirit had stayed with me it would have been unshakeable, but it didn't last long – my mood was quickly altered by what followed, as I'll explain.

'I was in that joyous state till about midday, when I was suddenly struck by a dazzling light. I peered ahead and there to my right I saw the most fabulously rich pavilion you could ever find. It was held up with silken ropes and handsome pegs which were firmly hammered in, for it was very hot and the gold-embroidered door of the tent was shut tight. I rode straight up for a closer look and opened the door; I ducked my head inside and saw three perfectly made beds, with the prettiest, loveliest sheets and coverlets. One of them was spread with the most exquisite blanket any man beheld, of Alexandrian purple lined with ermine; and on it lay the comeliest girl: I'd never seen one so beautiful. I dismounted at once and tethered my horse, laid down my lance and shield and went inside. I tell you, the beauty of the outside of the tent was nothing compared to what I found within! And it was perfectly arrayed, strewn with fresh flowers. I sat down right beside the girl's bed, and no man of woman born could describe her beauty – her shining, alluring face, her gorgeous lips and chin: everything about her was perfect. I was so stunned by her beauty that I loved her more than anything on earth, and I took off my helm – the feelings I'd had on leaving the hermitage were quite forgotten! I gazed at her entranced as she sweetly slept; but I didn't dare wake her, fearing she'd be alarmed – though I kissed her so softly that she didn't wake: she just said, without opening her eyes: "Dear sir, let me sleep."'

And at that point, sirs, Sir Gawain stopped; he told no more of his story, but held his hands out to the king and said:

'In God's name, sire, eat! If I told you the whole story I'd be worn out! And it would soon wear *you* out, too, my lord: the cock would have crowed before I'd finished – and I promise you, we're going to have trials and troubles enough tonight!'

But the king replied: 'Don't make me break my vow, dear nephew! You've still not said why you've donned your helm, and I vowed I wouldn't eat until I knew.'

'Sire,' said Gawain, 'I'll tell you the whole story, but by all the saints, I don't think any good'll come of it!

'For a long while, sire, I didn't move from the bedside of that beautiful girl; and I was so afire with love that I couldn't help embracing and kissing her: oh, how my heart was taken! And the fact is, my kisses woke her: she opened her eyes and looked at me and said:

'"Who are you? What are you doing here? You're not my brother or my father!"

'And I said: "No, damsel: I'm your lover!"

'And she replied that she'd never had a lover, and that it was very wrong of me to claim to be so because she was hoping for another if God would grant her prayers.

"Now be gone!" she said. "Have pity on yourself! If you don't get going you'll be cut to pieces! The two finest knights in the world are my two brothers, and the third's my father – he's still stronger and braver than any knight who ever lived, and he'll be rightly furious if he finds you in his pavilion."

'So, dear lord, the girl my heart loved above all others pleaded with me to leave. I begged her, I implored her – and then I told her my name; and when she heard it she said:

'"I've heard my brothers talk of the king's nephew, and I'm sure he wouldn't be so rude as to leave before they and my father come! They'd be delighted, overjoyed, to entertain and honour him and give him lodging – he's a knight of such valour and renown!"

'It would take all day, sire, to tell the whole story. But she'd got me in such a state that I had to disarm! And I went and lay in the bed beside her, quite besotted, ready to take my pleasure. I covered her eyes and face with kisses, a face lovelier than a lily, and then her lips and cheeks. And, sire, as truly as I'm sitting beside you, I went much too far, and deflowered her by force – not even her tears would stop me. She was in desperate distress – I've never seen a living soul grieve so piteously. I was nearly wild with anguish at the sight of the one I loved fainting and swooning, and nothing I could say consoled her: I was distraught. So there she was, distracted, collapsed in my arms, when up rode a knight, fully armed, the most impressive you ever saw. He called out in a fury:

'"Who's in there with you, sister? This horse belongs to some stranger! He's got a nerve breaking into my tent – especially when you're in there! – how dare he?"

'She heard him, and cried: "Oh, dear lord God, who'll rescue me from this knight who's brought me utter shame? I can't hide it from you, brother: I'll know nothing but shame and misery evermore – nowhere in the world will I be honoured for the rest of my days! My good, dear brother, the bright future that lay in store for me is gone! And the love between us is sundered!"

'The knight was not best pleased by this. He drew his sword and slashed through a panel of the tent, making an opening wide enough to see me – and to ride straight in! I was trapped – I didn't know what to do! And I remember how ashamed I felt – I knew I was in the wrong. Please eat now, sire, I beg you: if you make me carry on it's going to get worse!'

But the king said: 'Tell your story, good nephew! Don't stop now!'

'Sire,' said Sir Gawain, 'the knight advanced in fury, clutching his sword, and boomed: "Dear lord God, how shall I kill this wicked man? I know if I kill him when he's unarmed I'll be reproached for evermore!" Then he cried: "You wretched little rogue! What kind of low-born scum are you?"

'I told him, sire, I was your nephew and my name was Gawain, but he didn't believe me! Instead he said: "Don't give me that! Sir Gawain would never behave so basely! Damn you for even thinking it! You're a knight, are you? Not a chance: you're a vulgar lout! You're a slave indeed if you behave like one – and that's what you've done, wickedly stealing the honour of the finest, loveliest, brightest creature ever born! You've robbed her of her shining future! It's a wonder you're still alive, that I didn't kill you the moment I came in!"

'And with that, sire, he was about to strike; but he stopped himself and said: "I'd arm, and sharpish, if I were you! Anger could get the better of me – by all the saints of Christendom, I might cut you down unarmed!"

'I have to confess, when I saw him so enraged with me I armed without another word! Then I went up to the girl and said: "My fair, dear love, your brother doesn't believe a word I say! I am Gawain, King Arthur's nephew: no man in the world is dearer to him. I faithfully swear you'll have no other husband: I'm ready to make the pledge if you'll accept me! For God's sake, ask your brother to wait till your father comes: I'll do whatever they wish!"

'Well, sire, she spoke sensibly then; with great composure she said: "My good, dear brother, I pray you in God's name have mercy on me, and let me change my status and marry, now that I'm dishonoured in the world's eyes."

'"I'll do no such thing, sister, truly; I'll see you given a noble marriage – that's not going to change because of this wretch: he's going to die right now!"

'He poured contempt on me, my lord – and God help me he was right! He bombarded and battered me with abuse! Then his beautiful sister said: "My good, dear brother, listen: if you really mean me to have a husband, let me have Sir Gawain. He can be sure I'm innocent of any folly or wrongdoing with any man but him, actions for which I feel grief and shame. Another would reproach me for what I've done, and he'd be right, so I don't want to leave him for anyone else: it might well turn out worse for me."

'That was the way she reasoned, sire, the girl who'd won my heart. And when her brother heard this he responded in a rage, saying: "You whore! How quickly the heart of a woman turns! This isn't Sir Gawain! I'm going to kill him with my own two hands!"

'And he lunged forward and dealt me a blow that almost did for me, and cried: "Mount, you wretched slave! If you'd been without your helm that blow would have killed you!"

'Well, my lord: I went to my horse and mounted, and politely asked him to let me go. But he wouldn't listen; no, he cried: "I challenge you! So help me God, you've no more mortal enemy than I!"

'And with that, sire, we charged at each other, and he hit me so hard that he drove me to the ground; but I dealt him a blow that pains my heart still: a full yard of my lance I thrust through his shield and clean through his body, leaving him dead in the middle of the field. I was horrified, for the damsel was beside herself with grief at seeing her brother killed: she fell unconscious – so long that I thought she'd died. I uncovered her head and splashed water on her face, and hugged her so tight I almost killed her! God help me, uncle, I wouldn't have let go of her for all the gold I ever saw, even if it meant being cut to pieces. And it wasn't long before another armed knight arrived clutching a mighty lance. He started weeping bitterly, bewailing Meliant de Lis[96] and crying:

'"Ah, dear son! Whoever killed you has dealt me a grievous blow! I want nothing more than to avenge you and die!" Then he lingered over the body no longer; he rode forward and fixed his gaze on me and said: "Vassal! You've killed my son and broken into my tent, that's certain! And for all I know you've deflowered my daughter, loved and esteemed by everyone! How dare you sit there and indulge yourself, caressing her in your arms?"

'The damsel recovered consciousness when she heard her father's voice, and told him the whole story from start to finish. When he heard, he almost killed me on the spot. But do you know what he did, that worthy knight? Before he would attack me he told me to arm from head to foot. I kept insisting that I was your nephew Gawain and offering to marry his daughter, but he was deaf to it all; he didn't want to know, and challenged me outright and charged without more ado. What can I say? I did to the father as I'd done to the son: I killed him – a sinful deed that still weighs upon my heart.

---

[96] Meliant made a notable appearance at a tournament in Chrétien, above, pp. 44–8.

And it didn't do much for that sweet girl's grief: she passed out completely. I couldn't leave her: I loved her more than my own life. I can't help weeping as I think of it: the pain of it grips my heart – it'll be the death of me. I shan't waver from the truth of the story, sire, but I'll keep it short. Another knight, fierce and mighty and fully armed, came galloping up on a great destrier; and truly, his grief was terrible, it knew no bounds, as he wailed over the bodies of his brother and father, crying:

'"This is torture – it'll be my death! Lord God, this morning I left them in the flower of health. Why don't I just kill myself, finding them here now dead? Dear God, where's he gone, the rogue who committed this wicked deed?" With that he left the bodies, saying: "I'll never know a moment's peace till I've avenged them!"

'Sire, I was slumped against a bed in distress, my elbow resting on a pillow, holding that adorable girl in my arms in a dead faint; and my lord, the knight came up to me, raging, bursting with hatred, and roared:

'"Tell me, vassal, who committed this monstrous crime, the foulest ever? The girl in your lap looks as if *she's* dead, too! Tell me how you found them – and what happened here? If you know who killed them tell me – I've got to know, and God will bless you for telling the truth."

'God help me, when I heard this my heart nearly stopped; my blood ran cold; I was overcome with anguish. I'll be honest, it was the only time in my life I've fainted. The knight stared at me, bewildered; and when I came to he addressed me again, asking who I was, to be grieving so. So, sire, I told him I was his greatest foe in Christendom, for truly, I'd committed the heinous sins of killing his brother first and then his father. He said:

'"Lord God above! How's that? You're bold indeed to stay here after killing them, admitting your guilt! God help me, I can't believe you're that mad! Tell me who it was!"

'So I told him exactly how I'd killed them. His sister, still collapsed in my arms, revived then and spoke out, confirming all I'd said. And then, sire, I craved his mercy and offered him the homage of a hundred men, and a hundred monks and a hundred nuns, and to have you free a hundred serfs in a single day! And if it pleased him I would marry his sister. I promised him all this! And he replied in reasoned, measured fashion, saying:

'"I was the last to arrive here. Had I been the first instead of my brother, he and my father would still be alive, for I'd have looked kindly on your request: I wouldn't have denied you my sister, truly, but given her to you there and then. But as it is, rightly or wrongly you've killed my father and brother, and I can't accept peace terms – I'd be shamed for evermore. And truly, I'd rather die with them than languish in this world in shame."

'With that he bade me take up arms, which I did at once, not daring to refuse. Then I went to my horse and mounted swiftly: I have to admit I was in awe of him, seeing what a wise and valiant knight he was. He drew back to one side of the field and I drew back to face him – filled, God save me, with anguish and alarm. Then we charged full tilt and met in such a fearsome clash that we brought each other down, and then started exchanging mighty blows with the edges of our swords. But I shan't lie: he ended up doing me more harm than I did him. He was wearing me down and had the upper hand when I suddenly thought of a good way out: I asked him to tell me his name, my lord, and he told me truly his name was Bran de Lis; the brave and worthy Norroiz de Lis[97] had been his father and Meliant his brother.

---

[97] He is named here 'Yders de Lis', but this is a scribal confusion: the damsel's father is earlier (pp. 128, 130) named Norroiz.

'"If you'd killed me," he said, "you'd have vanquished the three finest knights in any land – but your battle's not over yet! With a little help from God I know I can take complete revenge! This combat of ours won't last much longer – one of us is going to die."

'But I replied: "Let's not settle it this way, sir: if you defeat me few will believe it – in this land they'd find it hard to believe that anyone had beaten me! It would be better, I'd say, to fight before people who could witness which of us had won. Let it be at your court on a day we agree, or at King Arthur's."

'To cut a long story short, he agreed, on the following condition: that he'd do battle with me at the first place we met – and he'd fight me in whatever state he found me, whether I was armed or not! We exchanged oaths to that effect.[98] And truly, by the faith I owe you as my uncle and my lord, since that day I've never heard a word about him anywhere I've been – until just now: when I sat down to dine I jumped up in alarm (and none too happily – I'd gladly have eaten if I dared!), because I thought I'd seen, hanging on a peg there in that chamber, the very shield that Bran de Lis had borne on the day we fought – I was sure of it. I promise you, my dear lord king, I've told you the absolute truth, so help me God. And I can see a stump of lance there with my pennon! I'm sure he lives here, sire! That shield of his is a worrying sight – that's why I left the table: I'm afraid of an attack! I fear him more than I can say: I've never seen a knight so fit to endure the fiercest battle, and I know what his blows are like! So there, my lord: now I've told you why I donned my helm. Need I say more? Not for all your land would I want to meet him unarmed, believe me! So I beg you, sire, in God's name, let's eat up quickly and be gone – if I have to hang around, the meal might cost me!'

But the king replied without hesitation: 'Dear nephew, sit down quietly at the table – there's nothing to fear – the knight won't come. And if he does, I promise you, he'll do as I ask. We'll be upset if you don't join us!'

'God help me, sire,' said Gawain, 'nothing you can say will make me eat!'

'I'm wasting my breath,' the king said then. 'It seems you've made up your mind.'

And all the others started eating quickly.

But a moment later they saw a dog come bounding through the door of a chamber and straight towards the king's table, trailing a long leash. It was wearing a big, gold-braided collar studded with precious stones, red and ivy-green. The dog itself was white as snow and whiter than the newest ermine, and far from an ugly specimen: it was a handsome, strapping hound indeed – the king couldn't take his eyes off it. It barked at the knights at the table, not recognising them. Kay was eyeing it admiringly, too, and said to the king:

'If you'd grant him to me as a gift, my lord, I'd keep this dog and take him with me to be a companion for Hudens.'

'Seneschal,' said the king, 'he's yours! Go and take him.'

Kay leapt straight to grab it, but the dog sped back towards the chamber.

'Stamp on the leash, Kay,' said the king, 'and stop him! There he goes, into the room!'

Kay went racing after it, but the dog didn't dally. It charged off through a panelled chamber, its long leash lashing Kay on the heels as he tried and failed to step on it; he was desperate to catch the dog, but he couldn't get a foot on the leash to stop it, and found himself dashing from room to room – five in all – and finally into a garden thick

---

[98] Above, p. 130.

with laurel and pine. This garden was filled with a vast crowd of people – more than a city-full, I'd say! – and by God, they were enjoying themselves, sporting on every side! Some were at sword-play, some sparring and tumbling, others playing dice and chess, and others simply watching. You've never seen so many gathered in one place in all your life – it would be tiresome to describe them all; they'd been celebrating the feast day of a saint of those parts. And in the middle of the garden, in the shade of a laurel tree, a knight was taking off his armour. He was imposing, tall and bold and strong, and surrounded by the finest and most valiant knights, honouring and attending him, kneeling to help with the disarming. The dog chased by Sir Kay bolted straight to the knight and took refuge between his legs, barking at its pursuer. Kay stopped dead – he didn't take another step. At the sight of the huge, festive crowd he wanted to turn back; but the knight called out to his men:

'There's a stranger among us, I don't know who!' He was looking towards the chamber, where Kay was trying to sneak off. 'There he is! Go, quickly, and bring him to me!'

They had him in an instant, and led him before the knight. And the moment he set eyes on him he realised who he was and said: 'Welcome, Sir Kay! My very dear friend! Where is your lord the king?'

'Inside, seated at table, sir, and a company of worthy knights with him; they haven't finished eating yet.'

'Is his nephew Gawain there?' said the knight. 'I'd very much like to be sure.'

To this Kay replied: 'The finest knight in the world is with the king, indeed he is – he wouldn't go anywhere without him.'

When the knight heard this he was so overjoyed that he almost took wing. Half-armoured as he was he jumped straight up, elated, and let them remove no more. Over the armour that he still had on they threw a short mantle, but he wouldn't stop to let them fasten it despite their pleas; and in his jubilant haste he had one mail legging, half-unlaced, dangling to the ground, but he wouldn't let them tie it! Off he ran towards the hall, and the whole crowd, seeing him go, rushed after. He didn't wait: from room to room he ran and into the hall, the mighty press stampeding behind, alarming the king with the thunderous din. The knight strode forward, beaming, and greeted the king most graciously; and he bade his men bring candles quickly, the light being now quite dim, and they hurried off to do so. Then he called for three more courses, and Arthur was served as befitted him, that worthy, noble king. The knight was in soaring spirits, and said to him:

'God has done me great honour, sire, in bringing you here: I've never served you before. What a pleasure and delight it is to give you lodging! With all goodwill I bid you and your company welcome – all of you, that is, but one, and I can't see him.'

At that moment into the hall came the men who'd gone for the candles and torches, and where it had been dark and dim, now it was filled with light. The huge crowd, flocking to see the king of whom they'd heard so much, were packed so tight that there was nowhere to sit: the hall was just a sea of heads – despite its being so broad and long that it hadn't been full for three hundred years. The knight was fuming – it meant he couldn't see Sir Gawain: he didn't know where he was. Hot and bothered, he struck out with the cane in his hand to part the press, driving them up on the tables and window-ledges, to the galleries and half-way up the walls – but he couldn't get them to leave the hall! When Sir Gawain saw the crowd scatter, leaving him now with no hiding-place, he mounted his horse at once. Now the knight could see him at last – and how furious he was to find him armed! Hunched with rage, he threw his stick aside, and after a moment's fuming he looked up and strode to Gawain and grabbed his reins and said:

'Let me remind you, sir, what we agreed after you killed my father and my brother Meliant de Lis: I was so enraged that I did battle with you there and then, in the middle of a glade. Our combat lasted a long while, but because there were no witnesses to testify who'd won we stopped and agreed that I'd fight you again in whatever state I chanced to find you. Will you keep that promise? Tell me! It pains me that you've got off lightly – I haven't found you unarmed as I'd have liked! I could kill myself for making the deal that day: if I hadn't accepted the truce I'd have slain you for sure! I'm sorry I ever did it! I'd gladly have died once I'd destroyed you – that's how much I hate you! And now, because our battle was postponed, suspended, it's going to last all the longer. But that was our pledge, was it not? Speak up, by God!'

And Sir Gawain agreed to do battle. Then the knight sent for more candles, for by now, outside, the stars were shining. He had plenty brought, and gave them to the whole crowd to hold so that everyone could see perfectly, the length and breadth of the hall. Then the knight had a servant bring a huge carpet, and he sat down on it in the middle of the hall and called for all the arms a knight could need. There was nothing he craved so much as this battle. He donned one mail legging and laced up the other that was hanging loose and pulled on his gauntlets. Then he came before the king and said:

'Eat heartily! Don't worry about a thing! You can see what a bold, fit, hearty knight I am! And your nephew's in good shape, too, I'd say! I don't know if he's explained why things have come to such a pass that one of us must die before we're done. Who'd have thought this morning that one of us was so near his end?'

The king's eyes filled with tears, and the knight, seeing this, said haughtily: 'I tell you, lord king, I don't think half as much of you now! What's this pitiful snivelling? By all the saints, you're like a dog that whines before it's been hit! I've never seen a man weep for no reason: it's a sure sign of your feeble heart!'

The king showed no anger as he replied: 'You can say what you like, Sir Bran de Lis: I know you're in a rage. But you shouldn't wonder at my distress – if I lost my nephew he'd be irreplaceable. If either of you were to die it would be a grievous loss and sorrow. My dear, most worthy nephew's made you a host of generous offers by way of amends; accept them, for God's sake, and you'll earn the praise and thanks of your people and of my companions here, the most valiant in the world! They'll all pay homage to you – they'll make their vows here all together. For the sake of peace and concord I'll found two abbeys of good men who'll pray for the departed evermore, especially for your slain father and brother: if it please God their souls will rest the better. I do believe, truly, this peace will be much to your honour.'

'King, I'd think myself cursed if I failed to avenge my brother and my father, who loved me dearly.'

With that the knight returned to the carpet to finish arming. He armed superbly from head to foot. Then he mounted, and slung his shield round his neck by its gold-braided strap, and called for a stout lance with a sharp, shining head. I tell you, there was no knight in Christendom more finely armed. He set himself in the stirrups and then called to Gawain, saying:

'I am lord of this place by right of inheritance! But I shan't claim any advantage: no, sir – I invite you to choose which side of the hall you wish, and I shall take the other.'

Sir Gawain heard this but hardly moved – he just drew back a little, as did the knight without another word. Then you'd have seen the crowd fall silent – you could have heard a pin drop. The hall was as brightly lit as if it had been midday. They set their shields in place, and then charged with all the speed they could summon from their mounts and met in a fearsome clash, striking each other's shield so hard that their lances split and smashed them. Clean through went the sharp iron heads, but they couldn't pierce their fine-meshed mail; and the force of the thrusts made the shafts bow and shatter into shards. Horses and riders didn't stop but met head on in a mighty collision, bringing all four crashing down. Their fine chargers lay sprawled beneath them, but both knights leapt straight to their feet on the flagged floor; and unsheathing their good swords they exchanged such blows on their shining helms that they battered and stove deep hollows. The king and all the others watching were filled with awe and fear. The mortal foes were unrelenting; I swear such passionate combat between two knights was never seen. They sent sparks flashing from their helms; they smashed away the bands and rivets: they meant business! Every blow that landed on a shield sent pieces flying, and they were so intent on dealing wounds that they wouldn't end this first onslaught till they both were covered in blood. But they were finally so overcome with heat that they had to pause a little to recover breath. Their combat had been so fearful to behold that all who loved them were filled with grief and pity and prayed on their behalf to God. The king wouldn't watch at any price: never had he feared so for his nephew.

Now, beyond the high table was the door to a chamber. And through it now, so the story says, a damsel appeared, so fair of face and body that she had no equal in all the world. Dressed in a rich red gown of new samite embroidered with lions, she was elegant and graceful and beautiful indeed; she was probably about twenty years old. As she entered the hall everyone who saw her was stunned by her beauty. She leaned on the end of the table and watched the two knights, intent on killing each other: they'd joined again in battle so fierce, so resolute, that truly they couldn't last long. With their whetted blades they rained such blows on their helms and shields that the shields were in pieces and the helms stove in. Blood was seeping through their hauberks and flowing across the flagstone floor. But the damage wasn't equal: every lace on Sir Gawain's helm was broken and it lay now at his feet, leaving his head quite bare; he was protecting himself as best he could with what was left of his shield. His enemy was pressing now, delivering a barrage of blows – but Gawain gave as good as he got; and then, being at a disadvantage with his helmet lost, he kept as close to his foe as he could, not giving him striking distance. So they thumped and battered, shoved and dragged, in a desperate effort to wound and wrong-foot and bring the other down. What valiant, worthy knights they were! How equal the contest would have been – if only Sir Gawain had had his helm! For just a moment Bran de Lis gained distance enough to deliver a blow – fearful, grievous, mighty – right on Sir Gawain's head; but first it landed on his shield – had it caught him fully, undeflected, the battle would have been over for sure: he would have been killed outright. In a towering rage Bran cried:

'Take that for my father! You'll have another in a moment for my brother, please God! If I can, I'll make it a mortal blow for you and a joyous blow for me!'

Sir Gawain's blood was streaming to the floor; and as he stood there, sword in hand, it was filling his eyes, too – he could hardly see, and wanted a respite; but Bran wouldn't have it: he kept pounding him with blows. Gawain replied as fiercely as he could, but he was in a bad way, driven hither and thither whether he liked it or not.

Then suddenly the damsel, so comely and fair, ran back into the chamber; she returned a moment later carrying a child, and stood him on the table. He was clad in a tunic of green samite, warmly lined with ermine and cut perfectly to his size. A more handsome child was never seen, with a shapely face and green eyes, bright and laughing. He was tall and strapping for his age, being five years old at the most; and judging by his rich apparel, he was obviously much loved. But all the while, sirs, the combatants were intent on wounding and killing each other, and everyone watching was aghast to see them exchange such perilous blows. Both were weak with heat and fatigue, and Sir Gawain tried to withdraw for a moment to wipe the blood from his eyes and face – but he couldn't: Bran de Lis kept battering and pounding, bent on maiming and slaying, driving him ever backward. He couldn't have met a more dreadful foe. The king was distraught, horrified; he couldn't bear to look. It was now that the fair damsel took hold of the child on the table before her and whispered to him:

'Hurry, dear son, to that mighty knight. He's your uncle, truly, and I'm his sister. I couldn't live if he killed or crushed your father: that's who he's fighting!'

And she set the boy down and he ran straight to his uncle and took hold of his leg and kissed him, saying: 'Dear, kind uncle, my mother begs you in God's name not to kill my father: truly, sir, she'd die of grief if you slew him!'

The king was filled with pity, and all who saw and heard the child were overcome with sorrow and compassion – all except Bran de Lis. He responded in a fury:

'Get out of here, you son of a whore!'

And he pulled his leg from the little child's grasp so violently that, whether he meant to or not, he struck him full in the face and laid him out flat on the flagstone floor: he skinned his forehead and, by God, was bleeding so profusely that he passed out. The king rushed from the table and gathered him up, and kissed his eyes and lips and cheeks more than twenty times. He was so upset and angry that nothing could have stopped his tears. He kept kissing the child most tenderly, heedless of the blood, for he loved him dearly, and thought he would be some consolation at least for the loss of Gawain, who he was sure was finished. Then he said:

'Sir Bran de Lis, what a handsome little child this is! To kill such a lovely boy would be the wickedest deed! How could you refuse his plea? It wasn't unjust or shameful – it was an appeal to your heart! You're hard indeed and cruel, treating the dear child so harshly you nearly killed him! He's my support and comfort from this day forth – I wouldn't lose him for anything.'

'My dear lord king,' said Bran de Lis, 'you're less impressive than I'd been led to believe! You're far too worried and upset! You shouldn't be so dismayed at the loss of a single knight! It's the sign of a wretchedly feeble heart!'

While Bran de Lis was busy talking, Sir Gawain was wiping the blood from his eyes which had been such a trouble to him, and taking the chance to rest a little and staunch his wounds. The king, clever man that he was, was keeping Bran talking to let his nephew recover breath. Once it was past midnight, Sir Gawain's strength and vigour were renewed, waxing ever stronger as day progressed till it doubled by the time noon came. And as his strength began to surge, and he saw the king and his beloved and the huge crowd watching him, he felt greater shame than he'd ever known in his life. He stormed back to attack his foe, who responded just as furiously, saying:

'All credit to you for attacking me so!'

Then you'd have seen them deliver mighty, raging sword-blows, nearly battering each other down. Sir Bran de Lis aimed a massive blow at Gawain's head; he deftly blocked it with his shield, but it landed with such force that it split the shield in half. Gawain was aghast, but returned a fearsome blow to his enemy's helm: it snapped every lace and sent the helm flying across the hall, leaving Bran's head exposed; and before he'd time to take this in another blow landed on his mail hood, bringing blood streaming from his head. Now the scores were levelled! It was impossible to say who had the upper hand, and they assailed each other with rage and fury – in no time both were covered in blood – as they desperately tried to gain the advantage. Everyone watching was filled with pity and would have dearly loved to part them if they'd dared. And now that noble knight Gawain, who'd offered Bran so many boons and honours, all of them rejected, summoned all his strength and drove his enemy back across the hall. He landed a blow that made him stagger, and a violent barge that almost knocked him down; he sent him reeling right back against a table. Seeing this, the damsel went and took her son back from the king, and rushed straight into the thick of the fray before the knights had realised – she almost got the child killed!

'Beg your father, in God's name, to have mercy on your mother and spare my brother's life – it means more to me than my own!'

The boy didn't say a word – he just looked at the flashing swords and started laughing. Everyone watching was awe-struck: a moment before they'd seen him bleed, and now he was roaring with laughter! Sir Gawain realised and took a step back; but the battered Bran attacked him like a mad thing and almost dealt him a grievous wound, as Gawain wasn't expecting it. Then the damsel, holding the child, dashed between them and cried:

'God help me, now we'll see which one of you will kill him! I'm keeping him between you – you'll have to cut him to pieces before I take him away!'

They kept brandishing their swords at each other but did no more damage – they couldn't get near one another for fear of hitting the boy and his mother. And still the child was laughing! He was reaching out for the shining blades because he could see his reflection in them: he pointed it out to his mother. Whenever the swords came within reach he'd jump and try to grab them, heedless of how sharp they were, as he saw himself mirrored in the shining steel: that was why he was laughing in delight, sweetest child in the world that he was. He kept pointing with his finger, showing his mother, until she pulled his hand away. Many a man wept to see him, and the cry went up throughout the hall:

'Go, good king, and stop this battle – we'll all support you – we can't bear it any longer!'

The king leapt from his seat that instant and took up his shield and sword. All his companions followed him, and knights came running from every side to part the combatants. Whether they liked it or not they were forced apart, and the king said to the knight you've heard so richly praised:

'In the name of God and His saints, sir, don't reject the offer he made you – it's hardly ungenerous! I promise you, by way of amends I'll do you a greater honour still – I'll become your liegeman!'

And everyone cried aloud: 'By God and His cross, sir, you can't refuse! What a noble offer the king has made!'

Bran's silence made it clear that he approved and was willing to accept. And so it was that peace was agreed and the battle ended. And Sir Bran de Lis spoke wisely when he said:

'Sire, it isn't right that you should become my liegeman – I should rather pay homage to you. But the peers of the Round Table, the most esteemed knights in the world, shall swear their loyalty to me: the deal was that they would declare themselves my vassals! I was offered other boons, as well: abbeys of monks and nuns, and your freeing of a hundred serfs!'

GAWAIN'S CHILD INTERVENES

'Truly,' said the king, 'I'll do all in my power – even more than I've said!'

'Sire,' said Bran, 'my thanks!'

And he paid liege homage to King Arthur, who accepted him gladly, and promised him lifelong loyalty, love and companionship. Then Sir Gawain was brought forward, and he humbly knelt at Bran's feet and asked him to forgive him his past animosity, saying:

'Sir, grant me your goodwill henceforth.'

Bran took him by the hand and raised him, saying: 'Sir Gawain, I forgive you all resentment; from this day forth I'll be your loyal friend, despite the wrongs you've done me in the past.'

They were both terribly weak, drained of all strength; they'd both lost so much blood that they were struggling to stand. But Bran de Lis accepted all the king's terms; he received Sir Gawain's homage and graciously kissed him and forgave him all ill will, and received the homage of all the others after; and so peace was concluded and affirmed by both parties.

Sirs, it would be gracious to acknowledge the debt this romance owes, if the tale is pleasing to you, by saying a Paternoster for the soul of the man of Laon;[99] and so indeed we should for all the departed.

As I say, sirs, the battle was ended that night; peace was made and conflict turned to friendship. And without more ado the wounded knights were taken to a chamber, the most elegant and beautiful, I think, that was ever beheld by knight or maiden: it was superbly painted in gold and silver and many other colours, depicting the story of Troy and of Hector, and how Paris abducted Helen and all the grief and suffering that followed. There were two beds in the chamber, richly covered, and on these the knights lay down. The whole room, I promise you, was gorgeously arranged: its floor was strewn with every herb in Christendom, and it was lit with four score candles, placed with such care that their light caused no discomfort. The surgeon examined the knights and declared they need fear no mortal wound: in a fortnight he would have them healed and well. Never in your life have you seen such joy as Arthur and the barons displayed at the news.

That night the king told Bran de Lis of his mission: to find Girflet, tragically lost and believed to be a prisoner at the Proud Castle.

'He is indeed, good sire,' said Bran. 'He was captured in battle: I know that for certain. As soon as Sir Gawain and I have recovered I'll go there with you: I think I'll be of more use than anyone if you mean to rescue him.'

The king said he'd gladly wait till he was fit to ride with them, and he and his companions stayed at the castle of Lis for a whole fortnight. They had as much as they could wish of every kind of bird and fish and meat and game in the world; and the king was reluctant to leave Bran's side as he supplied him with information about the great Proud Castle and said:

'We'll take servants, squires and sergeants with us, sire, and my pavilion, too – it's huge! And we'll choose the best of my hounds to take: the castle's surrounded by forests where we can go and hunt when you fancy – we'll be able to catch plenty of deer and other game!'

---

[99] '*Loënois*'; another MS gives '*Lodonois*'. Both are probably the adjective derived from *Laudunum*, the Latin name for Laon in Picardy. This curious sentence, appearing so abruptly in mid-episode, caused all the scribes a good deal of difficulty, and most omitted it entirely. I take it to be a reference to the anonymous author of the original, but I, like the evidently struggling scribes, may have misinterpreted it.

But Sir Gawain paid little attention to this: his thoughts were entirely on his love. Nor had she forgotten him: she was ready to attend to him at any hour he needed, giving him every innocent comfort. And Gawain didn't fail to show his feelings for his sweet son, kissing him often. He'd gladly have stayed for a long, long time, and little wonder: he was completely at ease; he had everything he wished – and no one, I'd say, who's free of toil and pain has any right to complain.

The Jousts at the Proud Castle

At the fortnight's end the king prepared to ride – he'd no desire to tarry longer. They had everything they needed, and as many sergeants and squires as they cared to take: they were ready to go and took to the road early one Tuesday, and that excellent knight Sir Bran de Lis went with them.

They rode for seven long days and passed through many a forest, till they came at last to their longed-for destination and saw, right there before them, the great Proud Castle. In a meadow beside a thick, fair grove of leafy olive trees, the men who'd ridden ahead had already pitched the king's pavilion and a host of tents around it. The king and his company arrived there and dismounted and disarmed, all in the highest spirits. They advanced no further – no one would dare attack the castle – but their arrival in the country was well known: they hadn't been there long before the people in the castle rang a bell, the biggest ever seen, that echoed for fully five leagues all around, rousing the whole land. As soon as they heard it the king asked Bran de Lis what it signified. He knew well enough, and said:

'It's a signal to all the surrounding land that the castle's being besieged. There won't be any lances or shields along the ramparts till it sounds.'

And even as he said this, they saw more than three thousand pennons of different kinds appear atop the walls, and just as many shields displayed along the battlements. And a moment later you'd have seen knights on palfreys and destriers emerge from the forests and on to the plain and ride in huge companies straight to the castle and in through the gate. The king and his companions gazed in admiration.

I shan't describe the castle in detail – it would take too long; but no man in all his travels ever saw such impressive walls and handsome halls and soaring towers and defences.

Food was prepared in the king's pavilion, and he went and supped with great pleasure. At supper all agreed that the knights they'd seen riding to the castle had gone there to oppose the company from court. Anyone seeking tests of chivalry would be sure to find them here! They ate in a very buoyant mood as they talked of the men in the castle.

As soon as the king had taken his seat, Lucan the butler had served him wine in a golden cup and said: 'I crave the first joust in the morning, sire, as befits my position.'

'The first favour asked of me here,' said the king, 'I shan't refuse! I gladly grant it.'

When they'd all eaten they washed and then called for their arms to be brought at once. They checked the fit of their chausses, stretching their legs and flexing their feet, and made their squires practise donning their hauberks, fastening and untying the straps; they wanted to make sure they'd be perfectly armed. You never saw such a cheerful company, in merry banter with the king; they asked him in jest to give each man his allotted day to joust, saying it would settle their nerves, but the king refused, saying he preferred to let them sweat! They spent a long while laughing and joking with the king, and then, as midnight drew near, they drank before taking to their beds.

Next morning they rose at dawn and went to a chapel in a meadow at the edge of the grove; all the slain knights, both from that land and elsewhere, were buried there. And as soon as the priest had said mass they returned to the pavilion where the king and all his company took dinner together. After a pleasant meal they rose at once and helped Lucan the butler to arm, most expertly and handsomely: the tunic he wore above his hauberk was of purple silk from Bonivent[100] richly embroidered with gold. They brought him his horse and shield and he mounted, full of eager confidence. Then he took up his lance and shield and thrust in his spurs with all his might and galloped away, straight for the Proud Castle, and didn't stop till he reached the field where all fought who came there seeking combat. The field was defined by a spreading olive tree at each of its four corners; once a knight had entered the field, whoever was first to leave the bounds of these trees was deemed a defeated coward.

The well-armed Lucan had barely arrived before he saw a knight ride boldly from the castle, mounted on a swift warhorse and superbly armed and equipped. He galloped straight to the field; and they lowered their pennons at once and thrust in their spurs and charged at each other and delivered mighty blows to their shields. The knight hit Lucan so hard that his lance flew into pieces, but the butler struck such a weighty blow that he sent him tumbling into the grass far behind his horse. He seized the knight's mount and rode away, leaving him standing in the middle of the field, and made his swift and triumphant way back to the king's pavilion. But Sir Bran de Lis said:

'Truly, butler, the siege would have been over if you'd taken him captive! Your work would have been done! You'd have put an end to the whole sorry business!'

'How's that, sir? Explain!'

'Listen, friend: you managed to unhorse one of their finest knights! You should have pressed home your advantage with might and main and taken him prisoner! If you'd brought him back here to us, Girflet would have been set free!'

When Lucan heard this, I tell you, he was less than pleased. He didn't stay a moment longer: he left the knight's horse and set off for the field. The king kept calling him back, but he ignored him and rode swiftly on – he'd no intention of returning. He'd only just reached the field when through the castle gate, armed, with pennon unfurled, rode a fine figure of a knight. On to the combat ground he charged, and when Lucan saw him he charged likewise and struck his shield so fearsomely that his stout-shafted lance was shattered, while the knight's lance smashed through Lucan's shield and struck him in the arm and bore him to the ground. The butler climbed to his feet again and tried to pull the stump of lance from his arm, but the knight returned to the attack; Lucan mounted such resistance as he could, but wounded as he was, pierced by the lance, his defence was weak.

'I surrender as your prisoner!' he said. 'I can fight no more.'

And without more ado he surrendered his sword to the knight, who hurried to help him, for he was bleeding heavily; he tore a strip from his surcoat and bound the wound tightly to stop the flow, and then led him away to the castle.

The king was distraught, but Sir Gawain said: 'By the high Father in heaven, as long as the butler's safe and has no mortal wound I'm happy to see him captured, for now the valiant Girflet, who's been a prisoner here for four years, will have news of us and be given heart. Now, thank God, he'll have a fellow captive who'll let him know we've come to rescue him – and rightly so: there was never a finer knight. And the butler's a

---

[100] Benevento?

worthy knight, too – it often happens that a knight's unhorsed and wounded: you won't hear me blame him for that.'

And Sir Bran de Lis added: 'By God, sire, he unhorsed one of theirs – and I don't know of many finer. There are a good three thousand knights in the castle – not counting the paid troops – but they won't be feeling comfortable!'

The king had great respect for the lord of Lis, but he was annoyed that he'd berated the butler for not bringing back the knight: he was convinced that Lucan had been captured solely because of what Bran had said.

Then Bran came to him with a request, asking by the love he owed him to grant him the next day's joust. He pleaded earnestly, but the king absolutely refused: he knew he'd be angry, but said that if he were to lose him it would be a grievous loss indeed – he was the only one with knowledge of that country.

'Oh sire!' said Bran. 'You mustn't think that way, expecting the worst! Have no fear, it'll never happen, please God! And the first favour I crave you should grant without demur! So I pray you, kindly grant me tomorrow's joust before anyone else requests it.'

'Since you insist,' the king replied, 'let it be as you wish.'

Then they retired to the pavilion to eat – but they were short of a butler.

He was inside the Proud Castle; he'd been taken straight there. They'd led him captive to the very same room where the good Girflet, the son of Do, had been so long; and in all the time he'd been imprisoned, Girflet had never felt such joy as he did at the sight of Lucan. He jumped up and kissed him and said:

'Tell me, dear friend, where were you taken prisoner?'

And Lucan told him the whole story, and how the king and his company were laying siege to the castle and encamped outside. 'And he says he'll never leave until you're rescued!'

Girflet was overjoyed at this; and he said: 'Sir Lucan, I long to hear news of the finest knights in the world, those of the Round Table. I've not seen them or heard a word of them for an age! How are they, good sir? Are they all still alive and well?'

'By all the saints, no, my good, dear friend. Many fine knights have died since the day you were captured – some passed away and others slain – but many good, renowned knights of proven valour have come to take their places.'

'Ah, God!' said Girflet. 'How the court and noble household will have changed! I dare say I'll know few of the ones you mention.'

'Good sir,' said the butler, 'there are many worthy knights indeed. And I swear they're so eager to see you that they won't stir from this place till they've recovered you!'

Just then their captors came with food, and they ate a long, hearty and cheerful meal. They spent the night in fine spirits, and it wasn't a long one, for Pentecost was past and it was around the feast of Saint John[101] when the nights are the shortest of the year. They were both surprised to see day break: they'd been engrossed in pleasant conversation.

And God! What a beautiful morning it was: the sun was shining bright and clear, the weather balmy. As soon as it was time the king rose in his pavilion and all his companions likewise. The first thing they did was to hear mass at the chapel, and then food was prepared – an early meal is good for revitalising the brain! They had a

---

[101] i.e. John the Baptist, now June 24th.

fine dinner, all sitting together and eating a hearty meal of the roast venison and other game they were hunting in profusion.

Once they'd dined, a chamberlain carried in a hauberk, bright as snow, and laid it on a fine Grecian carpet in the middle of the tent. Another brought a pair of chausses and laid them alongside, and Bran de Lis went and pulled them on and found them strong and comfortable. And then, as prime was rung inside the castle, he donned the hauberk and his tunic on top – of white silk it was, embroidered with gold: no man will ever see one finer. Then the king laced the ventail and with his own hands set the helm upon Bran's head; Sir Gawain tied the laces, and King Yder girded his sword, the finest ever seen: Bran had impressive squires indeed! Then his destrier was brought to him, and he mounted and took up his shield and hung it proudly from his neck, gripped his pennoned lance, thrust in his spurs and rode straight to the field that he knew so well. Through the gate he saw a knight come riding swiftly on his charger, finely armed; to the field he came, shield slung from neck. As soon as they saw each other they launched into a fearsome charge, and truly, they smashed through their shields with a force that made their lances shatter. Sir Bran de Lis pierced the knight's shield and struck him in the shoulder. They brought each other down in the collision, but they didn't stay there long: they leapt up in an instant, drew their swords and dealt each other mighty blows on their shining helms. They both fought valiantly indeed, but the knight was gravely hampered by his wound while Bran de Lis was fit and strong and sustained the assault, not allowing him a moment's rest; the knight couldn't resist and was driven back till one blow brought him to his knees, and before he could regain his feet Bran made him yield as a prisoner.

He led him back to the pavilion – but saw him remounted first, not wanting to make him go on foot. The king and all his company graciously came the range of a crossbow shot to welcome Bran's return; and when he saw them pay him such great honour he dismounted and thanked them deeply, and then delivered his captive to the king.

'A delightful gift!' said Arthur.

They returned to the pavilion, taking gentle care of the wounded knight. The king had a litter of branches made and finely blanketed, and in it they laid the knight, who badly needed rest. Then the king and his companions joyfully disarmed the lord of Lis in the pavilion and swiftly had him dressed, and spent the whole day in celebration. Later, in the cool of the evening, they went and made merry in the shade of an olive tree. Those valiant, illustrious knights sat all around the king and listened to the castle watchmen sounding their horns and pipes: they were having a high old time – you could hear them play every instrument on God's earth that a watchman might ever use! The king made his knights keep quiet – he was enjoying the watchmen's lively racket up on the castle walls. But Kay, sitting beside the lord of Lis and listening to it all, couldn't hold his tongue – he couldn't help himself: he had to say what was on his mind.

'By Saint Denis, sirs,' he said, 'I think tomorrow's joust has been forgotten: it hasn't been allotted. It seems none of the king's lords or companions cares to ask!'

'There's no need,' the king replied. 'I'm giving it to *you*!'

'By Saint Martin, sire,' said Kay, 'I'd rather tackle a spit-full of meat, dripping with fat, than have to joust in the morning! I'm not going to thank you for it, but I'll do it if you wish, sire – I'll bet Sir Gawain'll be pleased!'

Everyone had been enjoying this, and when they'd had a good laugh about it they returned to the pavilion and drank and then took to their beds, wanting nothing more. And so they passed the night.

As soon as it grew light next morning, before the bell rang for prime, the king heard mass; then, once they'd dined, they armed the seneschal, and he mounted and took his shield and rode swiftly away. The moment he reached the field he saw an armed knight come spurring from the castle. Without a moment's pause they charged and met with blows that brought each other down; but they leapt straight up and attacked ferociously with their well-honed blades, battering each other's helm. The knight aimed a furious blow at Kay, who parried it and returned a deep cut into the top edge of his shield; but as he pulled the sword free it broke, and the knight, seeing the broken blade, pressed home his advantage and sent Kay reeling back, forcing him beyond the boundary marked by the four olive trees at the corners of the field. At that point the knight abandoned him and returned to his horse and mounted at once; then he rode up to Kay's horse and, seeing what a prize it was, decided to have it and led it away. Kay strode back to the battleground and cried:

'You've surrendered the field to me!'

But the knight seemed to take not the slightest notice. Kay stood there for a good while before heading back to camp. Back he went, not realising he'd been outdone: he thought he'd won all the credit, but his opponent had won a great deal more! The king's companions said:

'By God, sire, let's go and meet Kay and give him a ribbing – he's ripe for it!'

The king agreed and off they went; and the king with his ready wit was the first to address him, calling out in the hearing of all: 'Where have you been, Kay? A long way, was it? Been busy?'

Kay was ready to curse but stopped himself and said: 'It's no use, sire! You can't mock me: in faith, I've defeated one of their knights – though he took my horse. The field and all the honour are mine – he ran away, without a doubt!'

Everyone was struggling not to laugh.

'Do you need any help?' asked Tors the son of Arés.

'Are you hurt, seneschal?' said others.

'Looks like you're limping,' said Gawain.

Then Sir Yvain said: 'Give me your shield, Kay. You fought a mighty contest – I saw you deal some amazing blows! What a performance! Praise be to God!'

Kay handed him the shield and he took it and slung the strap round his neck. Everyone was mocking Kay and he knew it. He said to Yvain:

'Since you have my shield, sir, I give you tomorrow's joust, along with everything I've won today – including the field! You'd do well to treat me with respect: you can be sure I'll pay you back in kind as soon as I get the chance!'

No one who heard this could help laughing. Amid much mirth they led him back to the pavilion and disarmed him, and Bran de Lis said:

'My dear Sir Kay, it looked as if you were the first to cross the boundary marked by the olive trees; and whoever does that, the people in the castle deem a loser!'

'Let them!' Kay replied. 'By God, sir, as far as I'm concerned you can go in or come out as you please! What's the problem? It's a field! People go in, people come out!'

At this they were helpless with laughter.

The Rich Soldier

Just then the bells in every church in the castle tolled, a peal so loud that you wouldn't have heard God's thunder. The king asked the reason for this mighty ringing, and the lord of Lis said:

'I'll explain, my lord: it's Saturday, and as soon as noon is past no one in the castle will do work of any kind. Rather, the mother of God is worshipped and honoured there more than anywhere else in Christendom, truly; everyone will go to church – ladies, knights, burghers and all the other folk – in their finest dress. It's an impressive sight! They all go to hear vespers in honour of that high lady, and from now till terce on Monday the bells peal thus for every mass. Only then do most tradesmen return to their work; and I assure you, you won't have any battles in the meantime, so you could spend tomorrow hunting if you wish.'

The king agreed enthusiastically. They spent a merry evening, and then rose next morning and made their way to the woods together, and the huntsmen's horns rang throughout the forest all day long.

Two hounds separated a big stag from a herd and took off in pursuit, and Sir Gawain followed and went way off track: on and on he chased them till they reached a glade where they finally trapped the exhausted stag and made the kill. He skinned the beast and gave the hounds their share; then he butchered it deftly, and trussed the back and flanks behind him and mounted and turned back. He sent the hounds ahead of him, knowing the country as they did, and they ran on with him following, keeping up a steady pace.

As he rode along after them he heard, quite close, the loud cry of a goshawk. He turned and headed towards it swiftly. Down a faint, shadowy track he rode, pressing his horse ever onward, till he came upon a fortress, the finest he'd ever found on any of his travels. It stood in a glade, and one more handsome and impressive he couldn't have imagined: there were halls and a mighty tower within and an imposing palisade all round, and a fine drawbridge over the deep, water-filled moats. At the foot of this bridge stood a pine tree, and beneath the pine sat a knight, fully armed, the biggest and most fierce in aspect ever seen or encountered in any land. He was wearing a purple haqueton.[102] When Sir Gawain saw him he rode towards him as fast as he could; but the knight didn't stir at all: he was hunched over, deep in thought. Gawain was taken aback by his size. He hailed him politely, saying:

'God save you, sir knight.'

But the knight made no reply, loud or soft, he was so lost in troubled thought. So Gawain said again: 'God bless you, knight!'

But the knight was silent; he said not a word. A third time Gawain hailed him, and a third time he said nothing. Gawain planted himself right in his way, but he neither heard nor saw him.

'God,' said Sir Gawain, 'you created man with your own hands, but what was the point of making this one? None so handsome, huge, well-built was ever born, but he's deaf and dumb and blind! Truly, if I had company I'd carry him off to the king if I could: he'd be intrigued to see such a specimen!'

And it occurred to Gawain that he could take him with him on his horse, and dismount if it got too much and accompany him on foot. Without more ado he unpacked the butchered venison and dumped it under the tree. Then he leaned over the front of his saddle, took the knight by the armpits and began to haul him up. The knight beat his hands aside and leapt angrily to his feet and cried:

'How dare you, vassal? Intruding on my thoughts like this! I could beat you to death with my fists! If I had my sword your blood would be on it! I'd get going, and sharpish, if I were you, and leave me here to die!'

---

[102] The padded tunic worn beneath mail. 'Purple' describes the rich cloth, not the colour: see Glossary.

And he sat down again beneath the tree, as rapt in thought as he'd been when Gawain found him. So Sir Gawain trussed his venison behind him again and turned away, leaving the knight lost in his mournful musing.

He hadn't gone half a league before he met a damsel coming down his path; she was fair and comely indeed, and riding a big, dark palfrey – no count or king ever had finer – and every part of its harness and its covertures was priceless. Her apparel was indescribably rich – her gown was covered in golden thread. The whip she held was of gold and ivory, with thongs of fine silk, knotted with gold, of Moorish make; she was lashing her mount repeatedly, and rode straight past Gawain without saying a word. Sir Gawain was amazed by the palfrey's speed, and when he saw the damsel pass without speaking he turned and spurred after her, calling:

'Stay a little, damsel!'

She'd no desire to talk and hurried on, but Gawain soon caught up with her and said: 'Ah, damsel, stay! Stay! Tell me where you're going.'

'I can't stop, sir! Let me be, by God! I've killed the finest knight in all Christendom, truly I have – no man could ever find his equal!'

'What?' said Sir Gawain. 'You mean you've killed him with your own hands?'

'I have! I won't deny it! I promised to be with him at noon – I'll have killed him by failing to keep my word! There was no finer knight on Earth! My dear sweet love was waiting for me at a tower up ahead.'

'Truly, damsel,' Gawain replied, 'he's alive, I promise you! He nearly hit me with his fist just now! There's no emergency!'

'Oh, good sir, was he angry or distracted?'

'He was indeed!'

'He'll die! Oh, sir knight, you mustn't keep me!'

And off she rode that instant, furiously lashing her palfrey. Sir Gawain watched her go, regretting he hadn't asked her about the knight: he didn't know the first thing about him – his name, which land he was from or where he'd be going next.

He set off once more for the Proud Castle, and rejoiced when he caught sight of it again. His companions spotted him from the pavilion as he emerged from the woods; they'd been very worried about him, and were mightily relieved to see him back. He rode up to the pavilion and dismounted. He'd hardly arrived before he launched into his tale and told them all about the knight he'd met, saying a bigger, more fearsome knight was never seen, 'and when he found he was without his sword he nearly killed me with his big, square club of a fist!'

Hearing this, Bran de Lis said to the king: 'That knight, sire, is the Rich Soldier, who keeps such a fine, impressive, well-schooled household. He loves that damsel so dearly that he calls her both "maiden" and "lady",[103] and everyone says he'll die if he fails to have her. God gave him mighty strength and courage, but his love for the damsel has taken such a hold that his courage and strength are much reduced!'

While they were talking, they noticed a vast dust-cloud rising towards the forest: a huge crowd of people – more than twenty thousand – were heading that way. Not a single man or boy, woman or child, knight or townsman remained in the castle! Anyone fit to go was eagerly making for the forest. It was far into the night before they returned. The king asked what was going on, and Bran de Lis replied:

---

[103] i.e. he hopes and intends to make her his wife.

'They've gone to meet and honour their lord, sire. Never before has he had the chance to take his beloved to the castle. I tell you, sire, every one of his men will dub three new knights in his honour before the evening's out, by way of celebration, and he's told them it'll please him greatly.'

What more should I tell you? There was such jubilation in the castle that night, with candles blazing in every tower and house and chamber, on walls, in trees, on belfreys, that it seemed to the king's men, camped outside, that the castle was afire. And songs rang out with beating drums as the celebration echoed on till midnight.

The king then retired to bed; and in the morning he graciously granted that day's joust to Sir Yvain – since Kay had given him his shield – and no one argued or protested. And as soon as they'd dined they armed him splendidly and he mounted swiftly and took up his shield and lance; he didn't dally but rode straight to the field without once drawing rein. Out from the castle rode another knight, finely armed, mounted on a strong, swift destrier. He thrust in his spurs and clashed with Yvain; his lance snapped and shattered, but Yvain's held firm long enough to drive him to the ground. Yvain then attacked him with his sword of steel, striking in earnest: as the knight tried to rise he beat him back to the ground, giving him a torrid time; he tried to mount a defence but it was hopeless: whether he liked it or not he had to yield as his prisoner. Yvain led him back to the pavilion and delivered him to King Arthur who received him with delight.

Such were the spoils that day; and let me tell you, the captive was one of the newly-dubbed knights – he hadn't yet had time to make himself as rich as the Soldier and his household! And when they'd disarmed him and the king saw how young he was, the king said:

'Where are you from, dear friend? From what country?'

'From Ireland, sire,' he said. 'I was the son of Count Blandigan. Truly, sire, I've served the Rich Soldier's beloved for seven years, cutting her meat at table, and my lord for love of her knighted me yesterday. In return for my service he granted me the joust – but I have to admit he wouldn't have done so if my lady hadn't begged him to, for it upset many worthy knights in the castle!'

'Do you know, friend,' said Sir Gawain, 'who's to joust tomorrow?'

'I know exactly who's to have the next joust: the Rich Soldier himself. And I'll tell you why I'm so sure: the custom in the castle is that the girls and ladies and damsels rise each morning and go up and watch from the walls, and whichever of them is the first to spot a knight approaching to do combat goes at once to arm her sweetheart – there's no argument. Well, last night my lady begged them that, for love of her, none of them would go up to the walls and watch the field tomorrow. So I've a good idea who the joust will fall to!'

Sir Gawain instantly rose and came to the king and asked to be granted the next day's joust, but Arthur refused, saying:

'Gawain my dear nephew, you'll not go tomorrow – in fact you'll be the last before me. First let all my companions go one by one.'

'I'd consider that shameful, sire, when I ask in all courtesy. If tomorrow's joust is denied me now, then God curse me if I ever joust here at all! I'll leave and go off alone instead!'

'Then have it!' said the king.

'Thank you, sire!' Gawain replied.

And so they passed the night, and in the morning, at the crack of dawn, Sir Gawain got up and woke Sir Yvain. He rose at once, and they slipped out quietly on their own and chatted together in the morning dew; for what a morning it was: pure and bright and clear, the most perfect summer's dawn. Gawain washed his face and feet and hands in the dew, as did Sir Yvain. Then they returned to the pavilion, where a rich cotton tunic with strips of fine purple* and samite was brought to Gawain and he donned it at once, and they deftly fastened the sleeves around his arms. By the time he was dressed his uncle the king was up, so they went to the chapel, and when the mass of the Holy Spirit was over they returned to the pavilion and dined.

Then Gawain called for his arms, and sat on a gorgeous carpet spread on the grass inside the tent; and all the knights stood in attendance, without cloak or mantle, until he was fully armed. The king himself gladly assisted, loving him dearly as he did, until he was armed as necessary both for attack and defence. There was nothing for it now but to be about it; his horse was brought to him, handsomely caparisoned, and he mounted briskly. What a fine figure he was! A finer figure of a knight, indeed, I can't imagine. King Arthur gave him his good sword Escalibor: he girded it himself as he sat in the saddle – loosely, so it didn't constrict him. Then he took up his shield and lance and set off at once and rode swiftly to the battleground.

According to my source, he hadn't been there long before a horn rang out atop the castle's central tower – such a resounding blast it was that the ground shook for a league in all directions. Sir Bran de Lis said to the king:

'We'll soon see the Rich Soldier, sire, ride out on his destrier! That horn sounds only when he's arming, and I can tell from the length of the blast that he's fastened his spurs!'

The horn rang out a second time, and Bran told them: 'Truly, sirs, now he's donned and laced his hose of mail!'

There was then a long pause before it sounded again, so loud this time that the whole surrounding country trembled, and the lord of Lis said: 'Now, my lord king, the Soldier's donned his hauberk and laced his shining helm!'

And then it sounded loud enough to carry a wondrous distance, and Bran said: 'My good lord king, he's mounted now – that'll be the final blast today!'

So he told them all about the knight; and there was a great commotion inside the walls as the lord of the castle rode through the streets, followed by so many people that they could hear them from the pavilion even before they saw them. The crowd escorted him to the gate and out he rode, and the king and his company saw him now, draped right down to his spurs in a rich cloth from the East.[104] Out he rode at speed, his splendid pennon unfurled; and so many people climbed to the walls to watch the battle between the two brave knights that they lined every inch of the battlements – it was an incredible sight. He rode proudly to the field where Gawain was awaiting him; and as soon as he caught sight of him he set his shield in place and faced him. Their lances were levelled, their shields set firm, blazons displayed, and they spurred their horses to a furious charge. They didn't pull out of the clash; they struck each other on their shields so hard that their lances shattered down to their fists, and then collided so violently – horses, bodies, shields together – that they were laid out in the grass whether they liked it or not, their horses sprawled on top of them. But those valiant knights leapt up at once and drew their swords and went at each other in a rage. What a fearsome contest followed then, as the vast crowd looked on. They dealt each other such blows to the helm that

---

[104] *'siglaton'*.

they were stunned and reeling. The king feared for Gawain, while the men of the castle were praying earnestly to God that their lord would return safe and sound. But the knights were unsparing with their whetted, burnished blades, and the rain of blows was strength-sapping, the more so since it was the hottest day there'd ever been, before or since: the heat as much as the combat drained them.

But you must know that when it reached midday Sir Gawain's strength and vigour always doubled; they waned by the time that evening came, and then began to wax again once midnight passed and continued till its zenith at noon. Truly, this had served him well before, in his combat with Bran de Lis; you won't deny that: you've heard me describe that contest – otherwise you might not believe me – and you'll remember what happened when midnight passed. And now, on this day, with the battle raging long, they'd reached the hour of noon; now Gawain waxed in strength against the Rich Soldier, dealing him huge and repeated blows. But the Soldier struck back vigorously, with power and fury – it was impossible to tell who was on top. Everyone watching was amazed that the battle was lasting so long, that they hadn't both collapsed with the heat in the middle of the field. But last the battle did through noon; then the Soldier began to flag and give ground – he couldn't stand the heat, and was so overcome with thirst that he nearly died. So what did Sir Gawain do? Seeing his opponent tire he pressed him all the harder, and when for a moment the Soldier staggered he strode in and gave him such a buffet that they both ended up on the ground. But Gawain leapt back to his feet in an instant and cried:

'Vassal, surrender as my prisoner or I'll kill you!'

But the Soldier was so stunned that he wouldn't have uttered a word if he'd been offered Paris; and when he did finally speak he cried: 'God! Someone kill me!', and then: 'She's dead! She's finished! I don't care who puts an end to me!'

Sir Gawain wondered what he meant. He seized the nose-guard of his helm and shook him, but seeing he would say no more he said: 'Yield, sir knight!'

But all he would say was: 'She's dead, for sure, the finest lady in the world! Ah, how I loved her!'

Sir Gawain, seeing he'd get no other reply, cut the laces of the Soldier's helm; but the Soldier's eyes were shut tight – he'd passed out, overcome by grief and heat. Gawain was infuriated that he couldn't make him speak, no matter how he shook and pummelled. He didn't want to leave him there for fear he'd be accused of weakness, but nor did he want to kill him – if he did, he thought, he would scupper their mission.[105] And if he went to the pavilion to fetch help to carry the prisoner back, he was sure he wouldn't find him when he returned – he'd have disappeared or fled! Gawain was at a total loss. He took off the Soldier's helm and sat down on the ground beside him. He placed Escalibor safely by his side and took the Soldier's sword. When he finally came to and saw Sir Gawain next to him he asked him his name. He didn't conceal it, and when the Soldier heard he was Gawain he said:

'Sir, now I know for sure: you are the most accomplished knight in all the world.'

With that he fell silent, and said no more. Sir Gawain looked at him and said: 'Before God, good sir, don't be upset by what I'm about to say: if you follow me to the king's pavilion, he'll gladly come to terms with you.'

The Soldier replied: 'I have a sweetheart whom I love, truly, more than my own life. If I hear she's died, I'll kill myself that instant. I beg you, sir, in all decency, courtesy,

---

[105] Literally: 'he would lose everything' – i.e. they wouldn't recover Girflet.

nobility, let me have her alive and I promise that no man of the Proud Castle, rightly or wrongly, will ever oppose you again. If you'll do this for me, sir, I swear on my honour to do whatever the king requests, and I'll have every man in the castle swear the same. But listen: if my sweetheart knew of this, so help me God she'd die that instant: she'd never believe I'd been defeated, truly! So for the love of God, and as a mark of your nobility, I beg of you a great favour: come back with me to the castle keep and kneel before my love and tell her you yield as her prisoner. We'll pretend it's true. And say I took you captive and vanquished you in the field. That way you'll give me back my life and my dear beloved! But if you won't do this, in God's name kill me here.'

Gawain recalled how he'd found the knight outside the fortress in the forest, downcast and distracted, and met the damsel on her way to him, convinced that he'd be dead. He knew she loved him so desperately that she'd die in no time if he were brought to shame – and he thought it would be a cruel deed to kill so great a knight. So he said to him:

'Have no fear, my good, dear sir: I shall indeed go with you to the Proud Castle and yield as the damsel's prisoner. You might very well betray me; but truly, I wouldn't have you or your beloved lose your lives, even if it costs me mine.'

The Soldier replied most nobly, saying: 'Sir, I'm your liegeman for the rest of my days.'

And he held out his hand and vowed to do the king's will, and Gawain accepted his oath. Then they both mounted at once and headed back to the castle.

The king was beside himself when he saw his nephew being led away, and cried: 'My nephew's been captured! I think I'll go mad!' He called to his men, saying: 'What's going on? Has he really been taken prisoner?'

'Yes, sire!' answered Agravain. 'And we can't understand it: we were sure he'd defeated the knight and had him at his mercy! It's the strangest misadventure ever! Before the knight got up again we thought he'd admitted defeat!'

The king couldn't listen to another word; he went and sprawled on a bed and flung his mantle over his head: no man was ever in such distress. In his mind, there was every reason to despair.

Meanwhile the people of the castle were flocking and thronging to the lord they thought they'd lost, and rushed to his sweetheart – who was in abject grief and torment – to tell her that he was on his way and bringing with him the vanquished Gawain. Then the Soldier and Sir Gawain arrived at the door and dismounted, and Gawain surrendered to her without more ado, saying:

'Lady, take my sword. This fine knight, your beloved, has outfought and overpowered me, that's the truth.'

Never in your life have you witnessed such joy as the damsel's then! And her lover said: 'My lady, you're to go with a hundred knights to the Castle of Dobliers – that's where I mean to stay a while. Have the chambers made ready and I'll join you there tomorrow – we can be fairly private there. I've had a taxing day today, so don't be surprised if I want to go and rest there a little in seclusion.'

'A fine idea,' she replied. 'It's a delightful place.'

So the damsel mounted and made her way there. Do you understand why he'd sent her off? So that she wouldn't hear what he'd *really* suffered that day! Once she was gone, word of what had befallen him spread throughout the castle. Then he gave orders for Girflet, son of Do, and Lucan the butler to be released. It was done at once, and when

Sir Gawain saw them he ran straight to Girflet and greeted him with the utmost joy, kissing him more than a hundred times. Then he seated him on a bench beside him and they talked together for a long while.

Once Gawain and the Soldier had been disarmed, they and Lucan and Girflet donned rich gowns – their like was never seen: of the finest cloth they were, fit for an emperor. Then the Soldier called for four horses, and they mounted and rode through the streets and headed out to the pavilion – just the four of them.

The king's companions saw them as soon as they left the castle.

'In faith, I can see four men coming,' said Sir Yvain. 'They're all knights, I'd say.'

'They look that way to me,' said Kay.

Soon they were close enough to recognise, and Yvain ran joyfully to the king and said: 'My lord! My lord! So help me God, Gawain's coming, riding side by side with Girflet and Lucan and another towering knight!'

But the king gave no response – he didn't show any sign of joy or make any attempt to rise from his bed. But he seemed to have regained his spirit a little as he said to his companions: 'Sirs, don't look downcast – retain a noble composure if you can. I think they've come to tell us to be gone, that our knights will be staying in prison. But I'm not leaving till I rescue them – or put up a fight at least!'

'Very good, sire,' they said; but the four knights had now arrived at the tent, and came before the king. You never saw such elation as the worthy, noble king displayed at the sight of Girflet: his heart was brimming with joy. I shan't beat about the bush: the Soldier told how Gawain had defeated him and saved the lives of him and his sweetheart – they owed him a very great deal.

I'm going to leave them now; but I must say this: Gawain should be admired and loved and honoured indeed, for vanquishing the knight in combat and then treating him with such great courtesy. That's all I'll say, and I'll move on – except to add that the king was now lord of the Proud Castle and all its land, and the Soldier supplied the king with everything he desired, earning his greater love and esteem. King Arthur entered the castle and spent a fortnight there. Then he set off back to Britain; all the people saw him on his way, but after escorting him a distance they turned back – except the Rich Soldier and seven other knights, for the Soldier didn't want to leave him, and carried on the journey with the others.

The Search for Gawain's Son

They rode on day by day in fine array, until they came to the castle of Lis. But what greeted them there was far from pleasant: they arrived to find sorry news indeed. As the king dismounted and entered the great hall, a lady told him that an unknown band of men had kidnapped his great-nephew,[106] that sweet and lovely child.

'He went one morning to play with the other children as he always did, on the road outside the town, and some people – we don't know who – came and carried him off! You never heard such anguish as there was in the town that day: more than twenty thousand collapsed in a swoon! Since then they've spared no efforts to find him, but no one's been able to bring him back.'

Everyone was dismayed by the news. As for the king, he spoke up at once, the first to declare that he would search the land for the boy and would select a band of companions

---

[106] i.e. Gawain's son.

to go with him. Sir Bran de Lis, who was very upset, promised to do all in his power to find him, and the Rich Soldier said he would take a hundred or two hundred knights or more and keep hunting till the boy was found: he was grieving and angry that the king should have returned to such news. Then the lord of Lis said:

'We'll be able to reflect and discuss this better once we've dined.'

'No one's going to argue with that!' said Kay.

And the knights said: 'Kay seems keen on the thought of dinner!'

King Arthur laughed at this; but then he took King Yder and Girflet and Sir Yvain and went to console Sir Gawain's sweetheart in her chamber, for she was in floods of tears. A good many more that I haven't mentioned followed them, the Rich Soldier included. They came to her and the king said:

'Take comfort, my dear, and dry your tears: we're going in search of my great-nephew, your son, and if it please God we'll find him.'

'By all the saints, sire,' the damsel replied, 'I was more worried about you than I was about him! I'd been told you'd be distraught! How could anyone be so cruel as to harm a child? No decent man would dream of it. In the name of God and Our Lord, I beg you, find the boy: it would win you great honour.'

'That's the best thing anyone's said, by God.' So said the king; and they returned to the hall and dined, and all agreed to set out next day in search of Sir Gawain's dear son.

But Gawain swore he wouldn't take part: he said searching for children wasn't his line. 'My lord king, I commend you to God. If there's anything else you want done in Britain, I'm at your service!'

And Sir Kay said: 'I'll go with you, by God! I'd just be a moaning bore if I had to go on a child-hunt! I'll leave that to the boy's great-uncle!'

'So be it,' the king replied. 'But by the love and faith you owe me, dear nephew, take Girflet with you: he's still suffering from his long imprisonment and it would do him good. I want you to take the queen my greetings, and tell her that a month from today, at the latest, she'll be sure to see me at the Glade of the Crossroads. Ask her to have my pavilion pitched at the four pines of the three sisters; I'll be there in a month with the Rich Soldier and his company of a hundred knights, for he very much wishes to see her. Bid her make every preparation for an honourable welcome, and send hunting parties into the forest so we find plenty to eat when we arrive! As for tomorrow, we'll all be leaving at first light, and we'll search for my great-nephew through forest and marsh: no matter where he's been taken in this land, he'll be found and rescued.'

They rested that night, and rose next day and scoured the surrounding country as they'd vowed the night before. Sir Gawain equipped and arrayed his men as splendidly as ever he could; he'd no desire to stay at Lis any longer and set off at once, taking his sweetheart with him and not forgetting the good Girflet and Kay and other knights, too. Girflet rode at their head, holding the reins of Sir Gawain's beloved: he was her constant escort, doing all he could to be of service. She was so beautiful and elegantly dressed: a lovelier creature was never born. As for the palfrey she rode, I shan't attempt to describe him as you'd struggle to believe me; but her saddle was covered in gorgeous silk and the champron* was made of finest gold.

They rode on day by day till they neared the court where the queen was residing – at the handsome, delightful Castle of the Elms[107] – and arrived there one Thursday. I don't want to hold things up by describing how joyfully the queen received them; but when

---

[107] *'Chastel des Ormiaus'* – literally 'young elms'.

the messenger who announced their coming told her of the damsel's beauty, you should have seen how the queen and her girls and ladies dressed their hair and adorned themselves! One had her hair combed, another the sides of her gown laced; a third said:

'How do I look?'

'Exquisite!' said a fourth. 'What about me?'

'Better still, I'd say!'

A fifth was asking: 'Be honest now: how's my complexion?'

'The most perfect in the world!'

And all this titivation, sirs, was prompted by the damsel's coming! Amid this frantic preparation the one endowed with all possible beauty[108] dismounted outside the hall with her great escort of knights. The queen and the ladies were thrilled and came to meet them, giving them a joyful welcome. And when they saw her beauty and her elegance, oh, what feverish talk was provoked! Then the queen led her to her chamber and honoured her highly – on account of the knight whose beloved she was. High rank indeed was conferred on her; she was treated with the utmost love and honour and respect by knights, maidens, damsels, ladies. That, truly, is how the good knight's sweetheart was received at court, and you can assure anyone who says otherwise that they're wrong! God send them shame for saying so! For that, I promise you, was the welcome given to the damsel, Guiolete.

Word spread quickly through all Britain that King Arthur had accomplished his mission and rescued Girflet from imprisonment at the Proud Castle, and that he was now returning safely home and would be at the Glade of the Crossroads on the day he'd appointed. The queen had the king's pavilion and many more transported to the glade, and there she went to spend a pleasant time, saying she wouldn't stir till the king arrived. She was accompanied by many counts and barons, and they pitched a great array of tents and pavilions there, as they went, quite properly, to stay and await their lord. The king's pavilion was set up right at the crossroads.

So the queen and a company of many fine knights waited for her lord to come, and they spent the time most agreeably. The huntsmen had great success in the forest, for the woods were teeming with game.

The Death of the Unknown Knight

One beautiful evening – a Tuesday, it was – during their wait for the king, the queen was playing backgammon,[109] her favourite game, with King Urien. Sir Gawain and many other worthy knights were seated around her, watching the game.

The light was beginning to fade when they saw a knight approaching, armed and mounted on a destrier; but he rode straight past without uttering a word. The queen was angered, saying the knight had shown her scant respect.

'He didn't so much as look at me or acknowledge me at all! I'd very much like to know his name and find out who he is.' And she said to Kay the seneschal: 'Mount, Kay, and bring him here to me.'

'Gladly!' And he went and armed at once: he was always eager to do the queen's bidding. He took off his costly tunic, lined with ermine, and swiftly armed and mounted and went galloping after the knight. He didn't shirk! He soon caught up with him and cried:

---

[108] Literally 'with the hundred beauties'.
[109] '*tables*': see note above, p. 133.

'Back you come, vassal! What possessed you to ride past the pavilions without asking leave of the queen and her knights? Come back at once!'

But the knight replied: 'So help me God, sir, it wasn't through any haughtiness that I failed to stop. You can't imagine a more urgent mission than mine! I can't turn back!'

'What a lot of nonsense!' said Kay. 'By God, vassal, if you refuse to return I'll kill your horse!'

'That wouldn't be doing me any favours!' the knight replied. 'I'm the most useless walker in the world, I truly am! And I've such a long way to ride tonight I can't tell you, so let me go, good sir. I promise I'll come and speak to the queen on my return – if God keeps me from being killed and sends me back alive.'

At this, Kay thrust in his spurs and charged to strike him. The knight saw him coming and let his horse go; he met him at full tilt, and sent him crashing to the ground with his legs in the air, so heavily that he almost smashed his ribs. Then he seized his horse and led it away, leaving Kay to trudge back to the pavilion in abject shame. There must have been a good hundred who were delighted but stayed tight-lipped! Then you'd have heard him tell the most arrant, outrageous lies about what had happened.

'Lady,' he said, 'that knight's an utter rogue! The dreadful things he said about you: I've never heard the like!'

'Come now, Kay,' said Sir Gawain. 'By all the saints, no worthy man would insult my lady. Let the knight go: just because he's taken your horse, don't start making up wild tales – that's shameful!'

'Go after him, Gawain,' said the queen, 'and bring him here to me.'

'Gladly, lady,' he replied; and his horse was brought to him and he mounted, quite unarmed, clad in a purple mantle and carrying a baton.[110] He rode swiftly after the knight, but he was going at quite a pace and it was almost dark by the time he caught up. He hailed him most courteously, and the knight drew rein at once. Gawain politely delivered his message, saying:

'Sir, the queen of all Britain and Ireland bids you come and speak with her.'

'Forgive me, good sir,' the knight replied, 'but as God's my witness I truly can't.' Then he asked him his name, and he assured him he was Sir Gawain; so he said: 'You can be sure, sir, that if I dared delay, there's no knight in the world for whom I'd more readily turn back. But I'm the only man this side of the sea who can accomplish the mission I've undertaken – which I can reveal to no one. Though you, I think, might be an exception: you might well achieve it. But no one would believe it at all.'

'For the love of God, sir,' said Gawain, 'with clasped hands I beg you return – I shall be your knight for evermore! Listen: Sir Kay is telling everyone at the queen's pavilion that you're a haughty rogue! The falsest of impressions, and I've rebuked him for it!'

'I couldn't care less about Kay: I'll be no worse a knight for his slanders. But for your sake, dear sir, I shall do as you wish, and my mission – more urgent than I can tell you – will have to be suspended.'

'We'll come straight back here, I promise you,' said Gawain, 'and I'll make amends to you in any way I can. I swear if I were the last man left alive I'd carry out your mission! You'll suffer no loss by coming with me.'

The knight replied most feelingly: 'I'm delighted to have met you, sir: I'm ready to go wherever you care to take me.'

And they turned their horses about. The knight left Kay's horse where it was – he

---

[110] i.e. as a sign that he comes on a peaceful mission.

didn't deign to take it with him, and Sir Gawain wasn't bothered! They set off swiftly for the pavilion, and rode back side by side. The sun had now fully set.

As they reached the queen's encampment and were passing the first of the tents, Kay flung a sly and sudden missile.[111] The knight cried aloud:

'Ah, Sir Gawain, I am slain! What a dreadful wrong, what a sin, that I should be killed while under your protection! Please God you'll do as you promised: if I die, don my armour straight away and mount this horse of mine and go wherever he takes you – don't attempt to change his course.' Then he said: 'God, why have they killed me? Truly, I've done no wrong!'

Sir Gawain stared at him in amazement, baffled by his anguished cries: he'd neither seen nor heard anyone strike or even touch him. Then he saw him slump unconscious over his horse's neck – and he started to bleed profusely, for he'd been struck right through the body: the shining head of a javelin was jutting forth. Sir Gawain, weeping, said:

'Ah, dear sir, whoever dealt you this blow has grievously dishonoured me!'

Then the knight toppled to the ground without uttering another word – and no one had asked his name or who he was, where he was from or what his mission. In moments a great crowd had gathered round, lamenting bitterly – not least Sir Kay; but Sir Gawain, flushed with rage and hatred, went and rammed into him, knocking him to the ground, and made his horse trample him again and again as he cried:

'You wicked, proven traitor! The truth about his death will be revealed, I'm sure of it! You're going to suffer!'

Kay vanished through the crowd as fast as he could. The knight was taken to the pavilion; Sir Gawain, distraught at his death, carried him with his own hands to the queen. Bowing to her, he said, in great distress:

'Here, lady, is the knight you sent me to fetch. He was coming without protest – so help me God and by my faith, to present him like this is an agony! Here, my queen, is his body – slain while under your protection! It brings dishonour on us all – especially me! No man ever suffered such shame as I have done tonight! It looks as if I betrayed him – but I've never been a traitor in my life!'

He gave orders for the dead knight to be disarmed. Everyone crowded round to look at him, and all who saw him grieved at the sight of his strong and handsome body.

'Dear Lord God,' they said, 'where can he have been born, to be so fair?'

No one recognised him, or knew which land he was from. But I'll come straight to the point: Sir Gawain donned the knight's armour and mounted his horse immediately, and the queen, weeping with distress and pity, asked him:

'What is it, sir? What are you doing? You mustn't keep it from me: why are you armed like this?'

'The truth is, lady, I must take up his work, even at the risk of dying, for that was my promise to the knight. That's all I can tell you! His mighty charger is to take me on this great mission – I don't know where or in which land – indeed I don't know what I'm looking for! Lady, you must investigate the knight's death. I don't know when I'll be back – but truly, I shan't be happy till I return.'

And with that he set off at once: no amount of pleading would make him stay. Knights,

---

[111] In other redactions, there is no indication at this point that it is thrown by Kay: instead the knight gives a sudden start as he is mysteriously stricken.

servants, squires, queen, maids, ladies, damsels, all were in tears, grieving desperately for their lord's dear nephew, having not the first idea where he'd be going. And so Sir Gawain departed, leaving the dead knight with them. At which point we should all say a *Pater Noster* for the deceased, and before I continue the story you will call for the wine.

The Black Hand

God save me, sirs, there's been a long digression in the story; but now you'll hear what you've long been waiting for.

The night turned foul and black as Sir Gawain galloped on, just as the horse took him. On he rode till he came to a great and handsome chapel at a crossroads. Inside he could see a gleam of light. The sky was pitch dark, and the wind was howling and the rain teeming down so hard that he couldn't have ridden on for all the gold of Bonivant.[112] So he rode inside to shelter and wait for the weather to calm and the wind to slacken. As soon as he entered he headed for the altar. On it stood a candlestick bearing a huge candle; it was burning brightly, and was the only source of light in the place. Sir Gawain had been there only a moment when he looked up and saw a hand reach in through a window to his left; no man on Earth ever set eyes on one so huge and strange and hideous, and it took hold of the candle and snuffed it out. Then a voice boomed, moaning so appallingly that the whole chapel shook, and Gawain's horse reared so violently that he almost threw him. Sir Gawain rode straight out of the chapel and went galloping on his way again through the howling wind and storm.

The awesome wonders he encountered all night long, as he resolutely carried on his journey, no man should tell, for they are part of the mystery of the Grail; and anyone who attempts to tell of them, except as they should be told, is guilty of grievous sin and wrong.

Sir Gawain rode on all night without stopping, in fear and alarm and trepidation, until the new day dawned. And then, when morning came, he looked about him and was amazed to see that he'd crossed the whole land, the whole country. He passed now into a great forest, and through it he journeyed all day long, from morning to nightfall; by the time he emerged the sun had run its full course through the sky. Then he looked ahead and saw the sea. He'd been awake all the previous night and ridden hard all day, and now was so in need of sleep that he could hardly keep himself upright. But his horse was tugging at the reins, so Gawain loosed his hold and let the horse go as he pleased, and he carried him straight down to the sea, just as darkness fell. The only way forward now was by a wide causeway that he found before him, stretching right out to sea; it was bordered on both sides by cypresses and laurels and pear and olive trees, their branches meeting overhead to canopy the causeway, and underfoot it was firm and flat, a track of solid stones and sand; but still it was a daunting prospect, for it was very dark. Sir Gawain crouched low in his saddle and peered along the causeway, and far off in the distance he saw a light like a burning candle. The horse was raring to go, but Gawain was reluctant: he could hear the sea pounding at the trees and the wind tearing at them as if it would rip them apart. He thought he'd wait for daylight before taking to the causeway; but the horse had the bit between his teeth and surged forward

---

[112] This is perhaps the same place as 'Bonivent', which I have suggested may be a version of 'Benevento', above, p. 199. The name also appears earlier, in the reference to 'Galehés de Bonivant': above, p. 110.

with such force that Gawain couldn't stop him, bearing him along the causeway whether he liked it or not. So Gawain abandoned all control, using neither reins nor spurs, and let the horse go just as he pleased. On he galloped, on and on till midnight – but still he didn't reach the light: he'd expected to find it long before. He had to keep pressing on.

The Grail and the Lance Again

And, sirs, he followed the causeway till it brought him to a great hall. He could see a vast crowd inside, and I tell you truly, the moment he dismounted he was greeted with the utmost honour: you never saw such celebration.

'Good sir,' they all said, 'we have long desired your coming!'

They led him before a roaring fire and swiftly disarmed him, and brought him a purple mantle which they draped on his shoulders with much ceremony. But then, having dressed him, they stared at him intently, and began to mutter to one another inaudibly. Sir Gawain, seeing them huddled together in earnest whispers, was seized with alarm and terror. They started to surround him, saying:

'This isn't the one!'

And suddenly, to his dismay, he found himself alone in that long, wide, lofty hall. The great crowd, of unprecedented numbers, was gone.[113] But in the middle of the hall sat a bier of extraordinary size. Sir Gawain gazed at it and raised his hand to cross himself, filled with awe and trepidation. The bier was draped with great reverence in red Grecian samite, embroidered with a cross of golden thread. And on the breast of the body which lay upon it was half a sword: the top half was missing. This broken piece of blade lay on the cloth, shining brighter than any ever seen. At the head and feet of the body were four candles, burning brightly in silver candlesticks bearing censers of finest gold.

For a long while Gawain stood there, all alone, fearful and bewildered: he didn't know what to do – he was at a loss, with no one to speak to.

'God,' he thought, 'where do I go from here?'

And just as he said this, he heard a loud sound of mourning coming from the door to the hall; he looked up, and the first thing he saw enter was a magnificent silver cross, inlaid with jewels and adorned with gold – there was none finer in any treasury. It was carried by a priest, an imposing figure, though the cross was taking all his strength; over his alb he wore a splendid garment made of rich cloth from Constantinople. Behind him came a great procession of canons, all of them dressed in gowns of richest silk. Without further ceremony they began the service for the dead, singing the vigils in ringing tones and censing the bier with the four censers that hung from the candlesticks. Then the hall filled with people, and I promise you, you never heard in all your life such mourning as they made around the bier. Sir Gawain prayed to God to protect him from trouble, as he stood among the crowd, behaving very properly and showing a bold front. As soon as the service came to an end they hung the censers back on the candlesticks. And thereupon all the people I've described – the vast crowd of mourners and the priests who'd sung – vanished. The lamenting was over, but the body remained. It's no wonder Sir Gawain crossed himself! And overcome by the wonders he'd seen – and having been on his feet for so long – he sat down and buried his face in his hands.

---

[113] These and the following sentences are badly garbled in the Long Redaction, and omit a crucial phrase indicating that the crowd disappears.

Then he heard a mighty, growing din, and he looked up again and saw the hall filled once more with the people he'd first seen. A score of servants carried cloths and laid them on the tables; and as soon as this was done, through the door of a chamber came a tall, powerful knight in the prime of life, with just a hint of grey, crowned with gold and holding a royal sceptre in his right hand, on which he wore a ring mounted with a gorgeous ruby. I tell you truly, in all Christendom there was no finer, nobler figure of a man. The cry went up:

'Bring the water for the king!'

He washed in basins of fine gold, and then bade that the water be given to Sir Gawain. Then he took him by the hand and seated him at his side for supper. And then, coming through a door, Sir Gawain saw the wondrous grail, which promptly served the bread, placing it swiftly before all the knights. Then it performed the butler's duty, serving the wine in great goblets of fine gold, setting them on every table for lords and retainers alike. Without more ado it served the next course to each table in great silver bowls. Sir Gawain gaped in astonishment as the grail served them so, with no other servant to be seen – he was utterly amazed: he could hardly bring himself to eat. When everyone had eaten as much as they pleased of the first course, it was instantly removed and replaced by the second. I shan't describe each of the courses, sirs, for that would be tiresome, but it was a long and leisurely meal, and all the while the grail served them with perfect, brisk and wondrous ease. And when they'd finished eating, they all vanished in the blinking of an eye.

Gawain, left there all alone, covered his face with his mantle, deeply troubled and disturbed by the wonder he'd beheld. He didn't know what to do with himself, or what would become of him. But despite his fear he summoned up his strength and courage and uncovered his eyes. Up and down the hall he looked, but he couldn't see a soul: he was alone with the bier – and a lance, standing upright in a silver vase. And this lance was bleeding, the red blood streaming all round the shaft and dripping into the vessel. From there it ran into a golden pipe, and on into another pipe of glittering green emerald that took it from the hall – though Gawain knew nothing of this: he had no idea what became of it. He was utterly amazed. Then the door of a chamber opened, and he saw two boys appear carrying a pair of burning candles, followed by the king holding the sword that Gawain had brought to the hall – the sword, that is, of the knight you heard about earlier, who was killed at the queen's pavilion. The king now called to Sir Gawain, bidding him rise from the table where he was sitting, and led him straight to the bier. There he began grieving bitterly for the one who lay dead. Through his tears and his weeping he said:

'Ah, noble body lying here! On your account this realm is a wasteland! God grant that you be avenged, to restore the people's happiness!'

Then he drew the sword. It was broken across the middle. He proffered it to Sir Gawain and the good knight took it. Sirs, the other half was lying on the dead man's breast; as Sir Gawain stood beside him the king took it in his hands.

'Good sir,' he said, 'if it please God, this sword will be repaired by you. Take it, put the two pieces of the blade together, and we'll see if they will join.'

And Gawain replied: 'Very gladly, sire.'

And he put the two halves together; but however hard he tried, he couldn't make the sword whole again. The king, crestfallen, laid the broken blade back in its place on the body. Then he took Sir Gawain gently by the hand and led him to a chamber, where he found a huge company of knights and ladies and other folk. They sat down before a bed, upon a rich, silken cloth patterned with wheels. Then the king said:

'My good, dear sir, don't be upset by what I'm about to say. The mission that brought you here will not yet be accomplished: you need to be a good deal more worthy. But understand this: if God were to enhance your prowess enough to allow you to return here, you might well achieve it. Sir, you've not repaired the sword, and the truth is that none can accomplish this mission unless he can repair it. I'm well aware that the one who undertook the mission is still in your land: I don't know what has kept him, but we've been waiting for him for a very long while. It was a brave and honourable deed to come here, truly, and if you desire any treasure we possess in this land you shall have it, sir, gladly, however precious it may be. And feel free to ask about anything you've seen: we'll tell you all we know.'

Sir Gawain had been awake and endured a great deal all the previous night: he was longing to sleep; but he longed still more to hear some answers. Forcing himself to stay awake he asked:

'My lord, I was amazed to see a lance that bled; tell me, for the love of God: the blood flowing down it, where does it come from? And I'd dearly like to ask about the sword and the bier out there in the hall: in God's name tell me the truth.'

The king replied: 'No man has ever sought to learn what you have asked, and I shan't refuse to answer. I'll tell you the whole story, dear friend, have no fear. I'll tell you first about the lance, and the terrible anguish and grief involved – and the immense honour. I promise you, sir, it is our healing and our salvation; for truly, it is the very lance with which the son of God Omnipotent was struck in the side on the day when He was stretched out on the cross. Since then it has been here always, and it bleeds unceasingly, as it will until the Day of Judgement, on which day, I assure you, without a word of a lie, all will see the Creator bleed as freely as He did then. The Jews and sinners who treacherously killed Him should be fearful indeed! But do you know what we shall gain? His blood will be our ransom! But it will not ransom sinners.

'But the other blow, sir – the blow struck with that sword which no one has been able to repair – has done us indescribable harm. No worse, no fouler deed has ever been done with any sword: it has been the destruction of many a king and prince and lord and lady and maiden and many a noble damsel. So now you know what disaster brought us here: the kingdom of Logres, the whole land, was destroyed by a single blow struck with that sword. And sir, I shan't lie to you about who it was who lost his life, or who it was who dealt the blow; and no man ever heard such a wondrous tale.

'But first, my friend, let me enlighten you about what you saw as you sat at supper in the flagstoned hall – a hall so long and wide that five hundred knights could comfortably feast together there. I know it troubled your heart. I refer to the grail that served the meal, coming and going all by itself from table to table and serving the knights with whatever they desired, copiously and effortlessly. And it's little wonder it has such power, for that grail is the vessel so loved by Our Lord that He honoured it with His holy blood on the day when He was crucified. Listen now, and I'll tell you the whole story.

'The truth is that Joseph had it made – Joseph of Arimathea, who was devoted to Our Lord throughout his life; and on the day when He died on the cross to redeem His people, the worthy Joseph straightway came with the grail he'd had made to the hill of Calvary where God was nailed to the cross. His heart was filled with anguish, though he didn't dare show it. But at Our Lord's feet, wet with the blood that flowed from them, he gathered every drop he could in that grail of finest gold. What a precious treasure!

And rightly he guarded it well, as you'll hear. He stored it away in a place of safety, known to not a living soul but him.

'Shortly after, he asked Pilate to give him the precious body of Jesus Christ as his wages – he wanted no other kind of payment – and Pilate gladly agreed. So the worthy knight Joseph carefully took the holy body from the cross, and gently wrapped it in a shroud he'd bought and laid it in a tomb. We know this to be true. I could say a great deal more about it, but it's not part of my story: I want to return to the grail, and tell you what happened to Joseph.

'He treasured the vessel, keeping it in a gorgeously carved cabinet with a pair of fine, tall candles before it. He went and lit them every day, and prayed and worshipped before the grail, honouring and revering the true blood of Our Lord, until his behaviour was noticed and remarked on by his people. They reported him to the wicked Jews, who hunted him down and imprisoned him for no other offence but that, locking him in a lofty tower enclosed by mighty walls.

'But he wasn't there for long! He prayed to his Lord to free him from the tower and to keep the grail safe and out of the hands of the Jews, and by His gracious mercy to lend it to him in times of need. The true God looked kindly on that worthy man's prayer: the long and the short of it is that He lifted the tower from the ground, high enough for Joseph to escape without hindrance or trouble – and the same with the walls! But rumour runs faster than the wind, and carried word of what had happened to the Jews; they were less than pleased – in fact they were enraged! Between them they agreed to be done with Joseph and drive him from the land. They let him know at once that he'd be exiled for his crime, he and all those close to him – including the outstandingly worthy Nicodemus and a sister of his. This Nicodemus had carved and painted an image of Our Lord, exactly as he'd seen him on the cross; and I'm convinced by those who say that Our Lord had a hand in its making, for none like it has ever been seen or ever been able to be made. Those of you who've been to Lucca know the image: you've seen and gazed upon it.[114] When he knew that he had to leave and flee the land, Nicodemus took the image, unbeknown to anyone, and smuggled it away at once, stowing it on board a ship and commending it to the Lord God in whose likeness it was made.

'Then he returned to Joseph, to whom God had appeared and told him to have no fear but to go in confidence, for he would find a land where he and all his company would be able to live in safety: he should go without misgivings. So Joseph and his followers fitted out their ship and boarded without delay, and kept sailing till they found the land that God had promised him. It was known as the White Isle – that's what it was called; it's a part of England, surrounded and hemmed in by the sea. There they landed and settled, finding good homes for themselves, and they had everything they needed and desired. No one made war on them or tried to deprive them of a foot of land.

'But in the third year, I believe, the people of the land massed together and attacked them repeatedly, inflicting dreadful harm; they fought back, with gains and losses shared. But at last Joseph was close to defeat, with food supplies exhausted; and he prayed to God the Creator in His mercy to lend him the grail of which I told you, the vessel in which he'd gathered the holy blood. Then he bade that the horn be sounded to summon

---

[114] The 'Volto Santo', a wooden image of the crucified Christ, arrived in Lucca in the eighth century and is still housed in the cathedral there. Frescoes in the nearby Basilica of San Frediano depict the legend according to which Nicodemus carved the image but fell asleep before he'd done the face, and awoke to find the Holy Face – the 'Volto Santo' – completed by an angel.

the water, and he and all his company went to dine; they sat at their tables in fine array, and the grail went among them all, serving bread and wine and other dishes in great plenty, whatever each of them desired. And so it was that Joseph held the land against his foes for as long as he had health and life.

'And at the end of his days he prayed earnestly to God to grant that his descendants be distinguished and ennobled by the grail. And God granted his prayer indeed; for the truth is that after Joseph's death possession of the grail passed to no man, however high his lineage, unless he was of Joseph's line. The Fisher King for certain was descended from Joseph, as were all his heirs; Greloguevaus[115] was one of his line, and so too was Perceval.

'Now you have some understanding of why it's to be so revered, the grail that serves all by itself. I've told you all I can at this time. The rest is secret: I can't and daren't reveal it to you, for you've not fulfilled the mission or repaired the broken sword – half of it still lies on the body of one who was most wickedly killed. The other half was being carried by the knight in whose place you've come here as his messenger: we don't know what's become of him. He clearly recognised you to be the foremost of your company, when he chose you to arm and mount his horse to carry out this mission, which is likely to be achieved by neither you nor any man in the world, but by God alone.

'Let me tell you now about the knight who dealt the other such a blow with that sword that he broke it in half. It was a grievous shame and sin, for by that blow the whole land and realm of Logres, which had been held in such high regard, was laid waste. Ah, what grief it caused! It's a piteous tale to hear; it'll make you – and me and anyone else who tells it – weep.'

And he started to weep indeed, and to tell the story through his tears. But, sirs, as he began to reveal the whole true story, he realised Sir Gawain was asleep. He didn't want to wake him: he let him rest, and didn't say another word.

Sir Gawain slept till morning, when he found himself in a marsh beside the sea, and all his equipment with him. He was alarmed and baffled: he couldn't see any house or wall, castle or tower.

'I'm in a fine mess here!' he said.

He armed and mounted. He realised he'd disgraced himself by falling asleep, and was desperately upset that he'd failed to ask who was to restore life to the land.[116]

'Ah, God!' he cried. 'The worthy, wise, courteous king was graciously explaining the marvels, revealing the mystery, and I fell asleep! Oh, how I wish I hadn't!'

And he vowed he'd suffer any hardship, and so devote himself to deeds of arms that, if God let him return to that king's court, he might repair the sword and accomplish the mission; then he would ask outright all about the grail and the bier, down to the last detail. Nothing would make him return to Britain till he was sure he'd enhanced his worth as a knight.

So he set off across the country; and no eyes ever beheld a land so richly endowed with rivers, woods and meadows. This was the waste kingdom, which the night before had been bare and void; but God had restored the waters to their rightful courses in the

---

[115] No two manuscripts give remotely the same reading of this name. It may be related to one of the twelve brothers cited in Perceval's lineage in *Perlesvaus*, a list which includes Gais le Gros, Gosgallian and Galerian. See *The High Book of the Grail (Perlesvaus)*, trans. N. Bryant, Cambridge, revised edition 2007, p. 2.

[116] Literally 'who was to people the land'.

land, and all the woods had turned green once more, the moment Gawain had asked why the lance bled. But I can tell you with all certainty: no more people had returned to the land, because he hadn't yet asked everything. Everyone he met riding through the country blessed him and called out:

'You've healed us, sir – and killed us! You should be happy and joyful – but also distressed! Happy for the blessings you've restored to us – we know it's thanks to you – but you should hate yourself for failing to hear about the grail and its purpose. No one can express the great joy that would have come from that, and you should grieve and rue it deeply.'

Sir Gawain roamed the land far and wide, performing many a deed of arms, and it was a long time, I assure you, before he would go back to Britain. The battles he won and the marvels he encountered I can't tell you now. I'm going to pass over them and return to the main story, and you're not going to hear about the knight who was killed at the pavilion, where he was from, or from which land; nor will you hear me speak about the king's arrival,[117] or about Sir Bran de Lis, so worried about the king's great-nephew, for I know for certain that they never found the boy. I need to attend to the main thrust of the story, so you won't hear me talk about who it was who'd taken the boy and raised and tutored him, and taught him above all to care for his arms and his fine charger, or about the noble damsel who took him into her household. But I shall tell you now about some of the funny, childlike things he said, which gave the damsel much amusement.[118]

The Challenge at the Ford

One day he and the damsel were out riding together, just the two of them, when they saw, crossing the heath not far away, a well-armed knight mounted on a destrier. The damsel called to the boy, bidding him:

'Go after that knight, dear boy, and find out his name – whether he wants to tell you or not – and where he's come from and where he's going. Do that and you'll have done well.'

'What if he refuses?'

'Strike him boldly!'

'How?' said the boy. 'Tell me.'

'Like this,' she said. 'Lower your lance, and with your other hand grip your shield tight.'

So he took his shield by the straps in the tightest grip, saying: 'I shan't let go for anything – I can't lose it if I hold it like this! These straps are a really good idea!'

The damsel laughed and said: 'You've got the hang of it, boy!'

He gripped it for all he was worth – he'd always slung it across his back: he'd never thought he might one day use it. Then he thrust in his spurs and galloped straight across the heath to the knight and fiercely demanded his name. But according to my source the knight refused to tell him. So the boy charged at him and killed him without a word being said. But I have to tell you, the knight thrust his lance through the boy's shield: fully two yards of the shaft smashed through and broke. The boy returned and drew rein over the fallen knight and promptly said:

---

[117] i.e. his arrival at the queen's pavilion at the crossroads as arranged above, p. 210.
[118] I have constructed this sentence, which makes good sense in the context of what follows, from phrases in both the Long Redaction and two different MSS of the Short, as no version on its own is satisfactory.

'You'll tell me your name right now, whether you like it or not!'

But the knight didn't make a sound. The boy was furious, and jumped down and said angrily: 'You *will* tell me! You have no choice!'

He'd never seen a corpse before. The knight didn't breathe a word, and little wonder – his soul had departed.

'Come to my lady, good sir, and tell her your name. She'll be most grateful.'

He was amazed when the knight made no reply, despite all his demands.

'God!' he said. 'Has he fallen asleep?' He propped him up against his chest and gently said: 'Wake up, good sir! Are you so worn out that you need to sleep?'

Then he dropped him again – he was heavy in his armour. The damsel was puzzled that he'd been gone so long; he stood up and saw her sitting there across the heath, not moving. So he climbed on to his horse again and said:

'Sleep, then. I'm cross that you haven't told me your name, I really am!'

He rode quickly back to his lady, and she said: 'Let's go.'

'So help me God,' he said, 'I didn't find out the knight's name.'

'Never mind, dear friend. Just pull that lance-stump from your shield.'

He pulled with all his strength and drew it out. He saw at once there was a hole left in his shield, and was so upset that he started howling. The damsel stared at him, amazed, and said:

'Are you wounded, boy? Don't hide it!'

'No, lady, I'm dying – dying of agony! The one who gave me this shield commanded me above all things to look after my arms and my horse – and that knight's gone and damaged it: he's put a hole right through it! By all the saints, I've broken his command, and he told me I'd be a useless wretch if I didn't care for the knightly calling!'

The boy was more distraught than I can say. But the damsel told him: 'My dear young man, don't worry about it being holed! I'll give you a much better and more handsome one!'

'I don't know about that,' he said. 'But I will when you give it.'

She laughed, sirs, at his childish words.

They carried on riding all day long, and as night began to fall they saw a knight go spurring by on a white-stockinged Gascon destrier. The damsel said to the boy:

'Go after him and bring him here. Use your shield as boldly as you like: I'll be giving you a new and much better one!'

'But lady,' he said, 'by the time you get it, this one'll be a disgrace!'

And with that he set off, letting his shield hang by his side, giving no protection to his body. He rode up and met the knight, but he refused to answer his request to ride back to his lady; instead he charged at him. And the boy struck him a mighty blow, through his shield and through his body, and sent him crashing to the ground, stone dead, without uttering a word. But before he'd ridden past him he toppled from his saddle,[119] for the knight had struck him full on his unprotected hauberk. The damsel, who loved the boy dearly, came spurring forward, and picked him up and lifted him on to her own horse as quickly as she could and told him to have no fear: she would see him safely healed.

'If you love me, dear boy,' she said, 'make sure you never joust with a passing knight without using your shield! You wouldn't have been hurt if you'd held it in front of you!'

---

[119] I have borrowed this from the Short Redaction which says 'he fell unconscious to the ground'; the Long says simply that 'he looked at himself [and realised] he'd been hit', which does not fit well with what follows.

He replied in anguished tones: 'By all the saints, lady, my shield would've been pierced and broken! If he'd hit it, it would've had another hole! He could have damaged it so badly it wouldn't have been worth a sou! In faith, lady, I'll get mended, I'll recover – but my shield wouldn't have got over that blow! It would've been crazy!'

The damsel vowed and promised that she'd give him a better and more handsome shield than that. And God! I can't tell you how much suffering and trouble that shield had cost! A magnificent shield it was, inlaid with gold and ivory, part of the treasure acquired by King Brandeval on the day of his wedding – and you never saw a more fearsome knight. It was destined, truly, to be won by whoever could wound him in the arm. And now this fine shield had been won by Sir Gawain's son: he'd defeated the king, and broken his arm, truly, when he jousted with him that day. But he was more worried about the shield than about the king, which made many noble men smile, I promise you.

I could tell you other stories, but not now: how he emptied a hall and his sweetheart gave him lodging; how he brought the floor crashing down when he was about to be cut to pieces; how he cut down a party who'd climbed on to the bridge; how – very young though he still was – he bounded up the staircase when he was disarmed, to the astonishment of all who saw him, including the king, and burst into the chamber like a wild man. He was a fine and handsome youth indeed, and his name was Lionel.[120]

But I'm only touching on this in passing: I want to move on to the last part of the story. The damsel took the boy away and they rode together to a pavilion beside a ford, its sides patterned with bands of gold. Here they drew rein and dismounted, and found servants and pages who gave them a joyful welcome. They stayed there for a long while, for the boy was set to guard the ford. I haven't time to tell you who appointed him and how, but I can assure you he fought many a fierce and testing battle there at the ford, and slew many a knight.

One day he sat on his destrier before the river, armed and ready, right up till noon; but he didn't see any knight appear, much to his surprise. But then he looked towards a forest and saw one coming, fully armed. Straight down to the meadow the knight rode on his charger; he was riding at a brisk pace, but his head was bowed and he was troubled, for he hadn't been to his own land for a long while. I shan't beat about the bush: the boy wouldn't let him pass and they had to joust. And truly, those valiant knights unhorsed each other in no uncertain manner, and then did battle with the sword, fierce and dreadful and mighty: such awesome, deadly blows were never seen or heard of. And to come straight to the point, I'll tell you their names – it's only right and proper: I know for certain that they were Sir Gawain and his son. Father and son fought face to face till they'd no helmets left: they'd battered them to pieces with their swords; and when Sir Gawain saw how young his adversary was he was amazed.

'Be at peace now, friend!' he said. 'And kindly tell me your name; don't keep it from me. You seem so young, but you couldn't be a more valiant warrior! So I'd like to know your name.'

[120] '*Lioniaus*'. This is the name given in the Short and Mixed Redactions. I have made the best sense I can of the passage represented by this paragraph, taking elements from all redactions. It gave all the scribes a good deal of difficulty; they don't appear to have recognised the references (the variants of each phrase are numerous), to the point where, in all MSS of the Long Redaction, the boy's name appears as '*li oisiaux*', which one would take to mean 'the Bird'. The incidents described are, however, reminiscent of the wild youth Lionel, nicknamed 'Unbridled Heart', in the Prose *Lancelot*, though he is not the son of Gawain.

'By the faith I owe God, good sir,' the boy replied, 'you can call me what you like! I've no idea what my name is – all I know, truly, is that where I was raised, in the rich hall at Lis, everyone in the castle referred to me as "his great-uncle's great-nephew"! That's what they were all told to say! My mother often said she didn't dare mention my father's name at the castle because of the wrongs he'd done her kinsmen.'

Sir Gawain didn't need to hear another word: he knew at once that he was his son. He rejoiced to see the courage in the boy; but he called upon him now to surrender as his prisoner. But he replied that he'd be dead before he yielded, and vowed and declared that he wouldn't make peace unless Gawain submitted as the captive of the damsel at the pavilion. And Sir Gawain did just that, for he loved the boy like his own heart and couldn't bear the thought that he might be hurt or wounded. He preferred to surrender, and vowed to do his will, saying:

'My very dear sir, let's go to your lady at the pavilion: I shall willingly yield as her captive.'

'Then we'll be friends,' said the boy, 'if my lady approves.'

So they set off, and rode straight to the damsel's tent, and Sir Gawain placed himself at her mercy, with clasped hands. She looked long at him, pondering, and said:

'I have to say, good sir, you don't seem to have been unduly troubled by this battle!'

'No indeed, lady, by the saints, but I surrender as your prisoner.'

'And I accept you so, sir; but tell me your name, for I'd dearly love to know it.'

'I shall tell you truly, lady. I shall hide it no longer: I am Gawain; King Arthur is my uncle.'

'Gawain!' said the boy; and he flung his arms about him and said: 'By the faith I owe my mother, that's what she used to call my father! I know that's right: his name was Gawain!'

And the damsel said: 'Good sir, there's no ruler in the world, however mighty, who wouldn't greet you with all honour!' She had them both disarmed so that she could see them openly; and as soon as she saw them without their armour she said: 'Truly, never in my life have I seen two figures so alike!'

'So help me God, lady,' said Gawain, 'it's exactly as he said, I'm sure of it.'

And he told the boy the whole story: how he'd sired him, and all about his mother, and how he'd killed her kinsman. The joy in the pavilion that night is beyond description – and I don't want to blather on pointlessly – but now you've heard how Gawain had chanced to find his beloved son, with the fair damsel at the pavilion.

As soon as he saw day break next morning he bade them prepare, and he led them back with him to Britain, heading straight for where he knew the court would be. King Arthur had been in residence for a month at Carlion,[121] alone with just his privy household, for he was grieving deeply for his nephew, not knowing if he was alive or dead. His mind had been beset by worry ever since he'd failed to find him on his return to the queen's pavilion – Gawain had been wandering through so many lands and realms before coming back to Britain that it would be exhausting to list them all. Every day they mourned him at court, convinced he'd been killed or taken captive. So you can imagine the joy that greeted his arrival at Carlion: he was nearly crushed by the crowd that flocked to meet him! They knew nothing about the damsel or his son, not realising he'd been found.

---

[121] '*Glomagain*' (Glamorgan); I have emended for the sake of consistency, as most later references say the events are taking place at Carlion.

The king was seated at dinner when he heard the news that Gawain was coming.

'Now I know God loves me!' he said, and leapt to his feet. Cups and goblets were left on the tables as everyone abandoned dinner, not waiting for each other, and through the house ran ladies and damsels and the queen and her maids, some with their hair undone, some without their gowns, as they rushed to greet Sir Gawain. He couldn't speak to them all or kiss each one, however hard he tried, as the ladies smothered him, weeping piteously! All who saw him were overcome. They led him up to the great hall and disarmed him at once, so overjoyed to see him that they could think of nothing else. But suddenly a man, unknown to anyone there, came into the hall and took Gawain's arms and horse and disappeared again. Gawain saw him go and was distraught: now he had nothing that had belonged to the knight[122] – neither his horse nor his sword, in fact nothing at all; for there was no sign of the man: no one knew what had become of him or which way he'd gone.

I wish I had time to pause and describe the joy at court, which doubled and redoubled when King Arthur asked Gawain where he'd been and who the supremely handsome boy was: when Gawain told him that he'd found his son and they realised who he was, everyone, I can tell you, joyfully welcomed and fêted him in honour of the worthy knight who'd fathered him. And one thing's for sure: the one then deemed the paragon of courtesy and fine chivalry was Sir Yvain, which is why the king entrusted his great-nephew to him, relieving him of other duties and earnestly entreating him to devote himself to instructing the boy in all knightly virtues; and Yvain did as bidden.

Then Sir Gawain told them thrillingly of the wonders he'd encountered. They marvelled indeed when he told them of the lance, and of the grail which served at table by itself, unaided; and he told them about the sword and the bier – and how falling asleep had cost him the chance of hearing all the mysteries explained.

At the end of his story he asked where Guerrehés his brother was, and enquired after the worthy Idier the son of Nu, and the king replied:

'They were so worried about you that they've gone to scour the whole wide world, as have many other good knights, and they've not been heard of since. God!' he cried. 'Bring them back to us!'

By now Sir Gawain was very weary, and little wonder. Night had fallen, and he went to his lodging and to bed.

And here this part of the story ends and another branch begins, which you'll hear me relate at once, and word for word. You all think you know exactly how the story goes, but by God you don't! It must be told with the utmost care and in the proper order, and you won't hear me tell it otherwise than in the right order, each part at the proper time, as presented in my true source.

The Swan-Boat

That night there was thunder and lightning and pouring rain; it was intensely hot, the sky plunged into darkness. The king couldn't sleep; he called two of his chamberlains to his bed and asked for a cloak of silk and fur. Dressed in just that and his breeches and stockings, tied round his legs to keep them secure, and a pair of fur-

---

[122] i.e. the knight killed at the queen's pavilion, whose arms and horse Gawain took to continue his mission, above, p. 213.

lined shoes, he made his way, lit by candles carried before him, to a little house beside the sea so that he could watch the storm. A path from a postern led down to the waves, beating at its walls. The king leaned at the windows and watched as the storm abated and the night grew calm and clear.

He hadn't been there long when he noticed a light like a star shining out at sea, and was startled to realise it was coming nearer. He pointed it out to his chamberlains, and asked them:

'Can you see something out at sea?'

'Yes, sire, there's no denying.'

'Where?'

'Right there. Dear Lord God, what can it be?'

While they were talking the light drew ever closer, until they were convinced it was miraculous. Then they saw it was a boat, the finest and most handsome there ever was, quite brand new and swathed and canopied in richest silk, but the only living thing they could see was the swan that swam before it; it was pulling the boat by a beautiful silver chain, attached to the prow and fastened to its neck by a golden collar. The swan swam on till it came below the house where the king stood watching. There it stopped, and started to cry and beat the water with its wings. The king gazed in wonder. Then he bade them open the postern: he wanted to go down to the boat. It was quickly unlocked, and he slipped out on his own and hurried down the steps and straight to the boat, now beached upon the sand. He saw how beautifully it was draped. To find out if there was anyone aboard he stepped on deck; and he saw that at each end of the boat was a burning candle, bigger than he'd ever seen. He ducked under the canopy, and this is what he found: spread out in the middle of the boat was the richest cloth there ever was, striped with fine gold, and stretched upon it lay a tall, stout knight, his body speared through the top of the chest. An ermine-lined blanket covered the body, up to the protruding stump of lance. The king was deeply saddened by the sight, for he'd never seen such a handsome knight lie dead. He stepped forward at once and lifted the blanket and looked at the knight; he was clad in a tunic of samite and silk of different coloured halves, divided down the middle.

'Ah, God!' he said. 'I've never seen such a handsome man of woman born, or one so finely clad: his tunic suits him splendidly.'

It was a perfect fit; and he also wore mail chausses, with golden spurs on his feet.

'And his belt is quite magnificent,' said the king.

And I tell you, I've never seen a pouch as exquisitely fine as the one that was attached. The king reached out and opened it. Inside he found a letter; he unfolded it at once and read it from top to bottom. And this is what he found: the letter sent greetings to the king and then, by God, entreated him most earnestly, saying:

"King, before he died the knight lying here requested that you leave his body in your hall, and keep it there till the lance which dealt his fatal wound is removed." It continued: "May the one who draws it out suffer the same foul, deep shame that Guerrehés did in the garden, unless he deals his killer the very blow that he dealt him, and with the selfsame lance-head in the selfsame place. Lay him, O king, in a fine tomb; his body is so well embalmed that it will not yield the slightest odour for a year or more. If the lance-head has not been removed by the time the year is out, then have him buried at the year's end without delay: you will hear no more of the matter and will incur no blame. But if he is avenged, his identity will be revealed to your court, and from which land and country he came, and how he was slain."

The king refolded the letter and replaced it in the pouch. Then he grasped the rich Grecian cloth at the dead knight's head, and his chamberlains took hold of the cloth at his feet, and they gently carried him out of the boat and up the steps and into the hall. The king bade them lay him on the top table, exactly as they'd found him when they boarded the boat. They propped his head upon a pillow, and covered him with his blanket, just as they'd found him. Then he gave an order to the chamberlains, warning them:

'Don't let anyone know what you've seen.'

Then he went back down to the house by the shore and leaned at the windows, and heard the swan crying and wailing and beating its wings on the sea. Then it abruptly turned the boat about, pulling it by the silver chain that ran from the prow to the collar at its neck, and sped away, snuffing out the candles that had shone so brightly: suddenly all was dark. The swan was wailing so piteously for its master that the king was quite amazed.

He returned then to his bed; but he lay awake all night, I tell you, till he finally fell asleep.

When the bells for divine service rang in all the city's churches, Sir Gawain was the first to rise and dress and prepare. Then he bade his companions do likewise, for he wanted to hear matins in the castle chapel. With a splendid escort of barons and knights on palfreys and destriers he rode up and dismounted before the door of the hall. He was the first to step inside; and how surprised he was, as were all his company, by the strange sight that awaited them. At first they thought the knight was sleeping.

'God!' said Sir Gawain. 'Who's this lying on the table?'

They all went up to look at him, and realised it was a slain knight; but no one recognised him by face or appearance, or could guess where he was from. They mourned deeply for that fine figure of a man.

Word spread throughout the city, and people came flocking to the great hall to see the mysterious knight. Sir Gawain left the body just as he found it, and said it wasn't to be moved until the king had risen. He went straight to the king's chamber and told him of the strange discovery in the hall. King Arthur, who'd been the first to find it, pretended to know nothing; he rose and donned suitably regal garb and returned with Gawain to the hall, and when he arrived at the table he looked at the knight and his blanket and his pillow, and the cloth he lay on and the wounds he bore, and drew back the blanket and said:

'God! I've never seen such a handsome figure of a man: look at his arms and his hands, his long, full fingers, his fine, straight legs and shapely feet. And I'll swear he's been in love with a noble maid indeed: see the splendid jewels he wears! And look at his belt, so rich and fine!'

And he pointed to the pouch, knowing full well what the letter within contained. He took it out and looked at it, and everyone asked him:

'What does it say, sire?'

The king was only too keen to answer, saying: 'I shan't keep it from you, sirs; it's only right that I tell you. This slain knight, the letter says, had utter faith that the Round Table would avenge his death: he trusted in them more than any others in the world. He has a lance-stump in his body and wants it to be removed, most certainly, though if it's not drawn out within this year then he may be buried at the year's end: that's what the letter begs most earnestly, and says that if it's done, we'll know all about him and where he's from. I'm sure he's of high lineage, by God – it seems so from the way he's dressed. The letter adds, strangely, that he wishes the man who draws the lance-head from his body to suffer the same disgrace as did Guerrehés in the garden, if he doesn't deal his killer the same blow, in the same place, with the same lance-head, as he dealt him.'

Tors the son of Arés replied: 'By the glorious saints, this dead knight doesn't know what he's asking! We've no idea which land or country under heaven we're supposed to go to seek revenge! Honestly! If the letter doesn't tell us, who's going to know the knight who slew him?'

'I don't know,' said Sir Gawain. 'And I don't understand: the letter bids us strike the one who struck him in the same place on the body, and with this lance-head when it's been drawn out. No man of woman born can do that. It would be a bold deed to try.'

So the matter stayed. A handsome tomb was found, of grey marble, and the body was laid inside in rich array. The king vowed he'd do exactly as the letter asked; but he didn't understand the reference to the shame that had befallen the good knight in the garden.

Guerrehés and the Little Knight

Sir Guerrehés had been searching for his brother Gawain, as he should. One day he was roaming along – it was past noon, and he hadn't met a soul for three days or more – when he came to the loveliest stretch of meadowland he'd ever seen. A river ran through it, and on its banks stood a castle enclosed by high walls of red and white, built of fine marble and lias. All around it were handsome figures of beasts, carved from regal ivory and bone, and the walls bristled with mighty towers; but I shall say no more about the castle: I haven't time to describe it further. Guerrehés pressed on towards it with all speed, for he was famished. Through the streets he rode, and never in his life had he found such wondrous riches and beautiful sights – but he couldn't see a living soul. On to the citadel he went, still seeing no one, and right into the hall where he dismounted. He made his way to a chamber, where he found four splendid beds of gold and ivory covered in the richest blankets. He'd led his horse in by the reins, and tethered him now to a bedpost; then he sat down on one of the other beds and laid his shield beside him and took off his helm, for it was very hot. He saw what a handsome, spacious room it was, with painted panels on every side, and it was lovely and cool, having been thickly strewn with fresh grasses just that day. Sir Guerrehés said:

'Well, it would be ungracious of me to leave you, sweet lodging, even though I can't see anything here for me or my horse to eat!'

Just then he glanced to his right and noticed a door. He got up and, keeping hold of his helm for comfort's sake balanced between his hands, he went to the door and opened it. He found himself entering a magnificent hall, more noble, grand and beautiful than the one he'd been in just before; but all he found within it were two beds covered in fresh blankets, the finest he'd ever seen.

'In faith,' he said, 'I'm going to see what else is here, so help me God.'

On through a third door he went, and passed into a chamber panelled in gold: none so beautiful was ever seen or described in words; in proportions it was perfect, unsurpassed. In this room there was only one bed, most elegant and fair, covered in a Moorish quilt of green silk adorned with so many bands of gold that the room was lit by its light alone. He noticed a window, and opened it and looked out; and there he saw a garden, and a fairer one I couldn't hope to describe. Guerrehés leaned at the window and looked up and down the garden and saw two pavilions pitched there; made all of silk they were, topped with the most splendid pommels ever seen. Inside one of these pavilions he could see a dwarf: he was the ugliest he'd ever come across, but very richly dressed, and he was carrying a silver goblet covered with a cloth, which he took through an open door into the other pavilion. Seeing this, Guerrehés guessed there must be people inside; so he climbed through the window – it was good and wide, and he could see no other way out – and into the garden. He was fully armed, with his sword at his waist, though his helm was in his hands. He went straight to the pavilion and stepped inside; and the first thing he saw, seated in a great silver chair, was the most beautiful damsel ever seen by man. Before the chair was a bed, on which was spread a rich cloth patterned with wheels, and the whitest, finest sheet imaginable, and a blanket of Alexandrian purple lined with ermine. And lying on the bed was a knight, tall and powerfully built, but wounded. He seemed to be in grievous trouble: he was bandaged in the same rich cloth, and a page was holding him in his arms, supporting his back, while the dwarf held the silver goblet before him. The goblet was filled with milk of almonds, into which the damsel had crumbled bread; and she was gently feeding him from a spoon from which the knight was eating as well as he could. Guerrehés stepped forward and hailed him, saying:

'God bless you, sir knight, and this page, too, and your dear friend.'

The knight looked up at Guerrehés and flew into a rage, dashing the goblet from the dwarf's hand, sending the milk flying, and cried: 'God! Someone get rid of this knight!'

And he flung himself round with such force that he split his wounds open, bleeding so profusely that the sheets were covered in blood. Sir Guerrehés said:

'So help me God, good sir, I'm sorry I came in if it's upset you so! I can't think why, but I'm ready to make amends!'

'God have mercy on me!' cried the knight. 'I'm dead if you don't get him out of here!'

'Don't worry, sir!' the page boy said. 'You'll soon be avenged – the little knight'll come and sort him out!'

As for the damsel, sirs, she was keeping quiet, not uttering a word.

Then in came the little knight, on a horse unbelievably small. There was nothing ill-formed about him – he wasn't like most dwarfs: his feet and legs and arms and hands and head and eyes and mouth and face were fine and shapely; he was a good-looking fellow for his size. But only half a foot of him showed above his saddle-bow, no more. He had a little shield of burnished gold, and a little lance likewise with a tiny pennon, and a very fine tunic. He burst into the pavilion as if in a rage, the very image of fury, crying:

'Where's that proven villain?'

And the moment his eye fell on Guerrehés he came forward and struck him on the head.

'You're lucky I didn't knock it off!' he cried. 'Go and arm at once!'

'Don't let him leave the garden till you've humbled him!' said the wounded knight. 'Pride drove him to trespass here!'

Hearing this, Guerrehés left the tent at once, and saw his shield outside in the garden along with his horse, brought to him by a page. He quickly donned his helm and mounted his horse, and took his shield and lance that the page held out to him, and said:

'I'll go now, sir, if you'll show me the way.'

'You're not leaving here,' the little knight replied, 'till you've been utterly humbled, you pitiful wretch of a knight! You're going to joust with me. And I shan't deign to arm, whatever anyone says. God! Why should my lord be upset by a rogue like you?'

Guerrehés said, very gently: 'I'd like to go, kind sir; you're a daunting figure, you know!'

But the dwarfish knight charged at him with all the speed he could summon, and when Guerrehés saw him coming he charged likewise; but I tell you, he let his horse go full tilt but missed his target; instead he struck the front of the little knight's saddle, with such force that his lance was smashed to pieces. He was amazed that he couldn't fell him or his tiny horse. And how did the dwarf fare with *his* blow? He sent Guerrehés crashing to the ground. Then he leapt from his saddle and – the strangest thing – trod on Guerrehés's head, nearly crushing it. Then he stepped back and asked:

'Will you yield as a captive?'

Guerrehés couldn't answer one way or the other – he was lying unconscious. The dwarf pressed down with his foot again, this time on his neck, and when Guerrehés felt this he held out his hand immediately and said:

'You have my word, sir – I'm at your mercy,[123] though I don't know why!'

Then the dwarf said: 'You must understand the custom established in this garden, which will be your shame and downfall! All the knights I vanquish here are condemned to the basest occupation in the world: they work as weavers, and no man of woman born will ever free them from it! They weave all manner of cloth and sheets of gold-embroidered silk, from which they make all kinds of rich pavilions: it brings in bags of money for my lord! I promise you, I've vanquished a hundred knights who now work as weavers. That was the fate they chose – because listen, vassal: no one does it unless they choose. What you'll do is leave here now and think it over for a year, and then come back to this garden promptly at the year's end – that you must swear. When you return here to me, you'll choose whichever of three options you prefer: if you wish to be a weaver, we'll gladly arrange it! If that doesn't appeal there's a second course: you'll do battle with me, and if you get through it, and I don't have you begging for the weaving job before we're done, then you'll be free to go and that'll be the end of the matter. If you don't fancy either option, you'll have to take the third, which isn't great: it's instant beheading! There, vassal: now you've heard the three choices. Will you give your solemn word?'

'Yes indeed, sir: I swear,' said Guerrehés, who couldn't wait to get away.

Then the dwarfish knight said: 'It was very wrong of you to come into this garden. You'll have to climb back through the window since you couldn't be bothered to look for a door. You'll find your horse in the hall in a moment – the page will bring him to you – and you can go then where you please.'

As soon as Guerrehés heard this he was off: he went straight to the window and clambered through. And there before him in the chamber, to his astonishment, he saw fully four score or a hundred girls making laces and ribbons and pouches and other fancies. And they all said:

'God! Where was he born, that proven villain of a knight?'

Sir Guerrehés heard this and hurried through the room – and what a terrible reception he got from them all as they hissed and hurled abuse at him. Overcome with embarrassment

---

[123] Literally 'you've killed me'.

he pressed on into the next chamber – and found it full of pages and damsels, many of them great beauties, all busily at work: the boys had gone there to keep them entertained. And the moment they saw Guerrehés they all cried out together:

'Feeble, craven rogue! The dwarfish knight has thrashed and humbled you! Shame on you, strapping figure that you are!'

He hurried on through the door, more vexed and embarrassed than he'd ever been in his life, and into the third chamber. He thought he'd escaped them now, but instead he found ladies and knights in every corner, some playing chess and others dice;[124] and they all said:

'There's the coward that the little knight trounced! Shame upon his vigour and his strength! He should be dying of anguish, letting himself be humbled by a poor, pathetic specimen like that, when he's so tall and handsome. Be off with you, you utter wretch, and may you never be seen and recognised after what's befallen you!'

Guerrehés didn't say a word; he scurried on through in abject shame till he reached the hall – and found it packed with all manner of people, crowding there together: boys and knights, townsmen, servants, squires. And the moment they saw him they started yelling:

'Behold the coward! Behold the basest villain who ever lived! He should be flogged and hanged – not having the heart to defend himself against the puniest creature in the world!'

The good Guerrehés nearly collapsed in anguish, but he pressed on through without saying a word and found his destrier in the courtyard and mounted without a moment's delay. He took up his shield and rode away, overwhelmed with shame. Out of the citadel he rode, and didn't see a soul. He thought he was free of them at last; but as he rode down through the town he found the streets filled now with burghers and common folk who all started mocking him, crying:

'Let's all jeer the craven wretch – he should've been hanged! But he's a fair old weight to carry now – he'll be burdened with indescribable shame!'

He rode on past the market stalls where they were selling meat and fish and wild birds and venison; and as the tradesmen saw him pass they all began to shout:

'There's the wretch defeated by the little dwarf! The whole world knows about it now! Come on – let him have it!'

And they started pelting him with fish-guts and pig's lights and offal: no man since the world's creation suffered such foul abuse as the people of the castle poured on Guerrehés, yelling and bombarding him. They were all saying that the whole world knew of his humbling by the dwarf; that's what vexed him more than anything.

Fully armed, he rode down through the town and out of it as soon as he could. In deep distress he galloped on to put as much distance as he could between himself and the castle. And then, with evening drawing in, he said:

'God, where can I go? In the castle I heard them shouting that the whole world knows what's befallen me! By all the saints, if that's true I'd rather be burnt and my ashes cast to the wind!'

What more need I say? He didn't dare face anyone: if he saw someone coming down the road he'd take off across the fields. He didn't look for lodging that night and didn't eat or drink a thing: he just kept riding, trying to put that land behind him.

Early next day he was riding along, his head bowed in troubled thought, when he ran into a party of sergeants and squires and pages leading a train of packhorses. But

---

[124] *'tables'*: see note 51, above, p. 133.

they greeted him warmly; they made no reference to his shame. He was mightily cheered and said to himself:

'God! What should I make of this? Lord, how happy I'd be if no one knew of my disgrace! If these lads had known of it they'd have heaped reproach on me; I don't think anyone beyond these parts has heard a thing.'

And he carried on till he was almost back in Britain. I haven't time to tell of all the places he took lodging, but he pressed on until, at the castle where he stayed one night, he heard certain news that Sir Gawain had returned to court safe and sound. He headed on and found the king at Tintagel, and was given the warmest welcome by the court and noble household: King Arthur and Sir Gawain greeted him with joy.

Guerrehés Takes Revenge

They told him at length about the body of the knight and the letter in his pouch – and all about its contents. He was very unsettled, and when they started asking if he'd ever been in a garden and suffered some deep disgrace he said:

'Not me! Who told you that?'

'The letter the knight has on him.'

'It's all lies!'

So matters rested for a long while, during which the king usually held court at Carlion with a host of princes and barons; and there in the hall, right in the middle, sat the tomb in which the body lay, its face uncovered. It was positioned in such a way that no one could enter the hall without seeing it quite clearly, and there and then, if he was brave enough, he could pull out the stump of lance. But no one wanted to try – and I can't say I blame them. But Sir Guerrehés was still fretting terribly about the dishonour that he'd suffered.

Then early one morning he and the other knights rose and went to wake the king and help him dress and prepare, for they were due to go hunting. As soon as he awoke he dressed and made ready; and as they made their way back through the hall the companions stopped beside the tomb and looked at the knight who lay inside. They all said that Guerrehés must really hate that body with its letter referring to his disgrace – had it not been for that, they'd never have heard of it. Guerrehés said to the body:

'Well, vassal, it looks like this stump's stuck in you for good! I don't think it'll ever be pulled out, and you'll never be avenged!'

As he was saying this, he brushed his hand against the stump. A shard hooked in his finger and, in full view of all the good knights, the length of shaft together with the head came clean out of the body. Sir Gawain was the first to see it, and in his dismay he angrily shouted:

'Guerrehés my brother, by our father's soul what possessed you to lay a hand on that lance? Isn't there some other knight here who could've pulled it out? That was a rash deed!'

'Enough, sir!' Sir Yvain said. 'There's no point chastising him now: it can't be helped. Best forget it!'

They took the lance head and stared at it: it looked splendid, as if it had just been polished! They all agreed it should have been fouled and stained after being in the corpse, but it was shining – you could have seen your face in it! When they'd looked long enough they returned it to the one who'd pulled it out, and asked him if he realised the burden he'd just assumed.

'So help me God,' Guerrehés replied, 'however onerous it may be, and whoever may stand in my way, I'll do all I can to accomplish it: no one will have cause to reproach me.'

And he went off with the lance-head to his lodging, in turmoil, and called for his lances. They were brought to him, and he had the head securely fitted to the stoutest.

Later that summer – around Easter it was – the valiant-hearted Arthur held a magnificent court at Carlion. He was seated at dinner at the high table, with Guerrehés, whom he dearly loved, close at hand. What had befallen him in the garden was still weighing on Guerrehés's heart, so much so that he'd lost his appetite, and nothing anyone said would make him laugh or smile. Kay the seneschal was watching him; and he came to the king and asked him a favour.

'Granted, seneschal,' Arthur said, 'but tell me what it is.'

'All I ask, sire, is that you make Guerrehés say what's on his mind. His head's been down all day: he hasn't laughed or joined in with the feasting at all.'

Everyone who heard this thought he was mad to make such a request, for the king was clearly offended. He briskly replied:

'I'll do no such thing, Sir Kay. It would be most improper to make a man reveal his thoughts unwillingly.'

The knights of the household rebuked Kay for having even thought to ask, but he told them he was determined to have the promised favour granted. 'By God, sire,' he said to the king, 'you should always keep your word, no matter what!'

'Very well,' the king replied, 'but I'm not amused. You're unkind and discourteous – and I tell you, this is the last time I'll ever grant such a request. Come, then, Guerrehés: tell him.'

I shan't beat about the bush: there was nothing for it – Guerrehés had to reveal his thoughts. Distraught, in torment, he said to the king:

'I'll tell you, my lord – and then, when my tale is done, you'll be rid of me and my company for the rest of your days!'

And without more ado he told the king, in everyone's hearing, of the shame and abuse he'd suffered, holding nothing back. Once he'd finished his tale he didn't linger an instant: he went straight to his lodging to arm; no words of prayer or blandishment from the king would make him stay. He armed and mounted his strong, swift destrier. Then he bade a page bring him the lance that was fitted with the head that he'd drawn from the body; he fetched it at once; and Guerrehés looked at the sharp and shining head and took the lance and set off.

He journeyed on until, on the day he'd vowed to be at the garden with the dwarf, he looked ahead and saw him coming, armed and mounted, looking like a monkey on a greyhound. Guerrehés knew at once it was the one he dreaded. And the moment they met, rather than any exchange of greetings, the dwarf said:

'By God, I was on my way to the king your uncle's court to summon you to keep your oath!'

Without another word they headed back to the garden. They rode into the castle and found the lord who'd had the grievous wounds. Now, to describe what happened in detail would be tiresome – it can be told as well in one word as in a hundred. So let me tell you in short that Sir Gawain's brother jousted with the dwarf and killed him, and the lord leapt to his feet in fury when he saw his dwarf struck down. He called for his arms at once and armed, swearing he'd avenge him, and mounted and took up a lance and shield and charged at Guerrehés, crying:

'I challenge you, vassal, as my mortal foe!'

Together they came and as they clashed their lance-heads met their mail; the lord's lance shattered, but Guerrehés sent his clean through the lord's chest; the head snapped off inside his body and he fell dead with the stump still in him. Nor could Guerrehés keep his seat: he fell heavily to the ground; but he jumped up again at once and looked across the garden and saw all the people running away – in moments there was no one to be seen. Praying to God for guidance, he grasped his sword of steel and strode up to the lord who was stricken through the body; he was already cold; his soul was gone. Then a girl appeared, comely of body and fair of face and richly dressed in silk embroidered with silver flowers. She came up to the body and looked at the wound and said to Guerrehés:

'Tell me truly, where did you get this lance-head? The one it slew was my dearly beloved. Is he buried, good sir, that gentle, noble, honoured knight?'

'No, damsel,' Guerrehés replied, 'so help me God.'

Then he bent down and looked in wonder at the wound, for the body was struck in the selfsame place as the one that had lain in the hall at Carlion for almost a year to the day. He was about to pull out the lance-head, but the damsel said:

'No, good sir, leave it! If it's removed we'll be cut to pieces in an instant! But he can't be avenged as long as it stays in his body.'

'Curse anyone who takes it out, then!' Guerrehés said.

The damsel begged him for the love of God to bring her a palfrey from the pavilion behind her, and to take her to her sweetheart lying in the king's hall, and told him to fear nothing more, for he'd avenged him truly. Guerrehés was overjoyed to hear that he'd taken revenge for the knight, and did exactly as she asked: he went to the pavilion and brought her the palfrey, already saddled, and swiftly helped her mount. Then he mounted likewise and they set off, leaving the body transfixed; and they found the castle empty.

They pressed on all day, never drawing rein, until at nightfall they reached the sea. Before them they saw a splendid castle standing on an islet. The damsel urged him to cross, and when they came ashore they went straight into the castle and she led him to a hall where he dismounted; and I tell you truly, never in your life have you seen so many knights and ladies, maidens and squires as were packed into that hall. And I've never seen a single man greeted with such honour as they all showed Guerrehés as he entered. The moment he dismounted he was helped from his armour; and supper was ready, so he washed and they seated him at the high table and served him with the utmost grace and honour. But he was puzzled to see many of them whispering together: they were sighing and grieving deeply for their lord King Brangemuer, who'd been dear to their hearts. But they were also talking of Queen Brangepart's joy that her son had been avenged.

When they rose from supper Guerrehés was heavy-eyed after all his riding and exertion, and having eaten and slept so little for so long; and if the story's to be believed he fell asleep on a patterned rug, right there in the middle of them all. And I tell you truly, in the morning when he woke he found himself below Carlion lying in the richest bed there ever was and ever will be, aboard the boat pulled swiftly by the swan. Draped just as it had been before, the boat was pulled to shore right below the little house.

It was the eve of All Saints, and there were many dukes and counts and barons feasting at Carlion, for the king was holding high court. News soon arrived that a swan had appeared below the house on the shore, with a splendid boat canopied in silk. The king guessed at once it was the swan that had brought the body of the knight they'd laid in the tomb; he said he'd go down to the sea and look at the mysterious boat, and down he went at once with a great company of knights. He was the first to go aboard, the others following; and he peered beneath the canopy and saw a damsel, in rich attire, sitting quietly before a bed. She rose to greet the king and came to him and said:

'I pray you, my good, kind lord, in God's name leave the boat now and let the knight sleep and rest just a little longer: he has no equal in all the world.'

The wise and courteous king replied: 'Damsel, the knight will have time enough to sleep and rest later.'

And he stepped forward and leaned over the bed and was astonished to find his nephew there. He showed his companions; then he woke the sleeping Guerrehés and kissed him and embraced him. No one could describe the joy with which his uncle, his lord King Arthur, greeted him and led him to the hall. And he didn't leave the girl behind: he took her with him, too; and as soon as she entered the hall she went straight to the tomb where the dead knight lay and began to mourn and weep most tenderly, saying:

'My dear lord and love, there is great sorrow in your land. Ah, gentle knight, now lying dead, you were held in such regard! No finer man was ever born, more generous-hearted or more loved! You've lain in this tomb all this while, till King Arthur's nephew struck your slayer the selfsame blow in the selfsame place through the chest. All the people of your land rejoice that you're avenged.'

So saying, the damsel knelt before the king and said: 'My dear lord, I must be gone: I can stay no longer. Here lies King Brangemuer – a finer heart than his was never born. Return him to us, and you'll make many people happy. Sire, Guingemuer begat him of a fairy[125] that he met. You'll surely have heard how he hunted the boar and was detained by my lady – you know what befell him. That lady is Queen Brangepart: she'll be overjoyed, by God she will, if you send the body to her. His death here was inevitable: he was mortal through his father, though not through his mother. That's why his name was composed from both of theirs, and it's only right that you should know: his name was King Brangemuer – "Bran" from his mother and "Gemuer" from his father. So his mother named him – and there never was a king more courteous. Now I've told you the truth, sire; and I should tell you, too, that he was king of one of the isles where dwelt no mortal man: such was his realm; his people are expecting him this month, and when he returns a great wonder will occur there in his land. So I pray you, sire, for the sake of God and love and nobility and honour, return this body to the queen: her joy will be complete if she sees the king her son return, and you may ask whatever favour you desire.'

And everyone said: 'It's only right. Do so, noble, gracious king.'

And he did, without demur. He gave orders for the body with its shroud to be carried to the sea, and he escorted it himself. The damsel commended the king to God and asked his leave, which he graciously gave; then the swan swiftly turned the boat about

---

[125] The word 'fairy' in many romances tends to imply a maiden or lady skilled in magic, as it does in the Prose *Lancelot* (c. 1220): '...the damsel who carried Lancelot off into the Lake was a fairy. At that time, the word "fairy" was used for all women who practised magic, and at that time there were many more of them in Britain than in other lands...'. Norris J. Lacy, ed. *Lancelot-Grail: the Old French Arthurian Vulgate and Post-Vulgate in Translation*, Vol. 3 (new edition, Cambridge, 2010), p. 19. But in a moment it will be clear that this fairy is not a mortal.

and set off for the land from which it had come. The king and all the people there, the maidens and the lords alike, watched it as long as they could, and when it was finally lost to sight they went back to the castle, to the hall, and turned their thoughts to eating. The water was brought, the king sat down and all the others after him, and they proceeded to have the merriest time – as befits a royal court at the feast of All Saints, as I mentioned earlier.

And so, sirs, you've heard how the swan and the boat sailed away from the strand, carrying the dead knight and with him the damsel, pale and wan, who had suffered so much grief for him and shed so many tears.

The Second Continuation

But I'm going to leave them now; from this point you're going to hear about the bold knight who went searching through many realms for the court that housed the bleeding lance. But he suffered so much toil and hardship before he succeeded in finding it that I couldn't possibly tell it all – he roamed very far and very wide: I'm turning now to Perceval.

Perceval, so the story says, had lost his memory to such a degree that he'd quite forgotten God. April and May passed by five times – that's five whole years – without him setting foot inside a church or worshipping God or His cross. That's how he stayed for fully five years. That's not to say that he abandoned the pursuit of chivalrous deeds: he sought out strange, taxing, daunting adventures, and encountered so many that he tested himself well.[1] But I'll say no more about that, for I told you earlier, and you'd be less than thrilled to hear the same again!

After taking communion and being cleansed of his sins, he took leave of his uncle, whose words he'd taken to heart.[2] Then he roamed through many lands and met with many challenges and adventures that aren't recorded. But early one Saturday he was riding along a cobbled road at the edge of a fair and pleasant forest when he came upon a wasteland; and for two days then he had to carry on across a barren heath without anything to eat or drink. On the third day he found himself on an open plain and kept riding, it seems, till terce.*[3]

The Lord of the Horn

Then, as he looked around, very troubled, away to the left he caught sight of a fine, strong castle; but there was no other building of any kind outside its walls, which were unassailably high and mighty – though they had no ditch surrounding them. Above the gate was an imposing tower, tall and strong and handsome indeed, but there was no other tower or turret, truly; and the gate was wholly of ebony, a wood which will never burn or rot. As Perceval looked at this castle he was struck by its bleak position.

He rode up to the gate and found it shut, but he sat and gazed at it for quite a while, for never in his life had he come across one so handsome. Only the most skilled of craftsmen could have made it: the nails were gold and the hinges silver, rich and beautiful indeed, and the locks and bolts were of fine, red gold. And fixed to the gate was a ring of purest gold on which a magnificent horn was hung on a strap of orfrey.* The horn was of ivory, whiter than snow, adorned with bands of gold. Perceval rode straight up to it and swore God should forsake him if he left without giving it a blast! He took off

---

[1] This is an almost exact repetition of a passage in Chrétien's romance, above, p. 54.
[2] i.e. in Chrétien, above, p. 56. The author of the Second Continuation is picking up Perceval's story from the exact point that Chrétien left it.
[3] An asterisk in the text indicates that the word appears in the Glossary, below, pp. 571–2.

his helm at once, and as soon as he'd bared his head he blew the horn with such force and power that the whole surrounding plain resounded. Moments later he heard people stirring and talking inside the castle.

'Did you hear that?' one man was saying. 'The horn has never been blown like that! Whoever gave it such a blast is a valiant man indeed! Bring me my arms at once!'

Perceval didn't know what to make of this: he couldn't see anyone at all. But then, through a crack in the gate, he chanced to glimpse a boy pass by carrying a splendid shield of fine gules* with a lion rampant of ermine; its strap was of orfrey, with handles bound with Grecian silk: it was superbly fitted indeed. The boy carried it into a great hall; and Perceval, I promise you, would have loved to hold such a fine and handsome shield. He stayed where he was, for he could hear people inside, but after waiting a while he blew the horn again, even louder than before. Then at once he heard a man say:

'God have mercy! This is tremendous: truly, the finest of all knights living in the world has sounded the horn – and he'll soon be tested!'

But that was all he said; and Perceval took the horn again and blew it a third time, with such a mighty breath that the whole castle echoed with the sound.

'By the Lord who never lies,' another man said, 'this one will vanquish every foe he meets!'

Perceval heard every word of this; and then he saw a knight emerge from the hall, fully armed, mounted on a magnificent destrier* caparisoned in Grecian samite emblazoned with snow-white lions, accompanied by a great train of squires, pages, knights and ladies. They headed straight to unbar the splendid gate; and when the worthy, valiant Perceval saw them coming in such numbers he hurriedly withdrew. In a field outside the castle stood a lovely almond tree, and he made his way there and waited quietly. Out of the gate rode the knight at speed, in splendour, bearing a golden crown atop his helm – it became him wondrously well, laden as it was with precious jewels: a splendid crown it was, and a sign that he was a king, which he was indeed – of Ireland and of Norway. The moment he rode forth, he and many others recognised the horse ridden by Perceval and the shield he bore, and his heart filled with pity and he said, impassioned:

'Dear Lord God! My beloved friend must be dead! Since he went to Britain I've had no word and seen no sign of him – but now I see his horse, I think, ridden by this knight who bears the very same shield as he! God, what a tragedy! Dear Lord, if he's dead it's a dire loss for the land!'

And he galloped into the field and challenged Perceval, who returned his challenge fiercely. They thrust in their spurs and lowered their pennons and launched into a mighty charge, and as they clashed they struck each other's shield with such force that they shattered their lances: the Lord of the Horn smashed and shivered his down to his fist, such were his strength and worth, and Perceval's blow was so fearsome that it bore him to the ground; and their mounts collided head to head and brought each other crashing in a heap. Perceval, finding his destrier down, leapt swiftly to his feet again and chopped the horse's head off with his sword, crying:

'You've shamed me! I've never been brought down before and it wouldn't have happened now but for you, you wretched nag!'

But enough of that! The Lord of the Horn returned to the attack and Perceval stood his ground; the lord assailed him in a fury, raining mighty blows, but Perceval defended awesomely. Shields were shattered, helms and hauberks* hewn: I swear there was never a more ferocious battle seen between two knights. Perceval realised he was up against a worthy knight indeed, brave and fierce and strong; he was daunted at first and nervous in response, thinking he was of lesser worth than his mighty attacker, who'd been a tried and tested knight before Perceval was even dubbed: he was much in awe of him. The knight was dealing prodigious blows whenever he had the chance, and Perceval realised he was dead if he didn't mount a better defence; so he launched his own sustained attack, raining huge and weighty blows. Each knight strove with all his might to ruin, wound, confound his foe, and the battle raged for ages until finally, I promise you, all those watching wept with pity for them both, distressed that they were powerless to part them. On and on they fought, till Perceval sensed the other knight was tiring, his strength waning; so he pressed him harder, harrying him and driving him back, till the Lord of the Horn cried:

'Enough, friend! No more blows! And don't hide your name from me – I pray you let me know it.'

He replied truthfully, telling him his name was Perceval.

'You're the finest, most renowned knight ever born of woman!' said the Lord of the Horn. 'By God, I'd be a fool to fight on! Have mercy, sir, and take my sword: our battle's over. My life and all I own are in your hands. I know of no more valiant knight than you, and you've outfought and defeated me. I didn't think there was a man alive who could beat me – and do me so much damage!'

'Thank you, sir,' said Perceval, 'for this honour. I'll gladly forgive you all ill-will if you'll go and yield to King Arthur on my behalf.'

The Lord of the Horn promised to go as soon as he was healed and recovered, for he was sapped of strength. And so they made their peace. Then knights and pages came running to the field and unlaced their helms and carefully helped them from their armour, and escorted them both to the castle and did all they could to make them comfortable, laying them side by side in two delightful beds. No man was ever so highly honoured as was the good knight Perceval: the lord provided splendid hospitality, placing the service of his guest before all else, for he held him now in great affection. No one could describe how he was fêted there.

He stayed at the castle happily, without a care, until one day he heard people talking of a marvellous pillar on the high peak of Mount Dolorous: how there were numerous hooks fixed in the pillar, but no one could tether his horse to it unless he was an outstanding knight. When Perceval heard this he said:

'God, what am I doing here? I swear I shan't rest till I reach that pillar! If I can, I'll know for certain whether I'm truly a good knight!'

The lord provided him with all he needed, and he armed at once and mounted and set off without further delay.

Meanwhile the Lord of the Horn headed straight to King Arthur's court to submit as his prisoner as agreed.

He duly made his way straight to Carlion where he was directed to the king, who'd assembled all the good, respected knights of his realm at the court at All Saints, as you heard earlier.[4] It was on the very day when the amazing adventure had occurred[5]

---

[4] Above, pp. 233 and 235.
[5] i.e. the adventure of the swan boat, above, pp. 233–5. This is my interpretation of a sentence which appears to be corrupt: as it stands it says simply 'on that very day, I promise you, this fine adventure occurred that the King of the Horn arrived...', which is not very satisfactory.

that the Lord of the Horn arrived at court while King Arthur was seated at dinner. He dismounted at once and went straight to the table and courteously said:

'God bless you, noble king, and all your company.'

The king didn't withhold a reply; he said: 'You are welcome!'

Then the Lord of the Horn said: 'I surrender to you, my good lord king, on behalf of the worthiest knight in the world, Perceval the Welshman by name. In no land or fief under heaven is there a knight to better or even equal Perceval: he is bold and valiant indeed. I yield to you in his name, and I tell you truly I am lord and king of Ireland. And he bids me tell you he will never return here, and will never, no matter what, stay two days in any one place, until, he says, he has found the lance that bleeds.'

When the king heard this news that delighted him so, he leapt to his feet that instant and embraced the knight and kissed his eyes and cheeks; never in his life had he been so cheered and pleased by any news. And he said:

'So help me God, sirs, I swear to you all I'm going in the morning as soon as it's light to search for that good knight: as long as I have health and life I'll scour every far-flung land and country till I find him! You're all proven traitors for not going in search of him long ago!'

All those good and valiant knights humbly begged the king's forgiveness, and vowed they'd go as soon as he wished and seek him everywhere: they'd carry on looking till they found him, no matter how far off he might be. But I'll say no more about them now, for they're not central to my tale: it's of Perceval I must tell you, word for word, omitting nothing.

As you've heard, Perceval left the Castle of the Horn.

The Castle of the Magic Chessboard

He rode on all morning, right across the heathlands of the Horn, until he came to a great, rushing river with banks so high that it was impossible to cross by boat. Something he recognised convinced him that this was the place where he'd first met the Fisher King, and he was instantly reminded of that noble man who'd given him lodging, and of the lance and the grail he'd seen pass before him but had failed to ask anyone about, which since had caused him so much grief. He longed to cross the river and go again to that king's court, for the country on the other side looked fair indeed and well peopled. He prayed to God to help him find some crossing-place, some ford or bridge.

On he rode along the river until it was past noon, when he saw on a slope on the further bank a handsome little castle, with a tower in the middle surrounded by impressive baileys. But since there was no place to cross he realised that if he wanted lodging he'd have to look elsewhere, so he pressed on along the bank till he caught sight of ancient earthworks approached by little used paths. He carried on, rather warily, and came upon a very old building, the ruins of a castle, though the gatehouse was still intact. So he rode up to the gate and passed inside. There he found a girl sitting beneath an almond tree, combing her hair. When he saw him she stopped her combing and said:

'By God, dear friend, I know you've been looking for a crossing-place – and cross you shall indeed, for you are a good knight!'

So she stood up and led him outside. Perceval, distracted by the sight of her and his eagerness to cross the river, asked her nothing. Outside the gate they found a handsomely harnessed mule, and the girl, most fair and comely, mounted and led Perceval down to the riverbank. Here she untied a little flat-bottomed boat, and the mule, who knew the drill, sprang in, making the whole boat rock and shudder.

'Come aboard, good sir!' said the girl.

Perceval gave his horse a tug, but the horse baulked, snorting and whinnying in alarm: it wouldn't board the boat for anything. The girl summoned him again, but he said:

'By all the saints, damsel, I can't!'

And then, from further off, a ferryman cried at the top of his voice: 'Stay off that boat, sir knight! The girl means to drown you! It's all she ever does! If you board that boat you're a dead man!'

It would take all day, sirs, to recount her many wicked deeds, and how she tricked people and bore them away to the court of King Brandigan:[6] you've never heard such shocking tales in all your life. But I tell you, she kept pressing him to board the boat, and when she failed to trick him she was enraged. The ferryman for his part kept appealing to Perceval to flee, and said he'd come and fetch him; and so he did, and ferried him across, telling him the dreadful truth about the girl. Then he showed him the exact, clear way that would take him straight to the court of the Fisher King. But truly, Perceval wandered off it, because there beside the river he saw the pretty little castle I mentioned before. He found the wide, handsome gates unlocked, and decided to go inside and explore its beauties.

To the first gate he came, and on through the bailey and straight to the tower. It was splendid indeed, and the surrounding buildings were a wonder, set in the vast shade of a pair of pines that stood in the middle of the courtyard. But there was no one to be seen. He dismounted and tethered his horse and propped his shield at the tower's foot; then he climbed up the steps to the hall. Inside he found racks of lances, and leashes and collars for hounds, and good, strong, burnished spears with stout, well furbished shafts. The hall itself was beautiful; and at the far end he could see a bed of carved ivory covered in sheets of Grecian silk: no count or king ever had finer. He strode straight up to this bed, expecting to find someone he could speak to; but he didn't see a living soul. He couldn't understand it. He sat down on the bed, puzzling, and took off his helm and gauntlets. He gazed at the hall, every inch painted, awash with bright colour, and said:

'This is a handsome place indeed.'

Then he noticed a door to his right; he rose from the bed and went to the door and found it open. Beyond it was a vaulted, panelled room, laid out like a bedchamber and filled with perfumes sweeter than would grace a king or an emperor, all perfectly fresh and new. And believe me when I say that in the middle of the room sat a chessboard painted blue and gold, of the finest Moorish craftsmanship, and the pieces were beautiful beyond description: of polished gold they were, adorned with emeralds and rubies that shed a brilliant light, for as you know, they're the richest jewels in the world. These chessmen were set up, ready to play. Perceval sat down on a grey silk cushion to look at them; and he started to move the pieces on the board. He thought he'd never seen such a magnificent chess set, and that it shouldn't have been left by itself, unguarded. He picked up a pawn and moved it forward a square – and with all due thought an opposing piece responded! Perceval stared and said:

'I don't believe it! What's going on?'

---

[6] A king of the Otherworld; his court is frequented by Morgan the Fay: see below, p. 303.

So he promptly made another move – and a response came just as swiftly! So what did he do? He took the opposing piece, the story says, and his was taken in return; and the fact is he was quite outplayed. I'm not going to describe their every move, but I promise you the game finished with Perceval checkmated. And instantly he saw the pieces set up on the board again, all by themselves! He played again, and again, until he'd been checkmated three times, whereupon he swept up the pieces in a fury, dropped them in the skirt of his hauberk and said:

'You'll never defeat another knight – it's not right!'

And he strode to the window, saw the great river below, and decided to fling them in the water. He was on the very point of doing so when a damsel appeared at the window and stayed his throw. She was clad in red samite woven and embroidered with fine gold, dotted with golden stars as bright as candles; and she was lovelier by far than any living creature. She was outside the window, on the river side, but her whole body was visible from the waist up; and she said:

'Sir! The chessmen are in my keeping! Don't throw them! It would be a shameful deed: you'll find none finer in all the world – they should be cared for.'

'You're right,' Perceval replied, 'and I promise I'll do as you wish if you'll come and join me here. It would be very kind, for I'm all alone, without company.'

She replied at once: 'Put the pieces back on the board and I'll come inside and join you – you won't be alone for long.'

He did as she said and replaced the chessmen; then he turned straight back, took her gently in his arms and lifted her through the window and into the room. Then they sat down beside the chessboard and spoke of many matters that I can't relate just now; but I'll tell you this much: he thought her the loveliest girl ever born – fair eyes, fair mouth, fair face, fair arms, fair body, fair hands and beautiful long, full fingers, and a more appealing countenance than any living being. Her nature and her beauty filled Perceval with such love for her that he began to sigh and said:

'God, how rapidly my heart is swayed and shaken!'

'What's wrong?' said the girl.

'What's wrong?' he said. 'I'm in agony on your account, my dear, my sweet!'

'On my account? What do you mean?'

'I mean I love you, dearest, more than my own life!'

And he took her in his arms and kissed her, taking such comfort as he could – he would have done more if he'd been able and she'd consented, but she wouldn't give way.

'Sir,' she said, 'I'll tell you truly what's in my heart. You must understand that no one has ever sought my love in any way: you're the first; and if you were to force your will on me you'd be cut to pieces instantly! If you really want my love, what you must do is this: go into the park beside this castle and hunt the white stag – you mustn't stop till you hunt it down. If you can bring me back its head, I'll do your will, without demur. You're to take my little dog with you: he's a fine hound – once he's sighted the stag he'll never lose him. Take good care of him for me – I wouldn't want him ever to be lost – if you lose my dog you'll never have my love! And you must go fully armed, in case of trouble.'

'I shall, my fair one!' said Perceval. 'Bring the dog here! Give him to me! I'll do just as you've said, this instant!'

The girl jumped up at once and went to her chamber; she'd barely gone before she was back with the dog, and she looked distinctly pleased. The dog was white as snow, with a long lead made of orfrey. She handed him to Perceval and he took him very happily and set off down the steps. May God see him safely back! He went to the foot of the tower where his horse was waiting and mounted at once, and with shield at neck and lance in hand he set off without delay – and without a bow or arrows.

The Knight of the Tomb

He rode straight to the park and started searching for the stag, and within half a league he found him. He was all on his own. With a loud halloo he sent the dog bounding forward, and I tell you truly, he ran the stag down and cornered him on a rocky height; and when Perceval saw the stag was trapped he didn't dally: he dismounted, jubilant, and swiftly struck off his head. But while he was dealing with the stag an evil-looking girl came riding across the glade, seized the dog without a word and swiftly rode away with it. Perceval looked up and saw her carrying it off; he was enraged, and mounted at once and went galloping after, crying:

'Wait for me, girl!'

'Not a chance!' she said. 'What would I gain by doing that? You can see me well enough – what do you want?'

'Give me back my dog, lady! It was very wrong of you to take him without leave: do the decent thing and return him now.'

'I'll do no such thing,' she replied. 'You took my stag without leave, and I'm most upset! The one who sent you here clearly didn't love you – she wanted to be rid of you! When she puts her mind to it she's good at turning the heads of fools! You know what I promise you? By the faith I owe the Creator, it's this: you'll never have this dog – not for a single hour of a single day!'

'With God's help I shall!' said Perceval. 'I want that dog! I'll *make* you put him down – I'll gain nothing by asking nicely!'

'In faith,' she replied, 'might isn't right! You can force me, sure enough, but it'll bring you nothing but trouble and you'll be shamed, a dishonoured coward! But listen: ride to the cleft in yonder rock and you'll find a knight there. Ask directly: "Vassal, what are you doing here?" Then you'll have the dog back, I promise you.'

Perceval was overjoyed at this and said to the girl: 'If that's all it takes let's go, both of us together!'

'Gladly!' she said. 'That's fine by me!'

So off they went at once, Perceval riding swiftly along bearing the stag's head before him. They reached the rock without drawing rein; and at its foot, beside a marble cross, where a cleft delved down into the earth, a vaulted tomb had been made with lime and mortar, well built and roofed, like a little cell. There was an arched wall to support the roof and make it secure, and in this wall were two little windows so that the one inside the tomb could see passers-by. And do you want to know what his life was like? He was all alone, both day and night, his horse his only company and solace. Winter and summer he was stuck there, unable to leave, for he'd promised his sweetheart, that girl so fair of figure, that he wouldn't move from there, regardless of heat or cold, until the coming of a knight who could vanquish him in combat. Five whole years had passed without any knight appearing, for it was such a wild land that hardly anyone ventured there. But truly, the one in the tomb was a knight of great renown; and he didn't want for anything: his sweetheart sent ample oats and hay for his horse – and she didn't neglect *him*, either! She always sent him plenty of food and drink and paid him frequent visits.

So the knight, as I say, stayed lodged in the tomb. And the moment he saw Perceval he armed superbly, expertly; and Perceval came to the window and called to him, crying:

'God save me, sir knight, what madness, keeping you stuck in this tomb! Come out and let me have a look at you! Then I'll be on my way, once you've told me why you've been shut up in here – you've had a tough time if you've been stuck here for long!'

While he was talking, decrying the knight's lot, the knight suddenly appeared, armed and mounted on his horse; and let me tell you, his arms and armour were entirely black – as black as the ripest berry. Don't ask me how he'd got out; but if the story's to be believed his shield hung splendidly from his neck – he cut a fine figure indeed – and he came up to Perceval and said:

'Who are you, sir knight? How haughty and proud you are! You had a nerve calling out to me – you made a big mistake!'

And he drew back and prepared to charge, and Perceval, seeing this, cried: 'By God, sir, if a battle's what you want you'll have it, I promise!'

And he took the stag's head and laid it down at the foot of the cross. The girl, too, placed the dog beside the head; then she turned to see how their battle would go. No more words were exchanged:[7] the knights promptly gripped their lances and shield-straps and set their blazoned shields to protect themselves. Then both knights thrust in their spurs and sent their brave, swift horses into an unstoppable charge, a charge so thunderous that they made the hillside shake and sparks fly from the stones. This was no sporting joust in lists below a castle; these two knights, the lesser of them a worthy warrior indeed, charged at each other from a mighty distance, lances levelled. All the force of the charge they put into their blows, their piercing lance-heads smashing through their shields, the shafts bending on the mail of their bright hauberks and shattering, shards flying skyward. The horses didn't stop, and the knights collided, bodies and shields together, with such force that they sent each other crashing over their horse's rumps. So violent was the clash that they skinned their right knees and their faces, and lay stunned and battered on the ground, showing no sign that they'd ever stand again. But they'd no desire to stay so, and hauled themselves to their feet as soon as they could, pulled the broken lances from their shields and drew their whetted swords. They advanced on each other in a fury, and exchanged such fearsome, weighty blows on their shining helms that they smashed off the golden hoops[8] and stove the helms in deeply. Down came blades on shields, cleaving off chunks of wood and leather with every blow that landed, for they were holding nothing back. Up came the swords and down again as they rained blows thick and fast, till they were both exhausted, bathed in sweat and gasping for breath.

While these mighty warriors were locked in mortal combat, battling with all their strength, a knight in full armour rode across the field towards them – and away again with the stag's head and the dog! Perceval was not best pleased; in fact he was distraught! Clutching his sharp and shining sword of steel, if he'd been mounted he'd have gone straight after the one who'd robbed him – but the Black Knight was coming to the attack. Ablaze with bitter fury, shaking with anger at the loss of his dog, Perceval sprang to face him. The Black Knight dealt him a tremendous blow on his shield; it didn't cut through to his helm but he bowed under the blow's weight. Incensed, he struck straight

---

[7] The rest of this paragraph is an almost exact repeat of Sir Gawain's battle with Bran de Lis in the First Continuation, above, p. 129. Many phrases used are identical.
[8] The reinforcing bands around the helmets.

back – and mightily, smashing through helm and chainmail hood and doing grave damage, cutting off an ear and into the cheek. Horrified by this fearful wound the Black Knight didn't linger: he fled at speed to the cell-like tomb and back inside as fast as he could. Perceval was furious at seeing him go, and pursued him to the arched wall where he stopped in his tracks, bewildered; he started shouting to him to come out and tell him what had become of his dog: had he been taken to some place in the forest, or to some city or castle or fortress, and what was the name of the knight who'd taken him? He'd never know a moment's peace till he recovered that dog! Three times he called, loud and clear, but there was no response of any kind. He was beside himself with anguish: he knew he was wasting his time.

'In faith, this is some kind of magic! There's no one here to speak to – but the knight I beat, I saw him go in!'

He turned away, bemused, distressed, and returned to his horse and mounted.

'God!' he said. 'He's done me no favours, the knight who carried off my dog! If I go back to the girl, what shall I say? What shall I tell her? In faith, she'll abuse me and think me an utter wretch – I'll be shamed in the eyes of all! I'd better go after him – what a disservice he's done me, what a problem he's caused! If I don't get that dog back fast I'll be disgraced for sure! If she doesn't see me coming back she'll say I've taken her dog and lost it! What chance will I have then of enjoying her love as she promised? No chance at all! She'll think I've been killed or captured!'

So Perceval set off across the hillside, wanting nothing other than to catch the knight; he galloped in pursuit, determined to recover the dog and the head which he knew the knight had taken. Into the forest he rode, up hill and down dale, pressing ever onward after him. He hadn't gone more than a league, it seems, when he ran into the girl who'd tried to take his dog. He didn't want to slow down for her, and rode straight past without a word; but a bowshot further on he thought it had been wrong of him to say nothing to her, and turned his horse about and rode smartly back. He soon reached the girl; she'd sped up and was riding fast but Perceval caught up with her and gave her courteous greeting. But she made no reply – she seemed very aggrieved. So he greeted her again – but again she said nothing, not a single word. Instead she gave her palfrey a lash, wanting to be off; Perceval reached out to take her bridle, but she said:

'Away with you, sir knight, away! What are you doing, grabbing my reins? You're not noble, kind or courteous: you nearly killed me when I took your dog today, but now a fine knight's carrying it off – he's obviously no friend of yours! Your sweetheart will be most upset that you let him have the dog without her leave and without discussing it! She won't appreciate it at all! But you could try and lie by her side tonight, as a reward for catching the stag!'

Perceval was most put out, hearing her taunt him so; but he replied politely nonetheless, asking her to tell him, if she could, the name of the knight who'd caused him so much trouble – and the name, too, of the Black Knight he'd defeated – and in return he'd never fail to help her.

'That's not much of a deal!' she said. 'Heaven and earth will join together before I tell you their names! You're not so high and mighty that I should!'

Perceval realised he was wasting his time dallying with the girl. He turned his horse's head about and swiftly rode away, swearing by almighty God that he'd never thought to find such spitefulness in a woman. On he rode without more delay, pressing on through the great, thick forest, turning over and over in his mind the strange things that had happened.

On and ever on he rode, until he heard the blast of a horn. He spurred straight towards the sound, hoping to find someone who'd give him news of the one he sought; and as he did so he saw, in a patch of cleared ground, a huntsman with two dogs: not great hounds but little ones, whiter than may blossom. And piled behind him on a second horse was game in plenty, I promise you, as he made his way homeward, tired from the hunt. When Perceval caught sight of him he hailed him and said:

'Sir hunter, by the love and faith you owe your sweetheart, tell me, I pray you, the way to the court of the Fisher King!'

'By the Saviour, sir,' the huntsman replied, 'I've never heard of such a place, and I've roamed this forest and the country round about and roved the hills and vales for thirty years!'

'Then tell me, good sir,' said Perceval, 'if you know anything of a knight carrying a stag's head and fondling a dog: he may well have come this way.'

'By God, sir, no: if he passed this way in the last two days I'd have seen him – I've been here since the day before yesterday.'

'There's nothing for it, then,' said Perceval. 'I'll just have to go and find lodging.'

'There isn't any, my friend,' the huntsman said. 'By Saint Thomas, I don't know of any house or cottage within thirty leagues of here – except the cell of a hermit who lives in this forest. If you want to find lodging tonight I'd go straight there. But if you want to come with me I'll look after you and serve you gladly, seeing as you're a knight. And tomorrow I'll see you on your way as best I can.'

Perceval accepted the offer gratefully, and accompanied him to a tent: there's no surprise in that – when the need arises we all do the best we can. And that night the good Perceval had venison in ample quantities, and his horse had plenty of oats. The huntsman took good care of him and he slept comfortably all night till dawn. And in the morning when it grew light Perceval armed swiftly, without delay, and mounted and took his leave of the huntsman who'd honoured him so. The huntsman told him to take the path to the right if he wanted to get out of the forest.

'Gladly, if you say so,' said Perceval.

The Murdered Boy

He pressed on till, about midday, he met with an adventure which really must be told, so tell it I shall. As he followed the huntsman's directions and was about to turn to the right, he heard a cry away to his left and headed off towards it. He'd gone no distance when he ran into a boy in headlong flight, his face covered in blood. And without a word of a lie, he didn't have a shred of clothing worth a light: his tunic had lost its skirt and collar and was torn to shreds that dangled to his heels as it snagged on branches – he was fleeing through the thickest bushes he could find. He was smothered in blood – not an inch of him was free of it – and he was running for all he was worth. He'd been hit by a javelin. As he raced along, clearly desperate for help, Perceval saw him from a distance and spurred after him to find out what was wrong.

'Boy!' he cried. 'Boy! Stop a moment! Tell me why you're fleeing in such alarm!'

The boy made no reply at all: he just went racing on, so fast that Perceval had never seen anyone run at such speed – or bleed so badly. Then he saw a hound come bolting after him, baying and howling as it caught his scent and catching up fast; next he saw a knight in full armour come spurring by, carrying neither shield nor lance but galloping on with amazing speed – and clutching a sword scarlet with blood to the hilt.

'In God's name,' cried Perceval, 'stop a moment, and tell me why you're chasing that boy!'

But he galloped on past without a word of reply; and truly, he didn't slow down till he reached the boy and struck him with his whetted sword and killed him instantly. Perceval arrived too late to stop him, and cried:

'Knight! If you had any decency you'd never have done such a bloody deed! And it was outrageous and haughty to ignore me just now and refuse to speak!'

But the knight replied: 'I swear I've never clapped eyes on such an idiot as you. Stop to explain my business to everyone I meet? God! How stupid would that be? You're a pain and a waste of space – get out of here and leave me be! You're a fool if you hang around, I swear! Off with you – be on your way!'

'I'll thank you, sir,' said Perceval, 'to calm down and stay your anger; speak to me properly, and kindly explain what wrong this boy had done.'

'By God!' said the knight. 'You've little respect for me, I see! Ignore me, will you? Well, that's too bad – you'll pay for it!'

And he dealt him a blow on the helm that stunned him and made him buckle over his horse's neck. Perceval, ablaze with rage at the blow, propped his ashwood lance against an oak, but keeping his shield in place he drew his sword from its scabbard and assailed the knight, landing three blows in quick succession. In short, he overcame the knight and avenged the boy by cutting him to pieces, for the knight wouldn't ask for mercy: Perceval kept bidding him to, but he absolutely refused. Perceval regretted it deeply: if the knight had asked for mercy he wouldn't have touched him.

So Perceval left them both, upset and frustrated that he didn't know who they were or where they were from. But that's the way it was. And he left them there and carried on through the wood until he came upon a hermitage, and there he spent the night. The holy hermit gave him barley bread and herbs and fruit, and Perceval told him all about what had happened with the knight and the boy. And in the morning when it grew light the hermit went and found the bodies, and buried them in his chapel where he spent long hours in prayer.

The Search for the Stolen Dog

Perceval took to the road again, and didn't stop riding until about noon. And then, I tell you truly, he met a very aged knight with a sparrowhawk on his wrist and two retrievers[9] before him, mounted on a handsome and perfectly white mule. He was on his way to the hermitage; and with Perceval still musing on the previous day's events, this knight, ambling along, hailed him first. Perceval replied politely, saying:

'God bless you, good sir, and grant you health and happiness.'

'Where have you come from?' the knight asked. 'And what brings you here? And do you realise the wrong you've done me and my kin? A dreadful wrong indeed!'

'How have I wronged you?' said Perceval. 'Tell me, dear sir!'

'I shall!' said the knight. 'I'll tell you straight! About nine or ten years ago you slew my brother, and a finer man I never saw! He was the Red Knight: you struck him through the eye with a javelin, killing him,[10] and no vengeance has been taken with lance or sword!'

---

[9] *'chiens a oisiaux'*: literally 'bird-dogs'.
[10] i.e. in Chrétien, above, p. 11.

'By all the saints,' Perceval replied, 'I'm sorry I killed him! But it was with King Arthur's leave, sir: honestly, he granted me the Red Knight's arms.'

'That's true,' said the knight, 'and you're forgiven, since you've admitted it. We'll say no more about it from this day forth. But by the Saviour, I know you're looking for the lance that bleeds at the Fisher King's court, and due to suffer much before you find it. So it may have been you the other night who found his daughter, a comely damsel, at a castle up ahead. I met her on her way to his court; and she mentioned a little dog that she'd arranged for a girl to carry off, along with a stag's head, because she wanted to test and trouble a much-praised knight who'd been to the court of the Fisher King but failed to ask the question he should: who was served from the grail. So while he was dealing with the stag he'd killed, this girl robbed him of the dog. He asked her to return it, but she gave it back only when he agreed to go to a vaulted tomb where a knight would fight anyone the moment he was called. But while he was embroiled in combat with him, he laid the dog and the stag's head on the ground there in the field, and another knight, passing by, carried off both dog and head! All this was the damsel's doing![11] When he finished his battle with the knight of the tomb he asked the girl if she knew what had happened to his dog, but she'd tell him nothing, except that it had been taken by a man who felt no love or pity for him or anyone close to him; and with that they parted. I heard all about it from the damsel herself, who made it clear that if it hadn't been for the business with the grail she'd have given the knight no trouble or grief. So saying, she went on her way.'

Perceval was so delighted at hearing this that he failed to ask anything about the one who'd killed the boy – the knight he'd slain with his own hands: either which land he came from, or where he'd been or where he was going. So he was none the wiser. All he said to the old knight was:

'God send you honour, sir! Please direct me to that castle, so I don't lose the way; if I could only find the girl, no knight would ever have been happier than I!'

'Trust me, friend, and just keep to this highway.[12] Eventually you'll come to a spring; leave the road then and set off across the meadows. Don't be alarmed by anything you see along the way: no matter what you're confronted with, you won't find the castle if you give way to fear.'

'God protect you from all ills, sir,' said Perceval, 'and grant you a good and happy life.'

With that they went their separate ways. So Perceval rode on alone along the good, broad, well-made road that the knight had shown him, but was very troubled when he saw no sign of the spring he was so eager to find – but he hadn't yet gone far enough. Then, most unfortunately, he became so distracted, so deep in thought about his quest and all he'd been told, that he wandered off the path before he reached the spring. Now his mission was going to be even harder, even more taxing than he imagined! Off he rode the wrong way, leaving the straighter path, preoccupied and lost in thought until he'd gone a fair distance.

'By God,' he said, 'I think he was having me on when he sent me this way! There's no sign of any spring! But maybe I missed it while I was busy musing.'

He pressed on, going ever further from the proper path, till evening was closing in; and he saw no sign of the meadows or anything else the knight had mentioned. Then

---

[11] i.e. the Fisher King's daughter arranged it all.
[12] Literally 'metalled road'.

he caught sight of a newly built tower, and a white castle came into view; he headed straight towards it, thinking it was the one the knight had meant.

'There it is!' he said, and thrust in his spurs. The sun which circles all the Earth had almost completed its course; and Perceval rode to the tower.

It was a fine summer's evening as he neared the fortress. He saw its imposing walls, its lofty towers and mighty keep and splendid halls and fine apartments, as impressive as any from there to Limoges. He didn't draw rein till he reached the castle, and rode in through the gate.

He found every door wide open but he couldn't see a living soul. He carried on to the hall, every inch a fair building indeed, and rode inside. Then he dismounted without more ado – but still he saw no knight or servant, no one to ask about anything. He laid down his shield and looked around, and to his right he saw the door to a chamber open wide. And propped in the doorway was a Danish axe. It was a sight that made Perceval far from easy, but he strode up, took the axe and entered the chamber. It was panelled throughout but completely empty, though it was all the lovelier for being newly strewn with fresh, green grass. The puzzled Perceval then noticed a window and went straight over and looked out; and there he saw the most beautiful meadow that ever eyes beheld, enclosed in a high wall of solid stone. In the middle of the sward was a spring of clear, sweet water, beside which stood the fairest tent that ever was seen. Before the tent was a tree that yielded a gorgeous scent in every weather: a cypress it was, my sources say. And stretched beneath it lay a mighty, fierce, colossal lion. Perceval stared at the beast, and then decided to go to the tent and see if he could find anyone there; but much to his annoyance the window was too narrow to climb through. He turned back, eager to find a window wide enough to let him out to the meadow, and returned to the hall where he'd first dismounted; but he didn't find his horse where he'd left him tethered, though his shield was still lying there – it hadn't been moved.

'By God, this is strange,' he said. 'I left my horse here quietly tethered, and now he's nowhere to be seen. If only I could get out to the meadow I might find someone who can explain what's going on.'

He bent down and picked up his shield and set off, eager to reach the meadow: he wasn't too worried about his horse. He hurried through a vaulted chamber and came to a flight of stairs; down them he went and saw the meadow before him. Towards the tent he ran at once, sword in hand, shield slung from neck; but the lion heard him, leapt to its feet, and with a mighty bound it raced at him and plunged its claws into his red shield. Perceval was shocked, and little wonder, for it ripped the shield from his neck, tearing the silken, gold-embroidered strap asunder; but undaunted, he delivered a mighty blow with his sword, holding nothing back, and the steel blade clove the beast's head in two; and so he was avenged upon the lion.

He hurried to the tent and went straight in, and there he found a maiden, comely indeed: Nature had excelled in her making. There he stood with drawn sword, and the maiden, seeing this, cried in terror:

'Help! Holy Mary, help!'

And as she did so Perceval saw a knight lying in a bed, blanketed in samite; the commotion woke him, and he was enraged to hear his sweetheart cry and to see a knight standing armed there in his tent clutching a naked sword all covered in blood.

'How dare you come marching in here?' he cried. 'It was rash indeed, and you'll regret it!'

He sprang to his feet in fury, and Perceval said: 'There's no need to talk like that, good sir! I've come in with a drawn sword but I've done you no wrong: I came here only to look for lodging! But I saw a lion in the meadow, huge and fierce, and it attacked me and I had to defend myself – and I killed it, I'm pleased to say! That's the reason my sword was drawn.'

'Is that right?' said the knight, proud and fierce and brimming with hostile rage. 'Who told you to kill my beloved lion? I'll avenge the beast, by God I will! Bring me my arms! I'm going to do battle! Don't dally, girl! Quickly, call two pages!'

'Gladly!' she said, and summoned two squires, who hurried to serve their lord. He bade them saddle his horse and bring him his hauberk, shield and lance.

'And one of you go and fetch this vassal his horse – look sharp!'

No sooner said than done: they brought Perceval his horse and he mounted at once; and the knight, so keen to avenge his lion, vowed and declared he'd pay for it. Now he was armed, and his steed was brought forward; he mounted. By the time they were both in the saddle the sun was almost down; but Perceval picked up a lance he found at the door of the tent – it was stout and sharp, with a steel head; and without a pause or further words they let their horses go and gave them free rein and spurred them on with all their might. They exchanged such blows that they smashed through their shields and brought each other down. The knight was distraught that his love had seen him fall, but he kept his composure and leapt to his feet and drew his sword at once. Equally undaunted, Perceval came to the attack, fierce and brave as a leopard, and dealt him a blow with his silver-pommeled sword of steel, holding nothing back; it didn't catch him full on the helm but landed so hard on the rim of his shield that it clove clean through it – a telling blow, he thought. But the knight returned a furious blow atop his bright, bejewelled helm, so weighty and so stunning that it almost brought him down. But Perceval wasn't slow to renew his assault – and the knight attacked back and they exchanged tremendous blows: it was a very even contest, for both were valiant knights indeed.

The battle raged on as night drew in. The knight was tiring now, and Perceval was suffering from all his riding and lack of food. How he must have regretted this reception from his host! No warm welcome, but a hefty fight with blades of steel! It struck him that if he let his host have his way he'd be in trouble, so he delivered a blow to the helm that smashed away the golden band and cut and split clean through to his chainmail hood, and there it landed; the knight collapsed face down in the field, quite stunned – you could have walked a league in the time it took him to revive. Perceval strode up and seized him by the helm and unlaced it and threatened to kill him, but the girl ran up and fell on the knight in a dead faint. Perceval calmed and reassured her, as she tenderly begged him for God's sake not to kill her love, for he was clearly beaten. Then the knight with a sigh returned to his senses, and Perceval opened the hood of his hauberk. The fine steel rings of mail had left their stamp on his forehead, and Perceval called for water to be brought from the spring. The girl, so distressed, made her way down to the spring and filled a golden cup and returned to Perceval and asked him to pull off the knight's hauberk; she didn't dally but bathed his face herself, and the knight, his heart revived, was back on his feet. He looked long at Perceval, and then begged him to tell him his name in all courtesy, now that he'd vanquished him in battle; and Perceval boldly answered:

'First you'll promise to go to King Arthur, at Cardoil or Carlion, and surrender as his prisoner.'

'Very willingly,' he said, and made his vow as bidden; then he asked in whose name he should submit.

'In the name, my friend,' he told him, 'of Perceval the Welshman, who not long ago spent a good five days with him in the forest.'

The knight told him he'd won great honour by defeating him in combat, for he was much praised and renowned – it could bring him only credit. Then Perceval asked him his name and the name of the mighty, handsome castle, and he replied:

'My name is Abrioris of Brune Mons.'

Then four servants came, tall, handsome and ready, and disarmed the knights and brought them scarlet[13] mantles lined with vair;* then they led their fine steeds away to stable them and make them comfortable. The knights and the girl – a fair and comely damsel indeed – strolled happily together through the fresh, green meadow, followed by knights and servants and squires from the castle; and when they were all together Abrioris called for tables to be set up in the meadow so that they could eat beside the spring, fair and clear and sparkling. The servants knew their business and set about it swiftly, and the water was presented[14] and they all sat down. I shan't give details of the various dishes, but you may be sure they had plenty.

As the knight, the master of the house, sat at his right hand, Perceval said: 'I'd like to ask you, sir, about a knight who has insolently done me shameful wrong.' And he told him of the outrageous theft of the dog. But the knight said simply that he knew nothing about it, and they let the matter rest.

While the servants cleared the tables they rose and walked to the hall, talking of this and that, and the three of them sat together on a carpet of samite from Thessaly. There's little more to say: they called for wine, the beds were made – and they'd no complaints, for they were splendid and covered with fresh, new sheets – and they lay down in the greatest comfort and slept soundly all night till dawn.

Then Abrioris went to Perceval's bed to see if he was awake, but finding him still asleep he went straight back.

A little later Perceval woke and donned his clothes and shoes alone, and came to his chamber door and saw it was a lovely morning: the fresh dew sparkling on the grass made his heart rejoice. He went back to the splendid hall, and found the knight there with two squires. Perceval was the first to give greeting, saying:

'May Our Lord give you good day, dear sir. Please have my arms prepared and my horse brought straight away and I'll be gone. Make no delay: I've dallied too long already.'

'No, good sir!' the knight replied. 'Stay here for a couple of days and then go when you wish – I'll leave with you, and won't stop till I find that renowned king's court at Carlion or Winchester.'

'It's really not possible,' Perceval said. 'I can't stay here a moment longer. But you stay if you wish: wait a week and then begin your journey.'

'No, by God!' said Abrioris. 'I'll not linger after you!'

'Then bring me my arms and I'll prepare,' said Perceval; and they handed him his fine Cornish hauberk, a page boy assisting him to don it. Another boy hurried to the chamber of the fair and comely damsel and told her to make ready without delay; she happily agreed, and while Abrioris armed and had a big, grey horse saddled for him,

---

[13] 'Scarlet' refers to the material rather than the colour: see Glossary.
[14] i.e. for the washing of hands.

she dressed herself in her richest clothes. As soon as she was ready she came to the hall, and Perceval rose to meet her, saying:

'God keep you, fair damsel!'

'Good sir,' she replied, 'I wish you a fine day blessed with joy and health!'

Then their horses were led forward and all three mounted and set off. They passed through the gate and over the bridge and rode on into the forest. They came to two broad roads that parted at a cross, and there they went their separate ways, Perceval turning to the right while Abrioris took the path to the left and headed for Carlion, his rose-cheeked sweetheart at his side.

They rode on until, at prime* on the seventh day, they arrived at Carlion. The king and all his barons had gone to relax in a garden outside the town, and the queen with them. Abrioris entered the town and saw a page and asked him where the king was, and the boy replied:

'Before God, sir, I left him a moment ago in yonder garden.'

'Tell me, friend, is Sir Gawain there? And Lancelot and Sir Yvain, the son of good King Urien?'

'Indeed, sir, no,' said the boy. 'The king's retinue is small at present: he has only two thousand knights. But Lucan the butler's there, and so are Kay and Taules de Rougemont, and they're all knights of high renown.'

At that Abrioris turned about and the squire left them, having given them sound directions. Abrioris made his way to the garden, fully armed upon his destrier and his comely sweetheart by his side. The king was sitting beneath a new-planted tree, and the fair-complexioned queen beside him. Abrioris dismounted while the Bold Ugly Knight helped the damsel from her palfrey. He walked straight up to the king and hailed him in the name of God the king of majesty, and the queen returned his greeting; then he explained his purpose, saying:

'Good lord king, on behalf of Perceval the Welshman, that knight of great renown, I surrender as your prisoner. And he also sends this fair and comely girl to my lady the queen.'

The king was delighted, you may be sure; he rose the moment he heard Perceval's name and went and embraced the knight, saying:

'You are welcome! Tell me, how is he faring, my much-loved friend, that most accomplished knight? Is Perceval in good spirits?'

'Indeed he is! And I don't believe there's a knight as fine in all the world!'

The king bade two pages help him from his armour without delay, and they did so at once, leaving him clad in an haqueton* covered with rich oriental cloth. The king seated him at his side, and the radiant queen welcomed him with joy and honour and asked him if Perceval was well.

'Lady,' he replied, 'by all the saints the pilgrims worship, I left him on Tuesday morning as safe and sound and hearty as could be; and he sends you my beloved.'

'By God who created all, for Perceval's sake she'll be honoured indeed!'

Then she stood and addressed the king, beseeching him to excuse the knight his imprisonment. It didn't take much persuasion: he gladly absolved him, for which he thanked him deeply; then the king asked him his name and he courteously replied:

'Sire, my name is Abrioris.'

'Dear friend,' said the king, 'I would have you be a member of my household for the rest of your days.'

And so he remained. And he was highly honoured at court, and became one of the Round Table, the most esteemed of knights in all the world.

The Dead Knight Odinial

Now we'll tell of Perceval, who didn't stop riding through the great, thick forest from early morning till prime and well past terce. It was almost noon indeed when he saw, beneath an oak, a knight lying dead, with his horse and shield tied to a branch. He'd been struck through the body with a lance, the point protruding nearly an arm's length; and a sword had cut through his helm and into his head. Perceval drew rein and gazed at him for a long while, grieving and mourning him, for he was a fine and handsome figure. Then he commended his soul to God and turned away, and rode swiftly on till he passed into a broad and beautiful glade in the middle of which was a clear spring with water colder than marble. Above it stood a lovely tree, beneath which sat a girl who seemed the very queen of beauty. But she had her head in her hands, and seeing her all alone, Perceval hailed her, and she replied at once with a deep and troubled sigh.

'In God's name, my dear,' he said, 'tell me why you're so upset.'

And she told him very readily she'd lost her sweetheart, whom she loved so dearly that she'd rather suffer herself than have any harm befall him. Perceval felt very sorry for her, and gently asked her how long her love had been gone.

'Since yesterday evening,' she said. 'He left me here beneath this tree and I haven't seen him since, though he was supposed to return in no time.' And she gave another deep sigh.

Perceval looked long at her and saw how fair she was – and how red were her cheeks, flushed from grieving, which made her all the lovelier. How pleasant it would have been to engage with her, if anyone were bold enough! But such thoughts weren't in Perceval's mind: instead he asked what shield her sweetheart carried. It was quite new, she said, and gold, with three silver lions rampant.

'My dear,' he replied, 'your lover is lying dead in this great forest.' And he told her there and then about the knight he'd found, speared through the body and with a sword-cut to the head. When she heard this she collapsed in a swoon, apparently not breathing, so overcome with grief she was almost dead. When she came to, Perceval asked her lover's name. She was utterly distraught, but managed to tell him that his name was Odinial and he was known as the Fair.

Perceval and the Giant

With that Perceval set off at once; he didn't stay longer, but took to the road again, escorting the girl neither onward nor back.

He rode on till he came to a river, deep and swift. He looked across and saw a handsome tower, though it was surrounded by no wall or ditch, or any fence, stockade or palisade. It was a comforting sight: if only he could reach the other side he could take lodging there, he thought, but he couldn't see any way to cross. He decided to ride downriver and find a bridge or crossing-place rather than turn back; so he followed the course of the river as it flowed downstream, and looking ahead he caught sight of a well-made bridge of stone. He rode straight on and swiftly across, and then back upstream, not stopping till he reached the splendid tower.

There was a tree by the entrance, the loveliest he'd ever seen, and he dismounted beneath it and went up the marble steps to the tower and in through the door. What met his eyes was the most beautiful, wondrously furnished house that ever a Christian man beheld. Perceval felt nothing but delight – though he could see no lady, knight or servant, not a living soul, to speak to. So he didn't disarm, not knowing what kind of place this was. Then, beside a lovely window, he saw a silver table, laid with a white cloth, and salt and knives, and golden goblets, rich and handsome, and a spread of food fit for a king. And water was ready in two beautiful basins of pure gold, finely wrought indeed, and the towel wasn't lacking – white it was, and soft and fine. What a welcome sight! Perceval's heart soared: he hadn't eaten for a long while and he was very weary. He quickly disarmed, and took a scarlet mantle that was hanging in the hall, and went to the door and down the steps and unharnessed his horse and left him to graze in the gathering dusk. Then he came back to the hall and took water from the golden basin and washed and dried himself with the towel. Then he sat down in the best seat and ate his fill – for there was plenty of everything: fresh meat, fowl and game, and copious wine: he drank as much as he wished. So there he sat, eating all alone, with no servant or squire to speak to, entirely without company.

And then, while he was busy eating, he looked towards the door and saw a girl. She was in a wretched state: thin and pale, jaundiced, wan, and as for her clothes, I swear they weren't worth tuppence. So poorly clad she came up to Perceval and greeted him and said:

'God help me, sir, I'm sorry you've had this meal: you're going to pay dearly for it – it's going to cost you!'

'Why, my dear?' he said. 'Who is there I should fear?'

'I won't hide it from you,' she said. 'The lord of this place is a giant, cruel and foul-natured. It was he who had this tower built, and any knight who comes to his house he kills!'

'Truly,' said Perceval, 'that's wicked and shameful indeed. But tell me now, in all honesty: are you and he close?'

'No indeed, sir! He's kept me in his house for two and a half years, much to my distress. I've no wish to do his will, but he puts me to endless shame – my life's not my own but I can't escape him. But come, make haste! Arm this instant! The giant'll be back at any moment and if he finds you here you're a dead man!'

'Truly,' said Perceval, 'if it's as you say he can't get away with it! If he wants to do me harm I'll take him on!'

'Don't say that, sir! To fight him would be folly! He's insanely strong, and such a size that no man can resist him! Arm now and be gone from here and see if you can escape!'

Perceval armed at once, swiftly donning his hauberk, lacing his helm and girding his sword; but he swore to God on high that he wasn't going to give up his lodging, whatever anyone said: he'd have to be driven out by force. He went and stood at the tall, broad window. The giant was only too pleased to see him, and cried out in a booming voice:

'What brings you here, vassal? You'll have good lodging tonight, but it'll cost you!'

And without another word he came storming towards the tower; he was furious to see Perceval's horse eating his grass, and gave him such a blow with his massive club that he smashed him in half. Perceval was filled with rage; he grabbed his shield and rushed downstairs, beside himself with anger, determined to avenge his good steed slain by the giant. He strode towards him, sword in hand, shield slung from neck. The giant thought he was mad to attempt to take him on; clutching his great, square, colossal club, he raised it aloft and aimed a blow at Perceval – but missed him as he dodged aside. It was as well he did: it would only take one blow to land and there'd be nothing left of him to mourn. Perceval was in awe of the club, but gripped his naked sword and aimed a truly mighty blow; he didn't find the target – the giant was too far off – but he caught him on the left hip: if the blow had landed properly it would have taken off his leg, but the sword turned and went flashing down, cutting through the muscle so close to the bone that it sliced the giant's heel clean off. The giant was wild with rage and grief as he realised he was wounded – his heart nearly burst – how he wished he'd killed the knight at the start! Determined to land a telling blow he wielded his club in fury, bent on killing him on the spot; the blow plummeted down; but Perceval was an agile swordsman and on his mettle and leapt back, and the mighty blow crashed down with such force that the colossal club was smashed to pieces. Perceval, exultant, rushed to attack him with his sword, and dealt him such an awesome blow that it sheared an ear from his head, severed shoulder and arm and cut into his side as far as the lung. The giant collapsed unconscious, and Perceval didn't hesitate but plunged his good sword right through his body. The giant was dead; the battle was over.

Then Perceval returned to the house he'd conquered; no one stood in his way! In he went and disarmed. There was no servant or squire to help him – only the girl; but she happily gave what assistance she could, and Perceval was only too glad to receive it.

'Now, sir,' she said, 'this manor is yours, to do with as you please. And I am at your mercy: in God's name have pity on me.'

'You've nothing to fear,' said Perceval. 'You'll not be harmed by me. But tell me: do you know if there's a horse here?'

'Yes indeed,' she replied. 'There's a black one in the cellar below. Some two months ago the giant killed a most worthy knight and put his horse down there in a big cellar; he's given him plenty to eat and drink – he's been there ever since.'

Perceval was pleased to hear this and asked for a candle; she brought one, ready lit, and they went down to the cellar to see this horse. When he saw him he was delighted: he was a handsome, noble steed indeed – he wouldn't have swapped him for all the wealth in the city of London!

Then he returned to the tower and undressed at once and lay down in a splendid bed, for it was now dark night and he was sorely tired – he fell asleep in no time; and the girl went to bed in a panelled chamber.

They slept without the slightest fear till morning when it grew light as the sun appeared, shining bright and lighting up the day. Then Perceval rose and made ready, impatient to be gone, and went to the horse and saddled him. The girl did all she could to help, and Perceval enjoyed her attention, not disdaining it at all. He said she should stay and be lady of the house and all the surrounding land; she thanked him deeply and said he'd saved her by ridding her of the giant who'd treated her so wickedly and slain so many good knights.

'You have much enhanced your honour,' she said. 'May Our Lord reward you for what you've done.'

Perceval armed without more ado and mounted his black destrier and took his leave; then he set off swiftly, his mount galloping away through the great, thick forest.

The Amorous Ford

It was a beautiful morning in the sweet season of Spring, and the bright sound of birdsong lit his heart. He rode all day without stopping till late in the afternoon, when he caught sight of a man and hailed him – a Welshman he was, running along on foot. He asked him where he'd come from, and he said he'd seen a crested serpent that morning that had scared him terribly. Then Perceval asked if he'd seen any man or armoured knight that day, or any castle, house or fortress.

'If you carry on the way I've come,' he said, 'you'll come to a place where you'll find a knight – and maybe a terrible surprise!'

With that he went running off, while Perceval galloped on the way he'd said. He pressed on hard over a lofty mountain and came to an open plain, the fairest ever seen, with grass growing long and green and a beautiful river flowing through it. On the bank of this river stood a tree, beneath which sat a marble block inscribed with tiny golden letters, and on the other bank, in the middle of the sward, was pitched a gorgeous tent of exquisite cloth from Antioch. Before the tent stood a destrier, completely white, I believe, and a white shield emblazoned with silver, and a lance, perfectly new and white. Perceval gazed at the tent, the river, the meadow, the white shield, the white destrier and the white applewood lance, and thought, rightly, that white portended only good. He decided to go and take lodging in the tent, for night was drawing in. So he rode down to the ford and splashed straight in, and stopped to let his horse drink. Then he glanced ahead and saw a knight busy arming, who called to him:

'By God, vassal! You've got a nerve, watering your horse in this ford! You've done great wrong! I challenge you forthwith!'

He mounted the white horse in an instant, and with lance in hand and shield slung from neck he came galloping forward. Perceval rode straight out of the ford where he'd been watering his mount, and set his shield and lance in position; then they charged at each other and exchanged tremendous blows on their shields, smashing through them and shattering their lances. From their sheaths they drew their sharp and whetted swords; on their helms they beat and pounded, thick and fast. Nor did they spare their shields: they hacked them both to pieces; never did two champions fight a battle so intense. The White Knight clutched his sword and dealt Perceval a ferocious blow that scythed through his shield right down to the boss, and nearly inflicted a grievous wound in his left arm; Perceval, incensed, struck him on his steel helm, making him buckle over his saddle-bow, then beat him from his fine Castilian charger and dealt him two or three more blows that left him battered. The knight desperately begged for mercy, admitting utter defeat, and Perceval, hearing this, replied at once:

'If you want to have mercy, vassal, you must yield as King Arthur's prisoner.'

'I'll do whatever you wish, sir. But I must know your name: what name do you go by?'

'My baptismal name, my friend, was Perceval. And it's only right that you tell me yours.'

'Indeed, sir, I shan't keep it from you. I'm called the White Knight, guardian of the Amorous Ford. By the faith I owe you, which is total, since I first bore arms – a good six years ago – I've not left this ford for three days together. I've given many knights grief for no more offence than watering their horses in the ford.'

'Then truly, friend,' said Perceval, 'you've long pursued an unworthy, unseemly and foolish venture! Explain the reason – if you can! Why have you spent all this time here, giving grief to knights who watered their horses?'

'Listen, sir, and I'll tell you if you wish to know. I'd gone in search of adventure and chanced to ride down here to the ford, and beneath this tree I saw an inscription on a marble block in golden letters. I read it through and understood it perfectly: it said in words of Latin that this was the Amorous Ford, the most wonderful in the whole wide world, and that no knight should enter it to water his horse. Listen on, and I'll explain why that was so.

'Some time ago, ten maidens, most fair and comely, stopped beneath this tree and stayed for eight whole years, never stirring from the place; and many great lords came from distant lands to seek their love, and stayed there with them for three months or four or five or six. News of this spread far and wide, and many knights came to test their prowess here. And when they came to the ford and watered their horses, the damsels' knights challenged them, saying that they'd done wrong, and as soon as they left the ford they made them fight – and if they defeated them they killed them on the spot, showing no mercy. But if they crossed the ford without watering their horses they did them no harm or shame at all – no more than if they'd been their brothers! Six years they spent like this, all the while guarding the Amorous Ford. And when the time came for the damsels to leave, they had the inscription I told you carved in the stone. And the inscriber added something else: that if any knight came and was brave and bold enough to guard the ford and could defend it for seven years, he would be accounted the finest knight then living in all the world.

'So that's why I've stayed so long. And now, sir, since you've vanquished me, you will defend the ford if it please you. You must stay here and guard the crossing and so enhance your valour: that's what the inscription says.'

'I've no intention of doing so!' said Perceval. 'Dear man, it wouldn't enhance my worth one jot!'[15]

With that, talking of one thing and another, they went to the tent where they'd spend the night. Two squires came and saw to their horses and helped the knights disarm, and clad them in short mantles of vair-trimmed silk – but that's enough description. Servants brought the water and then they sat at once to eat, for it was time. They were promptly served with an array of fine dishes: fresh meat, birds and venison; and they leisurely ate till satisfied, and the cloths were cleared away. Then they went to rest a little, while two fine beds were prepared for them with hay from the meadow, covered with elegant, handsome quilts and white sheets and pillows worthy of knights. When these beds were ready they took to them without more ado, and slept soundly all night long till day had fully dawned and the sun was shining bright.

Then they rose at once and called for their horses and their arms, and the squires who'd disarmed them brought them straight away. They donned their bright mail shirts and leggings, and fixed their broken shield-straps; then they mounted and exchanged no other words than to commend each other to God, and with that they parted.

The White Knight, I understand, went in search of King Arthur. He found him at Winchester, and told him all about himself and the Amorous Ford, and how the valiant Perceval had defeated him at the pavilion and sent him to yield as his prisoner.

'So do with me what you will, my good lord,' he said to the king.

'Truly, friend,' the king replied, 'you'll find it a good captivity!'

And he bade him disarm, and asked him about Perceval. When he said he was well and in good spirits the king was overjoyed, and excused him his imprisonment and

---

[15] Literally 'the value of a spur'.

declared him free, and retained him as a member of his household. And so he joined the company that was praised and highly renowned throughout the world.

The Fair Unknown

But now we'll return to Perceval, who'd left the tent the same morning and kept riding till he started down a path that wasn't wide, but narrow; and pressing on still further he left the forest and found himself in open country. But out of the woods he felt imprisoned: he'd been riding through nothing but woodland for a fortnight. He carried on all day and saw all manner of creatures: great antlered stags and boars and hinds and other wild beasts and game in profusion; for there was no city or castle within a three days' ride – the land all around was a wilderness of heath and briar. On he rode without stopping, and as night began to fall he found himself back in the forest; this was a comfort to him: he felt more secure in woodland than he did in a fortress behind strong walls. But he didn't know where to take lodging – and he could have done with food and rest. So he dismounted beneath a tall and leafy tree and laid down his lance and shield and unharnessed his horse and let him graze in the twilight on the fresh, green grass. It was a fine, clear night, and Perceval stretched out on the grass; but he ate and drank nothing – for he hadn't the wherewithal, much to his regret. To make matters worse he didn't dare shut his eyes and doze – he needed to keep watch on his horse. So he stayed awake all night till dawn; then he slumbered a little, his head propped on his shield, until day had fully broken and the sun was shining bright. Then he woke and rose, harnessed his horse and mounted; and with shield slung from neck he set off swiftly through the dense forest, fair and thick with green.

Then he looked ahead and saw a most comely damsel, beautiful indeed; she was sitting beneath a tree, her head dressed in a silk wimple. If I were to tell you of her beauty, how elegant her shape, it would take me all day to do her justice; but I'll tell you briefly what I know: her brows glistened bright as if they'd been gilded, her forehead was white and her nose most shapely, her eyes were pretty, shining, amorous, her cheeks a glowing blend of red and snowy white; she had a lovely mouth with perfect teeth as white as ivory, and a dimpled chin and a white throat and a neck more comely than a swan's; she had gorgeous arms and shapely hands with full but slender fingers; and what a graceful body, with small, firm breasts – she was perfectly lovely in every way, and dressed in a most becoming garment of rich silk from Otranto. Perceval rode up at a gallop and greeted her; she was undismayed and replied at once, returning his greeting.

'Dear girl,' said Perceval, 'is no one with you? Are you all alone here in the forest?'

She answered saying she thought her love was around there somewhere, a bold and valiant knight.

'So help me God,' said Perceval, 'he must be a worthy knight indeed to have a sweetheart such as you!'

She was so beautiful in his eyes that he was on the brink of asking for her love; but his attention was seized by something else: a fine figure of a knight approaching, mounted on a destrier and superbly equipped and armed. And the moment he saw Perceval he cried:

'You've done a rash and shameful deed, sir knight, in stopping here! I challenge you – defend yourself!'

And he thrust his sharp steel spurs into his mount, and without another word Perceval sent his own horse charging forward; and with their mighty, sharpened lance-heads they delivered shattering blows to their shields and brought each other down. But they jumped up in an instant and drew their blades of steel, shining, razor-sharp, and rushed to the attack in bitter fury. They exchanged such tremendous blows to their helms that they sent sparks flying and stunned one another; other blows smashed through their shields right down to the boss and hammered at their coats of tight-meshed mail. Both knights now shed crimson blood: they were cut and wounded, sorely battered; in awe of each other, they strove with all their strength to do the other down. I tell you, the knight was enraged beyond measure that Perceval was resisting so long; he drew back for a moment and asked him his name.

'My name will be kept from no man,' Perceval said. 'I'm known as Perceval the Welshman.'

When the knight heard this he was elated! He cast aside his sword of steel and kissed him more than twenty times and said: 'You've beaten me!'

Perceval was bewildered to be greeted with such joy, and: 'Sir,' he said, 'I'd like to know your name right now!'

And the knight said: 'My name is the Fair Unknown: that's what the Britons call me. My father is Sir Gawain, who loves you more than his brother Gaheriët – and he loves him a good deal!'

Now Perceval returned his joyful greeting, and declared *him* the victor! It seems they carried on arguing about who'd won till the damsel came and intervened. She made a great fuss of Perceval! Then the two knights mounted in highest spirits, and the damsel mounted likewise, on a black palfrey as fine as any ridden by count or king, and all three set off together.

Perceval was keen to know about his lord King Arthur, and the knight replied that he'd seen him in fine health just the other day: he was in residence at Cardigan.

'And how's Sir Gawain?'

'Very well, sir, but I didn't see him at court when I left the other day.'

'Where was he, then?'

'He'd gone to roam the land in search of adventures. I spoke to him three days ago: I met him here in the forest. He asked me about you, and bade me send you his greetings if I chanced to find you – and to pass on a request: that you be at the court at Cardoil this coming Christmas. I have to tell you honestly, he swore he wouldn't come to court unless he thought you'd be there to talk to!'

Perceval said he'd go indeed, provided he'd accomplished his quest, for he'd be more pleased to see Gawain than any man alive.

They carried on talking till they arrived at a most well-appointed house, not sited high upon a rock but in the middle of a lake, where a nobleman had sent two men out fishing in a boat. The three ambled on till they reached the bridge and hailed the nobleman; he came to meet them, and called four servants to take care of their horses. Then he gave the knights a joyful greeting and embraced the girl, so fair and comely, and had them both disarmed. Next he summoned a lovely daughter of his, and entrusted the girl, the sweetheart of the Fair Unknown, to her, and she led her to a vaulted chamber with painted panelled walls and ceiling where she saw her beautifully attired. Meanwhile the nobleman had two mantles brought to his guests, rich indeed, lined with squirrel-fur, and then led them upstairs to where dinner was laid ready. They sat down happily and ate all they wished; I shan't describe the various dishes, but it was a spread that would have been worthy of three counts!

Perceval asked their host his name – he seemed a worthy gentleman indeed; and he said:

'Elïadus; my father's name was Elidus – he was lord of all this land. Now you must tell me yours, for by his name one knows the man.'[16]

And Perceval told him his true name at once, and his companion's likewise, and they discussed it as they ate. The good man rejoiced in their company. And when they'd eaten their fill the servants cleared the table without more ado, and the knights rose and called for water and washed; then they went outside and sat on the bridge and looked at the lake and the surrounding land, and declared that no one could be lodged in a fairer or more comfortable place. They stayed there for a good while, talking of many things, before rising and returning to the house. The servants brought them wine and they drank while the beds were made. The Fair Unknown's sweetheart went to sleep in a chamber with Elïadus's daughter, while the knights stayed in the hall with their host, their beds made side by side, for he had no wife – she'd died two years before.

So they lay down and slept till they saw day break and the small birds sang in the greenwood. They didn't linger but dressed at once and donned their helms and hauberks and girded their swords. Elïadus, courteous man that he was, earnestly asked them to eat a little, but he was wasting his breath. Their horses were brought by the servants who'd tended them that night, perfectly ready for riding, and they helped the comely girl to mount. Then she took her leave of the noble's daughter who'd shown her so much honour, and the knights mounted their chargers and set off across the bridge and through the tall, strong gate, and on across the meadow, heavy with dew and filled with sweet-scented flowers of many hues; it was a lovely morning indeed. At the edge of the wood they came upon a spring, and beside it was a cross standing where the road forked and headed in two directions, the most beaten track going straight to London and Canterbury. To the Fair Unknown, for whom he felt much fondness, Perceval said:

'If you don't mind, sir, I'll take this highway, and you take the other.'

He embraced the damsel and commended her to God, and the knight likewise; and at the cross they went their separate ways, but not before they'd exchanged firm embraces and pledged each other their service. And with that the Fair Unknown departed, taking with him his sweetheart so radiant of face.

Perceval Returns to Blancheflor

Perceval rode on alone all day till noon, when he emerged from the forest and found himself in a land well cultivated on every side, abounding with wheat and oats like the fields of the abbeys of Cîteaux or Clairvaux. He wondered where he'd come to: it was a good two years since he'd seen a land so populous and prosperous and plentiful. Then he looked ahead and saw a splendid castle, with walls and battlements all whiter than new-fallen snow. To describe it truthfully, it had five imposing, handsome towers, one in the middle and four around; they were all identical except for their colour: the one in the middle was red, remarkable though it may seem, and the others were white as snow settled on a bough. The sea pounded at the foot of its walls, and on the other side flowed the Humber,[17] filled with salmon and pike and perch and sturgeon. Within its walls was a great township, nobly peopled with knights and serving-men, and merchants and burghers, liberal, courtly and well-bred, who traded in furs of white and grey, in silk and samite and the finest cloth, in Byzantine and English coin, in horses

---

[16] This line echoes the words of Perceval's mother in Chrétien, above, p. 6.
[17] '*Ombres*' or '*Hombres*'.

and vessels of gold and silver and every other commodity: pepper, wax, metal pots, cloves and zedoary* and all manner of rich and precious spices. There was an abundance of all these things, greater than was ever heard of in any castle or city; it all came by sea from Alexandria and Slavonia, from Babylon and Samaria,[18] from great Mecca and Cairo and Antioch and Caesarea, from Acre that stands beside the sea and from the barbarian lands – from everywhere came the vast array of riches in this city. And there were two abbeys in the town, most handsomely housed, and many fine churches, with lofty towers and splendid belfries, richly roofed in lead.

Perceval thrilled at the sight of this glorious castle, and spurred his horse onward till he reached the bridge. It was the most beautiful and perfect in all the world: the story says there was a tower at the entrance, tall and newly built, and beneath it a gate through which the highway ran, and the bridge itself stood on vaulted arches, and was constructed so that it could be raised at night; and it was fortified with barbicans at either end. Beyond the bridge, on the castle side, stood another tower with imposing battlements; and all around the castle were many other new defences and fortifications of wood and stone.

Perceval rode in through the gate, and gazed in delight at the many knights and their serving-men riding through the streets, and all the burghers and maidens and damsels, richly dressed. On through the town he rode, not stopping till he reached the palace, where four pages came running and helped him dismount and took his lance and shield. Then, without more ado, they led him to the splendid hall. A maiden came to meet him: she was of the utmost beauty, and accompanied by twenty knights. They greeted him and welcomed him with all honour, seeing what a fine and noble figure he was; and they seated him on a carpet embroidered with silver flowers, and disarmed him and dressed him in a silken mantle lined with ermine. The maiden gently nudged a girl and whispered to her secretly, so that no one else could hear:

'I've never seen any man in this mortal world who more resembled Perceval, the knight I love so dearly and who risked so much on my behalf, winning back my land for me and defeating my enemies Engygeron and Clamadeus.'[19]

'By God, my lady,' the girl replied, 'I do believe it *is* him!'

At that the maiden took him by the hand and led him aside, and they sat together on a cloth of rich silk patterned with wheels. He wasn't at all inhibited or lost for words: he was quick to ask her name and the name of the castle; the maiden was only too pleased at this – she didn't want him to stay silent.

'Sir,' she said, 'all who live in these parts call this castle Beaurepaire, and my name is Blancheflor. If it please you, sir, tell me yours.'

When Perceval heard this he gave a little sigh and blushed, and looked again at the maiden with the face so bright; he became so entranced that he couldn't utter a word. But then he recovered a little and turned his eyes away discreetly and answered, saying:

'Damsel, I shan't make a fuss about telling you my name, for that would not be courteous. My name, God bless me, is Perceval: that's what people call me. I was born and raised in Wales.'

When the maiden heard this her heart leapt in her breast; she couldn't help herself: she started kissing him more than a hundred times in one go! Then knights and girls

---

[18] '*Aumarie*'.

[19] In Chrétien, above, pp. 19–25. Strictly speaking (if seeking a consistency that clearly did not concern the author of this continuation or the scribe-redactors), the girl cannot know that his name was Perceval, as he didn't discover it himself till later, p. 32.

and squires came to see this knight beside their damsel; they stared at him, one and all, and the maiden told them:

'Sirs, this is Perceval, the good and loyal knight who rescued my land and won back my domain when Clamadeus was waging war on me: you're to consider him your lord.'

Then joy erupted in the palace: you've never heard the like! The news spread throughout the castle – ladies and maids came running and the whole town rang with joy; more than thirty thousand flocked to rejoice at the coming of Perceval. If I described the scale of the celebrations you wouldn't believe a word! The bells pealed in all the churches, censers burned throughout the streets, gold-embroidered silk festooned the windows: the whole place was a riot of decoration; and the festivities ran on all day and didn't end till far into the night, for the moon was shining bright, serene. Then the hall began to empty, as the townsfolk and merchants, women, boys and little children – those who didn't belong at court and had no business there – departed. But still it was filled with a brilliant light: there were candles burning everywhere in countless numbers.

Now Perceval was lord indeed: now he had all he desired; now his heart had no cause for grief – now it was filled with happiness and joy; now he felt no sorrow at all, for now he beheld his fair beloved, whiter than a flower on a sapling's branch; now he had the one who'd made him muse on the three drops of blood in the frozen snow.[20]

They called for the water, and the ladies and damsels and girls washed first and then the knights. The cloths and all things necessary were laid on the tables, in such a rich display as no man could describe in speech, no clerk in writing. So they sat down to feast, ladies, maidens, knights, in the greatest joy and merriment. And Perceval sat beside Blancheflor, whose cheeks were a finer hue than the new-born rose. There were so many dishes that it would take all day to list them! And Perceval was satisfied, for he was looking at one he'd never thought he'd see again in all his life. He thought it was amazing luck and chance that had led him to a place he'd never hoped to find.

They all ate at leisure, and then the cloths were cleared, and the gracious maiden had Perceval's bed made in a beautiful, panelled chamber. In the hall there was a riot of music ringing, a wonder to hear, and the merriment continued until midnight; then everyone at last departed, retiring to their lodgings in the town, leaving the great hall empty except for the household.

The servants led Perceval to lie in a rich and gorgeous bed. Blancheflor, as happy as could be, took to her bed in an adjoining chamber. The candles that had burned in every room, lighting the whole palace, were removed. And all those who'd been serving that night retired to their beds and fell asleep, being very tired and weary.

But though others might sleep, Perceval was wide awake, still marvelling at having found his love. Nor had Blancheflor's thoughts drifted: she rose at once and donned an ermine gown and slipped from her chamber; and all alone, with no chambermaid, she came to Perceval's bed; and drawing back the coverlet she lay down beside her love. And she said to him:

'Don't think it wicked or foolish that I've come here for your love: I've longed for you so much! And I promise you, I'd never take a husband if it meant being untrue to you.'

Perceval took her in his arms, hungry for the solace of her embrace: he had loved her for so long; he smothered her with kisses – a hundred in a row without a pause. I don't wish to reveal the rest of what followed; but if Perceval didn't fail to go further, Blancheflor

[20] In Chrétien, above, p. 37.

didn't object: gracious-hearted soul that she was, she wouldn't resist any desire of his. And so they took their pleasure; they didn't sleep much that night.

And they spoke of many things, plying each other with questions. Perceval asked his beloved: 'Do tell me, lady: when was this castle rebuilt? The walls look sparkling new, and the city and surrounding land seem filled with people.'

'Let me tell you, sir,' she said. 'The castle was in a terrible state after Engygeron had besieged it, as you know, for it was you who rescued it – along with me and all my land. But I couldn't at that time marry you: it wasn't yet your wish; so I remained alone, forlorn, while you went off to other lands – I don't know where – in search of adventures to enhance your honour. I didn't know whom to trust – I was very fearful after all I'd suffered. I was distraught: my troubled mind knew no rest; I truly yearned to be dead and buried, soul and body parted! My heart was in torment! But then those imprisoned by Engygeron were released and came back here, and when they heard the news the people of these parts who'd fled from the war returned to the city; it was a great relief and comfort to me, troubled as I was. And I took counsel with the worthiest, and at their advice I commissioned workmen and masons and carpenters to repair the walls and build new towers. So now you know! And in the morning, without more delay, you'll marry me and the land will be yours, and you'll keep it in peace, untroubled by war. There are a thousand knights in this domain, who'll all accept you as their lord.'

'Truly, my love,' said Perceval, 'I can't do that: I've undertaken a mission that I wouldn't give up for all the wealth of Frisia. But if God grants that I return, I'll come straight back to you.'

'Sir,' said Blancheflor, 'I don't know what'll come of this – or become of me! – but, no matter what anyone says to him, it isn't right for such a worthy man as you to abandon what he's vowed to do – especially to his sweetheart. I well remember that when you left me the other year you told me you'd go and find your mother, and once you'd seen her you'd return without delay. So I've been waiting for you ever since – however long that is – but I'll wait again, however painful it may be, for I'd rather suffer agony and have my heart made dark and sad than go against your will. I'll do exactly as you wish, since I can't keep you here by force or pleading! And even if I could it would be very wrong of me to do so and anger you, for a damsel should do nothing to displease and vex her love. If she's come to love him with a noble love that's true and sure, she should bear the pain that wrings her heart.'

So saying, she took him in a tight embrace and kissed him tenderly; then, with a sorrowful heart, she said: 'So that's that – you'll go. But stay here for just two days, and then return as soon as you wish: my heart will be waiting for you!'

Perceval agreed to this – but it pained him to delay: he was so eager to be on his way.

Then day began to break, and Blancheflor rose and kissed her love, grieving bitterly over what had been said – she so much wished him not to go – but she made no outward sign of it. She returned to her bed and lay straight down, and despite her troubled thoughts she fell asleep, very tired after being awake all night. And Perceval, too, fell fast asleep.

The weather was beautiful and calm, and the bright sun was streaming through the windows, filling the handsome hall with light. The bells rang promptly, summoning everyone to mass. Then you'd have seen knights and their servants hurrying to the palace – and what a splendid, elegant palace it was: there was none finer or better sited anywhere as far as Beauvais. The commotion woke Perceval; and Blancheflor, already up and dressed, sent a maid to her beloved with a gown of gold-embroidered silk, the richest any man ever saw. The girl came straight to his bed and presented it to him; he was delighted with it, and rose at once and donned the gown, superbly cut and sewn and embroidered, and then hurried from his chamber and into the great hall. Knights and squires and other folk were coming from all directions, and they hailed him, honouring him highly as their liege lord, and he returned joyful greetings to them all.

Then the fair Blancheflor appeared from her chamber, clad in indigo samite adorned with golden flowers and silver stars: a gown more elegant, beautiful or rich was never seen; and of the same cloth was her mantle, richly lined with ermine: no man of woman born ever set eyes on a lovelier damsel. Perceval came to meet her, and greeted her, and she him; then they went together to her chapel to hear mass. And without a word of a lie, all who saw them were stunned and said you could search every land and sea and never find such a handsome couple. They looked so fair indeed that people went more to see them than they did to hear the mass of the Holy Spirit.

When mass was over they made their way back to the hall, where the servants had the food all ready. The squires brought the water in basins of silver inlaid with enamel, and on every side the ladies and damsels and girls, so many of them so very fair, washed and then sat down at once, as did the knights in great numbers – fully five hundred, so we find recorded; but as for the dishes I shan't list them all, for you may be sure they had all they could ever wish. And when they'd eaten with great delight, they shared an array of nutmegs instead of fruit, and cloves and zedoary;* then they drank and the tables were cleared. Then merry-making started such as no one could describe: the festivities and gaiety lasted all day long without a break. There wasn't a word of sadness, of poverty or of growing old, only of joy and pleasure. And people who most commit themselves to being happy, and don't refrain from merriment, tend to find it's for the best.

Perceval finally stayed there for three days, for the love-sick Blancheflor begged him earnestly. On the fourth day she rose very early, distraught that he meant to leave; she broke down in tears before him, begging him most tenderly to delay his journey for one more day for her sake. But Perceval refused, saying he couldn't tarry longer. He called for his arms and armed at once, and then for his horse, which had been well groomed and richly fitted with breast-strap, reins and saddle, all brand-new. And that was that; he kissed his beloved, who was in agonies of grief and sorrow: her eyes filled with tears and her heart with sighs, and she stood there in silence, not saying a word. Perceval spoke to her most tenderly, saying:

'In God's name, my love, don't be so upset and sad at heart: by Saint Giles of Provence,[21] I shall return to you, my dear one, as soon as ever I can!'

Blancheflor said not a word in reply: her head and her heart were so gripped by grief that she wouldn't have spoken at any price, not if she'd been given a hundred thousand marks of purest silver.

The hall was filled with ladies, knights, burghers, townsfolk – more than four thousand in all – flocking there on hearing the news that gave them little pleasure. The most eminent spent a long while with Perceval, earnestly begging him to marry their lady, so fair and rich and prudent; he told them that he couldn't yet, but that they shouldn't be upset, for he'd return from his mission as soon as he could and then he wouldn't leave the lady or the land as long as he lived.

---

[21] A Greek hermit, Giles's legend and cult were centred in Provence, where the abbey supposedly founded by him – at Saint-Gilles-du-Gard – became an important object of pilgrimage, especially on the route to Compostela.

That was the end of their debate, and Perceval mounted his charger. He was handed a red quartered shield, newly made and painted, and he took it and hung it at his neck at once, and then took a lance of apple wood with a great, sharp head of steel; then he took his leave without more ado, commending them all to God, and rode from the castle and was on his way.

Blancheflor was left there, downcast, desolate, and all who were with her grieved bitterly for Perceval: knights, burghers, servants, ladies, girls and children, all were in tears, terribly distressed to see him go. To the one who suffered on the cross to set His people free from Hell, to the almighty king of all, they commended him a hundred thousand times.

The Handsome Knight and the Ugly Damsel

But I'll leave them now and return to Perceval, who was riding swiftly on. He swore whole-heartedly, by God and His mother and all the saints, that as long as he lived he wouldn't lodge in any one place for more than a night until he'd found the stag's head and the dog. And he vowed, too, that as long as there was breath in his body he wouldn't stop searching through forest and over land and sea until he'd learned the whole truth about the grail, and why the stout-headed lance bled and exactly what it was. He wanted to find out all about it from the good, rich Fisher King, who had honoured him so highly.

Pondering on all this he rode on without stopping till he passed into the forest; he felt more secure here – the forest was his fortress. He headed towards a mountain that was visible from a long way off; the path to it was wide, well-beaten, for it was the only path for a league around: the land all about was a forbidding, impassable wilderness of thorns. So he had no choice but to cross the mountain, which was very high and steep. Perceval struggled on till he reached the top; then he looked about and saw no castle, city, tower, town or fortress: nothing but forest, green and thick with leaves, the fairest in this world.

When he reached the foot again he set out along a path where he found many a handsome pine and many more trees heavy with fruit, and kept riding through the night, delighting in the forest. Then he looked ahead and saw a lady coming – or perhaps she was a damsel, I don't know; she was clad in a new silk gown cut in Cornish fashion, but I promise you she was the ugliest creature that man's eyes ever beheld. I tell you in all honesty, her hair was blacker than nightshade berry; she had a low forehead and flapping ears, bristling eyebrows joined together, and ink-black eyes buried deep in her head; her turned-up, snub nose was small enough, but the nostrils in it were vast and gaping, and her mouth, I swear, was a yawning maw with great, fat lips and big, yellow, ugly teeth and enormous gums; and she had a drooping chin and clumps of moustache. In every respect she was hideous – and thoroughly deformed, too: hunchbacked and twisted, with a neck blacker than iron; she looked like a demon from Hell. But, though loosely and lightly clad, she was dressed like a fairy, and mounted on a handsome palfrey, beautifully groomed, that carried her most agreeably. And behind her was a knight riding a big, white-stockinged horse; he was superbly armed and tall, fine, impressive, as handsome a figure in body and limb as was ever seen.

Perceval rode up briskly and greeted the damsel, and seeing her at close quarters was convinced she was a demon or a ghastly monster. He sat stock still, staring at her in wonder; she was mounted with great poise with one leg resting on the palfrey's neck.

Perceval couldn't help smiling, seeing the knight escorting such a hideous demon – for she really was foul, believe me! And the knight called out:

'By God, sir knight, you've a nerve, laughing for no reason!'

'Oh, I've reason enough!'

'What is it, then? You can't get away with mocking us so!'

'Don't be like that, friend! There's plenty to laugh at!'

At this the knight was furious and cried: 'Defend yourself – I challenge you!'

'If you insist!' said Perceval.

They set their shields in place before their breasts, levelled their ashwood lances and drove their horses forward to a charge. They exchanged mighty blows on the bosses of their shields, and brought each other crashing to the ground. But they leapt to their feet and drew their furbished swords, and aimed fearsome blows with their naked blades at their tight-meshed coats of mail. They defended themselves with great skill with their shields: they were able fighters and knew how to strike and parry blows. They assailed each other time and again without gaining a yard of ground, truly, for they were both knights of great valour. Then the knight struck Perceval on the helm with his sword of tempered steel; he'd have wounded him most terribly had the blade not shattered on the silver rim and flown to the ground. The knight was horrified. He stepped up to Perceval and humbly begged for mercy, saying:

'I yield to you, good sir. I admit defeat. It's pointless fighting on, when you've a sword and I have none.'

Then Perceval cast his sword aside and said: 'There! My sword's gone! Let's fight on with our fists as best we can!'

'I can't see there's any sense in giving up your sword! But you're a worthy and courteous knight indeed. And let me tell you, I don't fear you in the least!'

'I'm sure you don't,' said Perceval.

That was all they said; they attacked each other with their bare hands, tearing the laces of their helms and knocking them from their heads and beating each other in the face and teeth until they were covered in blood. They pounded and grappled and wrestled on till they both were short of breath. But the one who could endure more pain than any man in Christendom could see and feel that his foe was losing strength; he didn't want to pause and give him time to recover breath, no, he kept piling on the pressure till he begged for mercy in God's name, to do him no more harm and to spare his life, for he was helpless with exhaustion, and since he'd defeated him in combat it wouldn't enhance his honour to kill him needlessly – indeed it would be a great wrong. And Perceval replied:

'Have no fear: I've no desire to kill you, sir. But you must go at once to my lord King Arthur and surrender as his prisoner, or I'll never have mercy on you.'

'I'll go there gladly,' said the knight, 'and willingly.'

And he duly gave his word. Then he asked his name, and he told him: 'My name is Perceval, sir. And tell me yours – don't keep it from me.'

He'd no wish to refuse and said: 'I shan't hide it. I'm the son of the count of Galvoie, and I'm known as the Fair Bad Knight.'

'By God,' said Perceval, 'your name's half true and half false! You're not a fair *bad* knight at all, but fair and *good*! And tell me your sweetheart's name, and why you're with her.'

'I'll tell you, sir, and without a lie. I love her so much, with all my heart, that I couldn't live without her for a single hour. So help me God, in my eyes she's more beautiful than any lady or maiden in the living world – and so she is, I do declare! That's why I'm so jealous! I tell you, I don't trust any man with her! He could be my own brother – no, my father! – and still I wouldn't! I love and cherish her so much that I take her with me everywhere – though I have to ask her kindly. I won't deny it: the more I see her the more she pleases and delights my heart. My loving name for her is Rosete.'

'God take me to His side in Paradise,' said Perceval, 'it seems you really love her!'

'Too right I do!' said the knight. 'I love her more than all the riches in the world!'

'It would be a sin to part you from her.'

'Oh, God have mercy! I'd rather die than be forced to leave her! Not only is she endowed with beauty but with kindness, wit and spirit and courtesy.'

Not for all the wealth that God created could Perceval help but laugh. 'Well, that's enough,' he said. 'There's plenty of daylight left – you go your way and I'll go mine. But one thing I pray you: tell my good lord the king – who'll receive you with much honour – all about the love and passion between your sweetheart and yourself: keep nothing back.'

And the knight swore by all the apostles of Rome that there was no prince in all the world to whom he'd more gladly tell the truth. 'And I'd have no qualms about taking her to the court of an emperor – you needn't think otherwise!'

'My good, dear sir,' said Perceval, 'I meant no offence and take none.'

And with that they parted without another word.

The Fair Bad Knight kept riding through forests and over plains, through valleys and over mountains, never stopping, morning or night, till finally, after much toil and trouble, he and his beloved arrived at Cardigan. He'd be able to tell the king his news at once, for the king was in residence there. And in the chambers beside the hall were Kay and Lucan the butler, and Sagremor and Bedivere, Guerrehés and Sir Yvain, Gaheriët and Agravain the proud. Mordred, notably handsome and clever, he was there, too. They were all at the windows looking out towards the forest, along with nearly a hundred more. Sagremor was the first to spot the knight and the girl.

'Kay,' he said, 'yonder knight escorting that striking girl: he's about to have news for us, I'd say – he'll be coming to court to submit as a prisoner.'

'No doubt,' said his companions, 'but why's he bothering to bring *her*? What pleasure or honour can she bring him?'

'By the Saviour, sirs,' said Kay, 'you're quite wrong! She may seem beautiful to his eyes – if she didn't he wouldn't keep her with him. And maybe she's bewitched him! She looks more like a foul demon than a woman – so hideous and black!'

'How right you are!' the others said.

Having seen the girl, Kay ran to the queen's chambers and said: 'Come, lady! It's no good being here: you should be in the hall, making merry with your knights – there are three hundred of them, fine knights indeed, and they're all captivated by the beauty of a girl: they say there's none more glorious from here to Lombardy! What more can I say? Come and see!'

'Is she really so great a beauty?' said the queen.

'By the Holy Spirit, lady, I'll not say another word until you see her for yourself. Come this minute!'

So the queen rose and went straight to the great flagged hall. Knights came flocking to her side, and the king rose and seated her beside him. Then into the hall came the knight on horseback, and the girl with him; but before he uttered a word he dismounted and helped her down, the girl he so loved and adored. Then he came before the king and greeted him in the name of Perceval the Welshman, saying:

'My good lord king, Perceval, who feels nothing but love for you, sends me to you a prisoner – along with my beloved, so fair of face.'

When they heard him describe her face as fair, none of the knights could help but laugh, and the queen laughed with them; and Kay couldn't contain himself: cruel and full of bile as he was, he could have been offered a thousand silver marks but he would still have said to the knight:

'In the name of God, dear sir, do tell me: are there any more like her in your land? If I thought I'd find one I'd go and look! I can see what a strapping young fellow you are: did you take her by force? Did you have her for her beauty? You're not wrong there – good move!'

The king heard this and was furious; scarlet with rage he said, in the hearing of all: 'One thing's for sure, Kay: you'll never grow up! Curse the fruit that doesn't mature and the man who's committed to spiteful talk, who delights in it so that he can't resist and wants to mock the whole world with his foolish tongue! It's you I mean! Your tongue's deprived me of many a knight: it's always getting the better of you – always blurting out clever, cutting quips. You're insatiable, you never tire of it – you're so full of malice!'

That's how the king berated Kay. Then he turned his back on him and listened to the knight who told him the whole truth, regardless of his own honour or shame: how Perceval had vanquished him, and his name and the name of his beloved: he kept nothing back. The king listened with delight; then he summoned three squires and bade them disarm the knight, and called for a fur-lined mantle in which they duly dressed him. He declared him entirely free if he became thenceforth a member of his household, and the Fair Bad Knight agreed, so he stayed at court as long as he pleased.

And so did his sweetheart, whom he loved like his own life. And she came to be so beautiful, truly, that there was no damsel to compare with her in all the land. Perhaps – I don't know – she was enchanted.

Perceval Returns to his Sister

But I must leave them now; I want to return to Perceval. He rode a very long way that day, pressing on till nightfall. But he couldn't find any house to stay at and had to lodge in the forest – he had nothing to eat that night: it was very hard. His horse grazed on the grass around him, heavy with dew, till morning came and the sun began to shine. Then Perceval mounted without delay and rode on till nearly terce.

He passed into the Waste Forest where he'd been many times before, but he hardly recognised the place at all, it was so long since he'd been there. But then he looked ahead and saw a beautiful tree, tall and spreading wide; he held his horse still and pondered a moment.

'God!' he said. 'Where's this I've come to? I do believe I'm near my mother's house! But I don't suppose I've a brother or sister here, or anyone else who's close to me. It was by this tree that I met the knight who sent me on my way to King Arthur, who then granted me the red armour.[22] By God, I've no idea how I got here! There's nothing I'd like more than to discover the truth about my mother – God have mercy on her soul.'

---

[22] i.e. at the beginning of Chrétien's romance.

Then he wept most tenderly, seized by pity for his mother – it came quite naturally.

Off through the forest he rode swiftly on his charger, and turned along a path he'd learned so long ago, until he came to open ground and saw the house that had been his mother's.

'God, my aid, dear Father,' he said, 'I see what I've so longed for!'

So saying, he rode on and reached the bridge. A boy had seen him and came rushing from the house and greeted him at once; but Perceval didn't want to dismount: he rode straight on into the house where he found a good number of servants, looking bright and smart and well dressed.

'Welcome, sir!' they said to him, and received him with all honour. He dismounted then, and they disarmed him and brought him a mantle; but they didn't look at him closely or recognise him at all by face or manner: nobody remembered him.

Just then there appeared from a chamber a most beautiful girl, as white as a new lily and richly dressed. She came straight to Perceval and greeted him most nobly in the name of God the majestic king, and Perceval returned her greeting. He knew full well that she was his sister, but didn't want to let his feelings known so soon: first he wanted to ask and learn how long ago his mother had died, and if he still had sisters or brothers or uncles, or any other relatives or friends.

They sat together on a carpet beautifully woven with flora and fauna. The damsel bade a servant make haste with dinner; then she asked Perceval:

'Where did you sleep last night, sir?'

'Where I had little comfort or pleasure,' he said. 'In the forest.'

At this her tears began to flow. Perceval saw her sigh and said: 'What's the matter, dear girl?'

'Sir,' she replied, 'you remind me of a brother of mine. I haven't seen him since I was little, and I don't know if he's alive or dead, but in him lies all my comfort and I dearly hope to see him again. There's nothing more I can tell you about him, but whenever I see any knight my heart can't help being moved to tears.'

'Truly, my dear,' said Perceval, 'no one should be surprised at that. But tell me: do you have any sisters or brothers besides him?'

'That I know for sure, good sir. I've no other brother or sister, and it pains my heart, for I'm all alone in this wood. It's ten years and four months since my brother rode off into this great forest in search of sport, carrying three javelins that he always used to throw. It was early one morning, and he saw five knights, fully armed and superbly armoured, coming along his path. Child that he was, he asked them who had equipped them so, and they said it was King Arthur. I don't know if they said anything more, but when he came home no plea from our mother or anyone else was of any use: regardless of the grief and pain it caused he set off for the king's court. I don't know how he fared: I've heard nothing of him since. But when she saw him go from here my mother collapsed in a swoon; and she passed away and died of grief. That was a long time ago. An uncle of mine – a hermit who lives in the woods nearby – came and took her body to his hermitage. Since then I've lived here in this house, with good reason to feel heavy-hearted – which I do, and often. That's how it is – I've told you everything.'

Then Perceval wept for pity; she looked and saw him turning pale, and the tears streaming down his face, and said to him: 'Truly, sir, I'd be very glad to know your name if you'll tell me.'

'I can't keep it from you,' he replied, 'dear sister.'

But if his life had depended on it he couldn't bring himself to speak; all he could do was give a deep sigh. But then, after a long pause, he answered.

'Sister,' he said, 'I was baptised with the name of Perceval.'

When she heard him say his name she was so amazed, so taken aback, that if she'd been given all of Frisia she couldn't have uttered a word. Perceval took her in his arms and said he was her brother: it was on his account that their mother had died; and when she heard these words she kissed him, and all her troubles were forgotten as they rejoiced in their reunion. Just then the servants came to set up the table, and were shocked to see their lady kissing this stranger! They thought it shameful! But when she told them it was Perceval her brother, the whole household raised their hands in thanks to God: such an outpouring of joy was never seen.

Water was brought in two basins; then they sat down and the table was set. What more need I say? They had food in abundance – whatever their hearts desired, for the house was very well stocked – and drank a good deal of fine, strong wine, matured in the cask. And as they ate they spoke of many things and plied each other with questions. The girl couldn't stop gazing at her dear brother, and kissing and embracing him.

After a leisurely, unhurried meal they bade the servants clear the tables; then they rose and went together to take their ease in a garden at the foot of the bridge, for it was still only mid-afternoon.[23] Perceval told his sister he wanted to go to the hermitage and speak to his uncle – he hadn't seen him since his youth – and assume some penance for his sins: it was only right that he should; and he would go and see the tomb where his mother was buried, who'd lost her life solely because of him.

'That would be a good deed,' she replied. 'And take me with you – it'll be better to have some company, and I'll show you the best way through the forest.'

'I'll gladly take you, by God,' he said, 'so let's not dally.'

They had their horses saddled at once and led to the foot of the bridge, and the maiden – who in beauty resembled a fairy more than any other being – mounted; and Perceval armed from head to foot and laced his helmet on his head, slung his shield around his neck and climbed into the saddle, where he looked a worthy, valiant knight indeed. Then he set off, lance in hand, following his sister, who'd gone a little way ahead. On they rode together into the great forest, and followed the straightest possible path to the house of the good hermit.

But even though they were in their own land it seems they weren't free and clear of trouble: Perceval looked ahead, and in the distance, riding down a slope, he saw a mighty knight on a big dappled destrier, incredibly swift and strong. Perceval ambled on, his sister beside him, and the knight spotted him from far off, riding along the path, and thrust in his spurs and came charging towards him. His only words were the wild cry:

'I challenge you for the girl! She's beautiful – I want her!'

'Truly, sir,' Perceval called in answer, 'you might care to speak more courteously: she's my sister, and I'd never let anyone abduct her.'

'No,' said the knight, 'no one who was too afraid of you to take her! But I'm having both your sister and your horse! Unless you've the courage to defend her, leave her with me and be on your way – I'll let you go!'

Perceval felt nothing but rage. He drew rein and stopped and said to the knight in the utmost fury: 'I challenge you, sir knight, for the girl and the horse: I love her more

---

[23] Literally 'around none' – the ninth canonical hour, about 3 p.m.

than you think! I'm not so easily brow-beaten that I'll let you take her just because of your wild words!'

The knight was incensed. They drew their fine steeds back to gain ground for a stronger charge; then they let them go and drove in their spurs, their hearts as fierce as a lion or a cornered boar. The knight struck Perceval high on the shield with such force that he shattered his lance right down to his fist; but Perceval didn't fall, and he gave the knight such a mighty blow that he drove his lance clean through his body, so that fully two feet burst out behind. The knight was pitched dead from his charger as it galloped on. Perceval pulled the lance from the body; its head was covered in blood. He left the knight lying there on the ground and rode away. He gave the knight's horse to his sister to lead by the bridle; then they set off at a brisker pace than before, for the day was drawing to a close.

On they rode till they came to the hermitage deep in the woods. The moon was shining, bright and beautiful. Perceval called at the wicket-gate – the house was enclosed for fear of wild beasts. The good hermit, the holy man, who was devout indeed and led a most saintly life, was in his chapel in prayer to God, seeking His mercy; but the moment he heard their call he rose – he had no servant, page or porter, or any other company but God – and came straight to the gate and opened it. Perceval greeted him most courteously, as did his sister. The hermit saw that they needed lodging, but didn't recognise them. He made a sign to indicate that they should enter, that they'd be given shelter; but not for all the gold in the world would he say a word to them now that the sun was down and night had fallen. The wise and worthy Perceval dismounted, and took hold of his cherished sister and helped her from her palfrey. He left the horses to graze for the night in the grassy enclosure, and the hermit brought them a mixture of oats and barley. Then, it seems, he gestured to Perceval and his sister to ask them if they wished to eat, but they said they weren't hungry. So he left them and returned to his chapel – a beautiful place it was – and prayed for a long while to God.

Perceval slept on the grass outside, his sister beside him, until he saw day break next morning and the sun was bright and high. Then he awoke and went to the chapel, where his uncle was already dressed and ready to say mass. Perceval gave heartfelt sighs for the misdeeds and sins with which he was stained, and said his Paternoster, the only prayer he knew, long or short: his mother had taught it to him as best she could, with a good and willing heart, exceptionally worthy woman that she was.

The good hermit, filled with the Holy Spirit, said and sang the mass; Perceval listened attentively – and saw that he was assisted by an angel sent from Heaven by God. When the service was over the hermit didn't stay but left the chapel; and as soon as he saw the girl he realised she was his niece – but he didn't know it was Perceval: he hadn't seen him for a long while, so didn't recognise him. He greeted them both and said:

'What brings you here, niece?'

'Sir,' she replied, 'I'm so happy! God has sent me help by returning my brother to me: I thought I'd lost him! See, he's here: it's Perceval, who caused my mother such distress, as you know, dear uncle.'

The hermit gave a deep sigh; then he seated Perceval beside him and said: 'My good, dear man, your father and I were brothers. And your mother lies here: I had her brought here and buried before the altar.'

Then he rose and led them to his lovely chapel, and showed Perceval the tomb, draped in silk and yielding a fragrance of indescribable sweetness. Perceval began to weep as he remembered his mother. Then his uncle took him by the hand and sat him at his side and began to give him instruction. He gently urged him to tell him about his life in all honesty, and Perceval told him everything, omitting nothing: how he'd been in search of adventures and found many, tough and formidable; he told him of all he'd done since the king had dubbed him and granted him the red arms, and the worthy man was amazed. And amid much sighing he repeated the things he'd told him before, in every detail: how he'd gone and taken lodging at the house of the most worthy Fisher King, where the lance was kept along with the grail, so fine and beautiful, but had asked no questions and had left without learning anything about them. Then he told him of the girl and the game of chess, and the knight in the tomb, and the one who'd carried off the stag's head and the dog, and how he'd chased him through the great, thick forest without finding any trace of him. And he told him about the lion, in fine detail: how he'd killed it beneath the tree and sent the knight to King Arthur along with his fair and comely sweetheart. He told him all he'd done and how he'd fared, just as you've heard it in this book; he told him everything without a word of falsehood: he wouldn't have lied for a thousand marks of gold, not for all the treasure of Alexander the Greek or Porus, king of India.

Then the hermit asked him: 'Do you always travel with two destriers, nephew?'

'No indeed!' he said. 'Just one, that's enough for me! But yesterday, as night was falling, I met a knight out there in the great, thick forest who abused me most terribly and struck me so hard he broke his lance on my shield. I gave him such a mighty blow that my lance went fully two feet through his body! I left him dead on the ground and brought his horse back here. If you'd like to keep him, take him – he's right outside. He's keen and fast, but as meek as a lamb, and gives a smoother ride than any ship!'

'I've no use for him,' the hermit said. 'And you should be very unhappy about killing men like that.'

And that saintly, worthy, devout hermit begged him earnestly to be mindful of his soul, and of the One who made and will unmake us all. Perceval sighed deeply from the heart and said:

'God help me, sir, if only I had an explanation for the lance with the bleeding head, and for the grail, and the sword which can be repaired by one knight alone,[24] though I can't tell you who he is, or is destined to be: I haven't yet learned that much. But I'll find out in time; and when I know the truth, there's nothing you could say, dear uncle, that I wouldn't strive with all my heart to do to attain Paradise above: I give you my solemn word. But it must be so: I've vowed to see this through, and can't abandon it.'

'I don't want to say any more about it,' said the hermit. 'Not for now.'

With that they left the chapel and went to the hermit's little house and sat down, all three together. The good hermit brought them food – and it won't take me long to tell you all they ate: that morning the holy man, who loved them dearly, gave them white bread and a bunch of grapes. They'd been brought by the angel at Our Lord's behest, as they were each day, the hermit being such a worthy man that he lived solely by the glory of God. He set clear water before them and they drank their fill. It was the only thing ever drunk by the holy hermit, who was free of all vices, endowed with great

---

[24] Strictly speaking, Perceval doesn't yet know about the Broken Sword: it was introduced in the First Continuation when Gawain visited the Fisher King (above, p. 109). But it has now become a central element in the romance.

goodness and cleansed of the sins for which he often asked God's pardon; he never had wine, spiced or otherwise, or any other drink in his house, you may be sure.

When they'd eaten they rose, and Perceval said they should be on their way, for they'd a distance to travel before they'd be home. But before they set off the hermit gave them a lengthy sermon and much good instruction: about God and His Passion and Resurrection, and how He descended to Hell and broke open the gates through His divine power and set free all who'd been imprisoned, dragged there by the Devil with his determined might, ever eager as he is to ensnare us and bring us to our doom.

'Nephew,' he said, 'you must heed what I'm about to say: if you don't already know it you must learn it and believe it like a Christian. Honour and good may come of it: honour in this mortal world and good in the other, the spiritual, with the One who has all rewards and graces in His power. Anyone who fails to serve and honour Him is bound sooner or later to suffer deep disgrace before he meets his end. But God is merciful, and when He sees a man committed to evil and wicked deeds, He won't destroy him there and then, but allows him time to reflect and ponder in his conscience on the great wrongs that he's done; and when he's fully considered, and sheds tears from his eyes and sighs from his heart, and prays to the One who is king and lord to grant mercy for the wrongs he's done in this world, then God, being full of compassion, sees the sinner's heart, and if he's truly repentant He freely forgives him. But if he won't repent or expiate his sins, and continues to do the wicked things that bring him pleasure – but little profit! – Death will take him unawares and he'll lose his body and lose his soul. Lose them? Yes indeed! No one, however devout, however saintly, would dare ask God to give that man rest in Paradise – and such prayers would not be heard. No, he goes straight to stinking Hell, where he suffers such torment as no man can describe and no heart can conceive. Heed my words, dear nephew.'

'I do indeed, sir,' Perceval replied, 'and believe them utterly. And if it please God I shall be in Heaven yet, in His household with His glorious company.'

'God grant that it be so,' the hermit said, 'as my heart would wish.'

Then they stayed at the hermitage no longer; they took their leave and departed, riding swiftly away.

They took a path through the forest that brought them straight to their fortress home. By this time night was very near. The servants came running to help the maiden from her mount and take care of the horses. Then they entered the house and she called for food to be brought at once, while Perceval quickly disarmed; and the tables were promptly set and servants brought the water, and Perceval and his sister washed and sat down without another word. They had barbel, salmon, perch and pike in plenty, for they ate no meat that night. And when they'd eaten with great pleasure a bed was prepared for Perceval, a fine, deep bed of fresh-cut straw, with blankets and quilt of a precious cloth from Constantinople, the richest ever seen, and fine linen sheets and pillows, and coverlets of costly ermine; they decked the bed luxuriously and in no time at all. Then they returned to Perceval and removed his shoes and saw him to bed; he was soon asleep, for he was very tired. And his sister, who loved him deeply, retired to her chamber and prepared for bed without saying or doing anything more. And so they slept all night long.

At the crack of dawn, as soon as the sun rose, shedding its light over all the world, the good knight Perceval rose at once. A good many of the household came to serve him, needless to say; and although the fair-faced damsel rose early likewise and went straight to him, expecting to find him still in bed, he'd already been up a fair while, his chausses* were on and his knee-pieces laced and he was about to don his hauberk. She was dismayed by the sight and rushed to him and took him in her arms, saying:

'What are you doing, dear brother? I'm in despair: I don't know what I'll do if you leave me! There's nothing else for it: I'll die of grief unless you take me with you! If you don't, if you leave me here bereft, my days are numbered! I've been left here in this wood an orphan, as you see; are you going to leave me so, all alone, abandoned? You're my brother: it would be wicked of you!'

'Have no fear, dear sister, I'll return to you very soon. But I can't delay the mission I've undertaken. Be good now, and behave nobly, and stop your grieving – it'll do no good: it won't make me stay.'

What's the point of lengthening their words and conversation? He left his sister, distraught though she was to see him go – as were the rest of her household: they all wept together, inconsolably. He rode off without stopping, spurring all the way, until he plunged into the great forest.

The Castle of the Maidens

He didn't stop riding all day long till evening, but didn't see a castle, town or house of any knight where he could go for lodging: he had to sleep in the forest till dawn next morning when he saw the sun shine bright. Then he remounted his destrier and set off through the forest once more; but though he kept up a steady pace, in all that day he didn't find a single man or knight, any house or any living thing, and again he had to spend the night in the forest. What bothered him most was finding nothing to eat – that was the worst of all.

On the third day he made another long ride; and before mid-afternoon he came to a great river. He followed a cart track upstream, further than the range of a crossbow shot; but the river was deep and wide, and he couldn't see any way to cross. Then he looked into the distance and thought he could see a little bridge, but he wasn't sure. So he carried on to the top of a rocky height, and as he looked down to the plain below he saw the fairest meadowland and open country he'd ever seen in all his life. And then he caught sight of a splendid castle: all its walls and battlements were of coloured marble, red and yellow, and it had a handsome, lofty tower as perfect as a picture, and a great, imposing hall, as fine as any from there to Carthage. It was a well-appointed castle indeed. Perceval didn't dally, but spurred his horse straight on and over the bridge, and rode in through the mighty gate. And the moment he was inside, the gate shut fast behind him, all by itself; Perceval was baffled – he couldn't see a soul; and he was troubled to see the gate shut tight.

He went straight to the hall. At the door he saw four pedestals of copper, most handsome and beautifully wrought, inlaid with Arcadian gold; whoever had made them was skilled indeed: no columns of such fine workmanship were ever seen in any land. And on them was laid a table, the finest ever beheld by man: of intricately decorated brass it was, and six yards long but only five feet wide; and from it, on a silver chain, hung a steel hammer of wondrous kind, gilded with purest gold. Every inch of the table, too, was superbly gilded and richly engraved and worked. Perceval gazed at this gorgeous table, and the pedestals and the hammer, and saw how handsome and fine they were, and examined the patterning on the table and thought it quite superb, exceptional work indeed. Having studied the whole table he dismounted and tethered his horse to a column; then he entered the beautiful hall. But he didn't find a soul inside

– no knight, no maid, no lady, servant, page or squire. He started looking everywhere, but he found nothing to cheer or comfort him: there was no one – and no food!

'Dear me,' he said, 'here I am in a great house devoid of bread or anything else! I'd be better off in a peasant's or a carter's hovel if they had some food – it'd beat starving to death in this handsome tower! The Common Man[25] says, and rightly so, that if it's good enough, a man drinks more happily from a small spring than from a big one – and that he's better off aiming low and gaining much than aiming too high and suffering.'

So saying he went back through the door and down the steps to where he'd left his horse. Then he picked up the hammer; it was easy to wield, and he struck three blows on the table, with such mighty force that he made the castle shake and echo all around, the table making such a thunderous din that the whole hall shuddered. At this a girl appeared at a window: she was comely and fair but in disarray, her hair undone, and she shouted loudly:

'Sir knight! Sir knight! What do you think you're doing, hammering like that? What business brings you here? Come on, tell me!'

'Truly, my dear,' he replied, 'I've no desire to keep it from you: I came here simply to find lodging.'

'Well, by the saints, sir,' she said, 'haven't you struck it lucky? You won't have been so safely housed since Christmas! Aren't the walls here high and strong, the gate shut fast, and the great hall long and wide? And you can sleep at your leisure wherever you like!'

And with that she turned away without another word; Perceval was less than pleased and called to her loudly, crying: 'Stay a moment! Let's speak a while, I pray you!'

But answer came there none. Perceval felt very bothered: he didn't know what to say or do. He returned to the hall and went looking for the maiden everywhere, eager for a reassuring word. He searched every chamber, garderobe, cellar, solar, every room both large and small, every lodging, turret and kitchen, but the whole place seemed deserted: there wasn't a living creature to be seen. Back through the great paved hall he came and returned to his horse, where he'd first arrived. He paused a moment, thinking; then he grabbed the hammer and dealt the table three mighty blows, one after the other – the noise could be heard a league away, and the hall, so rich and splendid, quaked. Now another damsel thrust her head and shoulders through the window and called to Perceval:

'It's wicked of you, sir: you mean to kill us! If you give that lovely table three more hammer-blows like that you'll bring the tower down and kill yourself and us as well! There'd be no saving us!'

'By all-seeing, all-powerful God, my dear,' said Perceval, 'no threat or prayer from you or anyone – they can hate me as much as they like – will stop me hammering this table! If a hundred blows would wreck the tower and bring the castle down, I'll give it *two* hundred – or even more! You'd better watch out up there!'

So saying, he raised the hammer, and was about to test what damage could be done when the girl cried out: 'No, sir knight! Don't strike! Listen: if you want to leave I'll have the gate opened, I promise.'

'Nothing, my dear, will make me leave this place till morning! I don't know my way in these parts and it's evening now and almost dark, as you can see; I'm better off staying and resting here than fooling around in the forest.'

He left it at that; he said no more. The damsel couldn't help but smile, seeing him there with the hammer in his hand, ready to wreck the whole castle, unperturbed by

---

[25] Another reference to *Sayings for the Common Man (Diz au Vilain)*: see above, p. 159.

what she'd said and blazing red as coal, with a face fiercer than a lion or serpent. The gentle, courteous damsel said:

'Bear with me, sir, and wait a moment: I'll go to my lady and come straight back with news, I hope, that'll make up your mind one way or the other.'

'Go on, then,' he said, 'but don't hang about! I'll not stand waiting! Be off with you quickly – I've no more to say – if you're too long I'll call you back with the hammer!'

'I'm going, sir!' she said. 'In the name of the true Cross and the heavenly King, don't touch the table again!'

She vanished from the window: she knew what to do! She summoned three maidens in gorgeous attire and took them with her straight to Perceval, still poised over the table, hammer in hand. They greeted him most nobly, and one led his horse to a stable and gave him plenty of hay from the meadow and freshly cut oats, good and wholesome. The other three took Perceval and disarmed him in the hall, which he found richly hung with silken drapes of red and violet, yellow and blue, all embroidered with radiant gold, truly worth a fortune. He was utterly amazed: earlier it had looked completely different.

Just then a most beautiful, fair-haired girl appeared through the door of a chamber. She was carrying a splendid silken mantle, lined with white ermine, and with this she clad Perceval and said to him:

'Sir knight, you are welcome now to come and see my lady in her chamber. Or if you prefer, you may stay here in the hall and we'll bring you whatever you wish.'

Perceval said he would go and see the lady of the castle.

'Indeed,' she replied, 'I'm glad to hear that.'

So they led him to the chamber; it was paved with silver and lined with gilded panels: no man, I think, ever set eyes on such a wondrous place. And to complete the picture, there were at least a hundred damsels there, elegant, comely, beautiful, clad in rich attire and all dressed in one colour – indeed, they seemed all of one age, of one look, of one mind. They'd all removed their mantles and their wimples, revealing tresses of fair hair that shone brighter than fine gold. They were embroidering silk with golden thread, but when they saw Perceval they all rose and gave him a noble greeting as befitted a worthy knight. Perceval's heart lit up at this joyous reception! What more should I tell you? He sat beside the lady, her complexion a blend of lily-white and a more perfect red than a newly opened, dew-wet rose on a May morning. Perceval kept looking at the lady and the whole fair company, delighting in the sight of every one. He no longer felt hunger or discomfort of any kind; his every worry was forgotten; he was surrounded by more delights than he'd ever seen together in one place! The lady now addressed him, saying:

'Tell me your name, sir, if you will.'

Perceval didn't hide it but told her at once; and he told her, too, how he'd ridden through the forest for three days without finding any house where he could be given food or shelter.

'That may well be so,' she replied. 'To the left of here you could ride for a week before you'd find anywhere to have bread or meat.'

She gave orders for the tables to be set, and to be quick about it! Not that there were servants or squires – or knights – only damsels, most courtly and fair; but they set about it smartly, setting up the tables beautifully and then bringing the water; and Perceval and the lady washed and the others after them. The lady and Perceval ate together with the greatest pleasure. And before darkness fell there were so many candles lit in the hall that the light was brilliant, wondrously so. They had food in abundance: all manner of meat of game and fowl, and pike and salmon, fresh as could be; but to list every dish in detail would be tiresome.

When they'd leisurely eaten all they wished they bade that the cloths be cleared; and those praiseworthy damsels who'd served them so well cleared as swiftly. Then Perceval sat at the lady's side and asked the name of the castle and how it was that he'd seen no knights or servants, squires or pages.

'I shan't keep it a secret from you, sir,' she said, 'for you seem a good and honest man, and valiant and worthy. This castle, I promise you, is called the Castle of the Maidens. Perhaps you've heard of it? I'll tell you all about it if you wish, and without a word of a lie.'

'Truly, lady,' said Perceval, 'any loyal knight would gladly listen to the words of a fair lady! If you don't mind I'd like to know first why the gate was shut the moment I entered today. And that splendid table at the door: what's the point of the hammer? I'd like to hear about the hall, as well: I found it deserted earlier, and now it's completely full! My soul, it all seems very strange!'

'Sir Perceval,' the lady said, 'let me enlighten you. We live here in this wilderness, fully four days' ride from anyone. We've gathered together, all one in lineage, looks and age. And truly, we have all we wish and need. I had this castle built here for I thought it such a lovely place, beside the great river; and I promise you, no masons had a hand in its building, nor any labourer: it was built by four charming, fair and comely girls. And when any knight in search of adventures chances upon this castle, we know he's bound to be needing rest so we let him enter – and the moment he's inside, the gate is shut at once. Then he comes to the hall; and when he finds it deserted, then if he's a coward and easily daunted he'll imagine there's some trick afoot and turn back to the door, and if it doesn't occur to him to strike a blow with the hammer he'll have to keep a lonely watch all night – no one will come and see to him; and as soon as morning comes he can go where he likes – no one will bar his way. But if he's bright and noble-hearted, and strikes two or three blows with the hammer on the table, he'll be given fine lodging and all the comfort he could desire. Not that we have servants here – we have all we could possibly wish. If we choose to make the effort we have more than enough of everything.'

With that the lady ended her tale and said no more. Perceval had listened attentively, and had nothing more to tell of his own adventures; and by now the night was very dark and it was time to go to bed. I tell you truly, he was so very tired and weary that he fell asleep right there beside that gracious lady. She had a bed prepared for him, plush and perfect in every way, and over it two maidens spread a blanket bordered with orfrey and lined with fur. As soon as this gorgeous bed was ready, the lady gently nudged him awake and said:

'Go and lie down now if you wish, sir: it's high time. You're tired and weary – you should have been in bed a while ago!'

Then she rose and retired to a chamber with all her maidens, except two who stayed with Perceval till the good knight was abed and asleep. Then those maidens, so fair of face, left him and went to the chambers.

Perceval slept right through the night till the bright new day appeared with the rising sun. Then he awoke – and found himself under a tall and spreading oak, with his lance and arms and shield beside him and his horse all ready to ride, saddled and bridled: there was nothing to be said or done. Perceval was utterly astonished. He armed himself, donning his hauberk and lacing his helm without more ado; then with shield at neck and sword at his side he mounted. He looked about him now for the first time, and said:

'God help me! I slept last night at the Castle of the Maidens, and saw more beauties there than I've ever seen together in one place! And I'm sure there was a hall and a lofty tower, and mighty walls and battlements: it was a wonder! And now I can't see a house or cottage, wall or door or any living thing! I can only think it was done by magic! But of one thing I'm convinced: I had every comfort, and slept in the most gorgeous bed!'

That's what Perceval said to himself when he found himself beneath the oak. Then he set off on his way.

Recovering the Dog and the Stag's Head

On through the woods he rode till he came to a great valley where he found the biggest, loveliest glade from there to Ireland. Surrounded by the deep forest, the glade was a good two and a half leagues long, and right in the middle of the sward stood a great, spreading tree that Nature had made tall and broad and thick with leaves. A hundred knights could have sat in its shade – along with their servants! The sun at its summer hottest wouldn't have touched them! A bowshot beyond this tree was pitched a tent of wondrous splendour: of rich, red silken cloth it was, chequered with white on all four sides. The ropes, too, were of silk, violet in colour, made in India by a Saracen who charged a fortune. The pommel on top was of the purest, finest gold, which shone so brilliantly in the sun that the whole tent and the surrounding fresh, lush grass seemed all afire. Beside this magnificent tent were two lodges made in the Welsh manner, of interwoven branches. Perceval rode straight on till he reached the tent, and when he came to the door he stooped to peer inside and saw a rich bed covered in red samite thickly embroidered with golden flowers. But he could see nothing else. He turned his horse to the right and looked beneath the tree; and there he saw a girl dressed in an ermine-lined gown of silk of two colours: one half was white, the other red. Perceval headed straight that way; and hanging from the tree he saw the head of a superbly antlered stag.[26] He was convinced it was the head he'd lost – but there was no sign of the dog, which filled his heart with alarm and foreboding. He didn't know what he should or shouldn't say, but he greeted the girl. But his greeting didn't please her in the least – she realised exactly who he was – and she replied:

'God help me, sir knight, it's a great pity that a wretch lives as long as a worthy man! It's you I mean! Demons must have kept you from being killed or maimed out here in the wilds! But now your time has come: you won't get through today without shame and disaster – it's going to be a day of woe for you!'

'God help us!' said Perceval. 'What are you saying, dear girl? May the Holy Spirit guide me and send me joy and honour – I've seen nothing to scare me yet! But tell me – if you will and can! – the reason why I should be killed!'

'Don't you remember,' she said, 'taking my little dog? But I've got him back now, and have him still – you'll see him in a moment – but you won't have the nerve to lay a hand on him! And see: hanging there on the branch is the head of the stag you killed when you caught it in the park at the maiden's fair castle. That maiden loved her dog

---

[26] Literally 'with antlers of a dozen branches'.

more than anything in the world, and she hasn't heard a word about him since! She's been waiting for news all this while – and she'll be waiting for the rest of her life: she'll never get him back through you!'

But Perceval was delighted by all this: he'd found the dog again! He rode up to the tall and spreading tree and, without dismounting, quickly untied the stag's head from where it hung and laid it down on the green grass. The damsel was beside herself with fury; all she could do was cry:

'God! When will my avenger come?'

Perceval was jubilant; but just then he heard a hunting-horn ring out in the forest, twice, and he turned to see a stag come bounding forth, so exhausted from running, so hard pressed, that it was struggling to take another breath: its tongue was flopping from its gaping mouth. A dog was right behind it, viciously snapping at its leg, and galloping after, as fast as he could, was a knight clad in a hauberk whiter than a flower of hawthorn or sweet briar. On his head was a splendid helm of steel, and he was clutching a huge, sharp-headed lance. Thus armed, but without a shield, he was racing after the stag and the dog, at intervals giving great blasts on his horn that made the greenwood around him ring with the thunderous din. On ran the stag as far as the tree, but the dog was on him all the way, and the knight, following up behind, thrust his lance through the stag's right flank, with such force that the head burst out more than two and a half feet the other side. The stricken stag collapsed – he was well and truly taken, that's for sure. Then up stepped the damsel, calling to the white knight:

'Sir! God bless me, there's a knight beneath this tree who's upset me today, and very much!'

'How's that, sweet love?' said the knight, turning to look at her. 'Has he treated you other than decently?'

'It's not that,' she replied, 'no, God bless me; but the stag's head you're so fond of, he's taken it from the tree and dumped it on the grass – and he says it's his by right! And he's claiming that dog of yours, too: he says you stole it from him, snatching it from before his eyes against his will and without his leave! He's tracked you down now, he says, and will have the dog back if he can!'

At this the knight shook with rage; he left the stag and turned his horse straight at Perceval – who wasn't looking at all concerned: he was leaning on his lance.

'Vassal!' he cried. 'I see you've caused me great offence here! I hope you've someone to protect you!'

'Indeed I have!' said Perceval. 'This sword and this horse, this quartered shield, this helm of steel, this coat of mail, my body and my lance – they are my protectors, I promise you, against all my foes! But come: return my dog if you please, in peace, without strife; I've been searching for him for ages and don't need any more trouble.'

The knight swore by the blessed Virgin that he wouldn't be returning it at his bidding! But Perceval insisted he would – he'd have the dog back whether he liked it or not. He could see no friendly plea would be of any use: it struck him, not for the first time, how little kindness there was in a wicked heart, how little love in a proud one, how little humility in an arrogant man – and how often it proved their downfall.

'By God,' the knight said, 'I can see you've been well schooled and have a way with words – but you can give as much of a sermon as you like: it won't get you the dog you've sought so hard!'

'Truly, friend,' replied Perceval, 'I'm not expecting it to be freely given: I'll win it back with might and main!'

And he challenged him on the spot. The knight was incensed, blazing with rage. His shield was propped against the tree, and now he slung it round his neck; he was magnificently armed, and in his hand he clutched his lance, crimson with the blood of the stag he'd killed. They thrust in their spurs and drew apart; then, with shields in place and lances in rest they charged at one another and clashed so hard, horses, bodies and shields together, that they brought each other crashing down; they were both hurt and stunned and lay there a while, flat out. Their mounts had collided, chest to chest and head to head, with such force that they'd nearly smashed their brains out. So there they lay, the knights, in the middle of the field, and they had a struggle to find their feet. But out from their scabbards they drew their swords, gleaming bright and razor-sharp; and on their flower-blazoned shields they hammered blows. The fight was even indeed: they were both such worthy, valiant knights that barely any ground was given. With his blade of burnished, whetted steel Perceval struck the knight on his jewelled, gilded helm; had the blow landed fully it would have killed him, I'd say, but that fine sword with its silver guard was deflected to the right, and cut irresistibly through the noseguard and into the flesh, bringing the red blood gushing forth, drenching the hauberk and pouring to the ground. But the knight was undismayed: whatever he was given he'd promptly repay – at double the rate! Their swords of furbished steel sent sparks flying from their helms, and on their combat raged till they were weary from wielding blows and didn't know how they could carry on. But Perceval remembered the dog, and could see it now in the arms of the damsel who'd so taunted him; and the fierce anger he felt redoubled his courage and his valour.

'Truly,' he said, 'it's a shame and dishonour that this battle's going on so long!'

And in his rage he went at him and delivered three blows in quick succession; he struck and he hammered again and again, and cut through the helm and the ventail,* drawing blood. The knight carried on resisting, but in vain: Perceval assailed him with such fury that he laid him out flat – he collapsed on his shield. Perceval loomed over him, and struck him three times on the head, nearly killing him. The knight realised there'd be no respite and begged earnestly for mercy, to spare his life for the love of God; but Perceval said he'd never have mercy when he'd done all in his power to dishonour him.

'Sir!' cried the knight. 'You can do whatever you want with me, but it's sinful and wrong to kill a man!'

And Perceval took pity on him, and said he'd pardon him if he promised to surrender as a captive to King Arthur – and return the dog he'd taken with good grace; if he did so, he'd be spared and live. And he was to take the girl with him to court and present her to the queen, and tell her exactly what had brought it all about. He willingly agreed – not that he had a choice: the alternative was death. And so, it seems, on these terms peace was made, and they sat on the lush, green grass to rest.

Perceval asked the knight to tell him his name and the name of his sweetheart. He didn't withhold them; he said:

'My name, sir, is Garsallas: I was the son of the duke of Geneloie; and my beloved's name is Criseuz the Fair, and beautiful, courteous, prudent, generous, noble and gracious she is indeed. That's the truth about us; now, in whose name am I to surrender as a captive at the court of good King Arthur?'

'Don't you know, my friend?'

'Not at all, sir.'

'Submit on behalf of Perceval the Welshman: that's my name – and I hope it'll earn you a more joyful and honourable welcome. But tell me now, if you can, about the castle and the damsel who entrusted me with the dog.'

'It's no good asking,' said the knight. 'I know nothing about her, truly.'

'Then tell me, friend, about the knight who unhorsed me at the vaulted tomb. Tell me the truth, don't keep it a secret: your sweetheart sent me to ask why he stayed there – maybe he was forced to. All I know is I suddenly heard him coming up behind me, armed; I spun round and saw him, blacker than ink – his horse was black, too, and amazingly swift. We clashed with our lances and brought each other down: you saw it all with your own eyes – and it was then you stole my dog away without so much as a word! I defeated the knight in combat, but before I could take him captive he'd fled back to the tomb. I went after him and called to him, asking where I could find you, but for all my appeals he wouldn't come out or utter a word in reply. And amazingly, at no point since have I found any knight or boy, any lady or damsel who could tell me anything about him. So tell me, if you can, what became of him? Where did he go? I'd dearly love to know the truth.'

'I'll tell you, sir, and without a word of a lie. That knight is my brother – but we don't share the same mother: my father had two wives. As soon as he was old enough to bear arms he left home, and acquired such prowess, such nobility and strength that I've never heard of any to surpass him: he became so mighty, so redoubtable, he was the finest knight known in any land. For five full years he went in ceaseless search of adventures, and in those five years any knight he met, no matter how courageous and fierce, he defeated or killed in combat. That's how he spent five years, until he came by chance to the rich Isle of Avalon. In the Forest of the White Stone he found a maiden sitting by a spring of clear water; she was so wondrously beautiful that I don't believe her equal could be found in the whole wide world: God had made her with His own hand, so dazzlingly fair that any man who set eyes on her declared God had sent her from Heaven, from His own household. She was whiter than a lily. My brother was so stricken with love – which has mastery over every being! – that he couldn't have left her for all the gold in the East: he begged her for her love right there and then. And she, very aware of her own worth, granted him her love on condition that he'd fulfil her every wish, whatever it might cost him: this he had to swear. And he did: he promised her whatever she asked – the love-stricken will always do the bidding of the one who has him in her thrall, such is love's power!

'They didn't dally there long before they set off together; then they rode through the forest for three days, till they came to a fair, expansive glade in the middle of thick woods. It was already past terce, and they halted there.

'"Sir," she said, "we'll wear ourselves out with riding! I suggest we stay here, if it please you, in this meadow."

'He turned to her and said: "My dear, sweet love, if we stay out here in this great thick forest we'll have nothing to eat – and as long as we're stuck here I fear we'll never see a living soul, let alone a knight or an adventure!"

'"Yes, we will, sir," she said. "Let me tell you: the fine, brave, mighty knights of the good King Arthur's court pass this way, you may be sure. If you can stay here and guard this place for twelve years without losing your honour, you'll win more esteem and credit than any knight alive! And have no fear: we'll have everything we desire – you'll never want for bread and fresh meat and fish and wine in plenty!"

'He agreed to stay if she promised not to go but to be ever at his side. And she replied: "Most gladly!"

'The knight was weary; he dismounted, and she did likewise. My brother lay down on the thick, green grass to sleep – he couldn't have stayed awake for a hundred silver marks. He slept long and soundly, and didn't wake till none;* and when at last he rose he found himself in a castle, the most imposing, strong and handsome he'd ever seen.

'"This is amazing!" he said. "Where ever are we, my love?"

'"We've a house now, for a start!" she said. "And I'd say we've bread and wine and food enough to last till Saint Martin's Day!"

'"Are we really," he said, "still in that glade, so broad and fair?"

'"Indeed we are," said the girl. "Let me show you what's what, and what I've done!"

'And she led him through the gate – superbly made it was – to where their horses were grazing in the meadow on the tender green grass.

'"And now, my love," said that girl, so fair of face, "let me tell you what you must do to fulfil the vow you made me."

'"Tell me," he replied. "I'll listen, and I'll do everything in my power for you, you may be sure, for I love you like my own life."

'"Then look, my love: while you were asleep I built this house – with such craft and skill that no man will ever see it! No knight's eyes, however close he rides, will ever see the gate, I promise you! But at the gate, by that white wall, I've made a vaulted tomb – you can see it there, below the castle. That will be visible to anyone who passes; and they'll also see a mounted knight I've painted on the tomb – as you'll see for yourself; and above it I've written in tiny letters that if any knight comes to the tomb and says, loud enough to be heard, 'God help me, sir knight, it's madness: you shouldn't be in this tomb!', then you'll mount your charger and avenge those foolish words."

'He promised to take revenge indeed on anyone who came. I wouldn't lie to you, sir,' he said to Perceval. 'My brother stayed a long time with the girl, ten whole years, but at no point did any knight come who could vanquish him – until you arrived – and you know exactly what happened then! There, I've told you the honest truth, as surely as if it were laid down word for word on parchment.'

Perceval bowed his head in thought, rapt in wonder at the tale; and when he'd heard it all he asked the knight his brother's name. He replied at once:

'The Black Knight of Valdoire, from the Black Forest of Ardoire: that was his name originally; but later it was changed: he preferred to be called the Black Knight of the Vaulted Tomb – the tomb in that fair glade, long and broad.

'Now you know the lot! So I pray you, let's go and eat at my pavilion: it's high time. I know we've bread and plenty of wine at hand, and I think there are a couple of pies made from a rabbit I caught yesterday. And if you were happy to wait a little we could have some juicy skewers of venison, and other meat and game. What do you say, good sir? It's a fair while still till nightfall.'

But Perceval said he wouldn't dally: he'd go as soon as he'd eaten. So they went straight to the pavilion together. What more should I tell you? All three sat and ate most happily: they enjoyed it greatly but didn't linger, and as soon as they'd eaten and drunk they rose again. Perceval asked the knight to tell him anything he knew about the castle of the maiden who'd entrusted him with the dog; but the knight swore by almighty God he'd no idea how to find it. Perceval didn't know what to say, except:

'Give me back my dog, kind sir, and I'll be on my way, for I'll not rest till I've returned him to that fair and comely maiden: the dog is so dear to her.'

'There's no need for such haste, sir!' said the knight. 'Stay here till morning and the new day dawns: then your horse will be refreshed and you'll be rested; it's already past noon and the day's marching on, and the sun's ablaze, its rays spreading such heat – it's the hottest day I've seen this year! It would be a wretched idea to go just now! This forest is vast, and you'd have a tough and miserable night! Stay tonight, please, and leave in the morning – as will I, to find the king whose renown resounds through many lands.'

But Perceval resolutely refused, and the knight dropped the matter then and returned the dog at once – he didn't dare do otherwise, but if he'd been able to resist he wouldn't have returned the dog at any price. And Perceval, unwilling to stay longer, mounted at once with shield slung from neck, and took up his lance and the dog he cherished so. He had the stag's head tied to the back of his saddle; it was still as fresh as the day he'd caught the stag and killed it in the forest: it didn't smell and had no decay at all – nor would it ever till Judgement Day: as long as it was protected from damp it would never rot in this world but stay forever fresh as new. Then Perceval took his leave of the damsel and the knight and thrust in his spurs and rode swiftly away. He was jubilant at having found the dog, now carried in his lap before him: with the dog recovered he felt his troubles were behind him, that he was completely in control.

But now I want to return to the knight, who thought he'd die of grief at having lost the dog. What a blow it was to his honour and esteem! He was so stricken and gripped by shame that he thought he'd never find relief – he'd be better off dead! He was such a fierce and bitter man that, truly, if he'd dared he'd have gone after Perceval and challenged him again; but he knew he was so bold and worthy that it would be pointless to renew battle – instead he stifled his wrath and pretended to be at peace, impotent as he was to avenge the shame and the blow he'd suffered. So reluctantly he let it be and stayed there all that day, and slept in his tent that night till morning when the sun rose, bright and blazing. Then he and his sweetheart dressed and began their journey to the king's court. They found him and his household at Tinpincarantin, I believe. In short, the knight told King Arthur all that had happened, in all truthfulness, and presented his sweetheart to the queen who received her with much delight and joy. And the king took a great liking to the knight and retained him in his household and pardoned him his imprisonment.

Crossing the Bridge of Glass

Now settle down and listen, one and all, to the continuing story of Perceval, as he rode on alone through the great, thick forest. He had the antlered stag's head trussed behind his saddle and was holding the dog in his lap before him, stroking him frequently. He prayed to God, the mighty king, to lead him to the castle where he'd seen the handsome chessboard and the priceless chessmen.

'God!' he said. 'If only I could find my way back there and see the damsel, fairer than a siren, with her lovely face and sweetest breath, how happy I'd be!'

Frustrated and yearning so, he looked ahead and saw a mule approaching, whiter than snow frozen on a branch in January. It had a bridle of gold and a golden saddle – a lady's saddle, a fine one indeed and all brand new – and a saddlecloth of samite, the most gorgeous ever seen. The mule was on its own, and coming towards Perceval at quite a pace. The way was very narrow, no more than a stride across, and the white mule raced down and met Perceval right in the middle of the track, and stopped and stood motionless across his path. The day was already drawing to a close and night was about to fall. Perceval stared at the mule, standing there on its own, and saw the bridle and the saddle, wondrously rich: he'd never seen its like, he thought, in all his life, so handsomely was it crafted.

As he sat gazing at the white mule, and the harness and the saddle, he noticed a girl coming down the path: a comely and most graceful girl, but she seemed to be in a miserable state, plodding along on foot, with her dress hitched up. But to do justice to her beauty, you'd have to say no girl so lovely was ever born or beheld. Flushed as she was from walking, she glowed with such radiance that she seemed to have descended from Heaven – she seemed indeed a spiritual being. She was dressed in a delightful silken gown embroidered with golden flowers: none so rich or lovely ever appeared from any treasure-chest, and it was perfectly fresh and new. Perceval gazed at the girl in delight – and rightly so: a girl of such complexion should delight anyone. Then, in a loud voice, she cried:

'Give me back my mule, sir knight! She's made me so cross today! I dismounted beneath a tree to eat, and she promptly set off and I've not been able to catch her since!'

'I'll gladly return her, my dear,' said Perceval. 'Come here and I'll help you mount.'

But she swore by God on high that she didn't want any help from him, whatever he might say – she just wanted him to hold the mule still on the path, for once she had hold of the reins she could perfectly well mount by herself. Perceval did as she asked, and watched as she stepped up to the white mule, jumped straight into the saddle and briskly set off back up the path. Perceval rode at her side most courteously, and politely asked her where she'd come from and where she was going and where she'd be lodging that night – did she know of any castle or city where they could stay? – for darkness was already setting in.

'Sir,' she said, 'I'm not going to give you any illusions. If you've any business to pursue, pursue it; if you come with me another league and a half you'll be placing little value on your life. So turn back – I don't want your company any longer.'

'God bless me, fair one,' he replied, 'no business or mission of mine will keep me from escorting you.'

She was less than pleased at hearing this, and implored him by the faith he owed the Virgin to leave her be. While they carried on wrangling, oblivious of all else, night had fallen, smothering the light of day; it was dark indeed, for the moon had waned and didn't appear, the looming, leafy forest cast a deep, deep shade and there was no star to be seen in all the firmament. And the winds had grown so still that there wasn't the slightest breeze. The girl, riding the white mule beside Perceval, said she was completely blind, it was so pitch dark.

'My dear,' he said, 'it would make good sense to stay with me on this path till morning. I can hear you, but I can't see you at all: it doesn't make for an easy ride!'

She retorted that she'd never stay with him: she was annoyed that he'd been there so long, but didn't know how to get rid of him! 'If, good sir, you were as decent and noble-hearted as you should be, you wouldn't carry on like this! But unless I'm much mistaken you'll regret it before you see day dawn.'

And so saying she quickened her pace. Then the moon began to rise, shedding some light as midnight approached, and Perceval rode after her, eager to have her tell him exactly what was on her mind and why she forbade him to ride with her. While he was intent on this he noticed, far off in the distance, a glimmer of light like a burning candle. He kept peering at it, and soon he was sure there were five of them, burning so brightly that it seemed the great, deep forest was afire with their light on every side: it was surely supernatural. And that wasn't all: it seemed, too, that this blaze – bright red it was –

reached right up to the clouds. He thought he'd turn and ask the girl the source of this great and distant light, and he called to her:

'Tell me about this blaze I see!'

But she made no reply, for she was nowhere near: she'd left him and ridden off without a word. But Perceval wasn't bothered – in fact he smiled a little, not troubled or disconcerted in the least. Instead he vowed and swore to ride on to the light, come what may: no fear was going to stop him. So he pressed on a good deal faster than before. But suddenly the sky was plunged into darkness and a mighty wind struck up, bringing with it such violent, limitless rain that it seemed the earth and the whole vast forest would be swept away. Perceval was aghast; he covered his head with his shield and took shelter beneath a tree until this fearful storm had passed. He had to endure this wretched, dismal plight till it was almost dawn. But then the clouds dispersed, the darkness lifted and the weather began to turn fair, and Perceval's heart was lightened then and he set off on his way once more.

He looked ahead and all around, expecting to see the light as he had before; but there was no sign of it, and he couldn't remember in which direction it had been. He was frustrated and downhearted, but pressed on nonetheless until he came to a glade of the greatest beauty, though it wasn't very long or wide. It was now close to daybreak, and such a pleasant end to the night that Perceval hadn't a care in the world, despite all he'd been through, for trouble is soon forgotten when God restores joy to the sufferer. Sir Perceval decided to rest a little and let his weary horse graze. So he halted in the glade and placed his lance and shield beneath a tall, leafy tree. The grass was fresh and new, and he took off the bridle and then the saddle and set his horse free to graze and rest. For his own part he lay down with his head propped on his shield, for he was weak with tiredness. Soon he was fast asleep, with his dog beside him, lying quietly at his feet, not leaving him or straying off at all: it was as if he'd fed him all the days of his life! He made a fine companion.

So Perceval slept, and didn't wake till the sun rose, lighting up the day. A good part of the morning had already gone: it was almost terce and starting to get hot. So he rose at once, without delay, and saddled and loaded his horse and mounted with his dog. With shield slung from neck he set off swiftly through the wood once more, and rode on like this till about midday.

Then he looked beneath a lovely tree where the grass around was green and lush, and saw the girl who'd left him in the forest that night, and beside her the handsomely harnessed mule. He recognised her at once and rode briskly towards her, and greeted her most courteously in the name of God the almighty king. She returned his greeting, much to his surprise; and hearing her address him kindly he dismounted at once and said:

'If it please you, lady, I'd gladly know more about you – and why you left me last night when I saw the blaze of the bright red flame.'

'Don't be surprised, good sir,' said she, so fair and courtly, 'if we parted company: the sky was so dark that I couldn't see a thing; and I was afraid of running into a knight who'd made me swear not to accept the company of any man alive till I returned to him. I wanted to keep my word, and no one should blame me for that. But truly, since he left me yesterday I haven't set eyes on him; if you've seen him or heard news of him please tell me – don't keep it from me.'

'God bless me, no, damsel,' said Perceval, 'I've heard no word or mention of him. Tell me his name and what he's rightly called.'

'He was baptised, sir,' she replied, 'with the name of Brun the Pitiless. He's a fine and much feared knight, I promise you.'

'Indeed, fair lady, I've heard of him. I think I'd know him if I saw him. Now tell me, if you will: when you left me last night, were you caught in the storm that beset me so terribly?'

'No indeed, sir,' she said. 'I didn't see any rain or storm; the night was beautiful and fair, calm and still and serene – I never saw one more pleasant in my life! As for the light you saw, have you ever heard of the rich king fisherman? He lives near here beside a river, and he came into the forest last night: he loves the place. That was the source of the brilliant light you mentioned: the fire that burned so brightly was a sign that the grail, so beautiful and precious, in which the clear and glorious blood of the king of kings was gathered when He was hung upon the cross, was in the forest with the Fisher King, for the Devil can't trick or lead astray and into sin any man who sees its light. That's why the king has the grail carried with him, for he's a saintly, deeply devout man: he leads a good life indeed. He prays constantly to Our Lord – who never forgets a worthy man who repents of the wrongs he committed in his youth – to take him to His side in Heaven and to keep him from all misdeed and sin.'

Anyone who'd then seen Perceval's face would have said that no man was ever so distracted, short of losing his mind. He begged the girl to tell him more about the grail, and for God's sake not to keep from him the truth and all the secrets about the rich Fisher King: how he'd come to have the grail and from whose hand, and who'd given him the lance with the head that shed blood from its tip. And she, so charming and clever, was quick and astute in replying; she said:

'Sir, I can't tell you any more about that: I mustn't. If you were my lord a hundred times over I still wouldn't dare let another word pass my lips; for these are most sacred matters, and mustn't be spoken of by any lady, young or old, or by any girl or maiden – or by any man born unless he be an ordained priest or a man who leads a holy life, coveting nothing and treating others as he'd have them treat him: such a man could speak of the grail, and of the wonders which no one could hear without shaking and trembling and turning pale with awe. That's the truth of it. Now remount, sir, if you will, and come with me: you shall eat a little – it's high time, you know, when you've been through so much and haven't slept all night!'

Perceval agreed; he was only too glad to go, still hopeful as he was of hearing some mysteries revealed. He wanted to help her mount, but she wouldn't let him; she bade him mount his own horse at once, and then they set off together.

They rode on without stopping until they came to a deep valley. There they found a splendid pavilion, and a girl outside it, most comely and fair; there she stood, outside the tent. As soon as Perceval saw her he greeted her in the name of God, and she replied at once in the sweetest terms. The other girl, who'd brought Perceval with her, dismounted at the door, leaving her mule standing quietly. What should I tell you of Perceval? He dismounted and took off his horse's bridle, leaving him to graze freely on the green grass, young and fresh. He left the stag's head where he'd packed it on the saddle, but he was still holding the dog, and he carried him into the tent as the girl led him inside in most welcoming fashion. I needn't go into greater detail, but they had plenty to eat of whatever they wished, finding all the food that their hearts desired and the finest wines in all the world. They talked of many things as they sat and dined. The girl started asking about the dog she saw before her: in which land he'd found him, and why he kept carrying him, and if he'd ever caught any game; and why Perceval had the great stag's head, with its huge antlers, packed on his saddle. So he told her the whole story: how he'd caught the stag in the forest, how the little dog had been given to him at the handsome castle, and how he'd gone to the tomb where he'd found the knight. He told her everything that had followed: how he'd gone on to lose the dog but had tracked him down and won him back in combat.

'Whatever happens, lady,' he said, 'I promised the maiden who gave me the dog that I'd return him to her without fail. And since I'd hate to wrong such a noble and good-hearted damsel I'm taking her dog back to her. And if she keeps the promise she made me when I left to hunt the stag, I assure you I'll have no cause for complaint!'

'Truly, sir,' the girl replied, 'if it's as you say you should certainly return him to her. Do you know her name, or the name of the castle where you saw her before you set out on your hunt? And do you know the way?'

'God help me, no, I've no idea. But I promise you she's the fairest girl in the whole wide world!'

For the moment he fell silent and said no more. But when they'd eaten their fill and rose from the table, Perceval, longing to hear where the good king the keeper of the grail lived, asked the girl:

'Tell me, damsel, do you know the splendid court where that blessed king lives who guards the rich grail and the lance that sheds from its tip the drops of crimson blood?'

'Yes, before God,' she replied, 'I know it well, and I'll tell you how to find it – if you'll keep to the way and not stray from it.'

When Perceval heard this he set the bridle on his horse without a moment's pause, and with shield slung from neck and fully armed he mounted, beside himself with joy. Then he turned to the girl and asked her leave, but she said:

'Please don't go just yet: it would be discourteous to leave before you've told me your name. Tell me at once: I want to know.'

And he replied: 'God guard me from shame, damsel, my name is Perceval. Now show me the way to the Fisher King's court – and may God grant me joy and honour.'

'Gladly, sir,' she said. 'There are so many roads and paths that you'd never know which way to go. But if you'll lead your destrier by the reins and ride my mule, whiter than any living creature, she'll go straight to the glass bridge over the river Marsonde, which is swift and wide and deep. She'll take you there without any trouble. And when she reaches the bridge, cross it at your leisure and then let the mule return – she'll come straight back. But stay here till morning – you'll travel much better then.'

'There's no question of that, damsel,' he said. 'But truly, I'd be glad to hear about your friend Brun.'

'The fact is, sir,' she replied, 'a knight met me yesterday and told me that a girl had waylaid him seeking urgent help to save her lover who'd been taken captive and locked in a tower. His captor had promised that if she could find a knight brave and bold and fierce enough to do battle with him in the field and vanquish and unhorse him, then her sweetheart would be returned to her. So my dear Brun went off with her, for he's a strong and redoubtable knight indeed. God keep him from harm! But that's that: I can see you're determined to leave at once. So take this ring of mine: its stone is fine and precious indeed; I promise faithfully, as long as you have it on your finger my white mule will carry you safely, unerringly, wherever you wish to go. And you'll need have no fear of crossing the bridge of glass. But if by folly or mischance you come to lose the ring, be sure of this: the mule will stop – she won't take you another step – be it in forest or river, in glade, on heath, in city or castle. And if the ring falls into another's hands, the mule could likewise carry him wherever he wished. Come: put my ring on your finger.'

She offered it to him, and he bowed a little and took the ring and placed it on his middle finger, thanking her in the name of God.

'But listen, sir,' she said. 'I must have my mule and ring back as soon as we meet again, without delay or hesitation.'

'By God who made the firmament,' said Perceval, 'I wouldn't let you down, my dear, for all the riches in the whole wide world: you're so noble and good-hearted. Never in my life would I want to wrong you, truly.'

With that he took his leave, and left her in the pavilion of embroidered silk. Then he crossed the fair glade – it didn't take long – and entered the great forest, deep and beautiful. He still had the stag's head strapped to his saddle but was holding the dog as ever, cherishing him dearly as he did. The mule took to its path at a swift and steady pace, and Perceval's horse followed after. On he rode like this, following many roads and tracks. The mule kept to the right path, and Perceval didn't attempt to stray: he gave the mule free rein and she pressed steadily on, most agreeably and trustily. Perceval kept looking at the ring on his finger, and at the handsome, precious stone: he gazed at it intently all day long till evening.

And all that while he met with no adventure or anything worth relating – so says the true story of Perceval; but these days there are many brave fellows going round these courts as story-tellers who twist the good tales, distancing them from their sources and adding so many lies that the stories are ruined and the good books dishonoured. Those who hear them don't know what the proper stories are! No, when they have those minstrels in their houses for the night and they get them to tell a bit of some adventure – unrhymed![27] – they think they've heard the whole story, but they'll never hear it in their lives! Those rascals sell them a pack of lies – and they're great at padding and stringing them out! So let me tell you about Perceval.

He pressed on all day till the sun had set and the light of day was gone. But it's pointless to labour the story; he spent the whole night in the forest, with nothing to cheer or please him and nothing to eat or drink; he just guarded the white mule and his horse till day broke, bright and fair; then he harnessed them and mounted and quickly took to the road again, riding the mule, who knew her way exactly.

On he rode till prime, gazing fixedly at the ring with the holy stone. He didn't stop till he reached the river, and there he found the bridge of glass. He halted at once at the bridge's foot, and looked down at the river. It was half as wide again as a crossbow's range, and I tell you truly, it was awesomely swift, and so deep and dangerous that no craft or vessel in the world, no matter how big or broad or ribbed with iron or steel, could have survived its crossing. As for the bridge, its construction was so amazing that no tongue of man or pen of clerk could possibly describe it. It was made of glass, and two and a half feet wide. It was perfectly transparent: through it the water could be seen below, roaring like a tempest. But Perceval dallied on the bank no longer: he gave the mule free rein and she climbed straight on to the fragile bridge. He pulled his fine destrier after him by the reins, for he loved him dearly and didn't want to leave him behind. The white mule didn't falter: she walked on as surely and confidently as if she'd been on solid ground. But the destrier crossed with difficulty, most fearfully, and behind him the bridge, so perilous and daunting to cross, was crumbling all away: Perceval thought

---

[27] An interestingly scornful view of the prose romances.

it would collapse into the void, as it shook so furiously that he was convinced chunks were falling in the river. But he was undismayed: he had faith in the mule, who bore him fearlessly and calmly and safely to the other side, so that he felt no pain, discomfort, fear or doubt or dread. And once he was across he looked back at the bridge and was amazed: it was perfectly fine and whole.

'I was sure I could feel it crumbling!' he said. 'Truly, this is a fearsome bridge for any cowardly man to cross! It's a wonder anyone can venture on it and reach the other side without losing his mind and throwing himself into the torrent to drown!'

So saying, he stared at the bridge he'd crossed, still perfectly fine and in one piece when he'd thought his horse had smashed it apart behind him. It would have been a terrifying crossing indeed if he'd been a cowardly, fearful man. After gazing at this amazing bridge he turned away.

The Unfinished Bridge

At the edge of the wood he came upon a vavasor* in the prime of life, who looked a man of worth and intelligence. About his neck hung an ivory horn, finely adorned with chisel-work, and he was holding a spear and leading a pair of hounds. He was mounted on a splendid horse, handsome and strong and swift, and was lightly clad with his clothes hitched up, and finely shod in tall boots from England. You could have searched far and wide before finding a man of more impressive appearance. Perceval looked long at him and was then the first to offer a greeting; and the vavasor replied most courteously, saying:

'Sir, may that God who made us all grant you honour, health and happiness, and guide you on the path to attaining what your heart desires.'

'Kind sir,' said Perceval, 'may God hear you from on high! And may He grant you through His powers joy and honour, health and vigour, and keep you from coveting any other's fortune. Now tell me by what name I should call you – don't keep it from me.'

'I'll tell you indeed, sir: I am Briol of the Burnt Forest. And I'd gladly know yours; tell me at once.'

'Truly, friend, in my land I'm known as Perceval; I was born in Wales. Now by the faith you owe God, if you know a direct path to the court of the good Fisher King, it would be a kindness to tell me.'

'There's something,' said Briol, 'I should tell you first. If you want to go to that court, you'll need to be the most accomplished and respected of all knights; you cannot go there otherwise and achieve your aim. But if you'll trust in my advice you could improve yourself immensely and enhance your reputation, far more than I could ever say.'

'Then in God's name,' said Perceval, 'tell me at once!'

'Have you heard,' said Briol, 'of the bridge that no man can cross, or of the great tournament that's gathering at the Proud Castle, to which that good and wondrous king, the worthy and mighty Arthur, is to lead seven hundred knights to support the castle's men?'

'God bless me, no,' said Perceval, 'I've heard nothing about it, sir.'

'Come, then,' said Briol, 'I'll take you there; and tonight I'll gladly give you lodging at my house. When day breaks tomorrow we'll go together to the bridge which is like no other; and if you can cross it you may truly claim more glory and honour than your ancestors ever won.'

Perceval said he'd go with him indeed if he'd lead him to the bridge and promise to accompany him to the tournament. Briol agreed, and said that if Perceval could cross the great bridge he'd be his constant companion, even if it cost him his life; this he swore. With that they set off into the forest, and rode straight towards their lodging without a halt. They spoke of one thing and another as they went; and Briol looked at the stag's head strapped to the saddle of Perceval's swift mount and was curious, and asked him why he had such a huge and antlered stag's head packed upon his horse. So Perceval related the adventure as they rode along, just as I've told it to you, keeping nothing back. And he showed him the dog, which he loved and thought a splendid hound indeed; and he told him, too, about the mule, exactly as you've heard. But he didn't tell him about the fair and precious ring; he kept that secret – I don't know why. Yet Briol saw it on his finger and gazed at it in delight.

They rode steadily on till they caught sight of the towers of a castle and its splendid walls, built of limestone and white marble. I promise you, never was any house better fortified: it had a great tower and gate at the entrance and a most imposing drawbridge. But I'll say no more. They rode on and over the bridge and through the gate to the hall. A boy came down the steps with a horn in his hand, and as soon as Briol saw him he blew his own horn twice and the boy replied at once with a mighty blast, whereupon the courtyard filled with knights and members of the household. Briol bade them honour Perceval and serve him as their lord. Then they dismounted, and boys took their horses and led them to the stables. The wise and worthy Perceval asked only that they take good care of the white mule, which they did most willingly. Then two squires came, bringing a pair of mantles, and they escorted the knights to the hall where they disarmed Perceval and dressed him in one of the mantles before fastening the other on Briol. Then a lady appeared from a chamber, clad in richly dyed silk; it would take too long to record her beauty, but I'll say this much: she lacked neither breeding nor brain. She came to her lord and embraced him, and gave Perceval a joyful welcome; and all three sat together on a rich silken cloth. Then Briol left the lady with Perceval and went down to hasten preparations for dinner. He returned at once and went to a panelled chamber hung with silken drapes, where he found one of his daughters making a mantle-cord: she was as lovely as a siren or a fairy. She rose and greeted her father with all honour, and Briol took her by the hand and led her to the great hall and to Perceval, who was seated beside the lady telling her all manner of things in answer to her questions. When he saw the sweet-faced girl he rose at once and greeted her most nobly, and she, so radiant of complexion, curtseyed and sat down at his side. Briol, who loved and cherished her, said:

'Dear daughter, entertain and honour this lord, for he is a worthy and courteous knight indeed.'

Then servants came hurrying to set up the tables in that splendid hall, and presented the water without delay; then they all sat down to eat: it was high time, being late in the afternoon. The girl with the glowing complexion and faithful heart ate together with Perceval. They had food of the very finest kind, and wine from Poitou, the delight of all who like strong wine; but I shan't bother to list and describe their every dish, for they were served with all they could wish and desire. They talked of many things and recalled many a good tale. They were seated at table, it seems, till evening; then they rose together and went out to the bridge, the finest in the world, where they gazed at the water and watched the fishes swim, and at the forest and the meadow, most beautiful and thick with flowers. So they happily passed the time till night drew near and their beds were ready. Then they returned to the hall, lit now by many candles. Perceval, holding the girl by the left hand, asked her all about herself, and whether she had a sweetheart.

'Sir,' she said, 'it wouldn't be right for me to have a sweetheart yet: I know enough about it to be sure I'm too young, and have no need of one for now. Nor do I know enough to be able to talk of love without saying the wrong things, so I've no desire to try! But if I wished to yield my heart to love, then by Saint Giles and by three leaves of the Gospel, I'd have a handsome, gracious lover, a fine and high-born knight – but it's not yet my desire or wish: I'm in no hurry to have a lover or to be any man's sweetheart. But I do like being with people who've been in love and have experienced the pain one has to suffer before enjoying love's rewards! Yes, I gladly spend my time with them, to listen to what they have to say and to learn some useful lessons!'

Perceval was delighted by her words and smiled. 'Truly, sweet girl,' he said, 'I wish it were early morning again, so I could spend a good long time with you!'

Just then four servants came, bringing wine and fruit, and candles in great plenty, as many as they wished and needed. The knights ate the fruit and drank the wine with pleasure, and then the squires took Perceval to lie in the finest of beds. The lady had already gone to her gorgeous chamber, as had the radiant girl. According to the story Perceval wouldn't let any servant undress him or remove his boots – they would have taken too long: in no time at all he was abed and asleep, and he slept soundly all night without a thought for his sweetheart – unlike some I know!

All the boys of the household rose at first light, and Perceval rose early, too; but before he'd finished dressing Briol came from his chamber and nobly greeted him in the name of God the king of majesty, and then told a boy to hurry and get their horses ready. He didn't need a second command: he did as bidden promptly, harnessing the horses splendidly and bringing them to the hall.

'Sir Perceval,' said Briol, 'listen to what I have to say. We're going now, and I don't know when we'll be able to return. If you'll take my advice you'll leave behind the stag's head and the dog – and the mule you're so fond of – till after the tournament. All you need to bother with is your destrier.'

Perceval agreed at once to leave them. They swiftly armed with everything a knight should have; then the lady appeared from her sumptuous chamber, and with her came the girl so gracious and fair, and the knights greeted them most courteously the moment they saw them. Perceval rose to meet them, and the girl helped him lace his helm while the lady laced her lord's. Then, without much more ado, they mounted their horses and took their leave, and set off swiftly over the bridge.

They headed towards the forest, great and green and thickly wooded, and it didn't take them long; and once they were in the forest they pressed on over hill and dale, through glade and ford and mire and field and heath, until they came to the river and the bridge of great renown. If you'll attend awhile I'll describe it to you, briefly and exactly. It was made of wood, and built in such a way that from the bank it sloped upwards all the way to the middle, where it stopped – there was nothing more beyond – so that no one could ride across. A priceless pillar of shining copper supported it where it stopped. It was fully the length of a bowshot, and the river that rushed below was wide and deep and flowed faster than any in the world. Perceval saw all this and asked Briol in the name of companionship to tell him what he knew about the bridge: who had built it, and how and why it had come to be left unfinished.

'Sir,' said Briol, 'I can tell you exactly: if you care to hear I'll tell you the whole story in a nutshell.

'Once, some time ago, in the depths of this forest there was a strongly fortified house built by a mighty knight from another land. He had no wife or child or heir, but he was greatly feared and dreaded, renowned for his skill in arms; and he had an impressive household: a retinue of ten or twenty or thirty knights rode with him from his hall.

'Then one Christmas he went to the king's court: at Tinpincarantin, I believe it was, and it was great and splendid indeed. Now, the lord of the Proud Castle had also come to the feast; and as I understand it he challenged him to combat and the battle duly took place at court. After an exhausting struggle the Proud Knight was wounded and outfought and vanquished, and his kinsman Licorés of Baraguidan was deeply upset and pursued this knight of the forest and threatened him with war. The knight owned not a foot of land except his single manor here in the forest; and though he was very powerful his power was not to last much longer.

'One day at his house he discussed with his followers how he could deal with the men of the Proud Castle. One of his counsellors, a worthy knight indeed, said that because of this river, so swift and fierce, he would never be able to assail them, but if someone could find an ingenious way to cross it, the war would soon be won. For the moment nothing more was said.

'But before the month was out, the knight went hunting and came across a massive, ferocious boar. He started it in a thicket, and hunted and followed it so long that he was parted from all his companions and the light of day was gone. He lost track of the boar in the dark, and it fled swiftly away. But three of his dogs gamely kept up the chase: the darkness wasn't going to stop them! Finally they came near a house, tall and stone-built with a great gate at the entrance, but lacking any wall or ditch or tower or bailey: there was nothing to be seen but the gate and this big, expansive house. The boar rushed up and dashed through the gate. I don't know quite what happened, except that the dogs lost all sight of it and were utterly bewildered. The knight, galloping in pursuit, saw the great gate and the house and the dogs outside having lost their quarry; he was astonished: it wasn't like them at all! It was a lovely, tranquil night and the moon was beaming down, casting a bright and gleaming light. The knight called three times at the door of the great stone house, but he could have called all month and no one would have answered or come to speak to him. When he realised he'd have no reply he blew three long, loud blasts on the hunting horn that hung at his neck; the great, thick forest rang with the sound. As the horn's voice echoed away a girl appeared; she was fair and comely indeed, and dressed in an ermine mantle. My heart tells me that none more beautiful was ever born or beheld. She leaned at the window and called:

'"God help me! Who's that, making such a din? You've woken me from my bed!"

'He replied at once: "I'm a knight, lady, confused by all the paths and tracks – I'm completely lost! It would be a great kindness and courtesy to give me lodging."

'"God bless me, sir," she said very readily, "I'll gladly lodge you – say no more!"

'And she went straight to unlock the hall door. He dismounted, and there was a boy on hand to take his horse and see it fed with oats and hay. The lady, full of courtesy and kindness, graciously led the knight inside, and said she was sorry he hadn't come much sooner! The house was well strewn with grass and rushes, and brightly lit with burning candles. The knight hadn't supped and the lady called for food for him; he didn't refuse! They sat down together, and all I need tell you is that they had an array of fine wines and two excellent rabbit pies and other food befitting the hour. I shan't go on – too long a tale is tiresome. But the story goes that the lady asked him to tell her his name and what had brought him from his land. The knight was only too pleased to converse with her, and told her everything. He didn't make a long sermon of it, but briskly recounted what had happened at court: he told her all, and how he could quickly bring his war to a close if only he could cross the river; and how he'd followed the boar. When the lady had heard the story through she pretended it was news to her – but she knew all about it. And she knew, too, more than anyone alive about the magic arts and necromancy and ingenious devices. And the fact is she was overcome with love for the knight: without him she was helpless, bereft of strength and power. She asked his name again, and what he was rightly called.

'"Carimedic," the knight replied.

'"Listen, sir," she said. "If you'll grant me a favour I'll fulfil your wish to cross the great river, so swift and fierce."

'He was amazed, but vowed to do whatever she asked; it could be anything, good or ill – nothing would deter him. This high-born lady thanked him, and revealed at once that she'd loved him for a very long time; and now she wanted him to stay with her and take her for his wife, and Carimedic agreed. Then the lady rose and had the table cleared and the knight stripped of his clothes and boots; then she led him straight to her bed to lie with her: she strove to serve him in every way and did whatever he wished.

'In the morning when day broke and the shining sun appeared, Carimedic asked her to keep her promise about the crossing of the river. She said he'd cross it within three days as long as he waited for her there, and he agreed. So she left him and came straight here, and by her cunning use of necromancy she made the bridge you see before you: before the day was out she'd made the half on this side of the river. I don't know if anyone helped her, but I do know this: that very same day her lover Carimedic was killed by misadventure in the forest – a cruel and mighty knight struck him clean through the body with a lance. The lady heard the news that night and was consumed by anguish – I'd rather not describe her pain. She wouldn't build any more of the bridge, and declared in her distress that it would never be finished and no man would ever be able to cross it – unless he were the most praiseworthy knight in the whole wide world in combat and in chivalry, in largesse and in courtesy, in honouring and serving God and in respect for Holy Church, and in all the virtues that a man born of woman can possess. And so it remains – that's all I know. Many a knight has failed; they've come and tried to cross the bridge but to very little effect. But try yourself: if you succeed in crossing you can go to the great tournament without me. By the faith I owe you, I'll wait right here till I see you again. There's the bridge: try now.'

Perceval didn't hesitate: he rode straight on to the bridge; and the moment his horse stepped on to it, the bridge, never crossed before, let out a groan so hideous, so terrible, that it sounded as if it were splitting and splintering and collapsing utterly; but then the noise stopped; and at that very moment the foot of the bridge, fixed to the riverbank, suddenly tore itself away and swung right round and fixed itself to the ground on the other side. Briol saw and realised that Perceval was the finest, boldest, most awesome knight in the world, without a doubt. With all the breath he could summon he cried:

'Sir Perceval, you must go to the tournament on your own, without me: there's no way I can cross! Ride on now as fast as you can: it'll soon be past none.'*

Perceval heard him, and rode straight down from the bridge and set off into the forest. He rode on alone, rejoicing in his heart at having crossed the bridge where so many knights had failed.

The Tournament at the Proud Castle

He urged his destrier ever onward till he caught sight of the Proud Castle. The good, brave knights of King Arthur's household were already in the fields, drawing up in lines of battle. With the king, I can say for sure, were his nephew Gawain and King Urien's son, the gentle, noble Yvain; and Kay the seneschal and Lucan the master butler, and Sagremor and Bedivere, Gaherïet and Agravain; and Yvain of the White Hands was there, too, as was Yvain the Bastard and Tors the son of King Arés, and Taules de Rougemont, a knight of high renown, and King Lac's son Erec, and Lancelot of the Lake. In their company also was Elis of the ill-cut coat, the son of the Welshwoman; and Monendas, who was married to the Danish damsel who'd called the tournament together. Opposing them, at the other end of the field, was the mighty king of Ireland with three thousand of his Irishmen; and King Aguisial of Scotland was there with all his knights, as was the noble Brien of the Isles with a splendid company. The good Welshman Perceval rode down to join their side, wanting to joust against King Arthur's forces and perform such deeds of chivalry as everyone would envy.

The battalions and squadrons were all deployed, destriers stomping, pennons flying in the wind; helmets shone and shields shimmered; every knight had his lance in hand. Then Kay sprang forward and asked for the first joust, and King Arthur gave him leave to begin the tournament. Without more ado Kay rode forth in eager bounds; Perceval recognised him instantly and charged towards him, spurring his horse to a greater speed than a falcon swooping on a dove. Kay came to meet him bravely, and as the horses raced together the knights struck each other full on their shields; Kay's lance smashed in two that instant, but Perceval thrust his an arm's length through Kay's shield and pierced his fine and close-meshed hauberk, and as they met he crashed into him so hard that he sent him flying over his horse's rump and tumbling to the ground. He seized his horse and led it away, leaving Kay wounded a little and struggling to find his feet.

The two sides came together now, with a fearsome force that made the very earth shake. The king of Ireland clashed with Sagremor, and smashed right through his gold-striped shield; but Sagremor returned a blow that dashed him from his stirrups and brought him to the ground; but the Irish were at hand to help him up again.

The tourney now intensified, with everyone involved; many a knight shed blood as they clashed and brought each other down and rained blows on their steel helms with their naked swords. The most skilled in arms did wonders: Gawain was his usual self and captured the king of Scotland despite his reputation as a warrior; and on the other side Perceval was dealing awesome blows with his sword – the Scots and the Irish had a fine companion in him! Through the tournament the Welshman rode, his furbished sword of steel in hand, intent not on winning booty but on performing feats of chivalry.

The deeds of arms, assaults and mêlées raged on until vespers rang, when they broke up and departed. Then Perceval returned to the bridge and rode straight on; and it promptly swung round to the other side where it had been before. Briol saw this and, laughing, asked him how he was; Perceval cheerfully replied that he was in fine shape and spirits.

'Did the tournament take place?'

'Yes, and it was huge,' said Perceval. 'But let's turn our minds to other things: to board and lodging for tonight – I've eaten nothing all day!'

Briol replied most warmly: 'Tonight, I think, we'll have hospitality like Saint Julian's!'[28]

They set off then without delay, riding through the forest till they came to a deep valley. There they found a chapel and the cell of a hermit who lived a most holy and exemplary life in the woods, devoted to God; he was a wise and worthy man indeed, and a cousin of Briol's. They went straight to the wicket gate and entered. I shan't go into detail but they were made most welcome, and had such comfort as can be found in the woods, especially at a hermitage, until day dawned next morning.

Now let me tell you about King Arthur. He'd returned to the Proud Castle with all his splendid knights, who quickly disarmed and donned rich gowns and set off to the hall. King Arthur went to Kay to see if he was wounded; he sent two doctors to him, but they said he'd suffered no harm. The knights had been laughing a lot behind Kay's back: he'd been toppled from his horse in the very first joust in full view of a thousand knights or more! Even the king had made fun of him; and he asked them if they'd recognised the knight who'd unhorsed Kay, but they said they didn't know who he was and had never seen his shield.

'But I know this much,' said Sir Gawain. 'He's a worthy and valiant knight indeed, and he's won the vespers* prize for sure.'

Then a horn was blown to herald the water, and the king washed and took his seat and then all the worthy knights sat down to eat. But it would be tiresome and laborious to list the dishes; instead I want to tell you about the forces outside the castle – the Scots and the Irish who were camped out in the field, and many other respected lords who'd searched and scoured far and wide for the knight they'd seen at the vespers. Try as they might they could find no word of him, but all agreed he'd performed better than anyone. They spent all night talking of it – and in revelry – till morning came and the glorious sun blazed down. Then both sides – those in the castle and those without – made ready, and breakfasted on bread and wine. Without more ado their fine destriers were harnessed and caparisoned and pennons were tied to their smooth ashwood lances. The knights pulled on their chausses, laced their knee-pieces and donned their bright hauberks. Soon both sides were armed and assembled in the field. It was the most perfect expanse of ground ever seen, a sward of lush, green grass, as fine as could be for tourneying. There you'd have seen many a fine destrier, handsomely caparisoned, and so many lances and banners that it was a wonder to behold; and an array of shields – crimson, gold and red and silver – that lit up the whole country. Both sides now were ranged and deployed: they had only to join battle.

Sir Perceval hadn't stopped riding since early morning, pressing on till he reached the tourney. But he was completely unrecognised, for he'd left his arms with Briol who'd exchanged them for his own, and very fine they were. So he wasn't spotted by the knights who were looking out for him, longing to know from which land he came after he'd shown such prowess.

Battle now was joined; anyone with an appetite for clashes, jousts and mêlées, for seeing mighty sword-blows land on shining helms, would have sworn no combat was ever fought in any field in all the world with such ferocity, except in mortal battle. No knights ever endured so much; they had no thought at all for booty, only for doing great deeds. As for King Arthur, let me tell you, in the middle of the field, right between the lines, he felled the king of Ireland and seized his chestnut Spanish charger and

---

[28] A reference to the legend of Julian the Hospitaller (the patron saint of travellers seeking lodging), implying the generous offering of everything available.

handed it to Sagremor – and bade him return it to the king. You should have seen how the knights of Arthur's household charged! They smashed lances, shattered shields, dealt ringing blows to helms of steel! But their opponents fought back well – Brien of the Isles performed admirably, as did the Scottish king and his knights. The king of Ireland was remounted now among his men, and exhorted them to show their chivalry; they all vowed and swore to do just that. And what of Perceval? What wonders did he perform? King Arthur's nephew Guerrehés he struck from his Gascon steed in full view of all the Britons. Then Gawain, Lancelot and Yvain mounted a charge that made the battle-lines shake; what blows you'd have seen delivered then on helms and gilded shields! The poised and valiant Perceval gripped his sword of steel, vowing to drive them from the field or consider himself of little worth. He spurred his fine charger on and plunged into the thickest press; he felled two knights of high renown – companions of Gawain they were: one was the worthy Lancelot and the other the proud Agravain. Then he struck out to left and right: all could declare with certainty that the master of all knights had come! That was soon agreed by all, and rightly so, I'd say! Through the press he charged back and forth, unstoppable, driving opponents back on every side, and thanks to him the Irish were resurgent. Then the Scottish king clashed with Yvain; they smashed their lances utterly, but neither was unhorsed and they let each other be. The mêlée now was general.

King Arthur withdrew from the press and sat watching the feats of Perceval – not that he recognised him. He saw him holding his charger still in the very middle of the fray, and striking and repelling the very finest of his household; he saw that no one could prevent him doing exactly as he wished; he saw him carving the press apart with his naked sword; he saw him single-handedly restore the fortunes of the foe; he saw him display sufficient might to earn the whole wide world's esteem; he saw that if he'd wanted booty he could have captured steeds and knights at will. His courage and strength were such that he feared no man of woman born. Brien of the Isles and his men were at his side all day: what a fine companion they'd found in him! A wall, a fortress! Unless they suddenly lost their valour they'd win spoils from the tournament worth a thousand silver marks! After seeing all this, King Arthur called Sir Gawain to him and said:

'Nephew, on that black destrier there's a fine knight indeed! God bless me, I've never seen his equal in my life! At the tournament's close, dear nephew, go and find out his name and where he's from, and tell him straight to come to me: I command it. If he wished to remain a member of my household in company with you, I'd love him more than any man born! I'm amazed how many blows he's dealt this day – just as many now as he did at the start!'

'By the holy cross, sire,' Gawain replied, 'I'd say he's the finest knight in all the world!'

With that they both charged into the fray and delivered many a fearsome blow; they were the terror of all their foes; Sir Gawain showed his mettle and his chivalry indeed! By the time the Irish king arrived the king of Scotland's great battalion was broken and in retreat, and the Scottish king himself was unhorsed. But he was rescued and remounted and the pursuit was checked – thanks to Perceval coming to help his side: Gawain called on him to yield and abandon the fight, but Perceval was enraged by this and struck Gawain a blow that felled him and his charger together. What a battle followed then! Lancelot was furious and determined to avenge his companion Gawain; but he soon found himself in such straits that he'd have given a thousand marks of gold to escape, as Perceval gave him and the thirty peers a battering that confounded them utterly.

Monendas came unstuck, as well, he and all his men. But truly, they'd have won the day convincingly had it not been for Perceval.

It was now mid-afternoon. King Arthur and his household had struck many a mighty blow, but the opposing side had fought worthily and valiantly indeed, and with the help of Perceval – still unrecognised – they'd held their ground well. But at last the tournament broke up, with both sides very weary, and they all retired to their respective lodgings to rest.

Then King Arthur bade Gawain go and find the unknown knight. He did so very gladly, and went searching among all the knights for the one he had no chance of finding – for he was away and riding swiftly through the forest. When Gawain realised he wouldn't find him, he went and reported to the king that his search was fruitless: he had no news of him at all. That was that: they had to put up with it. But how they praised the knight! Inside the castle and in the camp outside, all were searching and asking for him. Brien of the Isles was most frustrated that he'd gone. They looked for him high and low, but there wasn't the slightest sign of him.

But that's enough of them; I want to tell you of Perceval. He crossed the great river unhindered, the bridge swinging round to the other side just as it had done before, and at the forest's edge he saw Briol, who'd dismounted and tethered his horse beneath a huge, spreading tree. He'd unlaced and removed his bright steel helm and was lying down to rest with his head propped on his shield. But he saw Perceval coming and realised who it was at once, and leapt up and donned his helm again and mounted without delay. With shield round neck and lance in hand he rode to meet him and greeted him most nobly in the name of God who is lord of all, and courteously asked him to tell him how he'd fared. Perceval recounted the whole day's work as they rode straight on to Briol's house.

Night was very near by the time they arrived. They exchanged few words as they dismounted and four servants came running and took their horses away to be well stabled. Then the two knights entered the hall, and before they'd disarmed the lady and her daughter came from a great chamber hung with oriental silks. Perceval was the first to see them; he'd just removed his hauberk, but still had on his shoulder-pieces of quilted cloth, and one of his chausses was unlaced and the other was round his ankle! But in this state he rose to meet them and embraced them, and that spirited lady greeted him with words of joyful welcome. Her modest and gentle daughter called for two handsome mantles of scarlet cloth, brand new, and had the two knights dressed. Then, without more ado, the candles were lit and orders were given for food to be brought at once. The servants weren't slow about it, and soon the tables were up and ready and the water brought, and the knights washed and took their seats. The fair-faced damsel with the faithful heart ate together with Perceval, and the lady with her lord. They had fine food in plenty, as much as they could wish, and there's no need to ask if they were sparing with the wine!

When they'd supped long enough they rose and their table was cleared. In the great, wide hall a bed was made for Perceval; but deeply tired though he was, he asked the girl earnestly about his mule and his dog: he was more eager to see them than anything, and they were brought to him at once. Once his mind was settled he lay down to sleep, for he was very weary, and by now it was far into the night; and all the others, too, took to their beds.

Perceval slept well that night, not waking till the sun had risen and the light was radiant. Then he dressed and made ready and called for his arms; a boy brought them for him and helped him to arm. He had his horse saddled and packed the stag's head behind, and the mule was ready, saddled and harnessed. There was no more to be said; but when Briol came and saw he meant to mount and leave he tried to hold him back, saying:

'I can't say I approve of this, sir! You've been hard at it for so long! In all that time you've not had a moment's rest, I know – nor has your horse! A single favour I beg of you, in the name of love and courtesy – and of companionship above all, and by the faith you owe God: stay here tonight, just till tomorrow; then you can go wherever you wish. You can surely grant me that.'

'Truly, friend,' said Perceval, 'I can't stay a moment longer; I'd perjure myself if I did. You mustn't ask me to stay and break an oath. You've shown me so much honour and kindness that I love you more than anyone, and be assured that if you ever need me I'll never fail you.'

Briol thanked him deeply for this, well aware that there was no finer knight from there to the city of Rome: he loved him all the more for that. And one should indeed value above all things a worthy man who proves his goodness – when God grants that you find such a man!

Then the lady came and greeted him most nobly, and she and the lovely maiden begged him to stay if he could. But he insisted that he couldn't, for the journey ahead of him was long indeed and he didn't know how he would reach the end. But enough; there's no point spinning the story out: Perceval mounted the mule without more ado and took his leave and set off; through the gate he rode, taking with him the stag's head and the dog he loved so much.

Trapped in the Tomb

He didn't stop till he entered the forest; then he pressed on hard all day till evening. Along a wide path he came upon a cross and a tree, and a tomb covered by a marble slab. He drew rein there and looked at the cross and the tomb and its marble slab – under which a knight was wailing loudly. He climbed from the white mule and leaned over the tomb. The knight inside was crying:

'Dear lord God, have mercy! Will I never be free from here?'

Perceval called back: 'Are you on God's side, friend?'

'Indeed I am, good sir! But I'm the most wretched, unfortunate knight ever born of woman!'

Perceval, amazed, said: 'Tell me how I can help you, friend. How can I lift this stone and let you out?'

'Oh, dear man, if you're willing to help me, all you have to do is cut a lever from that tree so you can raise the marble slab. That would do the trick!'

So Perceval did exactly as he asked, lifting the slab and holding it up till the knight was out; and a fine figure of a knight he was, in face and limbs and body. He was first to speak, saying:

'Sir knight, we must lower this heavy marble back in place.'

And he came up to the lever that was propping up the slab, stood next to Perceval who still had it in his hands, and without another word barged into him, knees and arms and ribs together, to send him tumbling into the grave. Then back down crashed the marble slab, so hard that the ground around it quaked, for it was truly colossal. And that was that! The knight cried:

'Now you'll have to guard this place, just as I've done all this while! Pursue folly and the chances always are you'll come to grief! I've bequeathed you a home where you'll have little comfort! I've a feeling you'll die before you ever escape!'

And he strode up to the mule and mounted at once, intending to ride off. But the mule stood firm as if tied to a stake. The knight was enraged, speechless with fury. He jumped from the mule and ran to the horse, and dumping the stag's head tied to the saddle he mounted at once. He took up neither shield nor lance, nor did he take any notice of the dog standing motionless by the mule; instead he beat and kicked at the horse, trying to ride away. But no amount of thrashing would make it stir.

'What's going on?' he cried. 'The nag won't move! Either it holds me in contempt or the knight's cast a spell on it! He's charmed the mule he brought, as well! She wouldn't take a step forward or back, not for anything!'

In a terrible rage he dismounted and strode back to the tomb. For a moment he paused. Then, with all his malice ebbing away, he raised the marble slab and said:

'Come out, sir. It would be wicked and wrong of me to do you harm. And I couldn't even if I wanted to: I know in truth you're the most worthy, refined, accomplished knight, the best endowed with chivalry, alive. And if you want to exceed and surpass the whole world in deeds of arms, follow this grassy path to the high peak of Mount Dolorous.'

Then Perceval stepped from the tomb and the knight jumped back inside without another word. The slab fell back on top of him, with a crash that made the ground around it shake. Perceval cried with all his might, calling on the knight to reveal his name and why he'd returned to the tomb; but the knight replied:

'You'll hear nothing more for now; but in time you'll know it all for sure – before the year is out.'

The worthy, valiant Perceval could see he was going to say no more, and returned to his horse and packed the stag's head on again; then he mounted the mule without more ado and picked up the dog and set off through the great forest.

It was a difficult path, thick with grass and thorns, but he didn't stop riding till none,* when he came upon a damsel sitting beneath a tall tree. She was dressed in a gown of samite, fresh and new, and on her head was a chaplet of leaves, very pretty and finely made. But she hadn't removed her wimple – indeed, she was so well muzzled she could hardly see! Perceval came straight up and greeted her, and she rose to meet him, took off her wimple and said:

'God help me, sir, I want my white mule back and my ring, as was promised when I gave them to you.'

Hearing this, Perceval dismounted at once and embraced her. She, bright girl that she was, asked him kindly to tell her if he'd been to the Fisher King's court and what he'd discovered: if he knew now about the lance and what the grail was, and if he'd asked about the sword that couldn't be repaired, and the other deep mysteries which would be revealed to no knight till the coming of the one endowed with every quality: that knight would be told the truth, and would then be so blessed and of such renown that he'd be deemed the finest of all knights living, now or ever in the past.

'Lady,' said Perceval, 'by God the lord of all, I shan't lie: I have to admit I've not been there. When I crossed the bridge of glass I met a most worthy man, and went with him that night and he gave me splendid lodging; and he told me about the high bridge that no one could cross, and of the tournament assembling at the Proud Castle. So by the faith I owe you, I got delayed! I'm sorry to say I didn't go to that esteemed king so full of goodness and honour and humility and kindness. But if it please God in whom I trust, I'll go there soon without being diverted.'

He climbed from the mule at once and returned her to that fair-faced girl; then he gave her back the ring. With barely a word she promptly mounted and, without taking leave, rode swiftly away, urging the mule ever onward, for dark night was setting in. Perceval was left bewildered – and lost: he'd no idea which path or direction to take if he was to find the way to the king called the Fisher. He decided to stay where he was and let his horse graze on the dewy grass till morning. So that's what he did: he stopped beneath the tree, and when he'd seen to his horse he stayed awake, reflecting deeply, until the new day had fully dawned and the sun was shining bright and clear.

The Magic Chessboard

He remounted without delay; and you may be sure he said his Paternoster, praying that God would put him on the path to the court of the Fisher King, who'd shown him so much honour, and to the castle of that fair-faced girl where he'd seen the handsome chessboard and the priceless chessmen laden with gold and precious stones imbued with holy, special powers to counter all ills.

Then, as he rode on, deep in silent thought, he heard a voice in a lofty, spreading tree, cry:

'Knight full of courtesy, Perceval by name, if you wish to find your way to the castle where you were given the little dog, listen to what I say: place him on the ground and let him go, and be sure to follow him swiftly wherever he goes, down every path and track he takes, till you see him enter the castle or some other house or fortress.'

Perceval heard every word the voice in the tree had said. 'God and Holy Mary help me: who's that talking up there?'

He looked up and down and high and low, but could see and hear no living thing. But he took hold of the dog and placed him on the ground; and to his utter delight he heard him bay three times, so loudly that the forest echoed long, before rushing off, head down as if following a scent. Perceval galloped after, and on they raced through wood and glade until, standing by a pool on a rocky slope beside a river, he caught sight of the loveliest castle he'd ever seen. Its walls were high and finely built of dressed stone, and its keep was tall and well fortified, standing at a bend in the river that lapped at the foot of its handsome wall. The castle in truth was too fair to describe. The dog went bounding on till he reached the gate, and Perceval galloped in after him, quite unhindered, for there was no one to be seen – no man or woman or any living soul. Perceval didn't draw rein till he reached the great flagged hall, where he saw the dog run up a short flight of steps and in; he dismounted then and tethered his horse to a ring he found fixed in a wall. Into the great hall he strode at once, and no man ever saw a place adorned so gloriously – it was an utter wonder. The floor was strewn with flowers, the ceiling a blaze of painted colours, the walls hung with gold-embroidered samite, green and red and every hue. I shan't go on, but in the middle of the hall was a bed of wondrous style: I can't tell you how gorgeous it was. And as Perceval approached he saw the dog lying on it, and before it he saw none other than the splendid chessboard on which he'd played before. Perceval stared, transfixed, at the magnificent chessmen.

'God!' he said. 'I'm back where I've so longed to be!'

He went and sat beside the gold-painted board; the pieces were neatly set up just as they should be. He picked up a pawn and was just about to move it when he glanced towards the door of a handsome chamber and saw a girl appear, of such radiant beauty that no fairer creature was ever born – she seemed a spiritual being. So charming was she, so beautiful, that Perceval was stunned; but he stood at once and came to greet her. She paused a moment before returning his greeting warmly; and when the dog heard her voice he leapt up to meet her, skipping and bounding and barking, and she stroked him and gave him the fondest welcome.

'Sir,' she said to Perceval, 'I've every reason to charge you with baseness, taking my dog without saying a word! Truly, if I'd known you were going to be so sly and deceive me, I'd never have granted the request you made me then. I'm sorry I ever lent you the dog and agreed to be your sweetheart – men have such faithless hearts!'

'My dear one,' answered Perceval, 'if you knew the misfortune, trouble and trials I've suffered since the moment I left you, I think you'd have pity on me! I promise you I caught the white stag in the park – I still have the prize part, down there outside the hall!'

And he went straight back to his horse and brought the head to the maiden who received the gift most gladly. Just then a boy appeared from a chamber and she told him:

'Go and see to the horse outside: take good care of him – stable him with my own.'

The boy did as bidden. The fair maiden and Perceval weren't left long before three other handsome, strapping boys came from a chamber and up to Perceval and promptly, smartly disarmed him from head to foot. His shield and sword and lance and all his other armour they stored securely away, and brought him a handsome, rich silk mantle trimmed with squirrel fur, while the servants set the table and brought them water for their hands. There's no more to be said than this: they had every fine, fresh dish they could have wished.

After they'd eaten, the damsel took Perceval by the right hand and they sat together at the window overlooking the great river.

'Sir,' she said, 'it's only right that you tell me your name, and exactly what kept you away so long.'

'By Saint Simon, lady,' he replied, 'my name is Perceval; I was born and raised in Wales. I'll gladly tell you all you ask, and without a word of a lie. After I'd caught the white stag and taken its head, I was on the very point of returning when some wicked-hearted girl appeared – I've no idea where from. I was there in the park, tying the stag's head to my saddle, and while I was busy with this she snatched your dog from before my eyes without a word, and then said she was taking him whether I liked it or not! I told her she'd do no such thing, no matter what she said! I was furious, beside myself with rage! But she just looked at me and said I was discourteous and that might wasn't right, but that if I was truly worthy and wanted to have the dog back in peace and friendship, without any trouble, I should go straight to a tomb nearby where I'd find a knight[29] and tell him that whoever had forced him to lie there was guilty of great folly and presumption. I swear I did exactly as she said; and I'd only been there a moment when a great knight, fully armed in black, appeared on a huge black horse and cried:

'"Vassal, you've made a big mistake!"

'There was no respite! We exchanged lance-blows and unhorsed each other, then drew our swords and combat began; and while we were at it another knight came riding

---

[29] Literally 'where a knight was painted'; see the reference to 'a mounted knight I've painted on the tomb', above, p. 282.

up, fully armed, and without a word he made straight for the dog, lying beside the stag's head that I'd left on the grass in the middle of the field. I was none too pleased to see him heading that way, and sure enough he took the dog and the head together and carried them off and vanished into the forest, much to my distress and fury. I was still locked in combat – the knight was fighting vigorously; but in the end he struggled to cope with the blows I dealt and fled to the vaulted tomb and dived straight in; I raced after him and called to him three times at the top of my voice – but couldn't get any useful reply, I'm sorry to say. So I rode off into the forest after the other knight: I didn't dare return to you having lost your dog, by God! I was determined to find him, and searched and scoured many lands; I suffered much toil and trouble and hardship, and at last I've brought him back to you! There – that's the whole story.'

'Really?' said the damsel. 'Is that truly what happened?'

'Yes indeed, so help me God! And now, if it please you, lady, I'd like you to fulfil the promise you made when you sent me to hunt the white stag.'

'You've deserved it, truly, my dear sweet friend, and I swear you shall have your reward, just as you desire.'

Perceval, joyously relieved, came straight up and kissed her twice, most tenderly and lovingly: those kisses tasted sweet, I'll bet, and perfectly in season! And he wasn't afraid to ask her now:

'The chessboard, lady, and the golden chessmen: may I ask who makes them play? I'd love to know, if you're willing to tell.'

'God have mercy!' she replied. 'Do you know what you're asking? It would be dark by the time the tale was done, and I fear you'd find it tiresome!'

'Indeed I won't!' said Perceval.

'Come then,' she said. 'Let's sit on the bed. I'll tell you the whole story in the proper order.'

So they left the window and sat on the gorgeous bed, and placed the chessboard in front of them and picked up the pieces. The worthy Perceval examined them closely as she began her tale:

'There was once a girl, most comely, bright and beautiful, who was very skilled in magic, having learnt it since her childhood. Well taught she was in every way: she understood the stars and all the powers of the moon and the heavens and the shining sun. She could explain every change in the weather. She was adept indeed – but I promise you, you couldn't find anyone more likeable or honourable. That was the girl, in a nutshell.

'One day she went into a wood and rode a long while till she came to a meadow where she found Morgan the Fay sitting with a knight. Before them was a chessboard with a superb set of ivory chessmen. I'm telling you the absolute truth; this is exactly what happened. The damsel rode up to the chessboard and dismounted from her splendid palfrey – no girl ever rode one more handsome, fine and swift, with a gorgeous saddle-cloth of scarlet embroidered with gold. Morgan and the knight rose to meet her; they greeted and embraced her joyfully, and then they sat down all together and spoke of many matters. Finally the damsel reached out for the chessboard and picked up a rook; she saw how beautifully carved it was, and inlaid here and there with gold to embellish the ivory. Morgan looked at the girl and said:

'"I pray you, my dear, take those chessmen – I'd like you to have them. Or I could send them to you with the board. They're beautiful, so handsomely carved, enhanced with inlays of finest gold. They were made with great skill at London, a city on the

Thames, and sent to me from there; and now I give them to you as a token of friendship. Take them – I bequeath them to you: they can remind you of me!"

'"Gladly, lady!" she replied. "And in return for your gift, I'll give you a handsome board and chessmen that I made myself. They're made in such a way that if anyone wishes to play a game, then as long as he be a loyal knight – or a worthy lady or damsel, wise and fair and courteous – he'll need no opponent: the pieces will move by themselves! They won't do anyone any harm, but they know exactly how to checkmate! And they'll reset themselves and start again unaided! Now they'll be in your keeping."

'Morgan said: "Many thanks!"

'Hardly had these words been uttered before a boy came galloping on a fine grey horse, right up to those two fair damsels, and dismounted. In his hands he was holding this chessboard, painted with fine gold. He came up to Morgan and greeted her, and presented her with the board and the chessmen on behalf of his noble damsel. Morgan took them and gazed long at the superb and handsome craftsmanship. She was very grateful to the damsel and thanked her deeply. I don't know quite what happened next and how they came to part, but they made their way back to their own lands.

'At that time, I think, I was at the castle of Sir Gawain's great-uncle King Brandigan – I was cousin of the queen, and still quite young, no more than ten years old. And one day Morgan – King Arthur's sister – came to stay; and the queen – my friend and cousin, who'd looked after me so long – asked me to go with Morgan when she left. I agreed, on the understanding that I could leave her whenever I wished, and that was promised.

'A week later she returned to her land and, in short, we spent fifteen years together until, one day, we went out to a meadow and pitched a tent on the green and flowery sward. Well, I got upset about something or other and asked her leave; she was reluctant to give it, but I insisted that nothing would make me stay with her a moment longer. So I took my leave and was about to go, and she invited me to ask for a favour and I'd have it at once, no matter how great. It didn't take me long to answer:

'"Lady, if you want to give me something, let it be your chessboard and its men; there's nothing else I want from you."

'She didn't refuse, and I left without another word. Then I came upon the river you can see below the windows here, and I loved the spot so much that I had this lovely place built – I've been here for ten years now. And with me I had this board and chessmen, the most handsome in the world, made just as I've described to you: I've told you the perfect truth. But come, let's get on – night is fast approaching.'

Then Perceval looked up and saw the door of a chamber open; and leaning in the doorway was a most beautiful maiden. Perceval told the damsel he'd like to go and see this chamber, and she said:

'Come, then.'

He didn't dally, but went with her into that sumptuous chamber – I shan't attempt to describe it: to record in detail the beauty and splendour, the luxury and elegance lavished upon that room would take too long! So I shan't hold up the story, either with truth or falsehood; there's really no point. As he entered, Perceval saw seven maidens sitting, alight with such beauty and intelligence that God might have made them with His very own hands – and so He did, I'd say. They were making orfrey with silk and gold, but when they looked up and saw Perceval they rose to greet him, and he replied most graciously.

He stayed there with them till night was setting in, but there was so much light in that chamber and the surrounding rooms that it was a wonder. Smart and handsome squires and servants promptly set up the tables, and the maidens took their seats along with Perceval and the damsel. I shan't describe the dishes they had, for they were plentiful; and when they'd eaten all they pleased the tables and cloths were cleared. They chatted of various things till the ladies retired to their chambers to lie down and rest, leaving Perceval in the great hall where the gorgeous bed was ready for him. The squires and servants removed his shoes and saw him into that lovely bed without more ado; then they left, taking with them all the lights.

But Perceval didn't fall asleep as quickly as usual: he was thinking of that damsel of fairy-like beauty. And as he was deep in those very thoughts she came to his bed and lay down and fulfilled her promise to him, just as he'd asked and she'd vowed to do barring some foolish failure on his part. They lay together all that night, until the day dawned bright and fair across the land.

Then Perceval rose at once. There was no squire or servant or maid or chamberlain present. The charming damsel rose, too, and Perceval asked her kindly to have his arms and his horse made ready, for he still had much to do.

'Oh, sir!' she replied. 'Stay here henceforth! You'll have everything your heart desires!'

Perceval said there was no way he could stay; but he swore by God and Saint Peter that as soon as he could, as soon as he'd been to the Fisher King's court, he would return. This he vowed and promised her and she accepted thankfully; and she said she'd see him on his way: she would show him the path that would take him straight there by the very next day – provided he didn't stray from it. Perceval thanked her deeply, and she called for his arms and had his horse made ready, and he promptly armed himself with hauberk, shield and lance and all he needed. Then they left the hall and went down the steps and found two horses saddled. Perceval mounted, and so did the damsel, white as the may, saying she would escort him till she'd set him on the right track.

Out of the castle they rode, and down a wide path till they came to the fierce and rushing river. There they found a boat tied and locked to a great, leafy oak tree on the bank. Perceval dismounted and helped the damsel down, and she took out a key she had and unlocked the boat.

'Step aboard,' she said, 'and take your horse with you; the boat will carry you safely – you need have no fear. When you reach the other side, follow the wide path and it'll lead you straight to the court of the Fisher King – keep to it constantly: you'll find it goes through a beautiful forest.'

Perceval said he would indeed, and commended her to God, the lord of all the world. Then he boarded the boat and pulled his horse in behind him. The boat flew faster than a sparrowhawk, over the river and ashore on the other side. Perceval sprang joyously on to the gravel and drew his horse out after him; then the boat returned to the charming girl, who was still on the further shore. She watched fondly as Perceval mounted his horse and rode off into the great forest; then she turned away and rode back to her castle and dismounted outside her hall. In she went at once; and there on her bed she found the chessboard and the chessmen and the dog, who went out of his way to cheer her. As for the stag's head, I'm not going to tell you what became of that – it would take too long; but I'll say this much: it was subsequently sent to the noble knights at court, and it was much fought over before all was done.

The Madness of Mount Dolorous

But I must leave all that: I want to return to Perceval, who left the broad path that the girl had shown him, that led to the good Fisher King. He set off down another track, tough and overgrown and thick with thorns. All day long he rode this way, and met no knight or girl or damsel who could give him guidance till it was almost dark. Then for the first time he spotted a knight – hung by his feet from a spreading tree. He was still fully armed, and his horse was tethered to a branch beside him. He'd been hanging there in agony for two whole days. Perceval saw him from far off, and wondered what was going on; he thrust in his spurs and his good charger carried him swiftly to the knight. He stared at him hanging from the tree, and the knight wasn't slow to speak, begging him to help him and to be quick about it, for if he delayed in the slightest he'd be beyond all help, he was in such pain. The noble, true-hearted Perceval rode right up close and took him down, gathering him in his arms and laying him in his upturned shield and setting him on the ground. Then he sat down at his side, unlaced his burnished helm for him and pulled back his chainmail hood to cool his face. The suffering knight let out a deep sigh and raised his head and opened his eyes and said:

'Sir, may God who suffered death for us grant you joy and honour: you've rescued me from agony and given me back my life. What more can I say? I'm your liegeman now for the rest of my days!'

Perceval took a good look at him and gently asked his name and how he'd come to be in such a plight.

The knight replied that his name was Bagomedés. 'And listen, sir,' he said. 'I was on my way to high Mount Dolorous. I promise what I'm about to tell you is true: in this wood here I met Sir Kay, King Arthur's seneschal, and there were three tough armed knights with him, worthy and valiant men to be sure. They were coming back from Mount Dolorous, and all four of them had lost their minds because they'd taken their horses past the crosses and tied them to the pillar on the mount. I'm sure you'll have heard of that great, unparalleled marvel: that no knight can tie a horse, palfrey or destrier to a ring in the wondrous pillar there, unless he be the finest knight in the world. Well, those four had come back completely deranged, and when they met me they didn't say a single word; I hailed them well enough, as befitted worthy men, but Kay – ill-natured as ever – and the other three attacked me and unhorsed me. I don't know what more to say: they did me indescribable shame and harm. Kay was at the forefront and the cruellest of them all, and he bound my hands and feet – he was merciless; and he hung me from this oak tree as you found me. If you hadn't come by I'd have been dead and done for: I was helpless. So thank you! You've saved me! Now tell me your name and where you're headed: what's your mission?'

Perceval said he was roaming the land in search of adventures, being very eager to test himself. Then he told him his name and said he would go without a doubt to the pillar on Mount Dolorous to find out if he'd ever be a knight of worth.

While they'd been talking night had fallen, and a beautiful, tranquil night it was. Their horses grazed on the fresh, lush grass at their feet till day dawned and the sun shone bright. Bagomedés was almost recovered and restored to health, and they harnessed their horses and mounted; then without more ado they took their leave, and with embraces and promises of mutual service they prepared to go their separate ways. Bagomedés told Perceval he'd go to the great royal court at Carlion and charge Kay with treachery, for he was now his enemy indeed. Perceval replied:

'If you're going to the court, my friend, give the king and the queen and her maids my greetings, and if they ask for news of me tell them I'm very well. And if Sir Gawain's there, and the worthy Yvain, you can be sure they'll entertain you with the greatest honour for my sake.'

'Thank you, sir,' said Bagomedés. 'You've done me such fine service that I should hold you dear above all others; and God grant that I see the day when I can repay you in some way – I'd be sorry if we didn't meet again.'

With that they set off and parted, Perceval heading straight for Mount Dolorous where many brave knights had found themselves in dire straits.

But here the story leaves Perceval for a little; first I shall tell you about others: how Bagomedés fared when he went to King Arthur's court, and how Sir Gawain and Yvain and Brien of the Isles and fully forty companions, all of them loyal and worthy knights of high renown, went in search of Perceval.

Revenge upon Sir Kay

Bagomedés rode into the forest at once, and spurring his horse he went faster than a swooping sparrowhawk or merlin, following a wide, clear path that led straight to a castle, well positioned and fine and strong with great walls and a lofty tower. At the gate stood a vavasor who cut an impressive figure indeed, and when he saw Bagomedés he came to meet him and had him dismount and bade two pages take his horse to the stable, though it was still not yet past terce. Two other boys ably disarmed him, and without more ado the vavasor called for the tables to be set. I'm not going to start describing the fuss they made of their guest at dinner, but they entertained him lavishly, for the vavasor recognised Bagomedés, and they had a generous spread and fine wines a-plenty.

As soon as they rose from table Bagomedés asked for his horse to be fetched and his arms to be brought at once, for he would arm; but the vavasor said he'd do no such thing – he should stay the night and wait till morning and set off at dawn before the day grew hot. Bagomedés insisted he must go that very day, and started telling him of the shame he'd suffered at the hands of Kay; when he'd finished his story he declared he'd never rest till he'd avenged the outrageous wrong that Kay had done him. The vavasor argued no more: he bade that his arms and his horse be brought at once and had him swiftly armed in his presence; and Bagomedés mounted as soon as he was armed and took his leave and set off swiftly, shield hung from neck and strong, steel-headed lance in hand.

He plunged straight into the forest, and fair it was indeed. There he met a girl on a handsome palfrey, iron-grey, and he asked her where she'd come from and where she was going. She didn't hide it, but told him she'd come from the court of the renowned King Arthur.

'Oh, tell me, dear friend,' he said, 'where he was when you left him.'

'I left him at Escavalon, sir, in the land of Wales. He'd just called for everyone to pack because he was about to leave: I heard he's to hold a great feast at Cardigan on Saint John's Day.[30] That's where you'll find him, I think, if you wish to speak to him – but you'll have to make haste and ride hard: the great court will be gathering now.'

He asked her if she'd seen Sir Gawain there, and Yvain and Kay the seneschal.

---

[30] At midsummer, on June 24th.

'I saw them, yes,' she replied. 'The other day Kay was out of his mind, and now he seems possessed by demons: he's intent on shaming everyone with his vicious tongue. I was on the receiving end myself, but no one should take any notice of his slanders.'

With that their talking ended, and they made their farewells and commended each other to God. Bagomedés set off swiftly, determined to avenge the shame and harm he'd suffered at Kay's hands. He found a well-made road leading out of the forest, and rode rapidly on over mountains and valleys, through tangled wastes and over plains, until he came on Saint John's Day to Cardigan where the great court had assembled. Lords of the highest renown had come from many a far-off land.

The king was seated in the hall at the high table; he was eating with the queen, a lady of very great beauty. Beside him was Sir Gawain, who was certainly no base-born man, and near him too were Queen Morcadés and the king of Cornwall: he was at the feast for sure, as was King Aguisial of Scotland, a fine and worthy man indeed; so was the king of Ireland, who wanted only tournaments and combat! In all there were seven kings at that table, and five archbishops and fourteen bishops; it was an illustrious company: elsewhere in the hall were lords and knights of great renown throughout the world, and those of the Round Table were seated with an array of beautiful maidens – fully three hundred in all.

Further down the hall sat the knights then known as the 'mamelots',[31] who were dressed in a way that ensured that when the king held court none of them would come to the table. They laid their cloaks and mantles on the floor and ate on those instead, and draped themselves in white tablecloths, so there was nothing to distinguish any of them. A 'mamelot' was a knight who had never saved his lord from death or capture, had never truly risked his life in the cause of prowess by taking on and vanquishing a knight at a ford or glade or hill or any other place of challenge, had never rescued a maiden, lady, girl or damsel and delivered her from a charge of shame at the court of the great King Arthur. If only he'd been known to have performed such a feat of prowess, he'd have been honoured with a place at the royal court with the rest of the illustrious knights, and held in esteem and respect.

Standing before King Arthur was Kay, having just served the fifth course. Merriment and celebration reigned throughout the hall. That king of highest honour was deep in thought; Gawain noticed this and said:

'My good lord king, it's not right or proper to look so troubled when you're holding court with all these worthy barons.'

The king replied in a passion: 'I can't help it, dear nephew! I'm so upset, so sad! And with good cause: there's no sign of the most true-hearted of knights, who's enhanced the reputation of my court more than any man alive. It's Perceval I mean: he's sent so many fine knights of worth as prisoners to me here. I've heard no cheering news of him for ages! It was him I was thinking of just then.'

'By God,' Gawain replied, 'you've every reason to think of him! There's no blame at all in that!'

And just as they were discussing this, the knight named Bagomedés entered the hall: it was on ground level, so he rode straight in and up to the king without dismounting. He greeted him most nobly on behalf of Perceval the Welshman, and then courteously hailed the queen and the whole illustrious assembly – except the seneschal. When the king heard mention of Perceval he was filled with joy and said:

[31] A word implying effeminacy.

'Dismount, dear friend, and disarm!'

But the knight's response was that he wouldn't dismount till he knew if he'd have redress there for the shame and injury he'd suffered at the hands of Kay the seneschal. The king replied that he'd willingly hear the case at his court, and would do all he could to see justice done. 'But dismount, dear friend, I pray you.'

So he stepped down and disarmed, and donned a short mantle brought to him by a boy. Around the tables there was much chatter among the knights and maidens, ladies and damsels, all openly saying that Kay wouldn't get away without a fight! The knight washed his hands and sat beside Gawain, and was generously served with whatever he wished.

After a leisurely meal the king bade that the tables be cleared. Then Count Quinable called the seneschal forward and asked him if he'd ever seen this knight in forest or glade. Kay swore by God and His powers and by Holy Mary that never in his life had he set eyes on him or met him anywhere. 'Nor to my knowledge have I done him any harm or shame, sir,' he said, 'not that I recall. And if he insists on being offensive I'll teach him not to sling insults at me, or accuse anyone else at the court of a count or king!'

Bagomedés strode calmly before King Arthur and said: 'Hear me, my lords – kings, counts, dukes and barons – and judge whether I'm lying or not. I was riding in search of adventure when Kay the seneschal met me in a dark forest. He had three other knights with him, and without uttering a single word they seized me and abused me and did me grave dishonour. It was Kay himself who decided to finish by hanging me from a tree. He didn't give the other three a chance to speak: they would rather have let me go, seeing I was a knight, but Kay, cruel blackguard that he is, wouldn't spare me in the least; no, he hung me from an oak tree by my feet – and I still had my helm laced on and my hauberk on my back! God help me, I daren't tell you how they beat me and abused me – it's not seemly for a knight to describe such foul things at court before so many people. But while I hung there in agony, the good and true knight Perceval came riding by, on his way to Mount Dolorous. I'd have died in moments if he hadn't taken me down. He stayed with me till I'd recovered a little; then when he left me I came straight here. There's nothing more to say; I present my gage* and challenge Kay here before these kings and all these lords, for he's full of treachery and cunning and spite. And if he chooses to deny my charge, I'll prove it in combat here at your court – I'll go nowhere else – on horse or on foot as he pleases.'

How the seneschal flushed with rage and malice! It wasn't a pretty sight! He cried to the king:

'Accept his gage, my lord! If he were mounted I'd go and arm now, but he's not in any hurry! Dear me, no! He didn't fancy fighting before he'd eaten, but now he's a bit more up for it! If he's so keen, let him go and arm! I'll do the same, and clear myself of this charge of treachery he's bandying about.'

'Kay,' said the king, 'I know you can't contain yourself and wouldn't let this matter rest for all the wealth of Lombardy or Cornwall. But don't be in such a hurry to fight – you'll have your battle soon enough.'

'It *can't* be soon enough, my lord! I can't wait to rebuff the outrageous, shameful charge he's made in front of you!'

'I wouldn't be so hasty,' the king replied. 'In seeking to avenge a shame, men sometimes increase it and make it worse! If you want the right result, you mustn't be so wild and rash that, when you need respite or a change of tack, you can't control the situation.'

'That's as may be!' said Kay. 'But I don't need lessons from anyone about what to do when I'm the victim of a shameful charge. Bring him his horse and let him arm at once! I'll do likewise, never fear! Then let battle commence – I can't wait!'

Gawain said there was no reason for the king to refuse. So their arms were brought and the knights duly armed.

Outside the city lay a garden with a beautiful sward, and that's where all the people went, for that was to be the battleground; but I shan't list the names of all those who were there! All the queens went up to their chamber windows, which gave a perfect view of the contest, and the girls went to sit there with them, and all the ladies too.

The knights were now clad in iron, and with barely a moment's pause they mounted their destriers and rode from the hall, not drawing rein till they reached the garden. The king arrived at once with all his barons and a great host of knights, fully five hundred of the finest. King Arthur had appointed those who were to guard the field, and they bade the contenders draw apart. They did so, creating a distance for the charge; then they set their lances in their rests and turned their mounts to face each other; then they thrust in their spurs and drove them forward, charging faster than a merlin or a noble falcon when it sights its quarry from afar and swoops from the clouds to make a better hit upon its prey. And to make a better hit as they approached, the knights lowered their ashwood lances and aimed at their painted shields – not seeking the gap between shield and breast but the shields themselves, which they struck with such might that nothing stopped the lance-heads smashing through, and the force of their horses' charge and the strength of the knights themselves made the lance-shafts shatter: if their hauberks hadn't stopped the heads one of them would have been maimed and even perhaps struck dead. Their chargers bore them past each other, galloping on a little way. King Arthur said to Gawain that the knights had jousted well indeed, and their steeds had matched one another for speed.

The knights promptly called for two new lances, and they were given fine ones, even stouter than their first. The queens, watching from the windows above, were saying they'd soon see one or other unhorsed, and they prayed that Kay would suffer shame and dishonour. 'He's bound to,' they said, 'sooner or later.'

Without more ado the knights drew apart and prepared to charge, filled with rage, blazing with fury. With shields clutched tight to their chests for fear of the lances, they let their horses go again, giving them free rein, and the fine destriers bore them wondrously straight and swift. The sharp-headed lances pierced their shields, and Kay's shaft shattered; but Bagomedés didn't fall – rather, he landed a blow that pinned Kay's shield to his arm and his arm to his body and sent him crashing from his charger to the ground. Then he threw his lance aside and unsheathed his sword of steel; spurring his destrier he swept past his hated foe three times before he found his feet again. But Kay struggled up and drew his sword, flushed with shame and sweating with rage at having all those ladies watching; and remembering the king's rebuke that day, he'd have given a thousand silver marks not to have been unhorsed and fallen. They were just on the point of dealing blows when King Arthur parted them, stepping in between. The brave Bagomedés said:

'Sire, you do me wrong! I'm not yet avenged for the shame he did me!'

But the king gently replied: 'Patience, my dear friend. This is a high and most solemn feast, and all the lords from my great land have assembled. I understand your desire for honour, but I tell you, to carry on your attack could bring you trouble – he's not defeated yet! I've seen a fallen man end up the winner! I pray you both, by the faith you owe me, let me settle this contest: I'll see your honour's safe; and my court will be all the happier and its dignity enhanced.'

Kay, who never knew how to hold his tongue, instantly replied: 'Sire! Sire! Let us fight on a little longer!'

But the king of Cornwall said: 'You're very wrong to say that, Kay! I know you'd kill him or take him prisoner if the king would let you, but we want the fight to stop if it please the knight. We're all committed to peace. You're too fired up!'

Then Gawain spoke to Bagomedés, it seems, entreating him by the faith he owed Sir Perceval who'd rescued him from his dreadful plight (as he'd said himself), to submit to the king's will; and Bagomedés promised to do so. So the king parted them and bade them disarm. I shan't mention their horses: they took some controlling.

They left the garden and returned to the splendid hall. The ladies were mocking and laughing at Kay for having come a cropper: because he was so cruel and abrasive, they were all delighted to have had revenge for the harsh words and treatment he'd dealt them many times. They came down from their chambers to the hall to join the king and all his lords. Kay was blazing redder than coal at his discomfiture, and when he saw the queen he didn't dare open his mouth. The queen began to laugh, as much as to say: 'God knows well enough who came off best!' Kay was so vexed and shaking with shame that he didn't know what to do!

The gracious-hearted king addressed the queen, saying: 'I've stopped the battle, lady. Now I want you to make peace between them, to the point where they'll be friends and companions for the rest of their days.'

'I'll make peace gladly, my lord,' the queen replied; and she came first to Bagomedés and embraced him, and asked him to agree to such companionship. He answered most good-naturedly:

'Lady, whatever pleases you I shan't refuse.'

'That's courteously said indeed!' the queen replied; then she came straight to Kay and put an arm around his neck and said: 'You'll grant what the king has bidden.'

'Lady,' he said, 'I won't argue.'

And so it was that the queen made peace between them. Their swords stayed in their sheaths and they embraced and kissed.

The noble, illustrious knights of the court made a great fuss of Bagomedés, and as for the king, he asked him to become a member of his household and a companion of his beloved nephew Gawain. He didn't take much persuading: he stayed with Arthur indeed, and was highly honoured at court and held in wide esteem through many lands; and Kay became a good friend of his, and from then on nothing would make him say a word against him.

Much of the day had passed and supper was ready and the tables set. The queens took their places after washing, as did the kings, archbishops, bishops and abbots, and the worthy knights, and the fair-faced girls who loved them dearly. And their attendants served them lavishly – I shan't draw it out by listing the dishes!

King Arthur started talking about brave Perceval, who was heading for Mount Dolorous to see if he could enhance his reputation. 'By God,' he said, 'he's a valiant knight indeed, worthy, loyal and good-hearted, endowed with all fine qualities. I tell you this: if he lives another three years he'll achieve more than any knight alive – and no one should feel envious of him, but pray to God to watch over him, that he may return to us safe and sound and full of strength.'

Then Gawain responded by saying: 'Truly, I'll go in search of him, no matter how far off he may be. I'll set off at the crack of dawn, and shan't stop till I reach the great Mount Dolorous.'

'And I'll go with you to look for him,' said Yvain. 'And I shan't stay in any place for more than one night – if God keeps me from capture or death or sickness – till I've been to that peak of such renown.'

Then Lancelot and Agravain rose, and so did Gaheriët and Gladoain, and Kay d'Estral of the great forest, and the kings of Scotland and Ireland, and Guerrehés and Sagremor, and the youth of the Circle of Gold, and Brien of the Isles and Lucan; the valiant Elis, the son of the Welshwoman, too; and Bagomedés said he would join their company, as did the knight of the ill-cut coat, a most experienced fighter, and Guirrez, who was very short and had suffered many troubles; and Licorrés of Cardigan, Count Quinable and Taules and Amaugin, and Carados Shortarm, a wise and worthy lord indeed, and Dodinel the Wild, and Erec, son of King Lac, never the most controlled of men; and Espinogre and Odinial, and Garsalas and Brun de Rumiaus, the Fair Bad Knight and the Bold Ugly Knight, and Yvain the Bastard and Bran de Lis, and the other Yvain, known as White-Hands. All these knights declared that they'd go in search of Perceval and wouldn't stop until they found him. When all had made their vows they rose from their tables and went to their lodgings to rest till morning. Finally Sir Gawain took his leave of his uncle the king and the fair-faced queen, who was reluctant to give it until he promised to return to court as soon as ever he could.

Then Gawain left and went to his lodging and slept till dawn, when he saw the sun rise, shedding its light over all the world. Then he swiftly armed and mounted Gringalet, shield round neck and lance in hand; and without further delay he rode from the city. He saw his companions waiting for him at a cross, armed and mounted on their horses, brown, white-stockinged, black and dun. The gold was dazzling on their shields, mirroring the sun – and little wonder, for they were forty of the finest knights in all the world, magnificently armed.

First to address Sir Gawain was Yvain, King Urien's son, endowed with all fine qualities; placing his hand on his horse's mane he said: 'We would all have set off already, sir, but weren't sure which way you planned to go.'

Gawain replied that he was going in search of Perceval; and if God kept him free from harm he would also seek the Fisher King who had honoured him so highly, for he longed to know who was served from the grail and uncover its mystery; he wanted to find out, too, about the body that lay on the splendid bier in the hall with a sword broken across the middle.

'I don't know what it signifies,' he said, 'but I saw it with my own two eyes. And you never saw anyone grieving like the mourners around that bier. I don't know what happened next – they vanished in an instant; so help me God, I didn't hear another sound of weeping or keening. And I never found out any more about it: I was so tired and weary that I fell asleep despite myself – I couldn't have helped it, not for a thousand silver marks! As soon as I could I lay down in a beautiful, luxurious bed, but when I woke next morning I found myself on a clifftop by the sea with my arms and my horse beside me! That's the last I heard of the Fisher King's court, and I can't wait to return.'

'It'll be a challenge,' said Sir Yvain, 'that's for sure.'

With that the companions parted, riding swiftly their separate ways, seeking adventure wherever they thought best.

For his part Gawain headed into a great, thick forest, accompanied by Yvain and Lancelot. The three of them rode together through the wood till they came to a broad expanse of open land through which a beautiful clear river ran. They carried on down to the water's edge and found the river fairly calm: it didn't need a bridge to cross, and cross it they did, though not before their horses had drunk. Then beneath a tall, spreading tree they found an old road that divided into three: each path was good and clear and wide but seemed to be little used. Gawain was the first to speak, saying to his companions:

'Let's part here, sirs, and each go a separate way. I pray that God may guide us to find what we seek; and let whoever first returns to court wait for his companions there.'

Each of them pledged to do so; then they parted without another word. In my source I haven't discovered what became of Sir Yvain – or of Lancelot, who kept to the broad path he took; nor shall I recount what happened to all the rest: you won't hear me tell about the paths and routes they followed. But I do want to tell you what the story records of Gawain. So hear the tale – it's worth the hearing; and to tell the story properly needs more time: if it were *all* to be recorded in rhyme it would be a task indeed! But the best of it is set down here – and the very best is yet to come: the story gets better and better.

The Little Knight's Shield

Sir Gawain rode steadily on through the forest, and fair and delightful it was indeed. He followed a wide grassy track till evening, when he took shelter for the night with a hermit in the wood, a wise and worthy man who led a most saintly life. He supplied Gawain with a whole bushel of corn and barley for his horse, grain that he'd grown himself, and prepared such a supper for him as he could – but I don't need to tell you the kind of bed and food he found at the hermitage: you know well enough that a man who's retired to the woods, committed to serving God to expiate his sins, has meagre comforts; but worthy hermits suffer such hardship to confound the Devil. Gawain lay all night beside his horse, resting his head on his shield, still armed apart from removing his treasured helm.

When day broke he made ready again; he harnessed his horse and mounted and took leave of the hermit, and spurred swiftly away from the hermitage. The great, leafy forest rang with joyous birdsong, and it was a beautiful morning, with dew so heavy that the tall trees on every side were dripping as if in pouring rain. Gawain was soaking; but the sun blazed down, breaking up the cloud, and it was turning hot with a sky so bright that there hadn't been such a lovely day for the whole of the previous month. Gawain rode on without a rest, his heart rejoicing at the glorious weather and at the sound of the birds, so clear and high: it was as if they were talking, telling each other of their love, as they warbled away in their high tongue. So sweet was their singing that Gawain was convinced that no one who heard it could help being stirred to thoughts of love.

Lost in his musing, oblivious to all else, he looked ahead and saw a tall, spreading tree. There was a shield hanging from a branch, and without a doubt it was silver emblazoned with a splendid black lion rampant. I'm equally sure that beneath the tree was a spring of lovely clear, pure water flowing down into a stream. Sir Gawain headed straight towards it; and there he saw a maiden sitting, clad in an ermine gown. In her bare white hand she held a comb of ivory, and was combing her hair by herself: she had no girl or chambermaid. And she was so elegant and comely that there was no lovelier creature born; her colouring was so perfect, the rose-red blending with the white, that Sir Gawain thought her a painted statue: had she been standing still, unmoving, he'd have been convinced she was! But he could see her combing and smoothing her hair, hair that looked like gold; so he knew she was a living damsel or lady! He swore there was no lovelier woman or girl or damsel from there to Rome. He greeted her most nobly, and she rose to meet him and returned his greeting with faultless grace, and asked him kindly to tell her his name. Gawain wasn't slow to reply; he said:

'Sweet friend, never in my life have I kept my name from lady, damsel, girl or maid or from any man born, and I've no wish to keep it from you!' And he told her at once that he was Gawain, King Arthur's nephew.

The damsel was overjoyed at this and said: 'I've heard a great deal about you, sir! That settles it: you're to come with me to a house of mine – I think you'll find things to your satisfaction!'

Gawain thought her so beautiful that he'd no wish to refuse or argue: he agreed very readily! Just a moment later they saw a knight approaching on a sorrel destrier – the finest and most handsome that ever was, so my source-book says – with saddle and harness superbly fashioned, inlaid with gold. The knight was unarmed, and approaching at a trot. Let me describe him to you, according to my source: it says he was born and bred in Wales – and so says the Count of Poitiers,[32] who loved this story and remembered it especially well – and was unbelievably small, but no creature of humankind was ever reputed to be more handsome. I tell you truly, he had blond, curly hair, and eyes and chin and mouth and nose, arms and haunches, legs and feet as perfect as anyone could wish, and he was splendidly dressed in a gown of green silk. But he was so tiny, sitting there on his horse, that he looked more than anything like a seven-year-old child. As Gawain stared at him he rode straight down to the spring and cheerfully dismounted and greeted Gawain and the girl most courteously. After returning his greeting Gawain asked him where he'd come from and where he'd spent the previous night; he replied:

'At a castle, sir, up ahead: a fine, delightful place it is, and I had a very comfortable time. If you care to go there you'll be received with all honour and provided with all you wish.'

The damsel didn't say a word, but she gave a little smile; and she told Gawain that the knight was her brother and the only member of her family she had, but through his prowess and quick intelligence he'd rescued her from many a plight, for he was a fine knight indeed, courageous, bold and daring despite his tiny size. Gawain, stunned by her beauty, gazed at the damsel and then back at the knight. She now told her brother that the knight they'd met was Gawain, praised, cherished and honoured by all for his abundant qualities. The knight was overjoyed by the news, and from his boot he drew a horn, beautifully made of white ivory, and blew four blasts that made the forest shake and the valley around the spring resound – yet this ivory horn, that yielded such a thunderous, ringing sound, was no more than a palm's width and a half in length. It brought three handsome pages rushing up, mounted on rounceys;* one of them was leading a mule whiter than snow on a branch; another carried a silken mantle, lined with finest ermine – there was none finer under heaven; and the third brought a handsome silken tunic – if I were to describe how it was made and adorned and told you what it cost, you wouldn't believe me in the least! These three pages rode smartly up and dismounted at the tree, and without a word each laid what he carried on the marble

---

[32] The MSS give several versions of this phrase but almost all refer to the count of Poitiers, and the clearest reading is the one translated here. It must surely be a reference to Richard Lionheart, who was count of Poitiers in the last decades of the twelfth century and had a reputation among minstrels, to whom he was always generous, for having a good knowledge of the romances (and a talent himself as a writer of songs).

block where the girl was sitting. The one who brought the mule left her standing quietly; then he turned back and rode away, as did the other two.

The damsel promptly donned the silken tunic and the fine mantle, too, and mounted the white mule, fitted with a superb saddle inlaid with gold and a brand new harness hung with little, jingling golden bells most pleasing to the ear. Her brother didn't dally but mounted his destrier likewise and said to Gawain:

'If you wish, sir, we'll head for our house: it's fast approaching noon, I'd say, and high time for dinner.'

Gawain asked him whether the shield was going to be left there hanging on the branch. The Little Knight replied:

'By all the saints, sir, no knight should take it down and hang it from his neck unless he's richly endowed with intelligence, strength, vigour, nobility and honour – and, above all, is possessed of a sweetheart who is utterly true and loves him like her own life and dreads harm befalling him as much as herself and wouldn't consider another lover, no matter how great his renown. A knight so blessed by God could certainly bear the shield and bestow it where he chose; but a knight less perfectly endowed who took the shield would be utterly dishonoured. But if he were so fortunate as to have all those qualities and a sweetheart as devoted as I said, then truly, from the moment he hung the shield at his neck it would double his worth, his courage, his strength, his force.'

'My word,' said Gawain, 'it's a shield with mighty powers!'

'Indeed it is!' said the girl. 'It's caused grief for many a knight, I think – they imagined it would work for them because of the faithfulness of their sweethearts, but they were sorely disabused! I must have seen a hundred come and take the shield, thinking they had perfect lovers so devoted to them that, even if they'd had the choice, they wouldn't have exchanged them for a king or a count or an emperor, however great their domains! How wrong they were! The moment they grabbed the shield's strap and slung it round their neck they realised their mistake – they were beaten and unhorsed that instant! They ended up saying that anyone who trusts in a woman's love, who stakes a farthing on it, is mad! That was how they rued the mess they'd brought upon themselves – all the worse for being vanquished and floored by my tiny brother! They could have taken the shield, you see, had he not been here to guard it.'

Gawain laughed at the damsel's spirited account and telling; and he laid a mail-coated arm about her, so delighted by her beauty that he couldn't take his eyes off her: he gave a little sigh.

Then the three of them set off, and hadn't gone far before they caught sight of the splendid castle. It had a handsome hall and a lofty tower and strong, battlemented walls all round, and a bridge, a gatehouse and good accommodation, a range as fine as any from there to Limoges; and it was surrounded by deep, imposing ditches: all in all it was as secure and well appointed as could be. Sir Gawain and the fair-faced girl rode up to the bridge with the Little Knight, who blew his horn so loud and clear that forest, meadow, water, walls and tower resounded with its blast. Four pages ran into the courtyard and greeted their arrival, and helped the lovely damsel from the mule. The knights dismounted at once and entrusted their horses to a boy. Then without more ado they entered the hall, where they seated Sir Gawain on gold-embroidered samite. What else should I tell you? They helped him from his armour and the damsel had a mantle brought for him, made of rich red Saracen cloth gorgeously lined with squirrel fur. Then the servants set up the table and prepared it for dinner, and after they'd washed all three of them sat down together. It would be a wearisome bother to list their dishes: I'll give myself a break and leave that out rather than bore the listener and tire myself. But they had plenty to eat and all the fine wines they could wish, that's for sure.

While they were seated there at dinner, they saw a boy come riding swiftly through the gate, mounted on a rouncey. He rode straight to the steps without stopping; then he dismounted and ran up to the hall and entered. He looked at the three of them eating together and recognised the Little Knight, and greeted him most courteously on behalf of Idier, the son of King Nu. He explained that he'd come from King Arthur's court, where there'd been all manner of talk about the shield.

'Kay the seneschal, who rates himself higher than anyone – in fact higher than any two together! – vowed before the king that if he ever came across that shield he'd bear it in a tournament and would never carry any other, and would go, lance at the ready, to seek chivalrous adventures far and wide. When my lord Idier heard Kay's boastful pledge, he promised the king and his company that he'd hold a tournament; and he undertook to have your shield sent to the king, as a test to the finest knights that day. So he fondly entreats you to come to the tourney, and to bring your shield to provide the test! It's being held on Tuesday, on the heath with the red cross. The king of Ireland won't be there, nor will the king of Scotland or Gawain or Lancelot or Sir Yvain or some sixty knights who left the other day in search of adventure. My lord thinks it's just as well, for they're the finest of the court! But all the rest are preparing for the tourney, every single one, and my lord Idier certainly is: day and night he's gathering more people to take part – he's called for King Claudas, who's sent a letter promising to be there; so has the king of Bralles, a firm friend of his. He'll win honour for sure: with Gawain absent, he'll have little opposition! So let me know what you think, and I'll go back and tell my lord.'

The Little Knight told him not to delay, for he'd gladly go to the tournament if the knight seated at his side agreed. 'And come what may,' he said, 'I'll take the shield and send it to the good, most worthy King Arthur. How about you?' he said to Sir Gawain. 'I want to be sure – I shan't go without you.'

Gawain said he'd accompany him to the tourney, and approved of him presenting the shield to the king. When the boy heard this he took his leave and left at once, refusing all invitations to eat, and rode hard all day till he reached his lord and reported the Little Knight's reply, which was much to his lord's delight.

Meanwhile Gawain, seated at dinner with the Little Knight, was amazed by all he'd heard, but the damsel begged him to forget all that and eat. She decided to have some fun and tease him a little, saying:

'Sir, may I be so bold as to give you a piece of advice? If I were you I wouldn't have such faith in your sweetheart's word as to feel you can joust in the tournament with that shield that's shamed so many knights! No man can fathom a woman's heart and nature: many's the man who thinks his lover's all his when it's not like that at all! A woman's like a child: quick to fall in and out of love, ever changing, ever fickle – it's a wonder, it really is! So if she calls you her sweet love, take my advice and steer clear of the shield: it's folly! A wise man learns from the experiences of others!'

He was taken aback by the maiden's words. 'Damsel,' he said, 'I'll preserve myself from shame if it please God.'

Then the servants cleared the tables and brought the water with all possible speed. Sir Gawain washed, as did the fresh-faced damsel of fairy-like beauty, and then the Little Knight, so brave and fierce. Once they'd washed and drunk they left the great hall and retired to a chamber. There was none fairer from there to Limoges: it was painted gold and blue, and adorned with the finest carvings ever seen. In the middle was a bed with a coverlet of samite stitched and embroidered by the damsel herself: Gawain was stunned and admired it very much. They went then and leaned at a window, which overlooked a pool and the meadow and the forest. Gawain said the castle and its surroundings delighted him: it was presented and furnished beautifully and should be pleasing to any worthy man. Like the courteous and good-hearted knight he was, the first thing he asked was his companion's name and how he should address him. With no desire to hide it, he happily replied in gracious fashion:

'The Little Knight of the Castle of the Great Forest, keeper of the shield that hangs on the spreading oak in the glade. That's how I'm known to many who haven't seen me but have heard reports. And my sister's name is Tanree: fair and radiant indeed she is, and of great intelligence, too. But sir, I swear by God who made the heavens, the object of so many prayers, I couldn't be more pleased by a hundred marks of purest gold than I am to have you lodge here at my house.'

Gawain thanked him deeply; then their conversation turned to other matters, many and varied.

After spending a good while at the window the three went and sat on the bed together. But the Little Knight didn't stay with them long: he hurried down to the hall and equipped himself with all he needed – hauberk, helmet, lance and shield, chausses and spurs and a fine sword of burnished, tempered steel – all of it made to measure. On a suitably sized horse he leapt without using the stirrup – it was quite amazing: he was so small, so tiny, yet so fit and agile that it would have been hard to find a more impressive knight in any land. Superbly armed, he passed through the gate and over the bridge and into the forest to the tree and the spring beneath the block of marble. There he dismounted and sat down to wait for someone to come and take the shield to test his prowess; so he did every day.

Meanwhile Gawain was at his sister's side, sitting on the bed. They exchanged many words – about love, nothing mundane! She was a bright and courtly damsel, and spoke most beguilingly, till her beauty set his heart afire and he began to woo her. He politely asked if she had a sweetheart, and she didn't lie: she told him that she'd been in love for more than a year with a knight from another country – a knight of very great renown and fame in many lands. Gawain burned to ask his name and which land he was from.

'He must be a valiant knight, I'd say, if he's worthy of your love!'

And he pressed her to name him. But she was hesitant: she kept looking at him and blushing with embarrassment, not knowing what to do. He couldn't bear the suspense, and kept on and on asking, begging her to reveal her beloved's name. Seeing him so desperate, the damsel blurted out the truth in the sweetest terms, saying:

'God help me, sir, and send me health and happiness: I've never loved any man of woman born but you! Your renown is such that I've loved you for a long while! But more's the pity for me, I'd say, for I'm sure you'll have a sweetheart more beautiful than me.'

Gawain heard this and leapt for joy. He took her in his arms and swore he loved her, and promised to be her true love – and she believed him utterly. So a compact was made, and their kissing and embracing carried on till Gawain plucked the flower. But there's no suggestion in the book that the damsel was upset at losing the name of maiden: she was only too happy and pleased. Had Gawain used force he wouldn't have been acting nobly at all, but recklessly and wickedly.

They carried on happily till evening was near; then the Little Knight returned, riding straight back to his house. He dismounted at once, and it didn't take long to disarm him and clad him in a short mantle cut to his size. Then he climbed upstairs to his sister's chamber. When Sir Gawain saw him he rose to greet him, saying:

'Welcome, sir! You've been a long time!'

The Little Knight told him he'd gone to the tree and waited on the marble block for a good while, hoping for adventure. 'That's my custom and my duty,' he said. 'I hope it didn't bother you: I left you in the hands of my sister, who's most charming – I'm sorry if she's been poor company!'

Gawain had nothing but praise for her entertainment! Then he asked if he'd seen or met any armed knight in the forest, or exchanged words with any girl or damsel. He said he'd seen and heard nothing at all and found nothing of interest anywhere, though he'd searched near and far and high and low: that's why he was back so late. With that they went downstairs to the main hall where many candles had been lit, for the sun had set and night had fallen. They had the merriest time they could have wished; but I shan't describe the supper or how well the beds were made: there were sheets and blankets of silk and samite and pillows and coverlets enough for twenty knights! Sir Gawain's bed was made with the costliest and most elegant of all. The damsel, who truly, deeply loved him more than her own brother, would have had no qualms about spending the night naked in his arms, kissing and embracing and answering his every desire – had it not been that both his bed and her brother's had been set up together as one. She was nearly beside herself with anger and frustration.

It was far into the night by the time the two knights went to bed. The head chamberlains left two big candles burning by a lovely window. Sir Gawain fell sound asleep, as did the Little Knight who was very weary. But that damsel so fair, she didn't sleep at all that night: she wished the household and her brother had all been in the East, I think! She suffered torment and frustration till it was almost dawn, when she managed to snooze a little.

The Tournament in the Blanche Lande

As soon as the sun appeared Gawain awoke, and thought he'd rise at once without calling anyone. But his companion was already up and ready, fully dressed and shod; and servants came from every side bringing their arms the moment they were bidden, and they armed without delay, with everything a worthy knight needs to protect and defend himself. Then they promptly called for their horses, and bade two pages mount and accompany them to the tourney. Then they mounted their destriers, impatient to be gone, and the four of them rode through the gate and over the bridge and away: they didn't wake the damsel, but left her quietly sleeping – Sir Gawain didn't feel good about this, but because it was so early he kept it to himself.

Through the great, thick forest they followed the most beaten path till they came to the spring beneath the lovely tree where the silver shield was hung; they bade one of the pages take it down and hang it round his neck, and then without more ado they carried on through the great, green forest. It was a beautiful morning: the sun was rising gloriously and the birds were greeting the fine weather by filling the woods with song, much to the delight of the two good knights. They rode on all day without stopping or eating till evening, when they came upon the house of a vavasor who greeted them with all honour and entertained them lavishly, providing them with a fine array of dishes in abundance, and well made beds with fresh new sheets.

When the next day dawned bright and clear they set out once again, but took leave of their host before departing. They journeyed on till, on the Monday, they caught sight of the great gathering lodged and camped on the edge of the Blanche Lande. The Little Knight asked Gawain what they should do: should they go to Idier the son of Nu, or send him the shield to give to King Arthur?

'Send it to him,' Gawain replied. 'We'll lodge here, then we'll have no bother – I don't want to be recognised or have anyone ask my name.'

So the Little Knight called his squire and said: 'Go straight to Idier and give him my shield, and tell him he's to send it to King Arthur at once, without delay.'

The boy thrust his spurs into his fine, swift horse and rode through the encampment till he found Idier, son of Nu. He knew him well, and greeted him on his lord's behalf, and promptly gave him the shield and told him he was to send it to King Arthur. Idier hadn't been more thrilled since the hour that he was born, and he called two squires and said:

'Go, quickly! Present this shield to my dear King Arthur on behalf of the Little Knight, who sends it to him in all sincerity; the condition is that the one who can joust with it twice without being unhorsed will be the winner of the tournament!'

The squires didn't dally: they set off at once, and crossed the fields and came to the forest where they found the king lodged in splendour with three thousand courageous, bold, redoubtable knights. They hailed the king and delivered the shield just as they'd been instructed; the king took it and gazed long at it, as did the lords around him. It created quite a stir – and would prove to be the bane of some of them by the time that evening came!

It was already past terce when the shield arrived, and Kay, in highest spirits, came before the king and said: 'My lord, you and your household should be armed by now!'

'No, Kay, there's no rush!' replied the king. 'There's plenty of the day left – it's not yet noon.'

'It seems you want it easy, sire!' Kay said. 'Give me that shield! I'll carry it all tournament long till nightfall – I don't care who it upsets!'

'I fear the upset may be yours, my friend!' said Arthur; and he laughed long about it with King Lot, who was at his side. But Lot added that, since Kay was so keen to have the first joust, it would be improper for the king to refuse and grant it to another. So Arthur agreed, and had the shield presented to Sir Kay, who duly set off, not in the least downcast but looking hugely pleased with himself. Without anyone's bidding he pulled on his chausses and laced his knee-pieces and donned his fine hauberk; his horse was brought and he mounted swiftly, and then hung the shield around his neck, that shield imbued with so much power. Then back he came before the king, who armed in turn, as did all the others without delay.

The king's party made a fine display, and so did the other side; there was no one with a faint or feeble heart, I'd say. The valiant Idier was mounted on a mighty, strutting destrier, shield at neck, sword at side, clad in mail with helmet laced, looking everywhere for the Little Knight. Suddenly he spotted him riding from the forest with Gawain, both of them with lances held erect. He galloped down to greet them, and they didn't dally but rode to join their side who were mounting, fully armed and ready to engage. The king likewise was ordering and forming his battalions. Oh, the array of destriers you'd have seen! Dun, white-stockinged, dapple-grey, all superbly caparisoned in silk from head to tail. And shields of gold, silver, blood-red, dazzling blue; and helmets hard and strong; and so many hauberks, so many lances, so many damsels' favours – wimples and sleeves of rich silk from the East; and fine steel blades girded at the left hip.

A fair part of the day was gone by the time the battle-lines were drawn. But now there was nothing else for it: Kay sprang forward, spurring his steed, charging towards the foe. From the other side came none other than the Little Knight, brave and fierce, charging on his strong, swift mount. On his shield were three eagles whiter than a lily, on a field blacker than any ink. The two knights clashed at a furious pace and delivered great blows to each other's shield – but they didn't break: it's amazing they weren't shattered, but the laths of their blazoned shields held firm. Kay had been determined to unseat the Little Knight, but even if he'd been four men he wouldn't have unhorsed him! Instead the Little Knight landed a blow that sent Kay tumbling, head over heels, right over the back of his saddle: shield still round neck, lance still in hand, he crashed down yards behind his horse. A good hundred knights had seen this joust, and every last one was in fits of laughter. The Little Knight seized Kay's horse and led it away. Three squires helped Kay to his feet and saw him remounted: the king had sent him another horse, with orders to the squire who took it to remove the shield from Kay's neck and bring it to him at once. The squire did exactly as bidden.

The battalions now engaged and the tourney began in earnest, with the smashing of many lances and the toppling of many knights. King Arthur had the shield now, and gave it to his nephew Mordred. Idier son of Nu saw this and set himself to face him; they were both fine knights, strong, bold, deft and skilled, and they spurred their steeds to a mighty charge and exchanged such blows on their blazoned shields that Mordred's lance shattered and flew into seven pieces. Idier struck the very boss of the shield and sent him flying over his horse's rump and crashing down; he seized his horse and led it away. Mordred struggled to his feet and flung the shield to the ground, hurling a hundred curses upon the one who'd sent it to the king!

Arthur now commanded everyone in turn to try the shield. There were some who took it who'd not yet struck a blow with sword or lance, but found themselves devoid of strength: the moment they hung the shield from their neck they seemed unmanned, and were toppled from their mounts in seconds! They might have been upset, but Kay was overjoyed! In short, they all had a go and ended up flattened – though one or two, seeing this, decided to steer clear.

The tourney ground was broad and long, and filled with vigorous fighting. The worthy, lauded Gawain was taking part, but had no friend or kinsman in support except the Little Knight, who served him fondly and well. And Gawain was carrying no shield, not wanting to be recognised: he'd left it where he'd camped out in the wood. Into the thickest press he plunged, unhorsing two knights who were close companions but didn't recognise him at all; then he struck out to right and left, and looked indeed the master of the tournament. And so he was, I'd say: he cut a swathe right through the press, charging back and forth almost unchallenged. The king and all his followers were forced to give ground to him; and they were on the point of fleeing when he suddenly left the fray: in the middle of his comings and goings he'd seen the shield lying on the ground in the distance, so he headed that way and picked it up and hung it at his neck. Then back into the press he rode. By this time Arthur had renewed his assault on Idier's men, and driven them back almost to their baggage train; some were even retreating into the great, thick forest. Gawain ran into the fleeing knights and stopped them there and then, and in no time at all he turned the tide. When the shield was spotted by King Arthur's men they thought they'd soon have Gawain down – but they couldn't have been more wrong! He sent them scattering, fleeing, willy-nilly; there was booty to be won then for anyone with an eye to profit.

The sun was down by the time the two sides parted and left the fray and returned to their encampments. Gawain, along with the Little Knight, slipped away from them all and returned to where they'd lodged: no one knew what had become of them. When they reached their camp they dismounted and disarmed and donned two splendid mantles of finely embroidered silk. Their pages had prepared plenty to eat: fine cuts of venison and two freshly caught rabbits, and three big kegs of excellent wine, strong and clear and well aged. They'd a good supply of candles, too; in fact they'd brought everything a worthy man could wish – they'd done their duty perfectly. And they'd strewn the shelter with flowers and sweet grass: there was plenty of the latter for their horses to graze. The pages had made a fine bed for their masters, too. When the knights had washed they sat down on the green grass. I don't know what more to say: they had no table, but were splendidly served at leisure with a fine array of dishes.

As for King Arthur, let me tell you: when he returned to his pavilions and dismounted with his household his supper was ready – his servants had hurried it along. They sat down to eat at once, as soon as they'd washed – and all I'll say is they ate and drank plenty. And as they ate they had plenty to say about the shield that Kay had carried: he'd have been on the end of some mockery had the most commended knights not come equally unstuck! That made them keep a lid on it!

King Arthur kept asking his barons if they knew the name of the knight who'd taken the shield and outdone everyone at the tournament, and the name of the little dwarf, too, who'd unhorsed Sir Kay with his stout lance – Kay the seneschal, who was incapable of speaking pleasantly and would never do anything commendable. 'And you can't expect otherwise. You won't make a silk purse from a sow's ear. You heard him bragging that he'd take the shield and carry it all day till evening, till the fighting was over – but he lost it in a flash! His knighthood was soon belittled by a dwarf!'

So said the king. Kay was as bitter as could be, and couldn't think of a reply. The others all kept quiet, too, saying nothing to the king except that the knights they'd seen arrive at the tourney with the shield were quite unknown to them. They carried on in this vein till they rose from supper.

I'll leave the king now and turn to Idier and his companions, who were camped elsewhere, in very high spirits. They'd sent people to scour the camp for the Little Knight – but he was lodged in the forest with Sir Gawain. They had to be patient till the morning, when they saw the sun rise, shining bright. Then destriers were clad in caparisons of every hue, and before terce the tourney recommenced. The king's men performed splendidly, but so did Idier's, and by the time evening came it was clear to all that the king's side had come off worse – because they'd been missing the lord of chivalry, the worthy and accomplished Gawain.

He'd risen early that morning, and set off at once with the Little Knight. Taking the shield with them, they'd ridden through the forest, over fields and plains, down paths and tracks, until, before the end of the second day, they returned to the house they'd left. The damsel greeted them joyfully; and when Gawain told her how they'd fared, and that they'd brought back the shield sent to King Arthur, the fair-faced damsel was thrilled, delighted.

Food was ready and they sat down to eat; I can't repeat all their conversation, but when they were done the servants smartly made their beds, and they couldn't wait to retire after supper – it was already far into the night. But the damsel went to bed far from happy: she could see her beloved but couldn't speak to him! She was furious that the two knights' beds had again been set up side by side – she cursed the servants who'd arranged them so! Her body was in torment all night long, till the blazing sun returned anew.

Then she rose at once and went straight to where the knights had slept, her fair face casting a radiant light around her. The knights were up and smartly dressed; the gracious damsel gave them noble greeting, and Gawain, his whole heart fired by her beauty, returned her greeting courteously and took her in a close embrace. Then he spotted a page and sent him to fetch his arms and his fine destrier. 'For I must go,' he said, 'at once.'

'By the holy cross where Our Lord was hung,' she said, 'be kind and stay here today!'

The Little Knight likewise begged him to stay, but for all their pleading Gawain would brook no delay, and the Little Knight desisted, not wanting to annoy him. He had his arms and destrier brought, and three squires deftly helped him arm, and splendidly. Once he was armed he took his leave without more ado and mounted and commended them all to God; then he rode through the gate and was gone. The damsel was downcast, distraught, and lamented:

'Alas! What a fool I am! I've a lot to learn! What possessed me to bestow my love where I'd no hope that it would be returned? And what hope *could* I have? It's obvious that before the month is out he'll have two or three more sweethearts, all more beautiful than I and all of them loving him just as much! He'll forget me, there's no doubt. He has my heart in his keeping, but it means little to him – he's used to it – he won't lose any sleep! Love to him is cheap: he's such an awesome, valiant knight, so courageous, bold, handsome, courtly, that every lady, maid and damsel from here to Pavia will fall in love with him the moment she knows he's near! And how in God's name could he love and please them all? He's canny – he knows how to play the field and come off best! I've given him my love, but why should that make him give me his? My heart may be afire for him, but his remains unkindled! I can sigh and long for him, but I've had all I'm going to get!

'Oh, I shan't keep on. But it would've been only right and fair if he'd loved me when I loved him! And cared for me when I cared for him! That's how it should have been! If God would hear the prayers of worthy lovers, how everyone would bless Him!'

So saying, she turned back to her chamber and sat down on a bed.

Sir Gawain and the Pensive Knight

Meanwhile Sir Gawain set off through the forest, and pressed on at a good swift pace all day long till vespers; but he met with no adventure or incident worth the telling. As the sun was about to set he emerged from the forest, and away to his left he spotted a little castle, very well appointed, with a bridge and gatehouse and a tall stone tower and strong walls on every side, but just one set of living quarters, that was all. Gawain headed that way, and rode over the bridge and through the gate and straight on to the tower. Outside he found the vavasor whose home it was, and he seemed a most worthy man; Gawain greeted him courteously and was welcomed with joy and great honour. He lodged there that night, but took to the road again early next day.

It was a beautiful day indeed, the sun shining bright and clear, and he rode on through the early morning until, before the first hour had rung, he saw a fully armed knight who'd stopped in the middle of the path. He was sitting on a Spanish destrier, his head bowed as if he were fast asleep. When his horse caught sight of Gawain's it took fright and bolted away down the path; but to Gawain's amazement he saw the knight's head still bowed low. Perhaps, he thought, he'd had no bed the night before, or any other comfort, so maybe it was no wonder he was sleeping.

'In which case,' he thought, 'it would be wicked to disturb him. But I wish I could speak to him, that's for sure, and ask if he knows anything about the Fisher King – and if he's ever been to the pillar on Mount Dolorous.'

While Gawain was talking to himself the knight passed into a forest, and he set off softly after him, making no sound and saying nothing, but following the knight with the ever-bowed head till it was well past terce.[33] They came then to a valley, where the knight stopped; Gawain, still behind him, quietly halted likewise, and was sure the knight was about to address him, for he saw him raise his lance and then lower it to rest on his horse's neck. But he didn't utter a word; not a sound did he make. So Gawain didn't address him, either: he decided to hang around no more and to leave him to his slumber. So he rode on past without more ado. But he'd gone no more than a lance's length when he drew rein and stopped, thinking it would be to his eternal shame to leave without learning something about this knight he'd found. He turned Gringalet about and came back to face the knight, still sitting there stock still, as silent as a stone. Gawain didn't hesitate; he laid his hand on his shoulder and gently whispered:

'Speak to me, sir.'

The knight made no reply at all: it was as if he'd heard nothing. So Gawain nudged and shook him till he raised his head; then:

'Vassal,' said the knight, 'how rude you are, prodding and manhandling me! It's most discourteous! If you were thinking of your sweetheart as I am of mine and I snatched you from your thoughts, you'd be none too pleased! And nor am I! Leave me in peace, good sir – I'm not disturbing you!'

'At least tell me your name, my friend,' said Gawain.

But the knight made no reply: his head was slumped once more. Gawain was annoyed, but didn't know what to do. He started tugging at his arm again, bidding him say – by the faith he owed his beloved – what his name was and why he was so preoccupied. When he heard this mention of his sweetheart he wouldn't breach the faith referred to; his head came up at once and he said:

'Truly, sir, it's a wicked shame to put such pressure on a man! I shan't keep my name from you – it would be very wrong of me, for you've summoned me in my sweetheart's name! So I'll tell you: I'm known as the Pensive Knight of the Forest of the Maiden, and I've a rich domain by the Black Chapel. I don't know what more to say, except this: the other day a knight used outrageous force to steal my love from me, and my heart's distraught and rightly so. If I described her beauty you wouldn't believe me – so don't take it ill, good sir, if I was lost in thoughts of her! God help me, I love her as much as I ever did. The knight who has her is cruel and wicked indeed, and I don't think anyone could get the better of him and force him to return her. I couldn't take him on myself – he's too big and bold and strong, a fearsome fighter: no one can withstand him. That's why I'm so troubled and distressed. So now you see what's distracted me, and why I'm beset by grief and pain.'

Gawain promptly asked him if he knew which way he'd gone, and where he was most often to be found; he replied that he was still there in the forest.

---

[33] In other words Gawain followed him from before the first canonical hour (prime, about six o'clock) till well past terce (the third canonical hour, about nine).

'Then let's go!' said Gawain. 'Take me to him right now! You'll have her back, the maid you've praised so much, if I can manage it!'

These words cheered the Pensive Knight, and he said: 'Tell me your name first, if you will.'

The courtly Gawain replied: 'Friend, my name is Gawain, and I assure you it's never been concealed from anyone who asked it, nor will it ever be!'

The knight was beside himself with joy, and said: 'Your prowess clears the darkness from my heart! I know you'll avenge the wrong I've suffered, and all the pain, and return my love to me! Now the perfidious wretch who stole her will have his just reward!'

They left the valley and set off on their way, and before noon was past they came to a broad and lovely glade. In the very middle stood a tree, beneath which was pitched a pavilion superbly made of silk in a chequered pattern of red and blue – no count or king could wish for one more handsome in this world. Beside this magnificent tent sat an armed knight on a great dappled destrier, as fine a steed as was ever seen. Gawain, approaching at an amble, asked his companion if he knew the name of this knight outside the tent, and he instantly replied that it was the very one who'd taken such a liberty and wronged him so. So they rode swiftly on without another word till they reached the pavilion; and there inside they could see a maiden sitting on a rich carpet. She was comely indeed and beautifully dressed, and all alone, amusing herself by making a chaplet of flowers and leaves. After gazing at her awhile Gawain hailed her most graciously in the name of God the almighty king, and the damsel rose at once and returned his greeting courteously. The knight on the other side of the tent was riled, and confronted them directly without any word of greeting.

'What are you doing here?' he said to Gawain.

'I'll tell you,' he replied, 'as soon as you return this fair and charming damsel to my friend here: she loves him truly, and I want you to surrender her forthwith, if you please.'

'Damn me,' the knight cried, 'if I surrender her at your bidding! I've had her awhile and I'll carry on having her – she's much to my taste! I'll not give her up! If the knight could win her from me in combat, man to man, then he could have her, certainly – but that's the only way! If you feel compelled to help him, have a go – I won't object! You've come to the right place if you fancy a fight! If there were four of you I'd make you suffer, each in turn, and that's a fact!'

Gawain heard this and smiled. 'It would be a brave knight,' he said, 'who wasn't afraid of you! But come, be kind, and let the knight have his sweetheart back. Pride often ends in a crushing fall, and in the words of the proverb, a wise man learns from others' mistakes.'

But the knight swore by God and His saints that he'd never give her back. Yes he would, Gawain replied, whether he liked it or not; and without wasting his breath on threats he challenged him there and then. The knight was filled with anger, wild with rage. The two foes drew apart to gain space for a mighty charge, and then thrust in their spurs and made the earth tremble: no sparrowhawk or falcon ever swooped on its prey at greater speed than they summoned from their mighty steeds. They struck each other right on the bosses of their shields; the strong-glued laths, resplendently painted in gold and blue and red, couldn't withstand the lances' heads, but the bright, tight mail of their hauberks saved the knights from death. The lances shattered into shards, but neither knight lost his stirrups; they drew their swords of steel, sharp, shining, dazzling bright, and turned about and closed again and dealt blows on each other's helm that sent sparks flying. The knight struck Gawain in a fury and caught him full on his burnished helm, cutting through the circlet,[34] bright with gold; but the blade stopped there, mighty blow though it was, and Gawain was only a little stunned – and his rage redoubled! He'd go mad if he couldn't make him pay, and he returned a blow so terrible that it smashed clean through his helm; the honed steel blade was stopped by the fine mail hood, but the force of the blow sent the knight tumbling from his charger to the ground where he lay stretched out, unconscious. Sir Gawain jumped down straight away, unlaced the knight's helm and opened his mail hood. He recovered breath and opened his eyes and saw Gawain and cried for mercy instantly, saying:

'I'll never keep the knight's sweetheart, sir! I surrender her forthwith!'

'A thousand thanks!' Gawain replied. 'It would have been better, my friend, to have said that sooner! You wouldn't have suffered this disgrace!'

'You're right, sir,' said the knight. 'But arrogance, conceit and pride often bring senseless fools to grief! It's foolish not to moderate desires when bidden: it was folly, not valour, that made me fail to heed you. Have mercy now, in God's name: don't hand me to that knight you brought – I've caused him so much pain and grief, just through this business with his sweetheart.'

'I've no wish to see you dead so soon!' said Gawain. 'But you must promise to surrender as a prisoner at once, without delay, to the good King Arthur.'

The knight said he would gladly make this pledge – he would do whatever he bade him, promptly, without demur.

They stayed no longer, but headed back to the tent. On the way the knight asked Gawain his name.

'Where I come from, my friend, the Britons call me Gawain.'

The knight was thrilled to hear he was Gawain, and said: 'Oh sir, I know I could never have held out against you!' Gawain was quick to ask his name in return, and he replied: 'In Cornwall, sir, I'm called Brun of the Glade.'

The Pensive Knight was already in the pavilion with the damsel; he didn't want to know about King Arthur or his men – or her brother or her parents or anybody else; all he wanted was to kiss her sweetly and embrace her tightly a hundred times! And she kissed and embraced him likewise – she hadn't forgotten him: she loved him with her whole heart.

The two knights now arrived and dismounted outside; they laid down their shields and tethered their horses and entered the pavilion which was strewn with fresh grass. The Pensive Knight and the damsel rose to greet them, and both knelt humbly before Sir Gawain. The knight said most sincerely:

'I am entirely yours, sir; you've freed me from the greatest pain and heartache.'

The good and courteous Gawain raised them to their feet and said to Brun: 'Sir, hand this charming, comely damsel back to this knight.'

'I shall do as you wish, sir,' he replied, and took her by the right hand and placed it in the right hand of the knight. And Sir Gawain bade them kiss each other there and then.

After that the damsel spread a cloth upon the lush green grass and laid out bread and wine a-plenty. The knights disarmed and sat down to eat, and that was that.

It wasn't yet past none,* and when they'd eaten they armed once more, and their horses were at the ready – they hadn't strayed at all; but Brun asked Gawain to do him the favour of lodging with him that night.

---

[34] i.e. the reinforcing band around the helmet.

'Truly, my friend,' Gawain replied, 'I can't: I've a long journey ahead of me and I'm not even sure which way to go.'

And without more ado or further words Gawain and his first companion mounted their fine destriers, and the elegant, comely damsel mounted a handsome, finely harnessed palfrey fit for the daughter of an emperor. Then they set out on their way. Brun escorted them a fair distance, and promised that in the morning he'd head straight for King Arthur's court and fulfil the pledge he'd made; then he took his leave and left them and returned to his pavilion.

Next morning he set out on the high road without delay, and rode on till he found the king at Escavalon where he'd assembled a great body of lords. Brun came before him in the hall and greeted him in Sir Gawain's name; the king was overjoyed at this and asked all about his nephew. He honoured the bearer of the splendid news most highly, pardoning him imprisonment and inviting him to stay as a member of his household, which he gladly did, joining that select company of knights and becoming not the least illustrious. So as I say, and my words are true, Brun joined the court, you may be sure.

Meanwhile Gawain and his companions rode on till evening, when they came to a wide track that went off in two directions. Gawain said he'd take the right-hand path, and the Pensive Knight said he'd go with his sweetheart to the left and make for the Black Chapel. Sir Gawain embraced the damsel tenderly, and promised that if she ever needed him he would go and assist her anywhere; she thanked him deeply and graciously. Then the knight said:

'So help me God, sir, I want you to know that I'm ever yours – and so I should be! But God! How can I repay you even a sixth of the favour you've done me? I can't imagine ever being in a position to render you the slightest service, much as I'd like to! Not three days ago I was locked in despair, but thanks to you my joy's a hundred times greater now than my sorrow ever was! You've swept away all my grief and woe and replaced it with utter joy! I don't know what more to say: may God who is lord and king of all bless you for what you've done.'

With that they left Gawain and set out on their way.

Most of the day was past and it was very nearly dark. Gawain pressed on a little faster than usual, hoping to find a hermitage in the forest where he could shelter. But for all his spurring he came across no house to lodge at; he dismounted beneath a tall and spreading tree and took off his horse's reins and let him graze. It wasn't the most comfortable of nights.

The War against King Carras

When day broke next morning he mounted and set off without delay. He rode hard till noon; then on a hilltop up ahead he spotted a knight, fully armed and splendidly equipped and mounted on a handsome, white-stockinged destrier. And he had, I believe, a shield painted gold and blue. He looked a most assured knight, strong and bold and sharp. Gawain headed towards him, and he likewise rode down to meet Gawain. As soon as they were within earshot the knight hailed Gawain and politely asked his name.

'I've never concealed my name,' he said, 'nor shall I now. I was baptised, my friend, with the name Gawain.'

When the knight heard this he seemed overjoyed, and Gawain immediately asked him his.

'Sir,' he said, 'I am Ginglain, your son, whom King Arthur named the Fair Unknown!'[35]

Gawain was filled with joy and said: 'My boy, I didn't recognise you! And I wasn't expecting you, that's for sure! When did you last see my lord?'

'A fortnight ago tomorrow, I think.'

'How is the king? Is he well?'

'Indeed he is, sir. But he bids you, no matter what your business, to return to him at once, without fail: he's greatly troubled and perturbed about King Carras, lord of Recesse, who never ceases, day or night, to seize and bind his men and reduce his castles to ashes. He's truly alarmed, and has sent men to look for you everywhere: he's assembled a mighty army and wants you in command. If he had you with him he'd move against King Carras, I know, and wage war on him and capture all his land! He hates him deeply, and has warned him that he won't be mounting a cattle raid – it's Carras himself he's after!'

When Gawain heard this news his heart burned with rage and anguish. He told Ginglain that he'd go to his uncle's court, but had been hoping and doing his utmost to find the Fisher King.

'I wouldn't have been away so long,' he said, 'if I'd learnt the truth about the knight who rode past the tent of my lady the queen.[36] Kay tried high-handedly to drag him back, but he trusts too much in bullying and it didn't work! Instead I coaxed the knight back with gentle words, and promised that if he couldn't complete his mission I'd mount his horse, without demur, and complete it for him. So we headed back to the queen's tent, but before we got there he fell dead from his charger! So I mounted at once and rode on till, about midnight, I came upon a chapel in a wood. I hurried inside as soon as I could, for the night was so pitch-dark and stormy that it seemed the sky was being rent asunder and the whole vast forest torn down. So into the chapel I went, and a pleasant and beautiful place it was. The altar was completely bare except for a single candle burning, shedding a brilliant light. But I hadn't been there long when I saw, I swear, a man's hand appear from the altar, blacker than ink, and it snuffed out the candle instantly. I saw it! So I got out of that chapel! It had filled me with fear and dread!

'I kept riding until, on the third day, I came to a splendid castle with handsome walls and battlements – but I didn't find a living soul. What I did find, in a magnificent hall, all hung with cloth from Thessaly, was a body on a bier, shrouded in sumptuous purple. I looked at it a moment, and then suddenly saw a crowd of people thronging round, lamenting and wailing bitterly – it was amazing. They didn't say a word to me or address me in any way. And all at once they vanished: I'd no idea what had become of them or which way they'd gone. I was left there, quite bewildered, till a knight suddenly appeared from a chamber. There were three servants with him who welcomed me with the greatest respect and helped me from my armour and took care of my horse; no knight was ever shown more honour, truly. Then they led me to a chamber painted with flowers, that's all I know, and knights rose as I entered and so did their lord – who was a king, I can assure you: his countenance made that clear. Then without more ado we all sat down to eat; I dined with the king himself: he insisted. And I saw a boy carrying a lance with a steel head, and from the tip it shed a drop of blood. Another boy held a naked sword that was broken across the middle, and he presented it to the king. The king bade me

---

[35] Perceval met him earlier in this Continuation, above, p. 259.
[36] i.e. near the end of the First Continuation, above, pp. 211–3.

put the pieces together, which I did, but I couldn't make them join. The king bowed his head and said I wouldn't fulfil my purpose in coming there. I was filled with shame as you can imagine, and my cheeks flushed red; but I saw something else that brought me great comfort, for there was also a grail, the richness and the like of which no man ever beheld, inlaid with many stones of power and fabulous worth. I saw it carried back and forth by a girl, most elegant and beautiful, her bearing very modest and composed. I watched her closely as she passed, not knowing where she was going or what was done with the grail. Through the hall she came and went, past every one of the knights as they ate, and before daylight failed I saw her pass before me, from one chamber into another; I watched it all in rapt delight. And the king said:

'"If you wish, dear sir, ask me about any of the things you've seen and I'll reveal the truth about it."

'So I asked about the lance and why it shed crimson blood in such profusion. He replied at once that it was the very lance with which Our Lord was struck when He was stretched upon the cross. But that was all I asked – my mind had gone: for some reason I was very sleepy after eating. So the king had a bed prepared for me, where I lay in sweetest sleep till morning came. Before the sun was fully up I woke to find myself lying on stony ground, much to my amazement. I armed at once – I'd no desire to stay – and set off swiftly, wanting to find out about everything I've told you. God bless me, that's why I'd left my land! Though it was also to look for Perceval, who I heard had gone to the pillar on Mount Dolorous in search of adventure.'

Ginglain replied that it wasn't a year since he'd spoken to Perceval in the forest of Mombranlant. 'And he pressed me for news of King Arthur and his men, and especially of you. And he said that, if he could help it, nothing would stop him seeing you and the king before the parting of the court that's to be held at Christmas.'

'I hope he does, so help me God!' said Gawain. 'Then I'd return with him to seek the king I spoke of. I'm certain that through Perceval I could learn and know and understand something about the lance and the grail.'

With that they set off down a forest path, wide and well beaten. They carried on along it, day and night, hour after hour, until very early one Monday, at the beginning of a new week, they rode wearily into Cardigan to a joyous welcome. But King Arthur wasn't there; he'd gathered all his knights at Escavalon: he had many kings, princes and lords in his mighty company. So before day was fully dawned Gawain was on the road again, riding night and day till he reached Escavalon. King Arthur and the queen and the lords were overjoyed, and the king explained why he'd gathered his forces. Gawain replied:

'Truly, King Carras has committed a great outrage, and so has his brother King Claudas, lord of the Desert. They won't get away with it, I swear! Bid your men arm and form their battalions, then we'll ride at once to your enemies' lands! We'll burn their cities, towers and castles to the ground! And if King Carras can be taken, then do with him as you will!'

The king agreed, and called for the trumpets and the great brass horns to sound; then the army made ready and formed their squadrons, and at daybreak they struck camp and set off through the forest. On they pressed, regardless of the terrain, not holding back with bridle or rein, till they all arrived together in their enemies' land. They fired all their castles, brought down many a mighty wall, and cornered their prey on every side. The long and the short of it is: they laid waste all the land. King Carras had mustered a great host of men and knights, but when he heard that Arthur was burning his land he could see no way of defending himself, and was well aware that if Arthur caught him he could expect no mercy. His only recourse was to take refuge in a castle by the sea, well walled and fortified, and there King Arthur laid siege to him.

He besieged him for two months or more, it seems, but he couldn't take the castle. He was enraged, and swore by God and all His saints that he wouldn't leave till he'd captured and destroyed it. This was made known to King Carras inside; he was less than happy, you may be sure, but he made no outward show of it. He sent word to Gawain, asking him to meet him, if he would, at the gate, which was great and strong. Gawain went at once, and King Claudas spoke with him, begging him to assist in making peace with his uncle: thenceforth he would be forever at his command and serve him unconditionally. Sir Gawain replied that he'd do all in his power to help him, and returned to the king and told him what Carras had said. When Arthur heard this he said:

'I'll agree to this, dear nephew, but first I'd like the counsel of my lords and yourself.'

'Our advice, sire,' he replied, 'is to accept his offer of peace at once. Sometimes what you think is winning can prove to be a loss – we've seen that often. If we'd done battle, someone would have been killed for whom you'd have grieved for the rest of your days. You should never give your temper such free rein that you can't pull back when need be to avoid grave loss. You'll have complete power over King Claudas of the Desert, too.'

'Nephew,' said the king, 'let it be exactly as you wish.'

Then the worthy Gawain summoned King Carras at once, and he came with all speed and fell at Arthur's feet, but he was quickly raised again by the king's own hand: he forgave him for his hostility and allowed him to keep his land.

With that the army was disbanded, each man returning to his own country, and King Arthur retired with his privy household to Escavalon. But as he dismounted at the block he felt downhearted and forlorn, reflecting that he was left now with a company of only three hundred knights. He swore to God that he'd never had so few in all his days, now that his great court had broken up. So Gawain stayed with him, and the story says no more about him for the moment. But now, if you wish, you can hear the continuing story of Perceval.

The Pillar on Mount Dolorous

Gauchier de Dondain,[37] who set these events on record for us, tells how the good and loyal knight Perceval rode for nearly a fortnight after leaving the tree from which he'd freed the hanging Bagomedés, but met with no adventure or anything worth relating till he passed into a very lovely wood. There, high up in a soaring tree, he saw a child sitting on a branch, beyond the reach even of a lance. In his hand he was holding an apple. And I tell you truly, you could search from here to the city of Rome and you wouldn't find a more beautiful being. He was very richly dressed, but looked no more than five years old, too young to be without his mother. Perceval looked long at him, then turned

---

[37] The author's identity cannot be certain. He may, as has often been assumed, have been Wauchier de Denain, but if so it's perhaps surprising that the name of such a prolific author of saints' lives was not recognised by the scribes: the variant forms they give of his name are many. They do include the persuasive 'Gaucier de Donaing', but they also include Gautier de Dons, Gautier de Denet and Gauchier de Doulenz. One scribe didn't register it as a name at all and constructed a different sentence featuring 'Chanter dou douz tanz' ('To sing of the sweet time').

his horse towards the tree; he stopped beneath it and hailed the child, and the child was quick to return his greeting. Perceval asked him to climb down, but he refused, saying:

'You've no authority over me, good sir. By the faith I owe glorious God, you may be a knight but I owe you homage for nothing of mine – and if I do I renounce all rights to it and yield it to you. Many words have reached my ears and truly had no effect on me – yours affect me not at all.'

'I've the feeling,' said Perceval, 'that you could direct me on the right path.'

'Perhaps,' the child replied. 'But I don't think I'm yet so learned that I can answer all the questions you might ask.'

'In faith,' said Perceval, 'none of the things I wish to ask requires great thought before you reply. I'd just like to know your name, and where you're from, from which land, and why you're sitting on the branch like that, and if you can tell me anything about the Fisher King.'

The child replied that he'd answer no questions, truthfully or otherwise. 'But one thing I do know: tomorrow you could go to the pillar on Mount Dolorous, where I think you'll have very pleasing news.'

With that he stood up on the branch and climbed swiftly to a higher one; with barely a moment's pause he climbed from branch to branch to the very top of the tree, wondrously high though it was. Perceval watched in speechless amazement: he couldn't say a word – he sat there stunned; and unseen by Perceval the little child went and vanished from the tree. Perceval kept peering upward, expecting to see him; but when it was clear there'd be no more sign he set off on his way again.

The day was drawing to a close. That night he took shelter at the house of a hermit who welcomed him gladly and provided him with all the sustenance and comfort that he could.

When morning came, Perceval armed and took to the road before the sun was fully up. He drove his horse onward and kept spurring hard till it was almost noon; then he spotted Mount Dolorous far off in the distance, for it was very high. So he pressed on again till he reached the foot of the mountain, the most beautiful in all the world. There he stopped awhile and dismounted: he could see his horse was tired and sweating after keeping up such a pace, so he took off the harness and saddle and left him to graze and rest. Then he saw a girl approaching, coming down the mountain. She was riding a dark grey palfrey which bore her swiftly; none more handsome or finely harnessed was ever seen, and Perceval gazed in admiration. The damsel rode straight down and hailed him, and he returned her greeting. Then she said:

'In God's name, sir, have mercy on yourself and me!'

'What ever do you mean, dear girl?'

'I mean, sir, don't go up this mountain! It would be utter folly! No one who goes to the top returns alive – except to live in torment evermore! My love went there this very morning – one of the worthiest knights in all the world – and I don't know what's become of him! He went to the top and it was the last I saw of him! My heart is black with grief! I met a lady yonder who told me he'd lost his mind and come rushing this way like a man turned wild! And here am I all alone and lost in this distant land: I don't know what to do or say; my heart's filled with despair and woe. If you'll turn back and avoid this mountain, I'll gladly go with you and serve you exactly as you please.'

But Perceval wouldn't lie to her; he vowed and swore he wouldn't leave, much to her distress: she was terrified of the great forest, so vast and lonely – she dreaded the thought of crossing it. But off she rode and vanished into the wood.

Then Perceval harnessed his horse again, and rode, all alone, to the top of Mount Dolorous. There he gazed at the pillar and its magnificent workmanship: it was made and overlaid with copper and polished from top to bottom – and was as tall as a crossbow bolt could fly. It was surrounded by fifteen crosses, all at least ninety feet in height. Human eyes have never beheld such an amazing creation as this, described in the story set down in writing at Fécamp. Perceval stared at these marvels, awe-struck. Of the fifteen crosses five were red, five were whiter than snow on a branch and the other five, I promise you, were a beautiful shade of blue; yet the colours were purely natural. They were made of solid stone, to last forever. Perceval rode past these crosses of wondrous beauty, and looked at the pillar, so tall and shining bright, and saw a ring attached to it. I don't know if it was silver or gold, but it was worth a tower full of treasure. Around it was an inscription in letters of fine silver – and in Latin, not a word of any other tongue – warning that no knight should presume to tether his horse to the pillar unless he could rightly claim to be the finest knight then living in the world. Perceval couldn't read it, but had heard as much from the knight who'd pushed him in the tomb – he'd told him all about it;[38] so he dismounted and took the reins and tied them to the ring. Then he left his destrier standing quietly, and leaned his shield against the pillar along with his sharp, steel-headed lance. He stood there, quite still, and took off his helm to see and hear if anything was going to happen.

Suddenly a girl appeared, riding a white mule; never in any land, near or far, have I heard of a girl more gloriously attired, and it would take me the longest summer's day and the next to do justice to her beauty, so I'll keep quiet rather than speak my mind and risk your disbelief! This girl of otherworldly beauty rode steadily up and dismounted on the thick green grass in front of Perceval. She greeted him most graciously in the name of God who never lies, and bowed to him most humbly and sincerely. Perceval returned her greeting, gazing at her in wonder. The damsel said not another word; she walked straight up to the fine destrier tethered to the ring and stroked his head and neck with her mantle, giving him the kindest and most gracious of welcomes. Perceval was upset by this: it seemed shameful to him that such a beautiful and charming girl should be bothering with his horse! He feared he'd be reproached for it – a knight shouldn't let a fair lady serve him so: there's a far more pleasing service she can offer! So he stepped up to her and said:

'You mustn't do that, damsel!'

But she swore that it was heart-felt, saying: 'Sir, I know beyond all doubt and fear that the whole world should worship and honour and bow to you and your horse alike, more reverently than to any saint, for no knight in this world can equal you, who have brought your horse to Mount Dolorous and tethered him to the ring fixed in the pillar. You can now claim to have greater honour than any knight of woman born has ever had in all his life.'

'Say what you like, dear girl,' said Perceval, 'but there are a good many finer than I about! It would be very wrong of me to think myself the best!'

'Sir,' she replied, 'you speak most honourably and courteously. But enough: you must come to my pavilion. You'll be treated with all possible honour, before God you will!'

Perceval happily agreed, and they both mounted and set off. They rode straight down

---

[38] Strictly speaking the knight told him very little, only that 'if you want to exceed and surpass the whole world in deeds of arms, follow this grassy path to the high peak of Mount Dolorous' (above, p. 299).

to the tent; big and rich and beautiful it was, pitched in a glade at the mountain's foot, in the shadow of a fir. They dismounted as soon as they arrived, and out of the tent came knights and ladies and maidens, many of them fair indeed, and all greeted Perceval; then two squires disarmed him from head to foot and the fair-faced damsel who'd brought him there gave him a rich mantle of green samite lined with squirrel fur. The squires promptly set up the tables and everyone sat down to eat – but I'm not going to list their dishes: they had plenty, for sure; I'll leave it at that.

After they'd eaten, the cloths and tables were briskly cleared. The day was drawing to a close and night was fast approaching; and quite a dark night it was. On the grassy sward, so pleasant and long and broad and fair, Perceval and the damsel sat alone while the squires made the beds in the pavilion. Perceval was questioning her, asking her kindly to tell him her name and where she was from, and why she'd pitched her tent there by the mountain, so forbidding and so strange. She said:

'Good, noble sir, I think I can answer that in few words. My name is the Damsel of the High Peak of Mount Dolorous. I've a castle nearby, beyond the mountain, and finely appointed it is; but I came to lodge here about a fortnight ago because a boy came and told me that he'd lately been in Britain at King Arthur's court, and the very day he was there he'd seen Sir Gawain, Girflet the son of Do, Yvain, Lancelot, Sagremor, the brave and redoubtable youth of the Circle of Gold and some forty other knights, the finest present, all vowing to come to the pillar on Mount Dolorous. That's why I had my pavilion brought here: I wanted to see those knights arrive, the very cream of chivalry.'

'I can understand that!' said Perceval. 'But tell me now about the pillar, if it's no trouble to you.'

'Gladly, sir. So listen, then – the story won't take long. When King Arthur was born, he was the loveliest creature Nature had ever made, applying all her powers to his making. The king his father was told that three ladies had been present at his birth; the mistress of the three had said he'd be endowed with intelligence, valour, prowess, renown and honour, blessed with more fine qualities than any man in Christendom. When Uther Pendragon heard this his heart rejoiced – and rightly so: the boy was his son!

'Then one day he was in a house of his in the forest of Gloucester, leaning at a window overlooking a pool. He was gazing at the water and the meadow and the forest – very beautiful, it was – when a maiden in fine array appeared before him.

'"Sire," she said, "I went out riding the other day, and carried on till evening. In a lovely meadow, beside the stream from a spring, I found a maiden sitting. I sat down at her side to rest, and we started talking as one does of one thing and another, till she finally told me you had a son who would come to be held in greater awe and esteem than his father, who was a king and emperor. She said no more and I took my leave and stayed with her no longer. I've searched for you and now I've found you and told you what she said, to be sure you cherish the child who'll be of service to many people."

'Now, the king had a seer known as Merlin, and while the girl had been talking he'd been standing nearby, listening in silence. The king saw him and called:

'"Master, do you know anything about all this?"

'"Sire," said Merlin, "I know indeed he'll be a king of mighty prowess, and largesse surpassing any man in Christendom. He'll have many kings and princes and barons in his household, and a hundred more in his company capable of enduring the fiercest battle. I trust this won't displease you, sire!"

'Uther laughed with joy at this, for he believed Merlin more than anyone in his whole vast land. Then he summoned Merlin to tell him just one thing if he could: how he might identify the finest knight in all his land at enduring battle and combat, and the one endowed with most great qualities. Merlin said he would certainly tell him, but he needed a fortnight's grace. The king granted him this respite, and Merlin promptly left the court and rode on through forests, over mountains, heaths and plains, up and down, this way and that, until he discovered this high peak. Then he set to work and made the crosses and the pillar – by magic, by the art of necromancy. At that time my mother was still young, no more than twenty; and she joined him there, which proved a grave mistake, for she couldn't break away from him when she wanted to leave: instead she became his mistress, at his will. And he built for her the fine house I mentioned a while ago.

'When the time came for him to return to Uther, he found him at Carlion in the land of Wales; and there in his hall, in the presence of a hundred knights or more, and kings and counts and dukes, he told how he'd found a pillar to which none could tether his horse save the finest knight in all his land. Uther was thrilled by this, and took a number of fine knights of high esteem to the pillar – but they suffered grave misfortune there.

'Then Merlin left the court and came to live here with my mother – and in time he fathered me. You shouldn't doubt my words – I've told you the story as true as the Paternoster! But enough – night's upon us: let's go and sleep and rest. But first I'd like to know who told you the way here; tell me, good sir.'

'Lady,' he said, 'it was a knight I found in a tomb beneath a tall and spreading tree. He was wailing and crying with all his might, appealing to God and His saints and His merciful mother, holy Mary, for help. I listened a moment and then did all I could to free him from the tomb, heaving off the marble slab with my bare hands. I was still holding it when he clambered out and stood beneath the tree, and I was sure – by Saint Peter! – he'd come and help me lower the massive slab back down. But no! Instead he barged me into the tomb and left me there stunned – I didn't know what had happened! And the mighty slab crashed back on top: I didn't think I'd ever escape – I thought I was stuck there for good! That cunning knight hurled mocking abuse and then mounted the mule I'd been riding, the mule that was guiding me on my way; he wanted to ride off on her, but for all his spurring he couldn't make her move! He had to climb down and release me from the tomb; then he clambered back in; and it was then that he told me that, if I wanted to win honour, I should go straight to the pillar on Mount Dolorous. But that was all he'd say. So I set off and kept riding till finally I came here and met you.'

'So help me glorious God,' said the girl, 'if you'd killed and destroyed that knight you'd have done great good and won God's thanks: he's robbed and murdered many good men who've passed that way. He stays lying in that tomb till someone passes by, and then starts yelling as you heard till he lets him out; then he kills him and strips him of all he owns! He never does anything else!'

'Then he's a wicked man indeed,' said Perceval. 'But if it please God and the Holy Spirit, he'll have his just reward.'

With that he fell silent and said no more. But the lady said to him: 'Good sir, I've not yet asked your name.'

Like a courteous and well-bred knight he politely told her: 'Lady, by God and my faith, people call me Perceval.'

Then squires and servants came with wine, and Perceval and the lady drank. But they didn't talk much longer; the damsel retired to a lovely chamber prepared there in the tent, while the good Perceval lay in a luxurious bed, most beautifully made.

He slept right through the night, until God who is lord of all things made the radiant sun shine down and light up all the world. Then that bold and mighty knight arose and clad himself in all his armour; with helmet laced and sword girt, with lance in hand – stained only with dark, congealed blood – and shield hung smartly round his neck, he mounted his fine charger. The damsel mounted likewise and they set out from the tent.

They rode on through the valley till they found a good, broad path through the great, thick forest.

'Tell me, sir, if you will,' said the fair young lady, 'which land you'll head for now.'

He answered very feelingly: 'To the court of the Fisher King, if I can find the way.'

'But you can!' she said. 'Take this path right in front of you! Have no doubt – it'll take you straight there. If you ride fast you'll be there tomorrow morning – as long as you keep to the path.'

With that she took her leave, and Perceval commended her to God and rode swiftly on his way.

Perceval Nears the Grail Castle

He followed the wide, well beaten track till noon. Then a great swirling cloud began to churn the air, and thunder and lightning and rain swept down, so violently that Perceval could scarcely see for the mighty storm. All the animals of the forest shook with fear of the tempest, and even the hugest trees were torn down on every side. Neither storm nor gale abated until none;* but Perceval battled on, not stopping despite the fearful weather: he kept going till night fell. And when the moon rose, it became as calm and soft and tranquil a night as any man of woman born had ever known; the stars in the firmament shone so sharp that each one could be clearly seen.

As he rode on through the lovely moonlight, all his heart and mind were set on recalling what he'd seen before when the good king had given him lodging and he'd beheld the bleeding lance. He longed above all to discover what the grail was, so handsome and so glorious: the rich and precious grail, of which only a man endowed with every quality was fit to speak. He swore that if he ever found that house again, he would ask the king the truth about it all.

He was still musing on this when he looked ahead and saw, a little way off, a great tree thick with branches, right in the middle of his path. And on the tree, I promise you, were more than a thousand candles, bright as stars, it seemed to him: there were ten, fifteen, twenty, thirty on each and every branch. Perceval rode straight on towards this tree ablaze with candles – but with each approaching step the brilliant light was paling, fading; he pressed on faster, right up to the tree – and when he arrived he found not a single candle or light of any kind. But what he did find, just beyond the tree, was a chapel. He thought he'd never seen one lovelier or better sited; and inside, through the open door, he could see a candle burning. He dismounted, and left his horse standing quietly outside.

Into the chapel he went; he looked up and down, but saw not a mortal man or woman or any living thing. But on the altar, I promise you, lay the body of a slain knight. Over him was laid a rich, dyed samite embroidered with abundant golden flowers; and before him burned a single candle, no more, no less. Perceval found it very strange, and listened hard for a sound of someone coming. He stood there in a quandary for quite a while, not wanting to linger there but not wishing to leave. Then suddenly he saw a brilliant light – he'd no idea where it had come from. He stood there stock still, gazing at the light, until, inexplicably, it vanished. It was followed by a thunderous din, so loud it seemed the chapel was crumbling down, and from behind the altar came a black hand

and arm as far as the elbow; it snuffed the burning candle, leaving Perceval in utter darkness. Perceval fixed his mind on God and all he believed in – and all his faith was in God alone; he was filled with wonder at what he saw but he wasn't daunted. He'd have been finished long before, if he'd given his mind to wickedness: he'd been in far worse plights than this, but he was more secure than any man. The only light was the moon outside: around the body on the altar he could see no more than at the bottom of a well. He stayed no longer; he left the chapel and returned to his horse and mounted. It was close to midnight. He prayed to God in all His might to keep him from danger, and away from the chapel and the tree I mentioned he rode at speed.

Pondering deeply on these strange experiences, he rode on till he came to a fork in the path by a beautiful oak tree, tall and wide. There was fresh, green grass beneath it, long and thick, so he dismounted at once and unbridled his horse, and left him to graze and rest until the sun rose bright and fair. Then Perceval mounted and rode all morning, through the dewy forest in the shining sun.

Suddenly he heard a great horn ring out three times, loud and strident. He wasn't alarmed – it was a welcome sound; and he listened again and heard a smaller horn sound thrice, as if in reply. He didn't know what it signified, but he headed in the horns' direction and saw a pack of hounds approaching, chasing a mighty boar, and four huntsmen galloping after them on splendid hunting horses. Perceval rode to meet them and gave them noble greeting, and one of them drew rein and asked him where he was going. He said he was looking for the court of the Fisher King.

'By Lord God the Creator,' the huntsman said, 'we're all in his service; and if you cross the peak you can clearly see, you'll find his hall and fortified tower by the river, just a league and a half ahead.'

So saying he turned and rode away, leaving Perceval overjoyed at the news. Then he saw a girl approaching, heading straight towards him, most richly dressed in indigo samite embroidered with silver flowers. She was mounted on a big, dappled palfrey; her hair was fastened in a band but she wore no cloak or mantle; and in all her fine, pure beauty she rode straight down to meet him. Perceval greeted her at once, most graciously, in the name of ever-truthful God.

'May He give you joy and honour, sir,' she replied. 'But tell me, I pray you, where you lodged last night – or did you sleep in the forest?'

'Indeed, my dear,' said Perceval, 'I shan't tell a lie: I was in the forest all night.'

And he told her there and then about the tree and its brilliant light, and how he'd been to the chapel where the dead knight's body lay; and how before he left and returned to his horse there'd been the sudden light and the thunderous din and the black-fingered hand that snuffed the candle instantly, plunging the chapel into utter darkness.

'Truly, sir,' said the damsel, 'this is a sign that you're soon to learn the truth about the grail and the lance.'

Then Perceval told her how he'd seen the child in the tree, so young, so small that he couldn't believe he'd left his mother. 'If you could tell me why he wouldn't speak to me, and how he came to disappear, I'd be very pleased to hear!'

'Before God, sir,' that wise girl said, 'I couldn't. It would cause you trouble if I did. Please God I never utter a word to make you think me foolish; for everything you've told me is a presage of the holy secret of which you're soon to hear.'

With that she turned and rode away at speed: for all his calling after her, she wouldn't say another word. So off he set towards the Fisher King's court, following the path that the huntsmen had shown him, over the mountain-top.

Perceval and the Fisher King

He rode on until, unless he was much mistaken, he could see the castle standing by the river. He pressed on eagerly, and rode in through the gate, and servants came from every side and welcomed him with the utmost joy. But I'm not going to drag things out: they took good care of his horse and disarmed Perceval and dressed him in a fine mantle, and then led him through the great hall and straight to the chamber. Since the days of Judas Maccabeus none more handsome was ever seen. It wasn't painted as many rooms are: looking up you could see the ceiling illumined with fine gold and dotted with little silver stars, but there was no other decoration; on the walls there was no blue, vermilion, green or red or any other colour – instead they were lined on every side with panels of gold and silver. If the story tells us true there were images worked into the gold, inlaid with many precious stones that lit up the whole chamber. Anyone entering might well have wondered who could have created such a place; Perceval was amazed, for sure.

And there, seated on a spread of deep red purple,* he saw the illustrious king. In the name of God the king of Paradise he greeted him most highly, and the good king replied with his customary kindness and grace. But let's press on. He seated Perceval at his side. Perceval was longing to see the grail again, the grail for which he'd striven so long, and he yearned to see the lance with the bleeding head. His heart was set on it, but he didn't see them yet. The good king politely asked him where he'd spent the previous night, and he said it was in the forest. And he went straight on and told him of the chapel that he'd found, and how he'd gone inside and seen the knight lying covered by the fine silk cloth, and of the light and the thunderous din, and how he'd seen a single candle burning, and how the black hand had snuffed it out and plunged him into darkness, and how he'd left the place; he told him the whole story.

'And sire,' he said, 'so help me God, beyond the forest I found a little child sitting high up on a branch of a soaring, leafy tree, who vanished after saying just a word or two to me. He revealed nothing at all, I promise you, except about Mount Dolorous: there, he said, I'd find something that would be greatly to my liking. And that was true indeed! What I saw and heard there delighted me: it's a place of many wonders.'

The king heard this and sighed, and asked him if he'd seen anything else that had intrigued him.

'Yes, sire. Near the lovely chapel stands a lofty, spreading tree. Looking from a distance, I saw it covered in candles, all around and right up to the top. And strangest of all, the nearer I got, the fewer candles I saw – and when I reached the tree, I saw no candles at all, no more than were on my lance! Yet moments before, every single branch had been covered in them! That's the truth,' said Perceval, 'I promise you.'

The king, who'd been listening closely, said: 'Did you see anything else?'

'No indeed, sire; but if you don't mind I'd like to ask if you know about the child I saw in the tree, who vanished almost instantly. And what was the meaning of his climbing from branch to branch to the very topmost? Also, if it's no trouble, sire, I'd dearly love to know the truth about the dead knight lying in the chapel, and about the tree of candles. If someone would tell me I'd be thrilled!'

He said no more and sat waiting intently. The king said: 'You'll know soon enough, but first you must eat a little; then you'll be more comfortable, for I'm sure you're very weary.'

With that the wise and courteous king called for the tables to be set, and all the knights sat down. The king invited Perceval to eat with him, from his own bowl.

They hadn't been seated long when a girl, whiter than snow on a branch, appeared from a chamber. In her hand she was holding the Holy Grail, and she passed before the table. A moment later another girl appeared, as fair as any ever seen, dressed in white, embroidered silk. She was carrying the lance that shed blood from its head. And a boy followed after, carrying a naked sword that was broken in two across the middle, truly; and he laid it squarely on the table before the king. Perceval was in turmoil, not knowing where to start: what should he ask first? About the grail, or the lance? Or the bright, naked sword that was broken across the middle? The king kept bidding him eat well, urging him repeatedly. And back came the girl, holding in her hands the grail, so glorious and holy; and behind her came the maiden with the lance. Perceval leaned towards the king and said:

'Truly, dear lord, I'd gladly hear the truth about the grail that's passed before us twice – and about the lance that bleeds, as well, if it's no trouble to you. Who's served from it, and what's done with it? And when you've explained that, tell me about the broken sword, and if it'll ever be repaired and drawn in battle.'

The king replied: 'My good, dear friend, it's a very great deal you've asked me, but I'll tell you the truth about it all. I'll tell you first about the child, for that is the beginning. Know, then, with certainty, that he was a being divine; and the aversion that he felt for you, because of the deep and wicked sins with which you're stained, made him unwilling to tell you anything. But listen: he was giving an important lesson when he climbed from branch to branch to the top of the tree. Let me explain,' said the wise and courteous king. 'My friend, when God first made the world and all the creatures in it – the birds, the fishes, the animals – He made them with their faces ever earthward, searching for their food. But man He made quite differently: He raised man's face to see the vastness and the splendour of the heavens, and all the riches with which He'd adorned the world in its creation. And to keep man ever mindful of the One who'd endowed him with grace and beauty, like Himself, He didn't want to make man in anybody's likeness but His own. But now they repay Him by straying from His commandments and committing themselves to sin. The child who left the tree and mounted heavenward was showing you symbolically that you should turn your thoughts at once to the Creator up above, to ensure that at the last He receives your soul in Paradise; for you, my friend, have long been dabbling in folly. He's a fool indeed who forgets God for the sake of worldly gain, for he loses the honour and reward that God promises His faithful. As for the tree you wondered at, all lit up with candles, and the chapel and the body of the dead knight, and the lance and the grail, you'll hear me say nothing, good or bad, until you've eaten and are more relaxed.'

With that he fell silent: for the moment he'd tell him nothing more. Perceval was so on edge that he would neither eat nor drink, and the good king gently urged him again to take some food. Perceval was quite distracted, and all he could say in reply was:

'Sire, so help me God, before we've finished eating I'd like at least to hear about this sword laid on the table, truly I would, if I didn't think it would bother you.'

And the king said: 'My dear sir, I'll tell you now, since you wish it so, the truth about the sword. If some truly worthy man – a man full of chivalry, loyal and free of wickedness, who loved and feared God and honoured Holy Church which God calls His wife – if such a man took hold of the sword and set the two halves of the blade together, I think it would be made whole again in an instant. And here it is before you; I pray you, take it, and join the two pieces together. Then I'll tell you all about the knight at the chapel, and the wondrous grail and the lance with the royal head, and anything else you wish.

Have no fear: you'll hear their stories, which are harsh, cruel, daunting beyond belief. And when you do you'll be amazed. But first I pray you take hold of the sword, for by you, I think, it'll be repaired.'

Perceval agreed to try his hand, but said he wasn't good or worthy enough to mend the sword. He took the pieces and set them together at once, and the steel blade joined so perfectly that it looked as handsome, new and shining as the day that it was made – except that, just by the join, there remained a tiny notch, not big at all. The king, so kind and courteous, said:

'Listen, sir. You've devoted much to the practice of arms, I think – indeed I'm sure you have. And this test proves to me that of all men now living in the world none can surpass you in combat or in battle; but you've not yet done enough to have God bestow on you the honour and perfect courtesy, the wisdom and the chivalry, to enable us to say with confidence that of all knights you're the most endowed with all high qualities.'

Perceval was so taken aback that he didn't know what to say; and he sighed so very deeply that all those seated at dinner marvelled. But the king looked at him and flung his arms round his neck with the utmost joy; and like the courteous and gracious man he was he said:

'My good, dear friend, be lord of my house! I freely bestow upon you everything I have, and henceforth will hold you dearer than any man alive.'

At that the boy who'd brought the sword came smartly back, and took it and wrapped it in a silken cloth and carried it away. Perceval felt greatly cheered[39]

---

[39] One manuscript, Bern Burgerbibliothek 113, which contains only the Second Continuation, adds an independent conclusion here: see Appendix 3.

Gerbert's Continuation

as he spoke with the Fisher King, but he acutely felt himself a sinner, being unfit to know the truth about the grail. But with all due courtesy – and eagerness – he begged the king to tell him, if it was no trouble, where the grail he'd seen was being carried and who was served from it, and why the lance bled. The king's reply was instant:

'After dinner, my friend, you'll hear things that will delight your heart, but I'll say nothing about the grail or the lance, whose secrets you can't yet know. Your service to the one who'll enlighten you will be incomplete until the notch in this sword – it looks as if it's been chisel-cut – has been repaired and made good by your hands. But listen – I'll tell you this: I know of no man in the world who can learn the full truth but you. But take good care not to lose that prize through sin. If you do transgress and anger God, then confess, repent, turn your back on sin and do thorough penance. And of this you can be sure: if you succeed in returning here, you may well repair the notch; then you could ask about the grail and the lance, and then indeed, I promise you, you'd know the perfect truth, the secrets and divine mystery.'

Perceval sighed, and wondered what offence or sin barred him from learning the grail's secrets. But the king would reveal nothing more, except that he made him keenly aware that he was gravely burdened by the sin he'd committed towards his mother, who'd fallen dead at the foot of the bridge outside the gate on the day he left her; and he said that until he'd atoned for that sin – and others – the secrets of the grail would never be fully disclosed to him.

Then four servants opened a chamber door and carried the king away to bed. Others removed the table and all that needed to be cleared, and made a bed beside the fire – a handsome, gracious, elegant bed set upon a silver frame with exquisitely fine sheets. Perceval went and lay down, and once he was settled the others dispersed to their various rooms and lodgings.

At midnight bells rang out so loud and clear that Perceval, who'd been asleep awhile, started awake. He peered ahead and saw a light brighter than in the open fields on the fairest summer day; then he heard a song so sweet that he thought it the sound of ultimate glory, and was most upset when it proved short-lived, that beautiful, precious, mellifluous song of glory to God and His sweet mother. Perceval laid his head down again; but then he heard a voice call out to him three times, saying:

'Perceval, dear friend, I am sent to bid you go tomorrow and seek the house where you were born, and aid your sister who's in the hands of strangers, though they're treating her properly and well. I commend you to God; I must be gone.'

With that the voice departed, leaving Perceval deep in thought. He had a great deal more to undergo before he'd see the grail again, and he couldn't wait to get going, to accomplish the grail adventure from start to finish. But he laid his head down once more and after a while he fell asleep, and rested and slept till daybreak.

Perceval Breaks his Sword

When it grew light he awoke; and how astonished he was to see neither hall nor house: he found himself in a lovely meadow beneath a flowering bush. There's no man with sufficient skill to describe that meadow's beauty, however hard he might try; a river ran through the middle, and never, upon my soul, have I heard of one so beautiful. Perceval saw his horse was saddled and bridled, much to his bewilderment; so he set about arming, and then mounted and said to himself:

'What *is* all this? What's going on? What's happened to me is a first, I think, for any man on Earth! I clearly recall – by the Saviour I do! – taking lodging last night with the rich Fisher King; and I saw the grail and the lance that bleeds unceasingly – though it has neither vein nor joint! – and the broken sword that I joined together, except for the notch which is still to be repaired: that much remains to be done. But now I find myself here all alone! Now by your mercy, dear lord God, show me the way to my mother's house.'

With this prayer on his lips Perceval followed the line of the river as it ran through the lovely meadow; and he saw before him a battlemented enclosure, and was startled to see that half the wall was red in hue and the other half was white. At the sight of this twin-coloured wall he swore that before riding on he'd try to find out who was inside – if anyone. Around it he rode till he found a gate, and was heartened by this, thinking he could enter; but there was no way in: the gate was shut fast. He started hammering and calling for the door to be unlocked, but not a word came in reply; yet within he could hear euphoric sounds, with a host of pipes and organs, harps and hurdy-gurdies playing melodies so beautiful and sweet that Perceval forgot every trouble he'd had since the moment he was born. He called again:

'Come on, open the gate! Let me in to see your merry-making!'

But there was no response of any kind.

'So then!' he said. 'It seems they scorn my call!'

And without more ado he drew his sword of steel and hammered with the pommel on the gate; but at the third blow thunder and lightning crashed and raged so violently that it seemed like the end of the world, and his sword of finest steel broke clean in half across the middle. Perceval was distraught to see his prized sword broken in two, with one piece lying on the ground. Then suddenly, a moment later, a man appeared at the gate with a shaggy head of snow-white hair; he opened the wicket-gate a crack and saw Perceval all clad in iron and said:

'What do you want, young man, yelling and bawling and battering at our gate? Grave sin has driven you to bellow so, and the devil who prompted you has done you no favours! Now your blade needs mending – it's broken in half, I see! You've added seven whole years and a half to the toil you'll endure before you see the bleeding lance! And you can be sure of this: you'll not learn the secrets of the grail until you've done enough to earn forgiveness for all your sins and misdeeds, and washed them away with confession and true repentance and acts of penance to free you from all ills.'

'Ah, good sir!' said Perceval. 'Open your wicket-gate wide! I can see a shining light inside – a radiant light; it looks a glorious place to be: everyone's laughing with joy!'

There was no anger now in the worthy man's reply, as he said: 'You'll see no more till you return, young sir. But if you can find your way back here you may well witness all our joy, and know for sure the perfect truth about the grail and why the lance bleeds – those secrets that have caused you so much toil.'

'Ah, kind sir!' said Perceval. 'Tell me if my sword will ever be repaired and made whole!'

And the worthy man said: 'Yes. The one who forged it knows the hazard that has caused it to be fractured and broken; take it to him and it'll be repaired: he alone can do it.' Then he added: 'Wait – stay there a moment. I'll be back with something you'll find an asset, for I do feel sorry for you.'

He was gone at once, but was soon back at the gate holding a small and neatly rolled letter. It didn't look as if it would take long to read, but anyone who tried would have found it a daunting task: a year from now he'd still be at it, though the words were very brief. The worthy man came straight to Perceval and handed him the letter.

'Young sir,' he said, 'be sure of this: you'll never be undone or deceived by any demon,[1] nor will any man, however lost or wild his mind, fail to recover his wits if he lays this letter on his head; so make sure it never finds its way into the wrong hands.[2] You don't understand your journey; you're seeking something so sacred that it will never be attained by any man unless he's clean of all sins – and you are sorely stained with them. I promise you, if there were as much faith in you as a tiny grain of salt you could know and accomplish all you wish with ease. But a wicked man's efforts are futile, imagining he can achieve heavenly joy through earthly joy: no! In spite of all renown and prowess, wealth and courage, he'll not attain the glory that awaits us on the Day of Judgement! Perceval has seen quite openly the earthly Paradise; we, hereafter, shall enjoy the celestial Paradise where the glory is supreme. All men should yearn to achieve that ultimate, eternal, never-ending bliss. Go; you'll know no more for now. But remember the letter I gave you, friend.'

And with that he turned away.

The Forge on the Lake

Perceval had listened to the worthy man's words and was left with the rolled-up letter in his hand. He tore a strip from his silken surcoat[3] and said:

'Wherever I may go from here I'll keep this letter hung round my neck – I'll tie it on now.'

He did as he said immediately, then quickly picked up the pieces of his sword and slid them in his scabbard. He turned his horse about and set off swiftly across the meadow; and then, chancing to glance back, he saw no sign of the enclosure he'd seen before: he hadn't yet ridden the length of a bowshot, but all he could see was open ground.

He kept pressing on at a swift pace until, towards evening, he left the meadowland behind. Before him now lay a broad sweep of arable, finely cultivated, and on one side the ploughed fields and vineyards ran down to the banks of a river where stood an array of townships, populous and richly prosperous. Perceval was astonished and said:

'This is a marvel, truly; I'm amazed – and with good reason! Last evening when I came this way I found the land a deserted waste, and now it's abundant, flourishing!'

Such were Perceval's thoughts. Then he looked ahead and saw the tip of a fortified tower: it was two hundred feet high and a hundred wide, and stood beside a lake at the

---

[1] *'anemi'*: it may simply mean 'foe', but the word *'anemi'* often implies a demon.
[2] Literally 'make sure it isn't taken to an evil place'.
[3] i.e. to give him something with which to tie.

top of a tall cliff, surrounded by a wall sporting many splendid turrets, and inside the bailey stood a range of handsome halls; I'm sure there was no finer castle from there to Thessaly.[4] And beneath it, I understand, was a town of greater beauty, wealth and splendour than any as far as Constantinople, below which ran a fast-flowing river bearing the grandest fleet of ships I've ever heard of in my life. Then Perceval's eye fell upon a house that stood in the middle of the lake: in no romance or any lay have I heard of one so charming.

He saw a peasant sowing corn in a strip of field; he rode straight to him and eagerly asked him who was the castle's lord, and the peasant replied:

'Go there, sir: they're all waiting for you! They'll give you a fine old welcome!'

And with that he turned away. So off rode Perceval, leaving the good fellow behind. Everyone at the castle was filled with joy when they saw him coming, and hurried to meet him in processions, bearing crosses, crying:

'Sir, you've restored to us all we'd lost! Thanks to you we've recovered our meadows, our crops, our fields – all our resources and worldly wealth!'

And amid much jubilation Perceval was escorted to take lodging in the castle. Those who came to disarm him certainly didn't look like shepherds! And how happy they were! And when they'd disarmed him with grace and skill, a beautiful girl brought him a fur-lined gown and a tunic and mantle, and a splendid purse on a belt fastened with a golden buckle studded with rich jewels: when they'd finished dressing Perceval there wasn't a more handsome man in all King Arthur's kingdom – nor any as bold and strong.

Then out of a chamber stepped a lady, and Nature never made a creature of more beauty, wit or courtesy. According to the story she had a comely body and a charming face – please be patient while I describe her beauty, for I want to do it properly: she was young and tall and elegant, upright and shapely, with a good, firm body; she had fine, straight shoulders, arms and sides, with a nicely slender waist, and hips as wide as one would wish, perfect for bed-sport; her arms were long and smooth and full, her fingers long, her hands small. But I don't think I can do justice to the beauty of her head: her hair shone brighter than gold – it seemed indeed to be golden thread, it was so fair; and her forehead was whiter than snow. Don't think it tiresome if I tell you all this – I want to describe her qualities as best I can. Brown eyebrows she had, and sparkling eyes, wide and innocent and laughing, and voluptuous red lips; and a nose as shapely as one could wish. I don't believe you could find a more beautiful girl, for Nature, putting Her skills to the test, had used Her powers to the full in her making. The colour of her cheeks, I promise you, was a thousand times brighter than a rose on a May morning: white blended with red so perfectly that I marvel – as did Nature herself as She worked to create her. Truly, without a word of a lie, her chin was quite the finest ever made, her neck so beautiful and smooth… oh, I was rash indeed to try to describe her! I could spend a hundred times as long and still I wouldn't be half way there! But I'll tell you this much: the whiteness of her bosom surpassed all others – what a pleasing encounter it would make, as her breasts were firm and nicely round… but why go on? Let's just say no man on Earth ever saw a lovelier creature! She was dressed in two swathes of samite, one green and the other red, and on her head she wore a chaplet that wasn't made of coarse stuff but of the very finest and most handsome, emblazoned with two lion cubs. The girl's name was Escolasse. I tell you, to describe her in every detail is a vain task: no one could capture her beauty fully – it would tax the efforts of anyone!

---

[4] '*Tesale*'.

As soon as Perceval set eyes on her he stepped up to greet her; but she didn't give him time – she greeted him first, in beautiful French, at which she was most adept.

'Sir,' she said, 'you've restored us to prosperity and honour and freed us from utter misery through your valour and goodness, which no one can ever hope to match. Welcome to this house! And welcome you shall be – I'll see to that!'

And Perceval, that noble knight, returned her greeting, saying: 'Truly, lady, I'm delighted if I've been of service, but I don't know what it is I've done for you! I'd gladly hear if you'd tell me!'

'By my life, sir,' she replied, 'it's only right to record good deeds, and I've every reason to recall the favour you've done for me. By the Saviour, I know you've been to the house of the Fisher King and asked about the grail. What a blessing that has been to us! Every river and spring in this realm was dry, the land was waste and desolate, but now they're flowing and hale again! And when you asked, good sir, why the lance shed blood, you repaired the whole country: now it's rich and plentiful, abounding in all the things of which we were in dire want before. You've rescued us all! But, sir, when you were there the first time and saw the grail and the bleeding lance, you'd have learned their full significance if only you'd asked, and that noble king would have been healed of the wound that afflicts him constantly. But I still believe that, if you devote unswerving thought and effort, you may yet earn the right to know the perfect truth.'

With that their talking ended, but their happiness did not. The damsel took him by the right hand and led him to a window to entertain him till nightfall when supper would be ready. There Perceval leaned and looked down at the great, beautiful lake that lay below the castle, and in the middle he saw the house[5] – a splendid place it would be to live: it was a lovely spot indeed. And while the tables were being set for supper Perceval, relaxing at the window, saw the flame from a great furnace, bluer than azure, surging from a chimney on one side of the house. He asked the girl what kind of fire could fling forth such a flame, and she replied:

'I'll gladly tell you, sir, and without a word of a lie: listen, and I'll tell you now. In that house on the lake lives a very aged smith. A king gave him the house in return for three swords he forged: there's a forge in the house where he made all three. One of them consumed his efforts for a whole year, and it was sharp and strong, magnificently made; and he said that it would never be broken except by one hazard which he alone knew; by that hazard the fine sword would be broken, and it would never be repaired except by him. And that strange, deep blue flame has never gone out – yet no fire's kept there, for he's never wanted to forge again! If he were given a coffer full of gold he'd still refuse, because he knows that once he's repaired that other sword he won't live long. It's the truth I'm telling you, and I'll tell you this, too: at the foot of his bridge are two serpents in chains, and no man of woman born can pass through his gate and return with life and limb except his own household – though the doors are always open. Now hear, my friend, why the serpents were put there: it's so that, if someone came to this land to repair the sword, those evil beasts would kill him the moment he tried to enter. Unless he flew like a bird he'd be torn to pieces.'

When Perceval heard this he was overjoyed: it seemed he'd found the place where the pieces of his fine sword would be joined once more to make it strong and hard and tempered. He questioned the girl again, saying:

'Lady, tell me the name of this fair castle: it's a delightful place to pass the time.'

---

[5]   i.e. the house on the lake mentioned above, p. 342.

'It's called Cothoatre, sir; and the house below is called the Lake – it once belonged to King Frolac. Let's go and have supper now: it's time.'

So they went and washed, for all was ready, and sat down to sup at the high table. That night, I swear, Perceval was served most handsomely, and after supper when they retired to their beds he was given a rich and splendid bed; I've never seen a count's or prince's more impressive or more pleasing: it was spread with two sheets from Constantinople, and at each corner hung a little golden bell that rang so very sweetly and in such perfect harmony that it sounded like a melody. Any man, however ill, who lay upon that bed would have forgotten all his pains. Perceval sank into its glorious comfort; and the girl whispered sweetly in his ear that if he wanted pleasure she would lie there with him in the bed, for he'd richly deserved it. She looked so lovely to Perceval that he didn't know whether to refuse or accept; he trembled in body and limb – and remembered the quest he'd undertaken for the grail.

'I'm in a fix here!' he thought. 'Such a beautiful girl freely offers me her love – but I daren't accept! I think she means to deceive me – or else she's always forward in asking knights for love, and I'm not the first! But a man should always fear sinning, both in word and deed, if he wants to win through to Paradise.'

The thought made Perceval shiver, and he said to the girl: 'Fair damsel, I've no need of that just now. But truly, my dear, I refuse you only because it would be a dreadful sin to ruin your virginity or mine. And I've never really yearned for such pleasure in my life – I don't see what purpose it serves.'

The girl was filled with shame and said: 'As God's my witness, sir, I said what I said to fulfil your desires! Now that I see your wish is to shun the sport I offered, that is my wish, too!'

At that she left without another word, and went to her chamber, to her own bed, leaving Perceval turning this way and that, his mind fixed on the grail and nothing else, till finally he fell asleep until daybreak when the watch sounded the dawn.

Then Perceval rose at once, impatient to be off. The girl was present as he rose, dressed in a rich and precious cloth, and begged him earnestly to stay, offering to honour him highly if he'd accept her service; but no plea or promise would make him delay. She led him to a splendid, handsome chapel to hear mass, where they heard about Our Lady, the jewel of all women. After mass she had food brought to him – a roast salted capon; and after he'd eaten he quickly armed, girding on his broken sword, and mounted at once and took up his shield and lance. To see him on his way the girl mounted, too, and all her people with her. Perceval was very taken with an axe he noticed hanging on a hook; he went and took it, then rode down from the castle with the girl named Escolasse beside him. As he passed through the streets the people flocked and thronged, bowing low and crying:

'Sir, you've restored our joy, you've freed us from a woeful burden and returned us to prosperity! How can we help but grieve and sorrow, seeing you leave so soon?'

This was the cry on every side. But Perceval, axe in hand, rode on till he came to the gate where the serpents, huge and fierce and hideous and foul, were chained to the bridge outside the house. No man, I think, ever faced such a perilous passage. But he pressed on towards them swiftly – and then dismounted, and the damsel said:

'What do you mean to do, sir?'

'To repair my sword, damsel, by entering this house and overcoming the two serpents I see here in chains!'

'Oh, gentle knight, have mercy! Do you want to die?'

'It's no use trying to stop me. I want to know if there's a man here who can repair my sword: a long while ago I was told that if it were broken it would be mended here.'[6]

Everyone present hearing this begged him to have mercy, warning him to stay away. But their pleas were vain: he wouldn't delay for a single moment. The girl was weeping desperately, dissolving in piteous tears, and the people's lament was like none you ever heard. But Perceval advanced towards the bridge, shield before his face and a prayer he'd learnt upon his lips; and clutching the axe in both his hands he strode on to the bridge to meet the two demon beasts. When the serpents saw him coming they seemed to go wild, bristling and rearing, preparing to kill him; and I swear they plunged their claws into the sandstone slabs of the bridge. Burning and blazing in their hunger to kill, they rushed at him as fast as they could. Perceval waited till they'd reached the extent of their chains and then assailed them in a fury, brandishing the mighty axe, and struck one of them a blow that sent both its feet flying two full yards and made it recoil a lance's length, back across the bridge. The other flung itself at him and plunged its feet into his shield: no spear, however sharp, could have smashed through with such ease. When Perceval, alert as ever, saw its feet impaled, he thrust the beast backwards with his shield and threw the strap off over his head. There was nothing foolish in this: the beast was so hampered by the shield that it couldn't use its legs. It was a fine ploy, and Perceval, seeing the serpent struggling, wielded his axe and struck the monster between head and body, slicing clean through its neck to send the head, black and hideous, flying into the water. But the other serpent lashed its tail at Perceval, and sent him crashing down two yards behind. He leapt up, brandishing his axe, which was keen indeed, sharper than the sharpest chisel;[7] the serpent coiled into a ball and grasped so firmly with its two hind feet that it fixed them in a marble block, and then sprang out in a lashing attack; Perceval wielded his axe in fury and hacked through its throat and into its entrails and deep into the bowel, and out of its body a red smoke belched like a blazing fire. Then he took the shield that the serpent had seized and pulled it from its claws; he slung the strap around his neck and looked in wonder at the impact of the serpent's blow.

When the maiden and her people saw he'd killed the two huge and hideous serpents, their terrible lamenting turned to joy. They brought him his horse and he mounted; then on he rode, and he passed through the gate and found the lord of the house. Perceval greeted him with great respect, as was only proper, for he could see that he was very old.

'God save you, sir,' he said.

But hearing him, the old man, white with age, flew into a rage and cried: 'Curse your coming! I know exactly what you want! Did you enter here on wings?'

'No,' said Perceval. 'I overcame the two crested serpents: I battled with them till I slew them both, thanks and blessings be to God; now show me where I can find the smith who used to forge here.'

'What do you want with him?'

'God save me,' Perceval replied, 'I need him to repair my sword.'

When the lord heard this he leapt to his feet; he trembled and turned pale; he saw

---

[6] He was told this in Chrétien's romance, after his first visit to the Fisher King, above, pp. 32–3. Gerbert doesn't strictly follow the details in Chrétien, however, for Perceval broke the sword almost immediately.

[7] Literally 'sharper than a mortising-axe'.

the sword at Perceval's side which he himself had made; and he knew exactly where it had been broken.

'Sir knight,' he said, 'you've greatly sinned in breaking your sword, which I made long ago. You broke it at the gate of Paradise, I see, and truly, I must repair it, or it will never be repaired.' With that he unlocked a wicket-gate and said: 'Dismount, sir knight, and give me your sword. I'll join the pieces together, and there'll be no risk of it ever breaking again, no matter what blow is struck with it. This sword is meant for a worthy man, truly; it's never to be in a coward's hands.'

Perceval heard this and unfastened his sword and passed it to him at once. And the lord, not short of skill at all, blew on the ever-burning fire with a great pair of bellows; then he took the pieces and set to work, and reforged the sword so perfectly that there was no sign it had ever been broken. He burnished the blade immaculately and repaired the inscription on it; then he returned the sword to its scabbard and said:

'I'll tell you now, sir: you should be counted the finest knight in the world. You've been through many perilous tests, I know, and many winters and summers, too, for the sake of the grail – and have more to go through yet, I think. And I can tell you this for certain: I've not much longer to live.'

So saying, he handed him the sword. Perceval girded it and took his leave and mounted and rode away. He passed back through the gate and over the bridge, and the damsel Escolasse and her people came to meet him and detained him as long as they could, but try as they might they couldn't make him stay: he set off on his way, with the people escorting him and guiding him to a great road.

The Healing Letter

Then Perceval departed, and the damsel left him and headed back to her castle. Perceval, with his shield at his side, rode on without more delay; but he hadn't gone far from the castle when he heard the bells tolling in every church, for Trebuchet, who'd repaired his fine, sharp, solid sword, was dead.

All day, every day, Sir Perceval journeyed on over plains and hills and valleys until one evening, beneath a tree in the middle of a meadow, he saw two girls. They were very fair and comely – but in terrible distress: they were hung from the branches by their hair. And he saw two armed knights in combat so intense that they were beating each other to the ground over and over, raining blows to their heads with their whetted swords, faster than the wind. They were both suffering dreadfully, for they wouldn't rest an instant: they assailed each other so furiously that they hacked their shields and helms to pieces. But neither could be defeated: they were both so engrossed in their combat that they felt no pain or wound. They'd once been loyal companions and loved each other dearly, but now they were locked in battle, shedding blood from all over their bodies. Seeing them so embroiled, Perceval spurred ahead, intent on parting them; but now, battered and tired to the point of exhaustion, they both toppled over and fell unconscious, flat on their backs, and lay motionless as a pair of logs, apparently devoid of life. Perceval, longing to know what had happened there, rode up to the tree without delay and took the two girls down. They were weeping and wailing bitterly – they would gladly have died; and Perceval gently asked them to explain what had befallen them. One replied:

'I'll tell you all about it, sir, if you really wish to know. There's a terrible pillar on Mount Dolorous – Merlin made it by magic long ago and set it on the peak. May God, the maker of the world, confound the one who put it there! It was a wicked deed! The pillar's surrounded by fifteen crosses, but he walled up a demon inside it, and if anyone asks "Who's in there?" he'll go mad that instant, no matter how wise or sharp his mind, unless he's the boldest knight in the world and the most upright in word and deed. Those two knights went and called at the pillar and asked "Who's in there?", and they instantly went wild! They lost their minds completely and hung us by our tresses from the tree, as you saw when you took us down! We loved them dearly, but now they've killed each other in their madness – yet not a month and a half ago they were the best of friends! They've killed and destroyed one another through devilry and sin.'

'Tell me their names if you will, dear girl,' said Perceval. 'Before the day's out I'll restore them to their senses if I can – unless they're dead.'

'Sir, one is the worthy Sagremor and the other's Agravain – who's neither weak nor faint-hearted in battle! They used to be such good friends!'

When Perceval heard who they were he quickly stepped from his stirrup and dismounted. He took out his letter immediately and laid it on Agravain's head, and at once he returned to his senses. Then he came to Sagremor and promptly laid the letter on his brow – and he too was cured of his madness. But he was shocked to feel his wounds and hurts, and raised his head and saw Agravain, his heart weak from his wounds and loss of blood. They were both bewildered, not knowing how or why they'd come to be so badly wounded: they remembered nothing that had happened since they'd left the pillar where they'd lost their minds and gone raving mad. They clambered to their feet; and as they stood there, nothing surprised them more than the sight of Perceval: dismounted as he was, they thought he must be the wicked attacker who'd inflicted their wounds and injuries. Each clutched a sword drenched in blood from top to bottom, and were about to charge at Perceval with their naked blades when the girls came with hands clasped in prayer crying:

'Have mercy! This noble knight has cured you of madness! It would be wicked to do him harm!'

'They're like the cur,' said Perceval, 'who turns on his master when he's rescued him from the savage beast! So does the wicked man treat the Christian who's done him honour and kindness!'

Sagremor saw the fair girls pleading for mercy, and heard Perceval reminding them of the adage, and realised he must have done them some great favour. Then the girls told them all about their plight and misadventure, just as I've explained to you; and when the knights heard what had happened they both threw down their swords and fell on their knees before Perceval and begged his forgiveness as true friends. Perceval raised them to their feet and kissed them both, feeling pity and sorrow for their sad plight. The girls were much relieved to see their sweethearts healed of the torment inflicted by the demon, the madness that had caused them to fight; and Sagremor and Agravain couldn't wait to ask:

'In God's name, sir, who are you? What's your name? Do tell us.'

'I shan't keep it from you,' he replied. 'My name is Perceval the Welshman, truly. Now I've told you mine and the girls have told me yours: we're well acquainted! But we must look for lodging now – it's high time.'

'We're ready to do exactly as you wish.'

So they all mounted, and the girls likewise, and rode on together till they came upon the house of a vavasor.*[8] They asked for lodging out of charity, and the worthy man

---

[8] An asterisk in the text indicates that the word appears in the Glossary, below, pp. 571–2.

granted it and freely offered them all he had. The three knights rode in and dismounted, and the admirable gentleman, who needed no lessons in courtesy, helped the two girls down and bade the servants in the courtyard take care of their horses. His wife came running to the girls and embraced them and took them by the hands and talked with them most sweetly. Sagremor and Agravain, being wounded, were helped from their armour and taken to bed, while the girls disarmed Perceval and dressed him in a robe which the vavasor presented as a gift; and when he was dressed you wouldn't have found a more handsome man from the sea to Roncevaux.[9] But he was very much concerned about the two wounded knights.

The servants set up the tables before the fire: supper was ready, and they washed and took their seats, and were served with some five or six splendid dishes in great bowls of silver; they ate well indeed, and drank many a fine wine of every kind, fortified and spiced and syrup.

After supper the lord of the house spoke most charmingly with Perceval, and asked his name. Perceval told him, and then asked him his.

'Sir,' he replied, 'my name is Gaudin of the White Shield. I've lived a long while, but I swear that in all my life, so help me God, I've never had a guest I so wished to honour.'

'Thank you, sir,' said Perceval.

With that their talking ended, and they had the tables cleared and the beds made, and saw that the two wounded knights ate a little and quenched their thirst with some costly drink. Then Perceval went to his bed, and fell asleep at once. The girls lay down before their sweethearts: they wanted to watch over them, being very worried about their wounds. So they slept and rested, and passed the night away.

The Perilous Seat

When Perceval saw the day break he had no desire to linger. He called for his arms at once from the servant to whom he'd entrusted them; they were duly brought and he smartly armed while his horse was made ready. Then he came to Agravain, Sir Gawain's brother, and to Sagremor likewise, and fondly took his leave of the two knights and the fair and comely girls. And he asked a favour of his worthy host: to take care of the knights and do all in his power to restore them to health; he replied that he'd treat them with all the honour, help and sustenance he could. Then Perceval promptly mounted and commended them to God. His host asked if he wanted him to guide him on his way, but Perceval said that for now he'd no need of guidance; and with that he set off swiftly down a lonely path.

He rode all day and all the week that followed, and met with many a fearsome, harsh adventure, and passed through many lands and many dire and daunting straits. Then he entered the forest of Carlion and pressed on till nearly none,* when he heard the blast of a horn and the loud baying of dogs. Thrilled to hear the sound, he spurred his bay horse towards it, till he caught sight of a man just as he blew the horn three times; he headed towards him and called:

'In whose service are you, my friend?'

'King Arthur's, sir,' the man replied. 'He's coming this way now, and his barons with him: they're hunting the white hart of the Black Knight. And my lady the queen's coming, too, with a host of other ladies. But by my soul I swear the hart just can't be

---

[9]   The setting of the epic battle in *The Song of Roland*.

caught! It's making the king forlorn and wan: he'd promised it to the queen and vowed to hunt it down.'

And while he was talking the king rode up, and with him the king of the Irish, the king of Rodas and the king of Dinas Clamadas, the king of Duveline, too; and Perceval saw a host of girls and damsels coming with the queen; he was delighted by the sight of this fair company. But when King Arthur saw Perceval sitting armed upon his horse he didn't recognise him – and no wonder: his arms were so rusty and battered as to be indiscernible. At the sight of the queen Perceval rode straight to meet her, and said, like a worthy, gallant knight:

'Welcome indeed to my lady, the jewel of all in honour, wisdom, beauty, courtesy and goodness!'

'Good sir,' she replied, 'may it please God to send you all that your heart cherishes and craves. I'd crave and cherish knowing your name, and who you may or may not be! I don't recognise you by your arms.'

'My name shall not be kept from you, lady. I'm rightly known as Perceval the Welshman.'

When the queen heard this she reached out and threw her arms around his neck and said: 'What a joy to have found you, my dear, sweet friend, a knight of proven worth and prowess!'

And all the girls and ladies greeted him most nobly. Then King Arthur and all the rest rode swiftly up; and when the king realised who he was he was filled with joy and embraced him over and over. The lords thronged to see him and made a great fuss of him.

Then the king had him recount all the trials, woes and obstacles he'd faced in his search for the grail which he'd twice seen at the house of the Fisher King. He explained that he'd been refused the right to know who was served from the grail, and had been plainly told he wasn't worthy to know the grail's secrets, and on no account could he know why the lance shed blood – though he'd asked most earnestly. But he'd repaired a sword that was broken in half – though imperfectly: a notch remained in the blade, and until it was mended he'd know nothing about the grail. Kay, hearing this, said to Perceval:

'Well, you're no smith! You've undertaken a quest, sir, that'll cost you your skin! You've been humbled and shamed, over and over, all summer long, and achieved next to nothing! You're chasing after dreams and fancies! You're like a man who prances around all day, skipping and dancing, just to get attention! Yes, that's your game! To get people talking you go looking for what can't be found! How wise is that?! Think you're better than the rest of us, do you? You'll be old and grey before you see the light! Take my advice and spend a quiet winter with my lady here. The hundred devils of Hell have made you set your sights on a thing that can never be seen or known!'

The king was offended and enraged at Kay's words: he was abusing the knight he loved most in all the world. 'Sir Kay,' he said, 'your foolish tongue and your insolence are always troubling you. Your heart would burst if you didn't vent your spite.'

'Well, sire,' said Perceval, 'at least his broken arm has healed![10] If he comes unstuck with his cruel tongue he needs some sound advice; it did him little good when he had his collar-bone broken.'

---

[10] Perceval broke Kay's arm when he rudely interrupted his musing on the drops of blood in the snow (in Chrétien, above, p. 38).

When Kay heard this sharp retort he was deeply shamed and his face fell; and the king embraced his much-loved Perceval and abandoned the hunt.

They made their way back to Carlion. The cooks had the food prepared and everything was ready, with meat and poultry and fresh fish in abundance. And what an array there was of kings and dukes and counts and mighty lords, and so many ladies of high renown in company with the queen! It was she who sent a gown of richest cloth lined with ermine for Perceval to don, which he did most gladly, having already disarmed. As soon as he was dressed the king took him by the hand, and after washing they sat at the table, and the queen and her maids and the ladies and the damsels and the knights sat down all together, all dressed in short mantles as was their custom at court.

But Sir Gawain stood before the table, not moving. With him were Lancelot of the Lake, Yvain and Erec the son of Lac, and a good twenty of the finest knights to be found there or anywhere; they all remained standing. It was now that Perceval noticed, at the head of one table, a seat of most striking appearance. It looked priceless – it was made of gold, inlaid and studded with countless jewels and richly enamelled. But it sat empty. He assumed that it was placed there for the king, and that he was about to sit in it – but the king was already seated. Perceval was puzzled that no one went to sit there, and called to the king and asked him to explain, if he would, why nobody was sitting in the splendid seat.

'Are you expecting a king or prince to come and take it? I'd love to know why it's staying empty. All these knights are standing with nowhere to sit: I've been watching them for ages! So why? Why are they reluctant to take the empty seat?'

'Don't worry about that, Sir Perceval,' the king replied. 'It's of no importance.'

'It seems you don't care for me at all!' said Perceval. 'So God may keep you from errors in this world, in word and deed, so that your soul may be received in Paradise, tell me at once, without deception, the truth about that seat! I swear I'll never eat in this house till I know why no one sits there!'

When the king heard this he sighed deeply and began to weep, and all the barons with him. The queen and all her girls wept, too, and tore their robes in anguish. Even Kay, who'd been so rude to him, was wailing so bitterly it seemed he'd surely die: many were alarmed to see him grieve so.

'Ah!' he cried. 'Curse the one who brought that seat here: it's cost us so many worthy men!'

Perceval was bewildered by all the grieving, and said to the king: 'If I've done something wrong I'll gladly make amends, but I still want to know why no one will sit in that seat!'

And the king, with tears now streaming, said in a piteous voice: 'Ah, Perceval! I thought you'd bring me joy and comfort; now I'm to have only grief and woe!'

But Perceval kept pressing him to explain, and the king said: 'Oh Perceval, my friend, the one who sent me that seat cared little for me or my honour. The fairy of Roche Menor sent it by a messenger – and God send that messenger shame and woe! Before he'd tell me anything he made me swear upon my crown and my life that the seat would be placed as it is now on every high feast day, and said that one man would be worthy to sit on it: the one who was to win the praise and esteem of all the world and learn what no one else would ever know: the secrets of the grail and the lance. He alone could sit there without fear. There: now I've told you the truth.'

On hearing this, Perceval said: 'By Saint Leger, sire, you can surely tell me: has anyone sat there yet?'

'Yes,' replied the king. 'Fully six good knights of my court. But they weren't in it for long: the earth swallowed them up! May ever-truthful God keep *you* from trying!'

But Perceval said: 'I'm going to sit there right away, I tell you – and no one's going to stop me! God give me honour and joy.'

The queen heard this and fainted, and Sir Gawain railed against Death for not devouring him that instant! And meanwhile Perceval strode across and sat down on the seat. King Arthur stood, in floods of tears, and everyone else fell back as the seat let out a groan that filled the hall and made everyone leap in terror; and the ground beneath the seat cracked open, and split so wide apart that the seat was touching nothing at all – for two yards or more on every side the floor had collapsed, leaving the seat hanging still as if suspended in mid-air, moving neither back nor forth! But Perceval didn't tremble or turn pale: he felt no fear at all. And before the earth closed up again and the cavernous pit was covered, out came the six knights who'd been swallowed there: all six rose at Perceval's feet, and thereupon the earth closed up and covered the abyss. The adventure was concluded. The king went rushing to Perceval, as did every lord of the court. The seneschal Kay was so jubilant that he sang for joy and, laughing, declared in the hearing of all that he wouldn't be so glad to have a thousand pounds as he was at seeing Perceval safe and sound after sitting in the seat and the six knights back on the earth above.

'My word, Sir Kay!' said Idier the son of Nu. 'That's two courteous deeds you've done which should certainly be put on record! First you wept and were beside yourself when you thought Perceval would be lost, and now you rejoice and sing that he's still alive! It's much to your credit! You rarely speak anything but spiteful ill of anyone, I swear! But now you've behaved most decently.'

But Kay responded angrily to the banter: 'You're in no position to mock, Sir Idier. You thought you'd got it made when you went to claim that sparrowhawk for some wrinkled, wizened old hag.[11] You thought the world of her when you gave her your love and took her to the sparrowhawk to prove no fairer girl could be found. But what happened when Erec and Enide turned up? You left the sparrowhawk with them!'

Idier, hearing this reproach, said: 'That'll teach me to keep my mouth shut!'

But the king had no time for this and bade them end their quarrel, which they did without demur. Then he asked the knights who'd returned from the pit how they'd fared beneath the earth. They told him they'd suffered much pain and woe; and as for those deviants who prefer young men to girls:

'It's a wonder the earth doesn't swallow them up! A terrible fire's in store for them on Judgement Day! You can be sure of this: the fairy sent you that seat just to make known the reward awaiting anyone tainted with that vice. On the great Day of Judgement they'll be deep down in the pit of Hell, blacker than ink or iron! But the fairy was well aware that the one who's due to achieve the grail quest has such a fine, true heart that he'd free us from the abyss. No one could express one tenth of his goodness and valour. He's the one who'll learn about the lance and why it sheds blood from its head. Perceval, dear friend, you've rescued us from the foulest suffering and restored us to the greatest joy; we'd never have been freed had it not been for your goodness.'

King Arthur was overjoyed to hear the words of these knights as they returned to tell of what they'd seen; and he said: 'Those who're befouled by such a hideous sin may

---

[11] This refers to an episode early in Chrétien's *Erec et Enide*, vv. 550–1080.

well be appalled: I was appalled just hearing of it now! Anyone guilty of such a sin will be damned at the end – and may his body burn in a dreadful fire, for I abhor that brand of carnal pleasure. Blessed be the man who truly loves and cares for his wife or sweetheart and can call himself a loyal friend: blessed be that kind of loving.'

With that King Arthur sat once more beside Perceval, and all the knights together, and the queen with her maids; and they had all the dishes that they wished. And you can be quite sure that Perceval was served with all possible honour with everything he desired, and at the utmost ease and leisure.

The Faithless Lover

After they'd eaten they had the tables cleared and went to the windows to relax, gazing at the surrounding woods and meadows and exchanging tales and pleasantries. Perceval was sitting beside the queen, distracted, his thoughts still fixed upon the grail. Then suddenly he noticed a lady riding away across the meadows on a mule; and no woman ever lamented so: with every step she was beating her face and tearing her hair and crying:

'Alas! My heart's in such distress and turmoil! I'll never be happy again – nor do I deserve to be, fool that I am! Why did I ever believe the one who loved me more than his own life – those were his words, but they were a wicked lie! With his fair, sweet, loving show the false trickster deceived and betrayed me! Too late I realised he'll never be any good to me! You judge a craftsman by his works – and that's how in the end you know a true heart from a false! The false heart deceives with words and looks, but reveals its nature with its deeds. It dissembles with its gilded mask, its golden surface, but underneath it's dark and foul: when the gilding's stripped away its rottenness is seen in action. He's been false with me – and little credit will it win him. And I, alas, I've lost my love and am filled with grief and woe. What a fool I was to rush into things and bring this torment on myself! I thought I was bound for happiness, but haste is never wise. But how true is the saying: it's no good shutting the stable door after the horse has bolted!'

Perceval was amazed to see the lady grieving so, and determined to find the reason if he could. Without more ado he took off his ermine gown to leave just his haqueton,* and quickly had his arms laid out on a cotton spread, impatient to go and catch up with the damsel. When the queen saw him arming she began to weep; her face was wet with tears as she knelt before him and begged him in God's name to stop. But he said:

'God have mercy on my soul, sweet lady, I'd refrain from this if I thought it right – I should always do your will; but I have to tell you, truly, on my honour, I must go and search once more for the lance and the grail. And if you care at all for my honour you shouldn't ask me to do anything for which I'd be reproached.'

King Arthur, who loved Perceval dearly, hurried over when he saw him arming, and all the lords of the court likewise; they begged him not to go, but they could have offered him all of Germany and still he wouldn't have stayed. Many were weeping, distraught to see him go; but Perceval didn't linger: he mounted and took his leave of the king and the worthy barons and the beautiful queen and all the other people in distress on his account, thinking they'd never see him again. But their grief wouldn't make Perceval risk tarnishing his honour. And indeed, a man disgraces and demeans himself if he lets softness or idleness stop his pursuit of honour: faint-hearted softness strips a man of prowess, making him stay quietly at home and earn a reputation as a glorified watchman! It's brought shame on many a man – and will continue to, I tell you! It's the work of the devil and sin.

But Perceval wasn't inclined to be idle. Off he rode towards the great, dark forest, following the damsel who was pummelling her saddle repeatedly, hurting her hands. It took him a while to catch up with her, but then she, pale and wan, saw him coming and stopped. Perceval rode swiftly up and greeted her, saying:

'May God who was born of the virgin, damsel, calm your grief and anger and send you honour and joy.'

'May He hear your prayer indeed, sir!' she replied. 'I don't see how He can allay my sorrow, but may God who judges all guide you to achieve what your heart most craves – I've certainly failed in *my* desire! But I still haven't given up hope – if only I could find the one I've sought so long! So much hunting and no catch at all!'

Seeing her anguish and torment, Perceval gently asked her who it was she'd been seeking so long, and why. She said she'd tell him all about it, keeping nothing back; and she explained at once that a knight had sought her love and sworn he loved her with all his heart and would be forever true, sincere.

'I thought he meant it! He begged so sweetly and sighed so deeply! He wept! He implored and prayed for mercy, hands clasped, crying: "Kill me, lady! I'm pining to death!" On he went, insistently, till he got the better of me and set my heart afire; and when he saw he'd convinced me and won me over he pressed me to do his will. And I, innocent fool that I was, told him I'd do whatever he wanted if he gave me his word in all good faith that he'd truly marry me. That two-faced, faithless man swore he'd marry me next day. I gave him too much credit – in more ways than one! He had more from me that night than he can ever give back! I did everything he desired. What a fool I was! God save me, his word, his promise, meant nothing to him! I've taken the leap that senseless, reckless women do, stupidly flinging their bodies away! How unthinking I was, how rash, how I degraded myself, agreeing to do his will – and now he's broken his promise. He'd no respect for me at all – and yet I love him! I can't help myself, can't control my heart! But he's so hard and cruel: he won't even speak to me – he treats me like a stranger, as though he'd never met me! And there I was imagining he'd keep his word and marry me! I keep begging him to honour his vow – and all he says is that if he didn't fear reproach he'd do me shame and injury! He told me to get lost – that if I had any kinsman who could take revenge I should go and find him right away! I'm not short of friends, and set off at once to find a cousin of mine; but I've searched near and far and can find no sign of him: I've heard he's gone looking for the grail and the bleeding lance – he's suffered a lot in the quest.'

'What's his name, the knight you're so keen to find?'

'Perceval – I'm a first cousin of his. I've been searching for weeks and found no news at all – in fact I've given up: it's all in vain – tomorrow the knight who's brought me utter shame is marrying another girl: he's betrothed to *her* as well! I'll die of grief and rage! But no! I'll go and try to stop it, come what may! God grant I arrive in time – if he's already married her I think I'll kill myself on the spot! I love him so much I'd rather die than languish in hopeless desire!'

'Damsel,' Perceval said, 'it's a painful struggle, I know, to spend endless days in fruitless search for what your heart craves. The one who's taken against you has deceived and betrayed you indeed. Breaking his promise was a most disloyal act – but perhaps he was under pressure from someone else. What's he like, this knight?'

'So handsome, strong and tall, sir, that he fears no man in single combat. He's vanquished many fine knights he's met – and he's tireless, despite all his adventures! He's much respected far and wide.'

'If he's as valiant as you say,' said Perceval, 'he should be keeping his word to marry you! Ride on, dear lady: I'll go to him and see if he's the sense to respond to rebukes and reason, and abandon his folly and honour his pledge. He's acting like a child if he casts you off and takes another! With any luck he'll heed our reproach and change his mind directly. What a shame it would be, when he has so many qualities, and is outwardly so fine and strong, if his heart were less than good and true. Enough – let's ride! I'm not going to abandon you!'

She, still very upset, replied: 'Let's hurry then – though I fear it's hopeless!'

And with that they set off together, the damsel's mule going faster than a palfrey. On they rode through the wood, beside a marsh, until a little after sunset they came upon a splendid house, the home of a wise and courteous prince who never refused lodging to anyone and offered hospitality to all comers, hospitality worthy of the noblest men. Perceval rode up to the gate and entered, the damsel with him; and as soon as the master of the house caught sight of them he hurried to meet them with his wife and all his servants: they all came running. He kindly helped the damsel from her mule and set her down, and all the servants offered their service and greeted them with high honour. Perceval dismounted from his destrier,* many hands offering to hold his stirrup, and the lord led them straight to his hall and had Perceval disarmed. As for the mule and horse, needless to say, they were given more than enough oats and hay that night. To avoid being tiresome I'll keep things short: the worthy lord gave them the finest lodging he could, providing abundant food and wine, and after they'd eaten they went to rest and sleep – though the damsel couldn't stop worrying that she'd arrive too late for the one she loved.

At the crack of dawn she rose at once, and Perceval woke and rose likewise, and two servants presented themselves that instant and ably helped him arm while two others quickly harnessed the mule and destrier and returned to the hall. Then Perceval went straight to his horse and mounted; the damsel, still afraid they'd be too late, begged him to hurry. He did so, and took his leave and set off swiftly, the damsel right behind.

On they rode, past terce* till almost noon; and after riding far they caught sight of a castle, fine and handsome indeed, and saw all the people pouring forth, some singing and making music and others dancing, making their way to church in a loud and merry procession, with songs and refrains and the joyous drumming of a host of girls and maidens. Perceval didn't dally; he galloped ahead, the fair damsel following as fast as she could, spurring her mule onward, and they raced towards the church that stood right outside the gate. A tall and well-built knight they saw come riding from the castle, superbly mounted and dressed in a stunning scarlet robe. Behind him came a maiden with great pomp and glorious escort, arrayed in purple* spangled with gold and adorned with bands of orfrey,* and mounted on a white palfrey that bore her elegantly. This maiden looked charming enough, but Nature never made a creature of such outward beauty and inward spite and scorn; haughty and mean-spirited, she was the most hateful woman ever known to mortal man. With a knight at either hand she came to the church door and halted there.

'Help me, sir!' the damsel cried to Perceval. 'There he is, the knight I long to be mine, who pledged himself to me! He's about to marry that lady!'

'God forbid,' said Perceval. 'Don't let him even think of it!'

And on they galloped. Suddenly they saw a vavasor advanced in years who looked worthy and wise indeed, as he certainly was; Perceval steered his fine, swift destrier towards him and greeted him most highly in the name of God the divine Father, and politely asked him where the crowd was going amid such mighty celebration.

'I'll tell you gladly, friend,' the vavasor replied, 'so help me God I will – I'll give you the whole truth, word for word! We're heading for a church close by – over there beside that garden – for the marriage of our young lady: fair and comely she is indeed. The count is giving her to a knight, a most redoubtable warrior: no knight in this realm of Cornwall can compare.'

'You clearly hold him in high regard,' said Perceval. 'But if his loyalty matched his reputation he wouldn't marry any woman but the girl beside me – now or any other day! – for he's promised and betrothed to her.'

The vavasor turned at once and rode back to his lord and told him the story just as you've heard it; and the count called his knights together and said he'd proceed no further till he'd seen the knight who wished to stop the marriage. One of notable wisdom said:

'It's only right and proper, my lord, judging by what you've heard.'

They could see Perceval fast approaching on his tan, white-stockinged destrier, and beside him the damsel, in floods of tears. At that moment the priest appeared in the porch, dressed in his alb with his stole at his neck, ready to conduct the marriage. The damsel spurred her mule all the harder, and Perceval was right behind; but as they drew near they didn't create an unseemly fuss. They heard the priest pronounce the banns:

'If any knows why this marriage should not take place, let him say so now.'

Then the damsel, emboldened by love, sprang forward and said: 'I have come to oppose it, sir: he's already betrothed to me!'

The knight was crazed with rage, and said: 'By God! If I didn't fear rebuke I'd have two servants grab you and flog you to the bone! Hold your noise and be off with you!'

'If you please, sir,' said Perceval, 'speak and behave more courteously. If the damsel feels she has a right to you and loves you enough to challenge for your hand, you shouldn't be abusing her: if she didn't hold you dear, why would she be appealing so? She'd be gone! If you were pledged to her before another, you should wed no woman but her: do the right thing and take her now. If you take another it'll be a false and faithless deed. No loyal knight, I tell you, lies in order to deceive: such a man is a treacherous fraud.'

'*You*'re the fraud, sir, and a worthless fool! Be off with you!' cried the knight. 'I may have fancied marrying her once, but I'm not going to take a hysteric like her just because you come barging in! Be off before I give you a thrashing! By Saint Paul the martyr, if you keep throwing your weight around it'll cost you dear!'

'There's no point making threats, sir knight,' said Perceval. 'You can be sure of this: a chivalrous knight doesn't break his oath and deceive; and I'll prove here and now that you've no right to marry your intended.'

The knight blazed with anger and leapt forward, saying: 'Listen, you clown, you're playing with the big boys here! I've beaten many braver and worthier than you: you haven't got a chance – I'll kill you or teach you a speedy lesson! Maybe you've had enough of life and want it done with – that's why you want to take me on! I tell you now, it won't take long!'

Perceval was getting riled and said: 'If threats were sword-blows you'd have had my head off by now. But it's all just empty bluster.'

At this the knight's intended bride sprang forward, shouting at Perceval: 'If he can get the better of you, curse him if he doesn't hang you! I'll deny him my body and all I own if he spares you death!'

'Don't worry, my sweet!' the knight replied. 'I'll do whatever you want with him – I'll have him beaten in no time!'

Just then the count arrived and calmly intervened; he greeted Perceval who responded courteously with the gracious: 'Sir, may God who makes the flower bloom in May grant you a good day.'

'And may God who allots and bestows all blessings keep you, sir,' replied the count; then he asked him to explain exactly why the knight couldn't marry his fair daughter when her parentage was anything but base.

'A moment, sir,' said Perceval, 'and I'll tell you exactly what this girl says. The knight you see there, so highly respected, came to her and begged her in God's name to have pity and grant him her love and to love him truly, for he loved her with a pure heart and would do so sincerely and faithfully forever! She thought he meant it: he was pleading so tenderly, sighing and groaning, weeping and appealing with hands clasped in prayer! He kept imploring till he won her over and set her own heart aflame, and when he realised his wiles had worked he asked her to let him have his way. Innocent that she was, she said she'd do whatever he wished if he'd give his word that he'd marry her in all good faith. This false, disloyal man vowed to make her his wife the very next day. She took him at his word, and he took advantage – he took more from her that night than he can ever give back! She did his will entirely, and what a mistake she made: he had no regard for his promise or his word, so help me God.'

But the knight leapt before the count and declared that Perceval was lying, and that he'd prove it in combat. Hearing this, Perceval calmly replied:

'If you'll take my advice, my friend, you'll not resort to that: battle's not a game.'

But he swore upon his head and eyes that nothing would stop him 'teaching you what a foolish move it is to take the field in another's cause'.

'Rein in your anger,' said Perceval. 'Talking too much can lead to trouble, I've heard it said. Bickering is base and threats are foolish. We'll see who comes off best by the time we've finished: go and arm quickly.'

The knight readily agreed and sent for his arms at once, and outside the church, beneath two elm-trees thick with leaves, on a blanket woven with golden thread, he was swiftly armed; then he mounted a white-stockinged horse and with helmet laced he took up his shield, afire with rage and hatred. The count led them to a long, broad meadow. The knight, brimming with confidence, spurred his swift charger and sent it leaping forward; straight to the battleground he rode, his great, stout lance in hand, ready to prove he was in the right. And Perceval was ready to confront him. The crowd thronged all around: it was a fair field, surrounded by a great gathering of knights. The adversaries, trusting in their strength, cried their challenges and launched into a fearless charge; they delivered such blows to their shields that they smashed them apart and shattered their lances, and collided with such force that they almost killed each other, I'd say. So fierce was the clash that they flew from their saddles – they couldn't help it; and their mounts went tumbling and sprawling head over heels, the saddle-bows smashing in the fall. But the knights leapt up and drew their swords of whetted steel; they spent no time on idle threats: they started striking instantly; they gave no thought to accord or peace: they rained blows faster than the wind, with all the strength that they could summon; they didn't allow a moment's rest: both were determined to make the other yield – their courage, prowess and rage convincing them they could. Whenever they could get a hold of each other they'd grapple, heave and wrestle; I tell you, no man ever saw a fiercer contest. In their blazing wrath and passionate fury they smashed their helms and shields to pieces; but neither would admit defeat: the blows kept raining ceaselessly, each knight intent on vanquishing his foe. Body to body, chest to chest, shield to shield they clashed, inflicting all the damage they could: they'd have torn their hearts from each other's breast, I tell you! Soon they were all too familiar with the edge of the other's blade! They tested their prowess thoroughly, and neither showed any sign of yielding. Every blow they were given they repaid in full, for they were both of the utmost strength. At last sword-play gave way to wrestling as they took fast hold of each other. Both were strong in bone and sinew and strove with all their might: it was a fearsome struggle. But once Perceval had him in his grasp there was no way the knight could wrestle free, and he was crushing all the breath from him; he heaved and hauled him to the ground, and overpowered him utterly, forcing him at last to admit defeat and concede he could fight no more.

'In that case,' said Perceval, 'you must marry the lady who brought me here! If you won't go through with that you'll go through death, so help me God!'

And the one who had to make the choice said: 'I'll do whatever you wish, sir. Until today I thought myself of greater worth than any man, but now I know how wrong I was! I've met my match and better: I've seen that all too clearly. A man with too high an opinion of himself's a fool – keep going long enough and you're bound to come unstuck!'[12]

Just as he said this the count came up with a mighty throng, and asked Perceval kindly to tell him his name.

'Truly, sir,' he replied, 'my name is Perceval the Welshman.' And he whispered in his ear, so softly that no one else could hear: 'And the damsel's name is Ysmaine, and she's my cousin.'

When the count heard this his heart swelled with joy and he said: 'Bless you for coming here today, my friend! You're the worthiest knight from here to Rome! All that we'd built in this land and lost, you have restored to us!'

'If I've been of service in any way,' said Perceval, 'I'm very pleased, so help me God!'

When the damsel of the castle saw that Perceval had vanquished her husband-to-be, her heart was so black with anguish that it nearly split in two. She mounted, distraught, and rode away. The count with all courtesy asked Perceval if he'd come and dine with him, as he very much wished to do him honour. Perceval thanked him, but said he wouldn't eat till his cousin was married, whereupon the count set off and returned to his castle followed by all his knights, and once they were through the gate they closed it fast behind them. Then Perceval summoned the knight and led him to the chapel; and however much it pained him he made him marry his cousin, which he did, whether he liked it or not. Then Perceval asked him his name, and he told him:

'Truly, sir, I'm called Faradien.'

'Faradien,' he said, 'however weary you may be just now, you're to go to King Arthur's court in Britain and give my lord that noble king a thousand salutations on my behalf, and submit to him as his prisoner.'

'I'll go, sir, without argument, and I'll take my wife with me. In whose name shall I present myself, good sir?'

---

[12] A proverb, literally 'a pot keeps going to the well until it breaks'.

'You can say you've been sent by the knight who sat in the seat that had been so feared.'

At this Faradien leapt for joy and said: 'God save me, sir, my honour's not diminished by defeat at your hands – not in the least! I see that plainly now! My worth and reputation are more enhanced by merely having fought you than they would have been if I'd unhorsed every knight of the Round Table! For you are the finest knight in the world, as the perilous seat has shown. I shan't delay for an instant – I'm going to the court!'

And he hurried to his wife and helped her on to her mule; then he mounted at once and took his leave and rode away with his wife, who was first cousin to Perceval, the knight who'd vanquished him – though she still didn't realise: she'd seen him, even without armour, but hadn't recognised him at all. She'd arrived there fearful and in distress, but now her marriage to Faradien, regardless of the way it had been secured, had restored her to happiness. And away they rode together.

The priest, a man of great goodness, charitably asked Perceval to take dinner with him, for he'd find the country in those parts very wild by the time he'd passed through the forest. He accepted the invitation and went with him at once, for he was very hungry. The priest called to his clerk at the chapel door, and bade him stable Perceval's horse; then he led him to his house, which stood close by the church. They helped him from his armour straight away, and attended to him carefully: they washed his eyes and face, which were covered in blood, with a mixture of warm water and wine, and dried them with a white cloth. To keep him from getting cold the gentle, pious priest then dressed him in a surcoat lined with fox fur. He gladly accepted the care and comfort offered. They had plenty of good and fitting food: roach and pike and carp and barbel; it was a fine dinner indeed. And the count, courteous man that he was, sent four servants with a supply of wine as a gift to Perceval; they set off with a will and went straight there, and greeted him nobly on the count's behalf as he sat at dinner, and gave him what their lord had sent. He happily accepted it and welcomed the boys and asked each of them to return his greetings to the count with a thousand thanks. They went back in high spirits and gave their lord the salutations of the knight from foreign parts, who was being served and honoured by the priest with all sincerity – purely out of charity and for the love of God. But we've said enough about the count.

A Demon in the Shape of a Girl

I want to return to Perceval, who ate at leisure of the generous dishes, gladly provided by the priest; and they had fine wine, clear as teardrops. After eating, Perceval armed and mounted and took his leave. The priest, courteous soul that he was, commended him to God and blessed him with the sign of the cross and directed him along the path to the right.

Perceval rode hard, following the path through the forest all day, till he came upon a cross and a little church, old and ruined. He hurried on towards it and dismounted; he tethered his horse to a stake beside him, laid down his lance and shield, tidied himself and entered the chapel. He appealed earnestly to the mother of God, whose image was on the altar, praying to her to keep him from harm and mishap, and to grant that he might find the lance that bled unceasingly, and the holy grail. Then he returned to his horse and took off his bridle, and tossed him some grass instead of hay, scything it with his sword; and with his silken surcoat he wiped his horse's head and back. Then he lay down beneath a thorn bush, fully armed, and fell asleep that instant.

Suddenly a demon appeared in the shape of a girl, sitting on a black mule. A more beautiful woman was never seen in any land. She kept saying: 'When will I ever find my love? I've been seeking him so long!'

Perceval awoke and raised his head, startled by the voice. The evil creature dismounted and said: 'Perceval, sweet love, you've caused me so much toil! I've been searching for you for more than a year – and I don't know if it'll have been of use or pointless! I promise you, if you want to know the secrets of the grail and the bleeding lance I'll reveal them instantly – if you'll do my will entirely and lie with me! I desire and adore you so much – I'm dying for your love! If you want to know about the grail I'll tell you all, and you'll be free of the toil that you've suffered so long! Understand, my beloved, I'm the daughter of the Fisher King, and for love of you I've undertaken to reveal the whole truth about the grail to you tomorrow – for it's in my keeping! And have no doubt: you'll also know the truth about the sword that you repaired except for the notch. Just do as I wish, and quickly!'

Do you know why the demon was pressing him so? To make him sin: to violate his chastity and prevent him ever knowing about the grail. For the Devil goes wild when he sees a man committed to good. So the demon pressed him again, without pause, determined to deceive him. But Perceval said:

'It seems to me you've a lot to learn! You're mad, misguided, pursuing foolish ends! I've no wish to answer your desires: you're brazen in speech and frivolous with your love, unbecoming in a girl as comely and fair as you, so help me! Be mindful of your honour – and of God, and of the holy cross where He was crucified.'

So saying, he made the sign of the cross; and when the demon saw that sign upon him it flew off through the forest, creating such a tumult, such a tempest, that throughout the woods for a league and a half the beasts and birds all shook with fear.

The Meaning of the Broken Sword

Perceval, seeing this awesome sight, drew his sword at once and marked a circle around himself and his horse; then he laid his head down, fearing nothing, and slept securely till dawn.

When he saw day break he rose, not wishing to linger, and saddled and harnessed his horse, and went to the chapel to say his usual prayers and to seek God's guidance. Then he crossed himself and left the chapel and mounted, and kept riding all day long and all that week. It was very hard going, but on he pressed till he came to the passes of Valbone and the tall, wild forest that surrounded the mountain. He recognised it very well, for it was near that wood, while out with his javelins, that he'd met the five knights and asked the first if he was God or an angel![13] Yes, he knew those parts so well; for near that place, he realised, stood the house where his mother had lived. He wanted to go there right away, for when he'd returned the previous time and been recognised by his sister, he'd promised to take her away and rescue her from that wild forest.[14] So off he set towards the house, and was filled with joy when he saw the tall tree with the marble stone beneath. He rode swiftly on; but the bridge was raised, for his fair sister was at dinner – and grieving bitterly, weeping, lamenting terribly for her brother. She was despondent; she hated her life; when she pondered and reflected on her lot she found nothing to cheer her at all. Perceval rode up to the gate and called at the top of his voice.

---

[13] i.e. at the very beginning of Chrétien's romance, above, pp. 2–4.
[14] In the Second Continuation, above, pp. 268–74.

'God preserve us!' said his sister. 'Who's that, yelling so loud?'

She jumped up and went out to the courtyard, her household hurrying after her. And when she saw Perceval, and recognised him by his build and his horse and his arms, tears of joy streamed down her cheeks, and more than a hundred times she said:

'Dear brother, you are welcome, welcome indeed!'

She couldn't wait to lower the bridge, and released the chain and brought it down and Perceval rode across. His sister kissed him a hundred times in a matter of moments, before he could even dismount! Every servant offered a hand to take his horse, and they stabled him finely with plenty of fodder, for their labour had produced enough barley, oats and other feed to last a hundred horses for many months.

Once Perceval was disarmed, his sister had him dressed in robes worth at least a thousand silver marks, I swear. He washed his hands in a pair of basins of pure gold that had been prepared for him; then he sat down to dinner. His sister had plenty of game and capons to offer him; nor was the wine in short supply: it was plentiful – and clear indeed, as if it had been drawn from a pool in a great vase; the boys and servants had so much to hand that their cups were always full.

After they'd eaten, Perceval relaxed all day, and when evening came they sat down to supper – and a finer supper was never served to the highest lord in so small a company. When he'd eaten at leisure Perceval wanted to lie down and rest, for he was very tired and weary; his sister had a bed made for him in the hall, and a splendid bed it was indeed. Then down he lay, and the servants, who loved him dearly, lay down all around him. His sister went to her bed and slept in deepest happiness that night.

Perceval, afraid that he might stay too long out of pity and love for the household, arose when the new day dawned. His sister, already up and dressed, asked him why he'd risen so early, and where he had to go.

'By the faith I owe you,' he replied, 'I want us both to mount and ride to the hermitage in the wood – that holy hermit's house where my mother was buried;[15] it may be the last time I'll go: I don't know if I'll ever return to these parts or anywhere near.'

He bade that her mule and his horse be harnessed; then he swiftly armed, and when he was ready his horse was brought as soon as he commanded. The servants asked if his sister was going with him.

'Yes,' he said, 'but we'll be back this evening, if it please God.'

'God grant that it be so,' said each of the servants, weeping.

Meanwhile Perceval helped his sister on to her mule; then he mounted and set off with all speed. On they rode together through the forest till they reached the little chapel. There they found the holy hermit, who recognised them the moment he saw them and welcomed them with embraces and sweet words. Perceval went to his mother's tomb, and prayed to God in His gentleness to have mercy on her soul; then he wept, and said in a louder voice:

'Oh, dear mother, the sins I've committed against you have burdened me so much that I shall never expiate them or gain God's love, unless He will look on me with pity.'

He dismounted then, and told the hermit once again of all he'd suffered in the quest for the grail.

'My good, dear friend,' the hermit said, 'abandon all wicked vices. He's a reprobate and a hypocrite who thinks to win God's love and glory when he follows proud, immodest ways! No! It takes suffering, fasting, prayer and true repentance, and wearing

---

[15] Perceval and his sister visited the hermitage in the Second Continuation, above, pp. 271–3.

a hair-shirt in penitence, and unburdening oneself of every sin in confession to a priest. Such are the arms with which a knight should arm himself if he seeks to love God and to be valiant and worthy. A knight's sword has two cutting edges: do you know why? It should be understood, truly, that one edge is for the defence of Holy Church, while the other should administer earthly justice, protecting Christian people and upholding justice without deception or self-interest. But I tell you this: Holy Church's edge is broken, while the earthly edge cuts indeed! Every knight hacks and hews the poor and holds them to ransom, though they've done him no wrong at all! So *that* edge of the blade is very sharp, and a knight who carries such a sword is deceiving God! And if he fails to mend his ways, the gate of Paradise will be closed to him. God keep you, dear friend,' the hermit said, 'from such a sword, which would condemn your soul.'

After this sermon the hermit said a beautiful, glorious, holy prayer, most sweet and precious, that God might keep him from affliction.

Then Perceval took courteous leave at once, and the hermit with great affection blessed them both with the sign of the cross. Away rode Perceval and his sister through the great, lonely forest.

After leaving the hermit he rode on beside his sister, who loved him with complete devotion, until they reached their home again. They were joyously received by their servants, given the warmest welcome by everyone; they were overjoyed to see them back. But before the week was out their joy would give way to distress: they'd be torn apart by grief, as you shall hear.

Perceval was highly honoured by the household that night – but to avoid being tiresome I'll cut the story short and tell you what matters as briefly as I can. Nothing and no one would stop Perceval continuing his search for the grail and to learn why the lance shed blood – it had cost him so much already; but first, he thought, he would see his sister in more honourable state. So he rested at the house that night, but when day broke next morning he made ready to ride, having no desire to stay, and bade his sister do likewise. There's no point stringing out the story of their leaving, but I don't think such grief was ever seen among so many: all the servants wished themselves dead – they wouldn't have cared if they'd been cut down on the spot. They all wept and wailed to see Perceval take his sister away: they'd cared for her for ten years while she'd been bereft of friend or kin. Nearly in pieces, such was their grief, they cried:

'Alas! Most wretched! To be alive is agony, when we lose the one who was so kind to us, so precious!'

But Perceval didn't hesitate: he armed and saw his sister on to her horse and mounted at once; then away they rode. The servants were beside themselves with anguish to see Perceval leave and resume his awesome mission to seek the grail. They all collapsed in a faint, as if dead: they didn't utter a word. The maiden was very upset, abandoning them when they'd cared for her so tenderly, and she wept with pity.

Perceval Learns his Mother's Name

But Perceval didn't linger: out of the manor he rode and away. He bade his sister ride always before him, loving her dearly as he did – though she was more concerned for her brother than herself. He loved having her company.

They rode on till they came to a broad, fair stretch of meadowland. Suddenly his sister saw a knight approaching, armed and mounted, and he advanced on Perceval with such mighty force that it seemed he was bent on total destruction, charging faster than thunder on his awesome steed. With shield set firm and ashwood lance gripped fast in hand, he swept up to Perceval and addressed him with a fearless roar:

'Vassal, hand the lady over now! Don't madden me and make me attack you: if you do you're a dead man, I swear – you won't have a chance!'

Perceval was outraged by these words, but replied quite calmly, saying: 'Let me pass, sir.'

'Are you going to make me ask for her again?' said the knight.

'There's a pitiless strength about you, sir,' said Perceval. 'But I swear you'll never have her while I live, unless you win her from me in battle, man to man.'

'I ask no more, I tell you!' said the knight. 'Defend yourself – I defy you!'

'As I do you,' said Perceval; and with that they wheeled their horses away and drew apart, set their shields in place and lances in rests and charged. They clashed with such force that they smashed the painted covers from their shields and split them asunder; their hauberks* saved them, but the lances were strong and so fiercely thrust that when the blows landed full on their chests they sent each other crashing to the ground. But there was no discredit in being unhorsed, for their saddles and harness and breast-straps were all torn loose, and the horses hit the turf before the knights. Up they leapt and assailed each other furiously with their swords of well-honed steel. There was no love lost: they exchanged such fearsome blows, holding nothing back, that helmets, hauberks, shields were wrecked. It was a harsh and terrible battle, their blows so dreadful that they made each other reel, seeing stars, and the hot, red blood came gushing forth as their hauberks were pierced, their steel helms cloven, their shields so battered that they barely covered their fists. For a moment they paused to recover breath; then back they came, dealing mighty blows with their naked blades, awesomely sharp. Then Perceval launched two fierce attacks, landing three blows in quick succession, blows so ferocious that he fell face down before him. Perceval jumped back on the horse that had borne him in that fearsome charge – but he wasn't done: he returned to the attack, and would have killed him in moments had the knight not cried:

'In God's name have mercy, noble sir! Don't kill me – I'm beaten, I swear! I surrender to you, admit defeat! I'll do whatever you wish!'

Perceval, who wasn't hard-hearted but kind and compassionate, said: 'In that case you must do exactly as I say.'

'I'll obey your command, sir, without demur!'

'Go then,' he said, 'and without delay, and yield as a prisoner to King Arthur. This you must swear.'

'I'll go gladly, sir,' the knight replied. 'I know the way to the king's court well. And I'll go armed and in the very state that I am now.' And he asked in whose name he should surrender.

'You must make your promise first, in faith,' said Perceval. 'When you come to court you can tell the king you're yielding on behalf of the knight who gave them such a hard time at the tournament[16] and kept his name from everyone, even the most renowned, and met Gawain in combat and they both unhorsed each other – indeed, you must give the noble Gawain a thousand salutations from me. But come – tell me *your* name: I want to know.'

'Truly, sir,' he said, 'I am called Mordred.'

'Well then, my friend,' said Perceval, 'go now with God.'

Then they reassembled their horses' harness, fastening the reins and fixing the stirrup- and saddle-straps, while Perceval's sister rejoiced to see him emerge the victor. They

---

[16] i.e. the tournament at the Proud Castle in the Second Continuation, above, pp. 294–7.

mounted then without more ado, and collected their shattered shields and took leave of one another, though Mordred first gave his pledge that he would go to court.

Perceval and his sister rode on all week, till they caught sight of the Castle of the Maidens with its great array of turrets; and its marble walls, I swear, were greener than the leaves on the trees in May. Even from afar Perceval realised he'd been there before: he knew it was the castle where the huge steel hammer hung at the table of brass.[17] As soon as he set eyes on it he pressed ahead swiftly, hoping to take lodging there with his sister if he could, and they rode on together till they reached the castle. Perceval picked up the hammer and struck two blows upon the table; and instantly, I promise you, there appeared on a tower's battlements a lady and a maiden both dressed in white shifts – but they weren't alike in any other way, for one was young and the other of great age. The elder was a lady of great wisdom – and little wonder: if you knew exactly who she was you'd expect her to be wise indeed; the younger was very fair and comely, and her body like her garb was whiter than a flower on a sapling's branch. They saw Perceval outside and his sister with him, and the young one called:

'You're a great vexation to us, sir knight! Do you mean to torment us all to death? No knight has ever come here more than once after hearing us forbid it – but here you are back again! You're the first one ever to ignore our command!'

'I've come to ask for lodging,' he said, 'in the name of charity.'

The old lady heard his courteous request and kindly replied: 'Dear friend, tell us who you are, directly. I'll see you're given lodging, but first I want to know your name, truly, and your father's, too.'

And Perceval replied at once, saying: 'I'll tell you all I know, lady, if it'll earn me lodging! My name is Perceval, and my father's name was Gales the Bald,[18] so the Fisher King told me; but he also told me that I was too burdened with sin to know anything about the grail till I'd mended the notch in the sword – and it's since cost me a deal of trouble! I've told you my name, dear lady, and my father's, too; but I never knew my mother's: I wasn't bright enough – I was just an uncouth fool and called her nothing but "mother" all the time I was with her! And she called me "dear son". That's the truth, gentle lady, so help me God. And my sister was so small when my mother died that she could never have known her name, and I never heard my mother say it. Robbed of her inheritance as she was, she was so beset by troubles that no one ever discovered who she was or from which land: for all their questioning, no servant she ever had could get her to say where she was from, or anything about her lineage. I've told you all I know, I swear.'

At this the lady was filled with pity, and said: 'Dear friend, I'll have the bridge lowered and the gate opened for you at once, and see that you and your sister are admitted; for in faith, friend, I know exactly who your father was and your mother's name, for she was of my lineage.'

This wise lady went down to the hall where she found many a noble old lady and many maidens, at least four score, all of them dressed in camelin* with white veils on their heads. The lady happily gave orders for the gate to be unlocked and the drawbridge lowered, and Perceval and his sister rode in to find a great crowd of maidens in the courtyard. All of them thronged to greet his sister, and Perceval dismounted quickly and gently helped his sister from her palfrey. Then the lady offered him her arm, clad

---

[17] The text reads 'copper', but to be precise, the table was earlier described as brass, standing on copper columns (in the Second Continuation, above, p. 274).

[18] '*Gales li Caus*'. There is a reference to 'Galles the Bald' in the First Continuation (above, p. 151), but there he is not Perceval's father.

in a sleeve of orfrey, and led him to the hall filled with maidens, white of skin and pure and innocent in manner, dressed in white wimples and black camelin. He'd had to take his horse to the stable himself, truly, for there was no seneschal* or constable* in the castle – only ladies; but he'd found a good supply of hay and oats.

He was soon disarmed, two fair and comely maidens helping him from his gear. Indeed, no count or king was ever better served than he. The hall was brightly lit and there were fires blazing, too, for the weather was far from warm – you'll understand when I say it was close to All Saints. Perceval was far from unscathed – he was wounded from his combat and bruised from wearing armour; but he was in the right place to be quickly healed: the lady had an ointment with which she gently treated him, and his wounds were healed in an instant: it was the very ointment taken by the three Marys to Our Lord.

They did all they could to honour Perceval and his sister; they had all they wished for supper that night. After supper Perceval was eager to speak to the lady of the castle; he said:

'Lady, for the love of God please tell me my mother's name: I long to know it. Tell me if you will – and how you're related to her.'

And the lady, with an air of sadness, answered: 'Know then: her name was Philosofine, and her heart was devoted to God. She and I were first cousins, and we loved each other dearly. We brought the grail – a sacred thing indeed – to this land when we crossed the sea; but at the command of the king of kings it was carried away by angels, for the land was in a dismal state, filled with deeply sinful people, and taken to the house of the good Fisher King, the house you visited. Now you know the truth. We live our lives here in purity and modesty: the ladies remain chaste and the maidens keep their virginity. Sir, you've embarked on a most arduous mission – one that no man can accomplish: the quest for the grail. And it's sinful and very wrong of you to take your sister with you: the wise and proper thing would be to leave her here with us.'

'Thank you, lady,' said Perceval. 'I'll gladly leave my sister with you, and with a happy heart.'

With that their talking ended; the beds were made and they retired. Two fair and comely maidens showed Perceval to a chamber adorned with gold mosaic, and saw him into a gorgeous bed and then left him and departed. The ladies took care of his sister, honouring her in every way, before taking to their beds to sleep and rest.

In the morning when the sun appeared, Perceval rose at once and saddled his destrier and called for his arms. His sister helped him arm, but she was sorely weeping. Once he was armed that true-hearted knight mounted and took his leave of the ladies, damsels and maidens and asked them to take every care of his sister. Then the gate was unlocked and Perceval, who loved his sister dearly, took his leave like the courteous and well-bred knight he was. He asked one of the maidens to tell him their lady's name for the love of God, and the bright girl sweetly answered:

'Truly, sir, that is the holy lady Ysabiaus.'

When the good and worthy Perceval heard this he was overcome with joy;[19] and with tears in his eyes he set out once more on his quest for the grail.

[19] If 'Ysabiaus' is the Biblical Elizabeth, mother of John the Baptist, then according to the Gospel of Luke (Chapter 1: 26–40) she is a cousin of Mary, mother of Jesus. Since Ysabiaus and Perceval's mother are first cousins, this would mean Perceval was related to Jesus, explaining his joy at the news; it would also explain the earlier comment that she 'was a lady of great wisdom – and little wonder: if you knew exactly who she was you'd expect her to be wise' (above, p. 363).

A Stranger Challenges Arthur's Knights

I'll leave Perceval for a moment; I need to tell of Mordred, who'd vowed to go to court and surrender as a prisoner to Arthur, that king of mighty valour. On and ever on he rode till he came at last to Carlion, where the king and all his barons were feasting. He didn't tarry in the least, but presented himself at court before the king in the very arms and state he'd been when he'd left Perceval. He stepped down from his horse and addressed the king as follows:

'My lord,' he said, 'I submit as a prisoner – I can't say on whose behalf, except that it was the knight who came to the great tournament and went unrecognised. He outfought and vanquished me in hand to hand combat, overpowered me and wore me down – though it was a very tough contest! He made me swear I'd present myself as a captive to you, without fail.'

The king's nephew Gawain took charge of Mordred and asked him his name, and Mordred told him; and when the barons heard it they were amazed, wondering who the knight could possibly have been, so accomplished in arms that he'd won the prize at the tournament and now defeated and captured Mordred.

'The knight sends you greetings,' said Mordred to Gawain. 'He knows you well, so help me God, but says you didn't recognise him at the tourney, much as you longed to know who he was.'

Then, with Mordred standing there in the hall, in strode Faradien, and his wife with him. They came up to the king and Faradien said most courteously:

'I surrender to you as a captive on behalf of the one who sat in the perilous seat – that's what he told me. He vanquished me, I shan't deny it – nor should I be ashamed of being defeated by such a worthy knight.'

And he told the whole story, concealing and falsifying nothing, of how he'd made him marry his wife. 'And I'm your captive now: he sends me to you.'

'As God's my witness,' the king replied, 'you are welcome and will be held most dear for his sake, for it was our good friend Perceval who sent you here to me.'

Then the worthy, courteous King Arthur sat down to dine, and all his barons with him, most happily, and they were finely served. When they'd dined and risen from the tables, they spoke of the knight who'd fought Mordred to exhaustion, and guessed it had been Perceval. In such discussion they spent the day, heaping praise upon the knight.

Then the bell rang for vespers, and the service was sung most splendidly and graciously by the archbishop of Cyriant at the request and bidding of the archbishop of Carlion. The archbishop of Duveline was in attendance, too, who'd come to speak to the great King Arthur on behalf of another worthy king – William, king of part of Ireland. The bishop of Winchester, a learned man indeed, presided over the right-hand side of the choir, and the bishop of Lincoln, a very fine churchman, presided over the left. They sang beautifully, faultlessly, with voices loud and clear. The responses were sung by the archbishops of York and Berwick.

When vespers was over the people dispersed, but returned at matins with five kings and six queens among them; and when it came to the high mass, every duchess, countess and queen attended. The offering was surely immense – as was the crowd that thronged to follow the procession. The archbishop of Carlion chose not to preside that day; he gave that honour again to the archbishop of Cyriant who'd conducted the service before: he'd sung vespers and then matins, and now he sang the high mass. It lasted a good while; and when it was done they all returned to the great paved hall to dine. Kay had preparations so well advanced that the water was presented without delay, and the five crowned kings could wash at once. The feast, most fine and elegant, lasted long, but finally, when all had eaten, the tables were cleared away.

Just as Arthur was washing, a squire burst in and was shown to the king at once; he went down on his knees and hailed him in proper fashion and then launched into his message.

'Sire,' he said, 'I've been sent to you by a knight who's come to seek adventures here in your fine land. He's come from far across the sea, for no other reason than to test himself against the knights of your household, and he asks you to send one straight away – that's all he craves. He's waiting armed and mounted in the meadows below the castle. The arms he's brought to this country are all of gold, and his horse is a roan – to describe him as a fine steed wouldn't begin to do him justice!'

The king smiled at this, and called for Girflet the son of Do and bade him arm at once and go and joust with the knight. Girflet was thrilled, and armed and made ready in no time, and mounted and rode to the nearby meadow where the knight was awaiting him. The moment they saw each other, without any kind of threat or challenge, they set their painted, varnished shields before their breasts, lowered their stout and smooth white lances and spurred their horses to a furious charge. Girflet delivered such a blow that it pierced his opponent's shield, but his hauberk was strong and the mail held firm and the lance flew into a hundred pieces. And the knight knew his business, and returned a ferocious blow that pinned shield to arm and arm to body, and in full view of the king and all his people – counts, dukes, kings, queens, ladies, maidens – he sent Girflet crashing to the ground. They weren't best pleased. The knight rode up and caught Girflet's horse and gave him to a page of his – he'd brought five with him, handsome and well-mounted boys indeed – and sent him to present the horse to the watching ladies. Meanwhile Girflet struggled to his feet, distraught; his pages ran to fetch his palfrey and took it to him in the field; they helped him into the saddle and led him back to the city, crestfallen and ashamed.

Even before Girflet had been disarmed, Lancelot of the Lake was armed and mounted, ready to avenge him, having asked the king's leave. He raced with all speed to the meadow, and found the knight in no awe of him at all: the moment he set eyes on Lancelot he charged in no uncertain manner. Lancelot, so full of prowess, charged likewise and they met in a fearsome clash; with their stout lances they smashed each other's shield with ease, but their hauberks proved too good and they couldn't pierce the mail; instead their lances shivered and flew into shards, splintering like so much bark. Their charge was unswerving and they crashed together, face to face and body to body; they saw stars, broke teeth and noses; and every part of Lancelot's harness – breast-piece, stirrup-strap, saddle-strap and saddle-bow – was ripped and smashed asunder, and he went flying from his fine steed and crashed to the ground so hard it nearly killed him. It was a long time before he could stand. The watching Britons were appalled and aghast, dismayed and amazed, and said:

'Dear God! Who can he be, this knight who's good enough to unhorse Lancelot?'

They were deeply shocked and downcast. And the knight took Lancelot's destrier by the reins and sent him to the ladies – not that it gave them any comfort or joy! Lancelot's pages hurriedly saddled his palfrey and took it to him furtively, and he mounted and returned to the town. A good three thousand had seen this joust, and all of them were stunned, bewildered.

Yvain, son of King Urien, was now superbly armed, and rode straight to the meadow to avenge Lancelot of the Lake: he'd rather die than leave the knight's pride untoppled – he wanted to flatten him! But when he arrived in the field he found him in great shape: the moment he saw Yvain he charged with all the fresh vigour he'd shown at the start! Sir Yvain needed no instruction and attacked him in a fury. Their mounts were swift and they clashed at speed, exchanging blows that smashed their shields apart, such was the force behind them. Sir Yvain shattered his lance, despite its strength; and his opponent struck him with such might that he pierced gold shield and bright hauberk alike, for all that the mail was good and fine. He was wounded in the belly, right below the navel; the blow would have sent him dead to the ground without uttering a word had the lance not broken; as it was, it hit him so hard that it drove him from his horse and laid him out flat with his legs in the air. The knight galloped past and turned about, and took firm hold of Yvain's horse and sent it straight to the ladies. The Britons were not amused. Yvain hauled himself up, wounded and ashamed; his pages brought him his palfrey and helped him mount and took him back to his house; he was deeply upset, but there was nothing he could do.

When Sir Yvain fell, Sir Gawain armed at once and mounted Gringalet, and rode to the meadows with a blazing desire, I promise you, to avenge his companions.

When he and the knight caught sight of each other they made ready to joust, gripping their shield-straps and lowering their sharp-headed lances; then they spurred into a charge. They delivered awesome blows that went clean through their shining shields and met their strong, resistant hauberks – but that was it: their lances couldn't hold, and shattered right down to their fists. They collided head on in a fearsome clash, their fine, bold chargers likewise, with such equal force that all four together – knights and steeds – crashed down stunned into the grass. They lay motionless for quite a while, then clambered up; out came the furbished blades and together the two knights came to test each other. They knew how to handle a sword, and dealt one another giddying blows, dashing the hoops[20] from their bright and shining helms and smashing their shields from top to bottom. They hammered and battered – nothing half-hearted! – and seized hold of each other and wrestled. The knight was the wearier of the two – he'd already jousted heartily and exerted himself more than Gawain – and I'm sure he was a good deal less accomplished. Yet Gawain couldn't drive him back a single step; he was nearly wild with rage, and dismayed to see that, for all his earlier jousting, the knight seemed as keen and fresh as he'd been at the start. He looked back towards the palace, and when he saw the great array of ladies he started to sweat with shame! He attacked the knight with all his might, convinced he must be tiring. He assailed and hewed and pressed and harried, and soon had him gasping for breath.

It was just then that a minstrel came to the king and said with great composure, in the hearing of all the barons: 'So help me God, sire, I know that knight – I've been trying to think who he was: his name is Tristran, definitely; he's the nephew of King Marc of Cornwall. He's the one who slew the serpent and the tormenting Morholt,[21] and so won the fair Yseut. But it led to a love that has brought him much heartache: he was taking her back to his uncle when he drank a potion that made him fall in sinful love with her; and when King Marc became aware of the love between them he drove

---

[20] The reinforcing bands around their helmets.
[21] An Irish warrior who demands tribute from King Marc until Tristran kills him in single combat. In most versions of the Tristan story he is related to Yseut.

Tristran out and banished him from his land. I recognise him by his arms: when he found himself exiled from his uncle's realm he resolved to bear gold arms until such time as his tough and testing adventures in distant lands equipped him to defeat a knight of your court, whose renown has spread far and wide. It's him, without a doubt – banished by King Marc at the city of Lancïen, in the presence of the beautiful, noble Yseut and her maid Brengien.'

King Arthur was thrilled to hear this news. 'Listen, sirs, listen!' he said. 'That knight down there, fighting so bravely, is the famous Tristran! God has led him here to me – he's honoured me indeed! I can't let them fight any longer – I'm going to stop the battle.'

He went out to the field without more ado, accompanied by many a knight. He forced them to part, and asked Tristran his name; he told him the truth and the king greeted him with the utmost joy. Sir Gawain was elated to hear that he was Tristran, and took him back to his own house where they disarmed. Two chamberlains brought them a pair of tunics, one of silk from Aleppo and the other of costly baudequin,* in which they dressed most elegantly, tying them with silken belts with rings of glowing gold. The chamberlains presented them with handsome clasps; Sir Gawain took one to fasten the neck of his tunic, but Tristran didn't take his, saying he wouldn't wear a brooch or a ring on his finger till he'd placed one on the hand of a certain lady in another land. Instead he fastened the tunic at his fine, white neck with a silken lace. Then they were given two splendid mantles lined with ermine, made of the same silks as their tunics. Then the squires ran to fetch palfreys; the knights mounted, and hand in hand Tristran and Sir Gawain rode together to the court where they were given a glorious welcome. The king greeted Tristran joyfully, and implored him to stay.

Tristran's Disguise

Everyone fêted Tristran, even those he'd unhorsed. But there were certain ladies and girls, I think, who would rather he'd been strung up by the neck than come barging in to topple their sweethearts so shamefully before such a great and illustrious company!

Tristran, I can tell you, was adept at every game and pastime – chess, backgammon, dice. At hunting in wood and river he was more skilled than any man; if he turned his hand to juggling tricks he surpassed them all; when it came to swordsmanship no one could compare; as for wrestling, he threw and pinned down every knight at court! He was tested by the finest and beat them all!

When Sir Gawain saw him getting the better of everyone, he wanted to try his strength against him in a wrestling bout. In private, in a chamber in his house well away from watching eyes, they went and wrestled with all their strength. They strained and flushed, took many a tumble, for both were strong and tough indeed. But Tristran was the better wrestler, and with a deft sweep of his knee he brought Gawain down and had him pinned beneath him: he fell on his belly with such force that he nearly crushed him. Then he jumped straight up again, and with a good-natured laugh he pressed his hand on the clasp at Gawain's breast and said:

'What do you make of my wrestling, Sir Gawain? You've seen enough to judge! You had me down just now, but you're the boss!'

Gawain stood up and smiled, and said to Tristran, with warm affection: 'Yes, I had you down – right on my belly! I tell you, I'm never going to take you on again – you nearly finished me! You're a far better wrestler than I!'

And off they went, laughing and joking.

Tristran was loved by everyone; and the worthy Gawain, so wise and full of prowess, took him far and wide to compete in all the tournaments – he wouldn't go anywhere without him. And the valiant Tristran surpassed all others – no one, in short, could compare with him except Sir Gawain.

But finally his thoughts returned to Yseut. He longed to see her, and was determined to devise some way of doing so, and soon. He fondly begged Gawain to ask his uncle the king to let him leave court with him and a dozen other knights. Sir Gawain happily agreed and went straight to the king with Tristran's request. The king didn't refuse; he granted permission, though not without a tender plea that he stay at court. But Love had Tristran in its thrall, had such a tight grip on his heart that not even a thousand marks of gold would have kept him from going to see Yseut: his love for her was a blissful torment.

I'll quickly name the knights he chose: Gawain first of all, and Kay the seneschal and Yvain and Sagremor and Agravain; and Lancelot of the Lake, and Cligés and Erec the son of Lac; and Carados, Bliobleris, Gorvain, Cadrus and Meraugis.

That night, after supper, the knights and lords and peers went to their lodgings to sleep; but the moment he saw the dawn Tristran, so eager to see his beloved Yseut, went straight to rouse his companions and bade them make ready – by dressing down. He'd prepared for each an ill-fitting robe of squirrel-fur and silk, while for himself the wily Tristran had a gown of brand new scarlet* with sleeves that dangled way below his hands – he hadn't been sparing with the cloth! And each of them had a wide-brimmed, ill-made hat or a black cap fit only for a fowler, and a pair of great big rumpled boots. As for their palfreys, they fitted them with clapped-out saddles, reins and stirrups – even their spurs had seen better days. And each was swathed in a hooded cloak that covered him completely. They carried an array of instruments – horns, whistles, Pan-pipes, bagpipes; one had a harp, others had a viol, a flageolet, a psaltery or tabor, one a flute for sure, and another a Cornish pipe; and Tristran had a hurdy-gurdy – no one played it better than he.

In such attire and so equipped, they went straight to court and took their leave of the king and the barons at once. How the knights present all laughed at their get-up! The king mounted to see them on their way, but Tristran, who knew the way perfectly, made him turn back, not wanting any delay.

He pressed on day after day, drawn irresistibly by his heart, following an ancient road to the noble, mighty city of Lancïen. There King Marc had come with all his forces – and with his fine and worthy Queen Yseut; for all his noblest vassals had come, either willingly or duty-bound, for a tournament he'd agreed to fight against a king of great prestige, a proud and redoubtable king indeed: the King of One Hundred Knights.

There was a vast host at Lancïen immersed in handsome preparation, readying their coats and leggings of mail and fitting straps to their shields, amid a dazzling array of heraldry on surcoats and banners. All through the city they were busy: the tournament was to start in two days' time. King Marc was seated before his tower, the queen at his right hand. The queen watched the knights avidly as they went back and forth about their business, but she couldn't see the one for whom her heart yearned: Tristran, that is, her beloved. She hadn't seen him for a year and a half, and how it grieved her. With head bowed, she was consoling herself in thoughts of him; and it was at that very moment that he rode through the gate with his companions, and two by two, and hand in hand, they made their way up through the town.

Tristran, full of guile, well primed by Love, rode through Lancïen with his hurdy-gurdy hanging from his neck. His hat was torn in two places so that his hair poked through; he pulled one flap of the hat down over his face, pretending to be blind in one eye. In this guise he clattered through the town till he came before the king. He dismounted at the block and his companions likewise, and with his customary eloquence Tristran said:

'God save you, my lord king!'

And when she heard his voice the queen gave a great start: it was a voice she'd heard so many times, and she wondered if it could be him – but told herself it couldn't be: Tristran had two eyes, definitely!

'King of Cornwall,' Tristran said, 'engage us and reward us – we'll serve you well!'

'In what capacity?' the king replied.

'Watching your back, sire!' he said. 'And that's not all we can do – we'll show you.' And he called on his companions to take out their instruments, and they did as bidden instantly. They tuned them and played so perfectly, in such faultless, mellifluous harmony, that every knight present swore he'd never heard such sweet music.

'Sirs,' said King Marc, 'you can keep watch on my house indeed! You're hired!' And calling to Dinas he said: 'Come, show our musical watchmen inside!'

The king had summoned men from far and wide and there were many fine, accomplished knights with him that day; and they weren't idle: they were busily preparing their gear, eager for the tourney to begin so that they could test themselves. And meanwhile King Marc bade Tristran and his companions play and earn their pay.

Word of the tournament had been spreading since mid-August, and now many illustrious knights had come to enhance their reputations. The plain between the city and the woods was good and level, and at the forest's edge, where the woods began, was a fairer glade than any from there to Ireland, through which, I believe, ran a bright and babbling stream. It was beside this stream that the noble King of One Hundred Knights was first to pitch his tent. He was of high renown indeed, and so named because he was never seen without a hundred knights – and on that day he had a good deal more: to join him, with burning eagerness, had come Claudas of the Desert, who was never discouraged by any setback; and Taillar and Clair and Godroés were camped there with him beside a ford; so were the worthy Dorchin and Gogulor, Guirrés the Red and Escanor, and Brandoine and Tydorïan, Glador Eslis and Estorgan, and many another knight: the glade was filled with rich pavilions. They spent the whole day scouring and polishing their mail, while their squires were busy with pennons and favours and banners and caparisons and their pages groomed and harnessed their horses.

Inside the city, too, all the knights were preparing to tourney – and if you'll bear with me I'll name some of the lords who'd flocked to join King Marc: there was Idier the son of Nu, Claradus and King Bridas, Disnadaret and Moadas; and Jacob d'Estragueil came, and so did Jolies of Tintagel, and Brun the Pitiless and Brunamort, who'd rashly killed many a good knight at the Ford in the Wood and sent Marc many a hostage; King Elygos came, too, and Meliadus and Gosengos, and Dinas and Count Beduier. And all of them brought as many knights as he could to back the king. They were all well armed and equipped, with fresh caparisons and shields: this had been their way of life for a long while.

On the eve of the tournament[22] the knights who were raring to go rode out, with many a pennon on display and many a lion-emblazoned shield. The outsiders[23] boldly, keenly took up arms to challenge the knights of the castle, and combat began with a number of new-dubbed knights jousting between the opposing lines. First to spur his swift mount forward was Maudamadas of Galoee: brandishing his lance he rode between the lines, calling for a joust, and to meet him from the other side charged Gogulor. They dealt mighty blows on their golden shields, shattering their smooth lances and smashing and splitting their shields, forcing each other to stretch their stirrups to breaking point; they roared with proud rage and clashed with such force that they skinned their elbows, arms and knees. Now jousts began in a hundred places, right across the field; and the combat raged outside the gate all day long till evening. Those who won booty bore it away. There were many horses lost and injured. And it seems the knights of the castle had a hard time of it, being battered back into the river's shallows, and I assure you, if darkness hadn't quickly fallen King Marc would have been in trouble! But night separated them, both sides exchanging vows that next morning, once mass was sung, they would all be donning their helms again ready to resume the tourney.

King Marc was deeply vexed that his side had been driven back across the fords, and that night he told his barons:

'Sirs, the tournament proper begins tomorrow! Let's put our minds to fighting well! The worthy can redeem themselves – we made a poor show at the vespers!'*

There was much talk among the counts and peers of how well the Bold Ugly Knight had jousted, as had Guirrés the Red, and Tydoriän had won two splendid horses. Then they sat down to supper, and were served well, with a fine array of dishes. All the while Tristran found solace in being able to look upon Yseut: he was sitting in the hall with his companions about him, and they had plenty to eat and drink, for the king made sure they were well served. Tristran would have liked to repay the favour in the tournament if he could! And it pained him that Yseut hadn't noticed him: he felt terribly let down, and resolved to devise a way to speak to her. He kept looking at her with his one eye; then he picked up a flute and began to play most sweetly, and the tune he played was the lay of *Chevrefoil*.[24] Then he laid the flute down. The king and the barons had listened with delight; Yseut had heard it and was stunned.

'Ah!' she thought. 'Holy Mary! That must be Tristran, my beloved! He's come here disguised, for my sake, I'm sure of it! But no – what nonsense! Tristran has *two* eyes in his head – this man's lost his left. It can't be him, of course not – and he's nothing to me now: he's lied to me and betrayed me, teaching someone else the lay that he and I composed! But it *must* be Tristran – he's never been untrue to me! It *is*! I see it now, I'm sure it's him! And how could I think ill of him, when he's disguised himself like that for me? He's acted like a faithful lover, putting himself through so much for my sake.'

And so it was that Yseut recognised Tristran by the tune of the lay he played.

Now Dinas, who was seneschal, had the tables cleared. Meanwhile the pages tended the horses and provided them with oats, while the squires worked hard all night to put the knights' mail in perfect shape. At last dawn came, and the knights rose at once and

---

[22] The 'vespers': see Glossary.
[23] i.e. the party camped outside the castle with the King of One Hundred Knights, as opposed to the 'insiders' from the castle, siding with King Marc.
[24] Marie de France, in her *Chevrefoil* ('Honeysuckle'), tells how, to celebrate the joy he'd had from a secret meeting with Yseut, 'Tristran,who was a fine harper, composed a new lay… The English call it Goatleaf, the French call it Chevrefoil.'

asked the priests to sing their masses, so that they could go early to honour the pledges they'd made to those encamped outside. The bells were rung in all the churches, and the barons went to hear the divine service.

Beaten by Minstrels

After mass those illustrious princes armed; and what a display you'd then have seen: so many banners of different designs, so many helms and golden shields, so many destriers, dun, white-stockinged, so many fine knights armed and mounted, their ventails* laced; and out they rode in handsome companies, magnificently armed and equipped. Those camped outside were preparing, too, and when they were armed they mounted and left their lodges and tents without more ado. The companies and banners now assembled in the field, riding forward at a walk to gather together on their sturdy steeds, banners and pennons aloft, swords girded, lances gripped and shields set firm before their breasts. Both sides deployed in tight, serried ranks, with no gaps at all; then they cried:

'Don helms! Don helms! Come, Huet! Come, Aliaume! Come, Garin! Come, Fouchier! Bring me my helm – it's time to lace!'

In two hundred places this cry went up, and squires hurried to lace their knights' helms. And when they were laced, they spurred their horses to an earth-shuddering charge; and as the lines met lances shivered, shields shattered, heads and shafts went cleaving through; helms were dashed away, split open, knights went sprawling on the ground; some were wounded, others captured, many cried for mercy. Lances split and splintered, shields were smashed and riven, knights and horses plunged and tumbled, yelled and bawled their battle-cries. Any who sought a joust soon found a willing foe – no need to look far! They attacked each other boldly, dealing blows with swords and lance-stumps, battering helms with such a ringing, clashing din that the woods and heaths, the whole surrounding land, resounded.

The sword-play and the fighting raged on all day till after none.* So many fine feats were seen: Brandoine, a valiant knight indeed, launched punishing attacks on the knights of the castle, as did Gogulor; and I promise you Esclador performed such feats that they were praised by both sides, and Glador Eslis, bearing red arms blazoned with three white moons, worked wonders. They wrought such havoc among the castle knights that they sent them reeling back to the fields outside the gate. Gosengos, with a white shield and white caparison, hazarded much as he rushed to stem the tide, charging into the press and unhorsing Gogulor; Claradus and King Bridas followed him into the fray, as did Disnadaret and Moadas, and King Marc and his company now held their ground and the mêlée resumed, blows raining down from sword and mace and broken lance. But the pressure mounted on King Marc's side till evening, and he was on his way to defeat, I'm sure of it.

But I'll leave the tourney for a moment, and tell you about Yseut, who'd recognised Tristran by the tune he'd played. She took him to her chamber, where they partook of the pleasure that lovers do – but I'll omit the details, as I wasn't there.

Meanwhile Gawain was in the handsome hall, sitting beside the queen's maid Brengien; his companions were there, too, and had heard news of the tournament and were troubled to know that King Marc was in need of help. So Gawain came to Tristran and said:

'Sir, let's ask the queen – and quickly! – to lend us arms and give us mounts and harness; let's go out and help the king!'

'Quite right!' said Yseut. 'You shall have them!'

And she unlocked her storerooms and took out handsome arms and surcoats and saw them well equipped: she and her damsels armed them perfectly, and each was given a fine, swift horse and a brand new shield and lance. Tristran summoned his companions to mount, which they did; then that knight endowed with so many fine qualities kissed Yseut as they departed. All twelve thrust in their spurs and set off for the gate, splendidly armed – and each with his instrument hung from his neck!

To the tournament they came, and at the moment they arrived Idier the son of Nu had unhorsed Tydorïan, Glador Eslis and Estorgan; Jacob d'Estragueil was fighting well, as were Jolies of Tintagel, Brun the Pitiless and Brunamort, who'd killed many a good knight in his time; but despite that, King Marc's side were on the point of defeat and capture when the valiant Tristran came charging to their aid on his strong and well-trained horse, pennoned lance levelled. On his gold, lion-blazoned shield he struck Escanor of the Mountain and toppled him from his Spanish steed; then he struck Dorchin and sent him sprawling, felled Glador Eslis and Bran de Lis's brother: until his lance broke he jousted brilliantly. Sir Gawain launched a fine charge, too, driving through the press; Kay the seneschal plunged into the thick of the fray; Meraugis, Sir Yvain and Agravain all performed splendidly. I can tell you with all certainty that King Arthur's men were supreme in the tourney. They drove back the outsiders with such vigour and might that even the strongest recoiled, wondering who these knights could be who were putting them to flight. Then they noticed the instruments hanging from their necks and were aghast, mortified to think they'd been trounced by a band of minstrels!

Tristran returned to attack once more, and so did Sir Gawain and the others, lances in rest, with such furious force that in that charge they brought down more than twenty, all quickly taken prisoner. Tristran surpassed everyone, displaying mighty courage as he launched himself into the thickest press to help and support his side. His companions were right behind him, and sent the outsiders reeling back into the ford in the river, where Gogulor was unhorsed, along with the worthy Taillar and Godroés. And as they emerged on the other bank, King Marc fell upon them; he wouldn't have been as thrilled by a hundred marks as he was by routing the outsiders; he drove them all the way back to their baggage train.

'My lord,' Dinas said to him, 'I'd say it's your heralds who launched those attacks! Look – they've their instruments round their necks! They've turned the tournament your way!'

Tristran was scattering the mighty press, striking, battering, charging, felling. And Gawain was fighting so well it was a delight to behold: he knew how to land a blow! Truly, they drove the outsiders right back to the woods.

They had them in total disarray when, quite by chance, through the forest came Perceval, mounted on a black, white-stockinged nag, skinny, mangy, weary, lame. His helm was split and dented, the laces broken; his shield was pierced in several places, its strap cobbled together from an old saddle-girth; his hauberk was holed, misshapen, rusty – it hadn't been furbished for a long, long time; his lance was a makeshift effort – a stump of wood with the bark still on, though the head was well forged, with a sharpened tip; his silken surcoat was in tatters. For he'd been on the quest for the grail: he'd scoured many lands in search of it, but despite all his efforts he'd found no news at all. His stirrup-straps were tied to his saddle with string. So many countries he'd ridden through, so exhaustingly that his horse's head was bowed, its neck sagging. Perceval was trying to drive the beast on, but you could have whipped it skinless and it wouldn't have managed more than a walk! By Saint Sylvestre, he'd have been better off on an ass! It had once been a fine steed – but as the saying rightly goes: give your horse poor fare, you'll have an old mare.

'Ah, God!' said Perceval. 'I've been through so many harsh adventures, roamed my way through so many lands! Alas! I've had nothing but toil and trouble in this quest for the grail! So much hardship, such affliction, such trials I've suffered for the ever-bleeding lance! Dear lord God,' he said, 'it's so long since I've known ease or comfort! Sixty nights I've slept out here in the forests with little to eat, and my horse is nearly dead with hunger. Help me now, God: let me find relief somewhere – how I need it!'

On he rode down the forest path, bewailing his lot, urging his horse to such pace as it could muster, till he heard the various battle-cries ringing out from the tourney. He was mightily surprised, and pressed on towards the din – but what an effort it was! His horse plodded on at a walk – it couldn't manage a trot, let alone a gallop! But at last he emerged from the wood and saw the jousting and the mêlées of the two sides locked in combat – and could see the outsiders were in desperate straits. So he steered his horse that way – but no matter how hard he spurred, a walk was all it could manage. Sir Kay was the very first to spot him, and came spurring towards him; seeing him in such a state he wanted to pay him what he owed, to avenge the shame and injury he'd suffered at his hands. He cried, provokingly:

'Where are your companions, sir? How long have you been in these parts? Ah, you've been off with the Lombards! Slaying the slug, eh?[25] How brave of you! Did you kill that dread, horned beast with a spear or a club? The lords and knights will be thrilled that you've come! When they hear you've arrived they'll be delighted to have your company! But if you've come to the tourney to compete, Sir Audigier,[26] your horse has had it! The mastiffs are waiting for him to die – they'll keep him for when they're observing Lent: he's nothing but skin and bone! And what's happened to your helm? Looks like the hens have been at it with their beaks for the last two years! What devils possessed you to leave your land? Ah, I know! You want to avenge Forré – no, Morholt, that's it![27] Well, you'll have the chance before nightfall, if you're so inclined.'

Perceval looked at him again and saw the instrument hung around his neck and said: 'If I felt it was right to start fighting minstrels I'd give you such a blow on your shield that you'd think you'd had no shield at all! I'd lay you out flat with your heels in the air! But by the God who made the world I swear I wouldn't lay hands on a wretched crooner, not for a thousand marks – by the Saviour, it would be too demeaning!'

'By the apostle James,' Sir Kay replied, 'you're wasting your time: I'll have your horse whether you like it or not! Not to ride him, though – I'll have him skinned! The dogs can have the flesh and I'll have the hide and make a nice new travelling bag! No one'll take you seriously, riding around in that state!'

'I'd give him to you gladly if I had yours – I'm very happy to swap!'

'Getting cheeky, eh?' said Kay. 'You'll pay for it, right now!'

And with that he drew back, lowered his lance and prepared to charge. Perceval

---

[25] The Lombards were traditionally accused of cowardice, and 'slaying the slug' was a proverbially derisory act. See also Chrétien, above, p. 52, and note 21.
[26] The hero of *La Chanson d'Audigier*, a scatological parody of a *chanson de geste*.
[27] 'To avenge Forré' was an expression implying a delusional mission, and may have been a reference to a pagan king killed by Roland; 'to avenge Morholt' refers specifically to Tristran's killing of Morholt when he demanded tribute from King Marc – see above, p. 367, note 21.

had been in too many battles to feel any fear – but he did feel shame: it seemed he was being threatened by a minstrel, and would have to fight him whether he liked it or not! He didn't know what to do: he'd be sorry to hurt him! So he turned his lance back to front – the head facing back and the butt facing forward – and sat waiting for him, not moving an inch. Sir Kay spurred his horse to a furious charge, and gave Perceval such a blow on his tarnished shield that he smashed his lance right down to his fist. He almost felled knight and horse together as the clapped-out nag shuddered and buckled; but Perceval's lance met Kay full in the chest and sent him flying from his stirrups and tumbling to the ground. Perceval seized the fine destrier's reins and leapt in the saddle without using a stirrup; then he called down to Kay:

'Take my horse, sir, and see how the two of you get on! You'd do better sticking to music than abusing and bothering knights!'

With that he left him, and went charging towards the knights from the castle, who were in hot pursuit of their retreating foes. He spurred the tan, white-stockinged destrier and it bore him in a mighty charge, and with his rough-hewn, twisted lance he dealt Gorvain a blow that drove him from his saddle, then Agravain, Cligés and the valiant Lancelot. He won control of all four horses, and gave them to those he saw who'd lost their own. The outsiders, who'd been in total disarray, saw the tide of the tournament stemmed by the intervention of Perceval; they turned their horses about: from his example they took new heart, and boldly resumed the battle against the castle knights. Perceval the Welshman thundered into the Cornish and drove them back across the ford in utter confusion; he fought with all his might, and wouldn't change or swap his crude, bark-covered lance!

Tristran was furious when he heard what was happening; ablaze with rage he asked who the knight was who was wreaking such havoc – he wanted to take him on! He didn't have to look for long. Perceval kept heading for the fiercest fighting, and forced them all back to the castle gate. Tristran was there in the thick of it, with the good Sir Gawain fighting better than any on their side; and as Tristran turned his horse about he saw Perceval to the right, mounted on Kay's charger. The moment he set eyes on him he knew he was the one and was enraged; setting himself so firmly in the stirrups that he stretched the straps, he charged towards him instantly. Perceval saw him coming with lance and shield set expertly, with perfect poise and finesse; but it bothered him greatly to see a hurdy-gurdy round his neck! He thought it was another minstrel, come to send them up and make a mockery of it all! But Tristran, furious that they were being driven back, couldn't wait to meet him man to man, this knight in tattered garb who'd turned the contest the outsiders' way. He spurred his swift and willing horse with all his might, and Perceval charged to meet him; they both had lances levelled and came full tilt, and delivered blows to each other's shield that split them apart and smashed their lances into shards. And as they met they collided full on – horses, too – and Perceval sent Tristran crashing: everyone in the tournament saw him with his heels in the air and measuring his length in the grass. It was such a heavy fall that his heart nearly burst within him; he was so badly hurt that he couldn't stand. Perceval drew rein and was about to make him yield as his prisoner, but suddenly Lancelot, Sir Yvain, Sagremor and the worthy Gawain came galloping to the attack. Perceval, undaunted, drew his sword and responded with such force that even the bravest was driven back. He assailed them with a rain of blows, battering armour, smashing helms and cleaving shields. He defended himself so brilliantly that they couldn't gain a foot of ground.

Then Gawain looked and realised he was the very one who'd been at the grand tournament[28] and displayed such mighty courage, outfighting all others.

'And he gave me such a seeing-to that for the rest of that week my head and arms and neck – every bit of my body! – still felt his blows! Seeing him again it's all coming back: no one else could endure such combat – it's impossible. He wouldn't tell me anything about himself, not even his name. Why on earth is he dressed so pitifully? He was superbly armed at the grand tournament, but look at the state he's in now! Maybe it's not him – but it is, surely! His blows tell me so, much more than his garb! Never judge a knight's courage by the gleam of his armour!'

Then the noble-hearted Gawain called out to Perceval, saying: 'By Saint David, sir, I'd gladly be your friend! I've never seen a knight whose acquaintance I'd value more. You were much smarter when I saw you last – you had far more handsome gear! But if you've no objection, sir, I'd dearly like to ask your name.'

Perceval was startled when he heard him speak: he was sure it was Gawain's voice. He shook with rage to see the instrument hung round his neck! If it was Gawain, what possessed him to want to be a minstrel? But he knew how to make sure: he'd ask his name! He'd know as soon as he replied, for Gawain would never keep his name from anyone who asked it, regardless of any risk! So he said:

'If you please, sir, tell me your name first, then I'll tell you mine.'

And Gawain replied: 'I shall indeed – only too pleased! I'll never conceal my name if asked. My name is Gawain. Now I'd like to know yours indeed, for you seem a most valiant knight.'

'Truly,' said Perceval, 'I know without the slightest doubt, at no point in his life has Sir Gawain been a minstrel! But since you're keen to know my name I'll tell it, for so I promised. My name, good sir, is Perceval.'

'Perceval?'

'Yes indeed: the one who went in search of the lance and the grail – which I've seen twice, but failed to learn their secrets. I repaired a fine and precious sword that was broken in two, though there's still a notch to mend; but the king wouldn't answer any of my questions, nor will he tell me anything till the notch is repaired and restored: no one can know anything till then. He told me outright that I wasn't yet worthy to know the secrets of the grail.'

Gawain knew it must be Perceval when he heard what he had to say. He took off his helm and embraced him, saying: 'My good, noble sir, my uncle the king longs to see you more than any man!'

But Perceval replied: 'Unless chance takes me there I'll never set foot in Britain, no matter what, until I've accomplished the grail adventure, and that's that. But tell me now, why are you carrying that instrument?'

Then Gawain told him the whole story: how Tristran had taken them to King Marc and engaged as his personal spy.

'It's not a good idea,' said Perceval, 'keeping watch on people if they're true and loyal friends. It can all go horribly wrong: it makes even the wisest lose all sense, breeding suspicion and jealousy.'

So saying, he took off his helm out of courtesy and kissed Gawain; they delighted in each other's company.

---

[28] The tournament at the Proud Castle in the Second Continuation, as mentioned above, p. 362.

Tristran Forgiven

Tristran was filled with joy at hearing Perceval: all pain and sorrow were forgotten. Then King Marc and his knights rode up to join them and the tournament drew to a halt, and when Marc realised it was Perceval he greeted him with honour and celebration. The worthy and valiant Sir Gawain didn't dally; he promptly helped the Love-tortured Tristran remount, and then along with Sir Yvain and Perceval he asked a favour of King Marc, which he duly granted: when he realised they were Sir Gawain and Yvain he was sorry he hadn't honoured them more highly! Then Gawain told the king what the favour was:

'Sire,' he said, 'forgive Tristran your anger and your wrath.'

When King Marc heard this he sighed: he feared his nephew Tristran because he'd been told he was in love with his wife – though he didn't know if it was true. But he pardoned him his anger and placed his riches at his disposal, and gave him licence to do as he pleased – apart from visiting the queen's chamber: he was barred from there unless the king himself was present. Tristran graciously accepted. Then he told Marc how they'd come in disguise on hearing of the tournament, 'for I didn't want to upset you.'

'Dear nephew,' the king replied, 'henceforth we'll be at peace together.'

And with that they rode into the city. That night ransoms were exchanged for the prisoners on both sides. And King Marc fêted Perceval highly.

Next morning he presented him with handsome arms and a splendid horse; and without more delay King Arthur's knights saddled and mounted and set off, and Perceval went with them. Tristran escorted them a fair way, till they came to a chapel where paths and tracks and roads diverged towards many different lands. Then Perceval called to the others, saying:

'Sirs, I must leave you now, for I have to go in search of the grail. May God lead you happily home to your land! In the name of God who dwells in heaven on high, greet King Arthur for me – may God send him honour, strength, vigour and joy.'

Sir Gawain, hearing and seeing that Perceval was set on the grail quest, said: 'May the true God guide you, as He surely can! I shall go to the peak of Montesclaire.'

When Sir Yvain heard this he almost dissolved in grief, and all the barons lamented sorely, sighing and weeping.

'What will the king say,' said Lancelot, 'when we see him and tell him about you and Perceval?'

But Perceval kissed them and left them and set off down a valley. Sir Gawain set out swiftly, too, along a great road in another direction; he was to endure much hardship and many a trial before he'd see his uncle again, and Perceval was to come to his aid.

So Gawain and Perceval departed, armed and mounted, while the others returned to their own land by their various paths and ways, downcast and grieving at having lost Perceval and Gawain: they were woebegone. Tristran was unhappy, too, at being left behind – he'd loved their company dearly; but Brengien would comfort him, as would his beloved Yseut.

On the others rode until they came to Morguan, not far from Cardigan, and there they found their lord King Arthur, who'd greatly missed his men and his nephew – they'd been gone a long time. And he was about to hear them give him news that would fill his heart with woe. He was alarmed to hear about his nephew, and crestfallen to hear that Perceval, having suddenly appeared at the tourney, hadn't come with them to court. His heart's tears flowed from his eyes and down his face, washing the colour from his bright, red cheeks. It's little wonder that he feared for his nephew: he'd vowed to go to the peak of Montesclaire, from which no knight, however fine, would return alive and free. He was fearful, too, for Perceval, who'd undertaken the awesome adventure of the grail.

But you're going to hear me tell now about Gawain and Perceval – I'll leave the king and his great sorrow; and I'll tell something first of Perceval before I return to Gawain.

Gorneman and the Demon Knights

Perceval rode on all alone, deep in thought, passing through many lands and regions and encountering many a fearsome, taxing, tough adventure. He entered a vast forest, and pressed on and on till he emerged the other side; and then, looking ahead, he saw a castle standing in a plain. All its walls and battlements were built of dressed stone, but the barrier before the bridge was made of oak with its bark still on. Perceval hurried on, for night was closing in.

As he did so he saw, riding ahead of him, five knights, all fully armed; but their armour was battered, their gold shields pierced, their helms stove and split, their horses exhausted and their swords notched and bent. Four of them were wringing their hands and grieving bitterly, for they were badly wounded, with blood streaming from their bodies – they'd clearly been in a grim battle; these four were leading the fifth and lamenting for him desperately, for unless I'm much mistaken he had four lance-wounds in his body and two sword-wounds in the head: they'd bitten through his helmet to the bone. They certainly weren't galloping, but plodding along at a walk. Perceval was shocked to see them in such a state, and before he went any further he wanted to find out what had happened if he could. And what shocked him just as much was to see the surrounding land destroyed, laid waste and desolate: nowhere around the castle was there a house or any cottage to be seen.

He hailed the five knights courteously, and one, most gracious and kind in speech, replied:

'May God in His power keep you from harm and loss and send you perfect joy, as He most surely can.'

'Ah, worthy, courteous knight,' said Perceval, 'before I go, I pray you tell me what happened to you.'

'It was cruel and dreadful, sir. I swear no man ever suffered such dire misfortune. But come and lodge with us tonight and I'll tell you all about it, without a word of a lie; I don't know of any house or resting-place where you'll find lodging, except this castle, within a long day's ride of here.'

'Thank you, sir,' said Perceval.

So they headed to the castle and the gate was opened for them. The people of the castle saw the loss they'd suffered with the wounds to their lord, and cried:

'Alas! There'll never be an end to our lord's suffering! Ah, he's endured this strife and torment for so long!'

Such was their lament, but they took comfort in the coming of Perceval.

The four sons carried their father to the hall, and removed his armour and bandaged his wounds and treated him with an ointment – and themselves likewise, for they needed it: their bodies were far from whole – they were covered in wounds. But they were all more concerned about their father than themselves, though they hid their grief and worry as well as they could. And they showed their guest all possible honour, having him smartly disarmed and dressed in a mantle of scarlet lined with ermine; and they had his horse stabled at once. Then they bade that the table be set. The lord was laid in a fine and costly bed, close to the table, beside the fire. Perceval was served most generously: they had fresh and hearty meats – plovers and partridges and ducks in jelly, and plump and tender woodland rabbits – and an abundance of fish from sea and river. The lord, lying wounded on the bed, spoke a little, calling his four sons to him.

'My children,' he said, 'make your guest comfortable and honour him: if I could I'd welcome him with honour and joy, for he reminds me very much of the boy I once made a knight.'

When Perceval heard these words he realised this was the worthy man who'd bestowed on him the order that God established in the world to uphold justice and protect Holy Church. Looking at him again he recognised him by what he'd said, but nonetheless asked his name. And the worthy man replied at once:

'Dear guest, my name in proper French is Gorneman de Gorhaut.'[29]

At this, Perceval felt joy and sorrow: joy at hearing his name and sorrow at his wounds.

'It distresses me, sir, to see you wounded; I'll feel no pleasure or happiness, only anguish, till I take revenge on the one responsible: he'll find me a fearsome foe if I track him down! It's my duty to avenge you and I'll not fail – may the supreme king guide me – for I'm the very youth you equipped with arms and dubbed a knight: you girded on my sword. That's the truth; so tell me the whole story now from start to finish: explain why you've suffered all this harm, and I'll take revenge if I can – or lose my head.'

With a great struggle Gorneman heaved himself on to one elbow. Now he knew for certain that this was Perceval, whom he'd made a knight. He said:

'I'll tell you the terrible story right here and now. It's been going on for a long while – and still is; nor will it cease as long as this castle stands, and till I'm destroyed. Every morning, every day, I find forty mighty knights, well armed and carrying gold shields, fresh and new. They have big, swift, powerful horses and sharp, stout lances sharper than a chisel.[30] Every day my four sons and I have to do battle with them. They've killed all my people! Every morning they come and attack me at the gate – they're ruthless, full of malice; and I have to go and confront them with no support but my sons here. But sir, that's not the half of it: we have to fight them every day, I swear, till we've destroyed them and left them dead in the field; then we return home when evening comes, not daring to remain – and the following morning, by some miraculous power, we find them all quite safe and sound and the battle begins all over again! So we spend our lives in grievous torment, and have done for a long, long time – and will do so still, I'm certain. We're in despair! We fought them yet again today, but all our efforts will have been in vain: we'll find them there again tomorrow and battle will resume! But I can't fight tomorrow – my wounds are too grave. My sons will have to face that danger without me, and withstand their attacks.'

'My good, dear sir,' said Perceval, 'I swear by this hand I'll go with your sons tomorrow to defend both them and you: it's only right that I repay the great service and kindness that I once received from you. Till I met you I knew nothing of the world but what my mother had told me. And how little I still know! When I saw the grail and the lance that bleeds unceasingly, I was dreadfully cautious and asked nothing about them – it's caused

---

[29] Perceval had his first instruction in knighthood from Gorneman in Chrétien, above, pp. 13–16.
[30] Literally 'sharper than a mortising-axe'.

me a deal of pain and anguish! If only I'd asked I'd have learnt the whole truth, but I could know nothing after that. I hadn't the sense to ask! Since then I've searched and scoured and found the place again, and asked to be told the truth; the king would have told me, but first I had to mend a splendid sword that was broken in half, and when I came to join the pieces a notch remained. The king said I could ask as much as I liked, but I'd learn nothing till I repaired the notch in the sword. He also said I'd done something that made me unworthy of knowing the secrets either by word or sign, so he'd tell me nothing, and it worries me that I don't know what wickedness or sin of mine's to blame: I can't think of any sin, great or small, that I haven't confessed and done penance for – except one: I gave a pledge of marriage to a fair and lovely girl – she was your niece, I know: she told me so a long while ago; it's Blancheflor of Beaurepaire I mean. It's only right that I acknowledge that sin. I brought an end to a war being waged against her, and she loved me with a true heart and said I should take her and make her my wife; I promised to be her love and marry her and to do no wrong with any other. I remember now! I'm sure that's the sin that taints me most.'

Gorneman heard this and leaned towards Perceval and said, like the worthy man he was: 'Dear friend, seek God's forgiveness and set your mind on marrying the lady as soon as you leave here. God is so full of mercy that He grants the requests of all who pray to Him with a true heart. Go willingly to mass – it's the most glorious and precious service of all; and whoever hears it can see with his own eyes the body of Jesus Christ when the priest consecrates the host and holds it in his hands – the very body, no more, no less, that was born of the Virgin and hung upon the cross. If you firmly believe this, and go willingly to mass, and honour the promise you made the damsel when you undertook to marry her, if you do all this, I swear by my soul you'll repair the notch and learn all the secrets of the lance and the grail.'

Such was his eloquent lesson to Perceval, who listened intently and took in every word. He bowed his head and prayed humbly to God to grant by His power that he might deliver his host from those who were bent on destroying him and his land, who'd cast them into such dire peril and inflicted so many wounds and injuries.

Then they washed and took to their beds.

Perceval lay down but couldn't settle or rest, being so worried about his host; he'd be distraught if he couldn't free him from his suffering and torment.

When day broke everyone in the castle rose. The four brothers were quickly up, despite their grievous wounds, and Perceval was out of bed at once, deeply concerned for them. Seeing the four of them armed to meet the onslaught of the forty, who'd already come and were waiting for them at the foot of the bridge outside the gate, he called for his own arms to be brought. They were, at once; they were presented to him on a carpet of costly silk, and two boys hurried to lace his chausses,* and knelt before him to arm and equip him. Now all five were fully armed, and there was nothing to mock in their appearance. They reverently heard the mass of God and His sweet mother, most worthily conducted; then each of the sons took his leave of his father, who was still sorely wounded.

'My sons,' he said, 'may it please God to bring you back – I ask nothing more than to see you again, safe and sound.'

Then Perceval mounted outside the chapel door, and gently called to the four knights, suggesting bread and wine should be brought for them – though I suspect they'd soon need more than that! – and that each should eat a sop. One boy brought good, clear wine in a large cup, and the other cut bread and dropped it in the vessel

– which wasn't made of pine or aspen but of the finest silver. Each knight ate and drank of the wine just once, that's all; then the gate was opened and they all rode out, their helmets laced.

The knights came charging at them like wild things; Perceval, lance raised, rode full tilt to meet them, all the brothers following as fast as their horses could go. With a thrust of his lance of apple wood Perceval struck the first knight such a blow that it pierced and smashed clean through his shield, ripped and tore his mail asunder and sent the lance-head right through his body; may his soul be sent to the devils of Hell! Then he struck another so fiercely on his gold-striped shield that none of his armour was of any use: head and shaft plunged through his body – his soul had left it before it hit the ground.

But the match was very far from even: there were still thirty-eight against five in the contest, and all thirty-eight were more than keen. Perceval killed eight with his lance, I think, before it broke; then they harried him hard indeed, smashing his shield to pieces and hammering at him with their blades of steel like smiths on an anvil. Perceval, foaming with rage and fury, drew his sword and beheaded one of the fiercest foes: he was giving them awesome treatment! And the four brothers were proving their worth, launching themselves full tilt into the thickest press – Perceval needed their help as he drove in among them. He struck one knight a blow that smashed off his helmet along with an ear, his sword turning red as it plunged into brain; he clove another head to the nape of the neck; in all he severed seven heads. But he was sorely hurt and wounded, for they were all hammering, raining blows, smashing rings from his hauberk and splitting his helm. The four brothers weren't half-hearted: all were dealing mighty blows. Yet if they'd been wounded badly before, now they were even worse: all four had their helmets split, their shields smashed, their hauberks pierced and were covered with more, fresh wounds. One had taken a sword-blow to the head that had cut through to the skull; his three brothers pulled him out of the fray and covered him up in a sheltered spot before returning to the fight. So now there were only four of them; but they battled on and battered the enemy till only twenty of the forty knights remained, and they withdrew a little to regroup and arrange their arms. But Perceval charged into their midst, his shield set firm before his breast, and the three brothers were fired up and galloped right behind him, determined to do well. So battle was joined anew. Perceval wielded his keen sword so awesomely that the brothers recovered heart and the will to fight, seeing his noble display; and he kept dealing blows and sustained the assault till the afternoon passed and evening drew near. Charge after charge he mounted, bent on slaying the foe, and the three brothers were right behind him, though the fourth was helpless and watched the combat motionless. Perceval assailed and hewed the enemy with his brand of steel; but they, with little fear of death and little love for Perceval, rained a storm of blows upon him – and not with the flats of the blades but with the edges! They injured and wounded him fearfully. And the three brothers fared no better: such were their wounds that the enemy cast them to the ground with their guts spilling out. Then they turned on Perceval in a terrible assault – though only four of them now were left alive. They were sure they'd bring him down, but he attacked them back with furious sword-blows, beheading one and cleaving another's head to the chin. But at that the last two cried aloud:

'Oh, Perceval, it's useless! Tomorrow the attack will begin again – you've exhausted yourself for nothing! In the morning, before you even wake, we'll all be back at the castle together to do battle all over again – of that you can be sure!'

'Damn you all!' cried Perceval. 'But come what may, before I leave here the battle will end for you as it has for your companions!'

'We don't fear you in the slightest – nor do we fear death.'

At that Perceval, sword in hand, spurred his horse forward and beheaded one and hacked an arm from the other and sent him crashing from his horse: all were now dead and slain.

He made his way to his companions and did enough to enable them to mount, bandaging their wounds which were giving them great pain, for they kept splitting open and bleeding. Then they began to say:

'We can go home now, good sir, and give you and your horse rest and comfort for the night. Tomorrow, if you wish, you can be on your way again. I don't think any of us will see beyond midday. And even if we do survive we'll only have to face the same dismal plight: those last two knights told you how it is – tomorrow the battle will begin again! It's no fun, this game! We won't have the strength to escape this time – and we don't know what'll become of us: they're bound to take us captive. They say they'll destroy us and burn our castle to ash. That's the dread fate and the torment we face in the morning.'

Perceval replied with all sympathy, saying: 'God save you from that! It's high time you returned to the castle for the night; but please tell me how it is that they come back to life – do you know?'

'God help me, sir, we've no idea. It's too dangerous to find out: anyone who stayed to see would die without question!'

But Perceval said: 'So help me God, however terrible the danger I'm not leaving here till I find out how they return to life.'

'Oh, sir!' cried the brothers. 'Do you want to die? Neither we nor our father ever dared do such a bold deed!'

'Nothing will make me leave,' he said. 'Go home now.'

They could see their words and warnings were in vain, and rode away, silent and grieving for Perceval. He dismounted and sat down on a rock, while the wounded brothers spurred on towards the castle without once drawing rein. They crossed the bridge and rode in through the gate, each with a grievous wound for which they expected no cure by any medicine or potion. Once they were disarmed they told their father of Perceval's great feats of prowess, of the jousts and the charges that he'd made in the battle.

'We'd have been slaughtered on the spot, without a doubt: our strength would have been worthless – nothing would have stopped them beheading us all. But Perceval overcame them! But now he's stayed behind to find out how they return to life: what a grievous loss and pity, that one so full of chivalry should stay to meet certain death! No words of ours could persuade him to come back! As for us, we're finished: in the morning our end will come – we're powerless to defend ourselves. And our hearts should break and burst with grief for the death of the bravest man who ever lived and sat astride a horse!'

'Ah, Perceval!' cried Gorneman. 'What a loss it'll be if you die! If you stay out there, no one can save you!'

Tears streamed from his eyes and down his face. They didn't stop grieving for Perceval all night.

But I'll say no more about their anguish; I want to return to Perceval. Holding his horse by the reins he was sitting on a marble stone beside a tree, overlooking the dead.

He'd no wish to sleep, but his body began to shiver with the cold, and he said if he carried on like this he could certainly come to harm. So he started moving about and jumping up and down, and stayed awake like that till after midnight. He can't have enjoyed it very much – he wasn't used to spending the night like that! But he was about to witness a wonder.

The Healing Balm

The moon was shining brightly – which didn't bother Perceval: he was only too glad of it. He sat down on the stone again; and then, peering ahead towards the foot of a slope, he saw a light appear, accompanied by such a tremendous groan that the very ground shook and trembled. Perceval was alarmed by this weird sound, and raised his hand and crossed himself in the name of the heavenly Father: it's the sign the Devil fears most, you may be sure. The groan was the sound of an opening door; and coming through the door, the source of the light that was pouring all around, he saw a woman, old and huge. She was carrying two casks of fine ivory, bound by hoops not of silver but of gold, pure, gleaming red. The like of these casks was never seen: they were inlaid with an array of precious stones – without question, all King Arthur's riches wouldn't have matched their value: you'll hear perfect proof of that before the end of this story, which has yet to be fully told. And I can tell you this most certainly: never was such a hideous creature described as this old woman with the casks. Her eyes were fouler than any beast's: one was buried in her head, and it was tiny and bright red; the other seemed stuck out on a stalk, and it was huge and dark as dregs. She was all wizened, with a thin, scraggy neck, a hairy face and a tiny, pointed head, and she was twisted and hunched and limped back and forth with knocking knees. No man could create such an ugly woman in portrait or in carving! Her tresses, I swear, were like the tails of two skinned rats. Her nostrils were so wide you could have shoved your fists up them. Never was iron or steel blacker than her neck and face and hands. Her chest was all bony and dry: she'd have burned like tinder if you'd set her alight. An uglier creature never lived: her mouth was an amazing size, splitting open from ear to dangling ear; her teeth were long and broad and yellow, her lips were fat as saddle-straps; her body was twisted, her back bent. An ugly lass, to say the least! To complete the picture, she had one hip jutting out behind her, the other half-way to her armpit. And her cheeks were swollen as she hobbled along, puffing furiously – and at every step, I swear, she seemed to be limping on both legs.

Perceval watched her for a long while, hot and panting from her exertions. 'God,' he said, 'what foul demon spawned such a loathsome creature? Is it by some charm or magic that she's so hideously shaped? She looks as if she's been hanging in the smoke of Hell-pit: she's blacker than any iron!'

That's what Perceval thought of her, but he was quite undaunted. He could see the casks hanging from her neck, and wanted to know more about the old woman; so he stayed where he was for now, deciding to wait and see what she would do. So he sat there in silence; and the old woman, thinking she could go about her business undisturbed, hobbled up the path and in among the dead, and put down the casks that were hung around her neck. The ugly, twisted hag now picked up the head of one of the dead lying there in the field – beheaded by Perceval that night – and placed it atop the headless trunk; then she took one of the casks, worthy only of the greatest lord or noble, and Perceval watched with rapt attention as she pulled out the stopper and poured into her palm a drop of liquid clearer than any rose water. She dabbed her finger in the drop and rubbed it on the lips of the knight whose head she'd put back in place; and in an instant his veins and joints all surged with life, every one of his wounds was healed as if he'd never been hurt at all, and he was up on his feet again before you could count to three. The potion had the power to restore the dead to life, for God, who delivers those He loves from Hell, was anointed and embalmed with it when He was laid in the sepulchre. The old hag replaced the heads of four and brought them back to life, just as she intended; she rubbed the potion on another's lips and up he leapt. Perceval was dismayed by what he saw, and told himself he'd soon be in a sorry plight if he dallied any longer. So he jumped on his horse, took up his shield and drew his sword, thrust in his spurs and rode up to the hag crying:

'The potions you've used to restore them to life will do you little good!'

The old woman was astounded – and alarmed. 'What foul devil,' she cried, 'has sent you riding here so late? Your name is Perceval – I know you well; and I've always known I needed to fear none but you. For by my life, no one but you will ever succeed: no battle or assault, sir knight, can stop you succeeding in the quest you've undertaken for the grail. You don't yet know who's served from it or what's done with it, but all will be revealed to you, as will the reason why the lance bleeds – all those things that have caused you so much toil and trial and hardship. You're rightly called "Perceval", for you've *pierced the vale*: you've penetrated the place where the balm is kept – which will be wholly yours if you can defend it from these knights who're about to attack you. Guard the casks as securely and as finely as you can, for no man of your lineage has ever possessed such a precious relic. But let me tell you this: you'll learn nothing about the grail – not the merest jot – as long as I'm alive, I swear it!'

'Damn your lingering life!' cried Perceval. 'It's made me endure so much! Now answer me this: why has Gorneman been attacked and assailed so many times?'

'By God,' she replied, 'that's a very shrewd question! Such was the command of the King of the Waste City, who cannot and will not believe in God. These strange and terrible men who lie here dead before me, he sent demons and devils to deliver them to my door – the door you heard groan open – and bade me post them on this mountain to wreak the destruction of Gorneman. He wanted to destroy him utterly because it was he who made you a knight, and because through his guidance you'll do a deed that will undo the Devil's work: by you God's friends, whom the Devil has been working to destroy, will be restored to joy and well-being. And truly, with the potion in these casks I'm restoring to life all the dead lying here, until Gorneman is finished! So now I've told you the reason why the sodomite tyrant sent me here – he wanted to stop you learning anything about the grail! You could toil for an age and never set eyes on it!'

'Oh, God!' cried Perceval. 'So many Aprils, so many Mays, I've sought it and achieved so little! I've not been able to learn a thing!'

'Nor will you, truly,' said the hag, 'as long as I'm alive.'

'Glorious God,' thought Perceval, 'what an evil old woman this is. I don't know if she's saying this out of boastfulness or trickery – or even if it's true.'

And just as he was thinking this the hag bent down to one of the dead and anointed him – and up he leapt. Then Perceval spurred towards them, clutching his whetted sword; he struck off the old woman's head and her body crashed to the ground. The six who'd been restored to life rushed at him in a mortal fury, and they and he rained blows upon each other's helms with their furbished swords. Perceval set his dark grey shield against their blows, and beheaded three, but the other three came back to the attack. They didn't have to chase him far – they found him right at hand! And over and over they cursed him for having killed their lady. Perceval didn't spare his blows and cut one of them clean in two; but the other two kept fighting back and wounded him and killed his horse beneath him and brought him to the ground. They smote at him and battered him, but he leapt to his feet and attacked them in a fury. He wasn't making idle threats: with his keen sword he clove the head of one and dealt a death-blow to the last.

He sat down then and rested for a long while beside his horse, who lay dead before him on the battleground. His ice-bright sword was smeared and stained with blood. Then he picked up the worthy, precious casks and said:

'Ah God, dear and glorious Father, how beautiful and richly wrought these vessels are! Their like has never been seen: I'm sure they're worth the king of Cornwall's whole estate! But I don't care a jot for the gold and jewels – though they're worth all King Arthur owns in land and treasure; I'm going to see if I can do as she did with the potion and restore these knights to life and health – yes, that's what I'll do: if I could revive them as instantly as she did I wouldn't exchange these casks for all the wealth the mightiest prince could muster! Before I leave I'm going to see if I can revive one of the dead.'

So saying, he picked up one of the priceless casks, poured a drop of the balm in the palm of his hand and gently moistened his finger in the drop. Then he said:

'By the faith I owe God, I'll try it on this one, who fought best of all in yesterday's battle and wounded me the most – because he's first to hand, not because I'm any fonder of him!'

He didn't dally: he came up to the knight and gently dabbed the potion on his lips. Up he jumped at once, feeling no ill! He saw Perceval standing there and took a step towards him. He was still holding his drawn sword. He dealt Perceval a blow that cut right through his helm and the hood of his bright hauberk and bit into his forehead, drawing blood.

'Damn the eyes,' cried Perceval, 'of anyone who heals you ever again, or tries to heal you when you're dead! What was I thinking of? As the proverb says: who seeks folly finds it! Men often do well-meaning deeds that lead to grief, as I've done here: if he'd asked me for mercy I'd gladly have helped him – but now I see he doesn't care about my forgiveness: he's repaid me wretchedly!'

At that moment the knight returned to the attack, mounting such a fierce assault that he inflicted grievous wounds. Then Perceval recovered heart and courage and vigour and power, and fought back so ferociously that he robbed the knight of strength and breath and drove him wherever he chose. The knight reeled back, struggling to defend himself, but refused to cry for mercy – it would certainly have been granted, but he was sure he'd done Perceval too much harm to be forgiven: he was too full of despair to have the capacity or heart to appeal for mercy. Now you can see that a sinner who abandons hope, who cares not a jot for confession and doing good and thinks he's committed too many sins to have forgiveness, is a fool to give way to despair; for God is full of pity and mercy for any man who seeks accord with Him and craves His forgiveness with a sincere heart and seeks His peace and love. But the knight didn't dare to cry for mercy, and the flower of courage and prowess bore down on him and dealt him a blow with his keen sword that severed his head, and his body collapsed on the ground.

Now Perceval delayed no longer: he sat down and picked up the casks and gently, carefully poured out a little of the balm and said:

'It's daft to look after others and forget yourself! If I can, God willing, I'm going to heal myself of my wounds.'

He had a drop of balm in his hand, and softly, gently he dabbed it on his lips – and that instant he was as fit as a fish!

'I wouldn't swap this potion for the world!' he said. 'It's healed and cleansed me of my wounds!'

He longed now to see the dawn: he couldn't wait to go and heal Gorneman and his four sons. He stopped the casks – not with hemp or oakum but with two rich rubies, finely cut to fit; and the bungholes in the handsome casks were lined with sardonyx. Emeralds and chalcedony, sapphires, diamonds and topaz were thickly inlaid in the golden hoops and collar-bands. But what of that? It would be tiresome to listen to how rich they were, but I can assure you no one could have wished for finer, and Perceval rejoiced till dawn at having won those precious, priceless casks.

Meanwhile Gorneman, who loved him dearly, was fearful and dismayed. When he saw day break he rose and had a palfrey saddled, and told his sons there was no time to lose.

'Up! Get up! Hurry now and stir yourselves and mount and let's be off!'

'We can't, sir, truly: we're too badly wounded! We're about to be condemned to torment – there's no escape! The wild demons will be attacking soon – they're bound to have killed our dear friend Perceval! Ah, we're about to face a grim battle, for sure – and it'll be the last! There'll be no way out for us this time – we've too little strength or power left.'

Gorneman swooned, seeing his sons so broken; he was pale and white with grief. His heart nearly failed when he thought of Perceval, and he shook in every limb with rage and anguish; he would gladly have died – and they all thought he was dead indeed. The castle rang with lamentation: everyone of every degree was stricken with grief.

But suddenly, at the foot of the bridge, there was Perceval, calling and hailing. His voice was heard by a girl as she wept, and she was filled with alarm. 'Oh, Holy Mary!' she thought. 'Who's that calling?' And she came to the battlements and cried: 'Who's there, in God's name?'

The noble Perceval replied: 'Young lady, I am Perceval. I've put an end to the torment your people have suffered. Come, open the gate for me.'

At this she ran straight back to the hall and told them the news that Perceval was at the gate below. When Gorneman heard he'd returned he was so elated that his wounds were quite forgotten! He ran to the gate and bade that it be opened with all speed, and as Perceval entered they welcomed him with abounding joy. Gorneman was filled with wonder when he saw him carrying the casks.

Perceval was greeted with joy unparalleled in so small a company, and up to the hall they led him with all ceremony and honour. Then Gorneman said:

'Tell me what's happened to your horse. Why have you returned on foot?'

'He was killed,' Perceval replied. 'But thanks be to God I've won more than I've lost.'

And he told the whole story from start to finish: how the hag had come and what had happened then – how she'd revived the dead, and how he'd robbed her of the casks and killed the knights she'd restored to life. He told them everything – and what the hag was like: that such an ugly creature had never been seen. And then he told Gorneman about the balm he'd brought, and Gorneman was filled with hope when he heard of the potion's power. Perceval longed to see them healed, and said:

'Please, dear sir, send for your sons.'

Gorneman, that kindly, virtuous man, had his sons carried to the hall and laid before Perceval on two wide couches, side by side. The knights were overjoyed when they saw their guest, but their wounds were so grievous they were fainting with pain. Perceval took his balm and poured a little in his hand; then he set about healing the wounded knights, dabbing a drop on the mouth of each. And I tell you, the very moment that it touched their lips they were all fitter than a river fish swimming in the Oise or Seine! Every wound was healed and they felt neither pain nor sorrow: now the rejoicing began indeed! If God had descended from Heaven and appeared in bodily form He wouldn't have been embraced more fervently than Perceval was by Gorneman and his sons. He took the casks and placed them at his side and sat examining them, while Gorneman gazed at him with gladness and great affection, and he and his four sons addressed him fondly, saying:

'Stay with us, sir, and take your ease!'

But he answered: 'It's no use: I'm not going to stay. I want to go to my sweetheart, your kinswoman Blancheflor. And truly, I'll be most grateful if your father will take me to her, for I mean to marry her. I'll live more chastely then; and the man who lives a virtuous life and keeps himself pure and preserves his chastity and virginity will find it to his advantage: as any priest will testify, he is loved and cherished in this life and his soul will be secure in the next. That's why I want to live chastely, sirs, to be of greater worth. And that's why I wish to take a wife, you see, to escape the mortal sins that torture and confound the soul. Mind you, there are things the priests and clerics forbid us to do – because they clearly see that, but for their prohibition, men would often do what they daren't! – which they go and do themselves! They pretend to be devout but they're deeply debauched! It's not for me to reproach them, but that's why I wish to take a wife, to lead a clean and wholesome life and to guard against falling into sin. I'm going to leave tomorrow morning, for sure.'

'I'll go with you,' said Gorneman, 'and keep you company and honour you in any way I can. In the meantime everyone here will gladly answer your every need.'

Perceval thanked him deeply. Then the table was set and they sat down to dinner. I can't describe all the dishes they had, but once they'd eaten and drunk the cloths were cleared and there was singing and dancing and revelling in Perceval's honour, and all day long they talked of joyful things. And when evening came they sat down to supper, and had five or six dishes of meat and as many of fish. And when it was time to sleep and rest, the servants didn't dally but made the beds smartly and handsomely. In a panelled chamber, painted with gold, magnificent and rich, they made a gorgeous bed with a coverlet of squirrel fur and a quilt of finest silk: I'm sure I'll never find a place that has its equal. And as soon as the beds were made they attended to the knights as they retired. Perceval had never seen anyone served better than he was that night, and to make him feel more comfortable the four brothers slept before him, and their father beside them. A minstrel softly played the lay of Guiron[31] on a Cornish pipe, and Perceval was soon asleep for he was very tired and weary, having been awake so long. Everyone in the castle soundly slept, no longer feeling alarm or terror; now they could sleep secure: their fear and dread were gone.

And I tell you this, truly: the two ivory casks that Perceval had won shed such a brilliant light in the room that it was as bright as it would have been at noon. Perceval

---

[31] *'le lai Gorron'*. If this is the *Lay of Guiron*, it is the lay composed by Yseut in Thomas de Bretagne's *Tristan* (c. 1170–5), where it is described as 'a sad lay of love'.

started awake and was astonished by the light, but he knew there was no danger: the light was coming from the casks – he knew it was good and holy. So after a while he fell asleep again, and slept till day broke and the watch sounded the dawn.

Then he awoke, but was still very tired – it was a long time since he'd had pleasant lodging; so he lay in bed all the early morning, till the bell was rung for mass to be sung in the chapel. Then Perceval called the servants, who ran to him and dressed him. Gorneman and his sons dressed, too, and they all went to hear the mass which filled their hearts with joy – for truly, the man who loves God and hears mass knows great joy indeed.

Perceval Marries Blancheflor

As soon as mass was over, Perceval, eager to go and fulfil his promise, said to Gorneman:

'Sir, please keep your word and come with me to Beaurepaire, to Blancheflor – who in my eyes is the flower of womanhood!'

'I'll be only too happy, I assure you,' Gorneman said. 'But if it please you we'll take a little breakfast before we leave.'

'Quickly, then!' said Perceval.

So Gorneman ordered plovers and pheasants and pies to be brought at once and the cloth spread on the table; then they washed their hands and ate. They didn't take long about it – they ate quickly indeed, and then ordered the table to be cleared, which it promptly was. Then they hurriedly went and mounted, Perceval on a strong, swift, spirited horse given to him by Gorneman. And he[32] wisely took both his casks – it wouldn't do to forget them. Then off they rode at a good deal more than a walk, a great crowd gathering to see them go.

I can't tell you every detail, but they pressed steadily on till they caught sight of Beaurepaire. It was quite the richest, most splendid city that anyone has ever seen, and excellently fortified: I can't imagine a more perfect palace or a finer town. A river bearing a fleet of vessels flowed along one side, and on another lay forest, great and thick and teeming with game. Then there were meadows and open ground, and farmland, fishing lakes and pasture, gardens and fine arable, and orchards broad and abundant. And on another side it was bounded by the sea, crashing at the wall's foot. Beside the river lay the vineyard, vast and flourishing: we've described this before.[33] As Perceval surveyed the land he recognised it at once, but Gorneman was bewildered: he hadn't been there since Clamadeus had laid waste the land and all the surrounding country,[34] but now it was as splendid a sight as you've heard from my description. The great wealth and splendour of the town have also been described to you before,[35] and it would be tiresome to repeat it so I'll say no more. I'll talk instead of Perceval, who sent two boys on horseback to tell Blancheflor he was coming, and that he was going forthwith to fulfil his pledge to take her for his wife.

They set off at speed, much faster than a canter, and rode on through the gate and found so many people thronging the streets that it seemed as if a fair was in full swing.

---

[32] The text reads 'Gorneman', but the 'his' that follows suggests this is an error: it should surely refer to Perceval.
[33] There is a lengthy description of Beaurepaire in the Second Continuation, though there is no mention of the vineyard. See above, p. 260.
[34] In Chrétien's romance, pp. 16–17.
[35] In the Second Continuation, above, pp. 260–1.

They pressed on till they found the damsel sitting at the palace door: she was dressed in samite, glittering with gold, gorgeous and most beautiful, and was surrounded by a great company of her people. The two boys sent by Perceval drew rein and dismounted and stepped towards the damsel; but they were so stunned by her beauty that they were incapable of speech – they said nothing to her: not a word could they utter. Had they been bequeathed all Lombardy they couldn't have made a sound; you could have walked right out of shouting range, I'd say, before they'd have spoken or a word had crossed their lips!

The damsel's head was bowed to the ground, lost in thought of Perceval like the lovesick girl she was.

'Oh God!' she was thinking. 'My love has been away so long! If he'd set his heart on me as I have mine on him, he'd be hurrying back! I've been waiting for an age – but I'll go on waiting, whatever anyone says, for his every wish is my wish, too. The hope I have in him comforts me in my pain. And I trust in the adage that a rich reward awaits those who wait in hope.'

The two messengers now recovered the heart and power to speak, and they stepped forward without more delay and swept back their hoods. They stood side by side and then knelt and said:

'Lady, your friend the valiant Perceval sends you greetings.'

She was utterly amazed. And when she heard them say he was coming with her uncle Gorneman, she was so lost in joy that if her fingernails had been pulled out she wouldn't have felt a thing! She sprang up like a startled deer, and was about to run off down the street all alone to meet him when her maids caught hold of her.

'Oh, lady!' they cried. 'All your dignity's lost when you're so carried away!'

'I can't help it!' she answered. 'Let me be! If you were in love you wouldn't blame me! But come, then: what should I do?'

She had the richest clothes prepared, quite the richest ever made in this world for any king or prince. And her people weren't idle: they lavishly adorned the streets with drapes of silk and samite – such glorious swathes hung from every window that it seemed like an earthly paradise; and they spread the ground with carpets, not caring that they might be ruined! Knights, clerics and burgesses all dressed themselves in silk and orfrey, and the burgesses' sons armed splendidly and set about a festive joust.[36] And I tell you, elsewhere bears and lions, boars and leopards were fighting in the streets. All the ladies and knights were celebrating joyously; and more than ten thousand rode from the town to meet Sir Perceval. The jousters had caparisoned their mounts with silks of every shade and kind, and there were scaffolds for spectators on every side. And the drummers weren't dressed in cheap stuff but in gold-embroidered samite, and rode fine palfreys with brand new harness, rich and handsome. The jousting was splendid, creating such a mighty, clashing din that the whole town shook and rumbled!

The damsel was mounted on a mule more richly harnessed than any ever was, and she was adorned with gold and jewels which alone were worth more than all the treasure of the king of Frisia; as she sat there on the mule everyone gazed at her in wonder. She was dressed in the gown of deep red purple* that had once belonged to Queen Brangepart,[37]

---

[36] '*bohordent*': see note 48, above, p. 131.
[37] '*Blanchepart*': I take this to be a reference to the queen mentioned in the First Continuation, above, pp. 233–4.

lined with new ermine. And what should I say of her beauty? You've heard it described in this story before, but I can say this much with certainty: never has any man – cleric, lay or monk – ever set eyes on such a beautiful girl; so Gerbert tells us in his account.

In her gorgeous attire her knights led her through the gate in great splendour, elegantly carried by her mule; and she had a great escort of ladies: as she came to the open ground her company was dazzling.

Gorneman called to Perceval, saying: 'My niece, your sweetheart, can't be ill-disposed towards you, welcoming you so magnificently!'

And when Perceval caught sight of Blancheflor, who longed for him so much, he said to Gorneman: 'Let's head that way, sir!' And he turned his horse towards Blancheflor.

At the sight of him she flushed, then turned pale and sat motionless, overcome with shyness. But that's often the way: when a girl fired with love sees the object of her passion right before her, she'll change colour and be confused and at a loss for words. Perceval was worried when he saw her so subdued; he spurred his horse towards her and greeted her ten times, rapidly; and she, sighing, returned his greetings sweetly more than thirty times over, and gazed at him adoringly like the lovesick girl she was. Then she greeted her uncle and her cousins. Perceval took her by the hands, and then embraced her, for he loved her deeply; and he called her his very sweet love, and she called him her beloved sweetheart; and then he began to embrace her round the waist, for Love was spurring him.

Now you'd have seen the crowds on horseback throng to greet Perceval with cries of: 'Welcome to the one who delivered us from ruin, misery, poverty! You brought us great wealth, great peace and great honour!'

Such was the greeting from all, of every degree. The girls and ladies danced in celebration, richly dressed in ermine and silk from Otranto: there were thirty or forty rings of dancers! But I want to move on: I've another matter pressing! They crossed the bridges to the town and passed through the imposing gates, and I don't believe any prince or king or emperor ever received such a glorious welcome from any people as did Perceval. No, no one could hope to be better served: everyone, princes and lords alike, honoured him. And when the time came the cooks prepared supper, and Blancheflor didn't dally but arranged everything perfectly like the bright and able girl she was. Then when night fell she sent messages to all her vassals bidding them come without fail at the crack of dawn.

When supper was ready the main horn was sounded, and the knights and ladies and lords washed their hands and sat down to eat. The dishes weren't scanty: there were cartfuls of wine and wagonloads of meat! Everyone had all he could want – and fish from sea and river. But I can't list the dishes – it would be tiresome to describe them all, so I'll move on. That night there was no guard or doorman: anyone who wished could enter, and carry off as much wine and meat – and candles, too! – as he liked! Town and castle alike were ablaze with light, as bright as if all the houses had been on fire!

When they'd eaten their fill they had the tables cleared. Then Perceval stood and spoke, addressing the knights who held land as Blancheflor's vassals.

'Sirs,' he said, 'I've come to ask to take your lady as my wife in good faith – as I should: I want to do this, with your agreement and hers, because it seems to me I'll benefit more from being joined in the sacrament of marriage than from putting my body, and she her beauty, to foolish use.'

When the lords heard this they said: 'Noble sir, if you do you'll have brought us joy forever! If she is your lady and you are her lord, we'll never know sorrow or pain again!'

'I shall do so tomorrow,' said Perceval. 'I swear it by this hand.'

The girl heard this and sighed with joy: she wouldn't have exchanged him for the empire of Greece or Rome and the most handsome man who ever rode a horse!

Now the rejoicing was greater than ever; but I've no wish to go on about their celebrations. They had the beds prepared. In a gorgeous chamber hung with tapestries and dazzlingly painted with gold, six beautiful, soft beds were made with fine and costly sheets. Perceval lay down in one and in the others, so the story says, lay Gorneman and each of his four sons, at a comfortable distance from Perceval, neither too close nor too far away. And I tell you, over his bed was spread a rich coverlet more speckled than a goshawk's feather shed at the fifth moulting. The fairy Blanchemal had made it on the isle of Gernemue, and no one who slept beneath it would suffer madness, gout or any ill, nor could his heart be smitten with base thoughts of harming others.

Meanwhile the maiden Blancheflor lay down in a rich and lovely chamber with her maids around her. Much to her delight they fell into a happy sleep, but she did not: Love was calling and goading her, allowing her no rest; she began to think such sweet thoughts of Perceval that she resolved to go and speak with him, and nothing was going to stop her.

'But no, I daren't!' – 'Why not?' – 'Because he'd love me less for doing so: he'd reproach me for it and think me forward!' – 'But if I don't he'll think me cold: I've always gone to him before. He'll think I'm staying aloof out of excessive pride, that I'm feeling very sure of myself now that he's promised to marry me! Even if it means he tells me off, I'm going!'

She sat up in bed, donned her shift and a mantle and slipped away from her maids and into the hall and on. She no longer cared who saw her or what anyone might say: Love had so emboldened her that she was convinced what she was doing was for the best. To Perceval's bed she came, naked beneath her shift and mantle, and leaned upon the edge. Perceval, who'd heard her coming, took her in his arms and hugged her tightly beneath the sheets and sweetly kissed her. They took great comfort in each other; and they could feel at ease with their kissing and embracing, for it went no further: they preferred to wait till they could be together without sinning.

And that was how they spent the night; she found great solace in their kisses and their whispers. And then, when she saw the dawn, she crept back to her bed and lay happily till the day was bright and clear.

Then the tourneying and jousting and commotion began again. Every lady and burgher's wife dressed herself in a brand new gown, and the chief seneschal called on everyone to start celebrating in earnest. The town was already full of the knights summoned by Blancheflor from all over the land, and they started the festivities anew, revelling whole-heartedly. Hearing these sounds of revelry Perceval rose at once and donned a finely tailored robe prepared for him, of deep red silken cloth. He was a strikingly handsome knight, with blond, curling hair and shining eyes; a bright face he had with arched brown eyebrows, a straight nose and a forked chin; and he had a small scar on his forehead that suited him so well that it was a delight to see. His body was slim and upright, with perfectly shaped shoulders, long, stout, strong arms, powerful in bone and muscle; his hands were white, straight-fingered, shapely; his legs were straight, too, and his feet well arched.

'God!' they all said. 'What a handsome, tall and gracious knight is Perceval!' So said everyone.

Blancheflor had risen now, the worse for having been awake so long: she'd hardly slept at all that night, having been with her love and awake the whole while. Her maids dressed her richly and with care, in garments resplendent with gold and jewels. Her clothes weren't those of a beggar or bumpkin! Her gown was of blood-red purple covered in stars and fringed with bright and dazzling gems, each appearing to the eye to be aflame: yes, the border of her gown was ablaze with jewels, redder than a tongue of fire; and her mantle was lined with white ermine to the very edge.

It wasn't long before the common folk were thronging outside the palace amid peals of celebration. They gathered outside the panelled hall and then moved on to the church, where the Archbishop of Landemeure was arrayed in his vestments, ready to begin the divine service. He was well rewarded at the offering. His two attendant ministers were the bishops of Lumor and Lumeri. God! There were so many crosiers and mitres of abbots and bishops – and this was before any mass had been said. Bishops, prelates, abbots, monks, all were eagerly awaiting a glimpse of Perceval, who was riding through the street with Blancheflor behind him and a vast crowd of people following after. Everyone who saw them was stunned by their beauty, and raced on to the church to find a place for a better view.

Perceval dismounted right outside the door and ran to the girl with outstretched arms to help her down, while her uncle Gorneman hurried forward, too, to be at her right hand. As they stepped inside the church they crossed themselves on head and breast – for be sure of this: it is a sign much feared by the Devil, for God was placed upon the cross and through His death He redeemed us all.

The archbishop conducted the service smoothly and in good time; he took them by the hands and promptly joined them in lawful marriage. So Perceval took his wife, who was always a most virtuous woman, as he was a most worthy man – and he was well rewarded for it, for as we find in written record, he completed the adventures which none but he could ever achieve, and none but he was ever worthy to learn the truth about the grail. But he was to suffer much toil and torment before he could learn it and accomplish the quest.

The people were elated when Perceval took his wife; and back they went to the palace where minstrels played lays and all manner of tunes and songs upon the hurdy-gurdy: the merriment was boundless. Then the tables were set and everyone sat straight down to feast. They were all served together in great silver bowls – I've never seen richer ware; but I shan't go on about the various dishes: they had so many spread before them that it would be tiresome to describe them all, so I'll leave it at that.

After they'd eaten they went to dance. The minstrels sang and played their hurdy-gurdies, harps and pipes: each according to his special skill came forward and performed his turn; and story-tellers told splendid tales to the ladies and the counts. After they'd played for a good long while they were well rewarded for their pains, as pages and knights took off garments to share among them – tunics, surcoats, fur-lined gowns; some of them received five pairs of gifts, or six or seven or nine or ten: they arrived poor beggars and left rich men! But as we all know, such practice is a thing of the past: we've seen a good many celebrations for a knight – either at his marriage or his dubbing – where lords (not for the first time) have promised the minstrels their gowns on a certain day, but when they came to collect they left empty-handed, for the lords had used them as payment to their servants, tailors, waggoners, barbers! Damn any lord who makes such pledges! May he never share in prayers or in the mass who parts with his garments in such a way, who promises to reward a minstrel well and does no such thing but feeds him a pack of lies – his pledges are pure fantasy! The world's becoming a stingy place, because no one's respected if he isn't rich. But I attach little value to wealth – it does no one any good: a curse on worldly riches. But I'm supposed to be telling of Perceval! So I'll leave this matter and say no more: I'll shut up and get on with the story.

What joy there was at Beaurepaire! Day waned and night returned, and the ladies, lords and knights sat down again to supper, with dukes and counts, archbishops, princes, prelates, bishops, clerics, burghers and other folk. And what an excellent supper it was, with such a dazzling array of candles blazing that they lit the hall, the palace, the whole great city! But I'll leave the description at that – I don't want to recount everything: I'll take you straight on to their going to bed.

In Blancheflor's chamber, shining and ablaze with gold, they'd had a gorgeous bed prepared: it would be a delight and pleasure to hear it described – but I don't want to spend my time on that! The archbishops of Rodas and Dinas Clamadas and Saint Andrew's in Scotland each took a cross, not a crosier, and went to bless the bed – they needed no instruction! And those who made the responses were no common clerics – I'll name them: one was the bishop of Cardoil, another the bishop of Cardigan; there were the bishops of Cardiff and Morguan, too, of Saint Pol de Léon, of Carlion, of Lumeri and Lumor (the last two being brothers of Sagremor), and the bishop of Saint Aaron in Wales. The dioceses of all these were under Blancheflor's suzerainty then; for indeed, in all Britain no king or queen, however mighty, with the sole exception of Arthur, had as fine a land as Blancheflor at that time – and she'd made Perceval her lord and the lord of her whole domain.

When the bed had been blessed on every side, and the sign of the cross made over it – with crosses and with fire – Perceval and Blancheflor lay down together, while the people departed and went their separate ways. The chambermaids left, too, feeling no worry for their lady: they knew she'd come out the winner from this engagement! They lay together beneath the sheets, arm against arm, skin against naked skin. And Blancheflor began to shake and tremble, and so did he, like an aspen leaf, for they felt unsure: they were both afraid that through bodily pleasure they might lose what the elect have in the bliss of Heaven, and they wanted to save themselves from the perils and dread torment of Hell. Perceval sighed and groaned as he held Blancheflor in his embrace. She, brought up to be ever mindful of goodness and honour, spoke like a lady of true decency and prudence, afire with love for God; she said:

'Perceval, my dear love, let's take care that the Devil has no force or power over us. Chastity is a holy thing, that's plain; but just as the rose surpasses other flowers in beauty, so virginity surpasses chastity, I tell you truly. And the person who possesses both will be decked in all honour, and doubly crowned before God in Paradise.'

When Perceval heard her words he agreed entirely and said: 'My sweetheart, for the love of God let's not cast away our lives in wickedness, for I believe virginity surpasses all: as topaz is worth more than crystal and fine gold more than other metal, so it is with virginity. And chastity, too, is of very great worth; and whoever possesses both will surely win, it seems to me, the delight and joy of Paradise.'

With that they rose from their bed and went down on their knees with clasped hands and faced the east. They both had their hearts turned to God in all sincerity, inspired by abstinence and goodness and loyalty and faith, which instructed and bade them not to sully virginity but to be full of charity and humility, avoiding pride, and to remember God; for then they would win everything. And they both begged Jesus to keep them in such a state that they might come to a good end, to preserve them in chastity, with their virginity inviolate. They lay back down together then, but didn't touch each other in such a way as to have carnal love: they fell asleep without delay.

They slept for a long while. Then as day began to break Perceval stirred drowsily and stretched a little; and listening, he heard a voice and saw a brilliant light. The voice said:

'Perceval, dear brother, think truly upon God. You have married your wife, who is full of goodness. Now know in truth that I have come from God to declare to you that no man should touch his wife except in a virtuous way and for two things only: to beget children, and to avoid sin. That is right and proper. But when young people are together they often think that whatever carnal pleasure they enjoy is for the best! But truly they are doing wrong – and harm to themselves. So help me God, they'd do better to plunge in cold water and purge the poison from them! Preserve your virginity and fill your heart with charity, and all honour will come to you. I tell you this: from your line will come a girl who'll be most comely and most fair; she'll be wedded to a mighty king, but wrongly and unjustly she'll be threatened with burning and death. But she'll bear a son who'll rescue her from this dire fate; and other sons will be born of her who'll conquer many lands. One will at first have the shape of a man, a fine and handsome figure indeed, but later he'll turn into a bird, much to the distress of his mother and father. And let me tell you, a fine adventure will befall the eldest of the brothers, marrying a girl whose land he'll win back in battle. And he'll beget a daughter who'll bear the choicest fruit, most pleasing to everyone, for she'll have three sons who'll conquer Jerusalem, the sepulchre and the true cross. But Perceval, if you now give up your search for the bleeding lance and the grail, for which you've striven so hard, then I promise you this: you'll have lost your valour and your strength and all the rewards that are to fall to you and your line. I can tell you no more; I commend you to God.'

And with that the voice was gone, leaving Perceval deep in thought for a long while.

He waited as the day broke until it was time to rise. Then a number of boys came to dress and make him ready before returning to the hall. The ladies had risen also, and duly dressed Blancheflor most graciously. And truly, she went to bed as a maiden and rose as a maiden.

Perceval and all the lords went to church to hear mass, and after mass he summoned all the knights and lords to him and received the fealty and homage of those who were to be his vassals, and they accepted him as their lord most gladly and with goodwill. Then:

'Sirs,' he said, 'I bid you always do for Gorneman as you would for me. I am asking him to be my bailiff, guardian of my wife and land; for I have to go in search of the grail, which I've already sought so long. I've no wish to tarry longer: bring me my arms and my horse!'

When Blancheflor heard his words she almost died of grief: he was leaving her so soon! She'd thought he'd be staying in peace with her now, as a worthy man does with his wife. But she loved him so deeply that she didn't dare contradict his words or actions: she would agree to whatever he said. Chrétien de Troyes, who began the story of Perceval till death overtook him and prevented him completing it, tells us that Blancheflor loved him with such a pure heart from the moment she first saw him and recognised his courage, that her love never wavered however far he might be from her: his absence never made her less enamoured, so much was she in love with him. And now he'd married her, as Gerbert has explained, who has continued the work where other poets[38] left it; Gerbert has now added his part according to the true source – and may God grant him strength and victory in quashing all wickedness, and that he may complete the story of Perceval that he's undertaken following the guidance of the book in which the

---

[38] '*trouvères*'.

matter is set down. Gerbert has composed and recorded it for us from the point where Perceval, who suffered such toil and trials, repaired the good sword and asked about the grail and the meaning of the bleeding lance. That's where Gerbert took up the story, judiciously treating the material that I'm recounting here – he even cleverly dealt with the tale of Tristran's trouble; and I've changed and omitted nothing.

Dragonel the Cruel

The story says that the worthy, wise and loyal Perceval called for his arms, not wanting to delay any longer resuming his search for the grail. On a silken carpet Gorneman's sons armed him according to his will and bidding; all the while the girls and ladies were sobbing and weeping bitterly. He then set free the serving-women, releasing them from all demeaning duties. And when he was armed to his satisfaction he didn't dally but mounted a horse blacker than a berry and set off on his way. The lords, in tears, escorted him, as did Blancheflor, in a fainting daze.

But Perceval forgot his balm! He was so eager to be off that he'd forgotten his casks! This was the work of the Devil, the result of sin. But away he rode, and kept on riding – and before he was to see the grail again he'd suffer wounds that he'd barely survive: he'd be needing those casks – without their healing power he wouldn't be healed at all. You'll hear how he came to recover them and where he found them, but before then he was to go through many trials.

He rode all day till late in the afternoon; then his wife turned back, upset, forlorn, saying: 'Ah, holy Mary! I thought I was to live in happiness, with my dear sweet lord staying at my side – I've given my heart to him entirely! But now he's going in search of the grail, and he doesn't know where or in which land! I don't know if I'll ever see him again!'

Now Perceval rode swiftly on through a lonely forest, until he came upon a spring and beside it a little chapel and a hermit's cell. Needing lodging as he did, he headed towards it. The aged, white-haired hermit was at the chapel door, and Perceval graciously hailed and greeted him, and asked him in God's name to say if he knew of any town or tower or castle thereabouts where he might spend the night.

'If you've no objection, sir,' the hermit answered, 'you'd do better to stay here with me. I swear I know of no keep or city, tower or manor or fortress – or any house, noble or humble – from here to Port Molain, which is fully twenty leagues away. And it's fallen into wicked hands: if the lord there catches anyone he's sure to suffer shameful treatment. I swear to God, no one who goes there returns a happy man! So if you wish I'll give you lodging here tonight.'

'Say no more,' said Perceval. 'I've no doubt you're right. I accept.'

He dismounted without more ado, and the good hermit reached out and took his horse and showed Perceval through the door and under his roof. The holy man brought the horse cut grass – he had no corn or oats to offer. Perceval took off his arms and gave them to his host to care for – which he did, along with the fine horse: he took off his saddle and saw him settled. Then he provided his guest with such fare as he had: spring water, cress and barley bread; but you could have put a knife to Perceval's throat and he wouldn't have eaten a crumb! He spent the night with no pleasure or comfort: both he and his horse had little to eat and the hardest of beds.

He rose as soon as he saw the dawn, and the hermit quickly led him to the chapel and brought him a psalter, and at Perceval's urging he sang matins, prime, terce and the midday service, which Perceval heard most gladly and attentively. Then the hermit donned his vestments[39] and stood before the altar to say the *Confiteor*.

It was then that a knight came riding up on a chestnut horse, superbly armed in brand new armour; and with him he brought a maiden – and he was beating her fearfully with a stick. She was crying aloud:

'Alas! I'm dying! He's cut my skin and broken my bones, this false, treacherous, faithless traitor! An agonising death he's dealt me! But he's battering me in vain – I'll never be his love!' She wept and wailed, wringing her hands and tearing at her hair, as she cried: 'Alas! How wickedly he tore me from my sweetheart! But I swear if he tries to take me I'll kill myself! I'll never lie with him a single night! I'd rather he killed me than let him lie with me: he's slain the one I loved!'

'I tell you,' cried the knight, 'you *will* be mine, or you'll die at my hands!'

'Do it, by God!' she said. 'I'd rather be hanged than have you as a husband!'

At this he nearly burst with rage; he raised the stick and battered and beat her terribly till she was smothered in blood. She wept and cried:

'Ah, holy Mary, help this wretched maiden! Why am I still living? I'd rather be dead!'

The knight jumped from his horse and pulled her down and gave her more than a hundred blows. Then he strode into the chapel and yelled to the hermit with outrageous nerve:

'Look sharp, priest! Come and wed me to this lady! If you don't, God help me, you'll pay for it, and dearly!'

The hermit heard the threat but calmly answered: 'Good sir, by the faith I owe Our Lord's body, I'll marry you gladly – if the lady is willing.'

'No, by Saint Paul!' she cried. 'I'd rather be strung up by the neck and torn limb from limb!'

At that the knight grabbed her by the hair, blonde as wool, and then crushed her in so tight a grip that she could scarcely breathe. She wept and groaned and wailed and howled. Then Perceval stepped forward and confronted this reckless, senseless knight, saying:

'By Jesus the king, this is rash and crazy, beating the damsel so! And it's madness, trying to force her to marry you! Let me tell you: those who take willing wives, and serve them well and treat them kindly and strive to please them, they often have trouble and strife enough! So if you try and wed her by force it'll do you no good at all! God in Heaven, you're out of your mind!'

'What're you on about?' said the knight. 'What's it to do with you?'

'Don't be dismissive, friend,' replied Perceval, 'if I give you sound advice. When you've acquired wisdom and you fail to pass it on, you're letting down God and the world. If you wish to serve and love God you should deplore wrongdoing and seek to do the right – and encourage others to do likewise. So listen: a man who dishonours a woman is base and wicked, for it was through a woman that the world was redeemed in an hour – a woman was the first bridge by which God crossed into Hell and rescued His friends, leading them out of Hell's gate: by Him was Hell's hold broken. Anyone who harms or shames a woman is inflicting the like upon himself. The worthy man says, citing the wise adage, that a base heart is ennobled when it heeds the right. By God, sir knight, a man is making a big mistake if he chooses folly over wisdom and shame over honour! Now leave the damsel be.'

---

[39] Literally 'God's arms'.

'Prattle on and you'll pay for it!' said the knight. 'By Saint Peter you will!'

'You're harder than stone!' said Perceval. 'I'll say no more. But I can't fight you at the moment – you're too well armed.'

'If you love her so much that you want to defend her against me,' the knight replied, 'go quickly and get your arms, and we'll settle this outside at the chapel door.'

'By Saint Amand,'[40] said Perceval, 'I ask for nothing more!'

So saying he strode out of the chapel and called to the hermit to fetch his arms. The hermit hurried back with them, and Perceval took them and the damsel gladly helped him arm to his satisfaction. Then they mounted their chargers and drew apart to confront each other. Before the combat was over they'd be in need of treatment! Their horses bore them in a furious charge, and they exchanged mighty blows with their lances on their burnished shields of gold; leather and wood and paint and varnish they pierced like needles – it was nearly disastrous: if their hauberks hadn't been so strong nothing would have saved them from death. As it was, their lances splintered to their fists, but as they passed they collided with such force that their shields smashed and shattered, they stretched so hard upon their stirrups that the straps snapped, and as they rode on past and turned about, they were gasping with rage and frustration. Perceval had been in many a battle, and he drew his sword now and rode back at his foe, and his foe towards him, in a fury. They dealt each other fearsome blows with their strong, sharp blades; they were so fired up that neither wanted respite. They didn't stoop to striking the horses, but they didn't spare each other's body, raining ferocious blows. But truly, they fought for an age with little gain: their helms were smashed, rings were sent flying from their mailcoats; they almost did for one another as they struck each other in the face. But Perceval's special gift was that the more he strove and the harder he fought, the more he gained strength and vigour; and now, recovering force and breath, he assailed the knight with such might and fury that he sent him tumbling over the back of his saddle. Then he wrapped his arm around his neck, tore his helmet from his head and started punching him in the face, breaking open skin and flesh. The knight was in agony – and powerless to save himself – and blood was pouring all over his face.

'Ah, noble knight, have mercy!' he cried. 'You've vanquished me! Show pity, for God's sake, if you've any in your heart – I'm begging you for mercy in God's name! You should heed my plea – you've surely heard that when a man forgives another's wrongs he's doing himself a kindness and a favour: he's saving his own honour; it's to his own benefit. And you've heard what the scriptures testify: that God our Father, Jesus Christ, forgave Longinus for His death when he asked for mercy, and bestowed upon him sight and light and understanding. If there is pity and compassion in you, and you heed the One who watches over all the world, I'm sure you'll show me mercy.'

Then Perceval, hearing him plead for mercy so fervently and eloquently, with hands clasped, remembered how Gorneman had begged and bade him not to kill any knight who dared to ask for mercy; and he said:

'You'll have mercy – on this condition: that never again in your life will any girl be abused by you, or any damsel molested.'

And the knight, so desperate for mercy, agreed to make this promise. Without more ado Perceval led him to the chapel door, where the hermit brought him a psalter and

---

[40] Like a number of other less familiar saints cited in *The Story of the Grail*, Saint Amand has particular connections with Flanders and Picardy.

the knight laid his right hand upon it and vowed unreservedly to do everything that Perceval and the hermit said.

'Now tell me your name,' said Perceval. 'I wish to know it. And you're to go to Cardoil and surrender as a prisoner to King Arthur – God guard and protect him. Tell him you've been sent by the knight who armed and set out after the lady who was crossing the meadows in deep distress.'[41]

'I shall, sir,' said the knight, 'and I'll tell you my name: I'm known as Dragonel the Cruel.'

With that he took his leave and set off without further delay.

Then Perceval dismounted and entered the chapel, and the hermit conducted a sweet and precious service in honour of a glorious martyr. When he'd sung it and said his prayers and completed the rites he promptly removed his vestments and left the chapel, and called Perceval and the lady after him and led them inside his cell. He brought them barley bread and cress and spring water for their breakfast, and said:

'You've had many a finer meal than this – and will again, please God! But once you leave here you'll find nowhere to eat: there's nothing but woods and plains, deep valleys and high mountains.'

When Perceval heard this he ate at once, and so did the lady – not that she thought it much fun: when she tasted the barley bread she said:

'Oh dear! I've never eaten anything like it – it's grating my throat! God send us a better supper than our breakfast – this is dreadful stuff!'

But Perceval said: 'Dear lady, this hermit will deliver a finer soul to God than we shall. We live fortunate lives, with all the foods we fancy, but the body cares only that it has enough to sustain it. This man is more deserving of glory, I'd say, than many people, who don't live good and proper lives but hunger for every bodily indulgence, with no thought for their souls till death draws near.'

'You're right,' she said. 'It's time to go now, sir; let's take our leave and mount and be on our way.'

Perceval readily agreed, and took her in his arms and set her in her saddle, and then mounted and asked the hermit's leave. He commended them to God, that He might send them joy and guide them to safe lodging, as He has the power to do; and with that they rode from the enclosure.

So Perceval took to the road, and the lady, still grieving for her sweetheart who she feared was dead, strove to keep up with him.

'Come this way, sir,' she said, 'along this broad path to the right, by God the glorious king of heaven, that I may see my beloved. I long to know if he's alive or dead: I hope I find him with enough life left that I may speak to him. I'll never leave his body: if he's dead I'll stay with him till I die myself.'

Perceval felt deep pity for her; and he escorted the lady till they found her love beneath a tree, lying on the ground against a marble stone, with dreadful wounds and injuries. The damsel jumped down and left her palfrey and ran to her beloved, and kissed him on the lips more than twenty times till he felt her sweet breath and opened his eyes and spoke, saying:

'Ah, God! Who's that, touching my lips so gently and so sweetly?'

'It's your sweetheart, my dear love, whose heart is wholly yours, so help me God!'

---

[41] Earlier in Gerbert's Continuation, above, pp. 352–3.

On hearing this he surged with joy. Then he raised his head and saw Perceval sitting armed upon his horse and was filled with fear, not knowing who he was. His sweetheart saw his alarm, and told him that the knight he could see had vanquished Dragonel; at this he was elated, and joyfully clambered to his feet. When Perceval saw him standing and caught sight of his wounds he made a move towards him – and suddenly remembered his forgotten casks. He was distraught: if only he'd had them he could have healed the knight in an instant! He was especially worried about an agonising wound in his side; but the damsel staunched it with an amethyst and then bandaged his body all around with a length of fine white cloth that had been belted about her waist. Struggling to his feet again, the knight begged Perceval to recover his horse, which Dragonel had driven off and tied up somewhere in the woods. Perceval went and found it, and brought it back to the knight and held the stirrup to help him mount. Then he said:

'Go straight to Beaurepaire, good sir, to the kind and gentle Blancheflor, my beloved and my lady; and tell her without fail to remember my casks and to care for them till I return as much as she cares for me and my love! And tell her to let you drink of what's inside: before it's even passed your lips you'll be healed – you needn't have the slightest fear! Go now with God, for I must hurry: it's no good being out in the wilds – the sooner I'm gone the better. But tell me your name, truly, and your sweetheart's.'

'I shan't keep it from you, sir. My name is Arguisial of Carhais, and my beloved's name is Rohais.'

The Knight of the Cart

Without any further questions they commended each other to God. Arguisial headed for Beaurepaire, while the good and valiant Perceval set off through the ancient forest.

All day long, deep in thought, he followed a narrow, solitary path until, as the sun began to set, he emerged from the forest and looked ahead and saw a splendid castle, with six small towers and one that loomed great and mighty. Beside it flowed a fine, broad river bearing a fleet of ships, and below the castle lay the town, well fortified with walls and turrets. Nowhere from there to Tours had finer defences, and the keep stood proud upon a rock: I don't think an arrow from an archer's bow could have reached its battlements, so lofty was the crag.

As Perceval rode from the forest and headed for the town he met a maiden coming out of the gate. She was wiping her eyes on her tunic, in floods of tears, in terrible distress.

'Ah, Holy Mary!' she said. 'My heart will break! I'll never know happiness again – how could I, when my love this day is suffering such shame and wicked, wanton harm? A curse on the founder of this city's custom!'

'Oh, tell me, damsel, if you will,' said Perceval, 'what custom do they practise here, to cause you such distress?'

Unable to control her grieving, continuing to weep and sigh, she answered: 'Sir, it couldn't be worse. I urge you to turn back and avoid grave shame: no knights who chance to pass through this gate have anything left when they leave! The lord of this place takes all their gear – there's no stopping him! If any knight tries to keep his arms, to stop them being taken, he has to joust, I promise you, with four formidable knights. And it's pointless! Even if he manages to defeat all four he'll still have to fight the lord himself – and he's invincible! His record stands at forty-four that he's shamed and wronged! And robbing them of their gear is the least of it: the degrading abuse he inflicts on their bodies is dreadful – no man can imagine the shame they endure. My sweetheart, in all innocence, was passing through the town just now and found himself having to confront the four; and in jousting with them he unhorsed three, but as he met the fourth – ah, dismal luck! – his mount stumbled, the reins slipped from his hand and his horse fell beneath him. They rushed and stripped him of his arms. I love him so much, I couldn't bear to see what they'll make him suffer! So I left, distraught and anguished. Ah, gentle knight, turn back if you want to avoid disaster! If you've any sense you'll go!'

'Truly, damsel,' he replied, 'my horse and I have had a hard day's ride. You tell me there are troublesome folk in the town – they should beware, as should everyone, of doing wicked deeds; but if I turn back I don't know where I'll go for shelter, and my horse has eaten nothing but a little hay for the last two days, and I'm expiring with hunger myself! No fear of combat is going to stop me going in.'

Just then he heard a racket and commotion in the city, and he rode on to the bridge and through the gate. The very first people he met were rude and coarse, yelling:

'Ah! You're going to be sorry you ever came here, pal! You'll leave here stripped and horseless! What a good move this wasn't! The Devil must have prodded you this way! It's grief and woe for you – you can't escape it! It'll do wonders for your reputation! Shame and humiliation are heading your way!'

Perceval held his tongue, not saying a word; he just rode on by. But all through the streets the town was packed with people, two ranks deep, and every one of them was clutching handfuls of offal or old shoes, or bundles of rags or matting plastered with mud and filth; and all were yelling:

'This way! On you go!'

Perceval kept riding till he reached the castle. There he found a little wagon sitting on a stretch of grass, and he'd never seen one better fitted, mounted on four wheels, sturdily riveted and handsomely covered; and five shields of various devices hung from this fine wagon's side. Beneath the tower stood a tree to which were tethered five destriers, superbly harnessed and caparisoned, and beside them was an array of lances, big and stout and strong and white. Perceval rode up to the wagon and found it set with yoke and collar and traces at the ready. And inside it lay a foul, ill-tempered cripple: no one could make him hold his tongue – he was so full of spite and bumptious malice that he was always taunting and stirring up trouble. When he saw Perceval approach he grabbed his garishly painted trumpet – it was nicknamed 'Horrid Neighbour' – and put it to his lips and blasted, and it blared out loud and clear throughout the castle and the streets. Everyone came flocking the moment they heard it; and down from the castle came five magnificently armed knights, closely followed by ladies and damsels carrying their helms. They came swiftly down, and with them they brought a knight they'd stripped: he was barefoot, clad in nothing but a shift. A great gaggle of boys and rabble thronged around him, with no pity for his plight, showering him with mocking cries of:

'Look! Here's the knight of the cart!'

Abusing him disgracefully, they led him to the wagon and:

'Here you go!' the cripple said. 'I've a job for you – in the traces here! You'll find it a bit of a *drag*! You're going to pull me and my cart through the streets, by God you are! And you'll be pelted with old shoes and offal – I've blown my trumpet to get everyone ready. And I've got my old ox-bladder here, blown up good and big: you'll feel it round your cheeks if you don't keep pulling, right through the mud and flood and mire!'

The cripple shut up at last and grabbed the collar, and was about to shove it on the knight's neck and strap him in the traces when Perceval intervened and said:

'That's enough, cripple! Take off that yoke! Curse the wicked rogue who brought this custom to the city! By God, I've no respect for any knight who shames another!'

'You'd better get used to it, sir knight!' said the lord, coming forward. 'The same's in store for you before you go! You'll leave without a mount or arms when I've finished with you! But listen: if you're confident and valiant enough and have the strength and prowess to defeat four knights then you'll fight with me, and if you can vanquish me you can demand whatever you wish and everyone will obey you absolutely. But if you fail, you'll be foully showered with offal and old boots! Though if you had a hundred horses and were willing to hand them over you'd be let off all this trouble and shame!'

'I don't know why you're prattling on,' said Perceval. 'I'll defend my arms – I won't surrender them as long as I can fight. A knight should be mindful of who he is and of his name. Baseness must be dead in him once he's been bathed;[42] he should part company with any trace of baseness; and if he cannot tear it out and it stays rooted in his heart, tempting him with the thought of material gain, then he violates the order of chivalry. Why? Because a knight should be kindly, calm and good-natured when at home, offering hospitality – and when necessary bold and full of prowess and judicious in speech. That's how a knight should be, and shun all thoughts of wickedness; and it's certainly a wickedness to dishonour a fellow knight! Not for a moment should you be respected when you deny your house to passing knights, and steal their arms and horses, and make them suffer the indignity of pulling that cart with the cripple! No one with any sense should have anything to do with you: you live on robbery! You've no place in the order of knighthood – you shouldn't be called a knight at all! Come – I'll joust with anyone, like it or not. Bid a knight mount – he'll have a joust, by my life he will! And I tell you this: if I win these jousts I'll have this custom abolished – it's a wicked practice indeed.'

At this a knight mounted, threatening Perceval with all manner of hurt and shame. As soon as he was in the saddle he laced his helm over his ventail; then the cripple handed him his shield – of gold and blue stripes it was, trimmed with gules* and sporting a lion made of ermine. He didn't dally but rode up to the lances and took one, while all the people gathered round, eager to watch the jousting as they always did. The knight who'd been stripped went to the lances, too, and picked out five, straight and strong, none of them looking frail or crooked; then he hurried to Perceval and handed him the very stoutest, saying:

'May honour be yours, sir! For the love of God, think of the offal and old shoes and mud-fouled rags that are ready to be thrown! It's a terrible thought! For God's sake, be sure you joust well!'

'Don't worry,' said Perceval. 'Unless this wretched, foolish rabble impede me I'm not afraid.'

They set their shields in position and their lances in their rests and then charged towards each other, bracing themselves in their stirrups and letting their chargers go

---

[42] This refers to the ritual bath taken by a knight before his dubbing. See, for example, Maurice Keen's *Chivalry* (Yale, 1984), p. 7, where, quoting a passage from the anonymous *Ordene de Chevalerie*, he tells how Hugh, Count of Tiberias, knights Saladin according to Christian conventions and explains on bringing him to a bath that: 'this is a bath of courtesy and bounty ... and should recall to you the baptism of the child, for you must come out of it as clean of sin as the infant from the font.'

full tilt, and struck one another with passionate fury, bent on nothing short of destruction. The knight smashed and split Perceval's shield apart, but his splendid hauberk held: he was neither hurt nor wounded and didn't lose his seat; but the mighty knight's lance flew into splinters. Perceval delivered a blow that pierced the knight's shield and thrust upward to hit him full in the chest and send him crashing over his horse's rump to the ground, his legs in the air, almost shattering his body. Three times he fainted with the pain, for his collar-bone was broken and blood was gushing forth. Perceval, looking down at him, said:

'I don't know about the others but I've no more to fear from you today! Anyone else who wants to joust, let him come – he'll find me ready!'

'God lend you strength and power!' said the other knight who had a sorry fate in store if Perceval couldn't rescue him.

'Have no fear,' Perceval replied. 'God – and Faith and Loyalty – will support us and our right. If the others put up no better a show than this one we'll be leaving without loss!'

When the lord of the castle saw the knight, unhorsed by Perceval, lying stretched out on the ground he told another of the three to mount without delay. He did so, furious at seeing his companion hurt; he rode up to the cart and grabbed his shield, his blood seething with rage and malice, and seized a stout lance, his helm already laced. Then they turned their steeds to face each other without another word, both blazing with proud fury, and the horses charged at speed. They exchanged tremendous blows on shields, unflinching, sparing nothing, and the knight's shield shattered into pieces; but Perceval's blow was such that he brought down knight and horse together in a deep pool, the water whelming over them: the knight would have drowned if people hadn't rushed to drag him out. Perceval cried, to needle him:

'Had a good drink, sir knight? Which do you think's best, then: wine or water? You should know – you've drunk enough – flat out in it and face down! *You*'re not putting me in traces, or in a collar of leather or cloth: if I'm to be put in harness it'll have to be someone else who does it – we're finished with you!'

The lord was riled by this, and promptly ordered the third knight to mount. He did, and vowed that Perceval would pay! And the lord said:

'Let's see what you can do! Hit him high on the chin and send him flying! By the Creator, if he brings you down you'll be no friend of mine: you'll have lost my love for good!'

'If I don't send him tumbling,' said the knight, 'you can have my head!'

And he rode to the cart and took up his shield, convinced he'd soon beat Perceval – not that Perceval feared him in the least. They drew apart, braced their shields, and then charged at each other full tilt. The knight met Perceval with a blow that smashed off the top of his shield, striking him as if he were a quintain; but it shook neither him nor his mount at all: rather, Perceval, well schooled in jousting, caught him full on the chest with such force that he sent him crashing, flat on his face in a filthy mire, and such a splash he made that flying mud spattered the lord in the face and plastered the ladies' gowns – they were not amused!

'Well, sir knight,' said Perceval, 'you've lost your head if your lord takes you at your word! That'll teach you: only a fool pledges a foot, a hand, an arm, a head when he doesn't know he's going to win! Next time, friend, don't go promising what you can't achieve. Bragging never does anyone any good: deeds count so much more than words. And no one's perfect! But listen: you're not getting me hitched to the cart, that's certain, so wallow in the mud as long as you like – you can lie there till I hoist you out! Let your companion come and joust while you enjoy your reward: the bath you deserve – for the first bath you had, when you were knighted,[43] clearly meant nothing to you. A knight should be cleansed of all base habits, and have no rancour in his heart prompting him to shameful, wicked deeds. A man who wrongs another wrongs himself: shame and hurt another and sooner or later it's sure to rebound on you. You've got your reward for your patent cruelty – face down in that cesspool.'

The fourth knight heard this and nearly burst with rage. He rose to his feet and mounted: huge he was and mightily fearsome. He laced his helm and took up his shield.

The knight who'd found Perceval facing battle at the castle took hold of the edge of his shield and again urged him to be resolute, 'for truly, I've heard that the one who's coming to joust with you now has never been unhorsed in his life!'

'There's a first time for everything!' said Perceval. 'And it's going to be now – if my lance holds firm.'

The knight who was so eager to joust was named Aligrés. He picked up a mighty lance, enormously stout and strong, and set himself to face Perceval, swearing he'd be inconsolable if he failed to vanquish him. Then they kicked their mounts' flanks and rammed in their spurs. On their shields, flashing gold, they delivered such blows that heads and shafts smashed through with ease, and clashed with such force that they struck sparks from their helms. Both horses staggered and rocked back on their rumps, and both lances, despite their strength, were smashed to pieces. And the knight emptied his saddle, for Perceval struck him so hard, both body and shield, that he sent him flying from his horse to the ground. Everyone saw him, heels in the air in a tumbled heap. The knight who'd been stripped was overjoyed – he'd never known such glee!

Then Perceval said to the lord: 'Come and fight, sir knight – the four are all defeated! Hurry up – it's time for supper! If, please God, I escape your clutches I'll have something to eat – plenty, I trust!'

'Escape my clutches? It's as likely as you being pleased with an egg when you're hungry enough to eat an ox!'

'So you hope,' said Perceval. 'But first – God give power to my right hand – you'll feel the edge of my sword.'

Parsaman, the lord so keen for combat, leapt upon a dappled grey destrier, and fixed himself so firmly in the stirrups that he made the leather stretch. With helmet laced he rode straight to the cart and seized his shield and a strong lance, and Perceval picked up another. Then the lord, fired for battle, wheeled away with a flourish and turned to face him; raring for the joust they let their horses go, and both steeds flew faster than swooping birds. The lord delivered such a fearsome blow, and Perceval struck him likewise, that their shields split and their lances smashed to pieces. It was an awesome clash indeed: they collided chest to chest; I don't know who came off worse, but all four, riders and horses, came crashing down. Up leapt the knights to do combat, not stepping back but drawing their furbished swords, setting their shields above their heads and striding to the attack. Ah, God! How well their blades of steel became them, gripped in their right hands! I don't know which of them landed more or fewer blows, but both made the other feel their fury and their wrath: rings were dashed from both their hauberks, both their shields were hacked apart, both their helms were split and deeply stove. The blows had fired them to such a pitch that neither wanted respite – they were

[43] See note 42, above, p. 401.

both intent and bent on wounding, crushing. Parsaman was beside himself at failing to vanquish Perceval, and assailed him boldly, fiercely with his naked sword. But Perceval attacked him back that instant, dealing more than five blows to his head in quick succession, and a final one that sent him staggering, seeing stars. He reeled back, not knowing where to take refuge: there was no escape – Perceval was hot on his heels and raining tireless blows, till every strap and lace on his helm and neck was sundered. Perceval hammered with all his force and beat him to the ground, giving him such a battering that his face was black and blue.

'Ah, mercy, knight!' the lord appealed. 'You've vanquished and defeated me! I've been so cruel to passing knights, but never in my life again will I seek to do any harm – I'll gladly mend my ways!'

'Indeed you will!' said Perceval. 'If you want mercy you'll do exactly as I say: you'll never rob knights of their equipment or mete out abuse and injury; you'll never refuse them hospitality – you'll offer it freely to any knight; you'll return to this knight the arms you took; you'll give everyone free passage. Refuse any of this and your life is over!'

And Parsaman, in fear of death, said: 'I'll do whatever you wish and demand!'

So Perceval called for relics to be brought, and made Parsaman swear on the bones of Saint Amand that for the rest of his days he'd give free passage to all. His knights made the same oath – and they were never forsworn – as did all the burghers of the town.

Then they escorted Perceval inside and swiftly disarmed him and dressed him most nobly. And they stabled his horse who'd earned his fodder – and paid for it dearly! The horse was given every comfort. As for Perceval, he was honoured more highly than a king. He had all gear and arms returned to the knight he'd found in such a piteous state, and he sent to the gate to fetch his sweetheart. The lord didn't delay but did his bidding at once, sending two courteous knights to bring her back. They found her quite distraught, grieving bitterly, but they consoled her, saying:

'Lady, stop your grieving now and come with us; it's turned out much better than you think: you'll have your sweetheart safe and sound – he's been rescued by the knight who arrived just now. Your beloved has had uncommon good fortune!'

She was beside herself with joy; she wiped her eyes and face but kept on weeping, hardly able to believe what she'd just heard. But she went with them all the same, and was overcome with happiness when she found her love, who rejoiced likewise: he rose and came to meet her with outstretched arms and helped her down, and then bade that her horse be stabled.

The lord had the crowds who'd gathered in the streets dispersed and sent away, while squires and servants hurried to prepare the tables; then ladies, girls and knights quickly washed their hands and mingled and sat down together. It was a splendid supper, and Perceval ate heartily: he needed it! He ate a whole roast haunch of venison, hotly peppered! They all had as much as they wished to eat and drink: Perceval and the knight and his sweetheart were well served indeed.

And after supper the servants promptly made the beds, for Perceval wanted to be on his way first thing next morning. The lord surrendered himself, his castle, his land and all he owned to him. And the damsel and her beloved served Perceval at supper like a cherished friend, for he'd rescued them from misery, and then lay down before him in a pair of soft, well-made beds.

Perceval was refreshed by his much-needed sleep, and when he heard the watch sound the dawn he rose at once – as did the knight and his sweetheart, fearful that the rabble would do them harm if they dallied and departed after him. But they should have had more confidence: never again would the townsfolk tolerate the abuse of any knight.

Perceval, the knight and the damsel mounted, for their horses had already been saddled; and all the ladies, knights and squires did likewise and escorted them out of the town and on to a road before taking their leave and returning. Then Perceval and the other two rode swiftly away together, but they hadn't gone more than a league before they came to a fork in the road. A cross stood beside it, with a sheet of parchment fixed to it bearing letters of fine gold, large and small. They read as follows:

> Rider, take the wide path to the right:
> It is the way to Durecestre
> And leads to safety;
> The other, truly,
> Is called the Path Adventurous:
> To travel it is perilous indeed.

Perceval saw these letters and understood what they were saying to passers-by, for he'd learned to read; and he took the knight by the hand and said:

'Listen: I've spent many winters and many summers toiling to find the grail, and risen early many a day when I dearly longed to sleep. Now I must go this way, for it's the path to adventure. But you must go to the right, and take the straight road to Durecestre. But tell me first about yourselves: your own name and your sweetheart's – don't keep them from me. Then set out along that road.'

'My name is Semiramin, sir – it would be wrong to hide it from you; and my sweetheart's name is Roseamonde de Nobles Vals.'

'Go now with God, dear friend,' said Perceval; and with that he departed, while the knight set off down the other path with his beloved.

The Shield with the Red Cross

Perceval rode on all week with much discomfort, for the country was deserted and he often went hungry and thirsty. With faith alone sustaining him he kept going, until he saw two girls approaching; and he saw they were grieving terribly, pulling a knight behind them, lying in a litter. And as he drew near he saw that this knight had both legs burnt: that was why the girls were grieving, both dissolving in tears. Perceval hailed them, and asked them who the knight was, in such a piteous state, but they were too distraught to utter a word: both were lost in woe. So he rode on past, having no further questions, thinking only about his search for the grail.

He descended now into a valley, but he hadn't gone far before he came upon another knight with his head and neck burnt likewise; a squire, weeping dreadfully, was carrying him before him. Perceval gave him greeting and asked him how and why it had happened, but the squire turned away in tears without uttering a word. Perceval was bewildered about these people that he'd met.

He set out now along the path which no knight took and returned alive or without a grievous wound. The way, as I understand it, wasn't very well trodden or beaten. He came then to a lovely glade and there, at the edge of a dell, he saw a beautiful wooden cross: I don't think any finer was ever made. He could see two hermits at the cross: one was making a great commotion, clutching a fistful of twigs with which he repeatedly beat the cross, as heavily and fiercely as if he meant to knock it down – he went on thrashing till he ran out of breath. But the other hermit was on his knees with clasped hands, worshipping the cross a hundred times over without respite. Perceval watched them for quite a while, baffled to see one furiously beating the cross and the other intent on worshipping it and praying to God. Then he rode forward, determined to ask the hermit his reason and purpose in beating the cross – that the other should be worshipping it was no surprise. Down he came swiftly, and demanded to know if it was folly or wisdom that drove him to beat the cross. The hermit was about to tell him there and then – but Perceval's attention was seized by something else: out of a bush he saw a beast of amazing size appear. He was so astounded that he forgot about his question, as the beast, heavily pregnant, went rushing past him with her offspring baying inside her like a pack of yelping dogs. And their cries weren't soft: they could be heard as loud and clear as if they'd been out of her belly and chasing her, hunting her down! The beast fled away as fast as she could, and Perceval followed as fast as *he* could, at a gallop, forgetting his question to the hermits he'd found.

He chased the beast all day until he finally caught up with her: she was exhausted from running, and her brood had torn at her so fearfully that she was split in two. Out they leapt and attacked and devoured her, gnawing her flesh right down to the bones. And thereupon they turned raving mad: they went wild and slaughtered one another. Perceval was staggered by the sight: he'd never seen the like. He set off on his way again, having no desire to stay.

Night was near, and he hurried on in search of a house where he could stay and find lodging for the night and something to eat: he was certainly in need of it. Then night fell and it turned pitch dark. Perceval, who'd seen and endured much hardship, suddenly saw a brilliant light and headed towards it, thinking it a promising sign. He followed the path to the beckoning light till he came upon an open door covered with broom, and beyond it a yard enclosed by a fence; and inside a little house he found thirteen hermits. Very pale they were: they'd no great amount of food for their supper – they'd cut a loaf of bread into thirteen pieces, and each was breaking his piece before him. A servant holding a lighted candle stood before the foremost hermit, and began to serve him while another cut his bread – which was coarse, not made of wheat. They were startled to see Perceval there, sitting armed upon his horse; but he greeted them and asked for lodging out of charity.

'I've been seeking shelter for a good while now, without success.'

'You'll have little to eat,' said one of the servants, 'and so will your horse.'

'I'm sorry to hear that!' said Perceval.

Then the one who was lord and master of the hermits – and rightly so – asked Perceval to dismount, and the servants took his horse and led him to the stable where they gave him some new-mown hay. Meanwhile Perceval was disarmed and seated by the fire, where they served him well with what they had – but he ate little, I think, for there was nothing to whet his appetite: he found the bread inedible.

And then, just as they were about to clear the cloths, a girl came through the door, carrying a wondrously handsome shield: all white it was, with a red cross, and in the cross was a relic that certainly mustn't go unmentioned, for in it was embedded a piece of the holy wood on which the flesh of Jesus Christ, the son of God, was tortured. The shield was made by two Chaldeans who'd been converted to God; and they'd made it in such a way that no one could find the holy grail or the lance with the ever-bleeding head except the first to be able to take the shield from this beautiful maiden's neck. But it was at his peril that any man touched it or tried to take it unless he was the bravest in the world, both in word and deed, and confessed of all his sins; were he not, he'd instantly be destroyed in a hail of a thousand stones, and nothing could protect him. There was an inscription upon it to that effect for the benefit of all who saw the shield and were able to read.

The girl stepped straight in. She'd been scouring many lands, both day and night, but no one who read the inscription would lay a hand upon the shield: they didn't dare – it was too fearsome a test. Without a moment's hesitation Perceval ran to help the damsel from her horse. And first he took the shield from her neck: it weighed little, but was made of such fine stuff that it feared no blow from any lance. When she saw he'd taken the shield she threw herself to the ground: she knew now he was the finest knight in all the world, for confession, which washes sin away, had greatly increased his worth. Without anyone's bidding she went and sat at Perceval's side; and she had two casks of wine and two rabbit pies, wrapped up in a cloth, unloaded from her horse. The hermit bade them sit and eat on a cloak all by themselves. The pies and the pair of casks were set before Perceval, but:

'Dear friend,' he said to a boy, 'take these pies and casks and offer them to the monks to share.'

'Sir,' the boy replied, 'I've no wish to lie to you, and please don't take it as a joke: they don't eat meat and they don't drink wine. And I promise you by Saint Livinus,[44] they never talk while eating – except their king: whenever people come he'll talk, at their arrival and departure, too. But eat now with good cheer – you, too, dear lady; then you can go and talk to the king without fear of impropriety – and if you've anything to ask him he'll give excellent advice, and if you've seen anything that's puzzled you, ask him and he'll explain its meaning faithfully. In case you want to know his name, he was baptised with the name Elyas Anaïs, and now he's called the Hermit King.'

Perceval was overjoyed by this, eager to ask about the strange things he'd seen and not understood: about the hermits at the cross and the beast that had been split open by the storming brood who'd then devoured her, and why they'd all gone raving mad and slaughtered one another. He waited till he and the girl had finished eating before he asked, but then he addressed the king as soon as he could, saying:

'Sir, you've lodged me in your house tonight; I hope you won't mind if I pose some questions. Let me tell you about the strange things I've seen today, for they are wonders indeed.'

And he told him first about the actions of the two hermits: how one had worshipped the cross and the other had beaten it furiously; then he told him all about the beast, from start to finish. The Hermit King listened to every word and then bowed his head in thought; then he looked up again and said:

'Dear friend, you've set me thinking deeply with your question. Be sure to listen closely now; for a man who hears but takes in nothing is like a man who casts his net to catch the wind: if he hears good words and fails to retain them, he's the worse for it! Such negligence shows no respect for the one who's trying to inspire good. But it would take an age to train a buzzard[45] to catch a lark – trying to teach the bad to do good is just as futile! You're throwing your pearls away for sure if you spread them

---

[44] Like Saint Amand (above, p. 397), Livinus is a saint with particular associations with Flanders, specifically with Ghent.
[45] The buzzard is a notoriously difficult bird of prey to train.

before swine! Good-for-nothings have more regard for those who frolic and prance about – and why? Because they resent having any demands made of them: they'll always go more readily to cavort around than to hear wise words that guide us to courtesy, worth and honour. My dear friend,' said the Hermit King, 'measured speech is better than banter – it wins over many men. There's a great deal to say and hear in answer to your question, but if you'll pay attention I'll tell you all I can. So listen, friend, and I'll tell you about the two hermits.

'They both have good intentions: the one who was beating the cross was weeping bitterly, I assure you, lashing the wood in return for the pain and agony that Christ suffered on the cross when He submitted His body to death for our sakes – that's the certain truth; in return for His torment and suffering there, the hermit beat the cross over and over. That's what was happening: that's why he was beating it. The other hermit was worshipping it because the glorious flesh, so sweet and precious, was tortured there, pinned fast with three great iron nails, and thereby He redeemed from Hell those souls who'd served Him. God hadn't deserved to be crucified – that's why the wood of the cross on which He was nailed is sanctified. And be sure of this, my friend: the Devil fears the cross more than anything, because thanks to the cross he lost his prey! And anyone who worships God and prays that the cross may be his shield will never be vanquished by any demon: if he makes the sign of the cross upon himself, all malign spirits will flee, for they fear the cross so much, believe me, friend; and that's why the hermit worshipped it.

'Now I've explained the hermits' thinking. I'll tell you now about the beasts who bayed inside their mother and then killed her and destroyed her and ate her flesh, and because of it went mad and slaughtered each other instantly. Bear with me if it takes me a while to reply – and if anyone disagrees with me I'll prove right here and now that my words are true, by God I will. My friend, the beast signifies Holy Church – let me explain. You know of course that people should behave with proper devotion in church; but the moment the priest begins to sing mass, they start chattering about the price of grain and having to pay their tithes! Soon there's such a hubbub, such a racket in the church that the priest can't conduct the holy office – and if he asks them to be quiet they shout back:

'"Sing on, sing on, sir priest! Get on with it and have done! We want to go and feed our faces!"

'These people have no fear of God – or of their wicked deeds; they're more worried about their great fat bellies – yet they've no right to live any better than a mendicant friar! They don't care two hoots about sermons or preaching! They're symbolised by the brood who bayed inside their mother and then killed her and devoured her, for anyone who jaws his way through a service is indeed devouring Holy Church. And when it comes to the Sabbath and the priest begins prayers and announces the feast days, and pronounces the commandments on pain of excommunication, such people couldn't care less – no sooner heard than broken! Excommunication means nothing to them and they scorn the commandments: nothing will make them change their ways. Instead they babble to each other:

'"This priest's always going on! Damn anyone who heeds his words and stops looking after number one!"

'They turn their hearts from doing good: they're the brood who go wild and kill one another in ignorance. I say a man is truly dead if he doesn't heed the commands of Holy Church and has no fear of doing wrong. Listen, dear friend: when God made Adam in the beginning He forbade him the fruit of an apple tree, telling him not to eat it; and because he broke that rule he was cast out of Paradise, naked and poor, reduced to beggary; now he was doomed to die through the bite of that apple, and condemned to Hell for breaking that command. But God went through death Himself to rescue him from torment. So I tell anyone who asks that whoever spurns a commandment made in Holy Church and lives excommunicate is truly killing himself: as long as he remains excommunicate he's as dead as Adam who broke the rule with his bite of the apple. They're like the brood in the beast – that's what I say.

'Now you've heard the truth and my sermon, and I bid and implore you remember it well. If you abstain from sin you may win Paradise – and learn the true meaning of the grail you're seeking, and why the lance bleeds. I'm well aware you're my nephew – and you had a little sister, and after your mother's death she lived without a brother's help or guidance among strangers in a land where her friends could never find her; she's of royal descent, but the best and wisest of her line have been lost in wars: many worthy men have been dishonoured and demeaned and brought low and reduced to poverty.'

'That's true,' said Perceval, 'but I can tell you that my sister's now at the Castle of the Maidens, living with the damsels and my lady holy Ysabiaus.'[46]

Perceval's news delighted the Hermit King: he was very glad to hear about that good and saintly lady, and gave thanks to the Supreme King that she was still alive. His heart was stirred with joy and he felt great comfort, for she was very old indeed: according to him she was at least three hundred, and a good deal more, he was sure; so he was thrilled to know she was still alive, for he'd never met a lady finer or more devout: she often saw legions of angels winging softly towards the house of the Fisher King, carrying the holy grail, and in it the host with which they sustained the life of the father of that king whom Perceval had chanced to find fishing in the little boat.

The servants made a couch of fresh grass and hay, and on it the Hermit King lay down fully dressed, for he had no quilt; and all the other hermits lay propped against this couch to rest. Then the servants attended to Perceval and made him a bed – though it offered little comfort. They made another for the girl, but I assure you she didn't rest or sleep: she yearned to have Perceval for a lover and to have a son by him, for then she could boast and spread it abroad that she'd had pleasure with the boldest knight ever born of woman. She lay awake all night thinking of nothing else.

When night had passed and they saw day about to break, the hermits didn't dally but went straight to a fine, neat little chapel to say their hours. Then the Hermit King donned his vestments again and sang the holy mass. Perceval listened attentively, as did the girl who'd brought the shield. And when the hermit – who'd once been king of a great land – had sung the mass, Perceval called for his gear and armed, a boy kneeling to help him. The girl held before him the shield with the handsome straps, for no one else would go near it while they remembered the inscription it bore, telling of the shield's powers and of the relic it contained. Perceval had never had such a shield, or one so fine; now he feared neither weapon nor fire, for they could never harm him. He mounted and hung it from his neck at once; then he took his leave of the hermits and departed. The girl set off another way, commending him to God.

But Perceval hadn't asked her where she'd got the shield, and this was a grave mistake: he could never afterwards find out and it was to cause him a deal of trouble. When he'd ridden about a pebble's throw he suddenly thought:

[46] See above, p. 364 and footnote 19.

'By Saint Peter, I'm a fool! I didn't ask where it came from, this shield I've won, or who sent it to me!'

And he looked back the way the girl had gone, wanting to ask her about the shield; but he could see no sign of her. He spurred back along the path she'd taken, but couldn't find her. It was baffling: he kept searching for a long while but could find neither scent nor track. He thought she must have been whisked away by a fairy or a phantom! And he swore by the noble Saint Cosmas he'd keep going and see if he could eventually find some news. But he could hunt for an age and not catch her: he'd lost this quarry.

Then suddenly he remembered the knights he'd seen who were burnt, and said: 'What a simpleton I am, not mentioning it to the Hermit King! He'd have explained it to me just as he did the beasts! But I'm so thick and uncouth I can't take in a thing! My heart's too hard to absorb advice! Anyone trying to shake sense into a fool is mad!'

And he crossed himself at the thought of this strange wonder: he'd seen the girl sure enough, but now there was no sign of her – yet he could see three and a half leagues in all directions.

The Knight of the Dragon

Deep in thought he rode down into a valley and found himself in a wasteland, where he met a damsel in a state of dreadful grief. She was wearing her shift and other clothes inside-out, and was driving a cart covered with a cloth of gold – and goading and scolding the horses furiously, for she was fervently seeking vengeance for her lover. For two and a half months she'd been travelling like this. It looked as if her lover, who was laid upon the cart, had been burnt at the stake: his feet, legs, thighs and belly were all burnt; and the flames had attacked him above the waist, too: he was black and charred all over. She'd taken him to every one of his kin, but her grief was unrelieved: none of them dared attempt to avenge him – they knew they'd not succeed. She was riding backwards, facing the cart, and had vowed she'd eat no meat and drink no wine, and would continue to wear her clothes inside-out, till she had revenge upon the one who feared and dreaded no one and had killed her love, now blacker than a Moor: everywhere the fire had reached it had charred and blackened him.

She was sitting on the shafts of the cart, lashing the horses with a whip. Perceval rode up and greeted her most courteously in the name of God who was crucified. She jumped in surprise – she hadn't seen him coming – and turned round when she heard his voice. And then, when she set eyes on the shield, all the suffering she'd endured was lifted from her.

'Ah, holy Mary!' she cried. 'I've found the one I've sought so long! This knight will overcome the devil, the demon, who killed my love! He'll vanquish him! That shield that hangs from his neck is proof of it – any who dared take it as he has done has lost his head in an instant, but this knight is worthy to bear it!'

Perceval, longing to know more about her plight, asked her why she was dressed so. She turned to face him and told him her heartfelt story from start to finish: how the Knight of the Dragon, brother of King Maragon, had built a city in the isles of the sea, superbly fortified with towers and walls, and filled it with people who refused to believe in God and had no fear of doing wrong. And this lord, the Knight of the Dragon, devoted himself to evil – and to the Devil, who'd endowed him in return with such power that no one could withstand him in battle or any combat.

'The Devil brought him a terrible, ghastly shield, blacker than any berry: a dragon's head is fixed in it, by such demonic art that it burns and engulfs in flame anyone who fights him! Any man who challenges him is condemning himself to an appalling death: by the Devil's power the dragon will consume him in fire! He killed my beloved sweetheart with his blazing, scorching shield!

'He's been laying siege for some time now to the peak of Montesclaire. No one dares go out to face him; there are three hundred and ten knights inside the castle, but none has the courage to confront him. The evil tyrant, with a vast army, is besieging the lady within because he wants her for his wife. But she – the Maiden of the Circle of Gold, the daughter of King Esclador – swears she would sooner kill herself: she'll never spend a night with him. My love went to challenge him for her sake – he didn't hesitate; but the tyrant slew him. I'm tortured by love and pity for my sweetheart! And I've vowed that as long as my suffering lasts I'll not wear my clothes properly or other than they are now; I'll stay dressed as I am, and facing the cart, and go from court to court displaying his body till I find one to avenge his hideous death at the hands of that wild fiend.

'But you give me great comfort with that shield at your neck: you don't know, do you, who brought it or where it's from?'

'I never thought to ask!' he replied. 'But truly, I'd have gone and looked for her at once if I hadn't had another goal that makes endless demands of me. But I'm amazed by your story of the knight so full of cruelty, who carries the shield with the dragon. By the soul of King Arthur's father Uther Pendragon, I'll go and try my strength against him, whatever may befall me. God grant me a happy return, that I may avenge your love and end the knight's siege of the lady! No one who trusts in God should fear a man full of malice who neither loves nor believes in Him and isn't afraid of doing evil. I shan't stop until I've found this man and tested myself against him.'

'And I'll go with you, sir,' she said, 'and see which of you is victorious – and may God be at your side! Let's go – I know the way, and it's only right that I show you the best path. We'll reach the nunnery of Saint Damian[47] today, though I think it'll be late afternoon by the time we do. The people there are in dire distress, and I'll tell you why: they used to get their income and provisions from Montesclaire, but the Knight of the Dragon, intoxicated by the Devil as he is, will spare no one – he lets no food be taken to the abbey and is driving them wild with hunger. It's a grievous pity. They're eating roots and crab apples – and they've precious few of those.'

'It's some time,' said Perceval, 'since I've found anywhere to lodge in comfort. Let's go now, and may God guide us. I'll relieve the nuns' plight if I can; and if it please God, the peak of Montesclaire will be set free.'

With that he fell silent, not that he was ever very talkative – and indeed, no knight should ever talk too much or indulge in banter.

The girl turned her cart about to guide Perceval on his way – though she'd travelled with rather more pleasure on many occasions – and they pressed on till they reached the abbey. Seeing them coming, the blessed abbess rose and came happily to meet them. She was greatly heartened by the sign of the cross, sure that good fortune had come her way when she saw it on his shield; her heart, which had been so beset by cares, was filled with joy and her hunger and distress were forgotten the moment she beheld the cross. She hurried to meet them and welcomed them warmly, offering them lodging with the greatest kindness. Perceval wasn't slow to return his greeting to the abbess,

---

[47] '*Domin*': I am guessing that, since this comes shortly after a reference to Saint Cosmas (above, p. 410), Gerbert may have had in mind the twin physician saints Cosmas and Damian.

whose face was gaunt with hunger and deprivation – but truly, if she'd not been in such want she'd have been a fair and lovely woman. Perceval felt great pity for her.

They rode straight into the courtyard, and all the nuns came running when they heard of their arrival. They welcomed the damsel joyfully – she'd brought them instant hope of aid – and honoured Perceval highly, stabling his horse and then disarming him at once and dressing him as finely and as handsomely as they could. They all shed tears of sorrow that they couldn't offer a decent supper to Perceval and the damsel with the cart, but they'd no bread or wine or meat and no way of getting any.

Perceval went and hung his shield on a handsome pillar, while the damsel took her cart with her sweetheart's body to the chapel. Neither she nor Perceval had a bite to eat that night, and their horses had to make do with grass, for there were no oats to be had; and so they stayed till morning. And meanwhile the nuns were awake all night in worship and earnest prayer to God, that He might defend Perceval and the girl from harm.

At first light Perceval saddled his horse, and the ladies, weeping, armed and equipped him splendidly; and the girl hurried to her cart and made ready, turning the shafts towards the gate and hitching the horses; then she covered her sweetheart's body with a sheet, blackened by fire as he was, and laid him in the handsome cart before mounting one of the horses. Then she and Perceval took their leave of the abbess and the nuns and set off with all speed, straight towards the peak of Montesclaire.

But thunder and rain and lightning fell all morning until prime:* it seemed as if the earth would crumble into an abyss, so tremendous were the torrent and the lightning bolts. But the storm abated; and when he saw the weather clear Perceval looked to his right, and down in a valley, beneath a poplar, he saw four packhorses laden with provisions, driven loose by the storm and tempest. The men pursuing them were saying:

'God be praised we've escaped that perilous storm, so fierce and mighty! And may He grant us vengeance before this summer's out on the evil tyrant who abuses us and forces us to serve him: no matter what we do he never gives us cloaks or gowns – instead he strips and robs us of everything: corn, oats, meat, wine! May God, the truly divine, send us swift revenge, for there's no restraint, humility or pity in the tyrant: he's so full of cruelty that he kills anyone who prays to God! All the people are appealing to God for justice, for his destruction, that he may yet meet his master who'll rid the world of him, for no book could encompass all the evils of that man! Oh God, send him punishment for his dreadful deeds!'

Before any of them mounted they sat down to breakfast – knowing they'd have no dinner if they returned to the tyrant's camp. No one should be respected if he's supplied with food and fails to share it with the ones who've toiled to provide it! Perceval, who'd travelled all week with little comfort, turned that way and hurried towards them. They all stood up when they saw he was a knight, and he asked if they had any food to sell.

'Sir,' they said, 'you're welcome to come and eat with us and have whatever you wish – on condition that you then turn back! Take our advice and go no further: if you do, if you go beyond this mountain, you'll be killed by the one we long to see vanquished; the demon, the tyrant who's intent on doing evil, burns every knight he attacks with a shield given him by the Devil! In it the Devil fixed a dragon's head that flings forth fire to set ablaze all who challenge him: its engulfing flame sears and burns them instantly. Such a man is to be loathed indeed.'

'True enough,' said Perceval, 'but nothing will stop me trying my strength against him. But I didn't eat yesterday, this morning or last night!'

'Here!' they said. 'Dinner's ready whenever you wish – whatever the one it's meant for says! It's wrong that we have to pay him these dues – but we have no choice.'

The damsel with the cart came hurrying down, and Percival dismounted and went to meet her and took her in his outstretched arms and helped her from the cart. The men gave them bread and wine and fish and meat in abundance, and they sat beneath the poplar and ate and quelled their hunger. But the damsel, truly, had nothing but bread and spring water, despite all that was spread before them; and Percival, too, ate and drank little, for a knight shouldn't weigh himself down with food when he's about to do combat: it can greatly reduce his power. That's why Percival ate sparingly – though his horse had a good amount of oats and the carthorses had plenty.

As soon as they'd eaten they made ready again and set off on their way, straight towards the peak of Montesclaire. The damsel – her name was Claire – still carrying her lover in the cart, feared and fretted and grieved for Percival; and she told him to make the sign of the cross when he saw the Dragon Knight, for as soon as he drew near he'd see the fire and flame come belching forth, the most searing that ever was.

'But the cross will aid you against the scorching fire: your shield is a sign of that.'

'I'd trust no monk,' he said, 'more than I trust you. But enough: let's hurry – I can't wait to see this man!'

So they pressed on swiftly and made their way to the mountain top; there are a good many less beautiful, in Asturias and Ricordane.[48] A great, wide river called the Gordane ran through the valley below, and beyond the river stood the castle of Montesclaire, of wide renown – and rightly so, for it was a handsome, splendid place indeed: it hadn't been built by a stingy miser! Anyone who's seen Coucy[49] might say it was modelled on Montesclaire with its fine, strong walls and towers.

The Knight of the Dragon was camped before the main gate, to stop any supplies getting through. He'd besieged and blockaded them so long they were white and pale with hunger; but no one could get rid of him: there were some three hundred knights inside who'd endured the siege and the suffering for a long, long time, but none dared don a helm and go and do battle with him, for he feared no one; such was his faith in the Devil that he'd vowed and sworn he'd burn them all with the dragon unless the maiden of Montesclaire surrendered to him her body, her land and her people. No amount of gold or silver would buy him off: he would seize and burn them all with the fire that burst from the dragon's maw.

The people had endured the siege so long that they were dying of hunger, and said that if they stayed there any longer they would starve to death indeed; they'd have to surrender the castle next day if no help arrived. This seemed much too soon to the maiden, who was sure that aid would come: she was constantly expecting Gawain to keep the vow he'd made long before.[50]

'He'd be a fine champion if he came,' she said. 'And the one called Percival, who's so long sought the grail and the bleeding lance: if he chanced to come this way, perhaps I'd have help from him.'

But with that she suddenly ran to the windows of the hall, bent on flinging herself to her death, not wanting to live longer, for then she'd be free of her pain and torment.

---

48   The region of central France between Clermont-Ferrand and Le Puy.
49   Coucy-le-Château, a very fine castle in Picardy. As its building began in the 1220s, this was a topical as well as a local reference (and possibly helps to date Gerbert's Continuation).
50   Strictly speaking, the vow that Gawain made in Chrétien (above, p. 41) he fulfilled in the First Continuation (above, pp. 112–16); but earlier in Gerbert (p. 377) he did again say he'd go to Montesclaire.

She was about to hurl herself to the ground when her men, who loved her dearly, pulled her back; and then, as she turned her head, she saw Perceval riding down the mountain, and the white shield with the red cross hanging at his neck; she was amazed and said:

'Ah God, dear heavenly Father, who can that knight be, coming down the mountainside? And I can see a cart before him, richly draped. Ah, it's driven by the girl with her clothes inside-out! Holy Mary!' she cried. 'Now send me help! I can see good King Arthur of Britain's court has failed me: he has no knights of sufficient strength – not even one or two or three or four – to dare come and challenge my besieger; and truly, I'd rather be killed than let him lay a hand on me! But the sight of that knight riding down the mountain gives me hope: the most handsome knight in arms in all the world, I'd say!'

Perceval and the damsel halted a moment; and it wasn't long before he looked ahead and saw, on the plain at the mountain's foot, the army camped in the fields, besieging the town and the castle and the keep. They'd launched many fierce assaults and attacks on those within, but had inflicted little damage on the walls and towers and ditches; but there was no one in the castle brave enough to come out of the gate and face the knight with the dragon's head in his shield, for all who did were burnt and vanquished instantly. Perceval looked at the army and the plain filled with their tents and lodges and huts made with branches that they'd gathered in the forest; and beyond the host he saw a tree, fairer than any from there to Calabria, planted in the meadow and thick with branches. From it hung a massive bell: there aren't four men in Scotland with the strength, if they tried to ring it, to move its tongue more than an inch! As soon as the bell rang, everyone in the castle knew there was to be battle outside the walls.

The fair damsel who drove the cart called Perceval to her and told him he should go to the tree and not hesitate to ring the bell. 'Then you'll see the army rush to the alert and the Knight of the Dragon will come. They'll let the two of you join battle and will do you no harm, I promise you: he's made them all swear that any man who can defeat him will have nothing to fear from any of them.'

'My word,' said Perceval, 'he's decent enough in that respect, at least! I commend you to God – I'm going at once.'

And with that he turned and left her and galloped straight off to the tree, and she raised her right hand and blessed him with the sign of the cross in the name of the heavenly King; and there she stayed in floods of tears.

Perceval rode up to the tree where the bell hung, and swore by everything most holy that he'd try his strength and ring it if he could. So he prepared to sound the bell, and gripped the rope and pulled; and the bell rang out so loud and clear that the whole castle echoed and the army leapt to the alert – its peal reached every plain and hill and valley for three leagues all around. The knights and maidens in the town heard the sound and climbed up to the walls that instant – even the limping and the lame came and ranged along the walls, all finding a place to prop themselves; and the lady, with her maids around her, hurried to the top of the tower.

The Knight of the Dragon was making ready, wondering who the man could be with the courage and strength to ring the bell so loudly and with such force. 'It'll be one of King Arthur's knights,' he said, 'come here to prove his mettle. But he's going to die a foul death!'

He had a cloth spread inside his tent and was armed without delay. They came running to lace his shoes – of fine and costly mail they were – and his strong chausses, triple-plied, tied with superb iron belts; and a young man fastened his golden spurs. Over his haqueton he donned a hauberk, edged with gold and damask; it was light and strong and tightly meshed, forged from iron purified five times over. Then he girded his sword at once: it was sharper than a sickle – and had harvested many heads! He kept swearing that the man was mad to want to come and challenge him, and that he'd soon show him the power that lay in his shield! Ablaze with rage, his heart filled with wrath, he mounted his horse and started hurling threats at Perceval. He had a strong, tough, costly helm fitted without more ado – four boys laced it over his mail hood and skullcap; but they felt more fear than love for him, and were whispering prayers for the downfall of that faithless, evil tyrant who'd abjured God.

Chafing at all the time it was taking, he slung his shield round his neck at once – black as any berry it was; and with the shield in place, convinced that the demonic head would engulf all foes in fire, he feared no one any more than a cabbage-leaf! He didn't care about the women and children left bereft by all his killings – but if he didn't completely mend his ways he'd soon have his just deserts, in the shape of measureless, indescribable torment. A man who serves the Devil should feel alarm and dread indeed, for in the end he gets what he deserves: everlasting Hell.

He took up his lance with its piercing head, thick and stout and strong, and rode from camp. The men of his host came with him – but didn't follow too closely: they drew up around the field. His heart full of rage, he thrust in his spurs and yelled terrible threats at Perceval: he was so cruel and full of witchery that he thought he'd have him burnt in no time. But there's many a gap between thought and deed: he might soon rue the day he met this foe! He charged at a gallop, and when Perceval saw him coming, and his shield blacker than the crudest ink, and the fire bursting from the dragon's mouth and scorching the meadow, he sat firmly on his Aragonese destrier and set his shield before him. The demon in the dragon's head, hurling the fire and flame, now saw the cross and was filled with dread, for Jesus Christ the King won the battle on the cross and so broke into Hell and freed His friends who were suffering dire torment; and in terror of the cross on which Christ was crucified, the demon howled and bellowed like a bull. The people of the castle wrung their hands and tore their hair and wailed with fear for Perceval; but he spurred his horse and charged at the Knight of the Dragon with all the speed his horse could summon – as fast as a buck or a stag. They could both be sure of a fearsome battle! The Knight of the Dragon blazed with excitement when he saw Perceval, so fearless, charging with such speed and fury; and as they closed they levelled their lances, aiming to strike with all their might with the sharp steel heads. But the foul and ghastly fire that burst from the dragon's maw burned the whole of Perceval's lance – even the head! – for it was the fire of Hell, which consumes whatever it touches. The knight with the dragon on his grim, dark shield met Perceval with such a ferocious blow that he smashed his lance into ten pieces; but it didn't do a farthing's worth of damage to his shield! The horses were running straight and swift, at such unstoppable speed that they collided head to head. Now hear what great good fortune God bestowed on Perceval: as the horses crashed head on, the fire, so the book informs me, seared and scorched their heads and necks – and they'd both been handsome beasts; and the knights, too, met with such force that they almost crashed head to head and their shields, for certain, smashed together. Both the watching host and the people in the castle were terrified, and when they saw the fire erupt they were sure Perceval was burnt along with his horse. But he wasn't – just listen to this wonder: the wood within the shield's red cross, which came from the true cross on which God was crucified, protected him from the scorching fire and he suffered no harm at all; and when the cross clashed with the demon it created mighty chaos: the cross's power made the demon leap from the dragon – it had no strength against the cross and dared abide no longer! It flew away in the shape of a black, black crow, accompanied by such claps and bolts of thunder that Perceval and the Knight of the Dragon were both knocked senseless, and stayed so for a long while.

The people of the castle were overjoyed to see the demon flee in the form of a crow; and the men of the Dragon Knight's army began to talk and said:

'It's no fiction that a man who serves the Devil will end up damned! Ah, what a wretch he is who forgets the good of his soul for the sake of worldly pleasure! The man who covets earthly gain, and fails to cleanse himself through confession, and refuses to do penance and repent to God, has surely lost both body and soul! But God is merciful when He sees a sinner abandon evil and embrace good for fear of His disfavour; and when he goes to confession and clasps his hands in prayer, then, if he does the penance demanded of him, he is remade. The Holy Spirit needs to intervene: in all the world there's no weightier burden to bear than sin, and it'll be the death of all who fail to shed it. Misdeeds will always be revealed! This lord of ours, who's committed so much evil, can clearly see now – if he will – that the Devil has betrayed him: now the Devil's ways are plain!'

The Knight of the Dragon recovered his strength; but Perceval leapt up even sooner. They saw their horses were burnt and charred, but the demon who'd sent the blaze from the dragon's maw was gone – there were no more flames or fire; Perceval rejoiced at this, but the Dragon Knight was distraught. Both now sprang to the attack, clutching and drawing their swords of steel and exchanging such fearsome blows that, whenever they found an opening, they drew blood and stained the grass: soon the ground was crimson. The Knight of the Dragon was taken aback when he failed to get the better of Perceval, but however much he battered his shield he couldn't breach it. He was frothing with rage, so incensed that he charged to grab him with his bare hands; but Perceval, stout and strong in bone and sinew, pre-empted this and seized him in a mighty grip. They grappled and tore at each other – no one could tell who was coming off worse! – and neither would relent or yield an inch: so fierce and equal was the fight that neither could escape his foe – they were both so in awe of each other's strength that when either had a hold of his enemy he wouldn't let him out of his grasp. They both stood firm and upright, and dealt each other such ferocious blows that both of them were stunned.

The people of the castle watched it all, and some were prostrate on the ground, praying to the King of Glory to give strength and victory to their champion. The Maiden of the Circle of Gold was wringing her hands in dismay, and appealing to Holy Mary to beg Her dear son to protect the knight who'd joined battle for her:

'For truly, my mind's made up: if he's killed in the fight I'll throw myself from this tower!' She was in utter turmoil.

The battling Perceval and the Dragon Knight struggled and strove and drove themselves on and struck with their fists and their swords alike till they hewed straps from their mail collars, slashed the laces from their helms and were finally so exhausted that they collapsed on the ground. But ill luck befell Perceval: as he landed his sword slipped from his grasp, and the knight who was bent on evil – and had already done so much – seized it and leapt back to his feet, clutching both their naked swords, and advanced on him. Perceval scrambled up at once, and almost died of anguish when he saw his sword in the knight's hand. He came at him boldly, raising his shield to protect himself, but the knight had little fear of him now and began to show it: he knew how to use a sword, and dealt him such a blow in the side that he cut away a great chunk of flesh and the blood began to pour. But before he could step back Perceval seized hold of him, and in the winking of an eye he prised the steel sword from his grip and cried:

'Hang on to yours, knight – I've got mine!'

The Dragon Knight, with his fierce, bold heart, answered: 'True, but it's cost you – take a look at your side: it's gushing blood! I tell you, neither your white shield nor the cross will save you now!'

'We'll see who comes off best today!' said Perceval, and he sprang to the attack. The Dragon Knight didn't shrink from him, but assailed him with his sword, and they threw themselves boldly into the fray and dealt each other cruel and mighty blows. They split open helms, smashed rings from hauberks, beat and pounded, smote and hammered. The Dragon Knight was amazed that he could do no damage to the shield with the red cross, and sensed that Perceval was stronger and fitter than at the start.

'Knight,' he roared, 'if it weren't for that shield of yours you'd have been finished long ago! You work by enchantment, not chivalry! You must do, to have overcome the one who threw fire from my shield! If you weren't bewitched you'd never have survived against me! But listen: if you're brave enough to lay down your shield I promise to lay down mine. And I tell you, if you dare do this you'll win a hundred times more praise if you then go on to vanquish me! Here: since I made the challenge I'll lay mine down first.'

'Gladly,' said Perceval. 'Let's do it now.'

And they both took off their shields and laid them down in the middle of the field. They clutched their swords of tempered steel, gleaming, sharp, and advanced upon each other, and aimed and dealt the most awesome blows: the wounds inflicted would surely never heal. Both knights almost burst with anger at failing to defeat the other – they'd made it clear there was no love lost!

On the sword-fight raged, so long that even the stronger weakened: the flesh of both was black and blue from the blows that they'd exchanged. But Perceval, naked sword in hand, launched himself at his foe once more, and with a backward cut caught the knight in the side, so hard that he slashed mail rings from his hauberk – it wasn't worth a farthing against that sword! – and sliced so deep into his flesh that the bowels came spilling out. But the Knight of the Dragon was tough and strong; when he felt the blow he summoned all his strength – before Perceval killed him he'd sell his life dearly if he could! – and flinging down his sword of steel, resolved to win or lose all, he ran and seized Perceval round the waist in an agonising hold. Perceval likewise gripped the knight as he drew him tight into his grasp; but the knight didn't loose his hold at all – his strength was great indeed. Both knights strove with might and main for the honour of victory.

Suddenly a girl came galloping up on a piebald palfrey, summoning all the speed she could; but she wouldn't address the fighting knights as they pummelled each other with their fists – instead she dismounted, picked up Perceval's shield and mounted again that instant. Perceval, embroiled in battle, suddenly saw she'd hung the shield from her neck and was carrying it off. He was none too pleased – he was furious! He had the Dragon Knight now with his back bent double, and he couldn't resist, for his wound was giving him terrible pain, splitting open and pouring blood; and Perceval kept pounding him with his fists till he battered him to the ground and laid him out flat. Then he reached out and picked up his sword again; and blazing mad at the theft of his shield, beside himself with rage and fury, not knowing who the girl was who'd taken it, he said to the knight:

'Beg for mercy!'

'Not from you!' the knight replied. 'I know you've wounded me mortally: even if you have mercy on me I'll die. What a fool I was to pay homage to the Devil – he's sent me to my downfall here! I see now he's deceived me, and I must submit to death.'

'But if you could be healed,' said Perceval, 'would you believe in God and His great power?'

'Yes,' said the knight, 'but it's impossible! No doctor in the world could heal this wound!'

'What reward would you give,' asked Perceval, 'to the man who cured and healed you?'

And he answered: 'My whole kingdom!'

'Then by my soul,' said Perceval, 'heed my advice and you'll be restored to happiness and health and healed of all infirmity before you see the sun go down.'

'Go on then, sir,' said the knight. 'I wish for nothing as much as my health.'

'You'll have it,' said Perceval, 'if you do as I say.'

'I shall – I'll not resist.'

'Then listen, friend. Don't delay, but call for the priest and make confession: cleanse yourself of the wrongs you've done in this world and be repentant, for your soul is a hundred thousand times more wounded than your body! If you'd died now unrepentant, all penitence thereafter would have been in vain. Trust in holy confession, let your heart be repentant and contrite, and I tell you in all truthfulness your soul will then be saved; if you don't it'll perish and be damned with your body at the judgement, and suffer the agonising torment of Hell – from which God defend us! My dear friend, make amends now and beg God for mercy and forgiveness and vow never to sin again. Do you know what you'll have in return? Joy and health in Paradise and everlasting bliss, free of all suffering. Even the greatest joys in this world fade and die; this world is a battle: no one living in it is at rest. Covetousness and violence strive constantly to possess us all – both knights and clerks! The latter go to Paris to study ordinances and books of law until they're judicious and wise; then they become lawyers and uphold cases for money, and then they truly sell their souls, and it'll send them all to Hell! What a fate they have in store! And the judges, the men of power, plunder and rob the people till they're stripped of gold and silver. And knights are becoming lawyers, too, coming and going to lawsuits every day! When a worthy man, with wealth worth grabbing, is involved in a case, the jury all corrupt him, happily offering their support for money; then if he pleads well and wins the case they promptly expose him, making him repeat his pledges to them, putting him in transgression of the law! So he's charged on his own testimony and piled with fines! A knight does himself no favours by bringing a lawsuit against another! Such tribulations they cause each other! They run the risk of boiling in the vast cauldron of Hell! And none of them will be litigants there! There they'll have justice for their wrongs! But you can have health in soul and body now, for God who is merciful will heal you of the deep wound that afflicts your soul, so grievously hurt by sin: you'll be saved from it entirely if you truly repent and sincerely confess. Confession is right and holy when nothing is concealed or feigned. Think upon your sins for God's sake; true confession is a doctor that saves you – without cauterising or surgery! – from the ever-burning wounds of Hell. Bind yourself firmly now to good, and heal your soul of the wound in your side.'

The Knight of the Dragon realised Perceval wasn't deceiving him but advising him for the best. 'Come, then!' he said. 'Bring me the priest at once – I need him to come and help me as you said: I'm going to die of the wound in my side – it's inevitable.'

So Perceval sent a knight from the army to the castle to fetch a priest. He came at once, and the Knight of the Dragon, reflecting deeply on his sins, sat with the priest beside him, and there and then began to make confession; he cried and lamented, fearing terribly for his soul and weeping bitterly for his sins. He sighed from the heart and wrung his hands and gazed to heaven; the hardest heart in the world would have felt pity at seeing him. The priest didn't dally; when the knight had confessed every sin he could think of he gave him absolution – and good instruction; and this new knight of God crossed himself over and over and lay down facing the east, and died while praying to God. The soul departed, the body stretched out.

Perceval delayed no longer; he summoned the men of the knight's army, who came and quickly disarmed the knight and wrapped him in a shroud. They were overjoyed that he'd confessed his misdeeds. And all the people of the castle came thronging forth to meet Perceval, and brought him a horse, big and handsome, swift and strong, splendidly harnessed and finely saddled, that had cost more than a hundred pounds. Every girl and lady in the castle came to greet him and gave him a glorious welcome. The Maiden of the Circle of Gold rejoiced like no one ever since; she wiped her eyes on her tunic, weeping as she was with joy and relief, and more than a hundred times over she blessed the hour that Perceval had come to her land, for he'd restored her to happiness.

'You've rescued me from dire peril: the Knight of the Dragon, now dead, would have wrought my ruin! I can never thank or reward you enough, but if you wish you can take my person, my land and my wealth: everything is freely yours – you've fully earned it. But by God and Saint David, send us something to eat!'

Perceval heard her and summoned the army's leaders at once. They heeded his every command and refused him nothing, for their lord had made them promise faithfully that any man who could vanquish him would have their full and prompt obedience. His order was carried throughout the army: all the food they had was to be taken to the castle. No loaf or cake or cask or barrel or cow or sheep or pig remained! Everything was transported there, so that everyone, nobles and commoners alike, had enough and to spare: now they were rich and prosperous!

Then the men of the army took their lord, who'd wronged so many people, and made him a strong and sturdy litter from two poles, and laid him in it, wrapped in a costly woven cloth. And because he was confessed they treated him with honour, covering his body with sumptuous silk, most rich and rare. Then they lifted him on to a pair of horses, and Perceval bade them take him back to their own land and bury him with honour. They departed, taking their lord with them, while the people of the castle rejoiced and fêted Perceval.

He mounted the horse they'd given him, and without more ado he went to take his leave of the maiden. She thought she'd die of grief when she heard he meant to go; she pleaded with him, saying:

'Stay, good sir: I'll see you're honoured here as highly as can be!'

'No, truly, damsel, I'm not going to pass your gate: I'm going straight after the girl who took my shield. I shan't stay anywhere for two days together till I've recovered it and found out why she carried it off – if God keeps me from harm and illness or capture.'

With that he took his leave and rode away.

But he hadn't gone far, it seems, before he ran into a fair, most comely girl. Leaving her horse standing quietly she dropped to her knees on the path before him and said:

'God bless you, gentle sir. You've taken revenge on my sworn enemy, who killed my love who lies in the cart, blackened by fire and covered with the cloth of gold. I wore my clothes inside-out, but now I'm wearing them properly, for thanks to you my vow is fulfilled. I'll have my love buried at the abbey of Saint Souplis, in the castle of the fair Maiden of the Circle of Gold. Wherever I retreat to then – to some wood or other wild place – I'll build a hermitage and pray for my love, and also for myself, but especially for you, that God in His power may grant you honour and joy and guide you to find what your heart desires.'

'May it please Him to grant me that indeed,' said Perceval. 'Rise now, damsel, by the faith you owe God, for no knight should let a girl stay kneeling so for long. God guide you to such prayer as brings salvation for your soul. But if you will, dear girl, tell me now, in God's name, if you've seen a lady pass by with a shield: it's maddening – I don't know which way she went.'

'She's heading yonder, sir,' she replied, 'towards that great forest.'

Perceval set off without delay, commending her to God. He asked her nothing more but rode straight on, determined to track down the girl who'd carried off his shield.

Meanwhile the damsel made for the gate of Montesclaire with the cart she'd driven for so many weeks. It was no trouble to her now: she passed through the gate and pressed on to the abbey, where she had her sweetheart buried with all due honour. But she didn't linger; she departed at once, weeping all the while, and journeyed on till she came to the wood of Claradeure, on a wild, forbidding mountain, where she found a ruined chapel and an old hut standing beside a spring. A hermit by the name of Heracle had lived there for more than a hundred years but had lately died. And there she stopped, the fair damsel – who rapidly lost her bright and rosy hue, and little wonder, exposed as she was to wind and weather and so often forced to go hungry: it was bound to make her pale. There was nothing to eat but roots, wild apples, beech nuts and acorns that she gathered in the wood – but she had no appetite for anything else. And so she spent her life in penance for her beloved. Jesus grant protection and a good end to all women who love faithfully, like this damsel, who loved with a pure heart and ended her life in service to God. But I'll leave her now: I want to tell of Perceval.

Mordrain

The story says that after leaving the fair damsel who retreated to the hermitage, Perceval, who suffered such toil and trials, rode on for a whole week as chance took him. On and on he pressed, without encountering any adventure, till he entered a vast forest where the girl who'd taken his shield had gone; but however hard he rode he could see no sign of her.

Then suddenly he heard the ringing of a bell; he steered his ever-willing horse towards the sound, and found himself descending through the great, dense forest to a valley, where he came upon a handsome abbey standing by a river. He rode up to the gate, and found one of the monks sitting on a stool. He greeted him with all due courtesy, and the monk at once replied likewise, having a kind, sincere and compassionate heart.

'Sir,' he said, 'you're welcome to stay here if you wish: you'll have good lodging.'

'Thank you,' said Perceval. 'If I carried on I don't know where I'd stay.'

And he went up the steps, fully armed as he was, and through an open door and straight into a hall. Monks came hurrying to welcome him and helped him to disarm; they realised he'd been travelling a long while and were eager to serve and honour him. They took his horse straight to the stable and showed Perceval all possible respect, ushering him to a chamber where they provided him that night with everything he wished. After he'd eaten Perceval lay down in a well made bed and refreshed himself with a good night's sleep till the bell rang for prime next morning.

Then he rose and went to the chapel to hear the divine service. He was surprised to be confronted by a beautifully wrought screen, covered with a fine iron grille. Through it he could see a handsome altar, the most splendid ever beheld, gorgeously draped with the richest cloth; it was a truly glorious sight. Before this altar stood a priest dressed in an alb and chasuble, beautiful and perfectly fitted, and on his head sat a mitre; and to assist him in the service he was attended by an angel. As Perceval stared, in the middle of the chapel he saw a lovely bed. Delighted by these sights Perceval made to enter – but there was no way in: he could see no open door. The bed, he saw, was covered with sheets of perfect white, and he was sure there was a man or woman lying in it, but to his surprise there was no one around who might tell him who it was. He knelt before the screen and grille and saw the priest arrive and conduct a most holy service. And when it came to the sacrament and he raised the body of God on high, the one who lay on the bed suddenly sat bolt upright. Perceval, enthralled, saw the figure bare from the head to the navel, with a fabulous crown of finest gold poised upon his head. As Perceval gazed, rapt and wondering, the figure stretched both hands towards the body of God and cried:

'True father of the world, true God, be mindful of my prayers, for in you is all my hope!'

He said no more, but he kept his arms thrust heavenward. Perceval had heard his words and pressed closer to the grille to peer at him in fascination; and as he did, he saw that his body, arms and head were covered in wounds, and so was his face, and the wounds were bright red as though they were fresh: Perceval was amazed. When the priest had finished singing and brought God's body to the figure on the bed, he received it with deep devotion. Then the priest took the crown from his head and placed it on the altar, whereupon the figure lay down once more and covered himself completely with the white sheets so no part of him could be seen. Perceval, who'd been watching him intently, looked back now towards the altar; but the priest had gone – he didn't know where: he could see no sign of him. He was filled with wonder, feeling sure that it all had deep meaning.

He left the chapel and returned to the hall, and asked for the monk who'd offered him lodging. He came as quickly as he could, and Perceval told him everything he'd seen in the chapel, just as you've heard described.

'I yearn to know what it meant!' he said. 'It's clearly of great significance. I'm all ears! I have to know! In God's name, sir, tell me the truth!'

'Listen now,' the monk replied. 'Make yourself comfortable here beside me, and I'll tell you a story that any king or duke or prince or count should delight to hear. It's a story well worth telling, one that brings those who're willing to renounce evil to a firm belief in God. Hear now this true and wondrous tale: I can vouch for its veracity.

'More than forty years after Christ's crucifixion, there was a heathen king on the coast near Jerusalem – and I can name both him and his city: Evalac was his name, and his city was called Sarras; at that time it was a finer citadel and town than Arras, and possessed a mighty fleet. From the city's name came the people's: Saracens; and this Evalac, as I say, was their lord and king. But Tholomé, a king of Syria,[51] waged war on him and laid waste all his land. But Joseph of Arimathea, a man full of goodness, who

---

[51] 'Sire'.

for five years, winter and summer, had been a soldier of Pilate (to whom Judas delivered Jesus Christ who was then hung on the cross), this Joseph came to Evalac with his brother-in-law Seraphé and a company of twenty knights. He found Evalac ablaze with rage and anguish, but told him that if he did what he was about to say he'd restore his land to him. Evalac agreed, and Joseph promptly won him over and persuaded him to renounce his false religion; and because of his faith in the King of Glory, Evalac grew in strength and was victorious, utterly crushing the fearsome Tholomé. When it came to his baptism, they made Evalac change his name: in his new faith he was called Mordrain; and he and Joseph were loyal friends.

'Not long after, Joseph came here to this land – not as a beleaguered exile but with sixty other good and godly people, including two fine, fair ladies devoted to God. One, named Philosofine,[52] brought with her a trencher that shone brighter than the moon, and the other brought a lance that bled unceasingly. And Joseph had a vessel, the most beautiful ever seen by man. He converted the people of the land to God and to righteous ways.

'But they had a most cruel and wicked king by the name of Crudel, and the moment he heard about Joseph and his company he had them seized and taken away and foully treated for baptising his people. His henchmen urged him to throw them in prison, which he did, in dreadful conditions, with nothing at all to eat. He thought they'd be driven mad with hunger and thirst and despair. And there they lay, on scraps of straw, for fully forty days, and in all that time, I promise you, they had nothing to eat or drink.

'But their health and colour never faded, for Joseph, that saintly man of great renown, had the holy grail in his keeping, and when it was displayed to them they were surrounded by such radiance and provided with such abundance that their every need and wish was answered. So there they stayed, in no distress at all, till forty days had passed.

'Then word reached King Mordrain that Joseph was imprisoned, and as soon as he heard the news he summoned his people and assembled his army and all his ships; a huge fleet put to sea, and they sailed on till one day at dawn they reached King Crudel's land. They set ablaze every house and croft, took captive every man they found; and when King Crudel heard this he was incensed and mustered his forces and marched to confront them. In the battle that ensued there was great slaughter; many a noble man's son was slain. And the two kings clashed in person; they unhorsed each other and battled on till both were exhausted and couldn't take another blow. What more should I tell you? If I were to recount King Mordrain's feats of arms in detail it would be wearisome to hear; in short, he beheaded Crudel, and few of King Crudel's men escaped. And after winning this great victory he went fully armed, shield hung at his neck, straight to the prison where his dear friend Joseph had been held so long and set him free. Joseph was overjoyed and filled with loving gratitude. But then, when Mordrain removed his armour, they saw that his head and body and arms and face were covered in wounds, so many that any man who saw him and the state of his wounds would have expected him to die within the hour: they were a mass of crimson blood. But listen to this wonder: he felt no pain, and his armour, truly, was nowhere pierced or broken. His men, thronging round, were baffled: no one could find a single hole or rent through which he could have been wounded. But wounded he was. But listen on, and you'll hear what happened then.

---

[52] Earlier in Gerbert's Continuation we are told that this is the name of Perceval's mother: above, p. 364.

'In the morning Joseph came to the king and had a handsome table brought before him, a delight and pleasure to behold, and had it draped in the manner of an altar. On it he placed the grail and began a most sweet and reverent service; and by all accounts King Mordrain saw the grail, that holy, spiritual vessel, and stepped straight forward to gaze into it and discover its great wonders. But this was not a wise move, for no heart could conceive, no tongue relate, no eyes behold the great wonders of the holy grail. And at that moment an angel descended from heaven clutching a sword more than six feet long, and it was all aflame; King Mordrain was stunned and stopped in his tracks, stock still. And a voice rang out, saying:

'"Mordrain, you have done wrong, and now bear a burden from which you will never be free: for the rest of your days your wounds will stay fresh as new. And I tell you, you will never be healed, nor will you pass from this world, until the coming of one who will be called a true knight, so beloved of Christ that he will be fully confessed and purged of sin; only then will your burden be lifted, and you will die in his arms. Meanwhile you will lie in this bed, beneath these sheets – such is Christ's command – and must expect to taste no food but the bread of life."

'Come the summer, the king will have been like this for three hundred years. There: now you've heard the truth. And we've been told that the one who's seeking the grail and the bleeding lance is already in this land; all the king's wounds would be healed if he came: may God in His mercy guide him here!'

Perceval was amazed to hear the monk's revelations about Mordrain, the king he'd seen, and very upset that he hadn't brought an end to the adventure and healed the king. He would gladly have set about it if it were God's will and he could have entered the chapel, but to his great frustration he could find no door or window to let him in. With sorrowful sighs he prayed earnestly to God to give him the means to recover soon his lost shield – its loss weighed terribly on his heart – and to find the lance and the holy grail, and to release from pain the king who lay wounded in the chapel. Then he called to the monk and asked for his arms and equipment to be brought.

'Rest here tonight, good sir,' the monk replied. 'You needn't worry: you and your horse will be well provided for.'

'I can't stay, truly, sir,' said Perceval. 'I've embarked upon a mission I can't neglect.'

So the monk went straight to fetch his arms, and brought him bread and cheese to eat and wine to drink. Perceval ate hurriedly, then armed and mounted at once, and with no desire to linger he rode through the gate and was gone.

But before the end of that dark night he would find himself in mortal danger: unless God who sent His son to earth to save sinners chose to protect him, he would never see bright day again.

The Ivory Chest

Perceval rode on without stopping, fearing and suspecting nothing, unaware of the dire trouble brewing and about to strike. As he emerged from the forest he looked to his right and saw a city, mightily defended by walls and towers and sea: I couldn't guess or tell its wealth and riches. At the entrance to the city stood a castle on a hill, the best constructed in all the world, with walls and fortified towers all of finely hewn sandstone. The keep was tall and handsome, with an array of marble columns in the windows on every side: there was no fairer tower in the world; and I promise you, at every window and battlement in the castle there hung a shield. King Arthur would have needed to spend every penny he owned before he captured that castle and took those shields down! The lord of the castle was a man to be reckoned with indeed.

Perceval headed straight towards it; he'd have done better to avoid it, but many a man, I've heard it said, goes merrily into trouble! Through the gate he rode – he was carrying no lance or shield, but was armoured and his sword was at his belt. A lady, loosely clad because of the heat, came to meet him with an escort of more than twenty knights, and with her she brought a child who seemed to give her great delight. He was certainly a handsome child: it would be hard to find one fairer; he was two and a half years old and her only son and heir, and there was no one she would trust to look after him. Perceval watched as she came down from the castle, dressed only in her bliaut,* without a cloak. He quickly dismounted and greeted the lady and her escort most politely like the courteous knight he was, and then asked if he might have lodging. The lady, esteemed and praised both far and wide, being endowed with all graces, replied eloquently, saying:

'As is the established custom of this castle, you shall have such lodging as we can offer, sir, and may God who dwells in heaven on high send you all joy and keep you from harm and woe.'

Without further words the lady and her knights happily led him into the castle amid much good cheer. Perceval was delighted to have found lodging. He was quickly helped from his hauberk and his arms were laid on a table, while a boy took his horse to the stable and unharnessed him. The lady had a tunic and surcoat brought for her guest – but I've a feeling he'd pay a high price for them before he left. So Perceval dressed. No sooner had he done so than he looked round and noticed, in the middle of the hall, a chest – and no common sort but one made of finest ivory: no man, I promise you, ever beheld one so fair, with bands of gold and silver studded with all manner of fabulous, precious, priceless jewels. It was curtained with gorgeous silk from Palestine,[53] and around it, in splendid golden candlesticks, stood four ever-burning candles; and I can tell you in certain truth that its lock was peerlessly fine, with a key hanging from it of exquisite gold. All the riches of the duke of Austria[54] couldn't buy a chest as magnificent as this. When Perceval saw it he said he'd never set eyes on one so fine, and longed to know if it was a reliquary. He had to ask, and drew close to the lady and said:

'Tell me, lady, what relics lie in that chest? It isn't covered with linen but with silk of richest hue.'

'God love me, sir, I can't tell you: no one has been able to discover that since the day it came here. Let me tell you what happened: this is the true story.

'More than ten years ago, I'd say, on the sea down below us a swan came swimming to the shore. It was pulling a barge by a silver chain attached to its neck, and crying so loudly that it roused the whole city. My husband and his brothers ran down to the shore with a great company of knights, and aboard the barge they found this chest and the candlesticks, and the candles burning brightly, and a message in French in tiny letters telling the reader that the chest – the very one you see there with your own eyes – should be brought here and kept in its present honoured state. And the message added, and insisted it was true, that no one would be able to open it but the finest and most renowned

---

[53] 'Palatyne'.
[54] A notable figure, Duke Leopold V having been the famous captor of Richard Lionheart (and recipient of a huge ransom for his release) as he returned from the Third Crusade.

of all knights living; and when he'd opened it and revealed what was inside, my husband and his three brothers – who're very worried about their father, who went to Arthur's court and never returned – would feel both happiness and sorrow when they saw what it contained. They yearn to know why it'll cause them sorrow and joy; so they go each day and guard the main route through the forest – in fact all seven main paths – and many knights with their wives and sweethearts go with them for amusement's sake; they do this every day but Sunday, truly; and when a knight chances by in search of adventure to enhance his honour and renown, they stop him and bring him here to see if he can unlock the chest. But I swear not a single one has done it, though at least a hundred have come and tried in vain. Yesterday they caught Sir Gawain, a knight of the highest worth – though before they took him he defended himself most valiantly and did them a deal of damage! He'd have done still more had the smarter knights not taken him to the ladies – he put up no resistance then! And they brought him here to see if he were worthy enough to open the chest and reveal what it contains – but he couldn't. And my husband swore by his life that Gawain would remain a captive because he was of good King Arthur of Britain's household. He'll stay so till we find the one who can open this mysterious chest. Then he and his fellow prisoners will be set free, to honour and praise the one who has tried and triumphed. There – now I've explained the position and the castle's custom; and may God grant you a joyous outcome, that you may leave exultant!'

'God hear your prayer indeed!' said Perceval, as he sat forlorn and distressed about Gawain, held imprisoned.

At that very moment the lord arrived, fully armed and lance in hand, with all his company; his brothers and the rest were likewise armed impressively, and each had his wife or lover at his side, except the lord himself, who didn't want his wife to leave his son, for he loved and adored him more than anything in the world. The knights came merrily up to the hall, while pages and squires took charge of the whinnying horses. Perceval wouldn't stand; he sat and waited till they'd all poured into the hall. Each of them had a sword at his belt, his helmet laced, a lance in hand. The lord was at the forefront – his name was Leander; his brothers were Evander and Marmadus,[55] the duke of Catenouse, and the fourth of them was called Meliadas: that was his proper name. They were fierce and strapping figures, and haughty, too, and bold and brave and tough and strong: the least worthy of them would have had no fear of the finest, most battle-hardened knight. The lord strode straight to Perceval, giving him no welcome – in fact he didn't deign to speak to him at all, except to tell him to go and see if he could open the chest.

'You must,' he said, 'before you get anything to eat or drink! Come on, up you get! You've got to do this first!'

'I remember what the lady said: she's explained already. I shan't refuse.'

So said Perceval, and he rose and turned towards the chest; but he'd have done better to take two steps back than one step forward: unless God, the true Father, watches over him, many a man pays dearly for his courage. But he stepped calmly up to the chest, took hold of the key and slipped it in the lock. The four brothers and their company were gathered all around. Perceval turned the key just once; it connected with the bolt; the chest was unlocked and he opened the lid. The lord at the front and his brothers and the knights and many of their wives pressed forward in a mighty throng, all desperate

---

[55] At this point he is called 'Enardus', but subsequently Marmadus.

to see what lay inside. The lord looked first – and saw a slain knight lying there, his body richly covered with the finest cloth. And as the chest was opened, such a beautiful fragrance wafted forth that they were all amazed, and the knights and ladies, more than five hundred, swore upon their souls that neither musk nor incense smelled so sweet. They weren't looking at the chest that had come on the barge: most eyes were on the body. It was shrouded by the sheets, but they could see the right arm and the hand quite openly, and in it was an unsealed scroll, written in letters of gold. The lord took the scroll from the hand and gave it to someone to read; had he read it himself he'd have been stricken with the greatest anguish of his life. The one who'd read it said to him:

'Sir, look beneath the sheet and see if you knew the one who lies there when he was alive: this letter says he was slain by the man who just opened the chest!'

And the lord drew back the great, rich, purple sheet and looked straight into the dead man's face. He knew at once it was his father, his eye and brain pierced by a javelin; after looking for a moment he was sure, and cried:

'My brothers, it's your father who lies here dead!'

He collapsed upon the body in a swoon, and his brothers fainted likewise; and when they came round they cursed their lives, and said as they rose:

'Does this explain the prediction that we yearned to understand? Is this the joy-and-sorrow we were told we'd feel?'

'We should feel grief indeed at the sight of our father, lying here slain; but as for the joy, the only joy I can see will lie in vengeance!'

'But alas! How can we ever have revenge? Our father was king of this great realm – if I slew his killer with my lance a hundred times we'd still not be avenged!'

The lord and his brothers collapsed a second time, and lay there for a long while in a faint; and Perceval, seeing the lord's passionate grief, thought coming there had been a big mistake!

'Oh!' he thought. 'Was any man ever in such a plight? If God wants me dead I'll have to accept it – there's no way out! I think Judgement Day's arrived for me! I've no weapon, no armour – I hope God wasn't expecting me to do a final worthy deed for my soul's sake!'

He saw the lady who'd offered him lodging standing there beside him, along with her much-loved son; and he also saw the brothers and the other knights recovering from their faint, and all bent on cutting him to pieces! He was horrified: he couldn't see any escape! He wished he'd been in Nijmegen, or Brindisi or Barletta![56] He was faced by a sea of foes: every knight and servant present was filled with mortal loathing! Then he spotted an axe with a willow handle hanging on a wall; it was sharp and honed, so he sprang and grabbed it. Then he seized hold of the lady's son and, wrapping his surcoat round his own left arm,[57] he gripped the boy beneath his armpit and picked him up, taking care not to hurt the child, noble soul that he was, while in his other hand he brandished the axe with its massive blade and its handle six feet long. He was determined to put up a fearsome fight before he was killed or captured, and like the valiant man he was he made a stand in the centre of the hall, and before he could be silenced he swore by God he'd sell himself dear. The lord cried back:

'Truly, knight, you're wasting your time! I'm not letting anyone kill you but my brothers. They'll avenge their father's death, treacherously slain by you – treachery

---

[56] *'a Nimaie ou a Brandis ou a Barlet'*.
[57] i.e. to protect the arm that will be wrapped around the boy.

alone must have made you kill him: what other reason could there be? As a murderer you took his life, and I'll have you pulled apart by horses – God damn me if I don't!'

'I deny treachery!' cried Perceval. 'Indeed I do! I'll vanquish any man, however strong, who lays that charge on me! I'm sorry I killed him, but it was his own fault, truly! I remember now: he hit me first, most haughtily – a mighty blow with his lance, it was, right across my shoulders! I was a simple, wayward fool and thought King Arthur had granted me all your father's arms as I'd requested – so help me God, I truly believed I was meant to have them there and then, so naïve was I![58] Kay told me to go and take them, so I thought I was doing nothing wrong when I told your father to take off his armour, and to be quick about it, or I'd strip them from him by force – I wasn't waiting! My words enraged him – he was fuming – and he didn't play around: he gave me a proper blow with his pinewood lance; then I threw a javelin at him that pierced his brain, and I'm sorry to say the blow was fatal. Now you think me your enemy, but I'm ready to make amends: I'll agree to anything you ask – short of death or loss of limb! You can plainly see I didn't mean to kill him – and he struck the first blow, truly. Noble sir, if you accept that I don't deserve to die, then spare my life – and have mercy, for God's sake, on this boy I'm holding: it would be a grievous sin to have him cut to pieces before you finish me – I'll be using him as a shield: it would be tragic to have such a fair child slaughtered so!'

The lady now fainted, too, distraught to see the son she'd carried in her womb in such dire peril; and when she recovered from her swoon she tore at her hair like a mad woman and scrambled to her feet, crying in terror:

'Oh, husband! Have pity on your child, in the name of God the son of Mary! Gentle lord, kill me rather than let me see him slain!'

Leander thought he'd go mad himself when he saw his son in such a plight; and the child was weeping and pleading with his little hands clasped, crying:

'Have mercy on me, dear father, and pity on my mother – she'll die of grief!'

Leander, too, would gladly have died at the sight and sound of his son, stretching out his hands and begging for mercy; he didn't know what to do or say, overcome as he was by rage and anguish – rage at his foe, and anguish at the thought of hurting his dear child, which he couldn't avoid if he were to attack his foe. And pity wouldn't let him strike his son: he'd rather have had his own heart torn from his breast! So he was inspired to a bold and gallant move: not wanting anyone to harm his child he ordered his people to back away and then said to Perceval:

'I'm going to offer you two options. The better of them is perilous enough, but the choice is yours. I'll have your arms returned to you and you can arm at your leisure, just as you please; then there are four of us brothers: you'll fight me first, and if you defeat me you'll take on the next, and if you beat him the third'll be ready, shield at neck, and if you vanquish or finish him you'll have to fight the fourth; and if you overcome him, too, I promise you'll suffer no wrong – rather, all the knights I hold captive will be surrendered to you. You can trust me as you would a white monk,[59] so help me God. If you prefer to stay and be attacked right now, just as you are, so be it, but it would be dreadful if the child were slain with you.'

'By the Holy Spirit,' Perceval replied, 'I'll take the first option: have my arms brought here. If you won't forgive me and there's no other way I'd rather do battle than die.'

---

[58] Perceval is referring to his killing of the Red Knight for his armour, in Chrétien, above, pp. 10–11.
[59] i.e. a Cistercian.

The deal done, Leander, a most feared knight, had Perceval's arms brought to him and his horse led to the courtyard. Perceval put down the child and hurried to his horse and saw to the harness, ensuring it was good and tight; then he fastened his mail chausses with their fine iron buckles, and fixed his perfectly fitting spurs, and stood and donned his strong, resistant hauberk over a haqueton of cotton and silk, and laced his ventail and girded his sharp, trusty sword over his surcoat, which he hitched about his waist; and he adjusted his spurs so they'd be tighter to his horse's flanks. All eyes were on Perceval, who could be relied on to fulfil his duty. He mounted, laced his helm and hung his shield about his neck, and took up a sharp-headed lance with a strong, stout shaft of pinewood fully the width of a fist: he was ready to defend himself! Leander was well armed, too, and had called for a big, strong horse, swift and fleet and sure. May Jesus the true and glorious King aid Perceval now, for his quarters that night would be less than pleasant if he were vanquished and outfought! Leander was hungry for battle and mounted at once, helmet laced above his ventail, and took up his shield and lance. Blazing with rage and aggression he drew to one side, ready and set for combat; he was tall and mighty and raring to go, and swore he'd own not a strip of land for the rest of his days if he failed to kill or maim his foe – he feared Perceval as much as a crippled sheep! Perceval looked and saw how fierce he was, wildly belligerent.

'Ah, God!' he said. 'Dear Father and King, let not the wrongs I've done you weigh against me as I face this man! True and merciful God, protect me from harm!'

Leander didn't hesitate: his brain a seething fury, he thrust in his spurs and his horse leapt forward; Perceval, too, sent his mount surging, and they charged at one another with all the speed they could summon from their steeds. And as they clashed, I promise you, they drove their honed steel lance-heads clean through their shields: the wounds they dealt would take some treating as they tore through the mail right by their ribs – it was a cruel exchange indeed; and the lance-heads stuck in the backs of their saddles and flew into pieces with thunderous cracks; their strong, fleet horses ran dead straight and met head to head, nearly smashing each other senseless; and the knights collided so mightily that they, too, were all but stunned, and reeled, thinking they'd been struck by thunder, seeing stars. The horses staggered and pitched forward on their hocks, and both knights would have been flung to the ground had they not thrown their arms around their horses' necks. Those fine steeds struggled to right themselves again, but were too dazed and shaken now to stand. So the brave knights clambered down. They had no lance or spear – they'd been shattered in the joust – but they drew their swords from their scabbards and advanced upon each other, shields braced, ready for defence, without uttering a word, as if they'd taken a vow of silence. With their first exchange of blows they clove and smashed their shields to pieces, split their helms and sent mail rings flying from their hauberks, inflicting such damage that blood was spilling from many a wound as each sought to repay what he received with interest. No man ever witnessed such a ferocious, harsh and bitter combat. They were cutting one another to the quick, dealing agonising wounds in such terrible assaults that it's a wonder they didn't kill each other; the mail kept flying from their hauberks, their helms were now stove in. Nearly blinded by the sweat and blood and dust that filled their eyes, they dug their shields in the ground before them and drew back a little to take a rest. But only for a moment! Then they took up their shields and advanced upon each other once again, blazing with rage and courage. They rained blows on one another's head; if they delivered one that cost the other dear, they paid a high price in return – neither party profited from any transaction! The battle was intense and grim, and the turf was crimson with the blood that was gushing from their wounds.

Then Leander, tough, strong knight that he was, caught sight of his wife and the tears that soaked her soft, white cheeks. He wanted it over and done with now! He rushed at Perceval and found a chance to deal him a furious blow in his side: it nearly carved him open, cutting through mail and into white flesh; and down the blow flashed, right down the chausse, so close to the leg that the sword cut the spur-spike clean in half as if it had been no tougher than a pin. But the blade turned and plunged into the ground – had it kept going straight Perceval would have been in a bad way, maimed in the foot. Still, Leander thought he'd won the day as he saw Perceval reeling from the blow, and he insolently cried with the utmost spite:

'Yield, knight! Admit defeat! You've lived too long, and that's a fact: you treacherously slew my father, and it's only right that you pay for it: you'll be pulled apart by horses!'

'Truly, sir, you're very wrong!' said Perceval. 'I deny the charge of treachery absolutely. You've given me a daunting battle and a taste of your steel in my flesh: it's a grievous wound; but before we call a halt and part I want a portion of your flesh in return! When I've taken it and we're even, you might find your perspective's changed!'

Then it struck Perceval, with his level head, that he'd have a hard time beating all four brothers if he couldn't humble the proud Leander. So he strode to the attack and smote him with his blade of steel – a mighty blow it was – and then again; he had him in total disarray, his defences dashed; Leander had no answer and had to suffer an endless barrage of blows: he realised he couldn't survive, and as Perceval's assault intensified he was forced to abandon the fight and flee. But he could find no refuge good enough, and in awe of his blows he kept on running, till Perceval barged into him, he tripped in a rut and fell to his knees in the middle of the path. Every man of his court saw him – and so did his wife, who wailed and howled and tore at her hair, crying:

'I'll lose my mind, indeed I will, seeing my husband die!'

Leander heard her, and rallying his strength and courage he sprang back to his feet. Perceval continued his assault, splitting and staving his helm, but Leander mounted a strong defence, determined not to flee this time.

They carried on their fight till darkness fell around them. But finally Perceval struck him down, right at his wife's feet.

'Ah, gentle sir!' the lady cried. 'For pity's sake, and to repay my welcome, grant me a favour, I pray you – don't reject my plea: suspend this battle, please, until tomorrow.'

'By Saint Germain,' Perceval said, 'I'll gladly grant a permanent truce, if he's willing! But by Saint Martin, if he insists, we'll start again in the morning. Personally I'd much prefer accord! This penitent sinner says: if he would accept amends from me, I would be at his command. Forget killing and wounding – he'll gain little from my death.'

'There'll be no peace between us,' Leander said, 'as long as you live!'

'By Saint Remy,' said Perceval, 'that saddens me; God grant I may somehow win your love.'

So a truce was declared till the following morning, and with that their talking ended. Leander had the courtyard cleared and everyone sent back to his lodgings, while the combatants went to disarm. Leander, stained with blood and sweat, returned to the painted hall and disarmed in the light of the brightly burning candles. His three brothers examined his wounds and cleaned away the blood, and gently bandaged the ones that needed binding. His people paled when they saw his wounds – he was in a sorry state.

The lady, whose name was Ysmaine, graciously led Perceval to a fine and elegant chamber, and carefully disarmed him on a quilted carpet; her beloved Leander had asked her, by the love she felt for him, to forget all animosity and to serve Perceval and to treat his wounds as well as she could. So she tenderly removed his shirt and cared for him well, wiping away the blood from the wound in his side and padding it with cotton and carefully binding it with a band of silk. She was helped by a lady named Elie, who amply proved her worth, dressing him in a brand new gown of vair.* Then four servants came, courteous, smart and well instructed, and two of them lit three torches while the other two set the table with an array of delicious and wholesome food.

The lady undertook to care for Perceval that night. For companionship she bade a girl share Perceval's plate as they supped. Then she said:

'Relax, sir, and make yourself comfortable. I promise I'll look after you tonight and return your horse and gear in the morning. If harm or shame befalls you then, please don't complain to me! But I pray to God that my lord and you may come to make peace with honour to him and his brothers, and that he may forgive you for his father's death.'

'God hear your prayer, lady,' said Perceval, 'and grant you perfect joy in whatever you crave.'

'Eat now,' she said, 'with me, if you will. You shall have salmon, shad and perch, and strong wine to drink – anything you like: I'll not have you disappointed.'

After supper they made him a fine and comfortable bed. Perceval had his arms laid on a table at the end of the bed, for in the words of the proverb: 'if ye are prepared ye shall not fear':[60] a man surrounded by threats and perils should think how best to evade those dangers – it's only wise and sensible; that's why Perceval shrewdly had his arms laid out before him and then promptly went to bed – with his sword of furbished steel right at his side.

I should explain to you what the lady now did – with no eye to trickery or guile but with purely honest intent. To see more clearly in the house she had two lanterns lit – so that Perceval could see to arm if need be. Meanwhile a minstrel told him a strange adventure which seemed to have pleased others, and Perceval lay and listened to the tale, as did the lady, who stayed with him till he fell asleep, for he had many enemies there at the castle – not that he seemed to fear them. When she saw he was asleep she slipped away; leaving part of her sleeve to cover his head, she opened the chamber door and went down to the great, wide hall. The minstrel bolted the door again and prepared to sleep.

Meanwhile the lady went to her lord's chamber where she found him sitting with his three brothers and his barons all around him. They'd now bound his wounds, stained with congealed blood, and anointed them with a precious ointment which gave him much relief. The lady had him fed with a tasty, nourishing broth, and placed before him a beautiful little casket filled with cinnamon, cloves and nutmeg and the seeds of two pomegranates, red and full of goodness. She knew what she was about: she had them all ground together in a mortar and then dissolved in wine, and made him drink it to calm his giddy head. He'd recover in a couple of days and be as right as rain – as long as he didn't fight next morning. His people now went away to sleep in their various lodgings – chambers, halls, towers and other nooks and crannies – and Leander, too, retired to bed.

His three brothers lay at his foot in their beds, side by side. They all swore they'd never seen any knight before who could match Leander in combat.

'Brothers,' said Evander, 'he's clearly a valiant knight indeed, who pressed Leander so hard today and never relented – he seemed to grow steadily stronger! I'd say he was

---

[60] Literally "the man who is equipped suffers no harm".

fighting better at the end than at the start! Listen: if he can beat Leander I swear the three of us will all be vanquished! We won't be able to withstand him or survive his blows!'

They all concurred, and said they'd like to make peace with Perceval, if they could do so without reproach or blame. As the third hour of the night approached they went to sleep without further talk.

But things were about to take a different turn! For in the castle were four other brothers, wicked and cruel. God bring them to grief – they were worse than Ganelon![61] Rash and misguided, it was at their foolish prompting that the Red Knight first went to Arthur's court to demand his kingdom![62] Leander was well aware that it was their fault that he'd lost his father; he hated them for it, and would gladly have been rid of them even though they were close kin. But in any swarm of good bees there'll be some – don't worry, I shan't drone on! – who spoil and waste the honey that the good bees make and store; likewise in any family there are sometimes wicked-hearted men, perfidious, false and devious – though in the end their actions give them away. 'Children take after their fathers' – so the saying goes; but it isn't always true and I'll prove it: it's often the case that a worthy man has a son who squanders all he owns, gambling and throwing it away till he turns to thieving and ends up hanged. In such a case his deeds reveal his nature, and it certainly isn't his father's: the father was a worthy man, his son a disgrace. By God and Saint Gervais, you see it all the time: 'follow a wicked path,' it's said, 'and you know where it'll end' – a traitor will always end up betrayed. How little sense such people have: history shows how murderers have always finished at the end of a rope – the one who betrayed Roland and Oliver at Roncevaux[63] was pulled apart by horses. In the words of another proverb: 'the heart determines deeds'; the urge to do good is prompted by the heart – from a good heart springs goodness, from a bad heart evil. I'm saying this in relation to these treacherous brothers, who'd all vowed together to murder Perceval, to see him dead.

They lit wax torches, and as soon as that was done they swiftly armed; then each took hold of a long, fat, burning torch in his left hand and a sword of steel in his right. They were all convinced that if they slew Perceval they'd have the love and approval of Leander and his brothers: in avenging their father they'd win their deepest gratitude. So down to the great hall they went and straight to the door of the chamber where Perceval was asleep, suspecting no one; they barged at the door and split the planks with a splintering smash that echoed around the chamber. The minstrel heard the shocking sound and leapt from his bed and cried:

'In God's name, sir, get up! Up! I don't know who your attackers are, but alas, you're betrayed, I swear it! Oh, noble, honest knight, you proved your valour today – don't go weak and frail now! And you can depend on me – I'll back you as best I can – I shan't let you down, not as long as there's life in my body! And if my gracious lady knew what was afoot, we'd have nothing to fear from anyone, she'd see to that! And Leander and his three brothers, too: if they realised what was happening they'd have these dogs put down, not just locked up!'

Hearing he was attacked, Perceval jumped from his bed and snatched up his arms, blazing with rage and courage. On his back he threw an haqueton of padded silk and

---

[61] The arch-traitor, betrayer of Charlemagne's army, in *The Song of Roland*.
[62] i.e. in Chrétien's romance, above, p. 9.
[63] i.e. Ganelon, mentioned above.

a hauberk over that: what a mighty man he looked! Then he laced the ventail and girded his sharp sword. The minstrel proved his worth, rummaging around the room till he found a good steel helm and ran to Perceval and laced it on – he clearly felt nothing but love for him – and then picked up an axe and an old abandoned shield that he saw propped against a wall. Then they ran together to the broken door, and Perceval, striding forward, cried:

'Sly, villainous traitors! The door's about to open, but I'd watch out when you step inside – you'll find the doorman's a devil! You thought you'd take me unawares, but before you kill or capture me you'll pay a high price – on the edge of my sword!'

And he threw back the bolt and flung open the door. One of the traitors was ready with his shield above his head and marched in, expecting to deal with Perceval in no time, seeing as he was wounded; but as he was about to enter, Perceval, fired and ready to defend himself, met him with a blow to his shield that smashed it clean in half; his helm saved him from death, but the weight of the blow sent him crashing head first down a stair. The other three now leapt inside and launched themselves at Perceval, expecting to overwhelm him in an instant; they assailed him from the front and sides, raining blows upon him with their blades – but the minstrel came to his aid, striking furiously with his axe, and Perceval attacked them back. They were about to overcome the traitors when the one who'd fallen regained his feet, and filled with rage he advanced on Perceval and assailed him with all his might. The others now returned to the attack, dealing him blows both high and low, inflicting grievous wounds. But Perceval found new heart and courage and vigour and strength, and fought and strove so mightily that he saw his enemies off – not with empty gestures but with liberal gifts: he gave them all he'd got! The minstrel backed him all the way – he could see he needed his aid. He ran at a traitor and struck the rogue full on the helm; it would have cloven him clean in two had the axe not turned on impact and saved him from an instant death; instead it landed on the flagstone floor, with such force that it smashed and flew in half. Disaster! When the traitor saw it break he was exultant, and struck the minstrel with his sword, cutting through his shoulder and down through his side: to the floor he fell, defenceless. Perceval, enraged, covered himself with his shield and advanced on the traitor, sword drawn, and delivered a mighty slashing blow between neck and hood; it cut through hauberk, then through skin, through nerve and bone and blood-filled veins and sheared the head off: it was good and sharp, that sword! When the other traitors saw this they renewed their assault on Perceval, fierce and cruel, yelling to each other:

'At him! Shame on us if he escapes!'

'You haven't caught me yet!' cried Perceval. 'God preserve my right hand! I wouldn't change places with the bravest of you – not for the whole of Brittany! I don't fear you in the slightest: I trust too much in God and justice!'

The traitors sprang at him in a fearsome attack. Perceval confronted them and set his shield to meet their blows and fought back ferociously. One he dealt a blow that brought him to his hands and knees with blood gushing and welling from his nose: if he lived to see Saint John's Day he'd be in agony every day. The other two were shaking like leaves with fury, rage and passion, seeing Perceval resist so long; so again they launched a fierce attack, but they were making little headway till their injured brother returned to the fray and charged at Perceval: then they rained blows once more.

But I promise you, Perceval would have destroyed all three for sure had four sergeants not come running to their aid; they were clad in hauberks, and not straw hats but helms of iron – and were wielding axes! Butchers slaughtering cattle don't strike mightier blows than they, and they were nearly beside themselves when they failed to kill Perceval – they were giving it their all! But Perceval, undaunted, fought back mightily with his sword. His wounds were giving him dreadful pain, but still he mounted a fierce defence, cleaving shields and splitting helms: he stuck to his task most diligently!

The chamber echoed with ringing blows till they were heard by the lady who'd taken Perceval under her protection – but if she wasn't quick about it that protection would mean nothing! She rose at once and came to her lord and woke him and told him the shocking news of the attack on Perceval. Leander leapt up and called to his brothers who were lying side by side:

'Up, my brothers, up! We've made a truce with the knight till tomorrow – we'll be deemed base, false, wicked traitors if we let him be killed under our own roof! And in treacherous murder, too – I don't know who's attacking him!'

They sprang from their beds the moment they heard and swiftly took up arms. The servants, very shocked, lit the candles and ran through the palace rousing everyone. They jumped up in alarm; and when they heard their lord and saw his brothers armed and carrying great wax torches they thought they were bent on murdering Perceval in his sleep – and in their house! They all protested:

'Sirs! What a shameful way to avenge your father! You'll all be judged mad traitors – rightly so! We don't want to see you lose your good name: you agreed a truce with the knight till tomorrow – and the lady undertook to see no harm befell him. What a disgrace it would be to let her suffer blame – you love her, sir, and should keep her from such shame! Treachery shouldn't enter your head – you should despise the very thought, and deal in no uncertain manner with anyone who tries to harm the knight!'

'You're right, by God!' Leander said. 'I'll be grateful to you as long as I live – come, help me confront his murderous attackers!'

Hearing this they leapt from their beds and took up weapons – swords, lances, gisarmes* – and raced to the chamber to rescue Perceval. Leander was at the very front, and to his dismay saw Perceval with his back to the wall – not that he looked weak or craven: he was defending himself like a valiant knight, and although hard-pressed, of his eight assailants he'd now killed three. But when he saw Leander coming he didn't know what to do – he was sure *he*'d come to attack him, too! But then Leander yelled and roared:

'So help me Christ, foul murderers, you've done wrong! You'll be torn apart, limb from limb! What base villainy is this? I've taken him under my protection, and you've violated the truce. Your bodies will be broken in the morning, pulled apart by horses!'

Perceval now realised that Leander wasn't behind it; and the brothers charged forward, swearing upon their father's soul that they'd see the traitors hanged – they ran and seized them from every side and had them tightly bound.

'They'll have their just deserts in the morning!' said Leander. 'By Saint David they will!'

'Truly, brother,' said Marmadus, 'I say we hang them all – they've killed my minstrel, and wickedly attacked the knight whose safety we'd guaranteed. Your honour's lost if you don't execute them tomorrow!'

The lady, too, pressed her lord to put them to death next morning, for they'd clearly done great wrong.

'By God,' said Leander, 'I wouldn't defy your judgement for half the wealth of Baghdad!'

'Quite right!' said Meliadas.

And the traitors were taken and locked in a tower.

Then the lady came to Perceval and gave him the best treatment a wounded knight could have: she unlaced his helm, and his hauberk was removed and they cleansed and washed the blood from his wounds and bandaged him with a bolt of white silk that she took from a chest. They dressed the wounds, applying a gentle, soothing ointment, and laid him down in bed again; and Leander swore by his life that nothing should disturb him: until he was healed their fight would be suspended. Perceval said:

'I can't say you've kept your promise well: without God's aid and the help of the minstrel they slew – how his death pains me – I'd have been killed or taken captive, for they'd have caught me unawares, in my sleep. But the minstrel woke me and gave me my arms, and supported me bravely with an axe: his killers should be despised indeed.'

'I promise you,' said Leander, 'their sentence will be fitting.'

They removed the dead traitors from the room and had them dragged off to a foul place and dumped in a pit. But early next morning the minstrel was carried to Saint Augustine's church where his funeral was held; his body was laid in a rich and handsome tomb with the utmost honour, and with an inscription on the lid praying that Christ would receive his soul and exhorting everyone to cherish all minstrels for his sake. May God who created land and sea grant honour to those who honour minstrels!

After mass Leander bade that a fire be lit and had the five remaining traitors taken there and burnt; and their heirs were banished from the land forever.

Perceval stayed there till the month was out and he was healed and had recovered. Then Leander said he wanted their battle to resume – he wouldn't abandon it on any account; Perceval replied he'd prefer to make peace than have more fighting, but Leander said:

'When I remember how you slew my father, my blood boils and surges!'

His wife fell on her knees before him and said: 'Gentle husband, pardon this man your father's death without more contention. It's dreadful that two such worthy men as you must fight together! My fear is that, if you meet again in battle, his offer to make amends will weigh heavily against you: it's often the case that one who rejects an offer comes to rue it in the end! The man who accepts an offer that's to his benefit and honour should be respected and deemed wise.'

Leander could see that his wife meant well, but he wouldn't relent even for her sake; instead they both armed, he and Perceval, and mounted and rode to the courtyard where everyone gathered to watch the battle. Those in charge of the field of combat kept the crowd back in an orderly ring, and then without more ado drew lots[64] for ends, to see who'd have the sun behind him. Then the Red Knight's son issued his challenge to Perceval and promptly thrust in his spurs, and his horse sprang forward faster than a hound unleashed after a hare. Perceval wasn't light with *his* spurs either; both knights charged with their piercing lances and struck each other full in the chest: they'd have lost their seats had they not shattered their fine, white lances. So out came their swords that instant, and they dealt each other such furious blows that they sent chunks flying from their shields – they smashed them to pieces – and hammered at their helms so hard that shards flew from them likewise. On and on they fought, and no one could tell who would come out on top. But finally Perceval overpowered him and struck him to the ground, and dropped on top and held him down so tight that he pinned him motionless, still as stone. He pulled off his helm, unlaced his ventail, cut away the back

---

[64] Literally 'with two sticks' – presumably one being longer than the other.

of the hood and laid the edge of his sword-blade across his neck. Leander, prostrate, face down, knew he was dead unless he cried for mercy, but was sure it wouldn't be granted; he thought:

'God, father, what shall I do? By my life, I swear I'd sooner let him kill me than admit defeat!' But then he thought: 'I'd be better asking for mercy, if he'll grant it, than dying – what will I gain by death? Better plead for mercy and be defeated than slain.' So he put his hands together there and then, and asked for mercy and admitted he was beaten, saying: 'Good sir, have mercy on me, your accuser: I declared you my enemy, but if you grant me mercy I vow in all good faith to be your good and loyal man from this day forth, and to help you always, truly.'

And Perceval said: 'Will you and your brothers pardon me for your father's death?'

'Indeed we will,' said Leander; but Evander said: 'By my life, not I! I've no desire to make peace with you! You can say what you like but you'll have to fight me, and I'm not going to wait! One of us will die, either you or I: I'm never making peace!'

'Then God help me,' said Perceval, 'I'll kill your brother.'

Hearing this the lady rushed forward and flung herself on her knees before Evander with hands clasped, and holding back her tears she loudly cried: 'Oh, Evander, you can see your brother's in mortal peril! It should drive you wild to see him lose his head when it's in your power to save his life!'

But Marmadus said: 'I won't make peace at any price! I'd rather be noosed and strung up on a winch!'

Then up spoke Meliadas, saying: 'Don't be so unbending, brother! Do you think I find this any easier to bear than you? Of course I don't, so help me God. But we've lost our father, and if we lose our brother, too, we go from bad to worse! I'd rather have the heart torn from my breast than see Leander killed! Evander, my dear brother, have pity on your brother and on my lady here. It's better, they say, to choose the lesser of two evils. Do you really want our eldest brother killed and then have to avenge him? That doesn't make sense to me! And there's no reason to suppose that you'll outfight him, that you'll win! No finer, worthier knight than our brother was known in any land! We'd do ourselves a favour by making peace, I'd say. I've always heard it said that folly's better shunned than practised!'

Meliadas finally talked both brothers round: they wouldn't let Leander lose his life. The gracious lady bowed low in gratitude. Now hear what the brothers did: they came to Perceval, the edge of his naked blade still resting on Leander's neck, and:

'Sir knight,' said Evander, 'have mercy on our brother, and we'll come to terms with you and surrender all the knights we're holding captive; and you shall be our friend henceforth: no more enmity – we'll hold you truly dear.'

'Agreed,' said Perceval, 'but all three of you must swear to it.'

So the brothers gave their word, as did Leander. And when they'd made their oaths they disarmed and exchanged kisses: now they were at peace and could rest and take the refreshment that they needed.

Meanwhile Perceval had the captive knights released from their grim prison. They thought they were being led to their deaths, and wept and wrung their hands. But Sir Gawain showed no glimmer of fear; and the moment he set eyes on Perceval he ran to embrace him and started recounting, most eloquently, how he'd been caught in the forest and taken to try his hand at the chest, and then been thrown in prison.

'But now they've brought me out. That's my story. The lord will do as he likes with me – set me free or kill me. But whatever happens to us prisoners I feel sorry for you:

it's a terrible thing to have to watch a friend being put to death. Never mind *my* death – I'd be distraught to see *you* die; so truly, by Saint Laurent the martyr, if I knew for sure you'd be leaving safe and sound I'd suffer death more happily.'

'Sir Gawain, dear friend,' said Perceval, 'you're released – a free man! You'll live till God chooses otherwise! And all your fellow prisoners are free, thanks be to God.'

Then he told how he'd opened the chest and the four brothers had recognised their father, 'killed by me with a javelin'. And when Sir Gawain heard this, and how he'd made peace with the brothers, he was happier than he'd ever been in his life.

Then the people of the castle took the body of their lord in the ivory chest and, so the true story says, carried him to Saint Brandan.[65] I swear Aude's grief at Blaye[66] didn't compare with the lamentation of the Red Knight's sons and friends at his burial.

After the interment they returned to the palace, where the skilled and able cooks had prepared a meal – after grieving, I'd say, food is always needed. The knights and lords washed their hands at once and took their places up and down the hall. The brothers honoured Perceval and Gawain as highly as they could: they took them both by the hand and led them to the high table, where they were served with five or six main dishes and numerous entremets.

When it was finally time to clear the tables it was done; then the four brothers sat beside Perceval and Gawain and tried in vain to persuade them to stay awhile and enjoy themselves: they would have the other prisoners escorted to the very borders of their land. But Perceval insisted he couldn't stay, and Gawain said he had to go to the peak of Montesclaire to rescue the damsel there. Leander quickly answered Gawain, telling him the damsel was already safe and sound – though he didn't know who it was who'd defeated and slain the Dragon Knight. Perceval blushed at this; he didn't reveal it was he who'd vanquished the knight with the shield with the fire-throwing dragon's head that had burnt to death so many worthy men: he felt it would be boastful, and preferred to keep quiet than say anything untoward – he didn't want to be seen to brag. Instead he remarked it was a woeful shame when a man of noble qualities abandons his belief and faith and imagines the Devil will be an aid and strength: the Devil's only wish is to deceive, to snare people in sin! Joining company with the Devil will gain you nothing, ever! But whoever loves God with a true heart can't fail to come to a good end. 'But now,' he said, 'enough of talking: have our horses and arms made ready.'

They were brought to them and they armed, as did the other prisoners freed by Perceval; and their horses were brought by squires who saw to their saddles and prepared them well. Then Gawain and Perceval and the others mounted, for they had a long ride ahead of them, and as soon as they were ready they rode down from the castle. The four brothers mounted, too, and guided them to the main road that led to the high forest. They rode without stopping till they reached the forest's edge. Then Perceval thought once more of the grail and his stolen shield, and it pained his heart that he didn't know the meaning of the grail and of the lance that ceaselessly shed blood from the tip of its shining head. He was resolved to rest nowhere for more than a single day – provided he were safe and well – till he uncovered the mystery and recovered his shield: this he vowed to God and all the saints. Then he stopped, as he came to a stone cross where the road divided. With different paths ahead of him he drew rein and said to Gawain:

---

[65] '*Saint Brandain*'. This may be the Saint Brandan in Brittany; it may simply mean a chapel dedicated to the saint.

[66] In *The Song of Roland*, Oliver's sister Aude dies of grief at Blaye (on the Gironde, near Bordeaux) when she hears the news of Roland's death.

'Take the path you wish, good sir: I'd like it to be your choice.'

Gawain thought quietly and then replied: 'So help me God, dear friend, if I had my way and knew the shortest route to the peak of Montesclaire I'd choose that, by Saint Acaire.'[67]

'The path to the left,' Leander said, 'will take you straight there, without fail, round the side of that mountain. The middle path leads to Britain – it's the safest of the three, with fewer dangers and challenges than you'll find on the path to the right. By almighty God my maker, I've never heard of any knight who took *that* path and returned without grave harm and loss.'

'My mind's made up,' said Perceval. 'I'll follow the right-hand path till I see for myself why no one can return. You won't persuade me otherwise – I'm going to the right!'

'God protect you,' said Gawain, 'and keep you from all harm! Let's get going before night falls. And may God guide us both to win honour and find what we most desire!'

'God in His mercy hear you, good sir!' said Perceval; then he called out: 'Sirs, adieu!'

And with that he left them, and set out along the right-hand path. Gawain took the path to the left, leaving the other knights to follow the middle road. Leander escorted them no further: he was asked to stay, and returned home with his three brothers.

And now, for a while, the story leaves Perceval and the lance and the grail, to tell you of an adventure – and an awesome one it is – that befell Gawain.

The Hidden Knife

Sir Gawain kept riding swiftly on, mounted on his trusty Gringalet, determined to make good use of his time and efforts. On he rode till he came to a forbidding and daunting ford, with a pavilion pitched in the field by the river's edge. Night was now drawing in. Seeing the handsome tent Gawain thought there must be someone there, so he headed towards it quickly. Two boys ran straight out and greeted Sir Gawain brightly, and kindly offered him lodging on behalf of their damsel inside the tent: most gracious she was and beautiful – no man who saw her could take his eyes off her. Gawain returned their greeting, and courteously replied that he needed lodging sure enough, for it was almost dark, 'and I don't know where else to go!'

Ah, God! If he'd known what they had in store for him he wouldn't have stayed at any price! But destiny is what it is. Gawain, expecting to be given lodging, dismounted outside the tent. One of the boys jumped to it and took his shield and lance while the other took his horse. He was in for a terrible surprise if God didn't come to his aid. Then he took off his helm, and as he did so the damsel came to meet him and gave him the sweetest welcome.

'Well, my luck's in here!' said Gawain. 'Upon my soul, I swear by Saint David I've never seen a lovelier one than you, my lady – and I've seen thousands! Truly, you can consider me your knight from this day forth!'

And she, to tease and stir and rouse him more, said: 'I have to tell you, sir, I've never had anything to do with love. I don't know what a lover is – and I don't think I ever want to! I wouldn't know how to love a knight! But if I had to give my love to a man it would

---

[67] As noted previously, a number of the less familiar saints cited (e.g. Amand, above, p. 397, and Livinus, above, p. 407) had a particular connection with Picardy and regions such as Hainault. In this case, relics of Saint Acaire were kept at Valenciennes.

be to you, without a doubt! I find you very handsome, most appealing! In fact, listen: you shall have my love, exactly as you wish, if you'll lie quite still beside me all night long, naked in my bed; when morning comes you can do as you wish with me and let your body take its pleasure! But if your heart's so stirred that you can't wait till dawn to have your way, I swear you'll be in trouble! Let's see how you get on! It's in your hands!'

Her words made Gawain hotter and hotter. He found it hard to wait – bedtime couldn't come too soon! But he'd pay dearly for this pleasure, unless God intervened. The more he eyed the lady, the more Love fired and pricked him. The damsel, practised temptress and seductress that she was, gave looks and sighs to rouse him all the more, and said:

'Off with your arms, sir: come, it's supper time! It'll be just you and me, and my two cousins here, that's all – I've no servants.'

And the two boys took off his arms and outer clothes, and clad him in a gown of richest silk. But he'd rather have forgotten about supper, and been in bed with the beauty, side by side! But many men rush in to do what proves to be their downfall, and so it was with Gawain: he was well and truly hooked by Love – it had caught him by the eye! – and mad with frustration, convinced he'd never have what he so desired.

They had an ample supper, for she, to wind him up still more, kept serving him with everything on offer – and embraces and kisses on the side, which seemed to go down well. But unless God, the true King, watched over him, Gawain would be throwing away his body and his life, for the damsel, who only ever sought to seduce and betray, said:

'I feel nothing but love for you, sir – I can't help it! In the morning you can do as you please with me! It's night-time now – I pray you don't be upset at having to wait! When morning comes you can have your every pleasure! Lie down now in this bed – it's high time – and have no fear: I'll be coming to join you!'

Gawain couldn't wait to feel her naked at his side. He called one of the boys, who came running to remove his shoes and leggings, and the other brought a basin of hot water to wash his feet. They had no qualms about serving him and carrying on the deception. God! If Gawain had known the trouble that lay in store, he'd have given up this dalliance like a shot!

Meanwhile the damsel was asking him his name.

'I'm Gawain, lady, King Arthur's nephew and son of King Lot.'

When she heard this she flung her arms about his neck and said: 'Gawain, my dear, sweet love! I've waited for you so long! I pitched my tent here to await your coming – and now it's happened: you're here, thank God! Before you leave you shall take your pleasure with me – I've longed for nothing so much as to have you here with me. All I want is to feel you against me, naked body to naked body!'

How liberal was her lying! How different was her thought! She was bent on luring Gawain to his death – that was her only desire.

'Come, good sir, lie down in my bed in my fine silk sheets: I can't wait to be lying at your side!'

So to the bed he went, hungry to enjoy the one he thought a lover – but she was a mortal enemy, for Gawain had killed a brother of hers: he had no idea of this, but she was only too aware as she hurried him to bed. He took off his surcoat and tunic and lay down; but if God wasn't on his side he'd never rise from that bed again till he'd received his death blow: she'd deceived many men and delivered them up to death by cunningly secreting a dagger in her bed – as soon as she had a knight beside her, ready to have his way, that evil-hearted girl who knew so many wicked ploys would pull out the knife and plunge it in his body. She'd murdered fully twenty, I believe, in just this way; she was so inured to killing that she had no fear of sin. And now, she thought, she was about to avenge her brother's death; then she'd go to her father's castle in the remote, wild forest known as the Angry Mountain. What always happened was this: at the very break of day two brothers of hers would ride, fully armed, to their sister's tent, ready to assist her if they saw the need – they did it all the time. But once she'd murdered Gawain they'd take down the tent: it would be gone for good – there'd be no tent, no pavilion.

So there was Gawain, raring to go, waiting for the girl to come and lie with him, when suddenly he remembered to cross himself. So he did: he made the sign of the cross in the name of God the celestial King. And then, as he moved his hand to the right, he felt the point of the dagger, hidden by the girl beneath the quilt. The moment he felt its sharpened tip, he lifted the quilt and took the knife and – shrewd and clever man that he was – slipped it under a chest beside the bed, cursing whoever had forged the knife, for it was clearly there for no good purpose.

'Come here, my dear sweet love!' said the girl as she lay down by his side, naked beneath her shift. The two boys left the tent. Sir Gawain gently took her in his arms. Then she reached out under the sheets, expecting to find the knife – but Gawain, I think, would soon be giving her a lesson in the game of love! The evil girl nearly died of woe when she failed to find the knife – she didn't know what to do! And Gawain was about his business: he forced her beneath him and started the moves one makes with ladies one loves. She was wailing, helpless! Like it or not, she had to put up with Sir Gawain's sport! Her heart nearly failing, she said:

'It's no more than I deserve – I've brought it on myself, this calamity! I see it now: if you try to deceive another it's sure to rebound. Misfortune's mine for sure – what infamous shame that a mortal enemy should lie with me and force his will! I'd rather be flayed alive! He slew my brother, and I thought I'd have revenge tonight with my own hand, by treachery – but now I can truly vouch for it: anyone who tries to trick another will be on the receiving end – as I have been, alas!'

She sighed and wept and howled and wailed. But then she said: 'Sir, I won't lie: you'd better get up quickly or you're dead! Arm right now – my cousins'll be here and they'll show no mercy: they'll kill you on the spot! You've slain my brother and abused my body, but I don't want you killed now – though by the Holy Spirit, when I first lay down with you I'd have liked to rip your heart out with my hands!'

At that very moment her cousins burst into the tent, one of them clutching a naked sword, the other a pike;[68] they were bent on avenging Brun de l'Essart, the brother Gawain had killed. Both were holding a blazing torch so they could clearly see, and when Gawain saw them he grabbed the dagger he'd hidden and said:

'The fight's off! This won't do! If the first of you takes me on he'll cut me in half in no time – all I've got to defend myself's this knife! But God have mercy on me, whatever happens afterwards I'll throw this knife at whoever makes the first move!'

One did step forward, with sword on high ready to aim a blow at Gawain; and Sir Gawain raised the knife and flung it with such force that the whole blade was buried in his chest, piercing his heart and striking him dead. The sword fell from his hand and Sir Gawain snatched it up that instant. The other boy came rushing with his pike and thrust through the skin and flesh in his side; but before he could withdraw the pike Sir

---

[68] 'Pike' is a somewhat rough translation of '*falsart*': the 'faussart' was a shafted weapon with a blade like a sickle or billhook, derived from improvised weapons used by peasant levies.

Gawain dealt a blow that cut through the shaft and took the right hand with it. The boy fled away, not daring to stay longer with such a wound.

'Oh, sweet love, embrace me!' the damsel cried to Gawain. 'Love has taken hold of me: all hatred's gone – henceforth you'll have my total love!'

So saying, the white and tender damsel drew the pike from Gawain's side and bound the wound with a wimple. When she'd finished bandaging, Sir Gawain, son of King Lot, embraced her and held her close. He felt no hunger or thirst – he was really quite contented! All former ill-will was forgotten: if the night had been as long as midsummer day and about to start again, I don't think Gawain would have been displeased, and nor would she! Face to face and lip to lip they held each other in soft embrace, and lovingly shared a slumber there in the meadow.

But now let me tell you about the boy with the severed hand. He ran and stumbled on till he reached the forest, where he found the two brothers armed and mounted, firmly set in their stirrups. He stopped them and reeled off what had happened: that Gawain had just slain his brother and now was lying with their sister – 'and he's cut off my right hand!' They were so enraged, so filled with wrath and hatred, they were almost speechless; but the elder said:

'The traitor! By my life, if I find him he'll die a foul death! He'll be sorry he ever set eyes on our fair sister – and rue the day he lay with her, or ever laid a hand on her! A woman's beauty has betrayed and undone many men! But I'm amazed – by holy Baudri[69] I am – she didn't kill him with the knife; she must have given in to him and let him have his way, and then taken pity on him and spared him death. But he'll find it's a brief respite! What a nerve and affront, to sleep with our sister – and after killing our brother and now our cousin! He deserves to die for the least of his crimes!'

And they set off at a gallop.

Meanwhile Gawain, fast asleep, was dreaming. In a vision he saw two lions come bounding up and about to pounce, intent on killing and devouring him; but he struck one with his lance and it fell dead before him – at which point he started and awoke. The damsel, alarmed by his sudden shock, said:

'God save me, sir, I think you'd better arm if you care for your life! My two brothers will be here any moment, and they'll kill you if they can!'

Sir Gawain dressed and armed at once; and no sooner was he in armour and mounted on Gringalet than the two brothers and the wounded boy came charging up in a fury, and yelled at Gawain, King Arthur's nephew:

'I hope you've got protection! You'll regret ever sporting with our sister – we have you now!'

Gawain, surprised to see them there so soon, hadn't got his helmet on and, worse still, hadn't yet taken up his shield and lance. The damsel, naked save for her shift, ran to her brothers and fell to her knees before them saying:

'Have pity, sirs! It would be tragic to see such a fine knight slain! He's promised to take me as his wife as a sign of peace and accord!'

'Indeed I will, most gladly,' said Gawain. 'And I'll serve for three whole years in Outremer[70] for the sake of your brother's soul! Don't scorn this offer of mine! Let me

---

[69] This may well be Baudri the abbot of Bourgueil from 1079 to 1106 and bishop of Dol in Brittany from 1107 to 1120. A poet of some note, he also wrote an important account of the First Crusade.

[70] Literally meaning simply 'beyond the sea', Outremer was the term used to refer to the Crusader states established after the First Crusade: the Counties of Edessa and Tripoli, the Principality of Antioch and the Kingdom of Jerusalem.

live a little longer! If you'd wronged me as I've wronged you, and were willing to make the same offer, I'd accept it if those close to me approved. A man is well avenged on his foe if he sends him to Outremer – that's a perilous course for sure! So accept my offered amends – they're surely enough!'

'If you refuse,' their sister said, 'you'll regret it before you leave!'

But they swore they'd agree to no kind of peace, regardless of the risk of wounds or death. At this the damsel blazed with rage and seized her brothers' reins and held them tight, while Sir Gawain raced to get his helm and fastened it and grabbed his shield and lance – much to the brothers' fury! They were so incensed they almost cut her hands off! They hurled abuse and threats at her! Then she showed a woman's weakness: not daring to hold on longer, she released her grip and let them go. The elder brother charged at Gawain, and Gawain charged at him; they gave their steeds their heads and came at each other full tilt and split and rent their shields. The knight's lance bowed and shattered right down to his fist. Gawain, King Arthur's nephew, struck him with a force that pierced both mail and quilted haqueton: none of his armour could stop it cleaving his heart in two and sending him toppling dead. The other brother dealt Gawain a blow that breached his shield and dashed rings from his hauberk, and the lance-head pierced his side; but God was with Sir Gawain then, for it was only a glancing blow, and Gawain drew his splendid sword and rode up close and delivered a mighty, sweeping strike to the right that severed the brother's sword-arm, cutting it clean off at the shoulder. He fled that instant, cursing the hour he'd come there.

But he ran into a band of twenty knights sent by his father, concerned that the brothers hadn't returned. They were enraged and aghast to see their young lord butchered so – and their cousin, too, who'd lost a hand; and these two with their dreadful wounds cried:

'Sirs, go and avenge our brothers, killed by Gawain! He's bent on killing us all! Look what he's done to us!'

With that they left the two wounded men and went galloping off to the tent. The day by now was clear and bright, and the good, wise, bold Sir Gawain saw the party coming.

'Damsel,' he said, 'I think these fellows would have you and me part company, I'm sorry to say.'

Hearing this, she wept and groaned: 'Alas! What woefully brief bliss I've had with this brave knight! His prowess has driven all grief for my brothers and my cousin from my mind! I love him with my whole heart, truly! Gawain my love, I beg you: if you escape from here have pity on me and keep my heart – it's yours! Be you never so far, my heart will be with you, and if my body dared follow it would do so gladly!'

'I am and ever shall be,' said Gawain, 'wholly at your command!'

'I ask for nothing more!' she said, and the gentle Gawain bent down and embraced and kissed her. Then he laced his helm once more and took up his lance with its steel head, and commended the damsel to God.

The brothers were careering across the field, yelling: 'You're a dead man! If you'd forty heads you wouldn't keep the least of them! If you're not afraid you're a fool! You'll pay dearly for the fun you've had when we get you in our clutches!'

With that they came charging in a pack, and Sir Gawain thrust his spurs in Gringalet's flanks and cried:

'God keep you, my love! I'm going – God be your guard!'

As his horse sprang forward the damsel watched, thinking he was riding off, and followed him with her heart as well as her eyes, beseeching God to defend him from death and return him to her safe and sound. She stood there forsaken while Gawain cried that he was leaving. But he could never have contemplated flight – he'd do battle! Spurring Gringalet with all his might he lowered his sharp lance and struck the first on his gold-painted shield, piercing shield and hauberk, too, dunking head and shaft in blood like a skewer of meat in spicy sauce and parting soul from body. Down he fell and on charged Gawain, brandishing his lance as he met a second and struck him square to send him crashing to the ground with his legs in the air. His days of sampling wines were done: his face was twisted black and grim as his heart burst within him. The others were aghast, beside themselves with grief and rage; but they shook off their dismay – they were neither weak nor craven – and the two at their head met Perceval with thrusts so strong that they almost felled him; they dashed the shield from round his neck and drove his feet clean from his stirrups, dislodging him from his seat. Then one seized hold of his handsome reins and cried:

'You're captive now! You'll not escape!'

But Gawain drew his sword, sharp and honed, and with a slicing blow he struck him across the brow to send brain and scalp flying into the grass. Then he set off into the forest as fast as he could with the knights in hot pursuit; but they couldn't overtake him – their horses' hearts would burst first: barring a fall by Gringalet or some other mischance he'd no fear of being caught by anyone. As it was, Gringalet bore him through a soaring wood in swift and mighty bounds.

Not wishing to look foolish the knights turned back to the tent; they quickly took it down and laid each of the bodies on a bier. They didn't linger: they set off at once, taking the damsel with them, her cheeks soaked with tears from her passionate weeping. They thought the tears were for her brother, but she was more upset at Gawain having left her: her heart was close to breaking with misery and pain. In a blaze of grief she ripped her hair and gripped her throat so hard she almost throttled herself, and tore and clawed at every part of her body. Soon she was consumed with a longing to die: she cursed Death for delaying so and swore she'd put an end to herself and her awful grief.

'Come, lady! No more of this!' said the knights who cared for her dearly. 'Why do you hurt your beautiful face and tear your lovely hands? That won't avenge your brothers or cousins! The one who committed these dreadful deeds has foully wronged you and your father and all your line! If only we could have caught him he'd have paid the penalty! God send him every possible trouble and woe before the night is out!'

He was to meet with trouble even sooner than that, unless God intervened.

So off they rode with their lady, lamenting bitterly for the dead and wounded, their heavy, dark hearts steeped in woe. They headed for the house of Urpin of the Angry Mountain – a fierce, wild-natured man he was, with black hair and a red beard.

Meanwhile Gawain, riding through the forest, found himself descending a great valley; ahead of him, on a mountain top, he spied a strong, impressive castle with deep ditches all around, and an imposing tower in the middle surrounded by shields of many kinds: skilled masons indeed had built it – siege engines were no threat at all. Gawain headed towards it – not slowly but at quite a pace: he was famished! But he was heading into serious trouble unless Jesus smiled on him. He pressed on till he reached the gate, and saw the lord of the castle sporting in a meadow with his men. Gawain hailed him courteously, and the lord, a man of note, returned his greeting graciously, saying:

'God keep you, sir knight! You've obviously been working your horse – he's felt your spurs for sure! And good and hard – I can see blood flowing! But come: I'll gladly offer you board and lodging if you wish – it's time for dinner, I'd say. The food was almost cooked when I came out here for a little sport.'

'Thanks indeed, sir!' replied the worthy Gawain. 'I need it, that's for sure!'

With that he dismounted. There were more than a hundred knights and damsels in the castle, all thrilled at the news that a knight had arrived. They loved to hear passing knights tell of their adventures: the custom at the castle was that, after dinner, anyone who took lodging there would tell what had befallen him that day, agreeable or otherwise; then he'd be assured of an untroubled stay that night. But if Gawain had known the full picture, he'd never have set foot in the place.

A boy received his lance and another his helm and shield. But Gawain's stay was to be less than comfortable – relaxation wasn't in store. They briskly disarmed him and dressed him in a rich, green surcoat over the finely stitched haqueton that he wore beneath his hauberk – but I promise you, after parting with that hauberk he'd wish he'd been in Benevento![71]

The servants quickly set the tables, spreading them with fine white cloths, and brought the water without more ado; then the lord took Gawain by the hand and courteously seated him by his wife. They were served with five or six courses and an array of delicacies in between, and when all was done the seneschal cleared the cloths. Then the lord bade his guest wash first; and when everyone had washed they stood and changed places – though not all: doubtless those who were seated beside their sweethearts were anxious not to move! The lord, quite properly, sat at Gawain's side; and taking him by the right hand he said:

'If you don't mind, sir, you must now tell everyone what's befallen you in the past night and day, and give me your word to tell the whole truth; that is the custom here.'

Gawain, ever wise and courteous, politely replied: 'I am at your command, sir, but I'd ask you to care for your honour and mine – as you should, having given me lodging and shared food and drink with me. By your leave, good sir, I'd prefer to keep quiet: I'd rather not say anything untoward, and what I have to tell might well upset someone and rebound on me!'

'It's no good,' the lord replied. 'You're going to tell your tale before you leave, by my life you are!'

Gawain saw there was nothing for it, and he swore by his right hand he'd tell the truth. So in the hearing of all he told how he'd lain at the tent where the damsel had meant to trick him and murder him with a knife.

'At first she was bent on deceiving me: before morning she'd have killed me with her own hand, but I chanced to find the knife beneath the quilt and quickly hid it; then I lay down with the lady and had my way with her – much to her wrath! Then two of her cousins came to kill me, but I slew one and wounded the other – I cut off his right hand, I think – and so saved myself. Then I lay back down with that lovely girl – this time enfolded in her arms, in sweet embrace! By Saint Nicholas, I'd won her round and she'd given in! Her words then were so loving and beguiling that I hope to see her and hold her every day of my life! Then I fell asleep till morning – but neither Chance nor Destiny wanted me caught! The one who'd wrapped me in her arms – I love her with my whole heart and hope to do so forever – woke me and told me to arm, saying her brothers were coming and would try and kill me on the spot. And she was right – up they rode, both armed! But, thanks be to God, as we clashed I struck one dead and fought with the other till I cut off his arm, and so I saved my life. There – that's my tale! And then twenty more knights came and attacked me instantly: I'd have been overpowered

---

[71] *'Bonivent'*. See above, pp. 199, 214.

for sure if I hadn't turned tail – mind you, I was busy first: I killed three of the twenty – but what of that? I had no choice but to flee. So there – now I've told you all that's befallen me!'

When the lord heard Sir Gawain's tale he seethed with rage and hatred; he was nearly crazed with torment – everyone thought he'd lost his mind. He sprang to his feet and cried:

'It's plain as day: you've deflowered my daughter and killed my sons and nephews! I vow and swear to God I'll have you torn apart by horses! Nothing'll stop me! What I've heard from your own lips – oh, no wonder I'm incensed! Listen: you've nothing to fear for the rest of today and tonight, but tomorrow I'll kill you with my own hand! But no! I'll do it now, this instant! I can't bear to let you live another hour – I'm going to rid the world of you! I'll bury my sword's point in your body, or lop off your head!'

He called for his sword and it was brought; and at that very moment the party carrying the biers arrived at the door. The doormen opened and let them in, and when they saw the biers they all cried as one:

'Urpin! If you fail to destroy the man who killed your sons may God have no mercy on your soul!'

And wailing and beating their palms with grief they flung themselves to the floor. And Urpin, hearing their cries and seeing the biers, was overcome, too distressed to utter a word. Every lady, everybody in the hall, was swooning with anguish – and the father, who'd loved them more than his own life, passed out, too. When he came round they tried to console him, and the ladies threw their arms around his daughter, whose heart was faint. But when to her astonishment she saw Gawain, the colour began to return to her cheeks: she wondered how to let him know she'd come – if she could, she'd save him from death. Gawain saw the eruption of grief and the biers being carried in, and as they passed through the doors and into the hall the wounds on the dead bodies opened and the blood flowed freely and covered the floor with red. Everyone who saw it was aghast: the spilling blood told them that the killer was in the hall; and when Gawain saw it he realised they were the men he'd fought – he was in deep peril unless God was with him! He looked around the hall but could see no weapon, not even a stick, and he muttered to himself that only a fool ever blurts out stories that might get him in hot water!

'Never again will I tell a stranger anything that could rebound on me and cause trouble! Oh, I'd give a tower full of treasure to have my arms and hauberk now – then I might have a chance! I'm amazed they haven't attacked me yet – there are enough of them! I've no sword or lance or axe, and there they are, all filled with loathing, wanting to cut me limb from limb! I can't see any way out of this! God help me, I don't know what to do for the best. But as I hope to see God face to face, no one'll point a finger at me and accuse me of cowardice! What will be will be, and everyone dies at his allotted time!'

He rolled up his sleeves and strode forward and stopped and stood in the middle of the hall, proud as a lion. And Urpin, who'd recovered from his faint, came rushing at him, sword drawn, and was on the very point of beheading him when the damsel leapt forward and cried:

'God save me, sir, don't strike him yet! Never, please God, will you break this castle's custom:[72] it would be no credit to you if you broke your word. Hand him over to me

---

[72] i.e. to guarantee a guest's safety, after telling his story, till the night is out – see above, p. 443: 'anyone who took lodging there would tell what had befallen him that day, agreeable or otherwise; then he'd be assured of an untroubled stay that night'.

– I'll have him in my keeping and return him tomorrow; then your word and your honour will be safe. And I'll give him a hard time, don't you worry! God curse me if I let him escape! He'll be in deep trouble if he's in my hands – he has no worse an enemy than I! Torment's in store for him tonight!' And then she whispered: 'He'll be held captive in a way befitting a faithful lover with his sweetheart!'

And with that she took hold of Gawain and appeared to be dragging him by the hair – but it was a sly pretence, giving them all a false impression, and seeing it they were taken in and said:

'He's in for it now!'

So said they all.

The lord, shaking with grief and anger, had the bodies shrouded and then buried in the church of Saint Organe.

Meanwhile the damsel, having managed to trick her father, called two chambermaids – spirited girls with a bit of pluck – and bade them fetch some pies and wine! So Gawain ate at leisure, and had many an embrace and kiss from her – in lieu of side dishes! – and indeed a good deal more! He was served with all he wished! The sight of the damsel he loved and craved helped him forget all present cares, and she craftily ensured she could have him on her own, for she loved him more than any treasure. When they'd leisurely eaten their fill they lay down together in bed, in tight embrace, with the utmost pleasure. Kisses upon kisses they exchanged, oblivious of the world. They were completely at one, all animosity and discord forgotten. The maids guarding the door to the chamber saw them lying there, wrapped in each other's arms, and swore it was a better way to spend one's life than cracking heads and weeping and moaning! Any girl should crave a tender, gallant lover.

'Our lady's in clover now,' they said, 'kissing and caressing her lover, and he returning in kind! I don't know what else is going on but they're certainly kissing enough! The knight's forgotten his fears and cares, and our lady's well over her grief and upset! The rest can lament as much as they want – our lady's done with sorrow!'

They lay together till darkness fell, when they rose and washed their hands; then the maids set the table and brought bread and wine and meat and served them cheerfully – they felt very merry after all they'd seen that day! After they'd supped, Gawain and the damsel lay down once more, naked together beneath the cover. And she didn't scratch or punch or pinch or bite! For his part, Gawain gave not a thought to his mortal peril: whatever might befall him, he was wholly fixed on pleasure. Nor did he think about safety or escape: there wasn't a shred of cowardice in him, and practicalities were quite forgotten – he was leaving all to Chance: he couldn't see the point of worrying when everything was stacked against him. So there he lay with his sweetheart, kissing her and holding her tight: they couldn't get enough; they passed the night in bliss, without a care – except for the thought of daybreak.

Urpin was up at the crack of dawn, his mood of course still black, and woke his men. They rose and made ready to put Gawain to death – all were filled with hatred. Lord Urpin picked up an axe, well-honed and double-headed.

The damsel, lying at Gawain's side, heard the commotion and quickly donned her shift; then she set about a cunning plan: she told Gawain to get up and dress and brought him a sword of bright, sharp, burnished steel, sent to her father by a dear friend of his, the lord of Glimesi.

'My love,' she said, 'you've many enemies here and they'll be coming any moment. I know they'll be bent on killing you, so get ready! Draw the sword and come and grab me by the hair – but try not to hurt me too much! Pretend you'll cut my head off if they try and lay a hand on you: I think they'll spare your life to get me back.' Then she called to the maid Jolïete and her companion Violete: 'Quickly! Strip to your shifts, look sharp and do exactly as I say: open my chamber door and rush out all unkempt and dishevelled and yell in distress: "Holy Mary, our prisoner's escaped!"'

'That's a great idea!' the maids replied; and they were quick about it: they ran to the door, dressed only in their shifts, their hair undone, veiling their heads, flung it open and rushed out screaming: 'Help! Help! In God's name, sirs, quick – come and rescue our lady! The prisoner's escaped – he'd have cut off our heads if we hadn't fled! It was dreadful! Now he's going to behead our lady unless she lets him get away – but she says she'd rather be boiled in pitch or wax or let him have her head than see him escape!'

At this Urpin blazed with rage and strode into the chamber, clutching his axe in both hands; but when he saw Gawain there, gripping his daughter by the hair and forcing her down and apparently about to behead her with his naked sword, he stopped in his tracks and bade his men stay put: he was so terrified for his daughter he didn't know what to do. And Gawain, seeing him arrive, called out:

'If anyone lays a hand on me I swear your daughter's dead!'

Her father was aghast, but replied: 'It's no use! She'll not save you! By Saint Nicholas, no, you're not going to save your neck like that! I'm going to cut you down!'

When Gawain heard this he raised his arm as if to strike that lovely girl – though he wouldn't have done her any harm for a thousand silver marks! Then into the exquisitely painted chamber ran her mother; hearing her daughter was about to be killed she was appalled: in fear and dismay she turned the colour of wax and cried:

'Alas! I'll never know joy again! Oh, woe! My heart's in blackest torment: I've lost all three of my sons and now I see my daughter about to die! I'd rather be put to death myself than see my daughter slain!'

It looked as if she'd lose her mind as she saw her daughter doubled over and Gawain with his sword aloft as if about to kill her; she was going wild, screaming:

'Husband! So help me Christ, if you let him touch my daughter I'll put a dagger through my heart! Your loss will be double – daughter and wife together! For the love of God, consider: if your daughter should lose her head and I should kill myself, what pain and loss for you! So temper your wrath, have a level head – and take pity on us! Think: if this knight were killed or maimed or wounded it wouldn't bring your sons back, and what would you gain by his death if your daughter were also slain? You've no more children! A man who sees his house on fire rescues some timbers if he can – so listen, and tell me if I'm not talking sense: no matter what you do you can't recover your sons, so don't lose any more or you'll be worse off still – you may have lost your sons, but save your daughter and me at least, and limit your loss.'

The damsel reached out, imploring, saying: 'Mercy, gentle father! If you try to hurt him this knight'll kill me! In God's name, father, break off this blood-feud, all this discord; make peace and come to terms, for God's sake, and save me from death!'

Urpin was almost torn in two: rage and hatred forbade him to make peace; but the pity and love he felt for his daughter told him to do just that! He crossed himself and pondered what to do. He knew if he tried to harm Gawain then Gawain would promptly kill his daughter – there'd be no way to save her. But suddenly he conceived a daring plan: anger and hatred inspired him to an extraordinary and hazardous move. He said to Gawain:

'Wait, sir knight! Stay your hand and listen to what I have to say. You can have your horse and your arms again, on condition that you swear an oath to go and wait for me out there in the wood, at the cross at the valley's foot, and I'll come armed and mounted to do battle with you there. If you overcome and vanquish me you can leave in total safety, I promise and swear it faithfully; but if I win there'll be no redemption: I'll have your head. If you win, kill me likewise – I'll never plead for mercy, for you'll have none from me.'

Then Gawain answered, saying: 'God forbid, sir, truly. May He in His goodness grant that I make amends and peace with you.'

Hearing this, the lady said: 'Dear husband, in the name of God and His holy body, make peace with this knight! Give him your daughter as his wife by way of accord and settlement!'

'I'd sooner be strung up by the neck,' said Urpin, 'than let him have my daughter! I'll kill him first! He's in the wrong and I'm in the right, and my loved ones will be avenged!'

'I'm sorry you won't accept amends,' said Gawain. 'I'd gladly come to terms acceptable to your kin and mine.'

'God save me,' Urpin said, 'you're not wriggling out of this! One of us is going to die – that's my last word.'

With that he called for his arms and made Gawain swear to go to the wood and wait for him there. Then he had Gawain's arms returned to him along with his horse, saddled and ready. They armed together in that bright, fair chamber. The damsel wept uncontrollably – she feared for her father and her lover likewise: whichever one of them was slain, her heart would grieve for the rest of her days and her sorrow would never end. She was distraught and filled with fear, and prayed to God the son of Mary to intervene and make peace between them.

Without more ado they strode from the chamber. Urpin, tall and mighty, mounted his destrier, and Gawain leapt astride Gringalet without setting foot in a stirrup. No page or squire, nor any knight, was brave enough to follow them: their lord had forbidden it, which upset a good many.

Down from the castle they rode, and pressed on till they came to the cross in the glade at the bottom of a valley, a fairer and more level stretch of ground than any in all of Ireland. In that fine glade they halted, all alone. Each withdrew beneath a poplar, readied his shield and his trusty lance and issued his challenge; then they thrust in their spurs and their steeds leapt forward, racing faster than a stag in flight from a pack of hounds, their hooves striking the ground so hard that they sent sparks flying from the stones. As they neared they lowered their lances and dealt each other blows that smashed and split their shields apart. The strong, tight mail of their hauberks saved their lives, but they struck each other in the chest with such force and might that they'd have gone crashing flat on their faces if the lances hadn't broken. Before they could draw their swords they collided, dashing the bejewelled bosses from their shields. The thundering horses crashed together and staggered and buckled but righted themselves, but they and their riders were all so stunned they stayed motionless for quite a while. When they recovered their senses the knights advanced on each other anew, swords drawn, and rained so many blows that they smashed their shields to pieces, rendering them almost useless. Intent on striking, sparing nothing, they battered and stove their helms and splintered their shields – there was almost nothing left of them. Urpin covered himself with what remained, and summoning up his courage and strength, inspired and driven by grief and fury, he caught Gawain with a slashing blow in his left side that went through his bright hauberk and cut away two fingers' widths of skin and flesh. The wound wasn't deep, but Gawain was incensed to see the blood come oozing down.

'Your kin,' said Urpin, 'will never see you alive again! You made a big mistake lying with my lovely daughter – no man ever bought pleasure with a girl so dear: my sharp steel blade is going to have your head! You can't escape me any more than you can leap from here to heaven!'

And back he came to the attack. The fine, accomplished Gawain blazed with rage when he saw the blood flow from his wound, and saw Urpin pressing home his attack and heard him swearing he'd cut off his head if he got the better of him. On and on went Urpin's wild assault; but Sir Gawain dealt a blow to his head with his furbished sword that stunned and blinded him – he couldn't see a thing as blood gushed and poured into his eyes and down his face. Urpin was beside himself when he felt this wound to his head; but he recovered as best he could, and he and Gawain, covering themselves with what was left of their shields, traded blows once more. The shields, their leather and wood held together with glue, were now destroyed, and their hauberks were rent and seeping blood all over. But Urpin, heedless of his wounds, charged again at Gawain, and Gawain at him, aiming blows this time at each other's face, and though they missed they shaved each other's chin and throat with their blades of steel. They seized hold of one another now, trying to wrestle each other from the saddle; then they started pounding with pommels and blades, severing their helmet straps and staving and splitting their helms on every side. Finally Gawain hauled and hammered Urpin to the ground, battering him so ferociously that he almost finished him. Urpin heaved himself up to face Gawain – but Gawain had turned away and dismounted, and dropped his reins and tethered his horse to a high branch of a bush. Only then did he return to Urpin, who said to himself:

'He has a courteous heart, that's clear, as well as fierce and bold. There aren't ten men in twenty thousand who'd have dismounted so and returned to fight on foot. That was an act of great valour; were it not for the wrongs he's done me, we'd make peace on the spot. But when I think of my children, my heart fills with such rage and grief that I can't help myself – I can't make peace: come what may, I can't! When I remember what he's done to my daughter, and how he killed my sons, my blood seethes and boils!'

And with that he and Gawain strode to the attack once more, raining all the blows they could to each other's head. Then they grappled again and started wrestling, and the battle-hardened Gawain seized Urpin by the ventail and dragged him to the ground, face down, and pinned him there till he almost crushed him. Urpin lay there, utterly distraught, and Gawain said:

'Crave mercy, knight.'

But Urpin replied: 'No, kill me! I've no wish to live on now you've vanquished me! Rid the world of me and give yourself one fewer foe! I swear to God, if I'd defeated you as you have me, no plea from you would have stopped me having your head.'

'You've made your feelings plain,' said Gawain. 'I'll kill you, then, here and now, since you refuse to ask for mercy. You clearly don't care for your life. But I'd have dearly liked to make peace, and come to terms with you and your friends and kin.'

'You're wasting your breath,' said Urpin. 'It's out of the question. Do with me what you must.'

The worthy Gawain was reluctant still, and gently insisted he'd gladly spare him if he'd just admit defeat and ask for mercy; but much to Gawain's sorrow Urpin preferred to die. So he raised the skirt of his hauberk. He was on the very point of driving his sword through his body when he looked beneath a pine and saw Bloiesine, Urpin's daughter, riding swiftly along the valley on a palfrey. She'd been fearing for her father; and when she saw what was happening she raced up to Gawain and leapt down and begged him for mercy a hundred times, to spare her father in God's name.

'Dear gentle man!' she said. 'Consider: if you ever had a sweetheart, then by holy God for the sake of her love don't kill my father! Have pity on him and spare his life!'

Gawain knew instantly what Bloiesine's words implied: that he should spare her father if he wished for her love; and he replied at once:

'My damsel, for the love you bid me remember I shall spare him: take him away.'

So saying, the good Gawain stood back, and Urpin, stressed to breaking point, passed out. Gawain, whose love for Bloiesine had swayed him to answer her plea, kissed her; then he went to his horse and mounted, and asked her to be mindful of his love and come to the court of the king his uncle: he'd see that she was honoured and served and would be her lover for the rest of his life; to this she gladly assented. With that Gawain commended her to God and rode swiftly away.

When her father regained consciousness she asked him if he thought he'd recover with the aid of potions; he said he didn't know: he was so distressed about his sons and his own defeat that he wanted the earth to swallow him up – he didn't care what became of him.

'Come now, father! Calamity strikes many a worthy man! By Saint Peter of Rome, try to console yourself – cast off this grief, as a worthy man should: he should have the strength to overcome misfortune. It's hardly wise to display your woe – it cheers your enemies all the more!'

Urpin, seeing the sense of her words, mounted without further delay and she did likewise. In short, they returned to their castle where his men were beside themselves with worry; they saw to his disarming and had his wounds attended to.

But I'm going to leave them now and return to Gawain, who rode steadily on through the forest till nightfall when, in the wood of Claradeure, he came to the hermitage and hut where the damsel who'd worn her clothes inside-out had retired to serve God in penance for her beloved.[73] Gawain lodged there that night – but he can't have enjoyed it much: there was nothing to eat or drink but crab-apples, acorns and juniper berries and water from the spring beside the chapel; and his horse had to make do with hay. He had an uncomfortable and hungry night and a very hard bed. But one thing did delight him: the damsel told him the story, and could assure him it was true, of how Perceval had taken revenge for her and raised the siege of Montesclaire and slain the knight with the shield with the dragon's head that flung fire from its maw. He was overjoyed to hear this, to learn that the worthy Perceval had accomplished the awesome adventure that had caused him to leave Britain – he'd vowed to go to Montesclaire himself.

'There's no point going there now: the challenge has been met by the knight whose deeds are winning such renown – and rightly so: he's an adept, worthy, bold and valiant knight, loyal in word and deed. I suppose he didn't tell me he'd done it for fear it would sound like boasting!'

Such were Gawain's thoughts. And in the morning, when he saw day break, he saddled and harnessed his horse and mounted and took his leave of the damsel. Then

---

[73] Literally 'in the hope of earning His love'; but there may well be a scribal misreading of a phrase more exactly relevant to her previous story: see above, p. 420.

away he rode, and pressed on till he came upon four thousand knights and as many ladies, counting all the girls; for the king had heard the news that his nephew was a prisoner, and had summoned all his bravest friends – by prayer and promise of reward – and vowed to go in search of him, and not to return to Britain till he'd freed his nephew either by entreaty or by force. So the king was on his way to find him. And when Gawain caught sight of the royal banner, and saw the great array of tents, he was beside himself with joy. He rode on till he reached the camp. He was recognised by the very first people he met; they all started crying:

'Welcome to the good, fair, worthy, noble knight who should rightly be esteemed and praised above all others!'

'God grant you all,' he replied, 'the best of fortune!'

On the briskly trotting Gringalet he rode to the royal tent; his uncle the king saw him and knew him at once from his arms and manner, and up leapt Sir Yvain and Bran de Lis and Lancelot and Sagremor and Kay – who'd been thinking he must be dead – and Girflet and Carados Shortarm. The king took him in his arms and kissed him tenderly, and so did all the barons; then he dismounted and they disarmed him. The queen and ladies gave him a joyous greeting, needless to say; and the queen had him dressed in a fur-lined gown that suited him perfectly. Then the king, in the highest spirits, sat down to supper and seated Gawain at his side and bade his barons sit where they all could see him.

After supper Gawain told how his dear friend Perceval had rescued him from dire, grim prison, and eloquently reported how Perceval had made peace with the sons of the knight 'who came to contest your land and carried off your golden cup – Yvonet brought it back after Perceval killed the knight with a javelin'.

Good King Arthur was delighted to hear his nephew tell of this pact, and kissed him and embraced him.

Next morning, as soon as they saw day break, they set off for Lincoln,[74] where the king intended to wear his crown and entertain his dukes and counts.

But here the story leaves Gawain and King Arthur – God send them honour and strength and protect them from all harm – and tells of Perceval.

The Worm in the Stone

At this point it says, in short, that from the day when he'd left Gawain, after inviting him to choose between the paths, he'd never rested in his search for the grail, so that he could ask and learn its origin and purpose, and find out about the lance he'd seen that shed constant drops of blood from its shining head. He'd already seen it twice, but had still not learned the truth about it or discovered its significance; but he was sure that if he could find it once again the truth would be revealed.

He rode on all that week, and encountered and accomplished many fearsome tests, till he came to a hermitage at the forest's edge. The hermit saw him coming and rose at once; Perceval rode up and greeted him with courteous words, and the hermit replied most kindly.

'If it's no trouble, good sir,' said Perceval, 'tell me for the love of God where I might find lodging.'

'By God the Spirit, sir,' the hermit said, 'I know of no house or castle ahead where anyone could live; they're all ruined and the people have fled: they'd rather have been

[74] 'Nicole'.

buried than stay in these parts – they couldn't bear the dire woes that befell all who came this way. I've never seen or heard of anyone who took this path and returned, and I've been here in this retreat for a hundred years or more. But please, be so kind as to stay here tonight and take lodging; then in the morning I'd advise you to turn back – it's the best thing you could do.'

'I wouldn't turn back for anything,' said Perceval.

When the hermit heard this he wept for pity. He led him inside his hut and helped him dismount and disarm, and dressed him in a surcoat of white cloth lined with the fleece of black lambs. Then he made the fire, and unbridled Perceval's horse and gave him hay with some barley he'd been about to boil and cook for his own meal. That day he'd hunted a young goat that lived in the wood, and had shot it with an arrow and tracked it down till he'd caught it and skinned it; now he cooked it by boiling and roasting. As soon as it was ready they sat down and had plenty of meat and a little bread. The hermit said:

'Dear friend, eat what's before you and drink water from the spring – I've no ale or wine to offer. I reckon it's more than a year since I had meat – and there's no pepper or garlic sauce! But at least you've the meat, so eat your fill: take what you like from the flanks and ribs and loin. And then, if my prayer has any power and your heart will assent, I beg you turn back.'

But Perceval replied: 'I won't hear of turning back – not for you or anyone.'

'Then God grant you a happy outcome!' the hermit said. 'I see you're determined to carry on, so I'll say no more.'

Straight after supper the hermit made him a bed, as comfortable as he could manage, of ferns and fresh grass – he had no straw to put on it, and no pillow or blanket to offer as he'd have liked. But Perceval went straight to sleep, having had a very hard day.

In the morning he made ready while the hermit prepared at once to sing the mass of the Holy Spirit, praying to God to aid his guest that day and keep him from all harm. But before going to arm and mount, Perceval decided he'd like to make confession. So after hearing the hermit sing the divine service, he politely called to him and sat down at his feet, downcast and sorrowful and troubled; he sighed from the depths of his heart, and then burst into a flood of tears as he thought of his sins that kept him from accord with God. Joy sprang in the hermit's heart when he saw him so contrite.

'In the name of penitence, friend,' he said, 'I bid you tell of your sins and conceal none: then you'll be at peace with God again, have no fear. You'll free yourself of a great burden if you make true confession. And you can be sure there's no hiding from God! If you came to be dealt seven mortal wounds and were healed of six but left the seventh untreated so it didn't mend, you'd surely die. Likewise, dear friend, a mortal sin concealed at confession and stowed in your heart will drag you down to the death of Hell, and no amount of charitable deeds done for your soul's sake will redeem you thereafter. For the love of God, don't let shame stop you confessing your sins! When our Lord God sees a soul in distress and in sorrow for his sins, and sweating with shame as he makes confession, then God, our Lord, wipes his heart clean, washing away the sins, erasing all misdeeds. Shame is the true remorse that helps so much to lighten the soul – it's plain to see.

'But don't be like the fox with his cunning heart, wily and deceitful! He's red, but he has a white throat! And let me tell you truly how the fox resembles the flatterer: as soon as a man begins to flatter, don't trust him – he'll stab you in the back while he smooths his oily words all over your face! For words are all they are! Flatterers, with their pretty speech, make people think their words are true, but when it comes to action, they're pure fiction! The words in their mouths are white enough, but the goodness isn't rooted in their hearts – they're empty, full of treachery. Such people resemble the fox indeed with his white throat! Flatterers lie to deceive – that's their nature – but it's not apparent from their nice white words; so on they go deceiving folk with their glib false promises over and over. You can have little trust in a man who lightly breaks a pledge. A man who won't keep his word, who lies quite freely, endlessly, will never be faithful to anyone; a man who won't keep faith or stop lying will show men no fidelity.

'Don't you stoop to such ways – they ill become a knight! In the order of chivalry there should be no deceit in pledges made – and certainly not in the hope of gain. But one often sees a knight, under solemn oath, act unjustly and dishonestly through covetousness, for profit. The truth is, he should never wear a sword again! No knight should ever fail to do his utmost to act justly: where he knows the right to lie he should advance it and not let it be swept aside, for that would be very wrong – a knight is made to do right. May God the true Father grant that all knights live correctly; and may *you* do so, dear friend, so that you may see God face to face, in His great glory, at the day of judgement.'

Then he gave him gentle absolution, and bade him do good, and blessed him with his right hand.

When Perceval had confessed every sin he could think of, the hermit quickly brought him some of the goat-meat – he'd cooked plenty the night before and there was still some left (though there was no wine or mead!) – and Perceval sat down at once and began to eat. He ate his fill, and drank cold water from a mug, and when he'd finished, and had no fear of hunger that day, he rose and went to harness his horse. He put on the saddle and bridle and then asked for his arms; the hermit helped him on with them, and as soon as he was ready he took his leave and set off. The hermit was left weeping and sighing for him deeply, and praying to God to keep him by His power from harm and loss. Unless God worked an outright miracle for him he'd never return – or see the grail or the lance with the bleeding head for which he'd suffered so much toil and pain and hardship. But there was no point expecting him to turn back – unless sent back by the true God who has the power to guide men's steps. No matter what he heard or saw, Perceval was not for turning.

On he rode down a narrow path, thick with tearing thorns and brambles. But he endured it all, and pressed on all day till late afternoon, when he found himself crossing a high mountain. Then he heard a foul and hideous cry – and then two more, as ghastly as the first. The one who'd uttered them was always bent on evil, and I promise you that was his one thought now. Perceval headed straight for the cries he'd heard; but when he reached the mountain's foot he sat still upon his horse and looked up and down, but couldn't hear a thing.

'So help me God, how very strange: this is where the cries came from, but there's nothing to be seen. I don't understand it.'

Then he noticed a block of red marble in the shadow of a tree. He rode up to it and dismounted, very puzzled, and sat down on the stone and invoked God and Saint Peter; and thereupon he heard a creature inside the stone cry:

'Oh, good sir! Free me from my pain and torment! I tell you, my dear, kind friend, I'm suffering dreadful torture, but you can rescue me!'

Perceval jumped up when he heard the voice, and leaned over the stone and said: 'I can't release you – this block's too huge! It baffles me how you ever got in! You'll never get out, I promise you, unless you tell me how to set you free. If I do, I bid you by all the power of God, tell me truly who you are and what you're up to.'

'Oh, I will!' the creature said. 'But free me from this torture! Step forward and stand firm, and pull out the spike that's skewering my body and stops me moving: then you'll see what'll happen!'

So Perceval went up to the stone and found an iron spike, stiletto-sharp – that's no exaggeration: it was sharper even than that. He went ahead and drew it from the stone; and then, very slowly, from the little hole he saw a worm emerge, and these verses assure us it was fully six feet long. Suddenly it shot off faster than a crossbow bolt. Perceval was dumbstruck – he'd no idea what had become of it. But the air, he saw, was so full of fire he was sure the worm must be burning alive, and he heard thunder and a roaring wind: it seemed the sky was about to crumble into an abyss! He was afraid – and not a little! He realised a demon had deceived him – he was distraught and filled with dread. But the terrible storm didn't last long enough to boil an egg; and when Perceval saw the weather clear he sat down on the marble block beneath the tree and pondered on the worm.

Then he saw a beast approaching. It had the head of a man but the body of a snake. And at once it said to Perceval:

'I've come to do as I said. Ask whatever you wish – you bade me answer by the power of the One who created and made me. But we were undone by Lucifer's pride at our having been made so beautiful: his self-regard cost us dear! It angered God the Father, and He cast us down in torment from His holy, glorious heavens where the proud will never enter. Since you freed me from that stone I've destroyed a city and laid waste the land: within a day's ride on every side there's not a town or tower or castle where I've left a building standing – I've ruined and destroyed them all! You'll see for yourself if you ride on: if you carry on along this path you'll die crazed with hunger!'

'You're lying!' said Perceval. 'I swear by God you are! The creature that uttered those mighty cries and slithered from the hole was a tiny, slender thing! Your serpent's body is huge! And you've the head of a man, it seems. When I look at your face you seem gentle-natured – though your body's hideous, foul! So I don't believe you – you're not the one I freed from the stone!'

'Listen to me,' the demon said. 'I tell you this: in such a shape as I am now the Devil tricked Eve! He'd have striven in vain if she'd seen his body – he'd never have deceived her then! He hid his body so that Eve didn't spot it! That's why I've assumed this shape – I've tricked people far more easily like this! I'll do much more evil now I'm freed from the stone; Merlin put me there by magic, so I wouldn't be able to use my wiles to thwart the one who's seeking the grail – he'll never be able to find it now I'm out of the stone! He'll be wasting his time – he'll never achieve his goal!'

'By my life,' said Perceval, 'now I know you're lying! I'll not believe a word of it – unless I see you go back in the stone in the form of the thing I released just now! If you're that creature, turn into it again and return to the hole: then I'll believe you – and pick your brains on another matter. But you can't – you're no shape-changer!'

'Right! You'll see!' the demon cried, and turned into a worm and was back in the stone before you could count to four! Perceval dashed up and rammed the spike back in the narrow hole; the demon was so distraught that he screamed and howled, yelling: 'Mercy, kind sir! Let me out of here! I'll never do anyone harm or shame or wickedness again!'

'You can wail all you like,' said Perceval. 'Enemy of God, I'll never set you free! A fool let you out, but a wise man put you in again! You tricked me at the start – I tricked you at the finish! Your wiles have failed! You're always on the look-out for God-loving people to deceive, to snare them in sin. Tell me, why do you work so hard to trick them and cast them into torment? The more intent they are on doing good, the more you work against them.'

'True,' said the demon. 'I'm bent on leading the good astray because the wicked will all be mine! The usurers and hypocrites, the traitors and the sodomites, I let them be – because unless they mend their ways God leaves them all to me! But He won't let me claim the good. I've failed with you, and my comrades have attacked you many times. But I promise you this: they'll assail you often, in many ways and many guises, before your adventure's done! But if you succeed, you'll be a king of great riches – of which pride has deprived me. Be off with you now – I can't speak any more. Go where you will.'

At that Perceval turned away and mounted and set off. He began to climb a mountain, and when he reached the top he sat still on his horse and gazed up and down, and saw the whole country was scorched and burnt. He couldn't believe his eyes: there wasn't a castle, town or house left standing. He was amazed; and then, reflecting, he realised the demon had told him the truth: he had indeed destroyed the land.

Lugarel the Jealous

Then he spied a path into a forest, where all the leaves were burnt as if by fire: it was clearly the demon's doing. But he could see no other path, and he followed it all day till he emerged from the forest into a great valley. By evening he'd crossed it and passed into a meadow, and he rode on till he came to a poplar tree and a marble cross and a beautiful statue in the likeness of a girl. Perceval saw the sun was setting and decided to spend the night there in the meadow: he badly needed rest. So he dismounted and took off his horse's harness. But unless God, the true King, watched over him, it would have been better if he'd been unborn! At least he didn't remove his armour! He propped himself against the cross at the statue's feet. Now God protect him from harm!

As darkness fell the moon rose, which Perceval was pleased to see; it was a fair and pleasant night. But as he lay there in the poplar's shade he heard a voice crying out in woe, saying:

'When will I find the one who killed my love? My heart's in torment for her death! I've slain so many good knights, and I'll keep on till I take revenge on my sweetheart's killer! The pain in my heart will never be gone till I find him! And I'll kill everyone I meet until I do!'

Hearing the voice he got up and harnessed his horse again. He stood there in the middle of the meadow, beneath the tree, beside the cross, and saw a knight heading for the statue at a thunderous rate. He nearly went wild with rage when he caught sight of Perceval. He turned his horse towards him and cried:

'I defy you, knight! I swear you're going to die!'

'It would be a sin, good sir,' said Perceval, 'to kill me: I've done you no wrong at all!'

'You'd better believe me,' the knight replied. 'I'm in earnest! I'm driven so by grief and rage that I'll have your head off with my sharp steel sword!'

'No you won't,' said Perceval, 'not if I can help it. I'd rather my end didn't come so soon – I'd like to live a bit longer if it be God's plan! It's crazy, wanting to have my head!

What's the point? Even if you did it wouldn't do you much good! And I'll defend myself, of that you can be sure.'

The knight was beside himself, and cried: 'What? You dare to resist? Are you really that brave? By God, even if there were ten of you you'd be no match for me!'

'Self-control's never out of place,' said Perceval. 'So says anyone with sense. Moderate your anger and calm yourself. There's no one here but the two of us, and since you're so full of prowess there'd be little to gain by killing a single man – it wouldn't be much of a victory when you say you could have slain ten! But come: let me mount and let's each do our best.'

'Mount, then: I swear it's time for you to die!'

'You won't be bandying threats around,' said Perceval, 'by the time we've finished.'

Then he mounted and laced his helm, and slung a shield about his neck, given to him by the defeated Leander along with a good stout lance. Without more ado they charged at each other vigorously, as fast as their horses could run, and exchanged such mighty lance-blows that they smashed through their shields and drove the lance-heads full in their chests; they both lost their stirrups and went crashing down, one backwards, the other sideways – which was just as well: their lances were unbroken, and if they hadn't fallen they'd have been speared through the body. They both jumped up and recovered their lances, shields and horses. The knight called to Perceval:

'What? Didn't I kill you in the joust?'

'No,' he called back. 'Thanks be to God who saved me.'

The knight's heart nearly burst with rage at this – I don't think he was too pleased with himself so far! Back they came in another charge. Now God keep Perceval from harm! – for the knight, who had little fear of him, struck him with all his force, piercing his shield, his hauberk, too, making an ugly wound in his side, rending skin and flesh; but God, invoked by Perceval, protected him from death, and without a word or cry of threat Perceval struck his opponent in return, splitting shield and hauberk and thrusting more than a hand's breadth and three fingers' lengths of lance into his left side. The knight's horse reeled and staggered, and fell right across the path on to its hind hocks; it couldn't right itself, and the knight had no choice but to jump from the saddle and stand, sword in hand, and then advance in mighty strides towards Perceval. Perceval dismounted and threw his reins across the saddle, while the knight came rushing at him, bent on revenge. Both were strong and agile, both were armed with sharp-edged swords, and they began a cruel, dreadful, bitter battle that lasted till almost midnight. They hacked their shields to pieces and hewed their hauberks till they were covered in gashes, dousing their blades with blood; they cut the laces of their helms; they were tiring and almost devoid of breath. But Perceval could endure exertion better than any man alive; he summoned up new strength and vigour and launched a fearsome assault, driving the knight back, awe-struck that Perceval could attack with as much power now as at the start – his blows rained on and on. His own strength now was on the wane, so weakened by the blood lost from his wound that his eyes were swimming – he could barely see; his blood was pouring steadily, and he began to cry:

'Alas! I could have killed ten of his kind at the start! But it's true what they say, and many know it: fools come a cropper in many a scheme! My scheme's well and truly scuppered – I'm powerless. If I could die right here and now that's what I'd crave – I'd face death boldly rather than see defeat.'

Perceval felt great pity as he heard the knight's lament, and said: 'I'll not mince words: plead for mercy or die.'

'You'll never hear me plead! I'd sooner be slain!' And he lashed out and dealt Perceval a blow that smashed the visor from his helm – had it landed a little higher he'd never have needed a surgeon again.

'By all the saints!' cried Perceval. 'That's the last time I offer you a deal!'

'I couldn't care less!' the knight replied. 'You think you've beaten me? Not a chance! Defend yourself!'

So saying, he looked at the statue and remembered his sweetheart; then strength and courage returned to him and he attacked Perceval once more, dealing blows both high and low and many of them fearsome. He went at it like a man gone wild, and if he hadn't lost so much blood he'd have inflicted dreadful damage. But the blood was pouring from his side, making him weak and faint, and Perceval battered him till he laid him out beneath him and pinned him down, quite powerless, with blood emptying from his body, rendering him limp and feeble – and all the more distressed at having not been slain.

'Ask for mercy and admit defeat!' said Perceval.

'I'd rather die than admit I'm beaten!'

At this, Perceval cut the silk laces of his gold-veined helm and bared the knight's face and head. Then suddenly he saw a girl ride up before him crying:

'I'm at your service, knight! But don't harm him any more – give him to me and I'll soon repay the favour, and handsomely: you'll have your reward sure enough, have no fear. Please do as I ask. Nothing will make him admit defeat: you can cut him limb from limb and he still won't say it! Consider now: if on your many travels a maiden has ever been of service, return the favour by answering my request – I ask for mercy on this knight's behalf: let him lose neither life nor limb!'

'I do recall,' said Perceval, 'the maiden who gave me the shield with which I overcame the fire-breathing demon in the dragon's head. I'll always act fairly: for her sake I'll deliver this knight to you.'

'Many thanks, sir!' she said, and promptly turned her palfrey about and rode away.

Perceval stood when he saw her go, and called to the knight he'd fought, saying: 'What's going on? By God, I meant to speak to her before she left! Tell me: do you know her name, that girl, and who she is?'

'Not I, sir! I don't know who she is or where she's from – but Chance and Destiny brought her to my aid!'

'But come, you can tell me your own name, knight! And why I heard you grieving so, lamenting for your love.'

'Indeed I can, sir. I had a sweetheart, worthy and wise, in looks and body like the stone statue there. I loved her so dearly, by Saint Peter I did, that I took her with me everywhere, and whenever I came to a pleasant spot I'd pitch my tent and stay there more than a week in joy and delight. Nearly a year ago I found myself here – at the feast of Saint John, it was – and had my tent pitched here and strewn with flowers; then I sent my servants away and, in my sweetheart's presence, vowed to stay for a week and joust with anyone who passed, whether they liked it or not. In the course of that week more than twenty came, and I vanquished and outfought them all! But as the second week began I saw an antlered stag wounded with arrows, chased by a swift hound hot on its heels. I mounted and rode after, and finally ran it down – it was exhausted from running – and skinned and butchered it. While I was away and busy doing this, a knight strode into my tent where I'd left my sweetheart, and threatened to run her through with his sword unless she let him have his way. She refused. And he was true to his word: when she wouldn't submit he buried his sword in her body, and having done the deed he rode away. When I returned and saw her in that state I was distraught; she told me what had happened, holding nothing back, and bared her side to show me the wound – and the very next moment she died, without another word.

'I was filled with rage and grief – and had no idea where the treacherous knight had gone or who he was. Not knowing what had become of him, I'd gladly have been burnt alive to end my grief! As I wept and grieved my servants arrived, and when they saw what had happened they joined in my lament. But grieving solves nothing.

'I sent for a skilled mason and had my sweetheart buried here with this cross at her head and this statue carved in her shape and likeness: any man with any sense who saw it would say it was exactly like her. When all was done I told my people I'd come and keep watch here day and night for everyone who passed this way, and I'd kill them all with my sword till I'd slain the one who'd wronged me so – unless I was beaten. Well, you've beaten me, and could have killed me if you'd wished; but that girl took pity and for her sake you've spared me. When I'm given leave I'll go – who knows where? – and become a hermit, and expiate the sins I've done in cutting down and killing all those knights. All my love I shall turn to God.'

'Tell me your name now, if you will,' said Perceval, 'and your sweetheart's, too.'

At this the knight dissolved in tears, but replied with proper courtesy, saying: 'Truly, I'm known as Lugarel the Jealous. And I'll tell you the name of the one I loved so dearly.'

But as he was about to say it, he was so overcome by grief that his heart broke and failed: he slumped dead at Perceval's feet. Perceval didn't know what to do with the body – he was at a loss, not knowing where to look for someone to help bury him. So he stayed to keep watch over the body, but soon fell asleep. And when he awoke next morning he looked beside him and was amazed – and little wonder – to see no sign of the knight; instead, before him, beneath the tree, he saw a handsome marble tomb, with an inscription on the lid that said:

> Pray for the soul of Lugarel the Jealous.
> All true lovers should pity him,
> Given the events that led him to his death.

Perceval read this and was baffled, not knowing how it had come to be there; but he remembered defeating Lugarel and asking him his name and his beloved's. He made the sign of the cross over body and head, praying to God in His power to protect him from harm and trouble; then he looked towards the statue, admiring its beauty, before riding away without further delay.

The Maiden in the Spring

He pressed on till he came to a great, wide valley. There he found a pure and shining spring – and standing in it was a girl, the loveliest ever seen in this world. Her hair hung loose and she was naked from head to foot. Whoever had forced her to suffer so had a crazed and cruel heart: so thought Perceval. He rode up and hailed her; she bowed her head, blushing, and said:

'May the One who bestows and allots all blessings keep you, sir.'

'Dear girl,' he said, 'please tell me truly, if you will: why have you been made to suffer so, to stay there in the water?'

'I swear by my right hand, sir,' she replied, 'no man ever inflicted cruelty with so little cause! If I dared explain, I gladly would, but I couldn't do so safely. If I thought it was safe I'd tell you.'

'I swear to you, I give my word,' said Perceval, 'I'll do all in my power to relieve you of this.'

'Listen then, sir,' she said, 'and I'll tell you. The knight who put me here once asked me for my love; he kept pleading till I granted it, and he loved me passionately. One day we came out here to frolic in the fields, and he plied me with songs and verses, and after we'd cavorted and romped and played he started pressing me to say if there was any knight in the world as gallant, bright, handsome, free and courteous as he, or one with such a cultured, happy way with words; I said I'd heard of none as renowned and worthy of love as the one named Perceval, who's sought the grail so long. The moment he heard this, his heart was stricken with jealousy: he blazed with anger – he was furious. He told me I'd said it to humiliate him! He made me strip and forced me in the water! Then I heard him swear I'd spend the rest of my days here and never leave, unless Perceval proved his strength and rescued me in spite of him. That's all there is to tell. I pray you now, let me know your name.'

'My rightful name, fair girl, is Perceval the Welshman. And by all the saints of Rome, your penance is done – I'll have you out of there if I can, by God the true King! It was an outrageous wrong to force you in!'

Just as he said this the knight came riding on a dun, white-stockinged horse, and cried from afar:

'By Christ, knight, you'll pay for your fun! You'll be sorry you ever stopped there!'

'I can't believe, by God the King,' said Perceval, 'you're going to hurt me for so little.'

'Say what you like,' the knight replied. 'Anyone who tries it will pay the price!'

Then Perceval said: 'If there's no point being polite, prepare to joust.'

No more was said; they braced their shields and sent their horses charging forward, their hind legs raising clouds of dust, their fore legs cracking stones apart. They delivered mighty blows to each other's shield, rending leather, piercing wood; their hauberks saved them, but the lances were strong and stout, unbending: the heads smashed into their chests and sent them crashing from their steeds – not that there was any shame in this, for the saddle-straps and breast-straps had split asunder, and the horses hit the turf before their riders. Up the knights leapt and assailed one another with their swords so sharp, dealing each other blows so great that they cut into helms and shields and mail. By the time the first assault was over hardly a scrap of shield remained! They'd been hacked and smashed to pieces! Then the knight drew back a little and said:

'Step back a moment, knight, and tell me your name.'

'Truly, my name is Perceval. Now let me know yours.'

'I'd never lie,' the knight replied. 'I'm known as Brandin Hard-heart. I'm delighted to hear you're Perceval! Your labours are over: I'll never eat again until I've killed you!'

And Perceval responded boldly: 'In that case your fast will be permanent!'

With that they returned to the attack, one striking high, the other low; but I promise you, this sword-fight didn't last long: Perceval rushed at him with naked sword and dealt him a slashing blow that severed head from trunk. He commended his soul to Beelzebub: he'd done all manner of harm in the land.

Then Sir Perceval helped the damsel out of the spring, and brought a gown of shot silk and hung it on a tree before her. She was chilled to the marrow and couldn't wait to dress – but once she was dressed she was the loveliest creature ever seen. Perceval took her by the hand and seated her beside him, and asked her all about herself: her name and her family and where they were from.

'Truly, sir, my name is Dyonise of Galoee.'

'I hope you don't mind, dear girl, but I had little rest or sleep last night, so forgive me if I take a nap.'

'I don't mind at all, good sir. It would be unkind to object!'

So Perceval lay down and rested his head in her lap; he was asleep in an instant, and Dyonise stayed very still.

But he hadn't been lying there very long before she saw a youth approaching. Handsome and courtly and smart he was, and bright and pleasant in appearance; he was dressed not in scarlet* but in coarse woollen stuff, though he was mounted on a good, swift horse and shod in splendid leather shoes, and hung from his saddle was a sword with a hilt of finest gold. He rode up to the girl, her cheek resting on her hand, and greeted her politely; she replied:

'May God who never fails His own protect you, friend.'

She said this softly, keeping her voice down so as not to disturb the one who was sleeping in her lap. The youth, without more ado, asked her who was slumbering there; Dyonise answered:

'By the Creator, friend, he's the most faithless, cruel, dishonest man ever to be born of woman! Just now he killed my sweetheart, and I know he'll abuse and dishonour me the moment he awakes! I pray you have mercy! In God's name, dismount: with that sword hanging from your saddle you could easily behead him while he's sleeping! As soon as you've slain him I promise I'll go with you and answer your every desire!'

But to this the youth responded shrewdly, saying: 'Curse the man who'd lay a hand on the knight at your bidding – and go a single step with you – when he's done no wrong! Why should I trust you, so quick to bid me kill him? You might well say the same about me if you ran into someone else!'

While they were talking Perceval awoke: he'd heard their every word, but was undismayed. He stretched and stood up, and the youth came briskly and greeted him and Perceval replied with all courtesy, saying:

'May God who never fails His own protect you, friend – He hasn't let *me* down today!'

At this the girl leapt forward, realising her mistake, and blurted: 'Ah, gentle knight, have mercy! Trust me: I swear I said it to test him!'

'It's clear to me,' said Perceval, 'your beauty's wasted on you when there's no goodness to go with it! What a shame! Alas for your fair body and arms and face – how badly Nature erred in omitting goodness! It saddens me to see it. I'm not going to punish you, but I'll accompany you no further.'

No more words were spoken, other than to commend one another to God; they left Dyonise to set off on her solitary way.

The Brigands' Girl

Perceval didn't dally – he was desperate for some food – and rode on down a valley, spurring his horse quite frequently, until he met a pilgrim with a cask of wine and a well-cooked shoulder of pork in his bag. Perceval asked if he had anything to eat, and without hesitation the pilgrim said:

'I've plenty of bread and wine and cooked meat, by Saint Livinus,[75] and you're welcome to have some – you look as if you need it!'

At this Perceval dismounted, and the pilgrim spread his cloth – quite white it was, too – and Perceval ate his fill, though he'd no wish to drink more than a little.

Once he'd eaten he took his leave of the pilgrim and mounted and set off again, riding straight and swift through a deep valley. Then he drew rein and looked about; and ahead and on either side he saw the valley's walls so steep that he was hard pressed to see which way to go. Suddenly he heard a loud, pained cry: on and on it rang, and he looked that way and saw a girl, the loveliest creature that ever lived or ever was beheld by man, all alone, bereft of company. He wondered why she was crying so, and rode ahead and greeted her, and she replied:

'Ah, gentle knight, have pity! In God's name, take me away from here! For three days I've found nowhere to eat or sleep or rest!'

'What ever brought you here?' he asked.

'Ah, sir knight, please listen and I'll explain. Truly, I'm the daughter of Arguisel of Scotland; they call me Felisse of the White Close after the castle where I was born: Felisse is my proper name. And I'll tell you why I came here: one day I'd left the castle, White Close, and gone into the meadows to enjoy myself. Two knights suddenly appeared and grabbed me and threw me over a horse and carried me off at a gallop to the edge of yonder wood. Then they laid me on the ground and one of them demanded I let him have his way. So help me God, I'd rather have been torn limb from limb! But moments later two other knights appeared; they saw us from a distance and started crying:

'"By Christ, knights, what outrage is this? You'll pay for it!"

'And the one who was holding me left me and jumped on his horse and they started fighting. I don't know what the upshot was because I turned and fled through the wood – I'm so glad I escaped! I kept going till I found myself here. By the Lord who made the clouds, take me on your horse and carry me away from here: it'll win you some fine new friends!'

So Perceval stepped down. Ah, God! He didn't see he was being tricked! She was lying, that faithless, false-hearted girl! She would sit in wait for passers-by, and when anyone – knight or peasant – came that way she'd accost them and have them stripped of everything they owned: that was her plan for Perceval, who'd dismounted now; and while he spoke to her, unsuspecting, he saw five brigands come riding through the trees yelling:

'You're a prisoner, knight, indeed you are!'

Perceval realised he'd been ambushed but was quite undaunted. He leapt into the saddle and quoted a saying that came to him: 'So much mischief comes from woman!' But then he added: 'And everything that's good, in faith! From good women spring so many blessings, from the wicked all manner of ills and shame.'

To come straight to the point, they surrounded him and rudely cried: 'Come, knight! Before you leave you'll tell us what you're playing at – and you'll leave us that destrier and all your arms and gear!'

'In faith,' he replied, 'I'd say it was pretty base of you to attack me all together! Come one at a time, lance levelled! If you attack me all at once and win, what honour or credit will there be in that?'

---

[75] '*Lievin*': see note 44, above, p. 407.

'Don't waste your breath!' they cried. 'By God, you're for it! Defend yourself as best you can – you're going to need whatever you've got!'

But Perceval felt no fear. He drew back and prepared for a valiant charge; ablaze with anger, he braced his shield and set it before his breast. The others made ready to joust likewise, all five lowering their lances and letting their horses go. Perceval spurred his own, and met the first with a blow that smashed through his shield, through the folds of his mail, through his heart and struck him dead. Now he engaged the others: they delivered mighty blows to his shield that pierced and smashed it and rent his hauberk, wounding him a little in the belly; but they couldn't unhorse him – instead all four of their lances broke, so they drew their swords, sharp and honed. And Perceval drew his, and neither fled nor spared them: he dealt one of the four a blow to the helm, delivered with such might that the blade cut through to the teeth as if through silk, and the two halves of his head fell clean away. The others were enraged and came at him like wild things; but they came too close – Perceval, undaunted, struck one on the shoulder to send his sword-arm flying to the ground. At this the other two turned tail, and the girl yelled:

'Ahi! Ahi! How pathetic you are: three of you killed and you two beaten by a single knight!'

Hearing this they returned to the attack, and the battle was fierce and long. They split each other's helms and shields and hauberks; they inflicted many a wound; but finally Perceval caught one with a blow that clove his head down to the shoulders. The other stopped fighting and took to flight, and Perceval rode after, determined to catch him; he did all he could to get away, but Perceval sliced through his shoulder and down through his side to send him crashing to the ground, stone dead. He'd killed and slain all five: he'd escaped them through sheer prowess. He decided now to go back and destroy the traitress.

So back he rode – but to no avail: she'd fled.

'May she burn in hell fire! She could carry on wreaking evil!'

Perceval hunted high and low but couldn't find her, much to his vexation. Seeing his search was in vain he set off swiftly through the wood, still on the look-out for the false traitress who'd done so much wickedness and harm, but he could see no sign of her. He kept riding hard till he came to a broad, main track and set out along it at speed.

He pressed on all day without pause or rest, until around vespers he caught sight of a manor house of which all the walls were black. It was there that the traitress had taken refuge. Perceval headed for the entrance; but as he did so he heard a cry of:

'Stop! Stop!' It was a shepherd, tending a flock of sheep. 'I can't believe you mean to go in there, knight! If there were thirty-four of you, not one of you would come out alive! Don't think of going in, good sir, not for anything! By God, there's no point, unless you want to die! I'm not pulling your leg,' the shepherd said. 'Do yourself a favour and turn back, sir! The men inside are brigands, thieves, grave-robbers, murderers! There are fully two hundred in their band. They send a madwoman to keep watch for the good, valiant knights of King Arthur's table as they go in search of fearsome, tough adventures – and that crazy, wicked woman, bent only on evil, she went in the house just now! I don't know what's been going on, but she arrived on her own, without company.'

On hearing this, Perceval cried: 'By God! May she be damned!' And without another word he galloped off towards the gate. But if they trapped him inside, he'd be for it – it would end in grief for sure.

He found a hunchbacked dwarf at the gate with a strong, stout lance in his hands, who yelled: 'By the Lord who created all, another step forward and I'll have you! You'll know about it – it'll be a proper blow!'

Perceval spurred towards him but didn't want to soil his weapons; instead he steered his horse at him and trampled him under his hooves. The dwarf was in a dismal state, not just battered but pulped to death. The men inside were shocked and aggrieved to see their dwarf killed so, and alarmed, too, for – luckily for Perceval – there were only three of them; but they were armed and mounted and came to the attack. But at the first of them Perceval launched his lance and speared him: it was the last that anyone heard of him – a great length of lance plunged clean through his chest and sent him crashing to the ground.

'That should keep you busy!' said Perceval. 'You'd nothing on your mind a moment ago – now you'd better think about a cure!'

He was about to recover his lance when the other two came charging; they both struck him together, but Perceval sliced one through to the bowels with his keen-edged sword. The third had struck him on his red-hued shield, but the lance had smashed to pieces. Suddenly the mad traitress came rushing, clutching an axe and screaming at him:

'You made a mistake coming here, I swear! You've seen the best day you'll ever see! There's nothing you can do – your head's going to soak in your blood!'

And she raised the axe aloft, aiming to behead him; but he charged in close and sliced off her hands – which pretty much broke her heart. The third brigand, seeing this, didn't know what to do to save his life – which was now his only thought. He tried to flee to a tower, but Perceval overtook him and struck him on the head – like it or not, the sword clove him to his collar-bone and laid him dead on the ground. The girl was looking at utter disaster; with all hope gone, knowing her end had come, she went rushing off – without her hands.

'You can try and run away from me,' cried Perceval, 'but you won't be playing games with anyone again!'

And he seized her by the hair, headed for a foul mire and hurled her in. She came to a sticky end.

Then Perceval went and scoured the castle but didn't find a soul, much to his annoyance. So he set fire all over, burning the whole place to the ground; now the brigands had nowhere to hide – their refuge was no more. Then he returned to his horse and mounted, and set off down a well-made road.

But he hadn't gone the length of a bowshot before he caught sight of a fortress. He headed that way, and the lord of the house and a great crowd of his people came out to meet him, welcoming him with joy and vying to hold his stirrup. He leapt from his good charger and entrusted him to the mareschal,* who supplied the horse with hay and oats and bedding. The lord – a most worthy gentleman, he seemed – cheerfully asked him his name, and he had no qualms about telling him:

'My name is Perceval, sir.'

When the lord heard this he was thrilled beyond words. He had Perceval disarmed, and his wife quickly unlocked a cupboard and took out a brand new scarlet mantle lined with sable – they believed it was the finest sable in the world, and had been treasuring that gown – and with its fastenings of pure gold she draped it across his shoulders. The servants briskly set the table, and everybody washed. They had some five or six dishes (I shan't describe them all) and plenty of clear wines, fresh and new, and happily drank their fill. And when everyone had supped and was replete, the cloths were cleared and they washed again, and then spoke of many things. They honoured Perceval as the finest knight to be found anywhere – and so they should: they'd soon have suffered all manner of harm and grief and trouble had Perceval with his great valour and his sword not freed them from the band of which you've heard, destroying them and their stronghold, too.

The lord's gracious lady, attentive to Perceval's every wish, was the first to ask him how he'd managed to achieve what she'd long desired. 'How did you deal with those brigands, who caused us and others so much harm?'

'They'll never hurt you or anyone again,' he said. 'They're destroyed, I promise you, and so is their refuge. They'll be attacking and fighting no one from now on.' And he recounted his adventure in truthful detail: how he'd been misled by the traitress and attacked by the brigands but had fought his way out and killed them all. He told them everything. With that their talking ended, and cup-bearers brought the wine, and the lord of the house invited Perceval to drink first from a gorgeous cup of pure gold. Then he bade that a bed be made in a panelled chamber – a fine, deep bed of fresh straw – and Perceval was escorted there and helped from his clothes and shoes, and down he lay. I shan't go on about the coverlets and the pillows, but he had ample, as befitted one of his worth. And he was soon asleep, being very weary, and slept till the new day dawned.

When he saw day break he rose, and the lord came to him and said: 'I wish you a good day, sir!'

'And you good fortune!' Perceval said. 'Please have my arms and gear made ready.'

'There's no need to rush,' the lord replied. 'No need at all: stay here with us for a week at least – or a fortnight!'

'By Saint Damian,[76] I can't possibly,' said Perceval. 'No, I'll be on my way good and early, if God gives me strength.'

And he set about arming swiftly, and as soon as he was done he went down and they brought his horse; he mounted his fine steed, took his leave of the lord and lady and departed, heading swiftly for the forest, where he felt safer than in open ground. He prayed to God who made heaven and earth to guard him from mishap and protect him from harm that day.

The Hermit's Injunction

All day long he rode, till darkness began to fall. He turned towards a little wood, finding no house of any kind – he didn't know quite what to do. But just as he approached the shelter of a rock he heard a little bell ring. It was coming from a hermitage where two venerable men of great age dwelt, and it was there that Perceval headed now, following the sound of the bell. He rode up to the door and called, and one of the hermits came with keys to open up. Perceval took off his helm to uncover his face, and asked for lodging in the name of charity; the worthy hermit, who was holding a letter, was full of kindness and made a sign by way of welcome, to show that he'd be given lodging. So Perceval dismounted, and one of the hermits took his horse and saw him comfortably stabled, while the other set the table and laid the cloth with salt and knives and bread. As soon as he was disarmed the trusty hermit saw him washed and seated, and Perceval was delighted by the warmth of the welcome. But as for the food, he had

---

[76] *'Domin'*; see note 47, above, p. 411.

barley bread, roughly kneaded – and it won't take me long to describe the rest: herbs, lettuce and cress he had, and wild berries gathered in the wood. There was certainly no wine of any kind; he drank water from a bowl till he'd had his fill. And his horse had hay and a whole bushel of barley. Then he lay on a bed of fresh straw, covered with a woollen drape and blanket, with his gear around him close at hand, ever wary of danger. But after crossing himself he felt no fear.

So there he slept that night till morning, when he rose, stiff from the hard bed, and made ready as best he could. Then the hermit beckoned him and led him to the chapel where divine service was to be sung. Perceval heard it all with a devout, true heart, and when it came to the sacrament he clasped his hands on high and prayed to God to forgive him the sins he felt he'd committed; and when the service came to an end, the presiding hermit blessed him and gave him a short sermon which pleased him greatly. He confessed his sins as fully as he could; and when he asked for guidance, the hermit said that some men's way of life was madness.

'I don't consider any man wise who spends his life in such a way that he wastes his body and loses his soul. God didn't make knights to wage war and kill, but to uphold justice and defend Holy Church: God loves not presumptuous pride. If you want His love, dear friend, you'd better not grow up like that!'

'I'll do my best,' said Perceval.

'I'd advise it! But come: tell me your name.'

'My name is Perceval, sir.'

'It's a shame that a noble youth like you has chosen such a path: you'd be better devoted to the Church! Put your trust in God, and always remember that He suffered death for us in His sacrifice on the cross. Keep Him ever in your mind and you will win God's glory.'

And he bade him kneel and say his *mea culpa* and pray to God; and Perceval, very moved, said it four times, repenting deeply for his sins. The worthy hermit kindly gave him absolution and commended him to God. Perceval asked for nothing more: he'd made confession and heard the divine service; and he left the chapel and swiftly armed, and his destrier was brought to him and he mounted at once and took his leave of the hermits.

Through the gate he rode, and found a number of beaten tracks. He didn't know which way to go, so he gave his horse free rein and the horse set off to the right. Perceval prayed to the King of Heaven to guide him to the house of the Fisher King: he wanted nothing else.

He pressed on harder through the forest, and began to cross a great, wide glade. And he suddenly saw, storming towards him, a superbly armed knight: it would be hard to describe the splendour of his gear. Perceval didn't know who he was, but he looked magnificent, with an indigo pennon on his lance and his shield painted blue. With a steely, wicked confidence and a heart brim-full of wrath, he cried to Perceval to defend himself or he'd strike, and Perceval, seeing his demeanour, made ready to joust, come what may. They charged at each other and exchanged such mighty blows on their shields that their lances smashed like bark into a dozen pieces. So they went at it with drawn swords, squaring up and raining blows on each other's shield to send chunks of gold and blue and silver flying to the ground. The knight struck Perceval on his jewelled helm, dashing the main hoop[77] into his lap.

---

[77] i.e. the reinforcing band around the helm.

'Take that, sir knight, as an advance!'

'By God,' said Perceval, 'such a generous loan must be repaid: I'll return it at double rate!' And with a mighty flourish he struck him on his helm, adorned with painted flowers, and split it to the nasal. 'I don't think much of your headgear, knight – you might as well have been bare-headed!' And he caught him with a slashing cut that almost brought him down, and cried again: 'Take care how you dole out your blows today – they'll be returned with interest! I won't be in debit at the end of the day – I always clear debts as soon as they're due!'

So saying he aimed another blow, but the knight thrust out his shield to block it; and clutching his well-honed sword he struck Perceval with all his force. They went at it now in earnest, giving and returning ferocious blows without flinching or delay – whatever was given was repaid in full, both capital and interest! No fiercer clash between two knights was ever seen, I'd say, with swingeing blows and cuts and slashes. They fought on horseback till they brought each other down, then leapt to their feet and returned to the attack, both tireless; they cut the laces from their helms and sent them flying from their heads, then seized each other round the neck, ripping open their ventails, tearing at the rings of their bright mail hoods as they strove to throttle each other. The knight swore Perceval was a dead man unless he yielded, but Perceval said he was mistaken.

'You think I'm beaten? You've got the better of me? How wrong you are!'

'What!' cried the knight. 'You don't scare me in the least! If you were the last man in the world I'd finish you! You're done for!'

'Let's see what you're made of, then!' said Perceval. 'You're full of yourself, bragging about your prowess! It's going to be tested now – fight on, and we'll see who's the stronger!'

'I couldn't agree more!' the knight replied; and with swords gripped tight they locked in a wrestling hold, beating each other with fists and pommels, both utterly committed, shaking with rage, pulling, pounding, pushing, crushing, till they'd almost worn each other down. So many moves and blows they made, till Perceval landed four in quick succession that forced the knight down flat beneath him.

'You're finished!' he cried. 'So much for all your bragging!'

'I admit defeat – you've beaten me,' said the knight. 'I crave mercy. I'd have done better amusing myself at chess than coming to fight with you today! I ask your mercy, sir, in God's name: have pity on me.'

'If you want to have mercy,' he replied, 'you must promise to go without delay and yield as a prisoner to King Arthur; you're to surrender on my behalf. When you arrive you're to give the king and all his company my greetings. Before we part, this you must swear.'

He gave his word, promising to let no obstacle or trouble prevent him going, barring death alone. 'And when I reach the court, on whose behalf am I to surrender to the king?'

'On behalf of his dear friend Perceval. And tell me your name now.'

When the knight heard Perceval's name he was overcome with rage and joy beyond words, and I'll tell you why: he was furious that he'd been vanquished, but overjoyed that it was at the hands of Perceval. He reached out and embraced him, and addressed him thus:

'My reputation is undiminished by being outfought by you: God has honoured me with this fight! Madiex is my name, the Knight of the Ill-cut Coat. You've cut and hewn my armour to shreds, but it's nothing but a joy and comfort to know I've been vanquished by such a worthy knight! I couldn't care less about my loss, by all the saints of Rome! Good sir, I ask your leave.'

'Before God,' said Perceval, 'I'd gladly pardon you imprisonment if you wish.'

But Madiex said he wouldn't accept for all the gold in Cornwall. 'Just tell me to go to the king and deliver my message.'

'I don't know what to say!' said Perceval. 'Other than to commend you to Jesus.'

'And I commend you, sir,' said Madiex, 'to the glorious King of Heaven.'

And he mounted his horse by the left stirrup. They commended each other to God once more, and those were their last words. The Knight of the Ill-cut Coat set out swiftly on his way, taking the most direct path that he could.

The Black Giant

But I want to return to Perceval, who set out in another direction – though he'd no idea where he was going. He could see that night was drawing in, and started spurring harder, but didn't know where to look for shelter – he prayed to Saint Julian[78] to guide him to good lodging. Then he looked ahead and saw a handsome little castle; he turned his trusty horse that way, and he bore him swiftly. Along the way he met an elderly man of noble appearance who hailed and greeted him genially, and Perceval replied likewise. The gentleman led him to his home and invited him to stay the night; Perceval was only too pleased to accept, and thanked him warmly for his kind offer. So together they went straight to the castle, and in the courtyard, beneath an aspen tree, the gentleman climbed from his black horse and Perceval dismounted likewise. Then his horse was stabled while he was disarmed and dressed in a short mantle to stop him getting cold, and because of the cold the lord led him to the fire. He asked him his name, being eager to know all about him.

'By God the glorious King of Heaven,' said Perceval, 'I'm from Wales, and was named Perceval in baptism, truly.'

'Now I know,' said the lord, 'great honour has come my way! I'm delighted to welcome you.'

He bade that the table be set, and this was done; but I'm not going to rattle on about the dishes that were served – it would take too long! When they'd eaten they washed and drank and then took to their beds: they saw Perceval into a huge, high bed where he slept peacefully all night long till dawn.

The lord and all the household rose early; and when Perceval heard the watch sound the dawn he woke and quickly dressed and went to the hall and asked for his arms; and at the lord's bidding the servant who'd been in charge of them brought them without delay. Then he asked the groom for his horse, and he didn't dally but harnessed the horse and led him to Perceval, already fully armed. He mounted, took his shield by the straps and hung it round his neck, and then took his leave of his host who commended him most feelingly to God.

He rode from the courtyard, praying to God to keep him from trouble and harm and shame, and to grant that he achieve his quest for the grail, for which he'd striven so hard, for so many weeks and months, and suffered so much toil and hardship.

'I've taken so many blows! All the strange things I've encountered, the privations

---

[78] Saint Julian the Hospitaller – the patron saint of travellers seeking lodging.

I've endured – going without food, without sleep: all so far in vain. No matter what I do it all seems fruitless – and now I've no idea which way to go or where to turn! All I want is to find the house of the good Fisher King – but I fear I'm so much a sinner I'm wasting my time! But if chance should lead me back there, I'll ask to know the truth about the grail and the lance, and all about the bier and the silver trencher that I saw, so beautiful and fine.'

This he vowed. He headed now towards a great, thick forest and kept going that way: he was happier there than in open country. He pressed on hard. And then, roaming on through the forest as chance took him, he saw a giant, striding swiftly down a valley. He was holding a horse whose master he'd slain: in his pride and folly he'd recklessly killed that knight of high renown, and now he was pulling his destrier by the reins. Perceval couldn't understand what the giant was doing, and headed his way and said:

'Why don't you mount your horse, sir knight?'

The giant, brimming with haughty pride, told him he'd be sorry he'd ended up there, saying: 'You'll never see your home again!' And he tied the destrier to the branch of an oak and came striding at Perceval. In his hands was a club fully ten feet long and bound with iron; he wouldn't have swapped it for ten spears or as many sharp swords! Its bearer looked like a devil from Hell, as black as if he'd been dragged from a fire. He strode up to Perceval and said:

'Here – what can you tell me, boy, about the fellow who slew my brother? He's made me mad! I've been raging night and day!'

'I haven't a clue unless you tell me his name. What's he called?'

'They call him Perceval, that's his name; he's seeking the grail and has won the balm.[79] I've scoured every land for him since I heard he killed my brother – I was none too pleased! I'll not drink another drop of wine till I've cut him down or hanged him high! But I've hung around here too long without killing you – I'm amazed your heart's not quaking with fear! But come, look sharp, and tell me your name – I want to know.'

'I shan't keep it from you – I'll tell you now: truly, my name is Perceval.'

'Are you indeed? "The one who plumbs the depths"?[80] If you're "the one who plumbs the depths", your death lies waiting in my club, four palms thick! You'd better start saying your psalms – it's time for you to pray!'

'Never mind threats,' said Perceval. 'Let's go to it.'

He drew back a little, the length of a bowshot; then Perceval, so skilled at striking blows, so battle-hardened, brandished his lance with its piercing head and charged at the giant and dealt him a mighty blow full in the chest. He had a tough hide, four folds thick, that saved him from death for the moment, so the verses say, but the blow sent him crashing down. He was quickly back on his feet, and Perceval faced a fierce assault – he'd have to defend himself now – as the giant rushed at him clutching his club in both hands and crying:

'You've washed up in the wrong place, sonny!'

---

[79] i.e. the healing balm he won from the hag, above, pp. 383–5.
[80] '*perches les vals*' appears literally to mean 'pierces the vales', but the implication of this play on Perceval's name is not clear, and 'plumbs the depths' is an attempt to have it suggest something more specific. Interestingly, the author of the prose romance *Perlesvaus* (from which Gerbert borrowed a number of episodes), in changing the name of the protagonist, created a clear meaning by having the name 'Per-les-vaus' refer to his having '*lost* the vales' by being robbed of his inheritance: see *The High Book of the Grail (Perlesvaus)*, tr. Bryant (revised edition, Cambridge, 2007), p. 13.

And he attacked him like a man deranged, wielding his spiked club. He aimed straight for Perceval's head, but he ducked aside and the mighty blow landed on his horse's neck, making it crumple beneath him whether he liked it or not; but Perceval thrust in his spurs and the destrier sprang back up. Back to the attack came the giant, aiming to club his head off without the cut of a sword; he gripped his club and swung it aloft, but Perceval thrust his shield upward and deflected the blow; it fell on the saddle-bow; the destrier bore the brunt and paid the price, as the wicked giant shattered the poor beast's neck with his bludgeon. He collapsed on the ground, stone dead, and Perceval had to jump from the saddle.

'Wretched boy!' the giant cried. 'I'll make you pay dearly for my beloved brother's death!'

'By Saint Nicholas,' said Perceval, 'he killed my horse in a garden,[81] outside his gate – it maddens me that you've done the same! I tell you this: you'll pay in full for the harm and shame you've done me and my horse!'

'It's nothing compared to what you're *going* to suffer – right now! Your time is up!'

They both attacked, and Perceval landed a blow to the giant's head that might have been decisive had he not been wearing a cap of boiled leather that partly absorbed it – but all the same the blade carried off his nose and lip and his front teeth, filling his mouth with blood and sweat.

'That'll slow you down a bit!' cried Perceval, mocking him. 'You'd have been better off across the Rhône than coming here! What a fool you're going to look! Before you get out of here you'll be in the sorriest state you've ever seen! You'd have done better to flee across the sea, to Germany!'

These taunts enraged the giant. He was determined to pay him back in full, so gripped by fury that the very ground shook and quaked; and clutching his club, which was far from light,[82] he launched himself at Perceval, aiming to kill him with a massive blow unless God saved him. He had to dodge aside; the giant tried to bowl him over, wielding his weapon with amazing speed, dealing four flailing blows in quick succession: how he hated Perceval! But he couldn't touch him: Perceval showed his agility as he ducked and dodged and covered himself; the giant kept battering furiously, raging, blazing with wrath and loathing. Again he gripped his mighty club and, with all his strength behind it, he aimed a ferocious blow at Perceval's head; but alert as ever, he dodged and ducked; down swept the blow with dreadful might, but it missed Perceval and landed on a stone that lay between them, smashing off a chunk of club – three and a half feet of it! The giant nearly went wild with grief when he saw his club in two; and Perceval attacked him with his drawn sword, hammering and harassing him and landing a blow on his cheek that cut away more than a hand of flesh beside the ear.

'You've gone bright red!' he said to the devilish creature.

'I'll make you pay!' the giant cried. 'You wretched scum!'

He rushed at him, intending to grab him by the arms; but he wasn't quick enough: Perceval went at him with his sword, bent on killing him. The giant flailed with the stump of his club, faster than the wind, but none of the blows properly landed, and he was losing heart and spirit as he failed to take control. Then Perceval dashed and recovered his lance, lying on the ground; he was frustrated that the giant had lasted so long, and that he'd had to endure so much.

[81] In the Second Continuation, above, p. 254.
[82] Literally 'wasn't made of poplar'.

'God,' he thought, 'I wonder if I'm still any good at throwing? If I can't take him by surprise and bring him down with a throw, then I fear I'll have no chance. This vile rogue's making me look a fool! Shame on me if he lasts much longer! I used to be good with my javelins – I had such a good aim and throw: if I wanted to bring down a buck or doe or any other creature it was dead! And this haughty, wicked giant's as wild as any beast! By Saint Lazarus of Avalon, I'll see if a throw'll do any good against this foe who despises me!'

He took the lance and aimed at the giant, and head and pennon flew through his brain and sent him crashing dead. Perceval pulled out the lance, the head covered in blood, and held out his hands towards the east and thanked God that he'd killed the giant. Then he went to his horse and was upset to see him dead, for he'd been a good, strong steed; but he was consoled by the sight of the other, still tethered to the branch: a fine, powerful destrier he was, handsome indeed, and Perceval strode straight up and untied him and stepped into the stirrup and swung into the saddle, fully armed. Then he took up his lance, its pennon stained red with blood; and once he had all his gear in place he thrust in his spurs and rode away.

All through the leafy wood the birds were singing in their Latin,[83] and Perceval was delighted by their song. On he rode, elated by the testing adventure he'd achieved in overcoming the giant. But he went at a gentle, easy pace, for he was drained and very weary: the giant had given him a hard and taxing time. Deep in thought, he kept riding right through the forest till evening. Then he met a vavasor mounted on a splendid destrier who said:

'Welcome, sir!'

'May God the Lord of all the world,' Perceval called back, 'protect you from misfortune, sir, you and all who wish you well.'

The vavasor, a worthy man indeed, politely asked if he'd kindly tell him his name.

'I'm a Welshman, friend,' he said, 'and conversant more with arms than laws: please call me Perceval.'

'You'll be well lodged tonight, sir; I trust you'll not decline my invitation – it's sincerely meant.'

'I'm sure it is, and it's very welcome!'

'My word is my bond, by the Holy Spirit,' said the vavasor. 'Come now to our home and rest. I couldn't let you ride on by – it wouldn't be right!'

'Many thanks!' said Perceval; and talking together they carried on to the castle, which was handsome indeed: had Perceval been a duke or a count it would have been a worthy place to stay. They rode straight through the gate and dismounted at the foot of the steps, and servants hurried from all sides to receive their horses. Then the lord and Perceval climbed up to the hall together. I'd be hard pressed to describe the finery and comfort: Perceval sat on a sheet of flowered red silk to be disarmed, and then took a seat beside a fire of elm-wood, and the lord beside him – and the seats weren't padded with straw but richly upholstered with fine and elegant cushions. A mantle lined with squirrel fur the lord placed about his shoulders. Then the table was set without delay and they rose and went to eat; they were served with plentiful dishes – I've never seen so many; quite simply, I've never seen a duke or count better lodged than Perceval was that night, and he and his horse slept soundly all night till morning.

---

[83] The same phrase appeared at the very beginning of Chrétien (above, p. 2); it reappears now, just after Perceval has returned to using the weapon of his youth, throwing his lance like a javelin.

When the sun's rays flooded the hall with light, Perceval awoke, surprised to find he'd slept so long. He rose at once and armed smartly: a young squire was in attendance and laced his ventail, and Perceval asked him to call for his horse.

'You'll have him at once, sir: he's quite ready. You'll have a new shield, too, painted red,[84] and my lord has promised you a burnished hauberk – we've plenty here – and a surcoat of Syrian cloth; all this he sends you: he holds worthy knights in the highest regard, and does all he can to honour them.'

'God bless his custom, and may it burgeon! I shall hold him as a friend indeed, when he provides me with such fine new gear.'

The lord, that kind and generous man, entered the room where Perceval was arming, and when he saw him he hailed him nobly, saying:

'May God whose word is ever true give you a good day!'

'And may He grant that I see the day when I can repay these favours!' Looking first at the hauberk with its tight-meshed mail, he said: 'You've improved my gear for sure – every bit of it!'

'Before you don your helm, good sir,' he replied, 'wait just a little, if you will, and have a bite to eat: a sop of bread and a little paste,[85] and a cup of good wine, strong and fresh and clear. It'll set you up for your day's journey.'

Food was quickly prepared and they served it to him, fully armed – he didn't object! – with four good drinks of wine. When he'd eaten all he wished he took his leave of the vavasor, saying:

'Forgive me if I go now.'

The vavasor fastened the helm on his head, and Perceval, with no desire to linger, went straight to the door of the hall and down the steps to where his horse stood ready. Then the good knight mounted, shield slung from neck, and took up his lance and rode through the gate without more ado and set out along a great, wide road. But there we'll leave him for just a little, and tell what happened to the knight he'd vanquished in the glade.[86]

The Search for Perceval

The story, and it's true, says that the knight – the Knight of the Ill-cut Coat – rode in search of the king dressed and armed just as he'd been when vanquished. I'm not going to make a song and dance about his journey and where he stayed; he followed the various paths and roads to Duveline, where the king of Ireland was holding court and, to enhance its prestige, had craved and implored the presence of the worthy, courtly King Arthur. So there the Knight of the Ill-cut Coat, who'd tested his strength in combat with the good Welshman Perceval, found King Arthur; and clad as he'd been when defeated, he came before the king as he sat at table in the packed court. The moment he entered he was recognised by many of those who were seated with the king; and he went straight down on his knees before him and said:

'Sire, your friend sends me to you with a thousand greetings. And I want everyone at court to hear – I've no wish to conceal it – who it is that's sent me here a captive. It's only right, my lord king, that you and all your barons know his name. So be silent and

---

[84] '*sinople*': see Glossary.
[85] '*un pasté*': essentially related to modern pâté (and the origin of the word).
[86] Literally 'between two woods'; this is Madiex, recently defeated by Perceval in a glade (above, pp. 464–5).

I'll tell you; but first I surrender as your prisoner, entirely at your command – and I feel honoured that such a worthy man has sent me.'

'My dear friend, who is he, tell me, who defeated you in combat and sent you to me on his behalf?'

'Perceval, sire, showed me his tricks – to my cost! Some days ago – before August was half way through – I came upon him out in the wilds. In my foolish pride I attacked him, and he overpowered and almost killed me – he vanquished me utterly, and I placed myself at his mercy. He made me swear to come and submit as your prisoner without changing my clothes or armour, just as you see me now. So do with me as you will. In the presence of all your barons, sire, I've told you what I had to say, so help me God.'

The king leapt for joy when he heard him name Perceval, and said: 'You're in safe hands here, sir knight! You'll be made most welcome for the sake of the one who sent you. I'm beginning to fear I'll never see him again in this world alive and fit and well.'

'By all the saints of Rome and by the Creator, it's only a week since I left him in good health and heart.'

'As I pray that God grant I see tomorrow,' the king replied, 'it delights me to hear that! But come, disarm now, and have no fear: I pardon you your imprisonment, on condition that you stay here in peace henceforth as a member of our household.'

And the Knight of the Ill-cut Coat vowed to do so, upon his honour and his soul. Then he disarmed and a servant brought him a gown of Tyrian cloth lined with ermine, sent to him by the queen. He donned it swiftly; then Lancelot and Count Quinable took him by the hands and led him to a place at table, where they were served with a fresh array of dishes: loins of meat, and swan and other river birds, and roast capons, followed by fine dishes of pike and salmon and barbel. There was nothing mean or sparing about that feast! The whole court was superbly served, and no one had the least cause for complaint.

When all had leisurely eaten their fill the cloths were cleared; then they washed, and some rose and gathered about the king in impressive array: eight dukes there were, and three kings, and four archbishops, I believe, and fourteen counts. Up and down the hall fine tales were being told, and meanwhile some spoke with the king about Perceval.

'I'm amazed, sire,' said Idier, son of Nu, 'that Perceval never comes to court but sends so many prisoners – knights and barons – to do your bidding! By God, it's a disgrace we don't go and seek him, however far we have to search!'

Lancelot was the first to step up; he vowed and pledged by his right hand to go the very next day. Sir Yvain stepped forward after him, and Agravain keenly followed, and Guerrehés and Gaheriët, and Tors the son of Arés, and Sagremor and Calogrenant – always bold in deeds of arms – and Bedivere the constable and Lucan the butler. But it's wrong to list just a handful: there were forty-two who made the pledge, and all began their preparations, to be ready to leave at the crack of dawn.

The moment they saw day break they rose and set to work that instant. I shan't describe it blow by blow: as soon as they were armed they mounted and rode off through the gate and over the bridge, all of them finely armed indeed. Outside the gate two elm trees stood where roads led off to many lands. The knights repeated their oaths to search for Perceval and then set out, some this way, others that, some at an amble, some at a gallop.

But here I'm going to leave them and tell you about Perceval, who was riding through a wood. After leaving the vavasor who'd honoured him so highly, providing such fine lodging and supplying him with complete new gear and harness, he set out through the wood, listening to the song of the nightingale and all the other birds. He rode on, lost in thought, till he found himself in open country; and there, looking across the plain, he saw two knights approaching, fully armed, equipped with everything a knight should have. But neither was equipped with a courteous tongue: one was Gollain the Bald and the other was Kay the seneschal, much favoured by the king. They were thundering towards Perceval, crying:

'Knight! Knight! Yield as our prisoner!'

And Kay charged up and grabbed his reins and pulled him in while Gollain said:

'Vow to accept imprisonment, knight, that you'll make no attempt to escape!'

'This is most unjust of you both, by God!' he replied. 'There are two of you and only one of me! If one of you cares to joust with me, come and see if you can unhorse me – if I take on the first and he comes unstuck and I bring him down, let the other try to avenge him!'

And both of them said: 'I swear it!'

'And if I don't make you admit defeat,' said Kay, 'may God desert me!'

Perceval, undaunted, drew back ready to charge, and Kay did likewise: he couldn't wait to give him a hiding! They sent their fine steeds storming forward, and dealt each other awesome blows on their shields that shone with gold. Kay's blow was so fierce that his lance shattered; and Perceval's landed full on his helm, close to the visor, sending him tumbling over his horse's rear. He called out:

'You'd better try things differently, my dear Sir Kay! Your method doesn't seem to be working!'

Kay passed out with the pain, while Gollain cursed himself for not having yet avenged him; he dallied no longer and thrust in his spurs, shouting to Perceval to defend himself.

'By God,' he called back, 'I could say the same to you!'

In went his spurs and he galloped to strike him; Gollain clutched his lance tight and charged likewise and struck Perceval on his painted shield, but his lance broke and shivered and the shards flew skyward; and Perceval made no mistake but struck him a mighty blow on the shield, full in the chest, to send him and his horse crashing down beside Kay with such weight and force that he broke his right leg.

'Sir Gollain,' he cried, 'you and Kay the seneschal thought you'd catch me and haul me in. He'd be better off back at court, serving hot pies and the like to the king, rather than gallivanting around earning the kind of payment he's had from me! I'm glad I've not been taken captive – I'd take the two of you prisoner if I thought there was any point, but what good would it do me? I'd rather get on with my mission. I know you both, I'm sure: one of you is Gollain, known as the Bald, and the other's the seneschal from the house of good King Arthur – whose might may God preserve.'

Filled with anguished rage they said: 'You'd better tell us your name!'

'I'm telling you nothing more for now,' he replied. 'Look after yourselves – I'm off!'

And he rode away and left them. They were both in trouble, sorely hurt, but struggled back into their saddles; they were furious at not knowing who he was, the knight who'd outfought them so decisively and unhorsed them both.

'We didn't do him the slightest damage, and he wouldn't tell us his name! By God,' said Kay, 'I don't know what to say – except I'm very angry!'

'Nor do I,' said Gollain. 'I swear I've never been so cross – but I suppose I've got to bear it!'

And away they rode, subdued and silent.

The Repair of the Broken Sword

And Perceval set off, jubilant, and prayed to the Creator to guide him by the true and straightest path to the house of the Fisher King; and he said that if he could find that court, he'd press the good king to tell him who was served from the grail, which he'd seen so clearly, and about the trencher, and the lance, and the joining of the sword which he'd repaired with his own two hands except for the notch.

'God grant that I find that house, that court, for which I've suffered so much toil and pounded so many roads and paths.'

He rode on all day, following a well-surfaced road, but met not a single boy, youth, man or woman; so he turned into the forest, for that was his fortress. As day drew to a close he headed towards a huge, round tree – it would have measured two lance-lengths around the trunk – that stood in a lovely stretch of meadow where the grass was green and thick and lush. The tree was of the kind that is ever in leaf. Perceval dismounted from his charger and tethered him to the tree; then he drew his sword and cut some grass and said:

'Field and forest are mine when I can have no other lodging.'

He cut so much that his horse had enough and to spare that night; he removed his bridle and lay straight down at his side while the horse began to eat.

He slept till after cock-crow; into the early morning he lay with his head propped on his shield. At last he awoke and was astonished to find he'd slept so long; he leapt to his feet, harnessed his horse and laced his helm; then he sprang into the saddle, braced his shield and grabbed his lance which was propped against a branch. He thrust in his spurs and set off, heading for the great road that he'd left the previous evening.

Through the leafy wood he rode, praying to God with a true heart to guide him along the right path. He came then to a crossroads where the road split into three. A cross stood in the middle, thirteen and a half feet high, and in it was fixed a wooden hand that pointed when a knight came by, telling him immediately the way that he should go. It had set many back on the right path: such was this strange wonder. Perceval swiftly rode to the cross, and as he cantered up and reined in he bowed to the cross and then noticed the hand. He saw the three paths and didn't know what to do or which way to go, but the hand directed him to take the middle path of the three, and he had great faith in it: he decided that, come what may, he would take the middle way.

'And if it please God, it'll take me to the house where the good and gentle king resides – how I long to be there! I commend myself to the King of Glory: may He keep me from going astray today!'

So he crossed himself with his right hand and set out along the way the hand had pointed. He rode on all that day. On and on through the wood he rode, following that path, until night drew in and his head began to bow over his horse. Then, in a valley below, he caught sight of a great, wide river running through the vale, and beside it stood a delightful castle: there was none finer, I'd say, from there to Porpaillart.[87] It was the fortress he'd been hoping to see, and he headed straight towards it; he recognised the tower and the other buildings, and felt in his heart it was the house of the king. He pressed on with all speed, and passed through the gate and into the courtyard. A boy

---

[87] A city – usually described as being by the sea (it sometimes appears as 'Port Paillart') – which features several times in the epic *Guillaume d'Orange*.

came running to his stirrup, and servants appeared from all directions – they weren't in short supply in that house! – and welcomed him with the greatest joy. They took charge of his horse, and led Perceval inside and disarmed him and clad him in a costly mantle, showing how much they cared for him, fearing he might catch cold. Then they led him straight to the king, in a painted chamber adorned with gold mosaic: it would take an age to describe it all, I promise you – no one has ever seen the like, and Perceval was filled with wonder.

He greeted the king most highly in the name of God who never fails or lies, and the king, like the noble soul he was, said: 'Welcome, friend!' – for he had a generous and gracious heart.

But I shan't ramble on! The king, sitting on a couch most beautifully wrought, seated Perceval at his side. Perceval was longing to see the grail for which he'd laboured, and longed as well to see the lance with the bleeding head – his heart was set on it. But he saw nothing yet. The king politely asked him to tell, if he would, where he'd slept the night before.

'Indeed, sire,' he replied, 'I slept last night by a holly tree at the forest's edge.'

Then he reeled off the stories of the chapel he'd found, where he'd gone inside and seen the knight lying on the splendid cloth, and of the serpent he'd seen in the shape of a little worm who'd made the terrible storm of rocks and gales and thunder.

'He rushed back faster than the wind, and slipped back in his hole and that was the last I saw of him. I'd love to know more about it, sire, if you're willing to tell – and about the child I saw in the tree: it chilled my heart when he wouldn't speak to me; it pains me – and baffles me utterly: I've never seen such a thing. I'd be very glad to hear it explained – before God, sire, I would – whatever anyone could tell me!'

The king pondered awhile, and then said: 'You shall indeed. But eat a little first and you'll be more at ease.'

The tables were swiftly set, and the knights washed. The king had Perceval sit at his side and eat from his bowl, most generously and freely.

They hadn't been seated long in their groups of five and six when a comely girl, whiter than a flower on a sapling's branch, appeared from a chamber. In her hands she was holding the holy grail. She passed before the table. A moment later another girl came, the fairest ever seen, dressed in pure, white, shining silk. She was carrying the lance that dripped blood from its tip. And a boy followed after, carrying in his hands an unrepaired sword; gently, carefully, he laid it on a corner of the table by the king. Perceval, very much on edge, started saying to the king:

'By God and my faith, sire, I've been to your house twice before, but however much I asked about the affairs of this land you'd tell me nothing. That was wrong of you, I have to say! I asked about many things, and repaired a sword that was broken in half – you were overjoyed: it was such a fine and excellent sword.'

The king's reply was this: 'Before God, that's true, my good, dear friend. You've endured a great deal to bring this business to a close, but don't be upset or feel aggrieved. Just take hold of this sword and it will be joined and mended.'

Perceval agreed; he came straight to the sword and grasped it boldly. Then he looked and saw the notch in the blade and was distraught. He rubbed his hand up and down the blade – no one intervened or bade him stop – and then brandished it four times, so violently that he almost broke it. And thereupon the notch was repaired: he had joined it perfectly. He took it by the point and passed it to the king in full view of everyone. The king beheld it with a joy I could never describe.

'My friend,' he said, 'all your toil is well rewarded, now that God has granted you such honour that you are worthy to know the full truth about these things.'

Perceval was elated. Now he was free of pain and stress; instead his heart was brimming with joy: I can't describe his euphoria – he almost burst out singing.[88] The king looked at him and was deeply happy. Like the courteous and gracious soul he was he threw his arms about his neck and said:

'My good, dear friend, be lord of my house. I willingly bestow upon you everything I have, and henceforth will hold you dearer than any man alive.'

At that the boy who'd brought the sword hurried back and took it and wrapped it again in a silken cloth and carried it away. Perceval's heart was glowing

---

[88] Here the manuscript repeats the last lines of the Second Continuation almost exactly, to lead into the final continuation.

The Third Continuation

after what had befallen him: I'm sure I've never heard of joy to compare. The king called to him, saying:

'Eat, good sir, and may God who endured His suffering and death grant you honour and forgive your sins.'

Perceval sat down and ate beside the king, and with great pleasure: I shan't describe the meal in detail, but no duke or king or count was ever so well served. But although he'd deserved to be fêted so, he stayed with his head bowed. What should I say? At perfect leisure they had all the food and wine they wished – and no prophet or divine ever drank the like.

Just as they were about to rise from their meal, there passed before the royal table the lance and the grail, and a beautiful silver trencher, most handsome and fine, carried by a girl most gracefully. Once they'd passed the table with its sumptuous spread, they processed back to the chamber from which they'd come. Perceval, who'd watched them fixedly, gave a sigh and turned to the king and said at once:

'My good, dear lord, tell me truly now what you promised before we ate.'

'Come close, my friend, and listen,' the king replied. 'I'll tell you exactly, omitting nothing, whatever you wish to ask: I'm at your command.'

'Good sire,' said Perceval, 'I want to know the absolute truth about the lance and the holy grail and the trencher that I've seen: tell me first, if you will, where are they from, and who is served with them? As for the girls who carry them and passed this way just now, they're clearly not poor women of low birth: I'd say they were of high lineage.'

'Dear friend,' said the king, 'I'm not troubled or offended by your questions at all. I'll tell you first about the lance, indeed I will; I'll keep back nothing – and I know it to be true. It is, I promise you, the holy lance of which the scriptures tell us, with which Longinus struck Jesus Christ as He was stretched on the cross where the Jews had hung Him. The blood that springs from the lance's fine and shining head is the precious, holy blood that flowed from God's side when Longinus struck Him. It is the very lance, the very head, that mortally wounded the one who harrowed Hell. But the blow He was dealt on the cross was a blessing! Through death He outwitted the Devil and delivered us from Hell's torment and brought us joy! That death cleansed us, you should understand, of the ills brought upon us by Adam and Eve when they bit into the fruit.'

Perceval leaned on his elbow and listened to the king. He wept and sighed at the agony and shame that God endured; I don't think he'd have stopped if he'd been given the empire of Rome! But he quickly said:

'Sire, you've told me about the lance. But I long to know about the grail and the trencher, if it's right to ask.'

And the king, in whom kindness ever reigned, granted his every wish and said: 'I'll not break my word.' And with tears in his eyes, he began at once: 'My friend, when Jesus Christ hung on the holy, glorious, supremely precious cross and was pierced in the side, as soon as the lance-head was withdrawn the blood streamed down to His feet.

But Joseph of Arimathea, ashen with grief at the sight of God's suffering, intervened: he carefully held that holy vessel to catch the holy blood. And that vessel – which proved to be a blessing to Joseph – was covered with the silver trencher carried by the girl just now; it covered the vessel so that the blood wouldn't be left exposed. And that vessel, without a doubt, was the holy grail that passed us with the lance. Every word I've told you is true. If you wish to know more, I'll tell you just as faithfully.'

Perceval, eager to hear everything, sighed and said: 'Sire, I'd love to know, if you're willing to tell, how the holy grail came to be in this land. I long to know that more than ever now!'

'I'll tell you, friend, since I promised to. When God was hung on the cross as you've heard, Joseph took Him down with the help of Nicodemus – a smith, the finest ever. And for his pains, for having taken Our Lord from the cross, Joseph was promptly thrown in prison, locked fast in a foul and terrible dungeon: they wanted him to starve to death and rot there. He was left for forty days[1] without anything to eat or drink, but the Lord God sent the holy grail to appear to him two or three times a day, and through its sweet, sustaining power he stayed there in prison without suffering any pain or ill.

'Then Titus and Vespasian, although they were no Christians, set him free and took him to Rome. Joseph, you may be sure, took the lance with him and the grail followed after: God willed it so, and so it happened. And Joseph, trusting in God's guidance, came to settle in this land and established this domain and house;[2] and I am of his line. The grail stayed here when he died; since he left the world the grail has never gone from this place – and if it please God, the true Father, it will never make its home elsewhere.'

Perceval was thrilled by this story of the grail, and praised Our Lord and His works. Sighing in wonder, he listened with rapt delight. And he pressed the king further, saying: 'If you will, good sir, tell me about the two girls, so charming and fair. Forgive me if I'm tiring you: all the riches in the world wouldn't give me so much joy!'

'If I could, dear friend, and thought you wouldn't find it wearing I'd tell you everything! But it's past bedtime! But come: you're so dear to me that I'll answer all you ask – it's only right. So, you want to know about the girls you saw. The one who carries the grail is of royal descent, and a virgin – were she not, God save me, she'd never be able to hold it in her hands. The one who carries the trencher with such elegance and grace is also of high lineage, a worthy, wise and well-bred girl indeed. She's the daughter of King Goondesert, and the girl with the grail is my own – and she's certainly no disgrace to me. So there: you've heard about the grail and the lance, and it's brought joy to your heart, I'd say! Now it's time to rest: let's retire to our beds, if you will.'

'Ah! Good sir, please don't object: I'd love to hear how the sword I've twice[3] repaired was broken.'

'I'll tell you,' said the king, 'and God grant it may lead to a happy outcome. Listen and I'll explain. The sword you mended – which should give you joy indeed – is the sword that dealt the mortal blow, and a blow so wicked and treacherous there will never be: I and all this kingdom grieve for it still – you never heard of a blow so outrageous and cruel.

---

[1] Most MSS read 'forty years', but neither forty days (too short) nor forty years (too long) fits particularly well with the story as created by Robert de Boron in his *Joseph of Arimathea*.

[2] This is a very compressed rendition of the story of Joseph and his imprisonment, and of Titus and Vespasian, and of Joseph's coming into the West, deriving ultimately from Robert de Boron's *Joseph of Arimathea*. See *Merlin and the Grail*, tr. Bryant (Cambridge, 2001), pp. 23–44.

[3] So says BN MS fr. 12576, carefully making sense of its inclusion of Gerbert's Continuation.

'My brother Goondesert – worthier than an emperor, he was – was besieged in the castle of Quingragan: the mighty Pinogrés was camped outside with a massive force of knights and infantry. My brother sallied forth to confront him and fought magnificently, routing his whole great army, crushing and destroying them all. But old Pinogrés had a bold nephew who vowed and pledged to kill my brother that day, and – dire disaster! – he promptly did so. Dismayed to see their forces in disarray, this nephew cast off his armour and set out to trick the men of the castle: he found one of their dead and, wedded to wickedness as he was, quickly stripped him of his arms and donned them himself; then he returned to the battle clutching that sword, so very sharp, whose broken halves you've joined. Twice he charged into the fray and then headed for my brother, blade of steel in hand. My brother, sure he was one of his own, suspected nothing, and with his helmet off and his mail hood down he turned away to rejoin his household who'd served him so well that day. The one who couldn't wait to do the deed went straight and struck my brother on the head with the drawn sword, and clove him in two, right down to his horse's saddle. And with that tragic blow the fine sword broke in half. The killer dashed off, hilt in hand, then threw it down and returned to his men who showered praise upon him. And the men of the castle gathered up King Goondesert, cloven in two, where he lay dead on the field. The broken sword, abandoned by the killer, they carried off amid dreadful grieving along with the body of their lord, which they laid on a shield and took back to the castle, though they had no blanket or sheet to cover him. Then they washed and dressed the body as finely as they could and placed it on a bier and sent him here to me.

'As for the sword, the blade that had stricken and slain my brother, both halves had been recovered and were brought to me by my niece. She, all-seeing girl that she was, told me they'd wrought the death of her father, my beloved brother, but that if I kept the sword till the coming of a knight who took it in his hands and made the two halves join again, "then know this," she said. "By the one who repairs the sword, my dear father will be avenged." I, crazed with grief, took the broken blade she gave me and, that very instant, made a cut through my thighs, severing every nerve. Truly, I've been helpless ever since, and will remain so till I'm avenged, my good, dear friend, upon the false traitor who slew the finest of all knights born since God was crucified.'

Perceval had hung on his every word; and with a sigh, very moved by what he'd heard, he replied at once, saying: 'Truly, sire, that was a dismal deed. Now that you've told me this much, please tell me if you can: what was that nephew's name? Without knowing his name or the land where he lives it'll be a tough task: whoever is to take revenge will need to know his name, and since that challenge falls to me I'm desperate to know it. And I want to know what device he bears on his arms. I vow to you as a loyal knight that if I track him down and am fit to fight, the conclusion will be final: I'll deliver him to you dead or captive or die at his hand: there'll be no other outcome.'

'My dear friend,' said the worthy king, 'may the one who forgave Longinus give you the strength and power! Since you wish to know his name I'll not conceal it: the cruel villain's name is Partinal; he's lord of the Red Tower and the surrounding land. He bears splendid arms of silver and blue, emblazoned with two damsels in red. If vengeance is taken upon him, all my grief will be assuaged. But he's no respect for any knight alive; in God's name I pray you, don't undertake this mission unless you think you can take revenge.'

'My dear lord,' said Perceval, 'those of us who journey far and wide over mountains and valleys in search of honour and glory suffer many blows; but if it be Our Lord's will, I believe I can succeed.'

'Christ keep you from ill fortune,' said the king, who held him very dear. 'But now, please, go to your bed – it's long past time! I'm sure you're very weary and need to rest.'

'Truly, sire, I've no wish to sleep until you've told me about the candles I saw in the tree, and the knight I saw lying on the marble altar in the chapel – what was he doing there? I've been longing to know about all this! And the black hand that snuffed the candle – explain that! And the tumult and the lightning! Before I leave this table I dearly want to know!'[4]

The king, sincerely eager to fulfil his wishes, said he'd answer to his satisfaction; and without more ado he said: 'The truth about the tree is this: it's the tree of enchantment – the fairies gather there, and the lights that look like candles from afar are the fairies who seek to lead astray those who don't believe in God. And I shan't keep it from you: the fact that you approached the tree and then saw nothing is a sign that you're destined to accomplish the wondrous adventures of this land. The truth is, that tree you saw will never be seen or found again – no more will be heard of the tree or the candles – for you drove away the fairy ladies as you rode up to the tree: that's the last we'll ever hear of them! Now it's time to go to bed and rest awhile.'

'Ah, by the faith I owe Saint Paul, sire, if you don't mind I'd rather hear first about the chapel and the body on the altar!'

'I'll tell you all you wish,' said the king. 'That's what I promised, so it's only right. Since you'd have me tell about the chapel, it was built, truly, at the behest of Brangemore of Cornwall, the mother of that wicked, cruel king Pinogrés. She became a nun in that chapel, but for just one day, from prime*[5] till none,* that's all, for then she died: Pinogrés, her own son, burst in and beheaded her, burdening himself with a terrible sin. As soon as he'd struck her down she was buried beneath the altar. So it was she met her end; and since then not a day has passed without a knight being killed in that chapel: four thousand have been slain by the hand that takes them unawares – no one knows who their killer is, only that they're killed by the hand you saw as far as the elbow, with its black and swarthy skin; and it's the hand that snuffs the candle. That hand, and the tumult that attends it, kills them all: the hand alone, and no one else, is the cause of their woeful end.'

'As I hope to see tomorrow, sire,' said Perceval, 'that's amazing! But in the name of God and His powers, tell me if you will, I pray you: can this curse be driven from the chapel? The man who cast it out would have done a wondrous deed!'

'Dear friend,' replied the king, 'if any man did battle with the black hand, and took from a cabinet a white veil that's kept there, guarded by that cursèd demon, and soaked it in holy water and sprinkled it all around the altar and the body and the chapel, then by God the object of our prayers, no harm would befall him. But he'd have to be brave indeed to confront the hand! Only a man of the utmost prowess would dare attempt it.' With that he rose and said: 'Go now, friend, and rest: you're very weary, and I don't want you to suffer from lack of sleep. It's given me great pleasure to tell you all this tonight, but the beds are all ready – go now and sleep if you will.'

And Perceval stood at once and said: 'I'll do as you bid, sire, indeed I shall.'

---

4   Perceval is referring here to his series of mysterious encounters in the Second Continuation, above, pp. 333–4.

5   An asterisk in the text indicates that the word appears in the Glossary, below, pp. 571-2.

Then six fine-looking young men appeared smartly from a chamber, four to serve the king and two to serve his guest,[6] and escorted them to their beds. And I tell you, no man of woman born ever set eyes on such a fabulous bed as they'd made for Perceval. It stood in a panelled chamber thickly strewn with rushes, and on it the worthy Perceval lay in sheets of fine, white linen: you'd find none to match them anywhere in the world; and over them was a coverlet of samite fringed with ribbons. A bed more beautifully prepared was never seen, with two rich, red pillows at its head. And the bed itself was made of neither wood nor iron but of gold and silver, and had little feet fashioned by a goldsmith's hand with delicate figures and tiny birds. Its maker hadn't worked from any model, but had put his heart and soul into creating a work surpassing anything ever made by hand. The bed rested on four dogs sculpted in solid gold – you'll never hear of any to compare in any land: none more handsome could be found; and atop the peerless golden feet were four superb lion cubs, two carved from onyx and the other from rubies: no Arabian or Persian ever beheld such perfect work. And the cords supporting the bed were silver: I'm sure I've never heard of any so fine. In this bed Perceval lay that night, and slept till early morning when the cock crowed and the watch sounded the dawn.

Then he dressed before anyone came to his bed; but as he was leaving the chamber two boys came to meet him, saying:

'May the one who made Adam and Eve in His image send you good luck, a good day and good fortune!'

They were bringing water in a basin; one presented it so that he could wash and the other held a towel which he passed to him to dry his hands. Then two squires came with his arms, while two other servants went to find their lord who was just rising. As soon as Perceval saw him he went to meet and greet him, and the king returned his greeting warmly, and kindly invited him to stay and spend the day with him. But Perceval said he couldn't – he had to go; on no account could he delay. But he thanked him deeply for the service he'd received. Then he called for his destrier* and mounted at once and took his lance and shield, then asked leave of his host and commended him to God and rode out through the gate. His horse bore him swiftly, having a full belly and surging vigour: it was clear from his face and flanks and belly he'd been fed that night with all the oats he wished!

Perceval and Sagremor

Perceval entered the forest, which stretched for six whole leagues. On he rode till he saw an armed knight plodding along on a thin, exhausted nag incapable of a snort or neigh. He rode ahead to meet him, marvelling that a knight such as he, superbly equipped with arms and shield, should be so poorly mounted. But when the knight saw Perceval coming he turned his nag about, not wishing to be seen with such a wretched mount: it wasn't worth five sous – or even four! He wanted to vanish into the woods to hide his shame; but truly, Perceval's destrier – worth a hundred marks, so fine he was – galloped ahead and overtook him before he could get away, much to the

---

[6] Some MSS say 'three to the king and three to his guest', but other scribes remembered that in Chrétien four servants took the four corners of the Fisher King's blanket and carried him to bed (above, p. 30).

knight's distress and woe. But Perceval gave him courteous greeting the moment he arrived, saying:

'Welcome, my dear sir!'

And he, being a worthy knight, replied: 'God send you honour – all the honour I wish I had!'

'Do tell me, sir,' said Perceval, 'which land are you from, and what's your mission? And if you're willing to say I'd gladly know your name.'

'So help me God,' the knight replied, 'I've never concealed my name, sir. I'm Sagremor, known as "the Rash". Truly, by the faith I owe God and His power, I'm one of the companions of King Arthur's Round Table, and fine and wondrous it is indeed.'

'God in heaven, I'm pleased to hear it!' said Perceval. 'It's more than a year since I've met anyone from my lord's household!'

'By Saint Peter of Rome,' said Sagremor, 'who are you, sir? Tell me your name if you will – I long to know it!'

'I'll gladly tell you, sir: my name is Perceval – I'm from Wales, and brother of Agloval.'

Sagremor was overjoyed, and unlaced his helm and opened his ventail* and threw his arms around him. Perceval took off his own helm, too, and joined him in a warm embrace as they held each other tight. For some time they stayed silent, saying nothing, then exchanged more than seven kisses, one after another, before Perceval said:

'Where have you come from, friend? Do tell me.'

'In faith,' said Sagremor, 'I left our land to search for you, along with Gawain and Calogrenant and Yvain and sixty more. How thrilled I am to find you! I've been longing to see you – as have all the others. Fully armed, lances in rest, we all left Camelot together the other day at the king's command, and we haven't stopped anywhere since. Once we'd gone from Camelot we went our separate ways. I vowed on holy relics that if I had news of you on my return, I'd give a full and true report; everyone made the same vow in turn, and then set out in all directions. I don't know how they've been getting on – I haven't heard a word! But I'm delighted to have found you – I don't care about anyone else! I'd like to return with you to court now, if you will: the king'll be overjoyed, as will all the barons – he can't wait to see you.'

But Perceval at once replied: 'Bear with me a little longer, friend: I can't go back there yet – I'm committed to another mission that I must accomplish first. But on the eve of Pentecost, come what may, if I'm alive and at liberty, you'll see me at court for sure. But tell me now: why are you riding that clapped-out nag?'

'I'll tell you truly, sir, indeed I will!' said Sagremor. 'I'm sorry to say I slept last night in the forest, beneath an ash, with my shield for a pillow; I tied my destrier to a hawthorn, propped my lance against a pine and went straight to sleep – but when I woke at dawn I found this old nag tethered where I'd left my destrier! I don't know what became of him – or where the fellow who brought the nag had come from or where he went! All I know is he took my destrier, and he was worth a fortune! Having no choice I took this thing – I'll have to make do till I find a stronger, fitter mount: it's a pain not being able to go beyond a walk!'

'Don't fret, good sir,' said Perceval. 'Take mine.'

'Oh, no!' Sagremor said. 'I wouldn't dream of it! God help me, I'd sooner be without a horse for months and lie sick in bed!'

While they were talking they saw ten knights coming through the forest at speed. All of them were kin or neighbours, and the one at their head was carrying a girl before him on his dark bay steed.

'Perceval!' said Sagremor. 'That knight, holding the damsel – he's riding my destrier!'

'So help me God,' said Perceval, 'he won't go any further!'

The girl, ashen with distress, was crying: 'Ah, gentle knight, take pity! Rescue me from these men who mean to abuse and shame my body!'

Perceval levelled his lance at the approaching knights and prepared to joust; with shield braced and lance at the ready he called to the leading knight:

'Vassal, put down that girl: you'll take her no further, I promise you.'

Then one of the others sprang forward, shield set and brandishing his lance, and warned Perceval he was making a big mistake; but Perceval, strong and valiant, spurred his horse into a charge, and the knight left the rest behind and galloped to meet him. The fearless Perceval, victor of so many jousts, made no mistake, and met him with a blow that thrust the lance-head through his shield and hauberk* along with six full feet of shaft and sent him crashing irresistibly to the ground. He seized the destrier by the reins, its saddle now empty, and delivered it to Sagremor, saying:

'Mount, friend, and have no fear: come what may, the first lies dead at the edge of the wood.'

Sagremor leapt on the horse without use of a stirrup, thanked Perceval deeply for the favour he'd done him, turned to face the approaching knights and thrust in his spurs, the destrier responding with a mighty leap; he was aiming to strike the leading knight, but Perceval grabbed his bridle, saying:

'Calm down, good sir! Don't be so keen – stay here and don't move till you see the need!'

'Whatever you say!' said Sagremor. 'But I want to help!'

'There's no need yet,' replied Perceval, 'if God is with me.'

And he lowered his lance and launched into a charge. One of the knights, filled with rage and shame, sprang forward to meet him. Both, with lances in rest, braced themselves in their stirrups till they stretched the straps, and the knight gripped his shield and levelled his lance and dealt Perceval a mighty blow on his gleaming gold shield. But the lance broke and splintered, and Perceval struck back, piercing and splitting his shield below the boss; the hauberk couldn't stop the lance-head: it drove through to the heart, sending him crashing from his fine charger to the ground, stone dead. Perceval pulled the lance from the body and charged straight to meet another who was out to avenge his fellow; he galloped up and thrust his lance clean through his ribs and bowled him over, dead. Now all the others charged at him together. Sagremor didn't like the look of this and withheld his aid no longer! With his strong, unbending lance he struck the first he met, dealing a wondrous blow on his painted shield that pitched him dead from his saddle. The lance broke in two, but he gripped his sword and prepared to show what he could do. Seeing his companions slain, the knight holding the girl dropped her beneath a hawthorn tree and thought only of saving his skin: he fled away through the wood, lance in hand, shield on back. Sagremor spurred after him as fast as his horse could go, leaving Perceval in deep trouble. He followed the knight the length of a bowshot. He wouldn't turn to face him – he just kept galloping on. But Sagremor was hot on his heels. On and on he raced, with Sagremor spurring after, refusing to give up.

Meanwhile Perceval, left confronting five, had drawn his sword and was giving many a cut and thrust. They pressed from every side, bent on inflicting damage, filled with hatred; all five rained blows on him together: it sounded as if the wood were full of carpenters! They hadn't enough of their shields left to cover their fists, and their helms were all split open by the blows of Perceval's sword, which had cut through their mail hoods and battered the hoops[7] from their helms; the field was littered with rings of mail from hauberks and ventails, as Perceval sent them flying along with shattered gems.[8] Then he dealt a blow to one knight that struck him from his saddle and laid him dead; the other four surged forward to unhorse him, and one of them thrust his lance right through Perceval's charger's chest, the point bursting out of his spine: it struck the horse dead and Perceval fell – but misfortune strikes many a worthy man. When he realised he was down he was filled with shame and anguish; he leapt up, clutching his sword, and dealt the first knight a blow that felled him from his horse and parted soul from body; but with this blow, to Perceval's horror, the blade broke clean in two. But he wielded the half attached to the hilt and clove another knight down to the teeth, dashing him dead to the ground, and rushed to where he saw him drop his sword, snatched it up and leapt into the saddle of a riderless horse without setting foot in a stirrup. Seeing him returning, naked sword in hand, the last two didn't dare wait to face his blows and were off without saying goodbye, turning their backs on Perceval and taking to flight at speed, desperate to escape. Perceval, giving chase, cried:

'Wicked knights! Craven, perfidious cowards! You're both going to suffer! And if you die in flight, what dismal shame you'll earn! Turn back! How cowardly it is to flee!'

'What do you think?' said one of the rogues.

'Let's turn and face him, noble knight!' said the other. 'It's shameful to run.'

With that both wheeled their horses about, but Perceval charged in and struck the first with his sword and severed his head: his soulless body toppled to the ground.

'It's a disaster!' said the other. 'Our whole valiant company slain by a single knight – he's killed seven all by himself! God grant I see tomorrow, but I'd rather die with the others than flee like a coward.'

And he drew his sword, braced his shield and set to it with a will. He performed quite splendidly, landing an undefended blow on Perceval's helm, his fine steel blade dashing off flowers;[9] but the helm was strong and feared no sword-blow, and the blade glanced off, flashed down and cut through the neck of Perceval's horse: he fell dead, killed instantly. Perceval leapt to his feet, flushed with rage, and dealt the knight a slashing blow across the waist; no armour or hauberk could resist: nothing stopped the steel blade scything through the tender flesh and cutting him in two. The body's top half toppled over; the bottom half stayed in the stirrups. The charger bolted and crashed into a bush; what it was carrying was dumped on the ground and the horse was stopped in its tracks; Perceval grabbed it and jumped in the saddle – he had no squire or page to help him mount. But I assure you he had a wound in his leg that would need a good doctor if it was ever to heal: it was bleeding heavily, the blood pouring down to his spur – it would give him pain for months. It had been cut with a lance by the knight who'd killed his horse, but Perceval hadn't noticed at the time.

He looked round now but couldn't see the girl: she was hiding, terrified after what she'd been through; and not finding her where the roguish knight had left her, he said to himself that he wouldn't have lost her for half the wealth of the world. The girl, in dire dread, was huddling in the bushes. He called out at the top of his voice:

'You needn't hide from me, dear girl! You've nothing to fear on my account, don't worry!'

---

[7] i.e. the reinforcing bands.
[8] i.e. precious stones adorning their helms.
[9] i.e. enamel and other decorations.

Hearing this, the girl emerged from the bushes at once and ran to him and cried for mercy, begging him for the love of God on high to take her safely home to a castle of hers: once she was there she'd be happy.

'Damsel,' he replied, 'I'll carry you on my horse wherever you wish – it's only right I should. We'll go at once.'

He dismounted and picked up the broken sword and put it in his scabbard. Then he remounted without a shield or lance, took the girl in his arms and sat her on his horse's shoulders, saying:

'Tell me the way to your home, dear girl, and we'll go straight there.'

'Take that little path to the right, kind sir.'

And Perceval, worthiest of knights, did just as she asked and set out along the little track and headed for the castle.

As they emerged from the woods they came upon all the castle's people, in such distress that they looked as if they'd just seen their fathers killed. I promise you by Saint Peter, they numbered more than three thousand and seven score, burghers, villeins, knights; they were carrying axes, sticks and clubs and hurrying along together. Twenty knights were at their head, and when the girl caught sight of them she recognised them by their banners and called:

'Turn back, sirs! This valiant knight has rescued me! I hold him in high esteem indeed – he's peerless! By his own hand he slew all those knights who feared no man and carried me off by force. It's thanks to him I'm back! Go and prepare lodgings for him, and make sure he's well served: he's richly deserved it!'

The servants returned to the castle at once, while the knights welcomed Perceval and thanked him for the service he'd done. A moment later a boy clattered up with a little dappled palfrey, fitted with a gorgeous saddle made of solid gold and silver and adorned with birds and larks and lions; from what the story says I'm sure no one could ever wish for one so fine. To describe the saddle and its origins in full, the richest cloth or samite weren't worth a sou in comparison – the queen of Cornwall never owned the like: it was of finest silk, embroidered all in yellow, red and indigo; it had been made by a fairy in Apulia, with hands of exquisite white beauty. With this gorgeous saddle, embroidered and painted with fleurs-de-lis and tiny roses, the little dappled palfrey was fitted; and the reins and head-stall were of richest orfrey: no girl or maiden ever had finer – such a wondrous harness was never seen since Cain killed Abel. The boy who'd brought the palfrey came before the girl with great decorum, and just as courteously presented him to her. And a knight who dearly loved her gently took her in his arms and set her in the saddle.

The girl was only too pleased to ride at Perceval's side, and in happy conversation, gracefully borne by their splendid steeds, they made their way down a valley and came to the castle gate. They found it open, and crowding above it were ladies and damsels waiting to see their lady return; the moment they saw her they came thronging forth to meet her, holding hands two by two, and when they came before her every last one of them showered her with wishes of honour and good fortune. The damsel rode on, escorted by Perceval in the highest spirits, till they came to the steps of the great hall where he dismounted with great poise and took her in his arms and set her down. A servant arrived smartly and took charge of stabling the horses, while that delightful girl took Perceval by the hand and, holding him in the highest regard and fondness as she did, said very sweetly:

'You have put yourself to great trouble for me, friend, and done me a very great service.'

Hand in hand they went up the hall, and a handsome hall it was indeed. The damsel had her guest disarmed at once: one girl, most capably, took off his bright hauberk, another took his sword and another unlaced his chausses.* A young girl brought him a mantle of good length made of scarlet,* peacock blue, and hemmed with gorgeous ermine. Another came and closely examined his wound, and after careful thought she said:

'Don't worry sir: it'll heal well – you've nothing to fear.'

She gave him a sop of bread in wine, and then showed him to his bed in a rich and handsome chamber. It was set at the foot of the damsel's own bed – that damsel endowed with wisdom and courtesy. She took the utmost care of her guest, treating him with all honour and great affection and having his wound well probed and carefully tended. Perceval rested there for a month, not leaving the castle till his wound had healed.

Sagremor and the Robber Knight

Now I must tell of Sagremor, galloping after the knight – it wouldn't be right to abandon his tale! The knight fled down a valley till he spotted a brattice* half a league away. He spurred that way and – lucky for him! – found the gate was open. He galloped straight in. Sagremor, right behind, lance at the ready, galloped in after. There was a villein above the gate who kept watch and lay in wait for anyone who tried to attack his lord, and the moment Sagremor passed the gate he dropped a huge portcullis. It cut off the tail of Sagremor's horse, but he was such a valiant steed that he didn't so much as break his stride; Sagremor charged straight on and caught up with the knight at the foot of a stair where he'd dismounted and was preparing to fight. Seeing him on foot, Sagremor threw down his lance and said he wouldn't dream of being accused of attacking him on horseback – it would be shameful. So down he jumped and battle began that instant. The man who'd dropped the portcullis saw this and promptly grabbed a horn and blew it so loud that the whole house and all the surrounding woodland rang. At this a knight came down from the tower; superbly armed he was, with a hauberk and a jewelled helm and mail chausses and ventail, and a well-honed sword at his left hip. And clutched in his right hand was a massive, double-headed axe. Without a sound he strode at Sagremor, axe raised. He was aiming to strike – but no: Sagremor saw the blow coming and dodged aside; and the knight couldn't stop – so great was the swing – and the axe-blade plunged a foot and a half[10] into the ground. Sagremor gripped his sword with its chased blade, raised it high and brought it down, and before his foe could move he landed such a mighty blow on his shining helm that the blade sliced through to the brain: he struck him dead with a single stroke. Then he turned to the other and said:

'By God, vassal, you made a mistake when you found me sleeping in the wood and stole my horse! It's cost you your life, truly: there's no escape!'

But the knight was brave and strong and summoned up his courage and answered: 'You haven't beaten me yet – you've plenty more to do first!'

And he leapt at Sagremor, his good sword raised, but Sagremor thrust out his shield to meet it smartly. The knight, raging, struck the shield with his burnished sword and split it right across; the fine steel blade sent half the shield crashing to the ground and cut off the right-hand skirt of his bright and tight-meshed hauberk; right to the ground

---

[10] Literally 'the length of a foot and the width of a hand'.

flashed the sword of tempered steel – but it didn't meet flesh. Sagremor considered it a shame, an outrage, an affront, that the knight was resisting him so long, and advanced on him and dealt a blow that the shining mail couldn't withstand, sending the mail-sleeved right arm flying to the ground. The villein who'd dropped the gate saw this and gave his horn a mighty blast, and four of his fellows burst from a chamber and attacked Sagremor with all their force, while the knight, knowing he'd had it, rushed into the garden where there was a deep well; crazed with anguish he jumped straight in and plummeted down and with the weight of his armour he drowned in an instant. The worthy, nimble Sagremor faced his four attackers and fought back mightily: he dealt the first a blow that clove him from the head to the waist; his gleaming blade landed happily to cut the whole leg off another and leave him sprawling on the ground; he turned straight upon the other pair, but they didn't dare face him and fled swiftly up the stairs, their feet barely touching them. He swore they'd not escape – no matter how fast they ran he'd have them! – and after them he went, come what may, so hot on their heels that he caught them in the hall. The first he struck with his blood-stained blade, cut him clean in two and left him dead on the floor; the fourth knew his way around the place and dashed off; he jumped through a window and into the ditch – but so heavy was his landing that he smashed and broke his neck: there in the ditch he lay dead.

Sagremor didn't dally: he scoured every inch of the house. When he retraced his steps, the villein at the gate saw him and was terrified; he flung himself to the ground before him and crossed himself and begged for mercy, crying:

'Have pity on me, noble knight, I beg you in God's name! Be lord of this house – you've won the mastery! Here are the keys – I give them to you – I'll do whatever you say!'

'Enough, friend!' said Sagremor. 'The mastery you offer I bestow on you – you shall be lord. It's pointless trying to tempt me – I want no part of it. It's yours – that's fine by me! But listen: first you must swear on holy relics that you'll never refuse lodging to any passing knight – I want your solemn pledge.'

'As you wish, sir, I promise; and I'll keep my word.'

'And I'll trust you,' said Sagremor. 'Now bring me my good horse Morin – I trust in him, too! Then I'll be off – and with any luck I'll find somewhere to lodge tonight.'

'Oh, good sir, don't bother: you're better off here! You won't find anywhere as good as this, not today. You'll have everything you want – just ask and I'll do it! Absolutely everything! That's only right.'

'My word, friend,' said Sagremor, 'such generous promises – I can't possibly refuse! I'll lodge with you tonight indeed!'

The villein gave him fulsome thanks and set about disarming him and took off his helm, promising to be a fine host. He prepared a meal with a will, not stinting in the least; then he gave him water to wash his hands and Sagremor, delighted to see food before him, sat down to eat. The villein cheerfully served him with all the castle could offer – which was a lot: abundant food had been laid up there, and a plentiful supply of all the fine wine he could wish, for the castle had been the lord's main stronghold and was well stocked with wine and provisions. It couldn't have been better.

Sagremor sat at the table as long as he wished, eating at his leisure, with the villein giving him every attention, seeing he wanted for nothing. When he'd finished he gave him water for washing and cleared the table: his eagerness to please was wondrous! Then he made a bed for Sagremor in a chamber: a gorgeous, gracious, fine and lovely bed, with pillow and quilt and linen sheets of triple width; then back he came and said:

'Your bed is prepared, sir! You may retire when you wish! You've been up a long time – it's been dark for an age – and you need to rest. God willing, you'll sleep right through till morning.'

'Come, then, friend,' said Sagremor. 'Take me where you will.'

And he rose at once and the villein, so eager to serve, scurried before him with brightly burning torch in hand. Answering his every need, he set aside the torch as soon as they reached the chamber, went down on his knees at Sagremor's feet and smartly removed his shoes and helped him undress; then he saw him comfortably, gently into bed with all possible care, placing a rich and lovely pillow beneath his head, which he covered with a brand new nightcap of yellow, green and deep red silk. Then he took his leave, commending him to God, and closed the door behind him to leave Sagremor snug in that delightful chamber. He now went down to the stable and found Morin wandering loose; he took off his bridle and saddle, and once he'd unharnessed him he curried and brushed him well with a fistful of straw and provided him with oats and hay. Then he returned to his place above the gate, taking his flute and horn, and lay down and slept awhile.

But he woke at first light and dressed and made ready, and sweetly sounded the dawn. Then he came to the chamber where Sagremor was still undressed – and still asleep: he was very weary after all he'd been through, and slept on till the sun was blazing bright. But when he saw the sun he was up at once, annoyed at having slept so long. Seeing he'd risen the villein said:

'God give you a good day, sir!'

'And send you good fortune,' said Sagremor, 'for you gave me a very comfortable night! But go down, if you will, and ready my arms and my horse. I don't want to stay longer: I'll be off now, if it please God.'

The villein dashed away and brought Sagremor's arms and his silver-stirruped destrier to the foot of the steps. Sagremor came down from the hall and was thrilled to see Morin, a horse worth a hundred others. He stroked his flanks and smoothed his mane: he loved that horse – he didn't know of a finer, stronger, better-natured steed. He made ready and mounted without further delay; then he and his host commended each other to God, and with that he was gone from the castle.

Sagremor at the Castle of the Maidens

So Sagremor set off, fully armed, riding his dark bay charger. He passed into the nearby forest, preferring the forest to the open fields. He was worried and upset at losing Perceval – in fact he was quite distressed, sure he'd never find him again. He pressed on through the woods without stopping, searching this way and that, till he came upon the knights' dead bodies.

'Ah, splendid!' he said. 'Perceval did a good job here!'

Then he rode on through a valley till he emerged from the forest; and it turned out well: he found the loveliest path imaginable stretching away before him. He followed this beautiful path till almost none,* when it pleased God that he approached a castle arrayed with brattices,* strongly prepared to resist attack. Seeing this he guessed it was at war, and headed that way to find out why it was so well fortified. With Morin bearing him easily he made his way to the gate, but found it shut fast. From beneath his helm he called for someone to appear above; it was a girl who did, and seeing a mounted knight below she said:

'What land are you from, sir, and what brings you here?'

Sagremor looked up, and thought the girl above the gate was the loveliest creature in the world. Softly, sweetly, he answered her: 'So help me God, dear girl, I'm a wandering knight in search of adventures. I'm wondering what's going on here!'

The girl came down and opened the gate, and Sagremor rode smartly into the courtyard. An elderly, white-haired lady, delighted by his coming, came hurrying to hold his stirrup – but she was too late: he'd already dismounted, and went to greet her the moment he saw her.

'May the maker of the world,' she replied, 'be your protector, sir.'

While they were talking, three girls came down from a hall and served him thus: one ran and took his horse and stabled him and gave him oats and hay, another helped Sagremor from his armour, and the third gave him a mantle of scarlet lined with squirrel fur which he donned to keep from catching harmful cold after the heat of riding. The lady was most courteous and, overjoyed that he'd come, took him by the hand at once and led him up the steps to the hall. It wasn't only her hair that was white: her face, too, was pale and wan; but elated at his coming, she treated him as her guest and led him, hand in hand, to a chamber where they sat together on a gorgeous spread of silk patterned with wheels.

Sagremor didn't sit subdued but said: 'Before God, lady, if you're willing to tell I'd be glad to know why this castle's so well fortified and surrounded by palisades. There has to be a reason for your pallid cheeks, by God – something's going on: that's clear from your face!'

'I'll explain, sir – I shan't keep it from you. First let me tell you the name of this castle: it's the Castle of the Maidens – there are seven hundred fair maidens here, all of them noble and worthy indeed. But a knight of great repute and power has been in love with one of them since she was a child, and because I refuse to give her to him he charges me with exceeding pride and has besieged us here, camping his army there outside. He launches attacks every single day, but we daren't attempt a sortie. A sortie? God preserve me, no! There are only women here, and we don't know how to bear arms. And there's no bolder knight than he from Wales to Denmark! His name is Tallidés of the March, and he's valiant and strong indeed. I've sent to the good King Arthur's court for aid – please God! – against his great assault: he's outside my gate and attacking each day the moment prime is rung! But King Arthur's not short of men and, God willing, he'll come to the rescue. Tallidés and his knights will be out there again in the morning – God grant we come to no harm!'

The instant Sagremor heard this he said: 'Lady! Lady! This Tallidés you've gone on about, the fellow camped outside: would he accept a challenge to single combat? If you can arrange it I'll take him on first thing tomorrow! And I promise you this most faithfully: unless he can defeat me the castle will be delivered – or *he*'ll be delivered to Death!'

The lady was overjoyed, and with a deep curtsey she thanked him for his offer. Then the cloths were laid by those whose task it was; but there were no manservants there – indeed no men at all, be they knights, burghers or villeins, except a clerk and a chaplain who sang the divine service each day in a chapel in the castle: they were the only men. The tables were elegantly set, and laid with white cloths and knives and salt cellars. And the lady, so pleased to have Sagremor at her side, took him by the hand and said:

'It's time to eat, sir. You're in my house and should do exactly as I say! So we'll go and take our seats now, if you please.'

The valiant, worthy Sagremor rose at once, and the lady took his hand. Three girls came smartly forward, one with a basin of warm water for the washing of hands. They washed and then cheerfully sat down. What more should I tell you? They were served with a bounty befitting their station, but it would be tiresome to list the dishes. And there they sat well into the night, beside the chimney where the fire burned bright and free of smoke; then they went and relaxed and spent a pleasant while in the hall. And when it was time to retire the lady fondly said:

'You may go to bed, sir, whenever you like: it's high time.'

Sagremor replied at once: 'I'll gladly follow your wishes, lady.'

And that wise and courteous lady took him by the hand and escorted him to a chamber, doing her utmost to honour and serve him and repay him for his valiant support. She seated him in a chair, and according to his wishes a fair, most charming maiden attended to his undressing with the aid of that noble lady, who thought she was helping – which she was, though Sagremor was embarrassed that a lady of her station should serve him so. What more should I say? The maidens saw him comfortably into a splendid bed – all commented on the gorgeous carvings and embroideries – and commended him to God, and then left him and made ready to retire.

They slept in their beds till the new day dawned and the bells began to ring. Then they rose, and the white-haired lady went straight to Sagremor's bed to find him already up and dressed and shod. She greeted him at once with:

'God give you a good day, sir!'

And Sagremor promptly replied: 'May you have as good a day, lady, as I wish for myself! But tell me: when's this knight going to be here?'

'First, good sir, you must come to chapel and hear mass. You should do so gladly: you'll be the safer for it.'

'Let's hope so, lady!' said Sagremor, and they went to chapel and heard matins and then the mass. But just as the service was about to end a boy arrived at the door with news, crying:

'Take shelter! Take cover! Prepare for assault! Tallidés and his men are coming back, wild and raging, across the fields! Look to yourselves! That's all I can say – I've got to get back – I can't let my lord see me here: he's in a frenzied mood!'

With that the boy dashed off, nearly torn apart with anguish: he was the brother of the maiden that Tallidés was after, but he'd rather she were dead than see him have her. Seething and distraught, he slipped back to rejoin the besiegers without their knowing where he'd been.

Tallidés and his knights galloped to the gate, hostile and aggressive, and he cried in his roaring voice: 'Lady, give me the girl I've loved so long or your time is up! You'll watch in horror as your whole castle's reduced to ash and you're reduced to poverty!'

So said the knight; and Sagremor, returning with the lady from the chapel, said to her: 'You must send a bright, reliable messenger with our challenge to single combat. But she'll have to be sure of the knight's good faith and secure his pledge and promise.'

'Sir,' she replied, 'there's someone, I think, who can be relied on to relay your message, just as you command.' And she called to a fair, most comely maiden and said to her: 'If you'll be so good, my dear, you're to go and talk to Tallidés, exactly as this knight instructs.'

'Truly, lady,' the girl replied, 'I'll do as you wish and as the knight commands.'

'Then go, damsel,' said Sagremor, 'and parley on my behalf; tell Tallidés that if he – or one of his men – dares take the field outside this palisade and face a knight in single combat, then if he's good enough and jousts well enough to defeat the knight he can demand the girl and will have her – and do as he likes with the castle. But if he's outfought and vanquished by the knight, he must return to his land without any fuss or further attack on the lady, the castle or any of the maidens. If he's willing to accept these terms, I shall go and do battle with him.'

'Good sir,' the maiden said, 'I'll convey your message just as you command.'

She asked for her palfrey, and another damsel ran to fetch him; she brought him to her beneath a pine tree in the courtyard, and the maiden mounted. Then she rode to Tallidés and delivered Sagremor's message, word for word. Tallidés was delighted by what he heard, and responded with courtesy, beaming happily, saying:

'I tell you, dear girl, there's no brave knight in King Arthur's household – Gawain, Lancelot, Yvain, Gaheriët, Agravain – I'd fear to fight to crush your lady's pride! And there's no knight in the world, I swear, so great that I couldn't vanquish him! My life's been wasted if I daren't accept this challenge!'

And he stepped up to the girl and gave his solemn word that, if he were defeated in the battle, he'd do no more harm to the maidens of the castle or seek to wrong them in any way. So pledges had been duly exchanged, and the maiden departed and Tallidés returned to his men. He started to prepare for battle, arming magnificently – his arms were superb, but it would be tiresome to describe them, so I'll leave it at that. And when he was armed he stood and addressed his men, saying:

'By the faith you owe me, sirs, I want you to stay well back and keep your distance; I've accepted a challenge to battle today in which I'll achieve my goal with the edge of my whetted sword! By all the saints, if I see any one of you move, no ransom will save his head if I get my hands on him! If I vanquish this champion of theirs, I'll have my beloved girl – I ask no more; but if he defeats me I'll go back to my land, leave the castle alone and the girl in peace: never more will I trouble them, on my honour. Those are the terms I've agreed and I'll honour them, come what may.'

With that he donned his helm and mounted a splendid destrier and took up his lance and shield; then away he rode to the castle on his galloping steed. And he didn't have to wait long before Sagremor rode out, fully armed, on Morin; and the moment he appeared, with shield at neck and lance in hand, both knights levelled their lances and charged. They exchanged such fearsome blows that they smashed their shields above the bosses and, like it or not, they both went crashing to the ground, in full view of all those watching – and both sides were equally dismayed. But up they leapt as fast as they could and prepared to attack. Tallidés was a valiant knight indeed, and with his fine, burnished sword gripped in his right hand he swore by God the celestial king he'd have Sagremor's head: there'd be no escape. But Sagremor replied at once:

'Don't imagine you've beaten me, vassal, that you scare me with your rant! Only a feeble fool would be impressed! I'm not bothered in the least – I've been in greater peril than this, by God I have!'

And with that he strode to the attack. They dealt each other mighty sword-blows on their helms. They smashed their shields, dashed mail from hauberks and battered their helms to pieces – bits of helm and shield were flying to the ground, strewn everywhere. That's the way when warriors mean business! Mail rings from their bright hauberks were raining on the grass, covering the field. They struck and smote unceasingly in a truly fearful onslaught, wasting not a single blow – both had gaping, deep and dangerous wounds. But I don't want to bore you by dragging out the tale with long description: the fact is they fought and battered with all their might till Tallidés was forced to plead for mercy. Then Sagremor said:

'I'll not grant mercy unless, before returning to your men, you go to the castle, to the noble lady I first met last night, the lady you've caused such trouble: I want you to surrender as her prisoner.'

'Ah, sir, for God's sake offer me a better deal than that! Have pity and send me elsewhere! I can't see hope of freedom for me there – or safety: she wants me dead! Send me somewhere else, I beg you: you'd have to truly hate me to condemn me to imprisonment with her! She'd have my head if she had me in her power – and if I came to any harm it would be on your conscience. You may as well behead me *now*, good sir! Send me there and you're sending me to the slaughter!'

'Listen, friend,' said Sagremor. 'You've pleaded for mercy so you must do as I say. I've no wish to send you anywhere else. Just as you are, helm on head, go straight to the lady and tell her I've sent you. Declare the maiden free, renounce your claim on her forever, and promise to give her all the aid you can if you ever hear that she's in need. If you yield a prisoner on those terms I'm sure you'll suffer no wrong. And being sent by me will ensure you're treated well.'

'It seems I must go there, then,' said Tallidés, who had no choice; and he picked up his sword and offered it to Sagremor, who accepted it along with his pledge. Then Tallidés, with no confidence that he'd ever return, mounted and headed for the castle, helm on head. The gate was opened to him and he passed through and dismounted at the foot of the steps. A hundred maidens appeared without being summoned and came to meet him; he bowed to them all and made his way through the press till he saw the old, white-haired lady. His face wet with tears, he knelt before her and said:

'Lady, dejected and defeated, in the presence of these maidens I place myself at your mercy on behalf of the knight who vanquished me. He's the finest knight I know of in the world – I have to admit it, though it pains me! I submit as your prisoner on his behalf, and that's the end of it. Do with me as you will.'

When the lady heard him humbling himself before her she was elated; she stood and replied at once, saying:

'Good fortune befall the one who sent you here! He's brought joy to my heart! How is he, that splendid knight? In God's name, is he safe and well? Speak up!'

'Yes, lady, before God, he's in good shape, I'd say! And his strength and valour now render me your captive.'

'And what's become of him? Tell me, by God! I'm desperate to know!'

'I left him outside the gate, lady. I saw him, the finest of all knights, mount a handsome, dark bay charger and gallop off to the forest. He had no shield or lance – but that hardly matters when there's no knight to match him! He's sent me here a prisoner and set your castle free. My radiant beloved girl, who's caused me more heartache than I can say, I must renounce whether I like it or not. Renounce? My tongue may do so, yes – but my heart is filled with a grief that'll be the death of me. And I wish for nothing else.'

That courteous lady's mood was far from darkened by what she'd heard; she told Tallidés: 'So help me God, the one who sent you here, you'll find, couldn't have condemned you to a better prison! I'll grant you a favour for his sake and pardon you captivity. But you must swear to me that you'll never harm my castle or my land and never wage war on me again.'

'I swear it, lady,' he replied. 'But let me have my love, I pray you: she'll have no cause for complaint! If you were to give her to me I'd be your man forever more, by the faith I owe the apostle Peter! If only you'd give me the maiden I'd see her right! And I've paid a high price for her!'

'Didn't you renounce your claim, sir?'

'I did, lady, I can't deny it. And I submit to your will. But I hope you'll have mercy.'

Hearing his words the lady felt deep pity in her heart; she realised his love for the girl was true, and that, because he knew she doubted him, he wouldn't dare let her down.

'Tallidés, good sir,' she said, 'you know full well you've done me much harm and wrong and caused me all manner of grief and woe: you've burnt my castles, ravaged my land and besieged me here. Day and night you've done all in your power to hurt me!'

'I know, lady, I know!' he said. 'But I'll make amends for all the strife and injuries, indeed I will!'

'And I,' she said, 'tomorrow, out of love for you, will give you the girl you love so much, have no fear.'

When Tallidés heard the lady's words he fell at her feet and was about to kiss them, not caring what anyone thought; but she wouldn't let him, and bent down and bade him stand. But there's no point dragging out the tale! At the lady's bidding the knight summoned his men and they came at once; they were overjoyed to hear the news about the maiden, and made elaborate preparations for the festivities next day. I don't need to tell you more than that, for that was the end of the matter: they were married next morning before terce,* and Tallidés happily set out with his beloved, beaming, glowing, and joyously took her home to his own land.

Sagremor Rescues a Damsel

Meanwhile Sagremor, after defeating him, rode on till the sun was about to set. Then he looked towards a rocky crag and caught sight of a brattice;* so he headed that way on his fleet-footed horse. Before he reached the crag he came to a wide, deep ford, and on the opposite bank two knights had built a shelter of branches. Inside it was a girl, scantily clad and looking far from happy: stripped to her shift, she'd been laid out on a bed by one of the knights who was intent on having his way with her. She was weeping and bawling, cursing the hour and the day she was born. At the top of her voice, with all the breath she could summon, she cried:

'Holy Mary, revered Virgin, beloved of God, help me!'

She was raving, pleading, desperate. One knight was pinning her down, her white and naked breasts exposed, and Sagremor, hearing her cries, plunged into the ford that instant. The river was wide and deep, and the weight of his armour nearly dragged him down; but his charger bore him over without wetting stirrups or saddle, and with sword in hand and reins let loose he galloped towards the shelter. One knight came charging out on a swift horse, lance in hand, crying:

'It was a big mistake to cross that ford! You'll never return – you're going to die right now!'

He struck him without another word, his steel lance-head flashing through his side; but Sagremor galloped right up close and dealt him a sword-blow that severed his head and felled him to the ground stone dead. Then he charged towards the knight who'd thrown the maiden on the bed; the knight abandoned her and jumped up and was about to flee in terror, but Sagremor caught him with his keen-edged sword; the blade cut through to the brain, striking him dead right there in the shelter without the slightest sound or fuss. The sight was much to the maiden's liking! Pale and wan and stained with tears, she rose from the bed and came to Sagremor, greeting him most warmly, saying:

'May God in His power grant you all good fortune! I thank our Lord for bringing you here – I'd have been shamed and deflowered, there's no denying. You came in the nick of time – how lucky I was! All my joy would have ended if God hadn't brought you to my aid: that knight would have defiled me. You've rescued me and saved my honour, which would surely have been lost.'

'Don't worry any more, dear girl,' said Sagremor. 'Dress now and come with me. Is there any dwelling hereabouts? If there is we could do with a rest.'

'Indeed, sir,' she replied, 'I've a house nearby, a delightful retreat, and it's high time to rest, I'd say! Come and stay with me tonight if you will, at the house of my lord my father – it's a lovely place. You can see it up there on the rock, as fine a house as any from here to Antioch!'

Then she clothed herself in a lovely red gown and dressed her head in a wimple – neatly, not covering her eyes but leaving her face open. Thus clad, Sagremor sat her on the shoulders of his dark bay charger and took her straight to her house, not stopping till they reached the gate. It was open, and they rode inside and made their way to the hall. Beneath a green pine they saw a knight, wrapped in a swathe of silk to keep himself warm; he was surprised to see them there, the knight and the girl in front of his saddle, and he sprang to his feet and ran to them with a joyful, heartfelt cry of:

'Welcome, sir! And you, dear sister, you're welcome indeed!'

And he took her in his arms and set her gently down beneath the pine. Then three servants came running up and helped Sagremor dismount, and disarmed him with careful attention. The knight saw he was bleeding heavily from his side, and was shocked to see the wound, so clearly fresh. He called to his sister and said:

'By the faith you owe me, sister, tell me: do you know how he got this wound?'

She looked and was aghast and fell in a faint; when she recovered speech she cried out in grief: 'Alas! He's suffered a mortal blow for my sake! This noble, loyal knight saved me from two villains who would have robbed me of my honour if God in His goodness hadn't sent this valiant knight to rescue me. He slew them both, but they've wounded him terribly: if it proves fatal, it'll kill *me*, too!'

Her brother, most concerned, seated Sagremor at his side and said: 'You've serious wounds, but have no fear: my father knows more about treating wounds than any man, truly: there's no better doctor on earth. Quickly now!' he said to a servant. 'Go and find him – tell him to come to me here.'

'Thanks, good sir,' said Sagremor, 'but I'm fine! I'm not worried! The wounds don't bother me much!'

He sat beneath the pine – as handsome a tree as one could wish, in a perfect spot and always green – until the lord of the castle came, alarmed to find his daughter weeping, full of sighs. Sagremor and all the others stood with perfect, proper courtesy and said:

'Welcome, sir.'

And graciously the white-haired lord replied: 'God bless you. And I bid you,' he said, coming to Sagremor, 'welcome to my house. I consider you not my captive but my companion and guest. Where have you come from, friend? Do tell us.'

Sagremor knew exactly, and said: 'In faith, sir, from the Castle of the Maidens.'

Then the comely girl stepped up to her father and said: 'Hurry, sir! Look to his wounds! He's badly hurt!' And she told him what had befallen her, and how Sagremor had fought her attackers and rescued her. 'And it's cost him dear as you can see! He's been struck in the side with a lance – I fear he'll die! Truly, God couldn't deal me a greater blow than losing him! So help me God, if I thought he was going to die on my account

I'd take a knife to myself this instant – I couldn't bear to see it!'

'Don't worry, my child,' said the lord as he looked at Sagremor. 'I'll attend to him and see him fit and well in no time, if it please God.'

'By God the ever-true,' said the girl, very upset, 'do all you can, father, to return him to me safe and sound!'

'I'd try no harder,' he replied, 'if I were offered a thousand pounds!'

He led Sagremor to a chamber and they laid him on a bed. His wounds were thoroughly examined, and cleansed with wine with all possible care. He had four great gashes, through the least of which, truly, a soul could have passed and flown to the clouds with outspread wings. The lord knew all about wounds, and was distressed to see how bad they were; but he raised a bright smile and said:

'Don't worry, sir: you're not so badly wounded that you've anything to fear.'

'I'm not afraid!' said Sagremor. 'Not in the least!'

They treated the wounds without delay and bandaged them with a wimple that the sweet and lovely maiden gave her father: she did all she could to help. Once they'd finished, Sagremor fell asleep for a while, tired from his exertions; it did him no harm to rest, for sure, and he slept right through to midnight. The maiden lay beside his bed, and didn't eat or drink at all. About midnight he awoke and she, who hadn't slept a wink, said:

'By the crucified God, dear friend, how are you? Tell me – I've been so worried!'

And that loyal-hearted knight replied: 'Not so badly hurt as to stop me riding!'

The maiden, who cared for him dearly, called for her father, the lord of the house, and he came at once and skilfully replaced the bandages with fresh dressings. He tended him most diligently, applying a poultice and a fine ointment, too, and once that was done he had sustenance prepared for him: hot milk with almonds. God bless him for all his effort and attention: he did his utmost to heal the knight, for his beloved daughter's sake. Sagremor sipped a little of the almond drink and it did him a power of good. He bade the girl eat, too – she was still at his side and had gone hungry because of him; but she could eat but little.

Then they rested and slept till they saw the sun rise, when the lord of the house returned to tend his guest's wounds once more. He removed the old poultices and applied new, and replaced the bindings with a fine, fresh wimple. But there's no point going on: quite simply, Sagremor stayed like this for a good six weeks before his wounds were healed, the lord treating him every day and the maiden ever at his side, refusing to leave on any account while he was so weak and ill.

But I'm going to turn now to Sir Gawain. I'll leave Sagremor for a while, laid up in bed with the grave and ugly wounds inflicted by Tallidés outside the Castle of the Maidens: the wound in his side gave him a deal of pain. I'll return to him in due course, but now I'm going to give you an exact account of what's recorded about Gawain, King Arthur's nephew – I shan't interpolate a thing.

Gawain's Unfinished Mission

Gawain, says the story as it's been recorded, was staying with his uncle, who honoured him most highly. But he was very troubled and concerned about the knight who'd been killed at the queen's pavilion while under his protection:[11] it weighed upon him

---

[11] i.e. in the First Continuation, above, pp. 212–3.

dreadfully, stifling all joy. What's more, as for the holy grail he'd witnessed serving him at dinner, he realised that, had he not fallen asleep, he'd doubtless have learned all about the sword and the lance, and about the body deeply mourned by everyone in the hall, and the chapel and the black hand that had snuffed out the light of the candle.[12] His sin had cost him all this knowledge, and he feared he'd be reproached for it. It grieved and pained him terribly; he'd taken comfort in the thought that he might go and find the house again, the house of the king where he'd been served by the grail, but he hadn't deserved ever to return. All the same, come what may, he was determined to leave court and see if he could solve the mystery of the knight who'd been killed at the queen's pavilion – his name, and where he'd come from and what had been his mission. He wanted to know all about him, and on no account would he return to court until he had the answers. His mind was made up: he said that never in his life would he return to the land till he'd done all in his power to achieve his goal.

One day he was seated at dinner in a chamber with the queen – he was very dear to her and she to him – and she was lamenting the death of the knight killed in such a fashion in her service. It troubled her greatly, doubly so because it was such a mystery. As they sat eating and discussing the slain knight, they saw a maiden approaching on a fine, handsome mule; gracious and modest in her bearing, she was dressed in red samite, beautifully embroidered and shining in the sun, and her head was covered with a wimple. The mule was whiter than snow, with a gorgeous side-saddle of a perfect fit, the most splendid ever seen, the story says: both saddle-bows were of ivory, skilfully and beautifully worked; and the breast-strap, reins, stirrups and head-stall were adorned with bright gold engraved with birds and flowers: no girl or lady had ever ridden to court with a finer harness. In her right hand she held the reins, in her left, rather than a whip, she held a slender cane to goad the mule. She was coming at speed, clearly in an urgent hurry. The queen saw her in the distance, and pointed her out to Gawain, sitting at her side, and said:

'Dear nephew, see that comely girl approaching: to judge by her apparel she's a maiden of some note, and I'd say she has a message for my lord the king.'

The girl rode through the gate and was met by the seneschal, whose words were always so full of spite that everyone feared his tongue. Smiling, he said:

'Tell me, my dear, if you don't mind: do you wish to speak to the king?'

With great composure but a heart weak with sorrow she replied: 'Where is Gawain, friend?'

'Upon my soul, he's inside,' Kay said. 'You'll find him with my lady the queen, in that chamber on the ground floor. Are you hoping for help from him? Be careful if you are – don't take him too far away: he'll come back here, you bet he will, and let you down just when you need him most!'

She wasn't interested in gossiping, and pressed straight on without more ado, paying no heed to his words. She entered the chamber, still mounted on her mule, and in the hearing of everyone she launched into her tale.

'Gawain,' she said, 'I've come here in urgent need from very far away, to remind you of my dreadful grief: you'll soon understand. While under your protection, and because of your pride, the finest knight who ever rode a horse was slain: the most noble and valiant knight he was from here to Constantinople, the brightest and the shrewdest ever born, the wisest and most courteous and most loved of all his line; from here to Rome

---

[12] Likewise a reference to the First Continuation, above, pp. 214–9.

there was no braver, more loyal or generous-spirited man. He and I were brother and sister, that good, handsome, noble, kind-hearted man, loved by all – and feared, too, for his redoubtable prowess and might in arms, the worthiest knight to be found.'

And with that she toppled from her mule to the floor, her heart quite overcome. Then the one who was loved and esteemed by all jumped up from the table and gently gathered her up and carried her to the queen's bed, limp in his arms as if she were dead. She lay unconscious for quite some time; and when she came to, she earnestly, with no pretence, began to weep and lament for her brother. Tearing her hair and wringing her hands, she said:

'My dear, sweet brother, the traitor who slew you did a grave and wicked wrong!'

Thus the fair maiden grieved for the knight who'd been killed, and the queen was so stricken with sorrow she would gladly have died. She sighed and wept and cursed the hour and the day she'd gone to the scene of that dread adventure; she was in anguish. Gawain, too, was as distraught as he'd have been to see his uncle on a bier: he was grieving bitterly – as were all in the room, their faces stained with tears, unable to contain their woe.

But at last they calmed and dried their tears, and the girl, though struggling to speak, said: 'Gawain, I've come from afar to remind you of the pain I suffer night and day. When, to your delight, you led my dear, worthy, courteous brother back to the queen's pavilion, you promised to take up his mission and follow whichever path his horse chose,[13] allowing no one to divert you. You've failed to keep your word; you've broken your pledge. Oh yes, you went to the court of the good Fisher King, and pressed him to tell you how the one who lay dead on the bier had died, and who had killed him, and about the holy grail that served at the table, and the holy lance. And the good king would have told you the meaning of it all, there and then, had it not been for the grave sins with which you're stained. Your sin cost you those revelations – and you'll rue it forever: you'll never gain that knowledge. But if you're willing and think you're worthy, you'll come with me to fulfil my brother's mission: take his arms[14] and we'll go – just you and I.'

'Before God, dear girl,' Gawain replied, 'to please you I'd take the wildest, most perilous route in the world! But by the faith you owe God, tell me, if you know, why I failed to learn those secrets. I'd feel cheated not to know about the grail! The king told me about the lance with the majestic head – and would've told me all the rest if I hadn't nodded off!'

'It's as I've already said: you fell asleep because of your sin, Gawain, which barred you from hearing about the mysteries of that house. I'll say no more: it's not my place to speak of it. But let's be going, quickly! Time is pressing: if I don't reach my destination within the week I'll have lost my honour and my land!'

'Don't fret, dear girl,' said Gawain. 'We'll leave as soon as you wish. And if it's a six-day journey we'll be there in four! Let your mule feel your stick – don't hold back!'

'Don't you worry about my mule!' said the girl. 'She'll run as fast as any destrier, no doubt about that!'

Without delay or dallying Sir Gawain armed splendidly from head to foot. He took courteous leave of the king and the queen; then they mounted and took to the road.

---

[13] In the First Continuation, above, pp. 212–3.
[14] As Gawain did in the First Continuation, when the knight killed at the queen's pavilion had asked him: 'if I die, don my armour straight away and mount this horse of mine and go wherever he takes you' (above, p. 213).

Gawain Rescues Dodinel

They journeyed on till they came to a castle, impressively positioned, and just as the sun was going down they rode across the bridge. A knight came out to meet them; a most worthy man he seemed, but shaky with age. He offered them lodging and gave them fine hospitality that night, much to their delight, and they stayed with him till dawn next day when they took their leave like the well-bred souls they were and commended him to God. Then they set off without more ado and pressed on as fast as they could: all day long they rode, their speed never slackening. They slept that night in a forest without anything to eat or drink, and resumed their journey at the crack of dawn.

They came then to a glade where they saw a tent pitched. They rode up and dismounted and went straight in: it was now past noon and they were tired from riding. As they entered two damsels jumped up and gave them a joyful welcome. In the middle of this elegant tent, seated on a quilt, were two young knights and two charming girls, having a very merry time. When they saw Sir Gawain holding the fair girl by the hand they showed every respect and said:

'Welcome to you, good sir, and to your companion!'

'And God bless you!' replied Gawain, that valiant knight possessed of all good qualities.

The knights and girls invited them to sit with them; then six servants promptly appeared and set and laid the tables and brought water for washing, working and serving assiduously. The two knights took Gawain by the hand and, showing perfect manners, seated him in the middle of the table, and his companion sat opposite, which pleased him greatly. In short, they were richly served as befitted their station: they must have had sixteen or twenty dishes. And when they'd eaten and drunk as much as they pleased the masters of the pavilion bade that the cloths be cleared. After washing their hands Sir Gawain and the damsel took their leave, and he helped her into her saddle and then mounted his horse without use of a stirrup, took his lance and shield and rode out of the tent. He commended their hosts to God and set off across the glade, which was wondrously fair, carpeted with little red flowers.

They passed straight from the glade and into a forest. As it pleased God, their journey through the forest lasted till vespers; they took lodging that night at the house of a vavasor who honoured them most highly, and first thing next morning they set off once more.

On they rode. And then, at the edge of a wood, they saw a burning bonfire. Sir Gawain was eager to find out what it was; the girl was troubled and wanted to stop him, but reluctantly let him go. So Gawain, who feared not a living soul, set off towards the fire. Up they both rode – to find two youths holding a damsel, stripped to her shift, trying with all their might to throw her in the flames. All the people of the surrounding land – men, women, children, of every age and station – were gathered there and lamenting as if they, too, wished to die; and there were twenty knights, one of whom, fully armed, was hurrying forward, keen to see the damsel put to death. Gawain and his companion rode up to the crowd and asked why the girl was being treated so; in reply a knight declared that everyone should want to see her suffer, for with a sword of steel she'd killed the finest man in the empire of Rome – her brother: she'd wickedly, treacherously killed him by night so that she could have his land.

'I can't believe that's true!' said Gawain.

'It's exactly what happened!' said the knight.

Then two thousand or more of the common folk came flocking from the nearby town, all of them crying to Gawain: 'Not a word of what he says is true, sir knight! She had no hand in it at all! Before God, he was wickedly killed the other day by Dodinel the Wild[15] – we've no idea why. He's still held captive by this damsel! For God's sake have pity and deliver her from danger, or these wicked men will put her to death!'

At this Sir Gawain thrust in his spurs and cried: 'Be off with you, you wretched boys! Let the damsel go this instant!'

But the armed knight, a renowned fighter, came charging forward, incensed that Gawain should interfere. 'What grounds have you to defend the girl?' he said. 'Her treachery's inconceivable! No honest man can condone murder! I challenge you to combat to settle her fate – no one, by God, should want to see her live! She's the most faithless creature in the world, I swear!'

The girl, in terror of the fire, was begging for mercy with clasped hands. Gawain felt deep pity for her and told the knight:

'As long as I'm fit to fight I won't allow this damsel to be so cruelly treated. God have mercy on my soul, I'll defend her against you or die with her!'

'You're a fool, in faith!' the knight replied. 'Without a doubt you're going to die!'

Both knights had their helmets laced and shields braced and ready; clutching their lances they drew apart and then charged at each other full tilt. They exchanged such blows that their lances bent and bowed. The knight's broke and shattered – he'd tried with all his might to do Gawain damage; but Gawain, determined to save the desperate girl, delivered a thrust that sent him crashing into the fire; and before anyone could pull him out, so the book records, he was overcome by the heat and met his end: he was consumed in the flames and his soul departed. It really hadn't gone his way! So, as I say, the knight who'd wanted to destroy the girl died wretchedly in the fire – but he was bound to come unstuck, for he'd been wrong: the girl was innocent. And seeing her delivered, the common folk acclaimed Sir Gawain, crying:

'Oh, illustrious knight, may the Trinity[16] bless the hour that you were born! Your coming here today has restored our joy!'

They helped the girl, so fair and good, back into her clothes. Then she came to Gawain and thanked him and asked him to tell her his name, and the worthy knight replied:

'My name is Gawain, my dear, nephew of Arthur, that mighty king free of pride and vice.'

'To repay your service, sir,' she said, 'I bequeath you all I have: my land, my wealth, myself; for I owe my life to you and you alone.'

'I want nothing of yours, my dear,' Gawain replied. 'But the knight you're holding captive – please bring him here to me: I'd like to see him.'

'I'll do whatever you wish, sir.'

She bade that he be fetched at once, and I'll tell you how he came: escorted by twenty knights, fully armed from head to foot.

'Dear girl,' said Gawain, 'this knight is from my land. I ask no other reward from you: I wish to take him.'

'I don't know whether this is wise or foolish, but I give him to you freely, sir. But, God bless me, I'd rather you left him and took everything I own! It was he that killed my brother – everyone knows it!'

---

[15] He appears as one of Arthur's knights in the Second Continuation, above, p. 311.
[16] Literally 'the one who made himself three'.

'Don't you believe it, my dear!' Gawain replied. 'If there's any knight here who dares uphold the case, I'll challenge him forthwith!'

'Wait, sir, be calm!' she said. 'There's no need for that – I submit to your wishes completely. There's no more to be said: I hold you in such esteem and love that I'd do nothing to displease you.'

So Dodinel, accused of the death of the damsel's brother, was released. His horse, saddled and ready, was brought to him along with his arms, all in fine condition. He armed smartly, and thanked Gawain deeply for his rescue; then with lance in hand and shield at neck he made his farewell. For his part Sir Gawain, along with his companion, took leave of the damsel he'd saved from the fire and then departed.

But he hadn't ridden far before he found himself nearing a great, dense wood, and at its edge he saw three knights awaiting him: they were bent on killing him – they were nephews of the knight who'd been burnt in the fire, and had vowed to avenge their uncle or be cut to pieces. As soon as they saw Gawain coming one of them charged towards him, crying that if he didn't defend himself he'd kill him on the spot. Gawain saw him coming and charged to meet him. Both had levelled lances. The knight struck Gawain first; he was a fine knight, strong, bold and confident, but he was unlucky to be jousting with Gawain, who returned a thrust that sent lance-head, pennon and shaft clean through his body – it struck him dead and his soul departed. One of the others charged to his aid – but he shouldn't have hurried: Gawain made no mistake and dealt with him at once, driving the head of his unbending lance right through him to send him crashing so hard that he broke his neck. The third knight was beside himself with rage; determined to avenge his brothers he headed for Gawain, filled with utter hatred. But seeking to assuage a grief can sometimes make it deeper. He unfurled the pennon that was wound around his lance, and his horse surged forward in a thunderous charge. They struck each other on their shields with a force that smashed the wood beneath the bosses; but it was the knight alone who fell, sent sprawling in the turf. But he leapt to his feet at once and drew his sword and attacked Sir Gawain, still mounted though he was. But Gawain jumped down, not wishing to be so base as to fight an unseated knight on horseback; he too drew his sword and braced his shield. The knight, in anguish for his brothers, dealt him a fearsome blow with his keen, naked sword that slashed away the right skirt of his hauberk and sent it flying to the ground: had it met his flesh the steel blade would have been stained with blood, but it didn't wound him or do any harm. Sir Gawain set his shield before his face and swore he couldn't bear to see his foe resist so long; with his whetted sword he struck a mighty blow to his head; unluckily it turned in his hand, but it knocked him senseless: he collapsed and measured his length, flat on his belly. He'd passed right out; Sir Gawain unlaced his helm, but he lay unconscious, stunned by the bloodless blow.

The fair and gracious girl fanned him with the skirt of his burnished hauberk until the faint, stunned knight opened his eyes to see Gawain standing over him with his drawn sword, saying his end had come unless he surrendered as his prisoner. The knight had expected certain death; to save his skin he promised to submit to imprisonment wherever Gawain wished.

'As soon as you leave you must go to the damsel who lives in yonder house and place yourself at her mercy.' And he pointed to the manor just behind.

'You'll have sentenced me to death if you send me there!' he said. 'Kill me yourself, my friend, rather than make me go to her! Force me there and I'm a dead man anyway – she'll kill me, I know she will!'

'She won't, never fear! You'll be treated decently when she knows you're sent by me.'

'I'll go, sir, since I have no choice,' said the downcast, woebegone knight. 'But at least tell me your name before I do.'

'My name is Gawain, friend, the good King Arthur's nephew. I wish you luck! Give my regards to that charming girl.'

'I shall, sir,' said the knight; and with that he left the field, crestfallen and defeated. Mounted on his charger, shield at neck and sword in belt but without a lance, he rode straight to the castle and dismounted beneath a pine. Then he went up to the hall to find the fair damsel whom he feared like death itself. Shaking with dread and anguish, he fell to his knees before her and said:

'Fair lady, I submit to your mercy, armed as I am, in the name of Gawain, King Arthur's nephew, whose strength and might have crushed me and my kin. He slew two of my brothers at the edge of the wood – I loved no one in the world as much as them: he's left me distraught. But I duly surrender as your prisoner on his behalf.'

The moment she heard this the damsel leapt for joy and said: 'God save me, vassal, Gawain has done you no disservice in sending you here: for love of him you may go quite free, wherever you wish. And may Gawain have good fortune!'

Then the knight, overcome with sorrow, thanked the girl for his release and sent people to fetch his brothers' bodies; they were buried amid much grieving, both together in the same chapel.

King Margon

Gawain and his fair companion took to the road again, and journeyed on till they came to the sea, where the damsel had had a castle built, and wondrously strong it was. But as they drew near she was dismayed – and mortified – to hear a wailing loud enough to drown God's thunder, as all the people of the town, more than thirty thousand, cried together in one voice and breath:

'Ah, damsel worthy and wise! You'll never return in time! By the first hour tomorrow you'll have lost your town and citadel – by your sluggishness, your tardiness! We can hold out no longer!'

Such was the lament of the people of the castle: all were in utter despair. Then Gawain and the damsel, her hand clapped to her cheek in her shock at their cries, rode up to the gate and in without delay, for it was wide open, and found the courtyard packed with knights and ladies. She and the dauntless Gawain dismounted at the block beneath two laurel trees, and as they did so knights both young and old flocked forward; and when they saw Gawain bearing their lord's arms,[17] they gave way to loud and dreadful grieving: they were nearly crazed with anguish. But I'll say no more about their grief – to describe it would delay the story too long and it's not what matters. They helped him from those splendid, handsome arms, and the damsel bade that he be served that night most graciously.

After supper she explained the situation fully. 'Gawain,' she said, 'I've brought you here – my thanks to you – to help me in my hour of direst need: I've never faced so grave a threat. King Margon wants to put me to death – he's striving with all his might; let me quickly tell you why.

'He had a very fine son, a young knight, and he wanted him to be my husband; but

---

[17] Donned by Gawain as the damsel requested, above, p. 499.

I wouldn't let him have me at any price: I'd already promised my love to a knight I adored – I was sworn to him absolutely. Margon – to his shame! – wanted to force his son Quagrilo on me, but the one for whom my heart yearned was twice as handsome, courteous and bright as he – and such a fine knight that he feared no man! So Margon came and camped outside and besieged us here in the castle; and he swore that if he got his hands on me he'd rob me of my honour: that's what he said! Then my beloved sallied forth with three thousand knights who were here in the town; they slew great numbers of Margon's men and took thirty notable prisoners – but my dear knight was captured, too! I was so desperate to have him back that, wisely or not, I sent a message to King Margon offering all our thirty prisoners in exchange for him. Fool that I was, I sent his men back – and in return he hanged my love before my very eyes! No one can describe the grief I felt: I was utterly distraught. First thing next day I sent my forces back to battle, and not without success: they returned jubilant, bringing Quagrilo with them. I was so filled with venom that like a wretched fool I swore I'd take revenge on him for the sweetheart I'd adored. I had him dragged up there to that mangonel, and in his armour, just as he'd been when captured, I had him catapulted on to King Margon's tent! The king blazed with rage, and vowed he'd stay and besiege the castle till death overtook him if he had to – he wouldn't leave till I was dead!

'Then Rumour, always swift to spread bad news, brought word to my brother. He was incensed, and would have come quickly to my aid – had he not been tragically killed while under your protection! It was a wicked crime: treacherously, without any cause, my brother was slain by Kay!'

'My dear,' said Gawain, 'I could never be sure it was Kay who killed him – no one could.'

'It was, sir, have no doubt,' she said. 'I've read in the stars[18] that Kay killed him with his knife: he drew it from his mantle without anybody seeing, taking him unawares[19] and condemning me to grief. I wouldn't have needed to seek aid from a stranger if my brother had lived; but that faithless man, driven by spite, robbed him of his life when he'd done him no wrong.

'And now, good sir, King Margon and I have agreed that if I can present a champion tomorrow who can vanquish him in combat, he'll leave me and my land in peace; but if he's victorious against my knight, he wants me to place myself and all my bold, worthy, renowned men at his mercy. That's why I came and appealed to you, good and brave and courteous as you are; for you promised my worthy, noble brother that, against all opposition, you'd fulfil his mission and avenge his death!'[20]

'Truly, my dear,' Gawain replied, 'I shan't refuse. I made that promise and I shall keep it. I'll do battle with Margon tomorrow, if he dares. Come what may, nothing will make me shirk this challenge.'

She was filled with joy and gave Gawain fulsome thanks, feeling deep affection for him. Then she led him to a chamber where he slept till the new day dawned.

The damsel awoke in good spirits and came to his chamber, where she found him rising from his bed. She greeted him warmly and the valiant Gawain returned her greeting likewise, praying that God would grant her honour, joy and good fortune. They

---

[18] Literally 'I know well by astronomy'.

[19] In the First Continuation the killing is mysterious, though there is a reference first to a missile and then to a javelin: see above, p. 213.

[20] Strictly speaking, in the First Continuation Gawain vowed to take up the slain knight's mission but was not asked to avenge his death: see above, pp. 212–3.

left the chamber hand in hand and went straight to church to hear the service; then after mass they returned and swiftly helped him arm. Once he was fully armed they brought him a destrier, saddled and harnessed, and with sword girded he leapt on his back and sent him galloping round the courtyard, and saw that he was a splendid mount indeed. Then they brought him a shield and he slung the strap straight over his neck, and gave him a fine lance, its head half a foot long and immensely sharp.

At that very moment they saw Margon spurring towards them on his destrier, magnificently equipped with arms worthy of a king. Galloping up to the main gate, in his fine, clear voice he roared:

'Damsel, keep your promise or submit to my mercy – you and all your people! I mean to take revenge on you for Quagrilo, the good, noble son I loved so dearly! And vengeance I shall have today, please God! Your breasts will be hacked and torn from your body in agony! You'll not escape, by God, and your castle will be levelled to the ground!'

'Sir Gawain, my dear friend,' the damsel said, 'now you've heard the king's savage threats: if he has me in his power he'll put me to a dreadful death!'

'Sweet friend,' he replied, 'open the gate and lower the bridge. Have no fear: unless he knows how to defend himself he's going to feel how sharp is my lance.'

So the bridge was lowered and Gawain rode out to defend the damsel. When Margon saw him coming down from the rock[21] he spurred his destrier forward; he was worth a hundred marks, that horse: there was no steed swifter. Without a word or any challenge both knights lowered their lances and charged full tilt and struck each other on their shields, the lance-heads smashing them to pieces; but the lances bent and broke and shattered, their stirrup- and saddle-straps snapped, their saddles came loose and both knights fell from their chargers. But they leapt to their feet with drawn swords and attacked each other ferociously. But why drag it out? The fact is they battled on till Margon was forced to plead for mercy. Downcast, crestfallen, he cried to Gawain:

'Noble knight, have mercy on me! Don't kill me – I surrender! I can fight and resist you no longer. With your sword and shield you've outfought and vanquished a king, and should rejoice. For pity's sake hear my plea, and in God's name spare my life.'

'I've no great desire to put you to death,' said Gawain, 'and I don't intend to. Since you've asked for mercy you shall have it – on condition that you submit on my behalf to the mercy of the fair and gracious damsel of the castle, whom I hold in high regard and for whose sake I undertook this battle.'

'God help me, I'm not going to her!' the king replied. 'If she had me at her mercy she'd kill me, I know she would! If you've a friend or sweetheart somewhere else, send me there, for the love of God! If you've a lady or a lord it would be much to your honour to send a captive king to them! That damsel's so full of passion and resentment: if you only knew, you'd never send me there!'

So Gawain said: 'By the faith I owe God, friend, you're to go then to the court of good King Arthur, and surrender to him without fail as a prisoner on my behalf. But first you'll swear to me on holy relics that you'll leave the girl and her people and her land in peace, and never wage war on her again as long as you live.'

'I swear it here and now,' the king replied, 'exactly as you say.'

The king gave his oath and Gawain received it; Margon was less than happy, but he had no choice, and necessity is a powerful thing! Then he took his leave of Gawain, and first, with proper courtesy, said:

[21] The castle clearly stands on a crag overlooking the sea.

'I'll go straight to the court, sir. And when I arrive before the king whose prisoner I'm to be, on whose behalf am I to surrender? I need to know your name.'

'I'll tell you truly,' said Gawain. 'My name shall not be kept from you: it is Gawain.'

'Gawain?'

'Yes indeed, upon my honour. I am nephew of the great King Arthur, son of his sister and King Lot.'

When King Margon heard this, his downcast spirits surged and he said: 'God has honoured me greatly today! I'm vanquished by the finest knight now living! By your leave I'll go now and find my men and take to the road: I shall set out this very day to seek King Arthur – and when I find him I'll deliver your message perfectly!'

He went and mounted his horse at once, and Gawain mounted *his* horse, too – a very fine steed it was – and they went their separate ways. Gawain headed for the gate, victorious, armed astride his splendid charger, and dismounted in the courtyard beneath a pine. The gracious damsel and her household ran to his stirrups and asked how he was and what he'd done with King Margon.

'Fair damsel,' he replied, 'I vanquished him. He pleaded for mercy and I granted it, but he vowed absolutely that he would never again wage war upon you or your land. I've sent him to the king my uncle to surrender as a prisoner in my name.'

'Ah!' she cried. 'If only you'd taken his head! That would have been the better deed! God help me, it's a shame you spared him death! But what's done is done, so let's just hope he keeps his word!'

And she took Gawain in her arms in a tender embrace, and kissed his eyes and face, still armed though he was. Then she asked him how he was feeling.

'Fine, lady!' he replied. 'Thank God! So tell me: do you have need of my help elsewhere? I'm entirely at your service!'

'Dear friend,' the damsel said, 'you've filled my heart with joy and washed away my troubles – except with regard to the seneschal Kay, who slew my brother while under your protection: a wicked act indeed. If only I were avenged on him I'd be free of all my woes – and that vengeance pertains to you, too.'

'By the apostle Peter I swear,' said Gawain, 'either he'll kill me or I'll deliver him to you dead or a vanquished captive.'

'I ask no more,' said that girl so full of goodness.

But with that Sir Gawain mounted and told her he must leave.

'Oh, you can't mean it – don't say that!' she said. 'You'll surely not leave to travel or fight for months yet!'

'It's not possible, my dear,' Gawain said. 'Before God, I have to go: I'm mindful of a matter I must settle in Cardoil – it worries me that I've delayed so long. I really can't stay – I must be gone; I commend you to God.'

Seeing that no plea from her would stop him, she had a lance presented to him to which she'd tied a wondrously handsome pennon of red silk emblazoned with a white lion; she implored him to stain it with Kay the seneschal's blood, wherever he might find him. He promised to do all she asked, and took the lance with the pennon – which was later to bring him much regret and self-reproach. Then he took his leave and commended her to God, and she commended him to the celestial King; and seeing there was nothing else for it she bade that the bridge be lowered for him and away he rode, through the gate and over the bridge and off at speed to the forest. On his mighty steed he galloped, spurring all the way, till he plunged into the forest, which stretched ahead for more than twenty leagues.

Meanwhile Margon, his heart filled with shame and woe, had returned to his men and, with many a sigh, told them how Gawain, Arthur's nephew, had outfought and defeated him: he told them everything.

'Quickly now,' he said. 'Go and mount. A hundred knights will come with me: it's only right that a king should yield as a prisoner and avoid reproach.'

They willingly did as commanded: a hundred fine, bold, courageous knights leapt to their feet and hurried to arm, while squires and pages packed the tents and their gold and silver. King Margon had a splendid company indeed, and they set off and headed for the court with a great baggage train.

They rode on all that day and the next till evening came, when they found themselves in a vast expanse of meadowland where the grass was thick and lush. There, in the shadow of two bushy trees, was a spring with a bright, clear stream, and the king, very weary, thought it a delightful spot and gave orders to make camp beside the pure and lovely spring. Those whose job it was set about it, pitching tents and pavilions in that beautiful stretch of meadow. Then they prepared a meal, and as soon as all was ready they set up the tables, and the king took his place as he pleased with his hundred companions seated all around.

But as the first course was being served a hunchbacked dwarf rode up on a dark hunting horse, and asked a fine, noble youth carrying a silver trencher which man was the king.

'You can see him there, dwarf, seated at the high table. Dismount: I'll hold your horse.'

'I'll not dismount,' the dwarf replied. 'I'll say what I want in the hearing of all.'

And he held forth, so that all could hear, saying: 'Noble king, esteemed and honoured by men of every degree, I am sent by your sister the lady of Malehaut. She's frenzied, crazed with grief! Near here, less than a league away, Gorgaris is riding off rejoicing as he abducts her! And if he gets her to his castle she'll be hard to rescue – recovering her will be a fearful job! He's a hundred and forty knights with him, all of them fearsome fighters!'

King Margon leapt up and roared: 'To arms, my knights! Let's go and save my sister!'

Squires went rushing to fetch their arms and the knights swiftly armed and mounted their chargers. King Margon, raging, rode out at their head, following the dwarf who knew the country well and showed them the way.

On they galloped till they descended a high, high hill. Gorgaris, fearing nothing, was holding the lady of Malehaut's bridle, and that worthy lady was crying:

'Stop, good sir, stop this! You shouldn't hold my horse or my reins against my will! It's base of you indeed!'

'You can protest all you like, lady,' he said, 'but you'll change your tune! Before you get out of my clutches I'll have my pleasure with you!'

'Will you now?'

'Oh yes!'

'Indeed you won't! I'd rather die!'

While they rode on, arguing, down charged King Margon with his men, furious at his sister's plight, and he cried to Gorgaris: 'You're a dead man, vassal, by my life!'

Hearing the threat Gorgaris turned his horse about and spurred towards Margon, giving his mount free rein. They dealt each other mighty blows on their shields, ripping off leather and nails; Gorgaris's lance shattered, but Margon drove him from his saddle to send him sprawling on the ground. He jumped down and stood over him, and swore he'd lose his head unless he yielded that instant. Gorgaris realised he was helpless; he handed his sword to Margon and surrendered to save his life. Forty eminent companions of his were taken prisoner and forty more were killed, much to his distress. And sixty took to their heels, taking no part in the battle – no one ever knew what had become of them. The prisoners went into a wood and made biers to carry off their dead, and they were buried at Malehaut with due respect. And the wise lady made Gorgaris pay: she kept him as her prisoner for seven years.

As for Margon, he went to court and on Gawain's behalf surrendered as a prisoner to Arthur, most esteemed and praised of kings. Arthur received him with the honour due to a prisoner of his status, and told him he should be a member and companion of the Round Table.

'So tell us your name if you will, and it will be recorded with the others this very night.'

'By the faith I owe Christ,' he replied, 'my name is Margon. I am King of the Marches, truly, and honoured as master and lord thereof. I'm known also as the King of One Hundred Knights,[22] because I never venture from home without that many in my company, truly.'

'They're both fine titles indeed, I'd say!' said Arthur. 'And they'll be added to the list of my companions.'

And he summoned a clerk and bade him be sure to add the King of One Hundred Knights to the roll, and his bidding was done.

The king stayed happily at court with his refined, illustrious household. But let me tell you, throughout his life Arthur performed many feats of arms and vanquished many knights: he was a mighty king indeed, much loved, and greatly feared and esteemed as a warrior. I don't know what more to say, other than this: he was endowed with the utmost chivalry, wisdom and judgement.

Gawain's Battle with Kay

But we'll leave him now and return at once to Gawain, who'd passed into the forest as you've heard. He lay that night beneath two thick trees, all alone except for his horse; and all day long he'd had no rest or anything to eat or drink – and he was very tired, for Margon had given him a long, tough battle that day. So under the trees he lay till the sun's first light appeared next morning early, and the birds sang clear and sweetly in their Latin – so sweetly that Sir Gawain's spirits lifted and his heart was no longer weak and weary: he jumped to his feet, laced his helm and took up his lance and mounted without delay. He slung his shield round his neck and set off, cheered and buoyant.

On he rode through the forest till he drew near a manor with a handsome tower, well fortified with a wall and impressive palisades: the master of such a splendid place could feel satisfied indeed. Leaning at a window of the tower was a maiden of wondrous beauty. Watching Gawain approach she couldn't take her eyes off him, and she called to her seneschal and said:

'I can see a knight coming, finely equipped, but I don't recognise him; I think he's a wandering knight in search of adventure. Go down and meet him, quickly. If he's a knight of Arthur's household, bring him here a captive, tied and bound, and we'll

---

[22] A name that appeared in the story of Tristran in Gerbert's Continuation, above, pp. 369–71.

take revenge on him for the staunch-hearted Silimac,[23] my uncle, my father's brother, who was killed while under Gawain's protection! Be sure to show your prowess and courage today!'

'Don't worry, lady, I'll handle this!' the seneschal replied. 'By God, I'll give you no cause for complaint!'

And he called for his arms and his bidding was done at once, and fully armed and mounted on a mighty destrier he rode through the gate and over the bridge, shield at neck and lance in hand. He called to Gawain from afar, booming at the top of his voice:

'Vassal, if you're one of Arthur's men, tell me now!'

'By the Holy Spirit,' Gawain replied, 'I am indeed!'

'So much the worse for you!' said the knight from the tower. 'You're not leaving till you've jousted with me!'

'Good sir,' said Gawain, 'I hope no worse befalls me in my life! But I've no wish to fight; let me pass.'

'Dismissive, eh?' the knight replied – and he was a brave knight indeed. 'You won't think this a game or joke by the time we're done!'

'Let's see what you can do, then!' Gawain said, and he spurred his fine, sure-footed steed while the other knight charged on his, full tilt. The knight from the tower, unswerving, struck Gawain on his shield's boss, piercing and splitting it and thrusting the lance-head at his ribs. But the lance flew in half, and Gawain gripped his own lance by the white lion pennon, the pennon he was saving to be steeped in Kay's blood, and – not caring who was watching – dealt his foe a blow that sent him crashing to the ground. He stood now over him, sword drawn, and there wouldn't have been a long respite had a girl not come rushing up, mounted on a mule; a sweet and lovely girl she was, her head bare, wearing no wimple, and she was crying desperately:

'In God's name, mercy! Mercy, Gawain! I beg you have mercy on that knight! He's my cousin – don't kill him!'

When Gawain heard the girl address him by his name he stopped the blow he was about to strike and took a step back and watched her approach. She climbed from her mule and came straight to plead for mercy. And Gawain, realising who she was, took her in his arms: she was the damsel for whom he'd fought and humbled the mighty King Margon. He unlaced his helm and she, who cherished Gawain dearly, hugged and embraced him. And the knight, seeing the damsel there, jumped to his feet and greeted her with a joyous welcome, for she and he were first cousins. But let's get on: the girl in the tower, seeing this display of joy, came running down and was thrilled to see her aunt – for so the damsel was – and eager to know the knight's identity.

'Dear niece,' she replied, 'this is Gawain!'

She stared at him and for a long while didn't say a word; then she said: 'In faith, dear aunt, I can't believe you're greeting him with glee! We're all beset by grief because of him! If he hadn't taken my uncle Silimac under his wing he'd still be alive today! I'd like to make him pay and suffer! You shouldn't be fêting and honouring him!'

That gracious, good-hearted damsel went straight to her niece and took her by the sleeve and said: 'You're wrong. I know better than you who killed my brother. Neither the queen nor this knight is to blame in any way: I can assure you it was Kay the seneschal.

---

[23] This is the first citing of the name of the knight who was killed at the queen's pavilion in the First Continuation.

He's the cause of our misfortune; *he's* the cause of all our pain. But this knight has promised to assume the burden of revenge: he's given me his word. How relieved I'd be, how overjoyed, to have vengeance on the one who's filled my heart with grief and darkness.'

'Truly,' said Gawain, 'I shan't fail, I swear, to place him at your mercy.'

'Thank you!' said the damsel, so overcome with joy that she kissed his foot – not that he felt pleased or comfortable at that: don't think it.

All four rode happily over a drawbridge and into the tower. Gawain was graciously disarmed and then the knight, who bowed to Gawain and did all he could to serve him. Being seneschal of the house he saw to the setting of the tables, for it was time for dinner, and they all sat down to eat and had some five or six courses.

Then when they rose from the table Gawain said to the damsel: 'My dear, sweet friend, if it please you, I'd like to know your name, your brother's too; then I'll gladly take my leave.'

'Before God, sir,' the fair girl replied, 'I'm known as the Golden-haired Maiden.[24] My brother's name was Silimac: he was a fine knight of great renown – he had no peer from here to Antioch! He was lord of the Castle of the Rock – hence his surname: Silimac of the Rock. He was feared by all, and I loved him very dearly. In God's name, set your mind on avenging his death and you'll bring joy to my heart – a joy I'll never know, I swear, till his wicked killer is dead or at my mercy: he's filled my heart with such deep grief I'd gladly die.'

Gawain replied at once, saying: 'Dear girl, with the help of God and His power, at King Arthur's court I shall charge Kay with treachery, with the wrong he's done the family of the knight he killed. No one witnessed it, but you tell me it was revealed to you by magic so I ask nothing more of you but my arms: have them brought to me at once, for I've no wish to dally. But listen: give me the arms worn by the knight who jousted with me just now outside the gate.'

They were brought straightway by a fair and charming girl who did her utmost to arm him perfectly. And he was given a splendid, handsome destrier: no king or count, emir or emperor, ever had a finer steed. Then that nonpareil of knights – no man knew his equal – mounted without a moment's hesitation, and as soon as he was in the saddle they hung a strong, fine, handsome shield about his neck, emblazoned with two silver lions passant. But they gave him the lance he'd brought there with him, for its pennon with the white lion he was to stain and steep with Kay's blood. That must have troubled Gawain greatly, and indeed it did. He took his leave and set off swiftly towards the court, mounted on the splendid charger, and the Golden-haired Maiden who loved him dearly went with him.

There's little point in delaying matters by telling you of their route and each day's journey; quite simply, they kept riding till they arrived at court one Tuesday, around dinner time, just before midday. The king was seated cheerfully at dinner with a great company, and Kay the seneschal was serving the first course. Gawain approached the king just as Kay came away from the table. No sergeant or constable challenged or addressed him at all[25] – they all stayed quiet and still – so he stepped up to the king and said:

---

[24] '*Sore Pucele*', a name that appears in the First Continuation, above, p. 121.
[25] As they might well have done, not knowing that he was Gawain, who is in disguise, of course, having borrowed the arms of the damsel's cousin before setting out for Arthur's court.

'Hear me, great king, beloved and renowned throughout the world! On this swift steed I have come from afar on an urgent mission, to seek justice at your court. Justice is what I crave, and if it please you I shall have it without delay!'

The king said he would do right by him, whatever his request might be.

'Thank you, sire,' he said. 'Know, then, that I have come here with this damsel who charges your seneschal with murder, with the treacherous killing of the knight who was slain, as you'll remember, while under the protection of your nephew Gawain, whose heart still feels the pain and grief. He must either defend himself against me or submit entirely to this damsel's mercy.'

When the king heard this he replied at once: 'Dismount, my good friend, if you please, and come and eat. Have no fear; I promise you this: at first light tomorrow, without delay or respite, Kay will do battle or he'll be your prisoner.'

Kay was blazing, outraged; he could listen to no more! He took the challenge seriously and said to the king, in his usual tone: 'God help me, sire, with your consent there'll be no delay at all: I'll fight him now and crush his haughty pride!'

He called for his arms at once and his bidding was done, and he armed right there before the table where the king was dining. Then he mounted and grabbed a lance and slung a shield round his neck and swore he'd lived too long if he failed to defend himself against this knight who'd made such a base accusation.

The king was very fond of Kay, and when he saw him armed and mounted he quickly left the table, worried and distressed, and called his companions.

'Go, sirs,' he said, 'and take Kay and his accuser out to that fair meadow.'

To guard the field he appointed Gaherïet and Agravain, and Idier the son of Nu, and Yvain and Galegantin the Welshman, and the fearless King of One Hundred Knights, and they all obeyed his command at once.

So the mortal enemies took to the field. The accuser drew back more than sixty yards;[26] both knights gave themselves distance to charge; they gripped their pennoned lances, they braced their shields; they lowered their lances and let their swift and mighty chargers go. They spurred at each other full tilt, lances in rests, and struck with such fury that they split their shields. The seneschal broke his lance, but Sir Gawain met him with a fearsome thrust that smashed clean through the boss; and by God's will he drove the steel head and the pennon right into Kay's side, so that the white lion turned red with blood. The lance-head went clean through his body, with such force that it sent him crashing to the ground, in such a state that he couldn't move his hands or feet: he lay there stretched out as if he were dead. Gawain dismounted, sword drawn, unlaced his helm and threatened him with death. King Arthur was in the chambers above, watching from a window. The queen was at his side, distressed to see Kay fall; she said:

'God and Saint Martin curse the day that dawned on us this morning!'

All who watched were grieving, tearing at their robes and gowns, and those who were guarding the field were desperately upset: this was no game, no sporting contest – they thought they'd lost Kay and were distraught. Kay recovered his senses and heard the dismay of the king's people at seeing him sprawled on the ground; and he paled and quailed to see Gawain loom above him, threatening to kill him unless he yielded as a prisoner. But he said:

'In faith, you can do as you like; never in my life will I surrender! I swear I'd rather die than admit defeat and be deemed a coward.'

---

[26] '*un arpant*'; in medieval France the *arpent* was roughly equivalent to 70 metres.

'Then I'll kill you, by my life, never doubt it,' said Gawain, 'unless you submit to the mercy of that fair and gracious girl.'

'God deny me mercy,' Kay replied, 'if I ever surrender!'

'Then I'll wait no longer,' Gawain said, and he raised his sword of fine, tempered steel, a blade that cut with awesome ease, and threw back Kay's ventail as if he wanted to kill him – but far from it: he was horrified by the whole affair. He wouldn't have engaged in the battle for the whole of King Arthur's treasury: he was terribly afraid that Kay would have to die, and desperately wanted the king to intervene. He was shaking with anguish, weeping so deeply that tears were streaming to his chin, soaking his double-plied mail. And all the while, as he stood there in distress, he was holding the sword aloft as if about to deal a death-blow. Inside the palace, filled with wailing, the Golden-haired Maiden was leaning at a window feeling anything but anguish: to tell the truth she was brimming with joy, as well she might be, and couldn't care less about the crushing, crazing agony the others felt! Instead she cried aloud to her champion:

'In the name of the crucified God, dear friend, look to avenge my brother! Go on! Cut off his head! Heal me of my pain!'

'Oh God! Holy Mary, help us!' cried the queen. 'Dear Lady, flower and jewel that illumines Heaven, forever at the side of Christ your son, save Kay the seneschal from this peril: don't let that knight kill him!'

As the queen made her prayer she wept from the depths of her heart. Then the king came to the maiden with more than twenty knights, and with tears in his eyes he humbly said:

'Ah, damsel! Have pity on me, I beg you! Don't kill my seneschal – it would be a wicked sin! I implore you now, show charity, and I and all my men will be at your service! By the faith I owe Saint Peter of Rome, I'll come to your aid, from far or near, whenever I know you need me. Hear my prayer, fair maiden, and tell your knight to withdraw: he's a worthy, mighty warrior to be sure!'

She answered, saying: 'So help me God, good sire, I don't know what to say. I don't see how I can ignore and refuse your plea: I'd be sorely reproached.'

And she turned to the window and called, to the delight of all who heard her: 'Dear friend, stand back! I thank you, but I want you to do no more than you've done. The king here has implored me, and for love of him I'll answer his request. I release his seneschal, who has done me such grave harm and wrong.'

When Gawain heard her bidding he didn't hesitate: he stepped back at once and sheathed his sword. He went to his horse, stepped in the stirrup and leapt into the saddle, slung his shield about his neck and rode straight off, heading back to the tower as directly as he could. The maiden followed him briskly on her mule, having first commended the king and queen to God, and pressed on till she caught up with him.

Kay was left there, pale, ashen: he'd lost so much blood that all who saw him were shocked. They had him carried to the queen's chamber – he'd always been dear to her heart; and the king, who was very fond of him, summoned his doctors and bade them probe his wound, and asked them if he was in mortal danger.

'No, sire,' they said. 'We'll have him healed of this wound and return him to you fit and well within two months, we promise.'

One of the doctors folded a fine, fair wimple and bound the wound, and to come straight to the point they took such care of Kay that he'd completely recovered before two months had passed. The king and queen were much relieved, and the whole court celebrated.

Meanwhile Gawain and the maiden had ridden to the tower where they were given a joyful welcome by the household. They looked after them for a whole week; but on the ninth day the damsel departed and returned to the land from which she'd come, and Sir Gawain, bearing new arms, took to the road again, to seek out the adventures of the land. But he was still very troubled about the wound he'd given Kay: nothing worried him more.

Gawain and Agravain

He rode and journeyed on till one day after vespers, as evening was drawing in, he met his brother Agravain on a cobbled road at the bottom of a valley. He'd opened his ventail and removed his helm,[27] and Gawain rode straight up and they greeted each other face to face with the utmost joy, both sighing with delight. Then Gawain pressed him for news from court: was everybody safe and well? Agravain replied briefly that everyone was in good health and spirits, including the king and queen; but then he told him in detail of the mortifying shame that Kay had suffered.

'By my life,' said Gawain, 'I'm sorry to hear that – is he mortally wounded?'

'No, good brother,' said Agravain, 'he's recovered well: he's never been better! He had a miserable time confined to bed for eight whole weeks at Cardoil, but now his trouble's passed: he's healed and well and can ride and venture forth again, to the delight of all who love him.'

'His recovery should please everyone, dear brother,' Gawain replied. 'But who was it that wounded him?'

'I couldn't tell you,' said Agravain. 'I've no idea, truly. No one at court knew who he was: they were desperate to find out, but couldn't get the slightest clue to his name.'

While they were talking they saw five knights come galloping down the valley. Agravain spotted them first and pointed them out to Gawain, saying:

'I promise you, sir, those five knights would like to tear my heart out! They're after me – they hate me – all five of them are baying for my blood!'

'My good, dear brother,' said Gawain, 'you're a knight, a bold and worthy warrior and daring when you need to be – you've no need to fear or quail! And I'm going to joust with the one at their head, charging at us with lowered lance!'

'No, brother, no!' cried Agravain. 'Wait and see how I deal with them! God help me, I swear I'll unhorse the first unless my stout lance lets me down.'

But let's get on! The first knight came charging, yelling: 'You're going to die, vassal, right here and now! You're about to lose your life – that's all I want!'

Hearing his threat, Agravain thrust steel spurs in his charger's flanks – worth a hundred pounds, he was, that destrier: swift and agile, a wondrous mount – and unfurling the red pennon wrapped round his lance he galloped towards the knight who was charging full tilt, lance levelled, ready to strike. They met each other with mighty blows to their sturdy shields; the knight was one to be reckoned with, but his lance was the first to break, shattering on Agravain's shield, while Agravain's held firm long enough for him to thrust with all his force and send him tumbling to the hard ground. The knight was unhurt and didn't blench; he leapt to his feet and ran at him with drawn sword. Agravain jumped down, not wanting to attack him on horseback, and when the knight saw this he swore he'd regret dismounting! He came straight at him, and they exchanged

---

[27] i.e. his face is therefore visible, so Gawain recognises him at once.

fearsome blows on each other's shield. But I'm not going to make a meal of this! Agravain launched such a fierce assault that the knight was forced to swear he'd go forthwith to Arthur's court and surrender as his prisoner and submit to the king's mercy: overcome by fear, he had to do as Agravain bade whether he liked it or not. Agravain asked him his name and he didn't hide it: his name, he said, was Patriz of the Mountain. Then downcast, crestfallen, he mounted and set off down the valley towards the court.

Agravain now remounted, and one of the others came at him full tilt, galloping like fury; but Gawain charged to confront him and struck him with such force that he sent him crashing to the ground, quite stunned, in such a state that he couldn't even stand. Gawain jumped down and drew his furbished sword; the knight, flat on his belly, recovered his wits and saw Gawain standing over him and begged for mercy in God's name, saying he'd submit to imprisonment and go wherever he wished. Gawain answered instantly that he'd send him to Arthur's court; the knight made ready to go, but first Gawain asked him his name and he told him it was Gilain – so he was called in his native land of Cornwall.

'But I'd like to know yours, sir, so that I can rightly tell the king who's sent me.'

'Be off now,' he replied, 'and when you get there submit as a prisoner on behalf of Gawain.'

With that the knight courteously took leave and departed. As for the other three, they fled towards a forest, scurrying into a wood and cowering in the bushes. Gawain and Agravain, it seems, didn't bother to pursue them, not a single step; instead they set off together and carried on down the road.

They kept riding till they came to a castle on a rock. Agravain, who loved Gawain dearly, said: 'Brother, let's stop here and take lodging at this house, if it please you.'

'Truly,' said Gawain, 'I'll gladly do exactly as you wish.'

So they rode straight in, and a most affable knight came down from a hall to meet them and invited them to dismount and take lodging there. Those good knights stepped down and went up to the hall hand in hand. They were lodged there till the following day in comfort and great honour, without the slightest care. Next morning they took courteous leave of their host and left at once.

Meanwhile the two prisoners kept riding till they reached the court. They surrendered to King Arthur, one on behalf of his nephew Gawain and the other on behalf of Agravain. The king was overjoyed, and pardoned them imprisonment out of love for his cherished nephews.

The two brothers, who loved to ride and roam, pressed on and passed into a forest, but neither saw nor met any man or woman all day. They rode on without stopping till they came to a hermitage in the wood and sheltered there that night, and set off again next morning. They wandered on like this for a whole week and encountered many a test – but I've no wish to tell anything that's not important for my story: there's really no point. They journeyed on together for a week until – one Saturday, I believe – they arrived at court. The king came running to meet them, as did the queen and all the most distinguished of the barons. They embraced and welcomed and honoured the brothers highly: they were thrilled to see Agravain, but that was nothing compared with the honour they showed to Gawain – as was only right for a knight such as he, who surpassed all the knights of his line in valour and prowess.

The Chapel of the Black Hand

But here we'll leave Gawain and tell of Perceval, who, as you know, had been lying sick at the castle after rescuing the maiden against great odds, killing nine knights to save her. He lay there in bed for a month[28] without eating or drinking, which can't have done him much good. But it didn't seem to bother him, for before six weeks were out all his wounds had healed and he could ride again, and if anyone had wronged him he could have taken revenge without any risk. So, feeling fit and well, he took his leave and departed. He commended the maiden to God and thanked her deeply for the kind service and lodging she'd given him – he'd never had any so pleasant and so good: had he been a king or count he wouldn't have been better served. But he'd deserved it. And still devoted to his care, she presented him with a magnificent hauberk of gold and silver mail, fine and light but strong and very tough: it had been forged in Egypt by four fair girls who'd taken great pleasure in its making – they'd sent it from Egypt less than a week before; and now this true-hearted maiden gave it to Perceval, and it became him well. Clad in this new hauberk he rode out through the gate, carrying the broken sword, yearning and longing to find a smith who could resolder and repair it: he could think of little else.

With shield round neck and lance in hand he rode all morning till almost terce, and didn't meet a soul. He passed into a forest and kept riding till well past none,* and pressed ever on till he emerged from the wood. And thereupon the skies turned black and he was plunged in darkness; a great wind struck up and all was turmoil. The elements were dead against him! Thunder crashed and lightning flashed and rain came lashing down; whirlwinds and dust storms raged; hail and thunderbolts fell from the skies, so dense and fierce that it might have been Judgement Day. Perceval and his horse were being pounded; he had to keep his eyes shut and take shelter beneath his shield, and the hailstones made a hammering din astonishing to hear. It was a fearful storm indeed, the thunder and the lightning so intense that on every side the heavens seemed ablaze – I don't know how God could have conjured such a barrage. Everything the lightning struck was wrecked – the woods all around were crashing down. But Perceval could see no fortress, house or tower in any direction, and his horse was rearing in terror at the tumult and the raging din. Underneath his shield he didn't even know where he was going, but he opened his eyes a crack and there, away to one side, lit by a lightning flash, he saw a chapel. He turned his horse's head that way and, in fear of the storm, kept spurring him on till he reached the chapel, battered, lashed and soaked.

He was much relieved to be inside and dismounted at once, swearing to God he'd never seen weather like it. Then he glanced towards the altar and saw the body of a knight lying on it, with a candle burning at its side. And a moment later he saw, thrust through a window, a hand and arm as far as the elbow: it was black and hideous – and it snuffed out the candle. And the moment the flame went out the sky turned dread, pitch black: Perceval could see no more than if he'd been at the bottom of a well. He realised now this was all a trick: he'd been there before, just the previous summer; and he realised, too, that he had to fight the hand. Undaunted he prepared for combat – but the darkness was so total he could see nothing. Then in the glare of a lightning flash he saw the hand and leapt that way and hurled his lance at it – but the hand caught the lance in a mighty grip and broke it! Perceval stepped back and drew his sword and

---

[28] Above, p. 486.

sprang towards the hand – but at the very moment he was about to strike he saw a head loom in at the window, and its body right down to the waist; and as it burst in it thrust a blazing brand at him, fully twelve feet long, singeing his moustache and eyebrows. Perceval invoked all the names of God – he realised he'd seen the Devil and was afraid; he raised his hand and made the sign of the true cross on his forehead and his face. And thereupon he heard a monstrous boom come crashing from the sky, and a bolt of lightning rent the wall and window where the hand and head had appeared. Then Perceval looked up and saw a gigantic demon all ablaze, its arm as black as coal – he was sure it was the hand from the window. Then suddenly he remembered the veil – he hoped he wasn't mistaken – that the Fisher King had told him would be lying in a cabinet.[29] He went to fetch it – but the hand darted out and barred his way, and a terrible voice cried:

'Vassal, it was rash of you to come in here! And you'll regret it! I'm going to kill you with my own hand – in the morning you'll be lying on the altar!'

Perceval uttered not a word, but at God's prompting he raised his hand and crossed himself. With that a colossal thunderbolt crashed down, and the demon, looming in the breach of the riven wall, recoiled; and in terror of God's thunder and in fear of the sign of the cross – a sign he loathed and dreaded – the demon leapt high on to the chapel roof. The lightning fell so awesomely, so terribly, that no one who'd been anywhere near could have stayed there and survived: it struck a wooden beam and set it aflame, and the fire spread till the whole chapel was ablaze – nothing could stop it. But Perceval was undismayed by anything he saw; instead he made straight for the cabinet to get the veil. But again the hand barred his way and the voice roared:

'Stop this folly, Perceval! Don't believe the Fisher King! You're mad if you do! Be gone this instant or you'll die! I've struck down many who've tried to fight me – so many knights I've killed – there's one left dead here every day! Have some sense, and make sure you're not another!'

Perceval made no reply; instead he fixed his mind on what he'd come for, and headed for the cabinet to win the veil. The hand seized his left arm to stop him, but in his right hand Perceval held his sword and tried to strike; again and again he strove to land a blow, but to no avail: every blow missed, all his efforts were vain. He was locked in a dreadful battle now, with little hope of winning: the devil was fighting awesomely to stop him getting the veil, and looking for a chance to wound him. He had him by the wrist and was wrestling and shaking him, sure he had him at his mercy; but the one with faith in God made the sign of the cross with his sword before his face, to stop the devil harming him – and the moment he did so, the hand recoiled. At that same instant a colossal bolt of thunder and lightning burst from the heavens, the most immense and terrifying ever seen; Perceval was blinded and fell unconscious in the chapel – and he couldn't be blamed for that: no man ever born saw such a fearful day in all his earthly life. No rafter, not a single lath, was left unburnt: the fire from the lightning strike spread everywhere. The devil fled away in terror of the lightning and the miraculous response of God to the sign of the cross.

For a long while Perceval lay beside the altar, face down, unconscious, stunned by the mighty shock of the lightning bolt. But when he finally came to, he went straight to the cabinet, pulled open the door and removed the lid of the golden vessel that he found inside. With no one to obstruct him now, he took out the white veil as the Fisher King

---

[29] Above, p. 480. All MSS at this point read 'inside the window', but a few lines later they again refer to a cupboard.

had told him. Faithfully following the king's instructions – he'd told him exactly what to do – he unfolded the veil and spread it on the altar. He gazed at it and fondled it, then took a pitcher full of holy water and immersed the whole veil. Then he went out through the chapel door, the veil in his right hand, and like the fine, assured knight he was he processed around the walls sprinkling them with the holy water, as if it had been Ascension Day, Christmas, Easter or Pentecost. It was no trouble to him at all! Once he'd sprinkled all around he went back inside the chapel and knelt before the altar and prayed with deep devotion. He soaked the veil once more in the holy water, and prayed to ever-truthful God to bring him to salvation and to protect him from demons and from the Devil's endless wiles. After this prayer and appeal to God he went and sprinkled water all around the inside of the chapel, including the crucifix. He acted in earnest, in all sincerity; and as he sprinkled the water, the fire inside was quenched – and the storm outside, that had raged and done such damage that night, was stilled. Seeing the storm abate, he stopped sprinkling the water from the veil, and folded it and replaced and sealed it in the gorgeous golden vessel, which he put back inside the cabinet and then shut the door fast.

As soon as he'd done all he should he went to the body that lay on the altar. He looked carefully to see if he knew the knight, but he couldn't see for sure: the body was dreadfully blackened from the devil's foul assault – black as pitch, it was; he wasn't sure if he knew him or not. He thought he'd never seen such a hideous corpse, and wanted very much to find a priest to bury it – he'd gladly lend a hand.

He rested there till morning. There was no light at all till day began to break, at which point the candle came alight – and it has never gone out, nor will it ever till the world's end. The worthy Perceval slept there in the chapel till the sun was blazing red; then he awoke, and was amazed to see the candle burning: he stared at it bewildered, wondering how it had come to be alight. Then he realised and was sure that God had lit it, and gazed at it in awe. Then, to his delight, he noticed a bell in a little belfry – it occurred to him that if it were rung then someone would surely come. He decided to pull on the rope and make it peal, and he tugged and heaved till it rang out loud and strong. It wasn't long before a little old man in a grey cloak appeared – he was at least a hundred years old. Perceval went straight to meet him. This worthy man was old and grey, and endowed with a beard that reached his waist and hair so long that it reached his heels; his flesh was withered and hairy. Perceval greeted him at once and he returned his greeting instantly, saying:

'I wish you all good fortune, sir! You are the finest knight alive: more than three thousand knights have come and tried to cast out this dread wonder – and you've succeeded!'

'Good sir,' said Perceval, 'please tell me if you know where I can find a priest to bury this body. I don't want to leave it without burial.'

'I'm a priest, my friend, don't worry. And, before God, I've buried three thousand myself – I've counted them – all throttled to death by the black hand. But now the dread adventure has been brought to an end, and the achievement's yours: the evil is cast out and there's no more to be done: you've accomplished it completely! So come now: take the body by the head, if you will, and we'll carry him out and conduct the requiem.'

Perceval did as he asked, and they took the body from the altar and prepared it for burial. They laid the dead knight in a wooden litter – the most handsome in the world, I'd say – and draped him in a gorgeous sheet of silk chequered indigo and green: I can't imagine one finer. The worthy priest made careful preparations: he placed a golden cross at the body's head, and then lit two candles that he took from a coffer and fixed them in a pair of tall, golden candlesticks and set them beside the cross. It looked splendid, and when all was ready they returned to the altar; the old priest dressed it with a simple grace as he thought best. Perceval, quite untroubled now, gave him every help, doing all he asked quite perfectly. Then he rang the bell. It was heard by two brothers who lived nearby as hermits; they rejoiced at the sound and came at once, bringing the vestments that the old priest wore at the altar, and a finely engraved silver chalice. They went straight inside the chapel and dressed the old man and he, committed to doing good, began the high service. Perceval heard it with all humility and deep devotion, his thoughts turned entirely to God. When the service was done the priest came to the body in the litter and commended the soul to God's mercy.

Then the two brothers took the body and carried it from the chapel to a graveyard surrounded by a row of trees: there are many cemeteries in the world, but I don't believe there was ever one more beautifully enclosed. All the trees were elms, and from them hung the arms, lances and shields of all the knights defeated and killed by the demon. Perceval was amazed to see the arms on the trees and was eager to find out why they were there; but he thought it best to let the priest see to the burial before plying him with questions. He decided to do just that; and the priest went calmly ahead of the bier while the other two carried it behind him. They stopped beneath a tree planted outside the graveyard with no armour hung upon it, and set the body down. Beside the tree was a beautiful marble tomb, and they sprinkled it with holy water and laid the body inside, and covered it with a marble slab, huge and massively heavy, superbly carved and inlaid with niello.*

When all was done they turned back to find the knight's arms, and Perceval, anxious to know all about the graveyard and why the trees were hung with arms, put his questions to the priest. As bidden, the old man replied at once and told him the truth from start to finish.

'Good sir, dear friend,' he said, 'since you're so keen to know, let me tell you: in this great cemetery, beneath these trees, are buried all those who fought and were slain by the devil whose dreadful assaults you – worthy, noble knight that you are – have put to an end. The dead all lie in marble tombs, and on each tree are hung the arms and shield of the one who's buried there. The lovely, fair Queen Brangemore – God have mercy on her soul – was the founder of this place, and lies beneath that tree yonder. She was the first to lie in this graveyard, truly. And it was an accursed beginning: not a day has since passed without a knight falling victim to the hand you fought and, by the grace of God, defeated. The first to be laid to rest was Brangemore, as I said just now, and the one we've buried now will be the last, for the hand will never more harm anyone.'

'By the faith I owe Saint Peter of Rome,' said Perceval, 'that's an amazing story! But please tell me, if you will, where did all these splendid, handsome tombs come from?'

'So help me God,' the hermit said, 'I'll tell you indeed: since the queen was killed not a day has passed without a tomb, made to measure for the knight who'd died, being found beneath the tree where he was to lie: it's happened every day! And by the faith I owe Christ, the dead knight's name was written on each one!'

Just then the brothers arrived bringing the dead knight's arms; they put them on the trees, hanging up the hauberk by the sleeves. They hung the burnished chausses on the branches, too, along with the knight's shield and helm and lance.

Perceval said that before he left he'd go and look at all the inscriptions on the slabs.

'By God,' said the hermit, 'it'll be noon by the time you're finished!' And with that he left him and went to the chapel to disrobe.

Perceval spent all day till evening reading the inscriptions, and I assure you he found a good number of names he recognised. He covered every inch of the graveyard, but found no sign that any of the dead had been members of King Arthur's Table – that would have been the greatest sorrow of all. But finding none of Arthur's knights he returned to the chapel. As he entered he saw the three brothers come to meet him, and the eldest – the worthiest of them all, he seemed – said:

'If you will, sir, come and lodge with us tonight in the name of charity and the Trinity: it'll soon be dark.'

'I'll stay with you,' he replied, 'but I'd better fetch my horse and bring him here.'

'Truly,' the old man said, 'he's already in the house and all's provided: two basins full of barley and hay and a great litter of straw that's belly-deep!'

So Perceval entered the house, the worthy man leading him by the hand. They swiftly helped him from his armour and gave him a grey garment brought by one of the brothers – it was just as the sheep wears: fleece without dye or colouring; but Perceval gratefully donned it. Without more ado the brothers set up the table and spread the cloth, and laid it as best they could with barley bread and water. One brother presented the water to Perceval with all honour, and then they sat down to eat. They were far from sombre or subdued as they supped on the bread and water and on cabbages they'd cut in the garden; but that was all they had, and with it they quelled their hunger.

When they'd leisurely eaten their fill, one of the brothers cleared the table. Then the old priest, the eldest of the three, drew up close to Perceval and asked him about himself: who he was, and from what land, and what had brought him to those parts, and what was his name. Perceval answered all his questions, saying:

'By the faith I owe God in heaven, I'm a knight, sir, a companion of the Round Table, and I'm roaming the land to win esteem and honour.'

'To win honour?'

'Yes indeed!'

'And how do you do that?'

'I'll tell you, sir,' said Perceval, 'before God I will. As I go riding in search of adventures – and some I encounter are fearful! – I do battle with a host of knights: lots I kill, lots I defeat and lots I capture! And so I enhance my reputation!'

'My dear friend,' the hermit said, 'I can't believe what I'm hearing! You say you win honour and esteem by vanquishing knights? So help me God, you rather win the surest damnation for your soul! And I'd say that a man who loses his soul has lost everything!'

Perceval was dumbfounded by the worthy man's words.

'By Saint Peter of Rome,' he said, 'how then can I save my soul?'

'I'll tell you,' the priest replied instantly. 'If you want to save yourself you must abandon the paths you've followed so long and control your proud heart: unless you have pity on yourself it'll lead you to damnation soon, indeed it will! A man without gentleness and kindness in his heart cannot last long – he's sure to die sooner or later. And a man who's acted badly will pay dearly: if he dies in a state of sin, then all the honour and esteem he's roamed the land to win by vanquishing good people will be worthless! It's plain to see that a man who kills and murders others and devotes himself to doing ill wins only his own misfortune, grief and downfall: he'll be in Hell eternally, for as long as God is in Paradise! For a man who dies without confession can have no remission for his sins.'

Perceval was deeply shaken by the worthy man's words, and took them very much to heart.

When it was time to sleep the brothers made a bed for him and took him to lie down. He slept right through till morning.

He rose early, and heard the bell ring in the chapel, summoning the brothers. They all went there together, and the old priest sang the mass and everything pertaining to his office. After mass he called to Perceval, who went to him and confessed all his misdeeds; and as penance the priest emphatically charged him to beware of ever committing such a sin as to kill a man except in self-defence. To this Perceval gave his word. Then he took up his arms and set off, commending the worthy man to God.

The Devil Horse and the Demon Maiden

He rode out into open country but met no one at all. He passed from the open into a wood, and on he rode, head bowed in thought. Suddenly a knight came thundering through the forest, lance in rest, as fast as his horse could go; he struck Perceval as he passed and sent him crashing from his horse with a blow that smashed his lance to pieces. Still securely in his stirrups, the knight didn't mount another attack but grabbed Perceval's destrier by the reins. Perceval leapt up swiftly and drew his sword, and raced after the knight to recover his mount, distraught and furious at being felled. He chased his horse the length of a valley, as fast as he could, not slowing for a moment; but it was hopeless: the knight was galloping away so fast that a thunderbolt wouldn't have caught him. As he disappeared from sight Perceval was beside himself, and sat beneath an oak, enraged, downcast and very troubled. In frustration and upset he fumed to himself:

'This morning I unburdened myself of all my sins, wanting to make amends for the wrongs I've done, and now I've lost my horse! It's maddening! That knight who stole him has played a rotten trick on me – how it pains my heart! I'd gladly break my promise to that God-devoted priest: if I knew where to find the wretch who robbed me and left me without a mount – not even a nag! – I'd take revenge! No matter how remote the land, if I knew he was there I'd track him down this instant! But I'd need to know his name first – I've no idea who he is.'

So raged Perceval, propped against an oak tree in the forest, woebegone and furious. But as he sat fretting, wondering what was to become of him, he saw a destrier heading straight and swift towards him. It was blacker than any berry. Fitted with saddle and stirrups and harness it was a handsome horse indeed, and it raced down to Perceval at a mighty speed, head down, whinnying, pounding its hooves. Perceval, roused from his troubled thoughts, jumped up to catch it as soon as he saw it. The horse saw him coming and knew he meant to seize him and baulked and reared; but Perceval leapt forward, grabbed the reins and jumped into the saddle in an instant and took up his lance and shield. He was jubilant – and delighted with his fine new mount! – and set himself firmly in the stirrups. But the horse was bent on tricking him, intent on evil, and the moment it felt his weight upon its back it stormed away whinnying, destroying everything in its path, wrecking trees, smashing branches, till it reached a cliff above a great, deep river, wider than the range of a catapult, and was about to hurl itself in and bear Perceval to his death. Perceval gaped down at the river, never guessing he was on a demon's back; but at the prompting of God he raised his hand and crossed himself, and the moment he made the sign of the cross the demon, who abhorred that sign, desperate though it was to drown him, reared and flung Perceval from its back to the ground as it launched itself from the cliff and into the river. If a tower had been demolished and crashed in a heap it wouldn't have made such a thunderous din as the horse as it hit the water!

Perceval was deeply shocked: he realised now it was a demon that had borne him there, and he blessed himself with the sign of the true cross more than a hundred times. He was dismayed and alarmed indeed: he was in a tighter spot there than he'd been in the forest, for before him lay the awesome, perilous river that no one could cross without a boat – no man since God rose from the dead had seen so forbidding a crossing; and behind him soared a crag so high that from the top the whole world could be surveyed. He didn't know what to do or which way to turn: he didn't dare venture into the river or scale the crag, for he could see it was much too sheer. So he stayed there on the bank till nightfall, far from happy or content.

Then rain fell, heavy, thick and fast. And out of the clouds he saw a whirlwind with three heads appear – and they weren't exactly friendly: they were huge and hideous and all hurled searing fire, and each had a gaping maw with a demon's tongue and the teeth and face of a leopard. Perceval, horrified, turned his eyes away – and saw a boat coming down the river, draped in black samite. There was just one window on the boat, and it was open, and at it a girl was leaning, apparently tired of being aboard. The boat sailed swiftly to the bank where Perceval was sitting in a dreadful plight and glided to the shore, whereupon the rain and the whirlwind disappeared, and the girl stepped calmly and gracefully from the boat. When Perceval saw her coming he went eagerly to greet her. And the girl, adept at every evil, said:

'Perceval, my dear, I've come here from a distant land to find you! But it seems I recognise you better than you do me, indeed it does! We've met before and I know it's you, but you don't seem to realise who I am!'

'By my faith,' said Perceval, 'I really don't recall!'

The damsel came up and took him by the hand and said: 'You've never seen me, Perceval? Look closely!'

Then Perceval looked at her body, her face and her expression and was sure it was his beloved, the fair Blancheflor; and he said:

'Well met indeed, lady! How ever do you come to be here? I've never been so pleased to see anyone!'

And he took her in his arms and kissed her. Then they sat together while she, knowing just what she was doing, bade her retinue pitch a splendid, elegant pavilion and spread it with a sumptuous carpet; and they made a bed at once, the most gorgeous ever seen. It was high time for supper, and the servants – intent on leading Perceval to his doom – went to set the table, and I can assure you they spread it with the most delicious dishes imaginable. Once they'd stripped Perceval of his arms he was seated in the place of honour. But no grace or blessing was given by any priest or cleric. Perceval ate and drank his fill with pleasure – and he needed it: he'd had nothing to eat or drink all day and had been through a lot; but now that was all forgotten.

As soon as he'd eaten to his satisfaction, the damsel, seated at his side, bade that the table be cleared and called for hot water. The servants were quick to obey and went straight to fetch the water, and she and Perceval washed their hands and dried them on a towel provided by a maid. Then they began to talk together, and Perceval said:

'If you please, my love, tell me what brought you here, to such a strange and distant land.'

'I came to find *you*, my love! I needed you so badly, for a wicked knight, Aridés of Escavalon, is striving with all his might to harm and dishonour me! He's ravaging and laying waste my land, and wants to take me for his wife! He says you're lost, or have become a monk! But not for all the world's riches would I accept him or wrong you in any way: my life will be devoted to being your wife.'

'My dearest love,' said Perceval, 'he'll find mountains, crags and valleys no refuge: I'll harry him to his death! I vow and swear I'll never fail you!'

The lady thanked him, feigning deep affection. And when it was time for bed she said: 'My love, you may go to bed whenever you wish – and lie with me in mine if you desire, as you shall elsewhere if I have my way!'

Perceval said he'd do just as she wished; so she lay down in that gorgeous bed and Perceval lay beside her – with great delight, having not seen her for so long. And when he felt her naked body he wanted to make love there and then – and she was willing to let him do all he wished: she wasn't coy! Then Perceval glanced up and saw his cruciform sword, and seeing the shape of the cross he crossed himself – and so thwarted the demon with which he'd been about to take his pleasure! For it was a demon indeed, be sure of that, who in the shape of his beloved wanted to make him sin with her while saying she loved him dearly; but when he made the sign of the cross, miraculously inspired by God, the demon lying under him leapt up that instant and swept away the pavilion and the bed. Perceval was left there all alone, downcast and distressed; he raised his hands to heaven and gave thanks to God, saying:

'Dear heavenly Father who became a mortal man, I worship you, and thank you for aiding me! It was the very demon, there's no denying, who tried to drown me here last night!'

He hurriedly donned his clothes and shoes and armour, then looked down at the water's edge where the boat had landed – but it wasn't there: there was nothing to be seen. Then the moon rose, much to his relief and comfort, and now he spied the boat: it had left the shore and was sailing away; and a storm struck up, a storm so fierce that rain and thunder and lightning fell and hailstones, great and small, lashed down from the clouds and pounded the boat incessantly till it disappeared from sight amid howling wind and rain and lightning bolts. But once the boat was gone the storm abated, and Perceval sat down, much relieved, and reflected on all he'd witnessed. He knew for sure that the horse that had borne him there had been a demon in horse's shape, and that the girl with the pavilion who'd arrived there when the whirlwind struck had doubtless been the demon bent on luring him into sin and dragging him with him down to Hell. As he sat and pondered this he kept raising his clasped hands to heaven, praying for the grace of God in whom he trusted, saying:

'Dear Lord God, have pity! Bring me from this place, I pray you, safe in body and soul! I swear I'll act henceforth to earn your love!'

Such was Perceval's plea; and he continued to sigh and fret till dawn was near. There on the shore he sat, taking comfort in praying to God the sovereign Father to cast His divine power over him.

And as he sat praying, appealing to God to send him aid and steer him away from sin, he saw another boat approaching with sail unfurled, though it had no rudder or oars; and it was surrounded by the most ineffable joy. The boat he saw approaching as morning dawned was richly adorned with drapes; but there was no one aboard save an aged gentleman who seemed, for sure, a good Christian. The boat sailed up to Perceval, and he went to see what was on board; and the worthy man, fully aware of Perceval's plight and what had befallen him, stepped out and greeted him most kindly in the name of the high master. Perceval returned his greeting courteously, and said:

'In God's name, sir, we're alone here, you and I: please tell me who you are – I'd be very glad to hear. Do tell me the truth, sir, for I dearly wish to know.'

'My good friend,' the worthy man replied, 'I'll tell you the truth about myself quite freely. The master of the Trinity, who guides sinners back to the right path, has sent me here to cheer and comfort you: He doesn't want you to give way to despair – you've suffered much, so I bring you comfort on His behalf. Have no fear or doubt: Jesus Christ the Saviour, who created heaven and earth, has sent me here to find you. Come aboard with me now, and worry no more about anything you've seen.'

'Wait a moment, please, dear sir!' said Perceval. 'Tell me first about the black horse that bore me here, and about the damsel who made me lie with her here beneath this cliff, both of us together naked in a bed.'

'In faith,' said the white-haired worthy, 'I'll tell you no lie. The horse that brought you was the Devil, truly, who longed to bundle you into Hell with all his fellows. And when you were at the chapel and overcame the demon and the black hand, and confessed your sins to the priest and repented and assumed penance, I tell you, friend, the Devil was distraught, enraged: he realised he'd lost you! So, to make you return to him, he had you toppled from your horse in that valley in the forest – to make you despair. He'd have made you pay dearly then for climbing on his back: he'd have drowned you here – a wretched, dreadful end – if God hadn't taken pity on you by having you make the sign of the cross to work your deliverance. That saved you from the one who would have cast you to your death in this rushing river, had God not come to your aid. Having failed to drown you, the horse plunged in the water, baffled and defeated, his force and power outdone, nearly crazed with anguish! So he sent another demon in a boat in the semblance of a girl. She claimed to be your beloved Blancheflor, whom you left at Beaurepaire, but by Saint Peter it was a lie! She was a demon bent on deceiving you, to drag you down to the murk of Hell!'

'Truly, sir,' said Perceval, 'his deception would have worked, I know, if I hadn't made the sign of the cross! But the cross on which Christ was sacrificed saved me from the demon: I saw him battling away across the storm-tossed sea to where he'd come from. I don't know what became of him then – nor do I want to! So I was left here; and now I'll go with you wherever you wish – as is only right, since you say you're sent from God.'

'Don't hesitate, friend,' said the worthy man, concerned for him. 'You'll be under God's protection as long as I'm your escort. I promise I'll guide you happily to the road you have to take.'

With that they boarded the boat, and the wind filled the sail and bore them swiftly away.

The boat sailed calmly and joyously to port. At the harbour where they landed they saw a castle standing on a rock beside the shore, a strong and handsome castle, most imposing, positioned so that the sea beat on one side and meadows and vineyards and cornfields lay on another, and on another lay forest where tigers and leopards roamed great mountains and deep valleys.

'Good sir,' said Perceval, 'tell me if you will: what's the name of that splendid castle? Please enlighten me!'

'Dear friend,' replied God's messenger, 'it's the castle of Lindesore, and its present lord goes by the name of Sartuz de la Loje.'

'If you've no objection, sir, I suggest we go there: I'm sure he could provide us with good horses.'

'We needn't go to him for horses, truly,' said the messenger. 'You'll have any horse you care to choose: I've some fine and handsome steeds indeed, as many as a mighty count!'

And as they spoke they saw two boys come clattering from the castle, one bringing a palfrey and the other a white destrier, both fully harnessed and both of them white.

'Perceval my friend,' said the worthy messenger, 'take whichever mount you wish, whichever you prefer: they're both fine steeds, handsomely harnessed and whiter than snow. There's no need to look further: make your choice and take it.'

Perceval didn't wait: he stepped from the boat and took the destrier – a strong, swift horse and superbly harnessed: he wouldn't have exchanged him for a hundred pounds! He mounted quickly and took his leave. The messenger who'd brought him there commended him to God; then the wind swelled the sail and the boat made its way from port.

A Toll is Demanded

Perceval, in high spirits now, rode off down a valley; but he hadn't gone a league before he heard a horse whinny in the vale behind him. He turned to look, and saw a knight galloping wildly towards him. His gear was worthy of a king or emperor, his armour resplendent in the sun; but he hadn't come for a friendly chat: he was crying:

'It was a big mistake, vassal, not paying the toll to cross my lord's domain! It'll cost you your honour!'

Perceval turned his horse to face him and said: 'Vassal, vassal, I'm a knight, I assure you, and no one's ever asked me to pay a toll! Be sensible now: be off and about your business!'

'God damn me if I go without my due!'

'Off with you or you'll regret it!'

'I'm taking you back to the castle by the shore!'

'Are you indeed?' said Perceval. 'Not without a fight!'

'I'll fight, in faith,' the knight replied, 'right here and now, if you won't come willingly!'

And they charged at each other as fast as their steeds could go. The knight met him with a mighty blow that pierced and smashed his shield; the lance-head caught him in the side but didn't quite find flesh, and the shaft shattered from the force of the blow. In return Perceval struck him full on the shield and sent him crashing to the dust with his horse in a heap across him. It was quite a fall and he couldn't help passing out; but when he came to he sprang to his feet and said:

'Vassal, I'm on foot and you're on horseback. Dismount or your horse is finished!'

'What's my horse done to you, to make you want to kill him? Don't worry: I'd never attack you or try to overcome you while I'm mounted. That's never been my way.'

And he climbed at once from his snow-white horse and drew from his left side his fine, keen sword, its blade as bright as a burning brand, and took his shield by the strap and hung it smartly from his neck. Then the knight advanced in a fearsome attack. They exchanged unsparing blows on helms and shields, and Perceval – victor of many a combat, many a battle – landed one so fierce that neither helm nor mail could stop the honed steel cutting through to the head. The knight fell that instant and measured his length on the ground. Stunned by the blow he passed out three times. Perceval unlaced his helm to expose his head; then the knight in terror cried for mercy, and took his sword and surrendered it, saying:

'I beg you, vassal, in the name of courtesy spare my life! Anyone who pleads for mercy should receive it, truly: I'm begging you, don't falter – grant me mercy!'

'You shall have it,' said Perceval, 'on condition that without returning to the castle you go straight to King Arthur's court and tell him I've sent you as his prisoner, and explain exactly why. You'll be treated well when you give him news of me, so that's easy enough! And tell him I'll be at court at Pentecost unless captivity or sickness prevents me going – nothing else, apart from death, will stop me. But first you'll need to know my name and remember it well: in my own country I'm rightly known as Perceval the Welshman.'

The knight took this in and answered courteously: 'I'll do exactly as you wish, sir. When I arrive at court I'll tell the king the whole story from start to finish, I swear: it will be a pleasure and an honour.'

And he went to his horse and mounted without asking for further respite, and they kindly commended each other to God. He set off swiftly and headed for the king's court, no longer rash and aggressive, his attitude transformed.

Perceval and Dodinel

Perceval remounted the fine white destrier and set off to resume his mission. He pressed on across a plain right through till noon, buoyant, in good spirits, and then when noon was past he found himself in a beautiful stretch of meadowland. There, standing elegantly beside a spring, he came upon a gorgeous pavilion of red-dyed silk. He headed straight towards it, eager for somewhere to rest, and dismounted outside this magnificent tent. A maiden appeared and welcomed him most warmly with a greeting befitting a knight. She happily led him inside the tent and they sat together on a bed. Very cheerful now, he asked her:

'Tell me if you will, dear girl, and truly: do you have a husband or a sweetheart?'

The girl, endowed with wit and courtesy and goodness and honour, eloquently and sweetly answered: 'I do have a lover, sir: a valiant, loyal, wise and courteous knight renowned for great courage, truly. I don't think you'll find a finer knight in all this land – before God you won't! His name is Dodinel the Wild; he's a companion of the Round Table – and they're the finest knights and most acclaimed warriors in the world!'

'I know him well, lady, the knight you mention. He is indeed valiant and loyal, full of fine qualities – I'm pleased to hear you speak so of him. But tell me truly: is he in good health and spirits?'

'Indeed he is, sir, thanks be to God, and he'll be here at any moment.'

They stayed conversing happily, with ample time to talk of all they wished; and as they did so they saw a group of four maidens coming: they'd gone into the meadow to gather flowers – primroses and violets – and make garlands. When they saw Perceval sitting beside the damsel they all came up and greeted him, a greeting he courteously returned. Their lady, eager for the return of her beloved Dodinel, called to the girls and bade them take care of Perceval's horse at once and provide him with plenty of oats and hay. They did as bidden, and the damsel had Perceval promptly disarmed: it was much to her credit that she had him served and honoured so.

But just as they finished disarming him, a knight burst in on a great charger, fully armed, came up to the damsel without a word of greeting, reached down, swept her up

– she was clearly a prize he craved – and put her across his saddle-bow and galloped away that instant. As he carried her off she cried in distress at the top of her voice:

'Holy Mary! Sweet, crowned queen! Help me! Save me from dishonour!'

The girls were aghast to see their lady borne away – as was Perceval. He called for his horse at once; a girl quickly brought him and he leapt in the saddle – unarmed though he was – and snatched up just his lance and shield and sword and galloped from the tent and after the knight. He was racing away at tremendous speed, but Perceval spied him in the distance, at the bottom of a great, wide valley, and with shield round neck and lance in hand he set off in hot pursuit, roaring:

'Vassal! Put down that girl! You're going to pay dearly, so help me God!'

The knight saw him coming but wasn't worried – he had no armour – and went galloping on. But Perceval was catching up, and cried:

'By God, you'd better turn and face me or I'll strike you from behind! And if you die in flight it'll be to your shame, I swear!'

The knight could see he was right. He put the girl down and turned to attack his pursuer. With his wickedly sharp-headed lance he struck Perceval on the shield, smashing through the boss; but the head was deflected and didn't find flesh and the shaft broke and shattered, while Perceval struck the knight's shield beneath the rim and smashed it clean apart, and the force of his thrust laid the knight flat on the ground, so stunned and senseless that he couldn't move a foot or hand and fell unconscious. Perceval jumped straight down and strode to the fallen knight, unlaced his helm and threw open his ventail; then he drew his keen sword, stood over him and said he'd lose his head unless he submitted as a prisoner. The knight, out cold, made no sound, said not a word; after a moment he addressed him again, and the knight, in his befuddled state, opened his eyes, saw him looming there and replied at once, without a second thought:

'I've nothing to say, sir, except I surrender and crave your mercy! On my word and honour as a knight, I swear I'll accept imprisonment wherever you choose and will faithfully keep any terms you set.'

'And I,' said Perceval, 'place you wholly at the mercy of this damsel here, to do exactly as she wishes.'

'Ah, my good, kind sir, would you have me die? She wants nothing other than to have me slain! Noble knight, don't condemn me to death!'

'Then if you want to save yourself,' said Perceval, 'you must go to the good King Arthur's court and greet him as befits a king in the name of Perceval the Welshman. Tell him in all honesty that I've sent you as his prisoner, and that I'll be at court a month from today barring mishap.'

The crushed and woebegone knight replied: 'I'll give him your message, exactly as you ask.'

And he mounted and took his leave. He left the girl and rode away, in such distress at leaving her that his heart nearly broke in two, and all alone he set off for the court.

Perceval came to that lovely girl and gave her comfort, and carried her on his horse's shoulders right back down the valley to the pavilion. On the swift, white destrier they headed straight back to the tent.

Dodinel had just dismounted at the door and was standing there on the lush grass; he hadn't yet heard about the knight who'd tried to abduct his sweetheart – and wouldn't have believed that anyone would dare, or would even think of it while he was known to be alive! He was shocked to see Perceval coming with her in his arms, and asked the maidens where their lady had been, and who it was that was holding her! The maids, all bowed and weeping, now looked up; and they told their lord of the dreadful shame committed by the knight who'd carried her off in desperate tears, but how this other knight had chased after them, even though unarmed, 'and it seems he's rescued her – look: they're returning together!'

When Dodinel heard this news he was too upset to speak. Fuming with rage and anguish, he couldn't feel relief at her rescue; all he could say was:

'How could anyone be so bold? How did he dare take my beloved from my own pavilion? He's made a big mistake, by God!'

While he raged, Perceval set the girl down from his horse; then Dodinel swept her into his arms – but she, endowed as she was with sense and courtesy, said:

'It's not me you should be making a fuss of! You should be welcoming this knight, who rescued me from the hands of one so dauntingly strong that he feared no man! But he gained nothing by abducting me: this knight had stopped here at the tent, and he bravely overcame him and sent him as a prisoner to King Arthur's court – he's already on his way!'

When Dodinel heard his sweetheart's words he stepped straight up to Perceval, his wrath now quite forgotten, and said: 'Welcome, sir!'

And the courteous Perceval replied: 'God bless you, and may he send you all the happiness I wish you. I pray he will, truly.'

Then Dodinel looked at Perceval and realised who he was, and ran to him with outstretched arms and took him in a tight embrace, hugging and kissing him with the utmost joy – he couldn't stop!

'Perceval! My dear friend!' he said. 'We've been scouring distant hills and vales in search of you – I and many more, as we were bidden, for more than five whole months! We've been asking after you everywhere! The only place I had word of you was at the Castle of the Maidens where I lodged the other day; there I found Sagremor lying sick, and he told me he'd seen you but didn't know what had become of you: he'd left you embroiled with a band of eight knights! That's what he said! So thank God I've found you here! We'll go back to court together – we'll set off first thing tomorrow!'

'Dear friend,' said Perceval, 'tell them at court that I shan't be there quite yet, but I shall be at Pentecost, if God so wills and keeps me from harm.'

What more should I tell you? They couldn't have been happier: a servant set the table and they sat down to eat and were splendidly served, and they drank to their hearts' content.

They'd just finished their leisurely meal when a girl rode up on a well-harnessed mule; and before she even reached the tent she cried at the top of her voice so that all could hear:

'Perceval! I've come for you from far away, and with urgent cause! I've crossed so many lands to find you – and you alone! I'm sent by your beloved: she's suffering at the hands of a mighty and notorious knight, Aridés of Escavalon[30] – every day he attacks and assails her, ravages and lays waste her land! If you delay it'll be too late – she'll have to surrender unless a defender arrives by Wednesday at the latest! Every word I've said is true!'

When Perceval heard this he leapt to his feet and said he wouldn't stay another moment – he'd go with her at once, as soon as she'd eaten a little; but the damsel said she wanted nothing, so he ran to fetch his arms and quickly armed, and Dodinel went

---

[30] As the demon had told him, above, p. 520.

to get his own, vowing before God that he'd go with him. But Perceval told him not to, but rather to return to court with news of him: that he'd be there without fail on the eve or the day of Pentecost, provided he was safe and well. Then the white horse was brought to him, and he mounted and commended Dodinel and his sweetheart to God, and set off after the damsel across the lovely meadow.

On they rode and came to a great and beautiful forest. Perceval asked the damsel how his beloved Blancheflor was, and she said she'd have been well had she not been at war with Aridés, the knight intent on harming her.

Perceval Returns to Beaurepaire

They kept riding till late afternoon, following a wide and well-made road; but then Perceval, trying to avoid a stretch that was always foul and boggy, winter and summer, encountered a rut; and as he then rode down a slope he felt his cherished horse begin to hobble. He wondered what was wrong. He stepped down from his left stirrup and immediately saw a nail stuck in his hoof. He thanked God it was nothing worse, and the damsel said:

'Sir, there's a smith up ahead who'll take out the nail and your horse won't feel a thing. Mount now, and don't worry – it's not a league and a half to his forge; he's made many a good nail! I'll take you straight there – we'll be there in no time.'

'I'll walk, my dear,' said Perceval. 'I don't want to make him worse.'

'By the faith I owe the Saviour,' she replied, 'you won't do him any harm!'

Perceval agreed to do as she said; he remounted without more ado and they set off at a gentle pace, and rode on untroubled till they came to the house of the smith. He was an absolute master of his craft, and he gently, carefully drew the nail from the hoof and said:

'You can carry on riding with confidence, friend: your horse is completely healed – he'll have no more pain or trouble.'

Perceval was delighted and thanked him warmly, and said: 'Worthy sir, please tell me your name.'

And the smith replied most civilly, saying: 'My name is Trebuchet,[31] sir, and anyone who seeks me will find I'm known in many lands. You, I'm sure, have heard of me, for the sword that hangs at your left side was forged and tempered by me.'[32]

'That may well be so,' said Perceval. 'I've carried it a very long way and it failed me at a moment of great need; but I know for sure it will be repaired by you and you alone.'

'Quite possibly,' said Trebuchet.

Then Perceval drew it from its scabbard and gave it to the smith. He beat and hammered it, and in no time at all it was mended. Having carefully repaired it he handed it back to Perceval at once and said:

'With a sword like this, sir, a man could do real damage! It wasn't made by a common tradesman! Take good care of it – a finer sword never fell into your hands, by God – and before nightfall tomorrow you'll be needing it, I think. But I want you to promise me this: that you won't draw it unless you truly need, for no king or emperor ever had a

---

[31] The name appears here as '*Tribüet*'. Trebuchet is the smith who repaired the sword and then died in Gerbert's Continuation (above, p. 346) – an indication that Manessier was probably writing his Continuation without knowledge of Gerbert's work.

[32] Perceval was told of Trebuchet by his cousin in Chrétien, above, p. 33.

better sword, and my father[33] never forged one so fine: he made three, one of which you broke at the gate of Paradise[34] and my father had to repair it; and he could never make another, for in completing that adventure he then had to die.[35] Be gone now, and may God guide you back to the right path.'

Perceval was overjoyed and thanked Trebuchet deeply; and taking the sword in his right hand he looked at it more admiringly than ever and could see no sign of any join. He grasped it by the hilt and slid it back in the scabbard. Then he stepped into the stirrup and mounted without further delay; he commended Trebuchet to God and thanked him once more for his service to him, and promised to repay the favour well if the chance arose.

Then he turned and rode away. He followed the damsel's lead; she delighted in his company. They made their way to Beaurepaire, and journeyed on till they finally arrived; and I don't remember ever seeing joy to compare with Blancheflor's as she welcomed her beloved Perceval: she kissed him more than thirty times before he could dismount! All her worries vanished in an instant: she could think of nothing but rejoicing at his coming! She bade a girl go to her clothes-chests and bring him a magnificent gown of rich red scarlet trimmed with ermine, and a tunic and mantle, the most elegant ever seen. As he dismounted in the courtyard and disarmed beneath two elms, two charming girls came and did all they could to serve him; they presented him with the gown and he received it with his customary grace and courtesy, and when he was dressed I swear there was no more handsome knight in the good King Arthur's court.

Blancheflor and Perceval sat on a bed – overjoyed, I'm sure, to be alone together – and spoke of all that had happened. Blancheflor told her beloved about the harm inflicted by Aridés, who was burning her land, stealing her cattle, oppressing her people.

'My love,' he replied, 'I've come to avenge you. Tomorrow I mean to make him pay dearly for the trouble and harm he's caused – and he no doubt plans to cause still more.'

They spoke together for a long while, until they went to supper. And after they'd eaten they sat at a window and carried on talking till it was time to retire. Then Blancheflor, who loved Perceval so dearly, escorted him to a gorgeous bed – none finer was ever made for the duke of Austria;[36] and as soon as she'd seen him into it she left the chamber and came to her own bed. She lay down at once and slept till day broke and the watch sounded the dawn.

Then the fair Blancheflor rose without any attendant girl or chambermaid, and as soon as she was dressed she went straight back to the chamber where Perceval lay. He hadn't been awake for long that night: he'd been tired and weary and slept the whole night through. I'm sure Blancheflor wasn't sorry to find him fast asleep – she'd wanted more than anything that he should be well rested. After a while he awoke, and was surprised to see her up so early.

'By Saint Martin,' he said, 'I've overslept! I should have been up by now and out there at your enemy's tent, giving him his wake-up call! I've been lying here too long!'

---

[33] This and the following references to his father, suddenly making this smith the original Trebuchet's son, appear in just one manuscript – Paris, BN ms fr 12576 – because that MS includes Gerbert's Continuation, and the scribe realised he needed to account for the fact that Gerbert had already described the death of Trebuchet and the repair of the sword.

[34] In Gerbert, above, p. 340.

[35] In Gerbert, above, p. 346.

[36] A notable figure; see above, p. 424 and note 54.

But Blancheflor, untroubled, said: 'No, you haven't, sir, so help me God! Don't worry!'

Perceval didn't dally; he rose at once and dressed in fine array, and called for his arms which were promptly brought. Then he armed and mounted, with shield round neck and lance in hand and Trebuchet's sword, still blood-stained, girded on.

While the fearless Perceval was being armed, Aridés arrived outside the gate with more than twenty knights, and in a ringing voice he cried aloud:

'Blancheflor, surrender the castle[37] before I do more damage! Your beloved Perceval's been dead and gone for a year and a half at least, so don't try holding out! Either yield the castle freely or send a knight to defend it against me, man to man! And if there are more – two or three or even four – I'll crush them all with my mighty strength!'

'I don't know how you'll fare, vassal,' Blancheflor called in reply, 'but you're about to see the one who'll save me, if God grants him the power.'

With that the gate was opened, and Perceval rode from the castle, lance raised and shield braced, on his galloping white steed. He didn't have to wait long for Aridés to dismiss his men, saying:

'Give us space and withdraw a little – but don't leave, any of you: you're about to see a splendid joust!' They did as he bade, and he called to Perceval: 'Tell me truly, vassal: what's your business?'

'All being well,' replied Perceval, 'I mean to do battle and crush your pride! I'm going to bring it crashing down in full view of the damsels in the castle!'

'What the devil!' cried Aridés. 'You really think you're up to it? By the Holy Spirit, you'd do better to return right now than come here threatening me! If you've any sense you'll turn straight back before you come unstuck!'

'I'll have your head first,' said Perceval.

At that Aridés, outraged, sent his horse charging forward; Perceval wasn't slow to respond, spurring the white destrier to meet him. They clashed, smashing their shields with awesome blows; both lances broke, and their horses nearly killed each other as they collided head to head. But neither knight shifted body from saddle or foot from stirrup, and the swift, strong horses galloped on. Both knights, undaunted, drew fine, well-tempered swords from sheaths and returned straight to the attack. They struck each other fearsomely, dealing wicked blows to helms and hauberks. What more is there to tell? They fought till Aridés could take no more, and was forced to proffer his sword and plead for mercy. He said he'd do anything asked of him except go to Beaurepaire, for he was sure he'd be shown no mercy there; so Perceval, compassionate as ever, offered an alternative: he told him he'd die, come what may, unless he placed himself completely at the mercy of Trebuchet.

'He's a smith of high renown.'

'I know exactly who you mean, by God,' said Aridés, 'but a smithy's hardly a noble prison!'

'I don't know where else,' said Perceval, 'to send you in this land – I'm not from these parts. But listen, then: you're to go instead to the court of the good King Arthur – I can think of nowhere else.'

'I'm on my way!' said Aridés. 'If you want to send me there I'll go at once, and I'll faithfully take King Arthur any message you wish to send: you've only to ask – I'm yours to command!'

'Then go to the court without delay,' said Perceval, 'and greet the king in the name

---

[37] Literally 'tower'.

of Perceval the Welshman as the finest king ever born of woman since God was crucified. And place yourself at his mercy on my behalf, armed just as you are now.'

Aridés gave his word and set off at once, asking for no respite. He didn't even look at his men; they were all downcast at his defeat, and slunk away to their own land.

Perceval rode back to Beaurepaire. Blancheflor, in glorious attire, came down from the tower and ran to meet him with fitting joy and fulsome thanks. He dismounted beneath the elms in the courtyard, and the fair and noble Blancheflor disarmed him with every care and attention. She unlaced his helm and had him clad in a mantle of scarlet,* peacock blue. Once he was disarmed she took him aside to relax. Alone together they sat beneath a spreading olive tree, and looked now trouble-free. The gracious Blancheflor was eager to speak first, and asked him:

'How are you, my love?'

'God bless me, very well!' he replied. 'I've set your castle free and sent Aridés captive to King Arthur!'

'By God and His power, you've done a fine deed!' said Blancheflor. 'But by the faith you owe me I've another favour to ask.'

'Tell me what it is – I'll never fail you.'

'If it please you, sir, I'd love you to stay here with me till Pentecost – it's not a lot to ask!'

'So help me God, my love,' he said, 'that's a favour I can't grant: by the faith I owe the heavenly king, at Pentecost I have to be at the court of the good King Arthur, and he'd think ill of me if I broke my promise. But wherever I may be, near or far, I'll be back the moment I hear you need me, my dear, sweet love.'

'Thank you, sir,' she said, 'but it troubles my heart that since you married me we've never known each other[38] – I don't say that lightly.'

'I'm sure you don't, by Holy Mary,' said Perceval.

'And I very much fear, sir, that you've no desire to stay.'

Dinner had been prepared inside, and the constables and servants were setting up the tables. As soon as all was ready, Blancheflor took Perceval by the hand and they went to the hall together. The water was presented to them and they washed and took their seats, and dined as long as they wished.

Then Perceval, eager to press on with his mission, sought no further delay: as soon as the order was given to clear the tables he called for his arms; the servant who'd taken charge of them promptly brought them and he swiftly armed and mounted the white destrier, the finest in the world. His faithful beloved Blancheflor was there as he mounted. If she'd had her way he wouldn't have left so soon: she would rather he'd stayed had it been possible – but it wasn't; and weeping, she commended him more than a hundred times to the heavenly king. Then he took his leave and rode out through the gate on the white charger, which carried him as smoothly and as comfortably as if he'd been aboard a ship. With a joyful heart he headed for a great, fair forest; and that fearless knight kept riding till he reached it.

---

[38] Literally 'I've not been touched by your body', implying consummation of their marriage. This reference to their marriage is inserted only in BN ms fr 12576 as the scribe seeks continuity with Gerbert's Continuation, in which Perceval and Blancheflor had already married but remained chaste (above, pp. 392–4). This is another indication (see note 31, above, p. 526) that Gerbert and Manessier probably wrote their continuations with no knowledge of each other's work.

Perceval's Prisoners Submit to Arthur

But we'll say no more for the moment about what befell him there; I want to tell of the prisoners who'd been sent to the court of King Arthur.

Each of them made his separate way, pressing on till he came to court. The first to arrive greeted the king on behalf of Perceval the Welshman, and said:

'My good lord king, whether it be to my honour or my shame, in that knight's name I duly submit as your prisoner.'

The king was thrilled, quite overjoyed to have news of Perceval; and he stood, unable to hide his delight, and took the knight in his arms in a warm embrace, saying:

'Is Perceval in good health and spirits? Tell me all!'

'I assure you, sire, he was perfectly well when I left him after our combat. And he told me that come what may, whatever the cost, he'd come to where you hold court at Pentecost – nothing would stop him, barring capture or death or sickness: otherwise you'll see him there for sure. That's what he told me to tell you, and I've no doubt it'll happen!'

The king was elated, of course, much comforted at the thought of seeing Perceval at court; and he released the knight from imprisonment and retained him as a member of his illustrious household, making him a companion of the splendid, august Table. His name was Menandre de la Loje, and in time he came to win high renown.

While they were merrily discussing Perceval in the hall, they saw the second captive riding up a valley. Kay was the first to spot him, and hurried to the king and said:

'Sire, a messenger knight's arriving at your court: be sure to respond as he deserves! I don't know what he wants – if you like I'll go and ask what brings him here.'

'I'd advise you, Kay,' the king replied, 'to say nothing rude or offensive! Try to restrain your mocking tongue – it won't do you any good!'

While the king was reproving Kay the knight had dismounted at the foot of the steps. He came up and hailed the finest king in the world on behalf of Perceval, saying:

'Noble, worthy, loyal king, most illustrious king of all, I have to surrender as your prisoner in the name of Perceval the Welshman.'

The moment the king heard this he jumped up and said: 'The one who sent you, friend, has committed you to fine captivity and care! Is he well? How is he?'

'Yes, sire,' he replied, 'he's well and happy indeed, by all the saints! He's the finest knight I've ever seen in my life, of the greatest prowess and valour. And he told me to tell you that wherever you hold court at Pentecost you'll see him, without fail. As long as God keeps him from harm he'll be there: only death or sickness or capture will stop him.'

The king, with his great magnanimity, pardoned the knight imprisonment forthwith, and granted him a place as a companion of the fine, illustrious Table. The knight was not in the least displeased to accept this mighty favour! The king asked him his name and how he'd come to be Perceval's prisoner.

'I'll tell you, sire, in all honesty. The other day I rode into a pavilion, the reddest of red silk it was, and found Perceval and a maiden sitting on a bed. She looked so gorgeous, and unsuspecting, and Perceval was unarmed! I was fired with love and seized the girl, put her on my horse and carried her off before his very eyes! But what's the point of dragging it out – it's the story of my downfall and disgrace! Perceval won her back from me, and made me swear upon my honour to submit here as your prisoner and behave towards you as a loyal knight.'

'As I hope to be absolved of my sins,' King Arthur said, 'he deserves our love indeed! And you deserve no discredit for being vanquished by such a valiant knight: by Saint Peter of Rome, I'll love you no less for that. But tell me your name now – I trust you've no objection.'

'None at all, sire; I'll gladly tell you. Gavïen is my name: I'm of the line of the renowned Galïen.'

'A fine name indeed,' said the king, 'and you strike me as a worthy and honourable knight.'

So both these knights became companions of the Table, and spent that night and the following day in uninterrupted joy.

And then, on the third day about terce, the king was sitting at the windows of his castle of Norhorbelande when he saw Aridés riding over the open ground towards him. He dismounted beneath a pine tree in the courtyard and came straight up to the hall where the king was seated. He hailed him, loud and clear, and said:

'Sire, Perceval the Welshman, who has robbed me of all joy and honour, sends me as his messenger with greetings to you. He is the most astute and valiant of all knights living – and it certainly does him no discredit to have Aridés of Escavalon submitting to imprisonment on his behalf! It shames me to do so, but I'm compelled to keep my word and wouldn't wish to break it – though it pains me, too, nearly drives me wild, for I'm a son and nephew of kings! But I've no cause to be distressed – or reproached – when his prowess and courage are so renowned.'

The moment the king heard the name Aridés he recognised the knight and was overjoyed; he leapt up and embraced him, and unlaced his helm himself and said:

'My friend, the one who sent you as a captive to me was doing you no disfavour! Out of love for both him and you, by the faith I owe the apostle Peter, I gladly release you from imprisonment forthwith.'

Aridés thanked him profusely, and then told him the day that Perceval would come to court, barring mishap.

And so it was that the prisoners came to the king and delivered Perceval's messages. All three fulfilled his commands exactly, and the king, so full of noble qualities, retained each of them in turn as a companion. He honoured Aridés highly, and rightly so, recognising who he was; he made him a companion of the Table and had his name inscribed on his seat – indeed, those who inscribed the seats did likewise for the other two. But here we'll leave the king and his three new companions who stayed with him as members of his household: it's the last we'll say of them for a while.

The Coward Knight

We'll tell you now of Perceval, who rode into the forest on his white horse. There he met a knight mounted on a strong, swift charger; disconsolate, despondent or mad, I'm not sure which he was, but he had his shield and helm and hauberk hung round his neck and trailing back over his horse's rump, and his lance was strapped along his horse's flank. Perceval was astonished to see him like this, and rode up and greeted him as he approached. The knight responded graciously, for he was a courteous knight indeed, and the most handsome that you'd find in thirty thousand – Perceval thought he'd never seen a finer-looking knight in face and body: his face was bright and glowing, his body strapping, amazingly strong; yet for all that, he was more timid than a hare! Perceval drew rein before him, and asked if he'd kindly explain why he was riding in such a way. He made no bones about it: he wanted to avoid combat, he said, not wanting to get hurt! He wasn't keen on fighting and being unhorsed!

'I'd rather go about my business in peace than get beaten and knocked about – what good would that do? What's the point of getting mortally wounded or bedbound? There's no fun in that! As long as I ride around like this, no knight will do worse than call me names! You won't, will you?'

'God help me, no!' said Perceval. 'I'm sure I won't! It would be wicked to attack you in this state! Anyone who did would be a heartless, rotten coward! But I'm amazed you're not ashamed to go around like this – I'm embarrassed and ashamed myself just to talk to you! It's unworthy of a knight to carry on so. I'd rather die an honourable death than behave so basely – you're a disgrace to all knighthood! Come, arm and dress properly and follow me, and don't be craven and afraid: no matter what the circumstance, right or wrong, no knight should fear to meet another, even if it means his instant death, for no one should wish to live in this world in such a shameful state!'

Perceval kept ragging and upbraiding him till he finally donned his arms and agreed to follow him.

'But don't be under any illusions,' said the knight. 'If you're attacked I won't be getting involved, by God! I'll sit and watch – I won't draw my sword or take anyone on! Combat's not my thing – I've no wish to fight anyone: I want to live an ordered, peaceful life and avoid all that madness! It's mad indeed to endanger yourself so pointlessly!'

So it was that this handsome knight assured Perceval of his cowardice. All the same, Perceval persuaded him, not without some difficulty, to arm properly and follow him. So away he led him, and they set off together down a well-beaten path through the forest.

But they hadn't gone far before they heard a cry away to the right; it sounded distinctly like a woman's, and Perceval headed that way at once, hoping to find an adventure where his companion could be tested! They rode to where they'd heard the cry with all the speed they could, and saw a fire of faggots and thorns burning beneath a tall, spreading tree. Before the fire were two girls, stripped to their shifts, their hands tightly bound; two rogues had hold of them and were about to throw them in the flames, while ten knights, superbly armed, were ranged about the fire ready to stop anyone intervening and saving the girls from death. The girls were in desperate need of help, screaming and imploring Holy Mary to save them; and when they saw Perceval approach they didn't hold back but cried aloud:

'In the name of the true cross, noble knights, have pity on two poor souls, or these cruel, treacherous men will put us to a dreadful death!'

'Well, my friend,' said Perceval, 'do you hear these girls, weeping and begging us to have pity?'

'I hear them all right,' the knight replied, 'but don't imagine I'm getting involved! There are ten of them and one of you! You'll pay dearly, I swear, for your crazy courage!'

Perceval couldn't help smiling at this, but he felt great pity for the girls, and without more ado he set his lance in its rest and charged towards them on his swift, strong charger, crying:

'You're all going to die, you wicked, faithless knights, for inflicting pain and suffering on these girls!'

'You'd do better to be off,' one knight cried back, 'or you'll die a foul death, by my life you will!'

And he charged to meet him; but Perceval reached him first and delivered a blow that sent him crashing, dead: the body stretched out, the soul departed. Perceval pulled out his lance at once and said:

'I don't think this one's a worry any more!'

He didn't dally but drew back ready to launch a second charge, and went to meet another who was riding to the attack; it turned out well: he thrust the bright lance-head and two feet of shaft through his body to send him crashing dead, in agony, though his lance now broke and shattered.

While he was fighting and toppling the knight, his companion was watching, horrified: he didn't like this business at all! He was underneath an oak tree, cowering in his saddle. But one of the knights was galloping towards him, lance at the ready, shouting that he'd hit him if he didn't watch out! But he just sat beneath the oak, not moving a muscle, never imagining he'd be challenged when he hadn't interfered! He called to the charging knight:

'Don't go hitting me, sir! I mean you no harm! If my companion's bothering you it's not my fault! If he'd listened to my advice, by God, he'd have left you well alone!'

But the knight took no notice of a word he said: he charged straight up and struck his shield a mighty blow, piercing and splitting it and smashing his lance to splinters; but the coward didn't shift from saddle or stirrups. The knight who'd broken his lance turned straight about and drew his sword and attacked him anew, dealing a tremendous blow to his shield and smashing a chunk clean off. Seeing his shield being wrecked the coward knight protested, saying:

'Why are you taking it out on me? I've done you no wrong! You've broken my shield and hit me twice! But I'm not such a fool as to want to fight you!'

'You're wasting your breath, by God!' the knight replied, and came straight back and struck him such a blow on his jewelled helm that he cut through the hoop[39] and the mail hood beneath, inflicting such a wound to the head that blood came streaming down. The coward knight saw the blood flowing to his waist and was so upset, so outraged, that his heart was close to bursting. Brimming with fury, he told the knight:

'That was very wrong of you, by God, hitting me when I'd done nothing to offend! I'll make you pay, by God I will! You'll be sorry you ever touched me – you picked on the wrong man!'

And he drew his sword and attacked the knight, landing a surprisingly massive blow full on his helm of steel; it clove him to the shoulders and sent him crashing to the ground, stone dead. Then he sheathed his sword again and sat crouched in his saddle as he'd been before. But another knight came thundering at him, yelling that he'd had it! He should take cover or he'd strike! The coward knight was annoyed to see him coming and called back loud and clear:

'By almighty God, vassal, if you hit me I'll hit you back!'

'Let's see what you're made of!' the knight replied. 'Defend yourself or die like a coward!'

'I'll defend myself, I promise you,' he said, 'right now!'

And he grabbed his lance and drew back, ready to charge, and they came at each other full tilt, bent on delivering massive blows. The knight who'd come from guarding the fire struck him so mightily on the shield that the shaft of his lance bowed and snapped and flew into shards; the coward struck him back on his shield of blue, emblazoned

---

[39] The helmet's reinforcing band.

with a lion, with such colossal force that he thrust lance-head, shaft and pennon through his chest and drove him dead to the ground. He'd emptied his saddle, but smashed his lance to pieces; and seeing his lance was broken he drew his sword at once and said that – whether it was a mistake or not! – he'd go and help his companion: he'd be a coward and spectator no more! He charged into the fray and unhorsed the first he met, leaving him laid out dead on the ground, and carried straight on to attack the rest. What can I tell you? He and Perceval killed the lot and rescued the girls from their thuggish captors who ran off into the wood.

They helped the girls dress and then set off through the great forest, carrying the girls on their horses' shoulders. But the two rogues who'd fled were hiding at the edge of a valley at a fork in the path; there they lay in ambush, and one of them had a Turkish bow and was a very good shot. He nocked an arrow – poisoned, I believe – and as Perceval drew near he loosed it. It struck Perceval in the thigh and almost knocked him from his horse: the arrow plunged in right up to the feathers; the shaft broke, the head lodged fast. Seeing this the coward knight set the girl down, drew his sword and rode to the attack and killed them both in moments. Then he turned back and, to his grave distress, saw that Perceval was in trouble. He asked the girls if they knew of a house anywhere near, and they said they had a castle at the edge of the woods where they'd be given good lodging and Perceval's wound could be tended.

'We're almost there – if we called loud enough they'd hear us clearly.'

So he picked up the girl again and sat her before his saddle-bow across his horse's shoulders, and they set off along the path they showed them, very upset and concerned about Perceval's wound.

They pressed on till they reached the castle. Beneath a pine they set down the girls they'd rescued from the fire and then dismounted. A moment later four servants came hurrying down the steps and helped them disarm; and they served and welcomed them warmly for their damsels' sake when they heard how they'd have been sure to die had they not been rescued by the knights.

They took Perceval to lie in a ground-floor room and called a doctor to him; the doctor came at once and examined his wound, and immediately said he'd need to make a cut if he was to get the arrow-head from his leg. He bound the thigh with a strip of fine white cloth, and after making the incision and drawing out the head he applied ointment and dressings, taking every care. Once his leg was dressed and bandaged they laid him in a splendid bed; and the other knight, distressed for him, lay down close by and never left his side. And there Perceval stayed for a full two months, in considerable pain the whole time he lay sick.

The Vow to Search for Perceval

Now I should tell you about Sagremor the Rash, who was cared for at the castle[40] as perfectly as if he'd been a king's son.

He'd recovered and was fully healed of the grave wounds he'd received, and on the Thursday before Pentecost, heedless of any objection, he took courteous leave of the people there and mounted and left the castle, and headed for where he thought the king would be holding court, expecting Perceval the Welshman to arrive there on the feast day. But it would be months before he did: he was sick, in such a bad way he couldn't even stand.

---

[40] Where he'd been left wounded by Tallidés, above, p. 495.

Sagremor pressed on towards the court, mounted on his swift horse Morin; and on the eve of the feast he dismounted at Camelot, on a marble block beneath a tree. The king came to meet him with more than twenty knights, and they welcomed him with joy and honour befitting a knight of his worth. Then they asked him how he was and how he'd fared, and he gave them a clear and ordered account of all he'd encountered on his quest; and he told them about Perceval, saying:

'My lord, unless he breaks his word he'll be coming to your court tomorrow, for so he promised me!'

The king said he couldn't wait! He thought the time would never come when he'd hold him by the hand again – tomorrow couldn't come too soon!

They spent a happy and enjoyable night, and in the morning, at the crack of dawn, the king rose and went to lean at the windows above the hall, looking out towards the forest, longing for the arrival of his cherished Perceval and very afraid that some obstacle would prevent him coming to the feast. He stayed there as the sun rose and blazed and lit the day. He stayed there still, till he saw Dodinel the Wild galloping to court on a swift destrier; the moment he spotted him he called Sagremor and Kay and told them about the approaching knight and urged them to say if it was Perceval.

'No, sire, it's Dodinel,' said Kay, who recognised him clearly.

The king hurried straight down to meet him. Dodinel dismounted, sweating from his rapid ride, and hailed the king on behalf of Perceval. At the mention of his name the king asked when he'd last seen him.

'So help me God, my lord,' said Dodinel, 'a month ago exactly. And he told me he'd be at court without fail this very day, unless prevented by some misfortune – death or imprisonment or illness.'

'God help me, I don't know what to say!' the king replied. 'Have you news of our other knights since they went to search the land for him?'

'Yes, sire, I've seen Gawain and Agravain and Yvain and Gaherïet, and the Fair Brave Knight[41] and Mordred and Boort, and all of them asked me to tell you they'll be here at court to see you today without fail.'

'Excellent!' said the king, greatly cheered. Then back he went to the windows to look out to the forest; and in no time at all he saw, bearing handsome arms of gold, Agravain and Boort de Gaunes riding towards the castle. They both dismounted in the courtyard, and the king hurried down to meet them and welcomed them, of course, with joyous embraces. And while they were disarming they saw Gawain and Lancelot come riding through the gate together, and with them, I believe, some twenty more: I don't know how they'd all come to meet. They clattered up together and dismounted before the king beneath a pine; he greeted them with great decorum and all possible honour. Then he pressed them all for news of Perceval: if they'd seen him they must tell him what they knew! But they said they'd seen no sign of him and heard no word. But I shan't go on about all the words that passed.

The king now went to church to hear the service, and pleased his companions by taking them with him. When the service was done they returned together to the principal hall. By now it was well into the afternoon, and Kay said to the king:

'You may dine, sire, whenever you wish: it's high time, that's for sure!'

---

[41] Strictly speaking, Dodinel doesn't yet know about 'the Fair Brave Knight', the name which is to be given to the Coward Knight only later. This may suggest that the story of the Coward Knight was so familiar that Manessier knew his audience would recognise and understand the new name.

'My friend,' the king replied, 'tell the constables to set the tables.'

'It's already done, my lord,' Kay said, 'and the cloths are laid, and the knives and salt-bowls, and a great spread of dishes: the cooks haven't been sparing! Come, sire, and wash, and bid your barons be seated.'

'Come, sirs, come,' said the king. 'Wash and take your places.'

Then up and down the packed hall you'd have seen the barons and knights all wash and take their appropriate seats, with the good King Arthur at the head, at the highest table. Those keen to eat could do so handsomely: they were served with a feast befitting their station – half a dozen dishes or a score, I don't know, and an array of fine, delicious wines.

When they'd finished they went to relax and amuse themselves. But by the time the king rose from the table the sun was going down, and he was very upset and troubled that Perceval hadn't come: his absence surely meant he was a captive or had suffered some misfortune, and King Arthur's spirits sank. The companions were talking about it, too, and all said they feared that, since he hadn't come to court, Perceval must be sick or imprisoned. After much discussion they all vowed to leave next day and scour the land for him: so thoroughly would they search that they wouldn't return to court till a year from that day. There and then they all made their oaths: the first to swear was Lancelot of the Lake, then Gawain and Boort and Sir Yvain and Sagremor and the handsome, valiant Dodinel; and after them Gaheriet and Guerrehés made their vows. Twenty-five in all there were who took the oath, so the story says. What more should I tell you? They left Camelot next morning, and outside the town, where the road divided into four, the companions went their separate ways, each riding on as chance took him.

Boort Abandons his Brother

Boort journeyed on alone, downcast and worried at being unable to find his brother Lionel. Nothing bothered him more: it was at least two years since he'd seen him. Day by day he rode on, fretting, till one day, towards the middle of August, he was riding through a forest, still worrying about his missing brother, when he looked to his right and saw six well-armed knights, with shields round necks and helms on heads, who had Lionel stripped to his shirt and were dragging him along in a wretched state – and at great speed – and lashing him with whips so hard that blood was pouring down his back: Boort could see it streaming to his waist. He was aghast and furious; he swore it was an outrage. He brandished his lance, the gold-embroidered pennon fluttering in the wind – and then suddenly heard the anguished scream of a maiden, crying:

'Dear lord God, help me! Holy Mary, lady, save my honour!'

Boort turned in alarm to see a girl trapped beneath a huge knight, forbidding, fierce – he feared no one in combat; he'd pulled up her dress and spread her legs wide. He had ten knights with him, all ready to defend him if anyone tried to interfere, armed and mounted on their chargers, self-assured and fearless. The knight intent on raping the girl was pinning her down by force and about to have his way with her, and her screams were so loud, so desperate, that no man who heard her could have failed to feel pity. Boort, seeing her dreadful plight, hesitated to go and help his brother; he said:

'Dear lord God, have mercy! Guide me! What shall I do about this girl? I can see my brother in straits so dire I don't know what to do: those cruel knights who're dragging him off may kill him unless he's rescued; but the girl in the grip of that vicious knight is begging for help so piteously I'm ashamed not to intervene!' He dallied no longer:

he gripped and levelled his lance and said: 'Dear lord God, protect my brother by your grace – don't let those base, low villains kill him – for I can't forsake this lovely girl who's being so foully treated. I'll save her now or die, I swear!' And he charged to the rescue, crying at the top of his voice: 'Leave that girl, knight, or you're a dead man, by God!'

One of the knights sprang forward to block him, and Boort met him with a thrust so fierce that the pennon on his lance burst out of his back. The lance broke and shattered and the knight left his saddle. Boort drew his sword and struck another of the knights, splitting his helm and cleaving his head to the shoulders to send him crashing to the ground, stone dead. Then he turned to attack the others. What more shall I say? He killed the lot! Not a single one escaped! Having battered and slain them all, he came to the maiden and said:

'If you wish, dear girl, I'll escort you from the forest to safety.'

She, still shaken, terrified, replied: 'Most gladly, sir! While there's no one else to threaten us I beg you get me out of here! On a clifftop, less than a league ahead, there's a strong tower defended by walls and palisades: we'd be safe there – we wouldn't need to fear a living soul!'

The wise and worthy Boort, praised and esteemed by everyone, took the maiden in his arms and gently, gallantly sat her on his horse's shoulders and carried her straight to the tower, not stopping till they reached the gate. Then he set her down and commended her to God. But before he left he asked the people there to tell him if they'd seen a knight being hauled along, stripped and flogged, and they said the knights had passed that very way. They showed him where they'd gone, and Boort set off in swift pursuit, berating himself, saying:

'Dear God have mercy! I'd found the brother I longed to see – it was two years since I'd seen him and there he was! I deserve reproach if I've lost him – oh, misery! I fear those men who were flogging him with all their might will kill him!'

Boort rode on all day till nightfall, but found no sign of his brother. He lay that night in the forest without anything to eat or drink – not that he felt like eating – and set off again, still all alone, next morning at first light. He prayed earnestly to God for guidance, and that he might find Lionel his brother fit and well: that was all he asked.

He emerged from the woods into a beautiful stretch of open ground, and pressed his swift horse onward till he found himself on a cobbled road; and there – sitting in the middle of the road – he saw a most fair and comely girl. He carried on and rode up to her, to find she was holding in her lap the headless body of a knight. He drew rein before her and said:

'Dear girl, please tell me, if you can bring yourself to say: who killed this knight?'

Pale and in floods of tears, she answered: 'Six wicked, cruel, villainous knights who're dragging a knight along and flogging him, laughing as they go! It was they who killed my beloved sweetheart: he felt pity for the knight and tried to save him.'

'Which way have they gone?' said Bohort. 'Tell me, my dear.'

'By God the king of heaven, sir, they took that path to the right, the traitors!'

'God grant that I live to see this day's end,' said Boort. 'If I can catch them I'll make them pay!'

'May He give you the strength, sir!' said the girl. 'How glad I'd be!'

And Boort set off the way she'd pointed. But the path forked – and he chose the wrong way and lost his quarry. He carried on all day till evening, when he stopped and took shelter in a forest, tethering his horse to a briar. There he stayed till morning.

But at the crack of dawn he was up again and mounted and took to the road once more, so distraught that he'd rather have been dead than alive. For a whole fortnight he kept riding, this way and that way, scouring the land in grave anxiety.

But here we'll leave Boort and tell you about Gawain, who could never be accused of being faint-hearted; he was out in search of Perceval and the chance of winning honour and praise.

One morning he was riding across a new-mown meadow when who should chance to come passing by but the knights abusing Lionel. The moment he saw what was happening Gawain braced himself on his strong, swift charger and rightly cried:

'Ah, you wicked, cowardly traitors! You'll pay for this, so help me God! Your time has come!'

And he brandished his lance and sent his horse charging at the knights; he struck the first with such power that he smashed clean through his shield and sliced his heart in two – his hauberk was not of the slightest use – to leave him splayed out dead in the middle of the path. Without more ado he drew his good, keen sword and launched into a bitter, fearsome battle with the rest. The first he met he sent crashing to the ground, and the others promptly fled down a valley. He chased them to the edge of a wood, and dealt one of them such an awesome blow that it took off his head; the other three didn't hang around – they vanished into the forest, each his separate way.

Gawain rode back to where he'd left Lionel; he mounted him on a strong, swift horse and led him away, elated at being rescued. They rode to a nearby house that Gawain knew; they were given a joyous welcome there, for the people of the house loved Gawain dearly. But they were distressed to see his companion in such a state; they prepared a soft bed worthy of such a knight to make sure he could rest in comfort, and entrusted him to the care of a doctor who tended him well, dressing his wounds twice a day. He cared for him most diligently for a fortnight, seeing him bathed and nursed so well that he made a full recovery and felt quite free of pain.

At the fortnight's end Gawain had him finely clothed and equipped with a splendid set of arms. Then their horses were saddled and those worthy knights mounted and took their leave. They set out together and rode on till they came to a fork in the road. As they drew near Lionel invited Gawain to have first choice of which path he'd take, for they really ought to part, and Gawain said he'd head to the right. Then they embraced and exchanged kisses and went their separate ways, warmly commending each other to God. Gawain took the right-hand path and Lionel the left.

And Lionel's heart was seething: he couldn't forget Boort's failure to come to his aid, and the memory was so bitter it was nearly killing him. Never, he thought, would he be happy while he knew that Boort lived – if he ever found him he'd kill him himself, without a doubt! He couldn't purge the rancour rooted firmly in his heart.

He rode on and relentlessly on till well past terce, indifferent to everything. It was terribly hot; the heat was so oppressive that he took off his helm and opened his ventail to get some air, and like this he rode on, all alone.

Boort's Combat with Lionel

Boort meanwhile, downcast and anxious, had been riding non-stop for a fortnight, all over the land. Beside a hut at a forest's edge he met a grey-clad monk; and when he saw Boort he came up to ask who he was and what he sought.

'My one and only goal is my brother,' he said. 'I don't know what's become of him. The other day six armed knights were abducting him and flogging him, stripped naked – and it's much to my shame that I saw it happen and left him to be dragged away, and I've no idea where to: I don't know if he's alive or dead!'

This figure disguised as a worthy monk was one who robbed men of their reason; and he answered saying: 'I know nothing about that, sir, but I can tell you this: beneath that spreading tree lies one of the finest knights in the world – he's been there for three days or more. I don't know who killed him, but he's swelled up like a barrel. His name is Lionel – he's the brother of Boort de Gaunes. You can go and see him there right now, all jaundiced, wan, discoloured.'

Boort headed there that instant, and found – or so it seemed to him when he saw the body, limbs and face – his brother lying dead! Despair and grief together seized him, gripping his heart and crushing all hope and reason. He collapsed over the body, his senses lost, and lay a long while unconscious. When he finally came to he kissed the lips and face; more than a hundred times he touched the eyes, the hands, the chin, the cheeks: his grief couldn't have been more plain. After smothering him with kisses and embraces a hundred times and more, he sat down at the body's side, in such torment, so distraught, that he almost burst ablaze with anguish. He leapt up and in his distracted state took the body in his arms and embraced it so tightly that he passed out with the strain: he couldn't stay upright and collapsed to the ground. Ten times – or even twenty, I don't know – he fainted in utter distress. When at last he stood again he began his lament, saying:

'My friend, your killers have won no credit, slaying a man as fine as you! Dear brother, you feared no one. Your line is so diminished by your loss! Lancelot's heart will fill with grief when he hears of your death; it's a shameful affront to your whole lineage, by God! Wise, kind, courteous brother, worthy to be a king yourself, may you be blessed by the hand of the king of Heaven – and may your killers be damned and cursed!'

So saying, he raised his own right hand, inspired by God to make the sign of the cross above the corpse; and the devil, the demon who lay there, aiming with his wiles to trick and lead Boort astray, couldn't endure or face the sign: it sprang to its feet that instant, creating such a howling storm in its torment and terror of the cross that the woods on every side were ripped apart. But at this shattering sight and sound Boort felt nothing but comfort – he realised it had been a demon in disguise, bent on deceiving him. Greatly cheered and much relieved, he bowed to God and implored him to keep him from harm and shame. Then he returned to his horse and mounted and commended himself to God, praying and entreating Him to grant that he might find his brother well in mind and body, and his honour safe.

It was in this state of mind that he set out,[42] reflecting on what he'd seen. It was past terce when he emerged into a glade – and met his brother Lionel! He knew him as soon as he saw him, for he'd bared his head because of the heat. From a distance he called at the top of his voice:

'Well met, brother!'

To show his delight, in joyous greeting, he took off his helm and held out his arms;

---

[42] All MSS but one add 'one day', implying a passage of time; but this seems anti-dramatic, and is surely unintended after the deliberate, echoing references to a fortnight having passed for both Lionel and Boort.

but Lionel, intent on making him pay if he could, cried:

'I'm not your brother! You and I have no connection! By God, you'll be sorry you met me here, you wicked, faithless traitor!'

'What? Dear brother Lionel, what are you saying? By the Holy Spirit, I've never betrayed you or done you any wrong!'

'No wrong? Indeed you have!' cried Lionel. 'You saw me being dragged away and flogged and didn't have the courage to come to my aid!'

'Ah, dear brother! I went to save a fair and comely girl! A knight had her pinned to the ground beneath him and was about to take her by force!'

'Ah, faithless man!' cried Lionel. 'You preferred to rescue her than me! They were hauling me off to hang me – it was obvious! You made the wrong choice, truly – you're going to die right here and now: your time is up, I swear! Put on your helm – I defy you!'

Boort, beset by guilt at having failed his brother, pleaded with him, hands clasped, for mercy in God's name, to forgive him his wrath and resentment.

'I'll rather break your neck, by God!' said Lionel; and so saying, he laced his helm, fastened his ventail and drew his keen sword from its scabbard, and told Boort he'd kill him on the spot unless he quickly donned his helm. Seeing his brother so fired with rage, Boort didn't know what to do; but he laced his helm – and then dismounted and knelt before him, his face wet with tears, and with hands clasped in prayer once more he begged him in the name of God the son of Holy Mary to pardon him his fury. But Lionel sent his horse crashing into Boort's chest to lay him flat out on the ground; then he jumped down before him and pulled off his helm, and was on the very point of severing his head when Calogrenant rode up. He was dumbstruck, appalled to see Lionel astride the grounded Boort, and cried with all his might:

'Lionel! What's this? What are you doing? Noble, wise, valiant knight, do you mean to kill your own blood? It's Boort, your brother!'

'God grant I see the new day dawn,' he said, 'he's going to die! No one's going to save him!'

Boort was unaware of all of this: he was sprawled unconscious at his brother's feet. Lionel, who'd lost all sense and reason, opened his ventail. Calogrenant begged him desperately to have mercy on his brother, but he swore by heaven and earth, by God's whole creation, that Calogrenant should never have interfered and wasn't going to stop him.

'Well I promise you,' said Calogrenant, 'he won't suffer till I've tried!'

'Then you'll die, by God!' cried Lionel. 'You'll not save him!'

And he left Boort, who was just coming round, and attacked Calogrenant, dealing him an awesome blow on his polished helm; the blade flashed down and struck his shield, hacking off a huge chunk. Calogrenant was none too pleased to see it clatter to the ground; he stormed to the attack, swearing that since they'd come to blows he'd be unsparing: let Lionel do his worst! He landed a blow on Lionel's helm, cutting through the hoop and into the ventail, driving rings of mail into his flesh. Lionel was enraged that he'd wounded him, and responded with a blow of mighty force, smashing fifteen or twenty mail-rings from his hauberk, a blow so fearsome, dealt by a knight of such great prowess, that it brought Calogrenant to his knees. But Calogrenant wasn't short of courage: he was back on his feet in an instant, and without a word of challenge he struck Lionel on his helm of steel and sent gilded trimmings flying. The blade flashed down to his left thigh and sheared through the hauberk, cutting away a gobbet of flesh enough to feed a falcon. Blood poured down his chausses; Lionel was speechless with fury when he saw the blood flow; he flung himself at Calogrenant and delivered a blow with his sword of steel upon his shining helm, sundering the laces to send it crashing to the ground. Calogrenant, aghast to feel his head laid bare, said:

'Boort, if I must die for you I've no regrets: I couldn't lose my life for a finer knight.'

And as he said this, Lionel attacked him with a blow so fierce that it clove his head to the teeth and struck him dead. Boort had recovered consciousness and said:

'Brother, you've done a dreadful wrong! You've killed the good and worthy Calogrenant!'

'Ah, Boort! That's the least of it!' cried Lionel. 'I swear by Saint Peter I'm going to do the same to you!'

Boort, desperate not to fight him if he could help it, said: 'Dear brother, do the right thing now and have mercy on me.'

'You can plead all you like,' he replied. 'You'll not have mercy, by my life.'

'I've asked for mercy,' Boort said, 'but since it's refused, then – madness though it is – I'll defend myself against you.'

And he strode to his horse, standing quietly nearby, and mounted and relaced his helm and readied himself for combat. Then he turned his eyes to heaven and said:

'Dear Father, heavenly King, who deigned to be born on earth of the sweet virgin who was your mother and your servant,[43] forgive me, Lord, if I defend myself against my brother: it's not my wish.'

And thereupon, that very instant, a cloud descended in between them, so that neither could see the other; and with the cloud came a voice from heaven; to Boort it came and said:

'Beware! Do not touch your brother: you would kill him with your very first blow; be gone from him!'

The voice vanished without another word, and the cloud lifted so that they could see one another again. Boort should have been relieved – but not when he saw Lionel lying on the ground as if dead. He ran to him in dismay and called to him most tenderly, his voice filled with fear, saying:

'My good, dear brother, speak! What's wrong with you?'

Lionel hauled himself to his feet as he recovered from a swoon, and berated himself for what he'd done, crying: 'Dear Lord God, have mercy! I'm well enough, but I yield to you and beg forgiveness!'

'Dear brother,' said Boort, 'I bear you no ill will – there's no man in the world I love so much!'

And he soaked Lionel's cheeks and chin with his tears; they both took off their shining helms and kissed each other joyfully. And so they were reconciled, at peace once more.

But then began their lament for Calogrenant, lying there dead before their eyes; they were nearly crazed with grief: how they wailed and wept for him, mourning his goodness, his wisdom and his valour.

'I slew you while I'd lost my mind,' said Lionel. 'Calogrenant, noble, worthy, loyal knight, I've done a dreadful deed! I'd rather have been a prisoner for seven whole years, so help me God, than have killed you thus so sinfully, my good, dear friend! I robbed you of your life in a wicked fit of malice.'

---

[43]   Luke 1, v. 38: 'And Mary said [to Gabriel]: "Behold the handmaid of the Lord…"'

Such was Lionel's lament for the dead Calogrenant; and Boort likewise was so distraught he would gladly have died himself. But they had to stop their grieving: it couldn't bring him back.

There was a hermitage nearby where a wise man lived an ascetic life; and this holy hermit, following the will of God, was out foraging for food as he always did when he crossed the glade where the brothers were mourning their killing of Calogrenant. He watched them for a moment, and then came and asked who'd slain the knight they were lamenting so bitterly.

'Good sir,' said Boort, 'we did; we killed him this very day by terrible misfortune.' And he told him how it had chanced to come about.

'Indeed,' said the white-haired worthy, 'believe me when I tell you this was the work of the Enemy, the Devil. He'd possessed your brother, my good, dear friend, because he wanted to have you killed. Come now: let's see about burying the body.'

'May the Saviour reward you, kind sir,' said Lionel. 'I take it you're a priest and live nearby?'

'True enough: a priest I am indeed. I've made my dwelling in a little hut here in the forest; I've lived as a hermit for forty years. I'll go back with you now and sing the office for the dead; then we'll see to his burial.'

'We'll go with you, sir,' said Boort, 'and lay the body in the ground. So come: mount and ride this horse, I pray you.'

'I've no desire to mount a horse, sir, ever in my life,' the hermit said. 'No desire at all.'

Lionel, weeping, took Calogrenant in his arms and laid him across his horse, and carried him to the chapel, which was as lovely as you could wish. The hermit sang the office of the dead, and then laid the body to rest before the altar, with all the dignity he could. They laid a tombstone over him in which the hermit chiselled the following inscription:

> Beneath this stone lies Calogrenant, cruelly slain by Lionel;
> it was a most disloyal deed.

Having buried the body with all decorum, the two brothers turned to the worthy, holy hermit and took their leave, and rode away on their splendid chargers; but I've never heard anyone tell of sorrow as deep as theirs.

They rode on together till they came to a fork in the path; then Boort, sighing, said to Lionel: 'Take which path you like, dear brother: I need to go on alone. I don't know when I'll see you again, but come what may at Pentecost I'll be wherever the king holds court.'

He kissed him hurriedly, and with that they parted, one heading this way, the other that, saying no more than to commend each other to God.

The Fair Bold Knight

We'll leave them now and tell of Perceval, who lay sick at the castle for a long while, as you've heard. But once he was healed and recovered he took his leave of the ladies of the house, and rode from the castle with the knight[44] who'd never left his side all the time he was ill: he'd stayed with him day and night, I understand.

All day long they rode together till evening; and then, as darkness began to fall, they

---

[44] i.e. the former 'Coward Knight'.

rode across a stretch of meadowland and came to a most imposing castle: splendidly handsome it was indeed, in a fine position beside a river. And then they saw that before it was spread a great encampment.

'My friend,' said Perceval, 'I suggest we lodge tonight out here: unless I'm much mistaken there's a tournament gathering! If we go to the castle we may be recognised sooner than we need.'

The knight replied that he'd gladly do whatever he said. So they headed off into a forest, where they heard a bell tolling and took it to be coming from an abbey. On their fleet-footed steeds they followed the sound of the bell and carried straight on till they reached the gate. They entered and asked for lodging, and were given the finest hospitality.

In the morning, as soon as they saw day break, they made ready and went to the chapel and heard mass. Then they mounted and rode steadily through one vale and another to the castle.

Knights were already thundering forth: the two sides together numbered more than three thousand; lances were lowered and the tournament began.

In the first company to leave the castle were two of King Arthur's nephews: Gaheriët, wise and valiant, and Mordred; and with them were Lionel, mounted on a strong, swift charger, and King Baudemagus, courageous and wily and fired with great prowess. Baudemagus had challenged to the tournament the proud and redoubtable King of One Hundred Knights; they were both superbly armed and backed by valiant men, but good King Baudemagus had even better than the King of One Hundred Knights. Into the tourney they rode with their companies, and it was a mighty clash indeed. In the very first charge many knights met and many fell and many tumbled, many a riderless horse ran loose, many a shield was pierced and broken, many a fine hauberk sundered, for the knights of the Round Table, masters of every contest, were performing wonders, bloodying many a head: no one could withstand them. Perceval watched their fine display with the utmost admiration, and said to his companion:

'By God, my friend, this side's going to be overwhelmed unless we help them out! Let's give them our support!'

'Gladly, sir!' he replied, not wanting to refuse.

So Perceval and his companion charged into the fray to assail Baudemagus's strong and valiant knights. Perceval arrived full tilt, shield braced, lance levelled, steering his charging horse at Gaheriët, who came to meet him, knight of might and prowess that he was. Of all King Arthur's lineage there was none so brave, save Gawain; and with his dauntless heart, when he saw Perceval coming he spurred towards him and they met at a gallop, smashing their shields. Gaheriët broke the lance he'd taken from a squire, and Perceval landed a blow so fierce on his azure shield that he sent him tumbling over his horse's rump, and galloped on past leaving him flat on the ground. Then he lowered his lance once more and charged to meet another of Baudemagus's knights; he thrust the steel head, strong and sharp, clean through his shield and drove him from his saddle. But the shaft broke, so he drew his sword at once – and dealt many a cut and blow that day and toppled many knights: bright-helmed knights were left strewn in his wake, covering the field.

Meanwhile his companion charged to challenge Mordred, and delivered such a blow to his shield that he sent him sprawling; but on he galloped, not interested in taking him captive, intent only on winning more glory: he left Mordred lying on the ground, attacking him no further, not giving him another glance. He met another knight and sent him and his horse together crashing to the ground; before he finished his charge or broke his lance he'd unhorsed four. He enjoyed himself no end that day! He was thrilled by the fine blows he delivered in the tourney: he'd never dealt so many in his life! He was determined now to perform so well that no one could ever again level shameful accusations: he renounced cowardice completely. As soon as his lance broke he drew his sword and struck out to right and left.

'In faith,' said Lionel, 'it seems we've met a master!' Lionel had a strong, swift horse and a fine, sharp lance, and seeing this knight charging through the fray he cried to him to turn and face him straight away: he wanted to fight! He galloped full tilt towards him. The knight, unhesitating, came straight to meet him, spurring hard; he raced by way of a squire who was holding a good, undamaged lance and snatched it from his hand, and then charged at Lionel, lance levelled. They exchanged tremendous blows on their shields, smashing through the nailed leather, splintering their lances, and both knights lost their saddles as they brought each other down. But undaunted, like the brave and valiant knights they were, they leapt to their feet, recovered their steeds and mounted instantly, neither hurt nor wounded. They advanced with drawn swords, and would have done each other serious damage had the mêlée not engulfed them and driven them apart.

Meanwhile Gaheriët and his brother Mordred had quickly remounted, seized and levelled lances and prepared to take revenge: Gaheriët headed for Perceval, and Mordred for the handsome knight.[45] Both had found a new lance with a pennon of embroidered silk, and without any exchange of challenges they charged and delivered great blows to their shields with their steel lance-heads. Varnish and paint weren't proof at all! The heads drove clean through all four shields and hauberks, too, and into flesh; Perceval sent Gaheriët crashing and his companion toppled Mordred: both of them ended on the ground. Lionel and Baudemagus were dismayed to see them felled, and with keen-headed lances they left the fray without a word to their men; Baudemagus charged full tilt and hit Perceval, and Perceval, never one to shirk, struck too; so fearsome were their blows that they pierced and shattered their shields and smashed the backs of their saddles – but only Baudemagus fell: Perceval kept his seat and stirrups. Lionel for his part lowered his lance and went charging at the handsome knight, who fearlessly charged to meet him; they exchanged awesome blows right on the bosses of their shields – and pierced them, the lance-heads thrusting through to their flesh; Lionel's lance then shattered, but the handsome knight's didn't even bend, and he met his opponent with such force that he laid him flat out on the ground. But then he seized his strong, swift destrier and, courteous, well-bred knight that he was, presented it to Lionel, saying:

'Mount, good sir: I count you one of the finest knights I've ever seen in my life.'

So Lionel mounted – hungry for revenge! He might perhaps have incurred more shame if they'd jousted yet again, but darkness brought an end to the tournament. Downcast, outfought, beaten, Baudemagus and his men headed back to the castle, pursued and battered all the way to the gate.

Perceval, who carried off the prize, set off with his companion and rode straight back to the abbey, where they lodged that night in highest spirits.

Next morning, with lances in rest, they set out alone, without company or escort, and rode on till they came to a cross at a fork in the road. There they stopped, and without more ado Perceval said to his companion:

---

[45] The former coward, whose handsome face and figure were described when he first appeared above, p. 531: he was 'the most handsome that you'd find in thirty thousand – Perceval thought he'd never seen a finer-looking knight in face and body'.

'We've been together for some while now, and it's bad of me never to have asked your name. The noble man who knighted me taught me to share no one's company for long without finding out his name,[46] so I'd like to know yours.'

'By Saint Peter the apostle,' he replied, 'I shan't hide it: I'm known as the Fair Coward[47] – I was given the name on the day I was born!'

'So help me God,' said Perceval, 'that name doesn't suit you, truly! From now on you'll be called the Fair Bold Knight,[48] for you're handsome, wise and brave, a knight of worth and honour. I witnessed that at the tournament: I found you to be a fine knight indeed. And the men of the castle discovered that! They were vanquished and humbled by you and your shield! But enough: I'm heading off alone now – but I'll tell you my name before I go.'

'Ah, have pity, good sir, in God's name! You can't leave without me!'

'I must,' said Perceval. 'I shan't keep it from you: I'm bound for a place where no one else can go – I have to go alone.'

The Fair Bold Knight was downcast and distressed at hearing this: he loved his company so much that no one could describe his sorrow.

Then Perceval told him his name, not wanting to keep it from him, and said that, if he'd go to the good King Arthur's court, 'by God and His power, you'll find me there at Pentecost, come what may.'

'I'll be there, I promise you!' said the Fair Bold Knight.

And with that, Perceval took his leave and departed. The Fair Bold Knight was so upset his heart was close to breaking: if he'd had his way he'd have stayed his companion for the rest of his days. He was filled with sorrow and regret.

The Healing Grail

But I'll say no more about him now; I'll tell of Perceval. He rode right along a valley till almost vespers. In a hermitage beside a wood he lodged that night till the break of day next morning. Then the hermit didn't dally but went to his chapel and called Perceval to go with him, saying:

'Come to church, friend, and hear the service of Our Lord – it will be much to your benefit: you'll ride more safely.'

'Before God, sir,' said Perceval, 'I'll do so gladly.'

So they entered the chapel, and the good man said and sung the service with great dignity. Perceval listened reverently, and after mass he made full and free confession of his sins. The hermit, seeing his sincere contrition, gave him absolution, and by way of penance bade him never to ride, if he could help it, after compline* on a Saturday.

'I promise,' said Perceval, 'to avoid it whenever I can.'

'May God the true Father grant that you do,' the hermit said, 'and pardon all your sins.'

Then Perceval set off without more delay, lance in hand, shield hung from neck, fully armed on the white destrier, its belly good and full and its hooves securely shod.

He rode till terce or thereabouts, when he passed into a stretch of open ground

---

[46] Strictly speaking it was his mother, in Chrétien, above, pp. 6, 15.
[47] '*Li Biaus Mauvais*': a 'Fair Coward' is referred to in the First Continuation (above, p. 151), and Perceval meets a 'Biau Mauvais' (the 'Fair Bad Knight') and changes his name in the Second Continuation, above, p. 266.
[48] '*le Biau Hardi*'.

between Scotland and Ireland. It was a fine, broad expanse with no forest or river, no town or house or tower, no wood of oak or elm, for a good two leagues in any direction. It was here that he met a knight with tattered arms, holed in more than a hundred places, wrecked and battered: his name was Ector, and he was a companion of the Round Table, but truly, I promise you, when Perceval saw him in such a state he didn't recognise him. His horse was so scrawny it could hardly carry him. He'd been riding for two whole years – through woods and on highways alike – without ever finding proper lodging: he'd had many hard times indeed. He was pale and wan from the winds and weather he'd faced – one moment roasted, the next frozen stiff.

As soon as he saw Perceval he headed his horse towards him and summoned him to defend himself: he defied him! Perceval stared in surprise and was slow to respond, so he cried again:

'By the holy cross, vassal, you'd do better to guard against my lance than sit there like a coward!'

'Truly, friend,' said Perceval, 'you're a valiant knight, I'd say, but your armour's nearly falling apart – your hauberk's in shreds! You're clearly not afraid of death! Go your way, dear brother: you could do without combat, by God you could! And your horse is so frail he'd collapse beneath you at the slightest blow! I suggest you go about your business and I'll see to mine – I've plenty to get on with!'

Ector thought this offer of peace was a mark of contempt! He spurred his horse towards him, shouting that no one would make him forgo battle! Perceval saw he'd have to joust and spurred the white destrier forward, galloping like the wind. They levelled their lances and struck each other's shield with a force that split the wood and drove the steel lance-heads into living flesh. The shafts were strong and bowed without breaking, but the backs of their saddles smashed and the knights went tumbling over their horse's rumps and hit the ground together. But they were quickly on their feet again and strode to the attack, drawing their naked swords and exchanging blows that smote off pieces of their helms and ventails and sent mail rings flying from their hauberks till the green grass was littered all around. They were covered in deep gashes, three fingers long, and each was beside himself with rage at failing to defeat his foe. Their battle was so ferocious that their shields lost their bosses and their helmets lost their hoops; their swords did such damage to their hauberks that the blood began to pour. It was a grim contest indeed: blood now streamed from heads and sides and arms till the whole field was stained with it, the grass dyed red. They were battering each other so dreadfully it's a wonder they endured so long. At last they could take no more; they were forced to drop, unable to stay upright or fight on. They lay flat out, incapable of further effort, and passed out from the pain of their wounds ten times or twenty, I don't know.

They lay there all day long till darkness fell. Not a living soul came by that way, and neither of them said a word. But eventually they took deep breaths, inspired by God, who didn't wish them yet to lose their lives or be gone so soon; and Ector was the first to speak – though not without a struggle – saying:

'Friend, for the love of God who bestows all blessings, go now and bring me the hermit who dwells on yonder hill, to hear my confession, that my soul may be absolved.'

'Believe me, sir,' said Perceval, 'I haven't the strength to move. You've killed me, truly; but by the faith you owe God, if you die forgive me for your death: I greatly fear my soul is burdened with it.'

'As I pray that God will attend my passing,' Ector replied, 'I do indeed forgive you; but in return I ask a favour: you've harried me so hard today that I don't believe I'll last till midnight, so if you chance to go to King Arthur's court, tell Lancelot of my misfortune if you see him, and greet him, sir, on behalf of his brother Ector.'

'By the faith I owe God my Father,' said Perceval, struggling to speak, 'I haven't the strength to travel at all! For Lancelot's sake, and for yours – for I loved you dearly – I'm sorry I came this way today! But if you ever make it to the court of our lord the king, greet my brother Agloval – and good King Arthur – on behalf of Perceval.'

'By God and His power,' said Ector, barely able to reply, 'there's no chance of that: I've lost all strength. You've killed me – and I've killed you, for certain. It's a shame and desperate sorrow that we should die so – and I'm to blame for your death.'

And they both passed out again, their senses gone, their sight and hearing lost with all their blood.

They lay in this wretched, parlous state till it was almost midnight. But as midnight arrived a light appeared between them, the brightest light they'd ever seen. The dazzle made them open their eyes, and there amid the radiance they saw a royal angel all alone, holding in his hands the grail. Three times he circled them, then departed with the light in which he'd come. They didn't know what had become of him – only that the holy angel had risen heavenward, taking with him the holy grail. Perceval was filled with joy, exultant at this vision, and sat upright, feeling entirely well in mind and body. He thanked ever-truthful God and His power for this miracle, sighing from the depths of his heart. Then he called to Ector and asked him how he was, and he replied that he was healed by the Creator's grace, free of all pain and suffering.

'I'm entirely healed, thanks to the holy angel I saw who came to us – though I don't know what it was that he was holding in his hands; that troubles me – how I wish I did! All my desires would be fulfilled if I knew the truth about the holy vessel borne by the heavenly angel in the light: I've never seen the like.'

'Dear friend,' said Perceval, 'it was the holy grail of which you've heard so much.'

When Ector heard this he was elated, filled with joy and happiness. He stood at once and asked Perceval how he was.

'How am I? Truly, of the wounds so grave that I couldn't so much as move, of the agonising pains that had robbed me of all colour, I'm as free and as fit as I've ever been in my life!' And he jumped up and said: 'I'm so pleased to see you well!'

'And I to see you, so help me God!' said Ector.

And they embraced each other there and then, in joy and relief, and in the middle of that open field they forgave one another for all the grief and pain.

They stayed there happily till daybreak. Then they found their horses – they hadn't strayed – and each went to his own and mounted by the stirrup, and without more ado they kissed and commended each other to God. Ector set off in search of Lancelot, and finally tracked him down.

Revenge for the Fisher King

Perceval set out to fulfil his mission, praying to God to bring him face to face with Partinal.[49]

Through woods and valleys, over mountains and plains he rode, till he caught sight of a castle with five handsome, splendid towers. It stood beside a river surrounded by

---

[49] The lord of the Red Tower, the treacherous killer of the Fisher King's brother King Goondesert; the Fisher King hoped Perceval would take revenge: see above, p. 479.

farmland, woods and meadows: it wanted for nothing – and feared no attack from any force, being so well sited and so strong that no catapult or engine or assault could threaten it: it was so well defended by walls and palisades that nothing in the world – unless it descended from the heavens – could do it damage. The people of the castle were well off, that's for sure, for their guardian lord gave them such protection that no neighbour could do them harm – though every neighbour loathed them, for their lord was ruthless, wicked, vicious, full of utter malice: he was the cruellest man alive.

Of the five towers I mentioned, four were smaller than the one in the middle, which loomed impressively indeed, and glowed redder than fine gold: none of such splendour was ever seen. And when Perceval set eyes on it he whispered to himself:

'That's the Red Tower, in faith! It must be – I'm sure of it – the abode of the one who's caused such grief to the king who guards the holy grail.'

Perceval viewed the awesome castle and the Red Tower and surged with excitement. He rode on till he neared the gate, which was fine and impressive indeed. Planted before it was a green and bristling pine, the most beautiful he'd seen in all his life, and from it hung a most handsome shield, newly emblazoned with two fair and comely damsels in fine gold. As Perceval gazed at this shield, he realised it belonged to the one who'd done so much harm and wrong to the Fisher King. Elated, he rode up to the shield, longing to know why it was hung there. Just as he was thinking this a boy came out of the gate; Perceval saw him and called him over and said:

'Tell me, friend, what's the name of this castle, and who is its lord?'

'May God forgive me His wrath,' the boy replied, 'I'll tell you sure enough. It's called the Red Tower and the lord's name is Partinal. He's awesome in battle – so much so that no knight who comes this way and takes down his shield can withstand him. He's vanquished a hundred and four since he started – all of them valiant knights of renown – in only five and a half years! Anyone who touches the shield is attacked ferociously! Lay a finger on it and your time is up! Partinal has hung it here so that all wandering knights in search of adventure can see it clearly.'

'What price does he pay,' said Perceval, 'the man who takes it down?'

'By God who was crucified,' said the boy, 'he pays with his life! And no one should fancy that!'

'His life?' thought Perceval. 'By Saint Peter of Rome, he's a cruel, false knight indeed if he'd kill a man for so little cause; it's an offence to God.'

And with that he rode up to the pine, took the shield down by the strap, and battered it against the trunk till he smashed it utterly. The boy frantically blasted a horn that hung about his neck; Partinal heard it and was ecstatic: he knew someone was looking for trouble! He armed at once, and with helmet laced, and girded with a sword that had severed many a head, he leapt in his saddle without using a stirrup, took an ashwood lance, gave his charger free rein and rode out through the gate. But he didn't have a shield – he was expecting to find it hanging on the pine; and when he saw it smashed on the ground he nearly went wild with anger – he was incensed! But it didn't stop him charging at Perceval, crying:

'Vassal! Vassal! By my life, that was the finest shield you ever saw! You'll regret you ever came here – it's going to cost you your miserable head!'

Perceval heard the threat and thrust his sharp steel spurs in his charger's flanks. With lances levelled they came full tilt to meet each other and clashed with all their prodigious might. Partinal struck Perceval's shield and split it asunder, while Perceval – determined to joust well – thrust two yards of shaft clean through his shoulder. Neither knight could keep his seat: like it or not, both fell; but Partinal had come off worse with his grievous wound. He was undaunted nonetheless, and sprang to his feet with drawn sword. Perceval leapt up, too, ready to defend himself. Then you'd have seen a bitter contest – none so cruel was ever witnessed. Both of them were exceptional, battle-hardened knights, and assailed each other with their well-honed swords, every blow that landed making the bright blood flow. Attack after attack, blow after mighty blow and many a wound they dealt. But Partinal showed no fear: clutching his sword in both hands he performed so well that any man who saw him would have said there was never a finer knight; and Perceval likewise: all the people of the castle, of every degree, declared they'd never seen his equal and knew of none in all the land – such an accomplished knight was nowhere to be found.

Their combat lasted from prime till almost noon. So many awesome blows they dealt with their blades of steel: their hauberks were cut to ribbons – neither had a patch of mail left big enough to cover a hand – and both were now bereft of shield and helm. They were both in serious trouble now: time and again they sank to their knees or collapsed full length on the ground, as the people could clearly see from the windows of the hall and chambers, watching the battle from which neither knight would flinch.

But there's no point going on and dragging it out! Victory went to Perceval by the will of the king of glory. He brought Partinal to the ground before him and said the battle was over if he'd surrender as his prisoner. But the one who didn't believe in God said he'd never stoop to yielding captive to any knight: he shouldn't imagine for a single moment that he'd ever ask for mercy.

'Then may God never forgive me if I refrain from killing you.' Perceval raised his sword and threatened to slay him there and then if he didn't yield.

'I swear,' Partinal replied, 'I'll not surrender to my dying breath. If you want to kill me, go ahead: I'll never plead for mercy or submit to being a prisoner.'

'Then kill you I shall,' said Perceval, 'though it grieves me.'

And he struck him a blow that severed head from trunk. He left the body bleeding in the green meadow, and took the head and hung it from the back of his saddle, resolving to carry it to the Fisher King who'd honoured him so highly. So saying, he mounted at once and collected the shield he'd smashed against the pine and hung it from his neck; then he departed without more ado, leaving Partinal's corpse outside the gate, and carrying off his head.

Calm and unhurried, he headed for the house of the Fisher King. But he couldn't think how he'd ever find it: it was a year and a summer since he'd been to those parts, and he couldn't tell which way to go to seek the castle, not knowing the surrounding country well – though he'd been born there: he was a native of the Waste Forest. But he'd been a simple youth when he left his mother, and he hadn't returned there since.[50]

The Healing of the Fisher King

He rode on through the country searching, this way, that way, until he saw the tip of a bell-tower peep above a rocky crag. He headed towards it – and realised it was the castle he sought! Chance had led him there! He pressed on to the gate. The drawbridge was down and he rode in and dismounted in the courtyard beneath a pine. A servant ran straight to tell the king that a knight had arrived with a slain knight's

---

[50] This last phrase ignores episodes in the Second Continuation as well as in Gerbert.

head on his saddle; the king that instant sprang to his feet in joy and jubilation: he felt healed in body and spirit alike. In utter elation he hurried to the foot of the steps. Perceval came to meet him and presented him with the head, saying it belonged to the one who'd caused him so much grief.

'This is his head, you may be sure – and as further proof that I've vanquished and slain him, I've brought you his shield.'

The king saw the shield and recognised it instantly; and afire with joy he took Perceval in his arms and hugged and kissed him more than a hundred times, and said: 'You've brought me the greatest relief and comfort, taking revenge on the foe who'd caused me such distress. My sorrow and pain are turned to joy, as all can plainly see! By God the Creator, my woes mean nothing to me now! I'll fix this severed head on a pike up there on my highest tower, in honour and remembrance of the vengeance taken on the man who wrongly, wickedly, treacherously slew my brother.'

He bade that a pike be mounted on the tower's top and the head impaled upon it, and his bidding was done at once. Then they disarmed Perceval amid the greatest celebration ever seen, and he stayed there with the Fisher King, who loved him dearly and called him friend and son and honoured and served him highly indeed, as he had well deserved.

The king called for the tables to be set, and the servant appointed didn't tarry but set them and laid the cloths at once, along with the knives and salt. As soon as they'd washed they took their seats, Perceval sitting beside the king. Then the lance and the grail appeared, carried by the two maidens; they gracefully passed before the tables – which thereupon were laden with the most exquisite dishes. The maidens swiftly returned with the grail and lance to the chamber from which they'd come. They stayed there for some while. Then back they came into the hall exactly as they'd done before; and all those at the tables were revitalised and sated when they saw the holy grail pass by, and the holy lance with its shining head from which hung the drop of blood. And after them came a handsome youth holding a silver trencher wrapped in a cloth of rich, red samite. They passed before the tables and then straight back to the chamber. The Welshman watched so fixedly that his eating was forgotten. Three times the grail passed among the tables, so that Perceval and all those present saw it quite clearly. And after the grail they saw the trencher, following the holy lance, and they came right up to the end of the table where Perceval and the king were sitting; then they returned to the chamber once again, just as they had come.

Everyone seated at dinner ate to his heart's content, and when they'd finished they all washed and rose from the tables. The king, alight with happiness, took Perceval by the hand, and they went together to rest at a window of the hall. Then the king spoke to Perceval, saying:

'My beloved friend, you've suffered much to free me of the torment that would have afflicted me for the rest of my days – I would never have found relief had it not been for you. Yet your name's unknown to me! Your great service to me will be relayed through many lands, so if you don't mind my asking, I'd gladly know your name.'

'My lord king,' he replied, 'I've never hidden my name: it's Perceval the Welshman; I was born and raised in Wales, but since the day I received my arms I've never been to my native land.[51] I don't know my father's name, but my mother, I know, was lady of the Waste Forest. Against her will, with great resolve, I rushed off to the good King

---

[51] See note 50, above, p. 549.

Arthur's court to ask for arms. Since then I've roamed many countries and explored many lands.'

'And won great honour in the process, truly!' said the Fisher King. 'In God's name, tell me: Agloval the Welshman – isn't he your brother?'

'Yes indeed, sire, by Saint Peter!'

'How happy I am to hear it!' said the king. 'You're my nephew, for sure! Your mother was my sister[52] – the wisest, bravest, most noble-hearted lady of our line. In distress at your leaving she died on the bridge outside her gate. But I'm delighted and thank God to see you here, fit and well! And all my land I place in your hands: I relinquish it forthwith. Come what may, I shall make you king at Pentecost, so help me God! I'll brook no opposition: it shall be done as I have said.'

With a sigh, Perceval calmly said: 'Since you take me to be your nephew, sire, I swear to God I'll never wear a crown or be king as long as God grants you life: I've no desire to have your land. But no matter how distant I may be, whenever you need me I'll come at once: nothing will stop me, barring imprisonment or sickness or death. I don't know what else to say. By the faith I owe Saint Martin, I must go tomorrow morning to the good King Arthur's court, but I'll see you again very soon, if God who bestows all blessings gives me the power and strength.'

Everyone present was jubilant at the avenging of Goondesert, lord and king of the Desert, and all rejoiced at the healing of the Fisher King. And with what joy they hailed Perceval the Welshman, too, when the king, aglow with happiness, told them that he was his sister's son. The maidens, his two cousins, lionised and fêted him, and the celebrations continued, uninterrupted, far into the night till it was time for bed. Then the king, filled with love for his nephew, had him lie beside him; since that was his wish, the noble-hearted Perceval agreed, and slept there at his side till morning.

As soon as he saw the first glimmer of day he rose and called for his arms. The servant who'd looked after them had them ready; but they were battered, damaged dreadfully, so the king had a set of arms brought to him: blacker than ink they were, the arms he'd borne himself before he was maimed.

'If you will, dear nephew,' he said, 'bear these arms for my sake, and with confidence, for they are the arms of a king – my own.'

'I'll bear them indeed, dear uncle, and keep them out of love for you, so help me God.'

Then he armed at once and mounted the white destrier and took gracious, courteous leave; and through the gate he rode bearing armour blacker than a berry.

Perceval Returns to Arthur

Into a nearby forest he passed, and headed for court on that splendid horse. He pressed on right through the forest; it was late in the day, well past noon, by the time he emerged. On he rode, without meeting a soul, till he came to beautiful open country. There was no wind or hail or rain – the weather was as fair as May – and he rode calm and untroubled across this peaceful land.

Then he came to an expanse of meadow. Before him he could see two laurels, two pines and two olive trees, the loveliest he'd seen in all his life; and on each of the trees hung a shield. Although eager to press on, Perceval couldn't resist a look at these shields;

---

[52] This gives a different relationship to that established by Chrétien: see above, p. 56.

and as he drew closer he saw there was a lance propped against each tree, too. One lance was greener than any tree, as was the accompanying shield; another was white as snow, as was the shield on the branch above; the third shield, truly, was a brighter yellow than the flowers in the meadow, as was the lance below; the fourth was the indigo shade of hawthorn blossom.[53] Perceval was hungry for a closer look. The fifth shield and lance were painted red;[54] but the sixth shield was different from the rest, being striped with a mixture of all their colours – white, yellow, green, indigo and red – and the effect when caught by the sun was dazzling.

Perceval didn't dally: he headed swiftly that way, and saw a beautiful spring in the shade of the trees. Around this spring sat six knights, eating, each with his horse at his side. They were enjoying a happy, carefree meal amid much merriment. Apart from being unhelmeted they were all superbly armed, and truly, the gear of each of the knights exactly matched the shields. So there they sat, as I say, all six of them eating; and four girls were gladly, cheerfully serving them, with the respect befitting such worthy knights. These girls saw Perceval approaching swiftly, armed and mounted on the white destrier, and as soon as they caught sight of him they alerted the knights, who stopped eating for a moment to take a look. They couldn't have been more thrilled. The youngest of the six rose excitedly, laced his helm and quickly mounted, took up the white shield and lance with its bright, sharp head, and galloped towards Perceval, shouting that he'd regret he'd come! Perceval saw he had to joust and charged to meet him; they clashed, the knight with the white shield striking Perceval's shield so mightily that his lance bowed and smashed and flew into shards; and Perceval returned a ferocious blow right on the boss that shattered the shield and dislodged his saddle, driving the knight from his horse to the ground so heavily that his right arm broke. With lance raised, Perceval rode on by: thinking little of the knight he left him on the ground unconscious, attacking him no more. But one of the others leapt to his feet, laced his helm and took his shield and mounted his splendid charger; he charged full tilt at Perceval and struck his shield so fiercely that he split the wood beneath the boss; but his lance broke and flew into splinters, while Perceval landed a blow to his shield that sent him crashing to the ground and laid him out in the middle of the field. Again he rode on by, not stopping, leaving the knight unconscious. The third knight at the spring jumped up eagerly, laced his helm, mounted his horse, grabbed his shield and charged at Perceval, lance in hand. Perceval levelled his own when he saw him coming, and they exchanged tremendous blows. The knight's landed first – a fearsome blow to the shield – but he smashed his lance in two; and Perceval caught him beautifully, just below his shield's rim, splitting it apart and sending him flying from his horse with his legs in the air, head over heels. But why carry on and make it boring? He had a fine time, unhorsing all six with the same lance. And all six promptly submitted to imprisonment wherever he chose, and he ordered them straight to Arthur's court to place themselves at the king's mercy in the name of Perceval the Welshman.

'Greet him on my behalf as the very finest king in all the world, and be sure to tell him that I'll be at court at Pentecost, come what may, be it at Winchester or Cardoil. But I want to know your names before you go.'

---

[53] All the MSS say it is '*inde*' (indigo, violet) like 'a hawthorn flower'; this seems curious, but hawthorn blossom, though thought of as essentially white, can have a violet tinge, especially before it opens. This subtlety might perhaps be seen as an interesting indication of medieval sensitivity to colour.

[54] '*sinople*': see Glossary.

'I'll tell you truly, as you wish, good sir,' the eldest said. 'Listen and we'll tell you: my name is Salandre of the Isles and these five are my sons, and courteous and noble knights they are. The eldest is Dinolsoldre, most valiant and wise; Monastide is the second, the third Lactor, the fourth Enariste, the fifth Gorgone. They're all downcast, distraught at being vanquished!'

'By the faith you owe God,' said Perceval, 'give my message properly to the king.'

They promised to do so, and took their leave and set off for the court, arriving there on the eve of Pentecost. They gave the king their message – not without some anguish and regret! – and the king received them with heartfelt joy: he was delighted by their news and pardoned them imprisonment. The whole court spent the night in highest spirits.

Next morning, after mass, the king returned from church and sat at the windows of the hall, disheartened now and worried – upset about Perceval, very afraid that he wouldn't be coming to court. Then he looked across the meadows and saw, riding towards him at great speed, a swift white destrier bearing a black knight. The king called to Kay the seneschal and said:

'There's a knight riding fast towards the gate: he bears black arms – I don't know who he is.'

And Kay retorted: 'Truly, sire – this is no joke – it's the Devil riding a heavenly angel: Saint Gabriel or Saint Michael!'

Gawain heard this, as did Lancelot and Sir Yvain, Boort, Ector, Lionel, Gaheriët and Dodinel and the other worthy knights, and they all roared with laughter. But the king was not amused; he said:

'Ah, Kay! You've such a brash, abrasive, scornful tongue! Your mocking jests will do you no good!'

At that moment Perceval dismounted at the foot of the steps beneath an olive tree; the knights went to meet him, as did the king himself, who received him with the utmost joy and bade that he be disarmed at once. Then hand in hand they went up to the hall – the most handsome in all the world, it was – and spoke long together, in public and in confidence.

The king now summoned all the barons who'd come to court, and kindly asked them to relate as they should, on their word of honour, all that they'd encountered while they'd been away. Just as promised each knight gave his report, be it to his honour or his shame. Boort and Lionel told how they'd met and how Lionel, in his fit of rage, had killed the worthy Calogrenant. Each of them told everything, in full and honest detail. The king was most upset about Calogrenant, as was everyone. Then Perceval told how he'd seen the holy grail, carried right before the eyes of the Fisher King's court, along with the lance from which the red blood ran, and the handsome silver trencher; and how he'd repaired the broken sword. And he told them all about the chapel and his fight with the black hand, and how he'd put an end to the dread adventure that had left a knight stricken dead upon the altar every day. Then he told them about the tree of candles, and of his anger and despair at being unhorsed by the knight, and how the devil had appeared in the shape of a black horse and carried him to the sea, and would have drowned him there if he'd had the chance – 'but the sign of the cross outwitted him! It wouldn't let him hurt me!' And then he told of the maiden who'd sailed up in a boat and so assured him of her love that he went to lie with her in a pavilion she had pitched there to deceive him and seduce him; but how, when he crossed himself, she'd recoiled from the sign and from him and fled across the sea amid a raging storm. And he told how the worthy man had sailed up and brought him comfort and carried him over the sea and given him the white horse that he'd ridden to court. Then he recounted his battle with Ector, in every detail, telling of the wounds they dealt each other and how they were healed by the holy grail, revealed to them by God. He told, too, the whole story of how the coward knight had turned bold. And then he told of Partinal: how he'd beheaded him, and how the Fisher King had been jubilant and fixed the head on his highest tower, and how it had led to his being healed. And finally he told how he'd seen the various shields hanging on the laurels and pines and olive trees, and how he'd vanquished the knights who were guarding the spring. He fulfilled his obligation and told them everything.

Then the king, duly and properly, had the name and adventures of each knight set down in writing, just as they'd reported them; and the good King Arthur had the records sealed and stored for posterity in a cabinet at Salisbury.

According to my source, once each of the knights had told his tale they all took their places at the tables and were served with an array of splendid dishes. So they dined and made merry, eating with the utmost joy and pleasure. The feasting lasted for eight whole days, and throughout that time King Arthur wore his crown. It was a joyous time indeed.

In the midst of their celebrations a damsel arrived at court on a swift hunting horse; she dismounted beneath the pine tree and hurried up the steps to the hall. She greeted King Arthur first, honouring him as lord, then Perceval and the other companions up and down the hall. Then she came to Perceval and handed him a letter. He read it, and learned that his uncle had passed from this world and wanted Perceval to go at once to Corbenic and be crowned, to be the holder and guardian of his land and ruler of his kingdom: he entrusted the realm to him upon his soul and in the name of God and of the Lady who bore Jesus Christ. Perceval was very upset when he read this news, but the king and all his company rejoiced; and King Arthur – very happily, I'm sure – said he'd go to Corbenic and attend his joyous coronation.

The Grail and the Lance Depart

The king and all the companions had their baggage packed and loaded – for Perceval invited them all by name – and took to the road. They made their way straight to Corbenic, where the people of the land gave them a fitting reception, honouring them unstintingly.

The good Welshman was crowned on All Saints' Day. Fourteen crowned kings were present out of love for him, all of them kings of high renown. They sat together in order around the high table, and then the noble companions of the Round Table took their places. And it wasn't long before they saw, quite openly, the holy grail: through a door it came, carried by a maiden of graceful bearing. Straight after her came a boy holding a lance with a shining head from which there flowed a drop of blood. After him, in view of everyone, came a maiden, as graceful as the first, holding a silver trencher. Three times they passed before them; and as they did so every table was laden and spread with the most delectable dishes that any man could find or possibly describe, along with every kind of wine. Then the boy and the maidens returned to the chamber. The good King Arthur asked for an explanation! And Perceval the Welshman told them everything from start to finish, without omitting a single detail. The king stopped eating – as did all who heard: they listened in rapt delight.

This plenary court continued for a month, and every day the grail served them in its customary way. At the month's end the court broke up and King Arthur departed with all his companions, not stopping till he reached his land.

But Perceval stayed in his own realm, and for seven years he held it in peace, free of war, untroubled by anyone. He rebuilt castles and fortresses, and all his neighbours held him in awe and respect. He arranged most noble marriages for his two cherished cousins: the daughter of King Goondesert, who'd been lord of the Desert, he married to Merïen, lord and king of Lenval – there was no more loyal knight in all the earthly world; and the daughter of the good Fisher King, free of all vice, of perfect temperament, he married to the king of Maronne, which bordered Wales on every side. In the seven years that he reigned as king, Perceval achieved all these things.

And then he heard news that Agloval had died, which grieved him deeply: he'd loved him dearly – as he should, Agloval being his brother. He summoned the king of Maronne and bequeathed his land to him, placing it entirely in his hands, and retired from this world. In a nearby forest dwelt a worthy man in a little hermitage, living a reclusive life, devoted and intent on serving God, and it was there that Perceval went to dwell. And the grail and the holy lance followed him straightway, along with the holy silver trencher, as all the people were well aware. The worthy hermit welcomed him with the joy and respect befitting such a man, regarding him as king and lord and cherishing and honouring him most highly. And with great care and attention he instructed him in letters, and Perceval responded with such keen, devoted effort that after two years he made him an acolyte, then a sub-deacon and then a deacon, and pressed on with his training until, in the fifth year, he made him a priest. He had him sing his first mass one Saint John's Day, and Perceval vowed to God to give Him willing service for the rest of his days.

Perceval served God thus for ten whole years, and in all that time he ate and drank nothing but what God sent him in the holy grail, which he saw and which served him night and day. It stayed with him constantly, day and night, which was certainly no trouble but a source of delight. He lived there for a long while in prayer and humble worship, singing psalms, fasting and keeping vigil.

He served God at the hermitage for the remainder of his life. So well did he serve and love Him that God claimed him for His own: on the day he left this world God received him and bestowed His grace upon him. It was on the eve of Candlemas that Perceval peacefully left the world and ended his life; and God, ever eager to take the good to His side, set him in the bliss of Paradise, at His right, where the good long to be. On the day when, to his joy, God took his soul, he was carried off to heaven – of that you may be sure. And in full view of everyone, the holy grail and the lance and the handsome silver trencher went with him. After Perceval's death no man saw the grail on earth again, search as he might; nor will any man born ever see it so openly.

Perceval, beloved of God, was buried with all honour at the Castle of Adventures[55] beside the Fisher King. Those who saw to his interment laid him in a tomb of gold and silver, and on the lid they inscribed in fine letters:

> 'Here lies Perceval the Welshman,
> who brought to completion the adventures of the Holy Grail.'

---

[55] *Palés Aventureus*: the castle of the Fisher King.

Anyone who travels to that land can still see the tomb resting on four golden pillars: so Manessier testifies, who has brought this work to completion for Countess Jehanne, lady and mistress of Flanders,[56] that illustrious lady endowed by God with wisdom, virtue, beauty, courtesy, loyalty, nobility, largesse and the highest reputation. Having such abundant knowledge of her good graces, I have completed my book in her name. It was begun in the name of her forebear,[57] but no one thereafter set his hand to its completion. Lady, it is for you that Manessier undertook the task, beginning at the mending of the sword, and now has brought it to an end – and accurately, according to the source. He has told the whole story just as it is found at Salisbury,[58] following the testimony of the records under King Arthur's seal. Anyone who goes that way can still see the records there, all on sealed parchment.

Here ends *Perceval the Welshman*

---

[56] Jeanne, countess of Flanders from 1205 to 1244. She could best be described as 'mistress of Flanders' from 1214 to 1227, while her husband was held prisoner by Philip Augustus following his defeat at the battle of Bouvines; she ruled alone also between 1233 and 1237.

[57] Count Philip of Flanders, to whom Chrétien dedicated *Perceval* (above, p. 1).

[58] '...the good King Arthur had the records sealed and stored for posterity in a cabinet at Salisbury' (above, p. 554).

Appendix 1

The Elucidation Prologue

This is included in just one surviving manuscript – Mons, Bibliothèque publique, 331/206 – where it appears at the very beginning, followed by Bliocadran *and then by Chrétien's romance (omitting Chrétien's own prologue, of which it incorporates the last few lines).*

By noble command,[1] here begins the splendid telling of the most pleasing tale there is: the story of the Grail. But the Grail's secret none should reveal or tell, for before it's finished the story might disclose something for which an innocent party might suffer;[2] so it's wisest to leave it and simply pass on – if Master Blihis[3] is to be believed, no one should reveal the secret. So listen now, everyone, and you'll hear a tale to delight you, for in it you'll find the seven guards, who have charge of all the good tales that have ever been told throughout the world. Here you'll learn what sort of people the seven guards are and to what end they're to come.

You've never heard the story recounted or treated truthfully, yet how and why the mighty land of Logres was destroyed has been widely told – at one time it was hotly discussed. The kingdom went to ruin; the land was so dead, so desolate, that it wasn't worth a jot; the voices of the wells were lost, along with the maidens who dwelled in them. These maidens performed a vital service: no one travelling the roads, night or morning, ever needed to stray from his path to go and find food or drink; he had only to go to one of the wells. Anything he craved by way of fine food he would be given at once – as long as it was sought in moderation. A damsel would instantly appear from the well, and no one could have asked for one more fair! In her hand she'd be holding a golden vessel filled with meat and pies and bread; another maiden would come bearing a white napkin and a gold and silver platter containing the dish requested by the one who'd arrived seeking food. He'd be warmly welcomed at the well; and if the dish wasn't to his liking she'd bring others, most willingly and generously, according to his fancy. Together these maidens happily and graciously served all travellers who came to the wells for food.

King Amangon was the first to abuse their kindness: he behaved wickedly, despicably; thereafter many more did likewise, following the example of the king who should have

---

1 The MS reads '*Pour le noble comencement*' ['for the noble beginning'], but Thompson in the notes to his edition (p. 102) observes that 'the analogy of v. 480 suggests that the original may have been "*Par le noble comandement*"'. This is certainly a far better reading.
2 A clearer reading of this strange line might be gained by emending a couple of easily mistaken words to give: '…someone might get the pay-off before he'd reached the end!'
3 Thompson comments (p. 80) that Blihis, this supposed authority on the Grail, 'was probably not cited … by the original author of the *Elucidation*; he was brought in by the interpolator, who may have found the name in the work from which he copied the passage about the "seven guards"'.

protected the maidens, should have guarded them and kept them safe, untroubled. Instead he forced himself on one of the maidens, deflowering her against her will; then he robbed her of the golden vessel and abducted her and forced her to serve him ever after. No good was to come of it: from then on no maiden ever came from that well to serve a man who happened by in search of sustenance. And it was the same at all the other wells. God! Why didn't the other vassals of the land realise? When they saw their lord raping the maidens he found most beautiful, they did likewise, and carried off the golden vessels; and from that time forth no maiden appeared from any of the wells to serve. This is the truth, I promise you. And that, my lords, is why the land went into decline. And the king who'd wronged the maidens so monstrously, and those who'd followed his example, all met a dismal end. The land turned to waste: no tree ever bore leaf again; the meadows and the flowers withered; the rivers dried to a trickle. And from that time forth no one could ever find the court of the wondrous Fisher King,[4] which had made the land resplendent with gold and silver, gorgeous furs, rich brocaded silks and cloths and copious food of every kind; and birds, too: gyrfalcons, merlins, goshawks, sparrowhawks. In former times, when his court was to be found, the land so abounded with all these riches that everyone, rich or poor, was astounded by the wealth. The realm of Logres was blessed with all the riches of the world; but now the land had lost it all.

But then, in the days of King Arthur, the peers of the Round Table came; their like have never since been seen: such fine knights they were, so worthy, strong and brave, so bold and stout-hearted, that as soon as they heard what had happened they resolved to restore the wells. All together they swore an oath to protect the maidens with might and main, so that they'd come from the wells with their vessels once more. And they vowed to destroy the descendants of the men who'd so wronged the maidens that they'd stayed in the wells and ceased to appear: whenever they captured one, they had him hanged or put to death. They gave gifts of alms and prayed to God that He might restore the wells to their former state; and in return for their honourable aid to the maidens they hoped to request their service. But for all their searching, far and wide, they could never find the wells; they never heard any voices and no maiden ever appeared.

Yet they did encounter something startling: in the forests they found maidens as beautiful as you could ever wish, but with them were knights, heavily armed and mounted on their chargers: they stood beside the maidens and fought anyone who tried to carry them off, and many a knight they killed. There were many battles fought there for the maidens' sake, it seems. King Arthur lost many good knights in the process – but he gained many good ones, too, as you'll hear in the story. The first knight to be captured was named Blihos Bliheris;[5] Sir Gawain it was who vanquished him, thanks to his mighty prowess, and sent him to submit to Arthur. Blihos mounted and rode without delay to surrender at the court. The king didn't know him, nor did anyone else; but he was such a fine teller of tales that no one ever tired of listening to him. Everyone at court pressed him to tell about the maidens who rode through the forest – some had never been there, so they had good cause to ask. And the knight Blihos told his tales so well that they listened to him gladly: the knights and girls would stay up many a night to hear him and ply him with questions.

4   '*rice Pescheour*': literally 'the rich Fisher'; but '*riche*', a much-used adjective in the romances, implies splendour and nobility and generosity as well as wealth.
5   There is a '*Bleheris*' mentioned briefly in the First Continuation, above, p. 146.

'You're intrigued,' he said, 'about the maidens seen abroad in these forests; and you keep wondering where we knights were born. So let me tell you: we're all offspring of the damsels – there'll never be any lovelier in the world – raped by King Amangon. The wrong will not be righted till the world's end! The peers of the Round Table, in their nobility and honour, with their valour and strength, have been striving to restore the wells to help the squires and knights and lords and girls who go travelling in the land. But I tell you, they'll have to roam the forests far and wide till God grants that they find the court[6] from which will spring the joy that will suffuse this land once more. Those who seek that court will encounter such adventures as have never before been seen or related in this land.'

Blihos's words thrilled and delighted all who heard them, and not long after, all the good knights of the court met to discuss the matter: each knight was to make ready, then all would go in earnest search of the court of the wondrous Fisher, who was so skilled in magic that he could assume a hundred forms; some would seek him in one shape and others in another.

And Sir Gawain found the Fisher King during King Arthur's reign – he went to his court, truly; and later you'll be told of the joy he engendered there, a joy that restored the whole kingdom.

But before Sir Gawain found the court, a young knight discovered it first – very young he was, though there was none of greater courage in the world. And this young knight then came to the Round Table; and in prowess he surpassed all knights before or since in all the world. At first he was held in low regard, but later proved his noble worth; and this young knight, in his search for the court of the Fisher King, scoured the land till at last he found it, truly, and many of you know of him: he was Perceval the Welshman. He asked what was done with the grail, but failed to ask why the lance bled when he saw it or to enquire about the sword of which half lay on the body in the bier and the other half was missing – nor did he ask where everyone then vanished to. But he did ask who the dead man was, and about the splendid silver cross that led the procession. Three times a day, for three hours at a time, there were such dreadful lamentations in the Fisher King's hall that no man, however brave, could have failed to be daunted by the sound. When the service was done, they hung four censers on four splendid candelabra that stood at the corners of the bier. Then suddenly the wailing ceased and everyone disappeared: the long, wide hall was left empty, fearful. And from a vase that held the bleeding lance, the stream of blood flowed along a channel of precious silver. Then the hall was filled with a throng of knights and other folk, and the most gorgeous feast in all the world was spread before them. Then the unknown king emerged from a chamber in magnificent array, so splendidly dressed that no man could describe his robe or adornments: his finger bore a handsome ring, his sleeves were tightly laced, and around his head was a circlet of gold, encrusted with gems that were worth a fortune; and his belt and its buckle were beautiful. No one could ever have found a more handsome man living. Anyone who'd seen him earlier, dressed as a fisherman, might well have been surprised! Once the king was seated you'd have seen all the knights sit down at the other tables. The bread was promptly served, and the wine presented in great cups of gold and silver. And then you'd have seen the Grail appear through a chamber door, without any servant or seneschal to bear it, and start serving – by itself, most graciously – on to rich gold plates of fabulous worth. It served the first course to the king, then to

---

6   i.e. the court of the Fisher King.

the others all around; and the dishes that it brought them and the food that it provided were astounding. Then came the wonder to which no other can compare – but you'll never hear me speak of it! Perceval must reveal it later, in the course of the story. It would be a shame and a crime to ruin such a good tale and tell it other than in the proper order! When the good knight comes and three times finds the Fisher King's court, then you'll hear me tell, point by point, inventing nothing, the truth about what happened to the wells, what became of the knights, and what purpose the grail served; and I'll tell you all about the bleeding lance and why the sword was on the bier – I'll tell everything, omitting nothing. To anyone who's not heard about the lamenting and the disappearing, I'll explain it all, just as it should be told.

My lords, it's the proven truth that the court was found seven times in the seven branches of the story; but you don't know what that means. You must understand that the seven branches, truly, are the seven guards; each guard will tell for himself how he found the court: it shouldn't be told in advance. I must, however, set down here the names of the seven guards; I don't want to leave out any: I must list them all, and I'll begin with the last.[7] The seventh and most pleasing branch is all about the lance with which Longinus struck the King of holy majesty in the side. The sixth, without a doubt, is about the great strife, the great struggle. The fifth will tell of the tragic loss of Huden.[8] The fourth is the Story of the Swan:[9] the dead knight in the skiff who first came to Glamorgan was certainly no coward. Next is the third, about the goshawk that terrified Castrar; Pecorin, Amangon's son, bore the wound upon his forehead ever after. That's the third. The second, according to the good story-tellers, is not told in verse: it's the Story of the Great Sorrows, telling how Lancelot of the Lake came to a place where he lost his strength.[10] And then there's the last: having started I'd better go on and finish, and it won't take long – it's the Adventure of the Shield,[11] and a finer one there never was; this adventure led to joy, and to repopulation after the great destruction. These are seven genuine stories that all stem from the Grail. Through these adventures, truly, the court and the Grail were found again, and through them the kingdom was so restored that the rivers and the springs that had all run dry were flowing once more across the meadows; the fields were green and lush again and the woods all decked in leaf. On the day the court was found again, throughout the land the forests turned so dense and vast, so glorious and thick with growth, that everyone who travelled the land was amazed.

But then a band of men returned, brimming with malice: they'd come from the wells but weren't recognised. They built castles and cities, towns and forts and strongholds,

---

7 The passage that follows is less than coherent. Some phrases do have possible echoes of narrative strands in Chrétien and the Continuations, but in his edition (p. 68) Thompson comments that 'the surviving manuscript betrays a copyist who was so unfamiliar with the seven tales that he made many errors in copying, and preserved the passage to us only in a corrupt form', and concludes (p. 75) that 'it has all the air of referring to real stories… [but] must be a real prologue or rimed table of contents to some work now lost…'.

8 Huden is the name of Tristan's dog, and Thompson suggests (in his edition, p. 108) that it 'may be the substitution by the copyist of a familiar name (Tristan's dog) for a word which had become illegible'.

9 The MS reads '*Ciel*' rather than '*Cygne*', but an emendation is strongly suggested by the echo of the story of the dead knight in the swan-boat that arrives at Arthur's court (in the First Continuation, above, p. 225; note the reference just beforehand to Glamorgan, note 121, p. 223).

10 Thompson (in his edition, pp. 73–4) suggests a possible reference here to episodes in the Prose *Lancelot*.

11 There are several shield adventures in the Continuations; 'it is hopeless', writes Thompson (pp. 74–5), 'to try to connect this reference with any particular one'.

and for the damsels they built the splendid Castle of the Maidens; they built the Perilous Bridge;[12] and they also built the great Proud Castle,[13] and grandly placed in charge of it a body of peers from the company established out of haughty pride as a rival to the Round Table, as everyone came to realise.

In the Proud Castle each knight had his sweetheart – they led a merry life! There were three hundred and sixty-six knights in all, each of them the lord of twenty more; the total I'll not fail to give: the defenders numbered seven thousand six hundred and eighty-six. But all their mighty efforts were in vain; I can assure the world there's not a single one of them left! They rode through the land and made war on King Arthur; his good knights left the court to confront them, and when they captured one they kept him prisoner for sure – there was no question of release. King Arthur wanted to go and destroy and waste the castle; but at that point all who hated him attacked him and waged mighty war; there was no chance of venturing elsewhere. These wars raged on for a good four years, according to the story and the one who recorded it.

I'm gradually telling you each stage of the story, because the author wishes to reveal to all of you what purpose the Grail served – the service it performed was revealed to him by the good master.[14] That great service will not remain hidden: he will make it freely plain to everyone.

So as I've explained, King Arthur was at war for four years against the people of his land; but at last he won so conclusively that no vassal or neighbour failed thereafter to do his will, either willingly or by force; that is the certain truth: it is the general view that the war brought honour to the king and shame to his foes.

With the war won, the king's illustrious household left the court and went hunting in the forests, or along the lovely rivers if they wanted to go after waterfowl. As is the way of people, some devoted themselves to courting, some indulged in other pastimes. They enjoyed themselves all winter till the following summer came.

Now Chrétien will relate this instructive tale; and his labour will not be wasted,[15] as he strives by the count's command to put into rhyme the finest story ever told in a royal court: it is the Story of the Grail, of which the count gave him the book. Now you'll hear how he acquits himself.

---

12 Possibly the glass bridge in the Second Continuation (above, pp. 288–9).
13 See the First Continuation, above, pp. 179–80, 197–209.
14 This is presumably another reference to Blihis (above, p. 557), and given how oddly this paragraph interrupts the flow, may well be an interpolation.
15 These last lines of the *Elucidation* are an almost exact repeat of the end of Chrétien's prologue, above, p. 1.

Appendix 2

Bliocadran

This appears in the Mons manuscript after The Elucidation. *It features also in a second manuscript – London, British Museum, Additional 36614 – where it appears after Chrétien's own prologue.*

In the land of Wales were twelve most worthy brothers; you could have searched the length and breadth of the land and all the country round about and I don't think you'd have found a knight of such esteem or so richly endowed with wealth, allies, castles and strongholds, woods and rivers and meadows. And they were fine knights indeed, fierce and bold in combat, and often travelled to other lands to engage in tournaments and wars, seeking to win renown and reputation. But I shan't go on, for the long and the short of it is that misfortune strikes many a worthy man and that was all too true of them: eleven of the brothers were killed, leaving one alone to maintain their entire inheritance. He was a wise and worthy man, courtly, bright and eloquent, and known to all the people of the land as Bliocadran.

He was most distressed at the loss of his brothers and brooded a long while, lost in sorrow. But it's foolish and pointless to mourn forever – sometimes a man must feign good cheer, even when he's feeling only grief; [he certainly shouldn't let despair][1] make him abandon striving to achieve fine deeds. And Bliocadran would mope no more: he had his arms made ready and his steeds well shod – back to the tournaments he'd go! But his wife and all those dear to him said:

'Have pity, good sir! Stay! Don't go! It's madness! If you go you'll be leaving your land exposed, defenceless, and your people in misery, distraught!'

They pleaded so insistently that he finally promised not to leave at all. How delighted they were!

The lord remained with his wife, a most worthy lady, for a good two years without their having any children – and they'd had none previously – until at last God granted that the lady conceived. All the people rejoiced – they loved their lord Bliocadran dearly – and he, you may be sure, couldn't have been more elated, truly.

The lady carried the child till it was almost time for her confinement. Then one day, after dinner, the lord was leaning at a window, watching people come and go below, when suddenly a squire appeared, riding swiftly towards the castle on a rouncey.* Into the courtyard he came and dismounted at the foot of the steps. Seeing this, the lord sent servants to take charge of the squire's horse and called out:

1   In both surviving manuscripts there is an accidental omission at this point; the missing lines were presumably to this effect.

'Welcome, friend!'

And the squire, bright and quick to reply, called in answer: 'I'm glad to have found you, my good dear sir, proven knight that you are!'

'You must stay here tonight,' said the lord. 'Rest assured, you'll have good lodging and be made most welcome.'

'No doubt,' said the squire, 'but let me have some bread and wine and I'll eat right now – I've had nothing all day!'

'Say no more!' said the lord. 'You shall have all you like!' And he called to a knight and said: 'Take this squire and look after him: have some food prepared – he's eaten nothing today.'

The knight ushered him in, showing him every respect, and cheerfully served him a generous meal in his chamber[2] overlooking a garden.

When the squire had eaten his fill he bade that the table be cleared, not wanting to dally; and he left the chamber and was met by Bliocadran who politely said:

'God bless you, friend; now tell us your news, the most reliable you have.'

'Indeed I shall, sir,' he replied, 'and you can trust every word of it: you'll hear no lies from me! The king of Wales has proclaimed a tournament, ranging all the knights of his land and all those of Cornwall against the knights of the Waste Spring. He's no wish to delay: he's sending word throughout the land, summoning knights to come to the tourney with their retinue and to be there this very Saturday! Do come, good sir, in God's name, and see the host of knights and the mighty crowd that'll gather for the tournament!'

He replied that he would go indeed, God willing. With that the squire took his leave and continued on his way.

Bliocadran left it till the morning before summoning his knights, but he told his squires to make ready with speed, for he meant to go to the tournament. Then, when the knights were all assembled, he greeted them joyfully and without more ado had all his packhorses loaded and his gear all prepared, and he and his knights promptly set off. The people of the town begged Sir Bliocadran to stay at home, and his wife with anguished heart implored him likewise, most tenderly; but he said:

'Hush, lady – stop your grieving.'

And with that he departed, leaving them all in dismay and praying to the Creator to look after their lord.

Bliocadran and the knights he'd taken rode on till they neared the tourney ground; but then they turned to their right and took lodging at a castle, where he and all his men were given a delightful welcome. Next morning they were gone at once, and made their way to the tournament.

Once all the tourneyers had duly assembled they took up their arms and mounted. The opposition rushed forward at the speed of a crossbow bolt, but our men, in serried ranks, advanced towards the city at a walk. Bliocadran was at their head, his knights with him; he wanted to be the very first to begin the tournament. Suddenly, from the foes' front line, a knight came bounding forth; Bliocadran saw him from afar and thrust in his spurs. The knight spotted him straight away and charged to meet him; they clashed, and the knight's blow landed first, striking him so fiercely on the shield that the lance smashed and shattered; and Bliocadran returned a fearsome blow, right below

---

2   Both MSS read 'the hall', but this sounds odd and is inconsistent with a phrase a few lines later.

his breast, that sent him flying over his saddle-bow and crashing over his horse's crupper to the ground. Then he handed the captured horse to a boy who led him back to their baggage train and took off the harness and saddle. By now all the other knights had engaged and were jousting with might and main.

At no point that day did Bliocadran suffer loss; he performed so well that everyone sang his praises as they beheld his fine and valiant feats. Then he saw a young noble coming, tall and strong and well mounted; equal in courage they were, and they charged at each other, spurring all the way, and clashed with mighty blows. Bliocadran's was so fierce that it split and smashed through the young man's shield, but the hauberk held together and the lance flew into shards, as was seen from all around the field. And the youth's flashed over the rim of Bliocadran's shield and struck him full in the face – and right through it: the whole lance-head burst through the back of his neck. He couldn't help but reel from the blow – it was a mortal wound; and he fell to the ground unconscious. His men came rushing to gather him up, wailing with shock and grief; and they made a bier, and in it they carried him to the castle where they'd lodged the previous night. They did all they could to comfort him, laying him gently in a chamber well away from everyone; and they saw that he was shriven. He lived for only two more days – there was nothing they could do to save him. He was carried to a church, his knights all grieving terribly, tearing at their clothes and hair. There they held a fine service for him, and then took him away to be buried.

I'll say no more now about him – or the tournament; I want to tell you how the lady, left behind at home, had fared when he departed. Just four days later[3] she gave birth to a boy, and none more handsome was ever seen. He was taken to church and baptised and raised from the font; and in his christening he was given a name that was never afterwards made known to him, never used or mentioned in his presence.[4]

Then the lady sent a serving-man straight to her lord, wanting to let him know how she was and that she'd given birth to the fairest son ever. But the messenger arrived to find him dead and in the ground. He delivered the news to his lord's companions: they were glad to hear it, but too distraught about their lord to celebrate at all. The messenger returned the way he'd come – but they forbade him, rightly or wrongly, to reveal that their lord was dead: he was to say instead that he'd gone off with the king who'd summoned them to the tournament. And this indeed he did. He made his way swiftly back to the town and dismounted outside the keep where the lady lay in her chamber above. Everyone he met gave him a cheery welcome. Into the chamber he went and bowed to the lady and her attendants, who received him warmly.

'My lord sends you greetings, lady,' he said, 'and has never been so thrilled by any birth as this! He'd been worrying that he might receive bad news, and is overjoyed to hear that you and his son have come through safely. I tell you, he'd have been very glad to see you if he could; but the king has summoned him back to Wales – I saw them leave, truly, the very day that I was there, he and all his companions: they won't be back for a week.'

---

3   One MS says four days, the other three. Four makes the time of the child's birth probably coincide with the father's death.
4   The two MSS give different versions of these phrases about his name, and the syntax in both cases is confused: the lines evidently gave the medieval scribes as much trouble as they do a modern editor or reader. I suspect that the sentence as originally composed was an allusion to Perceval's mysterious sudden guessing of his name in Chrétien (above, p. 32), and have translated it accordingly.

The lady, lying in her bed, believed he was telling the truth about her lord and having seen him: he managed to speak so convincingly – not that he had any choice: he'd been given a strong enough warning!

The end of the lady's confinement came and it was time for her to leave her bed. A week later, the knights who'd gone to the tournament where her husband had been killed met together; and one of them, a man of substance, said:

'We're in trouble, sirs! We've not yet told our lady about her husband's dreadful death. And one thing's for sure: I'm not going to tell her at any price! But there's a good abbot not far from here: let's ask him in the name of charity to come and speak to my lady.'

So they had their horses saddled and brought to them and they mounted by the stirrup, and set off all together and made their way to the abbey. They greeted the abbot and the monks, and then told the truth about their lord and how he'd died, and how they'd kept the news from their lady; and they asked him in God's name to go and tell her and console her, for she'd surely be needing comfort. The abbot immediately called for his palfrey, and bade the knights stay where they were till he'd spoken to the lady.

'I want to tell her the news and then say my piece; you can return when I'm done.'

They all replied: 'Very well.'

The abbot set off with just two servants and two monks. They made their way to the castle, where the monks dismounted and climbed the steps, leaving the servants in charge of the horses. They found the lady lying on a bed in the hall, and when she saw them enter she rose to greet the abbot, saying:

'Welcome, sir.'

He, courteous man that he was, graciously answered: 'May ever-truthful God save and guard and bless you and your household, and care for all those dear to you.'

Then he sat down close beside her, and the two other monks likewise sat gently on the bed. The abbot was the first to speak, beginning an apt and eloquent address. He prefaced it by saying:

'You must dearly love the one who gives you health and keeps you safe from sickness, who redeemed us from our sins and was crucified for us and resurrected on the third day. For His sake, lady, you should strive always to serve and honour Him, and willingly accept whatever He sends. You know we all shall die – there's no escape: at the hour of God's choosing we all must go to that place of no return. And lady, I have news for you that I shan't keep hidden: your lord, that worthy man so wise and loved by knights and men of the church alike, is dead. Now, lady, pray for his soul, and may God give you strength and courage.'

On hearing that her lord was dead and buried, the lady collapsed in a swoon. But the abbot was quick to help her up and gave her words of consolation – hard though they were for her to take.

It was now that the knights he'd left behind arrived; and thereupon the mourning began anew as they, too, collapsed in grief – and when they recovered their senses they all lamented for their lord as if he'd died that very day. But the lady's grief was most intense of all, you may be sure: she was overcome, swooning and raving and crying:

'Alas, why do I live, poor wretch that I am, having lost my good lord who brought me so much honour?'

On and on she cried, and tore her hair and beat her breast and cursed the day she was ever conceived and born and raised to suffer such mortal woe. Ah, the howling and the wailing you'd have heard: even the most hard-hearted man would have been distressed at the sight. The hall was beset by grief and sorrow; joy was well and truly banished. The abbot had no wish to stay; he had his palfrey readied and then took his leave of the lady and commended the knights to God, but not before he'd offered words and prayers that stilled their grief.

The very next morning the lady had more than a hundred masses sung in all the churches to packed congregations of knights and ladies and townsfolk, shocked, distraught and downcast at the loss of their lord. And thus the lady long remained; but she found comfort in the lovely son she'd borne, devoting all her thoughts to him – though grieving still for her lord.

But that's the last I'll say of him – his story's done; from now on I'll tell of the lady and her child, and what befell her and how she fared.

Fully seven months had passed, I think, since the lady learned the truth of her husband's death. She stayed where she was till April came, caring for her son who was a source of great comfort.

And all the while she kept thinking how to keep him from ever being a knight or learning to bear arms – or even hearing of knights' existence! For he was her only solace, and if he were killed in combat like his uncles and his father, then she, his mother, would die of grief that instant – she wouldn't live another day. If she could so arrange it, she thought, she'd like to go and live in the Waste Forest – yes, she'd do that very thing, and soon! None of her men must know till her son was bigger and had grown in wit and understanding – in the meantime he must see no one except those she chose to take. That way, she thought, she could keep him safe and would have nothing to fear for the rest of her days.

She sent for a serving-man of hers, a steward she especially loved for his quick wit and resourcefulness; he had twelve children by his wife – eight sons and four fair and charming daughters, intelligent and sharp. The messenger sent by the lady went to this steward's house and found him at the bedside of one of his children; he told him to come quickly and not to dally – his lady had summoned him and wanted nothing to detain him. The steward set off at once, without delay, and he and the messenger went together to the lady's chamber. When she saw him she greeted him warmly with:

'Welcome, steward.'

And he was hardly mute; he answered: 'May almighty God watch over you, and grant you happiness and health. You sent for me, my lady: what is your wish?'

She took him by the hand and led him to another room and seated him beside her on a couch. With a troubled heart she said to him:

'In God's name, steward, my dear, kind sir, I pray you have pity on me and my son. You're a worthy knight and have been loyal to me, so I shall confide in you: I mean to leave this land and keep my son from being killed. I shall go into the Waste Forest and keep him there as long as God pleases. If you'd come with me you'd have my deepest gratitude and I'd never forsake you; bring your wife with you for the love of God and your soul's sake – and bring all your household, too: I'll be all the happier.'

So pressing and persuasive were her pleas that he willingly agreed to go wherever she wished – he realised he couldn't stay behind. Then he said: 'Lady, you'll have to be very careful: if people get wind of this they'll never let you go. Listen: summon your men and tell them you want to take your son on a pilgrimage to Saint Brendan in Scotland; ask them to behave responsibly while you're gone, and bid them vow to guard the land in your son's name, for you wish them all to acknowledge him as their lord and give him their protection. Take my advice and do this: issue this command to all.'

The lady gladly agreed to do exactly as he said. With that their discussion ended and they left the room.

She had no reason to delay: she sent messengers, all at once, to seek out and summon all the knights of her land, all the ladies, servants, townsfolk, everyone who owed her allegiance. By the fourth day they'd arrived, and when they were all assembled the lady addressed them, saying, with courteous and well-chosen words:

'Sirs, I've summoned you all to gather here and you don't know why. But now I shall tell you, truly: a long while ago I made a vow to take this son of mine to Saint Brendan in Scotland, to pray that God will give him power and strength and keep him safe and well. I mean to leave tomorrow, and wish to have your guidance and approval. I'll be leaving in the morning early, taking my steward with me; and because I wish no trouble or strife to strike my land, I want you all to swear to guard it for my son's sake, so that it may be his if he safely returns. Now you know my wishes: give me your response.'

The knights were all dismayed by this; they'd no wish at all to see her and her son go, and said: 'In God's name, lady, stay with us for this summer – or leave our young lord at least: if you were both to die together we'd be lost!'

She gently answered: 'It's no use pleading, believe me: I'm taking him with me, and I'll protect him as the beloved son he is.'

So they gave her leave; but:

'Who'll go with you?'

'I will! And I!'

So cried knights and serving-men alike, all dreadfully upset at the thought of her going and taking her son with her. But the lady had a nephew, a fine knight, wise and valiant, and she made all the barons present give him their word that they'd defend the land and obey his command until such time as God granted that she and her son should return: this she bade them all swear. When they'd given their pledges the knights retired to their lodgings to rest.

A full month earlier, the lady had taken her great store of gold and silver and sent it from the land; and servants had readied more than a hundred carts and wagons and loaded them with grain – oats and wheat – and sent them on their way with a train of horses and livestock: oxen, cows and sheep. But according to my source no man, truly, had any clue that she was leaving for good. And now she would brook no more delay, and left next morning at the break of day with her son and her steward, who brought all his household with him, much to the lady's delight. Those close to her saw her on her way; they grieved terribly at her parting, but she insisted they return.

The lady made her way straight to a castle overlooking the Welsh sea, a fine and pleasant place called Calfle by the folk thereabouts. There she gathered all the people who were to come with her; and then she hardly paused before pressing on with her baggage train – as rich as any king's or count's – and all her company. They didn't stop for a single day till they reached the forest; then they journeyed for at least a fortnight without seeing a town or even a house – nothing at all but forest. It was hard going indeed, on and on through the endless, desolate forest, till they reached an open glade dotted with leafy trees; it seemed to stretch for many leagues, and beyond it lay fair meadowland and a great river running from the woods – a lovely river, flowing with the force to drive a mill. The lady dismounted here at once, along with all her people, and they made camp there till morning when they rose. Then the lady called her steward and asked him if it was a good place to stay and keep her son in safety, and he replied:

'Truly, lady, there's no town or village or house within a hundred leagues of here – not a man or woman, it seems to me! This would make a splendid refuge. Let's have a house built here and make it our home: my sons will build it well, and there's plenty of timber in the forest here.'

'Do just as you wish,' the lady said, 'and I'll be happy!'

So the steward went straight to his sons and told them: 'Let's not dally, sirs – start clearing the ground and cutting timber: you're going to build a house and we shall live here: such is my lady's wish.'

They obeyed without demur. They set off into the woods at once, and worked so hard that within a fortnight they'd built a house enclosed by a palisade, ample and fit to accommodate the lady and all her household. And the servants prepared and tilled the ground, ploughing it and sowing it well with grain.

There they stayed for a long while, the lady watching over her son. And in time he learned to ride and became adept at throwing javelins, skilfully made by the steward's sons. For fourteen years the lady dwelt in the forest, and no man of woman born knew where; her people sent parties to search for her over land and sea but they could find no news of her at all, till they gave up looking, convinced that she and all her household had been lost at sea and drowned.

Meanwhile the lady gave her son to understand that in the whole wide world there was no other house – or man or woman – but there where they were in the forest; and he, simple lad that he was, believed it. She sat him down beside her on a bed and smothered him with kisses, calling him "dear son and lord" and saying:

'Go into the forest, my son, and kill stags and hinds as much as you like; but one thing I forbid you: if you ever see men who look as if they're clad in iron, don't go near them – they're evil, winged demons who'll devour you instantly! Stay well away – come home at once – and be sure to cross yourself. Trust me – this is sound advice. And say your creed as well, dear son, I beg you in God's name; then you'll have nothing to fear.'

'I certainly will, mother,' said the boy. 'If I ever see such men I'll gallop home, God willing – if I can escape!'

With that he stood and left.

The night passed and next morning he rose and quickly dressed, and saddled his horse as fast as he could and mounted. Then into the forest he rode, his three javelins in his hand, and all day long without a pause he searched the woods and the open fields but found no game at all. He said that next day he'd go hunting further afield than usual. With that he rode home and quickly dismounted. His mother came to meet him and kissed him a hundred times and more, and lovingly pressed him to say where he'd been and what he'd found; and he told her the simple truth:

'I've been in the forest, mother; I enjoyed it a lot, I can tell you – it was fun!'

For the moment that was that: his mother pressed him no further and the boy said nothing more.

Appendix 3

Independent conclusion to the Second Continuation in the Bern manuscript (Burgerbibliothek 113)

(*Above, p. 337*) *… and carried it away. Perceval felt greatly cheered.* Mightily pleased and much encouraged, he asked about the lance. The king said:

'I'll tell you, and without a word of a lie. Truly, it is the lance with which the son of God suffered torment when He was stretched upon the cross. With it He was struck in the side, bringing blood pouring down; Longinus washed his eyes with it and recovered his sight.'[1]

Then the worthy, loyal Perceval said he wanted to know for certain who was served from the grail and what it could be. At this the king leapt up, entirely healed and free of all pain, and said:

'Listen now, friend: tell me your name – don't keep it from me – I want to hear it.'

'As you wish,' he replied. 'I am called Perceval, truly. I was born at Sinadon, and my father's name was Alain li Gros.'

'Ah, Perceval, you are dear to me[2] indeed! Alain li Gros was my son! His mother's name was Enigeus, and her brother was Joseph,[3] to whom Jesus Christ was given when He was taken from the cross: Pilate granted Joseph the body as a reward for his service, and Nicodemus took Him from the cross and delivered Him to Joseph. His wounds continued to bleed, and Joseph placed the grail in position, and the wounds shed their blood into the vessel, truly. In the same vessel Jesus made the sacrament on Maundy Thursday.

'And now, dear grandson, before you learn more, it is only right that you should bear a crown of gold upon your head and be king, for I shall not live for more than three more days. Such is the will of the Creator.'

Then he went and fetched his glorious crown and vestments and carried them to his beauteous chapel. There he blessed and anointed Perceval and bestowed his crown upon him. Perceval was named and crowned king of three realms before the Fisher King died and was buried on the fourth day. And three thousand knights were present at the burial: such was the will of God.

---

1 This is a reference to the medieval tradition that Longinus, the centurion who pierced Christ in the side with his lance, had been blind.
2 Literally 'you are my friend'.
3 i.e. Joseph of Arimathea.

Glossary

Argent	Silver in heraldry.
Baudequin	One of a number of varieties of fine silk.
Bend	A common heraldic feature, a 'bend' is a diagonal stripe, usually broad enough to cover about a third of the shield.
Bezant	A coin originally minted at Byzantium.
Bliaut	A close-fitting garment, usually laced, with long skirts and sleeves.
Brattice	A *bretèche* or brattice was a battlemented projection from a tower or gatehouse.
Camelin	A garment made from goat's wool and silk.
Champron	The champron (*chanfrain*) was the armour protecting a horse's head in combat.
Chausses	Chain mail leggings.
Compline	Night prayer, the final office of the day.
Constable	The constable ('*connestable*') was an important member of a medieval household, effectively a 'security officer', organising protection and maintaining order.
Cottice	In heraldry, cottices are narrow stripes defining and running parallel to a shield's main device.
Destrier	The finest of all warhorses, very costly and by no means common.
Electuary	The medieval equivalent of a 'digestif', taken after a meal.
Gage	Usually an object of value deposited as a pledge; sometimes simply an oath.
Gambeson	The padded tunic worn under mail.
Gisarme	A pole weapon similar to a halberd, combining a hook with a point or axe-blade.
Gules	'*Gueules*' were pieces of skin cut from the throats of certain animals and used to decorate shields. The word 'gules' later came to mean the colour red in heraldry.
Haqueton	A quilted jacket like the *gambeson*.
Hauberk	A shirt or coat of mail, sleeved and usually reaching at least the middle of the thigh.
Mareschal	The servant in charge of the care and feeding of horses in a noble household.
Mark	250 grams of silver; in England a mark was worth 160 silver pennies.
Niello	A black alloy used as an inlay on engraved metals, especially silver or gold.
None	The ninth canonical hour, in modern terms about three in the afternoon.

Orfrey	Rich, elaborate embroidery, often incorporating cloth of gold.
Prime	The first canonical hour of the day, in modern terms about six in the morning.
Purple	*'Porpre'* (purple) was a fine dyed fabric, usually but not always of the deep colour that has taken its name.
Rouncey	The rouncey (*'roncin'*) was a tough, multi-purpose horse, lacking the *cachet* of the finest warhorse (the *'destrier'*), and costing only a fraction as much, but still a fine mount, used in combat by squires or less wealthy knights.
Scarlet	Scarlet was a fine and costly woollen cloth; it was produced in various colours (at more than one point in the text it is described as peacock blue) but most often in red.
Seneschal	In a medieval household the seneschal was an important officer, overseeing the administration of the servants.
Sinople	Although in later heraldry this word came to mean green, 'sinople' was originally a blood or brownish red, the word deriving from the red-ochre clay found around the Black Sea city of Sinope.
Terce	The third canonical hour of the day, in modern terms about nine in the morning.
Vair	Grey and white squirrel fur.
Vavasor	'Vavasor is sometimes thought to mean the vassal of a vassal … [but] it does not seem… that its original meaning had anything to do with a position in a "hierarchy of tenure"… Vavasor may generally have denoted something more like a social status: a vavasor seems normally to have been part of noble, military society, though near the lower end of it. The status seems to have varied from place to place and time to time…' Susan Reynolds, *Fiefs and Vassals* (Oxford, 1994), p. 23.
Ventail	The section of mail, attaching to the hood, that protected the mouth and neck.
Vespers	The 'vespers' were usually the hastiludes (a generic term for all martial games involving lances) that took place on the evening before a tournament. They were often considered to be a non-serious trial for the following day, but there is evidence that they could easily become a tournament proper. This, Juliet Barker observes, is reflected in Wolfram von Eschenbach's *Parzival*, where 'the vespers began in the morning of the day before the tournament and involved all those who were going to participate then. During the skirmishing tempers were lost and the vespers became a full-scale combat …[and] the tournament for the next day was called off because too many knights had been captured and the rest were too exhausted to fight again.' Juliet Barker, *The Tournament in England, 1100–1400* (Woodbridge, 1986), pp. 140–1.
Zedoary	A spice, related to turmeric and with a gingery flavour, used as an aid to digestion.

Index

If a character or place features frequently, references are given for the first appearance and most important subsequent episodes

Abel, *son of Adam and Eve* 485
Abraham *(Biblical)* 26
Abrioris de Brune Mons, *knight defeated by Perceval* 251–2
Absalom, *Biblical son of David* 42
Acre 261
Adam, *Biblical first man* 408, 409, 477, 481
Aeneas 77
Agloval, *Perceval's brother* 482, 547, 551, 555
Agravain, *Gawain's brother* 42, 69, 146, 208, 267, 294, 296, 311, 347–8, 369, 373, 375, 471, 509, 511–2, 535
Aguisial, *king of Scotland* 294, 307
Alain li Gros 569
Alardin of the Lake, *knight in love with Guinier* 139–55, 173–4
Aleppo 108, 368
Alexander, *the Great, king of Macedon* 1, 142, 272
Aligrés, *knight defeated by Perceval* 403
Amorous Ford 256–7
Anjou 164, 170
Antioch 256, 261, 494, 508
Apulia 485
Arabia 184
Ardoire, Black Forest of 282
Arés, *father of Tors* 121, 123, 149, 164, 179, 202, 227, 294, 471
Arguisel of Scotland, *father of Felisse* 460
Arguisial of Carhais, *knight aided by Perceval* 399
Aridés of Escavalon, *attacker of Blancheflor* 520, 525–9, 531
Arras 421

Arthur, *king of Britain* 4, 5, 8–12, 25, 36, 38, 40, 41, 78–83, 92–4, 118–26, 131–4, 154–5, 158–9, 161–4, 170–2, 174–211, 223–7, 232, 240, 295–7, 307–10, 318–20, 327–8, 349–52, 365–8, 377–8, 509–10, 530–1, 535–6, 553–5
Asturias 413
Ateine, *forest* 102
Aude, *beloved of Roland* 436
Audigier 374
Austria, duke of 424, 527
Autandre, *Arthur's niece, wife of Dinadaret* 120
Avalon 119, 281

Baghdad 433
Ban, *king of Gomorret* 5
Barletta 426
Baudemagus, *king* 543–4
Beaurepaire, *castle of Blancheflor* 16–25, 260–1, 388, 393, 527–9
Beauvais 263
Bed of Marvels 67, 70, 74, 76
Bedivere, *knight (and constable) of Arthur's court* 121, 146, 267, 294, 471
Beduier, Count, *supporter of King Marc* 370
Beelzebub 458
Beirut 27
Beneoiz (or *Boënet*), *drinking horn* 175
Berwick, *archbishop of* 365
Biau Desconneü: see Fair Unknown
Biau Mauvés: see Fair Bad Knight
Black Chapel 322, 325
Black Knight of Valdoire 282

Blancheflor, *sweetheart and later wife of Perceval* 17–26, 261–5, 389–94, 527–9
Blanche Lande, *site of tournament* 318
Blanchemal, *fairy* 391
Blandigan, Count 205
Blaye 436
Bleheris, *knight* 146
Bliobleris, *knight* 369
Bloiesine, *daughter of Urpin* 449
Boënet see Beneoiz
Bofois see Rumpus
Bold Ugly Knight, the 150, 151, 180, 252, 311, 371
Bonivant / Bonivent (Benevento?), 214
Boort, *brother of Lionel* 535–42, 553
Bralles, *king of* 315
Bran de Lis, *knight* 128–30, 148, 150–3, 190–1, 193–202, 204, 206, 210, 311, 450
Brandeval, *king* 222
Brandigan, *king* 241, 303
Brandin Hard-heart, *knight defeated by Perceval* 458
Brangemore of Cornwall, *queen, mother of Pinogrés* 480, 516
Brangemuer, *king* 233, 234
Brangepart, *queen* 234, 389
Branlant, *city* 121, 122, 130
Brengien, *Yseut's companion* 368, 372, 377
Bridas, *king* 370, 372
Brien of the Isles, *knight* 294, 296, 297, 306, 311
Brindisi 426
Briol of the Burnt Forest, *vavasor and host of Perceval* 289–91, 293–5, 297–8
Brittany 137, 155, 158, 159, 164, 170, 172, 178, 432
Brun de Branlant 120–2, 125, 130
Brun de Rumiaus 311
Brun of the Glade 324
Brun the Pitiless 286, 370, 373
Burgundy 164

Cadoalan, *king of Ireland* 143–54
Cador, *knight of Cornwall* 121, 138–71
Cadrus, *knight* 369
Caesarea 157, 261

Cahadis, *knight and supporter of Carados* 145, 151
Cain, *son of Adam and Eve* 485
Cairo 261
Calabria 414
Calogrenant, *knight of King Arthur* 471, 482, 540–2, 553
Camandans, *king of Norgoise* 121
Camelot, *residence of King Arthur* 482, 535–6
Canguin, Rock of, *castle* 75
Canterbury 260
Canterbury, *archbishop of* 134
Caradoc, *king of Verne, father of Carados* 121, 131–2, 136, 137, 154–5, 159, 161–2, 170–1
Carados (nicknamed Shortarm) 121, 132–75, 177, 181, 311, 369, 450
Carahés, *'on the border between Wales and England'* 178
Cardiff, bishop of 393
Cardigan, bishop of 393
Cardigan, *residence of King Arthur* 164, 259, 267, 306–7, 327, 377
Cardoil, *city, a residence of King Arthur* 4, 8, 132–4, 136, 148, 250, 259, 398, 504, 511, 552
Cardoil, bishop of 393
Carimedic, *knight of the unfinished bridge* 293
Carlion, *city, a residence of King Arthur* 35, 37, 41, 111, 138, 142, 143, 173, 175, 223, 231–3, 239, 252, 305, 332, 348, 350, 365
Carlion, (arch)bishop of 87, 365, 393
Carras, *King, lord of Recesse* 326–8
Carthage 274
Castle of the Elms 210
Castle of the Great Forest 316
Castle of the Horn 240
Castle of the Maidens 277, 363, 409, 489
Castle of Marvels 82
Charles Martel, *Charlemagne's grandfather* 134
Chastiaux de l'Angarde see Look-out Castle
Chevrefoil 371
Chrétien de Troyes 1, 394

INDEX 575

Circle of Gold, Maiden of the   411, 416, 419, 420
Circle of Gold, youth of the   311, 331
Cîteaux   260
Claire, *damsel leading Perceval to Dragon Knight*   413
Clairvaux   260
Clamadeus, *besieger of Beaurepaire*   19, 21–6, 261, 262, 388
Claradeure, *wood of*   420, 449
Claradus, *knight of King Marc*   370, 372
Clarinon, *knight defeated by Gawain*   102
Clarissant, *Gawain's sister*   70, 83–4, 87, 92–4, 144
Claudas, *King, lord of the Desert*   315, 327–8, 370
Cligés, *knight*   146, 149–50, 369, 375
Constantinople   134, 215, 273, 342, 344, 496
Corbenic, *castle of the Grail*   554
Cornwall   138, 139, 155, 158, 159, 164, 167, 308, 324, 355, 466, 512
Cothoatre, *castle of Trebuchet the smith*   32, 344
Coucy, *castle*   413
Coward Knight   531–4, 542–5, 554
Criseuz the Fair   280
Crudel, *king*   422

Denmark   178, 489
Dinadaret, *knight, adversary of Gawain*   117–20
Dinolsoldre, *eldest son of Salandre of the Isles*   553
Disnadaret, *Cornish knight*   370, 372
Disnadaron, *in Wales, a residence of Arthur*   24–5
Dobliers, *castle*   208
Dodinel the Wild, *knight rescued by Gawain*   311, 499–500, 523–5, 535
Dragonel the Cruel, *knight defeated by Perceval*   396–9
Dröés d'Avés, *knight*   43
Dublin (Duveline)   470
Dyonise, *treacherous girl*   457–9

Ebrox, *king of Gomeroit*   121
Ector, *brother of Lancelot*   546–7, 553
Egypt   513
Eliavret, *enchanter*   131–2, 154–6, 167
Elie, *lady of Leander's court*   430
Elis of the Ill-cut Coat, *knight*   294, 311
Enariste, *son of Salandre of the Isles*   553
England   132–3, 136, 138, 142, 155, 157, 164, 170, 171, 172, 218, 289
Engygeron, *seneschal to Clamadeus*   19–21, 24–5, 261, 263
Enide, *wife of Erec*   351
Enigeus, *mother of Alain li Gros*   569
Erec, *knight of Arthur*   294, 311, 350, 351, 369
Escalibor, *Arthur's sword*   51, 206, 207
Escanor, *knight defeated by Tristran*   370, 373
Escavalon, *city and kingdom*   5, 42, 46, 115, 117, 119–21, 178, 306, 325, 327, 328
Esclador, *father of the Maiden of the Circle of Gold*   372, 411
Escolasse, *lady of the castle of Cothoatre*   342–6
Espinogre, *knight*   311
Estregales, *king of*   144, 147
Evalac, *pagan king baptised as Mordrain*   421–2
Evander, *son of the Red Knight*   425, 430, 435
Eve, *Biblical first woman*   453, 477, 481

Fair Bad Knight, the   266–8, 311
Fair Bold Knight, the   545
Fair Coward, the   151
Fair Good Knight, the   146, 148
Fair Unknown, the   258–60, 326
Faradien, *knight defeated by Perceval*   357–8, 365
Fécamp   330
Felisse of the White Close, *accomplice of robber knights*   460–2
Fisher King   27–30, 31, 41, 55–6, 219, 286, 335–9, 474–81, 549–51, 554, 555
Forré, *heathen king*   374
Fortune   41, 131
France   120, 157, 164

576 INDEX

Frisia   263, 270, 389
Frolac, *king*   344

Gaheriët, *brother of Gawain*   69, 259, 267, 294, 311, 471, 491, 509, 535, 536, 543-4, 553
Galegantin the Welshman, *knight of Arthur*   509
Galehés de Bonivant, *vavasor, host of Gawain*   110-3, 116
Gales the Bald, *named as Perceval's father*   363
Galles the Bald, *knight of Arthur*   151
Galvoie   57, 71, 74, 79, 82, 85, 178
Gandon, *king of Veline*   121
Ganelon, *traitor in 'The Song of Roland'*—431
Garin, *Gawain's host at Tintagel*   46
Garsallas, *knight defeated by Perceval*   280
Gascony   84
Gaudin of the White Shield, *vavasor, host of Perceval*   348
Gaviën, *abductor of Dodinel's sweetheart*   531
Gawain, nephew of King Arthur: *major figure throughout; to locate specific episodes, see table of Contents.*
Geneloie, duke of   280
Gerbert, *author*   394-5
Germany   84, 164, 352, 468
Gernemue, *island*   391
Ginglain, *Gawain's son*   326-7
Girflet, *knight of Arthur's court*   26, 41, 80, 81, 88, 123, 147, 148, 151, 179-80, 199-200, 208-11, 331, 366, 450
Girl of the Little Sleeves, *daughter of Tibaut of Tintagel*   44
Glade of the Crossroads   210-11
Glade of Marvels   95-6
Gladoain, *knight of Arthur*   311
Gloucester   331
Gollain the Bald, *knight of King Arthur*   472
Goondesert, *brother of the Fisher King*   478-9, 551, 555
Gordane, *river*   413

Gorgaris, *abductor of the lady of Malehaut*   505-6
Gorgone, *son of Salandre of the Isles*   553
Gorneman de Gorhaut, *Perceval's instructor*   13-16, 18, 29, 378-94
Gorvain, *knight*   369, 375
Gosoain, *knight*   180
Greece   134, 391
Greoreas, *knight*   61, 104-5
Gringalet, *Gawain's horse*   54, 61, 95, 96, 107, 126, 186, 311, 322, 367, 437, 440, 442, 447, 450
Guerrehés, *Gawain's brother*   69, 121, 224, 225, 227-34, 267, 296, 311, 471, 536
Guigambresil, *knight, enemy of Gawain*   42, 52-4, 118-20, 147
Guinaloc, *a hound*   156
Guinevere, *Arthur's queen*   94, 134, 176, 211-4
Guingenor, *great-niece of Arthur, daughter of Clarissant*   144, 145, 146
Guiniacalc, *father of Alardin*   173
Guinier, *wife of Carados*   121, 138-42, 148-51, 154-77
Guiolete, *mother of Gawain's son*   211
Guiromelant, *knight, enemy of Gawain*   73-7, 88-94, 121, 144
Guiron, the lay of   387

Haughty Maiden (of Nogres)   58-63, 72-3, 76
Hector (of Troy)   197
Helen (of Troy)   197
Heracle, *hermit*   420
Herman, *son of Garin*   46
Hermit King   407-10
Hudens, *dog*   191
Humber, *river*   260
Hungary   152

Idier, *son of Nu, knight of Arthur*   144, 146, 151, 180, 224, 315, 318-20, 351, 370, 373, 471, 509
India   15, 278
Ireland   81, 121, 164, 178, 212, 238, 278, 546

Jeanne, countess of Flanders 556
Jerusalem 394, 421
Jesus 6, 54, 218, 380, 393, 397, 406, 415, 422, 477, 521, 569
Jolies of Tintagel, *knight* 370, 373
Joseph of Arimathea 115, 217, 421, 478, 569
Judas (Iscariot) 422
Judas Maccabeus 115, 335

Kahendin, *knight of Arthur* 41
Kay, *King Arthur's seneschal* 10, 12, 25–6, 36–40, 80–1, 84, 86, 94, 118–9, 121, 124, 126, 131, 134–5, 144, 146, 148–51, 175–6, 178, 180–3, 185, 191–2, 201–2, 209–10, 211–3, 232, 252, 267–8, 294–5, 305–11, 318–20, 349–51, 373–5, 472, 496, 502, 504, 508–11, 530, 535–6, 553
King of One Hundred Knights (later named as Margon) 369–71, 506, 509, 543
Knight of the Dragon 410–9

Lactor, *son of Salandre of the Isles* 553
Lancelot of the Lake 121, 252, 294, 296, 311–2, 315, 331, 350, 366, 369, 375, 377, 450, 471, 491, 535–6, 547, 553
Lancïen, *residence of King Marc* 368, 369
Lavinia, *wife of Aeneas* 77
Leander, *son of the Red Knight* 425, 427–37
Licorés of Baraguidan, *knight* 292
Licorrés of Cardigan, *knight of Arthur* 311
Limoges, *French city* 27. 107, 249, 314, 315
Lionel, *brother of Boort* 536–44, 553
Little Knight (1), 228–30
Little Knight (2), 314–21
Logres, *kingdom* 53, 120, 178, 217, 219
Loire, *French river* 13
Lombards, Lombardy 52, 267, 308, 374, 389
London 255, 260, 302
Longinus 397, 477, 479, 569
Look-out Castle 123

Lord of the Horn 238–40
Lore de Branlant, *girl besieged at Branlant* 124, 131
Lores, *lady to Arthur's queen* 78
Loriagort, *a destrier* 156
Lost of Loënois, *king* 121
Lot, *king of Orkney, father of Gawain* 121
Lucan the Butler 144, 147, 149–51, 180, 198–200, 208–9, 267, 294, 311, 471
Lucca 218
Lugarel the Jealous, *knight defeated by Perceval* 454–7

Maboagran, *nephew of King Urien* 180
Macarot of Pantelion, *knight defeated by Gawain* 96–8, 100–2
Madoc, *king of* 121
Madoc, *knight of Arthur* 147, 148
Maiden of the Ivory Horn 94–8
Maine 164
Malehaut, lady of, *sister of the King of One Hundred Knights* 505–6
Manessier, *author* 556
Maragon, *brother of the Dragon Knight* 410
Marc, *king of Cornwall* 367–77
Margon, *the King of One Hundred Knights* 501–7
Marguïs of Ireland 121
Marmadus, *son of the Red Knight* 425, 433, 435
Maronne, *king of* 555
Marsonde, *river* 287
Mecca 261
Meliadas, *son of the Red Knight* 425, 433, 435
Meliant de Lis, *knight* 42–8, 128n, 189, 190, 193
Melioirant, count of 181
Menadoc, *king* 121
Menandre de la Loje, *knight defeated by Perceval* 530
Meraugis, *knight* 369, 373
Merlin 331–2, 346, 453
Moadas, *knight of King Marc* 370, 372
Mombranlant, *forest* 327
Monastide, *son of Salandre of the Isles* 553

Monendas, *knight* 294, 297
Mont Saint Michel 161
Montesclaire, *mountain and castle* 41, 100, 107, 111–6, 377–8, 411–3, 420, 436–7, 449
Morcadés, *queen* 83, 307
Mordrain, *baptismal name of Evalac* 442–3
Mordred, *Arthur's nephew* 267, 319
Morgan the Fay 302–3
Morholt, *defeated by Tristran* 367, 374
Morin, *Sagremor's horse* 487, 488, 491, 535
Mount Dolorous 41, 239, 299, 305, 306, 308, 310, 311, 322, 327–32, 346

Nantes 132, 137, 138, 154, 155, 159, 161, 162, 163, 166, 170, 171
Nicodemus 218, 478, 569
Nijmegen 426
Norhorbelande, *castle* 531
Normandy 120, 135, 142, 158, 164, 170, 184
Norroiz de Lis, *father of maiden seduced by Gawain* 128

Odinial the Fair, *knight* 253
Oise, *river* 387
Oliver, *Roland's companion* 431
Orgueilleus de la Lande: see Proud Knight of the Glade
Orgueilleuse de Nogres: see Haughty Maiden
Orgueilleus del Passage a l'Estroite Voie: see Proud Knight of the Narrow Pass
Orqueneseles, *city of Guiromelant* 73
Orquenie, *city, a residence of King Arthur* 75, 77, 78
Otranto 258, 390
Oustreport, *port in Normandy* 158

Pancrist, *fortress built by Arthur* 123, 130
Paris, *abductor of Helen* 197
Paris, *city* 207, 418
Parsaman, *knight defeated by Perceval* 403–4

Partinal, *killer of the Fisher King's brother* 479, 547–9, 554
Patriz of the Mountain, *attacker of Agravain* 512
Pavia 58, 321
Pensive Knight 321–5
Perceval: *major figure throughout; to locate specific episodes, see table of Contents.*
Perilous Ford 72–3, 89
Philip, count of Flanders 1, 52n, 556n
Philosofine, *name of Perceval's mother* 364, 422
Pilate 218, 422, 569
Pinogrés, *king, uncle of Partinal* 479–80
Poitiers, count of 313
Poitou 164, 170, 290
Proud Castle 41, 179, 180, 197–211, 289–97
Proud Knight of the Glade 34–6
Proud Knight of the Narrow Pass (Proud Knight of Rogal) 74, 79
Pucele as Mances Petites: see Girl of the Little Sleeves

Quagrilo, *son of King Margon* 502–3
Quinable, count 82, 121, 308, 311, 471
Quineli, *city* 130–1
Quingragan, *castle of Goondesert* 479
Quinqueroi, *forest, home of the Red Knight* 9, 36
Quirier, *King Yder's nephew* 178

Red Knight (of the Forest of Quinqueroi), *enemy of Arthur, killed by Perceval* 9–10, 247, 427n, 431
Red Tower, *castle of Partinal* 479, 547n, 548
Rhône, *river* 468
Rich Soldier, the 144, 146, 148, 204–10
Rion, *'king of the Isles', defeated by Arthur* 9
Ris, *king of Valen* 143–54
Rohais, *beloved of Arguisial* 399
Roland 89n, 431, 436n
Roncevaux 348
Roseamonde de Nobles Vals, *sweetheart of Semiramin* 405

Rosete, *beloved of the Fair Bad Knight* 267
Round Table 69, 82, 130, 144, 177, 178, 196, 200, 226, 253, 307, 358
Rumpus, the (*Bofois*), *tower where Yverne is imprisoned* 155, 166, 170

Sagremor, *knight of Arthur* 37–8, 121, 145, 146, 149, 180, 267, 294, 296, 311, 331, 347–8, 369, 375, 450, 471, 481–95, 534–6
Saint Aaron 393
Saint Acaire 437
Saint Amand 397, 404
Saint Andrew's 393
Saint Augustine 434
Saint Baudri 440
Saint Brandain 436n
Saint Catherine 82
Saint Cosmas 84, 410, 411n
Saint David 376, 419, 433, 437
Saint Denis 103, 201
Saint Damian ('Domin'), 411
Saint Gabriel 553
Saint Germain 85, 180, 429
Saint Gervais 431
Saint Giles of Provence 264, 291
Saint James 374
Saint John (and feast of) 135, 200, 306, 307, 432, 456, 555
Saint Julian 15n, 98, 295, 466
Saint Ladre 117
Saint Lazarus of Avalon 469
Saint Leger 351
Saint Livinus 407, 460
Saint Luke 96, 98
Saint Marcel 100
Saint Martin 63, 106, 201, 282, 429, 509, 527, 551
Saint Michael 553
Saint Nicholas 443, 446, 468
Saint Organe 445
Saint Paul 1, 97, 139, 355, 396, 480
Saint Peter 20, 38, 168, 304, 332, 397, 410, 449, 452, 456, 482, 485, 510, 516, 517, 521, 531, 541, 545, 548, 551
Saint Pol de Léon (bishop of) 393
Saint Remy 429
Saint Richier 18
Saint Simon 301
Saint Sylvestre 374
Saint Thomas 183, 186, 246
Salandre of the Isles, *knight defeated with his five sons by Perceval* 553
Salisbury 554, 556
Samaria 261
Sartuz de la Loje, *lord of the castle of Lindesore* 521
Satan 64
Saxony 164
Scotland 414, 546, 566
Seine, *river* 387
Semiramin, *knight rescued by Perceval* 405
Seraphé, *brother-in-law of Joseph of Arimathea* 422
Silimac, *knight killed at the queen's pavilion* 211–3 (while unnamed) 507, 508
Sinadon, *birthplace of Perceval* 569
Slavonia 261
Solomon 87
Sore Pucele: see Golden-haired Maiden
Southampton 132n
Spain 164
Spring of the Laurel 111
Sword of the Strange Belt 41, 100, 111, 114–5
Syria 421, 470

Tallidés, *besieger of the Castle of the Maidens* 489–93
Tanete la Petite, *Arthur's niece, wife of Guigambresil* 120
Taules de Rougemont, *knight* 181, 183, 252, 294, 311
Thames, *river* 303
Thessaly 251, 326, 342
Thiérache 164
Tholomé, *king of Syria* 421–2
Tibaut of Tintagel 43–4
Tinpincarantin, *residence of King Arthur* 283, 292
Tintagel, *city in Cornwall* 43, 231
Titus, *Roman emperor* 478

Tors, *son of Arés* 121, 123, 149, 164, 179, 180, 202, 227, 294, 471
Tortain, *a boar* 156
Touraine 164
Trebuchet ('*Tribüet*'), *smith* 33, 345–6, 526–7, 528
Tristran, *nephew of King Marc of Cornwall* 367–78
Troy 197

Urien, *king* 69, 121, 180, 211
Urpin of the Angry Mountain, *father of Bloiesine, defeated by Gawain* 442–9
Uther Pendragon, *king, father of Arthur* 5, 74, 85, 331–2, 411

Valbone, *the passes of, near Perceval's home* 4, 359
Venice 88
Verne, *Caradoc's kingdom* 131, 136, 161, 171
Vespasian, *Roman emperor* 478

Wales 25, 133, 164, 178, 261, 289, 301, 306, 313, 332, 466, 482, 489, 550, 555
Waste Forest, *home of Perceval's mother* 2, 5, 26, 268, 549, 550, 566
Wauchier de Denain, *author* 328n
White Close (*Blanclose*), *castle of Felisse* 460
White Forest 121
White Knight 256–7
White Stone, Forest of the 281
William, *Irish king* 365
Winchester 251, 257, 552
Winchester, bishop of 365

Ydain, *cousin of Carados, beloved of Cador* 145, 147, 149, 154, 155
Yder, *king* 88, 121, 146, 180, 201, 210
Ygerne, *Arthur's mother* 74, 83–4, 94
York, *archbishop of* 365
Ysabiaus, *lady of the Castle of the Maidens* 364, 409
Ysave (de Carahés), *Arthur's niece, mother of Carados* 121, 124, 131–2, 136, 153, 154–6, 166
Yseut, *wife of King Marc of Cornwall* 87, 367–9, 371–3
Ysmaine, *Perceval's cousin, married to Faradien* 429
Yvain, *knight of Arthur, son of Urien* 26, 69, 82, 86, 88–9, 119, 121, 124, 133, 134, 135, 143–52, 155, 158, 164, 176–7, 179, 202, 205–6, 209–10, 224, 231, 252, 267, 294, 296, 306, 311–2, 350, 367, 369, 373, 375, 377, 450, 471, 509, 536, 553
Yvain the Bastard, *knight of Arthur, son of Urien* 69, 294, 311
Yvain of the White Hands 294, 311
Yvonet, *squire at Arthur's court* 9–12, 49–50, 87, 90, 450

ARTHURIAN STUDIES

    I ASPECTS OF MALORY, *edited by Toshiyuki Takamiya and Derek Brewer*
   II THE ALLITERATIVE *MORTE ARTHURE*: A Reassessment of the Poem, *edited by Karl Heinz Göller*
  III THE ARTHURIAN BIBLIOGRAPHY, I: Author Listing, *edited by C. E. Pickford and R. W. Last*
  IV THE CHARACTER OF KING ARTHUR IN MEDIEVAL LITERATURE, *Rosemary Morris*
   V PERCEVAL: The Story of the Grail, by Chrétien de Troyes, *translated by Nigel Bryant*
  VI THE ARTHURIAN BIBLIOGRAPHY, II: Subject Index, *edited by C. E. Pickford and R. W. Last*
 VII THE LEGEND OF ARTHUR IN THE MIDDLE AGES, *edited by P. B. Grout, R. A. Lodge, C. E. Pickford and E. K. C. Varty*
VIII THE ROMANCE OF YDER, *edited and translated by Alison Adams*
  IX THE RETURN OF KING ARTHUR, *Beverly Taylor and Elisabeth Brewer*
   X ARTHUR'S KINGDOM OF ADVENTURE: The World of Malory's *Morte Darthur*, *Muriel Whitaker*
  XI KNIGHTHOOD IN THE *MORTE DARTHUR*, *Beverly Kennedy*
 XII LE ROMAN DE TRISTAN EN PROSE, tome I, *edited by Renée L. Curtis*
XIII LE ROMAN DE TRISTAN EN PROSE, tome II, *edited by Renée L. Curtis*
XIV LE ROMAN DE TRISTAN EN PROSE, tome III, *edited by Renée L. Curtis*
 XV LOVE'S MASKS: Identity, Intertextuality, and Meaning in the Old French Tristan Poems, *Merritt R. Blakeslee*
XVI THE CHANGING FACE OF ARTHURIAN ROMANCE: Essays on Arthurian Prose Romances in memory of Cedric E. Pickford, *edited by Alison Adams, Armel H. Diverres, Karen Stern and Kenneth Varty*
XVII REWARDS AND PUNISHMENTS IN THE ARTHURIAN ROMANCES AND LYRIC POETRY OF MEDIEVAL FRANCE: Essays presented to Kenneth Varty on the occasion of his sixtieth birthday, *edited by Peter V. Davies and Angus J. Kennedy*
XVIII CEI AND THE ARTHURIAN LEGEND, *Linda Gowans*
XIX LA3AMON'S *BRUT*: The Poem and its Sources, *Françoise H. M. Le Saux*
 XX READING THE *MORTE DARTHUR*, *Terence McCarthy*, reprinted as AN INTRODUCTION TO MALORY
XXI CAMELOT REGAINED: The Arthurian Revival and Tennyson, 1800–1849, *Roger Simpson*
XXII THE LEGENDS OF KING ARTHUR IN ART, *Muriel Whitaker*
XXIII GOTTFRIED VON STRASSBURG AND THE MEDIEVAL TRISTAN LEGEND: Papers from an Anglo-North American symposium, *edited with an introduction by Adrian Stevens and Roy Wisbey*
XXIV ARTHURIAN POETS: CHARLES WILLIAMS, *edited and introduced by David Llewellyn Dodds*
XXV AN INDEX OF THEMES AND MOTIFS IN TWELFTH-CENTURY FRENCH ARTHURIAN POETRY, *E. H. Ruck*

XXVI CHRÉTIEN DE TROYES AND THE GERMAN MIDDLE AGES: Papers from an international symposium, *edited with an introduction by Martin H. Jones and Roy Wisbey*
XXVII SIR GAWAIN AND THE GREEN KNIGHT: Sources and Analogues, *compiled by Elisabeth Brewer*
XXVIII CLIGÉS by Chrétien de Troyes, *edited by Stewart Gregory and Claude Luttrell*
XXIX THE LIFE AND TIMES OF SIR THOMAS MALORY, *P. J. C. Field*
XXX T. H. WHITE'S *THE ONCE AND FUTURE KING*, *Elisabeth Brewer*
XXXI ARTHURIAN BIBLIOGRAPHY, III: 1978–1992, Author Listing and Subject Index, *compiled by Caroline Palmer*
XXXII ARTHURIAN POETS: JOHN MASEFIELD, *edited and introduced by David Llewellyn Dodds*
XXXIII THE TEXT AND TRADITION OF LA3AMON'S *BRUT*, *edited by Françoise Le Saux*
XXXIV CHIVALRY IN TWELFTH-CENTURY GERMANY: The Works of Hartmann von Aue, *W. H. Jackson*
XXXV THE TWO VERSIONS OF MALORY'S *MORTE DARTHUR*: Multiple Negation and the Editing of the Text, *Ingrid Tieken-Boon van Ostade*
XXXVI RECONSTRUCTING CAMELOT: French Romantic Medievalism and the Arthurian Tradition, *Michael Glencross*
XXXVII A COMPANION TO MALORY, *edited by Elizabeth Archibald and A. S. G. Edwards*
XXXVIII A COMPANION TO THE *GAWAIN*-POET, *edited by Derek Brewer and Jonathan Gibson*
XXXIX MALORY'S BOOK OF ARMS: The Narrative of Combat in *Le Morte Darthur*, *Andrew Lynch*
XL MALORY: TEXTS AND SOURCES, *P. J. C. Field*
XLI KING ARTHUR IN AMERICA, *Alan Lupack and Barbara Tepa Lupack*
XLII THE SOCIAL AND LITERARY CONTEXTS OF MALORY'S *MORTE DARTHUR*, *edited by D. Thomas Hanks Jr*
XLIII THE GENESIS OF NARRATIVE IN MALORY'S *MORTE DARTHUR*, *Elizabeth Edwards*
XLIV GLASTONBURY ABBEY AND THE ARTHURIAN TRADITION, *edited by James P. Carley*
XLV THE KNIGHT WITHOUT THE SWORD: A Social Landscape of Malorian Chivalry, *Hyonjin Kim*
XLVI ULRICH VON ZATZIKHOVEN'S *LANZELET*: Narrative Style and Entertainment, *Nicola McLelland*
XLVII THE MALORY DEBATE: Essays on the Texts of *Le Morte Darthur*, *edited by Bonnie Wheeler, Robert L. Kindrick and Michael N. Salda*
XLVIII MERLIN AND THE GRAIL: *Joseph of Arimathea, Merlin, Perceval*: The Trilogy of Arthurian romances attributed to Robert de Boron, *translated by Nigel Bryant*
XLIX ARTHURIAN BIBLIOGRAPHY IV: 1993–1998, Author Listing and Subject Index, *compiled by Elaine Barber*
L *DIU CRÔNE* AND THE MEDIEVAL ARTHURIAN CYCLE, *Neil Thomas*
LII KING ARTHUR IN MUSIC, *edited by Richard Barber*
LIII THE BOOK OF LANCELOT: The Middle Dutch *Lancelot* Compilation and the Medieval Tradition of Narrative Cycles, *Bart Besamusca*
LIV A COMPANION TO THE *LANCELOT-GRAIL* CYCLE, *edited by Carol Dover*

LV THE GENTRY CONTEXT FOR MALORY'S *MORTE DARTHUR*,
 Raluca L. Radulescu
LVI PARZIVAL: With *Titurel* and the *Love Lyrics*, by Wolfram von Eschenbach,
 translated by Cyril Edwards
LVII ARTHURIAN STUDIES IN HONOUR OF P. J. C. FIELD, *edited by
 Bonnie Wheeler*
LVIII THE LEGEND OF THE GRAIL, *translated by Nigel Bryant*
LIX THE GRAIL LEGEND IN MODERN LITERATURE, *John B. Marino*
LX RE-VIEWING *LE MORTE DARTHUR*: Texts and Contexts, Characters and
 Themes, *edited by K. S. Whetter and Raluca L. Radulescu*
LXI THE SCOTS AND MEDIEVAL ARTHURIAN LEGEND, *edited by
 Rhiannon Purdie and Nicola Royan*
LXII WIRNT VON GRAVENBERG'S *WIGALOIS*: Intertextuality and Interpretation,
 Neil Thomas
LXIII A COMPANION TO CHRÉTIEN DE TROYES, *edited by Norris J. Lacy and
 Joan Tasker Grimbert*
LXIV THE FORTUNES OF KING ARTHUR, *edited by Norris J. Lacy*
LXV A HISTORY OF ARTHURIAN SCHOLARSHIP, *edited by Norris J. Lacy*
LXVI MALORY'S CONTEMPORARY AUDIENCE: The Social Reading of Romance in
 Late Medieval England, *Thomas H. Crofts*
LXVII MARRIAGE, ADULTERY AND INHERITANCE IN MALORY'S *MORTE
 DARTHUR*, *Karen Cherewatuk*
LXVIII EDWARD III'S ROUND TABLE AT WINDSOR: The House of the Round Table
 and the Windsor Festival of 1344, *Julian Munby, Richard Barber and
 Richard Brown*
LXIX GEOFFREY OF MONMOUTH: THE HISTORY OF THE KINGS OF BRITAIN: An
 edition and translation of the *De gestis Britonum* [*Historia Regum Britanniae*], *edited
 by Michael D. Reeve, translated by Neil Wright*
LXX RADIO CAMELOT: Arthurian Legends on the BBC, 1922–2005, *Roger Simpson*
LXXI MALORY'S LIBRARY: The Sources of the *Morte Darthur*, *Ralph Norris*
LXXII THE GRAIL, THE QUEST, AND THE WORLD OF ARTHUR, *edited by
 Norris J. Lacy*
LXXIII ILLUSTRATING CAMELOT, *Barbara Tepa Lupack with Alan Lupack*
LXXIV THE ARTHURIAN WAY OF DEATH: The English Tradition, *edited by
 Karen Cherewatuk and K. S. Whetter*
LXXV VISION AND GENDER IN MALORY'S *MORTE DARTHUR*, *Molly Martin*
LXXVI THE INTERLACE STRUCTURE OF THE THIRD PART OF THE *PROSE
 LANCELOT*, *Frank Brandsma*
LXXVII *PERCEFOREST*: The Prehistory of King Arthur's Britain, *translated by Nigel Bryant*
LXXVIII CHRÉTIEN DE TROYES IN PROSE: The Burgundian *Erec* and *Cligés*, *translated
 by Joan Tasker Grimbert and Carol J. Chase*
LXXIX THE CONTINUATIONS OF CHRÉTIEN'S *PERCEVAL*: Content and
 Construction, Extension and Ending, *Leah Tether*
LXXX SIR THOMAS MALORY: *Le Morte Darthur*, *edited by P. J. C. Field*
LXXXI MALORY AND HIS EUROPEAN CONTEMPORARIES: Adapting Late
 Medieval Arthurian Romance Collections, *Miriam Edlich-Muth*
LXXXII THE COMPLETE STORY OF THE GRAIL: Chrétien de Troyes' *Perceval* and its
 continuations, *translated by Nigel Bryant*

LXXXIII EMOTIONS IN MEDIEVAL ARTHURIAN LITERATURE: Body, Mind, Voice, *edited by Frank Brandsma, Carolyne Larrington and Corinne Saunders*
LXXXIV THE MANUSCRIPT AND MEANING OF MALORY'S *MORTE DARTHUR*: Rubrication, Commemoration, Memorialisation, *K. S. Whetter*
LXXXV PUBLISHING THE GRAIL IN MEDIEVAL AND EARLY RENAISSANCE FRANCE, *Leah Tether*

www.ingramcontent.com/pod-product-compliance
Lightning Source LLC
Chambersburg PA
CBHW070753300426
44111CB00014B/2396